American National Biography Online www.anb.org

Free subscription with purchase of a new book!

Visit the online user's guide of *American National Biography* at www.anb.org/userguide

American National Biography Online offers **portraits of more than 18,300 women and men**—from all eras and walks of life—whose lives have shaped the nation. Originally published in 24 volumes in 1999, the *American National Biography* won instant acclaim as the new authority in American biographies. **Winner of the American Library Association's Dartmouth Medal** as the best reference work of the year, the *ANB* now serves readers in thousands of school, public, and academic libraries around the world.

The publication of the online edition makes the *ANB* even more useful as a dynamic source of information—updated semi-annually, with hundreds of new entries each year and revisions of previously published entries to enhance their accuracy and currency. The *ANB Online* features **thousands of illustrations**, more than **80,000 hyperlinked cross-references**, links to select websites, and powerful search capabilities.

- Over 18,300 biographies, including the 17,435 original biographies from the print edition
- New biographies added and others revised semi-annually—including articles on recently deceased notables as well as figures from the past who were not subjects in the print edition
- Over 900 articles from *The Oxford Companion to United States History* provide historical and social context to the biographies
- Over 2,500 illustrations with more added with each update
- Regular updates to the bibliographies

To activate your **FREE** subscription to *American National Biography Online*, go to https://ams.oup.com/order/ANBAHS1YRSCRIP and follow the instructions for entering your activation code.

Please note that your subscription will start as soon as the activation code is entered. This code must be entered before June 15, 2014 in order to be valid. This offer is only valid in the Americas and the Caribbean.

PN2I-792O-F5N8-RHN3

D0080496

OXFORD
UNIVERSITY PRESS

ANB Online is a dynamic, easy-to-use resource

Search

- By full text (words and phrases)
- By subject name
- By gender
- By occupation or realm of renown
- By birth date
- By birthplace
- By death date
- By contributor name

Your search results will display alphabetically. The first listing of results are biographies from the ANB Online. Some of the entries are followed by a camera and/or globe, indicating that there is a picture or online resource available. All online resources are carefully reviewed by our editors.

A Teacher's Guide to Using *ANB Online*:
Make ANB Online work for you with a Teacher's Guide designed to help you get the most out of this valuable resource.

- How to Read a Biographical Essay
- An Introductory Lesson: *Thomas Jefferson*
- Using the Image to Learn More about the Subject: *Abigail Adams*
- Using Biography with Primary Sources: *Plessy v. Ferguson*
- Using Cross-References to do Collective Biography: *The Cuban Missile Crisis*
- A Research Lesson: *Frederick Douglass*

Jump-Start Your Research: You can now jump-start your research by browsing through pre-selected lists of articles from the *ANB Online* and *The Oxford Companion to United States History*, encyclopedia content that supports the 19,000 biographies. Selected by Oxford editors, the 12 research topics cover American Literature, Arts in America, Black History, Civil Rights Movement, Civil War, Depression and New Deal, Frontier and Western Expansion, Gilded Age, Hispanic American Heritage, Native American Heritage, Women's History, and World War II.

Special Collections: A special search feature allows you to guide your research with specially selected collections that celebrate the diversity of American history: Black History, Women's History, Asian Pacific American Heritage, American Indian Heritage, and Hispanic Heritage.

The Oxford Companion to United States History: Over 900 articles from the acclaimed *The Oxford Companion to United States History* have been incorporated into *ANB Online* to enhance and enrich the study of history through biography. As big and as varied as the nation it portrays, *The Oxford Companion to United States History* explores not only America's political, diplomatic, and military history, but also social, cultural, and intellectual trends; science, technology, and medicine; the arts; and religion. The articles selected for inclusion in *ANB Online* expand the learning experience, providing context to the biographies and further illuminating the nation's history through defining events, social movements, ideologies, and even natural disasters and iconic sites.

www.anb.org

OXFORD
UNIVERSITY PRESS

Concise Edition

Of the People

A HISTORY OF THE UNITED STATES

James Oakes
City University of New York Graduate Center

Michael McGerr
Indiana University–Bloomington

Jan Ellen Lewis
Rutgers University, Newark

Nick Cullather
Indiana University–Bloomington

Jeanne Boydston
University of Wisconsin–Madison

New York   Oxford
Oxford University Press
2011

Jeanne Boydston
1944–2008
Historian, Teacher, Friend

Oxford University Press, Inc., publishes works that further Oxford University's objective of excellence in research, scholarship, and education.

Oxford New York
Auckland   Cape Town   Dar es Salaam   Hong Kong   Karachi
Kuala Lumpur   Madrid   Melbourne   Mexico City   Nairobi
New Delhi   Shanghai   Taipei   Toronto

With offices in
Argentina   Austria   Brazil   Chile   Czech Republic   France   Greece
Guatemala   Hungary   Italy   Japan   Poland   Portugal   Singapore
South Korea   Switzerland   Thailand   Turkey   Ukraine   Vietnam

Published by Oxford University Press, Inc.
198 Madison Avenue, New York, New York 10016
http://www.oup.com

Oxford is a registered trademark of Oxford University Press

ISBN: 978-0-19-539072-8

Printing number: 9 8 7 6 5 4 3 2 1

Printed in the United States of America
on acid-free paper

Contents

Chapter 6 ●● Conflict on the Edge of the Empire, 1713–1774   153

Chapter 7 ● ● ● Creating a New Nation, 1775–1788   183

Chapter 8 ●●● Contested Republic, 1789–1800   216

Chapter 9 ●●● A Republic in Transition, 1800–1819   248

Chapter 10 ●●● Slavery and the Nation, 1790–1828   **279**

Chapter 16 ●●● Reconstructing a Nation, 1865–1877   452

Chapter 17 ●●● The Triumph of Industrial Capitalism, 1850–1890   481

Chapter 19 ●●● The Politics of Industrial America, 1870–1892 **533**

Chapter 24 ⬤⬤⬤ A Great Depression and a New Deal, 1929–1940   **673**

Chapter 27 ●●● The Consumer Society, 1945–1961   760

Chapter 28 ●●● The Rise and Fall of the New Liberalism, 1960–1968   790

Chapter 30 ●●● The Triumph of Conservatism, 1980–1991   852

Appendixes

Maps and Features

Features

American Portraits

American Landscapes

America and the World

Preface

At Gettysburg, Pennsylvania, on November 19, 1863, President Abraham Lincoln dedicated a memorial to the more than 3,000 Union soldiers who had died turning back a Confederate invasion in the first days of July. There were at least a few ways that the president could have justified the sad loss of life in the third year of a brutal war dividing North and South. He could have said it was necessary to destroy the Confederacy's cherished institution of slavery, to punish southerners for seceding from the United States, or to preserve the nation intact. Instead, at this crucial moment in American history, Lincoln gave a short, stunning speech about democracy. The president did not use the word, but he offered its essence. To honor the dead of Gettysburg, he called on northerners to ensure "that government of the people, by the people, for the people, shall not perish from the earth."

With these words, Lincoln put democracy at the center of the Civil War and at the center of American history. The authors of this book share his belief in the centrality of democracy; his words, "of the people," give our book its title and its main theme. We see American history as a story "of the people," of their struggles to shape their lives and their land.

Our choice of theme does not mean we believe that America has always been a democracy. Clearly, it has not. As Lincoln gave the Gettysburg Address, most African Americans still lived in slavery. American women, north and south, lacked rights that many men enjoyed; for all their disagreements, white southerners and northerners viewed Native Americans as enemies. Neither do we believe that there is only a single definition of democracy, either in the narrow sense of a particular form of government or in the larger one of a society whose members participate equally in its creation. Although Lincoln defined the northern cause as a struggle for democracy, southerners believed it was anything but democratic to force them to remain in the Union at gunpoint. As bloody draft riots in New York City in July 1863 made clear, many northern men thought it was anything but democratic to force them to fight in Lincoln's armies. Such disagreements have been typical of American history. For more than 500 years, people have struggled over whose vision of life in the New World would prevail.

It is precisely such struggles that offer the best angle of vision for seeing and understanding the most important developments in the nation's history. In particular, the democratic theme concentrates attention on the most fundamental concerns of history: people and power.

Lincoln's words serve as a reminder of the basic truth that history is about people. Across the 31 chapters of this book, we write extensively about complex events, such as the five-year savagery of the Civil War, and long-term transformations, such as the slow, halting evolution of democratic political institutions. But we write in the awareness that these developments are only abstractions unless they are grounded in the lives of people. The test of a historical narrative, we believe, is whether its characters are fully rounded, believable human beings.

We hope that our commitment to a history "of the people" is apparent on every page of this book. To underscore it, we open each chapter with an **"American Portrait"** feature, a story of someone whose life in one way or another embodies the basic theme of the pages to follow. So we begin Chapter 8 on the United States in the 1790s with William Maclay, a senator from rural Pennsylvania, who feared that arrogant northeasterners and "pandering" Virginians would quickly turn the new nation into an aristocracy. In Chapter 23, we encounter 19-year-old Gertrude Ederle, whose solo swim across the English Channel and taste for cars and dancing epitomized the individualistic, consumer culture emerging in the 1920s.

The choice of Lincoln's words also reflects our belief that history is about power. To ask whether America was democratic at some point in the past is to ask whether all people had equal power to make their lives and their nation. Such questions of power necessarily take us to political processes, to the ways in which people work separately and collectively to enforce their will. We define politics quite broadly in this book. With the feminists of the 1960s, we believe that "the personal is the political," that power relations shape people's lives in private as well as in public. *Of the People* looks for democracy in the living room as well as in the legislature, and in the bedroom as well as in the business office.

To underscore our broad view of the political, each chapter presents an **"American Landscape"** feature, a particular place in time where issues of power appeared in especially sharp relief. So Chapter 2 describes the sixteenth-century Native American villages of Huronia, whose social spaces and sexual relations reflected distinctive ideas about individual freedom and female power. Chapter 21 details the contrasting understandings of democracy at the heart of the early twentieth-century battle over creating a new water supply for San Francisco by building a dam in the Hetch Hetchy Valley of California.

Focusing on democracy, on people and power, we have necessarily written as wide-ranging a history as possible. In the features and in the main text, *Of the People* conveys both the unity and the great diversity of the American people across time and place. Lincoln's "people" have shared a common identity as Americans; but at the same time they have been many distinctive "peoples." So we chronicle the racial and ethnic groups who have shaped America. We explore differences of religious and regional identity. We trace the changing nature of social classes. We examine the different ways that gender identities have been constructed and reconstructed over the centuries.

While treating different groups in their distinctiveness, we have integrated them into the broader narrative as much as possible. A true history "of the people" means not only acknowledging their individuality and diversity but also showing their interrelationships and their roles in the larger narrative.

Of the People also offers comprehensive coverage of the different spheres of human life—cultural as well as governmental, social as well as economic, environmental as well as military. This commitment to comprehensiveness is a reflection of our belief that all aspects of human existence are the stuff of history. It is also an expression of the fundamental theme of the book: the focus on democracy leads naturally to the study of people's struggles for power in every dimension of their lives. Moreover, the democratic approach emphasizes the interconnections between the different aspects of Americans' lives; we cannot understand politics and government without tracing their connection to economics, religion, culture, art, sexuality, and so on.

The economic connection is especially important. *Of the People* devotes much attention to economic life, to the ways in which Americans have worked and saved and spent. Economic power, the authors believe, is basic to democracy. Americans' power to shape their lives and their country has been greatly affected by whether they were farmers or hunters, plantation owners or slaves, wageworkers or capitalists, domestic servants or bureaucrats. The authors do not see economics as an impersonal, all-conquering force; instead, we try to show how the values and actions of ordinary people, as well as the laws and regulations of government, have made economic life.

We have also tried especially to place America in global context. The story of individual nation-states such as the United States remains a critically important kind of history. But the history of America, or any nation, cannot be adequately explained without understanding its relationship to transnational events and global developments. That is true for the first chapter of the book, which shows how America began to emerge from the collision of Native Americans, West Africans, and Europeans in the fifteenth and sixteenth centuries. It is just as true for the last chapter of the book, which demonstrates how globalization and the war on terror transformed the United States at the turn of the twenty-first century. In the chapters in between these two, the authors detail how the world has changed America and how America has changed the world. Reflecting the concerns of the rest of the book, we focus particularly on the movement of people, the evolution of power, and the attempt to spread democracy abroad. Whether they were right is the burden of this book.

To underscore the fundamental importance of global relationships, each chapter includes a feature on **"America and the World."** So Chapter 15 reveals how ordinary Europeans' support for the abolition of slavery made it impossible for their governments to recognize the southern Confederacy. Chapter 20 shows how Singer, a pioneering American multinational company, began to export an economic vision of a consumer democracy along with its sewing machines in the nineteenth and early twentieth centuries.

In a sense, Singer had arrived at Abraham Lincoln's conclusion about the central importance of democracy in American life. The company wanted to sell sewing machines; the president wanted to sell a war. But both believed their audience would see democracy as quintessentially American. Whether they were right is the burden of this book.

About the Concise Edition

We are very happy to present *Of the People* in this concise edition. As instructors ourselves, we know how important it is to offer teachers and students a choice of comprehensive and concise versions of a textbook. In preparing this concise edition, we have tried especially to help those instructors who need to teach the survey in a short term, who wish to assign readings besides a textbook, or who want to save money for their students-without sacrificing the main advantages of the full edition. Put simply, we have cut size and cost, not quality.

To achieve our goal, we have refocused *Of the People* as much as possible on the text itself. So, there are 75 percent fewer margin quotations and 60 percent fewer images than in the comprehensive edition. Knowing how much our own students rely on good maps, we have eliminated only percent of those from the comprehensive. And we have reduced the full text itself by percent. We have done that, not by cutting any basic points or arguments, but by trimming illustrative examples and streamlining our prose. As we came to realize, any authors who take the title of their book from Lincoln's famously brief Gettysburg Address should be prepared to shorten their sentences!

Supplements

For Students

Oxford University Press is proud to offer a complete and authoritative supplements package for students—including print and new media resources designed for chapter review, for primary source reading, for essay writing, for test-preparation and for further research.

Student Companion Website at **www.oup.com/us/ofthepeople**

The open-access Online Study Center designed for *Of the People: A History of the United States* (comprehensive and concise editions) helps students to review what they have learned from the textbook as well as explore other resources online. Note-taking guides help students focus their attention in class, while interactive practice quizzes allow them to assess their knowledge of a topic before a test.

- **Online Study Guide**, including
  - ∘ Note-taking outlines
  - ∘ Multiple-choice and identification quizzes, (two quizzes per chapter, thirty question quizzes—*different* from those found in the Instructor's Manual/Testbank)
- **Primary Source Companion & Research Guide**, a brief online Research Primer, with a library of annotated links to primary and secondary sources in U.S. history.
- **Interactive Flashcards**, using key terms and people listed at the end of each chapter, help students remember who's who and what's what.

American National Biography Online **www.anb.org**

Students who purchase a **new** copy of Oakes's *Of the People: A History of the United States* (concise edition) will find an access code for a six-month (Volume 1 or 2) or a one-year **free subscription** to this powerful online resource published by Oxford University Press.

American National Biography Online offers **portraits of more than 17,400 women and men**—from all eras and walks of life—whose lives have shaped the nation. More than a decade in preparation, the *American National Biography* is the first biographical resource of this scope to be published in more than sixty years. Originally published in 24 volumes in 1999, the *American National Biography* won instant acclaim as the new authority in American biographies. **Winner of the American Library Association's Dartmouth Medal** as the best reference work of the year, the *ANB* now serves readers in thousands of school, public, and academic libraries around the world. The publication of the online edition makes the *ANB* even more useful as a dynamic source of information—updated semi-annually, with hundreds of new entries each year and revisions of previously published entries to enhance their accuracy and currency. The *ANB Online* features **thousands of illustrations**, more than **80,000 hyperlinked cross-references**, links to select websites, and powerful search capabilities.

ANB Online **is also a great teaching resource, since it can be actively incorporated into classroom lessons.** To assist teachers in fully utilizing *ANB Online*, we have prepared a Teacher's Guide to Using *ANB Online*. Developed with the participation of librarians and teachers, the Teacher's Guide offers six lessons that highlight the importance and value of studying biography as an end in itself and as a starting point for doing further research into the lives of those who shaped the American experience.

Writing History: A Guide for Students Third edition, by William Kelleher Storey, Associate Professor at Millsaps College.

Bringing together practical methods from both history and composition, *Writing History* provides a wealth of tips and advice to help students research and write essays for history classes. The book covers all aspects of writing about history, including **finding topics** and **researching** them, **interpreting source materials, drawing inferences from sources, and constructing arguments**. It concludes with three chapters that discuss writing effective sentences, using precise wording, and revising. Using numerous examples from the works of cultural, political, and social historians, *Writing History* serves as an ideal supplement to history courses that require students to conduct research. The third edition includes expanded sections on **peer editing** and **topic selection**, as well as new sections on searching and using the Internet. *Writing History* can be packaged for free with Oakes's *Of the People: A History of the United States*. Contact your Oxford University Press Sales Representative for more information.

The Information-Literate Historian: A Guide to Research for History Students by Jenny Presnell, *Information Services Library and History, American Studies*, and *Women's Studies Bibliographer, Miami University of Ohio*

This is the only book specifically designed to teach today's history student how to most successfully select and use sources—primary, secondary, and electronic—to carry out and present their research. Written by a college librarian, *The Information-Literate Historian* is an indispensable reference for historians, students, and other readers doing history research. *The Information-Literate Historian* can be packaged for free with Oakes's *Of the People: A History of the United States*. Contact your Oxford University Press Sales Representative for more information.

Primary Source Documents

Our Documents: 100 Milestone Documents from the National Archives brings documents to life, including facsimiles side-by-side with transcripts for students to explore, explanations, and a foreword provided by Michael Beschloss. This primary source book can be **packaged for free** with Oakes's *Of the People: A History of the United States* (concise edition). Among the documents it contains are: Declaration of Independence; U.S. Constitution; Bill of Rights; Louisiana Purchase Treaty; Missouri Compromise; The Dred Scott decision; Emancipation Proclamation; Gettysburg Address; Fourteenth Amendment to the U.S. Constitution; Thomas Edison's lightbulb patent; Sherman Anti-Trust Act; Executive order for the Japanese relocation during wartime; Manhattan Project notebook; press release announcing U.S. recognition of Israel; President John F. Kennedy's inaugural address, as well as many more.

Other primary source books that can be packaged with Oakes's *Of the People: A History of the United States* (concise edition) include Chafe's **History of Our Time** and Bloom's **Takin' It to the Streets**, as well as ***The Boisterous Sea of Liberty: A Documentary History of America from Discovery through the Civil War***; and ***Documenting American Violence: A Sourcebook.***

For Professors

For decades American History professors have turned to Oxford University Press as the leading source for high quality readings and reference materials. Now, when you adopt Oakes's *Of the People: A History of the United States* (concise edition), the Press will partner with you and make available its best supplemental materials and resources for your classroom. Listed here are several series of high interest, but you will want to talk with your Sales Representative to learn more about what can be made available, and about what would suit your course best.

Instructor's Manual and Testbank. This useful guide contains helpful teaching tools for experienced and first-time teachers alike. It can be made available to adopters upon request, and is also available electronically on the Instructor's Resource CD. This extensive manual and testbank contains:

- **Sample Syllabi**
- **Chapter Outlines**
- **In-Class Discussion Questions**
- **Lecture Ideas**
- **Oxford's Further Reading List**
- **Quizzes** (two per chapter, one per half of the chapter, content divided somewhat evenly down the middle of the chapter: 30 multiple choice questions each)
- **Tests** (two per chapter, each covering the entire chapter contents: each offering 10 identification/matching; 10 multiple-choice; five short-answer, two essay)

Instructor's Resource CD. This handy CD-ROM contains everything you need in an electronic format—the Instructor's Manual (PDF), PowerPoint Slides (fully customizable), Image Library with PDF versions of *all* maps from the textbook, and a Computerized Testbank, which was made specifically for the concise edition.

A complete **Course Management cartridge** is also available to qualified adopters. Instructor's resources are also available for download directly to your computer through a secure connection via the instructor's side of the companion website. Contact your Oxford University Press Sales Representative for more information.

Other Oxford Titles of Interest for the U.S. History Classroom

Oxford University Press publishes a vast array of titles in American history. Listed below is just a small selection of books that pair particularly well with Oakes's *Of the People: A History of the United States* (concise edition). Any of the books in these series can be packaged with Oakes at a significant discount to students. Please contact your Oxford University Press Sales Representative for specific pricing information, or for additional packaging suggestions. Please visit www.oup.com/us for a full listing of Oxford titles.

NEW NARRATIVES IN AMERICAN HISTORY

At Oxford University Press, we believe that good history begins with a good story. Each volume in this series features a compelling tale that draws on a sustained narrative to illuminate a greater historical theme or controversy. Then, in a thoughtful Afterword, the authors place their narratives within larger historical contexts, discuss their sources and narrative strategies, and describe their personal involvement with the work. Intensely personal and highly relevant, these succinct texts are innovative teaching tools that provide a springboard for incisive class discussion as they immerse students in a particular historical moment.

Escaping Salem: The Other Witch Hunt of 1692, by Richard Godbeer

Sleuthing the Alamo: Davy Crockett's Last Stand and Other Mysteries of the Texas Revolution, by James E. Crisp

In Search of the Promised Land: A Slave Family in the Old South, by John Hope Franklin and Loren Schweninger

The Making of a Confederate: Walter Lenoir's Civil War, by William L. Barney

"They Say": Ida B. Wells and the Reconstruction of Race, by James West Davidson

Wild Men: Ishi and Kroeber in the Wilderness of Modern America, by Douglas Cazaux Sackman

The Gentle Subversive: Rachel Carson, Silent Spring, and the Rise of the Environmental Movement, by Mark Hamilton Lytle

"To Everything There is a Season": Pete Seeger and the Power of Song, by Allan Winkler

PAGES FROM HISTORY

Textbooks may interpret and recall history, but these books **are** history. Each title, compiled and edited by a prominent historian, is a collection of primary sources relating to a particular topic of historical significance. Documentary evidence includes news articles, government documents, memoirs, letters, diaries, fiction, photographs, advertisements, posters, and political cartoons. Headnotes, extended captions, sidebars, and introductory essays provide the essential context that frames the documents. All the books are amply illustrated and each includes a documentary picture essay, chronology, further reading, source notes, and index.

Encounters in the New World (Jill Lepore)
Colonial America (Edward G. Gray)
The American Revolution (Stephen C. Bullock)
The Bill of Rights (John J. Patrick)
The Struggle Against Slavery (David Waldstreicher)
The Civil War (Rachel Filene Seidman)
The Gilded Age (Janette Thomas Greenwood)
The Industrial Revolution (Laura Levine Frader)
Imperialism (Bonnie G. Smith)
World War I (Frans Coetzee and Marilyn Shevin-Coetzee)
The Depression and the New Deal (Robert McElvaine)
World War II (James H. Madison)
The Cold War (Allan M. Winkler)
The Vietnam War (Marilyn B. Young)

PIVOTAL MOMENTS IN AMERICAN HISTORY

Oxford's *Pivotal Moments in American History Series* explores the turning points that forever changed the course of American history. Each book is written by an expert on the subject and provides a fascinating narrative on a significant instance that stands out in our nation's past. For anyone interested in discovering which important junctures in U.S. history shaped our thoughts, actions, and ideals, these books are the definitive resources.

The Scratch of a Pen: 1763 and the Transformation of North America (Colin Calloway)

As if an Enemy's Country: The British Occupation of Boston and the Origins of the Revolution (Richard Archer)

Washington's Crossing (David Hackett Fischer)

James Madison and the Struggle for the Bill of Rights (Richard Labunski)

Adams vs. Jefferson: The Tumultuous Election of 1800 (John Ferling)

The Birth of Modern Politics: Andrew Jackson, John Quincy Adams, and the Election of 1828 (Lynn Parsons)

Storm over Texas: The Annexation Controversy and the Road to Civil War (Joel H. Silbey)

Crossroads of Freedom: Antietam (James M. McPherson)

The Last Indian War: The Nez Perce Story (Elliot West)

Seneca Falls and the Origins of the Women's Rights Movement (Sally McMillen)

Rainbow's End: The Crash of 1929 (Maury Klein)

Brown v. Board of Education and the Civil Rights Movement (Michael J. Klarman)

The Bay of Pigs (Howard Jones)

Freedom Riders: 1961 and the Struggle for Racial Justice (Raymond Arsenault)

VIEWPOINTS ON AMERICAN CULTURE

Oxford's *Viewpoints on American Culture Series* offers timely reflections for twenty-first century readers. The series targets topics where debates have flourished and brings together the voices of established and emerging writers to share their own points of view in compact and compelling format.

Votes for Women: The Struggle for Suffrage Revisited (Jean H. Baker)

Long Time Gone: Sixties America Then and Now (Alexander Bloom)

Living in the Eighties (Edited by Gil Troy and Vincent J. Cannato)

Race on Trial: Law and Justice in American History (Annette Gordon-Reed)

Sifters: Native American Women's Lives (Theda Perdue)

Latina Legacies: Identity, Biography, and Community (Vicki L. Ruiz)

OXFORD WORLD'S CLASSICS

For over 100 years Oxford World's Classics has made available a broad spectrum of literature from around the globe. With well over 600 titles available and a continuously growing list, this is the finest and most comprehensive classics series in print. Any volume in the series can be **packaged for free** with Oakes's *Of the People: A History of the United States* (concise edition). Relevant titles include Benjamin Franklin's *Autobiography and Other Writings*, J. Hector St. John de Crèvecœur's *Letters from an American Farmer*, Booker T. Washington's *Up from Slavery*, and many others. **For a complete listing of Oxford World's Classics, please visit www.oup.com/us/owc.**

Acknowledgments

The authors are grateful to our families, friends, and colleagues who encouraged us during the planning and writing of this book.

Nick Cullather: To Isabel and Joey for (occasionally) allowing me to work, and to Melanie for the 16 best years.

Jan Lewis: I want to express special thanks to Andy Achenbaum, James Grimmelmann, Warren F. Kimball, Ken Lockridge, and Peter Onuf, who either read portions of the manuscript or discussed it with me. And I am grateful to Barry Bienstock for his enormous library, his vast knowledge, and his endless patience.

The authors would like once again to thank Bruce Nichols for helping launch this book years ago. We are grateful to the editors and staff at Oxford University Press, especially our acquisitions editor, Brian Wheel, and our development editors, Angela Kao and Frederick Speers. Brian's commitment made this edition possible; Fred's vision helped us give the book a new direction. Thanks also to our talented production team, Barbara Mathieu, senior production editor, and Paula Schlosser, art director, who helped to fulfill the book's vision. And special thanks go to Linda Sykes, who managed the photo research; to Elaine Kehoe, our copyeditor; and to Mike Powers and Martha Bostwick, cartographers, and Deane Plaister, editor, at Maps.com, who created the maps; and to the many other people behind the scenes at Oxford for helping this complex project happen.

The authors and editors would also like to thank the following people, whose time and insights have contributed to the comprehensive edition and to the concise edition.

Supplement Authors

Laura Graves,
South Plains College
Instructor's Manual

Andrew McMichael,
Western Kentucky University
Student Companion Website

Jim Jeffries,
Clemson University
PowerPoint slides

Archie McDonald,
Stephen F. Austin State University
Test Bank

Expert Reviewers

Thomas L. Altherr
Metropolitan State College of Denver

Luis Alvarez
University of California–San Diego

Adam Arenson
University of Texas–El Paso

Melissa Estes Blair
University of Georgia

Susan Roth Breitzer
Fayetteville State University

Margaret Lynn Brown
Brevard College

W. Fitzhugh Brundage
University of North Carolina–Chapel Hill

Lawrence Bowdish
Ohio State University

Gregory Bush
University of Miami

Brian Casserly
University of Washington

Ann Chirhart
Indiana State University

Bradley R. Clampitt
East Central University

Cheryll Ann Cody
Houston Community College

William W. Cobb Jr.
Utah Valley University

Sondra Cosgrove
College of Southern Nevada

Thomas H. Cox
Sam Houston State University

Carl Creasman
Valencia Community College

Christine Daniels
Michigan State University

Brian J. Daugherity
Virginia Commonwealth University

Mark Elliott
University of North Carolina–Greensboro

Katherine Carté Enge
Texas A&M University

Michael Faubion
University of Texas–Pan American

John Fea
Messiah College

Anne L. Foster
Indiana State University

Matthew Garrett
Arizona State University

Tim Garvin
California State University–Long Beach

Lloyd Ray Gunn
University of Utah

Suzanne Cooper Guasco
Queens University of Charlotte

Richard Hall
Columbus State University

Marsha Hamilton
University of South Alabama

Mark Hanna
University of California–San Diego

Joseph M. Hawes
University of Memphis

Melissa Hovsepian
University of Houston–Downtown

David K. Johnson
University of South Florida

Lloyd Johnson
Campbell University

Jorge Iber
Texas Tech University

Michael Kramer
Northwestern University

Catherine O'Donnell Kaplan
Arizona State University

Rebecca M. Kluchin
California State University–Sacramento

Louis M. Kyriakoudes
University of Southern Mississippi

Jason S. Lantzer
Butler University

Shelly Lemons
St. Louis Community College

Charlie Levine
Mesa Community College

Denise Lynn
University of Southern Indiana

Lillian Marrujo-Duck
City College of San Francisco

Noeleen McIlvenna
Wright State University

Michael McCoy
Orange County Community College

Elizabeth Brand Monroe
Indiana University–Purdue University,
Indianapolis

Kevin C. Motl
Ouachita Baptist University

Todd Moye
University of North Texas

Julie Nicoletta
University of Washington–Tacoma

Charlotte Negrete
Mt. San Antonio College

David M. Parker
California State University–Northridge

Jason Parker
Texas A&M University

Burton W. Peretti
Western Connecticut State University

Jim Piecuch
Kennesaw State University

John Putman
San Diego State University

R. J. Rockefeller
Loyola College of Maryland

Herbert Sloan
Barnard College, Columbia University

Vincent L. Toscano
Nova Southeastern University

William E. Weeks
San Diego State University

Timothy L. Wood
Southwest Baptist University

Jason Young
SUNY-Buffalo

Concise Edition Reviewers

Hedrick Alixopulos
Santa Rosa Junior College

Guy Alain Aronoff
Humboldt State University History
Department

Melissa Estes Blair
Warren Wilson College

Amanda Bruce
Nassau Community College

Jonathan Chu
University of Massachusetts–Boston

Paul G. E. Clemens
Rutgers University

Martha Anne Fielder
Cedar Valley College

Tim Hacsi
University of Massachusetts–Boston

Matthew Isham
Pennsylvania State

Ross A. Kennedy
Illinois State University

Eve Kornfeld
San Diego State University

Peggy Lambert
Lone Star College-Kingwood

Shelly L. Lemons
St. Louis Community College

Carolyn Herbst Lewis
Louisiana State University

Catherine M. Lewis
Kennesaw State University

Daniel K. Lewis
California State Polytechnic University

Scott P. Marler
University of Memphis

Laura McCall
Metropolitan State College of Denver

Stephen P. McGrath
Central Connecticut State University

Vincent P. Mikkelsen
Florida State University

Julie Nicoletta
University of Washington Tacoma

Caitlin Stewart
Eastern Connecticut State University

Thomas Summerhill
Michigan State University

David Tegeder
Santa Fe College

Eric H. Walther
University of Houston

William E. Weeks
University of San Diego

Kenneth B. White
Modesto Junior College

Julie Winch
University of Massachusetts–Boston

Mary Montgomery Wolf
University of Georgia

Kyle F. Zelner
University of Southern Mississippi

About the Authors

James Oakes has published several books and numerous articles on slavery and antislavery in the nineteenth century, including The Radical and the Republican: Frederick Douglass, Abraham Lincoln, and the Triumph of Antislavery Politics (2007), winner of the Lincoln Prize in 2008. Professor Oakes has previously taught at Princeton and Northwestern Universities, and he is now Distinguished Professor of History and Graduate School Humanities Professor at the City University of New York Graduate Center. In 2008 he was a fellow at the Cullman Center at the New York Public Library. His current writing involves a history of emancipation during the Civil War.

Michael McGerr is Paul V. McNutt Professor of History in the College of Arts and Sciences at Indiana University–Bloomington. He is the author of *The Decline of Popular Politics: The American North, 1865–1928* (1986) and *A Fierce Discontent: The Rise and Fall of the Progressive Movement, 1870–1920* (2003). He is writing *"The Public Be Damned": The Vanderbilts and the Unmaking of the Ruling Class.* The recipient of a yearlong fellowship from the National Endowment for the Humanities, Professor McGerr has won numerous teaching awards at Indiana, where his courses include the U.S. Survey, Race and Gender in American Business, War in Modern American History, The Politics of American Popular Music, The Sixties, and American Pleasure Wars. He has previously taught at Yale University and the Massachusetts Institute of Technology. He received the BA, MA, and PhD from Yale.

Jan Ellen Lewis is Professor of History and Associate Dean of the Faculty of Arts and Sciences, Rutgers University, Newark. She also teaches in the history PhD program at Rutgers, New Brunswick, and was a visiting professor of history at Princeton. A specialist in colonial and early national history, she is the author of *The Pursuit of Happiness: Family and Values in Jefferson's Virginia* (1983) as well as numerous articles and reviews. She has coedited *An Emotional History of the United States* (1998), *Sally Hemings and Thomas Jefferson: History, Memory, and Civic Culture* (1999), and *The Revolution of 1800: Democracy, Race, and the New Republic* (2002). She has served on the editorial board of the *American Historical Review* and as chair of the New Jersey Historical Commission. She received her AB from Bryn Mawr College and MAs and PhD from the University of Michigan.

Nick Cullather is a historian of U.S. foreign relations at Indiana University–Bloomington. He is author of two books on nation building: *Illusions of Influence* (1994), a study of U.S.-Philippines relations, and *Secret History* (1999 and 2006), a history of the CIA's overthrow of the Guatemalan government in 1954. His current work includes *Calories and Cold War: America's Quest to Feed the World*. He received his PhD from the University of Virginia.

Jeanne Boydston was Robinson-Edwards Professor of American History at the University of Wisconsin–Madison. A specialist in the histories of gender and labor, she was the author of *Home and Work: Housework, Wages, and the Ideology of Labor in the Early American Republic* (1990); coauthor of *The Limits of Sisterhood: The Beecher Sisters on Women's Rights and Woman's Sphere* (1988), and coeditor of *Root of Bitterness: Documents in the Social History of American Women*, second edition (1996). Her most recent article is "Gender as a Category of Historical Analysis," *Gender History* (2008). She taught courses in women's and gender history, the histories of the early republic and the antebellum United States, and global and comparative history, and she was the recipient of numerous awards for teaching and mentoring. Her BA and MA were from the University of Tennessee, and her PhD was from Yale University.

Worlds in Motion
1450–1550

AMERICAN PORTRAIT

>> Malinche, Cultural Translator

We do not know what name her parents gave her. She was born to a noble family on the eastern edge of the great Aztec Empire in Mexico. Her widowed mother gave her away to people in another kingdom, who in turn gave her to another people, the Chontal Mayas. In 1519, when the Spanish conquerors arrived, the Chontals gave them 20 women in the hopes that this gift would induce the Spanish to move on to the West. When Indian peoples first encountered the European invaders, they used every stratagem they could think of simply to get the foreigners to move on.

A priest soon baptized her Marina. She was turned over to a Spanish captain as his mistress, and then to the Spanish conqueror Hernán Cortés as his translator. In her world and that of the conquerors, women could be handed from one man to another, little more than property. The Spanish had noticed that she could speak not only the Mayan language but also Nahuatl, the language of the Aztec Empire they intended to conquer. In time, she learned Spanish also, making all other translators unnecessary. From that moment, she was at Cortés's side until he had conquered all of Mexico. And that is when the Spanish started calling her Doña—or Lady—Marina, in honor of her importance. In Nahuatl, her name became Malintzin, which the Spanish heard as Malinche, the name we know her by today: a Spanish translation of a Nahuatl translation of a Spanish name given to a Mexican girl.

The first meeting of Malinche, called Marina by the Spanish, and Cortés.

Cortés never learned the Indian languages, and Malinche translated his words to the Aztec king Moctezuma. Both came from highly developed cultures with elaborate rules for politeness. Neither understood the other's rules, however, and Cortés and his men had to be held back physically when they breached Aztec custom by touching the king. Yet when Malinche spoke to Moctezuma for Cortés, she did not use the honeyed words the king expected of his subjects, nor did she cast her eyes down. Instead, she looked him in the eye, something not even his own lords would dare to do. She had courageously assumed for herself the arrogance of the Spanish conqueror.

continued

>> **AMERICAN PORTRAIT** *continued*

Malinche survived the great battle for the Aztec capital, Tenochtitlán, which she saw the Spanish level. After the Aztecs had been defeated Cortés took Malinche as his mistress. Soon she bore him a son, Don Martín, named for Cortés's own father. Cortés raised the boy as a son, although he soon married Malinche off to one of his friends. Before long, she gave birth to a second child, a daughter. Both of her children lived out their lives in the world of the conquerors, her son in Spain, her daughter married to a Spanish settler in Mexico.

Cortés needed Malinche's translating services for one more venture, however. One of his lieutenants had gone off on his own, conquering Honduras, and Cortés set out to subjugate him. Moving through the province where Malinche had been born, they encountered Malinche's mother. The older woman was terrified, certain that the daughter she had given away would now have her executed. Instead, Malinche forgave her and showered her with jewels and gold and fine clothing.

In the long period of encounter and conquest initiated by the Spanish arrival in the Americas, cultural translators, women and men such as Malinche who understood the languages and customs of the different worlds, would possess unique power. In translating one world to the other, they helped create a new world, one very different from any that had ever existed before.

Common Threads

>> In which ways might the Native American societies before the arrival of Europeans be considered egalitarian? What forces shaped their societies?

>> How did Europeans' preconceptions affect their actions in the New World? In which ways did they adapt to new circumstances?

>> What role did gender play in organizing Native American, African, and European societies? What role did gender play in conquest?

>> What were the unintended consequences of conquest?

The World of the Indian Peoples

When Europeans arrived in the New World at the end of the fifteenth century, several large and powerful states, such as the Aztec and Inca, had emerged, as well as a number of less complex social organizations, each with different traditions, cultures, and languages. This diversity had its origins at least 12,000 years earlier when people known as the Archaic or Paleo-Indians crossed from Siberia into Alaska. By the time of Christopher Columbus's voyage, there were hundreds of separate Indian cultures, speaking 375 different languages

Map 1–1 Indian Cultures, Languages When Europeans first arrived in America, there were hundreds of separate cultures, speaking 375 different languages. Boundaries between the groups were constantly shifting, as disease, conflict, and environmental changes caused some groups to prosper and others to decline. Much of the Eastern Woodlands region had lost its population to epidemics and emigration. *Michael Coe et al.,* Atlas of Ancient North America *(New York: Facts on File, 1986), pp. 44–45.*

(see Map 1–1). The total native population of America north of the Rio Grande may have been as high as 18 million (with that of Europe perhaps five or six times higher).

As early as the first century CE, distinctive regional groups, held together by exchange relations, had begun to emerge. By the twelfth century, there were several centers of exchange north of the Rio Grande (one at Cahokia and the other at Chaco Canyon), although both had begun to decline before the arrival of the Europeans. When Europeans arrived in North America, they encountered a continent that already had a rich and complex history.

The Archaic Indians

The first Americans were hunter-gatherers who followed the mammoth and other huge animals across the land bridge from Asia. These were modern human beings who stood erect, wore clothing, and made tools. Once dispersed in America, they lived in small bands of perhaps two dozen people who occasionally interacted with other bands. There were strict bans on incest, so men selected their marriage partners from women in other local bands. Social and political relations among the Paleo-Indians were probably highly egalitarian, except for differences based on age or gender. Work, for example, was assigned by gender, with men hunting large game and women gathering nuts, berries, and other foods. The Paleo-Indians did not plant or store food and lived close to the edge of extinction.

With the end of the Ice Age, around 10,000 BCE, America's Paleo-Indians had to adapt to a world without the huge animals that had been their prey. As the earth warmed, three dozen classes of animals died, not only mammoths and mastodons but also 20-foot sloths and beavers the size of today's bear. The Paleo-Indians learned to hunt smaller game across a much smaller region, and tribes became less nomadic. They established base camps, crafted more sophisticated tools, and began storing some food, which helped them survive shortages.

As the Paleo-Indians became more efficient in hunting and gathering, they began to adapt the natural world to their needs, for example by periodically burning undergrowth to create an ideal environment for deer. By 3,000 BCE, some groups were beginning to cultivate native plants. The population in North America grew to perhaps 1 million. Although the Archaic Indians still lived in small groups of probably no more than 500, they became less egalitarian.

Changes in climate during the Archaic period led to other, more significant differences among Native American societies. Whereas the moist Eastern Woodlands area (generally, east of the Mississippi River) was hospitable to agriculture, the Plains region (between the Mississippi River and the Rocky Mountains) was arid. Plains Indians lived in small, mobile bands and pursued big game such as bison, elk, bear, and deer.

Further west, in the desert regions of the Great Basin and Southwest, Indians subsisted on small game and seeds. They domesticated several crops, including maize (corn) and chiles. Some groups started building pueblos and cliff dwellings as permanent homes.

On the California coast and in the Pacific Northwest, Archaic hunter-gatherers made use of the abundant natural resources, particularly fish. They also began to develop striking artwork. South of the Arctic Circle, Native Americans began to build the boats, weapons, and tools necessary to hunt whales and seals. Out of these regions—Eastern Woodlands, Plains, Great Basin and Southwest, California and Pacific Coast, and Subarctic—developed the distinctive cultures that European explorers later encountered. By the time of Columbus's voyage, Indian peoples were as different from one another as the peoples of Europe.

The Indians of the Eastern Woodlands

The woodlands east of the Mississippi River gave rise to several distinctive Native American cultures, including the Mississippian mound builders, centered at Cahokia (near present-day East St. Louis, Missouri). By 700 BCE, Indians in this area had begun to cultivate crops, and by the twelfth century, agriculture had spread over much of the area east of the Mississippi and into the Southwest. These Mississippian societies were distinguished by increasingly complex crafts, extensive trade networks, and a growing capacity to support large populations from agriculture. All of them built mounds in which to bury their dead and as platforms for temples and other public structures. The mounds can still be seen at

Cahokia, although the structures themselves and the people who worshiped in them have long since disappeared.

These societies were increasingly hierarchical in their political and social organizations. Some offices were probably hereditary, and large cities such as Cahokia (with a population of between 10,000 and 30,000) dominated smaller ones. When powerful people died, they were buried with luxury goods gathered through trade. (Cahokians of lesser rank were buried in mass graves, however.) Because mound builders buried these goods with the dead, they had to keep trading for new supplies. They also made exquisite metal and stone objects to bury with their dead and to trade to distant tribes.

Before the arrival of Europeans, Indian cultures flourished and also disappeared for reasons that are not fully known. Spanish explorers encountered mound-building Indians in the Southeast in the sixteenth century, but by the time the English arrived a century later, the mound builders had disappeared. Although these tribes were aggressive, their collapse does not seem to have been caused by warfare. Instead, preindustrial cities were probably "population sinks," that is, areas where densely packed populations without effective sanitation systems became breeding grounds for lethal diseases. Preindustrial peoples around the world always lived close to the edge of extinction, and a serious drought or epidemic disease could wipe out an entire population.

As the Mississippian cities were collapsing, other Indian cultures were rising to prominence in the Eastern Woodlands. The Iroquois occupied the southern Great Lakes region, and the Algonquians covered much of eastern Canada and the northeastern United States, as far south as Virginia. These two groups spoke different languages, but in many other ways, their cultures were similar. The Iroquois and Algonquians south of Canada practiced a slash-and-burn method of agriculture: clearing and burning forests for corn and other vegetables, planting them intensively, exhausting the soil, and then moving on to more fertile regions, where clearings once again were burned. This method of agriculture could not sustain as large a population as the fertile river valley cultivation of the mound builders; nonetheless, farming became increasingly efficient, making hunting less important. Because almost all agriculture was the work of women, their prestige increased.

Iroquois and Algonquian societies were more warlike than the Mississippians, although scholars are not certain why. One theory suggests that as agriculture became more

Image of Community of Cahokia The community at Cahokia, at eye level, as envisioned by a modern-day graphic artist. The town was surrounded by a stockade, which enclosed the mounds, plazas, temples, and homes.

efficient and women's prestige increased, men resorted to warfare to maintain their own prestige. By the eve of European settlement, many Iroquois tribes had banded together to limit infighting and to resist external enemies. Political influence within these cultures depended almost entirely on persuasion rather than force. Requiring the consent of all concerned, women included, made the Iroquois cohesive: by the time the Europeans arrived, the Iroquois were able to subdue internal violence, direct it outward, and keep interlopers at bay for more than two centuries.

The Indians of the Plains

The popular image of the Plains Indian comes from Westerns: the warrior on horseback, hunting bison. Plains Indians, however, did not have horses until after the Spanish reintroduced horses to the Great Plains in the sixteenth century (they had died out at the end of the Pleistocene epoch). Like Indians east of the Mississippi, Plains Indians became agriculturalists after the end of the Archaic period: women raised maize and other crops, while men hunted buffalo.

After the Spanish brought horses to the Plains, these Indians became nomadic, abandoning their multifamily lodges for tipis that could be carried from one campsite to the next. As buffalo became a more important part of their diet, women's prestige decreased, and men's grew.

The Indians of the Deserts

The arid landscape of the West and Southwest also shaped Indian cultures. Over the centuries, Indians learned to make maximum use of native plants such as the piñon and to cultivate increasingly productive strains of maize. The population remained relatively small, but by about 200 CE, villages began to appear. At that time, Southwestern Indians began to construct pit houses, round dwellings carved about a foot and a half into the ground with walls and roofs constructed out of mud-covered wooden frameworks.

After 700 CE, as the population grew, Southwestern Indians moved into adobe pueblos, such as the ones built on the surface at Chaco Canyon (in present-day New Mexico) and those carved into the cliffs at Mesa Verde (in present-day Colorado). Similar to Cahokia, Chaco Canyon was the center of a large population and a vast trade network. These huge complexes must have required the labor of well-organized work forces. Pueblo Bonito, the largest town at Chaco Canyon, contained more than 800 rooms and required 30,000 sandstone blocks to build. The surrounding area included 70 towns and 5,300 villages, with a total population of perhaps 15,000. The trade network of Anasazis, as they were called, reached south to Mexico (the source of copper bells) and west to the Gulf of California, from which seashells were obtained.

Like the cities of the eastern mound builders, the Anasazi communities at Chaco Canyon, Mesa Verde, and several other sites simply disappeared, from Chaco sometime after 1100 CE and from Mesa Verde in the last quarter of the thirteenth century. Archaeologists are not certain why, but recent theories suggest a combination of prolonged drought, the need to fight off outsiders, and a new religion that pulled people to the south and east, away from the dry climate and hostile neighbors. There they would build the Acoma, Hopi, and Zuni pueblos.

The Indians of the Pacific Coast

Along the California and northwest Pacific coast, plentiful fish, game, and edible plants permitted the population to grow even in the absence of agriculture. In California, the variety of local environments meant that each of 500 local cultures could concentrate on its own specialties, which it traded with its neighbors. The lush northwest coast provided such an abundance and variety of food that Indians were able to build up surpluses and create magnificent works of art such as totem poles and masks. Periodically, these Indians held potlatch ceremonies in which they gave away or even destroyed all their possessions. When Europeans first encountered this practice, they found it bizarre and even dangerous, so contrary was it to their own customs of accumulating wealth.

The Great Civilizations of the Americas

Although the Indian peoples north of the Rio Grande River were primarily agriculturalists or hunter-gatherers, several of those to the south developed much more complex political economies, technologies, and urban cultures. The splendid Maya civilization, which had developed both a writing system and mathematics, had dominated southern Mexico and Central America from the fourth to the tenth centuries. Historians do not know for certain why the Maya centers declined, but a change in climate or ecology might have made it impossible for Maya agriculture to support so large a population.

Another great empire in the region was that of the Toltecs, whose influence extended from central Mexico as far north perhaps as the cliff-dwelling Anasazis of the American Southwest. After the Toltec Empire was destroyed in the middle of the twelfth century by invaders from the north, the Aztec people dominated the region until their own defeat by a Spanish and Indian alliance. Elsewhere, other peoples were on the move, sometimes trading peacefully and other times attempting to wrest control of a new region. The powerful and complex Inca Empire in Peru had just reached its high point when the Spanish arrived.

The Worlds of Christopher Columbus

Imagine a world in which most people live in small villages, eat the food they hunt or raise themselves, and never travel more than a few miles from home. At the same time, others are on the move, especially traders, warriors, and people displaced by war and famine. The traders search the boundaries of the known world for better goods and new markets. The warriors aim at conquest. They seize land that others inhabit so their own people can move in. The traders and the warriors set the world and its peoples in motion.

Columbus came to the Americas as a trader and became a conqueror. In the process he introduced the ways of the Old World into the New World, changing both of them forever. The modern history of America begins in 1492 with the movement of all of these peoples, from the Old World and the New, on American terrain.

European Nations in the Age of Discovery

In 1492, Europe as we now know it did not yet exist. Many of what later became major European nations—Spain, Italy, Germany—were collections of small principalities, each owing its allegiance to a local ruler. Spain and Portugal had only recently been liberated from the Moors, a North African people who practiced the Muslim religion and who had invaded the Iberian Peninsula in 711. France and England were led by a single ruler, who still struggled with local feudal lords for control of the nation. European nation-states were being consolidated, each under the rule of a single leader, a hereditary monarch. In fact, not until a nation was unified under a strong leader could it turn away from internal struggles to the world beyond. As the first nations to be unified, Portugal and Spain were the first also to begin to explore and conquer foreign lands. The Netherlands, France, and England, unified about a century later, then followed. Germany and Italy, not unified until the nineteenth century, lagged far behind. The consolidation of European nations unleashed enormous energy, which put the Europeans in motion. The traders charted a way, first overland to China, and then by sea to Africa.

The Political Economy of Europe

The world's peoples have always traded with one another. However, between 1450 and 1750 new trade patterns were established that changed the face of the world. Previously, powerful empires had dominated trade in their regions (see Map 1–2). In the middle of the fifteenth century, Islamic traders, for example, linked parts of Europe, Africa, and Asia. Because trade was a relatively minor part of the world economy, it had a minor effect upon the political and social structure of the world.

Once western Europe began to dominate world trade, after 1450, it began to shape not only the world economy but also global social and political structures. The nations of western Europe established trade networks linking Europe, Africa, Asia, and the Americas. The inequalities between nations were heightened as wealth flowed first to Spain and Portugal and then to England, France, and Holland. As western European nations became wealthier and their economies more complex, those areas of America, Africa, and (to a lesser extent) Asia that were conquered or colonized became dependent on western trade, supplying the raw materials that made Europe wealthy. Increasingly, their own populations were exploited, even enslaved, and made to turn out gold, silver, sugar, and tobacco to feed the insatiable appetites of Europe.

When Christopher Columbus sailed west looking for Asia, he was trying to reestablish a European trade that had been disrupted by the Black Death; the bubonic plague had arrived from Asia in 1347. In the middle of the fifteenth century, as Europe began to recover from the plague, its population began to grow, the economy began to expand, and merchants, especially along the Mediterranean, began to look for new markets.

Most Europeans were peasants, many living close to destitution. Still, an increasingly prosperous elite (both the nobility and the affluent urban middle classes) developed a taste for luxury items such as sugar, spices, fabrics, and precious metals. They were dazzled by the Italian Marco Polo's accounts of his journeys between 1275 and 1292 to golden cities in India and China. The desire for luxury goods sent European explorers off in search of new routes to Asia.

By the middle of the fifteenth century, new technologies made it possible for Europeans to travel far from home. Some of these innovations were adapted from elsewhere—for example, gunpowder from China and the navigational compass from the Arabs. Others came from Europe, including better maps; stronger metal for guns and cannons; and the caravel, a swift ship well suited for navigating the coast of Africa.

Europe was on the move by the end of the fifteenth century. The Portuguese had begun exploring the Atlantic coast of Africa, searching for a water route to Asia. Portugal had recently driven out its Muslim conquerors. A small nation (about 1.5 million inhabitants, compared to almost 10 million for Spain), it had been unified by a strong king almost a century earlier. The combination of political unity, a strong and expansionist monarchy, and an aggressive merchant class seeking new markets enabled Portugal to become the first of the modern European imperial nations. By 1475, Portuguese explorers had reached the thriving kingdom of Benin on the lower Guinea coast (the modern country of Nigeria) and had established trading posts along the northwestern coast of the continent. In exchange for European goods such as horses, cloth, and wheat, the Portuguese received African luxury products such as ivory, and especially gold, that could be sold in Europe (Map 1–2).

Earlier in the fifteenth century, the Portuguese had begun raiding the Sahara coast for slaves. Once they opened trade with sub-Saharan Africa, however, they discovered that they could exchange goods directly with African kings for slaves. The Portuguese then resold the slaves, primarily for use as servants, in Africa or Europe. Until 1500, in fact, the Portuguese were shipping only between 500 and 1,000 slaves a year, most of whom were resold in Africa. However, with the opening of plantations (first in the Canary Islands, which the Spanish had conquered by 1496), the slave trade became an important part of the Portuguese economy.

The World of the West African Peoples

Starting with the Portuguese, European traders reached the west coast of Africa in the fifteenth century. There they found powerful and well-organized kingdoms, much like

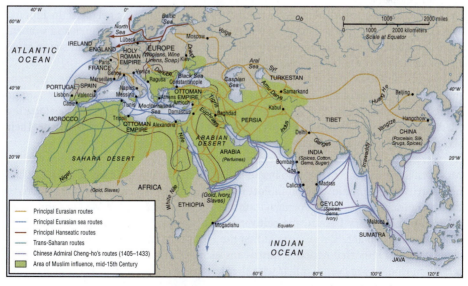

Map 1–2   World Trade on the Eve of Discovery   For a thousand years, world trade centered on the Mediterranean. European, Arab, and Asian traders crisscrossed much of the Eastern Hemisphere, carrying spices, silks, and cottons from Asia; linens, woolens, and wine from Europe; and gold and slaves from Africa.

the European states. Some of those states, especially those just south of the Sahara such as Mali and Songhay, had been influenced by Islam and had adopted its written language, Arabic. Others, such as the central African Yoruba kingdoms, were complex city-states that produced glorious works of art in bronze and ivory. The population density in Lower Guinea was higher than that of Europe.

Not all African peoples lived in states, however. Many were members of villages or family groupings without rulers or bureaucracies. Religious beliefs were similar among the African cultures, however, all recognizing a supreme creator and numerous lesser deities. Gender relations were similar, too, with most people living in extended, male-led families and clans, the basis for social order. Although men performed most of the heavy labor and women attended to domestic chores and childrearing, both men and women farmed. Men dominated government and commerce, but on occasion women from prominent families exercised power. Women were active as merchants as well.

Powerful kingdoms dominated commerce and welcomed trade with Europe, which supplied them with prestigious goods. Although Africans manufactured cloth, for example, European textiles found a ready market in Africa. In fact, those regions of Africa that already had thriving markets were the most eager to trade with Europeans. Soon African nations joined the international marketplace.

As in Europe, in Africa some kingdoms were increasing their dominance, whereas others were in eclipse. But such normal developments took on new meaning after the appearance of Europeans. In 1591 the defeat of the West African Songhay Empire by Moroccan invaders created an instability that offered unique opportunities for Europeans to profit.

Slavery Before 1500

The institution of slavery had a long history in both Europe and Africa. Slavery had been of limited importance in Europe, except in ancient Rome. The Roman Empire enslaved a number of the peoples it conquered, using them to raise food. At the height of the Empire, as many as 35 or 40 percent of its people were enslaved, or 2 to 3 million men and women. Unlike modern slavery, Roman slavery was not based on race, and Roman slaves came from many ethnic groups.

By the time Portugal began trade with West Africa, slavery had disappeared from northwestern Europe, although some slaves were being used in parts of Christian Europe along the Mediterranean. The Muslims who invaded Spain and other regions along the Mediterranean in the eighth century had brought their form of slavery with them. Their slaves worked as domestic servants and in the production of sugar.

Several centuries later, when they expanded their trade into regions controlled by Muslims, European merchants also began plying the trade in human beings. Slavery had been a relatively minor institution in Portugal, Spain, Sicily, Cyprus, and other regions of Mediterranean Europe. Once Portugal took over the Atlantic island of Madeira and Spain controlled the Canary Islands, the cultivation of sugar led to the creation of the much larger systems of plantation slavery. At first the Europeans enslaved native islanders, and soon after, they imported Africans. Europeans such as Columbus who traveled the Mediterranean would have been familiar with the slave trade and would have associated slavery with plantation agriculture.

As in Europe, slavery had been practiced in Africa from ancient times, although its character was different because of Africa's different political economy. In Europe, land was

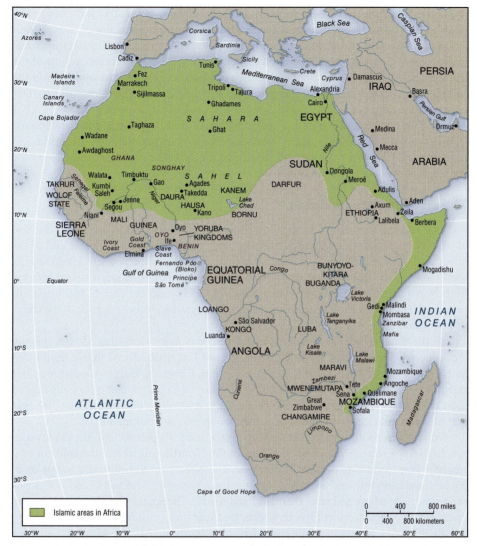

Map 1–3   Africa in the Age of Discovery Before 1450, Europeans knew little of Africa. Until that time, trade between Africa and Europe was controlled by Islamic traders whose empire extended across North Africa. In the middle of the 15th century, the Portuguese reached the western coast of Africa and began importing both trade goods and a small number of slaves. *Mark Kishlansky et al.,* Societies and Culture in World History *(New York: Harper Collins, 1995), p. 414.*

the primary form of private, wealth-creating property. In Africa, however, land and cattle were owned collectively, and the primary form of private, wealth-creating property was slaves. European law entitled the landowner to everything produced on the land, whereas African law entitled the slave owner to everything that the slave produced. The way to wealth in Africa was to acquire slaves, and in Europe, to acquire land.

In other ways, however, European and African slavery were similar. African slaves generally worked as domestic laborers, both in Africa and in other regions of the world where they were sold. Similar to European slavery, the status of the slave was not fixed by law, and the children of slaves might become free. African states sustained a vigorous internal slave trade. As the Islamic empire spread in the eighth century, Muslim merchants bought slaves in Africa, usually women and children, for export to other regions of the empire. The African slave trade thus had two components: an internal trade within the continent and an external trade run primarily by the Muslims. The Portuguese participated in both components.

Western and central Africans were accustomed to selling slaves, and they entered willingly into the global slave trade. By the seventeenth century, the high prices that Europeans were willing to pay for slaves stimulated the African slave trade and stripped the continent of much of its population.

The Golden Age of Spain

Portugal was the first nation in western Europe to achieve political unity and the first to embark on exploration in search of trade. Spain was the second. Until the end of the fifteenth century, the Iberian Peninsula was divided into five independent kingdoms. At one time, the entire Iberian Peninsula had been dominated by Muslims, who had invaded from North Africa in 711 and exerted a powerful influence in the region. Many Spanish people intermarried with Muslims, adopting their religion and customs, such as the seclusion of women.

At the time of the invasion, Arab civilization was more sophisticated than the one it conquered. Through the Muslims, Greek science was reintroduced into a region that had lost touch with much ancient learning. Muslim, Christian, and Jewish communities generally were able to coexist. Local leaders, however, for reasons that were political and economic as well as cultural and religious, contested Muslim rule and began a 700-year period of intermittent warfare known as the *reconquista*, or "reconquest."

Warfare was routine on the Iberian Peninsula, and it shaped society. The priests who proclaimed the *reconquista* a holy war against the Moorish infidel and the soldiers who waged it were elevated to positions of prestige. The surest path to wealth and honor lay in plunder and conquest, and a *hidalgo*'s (gentleman's) honor was defined by his capacity to vanquish the Muslims and seize their land and wealth. The Spanish hoped that the *reconquista* would be able to evict from their country those they considered infidels.

By the time Christopher Columbus arrived in Spain in 1485, the Muslims had been ousted from all of Spain except Granada. Castile and Aragon had recently been joined by the marriage of Isabel, princess of Castile, and her cousin Fernando, prince of Aragon. Although Isabel was only 18 when she married (and her husband a year younger), she had already shown herself to be a woman of boldness and determination. Because the match was more in Aragon's interest than in Castile's, Isabel was able to dictate the terms of the marriage contract, making it clear that she would play the leading role in governing. Having consolidated their power over their territories, Isabel and Fernando turned to the final stage of the *reconquista*.

By mobilizing their nobles against a non-Christian opponent, Isabel and Fernando were able to forge a Christian Spanish national identity that transcended regional loyalties. Herself exceedingly devout, Isabel had earlier inaugurated an Inquisition, a church tribunal authorized by the pope, to root out converted Jews and others who seemed insufficiently sincere Christians. By the end of the Inquisition, several hundred people had been burned at the stake and several thousand more imprisoned. When Spain finally conquered the Moorish province of Granada in 1492, militant Christians insisted on a forcible conversion of those Moors who chose to remain. The Christian conquest of the Moors led swiftly to the eviction of another religious minority, the Jews. Less than three months after the fall of Granada, Isabel and Fernando signed an edict calling for the expulsion of the approximately 150,000 Spanish Jews. The Spanish colonization of the Americas and the subjugation of their native peoples were simply the next chapters in the Spain of Isabel and Fernando, which defined itself by its ability to vanquish those labeled infidels.

It would be a mistake, however, to conclude that Spain was shaped by militarism and intolerance alone: In 1492, Spain was in the middle of its golden age. It was the most dynamic nation in Europe, and it soon became the most powerful. It welcomed and absorbed foreign influences, including Moorish art, science, and customs; Flemish art and architecture; and the Renaissance intellectual movement known as humanism, which was imported from Italy. Indeed, under the patronage of Queen Isabel, Spain became a center of humanism.

Spain's foray into the New World, both a commercial venture and a religious crusade, was also fueled by the humanist spirit of discovery. In establishing colonies in the New World, Spain spread her religion, her language, and her culture, creating a new political economy in the process.

Worlds in Collision

Christopher Columbus's voyages to the Americas marked the beginning of a new era. The world was made immeasurably smaller, and peoples who had lived in isolation from one another were brought into close contact. In this great age of European exploration, Bartolomeo Dias rounded the African cape in 1488, Vasco da Gama reached India in 1498, and an expedition led by Ferdinand Magellan (Fernão Magalhães, in Portuguese) sailed around the world between 1519 and 1522. These explorers were seeking not to discover new lands but to find faster routes to old ones. They were propelled by an expanding Europe's desire for trade and to spread the Christian religion. For the first time in human history, all of the world's great urban civilizations, from Tenochtitlán to Cathay, knew of one another's existence. Despite obvious differences in language, dress, architecture, art, and customs, Europeans, Africans, and Native Americans lived in political and economic organizations similar enough to make trade and diplomacy possible. Europeans drew the entire world into their trade network, and the Christian religion was spread by both force and persuasion.

Christopher Columbus Finds a Patron

Between 1492 and 1504, Columbus made four voyages to the New World for Queen Isabel and King Fernando of Spain. Born in 1451 in the Italian city-state of Genoa, Columbus first went to sea on merchant ships in the Mediterranean, later sailing to Portuguese outposts such as the Madeiras. Within a decade, Columbus had decided to seek support for a voyage to China and Japan, which he had read about in Marco Polo's book.

Columbus's ambitions were shaped by his reading and his extensive experience as a mariner. By his time, it was generally known that the world was round, but its precise dimensions had not been determined. Neither were Europeans certain about the lands to the east, but the search for wealth and national power fueled great curiosity about them. It was only a matter of time until Europeans headed west and bumped into America while attempting to circumnavigate the globe. Perhaps Columbus was the first (the Norse had planted a short-lived colony at Vinland 500 years earlier) simply because he mistakenly calculated that Japan was only 2,400 miles away from the Canary Islands, when in fact it is more than four times that distance away.

No private individual had the resources to finance such an expedition, so Columbus sought backing from the king of Portugal; when he turned him down, Columbus sought Spanish patronage from Isabel and Fernando. Even though scientists doubted his geography, the monarchs were intrigued by Columbus's vision of a western route to Asia.

The monarchy agreed to finance most of Columbus's trip (paying for it not, as legend has it, by pawning Isabel's jewels, but by the much more modern method of deficit spending) and granted him a number of powers and privileges. Columbus would realize his lifelong ambition of being made a member of the nobility. He was to be named admiral, viceroy, and governor-general of all the lands that he might find. After deducting for expenses, Columbus would keep one-tenth of the income from the enterprise, with the monarchy retaining the rest. The small amount spent on the voyages would prove to be one of the shrewdest investments in the history of nations.

Columbus Finds a New World

The obsessive quest for wealth took Columbus back and forth across the Atlantic four times between 1492 and 1504. He planted the Spanish flag on the modern islands of Cuba, Hispaniola, and Puerto Rico, as well as on the mainland at Honduras and Venezuela. The Spaniards who followed him onto the mainland eventually found among the Aztecs of Mexico and the Incas of Peru riches to match their most fantastic dreams. By then the patterns that shaped the next century of Spanish-Indian interaction in the Americas had been established.

Late-medieval Europeans tended to view the world in terms of opposites, which led them to exaggerate differences rather than see similarities or complexities. Columbus and later explorers typically described the lands they visited as an earthly paradise, even in the face of contrary evidence. By the time Columbus returned to Hispaniola on his second voyage, with 1,500 Spaniards, it was clear that his hopes of easy wealth and harmonious relations with the natives were not to be realized. Columbus had left 39 men on the island among the Taino Indian inhabitants and returned to find them all dead. According to the Taino chieftain, the sailors set off on a spree of gold seeking and debauchery, each of them "taking as many women and as much gold as he could," until they became easy victims for a rival Indian chieftain.

The Spanish could not see the death of their sailors as a predictable response to their behavior. Instead, they fit it into a growing view that all Indians could be divided into two groups: friendly, peace-loving, unsophisticated, "good" Indians, such as the Tainos, and fierce, savage, man-eating, "bad" Indians, for whom they used the Taino term "Caribs."

Historians and anthropologists have identified the Tainos and Caribs as two separate tribes. The Tainos, who inhabited the islands of Cuba and Hispaniola, were generally peace-loving farmers whose agriculture could sustain a population as dense as that of Spain. Taino farmers were accustomed to taking direction from their cacique, or leader; hence the Spanish could coerce the Tainos into working for them.

The Caribs were more aggressive. At the time of Columbus's arrival, the Caribs were moving north from the South American coast into the island chains of the Atlantic. If the Tainos were concerned with agriculture and religion, the Caribs focused on trade and warfare. Men and women lived separately, and because Carib men often obtained their wives by raiding other villages, they came to treat their own women as if they were captives of war. Because the Caribs were a maritime people with skilled warriors, it is not surprising that they came into conflict with another maritime people practiced in the arts of war, the Spanish.

Although the Spanish, like all the Europeans who followed them into the Americas, depicted themselves as civilized and the Indians as either gentle but primitive or savage and inhuman, the differences between Europeans and natives were not that great. Seven centuries of warfare with the Moors had made the Spanish a fierce people, and they believed that practices that later generations would condemn as cruel were justified for a people at war. Once the Spanish decided the Caribs were an enemy, they began to treat them harshly.

The Origins of a New World Political Economy

As early as Columbus's second voyage of 1493, it became clear that the vast treasures he had anticipated were not readily at hand. His crew, however, expected to be rewarded for their services, and the queen and king who had financed his expedition expected profits. Therefore, Columbus packed off more than 500 Indians to be sold as slaves and distributed another 600 or so among the Spanish settlers on the island of Hispaniola.

Once again a pattern of New World development had been established. The European quest for wealth led to the subjugation of native peoples. Generally, the Spanish rulers tried to restrain their New World colonizers and protect their new Indian subjects. In 1493, Pope Alexander VI confirmed Spanish dominion over all the lands that Columbus had explored and commanded the Spanish "to lead the peoples dwelling in those islands and countries to embrace the Christian religion." A papal bull (or proclamation) also

Taino Customs (Left) A young man introducing himself to the family of the young woman he wants to marry. (Right) The Tainos raising their crops in small, carefully kept gardens. These illustrations come from a manuscript thought to have been written by a Frenchman who traveled to the West Indies with Sir Francis Drake in the 16th century.

established the church's interest in the spiritual welfare of Native Americans. In the Treaty of Tordesillas of 1494, Spain and Portugal divided all lands already discovered or to be discovered along an imaginary line west of the Azores. The treaty formed the basis for Portugal's claim to Brazil, which her explorers reached in 1500.

As the monarch who had driven the Muslims out of Spain, Isabel took seriously her responsibilities to evangelize her Indian subjects. Isabel and her successors also had political and economic goals, all of which they attempted to reconcile by insisting that the Indians who inhabited the islands seized by the Spanish were vassals, subjects of the Spanish Crown. In this way, Isabel attempted to fit the Indians into the Spanish political economy.

Like other vassals in Spain and its growing empire, the Indians were technically free, although they could be required to both work and pay tribute to the Crown. Isabel instructed the governor to impose on them a European-style civilization. They were to be "made to serve us through work, and be paid a just salary," and in order to assure their salvation, "they must live in villages, each in a house with a wife, a family, and possessions, as do the people of our kingdoms, and dress and behave like reasonable beings." Humane treatment and freedom from slavery would depend on the Indians' willingness to abandon their religion and customs and adopt those of the Spanish. It is easy to be cynical about Isabel's motives, but her approach was considerably more benevolent that of other colonizers.

With the Spanish monarchy refusing to sanction the enslavement of friendly Indians, settlers had to devise an alternate means of getting labor from them. Out of this struggle a New World political economy emerged. For the first several years, the Spanish simply demanded tribute from the Tainos. Many of the Spanish found this arrangement insufficiently lucrative, and across the island of Hispaniola they began subduing individual caciques and compelling their villages to work for the Spanish. The settlers owned neither the land, which had to be obtained from Spanish officials, nor the Indians who worked for them. They possessed only the right to compel Indians to work. This system, called the *encomienda*, was unique to the New World. Technically it complied with Isabel's insistence that friendly Indians be made vassals of the Crown rather than slaves.

We do not know precisely how the system developed, although there is some evidence that Spanish men first seized native women as their concubines and that the village men subsequently worked for the Spanish, perhaps to remain close to their women. We often picture the encounter between Indians and Europeans as armed conflict between men. In truth, women often played a critical role in establishing a biracial society, as captives or as willing participants in a European way of life.

Columbus appears to have sanctioned this new system of labor, which received begrudging support from the monarchs in Spain. Although the system appeared to give due regard to their rights and spiritual requirements, Native Americans were subjected to overwork and abuse, even if they could not legally be bought and sold as slaves. Spanish settlers' desire to realize a profit in the New World led to a form of exploitation unknown in Europe.

The *Requerimiento* and the Morality of Conquest

Throughout Spain's New World empire, there were tensions between the colonizers, who wished to increase their wealth and enhance their power, and the Crown, which wanted to limit their autonomy. Moreover, both the Crown and the clergy continued to be troubled

AMERICA AND THE WORLD

>> Debating the Morality of Conquest

In 1550, Carlos V, the king of Spain, summoned two of the most important Catholic clerics in the nation, Bartolomé de las Casas and Juan Ginés de Sepúlveda, to debate the morality of conquest before the Council of the Indies. These two priests advocated two sharply different points of view. Las Casas, whose father sailed with Columbus on his second voyage and who himself later became an *encomendero*, was convinced by personal experience that "everything which has been done to the Indians is unjust and tyrannical." Sepúlveda was an eminent scholar and a nationalist whose defense of conquest had already won him the thanks of the municipal council of Mexico City.

The two adversaries did not meet face-to-face. Sepúlveda appeared first, resting his case on the innate barbarism of the Indians. Some people, he said, were born to be masters and others, slaves. He ridiculed the argument that the Aztecs were "civilized" because they built cities and engaged in commerce. So what if they built houses? This "merely proves that they are neither bears nor monkeys and that they are not totally irrational." War against such people could be justified "not only on the basis of their paganism but even more so because of their abominable licentiousness, their prodigious sacrifice of human victims . . . their horrible banquets of human flesh." Subjecting them to Spanish rule would be the most "beneficial" thing that could be done for them.

Then Las Casas was summoned for his rebuttal. He spoke for five days—in Latin— until the exhausted Council said they had heard enough. Warfare against the Indians was not justified, Las Casas argued. Instead, they could be won over by peaceful means, for they were "prudent and rational beings, of as good ability and judgment as other men and more able, discreet, and of better understanding than the people of many other nations." Las Casas denounced Sepúlveda's "deadly poison" and the greed of the Spanish, which "has led to such crimes . . . as have never been committed by any other nation, no matter how fierce it may have been." He feared that Sepúlveda's course would, in the end, provoke God to "pour forth the fury of his anger and lay hold of all of Spain sooner than he had decreed." The Spanish must convert the Indians, not conquer them.

Although the judges left without rendering a verdict, Las Casas's ideas prevailed. Las Casas had already helped shape the Laws of Burgos (1513) and the New Laws of 1542, which attempted to regulate the working conditions of the Indians and forbade any further enslavement of the native population. His influence can be seen in the next set of regulations, issued in 1573, written to govern Spain's future colonial ventures, which were to be called "pacifications" rather than "conquests." Henceforth, Indians were to be treated gently "so as not to scandalize them or prejudice them against Christianity." But because by that time Spain's New World empire was essentially complete, there were relatively few Indians left to conquer or to pacify.

continued

AMERICA AND THE WORLD *continued*

Sepúlveda argued for unlimited governmental power, but Las Casas's views were most useful to the monarchy. When Spain launched its overseas ventures, it was not even a nation itself. The century of Spanish expansion into most of South and Central America also saw the growth of national power in Spain. Las Casas's efforts on behalf of the Indians meshed nicely with the political plans of the Spanish monarchy for centralized state power. The *conquistadores* attempted to set themselves up as feudal lords, with almost unlimited control over the land and inhabitants in their possession, but with only limited obligations to the monarch. In insisting on humane treatment of the Indians, the Spanish monarchs were undercutting the authority of these local *encomenderos*. In this way, as well as by forbidding the establishment of local representative governments, the monarchy prevented the development not only of a New World feudal aristocracy, which might challenge its power, but also democratic habits of self-government and local autonomy—all in the name of humanity.

by the treatment of the Indians. To clarify the legal basis for the enslavement of hostile Indians, in 1513 the Crown issued the *Requerimiento*, or "Requirement," a document drafted by legal scholars and theologians. The *Requerimiento* promised the Indians that if they accepted the authority of Christianity, the pope, and the monarchs of Spain, the *conquistadores* (conquerors) would leave them in peace. If, however, the Indians resisted, the *conquistadores* would make war and enslave them. Henceforth, each *conquistador* was required to carry a copy of this document and to read it to every new group of Indians he encountered.

As with the *encomienda*, there is evidence that the *conquistadores* complied with the letter, but not the spirit, of the *Requerimiento* by mumbling it in Spanish to groups of uncomprehending Indians or reading it from ships, far from hearing distance. Moreover, the Crown provided no means of enforcement other than the good faith of the *conquistador* or *encomendero* (owner of an *encomienda*). Considering the profits that might be reaped by subjugating the population, perhaps what is most surprising is not the failure of the Crown to protect the Indians but that it kept trying.

The Biological Consequences of Conquest

Some of the most important changes produced by contact between Europeans and Native Americans were wholly unintentional. Each continent had its own diseases, its own plants, and its own animals. The arrival of Europeans tipped a delicate social balance in which everyone's effort was often needed to provide a food supply. The Europeans also introduced new diseases that spread rapidly. If the biological effects of human contact were felt immediately, however, the consequences of plant and animal exchange took much longer. New breeds of animals were introduced into the Americas, and plants were exchanged between the continents. The American landscape was changed, as domestic animals trampled grasslands and increasing acreage was turned over to the cultivation of Old World crops. This environmental transformation ultimately made possible the dramatic growth of the world's population, as new crops were cultivated.

Demographic Decline

Although the *encomienda* system satisfied Spanish settlers, it proved a disaster for the Indians. The agricultural methods of sedentary Indians such as the Taino could not produce the surplus necessary to support the Spanish. As soon happened to Indian communities throughout the Americas, the dislocation of their normal way of life proved deeply demoralizing, and the birthrate began to fall.

Within a few years after the appearance of Europeans, the Native American population began to decline, and the introduction of the smallpox virus to Hispaniola in 1518 hastened the process: soon no more than a thousand of the island's original half million inhabitants survived. Disease worked the same terrible destruction on the nearby islands of Cuba, Puerto Rico, and Jamaica. Disease followed the Spanish and other Europeans wherever they went in the Americas, making the work of conquest that much easier.

Europeans did not set out to kill off the Native Americans, but the diseases they brought with them did just that. Isolation had protected the native peoples from the diseases of the Old World, whereas centuries of trade had enabled Europeans, Africans, and Asians to share and acquire some biological defenses. Without such natural immunities, Indians were overcome by wave after wave of European disease, including smallpox, typhus, and influenza.

These terrible diseases challenged Native American belief systems. The Cakchiquel Indian Hernández Arana described the spread of a plague in his native Guatemala in 1521 that killed a substantial proportion of the community: "After our fathers and grandfathers succumbed, half of the people fled to the fields. The dogs and the vultures devoured the bodies. . . . Your grandfathers died, and with them died the son of the king and his brothers and kinsmen. So it was that we became orphans, oh, my sons! . . . We were born to die!" The shock turned Indians against their gods and prepared them to accept the god of the Spaniards.

The transmission of disease was by no means one way, although most diseases seemed to spread from the Old World to the New World. Historians have suggested that syphilis, or at least a particularly virulent strain, was carried back to Europe just after Columbus returned from his first voyage in 1493. The disease spread rapidly in the late fifteenth and early sixteenth centuries, from Spain to India, China, and Japan. Killing millions and incapacitating many more, syphilis became a legacy of the European age of exploration.

The Columbian Exchange

In what historians have called the Columbian exchange, plants and animals, as well as human beings and their diseases, were shared between the two worlds connected in 1492, eventually transforming them both. Along with the 1,500 Spaniards who joined him on

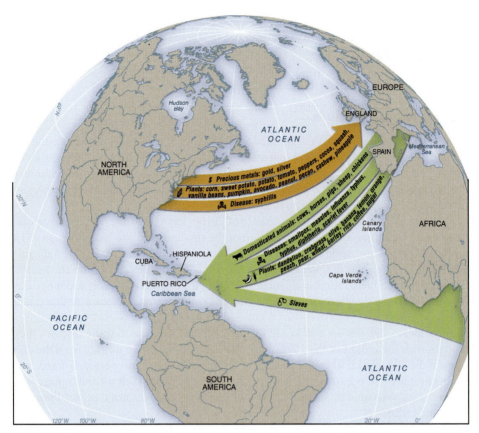

Map 1–4 The Columbian Exchange The exchanges of plants, animals, and diseases dramatically changed both the Old World and the New.

his second voyage, Columbus also brought pigs, cattle, horses, sheep, and goats, as well as sugarcane, wheat, and seeds for fruits and vegetables (see Map 1-4).

The introduction of these new plants and animals dramatically transformed the American landscape. Native agriculture was overrun by herds of Old World animals, which reproduced rapidly and destroyed both croplands and grassy regions. Indians adapted Old World life forms to their own purposes. American Southwestern and Plains Indian tribes took readily to the horse, which changed their way of life, making them more productive hunters and more dangerous enemies. Mounted Indians could easily kill more buffalo than they needed for their own subsistence, creating a surplus they could trade for European goods.

The Old World also was transformed by plants introduced from the Americas. Some plants that we associate with Europe came from the Americas. We might identify potatoes with Ireland, tomatoes with Italy, and paprika with Hungary, but none of these foods was produced in Europe before the sixteenth century. Moreover, the cultivation of American foods in the Old World, particularly potatoes and maize (corn), may well have made possible the dramatic growth in world population of the past five centuries (see Figure 1-1).

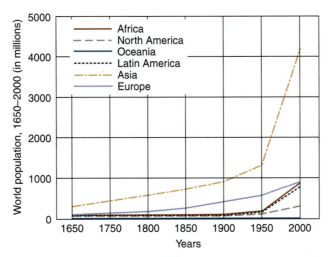

Figure 1–1   World Population, 1650–2000 These rough estimates of world population suggest the way that the colonization of the New World affected world population. The introduction of Old World disease led to population decline in the Americas, and the enslavement of millions of Africans led to population decline in Africa. At the same time, foods from the New World made possible the population increase of Europe and Asia. *Based on Alfred W. Crosby Jr.,* The Columbian Exchange: Biological and Cultural Consequences of 1492 *(Westport, CT: Greenwood Pub. Co., 1972), p. 166.*

Onto the Mainland

In a little more than a quarter of a century, the islands inhabited by the Tainos had been virtually emptied of their native populations. The Spanish began raiding the islands of the Lesser Antilles and seizing Caribs, transporting them back to the Spanish colonies as slaves. At the same time, other *conquistadores* pushed onto the mainland of America in search of treasure. Indians learned to tantalize the Spanish with accounts of glittering empires just a little further down the trail or up the river, just far enough away to get the Spanish out of their territories. Eventually, the Spanish found the Aztec empire in Mexico and the Inca empire in Peru, which rivaled the most fantastic images from literature and legend.

The First Florida Ventures

Ambitious Spaniards continued the search for paths to the Orient and cities of gold (see Map 1–5). Indians who resisted were treated brutally. As the Spanish moved rapidly in the quest for wealth, they disrupted local societies by purposefully spreading disease and undermining their political structures.

Juan Ponce de León was the first European explorer to set foot on the mainland that would later be called the United States. In March 1513 he reached the Atlantic shore of the land he named Florida, which he mistakenly thought was an island. He and his men sailed around Florida to its gulf coast, encountering hostile Indians who already knew about Spanish slave traders. On the west coast of Florida, he met the Calusas, the most powerful

Map 1–5 The Spanish Exploration In the 50 years after Columbus's first voyage, Spanish explorers traveled across most of the southern half of the United States.

tribe in the region. When Ponce de León returned in 1521, the Calusas attacked. He was wounded by an arrow and returned to Cuba to die.

In Florida, the diseases the Spanish brought with them struck the densely settled agriculturalists particularly hard. Later explorers routinely pillaged local villages and enslaved male Indians to carry their goods and females to serve as sexual partners, thereby destroying native populations in another way. Of the hundreds of small tribes, each with its own history, politics, economy, and culture, all that remains are the names that the Spanish recorded.

The Conquest of Mexico

Although the Spanish had continued to believe that vast and wealthy civilizations were to be found in the New World, until 1519 the only peoples they had encountered were small tribes who lived in villages of what the Spanish described as huts. They heard tales, however, of the glittering Aztec empire of central Mexico.

>> Tenochtitlán

When the Spanish reached Tenochtitlán, they found a city so beautiful that it "seemed like an enchanted vision." It may have been the largest city in the world at that time. In the center were Moctezuma's palaces, the public buildings, and huge temples sitting atop high platforms. All of these buildings were made of a glistening white stone, decorated in gold and surrounded by magnificent gardens, and all kept immaculately clean except for the blood from human sacrifices.

The society was arranged hierarchically, and the higher the status of the family, the better the housing. Aztec society was no more egalitarian than was Spain at the time. Nobles lived in well-decorated two-story stucco homes, whereas ordinary people inhabited more modest dwellings, with the those of the poorest built of wood and straw. Such houses were without any furnishings beyond reed mats for sleeping, a few cooking pots, and the stones on which the women in the family ground maize. Each home had several rooms opening onto a courtyard, where family activities took place, rather than on the street. Most people lived in family groupings—one or two families together—of 10 to 15 people. Married children often lived with the parents of either the bride or groom.

Work was assigned by gender. Every woman, whatever her age or class, spent much of the day weaving. Girls were taught by their mothers how to spin and weave and how to grind corn and prepare meals. Fathers taught their sons how to bring firewood and water back to the home and how to fish.

The heart of Tenochtitlán's economic life was the market at Tlatelolco, on the outskirts of town. It served 25,000 people daily, selling not only food, clothing, and household goods, but also luxuries such as feathers, gold, and precious stones. People sold their services, too, as barbers, fortune-tellers, scribes, and even prostitutes. Each kind of good and service was assigned its own section of the market, making it easier for customers to compare quality and price. The state regulated the market, setting an upper limit on prices and taxing each transaction. The state also assigned each group of artisans their own residential neighborhood, with separate districts for featherworkers, stoneworkers, gold- and silversmiths, and so on.

The Aztec people had moved into the valley of Mexico only two centuries earlier, but by the time the Spanish appeared, their empire encompassed perhaps 10 or 20 million people, a population possibly twice as large as Spain's. In several ways, the Aztecs resembled the Spanish: they were fierce, warlike, and deeply religious. Despite many differences in culture, the Spanish recognized in the Aztecs signs of a complex civilization. The Aztecs had built as many as 40,000 temples, and many of these buildings, like the palaces of the nobility, were quite splendid. Aztec society was rigidly hierarchical, with a nobility of warriors and priests at the top and slaves (usually captives of war or debtors) at the bottom. Sex roles were rigid, as well, with women of all classes expected to remain in the home. In separate schools, boys learned the arts of war, and girls practiced the skills of the homemaker. The Aztecs were literate, writing in a form of hieroglyphics on folded animal hide.

The capital city of Tenochtitlán was built on a lake, traversed with canals; Spaniards said that it reminded them of Venice. With a population of 200,000, it was more than three times the size of Spain's largest city of Seville. Its whitewashed stone pyramids, glittering temples, and clean, straight avenues stood in stark contrast to the typical cramped and dirty Spanish town.

The Aztecs believed that the universe was dangerous and unpredictable and that their gods must always be appeased. During a serious drought about 1450, the Aztecs feared that their god Huitzilopochtli was angry with them. When they offered him human hearts, cut out of the living with obsidian knives, the drought lifted. From then on, the pace of human sacrifice quickened. The more victims the Aztecs sacrificed, the greater their empire seemed to become, and the more they fought and conquered neighboring peoples, making them eager allies for the Spanish.

Hernán Cortés came with conquest in mind. He landed on the Yucatán coast with 500 men in February of 1519. After the Tabasco Indians were defeated, they gave him all their gold and 20 slave women, one of whom was Malinche, Cortés's translator. As Cortés marched toward Tenochtitlán, he picked up so many Indian allies that they greatly outnumbered his own troops. When they reached the Aztec capital in 1521, the ruler, Moctezuma, welcomed them, in the Aztec custom of offering hospitality to visiting emissaries. The foreigners soon placed Moctezuma under house arrest and Tenochtitlán under siege. Three months later, the victorious Spanish entered the city, but the proud Aztecs refused either to fight or to submit to the Spanish. Frustrated and angry, Cortés and his troops killed 12,000 and let their Indian allies slaughter 40,000 more. Then Cortés turned his cannons on the remaining starving masses. By the time of surrender, the once-glittering city was in ruins.

The Establishment of a Spanish Empire

The ruined city became the center of a Spanish empire, its economy based on silver, gold, and plantation crops. In the next decades, after the Spanish defeated another complex civilization, the Incas of Peru, as well as many other tribes of Indians, the Spanish ruled from the southern tip of South America to halfway up what is now the United States, excepting only the Portuguese colony of Brazil and some Caribbean islands. Finally, when the Indians' stores of gold and silver ran out, the Spanish began using slave labor to mine more.

After silver and gold, sugar was the next most important product of the New World, and as its cultivation spread, so did the demand for labor. By the second half of the sixteenth century, Indian laborers had been replaced by African slaves. In this way, Africans became yet another commodity to be transported across the seas, transforming the New World, robbing Africa of its population, and making the Old World rich. Once other European nations saw the great wealth the Spanish were extracting from their colonies, they established their own colonies that came into conflict with the Spanish.

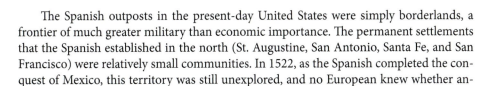

The Spanish outposts in the present-day United States were simply borderlands, a frontier of much greater military than economic importance. The permanent settlements that the Spanish established in the north (St. Augustine, San Antonio, Santa Fe, and San Francisco) were relatively small communities. In 1522, as the Spanish completed the conquest of Mexico, this territory was still unexplored, and no European knew whether another awe-inspiring civilization might yet be found.

Gender and Conquest

Every society has its own notion of the proper relationship between the sexes, and this is one of the ways it establishes order. When one society conquers another, not only do different gender orders come into conflict, but gender itself is one of the instruments of conquest. For Christopher Columbus, indigenous women were curiosities, objects of conversion, and commodities. On one island, the women "went around as naked as their mothers bore them"; on another, they "wore in front of their bodies a little thing of cotton that scarcely covers their genitals." Such women were "very respectful," and Columbus thought that with proper instruction in their own language, "soon all of them would become Christian."

Yet Columbus thought nothing of seizing friendly native women to bring back to Spain, believing they would ensure the good behavior of captive male relatives. Hostile women could be seized as the spoils of war. Columbus's men also seized native women on their own. Raping subjugated women is one of the ways that conquerors demonstrate their dominance.

Not all encounters between European men and native women were so violent, however.

In more complex Indian societies, such as those Cortés encountered in Mexico, indigenous people were accustomed to using marriage to cement alliances between prominent families, a practice among European nobility as well. Thus, after Cortés defeated the

Defeat of the Tlaxcalans Here, Malinche stands next to Cortés, receiving the Tlaxcalan women who have been presented to them as gifts by their defeated people.

Tlaxcalans, whose kingdom stood on the path to the Aztec city of Tenochtitlán, the Tlaxcalans handed over a number of women as part of the peace offering. A page from a Tlaxcalan codex (a pictorial account painted on a folding piece of bark or paper) illustrates the
ceremony. In the picture, Cortés sits in a chair, his officers behind him. In front of him is
the Tlaxcalan leader, also backed up by his nobles. Malinche stands next to Cortés, speaking to Tlaxcalan women. They include elegantly dressed princesses, intended as wives for
the Spanish leaders. Next are daughters of lesser nobles, and below them commoners,
intended as slaves.

Several decades later, the names and fates of some of these elite women could still be
remembered. Tleucuiluatzin, the daughter of Xicotencatl the Elder, was renamed Doña
Luisa and given to Pedro de Alvarado, Cortés' second-in-command. Although he had a
Spanish wife, he took Luisa as his mistress. She bore him three children. Their daughter
married another *conquistador*, and one of their sons died fighting in Peru.

The offspring of the Spanish conquerors and their noble Indian consorts created a
New World *mestizo* (mixed-race) elite in which rank was more important than ethnic
origin. In fact, the Crown encouraged intermarriage in order to speed the conversion of
the Indians and to assist the Spanish in ruling a conquered people. The first generation of
elite *mestizo* sons, including Malinche's son Don Martín Cortés, were brought up in their
fathers' households and sent to Spain for their education.

The necessity of forging alliances with conquered rulers ensured that Indian daughters who were given to the conquerors continued to hold high status, although sometimes
at great personal cost. After the defeat of the Aztecs, Moctezuma's daughter Isabel was
forced to become the mistress of Cortés, who was responsible for the deaths of her father
and husband. When he was finished with her, he passed her on to one of his lieutenants.

Conquest enhanced the power of the conquerors, including power over subjugated
women. Such was the power of the conquerors that they assumed they could have all the
native women they wanted, whether princesses turned over by their fathers or common
women seized by force.

The Return to Florida

The Spanish resumed their exploration of Florida with heightened expectations. There
were several ventures, the most significant led by Lucas Vázquez de Ayllón, Pánfilo de
Narváez, and Hernando de Soto. In 1526, Ayllón explored the South Carolina coast and
established a short-lived town on the coast of Georgia. Two years later, Pánfilo de Narváez
landed near modern-day Tampa Bay with 400 men and the king's commission to explore,
conquer, and colonize Florida. Eight years later, a Spanish slaving expedition found the
only four survivors of the failed expedition.

The Spaniard who left the greatest mark on the southeastern part of the United States
was a classic *conquistador*. Hernando de Soto had participated in the assault on the Inca
empire in Peru, which provided him with a small fortune and the belief that more wealth
could be found in Florida. He and his forces landed near Tampa Bay in 1539 to explore
and settle the region. His party spent four years exploring the southeastern part of the
continent, which was densely populated by Mississippian tribes. (Hernando and his company of 600 soldiers were the first Europeans to see the Mississippi River.)

Hernando de Soto came equipped for conquest. He took whatever food, treasure,
and people he wanted on his journey. Some Indian communities fought back fiercely,
whereas others attempted to placate the invaders. De Soto made his way through the South-

Timucua Indians, 1591 Here they celebrate the defeat of the enemy.

east, plundering and battling, his forces slowly diminishing. In May 1542, de Soto died. The remnants of the expedition, 300 men and one female servant, took almost a year and a half to return to Mexico.

The Spanish never found the great sought-after treasure, and because the land did not seem suitable for the large-scale agriculture of the *encomienda*, Spain never colonized most of de Soto's territory. Instead, military outposts, such as St. Augustine, were established to protect the more valuable lands to the south. To prevent rival nations from claiming the northern reaches of its empire, Spain did not disclose the geographical information it had secured from expeditions like de Soto's. This secrecy ultimately weakened Spain's claim to the region, because such claims traditionally depended on the right of prior exploration.

The impact of the expedition on the Mississippian Indians is difficult to determine. Their towns had begun to decline in the middle of the fifteenth century, before the arrival of Europeans. European diseases certainly hastened the process. The Spanish also disrupted the Mississippian political economy. Hernando de Soto's custom of capturing chieftains undermined their leadership, and losses incurred in battles made it impossible for the rulers to command tribe members to produce the food surplus and build the huge mounds that sustained the social order. After the appearance of the Spanish, no Indian civilizations would be able to match the power and sophistication of the Mississippians.

Coronado and the Pueblo Indians

As de Soto was attempting to conquer the Southeast, another group of Spaniards was setting out for the Southwest. They had heard tales of a city of Cíbola, supposedly larger than Tenochtitlán, where temples were decorated with gems. In May 1539, a party led by the Moorish slave Estevanico, one of four survivors of the Narváez expedition, reached the city, which was actually the pueblo of Zuni in New Mexico. The inhabitants recognized Estevanico as hostile and killed him. A year later, another aspiring *conquistador*, Francisco Vázquez de Coronado, arrived at Zuni with 300 Spanish, 1,000 Indian allies, and 1,500 horses and pack animals. They took the pueblo by force and later traveled west to the Grand Canyon and east as far as Wichita, Kansas, coming within 300 miles of de Soto's expedition.

Unprepared for the cold winter of 1540–1541, Coronado's party depleted the food supplies of the Indians near the Bernalillo camp. Some Spaniards literally took the clothes off the backs of their Indian hosts; when one Spaniard raped an Indian woman, the Pueblos rebelled. By the time the uprising was put down, 100 Indians had been burned at the stake, and 13 or so villages had been destroyed. This was the first of a number of Indian revolts; they continued until the Apache leader Geronimo surrendered to the United States Army in 1886.

>> Timeline

▼1434
Portuguese arrive at West Coast of Africa

▼1488
Bartolomeo Dias rounds Cape Horn

▼1492
Spanish complete the *reconquista*, evicting Moors from Spain
Jews expelled from Spain
Columbus's first voyage to America

▼1493
Columbus's second voyage

▼1494
Treaty of Tordesillas divides New World between Spain
    and Portugal

▼1496
Spanish complete conquest of Canary Islands

▼1497
John Cabot arrives in North America

▼1498
Vasco da Gama reaches India
Columbus's third voyage to America reaches South American coast

▼1500
Portuguese arrive in Brazil

▼1504
Columbus's fourth voyage to America ends

▼1508
Spanish conquer Puerto Rico

▼1513
Spanish *Requerimiento* promises freedom to all Indians who accept
    Spanish authority
Spanish conquer Cuba
Ponce de Léon reaches Florida
The Laws of Burgos attempt to regulate working conditions
    of Indians

▼1518
Spanish introduce smallpox to New World

>> **Timeline** *continued*

▼1521
Ponce de León returns to Florida
Cortés lands on Yucatán coast

▼1519–1522
Ferdinand Magellan's crew sails around the world

▼1521
Tenochtitlán falls to the Spanish

▼1526
Ayllón explores South Carolina coast and establishes fort in Georgia

▼1528
Narváez explores Florida

▼1534–42
Jacques Cartier makes three trips to Canada for France

▼1539
Estevanico arrives at Zuni

▼1539–1543
De Soto and his party explore Southeast, arriving at Mississippi,
    devastating the Indians and their land

▼1540–1542
Coronado explores Southwest

▼1542
The New Laws ban further enslavement of Indians

Conclusion

Within a half century after Columbus's arrival in the New World, both the world he had come from and the one he had reached had been transformed into a new, global political economy (see Map 1–6). Spain, the first of the major European states to achieve unity, dominated exploration, colonization, and exploitation of the New World. The wealth that Spain extracted from her colonies encouraged rival nations to enter into overseas ventures. Eventually France, England, the Netherlands, Sweden, and Russia also established New World colonies, but because Spain (along with Portugal, which claimed Brazil) had such a head start, rival nations would have to settle for the lands Spain left unclaimed. Spain and Portugal had demonstrated that great wealth could be obtained from the New World.

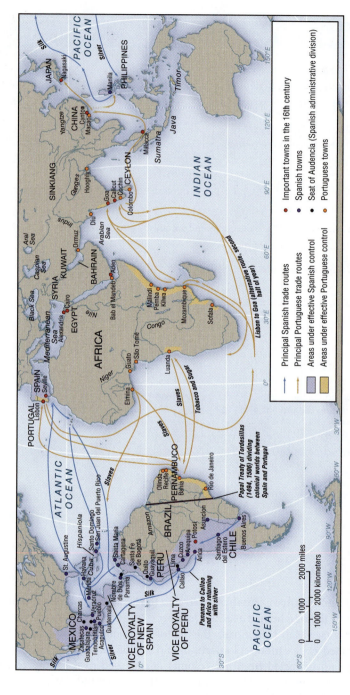

Map 1-6 A New Global Economy By 1600, both Spain and Portugal had established empires that reached from one end of the globe to the other.

In the shadow of this dream of unprecedented wealth, a new global economy was established, linking the Old and the New Worlds. Gold and silver extracted from its empire sustained Spain's rise to power, and the plantation crops of the New World would make many Europeans wealthy. From the beginning, the Spanish enslaved Indians to work the mines, farms, and plantations. As the native populations were depleted and the morality of enslaving native populations was questioned, the Spanish turned to African slaves.

Review Questions

1. Describe the development of Indian civilizations in North America from Archaic times until 1500. What were the major forces of change within these early populations?

2. What were the major similarities among European, Native American, and African societies? The major differences?

3. What were the forces that led Europeans to explore the New World?

4. What did the Spanish expect to find in the New World? How did their experiences alter their expectations?

5. What was the impact of European conquest on the population and environment of the New World?

For further review materials and resource information, please visit www.oup.com/us/ofthepeople

Colonial Outposts

1550–1650

>> Don Luís de Velasco Finds His Way Home

The Spanish gave him the name of Don Luís de Velasco. His own people, the Powhatan Indians of the Virginia coast, knew him as Paquiquineo. The son of a chieftain, he was a young man, perhaps still a teenager, when the Spanish picked him up in 1561 somewhere south of his home. The Europeans often abducted young Indians and took them back to their own nations so that they could serve as translators and guides. Sometimes the process worked the other way around, and Europeans who were members of trading or exploring expeditions were accidentally left behind. To survive, they learned the Native Americans' language and customs. If and when they were ever reunited with their countrymen, they were valuable as interpreters. In the early years of colonization, those who had learned the ways of another culture gained influence far out of proportion to their numbers.

Don Luís did not see his own people again for 10 years. First the Spanish took him to Mexico, where Dominican friars baptized and educated him. Later, Jesuit priests in Havana pronounced Don Luís "well educated," quite a compliment coming from a religious order known for its intellectual achievements. The young convert was taken to Spain, where he became one of King Felipe II's favorites, and then back to Havana, where he persuaded the priests to let him establish a Christian mission among his own people on the North American mainland.

In 1570, less than a week after the Jesuits and their Indian convert had settled in Virginia, Don Luís returned to his own people and customs. He scandalized the Jesuits by taking several wives, a privilege of Indian men of high rank. The Jesuits had expected Don Luís to act as an intermediary with his people, securing them supplies and favorable treatment, but they had misjudged him. Soon they exhausted their supply of food and had to beg from Don Luís. But Don Luís was being pressured by his own people to prove his loyalty. They were suspicious of someone who had been away so long and returned with arrogant foreigners who demanded food during a drought.

>> **AMERICAN PORTRAIT** *continued*

Don Luís had to make a choice, and he chose his native people. Powhatans killed eight of the nine missionaries. According to Indian custom, one of the victims, a young Spaniard named Alonso, was spared, although Don Luís argued for his death also. Knowing that the Spanish would someday return, he wanted no witnesses. As Don Luís predicted, the Spanish came back a year and a half later. They retrieved Alonso, ordered Don Luís to appear for an inquest, and began trying and executing other Indians when he failed to appear. Don Luís never returned to the Spanish. At these proceedings, Alonso acted as an interpreter.

In 1607 the English planted their first permanent colony on the mainland at Jamestown among Don Luís's people. Don Luís might well have been alive to greet these new foreigners. Throughout the seventeenth century, the English heard rumors about a Powhatan Indian who had spent time in the Spanish colonies.

The memory of the Europeans lived on among the Powhatans. Before they established settlements, the English, French, and Spanish all explored the North American coastline. In the process, Indians and Europeans learned each other's languages and customs. During this period of American history, no sharp geographic or cultural line separated the Indians and Europeans. Indians such as Don Luís lived among the Europeans, and Europeans such as Alonso spent time with the Indians. Even before permanent colonies were established each group knew the other moderately well. Although the customs and practices of the other group often seemed odd and even ungodly, they were never fully foreign.

Common Threads

>> Although they were all European nations, the empires of Spain, France, Holland, and England all developed in different ways. Why?

>> Why did each nation have a somewhat different relationship with Native Americans?

>> What did it mean for the English in North America that they came late to the business of establishing an overseas empire?

>> Chart the paths that each nation took toward offering greater freedom for some groups and less freedom for others.

Pursuing Wealth and Glory Along the North American Shore

The search for wealth and national prestige soon propelled other European nations across the Atlantic. In the minds of European leaders, wealth, glory, and power were almost inseparable. As the English explorer Sir Walter Raleigh explained the principles of political economy, "Whosoever commands the sea commands the trade; whosoever commands the trade of the world commands the riches of the world, and consequently the world itself." Most of the North American colonies established by European nations in the first half of the seventeenth century were outposts in the global economy. Despite significant differences, these colonies all shared certain factors: First, they were intended to bring in the greatest amount of revenue at the lowest cost. Second, success depended on harmonious relations with—or elimination of—local Indians. Third, colonial societies slowly developed their own distinctive patterns, depending on which route they followed to prosperity.

European Objectives

At first Europeans believed that Columbus had reached Asia by an Atlantic route. By the time they understood that he had discovered a new land, the Spanish were well on their way to conquering native peoples and stripping them of their wealth. Their success inspired other European nations to search for new sources of gold and silver in the regions Spain had not yet claimed. They also continued to seek a path through the Americas to Asia. Colonization was not a goal for almost a century, and even then colonies were designed to provide a quick return on investment, not to transplant Europeans onto foreign soil.

For many years the nations of northern Europe were unwilling to invest in permanent settlements. A foreign colony was costly. It involved procuring and provisioning a ship, providing a settlement with food and equipment, and resupplying it until it could turn a profit. Spain had been lucky: Isabel and Fernando's risk paid off relatively quickly. The northern European nations could not afford such expeditions, however, and, except for the most adventurous, exploration for its own sake had little appeal.

Tales of wealth and adventure in New Spain spread throughout Europe, nonetheless. Would-be explorers and *conquistadores* began to sell their services to the highest bidder. John Cabot, who sailed for England, was, like Columbus, born in Genoa, Italy. Before coming to England, he had spent time in Muslim Arabia, Spain, and Portugal, apparently looking for sponsors for a voyage to Asia. He found them in the English port city of Bristol, from whence he sailed in 1497. He landed in North America, possibly at Newfoundland, and claimed the territory for England.

Although England was slow to follow up this claim to American territory, soon both England and France sent fishing expeditions to the waters off Newfoundland (see Map 2–1). The population of northwestern Europe exploded in the sixteenth and seventeenth centuries, creating an increased demand for fish, and fishing expeditions to Newfoundland were relatively inexpensive to sustain.

The French colony of New France, planted in the St. Lawrence River region of Canada, grew out of the French fishing venture off Newfoundland. Early French explorers discovered neither gold nor a Northwest Passage to Asia. French fishermen, however, found that the Indians were willing to trade beaver pelts at prices so low that a man could make a fortune in a few months' time.

The Huge Geographical Barrier

At first, North America had seemed little more than an obstacle on the way to Asia. In 1522 Ferdinand Magellan's expedition had completed the first round-the-world voyage for Spain, proving finally that one could get to the East by heading west. Other nations

Map 2–1 North Atlantic Trade Routes at the End of the Sixteenth Century Hundreds of entrepreneurs from England, France, and Portugal sent ships to fish off the coast of Newfoundland to feed the growing population of Europe. The fur trade grew out of the Newfoundland fishing enterprise when fishermen who built winter shelters on the shore began trading with local Algonquian Indians (green lines). At the same time, European cities sent food, cloth, and manufactured goods to New Spain in return for gold and silver (red lines). After 1580, the Portuguese began transporting slaves from Africa to sell in Brazil and New Spain (yellow lines). *D. W. Meinig,* The Shaping of America *(New Haven, CT: Yale University Press, 1986), vol. 1, p. 56.*

then became interested in finding a way through, rather than around, North America. Two years after Magellan's voyage, the Italian Giovanni da Verrazano sailed for France. He explored the coast from South Carolina to Maine and was the first European to see New York harbor. To Europeans, however, all that Verrazano had discovered was a huge barrier between Europe and Asia.

On that "huge barrier" of North America lived Indians, some wary and some friendly. Unfamiliar with Indian customs, Europeans often could not distinguish hospitality from malice. When Algonquian Indians attempted to dry out one of Verrazano's sailors, who had almost drowned, by setting him near a campfire, Verrazano feared that they "wanted to roast him for food." In the early years of exploration, survival often depended on local Indians, yet because the French were looking either for treasure or for a Northwest

Passage, they tended to see cultural differences rather than similarities. Europeans noticed similarities only in search of trade or alliance.

Between 1534 and 1542, King François I of France financed Jacques Cartier to make three expeditions to seek a route through North America and to look out for any riches along the way. All three came to naught. On their second trip, the French sailed up the St. Lawrence River as far as the town of Hochelaga (near present-day Montréal). The Iroquois there spoke of a wealthy land to the west. Although the Iroquois may have been trying to deceive the French, it is possible that the shiny metal they spoke of was the copper that the Hurons to the west mined and traded. The winter was brutal. Even with food and care from the Indians, at the end of the winter almost a quarter of the party was dead. The French found that their survival depended on the native peoples.

Later expeditions failed as badly. The region was remote. The French quarreled with their Indian hosts and fought among themselves. Although their early attempts at colonization failed, the French were demonstrating that European claims to the Americas would rest on exploration, conquest of the natives, and colonization. Needless to say, this principle of European colonialism was established without the consent of the Indians who inhabited the land.

Spanish Outposts

Throughout the sixteenth century, European nations jockeyed for power on the continent. Because most of these nations were at war with each other, North America was often a low priority. But when the fighting in Europe abated, the Europeans looked across the Atlantic in hopes of gaining an advantage over a rival nation or finding a new source of wealth.

Soon the French and English, who found no gold or jewels along the coast, discovered an easier source of wealth—stealing from the Spanish. Every season, Spanish ships laden with treasure seized in Mexico and South America moved out of the Caribbean into the Atlantic and north along the coast until they caught the trade winds home. By the middle of the sixteenth century, French ships were lying in wait off Florida or the Carolinas. Because it was cheaper than exploration, preying on Spanish ships became a national policy.

To prevent these costly acts of piracy, King Felipe II established a series of forts along both coasts of Florida. At the same time, a group of Huguenots (French Protestants) established a colony, Fort Caroline, near present-day Georgia. For the new Spanish commander, Pedro Menéndez de Avilés, the task was to destroy the French settlement. On a September morning in 1565, 500 Spanish soldiers surprised the French at Fort Caroline. Although the French surrendered and begged for mercy, they were slaughtered. The religious and nationalist conflicts of Europe had been transplanted to North America (see Map 2–2).

Menéndez established a string of forts; one of them, St. Augustine, settled in 1565, is the oldest continuously inhabited city of European origin on the United States mainland. Most of Menéndez's ambitious plans for Spanish settlements were undermined by local Indians whom the Spanish alienated. After attacks by the Orista Indians in 1576 and by England's Francis Drake a decade later, the Spanish abandoned all of their Florida forts except St. Augustine. Spanish dreams of an empire in this part of North America had been

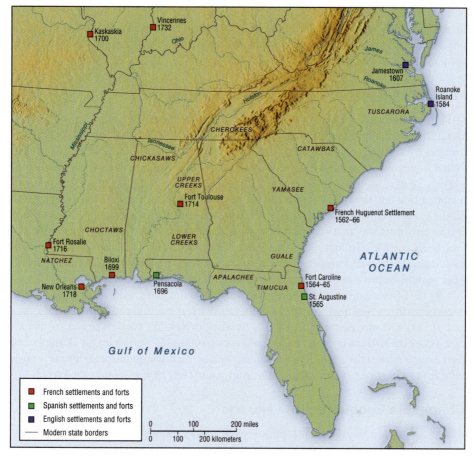

Map 2–2   European Colonization of the Southeast Beginning in the second half of the sixteenth century, the French, Spanish, and English established settlements in the Southeast. *Charles Hudson,* The Southeastern Indians *(Knoxville: University of Tennessee Press, 1976), pp. 430–431.*

reduced to a small coastal garrison. Although the Spanish would later establish other missions in Florida, their presence was peripheral to Spain's American empire.

New France: An Outpost in the Global Political Economy

The Spanish had given up hopes of an empire along the Atlantic coast of North America, but they had succeeded in scaring off the French. After the massacre at Fort Caroline, the French turned their focus to the St. Lawrence region. By the beginning of the seventeenth century the French had discovered a new way to make a profit in North America. French fishing crews, working off Newfoundland, traded for beaver pelts with the Abenaki Indians. These pelts found a ready market in Europe, where they were turned into felt hats.

A trade that began almost as an accident soon became the basis for the French empire in modern-day Canada. The French were drawing the Indians into a global economy, a process that dramatically changed not only the world of the North Americans but that of the Europeans as well.

The Indian Background to French Settlement

The French intruded on a region where warfare among Indian tribes had been widespread. Here, Iroquois culture groups were almost always at war, but casualties, unlike those in European wars, were generally light. These fights were blood feuds called mourning wars. When a member of a clan was lost in battle, his tribesmen, encouraged by his tribes-women, sought revenge on the enemy clan, either killing a warrior or seizing one and adopting him into the tribe to replace the dead clan member. The mourning war sought to fill the space in tribal society caused by the loss, either actual or emotional, of a member. If the clan's grief was particularly great, many captives might be necessary to repair the loss. Such warfare also focused violence outward. The cruelty that Indians practiced on their enemies shocked Europeans, whose own societies were quite brutal. Unlike in European society, violence and even crime *within* the clan was almost unknown.

By the fifteenth century, the mourning war was taking too great a toll among the Iroquois of northern New York. There, the five tribes living south of the St. Lawrence River and east of Lake Ontario, primarily in what is now upper New York State, created an alliance called the Five Nations or Great League of Peace (see Map 2–3). The league strengthened the Iroquois against their traditional enemies, such as the Algonquians and Hurons, a powerful Iroquoian tribe not a member of the league, and their new adversary, the French.

Champlain Encounters the Hurons

After Cartier's last voyage in 1541, the French waited more than half a century before again attempting to plant a settlement in Canada because they were preoccupied with a brutal civil war. In 1594, Henry of Navarre, a Huguenot, emerged the victor, converted to Catholicism, and in 1598 issued the Edict of Nantes, which granted limited religious toleration to the Huguenots. The French could once again look to North America.

The French had continued to fish off Newfoundland, sending ships to the mainland to trade for beaver pelts. The French Crown now realized that commerce with the Indians could increase its power and wealth. Several early ventures to establish a permanent settlement failed, but in 1608, Samuel de Champlain and a small band retraced Cartier's route up the St. Lawrence River and established a post at Quebec (see Map 2–4). Champlain, after several attempts, finally established the first French foothold in Canada, created a trading network along the St. Lawrence River, and learned how to live among people with a culture different from his own.

As the French government provided them with little support, Champlain's party depended on the aid of their Montagnais Indian (an Algonquian tribe) hosts. To survive in New France they had to adapt to Indian customs and assist their Indian benefactors in wars against their enemy. Killing the enemy in warfare was relatively easy for an experienced soldier such as Champlain. Indian forms of torture, however, seemed barbaric, not because Europeans did not engage in torture but because Europeans did not practice it against other soldiers, one's supposed equals.

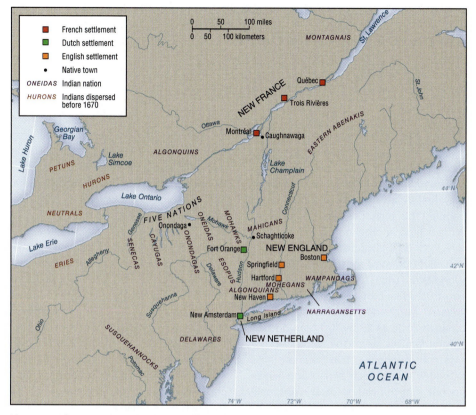

Map 2–3   The Iroquois Region in the Middle of the Seventeenth Century By the middle of the seventeenth century, the French, Dutch, and English had all established trading posts on the fringe of the Iroquois homeland. In the Beaver Wars (c. 1648–1660), discussed later in the chapter, the Iroquois lashed out at their neighbors, dispersing several Huron tribes. *Matthew Dennis,* Cultivating a Landscape of Peace *(New York: Cornell University Press, 1993), p. 16.*

Over the next several years, Champlain established a fur trade in the region, linking the French and the Indians in a transformed transatlantic economy. Peasants were brought to New France in 1614 to raise food for the traders; Catholic priests were sent to convert the Native Americans. The missionaries were more successful than the peasants. The persistence and adaptability of the missionaries and their ability to make Catholicism meaningful to Native Americans eventually gained them many converts.

After Champlain's original trade monopoly expired, his group competed with other Frenchmen in the fur trade. The French government was too busy with conflicts at home and abroad to support any of these outposts. To maintain a competitive edge, each summer Champlain pushed farther up the St. Lawrence River from his base at Quebec to intercept the Indian tribes who were bringing pelts to the east. Each winter he also sent some of his men to live among the western Hurons and Algonquians, to learn their languages and customs and to strengthen their trading partnerships. These Indians already traded widely in corn, fish, nets, wampum, and other items. As French traders and Huron and Algonquian hunters created a trade network, each group became dependent on the other.

>> Huronia

In the middle of the sixteenth century, over 20,000 Huron Indians lived in Huronia, a huge region bounded by Georgian Bay and Lakes Huron, Erie, Ontario, and Simcoe. Most Hurons inhabited triple-palisaded villages of 2,000 or so people. The palisades were sometimes 20 feet high in order to protect the Hurons from their Iroquois enemy.

The Hurons, like most of the Northern Woodlands tribes, lived in longhouses constructed out of bent tree branches covered with bark. These houses, sometimes as large as 25 by 100 feet, housed several families, all of the same clan. Inside the longhouse, two sets of racks extended along each side, upon which members of the clan slept at night: children slept in the upper "bunks" and adults in the lower ones. Fires for cooking and warmth were built in the middle of the floor. Europeans found the thick smoke oppressive, but it drove the insects away. There was no privacy; nor was there a concept of private property.

There were other village structures: sweat houses, where one went in the hope of sweating out an illness; small huts in which meat and fish were dried; and elevated racks on which the dead were placed prior to burial. The grounds were covered with garbage, including the carcasses of dead animals. The stench must have been familiar to Europeans who came from crowded cities, where offal and human waste were also tossed onto the streets. Edging each village were the fields where the women raised vegetables, primarily corn, squash, and beans.

The Hurons, like the other northern Woodlands tribes, were matrilineal and matrilocal. Shortly after puberty, Huron men and women entered into sexual relations, which either party might initiate. The relationship might lead to marriage, or either party might move on to another partner. When a couple married, the man moved in with his wife's clan in her family's longhouse. When the marriage dissolved, which was often, he would return to the longhouse of his mother and sisters, while his wife's brothers assumed the role of male teachers of the children. Each longhouse was supervised by a clan matron, who saw to the domestic and economic needs of her group; she also chose two men to lead the clan. Because the men of the clan spent much of their time hunting, trading, or engaging in warfare, most of the day-to-day responsibilities, including raising crops, making clothing, and rearing the children, were performed by women.

Huron children were brought up to participate in the world of the mourning war. Their parents trained them for "autonomous responsibility," to be independent men and women who were loyal to their clan. Babies were indulged by their parents, breastfed by their mothers until the age of three or four, and allowed to "toilet train" themselves. Parents did not believe in punishing their children when their behavior got out of hand. One Frenchman observed, "There is nothing for which these peoples have a greater horror than restraint. The very children cannot endure it, and live as they please in the houses of their parents, without fear of reprimand or chastisement." Another observed, "The mothers love their children with an extreme passion." Indian children prized their liberty and felt great loyalty to the group that had nurtured them.

Parents taught their children skills that they would need as adults. The girls stayed close to their mothers, perform- ing the easier household tasks, while the boys formed gangs that played competitive games and learned to hunt and make war, sometimes leaving the village for days at a time. In this way, the boys learned to be independent of their parents and loyal to their group. Huronia taught its children to love both liberty and the group.

Creating a Middle Ground in New France

Indians and French traders accommodated each other's cultural practices. Together they created a middle ground neither fully European nor fully Indian, but rather a new world created out of two different traditions. The middle ground came into being whenever Europeans and Indians needed each other and could not (or would not) achieve what they wanted through the use of force.

As the French drew the Native Americans into a global trade network, the Indians began to hunt more beaver than they needed for themselves, depleting the beaver population. Some historians believe that the introduction of European goods and commerce destroyed Native American cultures from within by making them dependent on those goods and inducing them to abandon their own crafts. Others have pointed out that the trade had different meanings for the French and for the Indians. For the French, trade was important for its cash value; for the Indians, trade goods were important both for the uses to which they could be put and for their symbolic value in religious ceremonies.

Indians integrated European goods into their traditional practices, breaking up brass pots, for example, into small pieces that could be made into jewelry. Iron tools enabled Indian craftspeople to create more detail in their decorative arts. The French were similarly drawn into the Indians' style of life. Traders and priests learned to sleep on the cold ground without complaint and to eat Indian foods such as sagamité, a sort of cornmeal mush in which a small bird or animal was often boiled whole. Many French traders found Indian wives. Indians such as the Hurons accepted *polygyny*, that is, taking more than one wife, so they were not troubled if the French had wives at home. Moreover, the Hurons were accustomed to adopting members of different ethnic groups, and the French were not averse to racial mixing. Both the Indians and the French believed mixed marriages strengthened trading and military alliances.

The French were drawn into their Huron and Algonquian allies' world as well. To keep the furs flowing east, they had to join war parties (usually against the Iroquois), finance their allies' battles, and purchase their loyalty with annual payments the Indians considered "presents" and the French the price of diplomacy. The French and their Indian

Map 2–4   French Exploration and Settlement, 1603–1616 Between 1603 and 1616, Samuel de Champlain and other French explorers made numerous trips up the St. Lawrence River and along the New England coast as far south as Cape Cod. They established several settlements, and they traded with local Indians and fought with them as well.

allies manipulated each other for their own benefit, and there were costs and benefits on both sides.

The arrival of the French stimulated competition among regional tribes for the positions of brokers between the French and the other Indians with furs to trade. The pace and nature of Indian warfare, which had always been fierce, now changed dramatically, for a new motive: control of the lucrative fur trade. Through diplomacy and the liberal dispensing of presents, French officials were usually able to quell the infighting among their allies. Once the Dutch and English established colonies to the south and made alliances with the Iroquois, maintaining the loyalty of Huron and Algonquian allies became the major French objective in North America in the seventeenth and eighteenth centuries. Because they were receptive to Indian customs, the French were the best diplomats in North America, and their Indian allies the most loyal.

An Outpost in a Global Political Economy

New France began as a tiny outpost. By the end of the seventeenth century, it had increased in both size and importance. Its population reached 2,000 in 1650 and 19,000 in 1714, and its primary focus remained the fur trade. In the 1630s, missionaries began to arrive in significant numbers, making the conversion of Indians to Catholicism the second most important endeavor in the colony. At the same time, the Huron population decreased dramatically, cut in half by epidemics that also killed many of Huronia's leaders. The result was internal conflict and political instability that left the Hurons vulnerable to their Indian enemies and increasingly dependent on their French allies. At the same time, the French depended on the Hurons and Algonquians to keep bringing them furs. The Hurons operated solely as middlemen, acquiring beaver pelts from other tribes.

By the middle of the seventeenth century, the local beaver supply began to diminish. Before the arrival of the French, the Indians had trapped only enough for their own use. The huge European demand, however, led Indians to kill more beaver than could be replaced by natural reproduction. As a result, Europeans (or their Indian middlemen) extended trade routes north and west, drawing larger numbers of Indians into the emerging global economy.

The European demand for beaver coats and hats was insatiable. To increase trade, the French expanded domestic manufacturing of cloth, metal implements, guns, and other goods attractive to the Indians. This pattern, in which the mother country produced goods to be sold or traded in foreign colonies for raw materials, was replicated in England and Holland. None of these nations found the treasures that Spain did in Mexico and Peru. Instead, they found new products, such as beaver pelts, for which there was a growing demand in Europe.

A new economic theory called *mercantilism* guided the growth of European nation-states and their colonies: its objective was to strengthen the nation-state by making the economy serve its interests. According to the theory, the world's wealth, measured in gold and silver, could never be increased. As a result, each nation's economic objective must be to secure as much of the world's wealth as possible. One nation's gain was necessarily another's loss. Colonies were to provide raw materials and markets for manufactured goods for the mother country. National competition for colonies and markets was not only about economics but also about politics and diplomacy. The nation's strength would depend on its ability to dominate international trade.

New Netherland: The Empire of a Trading Nation

In many ways, the Dutch venture into North America resembled that of France. It began with an intrepid explorer in quest of a Northwest Passage and a government unwilling to invest heavily in a North American colony. Unlike the French and Spanish, however, the Dutch government assigned the task of establishing a trading settlement almost entirely to a private company. And because Holland was a Protestant nation, there were no activist Catholic priests to spread their religion and oppose the excesses of a commercial economy. Even more than the French and Spanish colonies, New Netherland was shaped by the forces of commerce.

Colonization by a Private Company

Much like England, the Netherlands was rising to power as a merchant nation. The nation had secured its independence from Spain after a long and bloody war, which ended in 1648. Also like England, the Netherlands was Protestant, committed to a market economy, and sustained by a thriving middle class. Indeed, Amsterdam was the center of the world's economy. The Netherlands had neither a powerful aristocracy nor an oppressed peasantry. Its government and economy were dominated by prosperous merchants.

Holland was the home of the Renaissance humanist Erasmus, and his values of toleration and moderation permeated Dutch society. Jews expelled from Spain found a home in the Netherlands alongside strict Calvinists (Protestants who believed in predestination). The spirit of tolerance enabled the Dutch to put aside religious and political conflict and turn their attentions to trade.

It was an accident that the Dutch and not the British claimed the Hudson River valley. Henry Hudson, an English explorer, sailed several times for the English, attempting to reach the Northwest Passage by sailing over the North Pole. In 1609 Hudson persuaded a group of Dutch merchants who traded in Asia, the Dutch East India Company, to finance a venture. Sailing on the *Halve Maen* (*Half Moon*, in English), Hudson headed toward the Chesapeake Bay, which he believed offered a passage to the Pacific. He sailed along the coast, anchoring in New York Harbor and trading with local Algonquian Indians. He pushed up the river as far as Albany, where he discovered that the river narrowed, apparently disproving his theory about a water passage through North America.

> "The Dutch say we are brothers and that we are joined together with chains, but that lasts only as long as we have beavers. After that we are no longer thought of."
>
> IROQUOIS SPOKESMAN, 1659

The opportunity to profit from the fur trade soon drew investors and traders to New Netherland. Within two years of Hudson's "discovery" of the river that bears his name, Dutch merchants returned to the region, and in 1614 a group called the New Netherland Company secured a temporary monopoly of trade between the Delaware and Connecticut rivers.

The profitable trade drew other merchants to the region. In 1621 the Dutch West India Company obtained a monopoly of trade with the Americas and Africa that also entitled it to establish colonies in "fruitful and unsettled parts." In theory, the Company was to operate in the public interest. But both the wealthy merchants who were its commissioners and the ordinary Netherlanders they enticed to migrate pursued private interests above all else. The only way to attract investors or settlers to a remote colony was by the promise of profits. Within a few years, the Dutch West India Company established settlements at Fort Orange (present-day Albany) and New Amsterdam (present-day New York City) and purchased the entire island of Manhattan from local Algonquian Indians for a meager 60 florins' worth of merchandise. The first 30 families arrived in 1624 to serve the fur trade, either by trading with Indians (the Iroquois and the Delawares) or by providing support for the traders. All profits went to the Company, with the settlers given small salaries.

Until the Company was willing to offer better terms to settlers, the colony grew very slowly. There were 270 inhabitants in 1628, 500 in 1640, and fewer than 9,000 in 1664. It was difficult to attract settlers from a prosperous nation that, although by no means a modern democracy, permitted greater religious and political freedom than was customary in most European countries.

The Company tried to draw colonists to New Netherland. In 1629, it offered huge plots of land (18 miles along the Hudson River) and extensive governing powers to *patroons*, men who would bring 50 settlers to the new colony. It also offered smaller grants of land to individuals who would farm the land and return to the Company one-tenth of what they produced. Both approaches placed restrictions on land ownership and self-government, and neither was successful. In 1640, the Company offered greater rights of self-government and 200 acres to anyone who brought over five adult immigrants. This policy worked better. After a few decades, New Netherland had become a magnet for peoples from many cultures and nations. As the colony grew, it expanded up the Hudson from the island of Manhattan into New Jersey and Long Island and south to the Delaware River.

The ethnic diversity of the colony was increased even further when in 1655 it absorbed the small colony of New Sweden, a privately financed trading outpost on the Delaware that failed when it could not return a quick profit. The varied population of New Netherland was united by no single religion or culture that could have established social order. In most European nations at the time, social order was maintained by a combination of state authority and cohesive religious structures and values. Where the religious or government order was fractured, as in France, bloody civil war was the result. In New Netherland, however, both religious structure and government were relatively weak. The governors were caught between the Company, which expected to earn a profit, and the settlers, who wanted to prosper themselves. Peter Stuyvesant, governor from 1647 until the English takeover in 1664, was the most successful of the governors, but even he could not fully control New Netherland's disorder.

In one year alone, when the population numbered less than 1,000, there were 50 civil suits and almost as many criminal prosecutions. The rate of alcohol consumption seems to have been the highest of any North American colony. In 1645, there were only between 150 and 200 houses in New Amsterdam—but 35 taverns! There were also complaints of sexual promiscuity, especially between European men and Indian women.

Stuyvesant was unsuccessful in regulating either social life or the economy. He attempted to set prices on such commodities as beer and bread, but he was overruled by the Company, which feared that economic controls would thwart further immigration. In a pattern that would prevail in all of the Dutch and English North American colonies, commerce triumphed.

Slavery and Freedom in New Netherland

The colony, the Company, and the nation all wanted to make themselves wealthy through commerce. This desire led to the introduction of African slavery into New Netherland. The fur trade did not prove as lucrative as investors had hoped, and the Company found that colonists tended to abandon agriculture for trade. The Company decided that the primary function of New Netherland should be to provide food for its more lucrative plantation colonies in Brazil and the Caribbean. Earlier in the century, the Dutch had seized a portion of northern Brazil from Portugal and introduced a sugar-plantation slave economy, which it transplanted to islands in the Caribbean. By that time they had also entered the transatlantic slave trade. In fact, a Dutch warship dropped off the first 20 Africans at the English colony of Jamestown in 1619 in return for food. With its own plantation colonies needing slave labor, the Netherlands became a major player in the slave trade, transporting Africans to the colonies of other nations as well.

In the context of the lucrative Dutch trade in sugar and slaves, New Netherland was only a sideshow. Hoping to make the colony profitable, the Company turned to enslaved Africans. By 1664, there were perhaps 700 slaves in the colony, a minuscule portion of the more than half million Africans the Dutch ultimately seized from their homelands, but a considerable portion (about 8 percent) of New Netherland's population.

The Netherlands was perhaps the most tolerant nation of its day, and the Dutch Reformed Church accepted Africans, as well as Indians, as converts, provided they could demonstrate their knowledge of the Dutch religion. The Church did not oppose the institution of slavery, however. Moreover, the strict nature of Dutch Calvinism placed limits on the Church's tolerance. It insisted that its followers be able to read and understand the Bible and the doctrines of the Church.

The primary force for religious tolerance in New Netherland was, in fact, the Dutch West India Company, which saw it as necessary to commercial prosperity. When the head of the Dutch Reformed Church in New Netherland and Governor Stuyvesant attempted to prevent the entry of 23 Dutch Jews expelled from Portuguese Brazil, they were reversed by the Company.

The Company also advocated a policy of fairness to the local Indian tribes. They insisted that land must be purchased from its original owners before Europeans could settle on it. Because some settlers were coercing Indians to sell their land cheaply, in 1652 Stuyvesant forbade purchases of land without government approval.

It might appear puzzling that the Dutch, who encouraged toleration of religious minorities and justice toward Native Americans, would also introduce and encourage slavery in North America. The Dutch were not motivated, however, by abstract ideals. Their primary goal was profit through trade: religious and cultural toleration, amicable relations with local Indians, and African slavery all served that end.

The Dutch-Indian Trading Partnership

In the 40 years of New Netherland's existence, its most profitable activity was the fur trade. As the French had done, the Dutch disrupted the balance among regional Indian tribes. The arrival of the Europeans, rather than uniting the Indians, heightened long-standing local animosities. Tribes came to rely on their European allies not only for goods but also for weapons and even soldiers to fight their enemies.

The Indians and the Europeans were playing a dangerous game, one that required a constant low level of violence to prevent outsiders from encroaching on an established trade. Yet if the violence escalated into full-fledged warfare, it disrupted the very trade it was designed to protect. As a result, the trade frontier between Indians and Europeans was always filled with peril.

The Dutch began trading near Albany around 1614 and built Fort Orange there a decade later. This small outpost was in a region inhabited by the Mahican tribe, an Algonquian people who gave the Dutch access to the furs trapped by other Algonquian tribes to the north. The Dutch were assisting the Mahicans in their trade rivalry with the Mohawks (an Iroquois nation) when they were attacked—and defeated—by the Mohawks. The Mohawks, however, asked for peace: their objective was not to eliminate the Dutch but to secure them as trade partners.

By 1628 the Mohawks had defeated the Mahicans and forced them to move into Connecticut, establishing the Mohawks as the most powerful force in the region. The Dutch and the Mohawks abandoned their former hostility for a generally peaceful trading partnership.

By the 1660s however, New Netherland was in serious economic trouble. The underlying problem was an oversupply of wampum, beads made from the shells of clams.

Indians had placed a high value on wampum well before the arrival of Europeans, and the Dutch taught them how to mass-produce it. They also helped the Indians establish a trade in wampum itself, in which wampum was traded to the Dutch for European goods. The Dutch then exchanged the wampum for furs from the Mohawks and other Indians, shipping the furs to the Netherlands for more European goods. By the middle of the seventeenth century, perhaps as many as 3 million pieces of wampum were in circulation in the area.

By the 1640s English traders in New England had cornered the market in wampum, just when New Englanders were ceasing to use the beads as money. The traders then dumped them into the Dutch market by buying up huge quantities of European goods. Almost instantly the price of trade goods skyrocketed and the value of wampum fell, leaving the Dutch with too few of the former and too much of the latter. Competition among Dutch traders increased, pressure on Iroquois trade partners mounted, and profits fell. The economic crisis tipped the delicate balance of violence on the frontier and precipitated a major war.

The Beaver Wars

As the Dutch economic position faltered, the balance of power among many northeastern tribes collapsed. The Iroquois, dependant on the Dutch for guns, were now vulnerable. Western Iroquois tribes came under assault from the Susquehannocks, a tribe to the south, while the Mohawks faced renewed pressure from the Mahicans. Simultaneously, the Hurons had cut the Iroquois off from trade with the French to the north. Pressured, the Iroquois lashed out in hostilities, known as the Beaver Wars, which raged between 1648 and the 1660s. They attacked almost all of their Indian neighbors and pushed the last French-allied Hurons to the west.

This warfare was horrendous for all sides. As Indian fought Indian, Europeans gained the upper hand. The Iroquois won the Beaver Wars, but their victory was hollow. Although the Hurons had been dispersed west, the Iroquois could not secure the French as trade partners. Once the Hurons were gone, the French began trading with other Algonquian tribes to the east. Although the Iroquois remained a powerful force until almost the end of the eighteenth century, the Beaver Wars marked an important turning point. The Indians were never able to replace population lost to warfare, even by raiding other tribes. By the middle of the seventeenth century, the pace of European colonization was increasing, filling the land once hunted by Indians.

Even before the English conquered New Netherland in 1664, the Iroquois were looking for new trade partners. They found them in the English. The transition in New Netherland from Dutch to English rule was relatively quiet. The Dutch had established the colony hoping to make money through trade. Having failed, they had little incentive to fight for its control.

England Attempts an Empire

England came late to empire building, but by the time the plan was completed, that nation dominated not only North America but also much of the world. Although England's search for an overseas empire was motivated primarily by a search for wealth and power, it is impossible to separate these drives from the religious impulse. Every great imperial nation of this era—Portugal, Spain, France, and England—believed they conquered for God and country; nationalism was always tinged with religious fervor.

The Origins of English Nationalism

England did not achieve the political unity necessary for empire building until the second half of the sixteenth century. Between 1455 and 1485, England was torn by a dynastic struggle, the Wars of the Roses. King Henry VII and his son, Henry VIII, consolidated the power of the state by crushing recalcitrant nobles. When the pope refused to let Henry VIII terminate his sonless marriage to Catherine of Aragon, the king made Protestantism the official religion of the nation, banned Catholicism, and confiscated the land and wealth of the Catholic Church. Henry's daughter Mary, who reigned from 1553 through 1558, reinstated Catholicism, burning Protestants at the stake and throwing the nation into turmoil. Order was finally established under the rule of Henry's other daughter, Elizabeth I (reigning from 1558 to 1603), who reestablished the Anglican Church, subdued internal dissent, and strengthened the state her grandfather and father had consolidated.

Queen Elizabeth, although an ardent nationalist, was unwilling to risk her treasury on North American adventures. Others, however, were convinced that a New World empire could bring England wealth and glory. By the end of the sixteenth century, nationalists, such as two cousins both named Richard Hakluyt, were making the case for an overseas empire. The Hakluyts united nationalism, mercantilism, and militant Protestantism. They argued that if England had colonies for raw materials and for markets for manufactured goods, it could free itself from economic dependency on France and Spain. Moreover, colonies could drain off the growing numbers of the unemployed. The Hakluyts also believed that North American Indians could be relatively easily converted to English trade and religion, which they would much prefer to Spanish "pride and tyranie." The English could simultaneously strike a blow against the Spanish and advance "the glory of God." Although the Hakluyts' dream was never realized, their plans for an English mercantile empire became a blueprint for colonization.

Raiding Other Empires

England's first move was not to establish colonies but to try stealing from the Spanish. The English had neither the wealth nor the vision to found a colonial empire, and Elizabeth I was unconvinced by colonial propagandists. Most concerned about international power politics in Europe, she was willing to let individual Englishmen try to poach on the Spanish. Her goal was to weaken Spain more than to establish a North American empire.

As early as 1562, John Hawkins tried to break into the slave trade, but the Spanish forced him out. The English moved on to privateering, that is, state-sanctioned piracy. In 1570 Sir Francis Drake set off for the Isthmus of Panama on a raiding expedition. Drake was motivated equally by dreams of glory and by a conviction that his Protestant religion was superior to all others. Working in one of Hawkins's slaving expeditions, he had learned to hate the Spanish.

In years to come, Drake led the second expedition to sail around the world, crossed the Atlantic many times, helped defeat a huge Spanish fleet, the Armada, and became

AMERICA AND THE WORLD

>> The English on the Edge of Empire

Just as England came late to the exploration of North America, so it came late to the exploration of Africa. At the middle of the sixteenth century, England lacked the wealth and expertise of Portugal, Spain, or France. Indeed, the most powerful empire in the region at that time was the Ottoman one; it reached from Algiers in the west to the Persian Gulf in the east, covering most of North Africa and the Mediterranean and much of southeastern Europe and the Middle East. Its trade routes extended south across the Sahara into much of Africa. The Ottoman Empire was not only wealthy and powerful, but it also was, for its time, relatively tolerant. Many Jews who had been expelled from Spain found a new home in the Islamic empire to the east.

So dominant was the Ottoman Empire that the nations of Europe were, in important ways, peripheral to it. And England was on the margin of Europe. Hence, when it sought to expand, England would have to look to other marginal regions—for example, to Ireland, where the English had to subdue only the Irish themselves. In the middle of the sixteenth century, England sought out trade on the edges of the Ottoman Empire—the Muscovy region of Russia; Morocco; and Guinea, a West African nation where the Portuguese had already established a monopoly.

In fact, the English were latecomers to Africa, just as they were latecomers to North America. The Portuguese had been trading in West Africa for more than a century, and at first the English had trouble finding a foothold. In 1553, English traders made contact with an African leader in the city of Benin. Speaking in Portuguese, he told them that their trade goods were not up to his standard but graciously gave them a cargo of pepper on credit until they could bring back payment. Like the Native Americans the Europeans encountered in North America, Africans welcomed trade with Europeans and competition among them for the best price. The African environment, however, was not nearly as welcoming. Only a month after their arrival in Benin, the English were in such a rush to escape its deadly tropical fevers that they left several merchants behind when they lifted anchor.

In North America, Europeans brought diseases that killed millions of natives. In Africa, however, the situation was reversed: Europeans fell victim to tropical diseases. Not until the nineteenth century, when quinine came into use as a treatment for malaria, were Europeans able to colonize Africa. Until then, the continent was known as "the white man's grave." Europeans could not have established colonies even had they wanted to. Instead, they relied on their African trading partners. Within a century, though, the English had extracted so much gold from Africa that the new one-pound gold coin was called a guinea, after the region in Africa from which the gold came.

Because of the dominance of the Portuguese in West Africa, however, the English were slow to make inroads. On one early voyage, the English clashed with the Portuguese on the Guinea coast. They had to turn over one of their crew, a 15-year-old boy named Martin Frobisher, *continued*

AMERICA AND THE WORLD *continued*

as a kind of living security deposit. The Portuguese sent Frobisher back to Portugal, from which he returned to England. Later a privateer, he explored North America, looking for gold.

At about the same time, another Englishman, John Hawkins, backed by English investors, attempted to break into the Portuguese slave trade by force. On his first voyage, he simply seized a cargo of 400 Africans, as well as valuable trade goods, from a Portuguese fleet and took them to the Spanish colony of Santo Domingo to sell. Even after he bribed the Spanish official—trade with England was illegal—the profits were enormous. On his next voyage, Hawkins went directly to the Guinea coast. Rather than working through local African rulers, who were happy to sell other Africans as slaves, Hawkins tried to take slaves by himself. He seized ten Africans—and lost seven crew members. By

raiding Africans and Portuguese, Hawkins was able to amass another cargo to take to the Spanish colonies. By his third voyage Hawkins came to understand that Africans could be allies in the slave trade. He was approached by an emissary from an African king with a proposition: help the king defeat his enemies and share in the slaves taken as booty. Hawkins agreed and helped his new allies set fire to a town with 8,000 inhabitants. His reward was 250 captives. This voyage ended badly, however. This time the Spanish refused to purchase Hawkins's slaves and instead destroyed his fleet and killed 300 of his 400 sailors in a battle at San Juan de Ulúa (near Veracruz, Mexico).

In the middle of the sixteenth century, the English were outsiders, trying everywhere they could to force themselves into the empires that more powerful nations had established.

an architect of England's colonial strategies. He was the English version of the *conquistador*. His venture into Panama failed to produce any treasure, but it inspired a group of professional seamen, aggressive Protestants and members of Elizabeth's court, to plan for an English colonial empire. This group won the cautious queen's support. The success of Drake's round-the-world expedition (1577–1580) spurred further privateering ventures. He brought back to England enough treasure to pay for the voyage and proof that the Spanish empire was vulnerable. From 1585 to 1604, the English government issued licenses to privateers, sometimes as many as 100 per year. Each venture was financed by a joint-stock company, a relatively new form of business organization that was the forerunner to the modern corporation. These companies brought together merchants who saw privateering as a way to broaden their trade and gentlemen who saw it as a way to increase their incomes.

Rehearsal in Ireland

At the end of the sixteenth century, England embarked on a campaign to bring Ireland, which had long been its possession, under its full control. The conquest of Ireland between 1565 and 1576 became the model for England's colonial ventures. Ireland presented the monarchy with the same political problem that all early-modern rulers faced, that is, a set

Sir Francis Drake One of England's greatest adventurers, Sir Francis Drake sailed around the globe, defeated the Spanish Armada, and made a fortune stealing from the Spanish.

of powerful nobles who put their own interests ahead of those of the nation. Building the nation meant bringing the nobles into line.

England not only subdued the Irish leaders and their people but also forcibly removed some of them to make way for loyal Englishmen, who were given land as a reward for their service to the queen. By paying her followers with someone else's land and financing military expeditions from joint-stock companies, England made the conquest of Ireland relatively cheap. It showed a skeptical queen that establishing colonies on the edge of the known world was in England's interest—provided that the venture was paid for privately, by privateering, by charters to individuals, or by joint-stock companies.

The English conquest of Ireland provided not only practical experience in how to organize and finance a colonial venture but also a view of cultural difference that was applied to the Indians. Although the Irish were Catholics and hence Christians, the English thought that people who behaved as the Irish did must be barbarians. According to the English, the Irish "blaspheme, they murder, commit whoredome, hold no wedlocke, ravish, steal, and commit all abomination without scruple of conscience." Without a shred of evidence, the English also accused the Irish of cannibalism, a mark of the barbarian.

These attitudes were used to justify an official policy of terrorism. In two grisly massacres, one in the middle of a Christmas feast, hundreds of men, women, and children were slaughtered. The English governor, Sir Humphrey Gilbert, ordered that the heads of all those killed resisting the conquest be chopped off and placed along the path leading to his tent so that anyone coming to see him "must pass through a lane of heads." The English justified such acts by the supposed barbarism of the Irish people. These ideas, similar to early Spanish depictions of the Indians of the Americas, were carried to the New World, England's next stop in its expanding empire.

The Roanoke Venture

Roanoke, England's first colony in what became the United States, was a military venture, intended as a resupply base for privateers raiding in the Caribbean. In 1584 Walter Raleigh received a charter to establish a colony in North America. Only 30 years old at the time, Raleigh was the half-brother of the late Sir Humphrey Gilbert. Elizabeth agreed to let Raleigh establish a combination colony and privateering base north of Spain's settlement at

St. Augustine. Raleigh's scouts had found a potential site at Roanoke Island on the Outer Banks of North Carolina and had brought back to England two Indians, Manteo and Wanchese. Elizabeth gave the enterprise some support. She knighted Raleigh but refused to let the hotheaded young soldier lead the expedition himself.

The Roanoke expedition left Plymouth in April 1585 under the command of Sir Richard Grenville, an aristocrat and soldier who had fought in Ireland. Half of the crew of 600 were probably recruited or impressed (i.e., forcibly seized) from the unemployed poor of Britain. Little value was attached to their lives. When one of the ships separated from the fleet and found its supplies running low, 20 men were dropped off at Jamaica— only 2 of whom were ever heard from again—and another 32 were left on an island in the Outer Banks.

Roanoke was a poor port, dangerous for small ships and inadequate for larger ones. When the primary ship was almost wrecked and a major portion of the food supply lost, Grenville's fleet departed for England and fresh supplies. Colonel Ralph Lane, another veteran of war in Ireland, was left in charge as governor. He was supposed to look for a better port, build a fort, and find food for the 100 men left under his command.

Roanoke was established to gain an advantage over the treasure-filled Spanish ships traveling back to Spain. The men left on the island prepared for war—with Spain. The fort's guns were pointed out to sea, to protect them from Spanish ships. Raleigh intended to send another supply ship that summer, but the queen insisted he sail instead to Newfoundland to warn the English about a sea war with Spain. The first settlers of Roanoke were ill equipped to build a self-sustaining colony. Half soldiers and gentlemen and half undisciplined and

The arrival of the English at Roanoke, from a 1585 sketch by the artist John White.

John White's Watercolor of an Algonquian Village Much of what we know about Algonquian life at the time of the Roanoke expedition comes from the paintings of John White, who was a member of the Roanoke expedition. Here we see a small village, surrounded by a tall stockade.

impoverished young men, no one knew how to work. Unable to find gold or provide for themselves, the colonists turned to the local Roanoke Indians (an Algonquian tribe), whom they soon alienated.

The Roanokes were familiar with Europeans and ready to trade with them. The English tendency to use force and their need for more food than the natives could easily supply, however, led to conflict. Thinking that an Indian had stolen a silver cup, the English retaliated by burning an empty village and the surrounding cornfields, which fed both Indians and English. The Indians had to balance the benefits of trade against the costs of English hostility. After a failed ambush attempt, the Roanokes decided to withdraw from Roanoke Island, leaving the English to starve. When Lane learned of this plan, he attacked the Roanokes, beheading their chieftain Wingina. Indian-English relations deteriorated.

Not all the colonists, however, treated the Roanokes as an enemy to be conquered. Much of what we know about the Roanoke Colony and its Indian neighbors is due to the work of two sympathetic colonists. John White, a painter, and Thomas Hariot, who later became the greatest mathematician of his age, were sent to survey the region and describe its inhabitants and natural features. Their illustrations, maps, and descriptions provide the most accurate information about this region and its inhabitants before the arrival of large numbers of Europeans.

By June 1585, it was clear that Roanoke had failed in its mission. When Drake and his fleet appeared on their way back from a looting party in the Caribbean, the colonists decided to return to England. In their haste to leave they left behind three men on an expedition into the interior. They were never heard from again. Apparently, Drake also dropped off several hundred Caribbean Indian and African slaves whom he had liberated while picking up booty. Freeing slaves was one of his ways to hurt the Spanish. For the same reason, he had burned their outpost at St. Augustine. All of these abandoned people (the three Englishmen and the freed Indians and Africans) probably melted into the Native Indian population. Soon thereafter, Grenville dropped off 15 men at the empty colony and returned to England.

The English advocates of colonization were not yet ready to give up. The original plan for a military-style base had failed, and a new vision of colonization would now be tried. Raleigh's commitment was lukewarm, for Roanoke had already cost £30,000 without returning a cent. John White, the painter, remained enthusiastic and assembled a group of settlers that was the forerunner of all future successful English colonies. It included 110 people—men, women, and children who were prepared to raise their own crops—and one loyal Roanoke Indian, Manteo. (Wanchese had remained with his own people and was now an enemy to the English.) For their investment , Raleigh granted each man 500 acres of land. The new expedition arrived in July 1587. The plan was to pick up the men Grenville had left and proceed north to the Chesapeake, a better harbor. The pilot of the fleet, more interested in privateering, refused to take the colonists any further, however.

The second attempt to establish a colony at Roanoke was probably doomed by the poisoned relations with the Indians. White soon found that Grenville's men had been attacked by Roanokes. As the survival of the colony now depended on support from England, the colonists, who included White's daughter and granddaughter, sent White back to act as their agent in England. No European ever saw any of these colonists again.

The Abandoned Colony

No one had planned to abandon the little colony. It was mostly a matter of priorities. Raleigh assembled a supply fleet the next spring, but a sea war looming with the Spanish Armada prevented it from leaving. Finally, in August 1590, White arrived in Roanoke only to find everyone gone. There were signs of an orderly departure, and the word CROATOAN, Manteo's home island, was carved in a post. White assumed that was where the group had gone. Short of water and with a storm brewing, the fleet decided to return to the Caribbean for the winter and seek out Croatoan the next spring. They never got there.

The colony of Roanoke was not "lost," as legend usually puts it; it was abandoned. Serving no useful economic or military purpose, the people of Roanoke were entirely expendable. Because Raleigh's claim to the land depended on his sustaining a colony, he was better off pretending the colonists were alive than discovering they were dead or missing. In 1602, Raleigh sent out a search party that never quite made it to Roanoke. A year later Queen Elizabeth was dead, and her successor, James I, had Raleigh arrested as a traitor.

What happened to the abandoned colonists? In 1607, the English returned to the region, establishing a permanent colony at Jamestown, on the Chesapeake. In 1608, Englishmen heard that many Roanoke colonists had made their way up to Virginia and settled among the friendly Chesapeake Indians. Perhaps others went to Croatoan, leaving White the message carved into the post.

Those who moved north seem to have become victims of the Powhatans, a powerful and expansionist tribe. When the English arrived, their chief, also named Powhatan, ordered the slaughter of the Chesapeakes and the English who lived among them. There were reports that seven English people had escaped, and for years local Indians told tales about sighting a boy with "perfect yellow hair" and "white skin" among one tribe. The English at Jamestown came to believe that Roanoke's survivors were living 50 miles away, but they made no effort to find them.

Almost 20 years after abandoning Roanoke, the English finally established a permanent colony at Jamestown. By that time the Spanish empire was slowly declining. In theory at least, the English would be better able to support later colonies. As Roanoke

Portrait of an Algonquian Mother and Child by John White This beautiful picture illustrates the indulgence of Algonquian mothers and the sensitivity of the English artist who painted this one.

A cheife Herowans wyfe of Pomeoc. and her daughter of the age of 8. or. 10 yeares.

demonstrated, however, they had limited interest in colonies that did not return a fast, reliable profit. Moreover, because English settlers, with few exceptions, antagonized their Indian hosts, the English could not rely on the Indians for food. As a result, the English colonies would have to grow their own food. In addition, the English concentrated more on trade with the English inhabitants of the New World than with Native Americans. Consequently, the history of the English in North America is by and large that of the growth of the English population (augmented by Africans and European immigrants) and the steady decline of the original inhabitants.

Conclusion

European nations established colonies to achieve a political or economic advantage over their rivals. Most of these nations had only recently been unified by force, an experience that gave them the energy to establish colonies and a military model they could use for colonization. The distinctive experience of each nation, however, shaped its relations with the Indians it encountered, just as the distinctive experience of the Indian nations shaped their interactions with Europeans. The Spanish came prepared for a new *reconquista* and poured huge, well-armed forces into the New World. The French sent small numbers of military officers who quickly found Indian allies and became entangled in the Indians' own conflicts. The English used another military model, that of the pacification of Ireland. Some nations, in particular France and Spain, were comparatively willing to reach out to alien cultures by sending missionaries to convert the Indians. The Dutch also recognized that the goodwill of the Indians was vital for a flourishing trade. The English proved the least interested in accommodating Indian cultures and the most interested in transplanting their own. Out of these different experiences, a North Atlantic political economy began to emerge, shaped by the forces of trade and the quest for national power, as Europeans, Indians, and Africans were drawn into a global economy in which the nations of the world competed for advantage. The early years of American colonial history were shaped by impersonal forces that built empires and subjugated peoples. But they were also shaped by individuals. Some set out to find new worlds, whereas others were forced into them. Captives such as Don Luís de Velasco, Wanchese, and Manteo; explorers

>> Timeline

▼1400–1600
Five Iroquois nations create the Great League of Peace

▼1522
Giovanni da Verrazano explores North American coast for France

▼1534–1542
Jacques Cartier makes three trips to Canada for France

▼1561
Spanish abduct Don Luís de Velasco

▼1562
John Hawkins tries to break into the slave trade

▼1565
Spanish establish settlement at St. Augustine
Spanish destroy French settlement at Fort Caroline

▼1565–1576
The English conquer Ireland

▼1570
Don Luís de Velasco returns home to Virginia

▼1577–1580
Francis Drake sails around the world for England

▼1584
Walter Raleigh receives charter to establish colony at Roanoke

▼1585
First settlement at Roanoke established

▼1587
Second attempt to found colony at Roanoke

▼1590
English settlers at Roanoke have disappeared

▼1607
English establish permanent colony at Jamestown

▼1608
Samuel de Champlain establishes a fort at Quebec

▼1609
Henry Hudson arrives at New York, sailing for the Netherlands

>> Timeline *continued*

▼1614
Dutch begin trading in Albany region
French settlers arrive in New France

▼1621
Dutch West India Company established

▼1624
First Dutch families arrive at Manhattan

▼1648-1660s
Beaver Wars fought

▼1664
English take over New Amsterdam

such as Jacques Cartier and Henry Hudson; soldiers such as Sir Francis Drake and Samuel de Champlain; the poor dragooned into sailing for Roanoke and left there to die; Africans liberated from the Spanish only to be abandoned on the North Carolina shore; and Huron women who married French traders: all of them left their mark on the New World, even before the English planted their first permanent colonies in North America.

Review Questions

1. What were the key European objectives in exploring North America in this period? To what extent did England, Spain, France, and the Netherlands achieve their objectives?

2. What was the "mourning war"? What function did it serve in Iroquois culture? How was it adapted to new circumstances in the seventeenth century?

3. Compare the early encounters with Native Americans of the English, French, and Dutch.

4. Compare the approaches to colonization of the English, French, and Dutch governments.

5. What was the "middle ground," and how was it created?

6. Why was the colony at Roanoke established, and why was it abandoned?

For further review materials and resource information, please visit www.oup.com/us/ofthepeople

>> The Adventures of John Rolfe

John Rolfe was an adventurer. In 1609, when Rolfe was 25, he and his wife set sail for the two-year-old English colony at Jamestown. Their ship was blown off course and wrecked off the island of Bermuda. It was not until a year later that Rolfe reached Virginia, having survived a mutiny and the death of his infant daughter. Rolfe's wife herself died shortly after their arrival at Jamestown (not only were the date and cause of her death lost to history, but so was her name). Soon Rolfe was experimenting with tobacco, trying to find a strain that would produce a fragrant leaf in Virginia's soil. Walter Raleigh's men had introduced tobacco to England, where the addictive pleasures of smoking soon created a market. The English imported their tobacco from the Spanish West Indies, but with the founding of their colony at Jamestown, they hoped for their own source. Unfortunately, the variety grown by Virginia's Indians was "poore, weake, and of a byting taste." Rolfe tried planting West Indian tobacco seeds and produced a successful crop. By 1617, Virginians were exporting Rolfe's tobacco to England. Not as sweet as the West Indian product, it was a great deal cheaper. Tobacco was the economic salvation of Virginia, making many men and women rich and robbing others of their freedom. Like other colonies, Virginia achieved prosperity by feeding European cravings. Like other plantation crops such as sugar, coffee, and tea, tobacco was not a necessity but merely pleasurable and habit-forming.

Relations with the local Powhatan Indians were tense from the beginning. In the spring of 1613, the English captured Pocahontas, the favorite daughter of the chieftain Powhatan, and brought her to Jamestown. By summer, John Rolfe had fallen deeply in love with the 18-year-old princess. He asked permission of the English authorities to marry her, realizing that his countrymen would disapprove of his attachment to "one whose education hath been rude, her manners barbarous, her generation accursed." He thought people would gossip that he was marrying her just to satisfy his lust. He even feared that his love for Pocahontas was the work of the devil, and so he resolved to convert her to Christianity. In John Rolfe, the traditional ethnocentrism of the English was at war with

>> **AMERICAN PORTRAIT** *continued*

love. Love won out. Yet the marriage was more than a triumph of two people in love: it also established an alliance between two peoples that brought an end to warfare.

In 1616, Rolfe took his wife and their young son to England, where Pocahontas adopted the dress of an English lady and even met the king and queen. The Virginia Company used her as a sort of walking advertisement for their colony. Her transformation suggested to the English that Indians could easily be "civilized." Before Rolfe and his wife could sail back to Virginia, Pocahontas took ill and died. By the time Rolfe returned to Virginia, tobacco dominated the economy, and tobacco-planting settlers encroached on the Powhatans' land. On the morning of March 22, 1622, the new leader of the Powhatan Confederacy, Opechancanough, orchestrated attacks on all the plantations along the James River. By the time they were finished, nearly one-third of all the Virginia colonists—women and children as well as men—had been killed. John Rolfe was one of the victims.

John Rolfe had imagined that English people and Indians could live together in harmony. He was wrong. Once he developed a marketable strain of tobacco, the English could not be stopped from turning Powhatan lands into tobacco fields. European demand for tobacco doomed not only the Indians who were driven from their homeland but also generations of European indentured servants and, eventually, African slaves. A new kind of society based on plantation slavery took shape. Rarely in history has one person been so directly responsible for the demise of his own dreams.

Common Threads

>> After the failure at Roanoke, how were the English finally able to plant successful colonies?

>> Why did the Jamestown Colony almost fail, and why did the New England ones succeed almost immediately? Can the Chesapeake or the New England experience be considered more "typical" of what would become the United States?

>> How did the gender and family orders differ in the Chesapeake and in New England, and what impact did gender and family have in shaping these societies?

>> What were the similarities and differences in each region's relations with Native Americans?

>> What role did religion play in shaping the Puritan colonies?

The First Chesapeake Colonies

In 1607, 20 years after abandoning the Roanoke Colony, the English returned to North America. Their nation, strong and unified, was beginning a rise to wealth and power that would carry it well into the twentieth century. The English, however, had learned little from their failure in Roanoke, and although Jamestown was better financed, it was poorly planned. A combination of unrealistic expectations, flawed leadership, troubled relations with the local Powhatan Indians, and lack of economic viability almost doomed the colony. The key to survival was tobacco. With the development of this cash crop, in demand in Europe, Virginia began to prosper. Once John Rolfe had developed a palatable strain of tobacco, the needs became land and labor. The English settlers' desire for land led them into warfare with the Powhatans; their desire for cheap labor led them to import indentured servants, white and black, and African slaves.

Planning Virginia

When Queen Elizabeth died in 1603, she was succeeded by King James I, who signed a treaty with Spain, ending decades of warfare. With peace established, all those who had lived off privateering and warfare had to look for another source of income, from legitimate trade. They joined with old advocates of colonization to establish new colonies in North America. In 1606, James granted charters to two groups of English merchants and military men, one in London and the other in Plymouth. The Plymouth group could colonize New England, and the Londoners the Chesapeake region. Each operation was chartered as a private company, which would raise money from shareholders and finance, populate, and regulate its charter colonies. The Virginia Company raised more money from wealthy London merchants than any other colonial venture had. Although both the Virginia and Plymouth companies reported to a Royal Council, these ventures were largely private operations, subject to little governmental control.

Both companies eventually founded North American colonies, but the Virginia Company (named in honor of the recently deceased queen) met with success first. Just before Christmas 1606, it sent out three ships under Captain Christopher Newport, a one-legged veteran Atlantic explorer. When the ships arrived at Virginia on April 26, 1607, the 104 colonists learned that they were to be governed by a council of seven men. Unfortunately, two of them, Edward Maria Wingfield, an investor in the company but "an arrogant man of no special capacity," and Captain John Smith, a 27-year-old equally arrogant but considerably more capable soldier of fortune, despised each other. By the end of the summer, another council member had been executed because he was a double agent for the Spanish. The early years of Jamestown were marked by internal wrangling. External conflict soon developed , as the colonists antagonized their Indian hosts. Almost everything that could go wrong did.

The English hoped to find a land like Mexico, filled with gold and less glamorous raw materials. Whatever limited manufacturing was needed could be performed either by English criminals, sent over to work as their punishment, or by indentured servants, English men and women from the lowest ranks of society who agreed to work for a set period to pay their transportation expenses. The colonists expected to trade with the local Indians, who would be the primary suppliers of food.

The Company planned to get the colony up and running within seven years. During that period all colonists would work for the Company, which would give them food and shelter. At the end of that period, they would receive grants of land. The Company evidently thought the colony would need a great deal of direction, for more than one third of the original settlers were gentlemen, that is, members of the elite, a proportion of the colony's population that was six times higher than it was in England.

The Fort at Jamestown, as It May Have Appeared in 1607 The settlement at Jamestown was surrounded by a palisade, a high wooden fence.

The Company also sent skilled laborers, many with skills of little use in the colony, such as tailors, goldsmiths, and a perfumer. Some were thought necessary to support the gentlemen. Others were to work the gold and precious gems colonists hoped to find. Farmers and ordinary laborers, on the other hand, were in short supply.

Starving Times

Poor planning and bad luck placed the colonists on swampy ground with bad water. The salty water of the James River could be poisonous, and in summer it became a breeding ground for typhoid and dysentery. Some historians have argued that these diseases left the survivors too weak to plant food, whereas others note that many of the healthy seemed to prefer prospecting for gold. Whatever the reason, the colonists depended on the resentful Powhatans for food. Malnutrition and starvation made the effects of disease worse. These factors, along with conflicts with the Powhatan Indians, led to appallingly high mortality rates. By September 1607, half of the 104 Jamestown colonists were dead, and by the following spring only 38 were still alive. Although the Company sent over more colonists, they continued to die off at extraordinary rates. As late as 1616, the English population was only 350, although more than five times that number had emigrated from England (see Table 3–1).

Most died of malnutrition and disease. The lack of food was so great that over the winter of 1609–1610, the inhabitants were reduced to eating roots, acorns, and even human excrement. Archeological evidence shows that they also butchered their dogs and

Table 3-1 English Population of Virginia, 1607–1640

Population in Virginia Colony	Immigration to Virginia Colony
104 (April 1607)	104 (April 1607)
38 (Jan. 1608)	
	120 (Jan. 1608, 1st supply)
130 (Sept. 1608)	
	70 (Sept. 1608, 2nd supply)
200 (late Sept. 1608)	
100 (spring 1609)	
	300 (Fall 1609, 3rd supply)
	540 (1610)
450 (April 1611)	
	660 (1611)
682 (Jan. 1612)	
350 (Jan. 1613)	
	45 (1613–1616)
351 (1616)	
600 (Dec. 1618)	
	900 (1618–1620)
887 (Mar. 1620)	
	1051 (1620–1621)
943 (Mar. 1621)	
	1580 (1621–1622)
1240 (Mar. 1622)	
	1935 (1622–1623)
1241 (April 1623)	
	1646 (1623–1624)
1275 (Feb. 1624)	
1210 (1625)	
	9000 (1625–1634)
4914 (1634)	
	6000 (1635–1640)
8100 (1640)	total: 23,951

Source: Data from Carville Earle, *Geographical Inquiry and American Historical Problems* (Stanford: Stanford University Press, 1992) and Virginia Bernhard, "Men, Women, and Children at Jamestown: Population and Gender in Early Virginia, 1607–1610," *Journal of Southern History*, LVIII (1992).

Note: Although about 24,000 men and women immigrated to Virginia between 1607 and 1640, in 1640 the population stood at only 8,100. Most of the inhabitants fell victim to disease, although the Indian uprising of 1622 took 347 lives.

cats. One man killed his pregnant wife, ripped the fetus from her womb, then salted his wife's corpse and had it half eaten before his crime was discovered.

For centuries this starvation has perplexed historians. The land was fertile and abounded with game, and the James River teemed with fish. The colonists should have been able to raise enough to keep themselves alive. Captain Smith blamed the starvation on the laziness of the colonists, who preferred searching for riches to planting grain. Drought, disease, and malnutrition, however, were probably more to blame than laziness. Moreover, seeing so many die around them only increased survivors' sense of despair and depression.

Decisions by the leadership made the plight worse. Smith, an effective but hated disciplinarian, returned to England in 1609. The new rulers unwisely split up the settlement, sending a group of men down the James River to establish a fort and two other parties to establish settlements in spots inhabited by Indians. In both cases the English were attacked and suffered heavy losses. The survivors, "distracted and forlorn," had begun to abandon the colony when they were stopped by the arrival of Lord De La Warr, the new governor who came to impose harsh martial law.

Troubled Relations with the Powhatans

In Virginia, the English encountered one of the most powerful Indian tribes on the continent, the Powhatans, a confederacy of Algonquian tribes who, under their chieftain Powhatan, were bringing other Algonquians under their control. The English described him as an emperor who "ruleth over many kings." At the time Powhatan's confederacy included about 20,000 Indians, divided into about three dozen tribes. Each group, English and Indian, tried at first to get the other to accept the status of an allied but subordinate tribe. At one point, the English put a fake crown on the kneeling Powahatan's head, imitating the ceremonies in which feudal princes pledged allegiance to a king. For his part, Powhatan held John Smith captive and tried to bully him and other English leaders into acknowledging his supremacy. English bullying sometimes yielded food from the Indians, but it also increased animosity, as did English settlement on Indian land.

English leadership also made tensions worse. Some early leaders had hoped for a biracial society in which the Native Americans would become their loyal subjects and trading partners. Frustrated by their inability either to produce food or to get it from the Indians, Jamestown's leaders came to think of all Indians as enemies.

Lord De La Warr immediately set out to subjugate the Indians. He ordered Powhatan to return English captives. When Powhatan refused, De La Warr ordered an attack on an Indian village. The English killed about 75 inhabitants, burned the town and its cornfields, and captured the wife of a chieftain and her children. As the English sailed back to Jamestown, they threw the children overboard and shot them as they swam in the water. So opened the First Anglo-Powhatan War, the first of three conflicts between 1610 and 1646. The first ended in 1614, when the marriage between Pocahontas and John Rolfe cemented a truce. In permitting his daughter to marry an Englishman, Powhatan was adapting a means he had used to establish his powerful confederacy. He had an unusually large number of wives, selected from across his realm, as a means of tightening his dominion. Each of Powhatan's wives represented an important link between Powhatan's tribe and her own. After each of his wives had borne him a child, she and the child were

Powhatan and English Dwellings These are reconstructions of typical Powhatan Indian and English homes, ca. 1607. Both are dark and small.

sent back to her home village, allowing Powhatan to maintain a presence there. Sometimes, Powhatan also appointed his own son or son-in-law as chief of a village, undermining the customary right of Algonquian women to participate in the selection of leaders. By tradition, chiefs, or *werowances*, were the kinsmen of *werowansqua* (tribal queens). As Powhatan consolidated his personal leadership, he enhanced patriarchal authority in the tribes he controlled.

The marriage of John Rolfe and Pocahontas ushered in a brief period of peace. The English were so pleased with the new alliance that they soon asked for another one of Powhatan's daughters as a bride for one of their councilors. Powhatan refused, fearing that, as with Pocahontas, he would lose a daughter rather than gain a powerful and loyal English son-in-law. Powhatan had failed in his objective of turning the English into his vassals.

Toward a New Political Economy

The tide finally turned against the Powhatans, not so much because of diplomacy or the politics of marriage but because the English finally found a way to make money in Virginia. Rolfe's improved tobacco found a ready market in England, which stimulated the Virginia economy, transforming the colony almost overnight. Within three years, Virginia was shipping 50,000 pounds of tobacco to England per year. Suddenly Virginia experienced an economic boom. By 1619, a man working by himself was making £200 in one crop, and a man with six indentured servants could make £1,000, money only the nobility was accustomed to. Once fortunes this large could be made, the race to Virginia was on.

All that was needed to make money in Virginia was land and people to work it. In 1616 the Virginia Company, which had land but no money, offered land as dividends to its stockholders. Those already living in Virginia were given land, and anyone who came over (or brought another person over) was to be granted 50 acres a head. The Company was

Pocahontas, also known to the Powhatans as Matoaka and to the English
as Rebecca, wore English dress when
she accompanied her English husband John Rolfe to England.

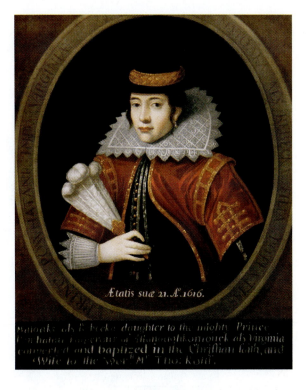

moving toward private enterprise, away from the corporate,
company-directed economy of
the early years. The leadership
of the colony also gave itself
grants, laying the basis for its
own wealth and power. It became far easier to obtain land
in Virginia than in England.

To attract settlers, the
Company replaced martial law
with common law, guaranteeing colonists all the rights of
the English people. The colonists were also granted greater
rights to self-government than were enjoyed by those who lived in England. The first
elected representative government in the New World, the Virginia House of Burgesses
(renamed the General Assembly after the American Revolution), met in Jamestown on
July 30, 1619.

These inducements attracted 3,500 settlers to Virginia in three years, three times as
many as had come in the preceding ten years. By accident more than planning, Virginia
had found the formula for a successful English colony. It was one all other colonies generally followed: offering colonists greater opportunities to make money and greater rights of
self-government than they had at home. These changes came too late, however, to rescue
the Virginia Company, which went bankrupt in 1624. King James I dissolved the Company and turned Virginia into a royal colony under his control.

Toward the Destruction of the Powhatans

As the new colonists spread out, establishing private plantations, English settlers claimed
all the Indians' prime farmland on both sides of the James River and began to move up its
tributaries (see Map 3–1). At the same time, the Powhatans became increasingly dependent on English goods such as metal tools. Moreover, as the English population began to
grow its own food, it had less need of Indian food, the only commodity the Indians had
to trade. The Indians slowly accumulated a debt to the English and lost their economic
independence.

After Powhatan died, his more militant brother, Opechancanough, decided to get rid
of the English. On the morning of March 22, 1622, the Indians struck at all the plantations

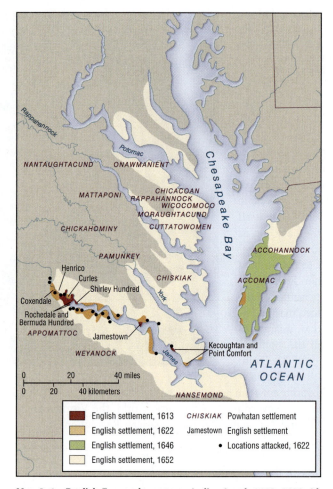

Map 3-1   English Encroachments on Indian Land, 1613–1652 After John Rolfe's development of a marketable strain of tobacco, the English spread out through the Chesapeake region, encroaching steadily on Indian land. Tobacco planters preferred land along the rivers, for casks filled with tobacco bound for England were more easily transported by ship. *Frederic Gleach,* Powhatan's World and Colonial Virginia *(Lincoln: University of Nebraska Press, 1997), and James Horn,* Adapting to a New World: English Society in the Seventeenth-Century Chesapeake *(Chapel Hill: University of North Carolina Press, 1994).*

along the James River, killing one-third of the colonists, including John Rolfe. The Second Anglo-Powhatan War, which continued for another 10 years, had begun. This war marked a turning point in English policy. Although some of the English recognized that the Indian attack had been caused by "our own perfidious dealing," most decided that the Indians were untrustworthy and incapable of being converted to the English way of life. Therefore, a policy of extermination was justified. Some were almost happy that the Indians had attacked; John Smith concluded that the massacre "will be good for the Plantation, because now we have just cause to destroy them by all meanes possible." Until this point, the English had claimed only land that the Indians were not farming. Now they seized territory the Indians had cleared and planted. In only 15 years' time, the English and Indians in Virginia had become implacable enemies.

Indian resistance made the English more determined to stay, and with the tobacco economy booming, settlers poured into Virginia. They spread across the Chesapeake to the Eastern Shore and north to the Potomac River. The aged Opechancanough, determined to make one final push, struck again on April 18, 1644, killing 400 and taking many prisoners.

The Third Anglo-Powhatan War ended, however, in the Indians' total defeat two years later. Opechancanough was killed. The English took complete possession of the land between the James and York rivers. Henceforth, no Indian was allowed to enter this territory unless he was bringing a message from the chief *werowance*. Any English person who sheltered an Indian without permission was put to death. The land north of the York River was set aside for the Indians, making it the first American Indian reservation. Soon, English settlers moved into that region, too. It was not the last time that the English settlers would break a treaty with the Indians.

A New Colony in Maryland

Virginia's original plan to make money from trading with the local Indians was not entirely forgotten. When tobacco prices dipped in the 1620s, trade became attractive once again. By the late 1620s, an outpost had been established at the northern end of Chesapeake Bay to obtain beaver furs from the Susquehannocks. Sir George Calvert, the first Lord Baltimore and a Catholic, saw the commercial potential of this region and in 1632 persuaded King Charles I, a Catholic sympathizer, to grant him the land north of the Potomac and south of the Delaware that was "not yet cultivated and planted." This territory became Maryland, the first proprietary colony, that is, a colony owned literally by an individual and his heirs. (Virginia was originally a charter colony, held by a group of private shareholders. Unlike royal colonies, in charter and proprietary colonies the English Crown turned over both financing and management to the shareholders or proprietors.) Maryland, named after the Catholic queen of England, remained the hereditary possession of the Calvert family until the American Revolution.

As the first proprietary colony, Maryland established a pattern for subsequent proprietorships. The proprietor had extensive powers to grant land and make laws by himself, but perhaps because Calvert knew he would have to compete for settlers with Virginia, which had a representative government, he agreed to a representative assembly. In 1649 that assembly passed the Act of Toleration, which said that no one would be "compelled to the beliefe or exercise of any other Religion against his or her consent." Even though religious toleration was extended only to Christians, Maryland was among the most tolerant places in the world. Moreover, this right was extended to women as well as men. (This experiment in religious toleration ended, however, in 1689, when Coode's Rebellion overthrew the proprietor, making Maryland a royal colony and, in 1702, establishing the Anglican Church. See Chapter 4.)

Although Maryland's population increased slowly, the familiar political economy emerged quickly. As in Virginia, attracting colonists required greater opportunities and freedoms—of self-government and of religion—than they enjoyed in England. During the conflict with the Powhatan Confederacy, the booming tobacco economy drew settlers to Virginia and, after about 1650, to Maryland as well. Although they had separate governments, Virginia and Maryland had similar political economies, based on tobacco. The defeat of the Indians made more land available for cultivation; the colonies needed only people to work it.

The Political Economy of Slavery Emerges

Chesapeake society in the first half of the seventeenth century was shaped by four forces: weak government, the market for tobacco, the availability of land, and the need for labor. Because government was weak, the forces of plantation agriculture were unchecked, and the profit motive operated without restraint. Those who could take advantage of these opportunities—male and female both—profited wildly, whereas the poor, both white and African, were without defense. Artificial distinctions such as social status counted for little in comparison with willpower, physical strength, and ruthlessness. Even gender roles were undermined, as women worked in the fields and wealthy widows controlled large estates. In this environment the political economy of slavery took root.

The Problem of a Labor Supply

Once the crises of the early years had passed, the Chesapeake's greatest problem was securing laborers to produce tobacco. As soon as John Rolfe brought in his first successful crop, the Virginia governor began pressing England to send him its poor. The Virginia Company also encouraged the emigration of women, for the young colony was primarily male. No matter how many colonists came, however, the demand for labor always outstripped the supply. By 1660, 50,000 Britons, mostly single men in their 20s, had migrated to the Chesapeake, but the population was still only a little over 35,000. Because of the poor water supply and disease, the death rate remained extraordinarily high.

The profits from tobacco were so great and the risk of death so high that landowners squeezed out every penny of profit as quickly as they could. Those with land and servants to work it could become rich overnight. Colonial officials, including members of the legislature, discovered a variety of ways to make themselves wealthy. Great wealth, however, could be achieved only by the labor of others, and the demand for labor was almost insatiable. Perhaps 90 percent of those who migrated to the Chesapeake in the seventeenth century came as servants, and half died before completing their term of service. In England, servants had some basic protections, but in Virginia, working conditions were deadly brutal. In 1623, Richard Frethorne, a young Virginia servant, wrote to his parents in England. "With weeping tears," he begged them to send food. "We must work early and late for a mess of water gruel and a mouthful of bread and beef."

Servants might be beaten so severely that they died, or they might find their indentures (the contract that bound them to service for a period of usually seven years) sold from one master to another. They found little protection from the courts. They were not, in fact, slaves. They would become free if they outlived their period of indenture; they retained all of the rights of English people, and their servitude was not hereditary. But they were far worse off than servants in England.

The Origins of Slavery in the Chesapeake

Other New World plantation societies in which labor was in short supply had already turned to slavery, so it was probably only a matter of time until the Chesapeake did so as well. Historians do not know precisely when slavery was first practiced in the Chesapeake colonies, but Africans first arrived in Virginia in 1619, when a Dutch ship sailing off course sold its cargo of "twenty Negars" to the Virginians. It is not clear, however, if these Africans were indentured servants or lifelong slaves. As long as life expectancy was low, it was more profitable for a planter to purchase an indentured servant for a period of seven years than a slave for life. Not until life expectancy improved toward the end of the seventeenth century were significant numbers of African slaves imported into the Chesapeake

All English plantation colonies followed the same pattern in making the transition from white servitude to African slavery. The transition was quick in some places and slow in others; in Virginia, it took about three-quarters of a century. This shift was made everywhere without debate. The primary factors dictating how English colonists adopted African slavery were the need for plantation laborers and the availability of African slaves at a good price. At the time that the English began to import African slaves into their colonies in the seventeenth century, the Spanish and Portuguese had been using enslaved Africans as plantation laborers for well over a century. The English were entering into a global economy already reliant on slave labor.

If there was any discussion about the justice of slavery, the English claimed that slavery was an appropriate punishment for certain crimes and for prisoners taken in just wars. No white people were ever enslaved in the English colonies, however. It was a practice reserved for "strangers," primarily foreigners of a non-Christian religion. Still, all the British colonies eventually practiced slavery, and it became critical to plantation economies. African slaves were even brought back to the British Islands, and by the middle of the eighteenth century, 2 percent of London's population was African.

Even before substantial contact with African people, the English and other northern Europeans probably harbored prejudice against dark-skinned people. By the second half of the sixteenth century, the English were depicting Africans in derogatory terms, saying that Africans were unattractive, with "dispositions most savage and brutish," a "people of beastly living" who "contract no matrimonie, neither have respect to chastity." Northern Europeans considered African women particularly monstrous, sexually promiscuous, and neglectful of their children. Although these views were not used to justify slavery, they formed the basis for the racism that would develop along with the slave system.

During the seventeenth century, African slavery and white and African servitude existed side by side. The Chesapeake was a society with slaves, but it was still not a slave society. The first clear evidence of enslavement of Africans in the Chesapeake dates to 1639, when the Maryland Assembly passed a law guaranteeing "all the Inhabitants of this Province being Christians (Slaves excepted)" all the rights and liberties of "any natural born subject of England." The first Virginia law recognizing slavery, passed in 1661, said that any English servant who ran away with an African would have to serve additional time not only for himself but for the African as well. Historians presume that such Africans were already slaves for life and hence were incapable of serving any additional time.

Such laws show the great familiarity that existed between white and black servants. Slaves and white servants worked together, enjoyed leisure together, had sexual relations

AMERICA AND THE WORLD

>> Christian Slaves in Muslim Africa

At the same time that Europeans were enslaving Africans and transporting them to the New World to labor on plantations, North Africans were carrying on a vigorous trade in European slaves. Between 1500 and 1800, the North African Barbary States, which were part of the Ottoman Empire, captured and sold as many as 1.25 million Europeans and sold them as slaves to other North Africans. This slave trade was an extension of the near-constant state of war between the Ottoman and Hapsburg empires. International law held that enemies captured in war could be enslaved and that enslavement was preferable to death. This was the rationale used to justify enslavement, even when the war was fought to obtain slaves.

Indeed, most of the European slaves captured by North Africans were used as galley slaves in corsairs, pirate ships that preyed on commercial traffic in the Mediterranean and the coastal regions of southern Europe. North Africans needed slaves in order to obtain more slaves: the mortality rate was so high—estimated as high as 20 percent a year—that the demand for fresh slaves was almost insatiable.

The treatment of slaves, particularly in the galleys, was brutal. There, as many as five men would be chained together at each oar of the corsair. They would row night and day, for days on end, always chained, and half naked and with no protection from the elements, so that their "flesh is burned off their backs."

The corsairs preyed on ships and also along the coastlines. The Mediterranean islands of Sardinia and Sicily were particularly vulnerable, but so also were coastal Italy and Spain. In some regions, such as Italy, whole villages were abandoned and moved inland by governments too weak to protect their citizens. Although most Christian slaves came from southern Europe, North African slaving expeditions also ranged north, not only seizing British ships but also raiding Ireland, Cornwall, and Devon, ultimately seizing perhaps 7,000 to 9,000 British men, women, and children.

Almost all the captives seized from ships were male, but when raiders went ashore, they took women and children as well. Still, the vast majority of European slaves—perhaps 95 percent—were male. In addition to serving as galley slaves, they worked primarily in heavy construction. Some became house servants. Europeans believed that some of the men, particularly young ones, were turned into male prostitutes and sexual slaves. Although it is true that, unlike Europe at the same time, North African cities had vibrant homosexual cultures that included European homosexual men, it is hard to know how widespread the practice of sexual enslavement was.

Although the number of Europeans enslaved by North Africans is just a fraction of the number of Africans transported to the Americas, the Muslim trade in Europeans provides a context for the African slave trade. First, both slave trades developed in an era when captives of war were often enslaved. Second, the basis for both slave trades was ethnic and religious, not racial. Only later was the African slave trade justified in racial terms. And the African slave trade developed differently in another way: North Africans were willing to ransom back Europeans and often seized wealthy Europeans in the hope of selling them back for huge sums. Europeans, however, never ransomed Africans. Once Africans were seized by European slave traders, they lost any hope of ever returning to their native lands. Finally, the trade in Europeans was essentially a premodern economic enterprise, neither requiring much capital nor producing much wealth. The trade in Africans, however, required significant capital investment and efficient organization. Plantation slavery was a modern business enterprise, which developed new methods of turning human beings into property.

with each other, and ran away together. As late as 1680, most of the plantation laborers were still white indentured servants. There is no evidence that they were kept separate from Africans by law or inclination.

As long as the black population remained small, the color line was blurry. Not until late in the seventeenth century were laws passed that restricted free African Americans. In fact, in 1660, Anthony Johnson, an African who had arrived in Virginia as a servant in 1621, owned both land and African slaves. In the 40 years that he had been in Virginia, slavery had become institutionalized and recognized by the law, but laws separating the races had yet to be enacted.

Gender and the Social Order in the Chesapeake

The founders of England's colonies hoped to replicate the social order they had known at home. As early as 1619, the Virginia Company began to bring single women to the colony to become brides of the unmarried planters. As in England, it was expected that men would perform all the "outside" labor, including planting, farming, and tending large farm animals. Women would do all the "inside" work, including preserving and preparing food, spinning and weaving, making and repairing clothing, and gardening. In English society, a farmer's wife was not simply a man's sexual partner and companion; she was also the mistress of a successful household economy. Both men and women were vital to the society the English wanted to create in the Chesapeake.

However, the powerful tobacco economy transformed both the economy and society of the New World. With profits from tobacco so high, women went directly into the tobacco fields instead of the kitchen. Children were in the fields as soon as they could work. Only when a man became wealthy did he hire a servant—often a woman—to replace his wife in the fields. As a result, for many years, Virginia society lacked the "comforts of home" that women produced, such as prepared food, homemade clothing, and even soap. Tobacco was everything.

Colonial society also weakened patriarchal controls. Chesapeake governments tried—but failed—to control immigrant women, insisting, for example, that a woman receive government permission before marrying and prosecuting for slander women who spoke out against the government or their neighbors. But colonial government was relatively weak, and, far from their own fathers, women found themselves unexpectedly free from traditional restrictions.

Although women without the protection of fathers were vulnerable in seventeenth-century plantation societies, where men outnumbered women three or four to one, women were often in a position of relative power. Local governments struggled to impose order by prosecuting women for adultery, fornication, and giving birth to bastard children. The public, however, was more tolerant of sexual misconduct than government officials were. When, for example, a ship's captain was executed for having sex with a boy on his ship (one of five recorded executions for homosexual activity in the period), the protests were so widespread that the protesters themselves were punished.

The first generation of women to immigrate to the Chesapeake region married relatively late—in their mid-20s. As a result, they had relatively few children, and it was many decades before Chesapeake society reproduced itself naturally. Perhaps half of all children born in the colony died in infancy, and one marriage partner was also likely to die within seven years of marriage. At least until 1680 or so, to be a widow, widower, or orphan was the normal state of affairs. Widows who inherited their husbands' possessions were powerful and in demand on the marriage market. Children, however, often lost their inheritances to a stepparent.

A Bible Commonwealth in the New England Wilderness

In 1620, 13 years after the founding of the Virginia Colony, England planted another permanent colony at Plymouth and, nine years after that, one at Massachusetts Bay. In many ways the Virginia and Massachusetts colonies could not have been more different. The primary impetus behind the Massachusetts settlement was religious. Both the Pilgrims at Plymouth and the much more numerous Puritans at Massachusetts Bay sought to escape persecution and to establish new communities based on God's law as they understood it. The Puritans and Pilgrims were middle class, and their ventures were well financed and capably planned. The environment was much healthier than that of the Chesapeake, and the population reproduced itself rapidly. Relations with the Indians were better than in the Chesapeake. Nonetheless, the Puritan movement was a product of the same consolidation and growth of national states in Europe and the expansion of commerce that led to the European exploration of the New World.

The English Origins of the Puritan Movement

In Europe during the sixteenth century, ordinary people and powerful monarchs had vastly different reasons for abandoning the Roman Catholic Church in favor of one of the new Protestant churches. In England, these differing motives led to 130 years of conflict, including a revolution and massive religious persecution. In the 1530s, Henry VIII established his own state religion, the Church of England, for political rather than for pious reasons. After many years of marriage to Catherine of Aragon, the daughter of Isabel and Fernando, Henry still did not have a male heir. With one of Catherine's ladies-in-waiting, Anne Boleyn, already pregnant, Henry pressed the pope for an annulment of his marriage to Catherine. In 1533, the pope refused the annulment, and Henry removed the Catholic Church as the established religion of England, replacing it with his own Church of England. He confiscated Catholic Church lands, which he redistributed to members of the English nobility in return for their loyalty. In one move, Henry eliminated a powerful political rival, the Roman Catholic Church, and consolidated his rule over his nobility. Replacing the Catholic Church did not bring stability, however. Henry's successors alternated between Protestantism and Catholicism. Under the reign of Catherine's daughter Mary, hundreds of Protestants left the country to avoid being burned at the stake.

When Mary's Protestant sister, Elizabeth I, ascended the throne, these exiles returned, having picked up the Calvinist doctrine of predestination on the continent. John Calvin, the Swiss Protestant reformer, insisted that even before people were born, God foreordained "to some eternal life and to some eternal damnation." Although the Church of England adopted Calvin's doctrine of predestination, it never held to it thoroughly enough or followed through on other reforms well enough to please the Puritans. And because the monarchs viewed challenges to the state religion as challenges to the state itself, religious dissenters were frequently persecuted.

What Did the Puritans Believe?

Like all Christians, Puritans believed that humanity was guilty of the original sin committed by Adam and Eve when they disobeyed God in the Garden of Eden. They believed that God's son, Jesus Christ, had given his life to pay (or atone) for the original sin and that, as a consequence, all faithful Christians would be forgiven their sins and admitted to heaven after they died. Unlike other Christian religions, Calvinism insisted there was nothing anyone could do to guarantee that God would grant the faith, by an act of "grace," that would save them from hell.

Protestants rejected the hierarchy of the Catholic Church, maintaining that the relationship between God and humanity was direct, "unmediated." Because every person had direct access to the inspired word of God through the Bible, Protestants promoted literacy and translating the Bible into modern languages. As Calvinists, Puritans wanted to "purify" the Church of England of all remnants of Catholicism, including all sacraments, rituals, and priestly hierarchy.

Finally, Anglicans had come to think that believing Christians could earn their way to heaven by good works, a doctrine the Puritans labeled Arminianism. Puritans, in contrast, believed that salvation was the free gift of God and that human beings could not force his hand. Individuals could only prepare for grace by reading and studying the Bible, so that they understood God's plan, and by attempting to live the best lives they could. Because they could never be certain of salvation, Puritans always lived with anxiety.

Puritanism contained a powerful tension between intellect and emotion. On the one hand, Puritanism was a highly rational religion. It required all of its followers to read and study the Bible and to listen to long sermons on fine points of theology. As a result, Puritans, male and female, were highly literate. On the other hand, Puritans believed that no amount of book learning could get a person into heaven and that saving grace was as much a matter of the heart as of the mind. The Puritan movement always struggled to contain this tension, as some of its believers embraced a more fully rational religion and others abandoned book learning for emotion.

Puritans believed that church membership was only for those who could demonstrate that they were saved. As they were persecuted for their faith, they came to believe that, like the Israelites of old, they were God's chosen people, that they had a covenant or agreement with God, and that if they did his will, he would make them prosper.

The Puritans first attempted to reform the Church of England. Once they saw that the Church would resist more reformation and move further from the Calvinist principle of predestination, some Puritans began to make other plans.

The Pilgrim Colony at Plymouth

The first Puritan colony in North America was established in 1620 at Plymouth, by a group of Puritans known as the Pilgrims, Separatists who had given up hope of reforming the Church of England. The Pilgrims had already moved to Holland, thinking its Calvinism would offer a better home. It was hard for the Pilgrims to fit themselves into Holland's economy, however, and they found their children seduced by "the manifold temptations of the place."

By 1620 the Pilgrims were ready to accept the Virginia Company of London's offer of land in America for any English people who would pay their own way. With the colony at Jamestown foundering and the Company looking for other opportunities, it filled the two ships in the expedition, the *Mayflower* and the *Speedwell*, with non-Pilgrims (known as the "Strangers") willing to pay their own way, Separatists, and Pilgrims.

The *Speedwell* had to turn back, but the *Mayflower* arrived at Plymouth, Massachusetts, in November 1620, far north of its destination and outside the jurisdiction of the Virginia Company. Because the Pilgrims had landed in territory that had no legal claim and no lawful government, 41 of the adult men on board signed a document known as the Mayflower Compact. The men bound themselves into a "Civil Body Politic" to make laws and govern the colony and also to recognize the authority of the governor. Although the Compact provided a legal basis for government until the colony was annexed by Massachusetts Bay in 1691, it was not a wholly democratic document. Some of the Strangers had been talking about mutiny, so the Pilgrims wanted to make their government secure.

Only one of the 102 passengers had died en route, but only half of the party survived the harsh first winter. Years later the second governor, William Bradford, remembered the Pilgrims' ordeals. The Indians, he claimed, were "savage barbarians...readier to fill their sides full of arrows than otherwise." And their new home was "a hideous and desolate wilderness, full of wild beasts and wild men."

In fact, the Plymouth Colony would never have survived had it not been for the assistance of friendly Indians. Like the French in New France and unlike the English at Jamestown, the Pilgrims established diplomatic relations both because they were better diplomats than the Jamestown colonists and because the local Indians needed foreign allies. Before the Pilgrims' arrival, Plymouth Bay had been inhabited by as many as 2,000 Indians, with ten times as many in the surrounding region. Then European fishermen and traders introduced some fatal disease—perhaps viral hepatitis, spread by spoiled food—which was carried along the trading network and killed 90 percent of the population. Indians "died in heapes as they lay in their houses," their villages filled with the skulls and bones of the unburied dead. So recently had Patuxet and Pokanoket Indians inhabited the region that the Pilgrims were able to supplement their meager supplies by rummaging Indian graves, homes, and hidden stores of grain.

The world was vastly changed for Native Americans who survived. Squanto, a Patuxet warrior, had spent the plague years in Europe, having been kidnapped by an English ship's captain. Much like Don Luís de Velasco (see Chapter 2), once back in Massachusetts, Squanto abandoned the English exploring party that had returned him. He found that his tribe, the Patuxet, had almost entirely disappeared. The once-powerful Pokanokets, led by Massasoit, were now paying tribute to the Narragansetts, who had escaped the deadly disease. Squanto persuaded him that the English might be allies against the Narragansetts. Thus in the spring of 1621, Squanto and Samoset, a member of another band, offered the Pilgrims their assistance and showed them how to grow corn.

From the Indian perspective, this assistance was a diplomatic initiative, enabling a treaty between the Pokanokets and the Pilgrims. By the time Squanto died in 1622, he had helped secure the future of the Pilgrims' Plymouth Colony. It grew too slowly for its investors, however,[who eventually sold their shares to the Pilgrims. Plymouth remained a separate colony until 1691, when it was absorbed into the larger, more influential Massachusetts. Plymouth demonstrated that New England could be inhabited by Europeans and that effective diplomatic relations with local Indians were critical for a colony's survival.

The Puritan Colony at Massachusetts Bay

Throughout the 1620s, other groups of English people attempted to found colonies in the region around Massachusetts. Most of them failed on their own, although one, Thomas Morton's community at Merry Mount, was actually crushed by the Pilgrims at Plymouth. Morton and a handful of English servants had adopted Indian customs, drinking and "dancing and frisking" with the local Indian men and women.

In 1629, the Massachusetts Bay Company, a group of London merchants, received a charter from King Charles I to establish a colony. The plan was similar to that on which Virginia had been founded. The investors in the joint-stock company would have full rights to a swath of land reaching from Massachusetts Bay west across the entire continent. Along with Puritans looking for a new home, the company included some who still hoped, against all evidence, to turn a profit from trade. The Puritans wished to make the colony entirely self-governing.

The expedition began in 1630, and by the end of that year Boston and 10 other towns had been founded. By the early 1640s, between 20,000 and 25,000 Britons had migrated to the Puritan colonies of Plymouth, Massachusetts Bay, Connecticut, Rhode Island, and New Hampshire. Although fewer than half as many migrated to New England as to the Chesapeake region, by 1660 both had populations of a similar size—around 35,000.

New England was able to catch up and keep pace with the Chesapeake for two reasons. First, New England was a much healthier region. Long, cold winters killed the mosquitoes that carried fatal diseases, the water supply was good, and food was plentiful. Second, Puritans migrated as families. Ninety percent came as part of a family group, a pattern almost exactly the reverse of that in the Chesapeake. In the healthy environment of New England, the population soon reproduced itself.

The Puritans came to stay. Before leaving England, they sold their property. Most were prosperous members of the middle range of society. Many of the men were professionals—craftsmen, doctors, lawyers, and ministers—people who profited from the changing English economy of the late sixteenth and early seventeenth centuries. Again, the contrast with the Chesapeake was dramatic. There, the vast majority of migrants were people with few skills and dim prospects.

The New England Way

The Puritans were men and women with a mission. Their first governor, John Winthrop, set out the vision of a Bible commonwealth in a sermon he preached aboard the *Arbella* in the spring of 1630, even before the ship docked at Boston. God, Winthrop said, had entered into a covenant with the Puritans, just as they had entered into a covenant with one another. Together they had taken enormous risks and begun an extraordinary experiment to see whether they could establish a society based on the word of God: "We shall be as a city upon a hill, the eyes of all people are upon us. So that if we shall deal falsely with our God in this work we have undertaken, and so cause Him to withdraw his present help from us, we shall be made a story and a by-word through the world." This broad vision shaped the development of New England's society.

This communal vision made early New Englanders relatively cohesive. Each town was created by a grant of land by the Massachusetts General Court (the name given to the legislature) to a group of citizens. The settlers in turn entered into a covenant with one another to establish a government and distribute the land they held collectively. This was by no means a democracy, for Puritans believed in hierarchy, and their vision was more communal than individualist. Nonetheless, there was considerably more economic equality and cohesion than there would be in the next centuries.

At first, the new towns divided up only a portion of the land that they held, reserving the rest for newcomers and the children of the original founders. The land was distributed unequally, according to social status and family size (see Table 3–2). Although New England society was relatively egalitarian, with only a small gap between the richest and poorest, the Puritans set out to create a social hierarchy. The rich and powerful were supposed to take care of the poor, and Puritan towns did assist all those who could not care for

 Table 3-2 Distribution of Land in Rowley, Massachusetts, 1639–1642

Rowley, 1639–c. 1642	
Acres	**No. of Grants**
over 400	
351–400	
301–350	
251–300	
201–250	1
151–200	1
101–150	
51–100	7
21–50	22
20 or less	63
no record	1
Total	95

Source: David Grayson Allen, *In English Ways: The Movement of Societies and the Transferal of English Local Law and Custom to Massachusetts Bay in the Seventeenth Century* (Chapel Hill University of North Carolina Press, 1981), p. 32.

Note: Between 1639 and 1642, the town of Rowley, Massachusetts, distributed a little over 2,000 acres to 95 families—an average of just 23 acres per family—even though the grant to the town was for many thousand acres. Although most grants were for less than 20 acres, some families received considerably more. The founders of Rowley wanted to re-create the hierarchical social order they had known in England.

themselves. Each town administered itself through a town meeting, a periodic gathering of the adult male property owners to attend to the town's business. In the past, historians pointed to the democratic elements in the town meeting as the source of American democracy. More recently, historians have emphasized undemocratic elements. Participation was restricted to adult male property holders, who were only 35 percent of the adult residents, once women are considered. In addition, the habit of deference to the powerful, prosperous, and educated was so strong that a small group of influential men tended to govern each town. Moreover, Puritans abhorred conflict, so great social pressure was used to ensure harmony and limit dissent. If democracy means the right to disagree and majority rule in open elections, then the New England town meeting was not fully democratic. However, even with all these restrictions, the New England town meeting was far more democratic than any form of government in England at the time, where the vast majority of men, not to mention women, were excluded from political participation.

Changing the Land to Fit the Political Economy

The Puritans' corporate social vision was generally compatible with a capitalist political economy. Although land was distributed to towns, once those towns transferred parcels of the land to individual farmers, they were free to leave it to their heirs, to sell it to whomever they pleased, and to buy more land from others. Any improvements on the land (from clearing away trees to building homes, fences, dams, or mills) remained the property of the owners. These practices followed English law.

The contrast with Indian patterns of land use was dramatic. Indians held their land communally, not individually. The entire group had to consent to its sale. Moreover, when Indians "sold" land to the Puritans, they thought that they were giving them the right to use the land only and to share the land with them. They might allow the Puritans to build a village, plant, and hunt, while they retained similar rights over the same parcel of land, including the right to allow it to be used by several groups of Europeans at once.

The Puritans' notion of exclusive land rights was a cornerstone of their political economy. Because a man could profit from the improvements made on his land and pass those improvements on to his heirs, he had incentives to make them. Moreover, not only the land but its products became commodities to be sold. Like other European colonists, the Puritans turned their Indian neighbors into commercial hunters. For centuries, the Indians had taken only as many beaver as they needed, but soon they were overhunting, which led to the disappearance of beaver in the region. The Puritans themselves cleared the forests of trees. They found a ready market for timber in England, as New England's trees were much taller and straighter than any known in Europe. The English navy came to depend on New England for its masts. Although the bounty of the land had seemed limitless, by 1800 much of southern New England had been stripped of its forests and native wildlife.

Prosperity did not come to Massachusetts immediately. For the first decade, the colony maintained a favorable balance of trade with England only by sending back the money that new immigrants brought with them in return for goods from the mother country. New England's rocky soil made it impossible to develop a cash crop such as tobacco. In the 1640s and 1650s, the government encouraged local manufacturing (to cut down on imports) and export of raw materials. Through government policy and individual initiative, New Englanders eventually profited from selling timber, wood products, and fish and by acting as merchants.

>> New England Settlements

When we picture a New England town, we think of a cluster of two-story, white-clapboard colonial homes with black shutters, arrayed around the town green, at one end of which sits a little church, its steeple rising above the village. Many such villages dot the New England countryside, but they date not from the colonial period but from the early nineteenth century.

When the Pilgrims and the Puritans after them moved to New England, they had to adapt to a new environment. Many of their preachers hoped that they would settle in small villages in which the houses were close to each other. In 1635, the Massachusetts General Court instructed that "noe dwelling howse shalbe builte above half a myle from the meeting howse."

This law, however, was an after-the-fact attempt to keep the population from dispersing. From the earliest years of Plymouth, the settlers spread out, seeking pastures for their cattle. It was by now too late to pull New Englanders back into clustered villages.

The only places in New England where settlers built their houses close to each other and to the church were more prosperous market and commercial towns. Many of the first New England settlers had lived in market towns in England, and they would have practiced their crafts and trades in the New World if they could have earned a living in that way. In New England, most of them turned to farming, and in particular raising cattle, which required large expanses of pas-

The Puritan Family

Like most early-modern western Europeans, Puritans thought of the family as the society in microcosm, or "a little Church, and a little commonwealth." There was no sharp distinction between home and the wider world. Although Harvard College was founded in 1636 (to train ministers) and the Massachusetts General Court established a system of public education in 1647, most early instruction and virtually all vocational teaching took place at home. Parents were required to teach their children to read the Bible.

The family was also the center of the Puritans' economy. Farmers, of course, worked at home, as did almost all craftsmen. Women also performed tasks critical to the survival of the family. Although tasks were assigned by gender, in the absence of her husband a woman could assume his responsibilities, selling the products he had made or even fighting off Indians. The family, like society, was a hierarchy, with the husband at the top and his wife as his "deputy."

Puritans lived in fear of lawlessness, and they used the family as an instrument of order. Puritans considered excessive affection and particularly excessive maternal love a tureland. Fortunately, New Englanders could spread themselves and their cattle out along the coast's many marshes and meadows. Even in Boston, the largest settlement, the farming population soon spread out. Boston's site was chosen because of its harbor, its water supply, and its defensive capacity rather than its farmlands. The original settlers sent their sons and servants to outlying areas to farm for them, and they eventually created new towns. The environment and the drive to earn a living were more powerful forces than religion or community. Over time, this impulse toward economic independence would undermine the forces of cohesion.

The first houses the settlers built were little more than huts, small one-room windowless cottages with chimneys made out of clay-covered logs. But even later homes were modest one-and-a-half-story, unpainted houses with low ceilings and very few windows. Although affluent people such as Governor John Winthrop began to build larger and more elegant homes as late as the end of the eighteenth century, most New England homes were still very small by modern standards. The typical house was just over 800 square feet, perhaps 40 feet long by 20 feet wide, with many only half that size, or even smaller. Considering that eight or nine people typically lived in such homes, living conditions could be quite crowded.

Only when the scale of economic development changed, so that town centers could sustain a variety of stores and shops, did New Englanders build homes around the village green and begin painting them white. The classic New England village is in fact the creation of the nineteenth century. Until then, most New Englanders lived in small dark homes scattered across the countryside, closer to their farmlands than to their neighbors.

danger. Children were subjected to strict discipline not out of cruelty but from deep religious convictions. Considering that Puritan women bore on average eight or nine children and that families were confined in small houses over long New England winters, this harmony was probably necessary for survival.

Despite the importance of control, Puritan households were hardly prisons. If Puritans believed that men were the natural heads of the household and that women bore particular responsibility for Eve's original sin, they also believed that both were equally capable of God's grace. Puritans distrusted the passion of love, which could lead to impulsiveness and disorder. They had great respect, however, for the natural affection that grew over the course of marriage.

So successful were the early Puritans in establishing tight-knit communities that only two years after their great migration to America had begun, the Reverend Thomas Welde could write proudly back to England that "here I find three great blessings, peace, plenty, and health. . . . I profess if I might have my wish in what part of the world to dwell I know no other place on the whole globe of the earth where I would be rather than here."

Dissension in the Puritan Ranks

The Puritan movement embodied tensions that created individual and social turmoil. Puritans had difficulty balancing emotion and intellect, the individual and the community, spiritual equality and social hierarchy, and anxiety over salvation and the satisfaction of thinking oneself a chosen people. The Puritans also had no mechanisms for handling dissent, which they interpreted as a replay of original sin. The migration to a strange land, populated by people they thought of as savages, as well as the pressure of thinking that the whole world was watching them, only increased the Puritans' desire to maintain a strict order.

Roger Williams and Toleration

The Massachusetts Bay Colony was only a year old when trouble appeared in the person of Roger Williams, a brilliant and obstinate young minister. No sooner had he landed than he announced that he was really a Separatist and would not accept appointment at a church unless it repudiated its ties to the Church of England. Massachusetts Bay was already walking a fine line between outward obedience to the laws of England and inner rejection of the English way of life, and an explicit repudiation of the established church was thought to be an act of political suicide.

Without a church of his own, Williams began preaching to those who would listen. Saying that the king had no right to grant land owned by the Indians, he questioned the validity of the Massachusetts charter and argued for strict separation of church and state, as well as strict separation of the converted and the unconverted. Williams went so far as to advocate religious toleration, with each congregation or sect governing itself completely free from state interference.

These doctrines were heresy to both Puritan church and state. In 1635, when Williams violated an order to stop preaching his unorthodox views, the magistrates decided to ship him immediately to England, where he might be imprisoned or even executed. John Winthrop warned Williams of his fate, giving him time to sneak away to Narragansett Bay, outside the jurisdiction of Massachusetts Bay. Williams and some followers established the new colony of Rhode Island, which was chartered in 1644. The colony, which became a refuge for dissenters of all sorts, was referred to by Massachusetts Puritans as "the sewer of New England."

Anne Hutchinson and the Equality of Believers

One of Puritanism's many tensions concerned the position of women. By insisting on the equality of all true believers before God and the importance of marriage, Protestantism and especially its Puritan branch undermined the starkly negative image of women that prevailed in sixteenth-century Europe. When Puritan ministers preached that women and men were both "joynt Heirs of salvation" and that women, rather than being a "necessary evil," were in fact "a necessary good," they were directly criticizing both the Catholic legacy and common folk belief.

Puritanism extended women respect, but it also insisted they be subordinate to men. In their hierarchical society, woman's position was clearly beneath that of man. Puritanism struggled to find the balance between women's spiritual equality and their earthly subordination: although most Puritan women deferred to male authority, others seized the opportunity that Puritanism seemed to offer. Without exception, the Puritan authorities put them back in their place.

Anne Hutchinson was just over 40 when she, her husband, and their 12 children followed the Reverend John Cotton to Massachusetts Bay. Cotton was a popular preacher who placed particular emphasis on the doctrine of predestination. Hutchinson pushed that doctrine to its logical, if unsettling, conclusion. She claimed that she had experienced several direct revelations, one telling her to follow Cotton to Boston. At informal Bible discussion meetings at her Boston home, which even the new governor attended, Hutchinson challenged the Puritan doctrine of "preparation": if God had truly chosen those whom he would save, it was unnecessary for Puritans to prepare themselves for saving grace by leading sin-free lives. Nor was good behavior a reliable sign of salvation. Hutchinson did not favor sin; she simply believed her neighbors were wrong in thinking that good works would save them. She accused them of the heresy of Arminianism. By claiming that the Holy Spirit spoke directly to her, Hutchinson opened herself to charges of another heresy, *antinomianism*.

Hutchinson's views were so popular that perhaps a majority of the colony's residents became her followers. Once she accused certain ministers of being unconverted, the colony leaders mounted a campaign against her and her allies. In 1637 they moved the site of the election for governor outside Boston, where her strength was greatest, so that John Winthrop could win. Then, after her most prominent ally among the ministers had been banished, Hutchinson was put on trial for slandering the ministry, convicted, and ordered to leave the colony. Followed by 80 other families, she and her family found temporary refuge in Roger Williams's Rhode Island. (She later moved to New Netherland, where she was killed in an Indian war.) The fact that Hutchinson's ideas came from a woman made them even more dangerous to the Massachusetts leadership. John Winthrop suggested that she might be a witch. Without any evidence at all of sexual misconduct, ministers asserted that Hutchinson and her female followers were driven by lust and that unless they were punished, it would lead to communal living, open sex, and the repudiation of marriage.

It is sometimes asserted that Puritans came to New England in search of religious freedom, but they never would have made that claim. They wanted the liberty to follow their own religion but actively denied that opportunity to others. Puritans insisted on their right to keep out nonbelievers. "No man hath right to come into us," John Winthrop wrote, "without our consent."

Puritan Indian Policy and the Pequot War

The Puritan dissidents were all critical of the Puritans' Indian policy. Thomas Morton had been "frisking" with the Indians, Roger Williams insisted on purchasing land from the Indians instead of simply seizing it, and the men in the Hutchinson family refused to fight in the Pequot War of 1637. The Puritans had been fortunate in settling in a region in which the Indian population had recently been decimated and in having the English-speaking Squanto's diplomatic services. The Puritan communities expanded so rapidly, however, that they soon intruded on land populated by Indians who had no intention of giving them exclusive rights to it.

Within a few years of the founding of the Massachusetts Bay Colony, small groups of Puritans were spreading out in all directions (see Map 3–2). The Reverend John

Wheelwright, Anne Hutchinson's brother-in-law and most ardent supporter, took a party into what is now New Hampshire. Others settled in Maine. In 1638, New Haven, Connecticut, was founded by the Reverend John Davenport and a London merchant, Theophilus Eaton, who purchased land from local Indians. Four years earlier, the first Puritan settlers had reached the Connecticut River in western Massachusetts. In 1636 the Reverend Thomas Hooker led his followers to the site of Hartford, Connecticut.

The Pequot War grew out of conflicts among Europeans about who would govern the fertile Connecticut River valley and among Native Americans about who would trade with the Europeans. Until the arrival of the English, the Dutch had controlled trade along the Connecticut River. They had granted trading privileges to the Pequots, which frustrated other tribes, who could trade only through these middlemen. When the English arrived, the Pequots' enemies attempted to attract them to the valley as trading rivals to the Dutch. The Pequots, afraid of losing their monopoly, made the mistake of inviting Massachusetts Bay to establish a trading post in the region. They were counting on their ability to control not only their Indian enemies but also the Dutch and English. As hundreds of settlers led by Thomas Hooker poured in, the Pequots became alarmed. They appealed to their one-time enemies, the Narragansetts, to join with them to get rid of the English. The Narragansetts, however, had already been approached by the Puritans to join them in fighting the Pequots. That is where the Narragansetts calculated that their long-term advantage lay.

The Pequots were caught in a rivalry for their lands between the parent colony at Massachusetts and the new offshoot in Connecticut. The Connecticut group struck first, avenging an attack by the Pequots, which in itself was in revenge for an attack upon their allies. At dawn on May 26, 1637, 90 Connecticut men accompanied by 500 Narragansett allies attacked a Pequot village at Mystic filled with women, children, and old men. The raiders knew most of the warriors were away from home. As his men encircled the village, the commander, Captain John Mason, set a torch to the wigwams, shouting, "We must burn them." Those Pequots who escaped the fire ran into the ring of Mason's party, which killed between 300 and 700 Indians, while losing only two of their own men. The Narragansetts' Indian allies were so horrified by the brutal attack that they refused to participate in it.

Deeply demoralized, the remainder of the Pequot tribe was easily defeated. By 1638, the Puritans declared the Pequot tribe dissolved, and in 1639 Connecticut established its dominance over the Pequots' land. In that year Connecticut established its own government, modeled after that of Massachusetts. In 1662 it became a royal colony.

Conclusion

At the middle of the seventeenth century, the New England and Chesapeake colonies could hardly have appeared more different. Although the forces of capitalism shaped each region, other factors—disease, demographic patterns, relations with the Indians, and, especially, the objectives of the founders—left their distinctive imprints. The early history and relatively quick settlement of New England was shaped by the extraordinary energy and cohesiveness of the Puritans, which made them uniquely successful. By contrast, New Spain, New France, and New Netherland were rough frontier societies for many decades,

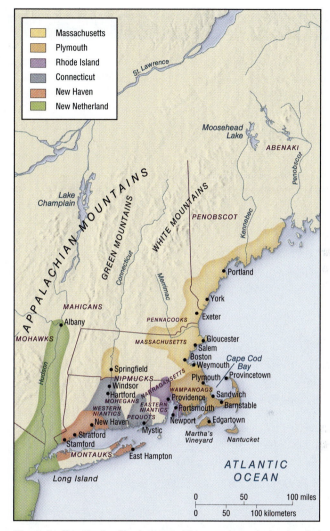

Map 3–2   New England in the 1640s This map shows the land settled by each of the New England colonies, the regions inhabited by Indian tribes, and the region of Dutch settlement. *John Murrin et al.,* Liberty, Equality, Power *(Orlando, FL: Harcourt College Publishers, 1995), p. 73.*

and the Chesapeake colonies were still raw outposts long after New England had achieved a secure order.

All of the North American colonies except those of New England were outposts in the transatlantic political economy, created to enrich their mother countries and enhance those countries' power. Had the Virginia Company known that the Puritans wanted to create a religious refuge rather than a money-making venture, it probably would not have given them a charter. So successful was New England in achieving a stable society that we sometimes forget that it was the exception and not the rule.

>> Timeline

▼1533
Henry VIII breaks with Roman Catholic Church, establishes
Church of England

▼1603
Queen Elizabeth I dies, succeeded by King James I

▼1606
James I grants two charters for North American settlement
to Virginia Company

▼1607
English found Jamestown

▼1608
John Smith named president of Virginia's council

▼1609
John Smith returns to England

▼1610–1614
First Anglo-Powhatan War

▼1612–1617
John Rolfe develops a marketable strain of tobacco

▼1614
John Rolfe and Pocahontas marry

▼1616
Virginia Company offers a 50-acre headright to each immigrant

▼1619
First meeting of Virginia General Assembly
First Africans arrive in Virginia
Virginia Company pays for transportation of women to Virginia

▼1620
Pilgrims found colony at Plymouth; Mayflower Compact signed

▼1622–1632
Second Anglo-Powhatan War

▼1624
Virginia Company dissolved; Virginia becomes a royal colony

>> Timeline *continued*

▼1625
James I dies, succeeded by King Charles I

▼1629
Massachusetts Bay Company receives charter to establish colony in North
  America

▼1630
Massachusetts Bay Colony founded

▼1632
George Calvert receives charter for Maryland

▼1636
Harvard College founded
Roger Williams exiled from Massachusetts

▼1637
Anne Hutchinson and her followers exiled
Pequot War

▼1638
New Haven founded

▼1639
First law mentioning slavery, in Maryland
Connecticut establishes its government

▼1644
Rhode Island receives charter

▼1644–1646
Third Anglo-Powhatan War

▼1647
Massachusetts establishes system of public education

▼1649
Act of Toleration passed in Maryland

▼1661
First Virginia law mentioning slavery

▼1691
Plymouth Colony absorbed into Massachusetts

Review Questions

1. What were the objectives of the founders of Virginia? Why did the colony survive, in spite of poor planning?

2. What were the objectives of the founders of the Puritan colonies at Plymouth and Massachusetts Bay? Compare the early years of these colonies to those of the Virginia Colony.

3. What role did gender play in the social order of the Chesapeake and New England colonies? Compare and contrast family life in the two regions.

4. Compare and contrast relations with the Indians in the Chesapeake and in New England.

For further review materials and resource information, please visit www.oup.com/us/ofthepeople

Continental Empires
1660–1720

>> **Tituba Shapes Her World and Saves Herself**

Her name was Tituba. Some say she was African, a Yoruba, others that she was an Arawak Indian from Guyana. Had she not been accused of practicing witchcraft in Salem, Massachusetts, in 1692, she surely would have been forgotten by history. Whether she came from South America or Africa, she had been torn away from her home and sent to work on a sugar plantation on the Caribbean island of Barbados, which the English had colonized almost 50 years before. Whatever her origins, Tituba lived in an African-majority society and absorbed African customs.

Tituba was probably a teenager when she was taken, again as a slave, to Massachusetts in 1680. She had been purchased by a young, Harvard-educated Barbadian, Samuel Parris. Parris's father had failed as a planter, and now he himself had failed as a merchant. In 1689 Parris moved his wife, their three children, Tituba, and her slave husband John Indian to Salem Village, where he had taken up a new profession, the ministry.

Three years later, all of their lives changed forever when one of Parris's daughters, Betty, and her cousin Abigail followed the folk custom of trying to see their futures in the white of an egg dropped into a glass of water. Soon several girls and young women were playing with magic. Then Betty began to experience strange and seemingly inexplicable pains, which spread to other young women. When neither doctors nor ministers could cure them, a neighbor asked Tituba to bake a "witchcake" out of rye flour and the girls' urine. This was "white magic," intended to uncover the identity of the witch who was thought to be bewitching Betty and the others. Their suffering, however, only got worse. Parris now questioned the girls: Who was bewitching them? This time the girls had an answer: two older, rather marginal white women—and Tituba.

continued

>> AMERICAN PORTRAIT *continued*

The three women were charged with the capital offense of witchcraft. Under duress, the first woman, Sarah Good, implicated the second, Sarah Osborne. Osborne steadfastly denied her guilt and was returned to jail. Finally, Tituba was summoned. As a slave, she was particularly vulnerable. Perhaps calculating the odds carefully, Tituba slowly began to embroider a story. She named only two names—Sarah Good and Sarah Osborne. She talked about a tall, white-haired man in Boston who made her sign a mysterious book and about conspiring with other, unnamed witches.

Responding to the hints of her Puritan interrogators, Tituba confirmed that she had made a covenant with the devil, the tall man in Boston. But she also added elements that came from African and Indian cultures, such as a "thing all over hairy, all the face harye & a long nose. . . ." Tituba's tales of witches' meetings, flying to Boston on a broomstick, and wolves and birds and hairy imps persuaded her interrogators that their colony was beset by witches. A children's game spiraled into panic, but Tituba escaped with her life. Having spent her life as a prisoner in other people's lands, she had combined their cultures with her own, crafting them into a strategy for survival.

Colonial America in the second half of the seventeenth century was remarkably unstable. Without secure colonial governments, colonial societies were torn by conflicting cultural and economic forces. In some ways, Tituba was a victim of these crosscurrents. She was in Salem because Samuel Parris failed as a merchant, unable to succeed in the world's economy. Tituba's freedom was sacrificed so that other, more powerful people could become prosperous. Instability, however, creates opportunity as it creates danger. By melding her own culture and that of her captors, Tituba became a cultural shape-shifter, and she was able to save herself when she faced accusations of witchcraft. Though more dramatic, Tituba's story is like that of many Americans of the late seventeenth century. Caught in the crosscurrents of cultural and economic transformation, they adapted their cultural inheritances to new circumstances.

Common Threads

>> What forces—political, economic, military, social, cultural—gave shape to the English empire? Which of these forces figured in the conscious plan of empire, and which shaped the empire nonetheless?

>> How did imperial politics—in particular the contest between England and France and England's larger geopolitical objectives—affect the lives of ordinary men and women in the colonies?

>> What is a slave society, and how did Virginia become one?

>> Which European institutions transplanted easily to North America, and which did not?

The Plan of Empire

Trying to make sense of the haphazard development of Britain's American colonies, the English political theorist Edmund Burke explained in 1757, "[t]he settlement of *our* colonies was never pursued upon any regular plan; but they were formed, grew, and flourished, as accidents, the nature of the climate, or the dispositions of private men happened to operate." In comparison, the Spanish and French governments more actively directed their colonies, but even then, the portions of their empires that would one day become the United States were so marginal that they, too, received relatively little attention. The British colonies were all private ventures, chartered by the government but little supervised or supported. So long as mainland colonies contributed little to the national wealth and cost the government less, they received the loosest of controls and were permitted to develop each in its own way.

The result was a period of significant instability at the end of the seventeenth century, as local colonial governments struggled to control their inhabitants, police their borders, and establish successful economies. In many of the colonies, elites vied for control, whereas in others poor people rose up against insecure leadership. As expanding populations and aggressive traders pushed against native populations, violence exploded. Elsewhere, the British, French, and Dutch—and their Indian allies—collided. In the midst of these struggles, colonists such as Tituba found themselves caught in—and taking advantage of—the crosscurrents.

Turmoil in England

In the middle of the seventeenth century, the British government was thrown into turmoil as Parliament and the king struggled over the future direction of the nation. Two issues were at stake: religion and royal power. The uneasy balance that Elizabeth I had established between Puritans and the Church of England collapsed under her successors, James I (1603–1625) and Charles I (1625–1649). Archbishop of Canterbury William Laud moved the Church of England away from the Calvinist belief in predestination, brought back worship that smacked of Catholicism, and persecuted Puritans, prompting Presbyterian Scotland to revolt.

Parliament refused to appropriate the funds that King Charles requested to quash the revolt. Instead, in 1628, Parliament passed the Petition of Right, which reasserted such basic freedoms as no taxation except by act of Parliament, no arbitrary arrest or imprisonment, and no quartering of soldiers in private homes. After years of stalemate, in 1642 Charles raised an army and moved against the Parliament, beginning the English Civil War, which concluded in 1647 with Parliament's victory. Two years later, Charles was beheaded. Oliver Cromwell, a Puritan, ruled as Lord Protector until his death in 1658. When Cromwell's son and successor proved an inept leader, Charles II was invited to reclaim the crown in 1660.

Although the monarchy had been restored, its authority had been diminished. Britain had been transformed into a constitutional monarchy in which the power of the Crown was balanced by that of Parliament. Britain also found a middle way between Calvinist Protestantism and Catholicism. When the Catholic King James II (1685–1688) tried to fill the government with Catholics and to rule without the consent of Parliament, he was removed in a bloodless revolution, known as the Glorious Revolution (1688). It brought Mary, James's Protestant daughter, and her Protestant husband, William of Orange (Holland), to the throne.

The Political Economy of Mercantilism

After the reassertion of Parliament's authority in 1688, the British state became increasingly strong and centralized. Britain then embarked on a course that would make it the world's most powerful nation by the early nineteenth century.

Throughout the political turmoil of the seventeenth century, Britain's economic policies were guided by a theory called mercantilism, which held that the chief object of a nation's economic policies was to serve the state. Mercantilism was developed to facilitate the consolidation of the new European nation-states, which required vast amounts of money to support their growing military and bureaucracies. Mercantilists considered the economy and politics as zero-sum games; one side's gain was another's loss. Wealth was defined exclusively as hard money, that is, gold and silver. With only a finite amount of gold and silver in the world, a nation could best improve its position by capturing a share of other nations' money. Mercantilism thus led to rivalry between nations. Between 1651 and 1696, the mercantilist British government passed a series of trade regulations, the Navigation Acts, requiring that all goods shipped to England and her colonies be carried in ships owned and manned by the English (including colonists). All foreign goods going to the colonies had to be shipped via Britain, where they could be taxed, and some colonial products (tobacco, sugar, indigo, and cotton, to start) had to be sent first to England before being shipped elsewhere. In mercantilist doctrine, the mother country was to produce finished products, and the colonies, raw materials. Hence, when the colonies began to manufacture items such as woolen cloth and hats, Parliament restricted those industries.

New Colonies, New Patterns

Lacking tight English control, each colony developed differently. In the second half of the seventeenth century, two important new English colonies, Pennsylvania and South Carolina, were established, and New Netherland was seized from the Dutch. As a rule, the most successful colonies offered the most opportunity to free white people and the greatest amount of religious toleration.

New Netherland Becomes New York

By the middle of the seventeenth century, the British were ready to challenge their chief trade rival, the Dutch, whom they defeated in three wars between 1652 and 1674. The Navigation Acts cut the Dutch out of international trade, and Britain began to challenge Dutch dominance of the slave trade. In 1663 King Charles II chartered the Royal Africa Company to carry slaves out of Africa to the British West Indies. Britain also made a move for New Netherland.

James, the Duke of York and King Charles II's younger brother, persuaded Charles to grant him the territory between the Connecticut and Delaware rivers (present-day

AMERICAN LANDSCAPE

>> New Amsterdam/New York

Today it is called Wall Street, and it represents the center of world finance, but in 1660, it was literally a wall that marked the northernmost edge of settlement on the island of Manhattan. Although some of the street grid remains—and today's Broad Street was once a huge canal—most of the other traces of the Dutch settlement of New Amsterdam have disappeared.

Lower Manhattan did not become a business and commercial center until the nineteenth century, however. Until then, it was a little urban village, first Dutch and then English. Even after the English takeover in 1664, the town retained its Dutch character and distinctive Dutch architectural styles. The original New Amsterdam was home to a variety of crafts- and tradespeople: not only the merchants, brokers, lawyers, and shipmasters one would expect in a commercial port but also druggists, painters, printers, tailors, and boardinghouse keepers. The homes and workshops were built in the Dutch style, out of red and yellow brick, with leaded-glass casement windows and terracotta tiles on the roofs. The comfortable feel of such homes was not unlike a middle-class home in Amsterdam.

Because buildings often functioned as both homes and workshops, they might contain not only the nuclear family but also the employees of the family business and slaves, both Indian and African. (In 1703, 40 percent of New York's households contained African slaves.) If New Amsterdam and its successor, New York, looked and felt like a European town, the presence of large numbers of Africans and Indians gave the little settlement a distinctive New World character.

From its earliest years, New Amsterdam was an urban village in a global economy, home to immigrants and natives, all buying and selling in a global market. The Kierstede family built its house at the corner of what today are Pearl and Whitehall streets, looking out on the East River. Hans Kierstede, a German religious refugee, came to New Amsterdam and served as its first surgeon. His wife, Sara Roelofs, had been born in Amsterdam and lived as a child near present-day Albany, where she played with the local Indians and learned their languages. In New Amsterdam, she built a backyard shed where Indian women crafted goods to sell in the market across the street from the Kierstedes' home. In 1664, Sara Roelofs Kierstede served as a translator when Peter Stuyvesant negotiated a treaty with the local Indians. The Lenape Indian sachem Oratam was so pleased with her translating abilities that he gave her some two thousand acres of land on the Hackensack River, in present-day Bergen County, New Jersey.

When archeologists excavated the family home late in the twentieth century, they found bits and pieces of the cultures that mixed on the island of Manhattan: pipes made in Holland and imported even after the English takeover; a German wineglass; a piece of a sword; hair curlers for curling wigs; whistles carved

continued

AMERICAN LANDSCAPE *continued*

from clay pipes and traded to the Indians for furs; and ceramic gambling tokens, similar to ones found at plantations in the South and the West Indies.

New Amsterdam was a crossroads of empire. There people—and goods—from both sides of the Atlantic, Europeans, Indians, and Africans, met and traded with each other, creating a new world made out of bits and pieces from each of their cultures.

Pennsylvania, New Jersey, New York, and part of Connecticut), which was occupied by the Netherlands. In 1664 James sent a governor, 400 troops, and several warships that easily conquered the small colony of New Amsterdam. In 1665 James gave away what is now New Jersey to two of his royal cronies, Lords John Berkeley and George Carteret, and in 1667 New York's governor gave the territory on the western side of the Connecticut River to Connecticut. New Netherland had become New York.

The new colony was part Dutch (in New York City and along the Hudson) and part English (on Long Island, where New England Puritans had migrated). The first governors attempted to satisfy both groups. The governors confirmed Dutch landholdings, including huge estates along the Hudson, and guaranteed the Dutch religious freedom. The governors also distributed 2 million more acres of land, most of it in enormous chunks called manors. The owners of these manors, like feudal lords, rented land to tenants and set up courts on their estates.

If religious toleration attracted diverse peoples to the region, feudal land policies and England's failure to restore self-government kept others away. Without an elective legislature to raise taxes, the governors, following English mercantilist policy, used customs duties to raise the revenue necessary to run the colony and send a profit to James. These attempts to regulate trade and direct the economy angered local merchants and harmed the economy. Eventually, James gave in to popular discontent and, in 1683, allowed New York to have an elective assembly.

At its first meeting, this group of English and Dutch men passed a "Charter of Libertyes and Priviledges," which, had the king approved it, would have guaranteed New Yorkers a number of civil liberties and the continuing right to self-government by their elected assembly. The charter expressed the principles of liberalism starting to spread through both Britain and the Netherlands. (Liberalism places an emphasis on individual liberty and holds that all human beings are equally entitled to enjoy the freedom and fulfillment to be found in their social lives—their work, families, and churches.) The charter would have guaranteed all freemen the right to vote and to be taxed only by their elective representatives. It also provided for trial by jury, due process, freedom of conscience for Christians, and certain property rights for women, the latter two items reflecting Dutch practices. However, the king refused to approve the charter on two grounds: it would give New Yorkers more rights than any other colonists, and the New York Assembly might undermine the power of Parliament. Without secure self-government, New Yorkers fell to fighting among themselves, and political instability in combination with feudal land holdings slowed New York's population growth.

Diversity and Prosperity in Pennsylvania

Pennsylvania demonstrated the potential of a colony that offered both religious toleration and economic opportunity. Its founder, William Penn, was a Quaker and the son of one of King Charles II's leading supporters. After his restoration to the throne, Charles had a number of political debts to repay, and giving away vast chunks of North America was a cheap way of doing it. As a Quaker, Penn was eager to get out of England. In 1661 alone, 4,000 English Quakers were jailed, and Penn was imprisoned four times. The Quakers were a radical sect of Protestants who believed that God offered salvation to all and placed an "inner light" inside everyone. Hardworking, serious, and moral, Quakers rejected violence and refused to serve in the military or pay taxes for its support.

Penn received his charter in 1681. To raise money, he sold land to a group of wealthy Quaker merchants, who received government positions and economic concessions in return. To attract ordinary settlers, Penn promised self-government (although stacked in favor of the merchant elite), freedom of religion, and reasonably priced land.

In 1682, when Penn arrived at Philadelphia (Greek for "city of brotherly love"), the colony already had 4,000 inhabitants. Penn had clear ideas about how he wanted his colony to develop. He expected the orderly growth of farming villages, neatly laid out along rivers and creeks, and mapped the settlement of the city along a grid, with each house set far enough from its neighbors to prevent the spread of fires. He created harmonious relations with local Indians.

Penn's policies attracted a wide variety of Europeans. Soon Pennsylvania was populated by self-contained communities, each speaking a different language or practicing a different religion. Pennsylvania's early history was characterized by rapid growth and prosperity. However, this progress undermined Penn's plans for a cohesive, hierarchical society. People lived where and how they wanted, pursuing the economic activities they found most profitable.

While moving away from the inequalities of the Old World, Pennsylvania replicated those of the New World. Many of its European immigrants were indentured servants or *redemptioners*, people who worked for a brief period to pay back the ship's captain for the cost of transportation to the colony. And by 1700, the Pennsylvania Assembly had passed laws recognizing slavery, although not unanimously. That slavery could take root in a colony where some questioned its morality suggests both the force of its power in shaping early America and the weakness of the opposition.

Indians and Africans in the Political Economy of Carolina

Like Pennsylvania and Maryland, South Carolina was a proprietary colony. One of the proprietors, Anthony Ashley Cooper, the Earl of Shaftesbury, and his secretary John Locke drafted the Fundamental Constitutions for the new colony. Locke later became a leading political philosopher, and the Constitutions reflect the liberal, rights-guaranteeing principles that he later developed more fully.

The Constitutions provided for a representative government and widespread religious toleration. At the same time, they embodied the traditional assumption that liberty could be guaranteed only in a hierarchical society. Shaftesbury and Locke tried to set up a complex hierarchy of nobles at the top and hereditary serfs at the bottom. The Constitutions also recognized African slavery, and Carolina was the first colony that introduced slavery at the outset. The Constitutions never went into full effect, for the first Carolina representative assembly rejected many of its provisions. Predictably, the attempt to transplant a British-style nobility failed. The only aristocracy that the Carolinas developed was one of wealth, supported by the labor of slaves.

The first settlers arrived at Charles Town (later moved and renamed Charleston) in 1670. The area had a semitropical climate, wonderfully fertile soil, and a growing season of up to 295 days a year. The region had once been explored by the Spanish, who still claimed it. It was inhabited by mission Indians, that is, Indians who had converted to Catholicism.

As happened so often when Europeans arrived, Indian tribes competed to trade with them, and rival groups of Europeans struggled to dominate the trade. In the colonial period, Indian wars usually pitted one group of Europeans and their Indian allies against another group of Europeans and their native allies, with the Indians doing most of the fighting. Such wars were an extension of Europe's market economy: Indians fought for European goods, and Europeans fought for a monopoly over Indian products. The English were particularly successful in achieving dominance because of their sophisticated market economy. London's banks had perfected the mechanisms of credit, which financed a fur trade in the forests half a world away.

As Carolina traders exchanged European goods for southeastern deerskins, they found an even more valuable commodity on the frontier: Indian slaves. In fact, un-

Trial of John Lawson In 1711, while exploring present-day western North Carolina for South Carolina, John Lawson and his party were captured by Tuscarora Indians. Lawson was put on trial and then executed. Notice his African slave, also bound and facing the Tuscarora tribunal.

til about 1690, slaves were the most valuable commodity produced by the Carolina Colony.

Carolina Indian traders quickly established control over the entire Southeast (see Map 4–1), pushing out the Spanish, the French, and even the Virginians. In 1680, in the Westo War, the Carolina traders sent their allies, the Savannah Indians, out to destroy the Westos, who were the Virginians' link to the Native American trade of the Southeast. The Carolinians vanquished the Spanish by sending in other Indian allies to destroy the mission towns. In this way, the Carolina traders eliminated their European rivals and established their dominance over all the regional Indians.

Peaceful relations did not last. In 1711, the Tuscarora Indians attacked settlers in western North Carolina, and the Tuscaroras were defeated in a short, brutal war.

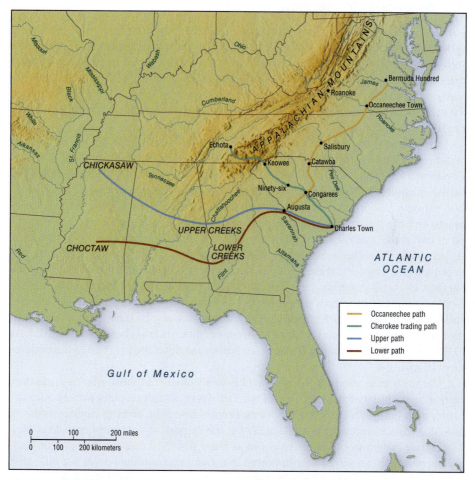

Map 4–1 Trade Routes in the Southeast Beginning in the seventeenth century, English traders from Virginia and later Carolina followed several paths to trade with Southeastern Indians as far west as the Mississippi. *Adapted from W. Stitt Robinson,* The Southern Colonial Frontier *(Albuquerque: University of New Mexico Press, 1979), p. 103.*

The survivors headed north, where they joined the Iroquois Confederacy. Although the Yamasees had been reliable trading partners for 40 years and had fought with the British in Queen Anne's War (see later in the chapter), South Carolina traders cheated them out of their land and enslaved their women and children. In retaliation, the Yamasees attacked with Indian allies before they were stopped near Charleston by the crumbling of the alliance. The Yamasee War (1715–1716) killed 400 white South Carolinians (a higher proportion of the population than was lost in King Philip's War in New England), forced the colony to abandon frontier settlements, and revealed the fragility of the entire South Carolina venture. When international war began again in 1739, the frontier regions were, as they had been a quarter of a century earlier, dangerous and unstable for settlers, traders, and Indians alike.

The Barbados Connection

Carolina was part of a far-flung Atlantic political economy based on trade, plantation agriculture, and slavery. Many of the early Carolina settlers had substantial experience with African slavery in Barbados, a small Caribbean island settled in 1627 that within a decade became a major source of the world's sugar. By then, it had an African majority and was Britain's first slave society. By the end of the seventeenth century, Barbados was the most productive of all Britain's colonies, its per-person income much higher than in England.

This income was not shared equally, however. Owners of the largest plantations became fabulously wealthy, and even lesser planters enjoyed a high standard of living. Conditions for African slaves, however, were brutal. As in their other slave societies, the British magnified differences between Europeans and Africans to enhance the distinction between landowners and slaves. Barbadians were the first to portray Africans as beasts, and the racism of Caribbean planters was intense. Slave codes were the harshest of any in the Atlantic world, prescribing that male slaves convicted of crimes could be burned at the stake, beheaded, starved, or castrated. When Caribbean slavery was imported into Carolina, these attitudes came with it. The Carolina slave code was the harshest in North America. Laws and attitudes separated whites from blacks, but differences among Europeans were minimized, as some restrictions against Irish Catholics and Jews were lifted after Barbados became a slave society. In 1650, Barbados allowed the immigration of Jews and other religious minorities, six years before England did. As in the Chesapeake, increasing freedom for Europeans developed alongside the enslavement of Africans.

The sugar plantations of Barbados and Britain's other Caribbean islands made their extraordinary profits from the labor of African slaves. British planters worked Africans harder than European indentured servants. Profits came from keeping labor costs down, as well as from the growing demand for sugar. It is important to remember that the New World slave system would not have grown as it did without European demand for plantation crops. African slaves were imported into Carolina from the outset, but only after 1690 did the colony develop a staple crop—rice—that increased the demand for slave labor. After rice became the region's major cash crop, African slaves became more valuable. By 1720, Africans composed more than 70 percent of Carolina's population. With a black majority, a lethal environment, and wealth concentrated in an elite, Carolina resembled

Table 4-1 Population of British Colonies in America, 1660 and 1710

Colony	1660 White	1660 Black	1660 Total	1710 White	1710 Black	1710 Total
Virginia	26,070	950	27,020	55,163	23,118	78,281
Maryland	7,668	758	8,426	34,796	7,945	42,741
Chesapeake	33,738	1,708	35,446	89,959	31,063	121,022
Massachusetts	22,062	422	22,484	61,080	1,310	62,390
Connecticut	7,955	25	7,980	38,700	750	39,450
Rhode Island	1,474	65	1,539	7,198	375	7,573
New Hampshire	1,515	50	1,565	5,531	150	5,681
New England	33,006	562	33,568	112,509	2,585	115,094
Bermuda	3,500	200	3,700	4,268	2,845	7,113
Barbados	26,200	27,100	53,300	13,000	52,300	65,300
Antigua	1,539	1,448	2,987	2,892	12,960	15,852
Montserrat	1,788	661	2,449	1,545	3,570	5,115
Nevis	2,347	2,566	4,913	1,104	3,676	4,780
St. Kitts	1,265	957	2,222	1,670	3,294	4,964
Jamaica				7,250	58,000	65,250
Caribbean	36,639	32,932	69,571	31,729	136,645	168,374
New York	4,336	600	4,936	18,814	2,811	21,625
New Jersey				18,540	1,332	19,872
Pennsylvania				22,875	1,575	24,450
Delaware	510	30	540	3,145	500	3,645
Middle Colonies	4,846	630	5,476	63,374	6,218	69,592
North Carolina	980	20	1,000	14,220	900	15,150
South Carolina				6,783	4,100	10,883
Lower South	980	20	1,000	21,003	5,000	26,003
Totals	109,209	35,852	145,061	318,574	181,511	500,085

Source: Jack P. Greene, *Pursuits of Happiness* (Chapel Hill: University of North Carolina, 1988), pp. 178–9.

the Caribbean islands more than it did the other English colonies on the mainland. In only a few decades, Carolina had become a slave society, not simply a society with slaves: slavery stood at the center of everything.

The Transformation of Virginia

At the same time that a newly vigorous England was planting new colonies, those established earlier were reshaped. In the final quarter of the seventeenth century, the older colonies experienced political and sometimes social instability, followed by the establishment of a lasting order. In Virginia, the transition was marked by a violent insurrection known as Bacon's Rebellion. Significantly, the rebels sought not to overthrow the social and political order but to secure a legitimate government that could protect economic opportunity. In its aftermath, Virginia became a slave society.

Social Change in Virginia

As Virginia entered its second half-century, the health of its population finally began to improve. Apple orchards had matured, so Virginians could drink cider instead of impure water. Ships bringing new servants arrived in the fall, a healthy time of year. Increasingly, they lived to serve out their periods of indenture and set out on their own to plant tobacco. However, most of the best land in eastern Virginia had already been claimed, and the land to the west was occupied by Indian tribes with peace treaties with the English. In addition, the government was controlled by small clique of men using it as a means of getting rich. Taxes, assessed in tobacco, were extraordinarily high, and as taxes rose, the price of tobacco began to fall. Caught in a squeeze, many ordinary planters went to work for others as tenants or overseers.

> "A white woman is rarely or never put to work in the ground, if she be good for anything else . . . whereas it is a common thing for to work a woman slave out of doors."
>
> VIRGINIA PLANTER ROBERT BEVERLEY

Still, servants kept coming to the colony, most from the lower ranks of society. Restless and unhappy, they joined in a series of disturbances beginning in the middle of the century. The elite responded by lengthening the time of service and stiffening the penalties for running away.

Bacon's Rebellion and the Abandonment of the Middle Ground

When the revolt came, it was led not by one of the poor or landless but by a member of the elite. Nathaniel Bacon was young, well educated, wealthy, and a member of a prominent family. Bacon made an immediate impression on Virginia's ruling clique, and Governor Berkeley invited him to join the colony's Council of State. For unknown reasons, Bacon cast his lot with Berkeley's enemies among the elite. The instability of elites created political factions in a number of colonies. When ruling elites, such as Berkeley's in Virginia, levied exorbitant taxes and ignored their constituents, they left themselves open to challenge.

The contest between Bacon and Berkeley might have remained minor had not Bacon capitalized on the discontent of the colony's freedmen (men who had served out their indentures). In 1676, Bacon's Rebellion was triggered by a routine episode of violence on the middle ground inhabited by Indians and Europeans. Seeking payment for goods they had delivered to a planter, a band of Doeg Indians killed the planter's overseer and tried to steal his hogs. Over the years, Europeans and Indians who shared the middle ground had adapted the Indian custom of providing restitution for crimes committed by one side or the other. Although this practice resulted in sporadic violence, it also helped maintain order. But this time, the conflict escalated, as Virginians sought revenge, prompting further Indian retaliation.

Soon an isolated incident escalated into a militia expedition of 1,000 men, an extraordinarily large force at the time. For six weeks the war party laid siege to the reservation of the Susquehannocks, a tribe drawn unwillingly into the conflict, who in turn avenged themselves on settlers on the frontier.

When Berkeley refused to fight the Susquehannocks, the frontier planters were infuriated. They complained that their taxes went to Berkeley's clique instead of being used to police the frontier. Planter women used their gossip networks to tell "hundreds" that Berkeley was "a greater friend to the Indians than to the English."

With his wife's encouragement, Nathaniel Bacon agreed to lead a wholesale war on "all Indians whatsoever." After his rebels massacred some formerly friendly Occaneecchees, Bacon marched on the government at Jamestown with 400 armed men, demanding to fight "all Indians in general, for that they were all Enemies." Berkeley agreed, then changed his mind, but it was too late. Bacon was in control, and Berkeley fled to the eastern shore.

By the time a royal commission and 1,000 soldiers arrived in January 1677 to put down the disorder, Bacon had died, and Berkeley had regained control. Twenty-three rebel leaders were executed, and the king removed Berkeley from office. After Bacon's death, support for the rebellion quickly dissipated.

After Bacon's Rebellion, the government remained in the hands of the planter elite, but the rebels had achieved their primary objective. The frontier Indians had been dispersed, and their land was now free for settlement. Those in power became more responsive to white members of society. Other factors also improved economic conditions: tobacco prices began to climb, and planters replaced servants with slaves.

Virginia Becomes a Slave Society

No one had planned for Virginia to become a slave society. With new colonies such as New York and Pennsylvania offering greater opportunity to poor whites, the supply of European indentured servants to the Chesapeake dried up just when more Africans were becoming available. Britain entered the slave trade at the end of the seventeenth century, authorizing private merchants to carry slaves from Africa to North America in 1698. Planters could not get enough slaves to meet their needs. In 1680, only 7 percent of Virginia's population was African in origin, but by 1700 the proportion had increased to 28 percent, and half the labor force was enslaved (Table 4–1). Within two decades, Virginia had become a slave society in which slavery was central to the political economy and the social structure. With the bottom tier of the social order enslaved and hence unable to compete for land or wealth, opportunity for all whites necessarily improved.

As the composition of Virginia's labor force changed, so did the laws to control it. Although all slave societies had certain features in common, each colony enacted its own slave code to maintain and define the institution. By 1705, Virginia had a thorough slave code in place.

All forms of slavery have certain elements in common: perpetuity, kinlessness, violence, and the master's access to the slave's sexuality. First, slavery is a lifelong condition. Second, a slave has no legally recognized family relationships. Because kinship is the basis of most social and political relationships in society, a slave is socially "dead," outside the bounds of the larger society. Third, slavery rests on violence or its threat, including the master's sexual access to the slave.

Table 4-2 Codifying Race and Slavery

1640—Masters are required to arm everyone in their households except Africans (Virginia)

1643—All adult men and African women are taxable, on the assumption that they were working in the fields (Virginia)

1662—Children follow the condition of their mother (Virginia)

1662—Double fine charged for any Christian who commits fornication with an African (Virginia)

1664—All slaves serve for life; that is, slavery is defined as a lifelong condition (Maryland)

1664—Interracial marriage banned; any free woman who marries a slave will serve that slave's master until her husband dies, and their children will be enslaved (Maryland)

1667—Baptism as a Christian does not make a slave free (Virginia)

1669—No punishment is given if punished slave dies (Virginia)

1670—Free Blacks and Indians are not allowed to purchase Christian indentured servants (Virginia)

1670—Indians captured elsewhere and sold as slaves to Virginia are to serve for life; those captured in Virginia, until she age of 30, if children, or for 12 years, if grown (Virginia)

1680—In order to prevent "Negroes Insurrections": no slave may carry arms or weapons; no slave may leave his or her master without written permission; any slave who "lifts up his hand" against a Christian will receive 30 lashes; any slave who runs away and resists arrest may be killed lawfully (Virginia)

1682—Slaves may not gather for more than 4 hours at other than owner's plantation (Virginia)

1682—All servants who were "Negroes, Moors, Mollattoes or Indians" were to be considered slaves at the time of their purchase if neither their parents nor country were Christian (Virginia)

1691—Owners are to be compensated if "negroes, mulattoes or other slaves" are killed while resisting arrest (Virginia)

1691—Forbidden is all miscegenation as "that abominable mixture"; any English or "other white man or woman" who marries a "negroe, mulatto, or Indian" is to be banished; any free English woman who bears a "bastard child by any negro or mulatto" will be fined, and if she can't pay the fine, she will be indentured for five years and the child will be indentured until the age of 30 (Virginia)

1691—All slaves who are freed by their masters must be transported out of the state (Virginia)

1692—Special courts of "over and terminer" are established for trying slaves accused of crimes, creating a separate system of justice (Virginia)

1705—Mulatto is defined as "the child of an Indian, the child, grandchild, or great grandchild of a negro" (Virginia)

1705—Africans, mulattoes, and Indians are prohibited from holding office or giving grand jury testimony (Virginia)

1705—Slaves are forbidden to own livestock (Virginia)

1705—"Christian white" servants cannot be whipped naked (Virginia)

1723—Free Blacks explicitly excluded from militia (Virginia)

1723—Free Blacks explicitly denied the right to vote (Virginia)

Note: Slavery is a creation of law, which defines what it means to be a slave and protects the master's rights in his slave property. Slave codes developed piecemeal in the Chesapeake, over the course of the 17th century. Legislators in the Chesapeake colonies defined slavery as a racial institution, appropriate only for Africans, and protected it with a series of laws, which, in the process, also created a privileged position for whites.

American slavery added other elements. First, slavery in all the Americas was hereditary, passed on from a mother to her children. Second, compared with other slave systems, including that of Latin America, *manumissions*—the freeing of slaves—in the American South were quite rare. Finally, slavery in the South was racial. Slavery was reserved for Africans, some Indians, and their children, even if the father was white. The line between slavery and freedom was defined as one of color.

Slave codes also defined gender roles. Two early pieces of legislation denied African women the privileges of European women (Table 4–2). A 1643 statute made all adult men and African women taxable, assuming that they (and not white women) were performing productive labor in the fields. In 1652, another law said that children were to inherit the status of their mother.

The same laws that created and sustained racial slavery also increased the freedom of whites. New World plantation slavery was developed in a world in which the freedom of most Europeans also was limited in various ways. In fact, two-thirds of the Europeans who migrated to British America before the American Revolution were unfree—servants or redemptioners. (When Africans are added, virtually all of whom were enslaved, the total increases to 90 percent.) The increase in freedom for whites was the product of several sorts of policies. First, it depended on the widespread availability of cheap land, which whites could obtain only by dispossessing the Indians who inhabited it. Second, it depended on British government policies, such as permitting self-government in the colonies, which were designed to attract immigrants. Third, it depended on specific laws that improved the conditions of whites, often at the same time limiting the freedom of blacks. For example, in 1705 Virginia made it illegal for white servants to be whipped without an order from a justice of the peace.

New England Under Assault

New England's prosperity led to problems, both internal and external. How would a religion born in adversity cope with good fortune? A combination of internal colonial conflicts and a growing population encroaching on Indian lands led to the region's deadliest Indian war in 1675.

Social Prosperity and the Fear of Religious Decline

In many ways, the Puritan founders of the New England colonies saw their dreams come true. Although immigration virtually halted as the English Revolution broke out, natural increase kept the population growing, from about 23,000 in 1650 to more than 93,000 in 1700. Life expectancy was higher than in England, and families were larger.

Most New Englanders enjoyed a comfortable, if modest, standard of living. By the end of the century, the simple shacks of the first settlers had been replaced by two-story frame homes. By our standards, these homes would still have been almost unbearably cold in the winter, when indoor temperatures routinely dropped into the 40s. Still, New Englanders were beginning to enjoy the prosperous village life their ancestors had once known in England.

For Puritans, such good fortune presented a problem. Prosperity became a cause for worry, as people turned their minds away from God to more worldly things. In the 1660s and 1670s, New England's ministers preached a series of *jeremiads*, lamentations about spiritual decline. They criticized problems ranging from public drunkenness and sexual license to land speculation and excessively high prices and wages. If New Englanders did not change their ways, the ministers predicted, "Ruine upon Ruine, Destruction upon Destruction would come, until one stone were not left upon another."

Most of the churches were embroiled in controversy in the 1660s concerning who could be members. The founders had assumed that most people, sooner or later, would have the conversion experience that entitled them to full church membership. By the third generation, however, many children and grandchildren of full members had not had the experience of spiritual rebirth. In 1662 a group of ministers adopted the Half-Way Covenant, which set out terms for church membership and participation. Full church membership was reserved for those who could demonstrate a conversion experience. Their offspring could still be "half-way" members of the church, receiving its discipline and having their children baptized. Those who wished to maintain the purity and exclusivity of the church resisted. Rather than settle this question, the Half-Way Covenant aggravated tensions always present in the Puritan religion.

Turmoil broke out as well in the persecution of Quakers, despite Charles II's having issued a protection order. In 1660, Massachusetts had executed the Quaker Mary Dyer, who had returned to Boston after her banishment. The Quakers had been brazen in their defiance of authority, not only returning to the colony when they knew it meant certain death but also even running naked through the streets or in church.

King Philip's War

Although New England's colonies developed along a common path, conflicts among them were intense and led to the region's deadliest Indian war. As in Bacon's Rebellion, the underlying cause of the war was the steady encroachment of English settlers on Native American lands. In the 1660s, Rhode Island, Massachusetts, and Plymouth all claimed the land occupied by the Wampanoags, Massasoit's tribe, now ruled by his son Metacom, known by the colonists as King Philip. By 1671, the colonies had resolved their dispute and ordered King Philip and his people to submit to the rule of Plymouth. No longer able to play one colony against another, King Philip prepared for war, as did the colonists of all the colonies except Rhode Island, which attempted to mediate. In June 1675 King Philip's men attacked the Plymouth village of Swansea.

During the next year, New Englanders attacked entire villages of noncombatants, and the Indians retaliated in kind. At the beginning of the war, New Englanders looked down on the Indians' traditional methods as evidence of depravity, saying they fought "more like wolves than men." By the end of the war, however, both sides committed brutalities, including scalpings and putting their victims' heads on stakes. That was the fate of King Philip. His wife and nine-year-old son were sold into slavery, along with hundreds of captives.

The New Englanders won King Philip's War, but the cost was enormous. The casualty rate was the highest for any American war ever. About 4,000 Indians died, many of starvation after the New Englanders destroyed their cornfields. The war eliminated any significant Native American presence in southeastern New England and killed 2,000 English settlers (one out of every 25). The Indians pushed to within 20 miles of Boston, attacked more than half of New England's towns, and burned 1,200 homes. It took the region decades to rebuild.

King Philip (Metacom's) Map, 1668
A map of the lands that Metacom (known by New Englanders as King Philip) sold in 1668. Note that Metacom's understanding of what it meant to "sell" land differed from English conceptions of property ownership. He insisted that the Indians who were living on the land could continue to do so.

The Puritans owed their victory to the Anglican colony of New York, its governor Edmund Andros, and his Mohawk allies. Andros worked effectively with local Indians, believing that the British Empire would be best served by maintaining peace among its colonies and the Indians, strengthening the British position against their true enemies, the French and the Dutch. Over the protest of New England, Andros encouraged the Mohawks to attack King Philip's forces. Once the Mohawks entered the war, the tide was turned.

Indians and the Empire

New England's relations with Indian tribes were not simply a local concern. They were of deep interest to the British Empire, as Andros's participation demonstrated. The British government had to balance the desires of its colonists against the empire's larger objectives. As the French expanded their presence in North America, using friendly Indians to check their advance became one of those objectives. In 1673 the French explorers Jacques Marquette and Louis Joliet had traveled down the Mississippi River as far south as the Arkansas River, and nine years later Réne-Robert Calelier, Sieur de LaSalle, reached the mouth of the river and named the surrounding territory Louisiana, in honor of King Louis XIV. Biloxi was founded in 1699, New Orleans in 1718, and the forts at Cahokia and Kaskaskia several years later. The French and their Indian allies controlled the Great Lakes region and the eastern shore of the Mississippi all the way to its mouth, while the British were confined to the East Coast.

This geopolitical reality dictated Britain's Indian policy. Andros saw a role for Native Americans as trade partners and allies in Britain's conflict with the French. He welcomed the Indian survivors of King Philip's War into New York and refused to send them back to New England for execution and enslavement, thus becoming the "father" who offered protection to his Indian "children." The British and the Iroquois, who dominated all the other tribes in the region, joined in a strong alliance known as the Covenant Chain, which enhanced the positions of both New York and the Iroquois. The Iroquois became the middlemen between other tribes and the merchants at Albany and were allowed to push as far north and west against French-allied tribes as they could (see Chapter 3.)

With New York dominating the British-Indian alliance, the New England colonies were effectively hemmed in. New York used the Mohawks to make a claim to Maine and blocked New England's movement to the west. Albany became the undisputed center of the Indian trade. In every way, King Philip's War proved exceedingly costly for the New England colonies.

The Empire Strikes

As Britain regained political stability at the end of the seventeenth century, it tried to bring more order to its "accidental empire" by making the colonies play a larger role in its governance. As the Glorious Revolution that removed King James II from the British throne secured constitutional government for Britain's subjects on both sides of the Atlantic, it also made Britain strong and stable enough to challenge France for world supremacy. Between 1689 and 1763, the Anglo-French rivalry drew the colonies into four international wars that shaped them in important ways.

The Dominion of New England

When James II ascended the throne, he decided to punish New England for its disloyalty to the Crown during the Puritan Revolution. There were also reports that New Englanders were defying the Navigation Acts by smuggling. In France, Louis XIV had centralized his administration and brought both his nation and his empire under firm control, and James decided to try similar tactics. In North America, he began unilaterally to revoke the charters of the colonies. By 1688, Massachusetts, Plymouth, Connecticut, New York, New Jersey, New Hampshire, and Rhode Island had been joined together into the Dominion of New England, and Edmund Andros was named its governor.

Before James II and Andros were deposed by the Glorious Revolution of 1688, they wreaked considerable havoc in New England, and Massachusetts, New York, and Maryland had all suffered revolts. James's attempt to strengthen rule over the colonies failed, but it marked a turning point: the colonies' last period of significant political instability before the eve of the American Revolution.

James's attempt to tighten control affected Massachusetts most seriously. He ordered it to tolerate religious dissenters; some feared he would impose Catholicism on the colony. He took away liberties that residents had enjoyed for over half a century: Juries were now to be appointed by sheriffs, town meetings were limited to once a year, and town selectmen could serve no more than two two-year terms. All titles to land had to be reconfirmed, with the holder paying Andros a small fee. Andros claimed the right to levy taxes on his own and began seizing all common lands. Some Boston merchants allied themselves with Andros, hoping to win his favor. This alliance revealed a growing rift in the region between those who welcomed commerce and a more secular way of life and those who wished to preserve the old ways. Most people in Massachusetts, however, despised Andros and feared the road he was leading them down.

The Glorious Revolution in Britain and America

The Glorious Revolution made it clear that Parliament, not an autocratic monarch, would henceforth play the leading role in government. It also determined, after almost a century and a half of conflict, that the Anglican religion would prevail. The Glorious Revolution ushered in a period of remarkable political stability that enabled Britain to become the world's most powerful nation.

In the next century Britain's North American colonies looked to this moment in British history as a model of constitutional government. Their understanding of events in Britain was shaped by political philosopher John Locke's *Two Treatises of Government* (1690). Since the time that he and Shaftesbury had written Carolina's Fundamental Constitutions more than 20 years earlier, Locke had become increasingly radical. The *Treatises* boldly asserted fundamental human equality and universal rights and provided the political theories that would justify a revolution.

The *Treatises* have become the founding documents of political liberalism and its theory of human rights. Locke argued that governments were created by people, not by God. Man was born "with a Title to perfect Freedom," or "natural rights." When people created governments, they gave up some of that freedom in exchange for the rights that they enjoyed in society. The purpose of government was to protect the "Lives, Liberties," and "Fortunes" of the people who created it, not to achieve glory or power for the nation or to serve God. Moreover, should a government take away the civil rights of its citizens, they had a "right to resume their original Liberty." This right of revolution was Locke's boldest and most radical assertion. Once news of the Glorious Revolution reached Massachusetts, its inhabitants poured into the streets, seized the government, and threw the despised Andros in jail. They proclaimed loyalty to the new king and lobbied for the return of their charter. Rhode Island and Connecticut soon got their charters back, but Massachusetts, which was perceived as too independent, was made a royal colony in 1691, with a royal governor. Although Massachusetts lost some of its autonomy and was forced to tolerate dissenters, the town meeting was restored. At the same time, New Hampshire became a royal colony.

The citizens of Maryland and New York also took the opportunity presented by the Glorious Revolution to evict their royal governors. In Maryland, tensions between the tobacco planters and the increasingly dictatorial proprietor, Charles Calvert, Lord Baltimore, had been building for several decades. Four-fifths of the population was Protestant, but the colony's government was dominated by Catholics, who allocated to themselves the best land. When Protestant planters protested, Baltimore imposed a property qualification for voting and appointed increasingly dictatorial governors. When news of the Glorious Revolution reached Maryland in 1689, a group led by John Coode, a militia officer, took over the government in a bloodless coup (known as Coode's Rebellion), proclaimed loyalty to William and Mary, and got the new government in Britain to take away Baltimore's proprietorship. In 1691, Maryland became a royal colony, and in 1702, the Anglican Church was made the state church, ending Maryland's experiment with religious toleration.

New York's rebels were less successful. A group of prosperous Dutch traders led by Jacob Leisler took over the government. Unlike Coode in Maryland, Leisler was not willing to cede power to the new king's appointees. As a result, the new governor put the rebel leaders on trial, and Leisler and his son-in-law were executed, their bodies decapitated and quartered.

This brutal conclusion to a bloodless revolt did not bring political stability to New York, however. Ethnic and regional divisions ran too deep. In the other colonies, by the end of the seventeenth century the elite had consolidated their position by both accepting British authority and providing opportunity and self-government for their fellow colonists. In New York, however, the top tier of the English elite competed with the second, Dutch, tier, creating political turmoil.

The Rights of Englishmen

Although the Glorious Revolution restored self-government to the North American colonies, the colonists and their British governors interpreted that event somewhat differently. Colonists felt it gave them all the rights of Englishmen. These rights were of two sorts: civil rights, from trial by jury to freedom from unreasonable searches, and the rights of self-government, including taxation only by their own elected representatives, self-rule, and civilian, not military, rule. The colonists believed that their legislatures were the local equivalent of Parliament and that, just as the citizens of Britain were governed by Parliament, so they should be governed by their own elective legislatures.

The British government held differently. First, it believed that the colonies were dependents of the mother country that needed a parent's protection and that owed that parent obedience. Second, the good of the empire as a whole was more important than that of any one of its parts. A colony was valued, as one British official put it, by what it contributed to "the gain or loss of *this* Kingdom." Third, colonial governments were subordinate to the British government. Finally, the British government had complete jurisdiction over every aspect of colonial life. The views of Britain and its colonists of how the empire should function radically diverged.

Conflict in the Empire

Between 1689 and 1713, Britain fought two wars against France and her allies, King William's War (1689–1697) and Queen Anne's War (1702–1713). At the same time, competition for the Indian alliances and the colonies' struggle over trade and territory made the European-Indian borderline uncertain and dangerous.

King William's War and Queen Anne's War followed a similar pattern in North America. Each was produced by a European struggle for power, and each resulted in a stalemate. The North American phase of each war began with a Canadian-Indian assault on isolated British settlements on the northern frontier (see Map 4–2). King William's War started with the capture of the British fort at Pemaquid, Maine, and the burning of Schenectady, New York, and Falmouth, Maine. Queen Anne's War began in North America in 1704 with a horrific raid on Deerfield, Massachusetts, in which half the town was torched and half the population was killed or captured.

The British colonies responded with massive retaliation, sending raiding parties into ambitious but ultimately unsuccessful attacks on Quebec. In 1690 Massachusetts governor Sir William Phips set out to seize Quebec in an attack by land and sea. The failed expedition cost 1,000 lives and £40,000 and drove American colonists away from the northern frontier.

Queen Anne's War followed much the same course. Canadian-Indian attacks on frontier villages were met with raids on Indian villages. Again, New England attempted a two-pronged attack on Quebec. When 900 troops (and 35 female camp followers) were killed as their ships sank in the St. Lawrence River, the commander canceled the expedition. Like King William's War, Queen Anne's War ended badly for New Englanders who had been eager to remove the twin threats of Catholicism and French-backed Indians to the north.

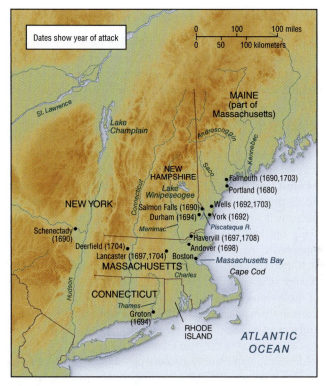

Dates show year of attack

0   100   100 miles
0   50   100 kilometers

MAINE
(part of Massachusetts)

St. Lawrence

Lake Champlain

Androscoggin

Kennebec

NEW HAMPSHIRE

Saco

Falmouth (1690,1703)
Portland (1680)

Lake Winipeseogee

NEW YORK

Connecticut

Salmon Falls (1690)
Durham (1694)

Wells (1692,1703)
York (1692)

Merrimac

Piscataqua R.

Schenectady (1690)

Deerfield (1704)

Havervill (1697,1708)
Andover (1698)

Lancaster (1697,1704)   Boston

MASSACHUSETTS

Massachusetts Bay

Charles

Cape Cod

Hudson

CONNECTICUT

Thames

Groton (1694)

RHODE ISLAND

ATLANTIC OCEAN

Map 4–2 Frontier Warfare During King William's and Queen Anne's Wars During these international conflicts, the New England frontier was exposed to attack by French Canadians and their Indian allies. *Adapted from Alan Gallay, ed.,* Colonial Wars of North America, *1512–1763 (New York: Garland, 1996), p. 247.*

The imperial wars merged with and were survived by long-standing conflicts with Indian tribes. In North America, European rivals almost never confronted each other directly but instead mobilized their Indian allies and made war on those of their adversaries. These tactics, in addition to an expanding colonial population and the Native American attempt to monopolize trade, made conflict on the frontiers endemic.

Massachusetts in Crisis

If the imperial wars provide a window onto international tensions, the Salem witchcraft trials provide a window onto a society in crisis, one coping with economic development, the conflict between old and new ways of understanding the world, and the threats presented by political instability, imperial war, and conflict with the Indians. In 1692 Massachusetts executed 20 people who had been convicted of witchcraft in Salem. Even in a society that believed in witchcraft, the execution of so many people at once was an aberration that revealed deep tensions.

The Social and Cultural Contexts of Witchcraft

Although the majority of New England's colonists were Puritan, many probably believed in magic. They subscribed to such tenets of Puritanism as predestation, but they also believed that they could use supernatural powers to predict the future, protect themselves from harm, and hurt their enemies. Although the ministry identified the use of magic with the devil, Tituba's folk religion and that of New Englanders were not incompatible. Before the development of scientific modes of explanation for such catastrophes as epidemics, droughts, and sudden death, people looked for supernatural causes.

In 1692, the inhabitants of Massachusetts were unusually anxious. They were without an effective government because they had not yet received their new charter. King William's War had just begun, with the French Catholics of Canada and their Algonquian Indian allies raiding the northern and eastern frontiers. Slaves reported that the French were planning to recruit New England's Africans as soldiers. These sources of stress increased underlying tensions, many of which concerned gender. Although men and women both attempted to use magic, the vast majority of those accused of witchcraft were women. Almost 80 percent of the 355 persons officially accused of practicing witchcraft were women, as were an even higher proportion of the 103 persons actually put on trial. Because most of these women had neither sons nor other male heirs, they could control property, which made them an anomaly in Puritan society. By the end of the seventeenth century, local land was an increasingly scarce commodity, and any woman who controlled it could be seen as threatening to the men who wanted it.

In addition, declining opportunity also disrupted the tight Puritan social order. Because land was scarce, it became difficult for young couples to start out. Consequently, the age of marriage increased, and the number of women who were pregnant on their wedding days began to climb, as did the number of women who gave birth without marrying at all. Courts increasingly shifted the burden of child support from fathers to mothers. By the end of the seventeenth century, New Englanders were more inclined than ever to hold women responsible for sin.

Witchcraft at Salem

In this context of strain and anxiety, on February 29, 1692, magistrates John Hathorne and Jonathan Corwin went to Salem to investigate accusations of witchcraft. By the time the investigation and trials ended, 156 people had been jailed and 20 executed. As in previous witchcraft scares, most of the accused were women past the age of 40, and most of the accusers were women in their late teens and 20s.

Most of the accused fell into categories that revealed the stresses in Puritan society. Many, like Sarah Good, were the sort of disagreeable women who had always attracted accusations of witchcraft. Others had ties to Quakers or Baptists. Several were suspiciously friendly with the Indians, whereas many of the accusers had been orphaned or displaced by the recent Indian wars, and they described the devil as "a Tawney, or an Indian color." As a dark-skinned woman from an alien culture, Tituba was also vulnerable. In addition, most of the accusers lived in Salem Village, an economic backwater, whereas most of the accused lived in or had ties to the more prosperous merchant community of Salem Town. The pattern of accusations suggested resentment, perhaps unconscious, about the increasing commercialization of New England's economy.

>> Witchcraft in Global Perspective

Set against the witchcraft panic that swept Europe in the sixteenth and seventeenth centuries, the trials at Salem appear relatively insignificant. In Europe, approximately 110,000 people were put on trial; more than half were convicted and executed, typically by hanging or burning at the stake. In comparison, fewer than 2 percent of those tried by the notorious Spanish Inquisition were put to death.

Yet even these numbers do not convey a full sense of the hysteria. Thousands more fell under suspicion, and entire communities were often paralyzed—900 executed in Würzberg during one seven-year period, 133 in one day in 1589 in Quedlingberg.

Witchcraft trials took place in every country in Europe during the period but were much more common in some places than in others. About half the prosecutions took place in the German states, and many of the others took place in regions, such as Poland, Switzerland, and France, that were facing religious and political instability during the Reformation and Counter-Reformation.

This was also the period in which modern nation-states emerged. As kings tried to consolidate their rule, they inspired witch hunts in order to impose conformity. Witchcraft trials were also common where the local prince was relatively weak. In such places, local magistrates could freely drum up a fear of witchcraft and conduct prosecutions. Moreover, an agitated populace might search for more witches, widening the scope of the original hunt. Such unchecked hysteria threatened to continue without end. In 1685,

officials in the German town of Rottenburg worried that every local woman ultimately would be executed. In the same year, two other German villages had been reduced to one woman apiece.

Almost everywhere in Europe, women constituted the majority of accused—and executed—witches. To be sure, the disproportionate number of women accused—as high as 90 percent in some regions—reflects an underlying misogyny in western European culture at the time. The *Malleus Maleficarum (The Witch Hammer)*, the guidebook for witch hunting, first published in 1486 but reprinted many times over the next several decades, claimed that the passionate and gullible nature of women made them vulnerable to the devil's wiles. Female witches were thought to engage in "carnal copulation" with Satan and to procure him children to eat. "Blessed be the most high who has so far preserved the male sex from such crime," the book concluded.

Such views found a ready audience. Some historians suggest that the witchcraft trials strengthened controls over women. The typical accused witch was unmarried and hence not under the direct control of a husband or father. Warfare and the plague had left an increasing number of women without husbands, and in some areas by the seventeenth century, as many as 20 percent of women never married.

Early-modern Europe suffered from many forms of dislocation: warfare, religious upheaval, economic depression, *continued* epidemic disease. Witchcraft prosecutions sought to restore order by rooting out subversion that seemed to come from within. In societies organized by gender—rather than other forms of hierarchy—women became the focus. The witch hunts in New England, though much less sweeping than those of Europe, reveal the same pattern: a period of political instability that made people anxious to establish control, particularly of vulnerable women.

By late September, accusations were falling on wealthy and well-connected men and women, such as the wife of the governor. Accusers were paraded from town to town to root out local witchcraft, and other people were drawn to Salem like medieval pilgrims Finally, the leading ministers of Boston, most of whom believed in witchcraft but had been skeptical of the trials, stepped in, and the governor adjourned the court No one was ever convicted of witchcraft in New England again.

The End of Witchcraft

Although they continued to believe in witchcraft, magic, and the occult, by the end of the seventeenth century most colonists believed that the universe was orderly and that events were caused by natural, and knowable, forces. By the eighteenth century, educated people took pride in their rational understanding of nature and disdained a belief in the occult as mere superstition. This change in thinking reflected a new faith not only in human reason but also in the capacity of ordinary people to shape their lives. More and more people, especially those who were well educated, prosperous, and lived in cities, believed that they could control their destinies and were not at the mercy of invisible evil forces. The seed of individualism had been planted in New England's rocky soil.

As individualism slowly spread and communities became larger, the cohesion of Puritan communities waned. In the eighteenth century new attitudes toward women freed them of their symbolic power to do harm.

The witchcraft trials also ended New England's belief in itself as a covenanted society with a collective future. Because Puritans had believed that God had chosen them for a mission, they read special meaning into every event, from a sudden snowstorm to an Indian attack. By the eighteenth century, however, they began to evaluate events separately, rather than as part of God's master plan.

Empires in Collision

As late as the middle of the eighteenth century, Native Americans still outnumbered Europeans on the North American continent. At the end of the seventeenth century in the territory that became the United States, Britain was the only European power with a substantial presence (see Map 4–3). The French and Spanish both had mainland outposts

Map 4–3   Colonial North America, East of the Mississippi, 1720 This map shows the expansion of European settlement. English settlement was concentrated in a strip down the East Coast from Maine to North Carolina, with pockets of settlement in Canada and Carolina. French settlements formed a ring along the St. Lawrence River, from the Great Lakes south along the Mississippi, and along the Gulf Coast. The Spanish had outposts along the Gulf and in Florida. *Adapted from Geoffrey Barraclough, ed.,* The Times Concise Atlas of World History *(Maplewood, NJ: Hammond, 1994), p. 67.*

north of the Rio Grande, but these nations concentrated their resources on more valuable colonies: for the Spanish, Mexico and Latin America, and for the French, the West Indies. Nonetheless, imperial ambitions brought European powers into conflict in North America, where they jostled against each other and the Native Americans.

France Attempts an Empire

After its civil wars of religion ended early in the seventeenth century, France was free to establish foreign colonies. After 1664, France's minister Jean Baptiste Colbert tried to formulate a coherent imperial policy, directed from Paris. He envisioned a series of settlements, each contributing to the wealth of the nation through the fur trade and fishing in North America and plantation agriculture in the West Indies. France tried to direct the development of its New World empire, but it could not control small settlements so far away.

Colbert attempted to control every aspect of life in Quebec. He subsidized emigration and had female migrants investigated to make sure that they were healthy and morally sound. To encourage reproduction, dowries were offered to all men who married by the age of 20. Agriculture developed and the population grew, more from natural increase than immigration. Colbert's attempt to make Quebec a hierarchical society on the Old World model failed, however. First, very few French men and women were willing to settle in the New World. Between 1670 and 1730, perhaps fewer than 3,000 moved to mainland North America (and only a few thousand more to the West Indies). Second, those who did move resisted being controlled from Paris.

Eventually, Native Americans were more successful than Colbert in shaping the fur trade, the mainstay of the Quebec economy. The French depended on their Indian trading partners to supply them with furs and serve as military allies. When Indians tried to trade their furs to the British, the French built forts—at considerable cost—to intercept them. French traders smuggled furs to the British in return for British fabrics that the Indians preferred. Moreover, to maintain the allegiance of their Algonquian allies, the French gave them gifts of ammunition, knives, cloth, tobacco, and brandy. When the declining revenues from the fur trade are balanced against the all these costs, it is questionable whether Canada was of any economic benefit to France, which maintained the fur trade more for political than for economic reasons.

It was for political reasons that France established outposts in present-day Louisiana and Mississippi, including Fort Biloxi (1699), Fort Toulouse (1717), and New Orleans (1718), all in the territory named Louisiana. (At the same time France built a number of forts in the north—Fort Niagara [1720],and Fort St. Frédéric [1731]—to guard against English encroachments.) When the French explorer LaSalle reached the mouth of the Mississippi River in 1682 and claimed it for France, the Spanish mainland empire was cut in two, and the British faced a western rival. British traders had pushed into the lower Mississippi region looking for deerskins and Indian slaves. When the French arrived, tribes such as the Choctaws and Mobilians looked to the French for protection from the British and their allies. Within several decades, the French had established trading posts as far north as the Illinois Territory. Further west, French settlement of the lower Mississippi Valley led to conflict with the Natchez Indians, whom they conquered and sold into slavery.

The early history of the Louisiana Colony resembled that of the British settlement at Jamestown. As in Virginia, the first settlers were ill suited to the venture, top-heavy with military personnel and pirates. Louisiana itself was so unattractive that it could not attract colonists, so France began deporting criminals to the colony. Debilitated by the unhealthy environment, colonists could not even grow their own food. Caught up in wars on the continent, the French did not adequately support the colony, so its survival depended on the generosity of local Indians. After African slaves began to be smuggled into the colony from the Caribbean, in 1719 France permitted the importation of African slaves, but the colony still foundered.

Unlike the Chesapeake, colonial Louisiana never developed a significant cash crop. Because the colony was not important to French economic interests, French mercantilist policies protected Caribbean plantations at the expense of those in Louisiana. Although Louisiana had a slave majority by 1727, it was not a slave society. Louisiana's economy was one of frontier exchange among Europeans, Indians, and Africans, rather than one of commercial agriculture. Marginal to France's empire, Louisiana was largely ignored, and Europeans, Indians, and Africans depended on each other for survival. They intermarried and worked together in an exchange economy. As late as 1730, Native Americans

Drawing of the *Savages of Several Nations, New Orleans, 1735*, by Alexandre de Batz Notice the array of foods, products, and crops produced by the Indians in the New Orleans area.

still made up more than 90 percent of the population, and social and economic relations remained fluid.

The situation could not have been more different in France's Caribbean empire. There, by the end of the eighteenth century, most of the native population had been killed by disease or war. It was soon replaced by African slaves. By 1670, the islands of Martinique and Guadeloupe were producing significant amounts of sugar with African slave labor. Between 1680 and 1730, 380,000 Africans were imported into those islands and the French colony of Saint Domingue on the island of Santo Domingo, where they outnumbered Europeans by an astonishing ratio of 7.6 to 1. By the middle of the eighteenth century, Saint Domingue was producing more sugar than any colony in America and would become the world's greatest producer of coffee. In a few decades, the French West Indies had been transformed into slave societies, in which slavery shaped every aspect of life. They were by far the most valuable part of France's New World empire.

The Spanish Outpost in Florida

Like France's colony at Louisiana, Spain's settlement at St. Augustine, Florida, was intended to be a self-supporting military outpost. Unable to attract settlers and costly to maintain, Florida grew so slowly and unsteadily that the Spanish considered abandoning it and moving the population to the West Indies.

When the British established their colony at Carolina, however, Florida again became important to Spain—and it gained a new source of settlers in runaway slaves. The British and Spanish began fighting, usually using Indian and African surrogates. Spanish raiders seized slaves from Carolina plantations, paid them wages, and introduced them to Catholicism. Soon, as Carolina's governor complained, slaves were "running dayly" to Florida. In 1693, Spain's king offered liberty to all British slaves who escaped to Florida.

The border between the two colonies was violent—and, for Africans, a place of opportunity. Africans gained valuable military experience and, in 1738, about 100 former slaves established the free black town of Gracia Real de Santa Teresa de Mose near St. Augustine. Mose's leader was the Mandinga captain of the free black militia, Francisco Menéndez. A former slave who had been reenslaved, he persisted in petitioning for his freedom. Spain freed Menéndez and other Africans like him and reiterated the policy that British slaves who escaped to Florida should be free. The persistence of Menéndez and the other escaped slaves established the first free black community on the North American continent.

Conquest, Revolt, and Reconquest in New Mexico

In the west, New Mexico developed into a colonial outpost on the far edge of a world empire, irrelevant to Spain's economy or political power. Early in the seventeenth century, the Spanish considered abandoning the settlement, but Franciscan missionaries persuaded Spain to stay so the priests could minister to the Native Americans. In the eastern half of the continent, Indians could play the European powers against each other, but in the west, only Spain was a presence, reducing the Pueblo Indians' leverage. When the Pueblo Indians rose up against the Spanish at the end of the seventeenth century, the survival of New Mexico was in doubt.

Spain had established its colony in New Mexico by conquest. Although Coronado's party had explored the region from Arizona to Kansas (1541–1542), it had not planted a permanent settlement. In 1598, Juan de Oñate was appointed governor and authorized to establish a colony. Like his great-grandfather Cortés, Oñate persuaded some local Pueblos to accept him as their ruler, and others he overcame by force. His harsh means proved effective, and the Spanish soon dominated the entire Southwest. In 1610 they established their capital at Santa Fe, and the colony, called New Mexico, began to grow slowly. The New Mexico Colony was to serve as an outpost against the French, just as St. Augustine was to defend against the English. The most important "business" in the colony was to convert the Pueblo Indians to Catholicism.

Franciscan priests established a series of missions in New Mexico. Although there were never more than 50 or so Franciscans at any time, they claimed to have converted about 80,000 Indians in less than a century. Most of these conversions, however, were in name only. The Indians deeply resented the priests' attempts to change their customs and beliefs. By forcing the Indians to adopt European sex roles and sexual mores, the Franciscans undermined not only Pueblo religion but also their society.

Spanish rule fell harshly on the Pueblos. Although Spanish law forbade enslavement of conquered Indians, some Spanish settlers openly defied it. More common was the *encomienda* system. Oñate rewarded his lieutenants by naming them *encomende-ros*, which entitled them to tribute from the Indians living on the land they had been awarded. Some *encomenderos* instead demanded labor or personal service. Women working in Spanish households were vulnerable to sexual abuse by their masters. Facing such burdens, the Indian population declined from about 40,000 in 1638 to only 17,000 in 1670.

A combination of Spanish demands for labor and tribute and a long period of drought left the Pueblos without the food surpluses that they had been selling to the nomadic Apaches and Navajos. Those tribes began to raid the Pueblos, taking by force what they could no longer get by trade. Under siege, Pueblos turned once again to their tribal gods and religious leaders.

When the Spanish punished the Indians who returned to their traditional religion, they pushed the Pueblos into revolt. A medicine man named Popé united the leaders of most of the Pueblos, promising that if the Indians threw out the Spanish and prayed again to their ancient gods, food would be plentiful. Indians would never have to work for the Spanish again, he said, and Indian customs would be restored.

Popé's revolt began on August 10, 1680, when the Spanish were low on supplies. First, the Indians seized all horses and mules, immobilizing the Spanish. Next, they blocked the

The Pueblo at Acoma The Acoma pueblo sits atop a mesa that rises 400 feet above ground. In January 1699, Spanish soldiers destroyed the pueblo and killed 800 of its inhabitants in retaliation for the killing of a dozen soldiers. All the male survivors over the age of 12 and all female survivors were sentenced to 20 years of servitude to the Spanish, and the men over the age of 25 each had a foot cut off as well. The pueblo was rebuilt after its destruction.

roads to Santa Fe. Then they destroyed all the Spanish settlements, one at a time. At day's end, more than 400 Spanish had been killed. The Pueblos laid siege to Santa Fe, forcing Spanish survivors to retreat to El Paso. In the most successful Indian revolt ever in North America, the Spanish had been driven from New Mexico.

The Pueblos held off the Spanish for 13 years, until 1696, but the struggles took a heavy toll. Contrary to Popé's promise, the drought continued. Warfare took more lives, and the population continued to drop.

The revolt taught the Spanish lessons. The new Franciscan missionaries were far less zealous than their predecessors. The *encomienda* was not reestablished, and exploitation was less common. Slowly the Spanish colony began rebuilding (see Map 4–4).

The population was divided into four groupings, from a small nobility at the top to enslaved Indians at the bottom. The nobility, a hereditary aristocracy of 20 or so families, included government officials. They developed codes of honor to distinguish themselves from lower orders. This nobility prided itself on its racial purity, considering white skin a clear sign of superiority. It scorned those of mixed blood, many of whom, of course, were the illegitimate children of elite Spanish men and the Indian women they raped or seduced. Aristocratic men placed a high value on the personal qualities of courage, honesty, loyalty, and sexual virility. Female honor consisted of extreme modesty and sexual purity.

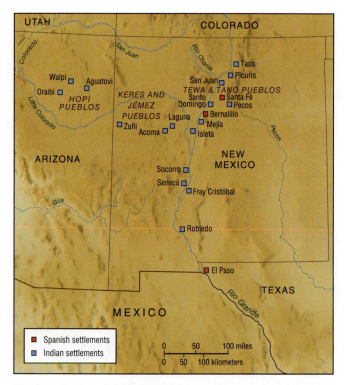

Map 4-4   Region of Spanish Reconquest of New Mexico, 1692–1696
This map includes the pueblos reconquered by the Spanish, as well as Spanish settlements. *Adapted from Oakah L. Jones, Jr., Pueblo Warriors and Spanish Conquest (Norman, OK: University of Oklahoma Press, 1966), p. 37.*

The second group was landed peasants, most of them *mestizos*, half-Spanish and half-Indian. In this highly color-conscious colonial society, the *mestizos* prized the Spanish part of their heritage and scorned the Indian. Next came the Pueblo Indians, living in their own communities. At the bottom were the *genízaros*, conquered Indians who had been enslaved. They were joined by Indians who left their tribes and moved to Spanish settlements. Often these immigrants were outcasts, such as women who had been raped by Spanish men. A century after their first conquest, the Pueblo Indians had begun to adopt the values of their conquerors.

Native Americans and the Country Between

Spain paid little attention to its impoverished outposts in New Mexico, leaving them vulnerable to the Indians to the east. When the French in Louisiana started arming their Comanche, Wichita, and Pawnee trading parters, New Mexicans—Spanish and Pueblos alike—were challenged.

The Indians of the Great Plains, however, profited from the conflict, obtaining guns from the French and horses from the Spanish. After the Pueblo revolt, the Spanish left behind hundreds of horses that Pueblo and Apache Indians passed on to the Plains Indians. By the middle of the eighteenth century, all the Plains Indians were on horseback, which transformed their lives dramatically. They became more effective buffalo hunters, thus making them better fed, clothed, and housed. Their new mobility gave them an increasing sense of freedom, too. But the horses—and the better living conditions they helped make possible—attracted other Indians to the Great Plains. In fact, most of the Indians we now associate with the Great Plains—Sioux, Arapaho, Cheyenne, Blackfoot, Cree—did not arrive there until the eighteenth century.

The result was increased warfare among the Plains Indians, and those with the best access to horses fared the best. For example, the Comanches came to dominate the southern plains, from western Kansas to New Mexico, where they intruded on both the Apaches and the Spanish. The Comanches raided the Apaches, taking not only their horses but also their women and children as captives, some of whom they sold as slaves—*genízaros*—to the Spanish. The Comanches cut the Apaches off from French traders to the east. The Apaches in turn moved west and south, bringing them into conflict with the Pueblos and the Spanish. In defense, the Spanish built a string of armed settlements in current-day Texas,

Eighteenth-century Spanish Illustrations of New World Racial Mixture In this case, the union of an Indian ("Yndio") and a "Mestiza" produces a "Coyote" child. The Spanish were much more attentive to color distinction than were the English, and they developed a large vocabulary so that they could make these distinctions with great precision.

De Yndio y Mestiza Coyote.

>> Timeline

▼1660
British monarchy restored, Charles II crowned king

▼1662
Half-Way Covenant

▼1664:
British seize New Netherland, renaming it New York

▼1665
New Jersey established

▼1669
Fundamental Constitutions written for South Carolina

▼1670
Carolina settled

▼1673
Marquette and Joliet explore Mississippi for France

▼1675–1676
King Philip's War

▼1676–1677
Bacon's Rebellion

▼1680
Pueblo Revolt in New Mexico reestablishes Indian rule
Westo War, Carolina defeats the Westos

▼1681
William Penn granted charter for Pennsylvania

▼1683
New York's assembly meets for first time

▼1685
King Charles II dies and James, Duke of York, becomes King James II

▼1686
Massachusetts, Plymouth, Connecticut, Rhode Island, and New Hampshire
    combined in Dominion of New England; New York and New Jersey added
    two years later

▼1688
Glorious Revolution

>> Timeline *continued*

▼**1689**
Leisler's Rebellion in New York, Coode's Rebellion in Maryland
William and Mary become King and Queen of Britain; Dominion of
   New England overthrown

▼**1689–1697**
King William's War

▼**1690**
Publication of John Locke's *Two Treatises of Government*

▼**1691**
Massachusetts made a royal colony
Maryland made a royal colony
New Hampshire made a royal colony

▼**1692**
Salem witchcraft trials

▼**1696**
Reconquest of New Mexico

▼**1702–1713**
Queen Anne's War

▼**1706**
Spanish establish settlement at Albuquerque

▼**1715–1716**
Yamasee War

▼**1718**
French establish settlement at New Orleans

but they could not withstand the Comanches, and even the New Mexican settlements were endangered.

Eventually, the new horse-centered way of life took its toll. Although some tribes grew stronger at the expense of others, all suffered from the increasing violence. European diseases proved deadly, as well. Under such pressures, gender roles changed. Men sought distinction as warriors, demonstrating success by the number of scalps or captives they seized. Yet so many fell in battle that they were soon outnumbered by women, which led to polygamy, as surviving warriors took multiple wives. As men's status as warriors and hunters rose, that of women—the agriculturalists—fell. Men also increased their status by seizing and selling female captives. In a warrior society, women were important markers of male prestige.

Conclusion

After a period of considerable instability, by the beginning of the eighteenth century, almost all of the British North American colonies had developed the societies that they would maintain until the American Revolution. For the most part, the colonies were prosperous, with a large white middle class. The efforts to replicate a European hierarchical order had largely failed. Each region had found a secure economic base: farming and shipping in New England, mixed farming in the middle colonies, and single-crop planting in the southern ones. The southern colonies had become slave societies, although slavery was practiced in every colony. For the most part, the colonies had figured out how to control their own populations, whether by affording them—in the case of Europeans—increased opportunity and political rights or by exercising tighter control, as was the case with enslaved Africans. These strong economic foundations, when combined with political stability, were the preconditions for the rapid population growth of the eighteenth century, when the British population on the mainland would far surpass that of the French and Spanish colonies. The French and Spanish colonies on the mainland were still little more than frontier outposts, although both nations still maintained imperial visions for North America. Native Americans remained a strong presence, but the competition among the European powers—and even the individual colonies—for the loyalty of the Indian tribes, their trade, and their land remained a source of conflict.

Review Questions

1. What was Britain's plan of empire? What role were the American colonies supposed to play in it?

2. Many of the American colonies experienced a period of political instability in the last quarter of the seventeenth century. Describe the rebellions and other examples of political instability, and explain what caused them.

3. What effect did political turmoil and the change of leadership in Britain have on the American colonies in the second half of the seventeenth century?

4. Describe Indian-white relations in the American colonies in the second half of the seventeenth century. What was the Covenant Chain, and how did Edmund Andros's vision of Indian-white relations differ from that of settlers in New England?

5. What were the primary causes of the witchcraft trials in Salem in 1692? What were the primary results?

6. Describe the causes and results of Popé's Rebellion of 1680, and describe New Mexican society in the early eighteenth century.

**For further review materials and resource information,
please visit www.oup.com/us/ofthepeople**

The Eighteenth-Century World

1700–1775

5

AMERICAN PORTRAIT

>> George Whitefield: Evangelist for a Consumer Society

In 1740 there were no more than 16,000 people living in Boston, but on October 12, some 20,000 people filled the Common to hear an English minister preach. Everywhere he went, the crowds were unprecedented—8,000 in Philadelphia, 3,000 in the little Pennsylvania village of Neshaminy. Those who could not see the evangelist in person read about him in the newspapers. If there was one binding experience for the American people in the decades before the Revolution, it was George Whitefield's ministry.

Born in Bristol, England, in 1714, George Whitefield would become not only a leading preacher of the Great Awakening of religion in the American colonies but also one of the most influential preachers in the history of Christianity. Because of the growth of the market economy, men and women on both sides of the Atlantic could now participate in a consumer culture that offered many ways to spend money and leisure time. To those schooled in a traditional Calvinist religion, the consumer society was both attractive and frightening. Could one serve God and oneself at the same time?

At 17, when Whitefield discovered he had no aptitude for trade, the career he had chosen, the boy from a poor family faced a personal crisis. Then, one morning, he blurted out that "God intends something for me which we know not of." Whitefield then prepared for the ministry. He enrolled at Oxford University, paying his way by working as a servant to wealthy students. He became friendly with the Methodists, a group of religious young men planning a mission to the new colony of Georgia. Under their influence, Whitefield turned his back on consumer culture. Now, "Whatsoever I did, I endeavoured to do all to the glory of God." Whitefield was determined to share what he had learned with all who would hear.

Whitefield helped create a mass public that broke down the boundaries of small communities in which each minister or priest had typically addressed only his own

continued

>> AMERICAN PORTRAIT *continued*

congregation. The crowds Whitefield drew were often so large that he preached outdoors, with a voice so loud that Benjamin Franklin calculated that it could be heard by 25,000 people at a time. Although Whitefield spoke directly to the heart of each individual, he also drew together entire communities in a way no one had ever done before.

Whitefield embodied the great contradictions of his age without threatening the political or economic order that sustained them. He appealed to men as well as women, to the poor as well as the rich, to slaves as well as their masters, and to those who were suffering from capitalism as well as those who were benefiting from it. Whitefield's strategy was to criticize the individual without attacking the system. In Philadelphia, he preached, "Do not say, you are miserable, and poor, and blind and naked, and therefore ashamed to come, for it is to such that this Invitation is now sent. The Polite, the Rich, the Busy, Self-Righteous Pharisees of this Generation have been bidden already, but they . . . are too deeply engaged in going one to his Country House, another to his Merchandize."

He censured the religious leadership, but not the church itself. Cruel slave masters were condemned, but not the institution of slavery. He showed people how to acquire the self-discipline that would enable them either to succeed in a competitive market or to bear failures with Christian resignation. He helped them experience religion as an intense personal feeling and find meaning in a time of rapid economic transformation.

A world traveler who called Georgia his home, Whitefield died in Newburyport, Massachusetts, in 1770, preaching to the end. Five years later, a band of Continental Army officers dug up his corpse. The body had decayed, but his clothing was still intact. The soldiers snipped pieces of it to take with them as protection.

Common Threads

>> What were the some of the choices that individual men and women made in the eighteenth century—for example, about where to live, how to work, what to purchase, what to believe—and how did those choices affect their society?

>> How did such choices make everyday life more democratic? What were the forces that worked against such democratization?

>> How were free Americans able to become wealthier even without significant technological innovations?

>> How did the consumer revolution affect American society and culture?

>> As the colonial population became more diverse and complex, with separate regional cultures and an increasing variety of beliefs and religious practices, were there other experiences that colonial Americans had in common? Is it possible yet, on the eve of the American Revolution, to talk about a common American experience or culture?

The Population Explosion of the Eighteenth Century

George Whitefield could speak to the hearts of the American colonists because he understood their world. As the colonies matured, they were tied into the North Atlantic world and brought dramatic changes. One of the most important changes was the increase in population, from both immigration and natural increase. This population produced products for the world economy and provided a market for them, as well, and its boom was both the product of American prosperity and the precondition for its further growth.

The Dimensions of Population Growth

The population in the American colonies grew at a rate unprecedented in human history, from just over 250,000 people in 1700 to more than 1 million by 1750. The rate of growth was highest in the free population in prosperous farming regions, but it was rapid everywhere, even among slaves.

Much of the colonies' population growth was caused by their unquenchable thirst for labor. They attracted an extraordinary number of immigrants, and when free labor did not meet the demand, unfree labor (slaves, indentured servants, and redemptioners) filled the gap. In fact, when the number of Africans who came in chains is added to the Europeans who came as indentured servants and redemptioners, 90 percent of the immigrants to the colonies between 1580 and 1775 were unfree when they arrived.

Increasingly, these immigrants reflected the broad reach of the North Atlantic political world. At the beginning of the eighteenth century, the population of the American colonies was primarily English in origin. By the beginning of the American Revolution, the population had changed significantly. There were small numbers of people with Finnish, Swedish, French, Swiss, and Jewish heritage, and large numbers of Welsh, Scotch-Irish, Germans, Dutch, and Africans. The foundation for American diversity had been laid.

Bound for America: European Immigrants

Much of the population increase came from immigration. In the eighteenth century, about 425,000 Europeans migrated to the colonies, with large numbers from Scotland, Northern Ireland, Wales, and Germany.

The largest number of European immigrants were Scotch-Irish, that is, Scottish people who had moved to Northern Ireland to escape famine in their own country. As many as 250,000 came to seek a better life and to escape the religious persecution they experienced as Presbyterians in an Anglican society. At first, Massachusetts invited the Scotch-Irish to settle on its borders, as a buffer between the colony and the Indians. Once the impoverished Scotch-Irish began to arrive in large numbers, however, the English inhabitants worried that they would have to provide for them. In 1729 a Boston mob turned away a shipload of Scotch-Irish immigrants, and in 1738 the Puritans of Worcester burned down a Presbyterian church. Thereafter, the vast majority of Scotch-Irish immigrants headed for the more welcoming middle colonies and the South.

Going where land was the cheapest, the Scotch-Irish settled between the English sea-board settlements and the Indian communities to the west, from Pennsylvania to Georgia (see Map 5–1). As their numbers increased, the Scotch-Irish pressed against the Indians, seizing their lands. Like the Scotch-Irish, most German migrants settled in the backcountry from Pennsylvania to the Carolinas. Between 1700 and the start of the Revolution,

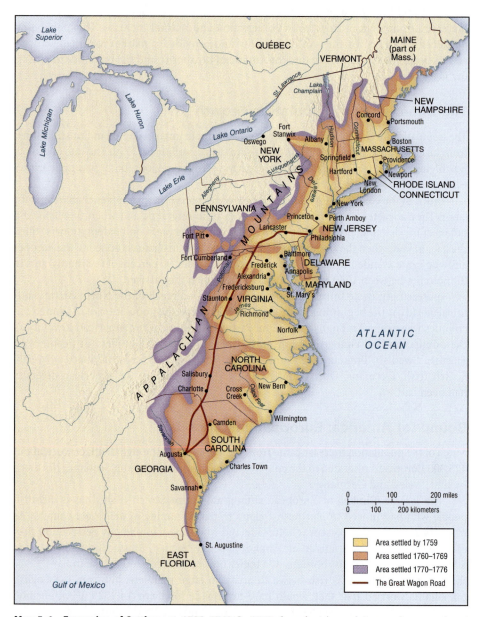

Map 5–1 Expansion of Settlement, 1720–1760 By 1760, the colonial population made up an almost continuous line of settlement from Maine to Florida and was pushing west over the Appalachian Mountains.

more than 100,000 Germans arrived, and by 1775, a third of Pennsylvania's population was German. Including not only Lutherans and Catholics but also Quakers, Amish, and Mennonites, Germans established prosperous farming communities wherever they settled. Indeed, colonies such as Pennsylvania that welcomed the widest variety of immigrants became not only the most prosperous but also the ones in which that prosperity was most widely shared. Unlike most seventeenth-century migrants, a large proportion of eighteenth-century migrants were artisans drawn to America by the demand for their labor. As African slaves became agricultural workers, especially in the South, the colonies needed skilled workers.

The majority of European migrants to the colonies were unfree, not only indentured servants and redemptioners but also the 50,000 British convicts whose sentences were commuted to a term of service in the colonies. Most English and Welsh migrants were single men between the ages of 19 and 23 who came as indentured servants. The Scotch-Irish migration included a larger number of families, and three-fourths of the Germans came in family groups. For all, the passage to America, which could take three months or more, was grueling and profoundly unhealthy. Once the migrants arrived, servants and convicts were sold for terms of service in auctions that resembled those held for African slaves (see Figure 5–1).

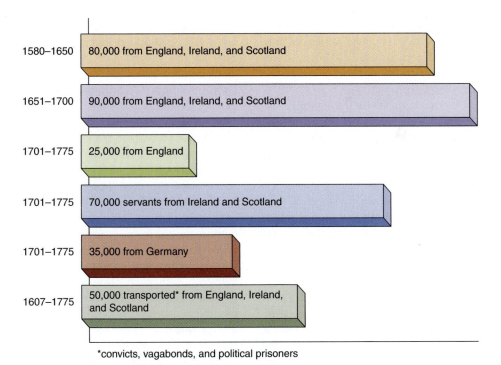

1580–1650   80,000 from England, Ireland, and Scotland

1651–1700   90,000 from England, Ireland, and Scotland

1701–1775   25,000 from England

1701–1775   70,000 servants from Ireland and Scotland

1701–1775   35,000 from Germany

1607–1775   50,000 transported* from England, Ireland, and Scotland

*convicts, vagabonds, and political prisoners

Figure 5–1   The Importation of Servants from Europe into British America, 1580–1775 By the time of the American Revolution, 350,000 servants had been imported into the colonies, most of whom came from the British Isles. *Richard S. Dunn, "Servants and Slaves," in Jack P. Greene and J. R. Pole,* Colonial British America *(Baltimore: Johns Hopkins, 1984), p. 159.*

AMERICAN LANDSCAPE

>> **The Slave Ship**

We do not usually think of a ship as part of a landscape, but the slave ship was one of the most important places in the eighteenth century. It was at once a floating factory, prison, and fortress. It was there that Africans were transformed into slaves.

Any ship, small or large, could be made into a slave ship. Because the cost of transporting slaves across the Atlantic was so high, accounting for three-quarters of the price of a slave, slave merchants tried to crowd as many Africans as possible into each ship—300, 400, or even 600. The English were particularly efficient, carrying twice as many slaves as crew members and half again as many slaves per ship as the other nations, thereby increasing the profits.

In order to maximize the number of Africans on each ship, platforms were built between decks, thus doubling the surface area upon which the slaves could be placed. With perhaps only four and a half feet between the platform and the ceiling, the Africans could not stand up. They were packed so tightly that they could not move from side to side. Even the smallest spaces were filled with children.

Packing so many human beings into such tight quarters created the risk of suffocation. But if the hatches were kept open, the Africans might escape confinement and overpower the crew. Hence, grates were placed over the hatches, and small air openings were cut into the sides of the ship. Later, some ships used large funnel tubes to carry air below decks.

Men and women were kept separate, divided by partitions. Male slaves were shackled and confined below deck for most of each day. Chained together and without enough room to stand up, many were unable to reach the large buckets that served as latrines. Some captains let the slaves lie in their own filth until the voyage's end. Heat and disease compounded the misery. One ship's doctor reported that the slaves' deck "was so covered with the blood and mucus which had proceeded from them in consequence of the flux, that it resembled a slaughterhouse." The women were left unshackled but were often prey to the sailors' lust. When slaves were brought above deck, some would jump overboard. Captains stretched netting around their ships to prevent such suicides.

In order to protect the crew in case of insurrection, slave ships often had thick, ten-foot-high walls—barricados—to separate the crew from the human cargo. Armed sailors patrolled atop the barricado. Ship captains gathered their human cargo from different regions, each with its own language, to make sure that the captives could not communicate with each other and foment rebellion. At the same time, the captains had to be careful not to bring together groups who might fight each other. With resistance from the enslaved the norm, ship captains used terror to maintain order. Flogging—a punishment for sailors, as well—was common. Some captains used instruments of torture, such as the thumbscrew, "a dreadful engine, which, if the screw be turned by an unrelenting hand, can give intolerable anguish." The object was not only to punish the disobedient but also to frighten their shipmates. That was surely the result after some of the Africans aboard the *Brownlow* rebelled. The captain dismembered the rebels with an axe "till their bodies remained only like a trunk of a tree when all the branches are lopped away," and he threw the severed heads and limbs at the other slaves, chained together on the deck.

Such terror hardened captain and crew. Few sailors signed onto a slave ship if they had better options, and one captain described his crew as the "very dregs of the community." The life of a sailor was hard enough; service on a slave ship—a floating prison—was even harder. Yet even the lowest sailor was superior to the enslaved. Even though many sailors were dark-skinned men from Asia, the Caribbean, or India, at sea, they were all known as "white people." Over time, both captain and crew became practiced in the ways of cruelty. Silas Todd was apprenticed to a slave ship captain at the age of 14 and hoped to become a captain himself. Then, ashore in Boston in 1734, he was "saved" in the Great Awakening. Had he not been, he later reflected, he might later have become "as eminent a savage" as the captains under whom he had served.

Bound for America: African Slaves

The increase in the African population was even more dramatic than that of Europeans. In 1660 there were only 2,920 African or African-descended inhabitants of the mainland colonies. A century later there were more than 300,000. The proportion of Africans grew most rapidly in the southern colonies, to almost 40 percent on the eve of the Revolution. By 1720 South Carolina had an African majority. Most of the increase in the African population came from the slave trade. By 1808, when Congress closed off the importation of slaves to the United States, about 523,000 African slaves had been imported into the nation (see Figure 5–2).

The African slave trade was a profitable and well-organized segment of the world economy. Until the eighteenth century, when demand from the New World increased, the transatlantic slave trade was controlled by Africans. Generally, Europeans were not allowed into the interior of Africa, so slaves were brought to the coast for sale. Many African nations taxed the sale of slaves and regulated the trade. Some nations supplied a steady stream of slaves, whereas others offered them intermittently, suggesting that participation in the trade was a matter of conscious policy.

Because African slaves were unwilling and sometimes rebellious passengers on the ships that transported them across the Atlantic, European slave ships needed larger crews and heavier weapons than usual. This resistance by slaves increased the cost of transporting them so much that the higher prices may have spared half a million Africans enslavement.

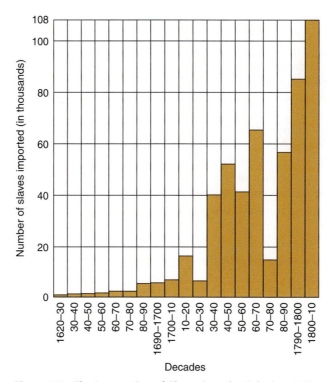

Figure 5–2   The Importation of Slaves into the Colonies, 1620–1810 The number of Africans imported into the colonies increased dramatically in the eighteenth century, and, except for an interruption during the American Revolution continued until the African slave trade was made illegal in 1808. *Helen Hornbeck Tanner,* The Settling of North America *(New York: Macmillan, 1995), p. 51.*

Most slaves were captives of war, and as the demand for slaves increased, the tempo of warfare in Africa intensified in response. In times of famine and epidemic, sometimes caused by the slave trade, desperate families might even sell their own children to a trader. The New World preferred male slaves, leaving most of the female captives to the African slave market, where they became domestic slaves or plural wives to wealthier Africans.

As bad as the voyage to America was for indentured servants, the trip for enslaved Africans was worse. Perhaps 10 percent died before reaching the African coast. Many had never seen an ocean or a white man, and both sights terrified them. They were confined in pens or forts for as long as half a year while waiting for a ship.

The voyage, or "middle passage," proved lethal to many more. As the slave trade became more efficient in the eighteenth century, the mortality rate dropped, from perhaps 20 percent to half that amount. Those who survived were ready to begin their lives as New World slaves.

The Great Increase of Offspring

Most of the extraordinary increase in the colonies' population, European and African alike, came not from immigration or the slave trade but from natural increase.

This group is being force marched by an African slave trader from the interior of Africa to a European trading post on the coast.

For European Americans, population increase was mainly due to the lower age of marriage for women and the higher proportion of women who married. In England, for example, as many as 20 percent of women did not marry by age 45, compared with only 5 percent in the colonies. The age of marriage for women in the colonies was also considerably lower, with women marrying in their late teens or early 20s, compared to the late 20s in England. Because more women married, and married earlier, they bore more babies, on average seven or eight each, with six or seven surviving to adulthood. As a rule, the more economic opportunity, the earlier the age of marriage for women and men, and the more children. In the healthier climate, more children survived to adulthood, but child mortality rates were high. Thanks to rapid population growth, the American population was exceptionally young.

In many ways, the African American population resembled the European American population. Slaves born in the colonies married young and established families as stable as slavery permitted. By the time they were 18, most slave women usually had had their first child. As in Africa, they might not form a lasting union with the father, but within a few years many settled into long-lasting relationships with the men who would father the rest of their children. Slave women bore between six and eight children, on average. With child mortality even higher for African Americans than for European Americans, between 25 and 50 percent of slave children died before reaching adulthood. Even so, the slave population more than reproduced itself, and by the middle of the eighteenth century it was growing more from natural increase than from the importation of slaves. Only a tiny fraction of the Africans sold into slavery ended up in mainland British colonies. Nonetheless, when slavery was abolished after the Civil War, the United States had the largest population of African descent in the New World.

The Transatlantic Economy: Producing and Consuming

In the eighteenth century, as the colonies matured, they became capitalist societies in an Atlantic trade network. More and more, people produced for the market, so that they could buy the goods the market had to offer. Throughout the Atlantic world, ordinary people reshaped their lives so they could buy more goods. Historians talk about two economic revolutions in this period: a consumer revolution—a steady increase in the demand for and purchase of consumer goods—and an industrious revolution (not industri*al* but industri*ous* revolution), in which people worked harder and organized their households (their families, servants, and slaves) to produce goods for sale so that they would have money to pay for items they wanted. Income went up only slightly in the eighteenth century, yet people were buying more. In the process, they created a consumer society, in which most people eagerly purchased consumer goods.

The Nature of Colonial Economic Growth

Throughout human history, population growth has usually led to a decline in the standard of living as more people compete for fewer resources. In the American colonies, however, population growth led to an expansion of the economy, as more of the continent's abundant natural resources were brought under human control. The standard of living for most free Americans probably improved, although not dramatically. As the economy matured, a small segment—urban merchants and owners of large plantations—became wealthy. At the same time, the urban poor and tenant farmers began to slip toward poverty.

All of these changes took place, however, without any significant changes in technology (such as the power looms that would be invented later in the century). Most wealth was made from shipping and agriculture. Eighty percent of the colonies' population worked on farms or plantations, areas with no major technological innovations. Virtually all gains in productivity came instead from labor: more people were working, and they were working more efficiently.

The economy of colonial America was shaped by three factors: abundance of land and shortages of labor and of capital. The plantation regions of the South and the West Indies were best situated to take advantage of these circumstances, and the small-farm areas of New England were the least suitable. Tobacco planters in the Chesapeake and rice and indigo planters in South Carolina sold their products on a huge world market. Their large profits enabled them to purchase more land and more slaves to work it.

Because northern farmers raised crops and animals that were also produced in Europe, profits from agriculture alone were too low to permit them to acquire large tracts of land or additional labor (see table 5–1). Northerners had to look to other opportunities for wealth. They found them in trade, exchanging their raw goods for European manufactured ones and selling them to American consumers.

The Transformation of the Family Economy

In colonial America, the family was the basic economic unit, and all family members contributed to it. Work was organized by gender. On farms, women were responsible for

Table 5-1 How Wealthy Were Colonial Americans?

Property-owning Class	New England	Mid-Atlantic Colonies	Southern Colonies	Thirteen Colonies
Men	£ 169	£ 194	£ 410	£260
Women	£ 42	£ 103	£ 215	£ 132
Adults 45 and older	£252	£ 274	£ 595	£ 361
Adults 44 and younger	£ 129	£ 185	£ 399	£ 237
Urban	£ 191	£ 287	£ 641	£ 233
Rural	£ 151	£ 173	£ 392	£ 255
Esquires, gentlemen	£ 313	£1,223	£1,281	£ 572
Merchants	£563	£ 858	£ 314	£497
Professions, sea captains	£ 271	£ 241	£ 512	£ 341
Farmers only, planters	£ 155	£ 180	£ 396	£ 263
Farmer-artisans, ship owners, fishermen	£ 144	£ 257	£ 801	£ 410
Shop and tavern keepers	£ 219	£ 222	£ 195	£204
Artisans, chandlers	£ 114	£ 144	£ 138	£ 122
Miners, laborers	£ 52	£ 67	£ 383	£ 62

Source: Alice Hanson Jones, *Wealth of a Nation to Be: The American Colonies on the Eve of the Revolution* (New York: Columbia University Press, 1980), p. 224.

the preparation of food and clothing, child care, and care of the home. Women grew vegetables and herbs, provided dairy products, and transformed flax and wool into clothing. Daughters worked under their mother's supervision, perhaps spinning extra yarn to be sold for a profit.

Men worked the rest of the farm. They raised grain and maintained the pastures. They cleared the land, chopped wood for fuel, and built and maintained the house, barn, and other structures. They took crops to market. Men's and women's work were complementary and necessary for survival. For example, men planted apple trees, children picked apples, and women made them into cider. When a husband was disabled, ill, or away from home, his wife could perform virtually all of his tasks as a sort of "deputy husband." Men almost never performed women's work, however, and men whose wives died remarried quickly to have someone to care for the household and children.

The eighteenth century's industrious revolution transformed the family economy: when people decided to produce goods to sell, they changed their family economies. Historians believe that increased production in this period came primarily from the labor of women and children, who worked harder and longer than they had before.

Sources of Regional Prosperity

The South, the most productive region, accounted for more than 60 percent of colonial exports (see Map 5–2). Tobacco was its chief cash crop. Next came cereals such as rice, wheat, corn, and flour, and then indigo, a plant used to dye fabric.

Map 5–2   Exports of the Thirteen Colonies, ca. 1770 Almost two-thirds of the exports from the colonies came from the South, and more than one-half went to Great Britain alone. Tobacco and grains were the most important exports of all. *Jacob Cooke, ed.,* Encyclopedia of North American Colonies *(New York: Scribner's, 1993), pp. 1, 514.*

Slave labor accounted for most of the southern agricultural output and was organized to produce for the market. When tobacco profits began to slip because of falling prices and the depletion of the soil, planters worked their slaves harder and, in the Chesapeake, began to plant corn and wheat. By diversifying their crops, planters were able to make maximum use of their slave labor force by keeping slaves busy throughout the year.

The work routine of slaves depended on the crops they tended. On tobacco plantations, where careful attention to the plants was necessary to ensure high quality, planters or white overseers worked the slaves in small gangs carefully selected and arranged to maximize productivity.

In the rice-growing lower South, however, slaves were usually assigned specific tasks, which they would work at until the job was completed. Rice growing required far less supervision than did tobacco planting. Because many Africans had grown rice in Africa and had likely taught Europeans how to grow it in America, rice planters let the slaves set their own pace. Once finished for the day, the slaves could use their time as they pleased. Many planted gardens to supplement their own diets or to earn a small income. Slaves trafficked in a wide range of products, from rice, corn, chickens, hogs, and catfish to canoes, baskets, and wax.

The inhabitants of the middle colonies grew prosperous by raising and selling wheat and other grains. The ports of Baltimore, Philadelphia, Wilmington, and New York became thriving commercial centers that collected grain from regional farms, milled it into flour, and shipped it to the West Indies, southern Europe, and other American colonies.

Farmers relied on indentured servants, cottagers, and slaves to supplement the labor of family members. *Cottagers* were families who rented out part of a farmer's land, which they worked for wages.

As long as land was cheap and accessible, the middle colonies enjoyed the most evenly shared prosperity on the continent. Most inhabitants fell into the comfortable middle class, with the gap between the richest and the poorest relatively small. Pennsylvania, which offered both religious toleration and relatively simple ways to purchase land, was particularly prosperous. The energy that elsewhere went into religious conflict here fueled work and material accumulation. Gottlieb Mittelberger, who endured a horrendous journey to Pennsylvania, described his new home as a sort of paradise: "Our Americans live more quietly and peacefully than the Europeans; and all this is the result of the liberty which they enjoy and which makes them all equal."

When land became expensive or difficult to obtain, however, conflict might ensue. In the 1740s and 1750s, both New Jersey and New York experienced land riots when conflicting claims made land titles uncertain. In the Chesapeake and southeastern Pennsylvania, increasing land prices drove the poor into tenancy or to the urban centers. Widespread prosperity led Americans to expect that everyone who wished to would be able to own a farm. When land ownership was not fully possible, tension and anger grew.

New England was also primarily a farming region. Here, however, male family members, rather than indentured servants, cottagers, or slaves, provided most farm labor. Although farms in some regions, such as the Connecticut River valley, produced surpluses for the market, most farm families had to look for other sources of income to pay for consumer goods.

Town governments in New England encouraged enterprise, sometimes providing gristmills, sawmills, and fields on which cattle could graze. The region prospered, and New Englanders came to expect their governments to enhance the economy. Agricultural exports were relatively slight, although both grain and livestock were sold to the slave plantations of the West Indies, which received more than 25 percent of the American colonies' exports (and more than 70 percent of New England's).

The other major colonial exports in the eighteenth century were fur and hides. By the eve of the Revolution, 95 percent of the furs imported into England came from North America—most of them provided by Indians, who traded them to European middlemen.

Merchants and Dependent Laborers in the Transatlantic Economy

Almost all colonies participated in a transatlantic economy. In each region, those most involved in the market were those with the most resources: large planters in the southern colonies, owners of the biggest farms in the middle colonies, and urban merchants in the northern colonies. The wealthiest never made their fortunes from farming or planting alone but always added income from activities such as speculating in land, practicing law, or lending money.

If some economic development was spurred from above, by enterprising individuals or by governments, much was also created by ambitious ordinary men and women. New

Drying Cod Men landing and drying cod in Newfoundland. Increasingly, fishing became a form of dependent wage labor, as merchants supplied boats and equipment and hired other men to fish for them.

England's mixed economy of grain, grazing, fishing, and lumbering required substantial capital improvements such as gristmills, sawmills, and tanneries to be profitable. By the beginning of the eighteenth century, shipbuilding was a major activity, and by 1775, one-third of the English merchant fleet had been built in the colonies.

The shipbuilding industry, in turn, spurred further economic development. In a process called linked economic development (because it ties together a variety of enterprises), shipbuilding stimulated other activities, such as lumbering, and the availability of ships enabled a flourishing trade. The profits generated by shipbuilding and trade were reinvested in sawmills to produce more lumber, in gristmills to grind grain into flour, and, of course, in more trading voyages. The growth of shipping in port cities such as Boston, Newport, New York, Philadelphia, and Charleston created an affluent merchant class, but trading was a risky business, and few who tried it rose to the top. One ship lost to a storm could ruin a merchant, as could a sudden turn in the market. With an average of 10 times the capital of colonial merchants, English merchants could weather such reverses. Because capital was scarce in the colonies, merchants took great risks, seeking to turn a quick profit during wartime (see Chapter 6) or gambling on a sudden spurt in the price of wheat. Bad choices or bad luck could ruin any merchant.

The seafaring trades led capitalist development. A wealthy, risk-taking merchant class emerged, as well as that other distinguishing mark of a capitalist economy, a wage-earning class. As long as there was a labor shortage in the colonies, workers had an advantage. By the beginning of the eighteenth century, however, rapid population increase led to a growing supply of labor. Although they were free to shop around for the best wages, workers became part of a wage-earning class, dependent on others for employment and income. Only a small portion of Americans were wage-earners on the eve of the Revolution, but they were a sign of things to come.

Consumer Choices and the Creation of Gentility

Under the British mercantilist system (see Chapter 4), the colonies were supposed to export raw materials to the empire and import finished products back, sending West Indian sugar, tobacco, wheat, lumber, fish, and animal pelts to Britain in exchange for cloth and iron. Yet within this general pattern, individual men and women made choices about what to buy.

On both sides of the Atlantic, demand for plantation products and consumer goods was insatiable. At first only the wealthy could afford such luxuries as sugar and tobacco. But as more and more labor was organized to produce for the market, ordinary people had the added income needed to purchase luxury products. Tea, imported into both Britain and the colonies from Asia, became, like tobacco and sugar, a mass-consumed luxury. By the time of the Revolution, annual sugar consumption in England had skyrocketed to 23 pounds per person, and tobacco consumption was about 2 pounds per person. Demand for these plantation products led directly to the traffic in African slaves.

As plantation products flowed to England, so manufactured goods came back to the colonies. Consumer behavior on both sides of the Atlantic was similar: people smoked tobacco; sweetened their tea with sugar; and bought more clothing, household items, books, and every sort of manufactured goods.

This consumer revolution was not due to higher wages. Instead, people chose to work harder and chose work that brought in money. They decided what they would do with that money—they chose to buy particular items. Increasingly, people bought items that their friends and neighbors could see and that they could use in entertaining them. In seventeenth-century America, extra income was spent on items of lasting value, such as tablecloths and bed linens kept folded away in a chest, to pass on to one's children. In the eighteenth century, men and women bought more clothing made out of cheaper, less durable fabrics. Until this time, most people had only a few outfits. The wealthy, of course, always had large wardrobes made from fine fabrics. In the eighteenth century, however, fabric prices fell, and clothing made from cheaper fabrics satisfied growing consumer demand. Then people needed new pieces of furniture in which to store their new garments. Chests of drawers, or dressers, first available to the wealthy in the 1630s and 1640s, had, by 1760, become a standard item for the middle class.

People became increasingly interested in how they appeared to others. Ordinary people began to pay attention to the latest fashions, once a concern only of the wealthy. By 1700, two new items made it easier for those with the time and money to attend to their appearance: the dressing table and the full-length mirror. For the first time, people could see how they looked, head to toe. Washing oneself and styling one's hair or periwig became standard rituals for all who hoped to appear "genteel."

In the eighteenth century, the prosperous on both sides of the Atlantic created and tried to follow the standards of a new style of life, gentility. Gentility represented all that was polite, civilized, refined, and fashionable. It was everything that vulgarity, its opposite, was not. Gentility meant not only certain sorts of objects, such as a dressing table or a bone china teapot, but also the manners needed to use such objects properly. Standards of gentility established boundaries between the genteel and the vulgar. Those who considered themselves genteel looked down on those whose style of living seemed unrefined and became uncomfortable when required to associate with social inferiors.

Yet if gentility erected a barrier between people, it also showed the vulgar how to become genteel. All they needed to do was acquire the right goods and learn how to use them. Throughout the colonies, ordinary people began to purchase goods that established their gentility. Even relatively poor people often owned a mirror, a few pieces of china, or a teapot. The slaves executed in New York City in 1741 (discussed subsequently) were probably conspiring not to burn the city down but to steal clothing and other fancy goods they could resell to poor people in the underground economy. This mass consumption

>> Consumer Tastes in Global Perspective

It is no surprise that Europeans got hooked on the products of colonial plantations: many of them were at least mildly addictive. The addictive properties of tobacco are well known today, but many of the other products of colonial plantations also were habit forming: coffee, cocoa, tea, and sugar (and its by-product rum). As consumer demand for such products grew in Europe, colonial plantation agriculture expanded.

Consider coffee. It originated in Ethiopia but was introduced into the Middle East by Arab traders around 1000 CE. The drink had made its way to the Ottoman Empire by the middle of the sixteenth century, and although some Muslim theologians disapproved of the drink, it soon became popular. European travelers to the major Muslim cities—Constantinople, Cairo, Alexandria, Aleppo—picked up a taste for coffee and began importing it into Europe. The first coffeehouse in London was built in 1652; 60 years later, there were at least 500. Coffeehouses in Europe quickly became what they were in the Middle East: places of male sociability.

By 1700, the prime coffee-growing region of Yemen could no longer meet the growing demand, so Muslim traders introduced coffee cultivation to India. Then Europeans expanded cultivation to their colonies in Jamaica, Barbados, and Indonesia, where the Dutch East India Company introduced both coffee planting and slavery. The French brought coffee cultivation to Martinique in the West

and widespread distribution of consumer goods created and sustained the consumer revolution.

The consumer revolution had another egalitarian effect: it encouraged sociability. Throughout the Atlantic world, men and women, particularly those with a little leisure and money (perhaps half the white population) began to cultivate social life. Many believed that the purpose of life was the sort of society they created during an evening shared with friends and family in their parlors.

To put all of their guests on an equal footing, people began to purchase matching sets of dinner plates, silverware, glasses, and chairs. Until the eighteenth century, the most important people at the table—the man of the house, his wife, and high-ranking men—got the best chairs. Children, servants, and those of lower social standing sat on stools, benches, or boxes, or they stood. Dishes, utensils, and mugs rarely matched. Matched sets of tableware and chairs underscored the symbolic equality of all guests.

The newest and most popular consumer goods made their way quickly to America—forks, drinking glasses, and teapots, each with its own etiquette. Such rules were

Indies, and the Portuguese took it to Brazil.

The history of tea drinking in Europe is similar; tea was introduced to Britain in the seventeenth century and eventually became more popular than coffee. By the middle of the eighteenth century, tea was an item of mass consumption. Most of it was imported—legally and illegally—from China or India.

Europeans liked their coffee and tea very sweet, so sugar consumption skyrocketed, too. The plantations of the New World, particularly the French West Indies, supplied this demand. The demand for sugar also created a demand for people to grow it: slaves imported from Africa. In fact, New World slavery came into being to satisfy Europeans' craving for tobacco and sugar, which were luxuries, rather than the necessities of life.

The history of opium, the highly addictive drug that also became popular in the eighteenth century, is somewhat different. Here, the British East India Company—the firm that sold tea to the American colonies—pushed the drug into China, in order to help rectify an imbalance in trade. As British imports of tea from China increased, the British needed products to sell to China, ones that would be as popular as tea. The Chinese were not terribly interested in the British goods, but they developed a taste for Indian fabrics and Indian opium. The East India Company secured a monopoly over Indian opium in 1773 and exported it to China, even though the Chinese had officially banned the drug.

The trade in addictive substances tied the continents together in the eighteenth century. A global trade network, organized by state-supported companies and sustained[in many cases by slave labor, supplied the world's consumers with the addictive substances they craved.

daunting for the uneducated, but once they were mastered, a person could enter polite society anywhere in the Atlantic world and be accepted. The eighteenth-century capitalist economy created a trade not only in goods and raw materials but in styles of life as well.

Historians debate the effects of the consumer revolution, but on balance it was a democratic force. Ordinary men and women and even slaves came to think it was their right to spend their money as they pleased. As one Bostonian put it in 1754, the poor should be allowed to buy "the Conveniencies, and Comforts, as well as Necessaries of Life . . . as freely as the Rich." After all, "I am sure we Work as hard as they do . . .; therefore, I cannot see why we have not as good a natural Right to them as they have."

The consumer revolution rested on new systems of production that eventually led to the Industrial Revolution and the creation of a working class. Even as men and women worked harder so they could buy the new goods, some worked harder voluntarily, but many did not. In the southern colonies, slavery expanded in order to produce the luxury goods that new consumers wanted to buy.

1. Hon.ble Peter Manigault
2. Taylor, an Officer
3. Demere — do —
4. Capt.n Massey

M.r Peter Manigault and his Friends.
Drawn by One of them (M.r Roupell) about the year 1754 from which this Copy is now
made in August 1854.
By his Great-Grand-Son Louis Manigault
                                              Charleston So. Ca.

5. M.r Isaac Godin
6. Cortmore, an Officer
7. Col.l Probart Howarth
8. M.r George Roupell

The New Gentility In 1750 in Charleston, South Carolina, Mr. Peter Manigault and his friends toasted each other, demonstrating their civility and their knowledge of the rules of polite behavior, including how to drink punch from a stem glass.

The Varieties of Colonial Experience

Although the eighteenth-century industrial and consumer revolutions tied the peoples of the North Atlantic world together, climate, geography, immigration, patterns of economic development, and population density made for considerable variety. Although the vast majority of Americans lived in small communities or on farms, an increasing number lived in cities that played a critical role in shaping colonial life. At the same time, farming regions were maturing, changing the character of rural life, and the growing population continued to push at the frontiers, leading to the founding of Georgia.

Creating an Urban Public Sphere

At the end of the seventeenth century, Boston, with 7,000 people, was the only town that was much more than a rural village. By 1720, Boston's population had grown to 12,000, Philadelphia had 10,000 inhabitants, New York had 7,000, and Newport and Charleston

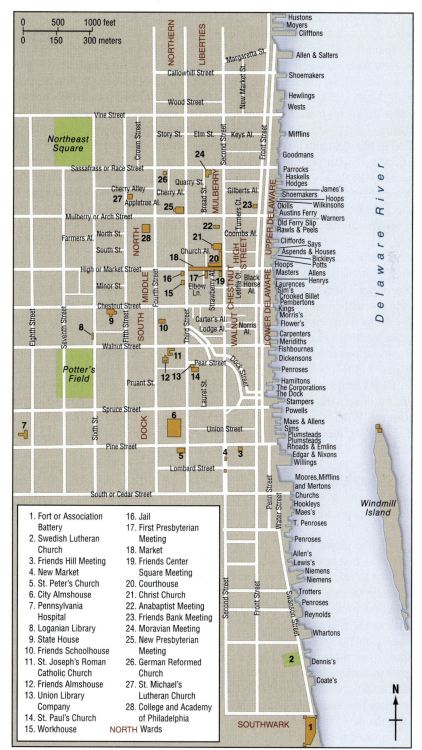

Map 5–3 Commerce and Culture in Philadelphia, ca. 1760 This map illustrates the close connection between commerce—note how many docks there are along the Delaware River—and culture. By 1760, Philadelphia was home to churches of many different denominations, as well as an array of enlightened institutions—a hospital, a college, and two libraries. *Lester Cappon, ed., The Atlas of Early American History (Princeton, 1976), p. 10*

The following text appears within the map:

0   500   1000 feet
0   150   300 meters

NORTHERN LIBERTIES

Northeast Square

Potter's Field

Windmill Island

Delaware River

SOUTHWARK

N

Legend:

1. Fort or Association Battery
2. Swedish Lutheran Church
3. Friends Hill Meeting
4. New Market
5. St. Peter's Church
6. City Almshouse
7. Pennsylvania Hospital
8. Loganian Library
9. State House
10. Friends Schoolhouse
11. St. Joseph's Roman Catholic Church
12. Friends Almshouse
13. Union Library Company
14. St. Paul's Church
15. Workhouse
16. Jail
17. First Presbyterian Meeting
18. Market
19. Friends Center Square Meeting
20. Courthouse
21. Christ Church
22. Anabaptist Meeting
23. Friends Bank Meeting
24. Moravian Meeting
25. New Presbyterian Meeting
26. German Reformed Church
27. St. Michael's Lutheran Church
28. College and Academy of Philadelphia

NORTH Wards

139

almost 4,000 each. Forty years later, other urban centers had sprung up, each with populations around 3,000—Salem, Marblehead, and Newburyport in Massachusetts; Portsmouth, New Hampshire; Providence, Rhode Island; New Haven and Hartford, Connecticut; Albany, New York; Lancaster, Pennsylvania; Baltimore, Maryland; Norfolk, Virginia; and Savannah, Georgia. By the eve of the Revolution, Philadelphia had 30,000 residents, New York had 25,000, and Boston had 16,000 (see Map 5–3). All of these cities were either ports or centers for the fur trade. Colonial cities were centers of commerce; that was their reason for being.

Social life in colonial cities was characterized by two somewhat contradictory trends. On the one hand, nowhere in the colonies was social stratification among free people more pronounced. By the eve of the American Revolution, each city had an affluent elite, made up of merchants, professionals, and government officials, and each city also had a class of indigent poor. On the other hand, cities brought all classes of society together at theaters, in taverns, and at religious revivals such as the one led by George Whitefield. This civic life became one of the seedbeds of the Revolution because it provided a forum for the exchange of ideas.

Affluent city dwellers created a life as much like that of London as they could. They imported European finery and established English-style institutions, founding social clubs, dancing assemblies, and fishing and hunting clubs. Although many of these associations were for men only, some brought men and women together. Such organizations helped the elite function as a class.

Urban associations reflected the ideals of the Enlightenment (see "The Ideas of the Enlightenment," p. 145). Some, such as the Masons, a European fraternal order with branches in all the major colonial cities, espoused the ideal of universalism, that all people were by their nature fundamentally the same. Other institutions advocated self-improvement. Whereas some urban institutions separated out the elite and others challenged the ruling hierarchy, still others brought together all members of society in a "public sphere." City dwellers could see stage plays in Williamsburg by 1716, in Charleston and New York by the 1730s, and in Philadelphia and Boston by the 1740s. Taverns brought all ranks even closer. By 1737, Boston had 177 taverns, one for every 99 inhabitants. (Between 30 and 40 percent were owned by women, usually widows.) Taverns became true public institutions in which people could meet and discuss the issues of the day.

Newspapers also played a critical role in creating a public sphere and extending it beyond the cities. The first newspaper was the *Boston News-Letter*, which appeared in 1704. By the time of the Revolution, 39 newspapers were being published, and the chief town in each colony except Delaware had at least one newspaper.

Strict libel laws prohibited the printing of opinions critical of public officials, or even the truth if it cast them in a bad light. John Peter Zenger, editor of the *New-York Weekly Journal*, was tried in 1735 for criticizing the governor. Zenger's flamboyant attorney, Andrew Hamilton, persuaded the jury that they should rule not simply on the facts of the case (Zenger *had* criticized the governor) but on whether the law itself was just. When the jury ruled in Zenger's favor, cheers went up in the courtroom. Although it would be many years before freedom of the press would be guaranteed by law, the Zenger case was a milestone in the developing relationship between the public and government officials. The verdict expressed the belief that in the contest between the two, the press spoke for the people, and hence it was the people themselves, not government, that would hold the press accountable.

City dwellers came to think of themselves as a "public" that had certain rights or liberties, such as making their views known and enjoying a fair price for their goods. At times, working people, acting as a public, and sometimes with support from the elite, used mob action to assert their political views. Mobs in both New York and Boston reacted violently to press gangs that scoured the waterfront for additional hands for the Royal Navy. By the time of the Revolution, city dwellers had a long history of asserting their rights in public.

The Diversity of Urban Life

Periodic downturns in the urban economy, especially after the middle of the century, led to increased activism by workers and the urban poor. Colonial politics had been premised on the deference of the less powerful to their social and economic "betters," but by the middle of the eighteenth century, the increasing wealth of those at the top and the appearance of a small class of permanently poor at the bottom of the economic hierarchy began to undermine the assumption of a common interest and that the wealthy and well educated could be trusted to govern for the benefit of everyone.

Although by today's standards the colonial population, even in the cities, was remarkably equal economically, in the eighteenth century it became more stratified. At the beginning of the eighteenth century, none of the cities had a substantial number of poor people. In New York, in 1700, there were only 35 paupers, almost all of whom were aged or disabled. Over the course of the century, however, colonial wars sent men home disabled and left many women widowed and children orphaned. Each city responded to the growth in poverty by building almshouses for the poor who could not support themselves and workhouses for those, including women and children, who could. In Philadelphia and New York about 25 percent of the population was at or below the poverty level, and in Boston perhaps as much as 40 percent of the population was living at or near subsistence. Many colonists feared that colonial cities were coming to resemble London, with its mass of impoverished and desperate poor.

All the major cities had slaves, and in some cities the black population was considerable. By 1746, 30 percent of New York City's working class consisted of slaves. After a serious slave revolt in 1712 and a rumored revolt in 1741, the white population responded with harsh punishments (but without halting the slave trade). In the wake of the 1712 revolt, which had left nine white men dead, city officials executed eighteen convicted rebels, burned three at the stake, let one starve to death in chains, and broke one on the wheel, a medieval instrument of torture. Six more committed suicide. The response to a rumored slave insurrection in 1741 resembled Salem's witchcraft trials: eighteen slaves and four whites were hanged, and thirteen slaves were burned at the stake.

New York enacted a stringent slave code after the 1712 revolt, and Boston and Pennsylvania imposed significant import duties on slaves. Nonetheless, the importation of slaves continued into all the port cities, where they were in demand as house servants and artisans. Almost all of Boston's elite owned at least one slave, as did many members of the middle class. Wealthy white artisans often purchased slaves instead of enlisting free whites as apprentices.

In Charleston, where more than half the population was enslaved, many masters let their slaves hire themselves out in return for a portion of their earnings. Such slaves set their own hours, chose their own recreational and religious activities, and participated in the consumer economy by selling their products and making purchases with the profits. Some whites complained about the fancy dresses of the black women at biracial dances attended by "many of the first gentlemen" of Charleston. Interracial sex in Charleston seems to have been common. Although white city dwellers were troubled by the impudence and relative freedom of urban slaves, urban slavery flourished.

The Maturing of Rural Society

Population increases had a different impact in rural areas than in cities. During the eighteenth century, some long-settled regions became relatively overcrowded. Land that had once seemed abundant had been carelessly farmed and had lost some of its fertility. This relative overcrowding, which historians call *land pressure*, led to a number of changes in colonial society, felt most acutely in New England. Population density increased, and with no additional farmland available, migration from farms to newly settled areas and cities increased. Both the concentration of wealth and social differentiation increased, dividing the farm community into rich and poor.

Such broad economic changes had a direct impact on individual men and women. Families with numerous children were hard pressed if the original plot of land could not be divided into homesteads large enough for each son. (Daughters were given movable property such as farm animals, household equipment, and slaves.) Some sons migrated to cities, looking for employment. Others worked on other men's farms for wages or, in the South in particular, became tenant farmers. Daughters became servants in other women's households. In such older regions, the average age of marriage crept upward.

As young men and women in long-settled regions had to defer marriage, increasing numbers had sexual relations before marriage. In some towns, by the middle of the eighteenth century, between 30 percent and 50 percent of brides bore their first child within eight months of their wedding day. The growing belief that marriage should be based primarily on love probably encouraged some couples to become intimate before they married, especially if poverty required them to postpone marriage. Young women who engaged in sexual relations before marriage took a huge risk, however. If their lovers declined to marry them, they would be disgraced, and their futures would be bleak.

The World That Slavery Made

The rural economy of the South depended on slave labor. Whites and their black slaves formed two distinctive cultures, one in the black-majority lower South and the other in the Chesapeake region. In both regions, the most affluent slave masters sold their crops on the international market and used the profits to buy elegant furniture and the latest London fashions.

Chesapeake planters modeled themselves after English country gentlemen, whereas low-country planters imitated the elite of London. Chesapeake planters designed their plantations to be self-sufficient villages, like English country estates. Because slaves produced most of the goods and services the plantation needed, planters such as William Byrd II imagined themselves living "in a kind of independence on everyone but Providence." But unlike English country gentlemen, southern slave owners were wholly dependent on both slave labor and the vagaries of the market for their fortunes. South Carolina planters used their wealth to build elegant homes in Charleston and other coastal cities, where they spent much time and established a flourishing urban culture. By the eve of the Revolution, the area around Charleston was the most affluent in the mainland colonies. In spite of their affluence, the southern planter elite never achieved the secure political power enjoyed by their English counterparts. In England the social elite dominated the government: not only the hereditary positions but also the appointive and elective ones. With noble rank inherited and voting rights limited to male property owners, the English government was remarkably stable. The colonial elite, however (in the north as well as the south), were cut off from the top levels of political power, which remained in England. The colonists were at the mercy of whichever officials the Crown happened to appoint.

Unable to count on support from above, the colonial elite needed to guarantee the loyalty of those below them. In Virginia, the elite acted as middlemen for lesser planters, advancing them credit and marketing their tobacco. In general, they wielded their authority with a light hand, and punishments for crimes committed by whites were light.

Although members of the Virginia gentry tried to distance themselves from their slaves, whom they considered "vulgar," some whites crossed the color line in a dramatic way, despite eighteenth-century racial views. Some historians believe that sexual relations between whites and blacks were common. Several prominent Virginians acknowledged and supported their mixed-race children. Some interracial relationships were affectionate; others were coerced. All the resulting offspring were in a vulnerable position; like all slaves they were dependent on the will of whites.

In the low country, the absenteeism of the planters combined with the task system to give plantation slaves an unusual degree of autonomy. As a majority, slaves in the low country were better able to retain their own religions, languages, and customs than were those in the Chesapeake. For example, the Gullah language, still spoken today on the Sea Islands off the coast of South Carolina and Georgia, combined English, Spanish, Portuguese, and African languages.

The mainland colonies' bloodiest slave revolt, the Stono Rebellion, took place in 1739, only a year after the founding of the Spanish free black outpost of Mose in Florida. The uprising was led by about 20 slaves born in Kongo (present-day Angola). The rebels were probably Catholics, for the king of Kongo, converted by the Portuguese, made Catholicism his nation's religion. Early in the morning of September 9, the rebels broke into a store near the Stono Bridge, taking weapons and ammunition and killing the storekeepers. The rebels moved south toward St. Augustine, killing whites and gathering blacks into their fold. Although the main body of the rebels was dispersed that evening and many were executed on the spot, skirmishes took place for another week, and the last of the ringleaders was not captured for three years.

The authorities reacted with predictable severity, putting dozens of slave rebels "to the most cruel Death" and revoking many liberties the slaves had enjoyed. A prohibitive duty was placed on the importation of slaves, and the immigration of white Europeans was encouraged. Although slave imports dropped significantly in the 1740s, by 1750 they rose to pre-Stono levels because slaveowners had neither the heart nor the inclination for the sort of systematic policing of their slaves that would have kept them completely under their control.

Georgia: From Frontier Outpost to Plantation Society

Nowhere was the white determination to create and maintain a slave society stronger than in the colony of Georgia. It is sometimes said that the introduction of slavery in North America was an unthinking decision, that the colonies became slave societies slowly, as individual planters purchased Africans already enslaved, and without society as a whole ever committing itself to slavery. Although there is some truth to this analysis, it is not accurate for Georgia, where the introduction of slavery was a purposeful decision.

The establishment of the English colony at South Carolina had, of course, made the Spanish nervous because of its proximity to their settlement at St. Augustine, Florida. With the French founding of New Orleans (1718) and Fort Toulouse (1717), Carolinians felt increasingly threatened. They were therefore eager for the English to establish a colony to the south, which would both serve as a buffer between Florida and South Carolina and, if extended far enough west, cut the French colonial empire in two.

The British Crown issued a 21-year charter to a group of trustees led by James Oglethorpe, who had achieved prominence by bringing about reforms in England's debtors' prisons. The colony, Georgia, was designed as a combination philanthropic venture and military-commercial outpost. Its colonists, who were to be drawn from Britain's "deserving poor," were supposed to protect South Carolina's borders and to make the new colony a sort of Italy-on-the-Atlantic, producing wine, olives, and silk.

Unfortunately, Oglethorpe's humanitarianism was not matched by an understanding of the world political economy. Because it was well known that excessive indulgence in alcohol was undermining the cohesion of many Indian tribes, Oglethorpe had banned liquor from the colony. However, without a product to sell, the colony could not prosper. South Carolina's wharves, merchants, and willingness to sell rum enabled it to dominate the trade with local Indians. Oglethorpe had also banned slavery for humanitarian reasons (making it the only colony expressly to prohibit slavery). As a result, Georgia farmers looked enviously across the Savannah River at South Carolinians growing rich off slave labor. The settlers were also angry that, contrary to colonial practice, women were not allowed to inherit property and that Georgia's trustees had made no provision for self-government. Georgia, despite its founders' noble intentions, lacked everything that the thriving colonies enjoyed: a cash crop or product, large plots of land, slaves to work the land, and laws of its own devising.

Never able to realize their dream of a colony of small and contented farmers, the trustees surrendered Georgia back to the Crown in 1752. With Oglethorpe's laws repealed and slavery introduced, the colony soon resembled the plantation society of South Carolina. Savannah became a little Charleston, with its robust civic and cultural life and its slave markets.

The Head and the Heart in America: The Enlightenment and Religious Awakening

American life in the eighteenth century was shaped by two movements, the Enlightenment and a series of religious revivals known as the Great Awakening. In many ways, these movements were separate, even opposite, appealing to different groups of people.

The Enlightenment was a transatlantic intellectual movement that held that the universe could be understood and improved by the human mind. The Great Awakening was a transatlantic religious movement that held that all people were born sinners, that all could feel their own depravity without the assistance of ministers, and that all were equal in the eyes of God. Although the movements might seem fundamentally opposite, with one emphasizing the power of the human mind and the other disparaging it, both criticized established authority and valued the experience of the individual. Both contributed to the humanitarianism that emerged at the end of the century, and both were products of capitalism.

The Ideas of the Enlightenment

The roots of the Enlightenment can be traced to the Renaissance and its spirit of inquiry and faith in science that led explorers like Columbus halfway around the globe. Men and women of the Enlightenment, on both sides of the Atlantic, contrasted the ignorance, oppression, and suffering of the Middle or "Dark" Ages, as they called them, and their own enlightened time. Thomas Jefferson described the earlier period as "the times of Vandalism, when ignorance put everything in the hands of power and priestcraft." Enlightened thinkers believed fervently in the power of rational thinking and scoffed at superstition.

People of the Enlightenment believed that God and his world were knowable. Rejecting revelation as a guide, the Enlightenment looked instead to reason. Jefferson's "trinity of the three greatest men the world had ever produced" included not Jesus Christ but Isaac Newton, the scientist responsible for modern mathematics and physics; Francis Bacon, the philosopher who outlined the scientific method; and John Locke, the political philosopher of democracy. The Enlightenment was interested in knowledge not for its own sake but for the improvements it could make in human happiness.

Enlightenment thinkers were more interested in what all people had in common than in what differentiated them. No passage in the Bible was more important to them than Genesis 1:27: "So God created man in his own image." It was the basis not only for overcoming Calvinism's belief in humanity's innate depravity but also for asserting the principle of human equality.

Humanity's duties were clear and simple. Chief among them, according to Benjamin Franklin, was "doing good to [God's] other children." In fact, people served God best not by praying, which, as Thomas Paine put it, "can add nothing to eternity," but "by endeavouring to make his creatures happy." Scientific inquiry and experiments such as Franklin's with electricity all had as their object the improvement of human life.

Although there had been some improvements in the quality of life, the eighteenth century was still violent and filled with pain. The Enlightenment responded to the pain and violence of the world in two ways. First, it attempted to alleviate and curtail them. Scientists eagerly sought cures for diseases. The Reverend Cotton Mather of Boston learned about the procedure of inoculating against smallpox (using a small amount of the deadly virus) from a scientific article and from his African slave Onesimus, who knew of its practice in Africa. An epidemic gave him an opportunity to try out the technique. The revulsion against pain and suffering also encouraged humanitarian reform, such as James Oglethorpe's reform of English debtors' prisons and, eventually, the antislavery movement.

Men and women of the Enlightenment also cultivated a stoic resignation to the evils they could not change and a personal ideal of moderation, so that they would neither give nor receive pain. The gentility and politeness of the urban elite was an expression of this ideal of moderation. Both gentility and the Enlightenment were espoused by the same set of people, the urban elite: professionals, merchants, and prosperous planters tied into the global economy.

The Enlightenment and the Study of Political Economy

Enlightenment thinkers began to study the connections among society, politics, and the economy. John Locke, the English philosopher, was the first to link these in a theory of political economy. He argued that there was a systematic connection between social institutions (such as the family), political institutions, and property rights. He began with the claim that each person has the right to life and the right to preserve that life. To sustain their lives, people form families, and to support themselves and their families, they labor. The basic right to life thus gives people the right to the product of their labor—property. To protect their lives and their property, people create governments. They give up some of their liberty but receive protection of their lives and property in return.

Locke also developed a new economic theory. His idea that money has no intrinsic value was a departure from mercantilism, which said that the value of money was fixed. In the second half of the eighteenth century, Scottish philosophers such as Francis Hutcheson and Adam Smith carried Locke's ideas even further, arguing that human beings should be free to value the things that made them happy. They developed a full-scale defense of consumerism.

Using happiness as their standard for human life, the Scots argued that people should be free to produce. Adam Smith's influential *The Wealth of Nations* (1776) was both a critique of mercantilism and a defense of free markets and free labor. For Smith and other Enlightenment theorists, the best incentive to hard work was the increased wealth and comforts it would bring. Human beings were happiest, they said, when they lived under free governments, which protected private property but left the market largely unregulated. These ideas became increasingly popular around the time of the Revolution.

Enlightened Institutions

The Enlightenment spurred the creation of institutions that embodied its principles. Humanitarianism led to the building of the Pennsylvania Hospital in 1751 and the Eastern State Mental Hospital at Williamsburg in 1773. In 1743 Benjamin Franklin proposed a society of learned men, modeled after the Royal Society of London, to study and share information about science and technology. He also helped establish the Library Company of Philadelphia in 1731, the first lending library in the colonies. Philadelphia acquired a second library in 1751 when the Quaker James Logan bequeathed his library, books and building both, to the city. By the time of the Revolution, Newport, New York, Charleston, and Savannah all had libraries.

The Enlightenment had a significant effect on organized religion as well. The Anglicans, in particular, were receptive to its ideals of moderation and rationalism. In England, John Tillotson, the Archbishop of Canterbury, preached a comforting and simple Christianity: God was "good and just" and required nothing "that is either unsuitable to our reason or prejudicial to our interest . . . nothing but what is easy to be understood, and is as easy to be practiced by an honest and willing mind."

This message became popular in the colonies, even among Congregationalist ministers, who abandoned the Calvinism of their forefathers. John Wise, the minister of Ipswich, Massachusetts, insisted that "to follow God and to obey Reason is the same thing." Arminianism, the belief that salvation was partly a matter of individual effort rather than entirely God's will, enjoyed a new popularity. Harvard University became a hotbed of liberal theology, and, in response, religious conservatives founded Yale University in 1701 to guarantee ministers a proper Calvinist education.

Origins of the Great Awakening

The problem with rational religion was that it was not emotionally fulfilling. In addition, rapid population growth had left the colonies without enough churches and ministers. Popular demand for more and better religion led to a series of revivals, known as the Great Awakening, that swept through the colonies between 1734 and 1745. At first, church leaders looked with pleasure on the stirrings of spiritual renewal. In the winter of 1734/1735, some of the rowdiest young people in Northampton, Massachusetts, who carried on parties for "the greater part of the night," began seeking religion at the church of a brilliant young minister, Jonathan Edwards. Everyone rejoiced at such signs of spiritual awakening.

The Grand Itinerant

When George Whitefield arrived in Philadelphia in 1739, the local ministers, including those of his own Anglican church, welcomed him. Whitefield drew audiences in the thousands everywhere he spoke. In the 15 months of his grand tour, he visited every colony from Maine to Georgia, met all the important ministers, and was heard at least once by most of the people of Massachusetts and Connecticut (see Map 5–4). He spoke to the entire community—rich, poor, slave, free, old, young, male, and female—acting out simple scripts based on biblical stories. The message was always the same: the sinfulness of man and the mercy of God.

In a calculated move, perhaps to increase his audiences, Whitefield began speaking out against some in the ministry, accusing them of being unconverted. He started with the deceased Archbishop of Canterbury, John Tillotson. Following his lead, Gilbert Tennent, on a preaching tour of New England, warned about "The Danger of an Unconverted Ministry." Tennent implied that some ministers were in it for the money and that true Christians should leave their churches for those of honest preachers.

Even sympathetic ministers were shocked by these accusations, which turned their congregations against them and split their churches. Some leading ministers, who already had reservations about the revivalists because of their emotional style, now condemned the revival. That only made the revivalists more popular and attracted larger crowds.

Cultural Conflict and Challenges to Authority

The Great Awakening walked a fine line between challenging authority and supporting it, which may well explain its widespread appeal. It antagonized the most powerful and

Map 5-4 George Whitefield's Itinerary In the 15 months between October 30, 1739, and January 18, 1741, Whitefield covered thousands of miles, visiting every colony from New Hampshire to Georgia, and stopping in some states such as Pennsylvania, South Carolina, and Georgia several times.

arrogant but did not challenge the fundamental structures of society. By attacking ministers but not government officials, the revivalists criticized authority without suffering any real consequences.

The Great Awakening appealed to all classes of people. Its greatest impact, however, was in areas facing the greatest change—in particular, cities (especially among the lower orders), the frontier, and older towns beginning to suffer from overcrowding. Here lived the people most disrupted by economic changes. Disturbed by an increasingly competitive society, men and women were attracted to the democratic fellowship of the revivalist congregation.

While criticizing the materialism and competitiveness of eighteenth-century society, the revival told people to look inside themselves for change, not to the structures of society. For example, a woman named Sarah Osborn blamed herself for her woes, which she saw as punishment for her sinful singing and dancing. After her spiritual rebirth, she trusted in God and accepted her poverty. Spiritual rebirth provided such people the joy and fulfillment that their world had been unable to supply.

The revival also walked a fine line in its treatment of slavery. Early in his travels, Whitefield spoke out against the cruelties of slavery and harangued slaveholders. At the same time, however, he maintained a slave plantation in South Carolina and pestered the trustees to permit slavery in Georgia. Like many slave owners after him, Whitefield argued that it was immoral to enslave Africans, but not to own them, provided that one treated them well and Christianized them. By linking humanitarianism, Christianity, and slavery, the Great Awakening anchored slavery in the South, at least for the time being.

Although it is hard to say whether slaves were treated more humanely on the plantations of evangelicals, beginning in the 1740s large numbers of slaves were converted to Christianity, and by some point in the nineteenth century virtually all slaves had become Christians. Although some may have converted to please their masters and to get Sundays off, blacks were attracted to evangelical religion for the same reason that whites were. It offered them a way to order and find meaning in their lives.

To a great extent, poor whites and slaves, especially in the South, had been left out of the society that more prosperous people had created. Evangelical religion placed the individual in a community of believers. It offered slaves the opportunity for church discipline and personal responsibility on almost the same terms as whites and gave some blacks the possibility of leadership in a biracial community. Africans grafted some of their religious practices, such as shouting and ecstatic visions, onto the revival, so that worship in southern Baptist and Methodist churches became a truly African American phenomenon.

What the Awakening Wrought

The opponents of the Great Awakening feared that it would turn the world upside down, but the leaders of the revival disciplined their own wildest members, such as New London's James Davenport. Davenport had led his flock through the streets late at night, singing at the tops of their lungs. They also made a bonfire to rid themselves of heresy by burning the books of their opponents and idolatry by burning the clothes they were wearing. The stripping party was stopped by evangelicals in the crowd, and Davenport was brought back to his senses by his fellow ministers. In general, the Great Awakening took colonial society in the direction in which it was already heading: toward individualism. Church after church split into evangelical and traditional factions, and new denominations appeared. Choosing a religion became a personal matter, and colonies with established churches tolerated dissenters. Religion, as a general force, was strengthened, making the colonies simultaneously the most Protestant and the most religiously diverse culture in the world.

The Great Awakening also spurred the establishment of educational institutions. Princeton, chartered in 1748 as the College of New Jersey, grew out of an evangelical seminary. Next came Dartmouth, Brown, and Rutgers, chartered in 1766, to advance "true religion and useful knowledge." Columbia College, chartered in 1754, represented the Anglicans' response. The focus of higher education was slowly shifting from preparation for the ministry to the training of leaders more generally. The Great Awakening diminished the power of ministers while increasing the influence of personal religion.

At the height of the Awakening, religious enthusiasm was both attacked and defended. Yet the conflict was hardly a battle of the pious against the godless or the well educated against the uninformed. Jonathan Edwards, one of the greatest minds of his age, drew from the Enlightenment, as well as from Calvinist ideas. For Edwards, however, reason and good habits were not enough, and reason must be supplemented by emotion, in particular the emotion of God's grace. By insisting that religious salvation and virtue were more matters of the heart than of the head, Edwards opened the way for a popular religion that was democratic, intensely personal, and humanitarian.

Conclusion

Eighteenth-century America was part of an expanding world market and a capitalist political economy. A growing population sustained a vigorous economy, one that produced for and purchased from the world market. As participants in an "industrious revolution," white Americans worked themselves and their slaves harder to purchase consumer goods. These new goods enabled people to live more genteelly and to cultivate a social life. Especially in the cities, this new emphasis on social life spawned an array of institutions in which people could acquire and display learning and gentility. The benefits of the economy were not shared equally, however. Slaves produced for the market economy but were denied its rewards. The increasing stratification of urban society and land pressures in rural regions meant many were too poor to profit from the expanding economy.

The eighteenth-century world spawned two different but related intellectual responses, the Enlightenment and the Great Awakening. Both were critical in shaping the eighteenth-century colonial world, and both paved the way for the Revolution. The Enlightenment led some to believe that rational thought and the scientific method would conquer human ills. At the same time, the Great Awakening reminded men and women that life was short and ultimately beyond their control. In different ways, then, the Enlightenment and the Great Awakening both encouraged the individualism that would characterize American life.

Review Questions

1. What were the primary sources of population increase in the eighteenth century? Compare the patterns of population growth of Europeans and Africans in the colonies.

2. What was the "industrious revolution"? How did it shape the development of the colonial economy? What were the other key factors shaping the development of the colonial economy? What effect did this development have on the lives of ordinary men and women?

>> Timeline

▼1701
Yale founded

▼1704
First newspaper, *Boston News-Letter*, published in colonies

▼1712
Slave revolt in New York City

▼1717
French build Fort Toulouse

▼1718
French found New Orleans

▼1731
Library Company, first lending library in colonies, erected in Philadelphia

▼1733
Georgia founded
King of Spain guarantees freedom to English slaves who escape to Spanish
  territory

▼1734
Great Awakening begins

▼1735
John Peter Zenger acquitted of libeling New York's governor

▼1739
Stono Rebellion

▼1741
35 executed in New York City after slave-revolt scare

▼1748
College of New Jersey (Princeton) founded

▼1751
Pennsylvania Hospital built in Philadelphia

▼1752
Georgia becomes a Crown colony

▼1754
Columbia College founded   *continued*

>> Timeline *continued*

▼1755
Philadelphia College (University of Pennsylvania) founded

▼1766
Queens College (Rutgers) founded

▼1773
Eastern State Mental Hospital built in Williamsburg

3. What were the primary changes in urban and rural life in the eighteenth century?

4. Describe the development of the eighteenth-century consumer culture and discuss how it affected everyday life.

5. What were the chief ideas of the Enlightenment? Why did some men and women find them attractive?

6. What were the sources of the Great Awakening? Why were some men and women drawn to it?

For further review materials and resource information, please visit www.oup.com/us/ofthepeople

Conflict on the Edge of the Empire

1713–1774

6

>> Susannah Willard Johnson Experiences the Empire

Today the town is Charlestown, New Hampshire, but then it was "No. 4," a small farming village on the northern frontier of Massachusetts. In 1754 Susannah Willard Johnson and her husband James lived there, having moved to the frontier during a break in the struggle between Britain and France for North America. At 24, Susannah had been married for seven years and had three children, with another due any day. James, a native of Ireland, had started his life in America as a servant indentured to Susannah's uncle. After working for him for ten years, James purchased the remainder of his time, married Susannah, and made his way by farming and shopkeeping. He also became a lieutenant in the militia.

The region's Abenaki Indians—Algonquians who were allied with the French and had their own grievances against the encroaching settlers—presented both danger and opportunity. At first the settlers at No. 4 were so frightened that they stayed in the fort. However, Susannah later reported, "hostility at length vanished—the Indians expressed a wish to traffic, the inhabitants laid by their fears . . ." James Johnson was part of the consumer revolution, selling goods to his fellow settlers and to the Abenakis, who gave him furs in return.

Susannah Johnson described her family's life as "harmony and safety" and "boasted with exultation that I should, with husband, friends, and luxuries, live happy in spite of the fear of savages." By the summer of 1754, however, the rumors of impending warfare with France would make the frontier village a target of France's Abenaki allies.

On August 30, 1754, just before daybreak, a neighbor coming to work for the Johnsons appeared at the door. As the Johnsons opened the door, the neighbor rushed in, followed by 11 Abenaki men. Soon, Susannah said, they were "all over the house, some upstairs, some hauling my sister out of bed, another had hold of me, and one was approaching Mr. Johnson, who stood in the middle of the floor to deliver himself up."

continued

>> **AMERICAN PORTRAIT** *continued*

The Abenakis tied up the men, gathered the women and children, and marched the party to the north. On the second day of her captivity, Susannah went into labor. Attended by her sister and husband, she gave birth to a daughter, whom she named Captive. Before they returned home five years later, Susannah and her family were held captive in Canada and sent to England as part of a prisoner exchange.

The French and Indian War had begun on the northern frontier, and the Indians were manipulating it to their advantage. In peacetime they traded furs for manufactured goods, but in wartime they seized British settlers, took them to Canada, and sold them to the French, who either ransomed them back to the British or traded them for prisoners of war. What to others might seem an imperial struggle was to Susannah Johnson a terrifying assault that took her from her home and family. The consumer revolution that gave settlers such as the Johnsons the opportunity to live a good life on the frontier was rooted in a struggle between France and England, two empires competing over both the markets the consumer revolution was creating and the lands it was populating. As families such as the Johnsons pushed at the frontiers, they became actors on a global stage.

Common Threads

>> What role did the colonies play in imperial conflict? That is, how did they shape that conflict, and how were they shaped by it?

>> How were Native Americans drawn into imperial conflict? To what extent were they able to shape it for their own purposes?

>> What did it mean for the American colonies to be peripheral—literally—to the British Empire?

>> How did the colonists adapt the available political theories to their purposes? What in the American experience made those theories attractive to the colonists?

The Victory of the British Empire

From 1689 to 1763, Britain and France were at war more than half of the time. These wars gave shape to the eighteenth century and created the international context for the American Revolution in several ways. First, the Revolution grew out of Britain's ineffective efforts to govern the enlarged empire it won from France in 1763. Second, France's support for the colonies in their war against Britain helped secure the colonies' victory. Third, once the colonies secured their independence, they entered a world still torn by conflict between Britain and France.

All of these wars were rooted in a struggle for world dominance between two powerful empires. To a great extent, colonial and imperial objectives coincided. Both Britain and the colonies would benefit from securing the empire's borders and from expanding British markets. Yet the imperial wars also exposed the growing divergence between the political economy of the colonies and that of the mother country. When the growing empire and its wars threatened to increase Britain's power over the colonists, raise their taxes to pay for the empire, and station among them a permanent army, the colonists resisted and finally rebelled.

New War, Old Pattern

England and France were at peace from the end of Queen Anne's War in 1713 (see Chapter 4) until 1739. It was an uneasy peace in the British North American colonies, however. In what is now Maine, New Englanders continued to fight the Abenakis, forcing them into a closer alliance with the French, who were attempting to stabilize relations with the Algonquians. The most common method was by providing "gifts" of trade goods.

Another round of international warfare broke out in 1739 and lasted nine years. In the War of Jenkins's Ear (1739–1744), Britain attempted to expand into Spanish territories and markets in the Americas. Urged on by merchants, and with the approval of colonists who wanted to eliminate Spain as a rival, Britain found an excuse for declaring war: a ship's captain, Robert Jenkins, turned up in Parliament in 1738 holding in his hand what he claimed was his ear, severed by the Spanish seven years earlier in the Caribbean. Once again, colonists joined in what they hoped would be a glorious international endeavor, only to be disillusioned. In 1741, 3,600 colonists, mostly poor young men lured by the promise of Spanish plunder, joined 5,000 Britons in a failed attack on Cartagena, Colombia. More than half the colonial contingent died.

Another ambitious move against the Spanish empire failed in 1740. James Oglethorpe and settlers hired by South Carolina, accompanied by Cherokee and Creek allies, failed to seize the Spanish outpost at St. Augustine and left the southern border vulnerable. When Oglethorpe's troops repulsed a Spanish attack in 1742, however, Spain's plan to demolish Georgia and South Carolina and arm their slaves was thwarted.

Just as the War of Jenkins's Ear ended in stalemate, so did King George's War (1744–1748), a conflict between Britain and Austria on one side and France and Prussia on the other over succession to the Austrian throne. A French raid on a fishing village in Nova Scotia met with a huge retaliation by the British. Troops from Massachusetts, supported by the British navy, captured the French fort at Louisbourg. Finally, a joint British-colonial venture had succeeded. But a planned attack on Quebec was called off when the British fleet failed to arrive. At war's end, Britain returned Louisbourg to France and warned the colonists that they had to maintain the peace. The British blockade of French ports cut off trade to Canada, including the all-important presents to Indian allies and trade partners. Without these gifts, the French-Indian empire began to crumble.

The Local Impact of Global War

Successive rounds of warfare had a significant impact on politics and society in British North America. Although the colonists identified strongly with the British cause, decades of warfare were a constant drain on the colonial treasury and population.

Wars are expensive. Generally, rates of taxation in colonial America were low, except when wars had to be financed. In a rehearsal for the conflicts that would lead to the American Revolution, the British government complained that the colonists were unwilling to contribute their fair share to the imperial wars. As a rule, colonial legislatures were willing to go only so far in raising taxes to pay for imperial wars or expeditions against

Indians. Then they simply issued paper money. Inevitably, the currency depreciated, making even worse the boom-and-bust cycles that war economies always produce.

No colony did more to support the imperial war efforts than Massachusetts, but the result was heightened political conflict at home. Royal governors, eager to please officials in London, pushed the colony to contribute to the imperial wars. As many as one-fifth of the colony's men may have served in the military in the middle of the eighteenth century. In 1747 Boston mobs rioted for three days to resist the Royal Navy's attempt to "impress" (force) men into service, and the local militia refused to restore order. For the first time, Bostonians began to speak about a right to resist tyranny.

Much more than in Europe, civilians in America became victims of war. By the eighteenth century, conventions of "civilized" warfare that held that civilians should be spared broke down in America for two reasons. First, without a transportation system to supply the army, troops often relied on plunder. Second, frontier Indians, adapting their traditional mourning war (see Chapter 2), routinely attacked villages, seizing captives to replenish their populations and to ransom to the French. Between 1675 and 1763, when frontier settlers such as Susannah Johnson were at risk, Indians took more than 1,600 New England settlers as captives, more than 90 percent during times of war (see Figure 6–1).

Almost half the colonists seized eventually returned home, but, as with Susannah Johnson's son Sylvanus, who had forgotten English entirely, Indian customs "wore off" only "by degree." Other captives died during the arduous march to Canada, sometimes

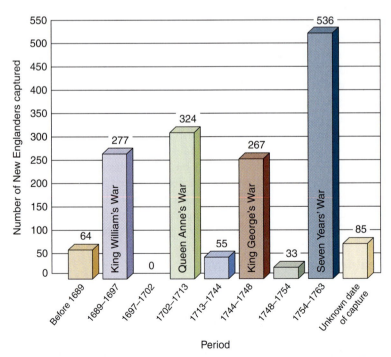

Figure 6–1 New England Captives During periods of war, the number of New Englanders taken captive by northern Indians and the French increased dramatically, with more than 90 percent of the captives being taken during times of war. *Alden Vaughan, Roots of American Racism (New York: Oxford University Press, 1990), p. 31.*

killed by Indians who thought them too weak to survive the journey. Many died of disease, and a few, typically girls between 7 and 15, remained with their captors voluntarily. Historians debate why this was so. Perhaps it was because Puritan culture trained girls to respond without question to those in authority. Or perhaps it was because, after the rigors of a Puritan upbringing, the relative freedom of Indian culture was inviting.

The French Empire Crumbles from Within

In the years after King George's War, a change in French policy offered a small band of Miami Indians the chance to gain an advantage over rivals. In the process, they started a chain of events that led to the French and Indian War.

Although King George's War had ended in a stalemate, it weakened the French position in North America. The costs of war had forced the French to cut back on their presents to allied Algonquian tribes, especially in the Ohio River valley. To raise revenue, the French sharply increased their charges for the lease of trading posts; in turn, traders raised the prices that they charged the Indians for trade goods. These changes significantly weakened the French hold over their Indian allies, creating political instability that was the underlying North American cause of the French and Indian War.

The Ohio River valley was home to small, refugee tribes (see Map 6–1). As long as the French provided liberal presents and cheap trade goods, they maintained a loose control.

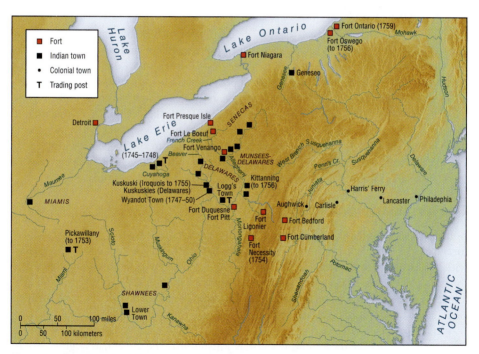

Map 6–1   The Ohio River Valley, 1747–1758 This territory, inhabited by a number of small bands of Indians, was coveted by both the French and the British, not to mention several competing groups of colonial land speculators. The rivalries between the imperial powers, among the Indian bands, and between rival groups of speculators made this region a powder keg. *Adapted from Michael McConnell,* A Country Between *(Lincoln: University of Nebraska, 1992), pp. 116–117.*

Once that control ended, however, each tribe sought to increase its advantage over the others, at a time when the British recognized the strategic and economic importance of the region.

The temporary power vacuum afforded a small group of Miamis, led by a chieftain called Memeskia, an opportunity to play one group of colonists off another. The chain of events that led to the French and Indian War began in 1748 when Memeskia's group established a new village, Pickawillany, near the head of the Miami River. Memeskia welcomed English traders from Pennsylvania, because their goods were better and cheaper than those of the French. He hoped to trade with the British free of political or military obligations.

Memeskia's move threatened not only the balance of power between Britain and France but also that between Pennsylvania and Virginia. The Pennsylvanians welcomed trade with the Miamis, for it gave them a claim to the western lands that Virginians sought. At the same time, Memeskia used his access to British traders to attract many small bands of followers to his village. Alarmed, the French shifted away from trade to force. In 1749, they sent a small expedition to cow their former Indian allies back into submission. When it failed, they began to raid dissident Indian encampments and planned to establish a fort in the Ohio River valley. With this change in French policy, Indians faced two options: to gather Indian allies (Memeskia's tactic) or to make alliances with the British (the strategy of an Iroquois chieftain named Tanacharison). Neither route promised real security, but the chaos these bids for advantage created drew the French and British into war.

In 1752, Tanacharison agreed to give Virginia not only the 200,000 acres claimed by the Ohio Company, a group of Virginia speculators, but also all the land between the Susquehanna and Allegheny rivers (today's Kentucky, West Virginia, and western Pennsylvania). In return, Virginia promised Tanacharison's people trade and protection from their enemies. Memeskia was isolated. With no European or Indian power dominant in the region, conflicts broke out, and the French pried off some of Memeskia's allies and conquered the rest. In a raid on Pickawillany, 250 pro-French Ottawas and Chippewas killed Memeskia. Their village destroyed, the demoralized Miamis returned to the French for protection. For the moment, the French regained power, but by shifting their policy from trade to force, they set a course that would lead to the loss of their North American empire.

The Virginians Ignite a War

Both France and Virginia now claimed the Ohio River valley, and they raced to establish forts to secure their claims. Virginia entrusted the job to a well-connected 21-year-old with almost no qualifications for the post: George Washington. Washington was tied to the powerful Fairfax clan, a British family that owned 5 million acres in Virginia and held a share in the Ohio Company. In the Anglo-American world, advancement came through such linked ties of family and patronage.

In the spring of 1754, the French and Virginians scrambled to see who could build a fort first at the forks of the Ohio (present-day Pittsburgh). The force that Virginia sent to the region, with Washington second in command, was pathetically small. Although the French army—numbering 1,000—was only 50 miles away, a combined Virginia-Indian band led by Washington attacked and defeated a small French reconnaissance party. The French and Indian War (known in Europe as the Seven Years' War) had begun.

The Virginians had bitten off more than they could chew. Washington's small fort was reinforced by British regulars but was quickly deserted by Indian allies, who recognized it as indefensible. The French overwhelmed the fort, driving Washington and his troops back to Virginia. Although war was not officially declared in Europe until May 1756, fighting soon spread throughout the frontier.

From Local to Imperial War

At the beginning of the war, the advantage was with the French. Although the population in the British colonies greatly outnumbered that of New France, France's population was three times larger than Britain's and its army ten times the size. More important, the more centralized French state was better prepared to coordinate the massive effort an international war required. The British government, aware that lack of coordination among its colonies could cripple the war effort, in summer 1754 instructed all the colonies north of Virginia to plan for a collective defense and to shore up the alliance with the Six (Iroquois) Nations. Pennsylvania's Benjamin Franklin offered the delegates, who met in Albany, a plan, known as the Albany Plan of Union, which every colony rejected.

The localism of the American colonies made cooperation difficult if not impossible. A deeply ingrained value, localism was suspicious of the centralized European state and its army of professionals.

Britain was now in its fourth war with France in less than a century. It had authorized Virginia's foray into the Ohio River valley and sent two regiments, under the command of General Edward Braddock, to Virginia in late 1754, hoping that the colonists could fight with only a little British assistance. But the disarray continued: colonial soldiers were reluctant to obey an officer from another colony, let alone one from the British army.

With four times as many troops as the British had in North America, superior leadership, and no intercolonial rivalries, the French dominated the first phase of the war, from 1754 through 1757. The British and colonial armies planned to besiege four French forts: Fort Duquesne (Pittsburgh), Fort Niagara (Niagara Falls), Fort St. Frédéric (Crown Point, at the southern end of Lake Champlain), and Fort Beauséjour (Nova Scotia).

Braddock was to attack Fort Duquesne with a combined force of British regulars and colonial troops, but without Indians. He had alienated the regional Indians, who rejoined the French alliance. After a grueling two-month march, on July 9, 1755, Braddock's forces were surprised close to their objective by a French and Indian force. Almost 1,000 British and colonial troops were killed or wounded; Braddock himself died from wounds suffered in the ambush. One of the survivors was George Washington, who had been serving as an unsalaried adjutant to Braddock to learn the art of war.

Two of the other three planned assaults ended in disappointment as well. William Shirley, who became the British commander in chief, led the attack on Fort Niagara himself and assigned Fort St. Frédéric to William Johnson, a Mohawk Valley Indian trader who was soon made superintendent of Indian affairs for the northern colonies. Well suited for leading Iroquois forays against the French, Johnson led a force of about 3,500, including 300 Iroquois. Their advance was stopped by the French and their Native American allies, but with equal casualties on both sides and the capture of the French commander, the British declared victory and elevated Johnson to the nobility. In the winter of 1755–1756 the British built Fort William Henry, and the French, Fort Carillon (which the British renamed Ticonderoga).

DEFEAT *and* DEATH *of* GENERAL BRADDOCK *in North America.*

Braddock's Defeat This detail depicting Braddock's defeat is from a drawing by an engineer with the British Army.

Hampered by rough terrain and intercolonial wrangling, Shirley's force never made it to Fort Niagara. The only outright success was at Fort Beauséjour, near the British colony at Nova Scotia. A British-financed expedition of New England volunteers easily seized the fort, and the British evicted 10,000 Acadians (French residents of Nova Scotia) who would not take an oath of loyalty. About 300 ended up in French Louisiana, where their name was abbreviated into "Cajuns."

Both the British and the French expected their colonists to carry most of the load of the war. Their defeats and continued intercolonial rivalries left the British vulnerable and the frontier exposed. The French began a cautious but successful offensive. First, they encouraged Indian raids along the frontier from Maine to South Carolina. Indians swung back to the French because the French appeared less dangerous than the land-hungry British. The price for French friendship, however, was participation in the war against the British. By the fall of 1756, some 3,000 settlers had been killed, and the line of settlement had been pushed back 150 miles in some places.

The French and their Indian allies seized Fort Bull in March 1756 and Fort Oswego several months later. A little over a year later, a massive French force attacked Fort William Henry. This loosely organized army of 8,000 included 1,000 Indian warriors and another 800 converted Algonquians accompanied by their Catholic priests. After a seven-day siege and heavy bombardment, the British commander surrendered on August 9, 1757. Louis-Joseph de Montcalm, the French commander, offered European-style terms: the British were to return their French and Indian prisoners, keep their personal weapons, and march back to Fort Edward, on the lower Hudson River, promising not to fight the French for 18 months. Historians still debate whether Montcalm knew what was about to take place. The Indians had expected, as was their custom, to be allowed to take plunder and captives. Denied this opportunity, they fell on the British, including the sick, women, and children, as they were evacuating the fort the next morning.

The massacre at Fort William Henry had significant repercussions. Still angry at being denied the spoils of war, Montcalm's Indian allies returned home, taking small-pox with them. The French would never again have the assistance of such a significant number of Indian allies. The British were outraged. The new British commander, Lord Jeffrey Amherst, declared the surrender terms null and void. Later, under his order, Delaware Indians who had been invited to a peace talk were given, ostensibly as presents, blankets that had been infected with smallpox. Historians are not certain whether these blankets were responsible for the outbreak of the disease among local Indians, but that was certainly Amherst's intent.

Problems with British-Colonial Cooperation

The British and the colonists blamed each other for their defeats. There was some truth in their accusations: unwillingness to sacrifice and disastrous infighting among the colonists and arrogance among the British. These recriminations, more than any side's failing, created problems. The colonists and the British had different expectations about their roles in the war. The colonists were not prepared for the high taxes or sacrifice of liberty that waging an international war required.

The British were dismayed by what they perceived as the colonists' selfishness, as they engaged in profiteering and trading with the enemy. Colonial governments were no more generous. Braddock's expedition to Fort Duquesne was delayed by the colonies' unwillingness to provision his army.

After Braddock's defeat, colonials deserted in droves. The British began recruiting servants and apprentices, angering their masters. Another serious problem was that of quartering soldiers over the winter. Under English law, which did not extend specifically to the colonies, troops in England could be lodged in public buildings rather than private homes. In the colonies, however, there weren't enough buildings in which to house soldiers without resorting to private homes. The residents of

Lord Amherst The new British commander, Lord Jeffrey Amherst, authorized germ warfare against the Delaware Indians who were fighting with the French. He invited them to a "peace talk" where they were given blankets infected with smallpox.

Albany took in soldiers only under threat of force. Philadelphians were rescued by the ever-resourceful Franklin, who opened a newly built hospital to the troops. In Charleston, soldiers had to camp outdoors, where they fell victim to disease.

Other problems arose from joint operations. The British army was a disciplined professional fighting force, led by members of the upper classes; service in it was a career. In contrast, colonial soldiers were primarily civilian amateurs, led by members of the middle class from their hometowns. Colonial soldiers believed that they were fighting by contract for a set period of time, for a specific objective, for a set rate of pay, and under a particular officer. If any of the terms were violated, the soldier considered himself free to go home.

The British, however, expected the same discipline from the colonists as they did from their own army. All colonial soldiers operating with regular forces were subject to British martial law, which was cruel and uncompromising. One regular soldier, for example, was sentenced to 1,000 lashes for stealing a keg of beer, which a merciful officer reduced to a mere 900! The British officers were almost unanimous in their condemnation of colonial soldiers. According to Brigadier General James Wolfe, "The Americans are in general the dirtiest most contemptible cowardly dogs that you can conceive."

Yet the colonists certainly believed that they were doing their share. Tax rates were raised sharply, tripling in Virginia in three years, for example. The human contribution was even more impressive. At the height of the war, Massachusetts was raising 7,000 soldiers a year, from a colony of only 50,000 men. Perhaps as many as 3 out of 10 adult men served in the military during the war, and only the Civil War and the Revolution had higher casualty rates.

The British Gain the Advantage

Montcalm's victory at Fort William Henry marked the French high-water mark. After a change of government in 1757, Britain resolved to win the war, as William Pitt became head of the cabinet. His rise to power represented the triumph of the commercial classes and their vision of the empire. Pitt was the first British leader who was as committed to a victory in the Americas as in Europe, believing that the future of the British Empire lay in the extended empire and its trade. Britain's aim in North America now shifted from simply regaining territory to seizing New France itself. Pitt sent 2,000 additional troops, promised 6,000 more, and asked the colonies to raise 20,000 of their own. To support so large an army, Pitt raised taxes on the already heavily taxed British and borrowed heavily, doubling the size of the British debt. He won the cooperation of the colonies by promising that Britain would pay up to half of their costs for fighting the war. As all of this money poured into the colonies, it improved their economies dramatically.

Now the British could take the offensive (see Map 6–2). In a series of great victories, they won Louisbourg on Cape Breton Island in July 1758; then Fort Frontenac in August; and finally, in November, Fort Duquesne, which the British renamed Fort Pitt. The only defeat was at Fort Carillon (called Ticonderoga by the British). There, Susannah Johnson's husband James was one of the casualties. The British seized Fort Frontenac, disrupting the supply lines from the French to the Ohio Valley Indians, who shifted their allegiance. The British also moved from a policy of confrontation to one of accommodation. In the Treaty of Easton (1758), 13 Ohio Valley tribes agreed to remain neutral in return for a promise

Map 6–2 The Second Phase of the French and Indian War, 1758–1763 This map shows British advances in Pennsylvania, New York, and Canada.

to keep the territory west of the Alleghenies free of settlers. Also, gifts to the Iroquois brought them back into the fold.

The British were now ready for the final offensive. Historians always argue about when and why a war is "lost": unless an army has been annihilated and the population entirely subjugated, which is rare, when to surrender is always a subjective decision. Political and military leaders must decide when the loss in lives and resources can no longer be justified, and the population must agree that further fighting is pointless. By 1759, some of the French believed that the war was essentially over. Casualties were extremely high, food was in short supply, and inflation was rampant. Most of the Indian allies had deserted the cause, and the French government was unable to match Pitt's spending on the war. It would take two more years of fighting and the loss of thousands more lives before the French surrendered, however.

In the summer of 1759, General James Wolfe took the struggle for North America into the heart of Canada, laying siege to Quebec. Quebec's position on a bluff high above the St. Lawrence made it almost impregnable, so for months Wolfe bombarded the city and tried to wear down its citizens, terrorizing those who lived on its outskirts by burning crops and houses. In mid-September, Wolfe ordered an assault up the 175-foot cliff below the city. In a battle that lasted only half an hour, his soldiers claimed victory on the Plains of Abraham. Each side suffered casualties of 15 percent, and both Wolfe and his French opponent, Montcalm, were killed. Four days later, New France's oldest permanent settlement surrendered to the British. By the time the British reached Montréal, the French army numbered fewer than 3,000 men.

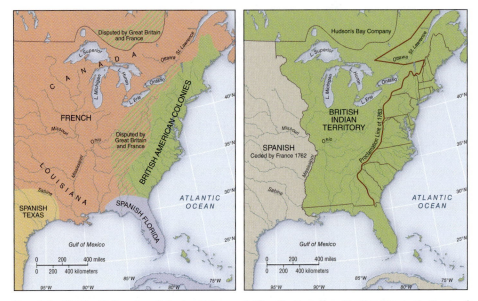

Map 6–3   The North American Colonies Before and After the French and Indian War In the Treaty of Paris in 1763, more American territory was transferred than at any time before or since. *Helen Hornbeck Tanner,* Atlas of Great Lakes Indian History *(Norman: University of Oklahoma Press, 1987), p. 54.*

The Treaty of Paris ended the war in 1763. By then, Britain had also seized the French sugar islands in the Caribbean and, after Spain entered the war on the French side, Havana and the Philippines. Pitt would have continued to fight, but the British public was unwilling to pay more to increase the size of the empire. The French, exhausted by war, surrendered all of Canada except for two small fishing islands in return for the right to hold on to the most valuable sugar islands, the most important part of their American empire. France even gave New Orleans and all of its territory west of the Mississippi to Spain as compensation for losing Florida, which the British claimed (see Map 6–3). (Britain let Spain keep Havana and the Philippines.) Britain staked its future on the mainland of North America, believing correctly that it would ultimately be more valuable than the sugar islands of the Caribbean.

Enforcing the Empire

Even before the French and Indian War, some in the British government urged tighter control over the American colonies. Colonists smuggled and even traded with the enemy throughout the war, and colonial assemblies sometimes impeded the war effort. Pitt had increased Britain's debt to pay for the war, rather than waiting for the colonial assemblies. Now, with the war over, Britain faced a staggering debt of £122,603,336. Moreover, there was a huge new territory to govern, one coveted by speculators and settlers and inhabited by Indian tribes determined to resist encroachment.

The American Revolution grew out of Britain's attempts to draw its American colonies more closely into the imperial system. Although various master plans for reorganizing the empire had been circulated, there had never been an overarching design or a clear set of guidelines. By 1763, there was a new resolve to enforce a vision of the empire and the role of colonies in it. In 1760 a new king, the 22-year-old George III, ascended to the throne upon the death of his grandfather. Reasonably well educated, the young king was determined to play a role in government. He changed ministers so frequently that chaos ensued. It is not clear, however, that more enlightened leadership would have prevented the war, for George's ministers pursued a fairly consistent policy toward the colonies. In resisting that policy, the American colonists developed a new and different idea of the purpose of government, one that propelled them to revolution.

Pontiac's Rebellion and Its Aftermath

Because the British had defeated the French and had entered into alliances with the Iroquois and the Ohio Valley Indians, peace in the West should have come easily. The British, however, soon made the same mistake that the French had made when they discontinued presents to their Indian allies 15 years earlier. Thinking they could impose their will on the Indians, the British instead found themselves embroiled in another war.

At the end of the French and Indian War, the western Algonquian tribes hoped the British would follow the practices of the middle ground by mediating their disputes, trading with them at good prices, and giving them presents. Lord Jeffrey Amherst, commanding British forces in North America, cut off the presents, believing them too expensive. He thought that threats of an Indian revolt were exaggerated and was willing to take the risk of war.

The war of 1763 is commonly known as Pontiac's Rebellion, named after the Ottawa chieftain who played a prominent role. It was the first battle in a long, and ultimately unsuccessful, attempt by Indians to keep the region between the Mississippi River and the Alleghenies free of European settlers. The Indians seized every fort except for Pitt, Niagara, and Detroit, and Detroit was under siege for six months (see Map 6–4). Casualties were high: about 2,000 civilians, 400 soldiers, and an unknown number of Indians. Tortures by both sides were horrific, and American colonists took out their aggressions on peaceful or defenseless Indians. In December 1763, a party of 50 armed men from the Pennsylvania village of Paxton descended on a tiny community of Christian Indians living at Conestoga Manor, eight miles west of Lancaster. They killed and scalped the six people they found—two men, three women, and a child—and burned their houses. Two weeks later, another group of these "Paxton Boys" broke into the county workhouse, where the remainder of the small tribe had been put for their own protection, and killed them, too.

Although colonial leaders decried acts of violence, they did little to prevent or punish them. British officials saw the failure of the colonists to maintain order on the frontier and protect innocent Indians as further proof of the incompetence of colonial governments. Even before Pontiac's Rebellion ended in a draw, the British had decided that peace with the western Indians could be preserved only by keeping colonial settlers and speculators away. The Proclamation of 1763 attempted to confine the colonists to the east of an imaginary line running down the spine of the Alleghenies. George Washington called the proclamation "a temporary expedient to quiet the minds of the Indians" and ignored it. Other Virginia speculators sought to take the territory by force. A pretext came in 1774

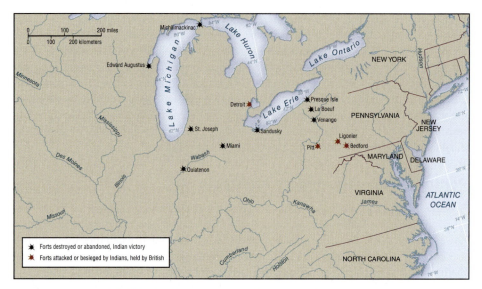

Map 6–4 Pontiac's Rebellion, 1763 The war began when the British abandoned the policy of the middle ground and cut off presents to the western Indians. In their uprising, the Indians destroyed nine British forts and attacked another four before the war ended in a draw. *Tanner,* Atlas of Great Lakes Indian History, *p. 49.*

when several settlers killed several Indians, and John Logan, a Mingo Indian, sought vengeance for his slain relatives. Rather than resolving this conflict in the ways of the middle ground, Virginia's royal governor sent a force of 2,000 to vanquish the Indians. Although the Virginians' success in Lord Dunmore's War ended Indian claims to Kentucky, Britain was still not ready to permit speculators or settlers to claim the land.

Paying for the Empire: Sugar and Stamps

On the edge of the British Empire, the colonies were important, but not nearly as important as Britain's domestic concerns. One of George III's highest priorities was to maintain the size of the army. During the French and Indian War, it had doubled, and it was filled with officers loyal to the king. Parliament in 1763 agreed to maintain a huge peacetime army, part of which would be posted in the colonies and West Indies. Colonists feared that the army would enforce customs regulations rather than police the Indians.

This large army, of course, would strain a budget already burdened by a huge war debt. George Grenville, the new prime minister, believed that the colonists should pay a portion of the £225,000 a year that the standing army would cost.

Under Grenville's leadership, Parliament passed four pieces of legislation to force the colonies to contribute to their own upkeep. The Molasses Act of 1733 had established a duty of six cents per gallon, but smugglers paid off customs officials at the rate of one and a half cents a gallon. At Grenville's urging, Parliament passed the Sugar Act (1764), which dropped the duty to three cents but established procedures to make certain it was collected. To discourage smuggling, shippers were required to file elaborate papers each time an item was loaded onto a ship. In addition, accused violators were to be tried in

AMERICA AND THE WORLD

>> **Paying for War**

For most of human history, the costs of war have worked as a check on war making: a country could not spend any more on warfare than it could pay for. Some countries plundered their neighbors. Others taxed their own people, but there are always absolute limits to how much money can be extracted in this way. Other countries borrowed from foreigners, which put them at the mercy of foreign creditors.

In the seventeenth century, the Dutch figured out a new method of financing government: borrowing money from its own citizens by selling them interest-paying bonds. The government then taxed its people to pay off the bonds and the interest, which enabled it to spread out the costs of war over a long period. The result was higher taxes in peacetime—but no excessive burden during times of war. Those who bought government bonds were literally making an investment in their nation and profiting from its success.

This was the method that Britain used to pay for its rise to power beginning in the eighteenth century. It raised astronomical sums of money: £31 million for King William's War, £51 million for Queen Anne's War, £73 million for the Seven Years' War. And with each war, the government borrowed an increasing portion of the costs.

As Britain's war debt increased—it was up to £122,603,336 at the end of the Seven Years' War—the country had to raise taxes to pay for it. The English were paying higher taxes than any other nation in the world except for the Dutch. In fact, at the time of the French Revolution—caused in part by unacceptably high taxes—the British were taxed at a higher rate than the French. Yet the political mechanisms of taxation were so efficient that the government was able to collect tax revenues with relatively little resistance.

This achievement is remarkable when one considers the relative unfairness of the English tax system. The burden fell on the middle classes, whereas both the poor and the affluent were relatively lightly taxed. There was widespread agreement that the wages and necessities of the poor should be taxed lightly or not at all. Instead, the burden should fall, in theory, on the wealthy. Indeed, in 1690, 47 percent of England's revenues came from taxes on land and other property of the rich, but the powerful landowners refused to pay higher rates. As the need for revenue increased, the proportion of taxes paid by the wealthy fell. By 1763, it was down to 23 percent.

In search of revenue, the English government levied excise and stamp taxes, which fell most heavily on the middle classes. By the end of the Seven Years' War, the public had come close to reaching its limit. Already unhappy with the tax on beer, it objected to one on cider to help finance the last year of war.

Parliament worried that it could not increase taxes on its own people any further, and so it looked for other sources of revenue in other parts of its empire.

continued

AMERICA AND THE WORLD *continued*

At just the time that Parliament tried to tax the American colonies to pay for the troops stationed there, it was also stationing more forces in Ireland—and trying, unsuccessfully, to get the Irish parliament to pay for them. When the East India Company conquered the huge Indian state of Bengal, King George III imagined that India's wealth was "the only safe method of extracting this country out of its . . . load of debt." In return for letting the East India Company govern Bengal, the government extracted a fee of £400,000 a year, which the Company demanded from the Bengalis. This crushing tax burden, which coincided with a serious drought, plunged Bengal into a famine that killed 10 million people, a third of the population. With strong traditions of local government, the American colonists and the Irish were better able to resist England's attempts to tax them.

admiralty courts in Nova Scotia, where the burden of proof would be on the defendant and the judgment would be rendered by judges rather than a jury.

To regulate colonial economies in the interest of British creditors, the Currency Act (1764) forbade the issuing of any colonial currency. British merchants had complained that colonists were discharging their debts in depreciated paper money. Moreover, the Sugar Act and the Stamp Act (passed the following year) required that duties and taxes both be paid in specie (silver and gold). The colonists complained that there was not anywhere near as much specie in the colonies as they needed.

The third and most important piece of imperial legislation was the Stamp Act (1765). The first direct tax on the American people, the Stamp Act sought to raise revenue by taxing documents used in court proceedings; papers used in clearing ships from harbors; college diplomas; appointments to public office; bonds, grants, and deeds for mortgages; indentures, leases, contracts, and bills of sale; liquor licenses; playing cards and dice; and pamphlets, newspapers (and the ads in them), and almanacs.

The final piece of legislation, the Quartering Act (1765), required the colonies to house troops in public buildings and provide them with firewood, candles, and drink.

Although the colonists objected to all of these pieces of legislation, the Stamp Act was the most troubling. By taxing newspapers and pamphlets, it foolishly angered printers and editors at a time when newspapers were taking the lead in criticizing the government and were perhaps the most significant public institution in the colonies. The Stamp Act also angered lawyers, for every time a lawyer performed the simplest task of his trade, he would have to buy a stamp. These laws fell hardest on the most affluent and politically active colonists, the merchants, lawyers, and printers. All of these pieces of legislation were an attempt to tie the colonies into a modern, centralized state. As the colonists framed their response to the new laws, they struggled with a question central to American history: Could the people share in the benefits of the modern state—in particular a trade protected by its navy and with borders secured by its army—without the state itself?

Rejecting the Empire

Colonial resistance to the imperial legislation of 1763 to 1765 was swift and forceful. A coalition of elite leaders and common people, primarily in the cities, worked to overturn the most objectionable aspects of the new regulations. In 1765, there was almost no thought of revolution, nor would there be for almost 10 years. Instead, the colonists rested their case on the British Constitution: all they wanted were the rights of Englishmen. Although in theory the colonists, as British subjects, were entitled to all of those rights, precisely *how* the British Constitution applied to colonists had never been clarified. The first phase of opposition, then, was a debate about the British Constitution, with the colonists insisting on their rights and the British government focusing on the colonists' obligations.

An Argument About Rights and Obligations

All along, Britain had maintained its right to regulate the colonies. Precisely what this meant became a matter of dispute after 1763. Did it mean regulation of trade? Taxation? Legislation? When Parliament passed these pieces of legislation, it acknowledged that the empire was a whole, that the parts existed for the benefit of the whole, and that Parliament had the authority to govern for the whole.

Britons were justifiably proud of their Parliament, one of the premier institutions of self-government in the world at the time. In principle Parliament represented all the elements in society: the king, the aristocrats (in the House of Lords), and the common people (in the House of Commons). It mixed and balanced these three elements of society, which also represented the three possible forms of government—monarchy, rule by the king; aristocracy, rule by hereditary aristocrats; and democracy, rule by the people—thus preventing both tyranny and anarchy and preserving liberty.

The British believed, and American colonists agreed, that their superb government was the product of centuries of struggle. First the aristocrats struggled with the king for more freedom, gaining it in the Magna Carta of 1215, and then the people struggled and won liberty, most recently in the Glorious Revolution of 1688. In this view, liberty was a collective right held by the people against the rulers and a limitation on the power of the monarch. A chief example of public or civil liberty was the right to be taxed only by one's own representatives. Taxes were a free gift of the people that no monarch could demand.

These ideas about the British government can be described as *constitutionalism*. Constitutionalism comprised two elements: the rule of law and the principle of consent, that one could not be subjected to laws or taxation except by duly elected representatives. Both were rights that had been won through struggle with the monarch. In the decade between 1765 and the outbreak of the American Revolution, the colonists worked out their own theory of the place of the colonies in the empire. A consensus formed on the importance of the rule of law and the principle of consent. Those colonists who became revolutionaries never wavered on these two points. In the decade between the Stamp Act and the beginning of the American Revolution, what colonists debated was whether particular pieces of legislation violated these principles and how far colonists should go in resisting those that did.

British officials never denied that the colonists should enjoy the rights of Englishmen. They merely asserted that the colonists were as well represented in Parliament as the majority of Britons. In fact, only one out of ten British men could vote, compared with about 70 percent of American white men. Yet British officials said that all Britons were represented in Parliament, if not "actually," by choosing their own representatives, then by *virtual representation*, because each member of Parliament was supposed to act on behalf of the entire empire. In Britons' minds, Parliament was supreme, and it had full authority over the colonists. In the decade between the Stamp Act and the beginning of the American Revolution, the controversy turned on only two questions: How forcefully would the British government insist on the supremacy of Parliament? And could colonial radicals put together a broad enough coalition to resist Britain's force when it came?

The Imperial Crisis in Local Context

While newspapers and pamphlets were filled with denunciations of the new imperial legislation, Americans were taking their protests to the streets and to the colonial legislatures. Everywhere, a remarkable cross-class alliance of prosperous merchants and planters and poor people joined to protect what they perceived as their rights from encroachment by British officials.

By the day that the Stamp Act was to go into effect, November 1, 1765, every colony except Georgia had taken steps to ensure that the tax could not be collected. In Virginia, the House of Burgesses took the lead. A young and barely literate lawyer, Patrick Henry, played a key role in the debate on the Virginia Resolves, the four resolutions protesting the Stamp Act that were passed by the Burgesses. They asserted that the inhabitants of Virginia brought with them the rights of Englishmen, that Virginia's royal charters confirmed these rights, that taxation by one's own representatives was the only constitutional policy, and that the people of Virginia had never relinquished these rights. In Boston, too, the protest united the elite with poorer colonists. Massachusetts was still reeling from the loss of life and extraordinary expense of the French and Indian War. Imperialists such as Lieutenant Governor Thomas Hutchinson wanted to tie Massachusetts more tightly to the empire. He advocated a consolidation of power, a diminution of popular government (e.g., by reducing the power of the town meeting), making offices that were elective appointive instead, and limiting the freedom of the press.

Boston's public, with its history of radicalism, was ready for a much stronger response to the Stamp Act than the Massachusetts House of Representatives seemed prepared to make. The *Boston Gazette* criticized the House's resolution as a "tame, pusillanimous, daubed, insipid thing." Once word of the more radical Virginia Resolves arrived, the *Gazette* rebuked the weak political leadership again. A group of artisans and printers who called themselves the Sons of Liberty began organizing the opposition, probably in concert with more prominent men who would emerge as leaders of the revolutionary movement, such as James Otis, John Adams, and his cousin Samuel Adams, the Harvard-educated son of a brewer.

In a carefully orchestrated series of mob actions, Bostonians made certain that the Stamp Act would not be enforced. When the militia refused to protect royal officials, including the collector of the stamp tax, the officials took refuge in Castle William in the harbor. Over several days, the mob systematically vandalized the homes of several wealthy government loyalists, including Hutchinson. Although the mob consisted mostly of artisans and poor people, it had the support of Boston's merchant elite, for no one was ever punished. The protest succeeded, and the Stamp Act was never enforced.

Samuel Adams This portrait of one of Boston's most effective political agitators in the years leading to the Revolution was painted by John Singleton Copley ca. 1772.

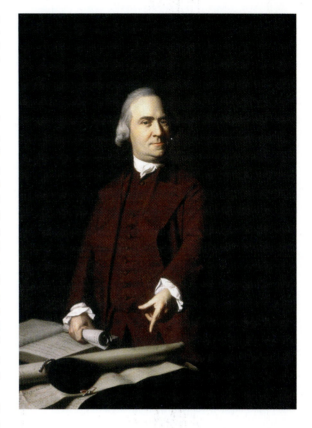

Not only did each colony protest against the Stamp Act, but a majority were now ready to act together. In October 1765, delegates from nine colonies met in New York in the Stamp Act Congress to ratify a series of 14 resolutions protesting the Stamp Act on constitutional grounds. At the same time, activists shut down colonial courts so that no stamps could be used, and merchants agreed not to import any British goods until the act was repealed. With 37 percent of British exports then going to the colonies, this was no idle threat (see Figure 6–2).

Facing this opposition, the British partly backed down. George Grenville was replaced by the 35-year-old Marquess of Rockingham, who preferred racehorses to politics. Parliament repealed the Stamp Act but was not prepared to concede the constitutional point, asserting in the Declaratory Act of 1766 that Parliament "had, hath, and of right ought to have, full power and authority to make laws and statutes . . . to bind the colonies and people of America, subjects of the crown of *Great Britain*, in all cases whatsoever."

Contesting the Townshend Duties

Britain gave up on trying to tax the colonies directly, for even some prominent Britons such as William Pitt sided with the colonists on that point. But between 1767 and 1774, those in power still tried to force their vision of empire on the colonies. In response, radical activists and thinkers formed a national opposition and took constitutionalism in new directions. By the time of the American Revolution, they had turned it into a new theory of government.

After a brief return to power by William Pitt, Charles Townshend, a brilliant but erratic man nicknamed "Champagne Charlie," became the third prime minister in as many years. His first act was to punish New York's assembly, which intentionally violated the Quartering Act. The assembly, denied the right to pass any legislation until it complied with the Quartering Act, quickly backed down.

The colonies refused, however, to comply with the next piece of legislation, the Townshend Revenue Act of 1767, which levied import duties on lead, paint, glass, paper, and

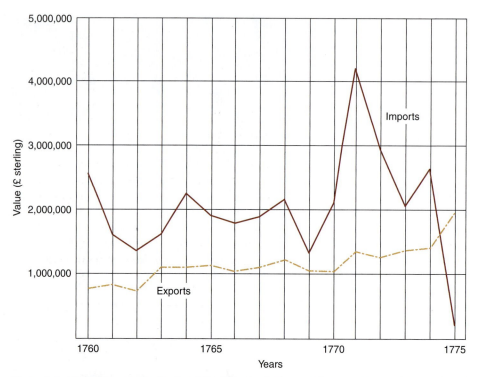

Figure 6–2 Trade Between England and the Colonies In the years between 1760 and 1775, colonial exports to England grew slowly but steadily, dropping off only after the beginning of the Revolution. On the other hand, imports from England—which always exceeded exports—rose and fell in response to political conditions. Colonial nonimportation agreements forced drops in imports after the imposition of the Stamp Act and Townshend Duties. But in both cases, imports increased after repeal, and the growth of imports after repeal of the Townshend Duties was dramatic and unprecedented.

tea. Townshend believed that the colonists objected only to taxes within the colonies, "internal taxes," but that they would accept an "external tax," such as an import duty. The revenue would be used to support colonial officials, making them independent of the colonial assemblies that had paid their salaries.

Resistance to the Townshend Act built slowly, as it was hard for colonists to make a case against all duties. Merchants were now complying with the new Revenue Act of 1766, which reduced the duty on molasses. Those colonists most troubled by the first round of imperial legislation, however, were convinced that the Townshend Duties were part of a design for tyranny.

A body of thought known as *republicanism* helped the colonists make sense of British actions. Republicanism was a set of doctrines rooted in the Renaissance that held that power is always dangerous, because "it is natural for Power to be striving to enlarge itself, and to be encroaching upon those that have none." Republicanism supplied constitutionalism with a motive. It explained how a balanced constitution could be transformed into tyranny. Would-be tyrants had access to a variety of tools, including a standing army, whose ultimate purpose was not the protection of the people but their subjection. Tyrants also engaged in corruption, in particular by dispensing patronage positions. So inexorable was the course of power that it took extraordinary virtue for an individual to resist its corruption. Consequently, republican citizens, it was thought, had to be economically independent; the poor were dangerous because they could easily be bought off by would-be tyrants. A secular theory with connections to Puritanism, republicanism asserted that people were naturally weak and that exceptional human effort was required to protect liberty and virtue.

Not only did people have to keep a close eye on power-hungry tyrants, but they also had to look inside themselves. According to republican thought, history demonstrated that republics fell from within when their citizens lost their virtue. The greatest threat to virtue was luxury, an excessive attachment to the fruits of the consumer revolution. When colonists worried that they saw luxury and corruption everywhere, they were criticizing the world that the consumer revolution had created. Although it is understandable why poor people embraced republicanism, it might seem perplexing that wealthy merchants and planters would also strongly denounce "malice, covetousness, and other lusts of man." Yet the legacy of Puritanism was powerful, and even those profiting most from the new order felt ambivalent about its effects on their society. Joining with poorer people in criticizing British officials and accusing them of attempting to undermine colonial liberties helped forge a cross-class alliance.

The colonial legislatures slowly began to protest the duties. Massachusetts's House of Representatives, led by Sam Adams, asked each of the other lower houses in the colonies to join in resisting "infringements of their natural & constitutional Rights because they are not represented in the British Parliament. . . ." When Lord Hillsborough, a hard-line secretary of state for the colonies, saw the request, he instructed the colonial governors to dissolve any colonial assembly that received the petition from Massachusetts. Massachusetts refused to rescind it, so Governor Francis Bernard dissolved the legislature. With representative government threatened, those colonial legislatures that had not already approved the Massachusetts petition did so now—and were then dissolved. In response, many legislatures met on their own, as extralegal bodies.

Not only did legislators assert their own authority, but ordinary people did so as well. In each colony, the radicals who called themselves Sons of Liberty organized a nonimportation movement using both coercion and patriotic appeal. Women were actively recruited into the movement, both to encourage household manufacture (an economic activity redefined as a political one) and to refuse British imports. In 1769 women in little Middletown, Massachusetts, wove 20,522 yards of cloth, and throughout the colonies women signed the nonimportation agreements. This politicization of ordinary people horrified conservative British observers. Although there were pockets of defiance, the movement succeeded in cutting imports dramatically. By the time that the Townshend Duties were repealed in 1770, Britain had collected only £21,000 and lost £786,000 in trade.

A Revolution in the Empire

The resistance to the Townshend Duties established a pattern that would be repeated again and again in the years before the Revolution. Each attempt to enforce the empire met with organized colonial opposition, to which the British government responded with a punitive measure. Ostensibly economic regulations such as the Sugar Act, the Townshend Duties, and the subsequent Tea Act, when rejected by the colonies, led to clearly political responses from Britain. Economics and politics became inseparable, as two visions of the empire came into conflict. Britain saw the colonies as a small but integral part of a large empire held together by an increasingly centralized and powerful government. The goal of the empire was to enhance its collective wealth and power, albeit under a system of constitutional government. Although they did not reject the notion of a larger empire outright, the colonists increasingly equated representative government with prosperity, not just for the empire as a whole but for its citizens in the colonies as well. Each round of colonial protest mobilized a larger segment of the population.

"Massacre" in Boston

Years of conflict with royal officials, combined with a growing population of poor and underemployed, had made Boston the most radical and united spot in the colonies. The political leadership had learned how to win popular favor in their ongoing strife with the governor and those who were loyal to him. The repeated attempts of the British government to enforce its legislation increased pressure on Boston and led finally to revolution.

In an attempt to tighten up the collection of customs duties, the British government, now led by Lord North, decided to make an example of John Hancock, Boston's wealthiest merchant and not yet a confirmed radical. In June 1768, customs commissioners seized Hancock's sloop, the *Liberty*, on a technical violation of the Sugar Act and threatened fines totaling £54,000 (most of which would go to the governor and the informer). All charges were dropped, however, after a riot of 2,000 "sturdy boys and men" sent the customs officials once again fleeing to Castle William for protection. Now Hancock was a radical.

After the *Liberty* riot, Governor Bernard called for troops to support the customs commissioners. Rather than restoring order, the arrival of the troops led to further conflict and a year and a half of tension. The Boston Massacre grew out of these tensions.

What angry colonists called a "massacre" was the culmination of months of scuffling between young men and adolescents and soldiers, perhaps inevitable in a town with so many men competing for work. On March 5, 1770, a fracas between a young apprentice and an army officer escalated as a crowd surrounded the officer, insulting him and pelting him with snowballs. Someone shouted, "Fire!" and the crowd grew. Seven soldiers came to rescue their terrified colleague, and they too were hit with snowballs and taunts of "Kill them." When one was knocked down, he screamed, "Damn you, fire!" and the soldiers fired on the crowd. Eleven men were wounded, and five were killed. One victim was Crispus Attucks, a 47-year-old free black sailor. The soldiers were later tried, but the only two convicted were later pardoned. The British withdrew their troops from Boston.

As long as the British were willing to back down, more serious conflicts could be avoided. The Boston Massacre was followed by a three-year period of peace. The Townshend Duties had been repealed—except the one on tea, which the colonists could not manufacture themselves—and the nonimportation movement had collapsed. Colonial trade resumed its previous pace, and in 1772, imports from England and Scotland doubled. Colonists were not prepared to deny themselves consumer goods for long. The Quartering Act had expired, and the Currency Act was repealed. As long as Britain allowed the colonists to trade relatively unimpeded, permitted them to govern themselves, and kept the army out of their cities, all could be, if not forgotten, at least silenced.

AMERICAN LANDSCAPE

>> Occupied Boston

For a year and a half, Boston was an occupied city. British troops began arriving in October 1768. They were supposed to maintain order and enforce customs regulations in a town thought dangerously out of control.

Republicanism, however, warned that tyrants used standing armies to deprive the people of their liberties. Hence the appearance of British warships and the disembarking of 1,700 soldiers in full "battle array" only increased Bostonians' anxiety. It was, however, the daily interactions between soldiers and locals that demonstrated why occupying armies so often antagonize just the people they are supposed to calm.

The immediate problem was where to lodge the troops. The Quartering Act required the town to provide housing, but Bostonians refused. Governor Bernard sent the soldiers to an old manufactory that housed the poor. The inhabitants refused to move. The army began renting lodgings wherever it could throughout the city. With the troops scattered, it was impossible for their officers to control them. Within two weeks, 70 soldiers had deserted. Policing civilians, especially your own countrymen and countrywomen, was not an attractive assignment. In order to prevent further desertions, an armed sentry was posted at the only land connection between Boston and the mainland, making Bostonians feel as if they were prisoners in their own city. The army executed one young deserter in full public view. Such harsh punishment shocked the Bostonians.

Still, in a city as small as Boston, filled with so many young soldiers, conflict between citizens and soldiers was almost inevitable. Liquor was cheap, and off-duty soldiers regularly became drunk and offensive. Prostitution increased, and inebriated soldiers assaulted local women. Because sentries could not distinguish between civilians and deserters in civilian clothing, all citizens had to be prepared to stop and identify themselves at the point of a bayonet. Moonlighting soldiers were also willing to work cheaper than Bostonians.

Some officers tried to keep soldiers under control, but there was no political mechanism for containing conflict. Patriots controlled the local justice system and used it to harass misbehaving soldiers. Any sentry who provoked a civilian could find himself before a patriotic magistrate, who made him post a huge bond, no matter how flimsy the charges. Yet even when the charges were truly serious, the attorney general—loyal to the Crown—would not prosecute. Without effective justice, gangs began to take the law into their own hands.

One of the confrontations was caused by John Mein, the publisher of a Boston newspaper. He printed the names of local merchants, some of them Sons of Liberty, who were violating the nonimportation agreements. Cynically, he wanted to demonstrate "that their Patriotism was founded on Self Interest and Malice." When patriots beat up two men who had the misfortune of resembling him, Mein

continued

appealed to Acting Governor Thomas Hutchinson for protection. Hutchinson said there was nothing he could do until a crime had actually been committed. Mein began carrying a pistol.

On October 28, 1769, a band of patriots fell upon Mein and his partner, throwing bricks at him and shouting, "Knock him down! Kill him!" The two men took refuge with soldiers in a small guardhouse that was soon surrounded by a mob of 200. When the partner's gun went off accidentally, the patriots assumed that Mein had taken the shot. Sam Adams got a friendly magistrate to issue a warrant for Mein's arrest for firing at citizens who

were "lawfully and peacefully assembled together." Certain he would be killed if taken into custody, Mein sent a desperate appeal to Hutchinson. By now the mob had grown to more than 1,000. Hutchinson knew, however, that if he used the army to rescue Mein, it would only "have set the whole province in a flame, and maybe spread farther." So Mein stayed in the guardhouse until he could be smuggled onto a ship leaving Boston.

The army that had come to Boston to maintain order learned that it, like many an army of occupation, was almost powerless in the face of a population that resisted its rule.

The Empire Comes Apart

Although the British government was controlled by conservatives who believed the colonists would eventually need to acknowledge Parliament's supremacy, the move that led to revolution was more accidental than calculated. The North American colonies were only part of Britain's empire. There were powerful British interests in India, where the British East India Company was on the verge of bankruptcy. Parliament decided to bail out the company, both to rescue its empire in India and to help out influential stockholders. The duty for importing tea into Britain—but not America—was canceled, and Parliament allowed the company to sell directly to Americans through a small number of agents. As a result, the price of tea would drop below that of smuggled Dutch tea. Also, only five men in Massachusetts would be allowed to sell British tea—relatives and friends of the despised Governor Hutchinson. Agents in the other colonies were also well-connected loyalists.

Radicals faced a real challenge, for they realized that once the cheap tea was available, colonists would be unable to resist it. In each port city, activists warned that the Tea Act (1773) was a trick to con colonists into accepting the principle of taxation without representation. In Philadelphia, a mass meeting pronounced anyone who imported the tea "an enemy to his country."

As might be expected, the most spirited resistance came in Boston, where Hutchinson decided the tea would be unloaded and sold—and the duty paid. Sam Adams led extralegal town meetings attended by 5,000 people each (almost one-third of the population of Boston) to pressure Hutchinson to turn the ships away. When Hutchinson refused, Adams reported back to the town meeting, on December 16, 1773: "This meeting can do nothing more to save the country!" (see Table 6–1). Almost as if it were a prearranged

Table 6-1 Major Events Leading to the Revolutionary War, 1763–1774

1763	Proclamation of 1763	Confines colonists to the east of an imaginary line running down the spine of the Allegheny Mountains.
1764	Sugar Act	Drops duty on molasses, but institutes procedures to make sure it is collected, such as trial at Admiralty Court (closest is in Nova Scotia), where burden of proof is on defendant and verdict is rendered by judge rather than jury.
1764	Currency Act	Forbids issuing of any colonial currency.
1765	Stamp Act	Places a tax on 15 classes of documents, including newspapers and legal documents, to raise revenue.
1765	Quartering Act	Requires colonies to provide housing in public buildings and certain provisions for troops.
1766	Declaratory Act	Repeals Stamp Act, but insists that Parliament retains the right to legislate for the colonies "in all cases whatsoever."
1767	Townshend Revenue Act	Places import duty on lead, paint, glass, paper, and tea; objective is to raise money from the colonies.
1770	Boston Massacre	Several citizens killed by British soldiers whom they had pelted with snowballs; grew out of tensions caused by quartering of four army regiments in Boston to enforce customs regulations.
1773	Tea Act	After Townshend Duties on all items other than tea are removed, British East India Company is given a monopoly on the sale of tea, enabling it to drop price—and cut out middlemen.
1773	Boston Tea Party	To protest Tea Act, Bostonians dump 90,000 pounds of tea into Boston Harbor.
1774	Intolerable Acts	To punish Massachusetts and Boston for the "Tea Party": 1. Port of Boston closed until East India Company repaid for dumped tea. 2. King to appoint Massachusetts's Council; town meetings to require written permission of governor; governor will appoint judges and sheriffs, and sheriffs will select juries. 3. Governor can send officials and soldiers accused of capital crimes out of Massachusetts for their trials. 4. Troops may be quartered in private homes.
1774	Quebec Act	Gives Ohio River valley to Quebec; Britain allows Quebec to be governed by French tradition and tolerates Catholic religion there.
1774	First Continental Congress	Representatives of 12 colonies meet in Philadelphia and call for a boycott of trade with Britain, adopt a Declaration of Rights, and agree to meet again in a year.

signal, the crowd let out a whoop and poured out of the meetinghouse for the wharf. There, about 50 men, their faces darkened and their bodies draped in Indian blankets, boarded three tea-bearing ships, escorted the customs officials ashore, and opened and dumped 340 chests of tea into Boston Harbor: 90,000 pounds, worth £9,000. Perhaps as many as 8,000 Bostonians observed the "tea party." John Adams, never much for riots, was in awe. "There is," he said, "a Dignity, a Majesty, a Sublimity in this last Effort of the Patriots that I greatly admire."

The British government saw only defiance of the law and wanton destruction of property. Parliament passed five bills in the spring of 1774 to punish Boston and Massachusetts. First, the Boston Port Bill closed the port to all trade until the East India Company was repaid for the dumped tea. Second, the Massachusetts Government Act changed the Charter of 1691. The Council (upper house) would now be appointed by the king, rather than elected by the House; town meetings were forbidden without approval of the governor; the governor would appoint all the provincial judges and sheriffs; and the sheriffs would select juries, who had until then been elected by the voters. Third, the Administration of Justice Act empowered the governor to send to Britain or another colony for trial any official or soldier accused of a capital crime who appeared unlikely to get a fair trial in Massachusetts. Fourth, a new Quartering Act permitted the quartering of troops in private homes. Fifth was the Quebec Act. It assigned to Quebec the Ohio River region, which the colonists coveted. In Quebec, there was to be no representative government, civil cases would be tried without juries, and the Roman Catholic religion would be tolerated. Together, these acts were known in Britain as the Coercive Acts and in the colonies as the Intolerable Acts.

At the same time, General Thomas Gage was appointed governor of Massachusetts and authorized to bring as many troops to Boston as he needed. Boston soon became an armed camp. The Port Act was easily enforced as Gage deployed troops to close the ports of Boston and Charlestown. The Government Act was another matter. Citizens summoned by the sheriff simply refused to serve on juries, and some judges even refused to preside. When Gage called for an election to the legislature, only some towns elected delegates, and a shadow "Massachusetts Provincial Congress" met in Concord in October 1774. The citizens of Massachusetts had taken government into their own hands.

The British had thought that Massachusetts could be isolated, but they underestimated the colonists' attachment to their liberties. The threat to representative government presented by the Intolerable Acts was so clear that the other colonies soon rallied around Massachusetts. In June 1774, the Virginia Burgesses sent out a letter suggesting a meeting of all the colonies. At about the same time, Massachusetts had issued a similar call for a meeting in Philadelphia. These two most radical colonies spurred the others to meet in early September.

The First Continental Congress

Every colony except Georgia sent delegates to the First Continental Congress, which convened on September 5, 1774. Only a few of the delegates had ever met any of their counterparts from the other colonies, so provincial were the colonies. For seven weeks these strangers met in formal sessions and social occasions. Together they laid the foundation for the first national government.

>> Timeline

▼**1715–1716**
Yamasee War

▼**1717**
French build Fort Toulouse

▼**1718**
French build New Orleans

▼**1720**
French build Louisbourg and Fort Niagara

▼**1731**
French build Fort St. Frédéric

▼**1733**
Molasses Act

▼**1739–1744**
War of Jenkins's Ear

▼**1741**
Attack on Cartagena fails

▼**1744–1748**
King George's War

▼**1748**
Village of Pickawillany established by Memeskia and his band
of Miamis

▼**1749**
French military expedition fails to win back dissident Indians
in Ohio Valley

▼**1752**
Tanacharison cedes huge chunk of Ohio Valley to Virginia

▼**1753**
French build small forts near forks of Ohio River

▼**1754**
Albany Plan of Union

▼**1754–1763**
French and Indian War   *continued*

>> Timeline *continued*

▼1755
Braddock's forces defeated

▼1757
British defeated at Fort William Henry, survivors massacred
William Pitt accedes to power in Britain

▼1758
Treaty of Easton secures neutrality of Ohio Valley tribes in return
   for territory west of Alleghenies

▼1759
British seize Quebec

▼1763
Treaty of Paris, ending French and Indian War, signed
Pontiac's Rebellion and Proclamation of 1763
Parliament increases size of peacetime army to 20 regiments

▼1764
Sugar Act
Currency Act

▼1765
Stamp Act
Quartering Act
Stamp Act Congress

▼1766
Declaratory Act

▼1767
Townshend Revenue Act

▼1768
Lord Hillsborough's circular letter
John Hancock's sloop *Liberty* seized
Treaty of Fort Stanwix

▼1770
Boston Massacre

▼1773
Tea Act
Boston Tea Party

>> **Timeline** *continued*

▼**1774**
Intolerable Acts (known as Coercive Acts in Britain)
Lord Dunmore's War

▼**1775**
First Continental Congress

With Massachusetts and Virginia almost ready to take up arms, and the middle colonies favoring conciliation, the greatest challenge was how to achieve unity. Since Massachusetts needed the support of the other colonies, it was ready to abandon any discussion of offensive measures against the British. In return, the Congress ratified the Suffolk Resolves, a set of Massachusetts resolutions that recommended passive resistance to the Intolerable Acts.

The delegates could now consider national action. Hoping to exert economic pressure on Britain, Congress issued a call for a boycott of all imports and exports between the colonies, Britain, and the West Indies. Then the delegates adopted a Declaration of Rights that for the first time expressed as the collective determination of every colony (except Georgia) what had become standard constitutional arguments. The colonists were entitled to all the "rights, liberties, and immunities of free and natural-born subjects" of England. Parliament could regulate trade for the colonies only by the "consent" of the colonies. Parliament could neither tax nor legislate for the colonies. Again and again, the Declaration reiterated the twin principles on which resistance to imperial legislation had been based: consent and the rule of law.

Finally, Congress agreed to reconvene in half a year, on March 10, 1775, unless the Intolerable Acts were repealed. The delegates had achieved consensus on the principles that would shortly form the basis for a new and independent national government.

Conclusion

Within a decade, the British Empire had come apart on its westernmost edge. The stage had been set decades earlier when Britain unintentionally allowed the colonies to develop more self-government and personal freedom than in Britain itself, without requiring them to pay a proportionate share of the costs of empire. As a result, the colonies created their own vision, one that linked democratic government and prosperity. Once Britain decided to knit the colonies more tightly into the empire and impose on them the controls of the centralized state, conflict was inevitable. At the same time, both Britons and Americans revered the same constitution, whose values and protections Americans invoked in their protests. That those protests would end in revolution was by no means a foregone conclusion. Revolution would require two key elements: Britain's unwillingness to compromise on issues of governance, and the ability of colonial radicals to convince moderates that there was no other way. By the end of 1774 that point had almost been reached.

Review Questions

1. What effect did the imperial wars of the eighteenth century have on the American colonies?

2. What were the reasons for the conflicts among the British, French, Spanish, and the various Indian tribes on the North American continent?

3. How and why did Britain attempt to reorganize its North American colonial empire? Why did the colonies resist?

4. What was the series of events that brought Britain and the colonies to the brink of war by 1774? To what extent were they the product of poor leadership? Differing theories of government? Different social experiences?

For further review materials and resource information, please visit www.oup.com/us/ofthepeople

Creating a New Nation

1775–1788

7

AMERICAN PORTRAIT

>> James Madison Helps Make a Nation

Why do some people achieve greatness? Perhaps it is not as much a matter of personal qualities as a match between the person and the times, an ability to understand and respond to the needs of the age. There was nothing in James Madison's childhood to suggest that he would become a leader of a revolutionary nation in a revolutionary age.

Madison grew up on the plantation his grandfather and his grandfather's slaves had cleared out of the Virginia Piedmont forest in 1732. Only a few months later, Madison's grandfather was killed by several of those slaves. One of the slaves was executed, but another, a woman named Dido, was given 29 lashes and sent home to work for the widow Madison. Perhaps James had his own grandfather in mind when he wrote later that men are not angels, and that is why government is necessary.

James went north to college, attending Princeton in New Jersey. After his graduation in 1771 at the age of 20, he suffered some sort of breakdown. Back in Virginia, Madison described himself as "too dull and infirm now to look out for any extraordinary things in this world. . . ." Short and slight of build, Madison was convinced that his poor health would lead to an early death. The event that drew this sickly, nervous young man out of his shell was the American Revolution. He became a leader in the nation that he helped create and whose Constitution he helped write. James Madison committed himself to the principles of liberty and order, and he devoted his life to establishing a government that would ensure both. Perhaps more than any other leader at the time, Madison understood how difficult reconciling these two principles would be.

Madison believed that strife and violence were deeply embedded in human nature, and he spent his adult life trying to create a government that would ensure peace without destroying liberty. He helped write the Constitution and then worked for the adoption of the Bill of Rights. His first political battle in Virginia had been on behalf

continued

183

>> **AMERICAN PORTRAIT** *continued*

of the Baptists, a dissenting Protestant denomination that demanded religious liberty. Madison was convinced that freedom of conscience was fundamental and that religion must be kept absolutely free from governmental interference. As a political thinker and leader, Madison came to advocate the great liberal principles of his age: the rights of conscience, consent, and property. Believing fervently in both human liberty and the rights of property, he could never reconcile himself either to slavery or to its abolition. He put his faith in the new government, hoping that just as he had learned to live with his own mental and physical disabilities, so the nation would rise above its internal conflicts and inconsistencies.

Common Threads

>> Which political theories did the American colonists use to justify their revolution, and how did they adapt those theories over the course of the next decades in the light of their experiences?

>> What does Britain's failure to defeat the colonies tell us about the limits of empire?

>> How did the doctrine of equality take on a life of its own?

>> To what extent has the conflict between the Federalists and the Antifederalists continued to shape American history?

>> In which ways was the American Revolution democratic? Not democratic?

The War Begins

By the end of 1774, conflict between the colonists and Britain seemed unavoidable. The British government, under the leadership of Lord North and King George III, seemed unwilling to make significant concessions. In the colonies, the radical opponents of British rule dominated politics. Despite these signs, no one anticipated eight years of warfare that would make the colonies a single nation under a centralized government.

The First Battles

Before he became governor of Massachusetts in 1774, General Thomas Gage had a long record of advocating force. He had called for the stationing of troops in Boston in 1768, leading to the Boston Massacre. Even before the Boston Tea Party, he recommended limiting democratic government in Massachusetts. Because he believed that Boston merchants and lawyers were instigating dissent among the poor, he wanted to isolate the colonial Revolutionary elite, by force if necessary.

In the spring of 1775, Gage received orders from England to act decisively against the colonists. He planned to seize the colonists' military supplies, stored at Concord, but alert Bostonians tipped off the patriot leaders once British troops began to march. On the night of April 18, the silversmith Paul Revere and the tanner William Dawes slipped out of Boston on horseback to carry the message that British troops were on the move. Militiamen from several towns began to gather.

The British soldiers arrived at Lexington at daybreak and ordered the militia to surrender, which they refused to do. Exactly what happened next remains unclear. The colonists swore that British soldiers opened fire, saying, "Ye villans [*sic*], ye Rebels, disperse; Damn you, disperse." The British major insisted that the first shot came from behind a tree. British soldiers lost control and fired, and the colonists returned fire. Eight Americans were killed, most while attempting to flee.

At the same time, the Concord militia had assembled and then pulled back about a mile, allowing the British to enter an almost-deserted town. Fighting broke out when a fire the British troops had set to the Concord liberty pole spread to the courthouse. To protect their town, the militia began marching on the British, who fired when the Americans drew near. In the exchange, three British soldiers were killed and several more injured. The British were forced back across the bridge. The entire battle took two or three minutes (see Map 7–1).

Once news of the fighting at Lexington and Concord spread, militias converged on Boston to evict Gage and his troops. More than 20,000 men soon were encamped in Boston.

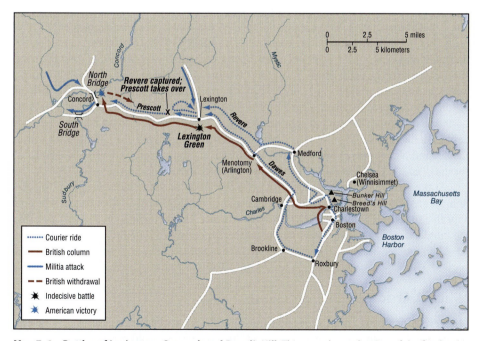

Map 7–1   Battles of Lexington, Concord, and Breed's Hill This map shows the sites of the first battles of the Revolution in and around Boston, along with the routes taken by Paul Revere and William Dawes to warn the colonists of the approach of British troops.

Gage declared that all the inhabitants of Massachusetts who bore arms were rebels and traitors, although he was willing to pardon everyone but John Hancock and Sam Adams, two leaders of the defiant Provincial Congress. Rather than backing down, the colonists fortified Breed's Hill (next to the more famous Bunker Hill) in Charlestown, overlooking Boston. On June 17, Gage sent 2,400 soldiers to take the hill. The cost was enormous: 1,000 soldiers and 92 officers killed or wounded (compared with 370 casualties among the colonists). The British learned not to make frontal assaults against fortified positions.

Other New Englanders were also taking matters into their own hands. A group under Benedict Arnold, an ambitious New Haven merchant, and Ethan Allen, the leader of the Vermont Green Mountain Boys, seized the crumbling fort at Ticonderoga on Lake Champlain and other small posts. In these heady days early in the Revolution, many colonists thought that this would be a quick and painless war.

Congress Takes the Lead

When the Second Continental Congress convened in Philadelphia on May 10, its greatest challenge was to maintain consensus. The most radical leaders, such as Sam and John Adams from Massachusetts and Richard Henry Lee from Virginia, were ready for war. However, many leaders, especially in the middle colonies, still hoped that war could be avoided.

Because Congress was an extralegal body, the elected colonial assemblies might easily have rejected its authority. But one after another, they transferred their allegiance from the British government to Congress. Although some moderates hoped for a negotiated settlement with Britain, they were caught between two sides that both anticipated war. The British refused even to acknowledge the petition sent by the First Continental Congress. That refusal, combined with Gage's attack on Breed's Hill, convinced the moderates that military preparations were necessary. Congress voted to create a Continental army and put it under the leadership of Virginia's George Washington. Not only was Washington experienced in military matters and widely respected, but his selection also helped solidify the alliance between New England and the South. Congress decided to attack Canada in the hope that a significant defeat would force the British to accede to American demands. To justify all of these actions, Congress also adopted the Declaration of the Causes and Necessities of Taking Up Arms, a rousing indictment of British "despotism," "perfidy," and "cruel aggression" drafted by Virginia's Thomas Jefferson.

At the same time, to preserve unity with the moderates, the radicals agreed to petition the king one more time. Without making any concessions, the Olive Branch Petition appealed to George's "magnanimity and benevolence." Nevertheless, on August 23, 1775, the king declared the colonists to be in "an open and avowed Rebellion." Although Congress had neither declared war nor asserted independence, the American Revolution had begun.

Military Ardor

Military ardor in the colonies reached its high point between the fall of 1775 and the spring of 1776. Colonists expected war, and they thought it would be quick and glorious. As a consequence, the first enlistments were for a term of only a year. Even if the war was not over by then, Revolutionaries were fearful of creating a permanent standing army.

In the summer of 1775, the Continental army marched on Canada. Victory would have either forced the British to the bargaining table or at least protected New York and New England from assault from the north. The contingent under General Benedict Arnold's command sailed from Newburyport, Massachusetts, to Maine and then marched 350 miles to Quebec. In November, after a grueling march, Arnold's forces prepared to assault Quebec, joined by troops under General Richard Montgomery, who had just seized Montréal. The battle was a disaster. Half of the 900 Continental soldiers were killed, captured, or wounded, including Montgomery. By the time the expedition retreated to New York in the spring, 5,000 men had been lost. The suffering was extraordinary, but it only increased American resolve.

Declaring Independence

By the beginning of 1776, moderates in Congress who still hoped for a peaceful settlement found themselves squeezed from both directions. The king and Parliament were unyielding, and popular opinion increasingly favored independence. Word arrived from Britain that all American commerce was to be cut off and that the British navy would seize American ships and their cargoes. Britain also began hiring German mercenaries known as Hessians, and Virginia's Governor Dunmore shelled Norfolk from warships. He had already offered freedom to any slaves who would fight for the British. Every prediction the radicals had made seemed to be coming true.

Public opinion also pushed Congress toward a declaration of independence. In January 1776, Thomas Paine, an expatriate English radical in Philadelphia, electrified the public with his pamphlet *Common Sense*, which sold 75,000 copies in a short time. In it, Paine liberated Americans from their ties to the British past so that they could start their government fresh. The idea of a balanced constitution that combined king, nobles, and common people in one government was "farcical," and monarchy was "exceedingly ridiculous." Paine had a message for Congress, too: "The period of debate is closed."

Thomas Paine Paine's *Common Sense* sold more than 75,000 copies in just a few weeks.

Most members of Congress either desired a declaration of independence or thought it inevitable. Most delegates also agreed that unanimity was more important than speed, so they waited through the spring of 1776 as, one by one, the state delegations received instructions in favor of independence. Then, under instructions from his colony, on June 7, 1776, Virginia's Richard Henry Lee asked Congress to vote on the resolution that "these United Colonies are, and of right ought to be, free and independent States." A committee of five, including Thomas Jefferson, Benjamin Franklin, and John Adams, was appointed to draft a declaration of independence. Adams asked Jefferson, a 33-year-old Virginia radical who could write stirring prose, to create the first draft. For four days, the delegates debated the draft and took preliminary votes. A clause that accused King George of forcing African slaves on the colonies was deleted. On July 2, the delegates voted unanimously to declare independence.

Many years later Jefferson insisted that there was nothing original about the Declaration of Independence, and he was not entirely wrong. The long list of accusations against King George, which formed the bulk of the Declaration, contained little that was new, and even some of the stirring words in the preamble had been used by the radicals time and again. Moreover, the Revolutionaries borrowed ideas from a number of British and European sources, including constitutionalism, republicanism, Enlightenment thought (see Chapter 6), and millennial Christian thought. The millennial strain in evangelical Protestantism suggested that the 1,000-year reign of Christ might begin soon in America if Americans would repent their sins, seek a spiritual rebirth, and defend their liberties.

However, in a different sense the Declaration of Independence was truly original. Jefferson's achievement was to reformulate familiar principles in a way that made them simple, clear, and applicable to the American situation.

The most important of these principles was human equality, that all people were born with certain fundamental rights. Second, and closely related, was the belief in a universal, common human nature. If all people were the same and had the same rights, then the purpose of government was to protect those rights. Just as people created government to protect their rights, they could abolish any government that became despotic. Third, government should represent the people.

It was many years, however, before the radical implications of the Declaration became fully evident to the American people. At the moment, more attention was focused on immediate political struggles. The Revolution succeeded because moderates and radicals were able to create effective alliances, reversing the pre-Revolutionary trend toward class and political conflict. To remain leaders of the opposition to Britain, elite Revolutionaries such as John Hancock continually appealed to poorer, more radical people and looked out for their interests, as well as their own. The result was a more moderate revolution than it might otherwise have been and a revolution that succeeded. Just as military fervor reached its high point in the spring of 1776, so did political unity, even if there were ongoing struggles over the meaning of the Revolution.

Creating a National Government

Although treated as if it were a legitimate national government, Congress actually had no more authority over the states than the states were willing to give it, and it had none whatsoever over the people. At the same time that Richard Henry Lee presented Congress with his proposal for independence, he also suggested that Congress create a permanent

Destruction of Statue of King George Here, a small crowd in New York City pulls down the statue of King George on July 9, 1776, a few days after independence had been declared.

national government, a confederation of the states with a written constitution. John Dickinson, a moderate, was assigned to draft the Articles of Confederation. He sketched out a weak central government with the authority to make treaties, carry out military and foreign affairs, request the states to pay its expenses, and very little else. There was no chief executive, only a Congress in which each state would have one vote. Term limits were imposed on representatives. Any act of Congress would require 9 votes (of 13), and the Articles would not go into effect until all 13 states had approved them.

With state jealousies strong, it took Congress more than a year to revise and accept a watered-down version of the Articles of Confederation. Not until March 1781, near the end of the war, did the final state ratify the Articles of Confederation, putting them into effect. By then, the weaknesses in a national government with no means of enforcing its regulations were becoming evident.

Creating State Governments

In 1776, all attention was focused on state governments, where the new ideas about liberty, equality, and government were put into practice. Americans were exhilarated by the prospect of creating their own governments. Between 1775 and 1780, each of the 13 states adopted a new written constitution.

Because the Revolutionaries feared concentrations of power, the powers of governors in the new states were sharply limited. In Pennsylvania and Georgia, the position of governor was abolished and replaced with a council. Governors were given term limits or required to run for reelection every year. Because royal governors had appointed cronies to powerful positions, the new governors also were stripped of their power of appointment.

The new state constitutions made the legislatures more democratic. The number of representatives was doubled in South Carolina and New Hampshire and more than tripled in Massachusetts. Many constitutions also imposed either term limits or frequent elections for representatives. As the property qualifications for holding office were lowered, poorer men sat in legislatures alongside richer ones. The admission of more ordinary men into government was one of the greatest changes brought about by the Revolution. Now the elite had to learn to share power and to win the votes of men they had once scorned.

Winning the Revolution

The British entered the war with clear advantages in population, wealth, and power, but with a flawed premise about how to win the war. Britain, arguably the world's most powerful nation, had the mistaken idea that the colonists could be defeated by a swift and effective use of force. It also assumed that Americans loyal to the Crown would support British troops, but they alienated Americans with their actions. Probably no more than one-fifth of the population remained loyal to Britain, but many more shifted loyalties depending on local circumstances. The war ultimately became a struggle for the support of this unpoliticized population.

Competing Strategies

British political objectives shifted during the war. The first goal, based on the belief that resistance was being led by a handful of radical New Englanders, was to punish and isolate Boston. This was the strategy of 1774 and 1775, with the Intolerable Acts and the battles of Lexington, Concord, and Breed's Hill. It failed miserably, due to the faulty assumption that well-trained British regulars were necessarily superior to untrained colonial rustics. However, if the British had a misplaced faith in their invincibility, the Americans had a misplaced faith in their moral superiority; but neither faith could guarantee victory. The result was a long war, as both sides tried to avoid decisive engagements that might prove fatal.

For seven years, the two armies chased each other across the eastern seaboard. Neither side had huge armies. Moreover, with no consensus in Britain about the strategic or economic value of the colonies, there was always opposition to the war and a limit to the investment that the British were prepared to make in it. Consequently, every battle presented a significant risk that troops who were lost could not be replaced.

Manpower was also a serious problem for the Americans. It was difficult to recruit enough soldiers into the Continental army. After a defeat in battle or near the end of the year when terms of enlistment were up, men left the army to return home. Any defeat demoralized the public, depressing enlistments. Hence there was limited incentive for the army to risk all in battle.

Early in the war, however, both sides hoped for a decisive victory. After the Americans failed in Quebec, the British pursued them back to Ticonderoga on Lake Champlain, where Benedict Arnold's leadership stopped the rout. The war then shifted to southern New York and the middle colonies. Having given up hopes of crushing New England directly, the British planned to isolate the region and defeat the Continental army under George Washington's leadership.

The British also sought to seize all the major American cities, and they did capture Boston, Newport, New York, Philadelphia, Charleston, and Savannah. The capture of these cities, however, did not bring about an American surrender. With 90 percent of Americans living in the countryside, the seizure of a major city did not strike the hoped-for psychological or economic blow.

The British on the Offensive: 1776

Preparing for an offensive in 1776, the new British commander, General William Howe, assembled a huge force on Staten Island: 32,000 soldiers and 13,000 seamen. Some of these soldiers were actually German mercenaries, the Hessians. Anticipating battle and hoping to protect New York, Washington moved his army south to New York (see Map 7–2). He had about 19,000 soldiers, too few for a pitched battle. Half his troops were in Manhattan while the other half, in Brooklyn Heights, dug in to protect Long Island. The British sneaked up behind the Americans in Brooklyn, inflicting heavy casualties, and on August 27, 1776, Washington pulled his remaining forces back into Manhattan. Had the British pursued rapidly, they probably could have crushed Washington's army, but Howe may have been more concerned with winning a peace than a war. After Washington re-treated, Howe invited members of the Continental Congress to meet with him privately on Staten Island. He was unable to recognize American independence, which was what the representatives insisted on, so his peace strategy failed.

Still hoping for peace, Howe began pushing Washington back out of Manhattan. Si-multaneously, he offered peace to any colonists in the region who would declare their loyalty, and thousands accepted. On November 16, the British forced the Americans out of Manhattan and pursued them to White Plains and then through New Jersey to New Brunswick. The British almost caught Washington twice in New Jersey, but on December 8 the Americans crossed the Delaware at Trenton, taking every boat with them to prevent pursuit. By Christmas Eve, Washington had only 3,000 soldiers, and General Charles Lee, the commander of the other half of the Continental army, had been captured. As Thomas Paine wrote, "These are the times that try men's souls."

Howe had captured New York and New Jersey and was poised to seize Philadelphia (which fell in September 1777). At the end of 1776, the British were close to achieving their objective. Then, on Christmas night, with morale in his army dangerously low, Washington took it across the ice-clogged Delaware and surprised the British garrison at Trenton at dawn, capturing 1,000 Hessian soldiers. About a week later, Washington evaded a British trap and sneaked behind the lines to capture an outpost at Princeton.

These American successes brought another 1,000 troops into the army. More signifi-cant, the British decided to concentrate their troops near New Brunswick, fearing the loss of any more garrisons, which were needed to defend the Loyalists. This strategic deci-sion revealed the weakness in the British position and demonstrated why, when victory seemed closest, it was very far away. Without enough troops to overcome the Americans' home advantage, the British needed to ensure that civilians did not aid the Revolutionary War effort. To assure the allegiance of Loyalists, the British had to offer them protection from American reprisals. However, the British were seizing the Americans' goods and

AMERICAN LANDSCAPE

>> The Winter at Jockey Hollow

It was the worst winter in a century. It snowed 28 times, and drifts covered the fences in the hollow of land tucked between Long Hill and the Watchung Mountains. It was snowing again on December 1, 1779, the day that General George Washington moved the Continental army into its winter quarters, four miles outside the New Jersey village of Morristown.

Washington chose Jockey Hollow because the low mountains and surrounding swamps protected it from sudden attack. The hilly terrain was covered with trees, which his soldiers, almost 11,000 of them, could chop down to build cabins. The water supply was good, and the many farms in the region could provide food.

The first order of business was to build cabins, but the winter was so harsh that the work proceeded slowly. Until cabins were built, the soldiers and the line officers had to sleep in their tents. The storm that raged for three days in early January was "one of the most tremendous snowstorms ever remembered; no man could endure its violence many minutes without danger of his life," Dr. James Thatcher reported.

Not until February were most men in the "Log-house city" of more than 1,000 cabins. They were all the same size and design, about 14 feet wide by 15 or 16 feet long, and 6½ feet high at the eaves. Each cabin had a stone fireplace and bunks for a dozen soldiers.

Both food and clothing were in short supply. Joseph Plumb Martin, a 19-year-old private from Connecticut, complained bitterly, "We were absolutely, literally starved. . . . I did not put a single morsel of victuals into my mouth for four days

and as many nights." Some officers gave their soldiers their own small rations of meat. Washington's requests to the Continental Congress had gone unanswered, but local farmers brought their produce to camp to sell at extortionate prices. Hungry soldiers, unpaid for five months, began foraging for themselves in the neighborhood. Washington threatened that unless the surrounding counties quickly sent supplies (for which he would issue IOUs) to his camp, he would organize a systematic forage of New Jersey. The problem was solved for the moment; but the large army quickly went through the new supplies, and by spring it was hungry again.

Some men began talking mutiny, "venting our spleen at our country and government, then at our officers, and then at ourselves for our imbecility in staying there and starving . . . for an ungrateful people who did not care what became of us, so they could enjoy themselves while we were keeping a cruel enemy from them." Officers were able to appeal to the troops' patriotism, telling them that they had "won immortal honor to yourselves . . . by your perseverance, patience, and bravery. . . ." Cold, hungry, half-naked, most of the soldiers stayed on. "We were unwilling," Private Martin said, "to desert the cause of our country, when in distress . . . we knew her cause involved our own."

The encampment at Jockey Hollow was a laboratory in which nationalism was created. The adversity bound soldiers and officers together; their suffering and sacrifice created a deep, enduring commitment to a shared destiny that became the foundation of the new nation.

property for the war effort. Then, once the garrisons were withdrawn, Loyalists were left alone and vulnerable to the reprisals of the patriots.

The British could control the American countryside only by maintaining troops there, but once the troops were withdrawn, civil warfare would break out. Thus, even though Washington's victories at Trenton and Princeton were small, they exposed the incapacity of the British to defeat the Revolutionaries unless they settled an army of occupation on the Americans, something they were not prepared to do.

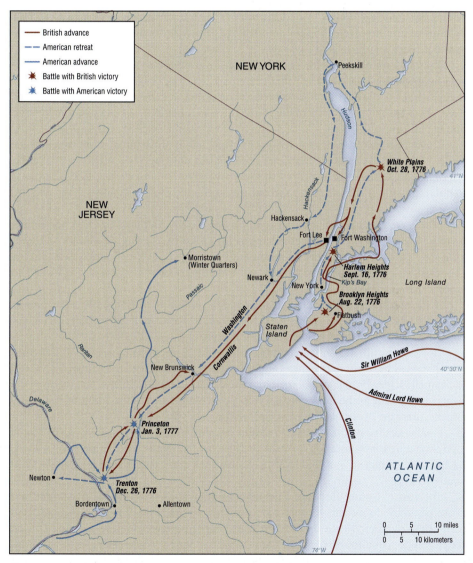

Map 7–2   New York and New Jersey Campaigns, 1776–1777 In the second half of 1776, British troops chased Washington out of New York and across New Jersey. As he would for the remainder of the war, Washington took care never to let the British capture him and his troops, leaving him free to attack at Trenton and Princeton.

A Slow War: 1777–1781

Washington settled in and enlisted soldiers for a long war. Lacking enough soldiers to confront the British head-on, he mostly led the British on chases across the countryside. Maintaining such an army year after year was expensive, but the Americans were unwilling to be taxed at high rates. Continental soldiers who were from the bottom tier of society suffered grievously; at Jockey Hollow, New Jersey, in the winter of 1779/1780, men roasted their own shoes to eat and even devoured their pet dogs.

In 1777, the British political objective was still the same: to isolate New England by seizing the middle colonies. American troops had the advantage in upstate New York by three to one, however, and they defeated the British under General John Burgoyne at Saratoga, stopping the British advance.

The victory at Saratoga convinced the French to enter into a formal alliance, negotiated by Benjamin Franklin, the American envoy. Winning French support was perhaps the major accomplishment of the middle phase of the war: the entry of the French tied down the British in other parts of the world and also brought America more than $8 million in aid.

The British had failed to isolate New England, and it proved impossible to pacify the middle colonies. As a result, the focus shifted from the least loyal section of America, New England, to the most loyal area, the South. British war aims shifted, too, in response to political realities at home. Now the war was needed to protect Loyalists from vengeful patriots.

Seeking to capitalize on internal conflicts and to rally southern Loyalists, the British invaded Georgia in 1778 and South Carolina in 1780. After seizing Charleston and trapping the American commander and thousands of troops, the British ranged out into the countryside, trying to rally the Loyalists and live off the land—the same strategy that had failed in New Jersey.

In the meantime, the Continental army and the militia worked together to wear down the British. The Continental army in the lower South was never large enough for a major battle and was defeated at Camden, South Carolina, in August 1780.

However, as the British marched through South Carolina and North Carolina, they were harassed by bands of irregulars and militia. Each hit depleted the British forces, and each small victory brought more men into the American ranks. This, in fact, became the American strategy as the Continental forces, now commanded in the South by Nathanael Greene, drew the British, led by Lord Cornwallis, on a wild chase.

Finally, Greene met the British at Guilford Court House in North Carolina in March 1781, inflicting heavy losses on the exhausted enemy. The battle was a draw, but Cornwallis, his forces depleted, retreated to Virginia. Greene's army retook almost all of the deep South.

The cost to South Carolina, however, was enormous. Most of the upcountry was crisscrossed by troops and stripped bare. As each side took control, neighbors attacked each other, plundered each other's farms, and carried away each other's slaves. During the Revolution, one-fourth of South Carolina's slaves simply disappeared. Some ran away, some died of disease, some were stolen by whites, and some followed the British, who in June 1780 promised freedom to all rebel-owned slaves who agreed to fight on their side for the rest of the war. Some were actually shipped off to slavery in the West Indies, but

AMERICA AND THE WORLD

>> Mercenaries in Global Perspective

In 1776, the Declaration of Independence warned that King George "is, at this time, transporting large armies of foreign mercenaries to complete the works of death, desolation, and tyranny, already begun." It charged that the use of such mercenaries was "scarcely parallelled in the most barbarous ages, and totally unworthy the head of a civilized nation." In fact, the use of mercenaries was the norm, rather than the exception, in eighteenth-century Europe, with some countries renting and others supplying them. Between one-fifth and two-thirds of the British, French, and Prussian armies were foreigners, typically Swiss, Dutch, and various Germans. Wealthy nations could buy other countries' soldiers, thereby protecting their own citizens' freedom.

The practice of using mercenaries had developed several hundred years earlier. Under the feudal system, a lord could command service only for defensive wars. Any lord who wanted to embark on a foreign war would have to pay for soldiers. As the pace of foreign wars increased in the seventeenth century (and feudalism died), so also did the practice of hiring foreign soldiers. Some nations soon became major hirers of mercenaries, and others became sources. John Smith, for example, was a mercenary before he joined the Virginia expedition. He fought for the Dutch against Spain and later for the Austrians against the Turks in Hungary.

Unlike these professional soldiers, less fortunate men were conscripted into their country's service only to be shipped off to fight another nation's war. This was the standard practice in the little German principality of Hesse-Cassel, whose renting of soldiers to other nations generated half of the government's revenues in the middle of the eighteenth century. The government claimed to conscript only "masterless servants and loafers," but as Hesse-Cassel grew dependent on the revenue from its mercenaries, it began to reach into peasant families, seizing their servants and younger sons. Because the law exempted from service men who owned homes, parents tried to give all their sons enough property to keep them out of the army. When inheritance laws were changed to keep parents from dividing their estates, parents began giving their daughters' dowries directly to their sons, sacrificing the girls' prospects for a good match to keep the boys out of the army. In this way, relations between the great nations reached deep into the lives of families.

American colonists rejected the use of mercenaries as "totally unworthy" of a "civilized nation." By the end of the eighteenth century, Enlightenment philosophers had begun to condemn the trade in soldiers—for that is what it was. Under new doctrines of nationalism, men were supposed to fight for patriotism, not for pay, and a nation that hired mercenaries began to seem less than "civilized."

many fought with the British. This use of slaves as soldiers, of course, outraged white patriots, but it hardly pleased the Loyalists either. Loyalist slaveholders did not want their
way of life undermined. Had the British been willing to wage a war of liberation, freeing all the southern slaves and using them as soldiers, they might have come closer to
winning the war. But the British were fighting to preserve social and political order, not
to overturn it. The British nonetheless disrupted the slave system significantly, and this
disruption was another aspect to the civil war that beset the region for most of the Revolutionary period.

The British southern strategy had failed, but the Americans were not yet ready to
win the war. Cornwallis moved on to Virginia in 1781, capturing Richmond, the new
capital, and Charlottesville, coming within a few minutes of capturing Thomas Jefferson.
Yet the British had been seriously weakened by the war of attrition. George Washington,
working closely with the French—who sent a huge fleet into the Chesapeake near Cornwallis's quarters at Yorktown—led most of his forces, accompanied by French troops, to
Virginia and laid siege. Trapped, Cornwallis surrendered on October 19, 1781. Although
the Treaty of Paris (see Map 7–3) ending the war was not signed for two more years, the
war was effectively over.

Securing a Place in the World

The United States revolted to escape from the British Empire and to turn its back on European power politics. However, to win the war, the new nation had to strike bargains

Surrender of British Army Here Cornwallis surrenders to Washington.

with those same European powers. These alliances and treaties set the stage for America's struggle for a place in the world order.

Early in the war the United States called on Britain's enemies—France, Spain, and Holland—for support, and it played these new allies off against Britain with the cunning of an Old World diplomat. Benjamin Franklin, Congress's envoy to France, now 70, arrived at court in 1776 dressed like a country rustic instead of wearing the expected silks and powdered wig. His appearance was a ruse, intended to make the French think that he was innocent and uncalculating. France entered the war in the hope of breaking up the British Empire and reestablishing itself as the world's most powerful nation. France and Spain both wanted the United States to be independent but small and weak.

The United States wanted to secure its independence, first and foremost, but it had no intention of remaining small or feeble. Americans sought a large chunk of Canada, the territory between the Appalachians and the Mississippi River, and the right to navigate the Mississippi. In return for French and Spanish assistance, the United States at first offered only the right to trade, vastly overrating the value in Europe of American trade.

Because America wanted France and Spain to fight for expanded American territory, whereas those countries wanted instead to keep the new nation small, it took three years, until 1778, to negotiate formal treaties. Franklin prodded the French by holding secret truce discussions with a British agent late in 1777 and then leaking reports to well-placed French friends. Although the alliance was an impressive accomplishment, it involved concessions. The Americans promised not to negotiate separately with Britain and to remain France's ally "forever."

The United States broke both promises, the first within a few years and the second in the 1790s. In April 1782, after Cornwallis's surrender at Yorktown but before France and Spain had gained their military objectives, Franklin began peace negotiations with the British. By November, a draft of the treaty had been completed, although Franklin assured the French that nothing would be signed without their consent. The agreement primarily served British and American interests, however. In the Treaty of Paris, signed in 1783, Britain recognized American independence, and the United States acquired the territory between the Appalachians and the Mississippi River and south of the Great Lakes (see Map 7–3).

In the long run Britain probably struck the shrewder bargain. The land it ceded was of little use. The Americans failed to press for commercial concessions, and by the mid-1780s, the British had forbidden Americans to trade directly with Britain or the West Indies. These restrictions seriously damaged the new nation's economy.

Neither France nor Spain gained much from the war. Although Spain won Florida, neither country achieved its other territorial objectives, and France was left with a large debt.

If America's allies were relative losers, so also were Britain's allies, the American Loyalists and Indian tribes that fought with them. The best the British could do for the Loyalists was to secure a commitment of no further reprisals against them and Congress's promise to consider making restitution. The British sold their Indian allies out by transferring their land (the territory between the Appalachians and the Mississippi) to the United States. Although a stunning achievement, the Treaty of Paris also set the stage for future conflicts.

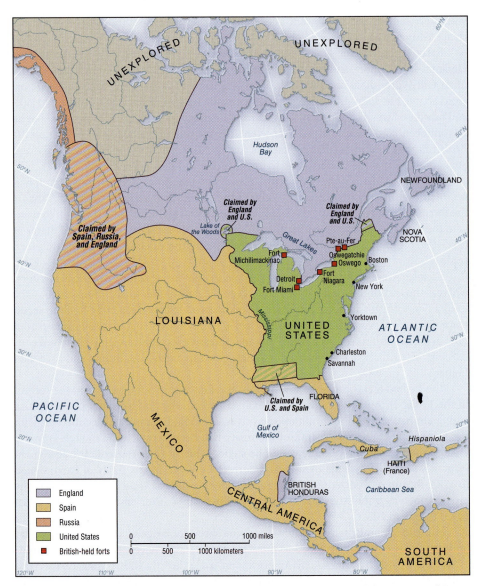

Map 7–3 The Treaty of Paris The Treaty of Paris confirmed the boundaries of the new United States, north to the Great Lakes, south to Spanish Florida, and west to the Mississippi. But it left the British in several forts west of the Appalachians, forts that they did not abandon until 1797. *Walter LaFeber,* The American Age, *2nd ed. (New York: W.W. Norton, 1994), p. 29.*

The Challenge of the Revolution

During and after the Revolution, Americans experienced all the upheavals of war: death, profiteering, and inflation, followed by economic depression. Other challenges were also presented by the new Revolutionary ideas about liberty and equality.

Radicals and moderates had compromised for victory, yet significant disagreements resurfaced once the fighting ended. One of the greatest challenges that Americans faced was designing political structures to contain these conflicts. The other great challenge came from the philosophy of revolution itself. Equality implied a transformed society. Followed to its natural conclusion, not only would the transformation lead to prosperity, but it would also necessarily challenge slavery and the subordination of women.

The Departure of the Loyalists

About 15 to 20 percent of the white population had remained loyal to the Crown during the Revolution, along with a majority of the Indians and a minority of slaves. Although sizable in number (almost half a million whites), the Loyalists were never well organized enough to threaten the success of the Revolution.

During the war, partisan fighting was fierce in contested regions such as the Carolinas and New Jersey, but there was relatively little retribution after the war. There were no trials for treason, mass executions, or significant mob actions directed against whites. Nor was there any significant resistance from the Loyalists. Perhaps as many as 80,000 left for Canada, Great Britain, or the West Indies. Among them were thousands of former slaves who had accepted the British offer of freedom.

The white exiles came disproportionately from the top tier of society, and their departure left a void. Confiscated Loyalist property represented a great deal of wealth to be redistributed, and people just below the top rung of society scrambled to take the Loyalists' places. The departure of the Loyalists enhanced the democratizing tendencies of the Revolution by removing the most conservative element in American society and creating an opportunity for many Americans to rise to power.

The Challenge of the Economy

Wars disrupt the economy in two ways. First, they interfere with production and exchange, hurting some people and creating opportunity for others. Second, because wars are expensive, they require some combination of increased taxation and deficit spending.

Those who suffered the greatest economic hardships and enjoyed the greatest opportunities from the Revolution were those most deeply involved in the market. During the war, trade with Britain and the British West Indies was cut off, and the British navy seized American ships and destroyed the New England fishing industry. After the war, Britain still excluded American ships from the West Indies. Congress, under the Articles of Confederation, was too weak to negotiate a better trade relationship, and merchants trading with Britain and the West Indies were ruined.

At the same time, other opportunities opened up. Merchants willing to risk seizure of their ships continued the trade with Europe and sold the goods they imported at astronomical prices. Privateering made other merchants rich, as did provisioning the Continental army. In 1779 alone, the army spent $109 million on provisions, fueling a wartime economic boom. The army's demand for supplies drove prices up. Prices for grain increased 200 to 600 percent and, in Maryland, 5,000 percent.

Enterprising Americans with a little capital to invest could rise quickly. Not everyone could take advantage of the Revolutionary economy. In fact, although the Revolution eliminated some of the ruling elite, it did not level social classes. Those who could not profit from the war had to work harder and struggle with rising prices. To meet the army's demand for cloth, women increased the pace of home production. Because there were set prices for cloth, women were unable to reap exorbitant profits.

Skyrocketing prices were hardest on those with limited incomes. While Congress debated price controls and some cities set them, aggrieved citizens sometimes took matters into their own hands. In Boston, a mob of at least a hundred women seized a hogshead of coffee from the merchant Thomas Boylston, who was hoarding it. Such conflicts pitted the community against the entrepreneur and raised serious questions about the purpose of the Revolution: Was it to create opportunities for the individual or to protect the well-being of the community?

After the war, opportunities for profit and prosperity for some increased, whereas a postwar deflation pushed others to misery. Speculation in land and currency offered the fastest ways to become rich. Entrepreneurs bought up paper currency and land patents at a fraction of their worth, counting on the day when they would be redeemed at their face value.

Even before the war ended, there was a clamor for land. Between 1776 and 1790, America's population grew by almost 70 percent, from 2.3 million to 3.9 million, almost all from natural increase. Colonists had long been pushing against the Indians to the west, and by 1783, the Wilderness Road had taken thousands into Kentucky; seven years later, 100,000 people were living in Kentucky and Tennessee.

With the demand for land so great, speculators who could corner huge tracts stood to reap extraordinary profits. Before the Revolution, seven men had secured a patent to 29,350 acres in upstate New York. By the end of the Revolution, three of them were dead; one—a Loyalist—had left the country; and the others were broke or close to it, all victims of the dislocations of war. William Cooper, a small-scale merchant and speculator, bought the patent in a possibly rigged auction for the bargain-basement price of £2,700. Yet his investment was worthless unless Cooper could get others to buy portions of the huge patent from him. After a few months, Cooper sold off thousands of acres not to poor farmers but to speculators who in turn sold farm-sized plots to their own townsmen, turning a profit by increasing the price.

All along the western frontier, farmers rushed to take the new lands, reversing the pre-Revolutionary trend to the cities. With the opening of new regions to the west, America would remain a farming nation for decades more, rather than industrializing rapidly along the rigid class lines of European industrial economies. At the same time, slavery expanded into new territories in the South, ensuring the persistence of inequalities based on race.

Even more than the dislocations of the Revolutionary economy, the financing of the Revolution challenged the American economy. Taxing the population was out of the question, not only because Americans had begun the Revolution precisely to avoid high taxes but also because Congress had no authority to tax. Instead, it simply printed more money. There was no increase in underlying wealth to back up this currency, and the more Congress printed, the less it was worth. By 1780, Congress had printed more than $241 million. In addition, Congress paid for supplies and soldiers' wages with certificates that circulated like money. These certificates put another $95 million into circulation.

The plan was for each state to raise taxes to buy up the Continental currency and remove it from circulation. However, the states were either unable or unwilling to buy up enough currency to maintain its value. Moreover, the states issued their own paper money.

Eventually, the states had to tax their inhabitants at rates far higher than had ever been seen before. Collecting taxes was difficult: people could not pay in hard money, and the Continental currency depreciated so rapidly that it was almost worthless (see Figure 7-1).

By April 1777, Continental currency was worth only half its face value, and by April 1781, only half a percent. By the end of the war, some creditors were refusing to accept paper money for debts owed to them, insisting on hard money instead. When trade with Britain resumed, imports increased sharply (because of pent-up demand for consumer goods), while exports fell (because restrictions kept American goods out of British markets). The result was severe deflation and a flood of cheap imports.

The weak central government was almost powerless to address these economic upheavals. In 1780 it stopped paying the army, which almost led to a mutiny at Newburgh, New York. Congress looked to each state to decide what to do about its debt and which element of its population to serve. Many states showed mercy to debtors. To help pay off debts, some states sold confiscated Loyalist property, whereas others tried to seize Indian lands in the west. Wherever states increased taxes to pay off state debts (as the postwar depression hit), hard-pressed debtors clamored for tax relief. In western Massachusetts, farmers led by Revolutionary War captain Daniel Shays shut down the courts to prevent them from collecting debts. This episode is known as Shays's Rebellion.

Figure 7–1 Depreciation of Continental Currency, January 1770-April 1781 At the same time that prices were rising, the value of Continental currency was falling dramatically. Between 1777 and 1781, it lost almost all of its value, becoming close to worthless.

Contesting the New Economy

Economic upheaval and popular uprisings against state governments led many Americans to question whether democratic government could survive. The process of rebellion that started in 1765 seemed to be starting again, this time directed against the new republican state governments. Americans now faced the same issue that had led to conflict with Britain: Were they willing to pay for a huge war? Could they avoid the perils of tyranny, on the one hand, and anarchy, on the other? Could they, in short, maintain democratic forms of government?

Shays's Rebellion was simply an extreme form of the protest that occurred in many states. It was an attempt by debtors to force the government to alleviate their economic distress, primarily by shutting down the courts so that their debts could not be collected, but also by passing legislation for the relief of debtors. By 1786, many western Massachusetts farmers had become used to the absence of government, and local courts had been shut down since 1774. Those who put down Shays's Rebellion did so in republican terms, faulting the Shaysites for inadequate virtue.

Such popular uprisings raised serious questions about whether the democratic governments created after the Revolution could contain anarchy. States that faced such uprisings learned that peace could best be preserved by going easy on the rebels. After Shays's Rebellion was put down, John Hancock was elected governor with the support of the Shaysites on a platform of amnesty for the rebels and relief for debtors. As a rule, popular uprisings by economically independent men (as distinguished from those by dependent laborers or slaves) have been punished very lightly in America, which may be a source of American political stability.

The relatively light punishments given to debtor insurgents and the generally inflationary policies of state governments quelled popular unrest, but the postwar depression and the inability of Congress to reopen trade with Britain devastated commerce. The huge national debt went unpaid, leaving numerous creditors holding worthless pieces of paper. Popular unrest had helped debtors but hurt those to whom they owed money. The nationalists, a group of commercial-minded political leaders centered in Congress and including James Madison, Gouverneur Morris, Robert Morris, and Alexander Hamilton, began to make a case for a strong national government that would actively advance commerce and protect private property. These nationalists were, in general, the moderates of the Revolutionary era. Radicals envisioned a weaker central government, a more localized democracy, and a hands-off approach to the economy. Whether these two visions of America could be reconciled was one of the greatest challenges of the Revolution.

Can Women Be Citizens?

The American Revolution raised questions that threatened and in some cases changed the social order. A revolution based on beliefs in human equality and a common human nature brought into question all social relations, including the role of women.

Many women were drawn into the Revolution as consumers. They had eagerly participated in the boycotts of the 1760s and 1770s and had increased home production. Many women identified with the goals of the Revolution and often led riots against merchants suspected of unfair dealings. Women could challenge the Revolutionary governments, as well, when they perceived interference with their rights as consumers and duties as homemakers.

If women were able to extend their traditional economic roles as producers and consumers to support the war effort, there was no consensus on expanding their political roles. Some women pointed out that the right to be taxed only by one's own representatives should apply to them, too. Under the principle of *coverture*, married women were generally denied the right to own property, but what was the basis for denying the vote to unmarried women who owned property? In 1776, New Jersey extended the vote to unmarried women who met the property qualification (although this right was rescinded in 1807). Although American Revolutionaries were not prepared to let women vote, except in New Jersey, they began to broaden their views of women's intellectual and political capabilities. The state laws that confiscated Loyalists' property, for example, often presumed that married women were capable of making their own political choices. This notion broke with the past, when married women were thought to have no political will separate from that of their husbands.

The Revolution challenged the idea that women lacked independent minds and could not think for themselves. The Enlightenment belief that all human beings had the capacity to reason led to significant improvements in women's education after the war. Reformers, many of them women, argued that if women appeared ignorant or incapable, it was only because of their inferior education.

Enlightenment ideas about women's intellectual abilities meshed neatly with republican ideas about the need for virtue and liberal ideas about the necessity of consent. If the nation's fate depended on the character of its citizens, both men and women should be able to choose intelligent, upright, patriotic partners. The Revolution also accelerated a trend for people to choose their own marriage partners and marry for love rather than for material interest. If women were to make such choices wisely, they must be educated well.

Yet once again the Revolutionary impulse had its limits. Discussions about women's citizenship and capacities implicitly applied only to prosperous white women. Moreover, almost no one advocated professional education or even knowledge for its own sake for women. Overly intellectual women were ridiculed as "women of masculine minds." Women's education was supposed to make them better wives and mothers and enable them to perform their domestic roles better. Because the family was still the bedrock of the nation, no one was willing to answer a question posed by Abigail Smith Adams in a letter to her husband, John Adams: What recourse was open to women who found that they were treated with "cruelty and indignity" at home?

The ideas of the Revolution presented a powerful challenge to the subordination of women, one that the Revolutionary generation was only partially prepared to meet. Women were recognized as intelligent beings who could make important choices in the market, about their families, and even about their political loyalties. They were partial citizens, and this revealed the limits of Revolutionary doctrines of equality.

The Challenge of Slavery

No institution in America received a greater challenge from the egalitarian ideals of the Revolution than slavery. Although slaves always resisted their enslavement, the world's first organized antislavery movement began before the Revolution with the Pennsylvania Quaker John Woolman, who in 1754 condemned slavery in humanitarian and religious terms. Within a few years, radicals in both the North and the South recognized that the institution was inconsistent with their ideals of freedom.

African American slaves saw immediately that the Revolution offered opportunities for freedom. The rise of egalitarian ideas and wartime disruption enabled thousands of slaves to claim their freedom. Some used a mix of Christian and Revolutionary principles of liberty to petition for "the natural rights and privileges of freeborn men." Others fought for their liberty by joining the Revolutionary forces; by the end of the war, three-fourths of the Rhode Island regiment and perhaps one-fourth of Washington's troops were black. Many more accepted British offers of freedom to slaves who deserted their masters. Tens of thousands of slaves ran away. This combination of Revolutionary ideals of freedom and African American activism presented a significant challenge to white Americans, and they met it in part. Every state north of Delaware eliminated slavery, either in their constitutions or through gradual emancipation laws. In addition, the Northwest Ordinance of 1787 prohibited slavery in the Northwest Territory (the future states of Ohio, Indiana, Illinois, Michigan, and Wisconsin). In the states of the upper South (Virginia, Maryland, and Delaware) legislatures passed laws making it easier to emancipate slaves.

If slavery was eliminated—sometimes slowly—in the North and questioned in the upper South, it still survived in every state south of New Jersey. Revolutionary ideals made slaveholders uncomfortable. Unwilling to eliminate it, they offered excuses, protesting that abolishing slavery was too difficult or inconvenient. Historians still debate whether the inroads made against slavery were one of the Revolution's greatest successes—or whether the inability to curtail it was its greatest failure.

A New Policy in the West

The new nation faced a major challenge in the West. It had to devise a policy consistent with its political economy, rejecting the old colonial models of Britain, France, and Spain. But how would the United States organize the new territory acquired through the war? There was no useful model for new territories and their citizens to become equal members of an expanding, democratic nation.

The Indians' Revolution

At the beginning of the American Revolution, most Indians regarded it as a fight among Englishmen that did not concern them. At the end of the war, all Indians were losers, as land-hungry Americans poured into the region beyond the Appalachians.

By 1776, both the British and the Americans were recruiting Indians. Within a few years, Indians on the frontier were drawn into the struggle, usually on the British side. They feared American moves onto their land; also, only the British could provide the customary "presents" that cemented alliances. Indians struck at American communities all along the frontier.

In retaliation, Washington ordered "the total destruction and devastation" of Iroquois settlements in New York and western Pennsylvania and the capture of "as many prisoners of every age and sex as possible." In 1778, an expedition under General John Sullivan systematically burned 40 Iroquois towns. One chief said that the Americans "put to death all the Women and Children, excepting some of the young Women, whom they carried away for the use of their Soldiers & were afterwards put to death in a more shameful manner." Such brutality undermined American efforts to keep Indian allies.

The End of the Middle Ground

The end of the Revolution brought neither peace nor order. The Indians who had won victories on the frontier were amazed when they learned the British had surrendered and given all of the Indians' land to the Americans. Needing land for settlers more than it needed diplomatic allies, the United States soon abandoned the middle ground (see Chapter 2). No longer able to play one group of Europeans against another, Indian tribes had little leverage.

Western Indians soon found themselves in the midst of a competition among whites for their land. Congress wanted to establish a national claim to Indian lands so it could sell them to pay off the war debt, whereas New York, Pennsylvania, North Carolina, and Virginia all attempted to seize land within their borders. Speculators moved in, knowing they could sell land at an immense profit. At the end of the Revolution, one-third of the men in western Pennsylvania were landless, and they believed that the Revolution's promise of equality entitled them to cheap land. Some of the poorest crossed the Appalachians into Kentucky and Ohio, even during the war, squatting on Indian-owned lands.

Those already on the frontier who both suffered from and inflicted violence maintained a visceral hatred of Indians, sometimes advocating their extermination. These settlers expected government to secure frontier land for them and to protect them from the Indians. Congress and the states moved quickly to force Indians, some with no authority to speak for their tribes, to sign treaties ceding their land.

Such treaties (15 were signed between 1784 and 1796) were almost meaningless. Native Americans refused to honor agreements made under duress and that did not include the customary exchange of gifts, and the states would not recognize another state's claims or those of the national government. Indian leaders were encouraged by the British and the Spanish. The Mohawk leader Joseph Brant took his followers to Ontario. Alexander McGillivray united the Creeks and secured military support from the Spanish in Florida. Not until well into the nineteenth century were American claims to Indian land east of the Mississippi secured and Indian resistance put down.

Settling the West

Establishing effective government in the West was one of the biggest problems the new nation faced. Many frontier regions (in particular Kentucky and the area north of the Ohio River, as well as portions of Vermont and Maine) were claimed by competing groups of speculators. The Articles of Confederation gave Congress limited powers of government in the West, but a national policy was necessary. Just after the Revolution, dissident settlers in New York, Pennsylvania, Kentucky (then part of Virginia), and Tennessee (then part of North Carolina) all hatched plans to create their own states.

Both state governments and nationalists in Congress believed that the Union was in peril. Yet it was difficult to reach a compromise among the competing interests. States wanted Congress to recognize their western claims, whereas states without any claims wanted all of the western lands to be turned over to Congress. Also at issue was which speculators' claims would be upheld, as speculators with dubious claims to the land were selling them to settlers at bargain prices.

The Northwest Ordinance, ratified by Congress on July 13, 1787, was a compromise among these competing interests. Finally realizing that they could not manage vast areas of territory, the large states yielded their claims to Congress. Because Congress validated the claims only of respectable speculators, it made losers not only out of unscrupulous ones but also out of anyone who had bought land from them at cheap prices.

The Northwest Ordinance set out a model of government for the western territories that reflected the liberal political philosophy of nationalists in Congress and established a

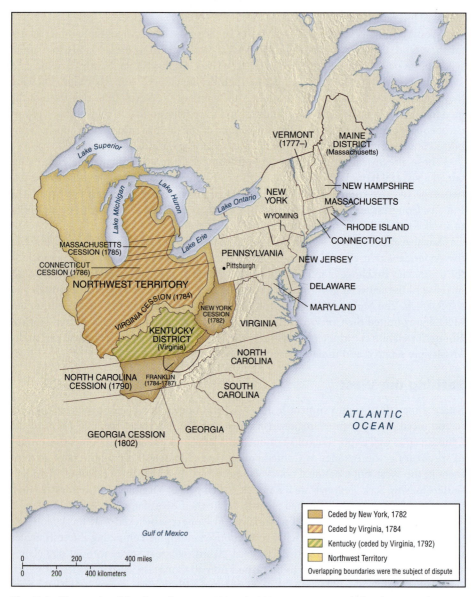

Map 7–4 Western Land Cessions Between 1782 and 1802, eastern states ceded to the national government the territory they claimed in the west. Under the principle established by the Northwest Ordinance, new states were carved out of this territory. Never before had a nation developed such a procedure for bringing in new regions not as colonies but as fully equal states.

process for the admission of new states into the nation. Rejecting Britain's colonial model of expansion, it declared that territories would be eligible to apply for statehood once they had 60,000 free inhabitants. There were other important breaks with the past. Slavery was forbidden north of the Ohio River, the first time that a line was drawn barring slaves from a particular region. Trial by jury and habeas corpus were guaranteed, as well as the right to bail and freedom of religion. Cruel and unusual punishments were barred. These were important principles that, except for the provision excluding slavery, would all appear again in the Constitution and Bill of Rights.

The Northwest Ordinance was designed to create an orderly world of middle-class farmers who obeyed the law, paid their debts, worshiped as they pleased, and were protected from despotic government and the unruly poor. The ordinance represented the triumph of the moderate Revolutionaries' vision of government.

Creating a New National Government

At the beginning of the Revolution, radicals and moderates had worked together to accomplish common goals. The years of war, however, slowly pulled radicals and moderates apart. Many moderates, particularly those who served in Congress or as officers in the Continental army, became nationalists. They worked with men from other states on national projects and came to think of the states as a threat to the success of the Revolution. Many of the radicals, meanwhile, retained a local, republican perspective. They dreaded a centralized government and feared that the Continental army would become a standing army that might take away their liberties.

This split between moderate nationalists and radical localists culminated in the battle over the Constitution, written by the nationalists to create a stronger central government and resisted by the localists, afraid it would subvert liberty. Almost all the problems that led the nationalists to wish for a stronger national government concerned the economy: paying the war debt, paying the soldiers, and improving commerce. The nationalists were deeply involved in the market economy as merchants, financiers, farmers, and planters. The localists, as a rule, were much less involved in the market and suspicious of those who were. As long as taxes were low and their creditors did not harass them, they were satisfied. The Articles of Confederation provided them all the national government and economy they needed.

A Crippled Congress

Nationalists in Congress soon realized that the national government was powerless to address the most pressing economic questions. By 1779, after printing $200 million in paper money that was dropping in value by the day, Congress had shut down its printing presses. It then gave the states the responsibility to provision the army. As legislatures dithered, the unclothed, unfed, and unpaid army threatened mutiny. Congress gave up trying to pay its war debt and passed that back to the states as well. Some states refused. States such as Massachusetts that raised taxes to pay off their portion courted armed upheavals such as Shays's Rebellion.

Congress was powerless to alleviate the economic distress. At the end of the war, British goods flooded in again to meet a consumer demand that seemed insatiable. However, there was no comparable British demand for American exports; in fact, Britain closed its ports to American trade. America could not close its ports to British ships, because the Articles of Confederation denied Congress the authority to regulate commerce. Additional foreign loans were out of the question. Congress could not pay back those it had already taken out. Even western policy, Congress's greatest triumph, presented problems. Once the states had ceded western territory to Congress (leading to the Northwest Ordinance), Congress discovered that it takes an army and a great deal of money to police a territory inhabited by Indians and coveted by land-hungry settlers. Congress lacked that money and could not pay the army it had.

Nationalist attempts to strengthen Congress failed, however, lacking the approval of the states. By the middle of the 1780s, several nationalists abandoned that reform in favor of a new and stronger form of government. James Madison and other nationalists began talking about calling a constitutional convention. But the challenge they faced was how to effect changes that the states did not seem to want.

The road to the Constitutional Convention in Philadelphia in 1787 ran through two earlier meetings. First, in 1785, at Madison's suggestion, commissioners from Virginia and Maryland met at George Washington's home, Mount Vernon, to resolve disputes about navigating the Potomac River. Madison suggested a further meeting of representatives from all the states in Annapolis, Maryland, to build on the accomplishments from Mount Vernon. When only 12 men from five states arrived, they called for another meeting, in Philadelphia, nine months later. In those nine months, Shays's Rebellion and the stalemate in Congress persuaded nationalists to consider strengthening the government. Over the summer of 1787, 55 men from twelve states met in Philadelphia to write one of the most influential documents in the history of the world.

Writing a New Constitution

The men assembled in Philadelphia were primarily moderate nationalists. Committed to the goals of the Revolution, they sought, in Madison's words, "republican remedies" for the problems of republican government. The 55 delegates met for almost four months during the summer of 1787, finally ratifying the Constitution on September 17. They deliberated in secret, in order to talk freely and achieve compromises.

Although there were sharp differences of opinion, there were also wide areas of agreement. Most of the delegates had considerable experience in state and national government. George Washington, a member of Virginia's delegation, was the most widely respected man in the nation. He was elected the presiding officer of the convention.

The delegates were young, with most in their 30s and 40s. No one was more important to the convention than James Madison, just 36. He came with a design for the new government already worked out. Known as the Virginia Plan, it became the outline for the Constitution.

The Virginia Plan was a blueprint for substantial change: a strong central government divided into three branches, executive, legislative (itself with two branches), and judicial, that would check and balance one another; a system of federalism that guaranteed every state a republican government; and proposals for admitting new states and amending the Constitution. The only alternative, the New Jersey Plan, was offered on June 15 and quickly rejected. It proposed a single-house legislature, with all states having an equal vote, and a plural executive, chosen by the legislature (see Table 7–1).

Table 7-1 Key Provisions of the Articles of Confederation, the Virginia Plan, the New Jersey Plan, and the Constitution

	Articles of Confederation	Virginia Plan	New Jersey Plan	Constitution
Executive	None	Chosen by Congress	Plural; chosen by Congress	President chosen by electoral college
Congress	One house; one vote per state	Two houses	One house	Two houses
Judiciary	None	Yes	Yes	Yes
Federalism	Limited; each state retains full sovereignty	Yes; Congress can veto state laws	Yes; acts of Congress the "supreme law of the states"	Yes; Constitution the "supreme law of the land"; states guaranteed a republican form of government; Supreme Court to adjudicate disputes between states
Powers of Congress	Conduct diplomacy and wage war; cannot levy taxes or raise army	All powers of Articles of Confederation, plus power to make laws for nation	All powers of Articles of Confederation, plus power to regulate commerce and make states pay taxes	Numerous powers, such as levy taxes, declare war, raise army, regulate commerce, and "make all laws which shall be necessary and proper" for carrying out those powers

The delegates agreed that the new national government would have to be much stronger: Congress would now have the power to collect taxes and duties, to pay the country's debts, to regulate foreign commerce, and to raise armies and pay for them. Once the delegates compromised on a method for choosing the president (by electors chosen in each state) and the length of his term (four years, eligible for reelection), they readily agreed to grant him considerable power to propose legislation, veto bills of Congress (subject to congressional override), conduct diplomacy, and command the armed forces.

The delegates vested judicial authority in the Supreme Court and inferior federal courts and granted them authority over the state constitutions as well. Although the delegates could agree rather easily on the structure and powers of the new government, they argued bitterly any time the interests of their states seemed in jeopardy. The most difficult issues related to representation: Would the numbers of senators and representatives be based on population or wealth, or would each state have equal numbers? If based on population or wealth, would slaves be counted? Large states generally wanted representation to be based on either population or wealth (they had more of both), whereas northern states did not want slaves to be counted, either as population or as wealth. The conflict between the large and small states was resolved by Roger Sherman's Connecticut (or Great) Compromise: Each state would have an equal number of senators, satisfying the small states. The number of representatives would be based on either population or wealth, satisfying the large states.

The Connecticut Compromise solved the conflict between small and large states, but only by creating another between slave and free states. The South Carolinians were adamant: whether slavery was called population or wealth, the institution must be protected. The argument was fierce, with several delegates threatening to walk out. Finally, the convention compromised. Representation in the House would be based on the entire free population (including women and children, but not Indians) plus three-fifths of the slaves, thus increasing the South's representation. The delegates recognized that the Three-Fifths Compromise was fundamentally illogical, but its acceptance was needed to make the Connecticut Compromise possible.

The Three-Fifths Compromise, or Clause, became the most notorious provision in the Constitution. Although the delegates were careful not to use the word "slave" (instead using bland phrases such as "other persons"), clearly they were establishing a racial line. The convention made two other concessions to slavery. First, it agreed, over Madison's vehement protest, that Congress could not ban the slave trade until 1808 at the earliest. In addition, the Constitution included a fugitive slave clause, which required states to return runaway slaves. The reopening of the slave trade did more to strengthen slavery than the other compromises on slavery. Madison predicted accurately that "twenty years will produce all the mischief that can be apprehended from the liberty to import slaves." Between 1788 and 1808, thousands and thousands of Africans were sold into slavery in the United States.

The nationalists were determined not to leave Philadelphia without a constitution, and they were willing to make whatever compromises seemed necessary. Those compromises were eventually achieved, and the convention adjourned on September 17. The delegates' work was not over, however. Now the Constitution had to be ratified.

Ratifying the Constitution: Politics

There was nothing inevitable about the nation, the Constitution, or the particular form either took. The Constitution was the creation of a small group of men who thought nationally, the Federalists. They then had the difficult task of getting the Constitution ratified by a nation that still thought about government in almost wholly local terms. That the Constitution would be ratified was by no means a given.

The Philadelphia Convention decided that the Constitution would go into effect once nine states had ratified it. They could not bind any states that had not ratified, but the nine signatories could go ahead. Small states were the first to ratify, because they most needed the union. For example, Georgia, the fourth state to ratify, was still in many ways a frontier region, vulnerable to Indian assault, its capital at Augusta an armed camp. The most serious opposition came from the large, powerful states of Massachusetts, New York, and Virginia.

The convention had concluded on September 17, and by December 7, Delaware had already ratified the Constitution. By January 9, 1788, New Jersey, Georgia, and Connecticut followed, with barely any dispute. The Federalists in Pennsylvania forced ratification by using strong-arm tactics. The Federalists in other states learned from these mistakes and more willingly made concessions to the Antifederalists (as the opponents of the Constitution were called).

In Massachusetts, as in Pennsylvania, considerable opposition came from the western part of the state among those sympathetic to Shays's Rebellion. In an inspired move that would be used also in Virginia, the Federalists made certain that the Constitution was debated section by section, enabling them to win point by point. And in another key strategic decision, the Federalists agreed that the convention in Massachusetts should propose amendments, not as a condition for ratification but as part of a package that recommended ratification. This concession, which made the Constitution both stronger and more democratic, was critical in winning ratification.

Only three more states were necessary for the Constitution to go into effect. The Federalists postponed or stalled the debate until the states most favorable to the Constitution had ratified it, as it would go into effect once nine states had ratified it. The Virginia ratifying convention was one of the most dramatic and divided. Patrick Henry, who had refused to attend the Philadelphia Convention, saying that he "smelt a rat," spoke in opposition. His impassioned speeches were rebutted by James Madison's careful and knowledgeable remarks. Having worn down the Antifederalists with logic, the Federalists carried the day, and the Constitution was ratified. The Antifederalists agreed to abide by the result, even though there had been threats of armed rebellion. The decision of Antifederalists to accept the Constitution and to participate in the government it created was one of the most important choices made in this era.

In New York, the Federalists stalled debate until news of Virginia's ratification arrived. Then they posed the inevitable question: Ten states had now voted in favor and the Constitution had been ratified; would New York join in or not? New York did, and eventually the Constitution was ratified by all the states. As a condition for ratification, several states had insisted that the first Congress consider a number of amendments. These amendments became the Bill of Rights.

Ratifying the Constitution: Ideas

The Constitution was the product of many compromises, and it did not precisely fit anyone's previous ideas. As the Federalists explained the benefits of the Constitution to skeptical Americans, and as the Antifederalists tried to explain what they thought was wrong with it, a new understanding of what American government should be evolved. Despite significant disagreements, this new understanding, which incorporated the Bill of Rights, was sufficiently broad that Antifederalists could join the new government.

Nonetheless, the differences between the Federalists and Antifederalists were profound. As a rule, the Antifederalists were more rural and less involved in the market, came from the western or backwoods regions, and were more likely to be veterans of the militia than of the Continental army. The Antifederalists were, above all, old-line republicans who warned of the dangers to liberty of corruption, tyranny, and enslavement, although now they spoke against the Federalists, not the British.

The Antifederalists believed passionately in the local community. They asserted that republics could survive only in homogeneous communities, where all people had the same interests and values. They believed that too much diversity, whether economic, cultural, ethnic, or religious, destroyed a republic. One Massachusetts Antifederalist criticized the Constitution because it would not allow states to stop immigration so as "to keep their blood pure." Although Antifederalists, like Federalists, generally supported freedom of religion, they also favored the spread of Protestantism as a means of ensuring morality.

At the same time, the Antifederalists were committed to individual rights, and it is to them that the nation is indebted for the Bill of Rights. They retained the republican fear of power, and they did not trust the person they could not see. If government were remote, then it would become oppressive, it would deprive the people of their liberties, and it would tax them. One of the most consistent complaints of the Antifederalists was not so much that taxation would be enacted without representation as that it would be enacted at all. If the national government needed money, let it ask the states for it (a system that failed under the Articles of Confederation). The Antifederalists displayed the same fear of centralized government and hatred of taxation that had led to their revolt against Britain. The Antifederalist contribution to American political thought was a continuing critique of government itself.

Federalists shared many of the beliefs of the Antifederalists, such as individual rights. Hence they readily accepted the Antifederalist proposal to list and protect those rights as amendments to the Constitution. They were also suspicious of government, most agreeing with Thomas Paine that "government even in its best state is but a necessary evil." The separation of powers and elaborate series of checks and balances that the Constitution created, as well as the system of federalism itself, reflects this fear. The Federalists divided power; unlike the Antifederalists, they did not deny it.

Their experience in the market economy, as officers in the Continental army and as members of the national government, provided the Federalists with a different perspective on political economy. They had come to believe that all people were motivated by self-interest. Unlike the Antifederalists, the Federalists were willing to accept self-interest and build a government around it.

The Federalists were convinced that no government could rest entirely on the virtue of its people. The challenge was to build a government out of imperfect human materials that would preserve liberty instead of destroying it. In *The Federalist* No. 10 (one of a series of 85 essays known as the *Federalist Papers*, written by Madison, Hamilton, and John Jay and published anonymously to influence the ratification debate), Madison explained that the causes of conflict "are sown into the nature of man." The only way of eliminating them would be either by "giving to every citizen the same opinions, the same passions, and the same interests" (the Antifederalist solution) or by destroying liberty itself. But "as long as the reason of man continues fallible, and he is at liberty to exercise it, different opinions will be formed." Toleration was the price of liberty and the necessary result of human imperfection.

In the Philadelphia Convention, the Federalists had been so intent on working out compromises and reconciling competing interests that they did not develop a philosophy to explain the profound changes they were proposing. That philosophy emerged from the ratification debates, in which it was met by the alternative philosophy of the Antifederalists. Both these bodies of thought, sometimes in harmony, sometimes in disagreement, constitute the legacy of the Revolution. This dialogue has continued to frame American government from their day until ours.

Conclusion

In rejecting the increasingly centralized British state, the Revolutionaries were clear about what they did not want. Over the course of the Revolution, they began to envision the kind of society and nation that they hoped to create. It would ensure individual liberty

>> Timeline

▼**1775**

Battles of Lexington and Concord

Fort Ticonderoga seized

Battle of Breed's Hill

Second Continental Congress convenes

Continental army created, with George Washington in charge

Congress adopts "Declaration of the Causes and Necessities of Taking Up Arms"

George III declares colonists in rebellion

Governor Dunmore offers freedom to Virginia slaves who fight for the British

Continental army attacks Canada

▼**1776**

Thomas Paine writes *Common Sense*

Declaration of Independence

Articles of Confederation drafted

British capture Manhattan

Washington captures Trenton and Princeton

New Jersey Constitution allows unmarried, property-owning women to vote

Washington captures Princeton

▼**1777**

British capture Philadelphia

American victory at Saratoga

▼**1778**

French enter into treaty with United States

British conquer Georgia

Sullivan expedition into New York and Pennsylvania

▼**1779**

Continental troops winter at Jockey Hollow

▼**1780**

British conquer South Carolina

▼**1781**

Articles of Confederation ratified

Battle of Guilford Court House

Cornwallis surrenders

▼**1782**

Franklin begins peace discussions with British

continued

>> Timeline *continued*

▼**1783**
Newburgh Conspiracy
Treaty of Paris

▼**1785**
Land Ordinance of 1785
Virginia and Maryland commissioners meet at Mount Vernon

▼**1786–1787**
Shays's Rebellion
Meeting at Annapolis

▼**1787**
Northwest Ordinance
Constitutional Convention

▼**1787–1788**
Federalist Papers published
Constitution ratified

▼**1789**
George Washington inaugurated

▼**1791**
Bill of Rights ratified

---

and economic opportunity. But this was a vague vision for the future. As the first modern nation created by revolution, the United States was entering uncharted territory. Winning independence from the world's most powerful nation, ratifying the federal Constitution, and planning for the admission of new territories into the federal union were all extraordinary accomplishments, unique in world history.

Yet there were many problems left unresolved. Not only was Britain still occupying forts in the Northwest Territory, but also the European nations were skeptical that the new nation would survive. Although the United States had more than doubled its size, much of the new territory could not be settled because it was inhabited by Indians who refused to recognize America's sovereignty. There were also disagreements among Americans themselves, particularly about the meaning of democracy. How could a nation founded on the principle of liberty practice slavery? How would individual rights be reconciled with the general welfare? Whose economic interests would be served? The American people had begun a great experiment whose outcome was far from assured.

Review Questions

1. Why was Revolutionary ardor highest at the beginning of the war?

2. What were American and British strategies for winning the war? What were the chief challenges the Americans faced in mounting the war, and how did they affect military strategy? What were the constraints on the British in waging a war on American soil?

3. What was the effect of the war on American society? How did Americans respond to the challenge presented by their doctrine of equality?

4. Which Americans believed a stronger central government was needed, and why? What were the compromises they made in writing the Constitution?

5. Describe the political philosophies of the Federalists and Antifederalists.

For further review materials and resource information, please visit www.oup.com/us/ofthepeople

8

Contested Republic
1789–1800

>> William Maclay Goes to the Senate

Pennsylvanian William Maclay had supported the ratification of the Constitution, and when the new federal government was launched, he was easily elected as the first senator from his state. But almost from the beginning of his brief service (he drew the initial short term as the Senate staggered its election cycles), Maclay's optimism about the new government began to fade. He recorded that disillusionment in a diary he kept until he left the Senate on March 3, 1791.

Some of Maclay's discontent arose from his own temperament. He had no tolerance for the inefficiency that came with setting up a government. He was impatient with long discussions over the proper wording of the enacting clause of legislation: should it read *be it enacted by the Senate and Representatives*, or simply *be it enacted by the Congress*? He was exasperated when the Senate suspended its other business while the two houses of the legislature set a protocol for communicating with one another.

But many of Maclay's irritations with the Senate also suggested basic disagreements over the nature of a republican government. For example, there were biases of region. Although Maclay had stature at home in central Pennsylvania (a wealthy landowner, he had served as a state legislator, a judge, and a member of Pennsylvania's executive council), many of his colleagues considered him a country bumpkin. They ignored him in debate and made him the brunt of demeaning pranks. Maclay nursed his wounded pride in his diary, in which he showed his own prejudices: easterners were power hungry, New Englanders were "insolent," and Virginians were panderers, especially to the new president.

Maclay also recorded what he saw as an alarming aristocratic bent in the new administration. He thought Washington's inaugural address was pretentious. It was a small irritation, but only 10 days later Vice President John Adams proposed calling the president "His Highness the President of the United States of America and Protector of the rights of the same"—a preposterous title for the executive of a republic, Maclay thought.

>> **AMERICAN PORTRAIT** *continued*

Maclay soon found more serious signs of antirepublicanism. He was convinced that the executive was trying to encroach on legislative authority. He thought the Judiciary Act of 1789 gave too much power to the courts. He was appalled by Treasury Secretary Alexander Hamilton's suggestion that the old depreciated Continental currency be redeemed at full face value, a trick to line the purses of speculators, he thought. And he viewed the national bank (proposed by Hamilton in 1790) as "an aristocratic engine . . . operating like a tax in favor of the rich."

On February 12, 1791, two weeks before Maclay left Congress, the Senate passed a bill leveling an excise tax on certain internal manufactures, including distilled spirits. One of Maclay's colleagues exulted that "we have a Revenue that will support Government." Maclay responded grimly: "I told him perhaps we might undo all. That the high demands we had made, would raise Opposition and That Opposition might endanger the Government."

His worries were well founded. The following July a group of Maclay's fellow Pennsylvanians met to petition for relief from the tax, which fell especially hard on western Pennsylvania distilleries. Their protest was peaceful, but the tax eventually sparked an armed confrontation between citizens and the new federal government. Before it was over, 30,000 troops had marched into western Pennsylvania against the Republic's own citizens, and national politics had dissolved into a battleground of warring parties.

Common Threads

>> What were the continuing disagreements about the power of a central government?

>> What were the conflicting values and ideas of citizenship?

>> How did the new nation negotiate with the European powers?

>> What was the status of slavery in the early republic?

The United States in 1789

William Maclay was not alone in his reservations about the new federal government. During the 1790s, differences in style and philosophy would give rise to such fierce disagreements and violent party divisions that, by the end of the century, some politicians wanted to repudiate the original federal compact. The Constitution had been ratified, but the process of ratification had revealed differences as well as shared assumptions. In 1789, the forces toward union and the forces toward fragmentation remained in a powerful tension.

Lands and People

The United States of America had come into formal existence as a republic with the Articles of Confederation in 1781, and its existence had been recognized in the Paris Peace Treaty with Britain in 1783 and again in the ratification of the federal constitution. Still, much remained unclear, unfinished, and highly contested when George Washington took office in 1789.

On the simplest level, the new republic lacked even clear external borders. Although the Treaty of Paris seemed to describe a very specific territory being ceded from Britain to the United States, things were much less clear on the ground. For example, the treaty prescribed a boundary beginning "from the northwest angle of Nova Scotia, viz., that angle which is formed by a line drawn due north from the source of St. Croix River to the high-

Map 8–1 Western Expansion, 1785–1805 Between the Treaty of Paris (1783) and the Louisiana Purchase (1803), Americans flooded into the territories that lay between the Appalachians and the Mississippi River. Then (as later) migration often followed rivers and valleys into the interior of the continent.

lands; along the said highlands which divide those rivers that empty themselves into the river St. Lawrence, from those which fall into the Atlantic Ocean, to the northwesternmost head of Connecticut River; thence down along the middle of that river to the forty-fifth degree of north latitude . . ." across the Great Lakes, down the Mississippi River, and across the border of New Spain to the Atlantic. But what exact spot marked "the source of the St. Croix River"? Where was the "middle" of the Connecticut River? These were not abstract problems: Britain and the United States would argue for years over present-day Maine, and Spain claimed a sizable chunk of present-day Mississippi and Alabama.

European empires were not the only ones challenging the territorial integrity of the new nation. There were also a hundred thousand or so Native Americans who lived *within* the boundaries of the republic, many of them crisscrossing large expanses of hunting and growing grounds in seasonal migrations. The United States had acknowledged the sovereignty of Indian nations in eight treaties before the ratification of the Constitution and again in Article I of the Constitution, granting Congress the power "to regulate commerce with . . . the Indian tribes." But the But the Native Americans rejected both European American ideas of fixed borders and the specific borders delineated in the Treaty of Paris. Most of the "United States of America" was still Indian land to them—the land of the Shawnee, for example, or of the people of the longhouses or of the turtle people. Even the states of the new nation disagreed on the division of lands within its borders. Many of the original boundary conflicts had been settled in the 1780s, but Virginia, Georgia, and North Carolina still claimed lands running to the Mississippi River (although North Carolina wanted to cede the land to the United States). Massachusetts, New Hampshire, and New York still fought over present-day Maine.

The new nation also lacked a clear cultural or ethnic identity. Most of the population was of European descent and most claimed English heritage. But almost half of the white population was of Scottish, Scotch-Irish, Irish, German, Dutch, Swedish, Welsh, or French descent. In Pennsylvania, the English were a minority, their numbers rivaled by the Germans, and they were a bare majority in New York. Being "European" did not necessarily give the white population common cause or even a common language. The Irish, Welsh, and Scots bore old animosities toward the English. England and France had just ended a prolonged war with each other (the fourth in a century), much of it fought in North America.

 Table 8-1 Americans in 1790

Population 1790: 3,929,000					
Northeast		**Northcentral**		**South**	
Whites	1,901,000	Whites	50,000	Whites	1,271,000
African Americans	67,000	African Americans	1,000	African Americans	690,000
Urban	160,000	Urban	0	Urban	42,000
Rural	1,807,000	Rural	51,000	Rural	1,919,000

Free African Americans	58,000
African American slaves	700,000

Religion also separated Americans as much as it united them. The English, Welsh, Dutch, Swedish, and many Germans were Protestant—but not the same *sort* of Protestants—whereas the Irish and most of the French were Catholic, at a time when Protestant-Catholic differences were cause for European wars. Many of these differences, submerged in the Revolutionary War, reemerged with independence.

Roughly 18 percent of the total population of 3.9 million consisted of enslaved Africans, African Americans, and Afro-Caribbeans (sometimes with mixed European or Native American heritage)—people or the descendants of people brought to the United States under coercion from hundreds of different cultures. In large areas of Virginia and South Carolina, slaves made up at least half of the population. Although slavery was embedded in the mid-Atlantic or southern states, it was not a wholly southern institution. In 1789 northerners still owned more than 30,000 slaves. New York City had the second highest number of enslaved people of any city, after Charleston, South Carolina. Northern merchants were active in the overseas slave trade, and countless shippers, merchants, and artisans in the North relied on business ties to the South. Some Americans spoke out

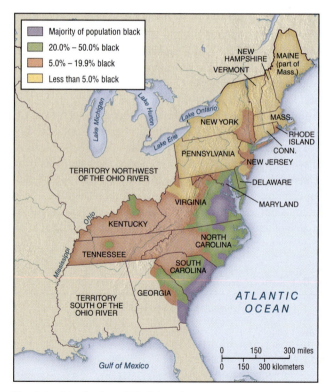

Map 8–2 Distribution of Black Population, 1775 At the founding of the nation, the overwhelming majority of African Americans lived in the South and were enslaved. In parts of the south Atlantic states, African Americans had long outnumbered whites. (Future states here are identified in parentheses.) *Lester J. Cappon et al., eds.* Atlas of Early American History: The Revolutionary Era, 1760–1790 *(Princeton, NJ: Princeton University Press).*

against the institution after the Revolution, but the Constitution implicitly recognized slavery as a part of the republic in the Three-Fifths Compromise and explicitly protected the institution for at least 20 years.

Ways of Living

The United States was overwhelmingly a rural nation. Ninety-seven percent of its almost 4 million people enumerated in the first census lived in the countryside, most of them on family farms of 50–100 acres. These farming families combined self-sufficiency with barter and trade, each family living, as one New Englander recalled, "as much as possible within itself." Men and boys grew grain for meal and flour; women and girls put in a family garden for vegetables, tended orchards for fruit, and kept chickens, a cow, or a pig for milk and meat.

And yet almost no families were entirely self-reliant. Rural households were tied to villages, in which they bought, sold, and bartered with small shopkeepers and independent craftspeople for what they could not produce. Even though the Goodrich family of Connecticut grew much of their own food and made their "own bread . . . soap, candles, butter, cheese, [and] cloth," they also traded in a general store and hired the services of a butcher, a shoemaker, a carpenter, a seamstress, and a spinner. Some households combined farming and craftwork: a farm woman might also serve as midwife or do specialized sewing for wages; a man might work as a blacksmith or mason when not tending his fields.

Not everyone who was technically free owned property. Perhaps as many as one-third of nonenslaved rural Americans were indentured servants or farm laborers, paid

A Farmer Plowing His Field Near the Moravian Settlement of Salem, North Carolina In 1789, most Americans lived in the countryside and considered farming the activity most likely to produce political virtue in the new republic. As this illustration suggests, by "farming," Americans meant not simple subsistence but a division of the land into cultivated, privately owned (and at least partly commercial) property.

(often seasonally) in wages and housing. Others, former servants or hired laborers who claimed a piece of land simply by their labor, became squatters.

For white settlers, constant outdoor hard work through the growing season was punctuated by indoor tedium in the coldest months. Most families seldom saw friends or government officials. Settlers traveled only rarely to the town centers where elections were held. Their typical encounters with government were run-ins with surveyors (and the sheriffs who protected them), appearances in local courts over boundary disputes, or petitions complaining that government had not done enough to drive off Native Americans. In New England, the cash-poor economy ran on paper debts, which merchants often sued poor farmers to collect. Adult men were liable for militia service, but their participation depended on needs at home, the prestige of the militia leader, and the aims of the call-up. Some—squatters, for example—avoided contact with the law altogether.

This isolation stood in stark contrast to the crowding of everyday family life. Most families lived in houses with only a couple of rooms. Women cooked in dangerous walk-in hearth fireplaces in the same small, drafty, earthen-floored rooms where their husbands repaired bridles, their daughters mended clothing or kneaded bread, and their youngest children learned their letters.

The roughly 5 percent of the free population living in port cities led very different lives. At one extreme were the few very wealthy: southern planter families, northern landed proprietors who kept city houses, and large merchants. These groups lived in big houses with imported furnishings and many servants. Most very wealthy Americans—and certainly the merchants—identified more strongly with their European counterparts than with their compatriots, many of whom they looked down on.

Below them was the large but amorphous "middling" group—householders who earned a relatively secure livelihood from a combination of household production (perhaps a small garden and a few chickens or pigs) and the income of a profession, craft, or small shop. Many did not own their own homes, and many lived in small, crowded dwellings where household labor and paid labor intermingled with family life. The poor made up the biggest segment of urban life, although this group, too, defied easy categorization. These men, women, and children made their livings as indentured or hired servants, as apprentices and shop helpers, as day laborers or piecework seamstresses, or in the make-shift occupations of the streets—selling food or salvaged coal, for example, or begging. Indentured and hired servants, apprentices, and journey craft workers sometimes lived with their masters and employers. But that older model of paternalism was giving way to the system of wage payment. Poor families were often packed into a single rented room or lived in crude hovels or in the nooks and crannies of alleys.

Most of the small but growing free black population was poor. In 1790, after the war and postwar emancipations, the community of free black Americans remained small—perhaps 60,000 at most, split between the northern and the southern states. Even in New England, enslaved African Americans outnumbered free African Americans. Lacking the money to buy land, most free blacks lived in port cities, working in domestic service, the trades, or day labor, or in small enterprises that required little capital, such as running a grocery out of their homes, cleaning chimneys, or selling soup in the streets. Free property-owning African American males enjoyed the right to vote in many northern and even some southern states in the first years of the republic, but few black men had sufficient property to exercise that right.

Second Street, Philadelphia As the view of this busy street scene in Philadelphia shows, social, commercial, political, and religious—"public" and "private"—life all commingled on the streets of the early republic's cities.

Most enslaved Americans lived in the South and most did agricultural labor on the lands of their white owners. But slaves also worked farmland in New Jersey, New York, and New England. The largest holdings—for example, the rice plantations of Georgia—ranged up to thousands of acres worked by several hundred slaves. But smaller white farmers often owned or rented the services of a slave—commonly in the South but also in New Jersey, Delaware, New York, and New England. Not all slaves worked in the fields. Some, like Jupiter Hammon of Long Island, New York, worked as a clerk in his owner's business and traveled to New York City. Others worked at crafts or as servants. Their lives had not been much improved by the Revolution, and in important ways they were far worse off. In southern states, fear of slave rebellion had resulted in tighter controls and harsher treatment during the war. State legislatures also made it more difficult for owners to emancipate slaves, and owners often emancipated only those who were old and deemed of little economic value.

Native Americans were still common sights even in more settled European American areas—showing up at farmers' homes or village stores to swap goods or beg food. Farther inland Native Americans more visibly claimed the landscape of the new republic, either in migrations to and from hunting and growing grounds or in settled communities that served French, Spanish, and American traders. The town of Kekionga ("Miami Town") illustrated the vibrancy of Indian economies in the late eighteenth century. Kekionga was strategically located east of Lake Erie on the Maumee and Wabash Rivers, near a British fort.

Maumee River Indian Towns This 1790 drawing suggests the complex economic arrangement of the Maumee River Indian towns and the diverse groups that occupied the towns.

The village was surrounded by huge cornfields and vegetable gardens, supported large herds of cattle, and accommodated guests of all backgrounds. Residents and visitors bargained for furs, tools, quills, beads, animals, food, and services.

Native Americans lived under systems of governance less centralized than those of the new government of the United States. Most Indian communities selected their leaders through consensus rather than formal balloting. Councils met as needed, and policy was implemented through the personal authority of leaders and the consent of their followers. Over the years, Native Americans had shared land and resources, reconciled differences, sustained elaborate trade relations, and supported powerful confederacies. Where native people differed from Americans of European descent was in their definition of an enlightened way of life. Eastern Woodland and Great Lakes Indians did not share European American views on the importance of privately owned property. Few Indian societies valued material accumulation for its own sake. Instead, they encouraged gift giving as a mark of rank. White American society seemed to native people to be driven by an "insatiable avarice" that clouded the heart and distorted the mind.

In so diverse a country, its people spread across hundreds of thousands of square miles, divided by mountain ranges and rivers, by languages and cultures, by long-established enmities, and by slavery, where was the glue to make a nation?

The First Emancipation Movements

Although slavery had existed in America for over 150 years by the time of ratification of the Constitution, its existence in the new republic was not a foregone conclusion. By 1789, many European nations were beginning to reconsider their involvement in the slave

AMERICAN LANDSCAPE

>> Philadelphia

Serving as the nation's capital in the 1790s, Philadelphia was the city where the new doctrines of freedom were given shape, in the new Congress Hall just west of Independence Hall, in humble homes, and in the president's mansion.

Philadelphia was America's biggest city and growing bigger by the day. Between 1780 and 1790, the population grew by more than 50 percent, to 42,520. After the Revolution, European immigrants began to arrive again, and people from the countryside flocked to the city. This rapid growth led to overcrowding, especially for the laboring class. Poor people were renters, living in rooming houses or back alleys, typically in overcrowded wooden buildings. Tailor William Smith and his wife shared their tiny home—550 square feet—with their three children and two boarders. Mrs. Smith cooked their meals in her fireplace.

The financier Robert Morris offered George Washington and his family the use of his home on Market Street. By the standards of the day, it was a mansion, two-thirds the size of the White House, which would be built several years later. Even with at least six bedrooms and four servants' rooms, a detached two-story kitchen, an ice house, a bath house, and a stable for twelve horses, it was not large enough for Washington's household. Washington added a two-story bow and rooms for his servants. When the Washingtons took up residence in November, they had with them about thirty people, not only the president and his wife Martha but also her grandchildren, his secretary and the secretary's wife, three more male secretaries, eight African slaves, and about fifteen white servants.

Philadelphia was also home to about 1,600 African Americans, two-thirds of whom were free and who created the nation's first significant free black community. James Oronoko Dexter, one of the leaders of that community, lived only a few blocks from Independence Hall, on the north side of Fifth Street, between Arch and Race, then on the edge of the city. This was a densely populated neighborhood filled with frame-and-brick homes and workshops of artisans, laborers, and merchants.. Dexter's two-story house, which he shared with his wife and family, was described in 1791 as "very plain." Dexter's wife Sarah worked as a washerwoman.

The center of the free black community was only two blocks from the president's house, and it was to that community that Oney Judge, Martha Washington's young chambermaid, turned when she wanted to make her escape from slavery. When Washington's term was ending, and the slaves were told that they would all soon return to Virginia, Judge decided to liberate herself. "Whilst they were packing up to go to Virginia," she later explained, "I was packing to go, I didn't know where; for I knew that if I went back to Virginia, I should never get my liberty. I had friends among the colored people of Philadelphia, had my things carried there beforehand, and left Washington's house while they were eating dinner."

continued

AMERICAN LANDSCAPE *continued*

Her friends put her on a boat bound for Portsmouth, New Hampshire, where, however, it was her bad luck to run into the daughter of the Washingtons' good friend, Senator John Langdon. *"Oney!"* she called out. "Where in the world have you come from?" The young woman could not understand why anyone would run away "from such an excellent place." "Yes—I know," Oney Judge replied. "But I wanted to be free, misses; wanted to learn to read and write."

Told his slave was in Portsmouth—where slavery was still legal, although unpopular—Washington asked a government official to send Judge back. The official did not see how he could do it "without exciting a riot or mob," and so Judge remained in New Hampshire. Several years later, however, one of Martha Washington's nephews turned up at Judge's house, where she told him, "I am free now and choose to remain so." When the nephew told Senator Langdon that he planned to seize Judge by force, the senator passed word to Judge so that she could go into hiding.

As the gospel of liberty spread through the new nation, slaves such as Oney Judge seized their own freedom, and along the way they had help from free blacks and whites both, expanding the landscape of American freedom.

trade. Even England, which led all other nations in slave trafficking by the late eighteenth century, outlawed slavery within its borders and by 1783 had begun what would become a 50-year-long drive to abolish both the English slave trade and the ownership of slaves by English subjects abroad (including in the British colonies). Although Napoleon would later resurrect slavery in the French colonies, in 1794 revolutionary France abolished slavery in the nation and all of its colonies.

Such moves might have been possible in the United States. Whether prepared to embrace a racially mixed society or not, many white Americans considered slavery an immoral and antirepublican institution. Many Christian denominations (notably including Quakers, Baptists, and Methodists) spoke out against it. None of the first state constitutions specifically recognized slavery, and many central and northern states took steps to outlaw it, either directly in their new state constitutions or in subsequent state supreme court decisions interpreting those constitutions. Vermont, Massachusetts, and New Hampshire enacted state constitutions with broad declarations of rights, although it took a series of court decisions in Massachusetts to apply that declaration to slavery. Pennsylvania had been home to an active abolition movement since at least 1775, when Anthony Benezet organized the Society for the Relief of Free Negroes Unlawfully Held in Bondage. African Americans were important abolitionist voices. In his 1786 *Address to the Negroes of the State of New York*, Jupiter Hammon, a slave on Long Island and the first published African American author, called on slaves to obey their masters, refrain from stealing, and cultivate humility. But he also noted that slaves would be welcomed in heaven (where "we shall find nobody to reproach us for being black, or for being slaves") and advocated gradual emancipation. As Phillis Wheatley (1753–1784), the first published African American poet, wrote in "On Being Brought from Africa to America," the subject of salvation spoke to the subject of slavery: "Some view our sable race with scornful eye, / 'Their colour is a diabolic die.'/ Remember, Christians, Negros, black as Cain, / May be refin'd, and join th' angelic train."

Although the process of emancipation in the North was sometimes slow and often contested, the first steps toward the elimination of slavery had been taken. By 1804, every state north of Delaware had placed slavery on the road to extinction. In the South, no state constitution specifically recognized slavery in 1789, and no southern politicians rose publicly as proslavery leaders—but there was no strong abolitionist organization, either. With slavery on the path to extinction in the North while persisting in the South, the distinctions between North and South became more pronounced.

Conflicting Visions of Republican Society

Agreeing on a structure for the new republic had not been easy. It had taken free Americans thirteen years to frame their government: a year to propose the Articles of Confederation, four years to pass them, seven more to fight over them and devise an alternative (the federal Constitution), and two years to ratify it. Even then, many Americans still opposed ratification, and two states (North Carolina and Rhode Island) had not yet ratified the Constitution when George Washington was sworn into office. Moreover, as William Maclay's experience in the first senate showed, supporters of the constitution did not necessarily agree on its meanings or on the principles of a republican society.

Still, there was a common ground of beliefs for many white inhabitants of the new republic. Most free Americans thought the success of the republic depended on the character of its citizens, by which they meant the traits that would enable citizens to protect themselves against either would-be tyrants or lawless mobs. For many these traits included industriousness, independence, and an ability to put self-interest aside for the larger good. Very often, these qualities were associated with certain types of economic life. When people grew too wealthy and used to luxury, many believed, they grew lazy and were willing to support corrupt governments for their own selfish purposes. Poverty, on the other hand, led to desperation, riots, and anarchy.

This consensus obscured real disagreements about the nature of a republic and about who really embodied its key virtues. In 1790, 97 percent of free Americans lived in nuclear households (parents and children) on farms or in rural villages, where they produced much of their own food, clothes, tools, and furnishings. For this great mass of the people, republican virtue was rooted in the land, and particularly in the working freehold farm. In *Letters from an American Farmer* (1782), J. Hector St. John de Crevecoeur had identified the new nation as "a people of cultivators scattered over an immense territory . . . animated with the spirit of an industry that is unfettered and unrestrained, because each person works for himself." Thomas Jefferson echoed this view in his *Notes on the State of Virginia* (1785). He thought that only the independent farmer could achieve true self-reliance, warning that "dependence begets subservience and venality, [and] suffocates the germ of virtue."

This emphasis on labor and the private ownership of land did not mean that rural Americans opposed manufacturing and trade. Farms were tied to villages that were tied

>> Transatlantic Talk About the Rights of Women

Abigail Adams's famous 1776 request to her husband, John Adams—that "in the new Code of Laws which I suppose it will be necessary for you to make I desire you would Remember the Ladies, and be more generous and favourable to them than your ancestors"—was not unique in the Atlantic world. Throughout much of Europe and in the new United States, the democratic revolutions of the eighteenth century provoked debate on the social status and political rights of women.

In France, in 1791, Olympe de Gouges, a butcher's daughter, published a "Declaration of the Rights of Woman and Female Citizen," a rebuttal of the omission of women from the revolutionary French manifesto, "Declaration of the Rights of Man." So far, de Gouge complained, the French Revolution had yielded women only "a more pronounced scorn, a more marked disdain." In a point-by-point rewriting of the earlier document, which presumably enumerated the claims of all citizens to "liberty, property, security, and resistance to oppression" (but without mentioning women), de Gouges inserted women into the new social and political contract of France. "[T]he only limits on the exercise of the natural rights of woman," she added, "are perpetual male tyranny." De Gouges insisted, "The laws must be the expression of the general will; all female and male citizens must contribute either personally or through their representatives to its formation; it must be the same for all: male and female citizens, being equal in the eyes of the law, must be equally admitted to all honors, positions, and public employment according to their capacity and without other distinctions. . . ."

Although England did not experience an outright revolution in the eighteenth century, there, too, agitation for political reform stirred debate on the proper role of women in democratic governments. In 1790, historian Catherine Macaulay published her *Letters on Education*, arguing that with the proper education women should be capable of competing equally with men in all aspects of social life. Two years later, in 1792, educator and radical journalist Mary Wollstonecraft published *A Vindication of the Rights of Woman*. Wollstonecraft agreed that women as a group tended to be vain and seemed to lack the reasoning ability required of citizens. But these deficiencies were artificial, she argued, the product of "the tyranny of man" in the family, society, and politics that had deliberately kept women in a state of "ignorance and slavish dependence." In fact, she asserted, women were the moral and intellectual equals of men and, if properly educated, were fully as capable as men of reason and of participation in "all political privileges."

These women were connected by historic circumstance: each lived in a society in which turbulent change was undercutting old assumptions that rank and property earned political power (including for a few women) and prompting new questions about whether females could be citizens of new democratic nations. They were also connected, however, by acquaintance and by expanding forms of international contact. Mary Wollstonecraft, who acknowledged a deep influence from Catherine Macaulay, followed closely in letters and newspaper accounts the growing repression in France that led to the execution of de Gouges. Abigail Adams corresponded with Macaulay (who had visited the United States in 1785), and, like many men and women in the United States, eagerly read Wollstonecraft's *Vindication*.

As the revolutionary moment peaked and passed in these countries, it became evident that women's status as citizens would remain ambiguous at best in the new democratic regimes. Various explanations for this failure are possible.

De Gouges died in 1793, a victim of the French Reign of Terror, and Wollstonecraft in 1797, following childbirth. In all three countries, moreover, the exhilaration of the revolutionary era was followed by a period of conservative retrenchment, during which the discussion of women's rights as *citizens* narrowed to a discussion of women's domestic contributions to the public welfare (as wives and mothers) and of their right to an education—a discussion confined, moreover, to white women from the prosperous classes. Nowhere did the call for rights for women become a wide-ranging call for universal rights, regardless of class or race, as well as gender. Meanwhile, in Europe and the United States, white male suffrage steadily expanded, but not until more than 100 years passed did women achieve suffrage in Britain, France, or the United States.

to larger markets in the port cities and overseas. Even Jefferson considered overseas trade essential to rural virtue, because it gave Americans access to manufactured goods without the blight of industrialization. As trade with Britain improved and the demand for American agricultural products grew both in Europe and in the plantation slave colonies of the West Indies, rural Americans agreed that a successful new nation required a booming free international trade.

The profits made by large merchants and landowners were another matter. Many of these wealthy families had begun their fortunes before the Revolution, with the help of the Crown, and they continued to dominate the economy. In Boston, wealthy merchant families made up 10 percent of the population but controlled 65 percent of the wealth, whereas the poorest one-third of the population owned less than 1 percent of the wealth. Great proprietors controlled the land. Both large landowners and merchants tended to support strong governments, which meant higher taxes for common folks.

Farmers, small shopkeepers, landless settlers, and craft workers saw the wealth of large merchant families and families with great landed estates as the moral equivalent of theft. "[N]o person can possess property without laboring," farmer and tavern keeper William Manning emphasized, "unless he get it by force or craft, fraud or fortune, out of the earnings of others." Manning viewed this distinction as "the great dividing line" of society.

Unsurprisingly, merchants and landed proprietors saw matters differently. They agreed that republican virtue resided in labor, but they meant *commercial* labor, which opened markets and expanded trade, nurtured invention, taught discipline, and contributed new wealth to society. Alexander Hamilton, the first secretary of the Treasury, was a chief proponent of this view. Born in the West Indies, he was raised by his mother, Rachel, a shopkeeper, who died when he was 13. Hamilton then entered the merchant firm of Beekman and Cruger as a clerk, becoming so valuable that Cruger paid for his college education. These experiences taught Hamilton that the merchant class (traders, investors, and financiers who took risks to generate new wealth, new markets, and new ideas) best embodied the qualities needed in republican citizens.

Just as farmers viewed merchants and financiers with distrust, so wealthy merchants and proprietors often regarded Americans of the middling and laboring ranks as their inferiors. Most people were undisciplined and gullible, Hamilton believed. Easily deceived by fanatics and demagogues, they required proper leadership. City elites dismissed their backcountry compatriots as "yahoos" and "clodpoles." To the rich, the rude huts of homesteaders, their barefoot children, and their diets of beans, potatoes, and coarse bread all signaled not the hardships of settlement, but rather the laziness of the settlers. The merchants and proprietors especially disliked the casualness with which country people treated debt. Rural people conducted trade in a combination of barter, cash, and promissory notes, with records kept casually and payments constantly renegotiated. Large-scale merchants and proprietors needed timely payment, preferably in hard currency, to pay off their own debts or to make new deals and investments.

Most white Americans denied that hard work produced republican character in slaves. They argued that because slaves could not own the property they produced, slaves' labor could never lead to self-reliance or the stake in the public order essential to citizenship. This view was rife with contradictions. As Thomas Jefferson, himself a slave owner, pointed out in *Notes on the State of Virginia*, slavery undermined the ambition of slave owners. "[I]n a warm climate, no man will labor for himself who can make another labor for him," Jefferson wrote. If slaves were of bad character, simply because of their status as slaves, then surely the institution of slavery was itself unrepublican.

Nevertheless, the unrepublicanism seemed to attach itself to slaves themselves, rather than to the institution. Northern states moved to abolish slavery, but they did so only gradually, often expressing concern about the ability of former slaves to adjust to freedom and democracy. The anonymous author of the antislavery tract *Tyrannical Libertymen: A Discourse on Negro-Slavery in the United States* (1795) argued that during the transition to freedom, younger slaves should be held in "a state of dependence and discipline," after which they should be resettled in the territories. Older slaves should be shipped to Africa. In the northern states, white craftsmen refused to work with free African Americans, white passengers refused to ride in stagecoaches alongside them, and landlords refused to rent them any but the worst housing. Meanwhile, the Naturalization Act of 1790 restricted naturalized citizenship to "free white persons."

Although most Americans believed free white women to be citizens of the nation in a general sense, women labored under severe legal disabilities and restrictive social prejudices. Under the English common-law principle of coverture, a married woman subsumed her separate legal identity under that of her husband. Although some individual women (usually wealthy women with access to special legal measures) did own property in their own names, as a category married women could not own property or wages, could not enter into contracts, and were not the legal guardians of their own children. Most women lost control of their property when they married and took little property other than their own clothing in divorce.

Social prejudice also made it difficult for most women to earn an independent living. Wives and unmarried women continued to ply their skills as midwives, seamstresses, hucksters, grocers, and milliners and in a variety of other trades. But the more lucrative male crafts and professions were closed to them, and most working women struggled to make ends meet.

A growing bias against the idea of female autonomy marked the final years of the eighteenth century. The earlier years of the century were by no means a golden age of female independence, yet age, wealth, and family appear to have mattered as much as gender in delineating individual status. And for a time it seemed that women (at least wealthy white women) might be among the beneficiaries of the Revolutionary spirit. Indeed, New Jersey granted single, property-owning women the right to vote in 1776 (but rescinded it in 1807), and women participated actively in the discussions both of their own new republic and of the French Revolution. In France and in England, women spoke out publicly against restraints on the natural rights of women.

In the wake of the creation of the new republic, however, attitudes toward women grew more conservative. As the *Apollo Magazine* put it in 1795, the exemplary woman married and asked no more than that "Her good man [was] happy and her Infants clean." Ironically, these hardening attitudes may in some ways have resulted from the experiment in democracy itself. In the face of social and political disorder, controlling the conduct of females may have seemed reassuring to some Americans.

The Culture of the Republic

Americans discussed these views, both the agreements and the disagreements, through a variety of practices—written and simply enacted.

Perhaps most important was the circulation of information through newspapers. Although fewer than 20 newspapers were being published in all the British North American colonies in 1760, by 1790 the new republic claimed 106 newspapers, and by 1800 more than 200. Most stories were strictly local, but editors also published official government documents and reprinted articles from other cities, states, and even countries.

The 1790s also saw the beginnings of an American fictional literature. In 1789, William Hill Brown published *The Power of Sympathy*, often considered the first genuinely American novel because some of its content was based on events in Boston. Other novelists also tried to develop distinctly American stories and themes. Actress and author Susannah Rowson's historical novel *Rachel and Reuben* (1798) imagined the lives of the fictional heirs of Columbus, and Charles Brockden Brown chose the countryside near Philadelphia as the setting for *Weiland* (1798), a tale of religious zealotry and the fallibility of human reason. In Connecticut, a group of poets known as the Hartford Wits produced a series of political satires celebrating New England as the model for national order and self-discipline.

News was easiest to come by in the cities, but a variety of information sources linked city to backcountry and region to region. Copies of periodicals and books found their way into the countryside, and comparatively high literacy rates produced a reading audience that went beyond urban elites. In shops, taverns, and homes, those who could not read listened as stories were read aloud. Where papers did not reach, travelers, peddlers, and preachers brought information and opinion.

In cities, prosperous Americans established salons (where local luminaries, male and female, gathered to discuss politics and culture), museums, libraries, and specialized societies of learning. Many of these reflected Americans' keen sense of themselves as involved in an important historical undertaking. The Philadelphia subscription library, founded in 1731 by Benjamin Franklin and others, became the de facto library of the government until 1800, when the capital moved to Washington, and the Library of Congress was founded.

For every occasion that drew American citizens together, however, there seemed to be another that divided them. Especially, strong attachments to place and great disparities of condition often transformed seemingly shared values and ideas into fodder for sharp conflicts.

William Maclay's disorientation when he left central Pennsylvania for New York City reflected the close identification most Americans felt with the places in which they lived, rather than with the nation as a whole. If anything, the process of ratification had underscored just how many differences remained among Americans. Advocates had won approval only by putting together a different coalition of interests in each state, not by drawing on a uniform set of interests across all the states. Even so, a bare nine states had ratified the document, and virtually all of these had made qualifications.

The localism of American society in 1789 was evident in daily life, as well as in formal politics. Never traveling far from home, ordinary Americans knew little about other parts of the country and tended to view them as quite different, becoming more exotic—and frightening—the greater the distance. Writing from Massachusetts to Philadelphia in 1776, Abigail Adams had asked John whether it was true that in Virginia the "gentery" were "Lords" and "the common people vassals." Travelers often described other parts of the nation as if they were foreign countries. The hard economic times of the era also nursed a suspicion of strangers. Describing these differences as an East-West contrast was also common in the early years of the nation. Rural revolts in the Carolinas in the 1760s and Shays's Rebellion in western Massachusetts in 1786–1787 had underscored the differences between backcountry farmers and eastern commercial elites, differences that settlers experienced as conflicts between "the people" and eastern governments. This sense of division and distrust persisted in the 1790s.

These disagreements ran deep and were not confined to formal politics or to polite discussion and debate. Newspapers often revealed sharp local bias in vituperative debates over the proper direction of republican politics. They were accompanied into the public arena by vitriolic political tracts and single-page "broadsides" that attacked individual politicians. Among these was William Manning's 1798 "Key of Liberty," condemning the predations of the "Few" upon the "Many."

Not all of the arguments took place in print. Wealthy city people met in parlors and salons to discuss the concerns of the day, and common Americans held their arguments outside courthouses and churches, on post office porches, at liveries and craft shops, and in taverns like the one run by William Manning. Travelers, peddlers, and preachers were sources of information and opinion.

The early republic was also an era of school building—primarily academies to prepare sons for professions or university training and daughters to participate in the discussions (if not the formal electoral politics) of republican society. More than 350 academies for females opened between 1790 and 1830. The first incorporated publicly was the Young Ladies' Academy of Philadelphia (1787). Intended for daughters of prosperous families, to educate them in "Reading, Writing, Arithmetic, English, Grammar, Composition, and Geography," its curriculum implicitly argued that women could flourish in a challenging academic environment.

Citizens also formed societies intended to provide relief to the needy. A group of prosperous Philadelphians established an almshouse to care for and house the poor (and to teach them the values of industry) and a penitentiary to reform criminals by isolating them from one another. Jewish organizations founded in New York in the late eighteenth century provided aid for the city's small Jewish community.

In a variety of occupational and manufacturing societies, masters and journeymen furthered their common interests, sometimes against what they perceived as the haughtiness of the merchants. Many of the trades of Philadelphia participated in the Federal Procession of 1789, for example—a sign to the elites that craft workers had their own expectations of the new republic. Promoting a different vision, Alexander Hamilton and his assistant secretary, Tench Coxe, formed the Society for Establishing Useful Manufactures in 1791, a joint-stock corporation meant to demonstrate the economic virtues of cooperation between the private sector and the government.

The Struggle to Form a Government

Concerns about the political economy of the new nation focused not only on the character of citizens but also on the character and operation of government. Here, too, questions of property loomed large. In *The Federalist* No. 10, James Madison had argued that the most common cause of internal conflict in a nation was "the various and unequal distribution of property," arising from selfish interests on the state and local level. He thought that an important benefit of the central government would be its capacity "to break and control" provincial interests. Most state ratifying conventions had expressed just the opposite concern: they were worried about self-interests controlling the federal government.

The States and the Bill of Rights

The Federalists had agreed to let the state ratifying conventions propose amendments to the Constitution, possibly to be added as a bill of rights. Two hundred of these had been suggested (see Chapter 7). Some Federalists originally opposed the idea of a bill of rights: if the Constitution did not protect liberty and property, no appended list of rights would help. At first James Madison had agreed, but when he ran for the House of Representatives, he pledged to secure additional safeguards.

Within a month of Washington's inauguration, Madison set about making good on his promise. Not all of the state proposals dealt directly with questions of property. For example, the ratifying conventions were adamant about the need for freedom of religion and freedom of the press, betraying a fear that the federal government would seek to amass power against the interests and freedom of citizens. To prevent this, states proposed amendments to limit the power of Congress to levy taxes and to protect the rights to bear arms, to trial by a jury, and against unreasonable search and seizure.

Madison never expected to incorporate all 200 of the state proposals in a bill of rights, and he never imagined that he could placate all of the groups critical of the Constitution. But he did believe that, with a few minor changes, moderate Antifederalists could support the new order. This goal guided Madison's selection of proposed amendments. He tended to reject proposals that altered the structure of the central government or strengthened the powers of the states at the expense of the federal government. Instead, he favored amendments that affirmed human rights within the structure already ratified (although the reference to a "well-regulated Militia" in the Second Amendment and the Third Amendment's restrictions on the quartering of soldiers reflected Americans' profound mistrust of standing national armies). The First Amendment protected citizens against congressional interference with freedom of religion, speech, the press, the right of assembly, and the right of petition. The Fourth Amendment protected the rights of citizens "against unreasonable [government] searches and seizures." The Fifth, Sixth, Seventh, and Eighth Amendments laid down the rights of citizens accused of crimes and established protection from "cruel and unusual punishments." The Ninth affirmed that the Constitution's silence on a specific right of the people "shall not be construed" as a denial of that right, and the Tenth ambiguously reserved all rights not delegated to the new government "to the States respectively, or to the people."

Congress eventually sent twelve amendments to the states for ratification. Two were rejected: one on Congressional compensation (adopted in 1992 as the Twenty-seventh Amendment) and one covering representation. The remaining ten amendments were declared in force on December 15, 1791.

Congress Begins Its Work

Although George Washington did not take the oath of office until April 30, his term began on March 4, 1789. When he was inaugurated, Congress was already in session. It was not a promising start: only 13 members of the House of Representatives and 8 senators were on hand when the first Congress convened.

Among Congress's first tasks was deciding what the president should be called, the task that had so enraged Maclay. Believing that the president needed an impressive title to demonstrate that the new nation was "civilized," a Senate committee recommended "His Highness the President of the United States of America, and Protector of the Liberties." But the House argued that the suggestion smacked of aristocratic pretension and in the end insisted simply on "the President of the United States."

Meanwhile, the Congress approved official advisors to the president (the cabinet). Washington's first administration reflected both his own close circle of friends and the political clout of the large states. The president was from Virginia, the most populous state, as were his secretary of state, Thomas Jefferson, and his attorney general, Edmund Randolph. For his secretary of the treasury he chose former aide-de-camp Alexander Hamilton of New York. Washington's vice president (John Adams), his secretary of war (Henry Knox), and his postmaster general (Samuel Osgood) were from Massachusetts. The Constitution had specified the existence of a third branch of government, a federal judiciary to have power over "all cases, in law and equity, arising under this Constitution, the laws of the United States, and treaties made," but had not offered much of a blueprint for its structure. Congress might have created a federal system that dominated state courts. Recalling the high-handedness of British courts, however, Congress passed the Judiciary Act of 1789, which created a federal court system with limited power. Under its first chief justice, John Jay, the Supreme Court remained a minor branch of government.

Political Economy and Political Parties

As Congress deliberated the structure of government, Secretary of the Treasury Alexander Hamilton turned to the problem of financial solvency. His fiscal proposals to Congress soon polarized views on the political economy.

The first challenge was to raise money for current expenses. Hamilton proposed that Congress place a tariff on imported goods and the foreign ships carrying them. The Tariff Act of 1789 passed easily. In the coming years the federal government would depend on tariffs for the vast majority of its funds.

Hamilton was also eager to pay off the enormous debt left over from the Revolution. He advised that the federal government should guarantee the payment of all remaining state and national debts incurred in the Revolution. Those debts existed as scrip and paper money the states and Continental Congress had used to purchase goods and services during the war. Hamilton suggested that the national government replace all of these obligations dollar-for-dollar with new federal bonds. To fund the plan, he proposed that the government sell additional bonds, the interest from which could be used only to pay off the interest and principal on the debt.

Madison and Jefferson were alarmed. Most southern states had paid their debts by 1790. Federal assumption would force them to help pay northern debts as well. Southerners were also unhappy about the possibility that the nation's capital (temporarily located in New York) might be moved permanently to Philadelphia. They preferred a site on the Potomac River in Virginia. At last representatives struck a compromise: Hamilton got his

 Table 8-2 Sources of Federal Revenue, 1790–1799

	Tariffs	Internal Taxes	Other (Inc. sale of public lands)
1790–1791	$4,399,000		$ 10,000
1792	3,443,000	$209,000	17,000
1793	4,255,000	338,000	59,000
1794	4,801,000	274,000	356,000
1795	5,588,000	338,000	188,000
1796	6,568,000	475,000	1,334,000
1797	7,550,000	575,000	563,000
1798	7,106,000	644,000	150,000
1799	6,610,000	779,000	157,000

Source: Curtis P. Nettels, *The Emergence of a National Economy, 1775–1815* (White Plains, NY: 1962), p. 221.

debt plan, and southerners got the nation's capital. The following December, Hamilton asked for a series of new taxes, including one on spirits, to generate revenue. This excise tax became law in March 1791.

Hamilton next recommended the creation of a national bank that would ensure a stable currency and enable the government to mobilize capital for development, two activities he considered essential to an expanding commercial economy. The bank would be chartered by Congress to collect, hold, and pay out government receipts; hold the new federal bonds and oversee their payment; and issue currency; and it would be backed up by government bonds.

The bank proposal passed Congress against the opposition of Madison, Jefferson, and other Virginians, who viewed the bank as an extralegal structure to support the interests of merchants and financiers against "the republican interest." Jefferson advised the president to veto the bill on the grounds that the Constitution gave the federal government no expressed authority to create such an institution, a position known as *strict constructionism*. Hamilton countered that every specified power in the Constitution implied "a right to employ all the means requisite . . . to the attainment" of that power. In granting the federal government the responsibility to coin and regulate money, pass and collect taxes, pay debts, and "make all laws which shall be necessary and proper" to these ends, the Constitution implied the power to create a bank. Washington accepted Hamilton's position and signed the bank bill.

Hamilton's final major recommendation to Congress was that the federal government subsidize domestic manufacturing. Jefferson and Madison were now convinced that the republic was being sold out to speculators and financiers. Hamilton had been using a Philadelphia newspaper, John Fenno's *Gazette of the United States*, to promote his views. In October 1791, Jefferson and Madison prevailed on their friend Philip Freneau to come to Philadelphia to establish a newspaper favorable to their position, and Madison began to use Freneau's *National Gazette* to publish essays in which he framed the rationale for the permanent necessity of political parties in a republic. There would always be schemers who placed self-interest above the good of the whole. Parties, according to Madison, arose in a struggle of the true "republican interest" against such dangerous conspirators, a struggle of "good" against "evil." He identified the two groups as "Republicans" and "Anti-Republicans."

In late 1792 and early 1793, sympathizers with Jefferson and Madison became known as Democratic Republicans, after the Democratic Republican Societies that opposed a strong central government and the "monied interests" who threatened "liberty and equality." The societies included some common people, but most members were from middling and even prosperous families. Washington blamed the societies for spreading "suspicions, jealousies and accusations of the whole government."

Hamilton and his supporters were no more tolerant of disagreement than were the Democratic Republicans. In the election of 1792, allies of Hamilton identified themselves as supporters of Washington's administration, advocates of the policies of the secretary of the treasury, or, increasingly, as Federalists, to suggest their commitment to union and the new government. As late as the election of 1794 most candidates resisted formal party alignment, and congressional voting patterns showed little sense of "party" discipline. There were several reasons for this, including the tendency of most citizens (including many partisans themselves) to associate political parties with corruption and a loss of independence. By 1796, however, the jumble of labels had sorted itself out to Democratic Republicans and Federalists, and congressional voting patterns revealed a distinct tendency to vote on one side or the other.

Controlling the Borderlands

For all of its symbolic importance as a source of republican order, the backcountry had so far been marked by constant conflict among owners and settlers and between Indians and Americans.

Americans fought over land prices and rights of ownership. Seeking quick revenue, the government sold large tracts of land to speculators and large proprietors, some of whom were federal officials. Alexander Hamilton and Secretary of War Henry Knox were both silent partners in the huge Macomb Purchase in New York. Proprietors subdivided their tracts for sale, but their prices were often too high for average settlers, who squatted on lands and claimed the rights of possession and improvement.

Squatters, proprietors, and governments shared the assumption that the land was theirs to fight over. The Treaty of Paris did not acknowledge Indian claims, and treaties promising Indians peace in exchange for land proved illusory (see Chapter 7). By the time Washington took office in 1789, the backcountries were in an uproar. Undisciplined federal troops and state militias roamed western lands in search of a fight, often attacking neutral or sympathetic Indian villages. Betrayed and angry, Indians banded together in loose confederations, retaliating against settlers and striking alliances with the British and Spanish.

By 1789, the Eastern Woodland and Great Lakes nations had been deeply altered by the westward pressure of white settlement. In the North, a group of battered Iroquoian villages traded large tracts of land for promises of security and called on tribes of the Northwest Territory to do the same. However, these peoples refused and effectively shut down settlement north of the Ohio River valley. In the South, the Creeks, trapped between white settlements and the Native American nations of the Mississippi River valley, allied with militant Cherokees to keep the Georgia, Tennessee, and Kentucky frontiers ablaze with war parties.

Washington had more reasons to worry about the western territories. By 1789, Spain was actively luring United States settlers into New Spain at the foot of the Mississippi River in order to weaken the loyalty of the West to the new United States government. In the Great Lakes region, Britain hung onto the string of forts it had promised to give up in the Treaty of Paris. Many Americans believed that Britain was biding its time to regain control of the lands south of the Great Lakes.

This turmoil took its toll in the East. The inability of the national government to control Native Americans angered states, would-be settlers, and small-business owners. Landowners complained that their property rights were not being protected, and small settlers complained of favoritism in land distribution. Understanding that both external relations and the domestic authority of the federal government were at stake, Washington turned immediately to the problem of the backcountry. Working with Secretary of War Henry Knox, Washington sought a more fair and consistent Indian policy. He also used the territories to demonstrate the power of the federal government.

Less than a month after assuming office, Washington submitted to Congress a report by Knox on Indian affairs. Knox argued that the United States should acknowledge a residual Indian "right in the soil" not affected by a treaty between Britain and the United States. That right could be extinguished, he insisted, only by separate dealing with the Indians; he recommended that the United States purchase Indian claims to disputed lands. In 1789, Congress appropriated $20,000 for negotiations.

In part, Knox and Washington shifted policy in the name of justice, but they also sought to avoid the costs of having to take the Northwest Territory by war. A change in tactics did not mean a change in ultimate goals, however. Although Knox tried to keep white settlers outside treaty boundaries, his policy did not recognize Native Americans' right to refuse to negotiate. Seeking to bolster the authority of the national government, Knox argued that Indian bands were not communities within state borders, but rather foreign entities, on the level of nations. Indian relations were therefore properly the business of the federal government. Knox in effect declared Indians aliens on their own lands, using federal policy to define Indians as the ultimate outsiders.

By 1790 continuing troubles in the Northwest Territory convinced Washington to project a military presence there. His first two efforts were dismal failures. In 1790 a combined Native American force led by the Miami war leader Little Turtle routed the United States Army, led by General Josiah Harmar. The next year a much smaller party crushed the troops of territorial governor general Arthur St. Clair. In 1792, Congress authorized "strong coercive force" (bigger, better paid, and better trained) and Washington turned to a seasoned infantry officer, Pennsylvanian major general Anthony Wayne. By the time Wayne found the Indians in 1794 at Fallen Timbers, near Lake Erie, his army was more than 3,000 strong. Facing a force of only 400 warriors, Wayne claimed a decisive victory.

According to the Treaty of Greenville, signed August 3, 1795, Indians ceded two-thirds of the later state of Ohio and a piece of present-day Indiana. In return, they received annual federal payments ranging from $1,000 to $500 per band. The annuities bought the United States influence within Indian communities and rendered the Indians more economically dependent. The treaty also tried to impose white ideas of work and economy by offering Indians annuities in the form of farm equipment, cows, and pigs.

Indian efforts at confederacy proved less successful in the South, where deep fractures existed within the Cherokee and Creek nations. Older leaders, wearied by constant warfare, and mixed-heritage populations familiar with white economic and social ways sometimes favored accommodation and entered into agreements they lacked the authority to make. At the Treaty of New York in 1790, Alexander McGillivray and other Creek leaders agreed to exchange lands belonging to the entire Creek nation for annual payments from the federal government and promises of U.S. protection for their remaining lands. A faction of the Cherokee nation signed a similar pact in 1791.

These internal disputes weakened Indian military efforts. When the government proved unable to stop settlers flowing into the future state of Tennessee, younger Creeks, Chickamaugas, Cherokees, and Shawnees repudiated the treaties and attacked the Americans at Buchanan's Station, near Nashville, Tennessee, planning to move on Nashville itself. Fearing reprisals, older Cherokee leaders betrayed the plan, and the assault was thrown back. U.S. Indian commissioners used military victories to coerce new land cessions and to insinuate white customs more deeply into Indian cultures, especially that of the Cherokees.

Resistance continued, in the North and the South, but dreams of a pan-Indian confederation were temporarily stymied. They would be resurrected at the turn of the century

Map 8–3   Major Indian Villages and Indian-United States Battle Sites, 1789-1800 During its first decade of existence, the new federal government struggled to assert control over the trans-Appalachian territories, claimed by Native Americans as their homelands and coveted by United States settlers and land
speculators.

by two Shawnees. One, Tenskwatawa, would become an important prophet. The other, his
half-brother, was named Tecumseh.

The West posed a domestic, as well as an external, threat to the federal government.
By 1791 western settlers were disenchanted with the seeming inability of the government
to protect their interests and had begun disregarding federal policy. They trespassed on
Indian lands, sent unorganized militias to enforce their claims, and traded illegally with

Indians. In 1791, western Pennsylvanians rejected federal authority explicitly, setting the stage for a direct confrontation.

The trouble began with the passage of Hamilton's excise tax. Living in a gateway to the Northwest Territory, residents of western Pennsylvania anticipated an economic bonanza from westward migration but were frustrated with the failure of the government to secure safe passage into the Ohio River valley. Hamilton's tax on spirits fueled their simmering anger over the question of republican fairness. Many Americans regarded excise taxes (internal taxes on specific goods) as unfair in principle. This particular tax seemed targeted specifically at western farmers, who found it easier to transport their grain in liquid than in bushel form.

Popular protests intensified at each new report of the army's failure in the Northwest Territory (efforts the tax was supposed to fund). Western Pennsylvanians vowed that they would not pay the tax and urged citizens to treat tax collectors with "contempt." Washington took the challenge seriously, and in August 1794 he sent 13,000 troops into western Pennsylvania. Against this show of force, the Whiskey Rebellion fizzled, but the government drove its point (and power) home. Remaining protestors were rounded up; twenty were sent to Philadelphia to face treason charges, and two were sentenced to death. Washington pardoned them both, but he had proven the authority of federal law.

Western Pennsylvanians were not without sympathizers, however. The congressional elections of 1792 were contests between the policies of Alexander Hamilton, on the one hand, and the beliefs of the self-named "republican interest," on the other, over what it meant to be a republican nation and society.

America in the Transatlantic Community

The internal turbulence the United States faced during these years was matched by conflict in the larger Atlantic community of which the new nation was inextricably a part. Washington would later summarize his foreign policy goals: "The great rule of conduct for us, in regard to foreign nations, is, in extending our commercial relations, to have with them as little political connexion as possible." But Washington's own experience, and that of his successor, John Adams, taught that commerce and politics were not so easily separated.

Other Revolutions

Just as the United States was launching its federal republic, France entered the throes of revolution. After years of fiscal mismanagement by the crown, high unemployment, and widespread malnutrition and starvation, the French bourgeoisie began a reform of the monarchy that soon led to wholesale grassroots revolution. In July of 1789, just eight weeks after Washington took the oath of office, the people of Paris stormed the Bastille prison in symbolic rejection of the power of the monarchy. The next month the new National Constituent Assembly abolished feudalism and promulgated the Declaration of the Rights of Man and of the Citizen, modeled on the American Declaration of Independence.

Initially, most Americans, including many Federalists, supported the French Revolution. As a part of its long eighteenth-century conflict with Great Britain, France had aided the Americans in their own revolution and had recognized the nation and its diplomats after the war. Americans now saw the efforts of the French people to overthrow monarchy as a reflection of their own struggle against Britain, and they read events in France as a confirmation that the United States would lead the world into a new era of democracy.

By 1793, however, as the Parisian mob grew more violent and moderate politicians lost power, many Americans lost their enthusiasm for the French republic. Although many, Jefferson and Madison among them, remained avid French partisans, others grew convinced that France was spiraling into chaos.

Part of their alarm may have derived from events on the French island colony of Saint Domingue in the West Indies. In 1791, its free people of color led an insurgency against the white planter class but soon lost control in the face of a full-scale revolution by the island's tens of thousands of slaves. Eventually, under the leadership of former slave François-Dominique Toussaint-Louverture, Saint Domingue would become the first black republic in the Americas.

Washington's response to the revolution in Saint Domingue was complicated. He did not support the revolutionaries, especially after the movement for equality for free blacks turned into a slave rebellion. Like other slave owners, Washington feared that support-ing the Dominguans would encourage slave rebellion in the southern United States. Still, he did not want to enter into an alliance with France (which opposed the revolution on economic grounds) that might seem hostile to the British. His compromise was to order supplies and ammunition sent directly to the island's white-planter ruling class.

Between France and England

Washington's efforts to avoid the appearance of pro-French partiality were soon tested. On February 1, 1793, France and Spain declared war on Great Britain and Holland. Ameri-cans were divided in their sentiments. Many Democratic Republicans (among them Jef-ferson and Madison) viewed with horror the possibility that America might join with its former colonial master against a fellow republic. Hamiltonians, meanwhile, believed that friendly relations with Britain best served American interests. Searching for a middle ground, President Washington endorsed neutrality.

Then, on May 16, Edmond Charles Genêt, citizen of France, arrived in Philadelphia, the temporary capital. France had several hopes for the Genêt mission. The revolutionary government believed it was the destiny of the French republic to free the oppressed people of Europe from their tyrannous monarchs. For his part, Genêt was to incite the European colonies in the Americas to revolution. He was also to press the United States for a new treaty allowing French naval forces and privateers to resupply in American ports. France's hopes were not entirely fanciful. The impoverished Washington administration had lent money to the new French government and recognized the republic as the legitimate gov-ernment of France.

But the French overestimated American support. Giving preferential treatment to French ships could only strain relations between America and England. Barely able to muster a force to the northwest, Washington was not about to risk a foreign war or to in-flame tensions on western borders. Washington considered Genêt's proposals reckless.

Genêt, however, did not believe that Washington's views represented the sentiments of Americans generally. In Philadelphia, he authorized the refitting of a captured English ship as a French privateer, and he encouraged American settlers in Kentucky to attack the Spanish.

Washington was furious. "Is the Minister of the French Republic to set the Acts of this Government at defiance, with impunity?" he fumed. Issuing a formal Proclamation of Neutrality, Washington disavowed Genêt and demanded that he be recalled. Disappointed by Washington's growing support of Federalist policies, Jefferson resigned as secretary of state.

To the Brink of War

Even without Genêt's provocations, by 1794 tensions with Britain were high. To the old issues of unsettled Revolutionary War reparations and British forts in the Northwest were added new charges that the British navy was harassing U.S. merchant ships. Still, Washington sought to avoid confrontation. In spite of restrictions on British ports, U.S. shipping had been steadily expanding, making it hard to argue that British policies were injurious enough to risk a trade war. Washington dispatched Chief Justice of the Supreme Court John Jay to England to resolve outstanding issues.

The heating up of French-British animosities enabled Jay to negotiate a treaty that reduced tensions between Britain and the United States. Britain agreed to open West Indies ports to some U.S. ships, and both countries agreed that (except for tonnage restrictions) their ships would receive equal treatment. They agreed to establish boards of arbitration to set the boundary between Canada and the United States, and Britain promised to evacuate its forts in the Northwest by June 1, 1796.

Most Americans knew nothing about Jay's Treaty until after it was approved, for the Senate debated it in secret. When Democratic Republicans learned of its contents and its ratification, they protested the closed deliberations and said the treaty would benefit the merchant class while taxing everyone to pay for its provisions. But public protest soon fizzled. News of Anthony Wayne's victory against the Great Lakes tribes cast the treaty's provisions for the evacuation of the British forts in a more positive light. Word followed that Thomas Pinckney had also concluded a treaty with Spain, opening the Mississippi River to U.S. navigation and permitting Americans to store goods duty-free in New Orleans. (Pinckney's Treaty also set the boundary between the United States and Florida at the 31st parallel.) Seeing the United States make peace with Britain, and fearful of an Anglo-American alliance, a weak Spain accepted the possibility of increased American encroachment across the river and sought peace with the new republic.

Wayne's victory and Jay's and Pinckney's negotiations seemed at last to open the territories to settlement. Western land prices soared, and the U.S. export trade boomed. By the time opponents in the House of Representatives tried to scuttle Jay's Treaty by denying necessary funds, popular sentiment had shifted to strong support for the treaty as a key to prosperity.

The Administration of John Adams

George Washington, reluctant to serve a second term, had been convinced to do so when Jefferson and Hamilton argued that no one else could bring the republic's fractious politics together. But Washington refused to run for a third term, and in 1796 the nation faced its first contested presidential election.

In his farewell address, published on September 19, 1796, Washington made clear his Federalist concern with social order and personal discipline. Having acknowledged the

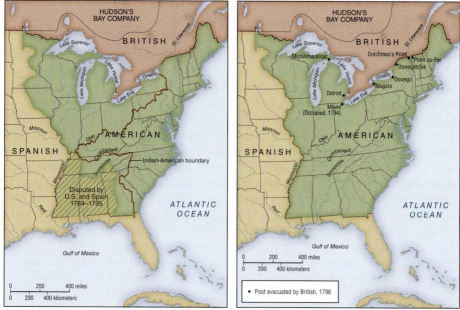

Map 8–4 Extension of United States National Territories, 1783 and 1795 The Treaty of Paris with Great Britain (1783) left the United States' borders with Spain (much of the western and southern boundaries) ambiguous. Those borders were clarified in the Pinckney Treaty with Spain (1795).

right of the people to alter their Constitution, he stressed the "duty of every individual to obey the established Government" until it was changed "by an explicit and authentic act of the whole people." Sounding themes that would echo through the first half-century of the republic, he warned against unlawful "combinations and associations" with designs on the rightful "power of the people," an image that, 30 years later, would drive the emergence of Jacksonian democracy.

Led by Hamilton (unable to run for the presidency, having been born in the West Indies), Federalists selected Vice President John Adams as their candidate. Adams had served in the Continental Congress, been a part of the committee to draft the Declaration of Independence, served as representative to France, helped negotiate the peace treaty, and served two terms as vice president. Thomas Pinckney of South Carolina was their vice-presidential choice. For president, Democratic Republicans supported former secretary of state Thomas Jefferson, along with Madison, the most visible opponent of Hamilton. New Yorker Aaron Burr was intended as vice president.

Although contested, the election of 1796 was not decided by popular majority. State legislatures chose two-fifths of the members of the Electoral College. Moreover, procedures in the Electoral College did not distinguish between votes for the office of president and vice president. The person who received the most electoral votes became president. The person who received the second highest number of electoral votes became vice president.

This procedure proved dangerously unpredictable in a new age of political parties. Although the Federalist Adams received a majority of electoral votes (71) and became president, the Democratic Republican Jefferson received the second highest count (68 to Pinckney's 59) and became vice president.

Benjamin Franklin once said that John Adams was "always an honest man, often a wise one, but sometimes, and in some things, absolutely out of his senses." Also cranky, defensive, and self-doubting, he was not the man to negotiate growing party rifts successfully. Against a background of partisan resentment, Adams confronted an increasingly hostile relationship with France. Unsurprisingly, Franco-American relations had been harmed by Jay's Treaty—which seemed to France to ally America with England—and by the French practice of plundering American ships. There was also the issue of Saint Domingue. By the time John Adams took office, the revolutionaries (now led by former slave Toussaint-Louverture) were seeking to resume trade with the United States as a step toward full independence. The abolitionist Adams had no qualms about supporting the revolutionaries and saw a number of advantages in allying with them. A trade deal with Haiti would further isolate the island from French control, it would help the United States economy, and it might prompt Louverture to close his ports to the French privateers attacking U.S. merchant ships. In June 1799, the Adams administration signed a three-way British-U.S.-Saint Dominguan trade agreement. Although that agreement was unratified when Adams left office, in the last months of his presidency Adams stationed U.S. warships outside Dominguan ports to help quash an internal rebellion of conservative free people of color wishing to reimpose slavery, while members of his administration discussed with Louverture the form that an independent Saint Dominguan republican government might assume. None of this pleased France, particularly not after the rise of Napoleon and the resurgence of French imperial ambitions in the late 1790s.

Even before his inauguration on March 4, 1797, Adams thought about sending a special envoy to France to resolve these issues. When Adams's cabinet objected, the president temporarily abandoned the plan. At the end of March, he learned that new American ambassador Charles Pinckney had been kicked out of France because the French government would "no longer recognize or receive" an ambassador from the United States. Adams decided to send a mission to France, appointing Elbridge Gerry, John Marshall, and Pinckney.

When the American mission arrived, French Foreign Minister Talleyrand made clear that he expected a bribe for his willingness to talk. Such arrangements were not uncommon in European politics, but to the starched and wary Adams, the idea was abhorrent. He turned over all documentation of the affair to Congress, identifying Talleyrand's agents by letters: X, Y, and Z.

The so-called XYZ Affair prompted a largely Federalist Congress to suspend commercial ties to France, empower American ships to seize armed French vessels, and expand the nation's military. In what became known as the "Quasi-War" (neither nation formally declared war), between 1798 and 1800 the United States and France skirmished on the seas, with the United States capturing more than 80 French ships. In the Convention of 1800, France and the United States agreed to end these hostilities. France agreed to return captured American ships, the United States assumed Americans' claims against the French for damages in shipping, and the earlier Franco-American Alliance was replaced by mutual most-favored-nation status.

The military expansion necessary for this conflict soon created tensions at home. Adams and Congress needed $2 million for it, which they found by imposing a tax on houses, land, and slaves. Each state had a specified portion of the cost to pay. The levy on houses, assessed according to the size of the house, fell especially hard on residents of states with few or no slaves or huge plantation estates and was particularly odious to German immigrants, whom it reminded of harsh taxes exacted by the kings of Germany. When the assessors reached eastern Pennsylvania, settled predominately by German immigrants, unrest became civil disobedience. Led by John Fries, men of the area raised a small army to chase collectors away, while women poured hot water on the assessors. When the governor tried to have the resisters arrested, Fries's supporters freed them. Adams sent a militia of 1,000 men to capture the leaders. Fries and most of the other leaders were arrested, tried for treason, and sentenced to hang. In the face of strong public sentiment, Adams pardoned the rebels. (This was the second uprising in less than a decade, and in both cases, the rebels were pardoned.)

The Federalists had also used the XYZ Affair and hostilities with France for domestic political purposes. Insisting that pro-French influence endangered the nation, in 1798 Congress passed the Alien and Sedition Acts, aimed at gagging the Democratic Republican opposition and preventing it from using the war issue to win the 1800 election. The acts required a 14-year naturalization period, the highest at any period in American history, and targeted immigrants, whom the Federalists presumed to be Democratic Republicans. The acts also empowered the president to deport any "suspicious" aliens and established a broad definition of sedition, intended to stop all Democratic Republican criticism of the administration's policies.

The Alien and Sedition Acts backfired against the Federalists. Twenty-five prosecutions were eventually brought under the Sedition Act (all against Democratic Republicans), and ten men were convicted. The acts were so transparently partisan that individuals convicted under them became martyrs to the Democratic Republican cause. A Vermont congressman who published criticisms of administration policies was reelected even as he served out his four-month jail term. But by targeting those believed to be "radical," especially newspaper editors, and warning immigrants away, the acts silenced the most outspoken opponents of the government.

Although Democratic Republicans insisted that the acts were unconstitutional, they hesitated to challenge them in the Supreme Court, both because the Court was dominated by Federalists and because Democratic Republicans did not want to set a precedent for giving the Supreme Court the power to rule on constitutionality. Instead, Madison and Jefferson encouraged the states to pass resolutions denouncing the Alien and Sedition Acts. Madison, now retired from Congress, authored a set of resolutions in Virginia affirming the rights of states to judge the constitutionality of federal laws. Jefferson, vice president of the United States, framed a more militant set of resolutions for the Kentucky legislature, saying that states might declare federal laws they deemed unconstitutional to be "without force" within their state boundaries.

Jefferson and Madison expected that other states would support the Virginia and Kentucky resolves, but they did not. Rather, voters simply returned the Democratic Republicans to power in the election of 1800, and the acts expired in 1801.

Before retiring, the Federalist Congress got off one more shot at the Democratic Republicans. Just as the session expired, Congress passed the Judiciary Act of 1801, which gave John Adams the power to expand the federal judiciary by appointing new judges, justices of the peace, attorneys, clerks, and marshals. He promptly filled these positions with good Federalists and then left office.

>> Timeline

▼1789
George Washington inaugurated
Judiciary Act of 1789
Tariff Act of 1789
John Fenno founds *Gazette of the United States*
William Hill Brown publishes *The Power of Sympathy*

▼1790
Alexander Hamilton's Report on the Public Credit
Assumption Act
Naturalization Act

▼1791
Excise tax (including tax on whiskey) passes
First Bank of the United States
Philip Freneau establishes *National Gazette*
Bill of Rights ratified

▼1792-94
Whiskey Rebellion

▼1793
Fugitive Slave Act
Edmond Genêt arrives in the United States

▼1794
Battle of Fallen Timbers

▼1795
Jay's Treaty
Treaty of Greenville
Pinckney's Treaty

▼1796
John Adams elected president

▼1798-1800
XYZ Affair and Quasi-War

▼1798
Alien and Sedition Acts

▼1798-1799
Virginia and Kentucky resolutions

▼1800
Jefferson elected president

Conclusion

William Maclay lived until 1804 and stayed active in public affairs in Pennsylvania. From time to time he added to his journal, underscoring the accuracy of his early forebodings.

Indeed, the first decade of the federal government's existence had demonstrated that the love of liberty and the love of order sometimes led in different directions, and they gave rise to very different visions of what constituted "good" citizenship. Democratic Republicans fumed at what they saw as the liberties Federalists had taken with the Constitution and their willingness utterly to abrogate civil rights. Federalists were more convinced than ever that Democratic Republicanism was a dangerous scourge on the land and the greatest threat to the republic. The 1790s had witnessed a steady escalation of suspicion and distrust, of which the Whiskey Rebellion, the Alien and Sedition Acts, and the Virginia and Kentucky resolves had been only the most striking illustrations. The political parties organized that fractious spirit, but they did little to defuse it. Meanwhile, even as Americans fought over the terms of the new republic's founding, those terms began to change.

Review Questions

1. What were the key elements of Hamilton's fiscal and economic policies?

2. What were the first two political parties in the federal republic? Who led each, and how did the two parties differ?

3. Who were "the Few and the Many"?

4. How did the Whiskey Rebellion reflect larger tensions in the early republic?

5. The constitution did not define "citizenship." What early laws and policies do you think gave practical meaning to the idea of citizenship? Do you think everyone agreed on who was included and who was not?

For further review materials and resource information, please visit www.oup.com/us/ofthepeople

9

A Republic in Transition

1800–1819

>> Washington Irving's America

One of the new republic's first successful writers, Washington Irving was born in New York City in 1783, the eighth surviving child of a prosperous merchant family. It was apt that his mother named him after George Washington, because much of Irving's career as a writer focused on the real and fictional history of his country. But Irving also spent much of his energy and time trying to negotiate the present and the young nation's economic, political, and social changes. His tales reflected some of that turbulence.

Although he and his family were of Federalist sympathy, Irving came of age just as Americans elected Thomas Jefferson to the presidency, throwing off the party of Washington, Hamilton, and Adams and ushering in a quarter of a century of Democratic Republican dominance. It was a change that Jefferson later described as "as real a revolution in the principles of our government as that of 1776 was in its form."

Accompanying this political upheaval was a profound economic and social transformation. Cash relations began to supersede barter and trade. Cities grew prosperous but also became more anonymous. More people worked for wages, fewer worked for room and board. Even farmers focused on commercial markets.

As a member of the merchant class, Irving benefited from many of these commercial changes. But he also felt their cost. Irving and his family were victims of the constant disruptions of American foreign trade after 1809, and, in 1817, they at last went bankrupt, forcing Irving to move to England to try to recoup their fortunes.

Irving had never cared much for business. He had become a lawyer (as did a growing number of Americans), but his real love was always the arts. Irving began publishing when he was only 19, contributing letters and essays to *The Morning Chronicle* under the pseudonym Jonathan Oldstyle. In 1807, he founded his own literary magazine, *Salmagundi*, using its pages to ridicule the provincial smugness of city

>> **AMERICAN PORTRAIT** *continued*

culture. It was in an issue of *Salmagundi* that Irving coined the nickname "Gotham" for New York City.

Irving's literary fame came from the series of stories published in 1819–1820 as *The Sketch Book of Geoffrey Crayon, Gent.*, which included both "The Legend of Sleepy Hollow" and "Rip Van Winkle." In "Sleepy Hollow" Irving poked fun at the clash of two cultures: the educated, scientific (and foolish) worldview of schoolteacher Ichabod Crane (who eventually became a lawyer in Philadelphia) and the old-world, old-fashioned (but also very wise) customs of the townspeople of Sleepy Hollow.

It was "Rip Van Winkle" that best captured Washington Irving's changing America. A simple fellow with a fondness for liquor and "an insuperable aversion to all kinds of profitable labour," Van Winkle fell asleep in the Catskill Mountains for 20 years and awoke to a world utterly unrecognizable. His village was "larger and more populous. There were rows of houses which he had never seen before, and . . . [s]trange names were over the doors—strange faces at the windows—everything was strange. . . . The very character of the people seemed changed. There was a busy, bustling, disputatious tone about it, instead of the accustomed phlegm and drowsy tranquillity." In the story, Van Winkle eventually understands what has happened, and although he slides comfortably back into his old ways, he is welcomed by and in turns welcomes the changes in his world.

Although the story was set during the American Revolution, it could have applied equally to the first two decades of the nineteenth century, when America experienced profound economic, political, and social changes. Ironically, the story appeared just as those changes ushered in the most severe fiscal panic in the republic to date, throwing farmers off their lands and drying up job opportunities in the cities. For many of those people, the story did not end so well as it had for Rip Van Winkle.

Common Threads

>> Why was overseas trade so important to Washington, Adams, Jefferson, and Madison? To ordinary farmers?

>> How did the way average Americans lived change over the first quarter-century of the republic?

>> How were the political debates of ratification and of the 1790s still playing out during Jefferson's and Madison's administrations?

>> What important changes in context and content occurred in U.S. Indian policy over the period of the first four administrations?

>> What roles did organized religion play in shaping the society of the early republic?

>> Was the market revolution important in the South?

A Politics of Transition

In his inaugural address in 1801, Jefferson strove to put the partisan bitterness of the previous decade behind American politics. He asked Americans to come together "in common efforts for the common good" and assured Federalists that he was committed to the rights of the minority. "Let us, then, fellow-citizens, unite with one heart and one mind," he encouraged. "Let us restore to social intercourse that harmony and affection without which liberty and even life itself are but dreary things." In some ways, Jefferson got his wish: over time many of the policies of the Democratic Republicans would so come to resemble the policies of the Federalists that it would seem as if the two parties had grown closer. In the daily battle of national politics, however, the Democratic Republicans and the Federalists seemed not to share any common ground at all.

Democratic Republicans in Office

Immediately on gaining office, Democratic Republicans set about closing the loophole in the Constitution that had almost cost them the election. With 53 percent of the popular vote, Jefferson had clearly defeated Adams. But in the Electoral College, the practice of balloting by party allegiance (rather than by office) had spelled disaster. Both Jefferson and Aaron Burr, the Democratic Republican vice-presidential candidate, received 73 votes. In the House of Representatives, Federalists threatened to support Burr to block Jefferson. Only after 34 ballots was Jefferson elected. Stunned Democratic Republicans rushed to pass the legislation that became the Twelfth Amendment (1804), providing for party tickets in national elections.

Meanwhile, Democratic Republicans sought revenge. They attempted to reduce the Federalist presence on the Supreme Court by impeaching Associate Supreme Court Justice Samuel Chase.

Chase was notorious for his open partisanship during the Sedition Act prosecutions, but it was unclear whether his behavior met the constitutional standard of "Treason, Bribery, and high Crimes and Misdemeanors." Democratic Republicans opted for a loose reading of the Constitution, but Federalists took up strict constructionism, arguing that the power to impeach had been narrowly drawn and should be used only in cases of clear criminal behavior. In the final vote, Chase was acquitted, and the Supreme Court remained Federalist, five to one. Jefferson's desire for a Democratic Republican court had to wait for vacancies in 1804 and 1807 and the creation of a new western circuit in 1807.

Before leaving office, the Federalists had tried to pack the courts with Federalists. The Judiciary Act of 1801, passed by the lame-duck Federalist Congress, increased the number of federal judgeships. Adams promptly appointed—and Congress confirmed—loyal Federalists. He also issued commissions for 41 justices of the peace, but they had not yet been acted on when he left office, and Jefferson ordered their appointments withheld. One of those "midnight" appointees, William Marbury, went directly to the Supreme Court, asking it for a "writ of mandamus," a court order compelling Madison to issue the commission. In a landmark decision, Chief Justice John Marshall, speaking for the Federalist-dominated Court, refused—but in a ruling that actually enhanced the Court's power. The provision in the Judiciary Act of 1789 (which Congress had reinstated after repealing the Act of 1801) that gave the Supreme Court the power to issue writs of mandamus was unconstitutional.

The Constitution had set out the powers of the Supreme Court, and no act of legislation could change them. Marbury was out of luck, but the principle of judicial review (itself nowhere mentioned in the Constitution) had been established, and henceforth, the Supreme Court would decide whether acts of legislation were constitutional or not. Jefferson had won the battle but lost a very big constitutional war.

Jefferson also set out to reduce the size of the federal government. Working with Secretary of the Treasury Albert Gallatin, he slashed the army budget by half and the navy budget by more than two-thirds. He also supported congressional efforts to reduce the $80 million national debt and to repeal internal taxes, including the hated one on whiskey. By 1807 the national debt had been cut in half.

These efforts at thrift were soon derailed by the politics of overseas commerce. The monarchs of the North African nations of Tunis, Algeria, Morocco, and Tripoli had long sought to dominate shipping on the Mediterranean, exacting tribute as the price of permitting ships to travel the Barbary Coast. As soon as the United States became a separate nation, it became liable for such payments. In 1794 the United States created the navy to protect American shipping in the Mediterranean, the very navy whose budget Jefferson cut.

Renewed demands for tribute in May brought the crisis to a head. Democratic Republicans opposed war as expensive and as tending to enlarge the powers of the federal government. Yet to pay tribute was to abandon the principle of free trade. Hoping for a small, contained war, Jefferson supported a Congressional appropriation for warships and gunboats "to protect our commerce and chastise their insolence—by sinking, burning or destroying their ships and vessels wherever you shall find them."

Results were mixed. Democratic Republicans managed to avoid new internal taxes, and they cut the national debt substantially. They were not, however, able to dismantle Hamilton's economic system, which provided the revenue to finance the country's defense. America's military intervention in the Mediterranean was not particularly successful. The warship *Philadelphia* ran aground off Tripoli and was burned by a raiding party led by Lieutenant Stephen Decatur before it could be taken.

The Louisiana Purchase

Many citizens, including Jefferson himself, had long presumed that white Americans would eventually settle west of the Mississippi River, but Pinckney's Treaty of 1795 (which had improved American access to the Mississippi) had removed any need for immediate action.

Napoleon Bonaparte changed all that. By the turn of the century, American-French relations had chilled. Ambitious to establish his own empire in the Americas and determined to prevent further United States expansion, in 1800 Napoleon acquired Louisiana from Spain. Jefferson worried that France would eventually send troops to occupy New Orleans. Hoping to block Napoleon, Jefferson dispatched Robert Livingston and James Monroe to France to purchase New Orleans and West Florida, too.

Bonaparte intended to fortify New Orleans, but he first diverted his troops to Saint Domingue to reverse the revolution there. Some 30,000 French troops died in the failed attempt. Defeated by the island's former slaves and by infectious disease, Napoleon was ready to unload his American territory. He stunned the American agents by offering to sell not only New Orleans but also the entire Louisiana Territory—883,000 square miles. (The Americans claimed that the purchase included West Florida, but Spain denied selling the territory to France. This issue was not resolved until 1819; see Chapter 11.) On April 12, 1803, the deal was struck. The United States paid France $11.25 million and agreed to satisfy American claims against France (from the Revolution) up to a value of an additional $3.75 million. For $15 million, or roughly 3.5 cents an acre, the United States obtained the Louisiana Territory.

In Jefferson's own "strict" reading of the Constitution, the purchase required a constitutional amendment. But this Democratic Republican belief in explicit powers ran counter to his Democratic Republican belief that the nation required land for expansion. Congress granted citizenship to French and Spanish inhabitants of the territory, ignored the status of Indians living there, rebuffed an effort to outlaw slavery, and authorized the purchase. Jefferson rationalized "that the good sense of our country will correct the evil of [loose] construction when it shall produce ill effects."

Long before Louisiana was in the hands of the United States, Jefferson began to plan its exploration. Jefferson appointed his trusted secretary, Captain Meriwether Lewis, and another officer, William Clark, to lead the expedition. Lewis was an ambitious soldier with some experience in the Old Northwest. Clark, who had commanded troops on the Mississippi, was a skilled surveyor and mapmaker. Their mission was "to explore the Missouri River, & such principal streams of it, as, by its course and communication with the waters of the Pacific Ocean, whether the Columbia, Oregon, Colorado or any other river may offer the most direct & practicable water communication across this continent for the purposes of commerce." The commerce Jefferson sought was not across the Pacific but rather with the Indians of the northern Missouri River, who traded chiefly with the British.

The expedition left St. Louis on May 14, 1804, on three boats containing 45 men and a dog, firearms, medicines, scientific instruments, tools, flour, and salt. The party traveled first up the Missouri River, closely observed by the Mandans, the Minnetarees, and the Hidatsas, who visited their camps and sent ahead stories of these curious people. In early November, the white men made their winter camp. When the expedition broke camp the following spring, a Shoshone woman, Sacagawea, her French-Canadian trapper husband, and their newly born child left with them. As a young girl, Sacagawea had been captured and adopted by the Minnetarees. Traveling with Lewis and Clark, she would return home. En route, her foraging and fishing skills enriched the party's diet, and she became an invaluable guide and interpreter. Native women such as Sacagawea and Malinche often served as cultural mediators.

Some encounters with Native Americans were less friendly. Far more dangerous than the Indians, however, were waterfalls and rapids, freezing temperatures and paralyzing snows, accidents, diseases (especially dysentery), and dead-end trails. The final portage across the Rocky Mountains in the fall of 1805 proved longer and more difficult than anticipated. Snow and hail stopped the expedition. Exhausted animals wandered off. Supplies ran out. The expedition members at last cleared the worst of the mountains and came to Indian villages, where they were fed and sheltered. On November 7, 1805, Lewis and Clark reached the Pacific Ocean.

Throughout their journey, Lewis and Clark had represented themselves as the envoys of a great nation with whom the Native Americans should now trade. To cement relations, they presented medals of friendship to Indian leaders. But they also kept an eye out for future settlements. According to Lewis, they found "a most delightfull country . . . fertile in the extreom . . . covered with lofty and excellent timber." After their return, in 1806, parts of their journals and letters, including detailed maps and drawings, slowly found their way into print, advertising what Jefferson called America's new "empire for liberty."

Other Americans had other plans for the territory. In 1805, former vice president Aaron Burr went to New Orleans to have a look at the new country. He immediately fell in love with it, and saw, too—or so he later claimed—that the United States might extend its sovereignty to include some of Spanish Mexico, where settlers were unhappy with high taxes and little government attention. By 1806 Burr had raised a force of several thousand men. Convinced that Burr intended treason and wanting to avoid trouble with Spain, Jefferson ordered his arrest. Burr was brought back to Richmond to stand trial before John Marshall, who happened to be presiding over the federal circuit. Prosecution proved difficult. Marshall interpreted treason in the narrowest sense possible, as requiring two witnesses to an overt act of war against the United States, but none came forward. Burr was acquitted, but he was also disgraced.

Embargo

In the fall of 1804, Jefferson's popularity was soaring. Internal taxes had been abolished, the national debt was falling, the United States had (seemingly) stood up to international coercion and, most amazingly, had acquired a huge western empire. Choosing George Clinton of New York as his running mate, Jefferson won reelection handily, and the Democratic Republicans took control of both houses of Congress. Faced with the prospect of federal surpluses, Jefferson again abandoned strict constitutionalism and began to contemplate a future role for the federal government encouraging "the great objects of public education, roads, rivers, canals, and such other objects of public improvement as may be thought proper." But Jefferson's second term had barely begun when his attention was riveted to developments in Europe.

A Philosophic Cock This 1804 cartoon caricatured Jefferson as a "philosophic cock" courting his slave Sally Hemings. Jefferson's Federalist opponents tried to tarnish his reputation by publicizing his relationship with his slave, but the voters reelected Jefferson by a decisive margin.

In his first inaugural address, Jefferson had counseled "peace, commerce, and honest friendship with all nations, entangling alliances with none." He remained committed to American neutrality, but by 1805 Napoleon's growing power in France and his expansionistic designs on Europe had complicated this policy. On the one hand, Jefferson knew he might need Napoleon's help to settle the unresolved question of West Florida, still claimed by Spain. On the other hand, France's increasing indifference toward American shipping rights raised the possibility that the United States might need Britain as an ally. Napoleon's victory over Austria in 1805 made France the undisputed master of western Europe. At the same time, English victories over the fleets of France and Spain had made England the undisputed master of the seas. The stalemate had dire consequences for American shipping.

Jefferson's hopes that Britain might respect the neutrality of American ships were dashed in 1805 when Britain again began seizing ships traveling between enemy ports, taking more than 200 American ships in that year alone. Then Napoleon declared a blockade of England and also began confiscating American ships. In June 1807 the British ship *Leopard* stopped the American frigate *Chesapeake* as it left Norfolk, Virginia. The captain of the *Leopard* demanded the right to search the American ship, insisting that it had recruited British deserters for its crew. When he was denied, he fired on the ship, boarded it, and took four men prisoner, leaving the *Chesapeake* to limp home.

Jefferson immediately ordered all British ships out of American waters and demanded reparation for the *Chesapeake*. In secret sessions, Congress passed an act that permitted only those American ships with the president's express approval to sail into foreign ports and prohibiting foreign ships from the American export trade. In effect, the United States had embargoed itself.

It was the most disastrous policy of Jefferson's career. Because enforcement was impossible, wealthy merchants enjoyed the large profits of smuggling. At the same time, small merchants, sailors, and shopkeepers who depended on steady maritime trade were thrown into crisis, and farmers in the South and West had trouble finding overseas trading outlets. As the economy settled into depression in 1808, the remaining Federalists charged that the embargo was helping Napoleon. Adding to American frustration, Napoleon then slyly claimed the right to attack U.S. ships in any continental port because, by Jefferson's own order, they could not be legal carriers.

The ironies of the embargo did not end there. As violations mounted, ever more repressive versions of the embargo were enacted. The final, fifth Embargo Act (signed January 9, 1809) swept away protections against self-incrimination and the right to due process and trampled on the right to trial by jury. By comparison, even the Alien and Sedition Acts looked tame.

As he himself acknowledged, the Embargo Acts represented the failure of Jefferson's agrarian political economy. His dream of a republic of farmers was dead, the victim of the principles of territorial expansion and free trade on which he had based it. Meeting America's need for manufactured goods solely by "this exuberant commerce," as Jefferson admitted in 1809, "brings us into collision with other powers in every sea, and will force us into every war of the European powers. The converting of this great agricultural country into a . . . mere headquarters for carrying on the commerce of all nations, is too absurd."

The anguish caused by the Embargo Acts exposed long-simmering dissension within Democratic Republican ranks. The most serious rupture came after the Louisiana Purchase. Although Jefferson insisted that West Florida was a part of the Louisiana Purchase, Spain denied ever ceding it to France. Napoleon hedged, but his ministers let it be known that the right price might convince them to lobby the American cause with Spain. Jefferson asked Congress for the money. To Jefferson's critics, this was the last straw. Loosely organized, his Congressional critics dubbed themselves the *Tertium Quid* (the "third something") to distinguish themselves from both Federalists and Democratic Republicans. By 1808, the Quids were threatening open rebellion. Although Secretary of State James Madison seemed the logical heir to Jefferson's presidency, Quids talked of throwing their support to James Monroe of Virginia or even Vice President George Clinton of New York. To avoid the risk of public brawling, in 1808 party loyalists met in closed caucus to select Jefferson's successor. They chose James Madison. In the election, Madison captured 122 electoral votes to Federalist Charles C. Pinckney's 47. Clinton won only 6. The Democratic Republicans again won both houses of Congress.

From 1801 until 1829, the federal government would remain under the control of a single party. By itself, that did not challenge Democratic Republican principles. Neither Madison nor Jefferson considered a two-party system necessary to American political life. Both, however, warned against the day when a small cadre of like-minded men would meet in secret to choose the nation's ruler. Democratic Republican ascendancy itself had now come to rest on just such a closed institution. Meanwhile, with American hopes for international prestige now a joke, and with commerce and agriculture in trouble, on March 1, 1809, Jefferson signed a bill repealing the Embargo Act. Three days later, Jefferson left the office he now described as a "splendid misery."

The War of 1812

Facing ruptures in his party serious enough to accept nomination by the kind of closed and antirepublican institution he himself had once condemned, James Madison took office on March 4, 1809. Madison had stood side by side with Thomas Jefferson on virtually every important political and ideological issue since the founding of the nation. Now he inherited his friend's presidential woes.

Madison and the War

In 1809, with Madison's approval, Congress replaced the embargo with the Non-Intercourse Act, reopening trade with all of Europe except England and France but authorizing the president to resume commerce with whichever of these countries dropped its restrictions and attacks on American shipping. The act set off a series of diplomatic feints by England and France, both pretending to change policies without making actual concessions.

France eventually won the game. In the summer of 1810, Napoleon's ministers officially told Madison that, as of November of that year, France would stop

> The distinction of Federalists and Republicans will cease; . . . the inquiry will be, are you for your country or against it?
>
> TENNESSEE CONGRESSMAN AND WAR HAWK FELIX GRUNDY

seizing American ships if Britain would do likewise. Probably correctly, Britain did not believe France would follow through on this policy. But Madison accepted the French declarations, and he altered American Non-Intercourse Act policy to apply to Britain alone.

Still, war might have been averted. A quarter of a century of European wars and Napoleon's continental policy—which closed continental markets to English goods—had taken its toll on Britain's economy. Although far more powerful militarily than the United States, Britain would have been happy to avoid the cost of an additional war. On June 1, 1812, in light of continuing British attacks on American shipping, Madison requested that Congress declare war on Great Britain. He listed several other reasons, including that the British were "impressing" American seamen into service and instigating Indian attacks in the Northwest. On June 4, the House voted to pass a war bill. On June 18, the Senate concurred. Ironically, unaware of events in the United States, England announced that it was revoking its maritime policy against United States ships.

The war vote in Congress went largely along party and regional lines. New England shippers remained firmly opposed, protesting that shipping was just beginning to recover and that American prosperity was dependent on Britain. Farmers and planters in the West and South were ready to fight to open up the seas. They suspected that the war might prove useful in other ways, too. Western migrants were convinced that Creek and Shawnee resistance was the work of the British, with its forts still along the Great Lakes. War with England could provide the excuse for an American invasion of Canada, both to grab more land and to wipe out the Indians. Even the Democratic Republicans were not fully unified, however. Led by Henry Clay of Kentucky and John C. Calhoun of South Carolina, the War Hawks (a group of fiercely nationalistic and expansionist young men who had come of age since the Revolution) wanted to respond to British insults. Moderate Democratic Republicans were more hesitant. They dreaded the cost of the war and doubted that the nation could gear up to take on such a formidable foe.

All of these tensions were reflected in the election of 1812. Maverick Democratic Republican De Witt Clinton rallied Federalist support and ran as Madison's opposition. He did not win, but his 89 electoral votes (to Madison's 128) constituted a higher proportion than the Federalists had enjoyed since the election of 1800.

Doubts about America's war readiness were soon justified. An ill-planned attempt to invade Canada in the summer of 1812 failed. Two thousand American troops surrendered at Detroit, and two advances failed when state militiamen insisted they were not required to leave the country to fight. Only Commodore Oliver Hazard Perry's dramatic victory on Lake Erie saved American honor in the north. On September 10, 1813, Perry forced the surrender of the entire British Great Lakes squadron. "We have met the enemy," he relayed to a relieved General William Henry Harrison, "and they are ours—two ships, two brigs, one schooner, and a sloop."

A comparable victory eluded Americans in the Atlantic. After initial successes, the tiny American navy was easily overwhelmed by superior British sea power. Americans turned to private schooners and sloops and by the war's end managed to capture more than 1,300 British vessels. Nevertheless, by 1813 the British navy had succeeded in blockading the American coast from the Chesapeake Bay to New Orleans, and, in the following year, to New England. The British fleet pummeled coastal cities and villages. On August 24, 1814, British troops invaded Washington, burned the Capitol, the White House, the

Treasury Building, and the Naval Yard, and terrorized civilians. The entire cabinet, including President James Madison, had already evacuated.

While Washington smoldered, the British turned to Baltimore. Through the night of September 13, its ships fired on Fort McHenry, the island citadel guarding Baltimore's harbor. Among the anguished observers was a Washington lawyer by the name of Francis Scott Key. Elated that the United States flag still flew over the fort at dawn, Key quickly scribbled the words that would in 1931 become the lyrics of the national anthem, "The Star-Spangled Banner."

In the South, Andrew Jackson used the war to suppress Indian resistance to U.S. settlement. After the militant Creek faction known as the Red Sticks had attacked a U.S. fort and settlers in Mississippi Territory, Jackson assembled a volunteer militia, including free African Americans and Indians. In March 1814, he defeated the insurgents at Horseshoe Bend, forcing them to sign a treaty ceding two-thirds of remaining Creek lands to the United States.

Federalist Response

For a time the war worked in favor of the Federalists. Although they did not win the presidency in 1812, they doubled their numbers in Congress. Angry at declining profits and frustrated by Virginia's domination of the presidency, in October 1814, emboldened Massachusetts Federalists called for a convention of the New England states "to lay the

Fort McHenry Fort McHenry is best known for its role in the War of 1812, when it successfully defended Baltimore Harbor from an attack by the British navy in Chesapeake Bay. It was this bombardment that inspired Francis Scott Key to write "The Star-Spangled Banner."

Map 9–1   Battles and Campaigns of the War of 1812 The War of 1812 was largely a naval war, fought along the Atlantic coast, in the Gulf of Mexico, and on the Great Lakes. Several land campaigns proved important, however: the British ground attack that ended the looting and burning of the capital and Andrew Jackson's trek overland to New Orleans.

foundation for a radical reform in the National compact." They planned to meet on December 15 in Hartford, Connecticut.

The Federalists meeting in Hartford were divided. Extreme Federalists, arguing that the Union could not be saved, lobbied for a separate New England confederacy that could immediately seek an end to the war. More moderate voices prevailed, and in the end, the convention sought amendments to the Constitution. The Federalists demanded restrictions on the power of Congress to declare war, an end to the Three-Fifths Compromise allowing slaves to be counted for purposes of representation, exclusion of naturalized citizens from elective federal office, and restrictions on the admission of new states. They also sought to limit the number of terms a president could serve and the frequency with which the presidential candidate could be chosen from a given state. The resolutions expressed a developing identification of the Democratic Republicans as the party of the South.

Federalists misjudged their strength and mistimed their efforts. By 1814, a weary Britain was ready to end the war. Emerging as the dominant power in Europe, Britain had little incentive to offer Americans more than simple peace. Signed in Ghent, Belgium, on December 24, 1814, the treaty that ended the War of 1812 was silent on the issues of free trade and impressment that had triggered the war. The Treaty of Ghent also sidestepped boundary disputes between Canada and the United States. British negotiators did agree to remove British troops from the Old Northwest, in effect acknowledging the failure of Indian resistance to white settlement.

Only Andrew Jackson's ragtag militia saved Americans from outright humiliation in the war. After the victory at Horseshoe Bend, Jackson's troops moved on to New Orleans, where a British fleet prepared to attack the city and take control of the mouth of the Mississippi River. Unaware that a peace treaty had been signed, on January 8, 1815, 7,500 British regulars stormed Jackson's position. In 30 minutes the battle was over, and, miraculously, the Americans had won. Establishing Jackson as a national hero, the Battle of New Orleans signaled the rise of a new star.

In 1815, the chief political importance of Jackson's victory was the lift it gave to American nationalism and the light it cast on the Federalist Hartford Convention, still meeting in Connecticut. Threatening secession was one thing in a failing war, but quite another in a moment of national triumph. Suddenly, the proceedings at Hartford seemed downright traitorous.

An Economy in Transition

The period after 1815 is sometimes referred to as the "market revolution" in United States history. Calling the cluster of changes that occurred over the next several decades a "revolution" suggests their importance: the decline of paternalistic employment arrangements (apprenticeship, indenturing, and the master shop) and the growth of labor contracts and wage dependency; the decline of relative self-sufficiency and the rise of longer-distance market exchange; and the decline of informal transactions (barter, for example) and the growing importance of formal contracts. These changes in American economic life were reflected in every aspect of society, from religion and politics to family life and everyday values. The term *revolution* slightly misrepresents the pace of this change, which was actually quite gradual. And yet, like Washington Irving's fictitious Rip Van Winkle, anyone who fell asleep before the War of 1812 and woke up 30 or 40 years later would have encountered a startlingly altered world.

International Markets

The economic transformation of the late eighteenth and early nineteenth centuries had many sources. One of the most significant was the gradual revival of overseas commerce at the end of the eighteenth century, much of this supported by conflicts in Europe. As Napoleon tried to spread the French Revolution (and his own power) throughout Europe, Europe remained at war—disrupting agriculture on the Continent and impeding European overseas trade. America shippers happily filled the gap.

This American shipping was of three kinds: export/import (exporting American wheat, rice, indigo, tobacco, and especially cotton to Europe and importing European

AMERICA AND THE WORLD

>> The United States in China

Although much of the history of the early republic unfolded in the Atlantic world, the Pacific Ocean was also an important stage for American political and commercial ambitions.

American traders had sent ships to China as early as 1784, when Robert Morris hired the *Empress of China* to sail out from New York to Macao, China. After the Revolutionary War, wealthy Americans were keen to purchase Chinese consumer goods—tea (boycotted during the War), porcelain, silk, and spices—and American merchants (barred from British colonial ports) were eager to find new markets. When the *Empress* returned a year later to realize a $30,000 profit, other American merchants jumped into the China trade.

From the beginning, however, Americans faced problems. First, although the Chinese were willing to trade with foreigners, they did not want foreigners in the country. Traders were forced to stay in designated areas, called *hongs*, where Chinese traders came to them to discuss possible deals. Fearing the settlement of foreign families, the Chinese insisted that any women on board trading vessels (not uncommon at the time) wait on the Portuguese island outpost of Macao.

The second problem was Chinese lack of interest in most products the United States had to offer. The ginseng market was quickly saturated, so American traders shifted to fur pelts obtained in trade with the Indians of the Pacific Northwest. From there they sailed across the Pacific, often stopping in the Sandwich Islands

(now Hawaii) to pick up sandalwood for the Chinese market.

Among the American merchants who eventually realized a fortune from this trade was John Jacob Astor, who migrated from Germany to America just after the Revolutionary War and, with his wife Sarah (a smart businesswoman and an expert in furs), set up shop in New York City, dealing mostly in furs from the Canadian Great Lakes region. But after Astor made $50,000 from his first venture in China— a staggering sum for the time—he envisioned a route that would carry New England manufactured goods to the Northwest Indians for furs to be traded with China. He established a trading post in present-day Oregon for that purpose in 1811.

In the meantime, the most successful commodity Americans could sell in China was silver, which the Chinese were willing to take in payment. But the United States had no silver mines, so obtaining the metal required either trading for silver with the Spanish South American colonies or acquiring it in European ports before heading off to China.

As early as the late eighteenth century, Americans found another trading medium: opium. Opium had long been chewed in South and Southeast Asia as a general analgesic, but the far more addictive practice of smoking opium became common only with the introduction of tobacco and contact with foreign merchants and sailors. Its trade monopoly in India encouraged English efforts to sell opium in China, but by the first decade of the nineteenth century Americans got in on the action. American ships were being specially designed to carry opium from India to Canton, and some of the early republic's great-est merchants—including Stephen Girard of Philadelphia and James and Thomas Perkins of Boston—amassed fortunes in part on the profits of drug trafficking in Southeast Asia.

manufactured goods to growing United States markets); re-export (carrying goods between two foreign ports with an intermediate stop in the United States, often to avoid French and English embargoes on each other's Caribbean colonies); and the simple carrying trade between two foreign ports (as U.S. ships became the main carriers between warring England and France). In addition to farm products and manufactured goods, American ships also carried people: political refugees from France and from Ireland's ill-fated rebellion seeking safety in the new republic and—before 1808, when the slave trade was officially ended—captives from Africa forced through the middle passage to slavery in the Caribbean and the United States.

American shipping tonnage tripled between 1780 and 1810, reaching almost 11 million tons annually. The American share of the traffic between England and the United States grew from 50 percent in 1790 to 95 percent by 1800. The value of the re-export carrying trade also increased from about $500,000 a year in the 1790s to about $60 million a year in 1807. By the first decade of the nineteenth century, American ships were in the harbors of India, the East Indies, China, the Philippines, Japan, and Hawaii and on the Pacific coast of North America and the eastern coast of South America.

The return of overseas trade fed an already rampant inflation (the result of a shortage of gold and silver and a surfeit of local and state-issued currencies of doubtful values). But it also created many jobs and helped alter the way Americans understood the terms of labor.

Merchants contracted for vessels (built at an astonishing rate), captains hired crews, and teamsters hurried goods to port. Some merchants also invested in port-city manufacturing. They gathered tailors, for example, into large central shops to turn out cheap clothing for sailors or to sell to planters for their slaves—even though the new merchant-manufacturers seldom recognized the traditional obligations of shop master to worker: food, housing, and training. Rather, they tended to hire unattached workers, apprentices, or jobless young men and put them to work at some single, specialized aspect of the craft. Some traditional shop masters became merchants, taking investments in ships to carry their goods to southern and Caribbean markets.

The growth of overseas shipping also spurred the development of business services in the early republic, particularly in port cities. The National Bank of the United States would be reauthorized in 1816. In the meantime, citizens formed insurance companies against the risks of loss in trading and local institutions for pooling capital for investment.

By 1810 there were more than 100 banks in the nation. Many of these banks, corporations, and insurance companies operated under special state charters that allowed them to function as legal entities. As the businesses mushroomed, so did new jobs for clerks and lawyers.

In the countryside, farming families shifted from a relatively self-sufficient model of agriculture to more commercially oriented enterprises. Farmers were willing to travel longer distances to sell their goods. Whenever possible, they expanded the size of their holdings. In Delaware, for example, families used the profit from women's dairying activities to finance new land to grow wheat for sale in the cities or in Europe. Farmers, like merchants and shop masters, tried to hedge their bets by reducing their costs and liabilities. They ceased using indentured servants, to whom they would have owed year-round room and board and a freedom bonus at the end of their term, in favor of hiring seasonal wage workers, to whom they had no responsibilities in the off-season.

The most significant boost to American commercial agriculture arose from the late eighteenth-century mechanization of the English textile mills and the resulting increased demand for cotton. The colonies had not been an important source of raw cotton, because the only variety that grew well in most of North America was extremely laborious and time-consuming to clean. Spurred by the new English markets, in 1793 Eli Whitney invented a mechanism that reduced the cleaning time of this short-staple cotton from a pound a day to 50 pounds a day. Almost at a stroke, Whitney's gin made cotton a viable cash crop for much of the South.

The invention occurred at a critical moment. American indigo was losing English market share to indigo from the East Indies. The tobacco trade was in decline. The market for rice was still strong, but rice cultivation required such large investments of land and labor as to exclude most farmers from production. Cotton gave the South a new commodity crop, and one that, unlike rice, could be grown on small farms without significant investment. Between 1790 and 1810, American cotton production increased from 3,000 bales to 178,000 bales a year. Increasingly after 1800, cotton was the largest single U.S. export commodity, making the development of the nation, not merely the development of the South, dependent on cotton and its labor system, slavery.

Crossing the Appalachian Mountains

After the Treaty of Greenville opened the Ohio River valley, the expansion of overseas markets fed a pent-up desire for new lands in Tennessee, Kentucky, and the soon-to-be-state of Ohio (1803). The Land Ordinance of 1785 had provided for sales to private individuals who could afford sections of 640 acres or more at a dollar an acre, but that was far beyond the reach of ordinary citizens. Sales were effectively restricted to speculators. Hoping to find a source of revenue, in 1796 Congress made matters worse by raising the price to two dollars an acre.

Finally, in 1800, settlers got some relief. The Land Act of 1800 reduced the size of the minimum parcel from 640 acres to 320 acres. For the first time, buyers were permitted to spread their payments over time. In 1804, the minimum size was decreased to 160 acres and the price reduced from $2.00 to $1.64 an acre. Even though the cost of the land and the journey were still prohibitive for many Americans and easy credit sometimes led to unmanageable debt, lower prices per acre, lower minimums, and the promise of credit opened the West to tens of thousands of settlers.

The unprecedented migration set off by the Treaty of Ghent quickly swelled the population of the trans-Appalachian region. Kentucky grew from 220,955 in 1800 to 564,317 in 1820; Tennessee from 105,602 to 422,823; and Ohio from 42,159 to 581,434. Equally important, settlement led to the organization of new states. After Ohio in 1803, nine years passed before the next new state, Louisiana, entered in 1812. But then the admissions came rapid-fire. Indiana became a state in 1816, Mississippi in 1817, Illinois in 1818, and Alabama in 1819. By then both Missouri and Maine were also eager to join the Union.

The westward migration was a remarkably diverse parade. The earliest arrivals were usually hunters, fur traders, explorers, and surveyors. Wealthy speculators (European and American) sometimes traveled to the backcountry just long enough to buy up the best parcels of land, then scurried home to sell them to investors or migrants. Single men (displaced mechanics, sons of poor farmers, husbands sent ahead to purchase land) trekked along dusty roads, sometimes on horseback, often on foot. Families soon followed. Some traveled in wagons, packing food and seed, a few household items, and perhaps a gun, herding a cow or a few pigs alongside. But equally common was the sight of a "man, wife, and five children, with all their household goods thrown in a wheelbarrow . . . walking to Ohio."

The backcountry roiled in "anxiety and confusion," one observer noted, as newcomers raced to claim their share of territorial lands. There were cotton lands in the South and huge expanses for grain in the old Northwest Territory—and favorable possibilities for transportation. Speculators were eager for huge returns on land investment, and migrants were eager to escape debt and taxes, oppressive jobs, and overworked soil.

Invention and Exploration

Western lands offered the potential for vastly enlarged markets within the United States. Settlers wanted to get their tobacco, wheat, corn, hemp, and cotton to coastal and European customers, and merchants and manufacturers were impatient to get their buttons, shoes, pots, pans, and farm tools to rural stores. Making that connection was still a backbreaking task, and the challenge of figuring out how to connect people to land and products to markets spurred some of the century's most important inventions.

The first improvements in transportation came from locally sponsored toll roads. Although states generally granted a special charter of incorporation for such projects, most of the capital came from local investors expecting to benefit from tolls. New York communities increased their road mileage from 1,000 miles in 1810 to more than 4,000 miles in 1820. To bolster the trade from cities such as Cincinnati, Pennsylvania extended an older highway that ran from Philadelphia to Pittsburgh. But the toll roads proved a poor investment. Only one (a short turnpike in Connecticut) paid profits, whereas many made no money at all.

The most important effect of road building in the post–War of 1812 era was the spur it gave to bridge building. The new bridges (such as one constructed over the Hudson River at Newburgh, New York) dramatically improved the time and cost of transport. They were heavily used and usually turned a good profit.

But it was the application of the steam engine to transportation that made the most dramatic difference. By the end of the War of 1812, the steam engine had begun to attract investors. There were some steam-powered overland rail carriers, but they remained fragmentary until the 1850s and conveyed only passengers, not cargo. The use of steam engines to power boats proved more successful. As early as 1787, James Rumsey of Maryland built a boat propelled by a jet stream, and John Fitch of Connecticut designed a steam-driven paddleboat. By 1790 Fitch was running a passenger ferry on the Delaware River. In 1804 Philadelphian Oliver Evans demonstrated a steam-powered river dredger.

This technology came together in August 1807 when Robert Fulton and his patron Robert Livingston (Jefferson's minister to France during the Louisiana negotiations) announced the Hudson River trial run of the *North River Steamboat of Clermont*, a 140-foot-long vessel with two steam-driven paddle wheels. Fulton wryly described the trip, 150 miles from New York City to Albany, as "rather more favorable than I had calculated." "I ran it up in thirty-two hours, and down in thirty," he boasted.

Although he had not invented the steamboat, Fulton had demonstrated its practical value for transporting people and goods. By 1817 steamboats were common in the coastal waters of the East and across the Great Lakes, but their most telling impact occurred on the western rivers: the Ohio, the Wabash, the Monongahela, the Cumberland, and especially the Mississippi. In 1809 Livingston and Fulton hired Nicholas Roosevelt to survey the river waters from Pittsburgh to New Orleans, and in 1811 they sent the steamboat *New Orleans* downriver from Pittsburgh. After carrying troops and supplies on the river during the War of 1812, in 1815 steamboats began regular private routes upriver on the Mississippi.

The steamboat powered the market development of the Mississippi River valley. Able to travel upstream as well as down, it knitted northern and southern regions together in an integrated economic system, with eastern manufactured goods and passengers flowing upriver into the Ohio River valley and northern grain, livestock, and manufactured goods flowing to downstream markets and out through the Gulf of Mexico, joined in Kentucky, Tennessee, and Mississippi by a swelling cargo of cotton. In 1811 the Mississippi River valley produced some 5 million pounds of cotton. Within two decades it produced 40 times that much, virtually all of it carried downstream to market on steamboats. In 1817 the overland route from Cincinnati to Philadelphia or New York took nearly two months. On steamboats, freight sent downriver from Cincinnati through New Orleans and on by packet to Philadelphia took about half the time.

The steamboat soon became a conspicuous and controversial symbol of American economic promise. Not only were steamboats fast and exciting, but they were also relatively inexpensive to own and operate, within the reach of small investors eager to have a chance at making their fortunes. Citing the importance of orderly and reliable service, however, state lawmakers often encouraged large enterprises, awarding monopoly rights to specific prime routes. In 1798, Robert Livingston had gained exclusive rights for 20 years over the waters of the state of New York by vessels propelled by steam, a monopoly he revived and expanded to include Robert Fulton in 1803. Fulton and Livingston failed to obtain sole rights to the Mississippi, but in 1811 they succeeded temporarily in gaining a monopoly on steamboat transportation at the mouth of the river. Their success provoked a storm of protest from competitors, who saw government favoring wealth at the expense of the small entrepreneur. In 1819 the monopoly was withdrawn, but many small operators remained convinced of the state's favoritism toward the wealthy. In fact, few got rich running steamboats on the Mississippi. The twists and hidden snags of the shallow river saw to that. Only in the East, where rivers were deeper and where steamboats became fashionable transportation for wealthy travelers, did investors realize large profits.

Even steamboats were limited by the existing waterways. Since the turn of the century, investors and inventors had sought to enlarge those water routes by linking them artificially with canals, but the early history of canals did not portend great success. By the end of the War of 1812, only about 100 miles of canals existed in the United States (the longest ran 27 miles between the Merrimack River and Boston Harbor). None earned much money.

Thus, when at the end of the war New York City mayor De Witt Clinton proposed building a canal to connect Albany and Buffalo, he was thought to have taken leave of his senses. The canal would run 364 miles, making it the longest canal in the world. It would require an elaborate system of aqueducts and locks to negotiate a 571-foot rise in elevation and would cost $7 million, the largest investment of the sort in the nation's history. Clinton argued that the canal would "create the greatest inland trade ever witnessed" and would tie the "most fertile and extensive regions of America" to the city of New York, making that city "the granary of the world, the emporium of commerce, the seat of manufactures, the focus of great moneyed operation." In 1817 he convinced the state legislature not only to authorize the project but also to pay for it entirely in state funds, a gamble that amounted to a $5-per-capita levy for the entire population of New York.

Begun on July 4, 1817, the Erie Canal was completed in 1823 and officially opened two years later. At 10:30 on the morning of Wednesday, November 2, 1825, the first boats cleared the final locks and made their way into the Albany basin. Bells pealed, bands played, a huge crowd cheered, and 24 cannons fired successively in a national salute.

Clinton's gamble paid off spectacularly. Passenger boats and transport barges produced revenues high enough for the state to pay for later stages of construction with the profits of early ones. Transportation costs from Buffalo to New York City fell from $100 a ton to about $10 a ton when the canal opened and dropped even lower later on. The Erie Canal set off an explosion of canal building that lasted up to the Civil War, but few later canals duplicated its success.

Early Industrial Society in New England

New Englanders had been experimenting with the idea of water-powered textile mills since the 1780s, when prominent Massachusetts merchants tried to convince the state legislature to support the creation of textile machinery in the United States. In 1790, émigré mechanic Samuel Slater had replicated the English water-powered carding and spinning machines in his mill in Pawtucket, Rhode Island. But Slater lacked the power loom necessary to turn yarn into finished cloth. It took Eli Whitney's invention of the cotton gin in 1793, some industrial sabotage, and the devastating trade losses during the embargo and the War of 1812 to finally propel Americans to devise a power loom and invest seriously in a domestic textile industry. Boston merchant Francis Cabot Lowell pioneered the shift.

A graduate of Harvard with a knack for machine design, Lowell traveled to England to see the loom for himself and surreptitiously to memorize its plan. Back home, working with mechanic Paul Moody, he duplicated the English model in 1814. With a special charter from the Massachusetts legislature, Lowell and his Boston associates (organized as the Boston Manufacturing Company) opened the United States' first fully mechanized textile mill in Waltham, Massachusetts. Within three years the mill had expanded and was paying a whopping 20 percent dividend.

Map 9-2 The Development of Regions and of Roads and Canals By 1830 internal development had fostered a growing transportation infrastructure throughout the United States. That development was regional in character, however. In the southern states, where natural waterways ran from deep in the interior to the coast, citizens saw little need to build additional linkages. In the North, where natural waterways seldom ran directly to coastal outlets, investors were far more willing to spend money on internal development, especially canals.

Lowell died in 1817, but under Nathan Appleton's leadership the company (now the Merrimack Manufacturing Corporation) raised more than $8 million to finance a second group of mills in East Chelmsford, Massachusetts. The new mills turned out their first finished cloth in 1823. A sleepy rural village of 200 in 1820, by 1826 East Chelmsford had grown to 2,600 and had incorporated as the city of Lowell, America's first industrial town. The mills relied entirely on the South for their raw cotton. Northern domestic purchase of raw southern cotton grew from 8 million pounds in 1800 to 31.5 million by the end of the war in 1815.

The Waltham system, as Lowell's approach was called, differed from earlier American manufacturing enterprises in several ways. The Waltham mill was the largest industrial undertaking attempted in America up to that time. It housed the full production process, from fiber to finished cloth. It relied on a new organization plan in which a professional managerial rank (separate from the owners) oversaw daily operations. Finally, to cultivate an appearance of benevolence (in contrast to the plight of workers in the English mills), the Waltham system required that employees live on site in subsidized and supervised housing.

For their workforce, the owners turned to the young rural women from Vermont, New Hampshire, and western Massachusetts. Textiles were traditionally women's work, and power-driven textile machinery was not necessarily identified with either sex. Moreover, female workers were cheaper than men, the result of their long exclusion from customary craft protections and their loss of the right to make contracts if they were married.

In the early years, parents and daughters both saw benefits in mill work for unmarried young women. Presumably, a daughter would leave her family anyway when she married. Having her work in the mills before marriage reduced the number of mouths to be fed at home. The residential system allayed fears that a young woman was compromising her respectability. Matrons supervised company-owned boardinghouses, where operatives lived together in single-sex settings. Strict rules of behavior guided leisure time, and factory bells regulated the workday.

The success of the mills underscored the paradoxes of American slavery and American freedom in the early nineteenth century. In the early years, at least, the women operatives enjoyed a financial and social independence virtually unknown under the parental roof. They lived together under the guidance of a female head-of-household. They returned home for vacation largely at their own discretion. Many of the young women kept all or most of their pay, enjoying (perhaps for the only time in their lives) a separate disposable income. They developed pride in their work and in their community and began to see themselves part of a long Yankee history of hard work and independence. All of this was made possible by the fact of slavery in the American South.

The final irony of this contradiction would play out only in the later years of the mills, after employers had cut pay and intensified production. In 1834 and again in 1836 the operatives turned out in defiant strikes—condemning the mill owners for reducing them, "the daughters of freemen," to the condition of slaves.

The Rule of Law and Lawyers

Before settling on a writing career, Washington Irving had first trained in the law. He was one of a growing number of young men to do so in the early nineteenth century, as the revival of commerce and the work of governments converged to make that occupation attractive. By 1815 lawyers made up about half the members of Congress.

Americans had long emphasized the importance of the written law to the preservation of the republic, but the law became important in new ways in the growing commercial economy. Overseas trade, internal expansion, the buying and selling of land, new inventions—they all required complex legal documents and lawyers to draw them up and execute them. The growing importance of lawyers reflected the growing importance of courts and of the judiciary. Again and again, judicial interpretation reinforced and set the course for market development. When the common-law tradition clashed with economic development, judges tended to side with the entrepreneurs. For example, as businesses experimented with the use of water power in manufacturing, they sought to erect dams and millraces that altered the flow of streams. English common law protected the use of waterways undisturbed by alterations upstream. But in 1805, in *Palmer v. Mulligan*, a New York court ruled in favor of the right of development, against customary common-law rights. For workers, the power of judicial interpretation became clear in March 1806, when striking Philadelphia bootmakers and shoemakers were found guilty of common-law conspiracy to restrain trade. Conservative newspapers applauded the verdict, but the Jeffersonian *Aurora* protested that there was nothing in the (written) Pennsylvania or U.S. Constitution to support such a decision. The unwritten common law, the *Aurora* insisted, would soon "reduce the laboring whites to a condition still more despicable and abject" than "the unfortunate Africans."

On the federal level, the power of the Democratic Republicans (and, later, the Jacksonian Democrats) in the executive and legislative branches was countered by the power of John Marshall (a Federalist) as the chief justice of the Supreme Court from 1801 until 1835. Between 1805 and 1824, the Marshall Court issued three decisions that brought the Constitution to bear in support of the new market-based economy.

The first, *Dartmouth v. Woodward* (1819), explicitly reinforced the principle that the rights of people were best protected through the rights of contract. The case concerned an attempt by the New Hampshire legislature to alter the original charter of Dartmouth College, given to the college by King George III in 1769 when the nation was still a set of British colonies. New Hampshire argued that the original charter was not binding on the current state government, but Dartmouth insisted that the charter was in fact a contract, protected under Article VI of the U.S. Constitution, which protected debts and engagements entered into before the Revolution. Acting to ensure the stability of contract in the broadest sense, the court ruled in Dartmouth's favor.

The case of *McCulloch v. Maryland*, also decided in 1819, centered on the Second Bank of the United States. The creation of the bank had been one of the successes of the new Democratic Republicans, who had managed to overpower their party's objections to national banks by attracting Federalist votes. The Second Bank had created a number of branches, one of which was in Baltimore. Viewing the presence of the bank within its borders as a threat to its sovereignty, Maryland attempted to assert its authority over the Baltimore branch by taxing it. James W. McCulloch, chief clerk of the branch, refused. Maryland appealed to the Supreme Court, arguing that because the federal government was a creation of the states, its branch institutions could be taxed in the states in which they existed. Marshall's court unanimously rejected this position. The federal government was superior to the states, the Supreme Court concluded. Because the power to tax was potentially the power to destroy, the states could not have the power to tax the creations of the federal government, whatever their location.

Gibbons v. Ogden (1824), the last in Marshall's long line of landmark decisions, concerned a disputed ferryboat monopoly in New York. Having exclusive rights to operate steamboats in the state's waters, Robert Fulton and Robert Livingston had, in turn, "contracted" a part of this right out to Aaron Ogden, giving him a ferry monopoly across the Hudson River from New York to New Jersey. At the same time, however, Thomas Gibbons had obtained a federal license to operate a boat line along a coastal route that came into conflict with Ogden's line. Who controlled these waters and therefore had the right to grant licenses, New York or the federal government? Consistent with its national view of power and development, the Marshall Court found in favor of the federal power. The decision noted that the Constitution had given to Congress (Article I, Section 8) the right "to regulate Commerce with foreign nations, and among the several States." Because the waterways under dispute did not fall clearly within the boundaries of a single state, state power was in this case in conflict with federal power. In such cases,the Marshall court found, federal power took precedence.

Ways of Life in Flux

When Irving's Rip Van Winkle woke up to his new world, he was saddened and confused to discover that all his old friends had either left or died. On the other hand, his wife had also died, and Van Winkle was happy to be freed from her company. Unlike Van Winkle, Americans at the turn of the century were not merely passive objects of the political, social, and economic changes affecting their communities. Those changes grew out of choices some Americans made—to invest in an overseas venture, for example, or to buy new lands in the West to grow wheat or cotton. Their choices affected their own lives and the lives of others and slowly added up to a far more market-driven way of life.

Indian Resistance to the Yeoman's Republic

Although he expressed benevolence toward Indians, President Jefferson believed that they must give way to American settlement. Not only did the territories represent the supply of land necessary to nurture republican virtues and stabilize republican institutions, but they also provided a western buffer against Britain, France, and Spain. Preferring peaceful American expansion westward, Jefferson fostered a growing Indian dependency on American agents that would, he hoped, lead them to sell off their lands.

Nevertheless, by the turn of the century, that westward migration was devastating native life and culture. As settlers occupied new lands, Indians lost their villages and fields. Thrown back on the fur trade, they overhunted dwindling grounds. By 1800 many of the pelts and skins brought to traders in the Northwest Territory had actually been hunted west of the Mississippi River, and the deer were all but gone in the Southeast. Protestant missionaries urged the Indians to adopt European American religious and social practices, including male-headed households and private ownership of property. Unscrupulous agents bullied Indian nations into signing away their land. When the Indians resisted, the agents made deals with leaders they knew to be of doubtful legitimacy, promising bounties and annuities for territory.

Native Americans resisted these assaults on their autonomy. Seneca communities accepted some missionary aid but refused to abandon their holdings, gender division of labor, and matrilineal households. The southern nations declined Jefferson's promise of new lands in the West and focused on constructing internal institutions Americans might recognize as "civilized." For example, the Cherokees adopted a series of laws that functioned as a constitution, established a congress, and executed individual land titles. Meanwhile, resistance to European American culture also took the form of a broad movement for spiritual revitalization. Ganioda'yo (Handsome Lake), who rose to influence among the Senecas after 1799, preached

Tenskwatawa (known as The Prophet) This is a copy of a portrait of the Indian prophet painted some time between 1822 and 1832; the original was destroyed by a fire in 1865 at the Smithsonian, where the portrait was displayed.

revival through a synthesis of traditional beliefs and Christianity, but for other groups revitalization meant cleansing themselves of European American practices. Cherokees revived the Green Corn Ceremony, celebrating personal bonds and repudiating material wealth.

This crisis of survival virtually ensured armed confrontation. As early as 1807, William Henry Harrison, governor of the Indiana Territory, heard rumors of "a general combination of the Indians for a war against the United States." Two Shawnee leaders, Tecumseh and his half-brother, Tenskwatawa (known as the Prophet), coalesced the diffuse anger into organized resistance. Tecumseh's struggles against whites in the Old Northwest and in the South helped him build a pan-Indian alliance. After 1805 Tenskwatawa became the leader of a movement that rejected white culture. About 1808, Tecumseh and Tenskwatawa founded a village in present-day Indiana on the banks of the Tippecanoe River. The Prophet remained there while Tecumseh traveled widely, encouraging organized resistance to white settlement.

By 1811, Tecumseh's success alarmed Harrison. That fall, Harrison marched an army toward Tecumseh's village on the Tippecanoe River. Although cautioned by Tecumseh not to be drawn into battle in his absence, on November 7, 1811, the Prophet engaged Harrison's troops and was defeated. The Prophet was discredited, but when war broke out between Britain and the United States the following year, Tecumseh was still able to amass a huge force for the British. He played a decisive role in the British victory at Detroit but was killed in battle in October 1813. His death marked the end of organized Indian resistance east of the Mississippi.

Winners and Losers in the Market Revolution

For many Americans, the more cash- and contract-based society at the turn of the century offered both new freedom and new wealth. Large merchants who were able to absorb the risks of war might realize enormous profits in transatlantic shipping. Owners of shipbuilding and related enterprises benefited from the prolonged boom in American shipping.

>> Religion in the Backcountry: Cane Ridge, Kentucky

Barton W. Stone was a Presbyterian minister, but one with a number of reservations about his church. In particular, Stone doubted the key Presbyterian doctrine of original sin, which directed that all humans were born sinful and were unable to act for their own salvation; salvation, orthodox Presbyterians believed, came completely through the grace of God. To Stone, as to a growing number of dissenting Presbyterian ministers, God had given humans a capacity to yearn toward salvation and required fervent belief and longing as a condition for grace. Religion without that longing seemed to Stone lifeless and cold.

Pastor of the Presbyterian Church of Cane Ridge, Kentucky, Stone worried especially about the deadness to God's grace in the people around him in the backcountry. The year was 1801, and many of Stone's congregants and neighbors were transplants from from Virginia and Maryland busy settling new farms, slaves newly forced from their families in the East, and drifters fleeing family and community. Most had few church ties and, in Stone's view, little interest in religion.

But by 1801 something was stirring in the backcountry. Prayer meetings scattered throughout Kentucky were drawing thousands of participants: 4,000 at Concord, for example, and 6,000 at Lexington. Stone went to investigate one in Logan for himself—and was amazed at what he found: "Many, very many fell down . . . in an apparently breathless and motionless state," Stone recorded in his journal, their trances broken only "by a deep groan, or piercing shriek, or by a prayer for mercy most fervently uttered." Then they rose up "shouting deliverance . . . men, women and children declaring the wonderful works of God."

Back in Cane Ridge, Stone began organizing a sacramental communion service to be held in August, sending out invitations by word of mouth across the region. Participants began to arrive on August 6. As one observer noted: "On the first Sabbath of August, was the Sacrament of Kainridge, the congregation of Mr. Stone.—This was the largest meeting of any that I have ever seen: It continued from Friday till Wednesday. About 12,000 persons, 125 waggons, 8 carriages, 900 communicants. . . . " The prayer meetings continued day after day and deep into the night. News of events at Cane Ridge spread "like fire in dry stubble driven by a strong wind." Soon, the roads were jammed "with wagons, carriages, horsemen, and footmen," as "between twenty and thirty thousand" people (women, men, and children, whites and blacks, Methodists, Baptists, Presbyterians, the churched and the unchurched, anguished sinners, and the merely curious) hastened to the scene. Cane Ridge was the climactic event of the western revivals of 1800–1801, but it fed waves of revivals that moved into upstate New York (later dubbed "the burned-over district" for the intensity of its meetings). In the first decades of the

continued

AMERICAN LANDSCAPE continued

nineteenth century, religious enthusiasm flamed brightly in the republic. In one sense, there is no surprise in this. Religion had always played an important role in American history. But why this particular outpouring of fervor, and why just at the turn of the century? And why the Kentucky frontier?

Some of the answers lay in the broader rejection of old Calvinist orthodoxies and hierarchical religious styles. The revival ministers preached a theology of self-striving surely welcome to people gambling everything they owned on their ability to make a better life for themselves in the West. And they preached that message with a directness, intimacy, and spontaneous passion that could not have been in starker contrast to the intimidating formality of most Presbyterian and Congregational churches. Ultimately, the Baptists and Methodists were the chief beneficiaries of this shift. Although Stone was a Presbyterian, he was dismissed from the Kentucky Synod for his nonconformist beliefs shortly after Cane Ridge and went on to help found the nondenominational Christian Resto-

ration Movement, which had no formal creed.

Why these revivals caught fire on the Kentucky frontier can be answered by the circumstances of frontier life in 1800 and 1801. The new sects were more willing than the Presbyterians and Congregationalists to send itinerant ministers into the field, wherever people lived. Those preachers often found people newly dislocated from family and friends, excited about their new lives but also isolated and homesick. Christian churches had often supplied sites of solace and community for Americans.

The anxieties of the frontier extended beyond the loss of the familiar. These settlers were part of a torrent of expansion across the Appalachians, advancing into territories still claimed by indigenous people and facing constant resistance from Cherokees, Chickasaws, Shawnees, and others. For European Americans, Christianity had long been a boundary of distinction between themselves and Native Americans and a marker of superiority. And it served that purpose again as migrants grappled with the consequences to others of their new opportunities.

Farmers able to expand their holdings and take advantage of trade networks thrived in the increasingly commercial environment.

The blessings of these new liberties were mixed. New, unskilled workers took jobs away from journeymen, but they were as quickly fired as hired. Wages fell. Near poverty, journeymen in Philadelphia, New York, and Baltimore began to form mutual aid societies, helping each other and laying the foundations for trade associations. But when they tried to organize for higher wages, they discovered that in the eyes of the law, these assertions of liberty amounted to a conspiracy against the rights of trade. When Philadelphia journeyman shoemakers demanded a bill of higher wages in 1805–1806 (in the first strike in United States history), they were arrested and required to pay stiff fines.

But craft masters paid, too. New opportunities in manufacturing lured entrepreneurs and merchants who organized bigger shops, hired cheap workers, and offered cutthroat competition. Initially, the traditional craft masters refused to associate with these new entrepreneurs. By the early 1800s, however, their solidarity eroded. Wanting to take advantage of economic opportunities or to cut costs, shop masters began to hire runaway servants with no questions asked or unskilled workers to whom they had fewer lasting obligations.

Americans described these changing relations of labor and society in the language of the Revolution. Elites fretted that the masses were unfit for republican self-government, whereas workers condemned the older structures of authority as repugnant to a free people. However, local conditions were also sources of new social instability. Apprentices ran away not to express allegiance to Jeffersonianism but to escape cruel masters or to seek higher wages. Masters did not hire untrained workers to affirm republican freedom but to protect profits by cutting costs.

Religion

These were years of ongoing religious upheaval, some of it evidence of a new freedom of belief and some of it expressing a sense of profound personal dislocation.

The new demands for personal liberty focused on religion, as well as work and family, as Americans increasingly objected to paying taxes to support state churches. Anglicanism had been disestablished in the South in the 1780s, replaced by the Protestant Episcopal Church. The Congregational Church was disestablished in New England in 1834, and new denominations began thriving in all regions.

Southerners were drawn especially to new evangelical Christian faiths, principally Methodism and the various forms of Baptist practice. In contrast to the more staid and ritual-based Episcopal Church, these sects stressed the personal, emotional nature of religion and the ability of individuals to struggle actively for their own redemption. Methodists rejected what they deemed artificial differences among Christians, pronouncing "[o]ne condition, and only one" required for salvation: "a real desire." Their system of itinerant preaching (preachers traveled among congregations, rather than associating with a single church) enabled the clergy to reach out to the dispersed and the displaced. Emphasizing inner truth, a plain style, and congregational independence, evangelical denominations offered a relatively egalitarian vision of the community of believers that was especially attractive to the poor, to enslaved and free African Americans, and to white women. Some congregations questioned the morality of slaveholding itself.

Even before Congregationalism was fully disestablished, it was plagued by breakaway movements from within and by competition from the evangelical sects. The most important splinter groups were the Unitarian and Universalist movements, which held generally positive views of human nature, embraced universal salvation, and offered an alternative to strict Calvinism. Everywhere, the far greater threat to established religion came from the Methodists and Baptists, who found converts among country folks and city workers.

This widespread religious turmoil was expressed in a series of highly emotional revivals at the turn of the century, sometimes referred to as the Second Great Awakening. These began in Virginia and western New England and spread quickly into newly settled areas of Kentucky and Tennessee. The most famous of these revivals occurred in August of 1801, in the tiny rural community of Cane Ridge, Kentucky, where thousands of men, women, and children, black and white, free and enslaved, came to watch and experience mass conversions. Eventually, the awakening spread to all parts of the country and to virtually all faiths. Yet many members of older denominations were displeased that revivals were led by unschooled preachers and encouraged unconventional beliefs and extravagant emotionalism. In 1803 to 1805 these misgivings led to schism, as the "Old Light" members of the Kentucky Synod purged "New Light" revivalists. Where Congregationalists and Presbyterians saw confusion in the revivals, Methodists and Baptists saw converts. In the first years of the nineteenth century, the number of Baptist congregations grew from about 400 to about 2,700, and membership in Methodist churches more than doubled, from 87,000 to 196,000. Eager for new members, Methodists founded the the national Sunday School Union and the first denominational publishing house in the United States.

Federalists often viewed this religious upheaval as a sign of the deterioration of both politics and morality. Thomas Robbins, Congregational minister of Danbury, Connecticut, regarded Methodists in New England as dangerous "infestations" encouraged by the Democratic Republican Party. The linkages were seldom so simple. Neither Jefferson nor Madison, the founding lights of the Democratic Republican Party, embraced evangelical faiths. Moreover, far from signaling a drift toward irreligion, this contentious fragmentation of belief at the turn of the century had the effect of securing the language of religion, especially Protestant Christianity, as an idiom of both identity and exclusion in the new nation. Even as they fought over the correct form of Christian practice, many Americans formulated their visions of the ideal political community in the language of Protestant Christianity and suspected those who disagreed with them not only of bad politics but also of bad faith.

The Problem of Trust in a Changing Society

Rip Van Winkle was not much bothered by awakening in a land of strangers. But real people often were. As old friends headed west for new lands, as young people slipped away from parents or masters, as newcomers swelled the port cities, many Americans grew skeptical about whom or what they could trust.

Particularly distressing to middling and wealthy Americans were signs that workers and children were forgetting their proper place. The customary discipline of the craft shop seemed to be crumbling. Apprentices demanded better treatment, refused drudgery work, or just ran away. In the larger port cities, unemployed young men gathered on the streets shouting obscenities, frightening children, hassling shopkeepers, and sometimes attacking strangers. Journeymen in Philadelphia and New York demanded better pay and threatened to take their skills elsewhere.

Household society seemed to be falling apart, too. Domestic workers told masters and mistresses that they should now be called "help" instead of "servants." Indentured workers balked at having their lives closely scrutinized. Even children seemed to have found a new "republican" determination to make their own decisions about whom to marry, where to live, and what work to pursue.

To their parents and masters and mistresses, it seemed that the youth and laboring classes were out of control. Indeed, in 1820, half the nation's population was under the age of 16 (compared with 26 percent under 18 in 2000). Parents threatened and cajoled. Masters offered rewards for runaway apprentices. Ministers warned against libertinism (especially young women's fashions, cut too daringly, they thought). Meanwhile, local authorities responded with laws intended to control apprentices and regulate public behavior.

For several reasons, these efforts were largely doomed. The Revolution and its aftermath had changed society. Young people coming of age at the turn of the century had been nurtured on the rhetoric of independence. The economic boom of the 1790s and the later market revolution offered them numerous alternatives to older structures of authority. Why should a young person remain on the family farm when there were jobs in nearby towns? Why not just leave the controls of indentures or an apprenticeship? Why languish in Philadelphia when New York beckoned?

Rumor and deception thrived everywhere in this landscape. On the brink of war in 1812, one Charles Redheffer told the Philadelphia city government that he had invented a perpetual motion machine. Philadelphians were riveted by the possibilities of steam power, but the city commissioners discovered that Redheffer was actually powering his machine through a hidden cranking device. Rather than simply crying foul, they responded with a hoax of their own, having a local engineer build a similar but even more cleverly deceptive machine. Redheffer fled Philadelphia for New York City, where he was exposed by Robert Fulton (who had his own interest in debunking the machine).

Meanwhile, the New England countryside was filled with treasure hunters who had heard countless rumors of long-buried riches. Some said pirates had buried it. Others said Indian bands—now long dead or departed—had hidden it. Some of these seekers were amateur scientists and historians. Some were charlatans, trying to make a quick buck off gullible visitors. Some were just the down-and-outers of New England's changing economy who still believed in miracles that might turn their fortunes around.

One of these was the treasure seeker Joseph Smith. Smith was born in 1805 to a family of poor farmers in Vermont and grew up in western New York surrounded by economic and religious uncertainty. Although the family moved constantly in a region bursting with development, economic security eluded the Smiths. Perhaps in search of some sense of constancy, Joseph was drawn to the religious revivalism that scorched upstate New York, and he believed in direct spiritual revelation. Occasionally Smith and his father used what they claimed were supernatural powers to hire out as guides in what an observer described as "the money digging business." In 1819, however, Joseph Smith's powers of divination took a different turn: he experienced the first of a series of revelations in which he claimed that God had instructed him to found a new church that would teach the true lessons of Jesus Christ. In a second vision a few years later, an angel gave him the location of golden tablets, buried near his home, which described God's intentions for the "latter days" of creation, now approaching. In 1830 Smith published his translation of the ancient writings on the tablets as the *Book of Mormon*. He formally founded the church now known as the Church of Jesus Christ of Latter-day Saints (or the Mormon Church).

The Panic of 1819

In 1819 Americans learned that the market revolution could produce dream-shattering plunges, as well as exhilarating rises. After he signed the bill chartering the Second Bank of the United States in 1816, James Madison promptly appointed an old political ally, Captain William Jones, as its director. Jones was a poor choice, speculating in bank stock and willing to accept bribes to overlook reckless local practices. By the time he was replaced, bank stock was at an all-time low, and the state banks had glutted the economy with unsecured paper money.

Jones's successor, Langdon Cheves, moved quickly to cut the supply of paper money (too quickly, given that Great Britain was taking the same measures). Cheves began to call in loans and to redeem the bank's holdings of currency issued by the various state banks. Dangerously overextended, the state banks were forced to respond with their own programs of retrenchment. As credit dried up and the value of paper money plummeted, the nation was thrown into depression. Without credit or sufficient circulating money, commodity prices crashed throughout the Atlantic community. The market in cotton, basic to the growing American economy, fell by almost two-thirds. Their mortgages unpaid, farms and businesses failed. And tens of thousands of workers lost their jobs. For three long years, the economy stalled. Visitors to America warned potential immigrants not to come.

Because the branches of the Second Bank of the United States reached far beyond the East Coast, so did the distress of the panic. When the branch in Cincinnati, Ohio, suddenly cashed in the paper money it held from local banks, for example, Cincinnati's booming economy felt the blow, as local banks scurried to collect enough debts to make good on the face value of their paper. Similar shock waves rolled through Kentucky and Tennessee and into the lower South.

Cheves had saved the monetary system of the United States but did not make many friends for the Second Bank. State legislators, who saw the national bank (not runaway local speculation or wildcat state banks) as the villain, scrambled to reduce its power. Fourteen states passed laws preventing the bank from collecting its debts, Kentucky abolished imprisonment for debt, and six states levied heavy taxes on bank branches (a practice soon banned by the Supreme Court in *McCulloch v. Maryland*, discussed earlier). After opening 18 branches in 1817, the Second Bank opened no additional new branches until 1826.

Conclusion

Washington Irving proved a keen and amusing observer of American life. He wrote about John Jacob Astor's fur company in the Pacific Northwest, about Native Americans, and about the customs of immigrant groups. He did not write about the American South, or about slavery—except in a piece titled "The Origin of the White, the Red, and the Black Men" to locate blacks at the lowest level of God's human creation. Like most white Americans of his day, Irving seemed neither aware nor concerned that the growth of the nation he so loved to chronicle was being powered by the enslaved labor of black workers and that his own comfortable life in New York was being sustained, directly and indirectly, by that labor.

>> Timeline

▼1800
Thomas Jefferson elected president

▼1801
Judiciary Act of 1801
Cane Ridge (Kentucky) Revival
Barbary War

▼1803
Louisiana Purchase
Marbury v. Madison

▼1804
Jefferson reelected
Lewis and Clark begin exploration of Louisiana

▼1805
Palmer v. Mulligan (New York)
Essex Decision (British Admiralty Court)

▼1806
Conspiracy trial of Philadelphia journeyman shoemakers

▼1807
First Embargo Act
Hudson River trial of Fulton's *North River Steamboat of Clermont*

▼1808
External slave trade becomes illegal
Madison elected president

▼1809
Non-Intercourse Act

▼1810
American cotton production reaches 178,000 bales

▼1811
Tecumseh at peak of influence
Battle of Tippecanoe River

▼1812
War of 1812 begins
James Madison reelected   *continued*

>> **Timeline** *continued*

▼1814
Federalist Hartford Convention
Treaty of Ghent ends War of 1812
Fully steam-powered textile mills established in Waltham, Massachusetts

▼1815
Battle of New Orleans

▼1817
Work on Erie Canal begun
Steamboats common on Mississippi River

▼1819
Panic of 1819
Dartmouth v. Woodward
McCulloch v. Maryland
Irving publishes "Rip Van Winkle"

▼1824
Gibbons v. Ogden

▼1825
Erie Canal completed

Review Questions

1. What was the market revolution? What concrete changes did it make in Americans' daily lives?

2. How would you account for the timing of the many innovations in transportation at the end of the eighteenth century and the beginning of the nineteenth?

3. By 1816, were the differences between the Federalists and the Democratic Republicans matters of politics, principle, or both?

4. What were the main themes of Jefferson's presidency?

For further review materials and resource information, please visit www.oup.com/us/ofthepeople

Slavery and the Nation

1790–1828

AMERICAN PORTRAIT

>> Lucretia Coffin Mott and the Free Produce Movement

Lucretia Coffin Mott was born in 1793 on the island of Nantucket in Massachusetts. In her adulthood Mott would become one of the most influential and powerful voices for social justice in the United States, a strong supporter of women's rights and a revered antislavery leader. That commitment was honed early in her life by the conflict between her Quaker ideals and the evidence all around her—including in her own family—of the iron grip of slavery on the young republic in which she lived.

Lucretia Coffin was the child of devout Quaker parents, Thomas and Anna Folger Coffin. By the late eighteenth century the Society of Friends had become one of the most outspoken communities of antislavery sentiment in the United States, and after 1774 many Quaker meetings had begun expelling members who owned slaves. Coffin spent her first 11 years in the tight Quaker community of Nantucket, imbibing Quaker beliefs about the dignity and equality of all people, female and male, white and black. She was educated in Quaker schools, including the Friends Boarding School at Poughkeepsie, New York, where she became an assistant teacher. It was there she met James Mott, who shared her Quaker beliefs and became her husband in 1811. When Lucretia joined her parents in Philadelphia in 1809, she moved into the heart of Quaker activism in the United States.

But Lucretia was also the child of a family deeply dependent on the northern merchant economy, which by 1809 had numerous ties, direct and indirect, to slavery. Lucretia's father, Thomas, was a sea captain engaged in whaling and in the China trade. Although the family neither owned nor directly trafficked in slaves, Thomas almost certainly carried food supplies for the Caribbean slave islands and for the West African slaving ports he passed on his way to China. Lucretia's mother, Anna, maintained a family store, where she sold goods acquired in Thomas's voyages. In 1804 the family had

continued

>> **AMERICAN PORTRAIT** *continued*

become successful enough to move to Boston, where Thomas had expanded his business to include trade in cotton. By the time the family moved to Philadelphia, in 1809,
other New England merchant families were beginning to experiment with the textile
mills (using southern cotton) that would soon power the northern industrial economy.
In Philadelphia, meanwhile, Thomas operated a hardware business with Lucretia's husband, James, whose customers were almost certainly southern planters.

Lucretia Mott later recalled that her "sympathy was early enlisted for the poor
slave, by the class-books read in our schools, and the pictures of the slave-ship," but
it may have been in Philadelphia, under the influence of radical Quaker preacher Elias
Hicks and others, that she began to contemplate her personal involvement with slavery.
Hicks had long insisted that opposing slavery meant not only refusing to own slaves,
helping to emancipate and educate them, and speaking out against the institution,
but also cleansing one's own life of the luxuries made possible by slave labor. Under
this influence, and the influence of English Quaker Elizabeth Heyrick, Lucretia began
to boycott commodities made by slaves, chiefly cotton and sugar. But it wasn't easy
to procure substitutes. In 1826 Lucretia and James (who had by this time divorced his
business from the slave trade) helped form the Philadelphia Free Produce Society to
make alternative choices available to members.

Lucretia Mott continued to fight slavery all of her life, but the free produce movement she helped found did not prove a very effective tool. Some of its activists simply
did not consider a boycott a strong enough or direct enough measure against the towering crimes of slavery. Most northerners came to understand that political action, not
consumer boycotts, would abolish slavery in the United States.

Common Threads

>> **What was the impact of the
cotton gin on American overseas
trade?**

>> **How did the economic develop-
ment of the South affect the economic development of the nation?**

>> **How did the social and cul-
tural development of the South
after 1800 affect the daily lives of
northerners?**

>> **How did the tariff affect the
South?**

Southern Slavery

Southern slavery took many forms in the antebellum years. Some enslaved laborers
worked as hired-out field workers or house servants, some worked in mines and mills,
some belonged to small farmers, although most slaves lived on plantations. But what

made all of them "slaves," no matter what they did or where they lived, was the fact that they were defined as property, treated as property, and defended as property.

"Property in Man"

By the time the first slaves arrived in colonial Virginia Europeans had been buying and selling African slaves throughout the Atlantic world for more than a century. For most of that time the trade was dominated by the Spanish and the Portuguese, but at the moment the first Africans were sold to Virginians, the Dutch were becoming dominant in the transatlantic slave trade. The first 20 slaves brought to Jamestown in 1619 had been purchased in Africa a few months earlier and were sold to the English colonists from a Dutch man-of-war.

Those first Africans were already property—slaves—when they arrived, and the English colonists who owned them had a common law of property into which the slaves could be fitted. Almost immediately slaves were showing up in the estate inventories of English settlers as part of the property to be passed on to the relatives of deceased owners. Because slaves were *human* property, masters had to enact slave codes to regulate the slaves' behavior, laws that had no bearing on nonhuman property such as houses and livestock. But slave law was at bottom property law.

In most slave societies—ancient Rome, medieval Islam, western Africa, Brazil, Cuba—large numbers of slaves were individually freed, a process known as manumission. For a time after 1620 the Chesapeake followed this familiar pattern: a good number of the African slaves were freed, and some of those who were freed became slaveholders themselves. By the second half of the seventeenth century the slave societies of Anglo-America, including the Chesapeake, stood out for the very low number of slaves who were freed.

Most property law was written to cover real estate, primarily land and houses, and was riddled with restrictions on how the owner could dispose of an estate. But slaves were moveable property, and their owners chafed under these ancient feudal restraints on real estate. At first they carved out legal distinctions within the law of "real" property, giving masters freedom to dispose of their slave property more easily. But by the end of the eighteenth century the slaveholders had a better solution. They rewrote the law entirely, transferring their slaves from the category of "real" property to the much more flexible category of "personal" property. In the nineteenth century only Kentucky continued to define slaves as a special category of real property. Louisiana devised a similar exception within its distinctive civil law tradition. But the effect was the same: in the nineteenth-century South, what made a slave a slave was his or her status as the personal property of the master.

This was important because slave economies need slave trades, and by defining slaves as personal property, the slaveholders gave themselves the freedom to buy and sell their slaves virtually without restraint. To be sure, Congress banned the foreign slave trade in the United States as of 1808 (the earliest date permitted by the Constitution). In anticipation of this action, between 1800 and 1808 slave traffickers delivered and southern planters purchased at least 40,000 Africans into American slavery. By the Civil War, the southern states had become dependent on a flourishing domestic trade in slaves.

The invention of the cotton gin in the 1790s provoked a boom in cotton production and with it the aggressive expansion of the South into the new cotton lands in the West. In response, eastern slave owners whose farms and plantations were no longer able to sustain profitable single-crop production began to supply slaves—selling their own excess labor "South"—to newer farms in Mississippi, Alabama, and western Tennessee and Kentucky. There is little evidence that slaveholders consciously "bred" slaves to increase profits. But there is abundant evidence that slaveholders were aware of the additional profits to be garnered from slave women who bore many children, and many went out of their way to encourage slave reproduction. Even as the United States withdrew from the Atlantic slave trade, a flourishing domestic slave trade arose to take its place.

The Domestic Slave Trade

Before 1808 most enslaved people who were forced to migrate south and west did so as a part of planter migrations. But by the 1820s, as many as one-third of all migrating slaves (about 15,000 people a year) went west as the property of traders. The internal slave trade was often a highly organized business, with firms employing 10 or 20 employees (bosses, clerks, guards, agents) in fine offices in Charleston, Richmond, and Baltimore. One of its features was the slave market.

The slave market had long been a southern institution, but its sheer inhumanity was laid visible anew as the prime symbol of being "sold South." The market was a ghastly collision of worlds: for potential buyers, sellers, and onlookers, it was a lively gathering place (like a club or tavern) for white men, whose easy camaraderie stood in stark contrast to the terror of the black people about to be offered for sale. Indeed, the amiability of the market helped potential buyers more easily to see themselves as rational, well-motivated businessmen, rather than purveyors of misery. And yet the truth of the transaction permeated the place—in the audible sobs of mothers and children, in the harsh calculations and coarse comments of attendees, and in the absence of white females, a powerful silent admission that what was occurring at the slave market was so nakedly brutal as to taint the purity of white women.

Some slaves were shipped south on a boat, but they were often driven overland. It was a "singular spectacle," one English visitor to Tennessee remembered. "In the early gray of the morning, [I came upon] a camp of negro slave drivers, just packing up to start. They had about three hundred slaves with them, who had bivouacked the preceding night in chains in the woods." Leading the convoy was "a caravan of nine waggons and single horse carriages, for the purpose of conducting the white people."

Former slave Frederick Douglass, born in Maryland, later described the terror that the threat of being "sold South" struck in the hearts of enslaved African Americans. After his owner died when Douglass was eight or nine years old, the enslaved workers were hustled together to be appraised and allotted—some to be retained by family members, some to be "sold at once to the Georgia traders." "I have no language to express the high excitement and deep anxiety which were felt among us poor slaves during this time," Douglass wrote. "Our fate for life was now to be decided. We had no more voice in that decision than the brutes among whom we were ranked. A single word from the white men was enough—against all our wishes, prayers, and entreaties—to sunder forever the dearest friends, dearest kindred, and strongest ties known to human beings." One in three enslaved children under 14 was separated from at least one parent as a result of westward migration. One in three slave marriages in the upper South was destroyed.

The journeys of 20-year-old Elizabeth Ramsey and her infant daughter, Louisa, were illustrative. Elizabeth and Louisa were sold from South Carolina to a Georgia cotton planter by the name of Cook. When Cook landed in bankruptcy, he fled to Mobile, Alabama, where he hired out both Elizabeth and Louisa as domestic servants. He later sold Elizabeth to a new owner in Texas and her daughter to a man in New Orleans.

Plantation Slavery

The symbol of the early nineteenth-century South was the cotton plantation, a large farm owned and operated by a single white family and worked by a large number of enslaved laborers, toiling up and down plowed rows planting the seed in the spring, hoeing the young plants in the hot summer sun, and picking the sticky cotton balls in the autumn. For good reason did this image seem to capture life in the slave South. Although slavery existed in America long before the cotton boom of the late 1790s, that boom vastly increased the demand for slaves. Cotton was a crop highly suitable to slave economies. It could be grown on large plantations tended by gangs of coerced workers who (thanks to the relatively short height of the cotton plant) could be kept under supervision at all times. Of the 1.5 million enslaved inhabitants of the South in 1820, probably three-quarters lived on plantations with 10 or more slaves.

The number of slaves on a plantation varied widely. Sugar plantations averaged 30 or more workers. Rice plantations were smaller, but still larger on average than cotton and tobacco farms. The wealthiest families of the South owned hundreds of slaves on several different plantations, often hundreds of miles apart. Owning large tracts of land and large numbers of enslaved workers was the highest symbol of status in the South. Cotton plantations proliferated in the new western lands. Meanwhile, the reopening of international markets gave new life to tobacco plantations in Virginia and North Carolina, rice plantations in South Carolina and Georgia, and sugar plantations in Louisiana.

For a slave, there was nothing worse than the hellish life of the sugar plantation. Masters there drove workers hardest, producing the highest rates of sickness and death in the South. The crop cycle for sugar was 13 months or more, which meant that the planting of a new crop overlapped with the harvesting of the old one—producing weeks of almost unbearably intense labor. Because sugar, unlike cotton or tobacco, had to be processed immediately on harvesting, sugar plantations had to have the boiling and pressing machinery to rush the cane immediately into production. For these reasons sugar planters preferred to buy strong adult men. Fewer women meant fewer slave families on sugar plantations. To top it off, this intense exploitation took place in the hottest, swampiest parts of the South. Higher rates of sickness and death combined with lower rates of reproduction meant that sugar planters had to restock their slave labor force frequently with newly purchased slaves. The cost of the sugar presses, plus the cost of buying large numbers of the most expensive slaves—strong young men—meant that only the wealthiest owners could afford to set up sugar plantations. The needs of the sugar parishes of southern Louisiana sustained the Old South's largest slave market, in New Orleans.

Rice cultivation was not quite as lethal, but it was also centered in the sickliest low-country regions of the South—the coastal tidewater regions of South Carolina and Georgia, where rice workers stood ankle deep in mud under the blazing sun in snake-infested, swampland fields. Skilled rice cultivators commonly worked by the "task" system, under which workers were assigned a specific task for the day and were able to exercise some autonomy over their labor.

>> Gowrie: The Story of Profit and Loss on an American Plantation

"Gowrie" was a plantation, 265 acres of fertile rice fields spread across a large island in the middle of the Savannah River, upstream from Augusta, Georgia, and over the border from South Carolina.

In 1833, Gowrie's land and enslaved labor force of 50 people became the property of Charles Manigault. Manigault had lost half of his paternal inheritance in the volatile markets of the early 1820s. By the end of the decade he was eager not simply to restore his wealth but also to establish his family among the ruling dynasties of the South.

For Manigault, Gowrie was the means to that end—an investment and a profit center, but never his "home." He never lived full time at Gowrie and never built a family seat there, preferring instead the elaborate mansion at Marshlands, his plantation seven miles from Charleston. Manigault ran Gowrie from afar, directing affairs through periodic visits and regular letters of instruction to his resident overseer, while he traveled abroad and enjoyed more cosmopolitan living.

For the enslaved workers who lived there, Gowrie held different meanings. It was, above all, a place of hard, forced labor. Rice cultivation began in the winter months, when slaves burned off the old stubble in 15 fields and leveled and plowed the land. Women seeded the rice between mid-March and early June. Then, "trunkminders" (aided by the tides of the Savannah River) opened the elaborate irrigation systems to flood the fields. As the seeds grew into young plants, the slaves periodically drained the fields (to allow for weeding and hoeing) and then reflooded them, until the final flooding in mid-July.

The flooding and draining reduced (but did not eliminate) the work of cultivation. However, it created the additional labor of building, repairing, and cleaning ditches, canals, traps, and drains. Men built the systems, while women hauled in the mud to construct earthworks and hauled away the muck that clogged ditches and canals.

But for its laborers, Gowrie was also home, and it offered slaves a few advantages over life on other types of farms. Because of the economics of scale, rice plantations were among the largest in the South and had unusually large slave populations—119 at Gowrie in 1849. The large workforce created a community of kin and friends unknown to slaves on smaller holdings. Moreover, the complexity of the work led most overseers to employ the task system—which provided slaves with a degree of autonomy in their labor. The breaks in the rhythms of cultivation allowed slaves time to plant their own gardens, yielding produce to improve their diets and perhaps some to sell. The slaves were all but forced to do this. Rice planters such as Manigault underfed their workers in the expectation that the slaves themselves would make up for it in their spare time by fishing, raising chickens, tending vegetable gardens, and exchanging their produce among themselves.

Gowrie was a harsh home. Tending muddy or flooded fields was dangerous and exhausting labor, and accidents were common. Constantly wading in the waters, rice workers were particularly subject to snakebites and to malaria. Being forced out in the unpredictably high tides, hurricanes, and floods to mend dikes and clear canals was part of the dangerous everyday labor on rice plantations. Manigault evidently did little to reduce these dangers. Health decisions were often left up to the overseer (who virtually never called in a doctor) and to a single elderly slave woman (who was hard pressed to care for such a large community).

While Manigault grew spectacularly wealthy, enslaved workers paid the price of a staggeringly high mortality rate, especially among children. None of the six infants who lived at Gowrie when Manigault purchased the estate lived to see adulthood. By January 1835, only half of the original labor force remained alive.

But sugar and rice were restricted by geography to relatively contained regions of the South. The vast majority of slaves worked cultivating cotton and, to a lesser extent, tobacco on farms and plantations in the drier inland regions. Growing seasons for these crops were shorter, and the plantations were more self-sufficient in foodstuffs. As a result, cotton and tobacco slaves were relatively healthy. On large cotton plantations, slaves were more likely to be organized in "gangs," set at repetitive tasks under close supervision. Cotton workers dragged their harvest to the gins that pulled the sticky cotton fibers from their bolls, continuing by the light of torches long after sunset. Tobacco workers were busier in the spring, carefully transplanting young plants and pruning off extra shoots.

Not all plantation slaves were field workers. On tobacco farms slaves tended the drying leaf. On sugarcane plantations, workshops were needed to wash, chop, and squash the stalks and reduce their juices to sugar. On big cotton and tobacco plantations, as much as one-quarter of the workforce was assigned to domestic service or to crafts intended to make the plantation more self-sufficient. Although white observers tended to view household servants as fortunate, their lot was not necessarily better than that of field workers. Constantly on call, their workday could last even longer than that of field workers. They were also more vulnerable to the whims and moody outbursts of owners.

More independent than the house slaves were the 5 to 8 percent of the workforce trained for craft work. Men became carpenters, ironworkers, and boatmen. A smaller number of women became spinners, weavers, seamstresses, and dairymaids. Because they worked in separate shops, craft workers often enjoyed a degree of autonomy rare for most slaves.

Some plantations were complex economic concerns, with many barns and outbuildings, batteries of craft workers, a village of slave cabins, and an elegantly furnished "big house." Planters such as George Washington and Thomas Jefferson devoted years to creating homes of luxury and ease—in Jefferson's case, in settings artfully arranged to conceal the slaves whose work created the luxury. But many plantation houses were less noble.

Northerner Emily Burke described the big house of a Georgia plantation as a husk of a building with unplastered walls, an old plank floor, and a roof like a sieve.

Other Varieties of Slavery

Although most enslaved African Americans were held on fairly sizeable plantations, some slaves worked in other settings. On large plantations that did not always require the work of all the slaves, and on older plantations whose soil was exhausted, planters made part of their income by renting out slaves to other plantations or to small farmers. Other enslaved people were hired out to nonagricultural work. By one estimate, a quarter of all Appalachian slaves were hired out, most of those to nonagricultural jobs. Other slaves hired out to work in stores, hotels, blacksmitheries, and cotton gin works. Frederick Douglass hired himself out as a skilled caulker on the Baltimore docks.

A smaller number of slaves worked in extractive industries or mills in the South. In Kentucky, Virginia, and West Virginia, for example, slaves worked in saltworks. White people held virtually all of the supervisory positions, but slaves tended and stirred the boiling kettles of brine and prepared the salt for drying and packing. As the industry grew, it supported an expanding economy in lumber, coal mining, boatbuilding, and shipping (down the Ohio and Mississippi rivers). Some of these related jobs (cutting lumber, operating boats and ferries, coal mining) were also done by slaves and some by free workers whose employment depended on a slave-based industry. In the southern Appalachians, the early 1820s saw the beginnings of a gold rush that peaked in the 1830s. By 1833 some 5,000 slaves (men and women) worked in gold mines in one North Carolina county—enough to raise concerns among local white people about the possibilities of rebellion. Slaves also worked as copper and coal miners and in copper smelters and iron forges. Neither slave owning nor plantation farming typified the experiences of southern whites, most of whom lived on small holdings of several hundred acres or less. These "yeoman" households owned no slaves, although they sometimes hired slaves from nearby planters. Living in rough and isolated homes, they produced as much of their own food as they could; planted small amounts of cash-crop tobacco, cotton, or grain; and often relied on nearby planters to sell their crops or purchase seed or equipment. They also relied on larger estates for labor when they needed to hire a slave for a brief period of time. Beneath these households, economically and socially, was a white underclass of tenant farmers and day laborers and a precarious free black population.

Although most white people did not own slaves, the institution of slavery influenced their material lives and personal values. A workforce of millions of unpaid laborers meant fewer stores and businesses in the slave states than in the Northeast. A large number of rivers flowing from inland regions to coastal ports reduced the need for expensive railroads and canals. All of this meant that the southern economy remained less developed than the North's, and this had important consequences for the southern whites who owned no slaves. By 1820 the South did have mills and factories, but most of the workers were slaves. For subsistence farmers, the relatively underdeveloped slave economy offered some measure of protection. For more ambitious farmers, slavery restricted economic opportunity to the accumulation of land and slaves. Small farmers could hire field slaves from larger planters more cheaply than they could hire free labor, and planters could put a slave to craft work for less than it would cost to hire a free artisan.

>> The Demand for Raw Cotton

The economic and territorial expansion of the United States in the early nineteenth century was propelled by the cotton boom. And the American cotton boom was propelled by the growing European (primarily English) demand for raw cotton.

Americans were not the only suppliers to British mills. Britain also imported large amounts of raw cotton from its colonies in India (and then returned the finished cloth to colonial markets for sale). But the voyage from India to England was long and difficult, and India production alone was unable to satisfy the voracious English demand. Moreover, American short staple proved both more durable than India cotton and cheaper because it was produced by slave labor. By 1800, American planters were producing over 36 million bales of cotton (compared to 1.5 million in 1790, three years before Whitney's invention of the cotton gin). By 1830, that volume had grown to nearly 366 million. By then, cotton accounted for roughly half of all American exports, a proportion that kept growing.

As the annual production of cotton increased, so did the number of slaves and the extent of slave territory. In 1790 there were approximately 700,000 enslaved people in the United States. By 1830 that number had nearly quadrupled, to 2 million. (It would double again in the next 30 years, to almost 4 million.) As the number of slaves increased, so did the price of each person—from an average of about $250 for a field hand in 1790 to $1,500 in 1825—a difference that remained fairly closely correlated with the volume of cotton production. In 1790 most slaves in the United States were held in Virginia, with North and South Carolina and Maryland ranking next in slave populations. By 1830, the number of slaves in Maryland was in decline, but slavery had expanded in Kentucky, Tennessee, Georgia, and Alabama, following the availability of the rich cotton lands in those regions.

Former slave Charles Ball later recalled that the greater British demand for American cotton not only bolstered the internal slave trade but also shaped the qualities planters looked for in the slaves they purchased. In 1805 Ball overheard another white man advising Ball's master to take his slaves to Columbia or Augusta, where "[P]urchasers were numerous and prices good; [and that] prime hands were in high demand, for the purpose of clearing the land in the new country—that the boys and girls, under twenty, would bring almost any price at present . . . and young niggers, who would soon learn to pick cotton, were prime articles in the market."

The international cotton market was not stable during these years. Any number of factors far beyond the control of American producers—the War of 1812, the collapse of credit in 1819, the volatility of world markets—could and did catalyze dramatic shifts in cotton prices. Between October and the end of December in 1818, for example, the value of cotton in American seaports dropped by 26 percent. As the steady growth of cotton cultivation indicates, however, planters' response to declining prices was not to cut back on cultivating cotton but to plant even more.

costume de Scrofuleuse... d'après Jean nièce de Martha church

African American Scrubwoman This early nineteenth-century drawing of an African American scrubwoman is interesting both because it individualizes the subject and because the subject, a worker, is presented in a style of almost classic reflection.

Because southern slavery was overwhelmingly agricultural, the South had fewer and smaller cities than the North. Even in the older seacoast states, less than 3 percent of southerners lived in cities. This number included planters taking refuge during the malaria season, slaves in domestic service for the urban professional class, and the free African American population. Traditionally, southern planters looked to Philadelphia and New York for services and luxury goods. When planters sought alternatives to this pattern of external dependence, they looked not to local villages or towns but to their own plantations, reassigning field workers to produce the butter, cheese, and tools they might otherwise have purchased locally. With a few exceptions, the economies of southern cities were based narrowly on the commerce of slaves and cotton.

Most white southerners lived in rural settings, continuing the patterns of domestic patriarchy that had emerged in the eighteenth century. They had long since accepted the modern notion that freedom and fulfillment were to be found in the private sphere of life, in families and private property. In this view, the good citizen was the patriarchal father who protected his family, stewarded his human and nonhuman resources, and was generous to his neighbors. Whether the farmer was engaged in producing cash crops or concerned primarily with self-sufficiency, his manhood was tied to the economic independence that came with ownership of land.

The slaves were thus another part of the master's property and were fiercely defended as such. But because the accumulation of slaves was a source of wealth in its own right, the economic interests of the master often dovetailed with the benign treatment of his human property. The most consistent calls for reform of the slave system came from efficiency experts who argued that the most profitable plantations were those on which the slaves were well fed, adequately housed, and decently clothed. That was the ideal, of course, but all too many masters were tempted to provide slaves with as little as possible. A rational system of incentives could motivate slave labor, but the whip was often easier. In any case, the proper maintenance of slave property only highlighted the fact that slaves were, after all, property.

Resistance and Creation Among Southern Slaves

For enslaved people, slavery was not merely a system of enforced and often harsh labor. It was also a system of daily survival, practically and emotionally. It was a struggle against poor food, poor shelter, and the constant threat of brutal treatment and separation; a decision to speak or not speak, a judgment to refuse or not refuse, a choice, usually, between unsatisfactory alternatives.

In all its forms, slavery was a steady assault on the selfhood and the family and community life of slaves. The killing of a slave was the most extreme example of this aggression. But maiming and branding were also common practices in the South—so common that inventors devised special instruments for them, and owners included descriptions of signs of torture in their advertisements for runaway slaves. In 1802 Virginian John Stevens let friends and neighbors know that his runaway slave Toney "has scars on his back [not for his good behavior] and one very noted scar on his breast as large as a man's finger and as long, like unto a gristle; he has been branded on both jaws, he being very crafty, and has laid poison oak on them, and has removed the brand and is now become a scar on each jaw."

The scarring, chaining, and beating were common. So, too, were daily casual humiliations. The early life of Elizabeth Keckley (who later purchased her freedom and founded the Contraband Relief Organization to support freed slaves during the Civil War) illustrated common patterns of dislocation. Born in 1818, Keckley scarcely knew her father, who belonged to a different Virginia planter. When she was 18, Keckley was hired out to a man in North Carolina, by whom, cut off from the protection of family and friends, she conceived a child. She later returned to Virginia to live with her mother, but was then forcibly taken to St. Louis. There, faced with the threat of having her aging mother hired out for service, Keckley worked for wages as a seamstress, "ke[eping] bread in the mouths of seventeen persons."

It was not unusual for enslaved women to bear children whose fathers were free and white. Undoubtedly, some intimate relations between enslaved women and free men were consensual, but most were not. In *Incidents in the Life of a Slave Girl*, Harriet Jacobs described the limited choices available to female slaves. Jacobs's master began making sexual advances when she was only 15: "[S]hudder[ing] to think of being the mother of children who should be owned by my old tyrant," and hoping to make him so mad that he would sell her, Jacobs entered a sexual relationship with another white man, with whom she eventually bore two children.

Some slaves chose rebellion. By the turn of the century the record of attempted revolts was long—and the recent successful revolution in Saint Domingue powerful enough to nurse constant fear and dread among white southerners. In the early years of the nineteenth century, enslaved Americans made two more dramatic strikes for freedom.

The earlier of the two was in 1800, in Richmond, Virginia, led by a 24-year-old young man, a slave named Gabriel. Gabriel grew up on the plantation of his owner, Thomas Prosser, where he was taught to read and was trained as a carpenter. When not needed on the plantation, however, Gabriel was sometimes allowed to hire out his own labor in the city, giving most of his wages to his master.

There, Gabriel negotiated his own hours, handled his own pay, and worked alongside free men. He watched as other young men—free men, but men no smarter, more skilled, or educated than himself—went west to new land and new opportunities. He may have heard other workers complain about the city's fathers (mainly merchants, and Federalist) and vow that a Democratic Republican victory would finally wipe away elite control.

Gabriel's plan was bold: to assemble in the woods outside of Richmond, enter the city and take control, and then spread through the countryside, freeing slaves.

By some accounts, the rebels intended to kill all the whites except those "friendly to liberty" and the "poor white women who had no slaves" and then (aided by the French or by Indians) to escape to freedom. By other accounts, Gabriel was willing to make peace with white southerners if they would free African Americans.

The conspiracy was discovered, but not before hundreds of slaves had been recruited, and 27 African Americans, including Gabriel, were executed. According to white witnesses, all went to their deaths with "a sense of their rights and a contempt of danger." It was a determination, Congressman John Randolph later cautioned, "which, if it becomes general, must deluge the Southern country in blood."

Eleven years later, that prediction seemed to come true in St. John the Baptist Parish, Louisiana, when perhaps 500 slaves marched on New Orleans, burning fields, destroying crops, and gathering weapons on the way. Louisiana had long been a cauldron of slave unrest, probably buttressed by events in revolutionary France and Saint Domingue and by the arrival in New Orleans in 1810 and 1811 of perhaps 10,000 refugees from the Haitian Revolution—whites, free people of color, and slaves. But the 1811 uprising was homegrown, led by a Louisiana-born slave of mixed racial background, Charles, who was owned by the wealthy Deslondes planter family.

The rebels made their way down the bank of the Mississippi River toward New Orleans. Armed chiefly with farm tools, they captured weapons and ammunition as they moved from plantation to plantation, destroying crops, burning buildings, and gathering recruits. West of the city, they were met by a planter militia and United States troops, who killed at least 60 slaves. Charles Deslondes and 15 other slaves were captured, tried, and executed, their decapitated heads raised on pikes along the road as a warning to any other slaves thinking of rebellion.

Slave resistance took many forms other than outright or attempted rebellion. Although masters and mistresses were ready enough to punish slaves without cause, individual slaves also set boundaries on that punishment. In his later *Narrative of the Life of Frederick Douglass, An American Slave*, Douglass recalled the day he reached his limit. Douglass had been rented out to Edward Covey, a poor farmer with a reputation for "breaking young slaves." Covey whipped Douglass regularly for six months. And then Douglass was done with it. He fought back, brawling with Covey for two hours until, exhausted and bleeding, the white man gave up. He never tried to whip Douglass again.

Most forms of resistance were less dramatic than Douglass's act of defiance. Feigned illness or ignorance, carelessness, a slow pace of work—all of these diminished the power of the master or mistress or driver, forcing him or her to adjust to the distinctive tempo or personality of the laborer. Field workers carved out implicit understandings with their masters about at least some of the terms of their labor. Task groups finishing early expected to be rewarded with free time. Individuals with particular expertise expected deference from drivers, overseers, and even owners. Throughout the South, a two-hour lunch break in the hottest part of the summer day was customary, and slaves had Sunday for their own work and families.

Slaves were also able to accumulate a certain status, based on age or expertise or their place in the slave community, that owners could not ignore altogether. Such a person was Harriet Jacobs's grandmother. In her memoir, *Incidents in the Life of a Slave Girl*, Jacobs recalled that her grandmother delivered "scorching rebukes" to her master, for which he dared not punish her.

To focus only on their acts of resistance, however, is to see unfree African Americans only in relation to the institution of slavery. Albeit with one eye always on survival, enslaved African Americans also established strong familial and community bonds, rich cultures, and a humanity that often outstripped that of their owners. Parenthood often came to slaves unchosen or, if chosen, still under circumstances choreographed by owners (who often tried to arrange partners). Certainly, some slaves—like some free people—were unable to navigate the responsibilities of parenthood successfully. Separated from spouses and children, many slaves never had the chance to try. All these conditions make the record of strong slave parenting all the more impressive. Parents taught their children to fish and hunt and cook. They praised their children. They told them stories about their grandparents and great-grandparents. White owners felt they were the masters of all their chattel, but African American parents made certain their children understood that, as Jacobs remembered her father's words, "You are my child, and when I call you, you should come immediately, if you have to pass through fire and water."

Enslaved Americans also created communities of custom, both formally and informally. Market women carried produce and handicrafts to county seats and gossiped while they traded with local whites. Men fished and trapped small game. Men and women perfected skills at cooking and storytelling, quilt making and wrestling, and gained reputation and status among their friends. Whites denied legal recognition to slave marriages, but slaves sanctioned their own relationships, combining African ceremonies with European wedding rituals.

As slaves built the economy of the South, they also left a lasting imprint on the culture of southern whites and blacks. Enslaved African Americans began converting to Christianity in the late eighteenth century, and many embraced the religious revivals of the early nineteenth century. Yet as they accepted Christianity, they made it their own. Slave preachers made selective use of Christian themes, emphasizing the story of Moses and the escape from bondage over homilies on the importance of absolute obedience. Newly arrived Africans provided a constant infusion of African religious forms, such as dancing, spiritual singing, chanting, and clapping, as well as distinctly African and Afro-Caribbean religions, such as voodoo. Slave religious practice became both the embodiment and the instrument of self-assertion. The call to "cross over Jordan" in the refrain of many slave songs symbolized the harshness of slave life but perhaps also the singer's intention to escape.

Slavery and National Development

By 1827, when New York finally concluded its long abolition process, few slaves resided in the North and Northwest. But in the North, as in the South, dependency on slavery was not a simple matter of owning or not owning slaves. A free American worker might never see a slave and yet be dependent on the shipping business that carried slave-produced goods or the manufacturing or farming enterprises that supplied planters' needs. An American proud of the country's growth might cherish elaborate shirts and petticoats without ever wondering where the cotton came from. A white American might never have seen a slave and yet believe that there was some natural association of African Americans with servility. As the example of Lucretia Coffin Mott suggested, the dependences were cultural, as well as economic, and they ran deep in the North, as well as in the South.

Slavery and Industrialization in the Northeast

The seagoing economy of the central and northern coast had always been entangled with slavery, carrying food to the slave islands of the Caribbean and slave-produced commodities to European markets. By the late eighteenth century, American merchants were second only to British merchants in the slave traffic itself. But in the early nineteenth century the northern economy began to develop robustly on its own, whereas the slave economy continued to depend on the northern and European markets for the sale of its cash crops.

In the North, cities such as Philadelphia, New York, and, later, Chicago began to stretch their economic tentacles deep into the surrounding countryside and its farms to feed a growing army of city factory workers and other wage laborers. Meanwhile, southern cities such as Charleston and New Orleans remained chiefly commercial ports with few signs of the economic development beginning to emancipate northern cities from their long-standing commercial dependence on the southern slave economy.

Boosters of the southern slave economy missed the signs of the North's slowly emerging economic independence because their own cotton economy was thriving. The slaveholders were shipping larger volumes of cash crops to the North, evidence, they thought, of increasing northern commercial dependence on southern slave society. In many ways the slaveholders were right. Northern and southern economies grew closer in the first half of the nineteenth century. Merchants in New York and Philadelphia began to specialize in consolidating shiploads of consigned cotton and sending it to England, where agents arranged for sales to English textile manufacturers. Those agents then put together shipments of consumer goods for sale in the United States, often to southern planters. The importance of this commerce to the economy of the north cannot be measured in voyages alone. Every voyage required a ship and a crew. The ships were made in Boston, Salem, Essex, and other New England towns, where local residents were employed in logging or as carpenters, caulkers, or sailmakers and on the rope walks. The crews were mostly New England bred but also came from around the world and included African Americans and Native Americans. Most of their clothing was cotton hand-stitched by New England seamstresses, and most of their food was grown by northern farmers, dependent on the merchants to sell their produce. Overseas trade also developed the business services of seaport cities. Insurance companies and banks in mid-Atlantic and New England ports catered to southern planters, providing agents for their sales, protecting their goods against the risks of oceanic trade, and holding their debts.

Northerners also benefited from southern consumers. Planters' annual shopping trips to Philadelphia or New York prompted merchants to import expensive English furniture and Chinese porcelain and encouraged tailors, seamstresses, milliners, and glove makers to keep up with the latest European fashions. Peddlers carried household goods into the southern countryside, and northern bookbinders sold religious tracts and prescriptive manuals to southern households. The symbiotic relationship of northern industry and the slave South are nowhere clearer than in the textile mills of early nineteenth-century New England that powered the Industrial Revolution in the North. The desire for such mills was an old story in the republic, but it took slave-produced southern cotton to make that aspiration viable.

The idea of water-powered mills probably existed apart from the idea of water-powered textile mills using southern cotton, and few could have predicted a southern cotton explosion in 1789, for example, when Massachusetts chartered a mill in Beverly. But even then southern plantations were producing some cotton, and mechanics were working on designs to clean cotton faster.

The cotton boom certainly propelled Francis Cabot Lowell and his associates to make their large investments during and after the War of 1812. Cotton, then, sustained the first major factory workforce in the United States. It also funded purchases of large tracts of land with rivers and falls and eventually supported industrial towns, with all their ancillary commerce, across Rhode Island and Massachusetts. Cotton built those communities dependent on the mills for their housing, their food, their shopping, and even their religion. The textile industry relied on the South not only for raw material but also for customers. Especially early on, most of the rough, coarse cloth produced by the New England mills was considered suitable only for sailors and day laborers—and slaves. To protect this southern trade, in 1816 Lowell lobbied for (and received) a strong tariff that taxed imported woolen and cotton goods.

The reliance was reciprocal. Just as southern cotton underwrote this aspect of northern industrialization, so too did the northern mills at critical moments save the southern cotton industry. The interruption of export trade before and during the War of 1812 was difficult for southern cotton growers, but it might have been even more harmful had the new northern mills not offered an alternative market for their crops.

The many linkages between northern and southern economies led some slaveholders to predict defiantly that the Yankees would never wage war on slavery because they were too dependent on the South. But this was an illusion. What the northerners wanted was cotton, whether it came from Egypt or Alabama, whether it was produced by wage laborers or by slaves. The statistics showing the importance of cotton to America's overseas trade impressed slaveholders. But what those statistics did not show was the far greater volume of trade and commerce within the northern states themselves that was dependent on the development of cities and industry at home rather than oceanic commerce. The textile mills needed the cotton produced by southern slaves, but the mill owners and shoe manufacturers of New England needed even more the northern customers who made their livings off wages in the factories and businesses of a rapidly developing northern economy. By 1860 the South was more dependent on the North than ever, but the North was not nearly as dependent on the South as it had once been.

Slavery and the West

Like other regions, the "West"—the area beyond the Appalachian Mountains tied together by the Ohio and Mississippi river valleys—was actually several Wests. Parts of the West were slave and parts were not: in 1819 slavery was legal in Alabama, Mississippi, and Louisiana and not legal in Ohio, Indiana, and Illinois. The free states tended to replicate Northern economic patterns: small freehold farms connecting to towns and small cities that served both as market and manufacturing centers and as transportation centers to the coasts. The slave states tended to reflect the economic patterns of the South: many small general farmers and some very large plantations whose owners tended to dominate economic exchange between the countryside and the coastal ports, with a relatively small number of town centers that served as providers of legal services more than as independent economic units.

In some parts of the western region, these differences were quite pronounced, dividing at the Ohio River. But the river valleys also united the economies of north and south and merged them into a single region. Farmers in the Northwest had long been frustrated by their lack of convenient access to eastern markets. The opening of cotton lands along the southern Mississippi resolved that problem, with growing new local markets for their grain and pork and lumber products. Northern cities along the Ohio provided transportation, business, and manufacturing services to customers and producers all up and down the river system.

Cincinnati was an example of the web of western development. Like other settlements on the Ohio and Mississippi rivers, Cincinnati's location helped it become a thriving trade center, shipping wheat, corn, rye, and livestock overland to Pittsburgh and downriver to New Orleans, and selling goods and services to local farmers. Even before the War of 1812, Cincinnatians had begun to reorient their trade from overland routes across Pennsylvania to water routes down the Mississippi. The outcome of the war guaranteed access to those routes down to the Gulf of Mexico and also opened the way for the newly invented steamboat to carry goods upriver. When it incorporated as a city in 1819 Cincinnati had 10,000 residents and the title "Queen of the West."

These economic connections sometimes led to political sympathies. Although technically free, Ohio entered the Union with a severe "black code" that barred all blacks and persons of mixed race from entering the state unless they could prove they were free, that required such people to purchase certificates of freedom from the county where they resided, and that required that employers verify their free status before hiring black people. Both Indiana and Illinois abolished slavery in their state constitutions, but both followed Ohio in passing harsh restrictions on free blacks. Even as a territory in 1813, Illinois prohibited free blacks from entering, under penalty of 39 lashes and expulsion—although out-of-state slaveholders were allowed to rent their slaves to work in Illinois. In 1822 proslavery sentiment was so strong in Illinois that voters tried to legalize slavery in the state, electing proslavery majorities to the legislature and just missing electing a proslavery governor. In a referendum in 1824, proslavery forces lost, but they took 43 percent of the vote.

Slavery and the Laws of the Nation

The men who wrote the Constitution had compromised on the issue of slavery, and it is the nature of compromises to produce ambiguities. After the Constitution was ratified, for example, both New York and New Jersey abolished slavery in their states—completing the process of emancipation in the North. Congress reenacted the Ordinance of 1787, prohibiting the importation of slaves into the Old Northwest and into the federal territories of the Old Southwest. And in 1807, the earliest possible date allowed by the Constitution, Congress prohibited the importation of any more slaves from the Atlantic slave trade. Under the new Constitution, the states were now free to abolish slavery on their own, and the federal government assumed the power to regulate and even prohibit slavery in the

Cincinnati Public Landing A gateway to the Northwest and the South, by 1820 Cincinnati was a thriving city. This view of the Ohio River wharf by John Caspar Wild suggests the complex economy that supported the city's prosperity: retail establishments, wagons carrying settlers west and bringing produce from the backcountry, and steamboats transporting goods and people up and down the Mississippi River system as far south as New Orleans.

territories. The Founders' misgivings about slavery were reflected in their deliberate decision to exclude the word "slavery" from the Constitution itself.

At the same time, however, the Constitution recognized and even protected slavery from federal interference in the states where it already existed. The Three-Fifths Clause, for example, gave white southerners disproportionate power in the House of Representatives and the Electoral College (in which the number of electors for each state was based on the number of senators and representatives). And although the Constitution implicitly recognized slavery as a matter of *state* law, Article IV made the protection of the slave owners' property a *national* obligation: "No person held to service or labour in one state, under the laws thereof, escaping into another, shall, in consequence of any law or regulation therein, be discharged from such service or labour, but shall be delivered up on claim of the party to whom such service or labour may be due." The article avoided the word "slave," but everybody referred to it as the "fugitive slave clause" of the Constitution.

The Constitution thus produced a patchwork of state and national laws, some of which restricted or abolished slavery and some of which protected it. In 1793, for example, Congress enacted a fugitive slave law that made it a federal crime to aid an escaping slave. But it left enforcement of the law to the states, and in the North accused runaways were often guaranteed the due-process rights of free citizens, much to the dismay of the slaveholders. The slaveholders objected because slaves were, by definition, not citizens. But northerners resented the Three-Fifths Clause for precisely the same reason. In principle, only citizens were supposed to be counted for purposes of representation. By counting as citizens three-fifths of the slave population, the Constitution rewarded southern states with enough extra representatives and Electoral College votes to help ensure the election of a string of presidents from the South. Their support for a limited federal government helped protect slavery from federal interference.

Local and state laws concerning slavery affected the lives of people in all the states. Northern states, for example, passed personal-liberty laws designed to protect free blacks from being kidnapped into slavery by bounty hunters in search of fugitive slaves. But northerners understood that the personal-liberty laws made it much harder for masters to enforce the fugitive slave clause of the Constitution. Southern masters deeply resented what they saw as northern-state interference with their rights of property. Conversely, when Charlestonians, fearful of the influence of free black sailors over South Carolina slaves, empowered sheriffs in southern ports to lock up free black sailors, they affected the lives and the employment of men from Boston and Nantucket and New York. The law not only specified the imprisonment of black sailors but also required a bond from their captains to cover the costs of incarceration. Under pressure from a planters' organization, the sheriff of Charleston imprisoned free Jamaican sailor Harry Elkinson. In court, lawyers argued that any treaty that interfered with the power of the state to guard against internal revolution must be unconstitutional. The court rejected this position, but South Carolina continued to enforce the act. By this time, black sailors made up roughly a fifth of northern seamen—a proportion far higher than their presence in the free population. Sailing was an important occupation for them and their families. The act in effect made hiring them a handicap to any captain using South Carolina's ports and jeopardized the sailors' employment. The South Carolina act was later copied by Louisiana, North Carolina, Alabama, Georgia, Florida, and Texas.

Free Black People in a Republic of Slavery

By 1815, some 200,000 African Americans lived as free inhabitants of the United States, most of them in urban areas. Whether they were more than inhabitants—whether they were citizens—varied from state to state and from North to South.

Free blacks faced formidable discrimination in all parts of the country. In the slave South, their very existence was a threat to the system, both in the possibilities of freedom they represented and in the avenues of communication they offered enslaved people. Southern and border states responded by tightening laws permitting individual emancipation, by increasing surveillance of slaves, and by regulating the movement and occupations of free black people. Southern courts increasingly argued that the "taint" of color followed African Americans out of slavery, assuming that free blacks lacked the privileges and immunities of citizens. Free blacks in the South were barred from militias, from the ownership of weapons, and from occupations that might bring them into contact with slaves, such as operating groceries or taverns. What's more, they lived in daily danger of being enslaved, especially as the demand for slaves in the new southern territories increased. It was worth a free black person's life to cultivate ties with the white community, should he or she need authority to ward off the greed of traders. Some border states—including Maryland, New Jersey, and Ohio—barred free blacks from settling within their borders.

Free blacks in the North suffered from similar discriminations, but their conditions varied from state to state. In New England, blacks could vote and send their children to public schools alongside white children. In other states, such as New York, free black men could vote only if they met a property qualification not required of white men. Elsewhere, blacks were barred from voting altogether. Most northern courts assumed that blacks were citizens entitled to own property, to make contracts, to move about freely, and, if accused of crimes, to have a jury trial. But some northern states, particularly along the borders of the South, prohibited free blacks from moving into the state, thus denying them one of the traditional "privileges and immunities" of citizenship. And as in the South, blacks were often segregated from whites in schools, churches, theaters, cemeteries, hotels, streetcars, ferries, and railways.

In the North and the South, however, the laws were not always a reliable measure of social practice. Often, free blacks and whites interacted every day in ways that defied state statutes. They did business with one another, attended the same churches, and helped one another in times of need. In some southern states the laws restricted free blacks from owning land and houses, but free blacks did so anyway. Periodically, states and localities would require free blacks to be licensed for certain jobs or to carry freedom papers with them at all times, but the laws were only erratically enforced. The threat of enforcement, however, was a constant source of pressure on free black communities across the South.

Within this complicated mosaic of formal and informal discriminations, free African Americans found ways to survive, to earn a living, and, once in a while, to flourish. By the 1820s, the self-help movement founded at the beginning of the republic had yielded many African American mutual-aid and benevolent associations. Organizing was most lively in Philadelphia, where free blacks established more than 40 new societies between 1820 and 1835, but the self-help impulse extended south to Baltimore and Charleston and north to New York and Boston. Although some societies were clearly limited in membership to relatively prosperous free blacks, self-help organizing crossed economic lines: coachmen, porters, barbers, brick makers, sailors, cooks, and washerwomen all formed associations.

Although the vast majority of free blacks lived in cities, a few lived in the countryside. Some of those owned their own land, but most worked as farm laborers or as sharecroppers (dividing their produce with the white landowner on a preagreed basis, usually not advantageous to the sharecropping family). Free black farm laborers often did not live on the farms they worked, but rather resided in nearby small towns, where they might find at least a few other free black men and women like themselves and where they were freer from white landowners.

The growth of white racial prejudice in the nineteenth century was reflected not simply in the spread of laws discriminating against blacks but also in renewed calls for the abolition of slavery. In 1816, a group including prominent national politicians, northerners, and slave owners formed the American Colonization Society (ACS). Styling itself a benevolent society, the Society (whose founders included Andrew Jackson, Francis Scott Key, Daniel Webster, and Henry Clay) determined that because of "unconquerable prejudice resulting from their color," African Americans could succeed only in Africa, which was declared their home (although by 1816 almost all United States slaves had been born in the republic). Made up of wealthy, influential white men, the ACS lobbied Congress for funds. It received $100,000 in 1819 and sent out its first emigrant ship in 1820. Dedicated to removing free African Americans from their native land to Liberia, in Africa, the ACS signaled waning white support for a racially integrated republic.

Even the federal government restricted African Americans from certain occupations. As early as 1798 the secretaries of war and the navy had each tried to bar African Americans from the military. In 1810, the federal government excluded African Americans from delivering the mail.

The Politics of Slavery

In 1817 a Boston reporter, observing the absence of the invidious politics that had plagued the first three decades of nationhood, declared that America had at last achieved "an era of good feeling." That sentiment seemed true three years later when President James Monroe was reelected with all but one electoral vote.

But all was not right with the new republic. Among the festering problems, becoming more apparent even in a time of seeming prosperity, was slavery, its existence ever more controversial. In 1820 the Congress defined the slave trade as piracy. Five years later a U.S. patrol seized the slave ship *Antelope*, sailing under a Venezuelan flag with a cargo of 281 Africans. Declaring the slave trade contrary to natural law, the U.S. Supreme Court freed most of the slaves. Because the United States had no jurisdiction over the laws of other nations and because slavery was legal in Spain and Venezuela, the Court returned the ship and the 39 captives held to be owned by Spaniards.

Free blacks and a significant number of whites continued to attack slavery as immoral and proposed to abolish it. A larger group of white people, though far from committed abolitionists, felt uncomfortable supporting the institution. Northern churchgoers were uneasy with their denominations' acquiescence to slavery, for example, and northern mill owners and merchants, so tied to the institution, nevertheless shied away from acknowledging that linkage publicly. And many northerners who thought very little about slavery at all were aware that the Three-Fifths Clause had helped ensure southern victories in seven of the first eight presidential contests. Had it not been for that clause, they believed, that single northerner, John Adams, would have been reelected president over Thomas Jefferson in 1800.

The Missouri Compromise

Land hunger had fueled the new American economy, having come to represent national, as well as individual, prosperity for many Americans. For decades northerners had been trying to block slavery's westward expansion, only to be thwarted by an increasingly aggressive block of powerful southern politicians. During the War of 1812, calls for national unity had silenced antislavery advocates. But when peace returned, a spate of proslavery expansionism provoked the most powerful reaction yet among northerners. Before the war, Americans had withdrawn from the despicable Atlantic slave trade, but with the war over, it was clear that southern expansionism was creating an equally despicable domestic slave trade. By 1819, when Missouri applied for permission to organize as a state, antislavery politicians had had enough.

The question of Missouri, though legally framed in terms of national political power on the federal level, was inextricable from the larger dispute over the morality of slavery. Northerners had long been unhappy with what they saw as the unfair advantage awarded to southern states by the Constitution's Three-Fifths Compromise. Admission of Missouri would extend that unfair pattern of representation in the House and create a new imbalance in the Senate, where each state had the same number of representatives regardless of population. In 1819 there were 22 states in the Union, 11 free and 11 slave. Admission of Missouri would give the slave states domination in any purely sectional disputes. (Florida, certain to apply later for admission as a slave state, would add to the disparity.) Meanwhile, the South continued to dominate the presidency.

There were other issues. Missouri was the first wholly new state to be organized from the Louisiana Purchase. (Louisiana had entered as a slave state, its slavery already established in the territory.) Missouri, northerners feared, would set a precedent for extending slavery into additional new states carved out of the territory. By 1819 many northerners also no longer believed that slavery would simply die on its own. Far from withering away, the institution seemed to be thriving. Americans had imported only about 5 percent of the Africans forced into slavery in the hemisphere, but by 1819 slaves in the United States were one-third of all the people of African descent in the Americas. Slavery seemed to be making headway even in free states. When Illinois had entered the Union in 1818, for example, it had entered as a free state but with a "black code" that limited the economic and civil rights of free blacks and provided for the continuation of slavery where it existed in the southern parts of the state.

The trouble over Missouri began almost at once. In the House debate, New York representative James Tallmadge proposed that Missouri be admitted under two conditions. First, no more slaves were to be brought into the state, and, second, slavery was to be gradually abolished after the state was admitted to the Union. Southerners unanimously opposed the amendment, whereas northerners voted unanimously for it. The more populous North carried the vote. But when the House bill reached the Senate committee charged with its consideration, the vote was reversed. The Tallmadge amendment died in committee, to be reintroduced in the next session.

By the time Congress reconvened, positions on both sides had hardened. Northern congressmen insisted that Congress had the power to prohibit slavery in a territory. Just as the Congress of the Confederation had earlier prohibited slavery in the Old Northwest Territory, now the federal Congress must prohibit it in the Louisiana Purchase. Southern congressmen responded that the Constitution provided no such power to Congress and that the states had carefully preserved their equality in joining the federal pact. In addition, they argued that in guaranteeing that no citizen could be deprived of life, liberty, or property without due process of law, the Fifth Amendment actually protected the right of slave owners to carry slaves into new states.

The struggle over Missouri was the culmination of decades of growing frustration on the part of antislavery northerners. Also, it accurately foreshadowed later congressional debates over slavery, as it did the use of racial politics as a weapon for silencing antislavery politics, a pattern lasting until the 1850s. Arguing for the continuation of slavery,

Senator Nathaniel Macon of North Carolina cautioned that in no place in the United States were free people of color truly welcome. No one rose to dispute him. Indeed, racism was codified in many northern state constitutions. Ohio and Connecticut excluded black men from voting. Vermont and New Hampshire barred black men from the militia. Rhode Island and Indiana prohibited black and white people from marrying, and Indiana also barred blacks from appearing as witnesses against whites.

The firestorm over Missouri was finally resolved when Maine applied for statehood as a free state. Under Speaker of the House Henry Clay's guidance, the two bills were linked, preserving the balance in the Senate. The compromise also provided that slavery would be permitted in Arkansas Territory but excluded from the rest of the Louisiana Purchase. The compromise passed narrowly in March of 1820.

Almost immediately, another problem arose when Missouri submitted a state constitution that barred free black people and free persons of mixed heritage from the state. This was a clear violation of Article IV of the Constitution, which provided that citizens of one state should enjoy the rights of citizens in all states. Here was another sign of an emerging sectional division over the issue of black citizenship. In 1821, during the second round of the Missouri crisis, that division was just beginning to show itself, as Henry Clay struggled to engineer a second compromise. Congress allowed Missouri to enter under the proposed constitution, but it demanded that the new state legislature promise never to interpret the clause to mean what it so obviously meant, that Missouri reserved the right to deny free African Americans their constitutional rights. The Missouri territorial legislature made the promise but withheld any power to bind the people of the state to what it said. Finally, in August 1821, President James Monroe greeted Missouri as the 24th state of the Union.

Antislavery in the 1820s

The Missouri Compromise was a devastating defeat for the opponents of slavery. For decades they had struggled to hold back the expansion of slavery and the growing power of the slaveholders in national politics. Disgusted by the increasing belligerence of proslavery politicians, antislavery northerners had campaigned to stop slavery once and for all, they hoped, by keeping it out of Missouri. But they had failed, and the consequences of their failure were soon apparent. Slavery's defenders had always used racial politics to try to stop antislavery politics, but their successes were limited and local until the 1820s. Impressed by the strength of antislavery sentiment during the Missouri crisis, southerners joined an emerging political coalition that came to be known as the Democratic Party. This coalition started from the premise that slavery would henceforth be excluded from national politics by means of an increasingly effective white racial consensus. It worked. By the late 1820s national antislavery politics was effectively dead.

With the collapse of antislavery politics, leadership of the movement passed to a small group of articulate abolitionists who took up the cause with more fervor than ever. Free black leaders in the North led the way. They began to wonder whether the American Colonization Society had become a cover for slaveholders who wanted to forestall abolition by insisting that blacks were unfit for self-government. Colonization, which began as a conservative means of supporting abolition, looked more and more like an effort by slaveholders to rid themselves of the troubling presence of free blacks. The transformation of the ACS was further evidence of the collapse of antislavery politics.

There was another, bigger, problem with colonization. By the 1820s almost all African Americans in the United States were American born. Although some later thought about migration to Haiti or to Canada, most claimed the United States as their own. They strongly rebuffed the ACS's attempt to recruit them for relocation efforts. Many earlier black efforts had focused understandably on self-help and community building. The emphasis on self-help grew in the wake of the Missouri debates, the organization of the ACS, and the racism of the early nineteenth century. It was a constant refrain from black abolitionists: "Too long have others spoken for us," John Russwurm and Samuel E. Cornish declared in the first issue of the first independent black newspaper, *Freedom's Journal.* In the 1820s, free blacks began to form their own all-black antislavery groups, beginning in 1826 with the General Colored Association of Massachusetts. Their protest was not timid. In 1829 David Walker, an early member of the Association, published a pamphlet titled *An Appeal to the Colored Citizens of the World*, calling on blacks to take resistance to slavery into their own hands by armed insurrection, if necessary. Walker's protest, like those of other black antislavery writers in this period, targeted the hypocrisies of white people. In his first article, he noted that a South Carolina newspaper article had labeled Turks "the most barbarous people in the world" who "treat the Greeks more like brutes than human beings." In the same paper, however, Walker had also found an advertisement for the sale of "Eight well built Virginia and Maryland Negro fellows and four wenches [to] positively be sold this day to the highest bidder!" "And what astonished me still more," Walker added, "was, to see in this same humane paper!! the cuts of three men, with clubs and budgets on their backs, and an advertisement offering a considerable sum of money for their apprehension and delivery." Many whites were furious, and southerners put a $3,000 bounty on Walker's head. Walker was undeterred: "Somebody must die in this cause," he added. "I may be doomed to the stake and the fire, or to the scaffold tree, but it is not in me to falter if I can promote the work of emancipation."

The defeat of the antislavery forces in 1820 also helped inspire a new and more radical abolitionist movement among a small but vocal group of white Americans. By the mid-1820s, popular clamor had prompted a few northern states to pass laws divorcing them from the national Fugitive Slave Act and making it more difficult for masters to recapture runaway slaves. An 1820 state law made it illegal for Ohio officials to enforce the federal 1793 Fugitive Slave Act and made kidnapping free people of color in Ohio punishable by fines of up to $2,000 and "seven to twenty-one years' imprisonment at hard labor." When proslavery forces tried to scuttle the act in 1826, antislavery workers—black and white—combined to pass another bill that essentially restated the first. Meanwhile, Quakers in Philadelphia and other northern cities began to try to wean themselves from dependence on slave goods.

With the defeat of antislavery forces and the triumph of racial politics, radical abolitionism emerged in the 1820s. Absent the discipline of party politics, the abolitionists were a contentious lot. But through the 1830s and into the 1840s they were the lonely voices of antislavery idealism in America, and from the start they made it their business to break through the racial consensus and put opposition to slavery back on the national political agenda. In the wake of disastrous defeat and in the face of overwhelming

>> Timeline

▼1791
Haitian Revolution

▼1793
Eli Whitney invents cotton gin

▼1800
Thomas Jefferson elected
Gabriel's rebellion, Richmond, Virginia

▼1807
First trip of Robert Fulton's *North River Steamboat
of Clermont*

▼1808
External slave trade illegal

▼1810
American cotton production reaches 178,000 bales

▼1811
Slave rebellion in Louisiana

▼1814
Treaty of Ghent reopens trade with England
Waltham mills open

▼1815
Steamboats begin regular two-way trips on the Mississippi

▼1816
Tariff provides protection to northern textile mills
James Monroe elected president
American Colonization Society founded

▼1817
New York begins construction of Erie Canal
(opened 1825)

▼1819
Missouri applies for statehood
Panic of 1819

▼1820
Maine becomes a state

>> **Timeline** *continued*

▼**1821**
Missouri becomes a state
Benjamin Lundy founds *The Genius of Universal Emancipation*

▼**1822**
South Carolina Negro Seamen Act

▼**1823**
Merrimack Manufacturing Company mills in Lowell produce first finished cloth

▼**1824**
John Quincy Adams elected president

▼**1825**
Antelope affair

▼**1826**
Lucretia Mott and others form Philadelphia Free Produce Society

opposition, abolitionists white and black alike never gave up. And in the long run, they would win.

Conclusion

One of the reasons the Founders had compromised with slavery when they produced the Constitution of 1787 is that they thought it was a dying institution. By then most northern states had abolished slavery, increasingly strong antislavery movements were making headway in the two northern states in which it remained, slavery's expansion into the northwestern frontier had been restricted, and the slave economy in the tobacco states seemed to be foundering. But the Founders underestimated slavery's strength in the deep South and could not have predicted that a new machine—the cotton gin—would soon revive southern slavery, making it stronger and more aggressive than ever. The result was a lethal paradox: As slavery became stronger, it also became strictly sectional. As northerners stepped up their fight against slavery's expansion, slaveholders stepped up their defense of slavery. By 1820 it appeared that the experiment in republican government would collapse over the issue of slavery. But a compromise, followed by a determined effort to keep the slavery issue out of national politics, established an uneasy truce that kept the Union intact for another generation. With slavery shoved to the sidelines, American voters turned to the contentious but less threatening issues of economic development and political democracy.

Review Questions

1. What were the provisions of the Missouri Compromise?

2. How were the Waltham and Lowell mills linked to the South?

3. How did the 1808 abolition of the foreign slave trade affect slavery in the United States?

4. What assumptions about American society were expressed in the American Colonization Society?

For further review materials and resource information, please visit www.oup.com/us/ofthepeople

Jacksonian Democracy

1820-1840

11

>> Harriet Noble

By 1824, the New York backcountry was abuzz with talk of Michigan Territory and the opportunities there for families willing to make the trip. The economy was at last bouncing back from the Panic of 1819. Markets for agriculture, in the east or down the Mississippi River, were reviving. Land prices had declined slightly, and families could buy in for smaller parcels.

"My husband," Harriet Noble later wrote, "was seized with the mania," and by September, the Noble family—Harriet, 21, her husband, 23, and their two young daughters—had joined the growing migration of Americans moving west. "Could we have known what it was to be pioneers in a new country, we should never have had the courage to come," Harriet recalled.

Harriet's husband had already made the journey once that year, with his brother, to scout out land for their families. Now the two families set out. First came a rough trip by wagon over bad roads to Buffalo. Next, after a four-day wait in Buffalo for a steamship that never showed up, a seven-day trip on a schooner across Lake Erie "entirely prostrated with seasickness," Noble recalled. And then, after days of trekking through the Michigan wilderness until "my feet were so swollen I could walk no further," they arrived at Ann Arbor: "some six or seven log huts occupied by as many in-mates as could be crowded into them." The Nobles jammed in with the others, so packed that they could not move in the night without stepping on someone's hand or foot. So

No pictures of Harriet Noble exist, but this one of Ann Allen, who moved to Michigan at the same time, suggests what Noble might have looked like in her 50s.

they survived for a month and a half, until the men managed to put up separate cabins. But that winter most of the community fell mysteriously ill. Deciding they had chosen an unhealthful place, the following spring the Nobles moved again, this time to Dexter, 10 miles west. They were fortunate enough to be able to take over a shell of a log cabin abandoned by discouraged settlers before them. That summer and fall Harriet and her

continued

>> AMERICAN PORTRAIT *continued*

husband worked together to put a roof over their heads and haul stones to set a fire-place. By the second winter, they had a roof, a floor, a fireplace, and a door. Provisions were always scarce. Waiting 15 days for her husband to return from Detroit with supplies, Harriet ran out of flour. "After being without bread three or four days, my little boy, two years old, looked me in the face and said, 'Ma, why don't you make bread; don't you like it? I do.'"

The difficulties continued into the next year: first Harriet and her husband were recurrently ill with fever and barely able to work. As they seemed to be recovering, her husband had his hand "blown to pieces" in a gun accident, permanently disabling him and forcing Harriet to do all the field work, the tending of the animals, and the laying by of wood. Not until the following spring, three years after their arrival, did prospects look up, when Harriet's husband was at last able to travel back east to get a nephew to help with the work.

Harriet Noble and her husband were the kind of Americans Andrew Jackson considered the heart of the democracy—ordinary citizens of modest means willing to risk their resources, even their lives, to gain new opportunities and forge new freedoms. They were the people for whom he and his generation had fought the Revolutionary War. Especially after he lost his first bid for the presidency in what he considered "a corrupt bargain" among the eastern and western elites, Jackson resolved that these Americans must be protected. Of course, settlers were not the only struggling common Americans by 1824. The port cities were awash with wage laborers trying to support themselves and their families on smaller and smaller paychecks. But Jackson was a man of the pre-market revolution era. He distrusted paper money and wages and banks. His was still a world of settlers to be protected against the rich and well connected. Convinced that he alone could provide that protection, he would do this even if it meant forcibly dispossessing tens of thousands of indigenous people, ignoring the decisions of the Supreme Court, threatening to send federal militia against state authorities, and, all in all, claiming for the executive branch of government an expanse of powers so unprecedented that his critics would label him "the tyrant."

Common Threads

>> Why was the Bank of the United States so controversial in the early republic?

>> How did the market revolution affect wage labor?

>> What actions and policies of the Democratic Republican presidents,

1800–1824, laid the groundwork for Jackson's breakaway movement?

>> Did the territorial expansion of the republic require the removal of Native Americans?

Common People and the Political Economy of Democracy

Americans had long associated republican virtue with labor, particularly with labor that afforded economic independence. In the early years of the republic, that virtue-producing labor was most often represented in the figure of the farmer. In the wake of the market revolution and the madcap dash across the Appalachian Mountains, that image had been fractured. In place of Jefferson's cherished yeoman farmer were the settlers and the urban workers.

Settlers

The migration into the backcountry, set off by the Treaty of Ghent in 1815, continued throughout the 1820s. After Maine in 1820 and Missouri in 1821, no new states entered the Union until Arkansas in 1835. But in the meantime the populations of the new states grew steadily, in some cases doubling and tripling in a single decade: Mississippi grew from 75,448 in 1820 to 136,621 in 1830, Illinois from 55,211 to 157,445, and Indiana from 147,178 to 343,031.

North or South, migrants wanted land. They also wanted easy credit and low prices—but they weren't always convinced that government was their friend in getting these. To be sure, the price of land per acre and the size of the minimum-permitted individual purchase had fallen steadily during the early nineteenth century. The Land Act of 1820 reduced the price to $1.25 per acre for a minimum purchase of 80 acres. In lowering the minimal outlay to $100, however, Congress also eliminated the 1800 provision that had permitted settlers to buy on credit from the government and added the requirement that land that wasn't promptly paid for would go back up for sale. This made small buyers even more dependent on easy credit from local or state banks. There were plenty of these institutions, but state and local bankers were often more interested in putting together big deals with land speculators than in making smaller loans to risky individual settlers. And when Langdon Cheves, the bank's director, called in National Bank monies in 1819, even those local sources dried up for a time. When local banks had tried to foreclose on mortgages in arrears, other settlers had formed vigilante committees to intimidate potential buyers and convince the banks that foreclosure was not in their financial interest.

The obstacles to land purchase for ordinary citizens had kept alive the practice of squatting, of claiming land simply by occupying it, demanding that a person's labor on it over time be recognized as a legal claim. As they had in the late eighteenth century, squatters harassed surveyors and ran off sheriff's deputies. Even when a small settler had a legal claim, if the land was good, or the area promising, the settler was likely to have to fight off high-powered lawyers and their clients. Backwoodsmen, squatters, and settlers did not always share the same interests, but probably all would have agreed with William Manning that "[N]o person can possess property without laboring, unless he get it by force or craft," and that "those that labor for a living and those who get one without laboring—or, as they are generally termed, the Few and the Many"—was "the great dividing line" of society.

Emigrants Crossing the Appalachians This early nineteenth-century engraving depicts emigrants crossing the Appalachians on their way to Pittsburgh, Pennsylvania. Harriet Noble and her family would have traveled in a similar wagon.

The Political Economy of Free Labor

Settlers were not alone in feeling abandoned to the wiles of the wealthy. Although farm labor would dominate the workforce for decades to come, by the second decade of the nineteenth century nonfarming wage labor was becoming more common. Especially in the cities of the coasts, growing numbers of people worked for wages in increasingly precarious circumstances. They had been hard hit by the war, and even improved prosperity afterward left many wage workers with barely enough money to meet their own and their families' needs. Few owned their own homes, and often multiple families crowded into a single apartment. Like the frustrated settlers, wage workers worried that the new political economy was keeping common working people dependent on the rich. Workers had stuck with Jefferson and Madison through the embargo and the War of 1812, but their patience grew thin. In 1817 Cornelius Blatchly, a Quaker physician from New Jersey, published a pamphlet titled *Some Causes of Popular Poverty*, arguing that property owners had become tyrants, enabled by law to steal from laborers the value that they produced and that rightfully belonged to them.

The Panic of 1819 strengthened that skepticism and gave rise to the beginnings of organized protest in the 1820s. Workers turned out in huge numbers to hear critics denounce the growing inequities of American life. Scotswoman Frances Wright, one of the most popular of these speakers, charged that the clergy conspired to keep workers shackled to superstition and inveighed against slavery and advocated for women's rights.

In addition, workers began to form unions and go out on strike. Printers, weavers, carpenters, tailors, cabinetmakers, masons, stevedores, and workers in other crafts turned out on strike throughout major cities, protesting poor pay and long hours. Strikers argued that the shorter day was essential if they were to have time to refresh themselves, to spend with their families, and to obtain the education necessary for newly enfranchised voters. Over time, these separate strikes merged into citywide and regional labor organizations. The first, the Mechanics' Union, was established in Philadelphia in 1827. Pledged to the 10-hour day, the union protested the exhaustion associated with industrialization and the "evils which . . . arise from a depreciation of the intrinsic value of human labor."

Suffrage Reform

At the founding of the nation, suffrage was restricted not just by gender and race but even more on the basis of property ownership and tax payment. Urban craft workers, who often owned little more than their tools and clothing, had objected to this state of affairs, demanding the vote on the basis of their military service, loyalty, and economic importance. Most of all, they had demanded the vote as the emblem of liberty. "Suffrage," as one editor insisted, "is the first right of a free people."

Territorial expansion also raised the question of suffrage. Settlers who owned little more than the mortgages on their land saw themselves as the chief embodiment of the republican spirit. They wanted their votes to count as much as the votes of wealthy speculators, bankers, and landed proprietors.

The new, less settled states led in expanding white male suffrage. Vermont entered the Union in 1791 (the first new state after the original 13) with virtually universal white manhood suffrage. Next year, New Hampshire dropped its last qualification, and Kentucky entered the Union without restrictions on adult white males. Tennessee, which became a state in 1796, required that voters own property but did not set a minimum value. Ohio became a state in 1803 without property requirements for voting, and all the six states admitted between 1812 and 1821 entered with universal white male suffrage (see Map 11–1).

In 1817 Connecticut became the first of the older states to abolish all property qualifications for white men. In 1824, when Jackson made his first run for the presidency, only Virginia, Louisiana, and Rhode Island retained any significant restrictions on white male suffrage, and only 6 of the 24 states retained indirect selection of the delegates to the Electoral College.

The struggle for an expanded male suffrage was fought openly on the landscape of race. Opponents of suffrage reform offered lurid visions of energized African Americans "rush[ing] to the polls in senseless and unmeaning triumph." As suffrage was extended to all white males, it was withdrawn from African American men in New York, Maryland, Pennsylvania, Connecticut, and New Jersey (where single, propertied women also lost the right to vote). In addition, every new state admitted after 1819 specifically excluded African Americans from the vote. Through suffrage reform, white Americans refashioned the vote as the domain of white citizenship. "The people of this state are for . . . a political community of white persons," one Pennsylvanian asserted bluntly.

The partial exception to this pattern was Rhode Island, where elites blocked universal white male suffrage throughout the 1830s. When, in 1841, white working men called a People's Convention to demand universal white male suffrage, they rejected pleas to include African American men in their demands. Spurned by white working men, African Americans supported the conservative opposition. When state conservatives later broadened the franchise, they repaid African American men for their earlier support by including them.

Opposition to Special Privilege and Secret Societies

Since the nation's founding, one strain of American political rhetoric had focused on corrupt insiders who enjoyed opportunities not available to other citizens. In the early nineteenth century, the emphasis on personal striving combined with the growing political assertiveness of white working men to reinvigorate those older fears. Politics became a symbolic battle of the virtuous "many" against the corrupt "few."

Early in the century, specially chartered corporations became visible symbols of affluence and the target of these suspicions. Created by special acts of state legislatures, these corporations were, theoretically, open to all Americans. However, the charters were granted on a personal basis to people of wealth, power, and reputation who were known to individual legislators. The movement to use charters to promote development accelerated after the War of 1812. States chartered companies to build roads, provide transportation, and establish banks. Local reactions to chartered projects were mixed. Many shared journalist William Leggett's bitterness that "[n]ot a road can be opened, not a bridge can be built, not a canal can be dug, but a charter of exclusive privileges must be granted for the purpose." Some of the specially chartered initiatives, especially banks, provided easy

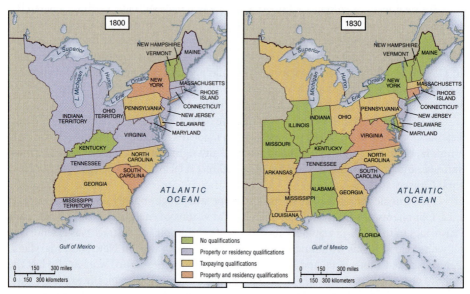

Map 11-1 Toward Universal White Male Suffrage As the western territories organized and entered the union, they formed a band of states in which there were no property qualifications on white male suffrage, and often minimal taxpaying qualifications. By 1830, Virginia and Connecticut were unusual in the nation for restricting white male suffrage based on both property and tax payment. At the same time, free black males and women lost the vote where they had enjoyed it.

credit to local farmers and workers. When the Panic of 1819 ended that bubble of easy credit, shopkeepers, farmers, and urban workers were devastated. They focused their anger on eastern bankers, especially the Second Bank of the United States, and grew suspicious that the new Republican leadership would increase preferential rules. By 1820 John C. Calhoun noticed the appearance, in "every part of the Union," of "a general mass of disaffection to the Government . . . looking out anywhere for a leader."

Corporations were not the only focus of hard feelings. The old Republican fears of special privilege extended to secret societies that might give their members special access to money and success. In western New York, where the opening of the Erie Canal had ushered in an economic boom and widespread social instability, tensions exploded in a virulent fear of Masons in the late 1820s.

The Masonic movement had originated to counter aristocratic power and protect craft masons, but in the eighteenth century a new Order of Freemasons emerged, made up of urban businessmen, professionals, and politicians who pledged to support one another. By the 1820s the Masons seemed to many working people to embody a dangerous antidemocratic spirit. This distrust was galvanized into popular opposition in 1826 by the mysterious disappearance (and presumed murder) of New Yorker William Morgan, who had written an exposé of the order's purported secret designs on public power. The story spread that Morgan had been abducted to Niagara Falls and then drowned. The outcry against this subversion of justice was magnified by the fact that public officials, including Andrew Jackson and Henry Clay, were also Masons. By 1827 New Yorkers had organized a separate political party to oppose the Masons. The Antimason Party spread from New York into other states, winning local elections in Massachusetts, Pennsylvania, and Vermont. In 1831 Antimasons held the first open presidential nominating convention, choosing William Wirt of Maryland as their candidate. Wirt carried only one state, and the party remained a minor player in national politics. Nevertheless, the battle against cabals illustrated the belief that American party politics was a struggle of common people against the monied aristocracy. This would become a staple of Jacksonian rhetoric.

Jackson and the National Republicans

By 1816, the party of Jefferson itself was changing. Jefferson had demonstrated that, as need arose, even Democratic Republicans could shift from strict to loose constitutional constructionists. Both Jefferson and party cofounder James Madison had flexed the muscles of the central government before and during the War of 1812. They had both loathed Hamilton's bank, and Madison had happily allowed its charter to expire in 1811. But that was before the war taught him the importance of a central bank for financing war. In 1816 Madison signed the bill to recharter the bank—on the same terms as the first!

Changes in the Democratic Republican Party

In the early nineteenth century the Democratic Republican Party fell under the influence of a new generation of politicians who came of age during the troubled years of the Confederacy. Having witnessed the effects of poor transportation and a weak federal military in the War of 1812, they believed that a strong, activist national government might well

Henry Clay Henry Clay was 44 when Charles Bird King painted this portrait in 1821, but he looks much younger. He charmed women and men both. Margaret Bayard Smith said that he had a "power of captivation, which no one who was its object could resist."

be the nation's best protection against localism and fragmentation. By the election of 1824, they would identify themselves as National Republicans.

This new brand of Republicanism was epitomized by four men: Henry Clay of Kentucky, John C. Calhoun of South Carolina, and Daniel Webster and John Quincy Adams of Massachusetts. Henry Clay (1777–1852) entered national politics as the champion of the large planters and merchants of Kentucky, who had turned to the federal government for support for projects (especially transportation) they could not win at home. John C. Calhoun (1782–1850) was first a representative and then senator and vice president. Although both Calhoun and South Carolina later became symbols of states' rights sentiment, in the postwar years South Carolinians believed that their international export economy (based on rice, indigo, and cotton) was best served by a strong federal government.

Adams and Webster, both New Englanders, illustrated the compatibility of National Republicanism with the old Federalist views. Webster promoted the interests of New England's banking classes. He was a strong supporter of protective tariffs after the War of 1812, as Massachusetts merchants shifted from importing to manufacturing. Born in 1767, John Quincy Adams was influenced by his father's Federalist views and was first elected to the Senate in 1800 by the Federalist Massachusetts legislature. Adams broke rank with his party when it opposed the Louisiana Purchase.

Led by Clay, the new nationalists fashioned a vision of a Republican political economy based on individual entrepreneurial and market development (including domestic manufacturing), guided by an active federal government. Not surprisingly, their platform, loosely called the American System, was devised to appeal to local interests and identities. In the West and South, that meant promoting a national subsidy to improve transportation, whereas in the Northeast, it meant a protective tariff for domestic industries. To protect federal credit and stabilize currency and internal credit, they supported a national bank.

The various elements of the American System came before Congress as separate bills after the War of 1812, each with its own supporters. The bills to create the Second Bank of the United States and to increase the national tariffs passed easily and were signed by President Madison. Authorized in 1816, the Second Bank of the United States was chartered for 20 years and located in Philadelphia, with the federal government providing one-fifth of its $35 million capitalization and appointing one-fifth of its directors. The tariff bill (with Lowell's relief included) was less protective than some nationalists wished.

Transportation subsidies fared less well. Madison was skeptical about the constitutionality of this form of federal intervention. In his annual messages of 1815 and 1816, he urged Congress to initiate a constitutional amendment to clarify federal power in this area. A torn Congress eventually passed a bill creating a federal fund for internal improvements. On his last day in office, Madison vetoed it. In 1818, the federal government opened a section of the National Road, a highway that connected Baltimore to Wheeling, Virginia (later West Virginia). Otherwise, federal transportation initiatives fell victim to questions of constitutionality and regional jealousies.

James Monroe and National Republicanism

In 1816, Republican James Monroe ran for the presidency against Rufus King, the last Federalist to vie for that office. In the flush of postwar victory and prosperity and in the aftermath of the Hartford Convention, the returns were lopsided in Monroe's favor: Monroe took every state but Maine, Massachusetts, Rhode Island, and Delaware and won 183 electoral votes to King's 34. He was the third Virginian in a row to hold the office—the fourth Virginian of only five presidents total.

Monroe's inaugural address sounded many familiar Republican themes: he praised the virtue of the American people and warned against corruption, greed, and the usurpation of power by foes of the republic. But in explaining the "principles" that would guide him in office, Monroe seemed almost to sound Federalist themes. Although he emphasized the primary importance of local and state militias, he suggested the need for a more vigorous national defense and a more aggressive foreign policy toward Europe generally. He also recommended federally subsidized internal improvements as necessary for a prosperous, cohesive nation. "The improvement of our country by roads and canals, proceeding always with a constitutional sanction . . . shall shorten distances, and, by making each part more accessible to and dependent on the other . . . shall bind the Union more closely together."

In office, Monroe governed with the nationalist bent suggested in his inaugural address. He asked former Federalist John Quincy Adams to be secretary of state (the presumed stepping-stone to the presidency). Together Monroe and Adams moved toward a new United States assertiveness in the Atlantic world.

Their first initiatives were a series of agreements clarifying relations with British colonies in North America. In 1817, Richard Rush (acting secretary of state while Adams was in Europe) and British minister Charles Bagot agreed to limit British and American forces on the Great Lakes. The Convention of 1818 extended that nonmilitarized border along the 49th parallel to the Rocky Mountains. It also formally acknowledged American fishing rights off the Labrador and Newfoundland coasts.

AMERICA AND THE WORLD
....

>> The Monroe Doctrine

In his annual address to Congress in 1823 (the forerunner of the modern State of the Union address) President James Monroe declared that "the American continents, by the free and independent condition which they have assumed and maintain, are henceforth not to be considered as subjects for future colonization by any European powers." Seemingly an affirmation of the United States' support for indigenous democratic movements among its neighbors and a reassertion of the young nation's role as the beacon of democratic hope everywhere, the Monroe Doctrine was actually not about democracy at all. It echoed an equally persistent, but quite different, strain of American foreign policy: the desire to avoid entanglement in European wars.

Equally importantly, the Monroe Doctrine represented the United States' willingness to isolate itself from democratic movements stirring within Europe. In 1820 angry unpaid Spanish soldiers (needed to fight the breakaway American republics) rebelled against their monarchy. The insurgence soon spread to Naples, Italy. After years of domination by the Ottoman Empire, in 1821 Greek revolutionaries had launched a conspiracy against the state that ended in civil war. By 1823 the bourgeoisie and commoners of France were growing angry with the assaults of the restored Bourbon monarchy on the franchise and the freedom of the press. Insurgences also occurred among the Poles, the Hungarians, the Czechs, and others. In Great Britain, the fall of Napoleon provoked agitation for parliamentary reform and the broadening of the franchise.

In his 1823 statement, Monroe acknowledged and broadly supported these democratic movements but declared that the situation in Europe was "eminently and conspicuously different" from that in the Americas: "Our policy in regard to Europe," he said, was "not to interfere in the internal concerns of any of its powers; to consider the government de facto as the legitimate government for us."

Even within the Western Hemisphere, the area Monroe specified, the doctrine was ambiguous. The Monroe Doctrine applied to the Americas—but only to Central and South America, and then only to new republics formed by mixed European-American populations. It did not apply to Canada: the United States would not support revolts against the British government there in the 1830s. And the doctrine did not apply to the black republic of Haiti. Moreover, even as Monroe informed Europe that that the United States would be the guarantor of the new American republics, some Americans were already coveting northern Mexico.

The abstract principle of democracy did not make the new American republics of special interest to the United States, nor did the specific examples of democracy they represented. They could as well have been insurgent monarchies, as far as Monroe's doctrine was concerned. The "interests" they activated in the United States were a coincidence of politics and geography. European efforts to recapture their brokenaway colonies might again bring war to the Americas and to the United States.

In 1819, the United States at last fixed definite borders to the Louisiana Purchase. After the purchase, Jefferson had attempted unsuccessfully to buy Florida from Spain. His successor, Madison, had simply declared that West Florida had been a part of the Louisiana Purchase all along. Taking the Florida peninsula had been left for James Monroe. With Spain too weak to prevent Seminole raids into Georgia and South Carolina, Monroe authorized Andrew Jackson to lead a raid into Florida, ostensibly to frighten the Seminoles. But Jackson wanted more. Without clear authorization, in 1818 Jackson's troops entered Florida, destroying Seminole settlements, capturing a Spanish fort (against orders), and executing two British citizens whom Jackson charged with supporting Indian resistance. Jackson had no need to conquer all of Florida. By May 1818 it was plain that the United States could take the territory whenever it chose.

In the Transcontinental Treaty of 1819, Spain ceded all of Florida to the United States in return for the U.S. government's agreement to assume private American claims against Spain of about $5 million. The Transcontinental Treaty also clarified the border between the United States and Spanish Mexico. The United States gave up claims not only to California (which few considered part of the original purchase) but also to Texas (which many did). The boundary gained in return ran in a series of ascending steps from Louisiana to the Pacific, defining the United States as a nation that spanned the continent.

In the 1820s, under Monroe, the United States began to view itself as American, not quasi-European, and as protector of the Americas against Europe. By 1815 a number of former Spanish colonies, including Argentina, Chile, and Venezuela, had revolted, and an independence movement was under way in Mexico. As these new republics won their independence, they turned to the United States for recognition and support, while the absolute monarchies in Europe sought to preserve and extend their territorial empires. France offered to help Spain regain its colonies in South America. Russia reasserted and strengthened its long-standing claims in the Pacific Northwest.

Disavowing any future new territorial ambitions for itself in the Americas, Great Britain offered to make a joint declaration with the United States warning other nations against intruding in the internal affairs of Western Hemisphere countries. An alliance with Britain would have enhanced U.S. diplomatic credibility, but many Americans suspected that Britain would use its position to squeeze the United States out of South American markets.

Secretary of State John Quincy Adams convinced Monroe to refuse the British offer and, instead, to act independently and issue a unilateral statement of support for the new republics. Adams hoped that being identified with this policy would help him shed the pro-British tag that was associated with many New Englanders.

In his annual message to Congress in 1823, Monroe enunciated the policy that has since become known as the Monroe Doctrine. Monroe asserted a special United States relationship with all parts of North and South America, with which, he insisted, "we are of necessity more immediately connected." "We . . . declare," he added, "that we should consider any attempt on their part to extend their system to any portion of this hemisphere as dangerous to our peace and safety." The Monroe Doctrine marked an important milestone in the development of American nationalism and internationalism. The United States asserted not only a new relation (as peer) to the European nations but also a new relation to the Americas. Surveillance over the nations of North and South America would be the domestic right of the United States.

The Election of 1824 and the "Corrupt Bargain"

In the usual order of custom in the young republic, Secretary of State John Quincy Adams would have been Monroe's presumed successor. But by 1824 the Republican Party housed experienced men who considered themselves next in line. In addition to Adams, there were John C. Calhoun (secretary of war), Henry Clay (speaker of the House), and William H. Crawford of Georgia (secretary of the treasury, who suffered a massive stroke in 1823). This group, which called itself the National Republicans, contained some of the nation's most experienced and respected leaders.

And then there was the outlier, Andrew Jackson. From his unpromising beginnings as an orphan of backcountry settlers, Andrew Jackson had gradually worked his way to wealth and to public prominence. After the Revolution, Jackson studied law in North Carolina and was admitted to the bar in 1787. That year, he moved west to Jonesboro, in today's Tennessee. There Jackson practiced law and made a reputation representing settlers with disputed land claims. He was a delegate to the Tennessee constitutional convention in 1796 and elected the state's first congressional representative. In 1797 he was elected senator but resigned to serve as a justice on the Tennessee Supreme Court until 1804. In that year, he bought land near the future city of Nashville, Tennessee.

Jackson became a national figure during the War of 1812, first as commander of the devastating campaign against the Creek nation and then as the hero of the Battle of New Orleans. His controversial but effective campaign against the Seminoles in 1818 and 1819 and his brief career as governor of the Territory of Florida completed his credentials as an unyielding champion of the western settler.

Still, when the Tennessee legislature nominated Jackson for the presidency in 1822, few politicians took the candidacy seriously, given his competition. But by 1824 voting Americans were beginning to pull back from the new expansive Republican vision. Among the viable candidates in the field, all but Jackson advocated a strong central government—a sign perhaps of how out of step the Republican leadership was with its constituents. An early indication of the storminess of the election came with the Republican nomination. Because James Monroe had not designated a successor, the selection was thrown to the Republican congressional caucus and was expected to benefit Crawford. But this time, the other candidates disowned the caucus as a corrupt and irregular institution so effectively that only 66 of a possible 216 Republican members of Congress even attended. Crawford did get the nod, but its value had been diminished.

In the election, no candidate claimed a majority either of the popular vote or of the Electoral College. The underdog Andrew Jackson came closest, with 43 percent of the popular vote and 99 electoral votes. Next was Adams, with 31 percent of the popular vote and 84 electoral votes. Crawford managed only 41 electoral votes, and Clay came in last with 37. (Calhoun had withdrawn.)

The election was thus thrown to the House of Representatives, where members had to select from among the three candidates with the highest electoral count. As the highest vote getter, Jackson was confident at first, but by late December he began to hear rumors "that deep intrigue is on foot." Those rumors were correct. Although Adams did not receive a single popular vote in Kentucky, and although the Kentucky legislature had directed its delegation to vote for Jackson, Clay overrode those instructions and also marshaled support for Adams in other states. Adams received the votes of 13 of the 24 state delegations. Jackson received 7 and Crawford received 4.

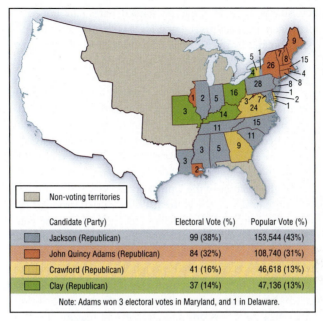

Candidate (Party)	Electoral Vote (%)	Popular Vote (%)
Jackson (Republican)	99 (38%)	153,544 (43%)
John Quincy Adams (Republican)	84 (32%)	108,740 (31%)
Crawford (Republican)	41 (16%)	46,618 (13%)
Clay (Republican)	37 (14%)	47,136 (13%)

Note: Adams won 3 electoral votes in Maryland, and 1 in Delaware.

Map 11–2   The Election of 1824 Almost all of Adams's electoral votes came from the Northeast, while Jackson's were spread through the South, the Midwest, and the Mid-Atlantic.

Jackson later charged that Adams had bought Clay's support with the promise of the post of secretary of state. Adams did give Clay that job, but Clay had had good reasons for allying himself with Adams. They shared similar political philosophies. In addition, Jackson and Clay vied for the same regional vote. Clay's support for him in 1824 would have helped Jackson build a stronger western base for 1828.

Jackson was furious. His supporters charged that the election had been stolen in a "corrupt bargain" brokered by insiders who debased the virtue of the republic and disregarded the clear will of the electorate.

The Adams Presidency and the Gathering Forces of Democracy

In many respects, Adams's choice of Clay made perfect sense. Since the postwar period both men had shared a commitment to the "American System": the preservation of a national bank, the levying of a national tariff, and the improvement of infrastructure.

Adams continued to support these policies in office, even using his first annual message to Congress in 1825 to lay out a grand vision for federal involvement in the political economy. He called not only for economic projects, such as transportation improvements, but also for the creation of a national university, a national observatory, a naval academy, and an elaborate system of roads and canals supported by federal expenditures. He urged Congress not to be "palsied by the will of our constituents." His opponents railed that this was clear evidence of his intention to benefit the wealthy at the expense of the common people and that this branch of the Republican Party (increasingly identifying itself as the National Republicans) seemed more Federalist than Jeffersonian.

John Quincy Adams was a wise and principled statesman, but he was never able to set an independent agenda for his presidency. He was shadowed by the political battle that began with his election and by his unpopular identification with banking and mercantile interests. Defensive and prickly in public, he did not build strong political alliances, and he misread the gulf developing within the American electorate.

And Jackson's supporters worked hard to discredit Adams, especially on the issue of the tariff. Early on, the federal government had depended on the tariff and on land sales for most of its revenue. By the end of the War of 1812, the importance of the tariff for generating funding had declined, but its role in addressing the growing regional economic differences had increased. The 1816 tariff was protectionist, but only very mildly so, working to give some recognition to the importance of domestic manufactures. But the Panic of 1819, brought on in part by the reliance of the United States on world markets, reenergized protectionists: a bill to raise tariffs on the entire list of imported products by 5 percent (even higher for cotton, wool, iron, and glass) failed passage by only one vote. It was broadly supported in the western and middle states and opposed in the South (where it was seen as favoring high-priced New England products), whereas New England split on the issue. But by 1824 New England was committed enough to industrial growth to become solidly pro-tariff. That year, when Congress proposed a tariff that included levies of 35 percent on imported cotton, wool, hemp, and iron, passage was a forgone conclusion.

Passage of the 1824 tariff was ominous for several reasons. First, of course, it was vehemently opposed by the South. Second, neither the North nor the federal government really needed it. In 1824 the federal government reported a surplus of funds, a year when New England manufactures were doing well enough not to need the help. The tariff had become the language of sectionalism, but the underlying conflict was over the power of the federal government. This was not a simple question of nationalism versus localism. Jackson, a nationalist willing to support some level of protective tariff, had even conceded that, "It is time we became a little more Americanized." The difference between Adams and Jackson was the question of federal legitimacy. In what actions could the federal government claim the authority of the American people? And in what actions did it overstep that authority? That conflict was now infused with the energy of a rising democratic spirit.

The Election of 1828

The campaign was personal and vicious. Adams's supporters tarred Jackson as an undisciplined liar and blasphemer. They accused him of having married Rachel Robards before her own divorce was final. Jackson supporters retorted that Adams was a Sabbath breaker, a closet Federalist, and an unprincipled hypocrite who disdained popular government. To make the point, Jacksonians began to refer to themselves as Jacksonian Democrats (or just the Democrats).

The Democratic campaign of 1828 ushered in a new era of national political campaigning. Earlier campaigns had been fought primarily on the local level and among a far smaller group of potential voters, but in 1828 Martin Van Buren coordinated a Democratic national campaign designed to appeal to a mass electorate. Van Buren oversaw the creation of a highly controlled party hierarchy of local and state societies linked to the national organization. He pioneered the use of carefully choreographed demonstrations and converted nonpartisan occasions (such as Fourth of July celebrations) into Democratic rallies by sending out Jackson supporters armed with American flags and placards.

Van Buren also used political imagery to evoke campaign themes. Trading on Jackson's nickname, "Old Hickory" (for the hardest wood in the United States), campaign workers handed out hickory canes at political events. Supporters also used editorials and campaign tracts to describe Jackson as the embodiment of the common man. Turning Jackson's obstinacy and lack of formal education into strengths, they argued that he was nature's product, with a "native strength of mind" and "practical common sense."

When the votes were counted in 1828, Jackson had won a clear majority: 56 percent of the popular vote and 178 electoral votes to Adams's 83 electoral votes. Although Adams had retained New England, New Jersey, Delaware, and northern Maryland, Jackson had solidly taken the South and the West, as well as Pennsylvania, most of New York, and even northern Maine.

Jackson was elected by a cross-section of voters who identified with his stance as an outsider to, and victim of, eastern elites. He was the candidate of westerners, migrants, settlers, and landowners who opposed eastern banks and congressional land policies, but he also drew support from urban professionals, shopkeepers, laborers, and craftsmen who believed that special privilege was denying them their chance of prosperity. A planter and a southerner, Jackson could claim the mantle of Jeffersonians. In that spirit, he favored limited government, feared concentrations of economic and political power, and seemed to share Jefferson's emphasis on the individual common American.

At the same time, the Jacksonians were vague about exactly where the heart of their new democratic movement resided. Structurally, they believed that it evolved from the states, which restrained federal power. At the same time, however, Jackson's strong conviction that he *was* the people and that his will was indistinguishable from theirs confused

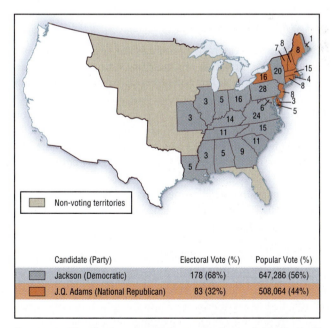

Candidate (Party)	Electoral Vote (%)	Popular Vote (%)
Jackson (Democratic)	178 (68%)	647,286 (56%)
J.Q. Adams (National Republican)	83 (32%)	508,064 (44%)

Map 11–3 The Election of 1828 In 1828, Jackson solidified his hold on the South and Midwest and even made inroads in the Northeast.

matters. The ironic result was a shift of power from the states to the executive during the presidency of the man elected to protect the common man.

The tendency to personalize political struggle characterized Jackson's presidency. He never forgave the National Republicans for publicly questioning the legitimacy of his marriage. Later, he viewed his battle against the Second Bank of the United States in the same highly personal terms: "The Bank," he informed Van Buren, "is trying to kill me, but I will kill it."

If Jackson understood himself as the embodiment of the people's will, he understood the new Democratic Party as its direct instrument. After personal loyalty to Jackson, party loyalty became the avenue to appointment and the justification for an unprecedented turnover in appointees. The overall results were mixed. Jackson expanded the powers of the presidency, but his conviction that he alone embodied the true virtue of the republic also led to personal pettiness, widespread patronage, and turmoil within his cabinet. His efforts to abolish the Second Bank of the United States created serious hardship for average Americans, and his hostility to Native Americans resulted in widespread death and impoverishment.

A Policy of Removing Indigenous People

The message of the new presidency was clear: reform. "As the instrument of the Federal Constitution," Jackson declared in his inaugural address, "I shall keep steadily in view the limitations as well as the extent of the Executive power." He advocated fiscal restraint, an end to government patronage, and a constitutional amendment to remove "all intermediary agency in the election of President and Vice-President."

Jackson and Native Peoples

For Andrew Jackson, the quintessential "common man" was the western settler, struggling to bring new lands under cultivation and new institutions to life. Pioneers confronted many obstacles in their trek west, but none loomed larger than the resistance of Indian peoples. The War of 1812 had ended intertribal resistance east of the Mississippi River. By 1828, most of the Great Lakes nations had been pushed out of Ohio, southern Indiana, and Illinois, but the Ojibwa, Winnebago, Sauk, Mesquakie, Kickapoo, and Menominee tribes retained sizable homelands in the region. In the South, in spite of repeated forced cessions, the Chickasaws, Choctaws, Creeks, Cherokees, and Seminoles retained ancestral territories.

Jackson's views concerning Native Americans had been settled in the crucible of the Indian wars of the 1790s. "Does not experience teach us that treaties answer no other Purpose than opening an Easy door for the Indians to pass [through to] Butcher our citizens?" he wrote in 1794. Congress should "Punish the Barbarians."

In these views Jackson was no different from many American settlers—some of whom had directly experienced the violence of white incursions into Indian Country, but many of whom formed their ideas long before they ever saw an Indian, basing their preconceptions on inflamed newspaper accounts in the new mass-produced "penny press." Most American settlers saw Indians only in passing. Some of these encounters were surely unnerving but usually of no harm to the settlers. The harm that Indians represented was more basic: they occupied lands recognized as belonging to them in treaties with the federal government. Despite recurrent wars and land cessions, western settlers were no happier with federal initiatives in the 1820s than they had been in the 1790s.

Tension ran especially high in Georgia. There officials complained that the federal government had not kept its promise to remove all Indians from the state, a condition of Georgia's 1802 agreement to cede its western land claims to the federal government. A few Creeks and most of the Cherokee nation remained. In 1826 the federal government pressured the Creeks to give up all but a small strip of their remaining lands in Georgia, but white Georgians were not satisfied. Georgia governor George Michael Troup sent surveyors onto that last piece of Creek land. When President Adams objected to this encroachment on federal treaty powers, Troup threatened to call up the state militia.

The election of Andrew Jackson emboldened Georgians to go after Cherokee land. They invalidated the constitution of the Cherokee nation within Georgia and proclaimed that the Cherokees were subject to the authority of the state of Georgia. When discoveries of gold sent white prospectors surging onto Cherokee land, Georgia refused to stop the trespassers or to protect the Indians. To the contrary, the state passed laws that stripped Cherokees of their rights and their land. Jackson quickly notified the Cherokees that it was his duty, as president, to "sustain the States in the exercise of their rights."

In fact, the states were not exercising their rights. In 1830 the Cherokee nation took the state of Georgia to the Supreme Court, arguing that the Cherokee nation was a "foreign nation in the sense of our constitution and law" and that, as a state, Georgia had no right to pass laws over the inhabitants of a foreign nation. Chief Justice John Marshall agreed that the Cherokees were a distinct political society, but he demurred that they were not a foreign state "in the sense of the constitution, and cannot maintain an action in the courts of the United States." But the following year, *Worcester v. Georgia*, which was *not* brought by the Cherokee nation, gave Marshall the opportunity to say more. He identified the Cherokee nation as "a distinct community, occupying its own territory, with boundaries accurately described in which the laws of Georgia can have no force, and which the citizens of Georgia have no right to enter but with the assent of the Cherokees themselves or in conformity with treaties and with the acts of Congress." Marshall concluded, "The whole intercourse between the United States and this nation is, by our Constitution and laws, vested in the government of the United States." Georgia had acted unconstitutionally.

Jackson refused to enforce this decision. He had long believed that the best policy would be to remove the Indians entirely from lands sought by settlers. The place he had in mind was across the Mississippi River. Because full-scale removal of the Indians involved shifting populations across state lines and into federal territories, however, it required congressional consent.

The proposed policy was not unopposed. "[I]f, in pursuance of a narrow and selfish policy, we should . . . drive away these remnants of tribes, in such a manner, and under such auspices, as to insure their destruction . . . ," Jeremiah Evarts, secretary of the American Board of Commissioners for Foreign Missions, warned, "then the sentence of an indignant world would be uttered in thunders." In Congress the Native Americans found unexpected allies. To the old Adams men, now led by Henry Clay, "removal" was the policy of states, forced on the federal government. For Congress to pass an act authorizing the policy would mean encouraging states to trample on federal powers.

The Grand National Caravan Moving East In this satirical cartoon, Jackson and Van Buren are on the left, followed by the devil, an army officer, and a group of caged Indians, who represent Indian removal. On the ground, a drunken Jacksonian proclaims, "Hail, Columbia, happy land."

Van Buren responded by forming a counterlobby, the Board for the Emigration, Preservation, and Improvement of the Aborigines of America, which argued that Indians were ill equipped for contact with white civilization and that removing them was humane. Among the proponents of removal was former president John Quincy Adams. In the end, the bill passed by only five votes and only after four months of debate.

The Removal Act

In 1830 Congress passed and President Jackson signed an act "to provide for an exchange of lands with the Indians residing in any of the states or territories, and for their removal west of the river Mississippi." In one sense, the act only made official and accelerated a policy that Americans had pursued since the founding of the nation. In his State of the Union address that year, Jackson praised the Removal Act as an act of "Philanthropy." He reminded Congress that for generations European Americans had been "leav[ing] the land of their birth to seek new homes in distant regions" and that new lands meant opportunity and liberty. "Doubtless it will be painful to leave the graves of their fathers," he acknowledged of the eastern Indians, "but what do they more than our ancestors did or than our children are now doing?" In fact, leaving "the land of their birth" was for Native Americans not an act of opportunity but rather an eviction from their very identity as a people.

In 1830 the Choctaws were forced from their lands in Mississippi to present-day Oklahoma. The Chickasaws and the Creeks followed in 1832. Then, in 1836, six years after passage of the Removal Act and four years after they had exhausted their judicial options, a small

AMERICAN LANDSCAPE

>> **Liberty and the Land: Cherokee Removal**

The Cherokees, one of the largest Indian nations the United States sought to displace, had lived on the rocky slopes and in the pocket coves of the southern Appalachians since long before the arrival of the Europeans, and their sense of themselves was intimately tied to the mountains. Their ancestors, Kana'ti and Selu, the first man and the first woman of the Real People, had migrated into this land when the land itself was newly created. They had been fed from game Kana'ti found in a deep cave and from the corn and beans Selu had produced by rubbing her stomach and armpits.

These beginnings were preserved in the daily life of the Cherokees in the early nineteenth century. They lived in settled agricultural villages in the Smoky Mountains, their communities anchored by the fields women cultivated. Men traveled far and sometimes for years at a time to find game, but they always returned to their mountain homes. Corn and deer remained at the ceremonial center of the culture. Men and women ritualized marriages by exchanging corn and deer, and each year communities celebrated the Green Corn Festival, when their elders recited the stories of their origin and migration into the mountains. Social and political life were governed by the principle of harmony and balance. Each village had a council hall large enough to hold the entire community, and decisions were achieved by consensus. For the Cherokees, where they lived was who they were. They had become Cherokee by entering the land of the mountains, and they remained Cherokee because they stayed there.

Two centuries of contact altered that way of life. Some Cherokees embraced racial slavery. Most grew more dependent on farming. Trying to accommodate white practices, Cherokees adopted a written alphabet. Yet they clung to their diminishing lands. Not until eight years after Congress passed the Removal Act did the U.S. Army arrive, in late spring 1838, to enforce the provisions of the Treaty of New Echota. They found a settled people unwilling and unprepared to move. They had not gathered their families together or set aside blankets and food for the trip. Their fields were newly planted, and their cattle were at spring pasture. Cherokees were rounded up, often at the point of a bayonet, and held for weeks in stockades. Corrupt land dealers took advantage of the circumstances to buy Cherokee lands cheap, and thieves stripped houses of furniture and equipment.

Gathered at three points (two in Tennessee, one in Alabama) for embarkation, the Cherokees went west in two waves. Under the supervision of the army, three groups totaling nearly 3,000 Cherokees started almost immediately, in the hottest part of the summer. According to a missionary eyewitness, the agent shipped the Cherokees "by multitudes," "[n]ine hundred in one detachment, and seven hundred in another . . . driven onto boats" to carry them up the Tennessee and Ohio rivers to the Mississippi. "It will be a miracle of mercy if one-fourth escape the exposure to that sickly climate." Hundreds did not.

With the death count mounting, the Cherokees requested authority to manage
continued

AMERICAN LANDSCAPE *continued*

their own removals and to delay them until the end of summer. After getting this permission, they did everything possible to survive the journey. Those permitted to return to their homes before leaving salvaged what remained. Some of the contingents included hundreds of wagons and thousands of horses, but others were far less well supplied. The wagons carried whoever could not walk, usually the sick and the aged. Others who could still walk bundled their goods in blankets on their backs .

Escorted by soldiers, the contingents sometimes looked like "the march of an army, regiment after regiment, the wagons in the center, the officers along the line and the horsemen on the flanks and at the rear." At least for the removals they organized, however, the Cherokees established their own internal police. To the meager stocks of salt pork and often moldy corn and wheat flour provided by military suppliers, the Cherokees added whatever they could hunt or forage along the way: turkeys, small game, occasionally deer, and berries. The later removals avoided the diseases of summer but faced the cold winds and ice storms of winter. Many migrants had only thin clothing and few blankets, and the cold was especially hard on elders, children, and the sick.

Removal did not annihilate the Cherokees, but it deeply wounded their society. The entire process claimed at least 4,000 (perhaps as many as 8,000) of the roughly 17,000 Cherokees who were initially rounded up. Those who arrived in Indian Territory found a land very different from the one they had known, drier and flatter. The United States government had promised to support the migrants during their first year in the West, but government subcontractors lined their own pockets by supplying insufficient and substandard goods. As deaths mounted and poverty, illness, and alcoholism increased, the hatred between proremoval and antiremoval parties within the Cherokee nation ignited into civil war, forcing Cherokees to reclaim the principle of harmony that lay at the center of their world. In the meantime, their ancestral lands had been cleared for white settlers and their African American slaves.

splinter group of the Cherokees (claiming to speak for the whole nation) at last agreed to removal. The Treaty of New Echota provided that within two years the Cherokees would leave the mountains for Indian Territory, in return for safe passage, $5 million, and food, shelter, equipment, and medicine for a year after their arrival. The Senate ratified the treaty in the spring of 1836. The pro-treaty Cherokees began to leave almost immediately. The overwhelming majority of Cherokees, who considered the treaty fraudulent, remained in the East.

Three years later, after their unsuccessful appeals to the Supreme Court and after several years of resistance, the Cherokees were removed from their eastern lands. In a forced march that became known as the Trail of Tears, they were driven off their homelands to Indian Territory in what is now eastern Oklahoma. Most people had delayed leaving until the last moment and had made few preparations for the journey. Many died of disease, malnutrition, dehydration, and exhaustion along the way.

Indians did not accept removal willingly. In 1831, the Sauk and Fox people (descended from Native Americans who had earlier been pushed across the Great Lakes region) were forced to relocate once again. In their new lands, however, they began to hear rumors of whites desecrating their former burying grounds. When Indians recrossed the Mississippi to rebury their dead and harvest produce from their old fields, white farmers and Illinois militia attacked them. The Sauk and Fox Indians turned to a revered old fighter, Black Hawk, who raised a band of 500 warriors. Attacked by state militiamen, they spent the summer fighting a series of skirmishes called Black Hawk's War. Finally, on August 2, 1832, the exhausted remnants of Black Hawk's band were cornered and massacred by the army.

More successful were the Florida Seminoles, also a diverse community including militant Creek warriors, known as Red Sticks, and runaway slaves. When federal troops arrived to remove the Seminoles in 1832, the Indians resisted with skill and determination. Unfamiliar with the terrain and vulnerable to malaria, the American troops were picked off by both disease and snipers. The war dragged on for seven years. Not until 1842 could President John Tyler proclaim victory.

History, Destiny, and the Disappearing Indian

American territorial expansion implied more than just a positive association between American citizens and the land. It also implied a negative association between the land and its current occupants. In this view, the land and the striving American individual could fulfill their joint destinies only if the Indians and their cultures disappeared.

Drawing on a tradition reaching back at least to Jefferson, proponents of dispossession based their argument on the character of the land itself: certain environments

The Trail of Tears This depiction by twentieth century artist Robert Ottokar Lindneux shows Cherokees being forcibly marched from their homelands in eastern states to Indian Territory in what is now Oklahoma.

were *naturally* fitted to certain groups of people and naturally unsuitable for others. Maximum progress came from fitting the people to the place. Native American dispossession was inevitable, they insisted—not only because white Americans were perfectly matched to the land but also because Indians were *not*. White Americans claimed to have tried again and again to help Native Americans survive but considered them incapable of taking full advantage of the land. Jackson spoke bluntly in his 1833 address to Congress. Native Americans, he declared, had "neither the intelligence, the industry, the moral habits, nor the desire of improvement which are essential" to realizing the potential of the land.

This understanding of manifest destiny as entailing the inevitable disappearance of Native Americans made its way into American literature in the 1820s, just as white Americans were considering Indian removal as an official government policy. Its venue was the historical novel. The depiction of Native Americans in antebellum historical novels represented a departure from earlier Indian captivity narratives, which often described Indians as almost incapable of human feeling and bent on the violent destruction of European American civilization. Although the historical novels of the 1820s did not romanticize all Native Americans, they did identify among the Indians individuals of high character—of integrity, intelligence, and great sensitivity—but who, significantly, were always doomed to extinction.

The most notable of these were James Fenimore Cooper's wildly popular Leatherstocking Tales—a series of novels that follow the life and death of the backwoodsman Natty Bumppo, the son of a Native American father and a white mother. Bumppo was a true friend of both Indians and whites. But, as Cooper made clear, Bumppo was tied to a particular moment. Like the wilderness, his life gave way to the arrival of white settlement.

Bumppo was by no means unique. In *Hobomok: A Tale of Early Times*, published in 1824, Lydia Maria Child (1802–1880) recounted the story of Hobomok, a Native American torn between friendship with the Salem settlers and loyalty to his own people. In the story, Hobomok falls in love with and marries a Puritan woman, who consents to the marriage only after she believes that her fiancé has been killed at sea. Mary and Hobomok have a son, and Mary comes to respect Hobomok for his character and courage, if not to love him. But Child makes clear that Mary's future, and that of her child, is with her own people. When Mary's lover unexpectedly returns, Hobomok graciously withdraws, and Mary and the boy return to white society. Carrying Hobomok's name, the mixed-heritage boy grows up to attend Cambridge and become the new American citizen—his name marking the passing of his father's way of life.

Although dispossession was a devastating experience for Native Americans, native cultures survived. For example, although during the 1820s European Americans sought to Christianize the Cherokees (four denominations established seven schools and sent almost 80 missionaries onto Cherokee lands), at the end of the decade there were only about 1,300 converts out of a total Cherokee population estimated at almost 16,000. Most were wealthy Cherokees who had already accepted European American ways. The remaining vast majority pursued the traditional practices and told and retold the stories of their forebears. Even when they incorporated aspects of European American culture into their lives, most Cherokees appear to have done so as a means of preserving their own heritage. Initially, Cherokees rejected the European American emphasis on literacy as a tool of cultural obliteration. When in 1821 Sequoyah invented the Cherokee syllabary (a system of written symbols representing the sounds of the spoken Cherokee language), most Cherokees were indifferent. Only as they came to realize how few whites could read the symbols did Cherokees begin to take an interest in the syllabary. By the mid-1820s perhaps half of the Cherokee nation had become proficient in Sequoyah's system, using it to communicate privately among themselves and to preserve the sacred stories of their culture.

But most Cherokees, like most Native Americans, preserved their culture simply by withdrawing from government officials and missionaries. They dealt with whites when they had to—for trade or for jobs—and they adapted to white ways as necessary. But the core of their lives lay elsewhere, in distant settlements and in practices and rituals from which whites were barred.

The Bank War

Jacksonians saw the Indians as the western barrier to progress, but when they looked eastward, they saw different obstacles: the special privileges and unfair advantages of the rich and well connected. Jackson had long associated this obstacle with Henry Clay, John Quincy Adams, John Calhoun, and the Republican caucus. By 1828 Jackson focused his anger on the Second Bank of the United States.

Jackson's Opposition to the National Bank

Jackson hated the bank for all the reasons southerners and westerners did: it was powerful and privileged, and wealthy easterners and foreign investors controlled its private stock. Also, as much as they liked easy credit, most Americans were suspicious of banknotes of all kinds. They had been stung too often by counterfeiters and deadbeats.

But Jackson also had very personal reasons for his opposition. Soon after his first election, Jackson heard rumors that the bank had used its power to buy votes for Adams in 1828. Declaring that the bank threatened "the purity of the right of suffrage," Jackson vowed to oppose it.

Nicholas Biddle, the bank's president, rebuffed Jackson's criticisms. Confident the bank enjoyed broad support, Biddle decided to force the issue before the next presidential election. Although the bank's authorization ran until 1836, on January 6, 1832, Biddle asked Congress to take up renewal early. Jackson may have felt Biddle's behavior to be a personal challenge, because he vetoed it in 1832. "The rich and powerful," he thundered, "too often bend the acts of government to their selfish purposes. . . . [W]hen the laws undertake . . . to make the rich richer, . . . the humble members of society . . . have a right to complain of the injustice of their Government."

The Democrats carried the bank veto proudly into the 1832 election as a contest of "the Democracy and the people, against a corrupt and abandoned aristocracy." The Republicans responded that Jackson's veto showed his tendency toward despotism. The Supreme Court had ruled the national bank constitutional, and Congress had voted to recharter it. Jackson had trammeled the authority of the other branches of government, assuming the sole right to determine the future of the bank.

Dismembering the Bank

Jackson won reelection in 1832, although by a smaller majority than in 1828. By 1833 he was ready to disassemble the Second Bank of the United States. He asked Secretary of the Treasury Louis McLane to select other banks into which the federal government could move its deposits. McLane balked, worried that the selection would be compromised by politics and that the state banks would lose all fiscal restraint. Impatient, Jackson replaced McLane with William J. Duane, and then replaced Duane with Attorney General Roger Taney. On October 1, 1833, the federal government began to distribute its deposits to 22 state banks. By the close of the year, the government deposits had been largely removed.

The deposits had been used to make loans to individuals and corporations around the country. To make the funds available, the Second Bank began furiously calling in loans and foreclosing on debts. In effect, Biddle was repeating the process that triggered the Panic of 1819. In six months he took more than $15 million worth of credit out of the economy.

As recession gripped the nation, the Senate passed an unprecedented resolution censuring Jackson for assuming "authority and power not conferred by the constitution and laws." Jackson's response underscored the new "democratic" politics of the times: "The President," he maintained (and no other branch of government), "is the direct representative of the American people." The expansion of white male suffrage (and the spreading practice of electing members of the Electoral College directly) made Jackson the first president who could claim to be elected directly by the voters. Congress, on the other hand, would soon become the power base of elites.

The first recession passed quickly as state banks tapped their federal deposits to churn out loans, and new wildcat banks took advantage of the glut of paper money. Much of the borrowing went for land sales.

The Specie Act

Correctly, Jackson believed that the excess of paper money in circulation had caused the recession. As soon as conditions improved, he implemented a hard-money policy. In 1833 he had announced that the federal government would no longer accept drafts on the Second Bank in payment of taxes, a move that reduced the value of the bank's notes. In 1834 Jackson declared that the "deposit" banks receiving federal monies could not issue paper drafts for amounts under $5 (later raised to $20), an action that reduced the small-denomination paper in circulation. In July 1836 he had the Treasury Department issue the Specie Circular, which directed land offices to accept only coins or precious metals in payment for western lands. This shut out actual settlers, who could not get together enough gold or silver for their purchases. Meanwhile, the Deposit Act, passed in 1836, expanded the number of "pet banks" to nearly 100 and distributed a federal surplus of more than $5 million to the states, on top of the more than $22 million already deposited in the state banks from the Second Bank of the United States. Underregulated and under local pressure, the state banks could not absorb these funds. They issued loans and printed money that vastly exceeded their assets. When the bubble burst in 1837, the nation faced the worst financial disaster of its young history.

The Growth of Sectional Tension

The growing fiscal strains in Jacksonian America were matched by brewing sectional conflict. Americans had not always viewed the differences between the political economies of the North and South as bad. Those regional differences had powered northern industrialization during the War of 1812 and had laid the foundation for the National Republican vision of robust nationalism after the war. But economic expansion brought old differences into open conflict. The immediate catalyst was the tariff, but by 1832 the tariff question had ignited a broader debate over the institution of slavery.

The Political Economy of Southern Discontent

Despite an apparent victory in the Missouri controversy, many white southerners had felt betrayed by northern criticisms of slavery. Economic and political frustrations in the 1820s nurtured that sense of mistreatment, leading the planter class, which had so far dominated the presidency, to see itself as the victim of the federal government.

White southerners read signs of shifting public attitudes toward slavery. Proslavery advocates in Illinois (where many African Americans were already held in indentures comparable to slavery) were unable to elect a proslavery congressman in 1820. In 1824 Ohio asked Congress to consider a plan for the gradual abolition of slavery throughout the United States. On July 4, 1827, New York completed its long process of gradual emancipation, an occasion celebrated by free African Americans as far south as Virginia. And news from England had it that abolitionist William Wilberforce was likely to get slavery outlawed in the British West Indies.

Most important, though, was the economy. By 1828 cotton prices were only about one-third of their 1815 levels. Many planters and farmers tried to compensate for falling profits by planting more acres, but worn-out fields kept production low. Large eastern planters often sold off slaves, lands, and city houses. Many smaller farmers, dependent on cotton as their cash crop to pay off debts, were forced to sell out. Although the Panic of 1819 hurt northern farms and businesses, most of the Northeast bounced back faster than the South, which focused planter attention on the 1816 protective tariff as a sign of government favoritism. They complained that the tariff was unnaturally driving up the prices of European imports, forcing strapped southerners to purchase expensive northern-made products and driving down southern export sales. "We have no objection to the North being enriched by our riches," one Charleston *Mercury* reporter wrote sarcastically in 1827, "but not from our poverty."

Of the slaveholding states, South Carolina was particularly insecure. Its white residents faced a growing African American majority (the result of white migration west) that heightened fears of slave insurrection.

South Carolina's Protest

Passage of the Tariff of 1828, the "tariff of abominations," led to nullification talk in South Carolina and created a new leader, John C. Calhoun. Like other South Carolinians, Calhoun had been disenchanted by the experiences of the 1820s and was a far less enthusiastic nationalist than he had once been. Yet he retained enough faith in the Democratic

Party to believe that Democrats would lower the tariff once in office and would see the injury to southern states from such national laws. To encourage both results, in 1828 Calhoun wrote the *South Carolina Exposition and Protest*, a justification for the theory of nullification, under which states might declare particular federal laws null and void within their borders. Although Calhoun published the pamphlet anonymously (still aspiring to the presidency, he was reluctant to associate himself too openly with the extreme position), he let his authorship be widely known, hoping for the support of radicals in his home state. In the *Exposition*, Calhoun argued that the federal government was the creation of the states. In agreeing to create a federal government, the states had ceded some of their powers, but only conditionally, and always reserving the right to do whatever was necessary to ensure their survival as "distinct political communities." A state had the right to assert its sovereignty in defiance of federal policies that might threaten its distinctive character. It was at such a juncture, Calhoun argued, that the states of the South had arrived in 1828. They had become the "minority" culture, their interests and institutions endangered by "the unrestrained will of a majority." The tariff would gradually drain away the money and the independence of the South, subjecting it to northern tyranny.

Much in America's history supported Calhoun's view. The states had existed before the federal Constitution. Representation at the Constitutional Convention and ratification of the Constitution had been by state, and representation in the federal government continued to be on the basis of states. Moreover, defenders of the theory included Thomas Jefferson and James Madison, in their resolutions opposing the Alien and Sedition Acts.

On the other hand, the Constitution's status as the supreme law of the land rested on the fact that it had been ratified by the *people*, acting through special conventions, *not* by the state governments, and subsequent suffrage reform had enlarged the popular participation of white men. Moreover, after the debacle of the Hartford Convention, states' rights arguments had the whiff of treason. And Calhoun went further than that convention had: he argued explicitly what the Federalists had dared only hint, that if all else failed, states retained the right to withdraw from the compact.

Among those who viewed the federal government as properly the creation of "the people," not of the states, and who regarded threats to withdraw from the Union as unforgivable, was President Jackson.

The Nullification Crisis

Other southern states, less economically pressed than South Carolina and more optimistic that regional political differences could yet be reconciled, did not rush to endorse the *Exposition*. But two events increased political tensions—a seemingly innocuous Senate debate over western land sales that sharpened the rhetoric over sectional differences and a slave rebellion in Virginia that came closer than any other to succeeding.

Eager to attract population, westerners had long lobbied for a reduction in the price of federal lands. Southern representatives offered to support the measure if the western states would join in opposing the tariff. When, in December 1829, Senator Samuel A. Foot of Connecticut advocated limiting land sales in the West, South Carolina Senator Robert Y. Hayne accused him of conspiring to keep labor prices low in the East and insinuated that the government was keeping land prices artificially high to build a slush fund "for corruption—fatal to the sovereignty and independence of the states."

Rising to defend his region, Senator Daniel Webster of Massachusetts countered that it was South Carolina, not the Northeast, that was a hotbed of disloyalty, pointing for evidence to the *Exposition*. The Revolution had been fought by *the American people*, Webster thundered, and *the American people* had created the federal government. Uncannily foreshadowing, Webster evoked the image of "a once glorious union" "rent with civil feuds, or drenched, it may be, in fraternal blood!" Such a fate must be prevented, Webster roared. "Every true American heart" must recommit itself to the founding spirit of the nation: "Liberty and Union, now and forever, one and inseparable."

Although he supported the federal Union, President Jackson did sympathize with southern complaints about the fairness of tariff levels, and he advocated tariff reform. The Tariff of 1832 lowered duties on many goods to 1816 levels, but not on textiles and iron. In this continued protection for the largest northern industries, South Carolinians saw a defiant reaffirmation of a special relationship between northern interests and the federal government.

By then, the South had been the scene of another slave insurrection. In the summer of 1831 an African American driver and preacher by the name of Nat Turner launched a rebellion in Virginia. The rebellion was put down, and Turner and other conspirators were executed, but unlike earlier plots, this revolt *had actually taken place.* Inspired by a millennialist fervor, for two days Turner and his followers had effectively controlled parts of southern Virginia, recruiting new allies, executing whites, and freeing slaves. Although the number of active insurrectionists probably never exceeded 70, 57 whites died in the uprising, more than in any previous slave rebellion. Southern whites took their revenge in a monthlong reign of vigilante terror, but the insurrection had left its mark. Southern whites lived in a state of constant fear, convinced that northerners and southern slaves were in league against them. In a 1832 convention South Carolina radicals voted 136 to 26 to nullify the tariffs of 1828 and 1832 in the state. The acts forbade the collection of the tariffs within South Carolina.

For Jackson, the act of nullification transformed the crisis from a question of regional interests to one of national union. "The laws of the United States must be executed," he declared. "I have no discretionary power on the subject; my duty is emphatically pronounced in the Constitution." He asked Congress for a law specifically affirming his responsibility to compel the collection of the tax in South Carolina, by force of arms if necessary.

Congress rushed to find a compromise. In early 1833 it passed a tariff that gradually reduced duties over the next decade but also passed the law Jackson had requested, known as the Force Bill. Jackson signed both the new tariff law and the Force Bill, a signal to South Carolina that nullification and secession would not be tolerated.

In 1832, with South Carolina virtually alone even among southern states, supporters of nullification had no choice but to withdraw their ordinance. At the same time, they voted to nullify the Force Bill within the boundaries of South Carolina. Jackson let the gesture pass, and at least for the time being, the constitutional crisis was over.

Conclusion

The political economy of the Jacksonian consensus was forged from belief in the efficacy of the individual, a distrust of unfair privilege, and a commitment to geographic expansionism. Few of these elements were new to Americans, but their meanings had shifted

>> Timeline

▼1824

John Quincy Adams elected president (the "corrupt bargain")

Rappites sell New Harmony to Robert Owen and return to Pennsylvania,
  establishing third community, Economy

Charles Grandison Finney begins preaching in upstate New York

▼1825

Owen establishes New Harmony labor reform community

▼1827

Antimason Party organized

▼1828

Andrew Jackson elected president

Virtually universal white male suffrage

Philadelphia workers organize the Philadelphia Working Men's Party

Protective Tariff of 1828 passes

▼1830

Shakers support 60 communities

Removal Act passes

Joseph Smith organizes the Church of Jesus Christ of Latter-day Saints

▼1831

Antimason Party holds first open presidential nominating convention

Cherokee Nation v. Georgia

▼1831–1832

Alexis de Tocqueville visits United States

▼1832

Worcester v. Georgia

Black Hawk's War

Jackson vetoes act rechartering Second Bank of the United States

Jackson reelected

▼1834

Female Moral Reform Society formed

▼1836

Deposit Act expands number of Jackson's "pet banks" and provides for
  distribution of federal surplus

since 1776. The republic was becoming a democracy. But the harmony that seemed to be expressed in the Jacksonian celebration of democracy was misleading. Consensus was always partial, and conflict always present and growing. African Americans and Native Americans were excluded altogether; workers and women were included only contingently. If Jackson the southerner, the settler, and the son of common parents was able to draw support from a wide variety of constituencies, he was not without his detractors. These included southerners who hated the tariff; workers who sought urban, not agricultural, utopias; reformers who opposed his policies; and merchants and entrepreneurs who wanted a more stable currency. Within 25 years of Jackson's election, workers were in the streets, hundreds of thousands of Americans were petitioning to end slavery, political parties were in chaos, and the nation stood on the brink of civil war.

Review Questions

1. What about Andrew Jackson's life or career would have appealed to voters in 1828?

2. What was so democratic about the Jacksonian Democrats?

3. Why did Jackson, a southerner, oppose the *South Carolina Exposition and Protest*? Why did other southern states not support South Carolina in the nullification crisis?

4. How did Native Americans fight removal?

5. Why might white Americans have found the image of the disappearing Indian comforting? Did it share any cultural attractions with the colonization movement?

For further review materials and resource information, please visit www.oup.com/us/ofthepeople

Reform and Conflict

1820–1840

12

>> Nat Turner

On October 2, 1800, just a week before the slave Gabriel was executed for conspiring to lead a revolt in Richmond, Virginia, a slave child by the name of Nat was born in nearby Southampton County. Nat was the property of Samuel Turner and was raised to be one of Turner's field hands. But he was a bright child and learned to read and write early. Deeply religious, Nat Turner spent whatever time he could in prayer and fasting and soon matured into a charismatic preacher and prophesier, respected by blacks and whites alike.

According to Thomas Ruffin Gray, who later interviewed him, by the time Nat was in his twenties he understood that he "was ordained for some great purpose in the hands of the Almighty." One day while Nat was working in his master's field, he heard a huge noise in the sky "and the Spirit instantly appeared to me and said the Serpent was loosened, and Christ had laid down the yoke he had borne for the sins of men, and that I should take it on and fight against the Serpent, for the time was fast approaching when the first should be last and the last should be first." The yoke he was to take up was the freeing of the slaves. Three years later, he interpreted a solar eclipse as a black hand covering the power of white people, and he began to plan revolution.

Three months after the eclipse, on August 21, 1831, Nat Turner led one of the largest uprisings against slavery in United States history. Gathering a group of over 50 people, slaves and free black people, for two days Turner and his followers controlled the Southampton countryside, killing 57 white men, women, and children.

Turner's rebellion enraged and terrified the white population of Virginia. The state eventually executed 55 African Americans suspected of taking part in the revolt. Several hundred more were beaten, mutilated, and murdered by white mobs. The legislature passed laws tightening controls on the movement and assembly of blacks and augmenting the power of slave patrols.

>> **AMERICAN PORTRAIT** *continued*

But Turner's rebellion also catalyzed a different response in Virginia in 1831: a prolonged discussion of whether the state should find a way of ridding itself of slaves and slavery. The discussion was not altruistic. Whites made up just under 58 percent of Virginia's population and lived in fear of another rebellion. Moreover, not all whites in Virginia supported slavery. The western part of the state had never been dependent on it economically, and many western Virginians associated slavery with the disproportionate legislative power of the eastern part of the state. And although the east was deeply proslavery in its plantation culture, that economy had been declining for many years, the result of long-exhausted soil. Maybe it was time to get rid of slavery.

The discussion was also not about human dignity. The proposals in the Virginia House of Delegates would have had slaves either sold out of state before they reached adulthood or freed in stages and removed "beyond the limits of the United States."

Still, most eastern Virginians remained committed to slavery. After months of debate (and the likely intervention of Vice President John C. Calhoun), the legislature abandoned the whole idea by a 67–60 vote.

But if Turner's rebellion seemed a failure in Virginia, it was having profound repercussions elsewhere. Northern abolitionists were following events in Virginia closely, looking for any chance that a southern state would voluntarily eliminate slavery, even through colonization. As it became clear that Virginia would not even undertake colonization, abolitionists prepared for an unprecedented massive and militant propaganda assault on the South.

Common Threads

>> How did African American activism change over time?

>> How did the market revolution shape the Benevolent Empire?

>> How did the conditions of paid labor change between 1789 and 1835?

>> Why did many white northerners oppose abolition?

Perfectionism and the Theology of Human Striving

There was nothing about the depth of Nat Turner's faith, or its centrality to his life and identity, that set him apart from many others in early nineteenth-century America. The profound revivals of the turn of the century were continuing into the 1830s and set the

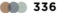

terms in which many people understood themselves and their world. Some Americans looked at the changes of the preceding decades and saw a nation on the verge of losing its moral compass. Convinced that the day of final reckoning grew near, they preached doom and withdrew from society into covenanted communities to prepare themselves for the end of time. Others remained hopeful that the nation could yet be redeemed. These reformers believed that it was the responsibility of each individual to work actively to perfect American society. Both reformers and separatists, however, shared the conviction that social life should be modeled on the principles of Protestant Christianity.

Millennialism and Communitarians

Separatist communities were not new to the American spiritual landscape in these years, and they never accounted for more than a minority of the American people. Nevertheless, they enjoyed renewed success in the 1820s. As a group, these religious communitarians sought to create more perfect societies on earth by withdrawing from daily contact with their neighbors and instituting tightly controlled spiritual, social, and economic regimens.

One of the earliest of these religious communities was the United Society of Believers in Christ's Second Appearing, a radical branch of Quakerism. This group was dubbed "Shakers" by its critics, for the "[d]ancing, singing, leaping, clapping . . ., groans and sighs" that characterized its services. Shakerism was rooted in the experiences of Ann Lee, a late-eighteenth-century English factory worker and lay preacher who believed that she was the second, female embodiment of the Messiah. Lee preached that believers should return to the simplicity and purity of the early Christian church, pooling their worldly resources, withdrawing from the vanities of society, and observing celibacy. The Shakers migrated to North America in 1774 and established their first community near Watervliet, New York. "Mother" Ann died in 1784, but by the turn of the century the Shakers had established a dozen communities in New England. Moving west, they established four settlements in Ohio and Kentucky. By the 1830s, membership approached 4,000.

Shaker beliefs required a community based on a "union of faith, of motives, and of interest" of all members. To ensure this perfect unity, Shakers organized themselves into "families" of 30 to 100 members, each of which was supervised by a panel of eight people (two women and two men to oversee spiritual matters, and two men and two women to oversee temporal concerns). The "families" within a community were guided by a ministry (also composed equally of men and women), and the individual communities submitted to the authority of a head ministry at New Lebanon, New York.

Their search for perfection led the Shakers to repudiate the values of the increasingly market-driven American economy. Although Shakers sold goods to outsiders, they rejected materialism and competitive individualism, allocating individual labor according to the needs of the community. This alternative political economy resulted in prosperity and innovation. Shaker gardeners developed the first American seed industry, and Shaker farmers produced bumper crops of grain and bred large and healthy herds of dairy cattle.

Women appear to have been especially drawn to Shakerism, probably because of the Shaker belief in the spiritual equality of women and men. This was reflected in the organization of the communities, with "sisters" and "female elders" supervising the women's lives and "brothers" and "male elders" supervising the men's. The Shaker practice of celibacy afforded women freedom from the dangers of childbirth.

Shakers Outsiders labeled members of the United Society of Believers in Christ's Second Appearing "Shakers" after the active twirling and shaking movements that accompanied their services.

Like the Shakers, the followers of German farmer George Rapp rejected the private ownership of property and practiced celibacy. Believing that "the kingdom of Jesus Christ is approaching near," they considered it the responsibility of the truly devout to amass great material wealth to put at the disposal of Jesus Christ on his return to Earth.

Rapp and several hundred followers arrived in North America in 1803 and migrated to western Pennsylvania, where they established the town of Harmony. They moved in 1815 to the banks of the Wabash River in Indiana Territory, where by1824 their membership numbered 800. There they grew fruit, grain, and cotton; grazed sheep; and erected a cotton and woolen mill and a distillery. Unfortunately, the climate that made the Wabash hospitable to agriculture also made it hospitable to malaria. After years of malaria scourges, in 1824 the Rappites sold New Harmony to the English social reformer Robert Owen and returned to western Pennsylvania.

The largest and most long-lived of the millennial communities of the early nineteenth century was the Church of Jesus Christ of Latter-day Saints, also known as the Mormons, founded by Joseph Smith Jr. in 1830. Smith preached that God had made known his intentions for the "latter days" of creation, now approaching, in golden tablets revealed to Smith by the angel Moroni. Christian in many ways, the Mormon Articles of Faith also included a belief "in the literal gathering of Israel and in the restoration of the Ten Tribes; that Zion (the New Jerusalem) will be built upon the American continent; that Christ will reign personally upon the earth; and, that the earth will be renewed and receive its paradisiacal glory."

Smith's preaching attracted rural followers, most of them displaced by the changing antebellum North. To them, Smith preached that it was God's will that they go forth into the wilderness to found the city of Zion, where they would reign over the coming millennium.

The opposition of their neighbors, who considered Mormon beliefs blasphemous, forced the Mormons to leave New York. Smith first moved his followers to Ohio, and then to Missouri. In 1839 a large group moved on to Illinois, founding the city of Nauvoo. By the early 1840s, Smith had begun to preach the doctrine of plural marriage. The Mormon community split, and anti-Mormon outrage flared anew. Smith was arrested and thrown in jail in Carthage, Illinois, where, on June 27, 1844, he was murdered by a mob (allegedly helped by a jail guard supported by leading citizens). In 1847, following Brigham Young, the Mormons left again, reaching the Great Salt Lake in the West. By 1850, hard work, irrigation, and careful cultivation had turned the desert into a garden paradise inhabited by more than 11,000 people.

Urban Revivals

Separatist millennialists were a relatively minor stream in the floods of religious organizing during the 1820s and 1830s. Far more numerous were the Americans who sought to perfect society by carrying the spirit of reform into their own communities. This massive evangelizing of America took many forms. Itinerant Methodists and Baptists continued to minister to newly settled churches in the backcountry. By the 1820s, however, even such great metropolises as Boston, Philadelphia, and New York became hothouses of evangelism.

The career of Presbyterian minister Ezra Stiles Ely reflects this shift in mainstream religious life. From 1811 to 1813, Ely was a chaplain for the Society for Supporting the Gospel, working with people who lived in public shelters. He led religious services, distributed Bibles, and prayed at the bedsides of the sick and dying, observing firsthand the growing poverty of American cities. After the War of 1812, he worked the shanties and tenements of New York's poor neighborhoods. He increasingly understood his mission to be not merely providing solace but also converting souls. Ely and other city missionaries believed they could only save people who were chosen by God, but they believed the elect were also among the poor.

The new urban missionary societies soon looked to the boomtowns of the West. The New York Evangelical Missionary Society of Young Men raised money to send missionaries to new settlements of western Pennsylvania, upstate New York, and Georgia. No one was more successful or controversial than Charles Grandison Finney, who became an influential advocate for a dynamic Protestantism based on personal responsibility.

Finney had originally trained in the law, but in 1821 he experienced a calling to the ministry. Although Finney's rejection of the Presbyterian belief in original sin worried his teachers, he developed into a charismatic preacher, and after ordination in 1824 he moved to upstate New York to begin his work.

By the 1820s, construction of the Erie Canal was drawing even the most remote farmers closer to East Coast markets and enmeshing them in relations of cash and commerce. Inhabitants of towns and small cities were at the center of the rapidly developing market economy. Some people were troubled by the swirl of development around them. Others, more alert to the possibilities for success, were attracted to the way the new economy appeared to reward industry, hard work, and personal ambition.

Charles Finney Charles Grandison Finney was one of the most popular revivalist preachers in nineteenth century America.

To this latter audience, Finney preached of the power of human spiritual striving. Instead of the stern God of Calvinism, he offered a God of Justice, who spoke to a humankind "just as free as a jury" to accept salvation or not. This theology gave great latitude to human effort, but it also placed a new burden on the sinner. If "a man that was praying week after week for the Holy Spirit . . . could get no answer," Finney insisted, it must be that the man "was praying from false motives," not that God had abandoned him.

Finney enjoyed immediate success in the Genesee Valley of New York. Drawn to his preaching were those most benefiting from the economic boom: the families of merchants and bankers and of grain dealers and mill owners, as well as young, ambitious employees in such businesses. Finneyite Presbyterianism gave individual ambition a new role in the process of salvation, a sign of the human potential for good. For America, Finney claimed a new and optimistic religion based on the power of the individual.

Finney's preaching alarmed the Presbyterian establishment in the East, which feared the emotionalism and unorthodoxy of the revivals and Finney's influence in the new western areas. Among the eastern leaders was Lyman Beecher, pastor of the prestigious Hanover Street Presbyterian Church in Boston. Like many New Englanders of his era, Beecher was convinced that America's future greatness lay in transferring New England culture and its orthodoxy westward. Finney represented a dangerous threat to that orthodoxy. In 1832, Beecher moved his family to the new boomtown of the West, Cincinnati, where he wrote *A Plea for the West*, in which he predicted that the final battle of the Christ and the Antichrist would take place in the American West.

The Benevolent Empire

"Every truly converted man turns from selfishness to benevolence," Charles Finney said, "and benevolence surely leads him to do all he can to save the souls of his fellow man." The new evangelical emphasis on personal agency soon fostered a broad impulse for social

>> The American Board of Commissioners for Foreign Missions

The soldiers of the Benevolent Empire did not confine their attention to the United States. In 1810, in the earliest awakenings of the antebellum reform spirit, the General Assembly of Massachusetts (the governing body of the Massachusetts Congregational Church) created the American Board of Commissioners for Foreign Missions, an umbrella organization intended to promote Christian evangelizing in "heathen" lands around the world. The action came at the urging of a group of young Williams College students, who had pledged their lives to the project of "send[ing] the Gospel to the Pagans of Asia, and to the disciples of Mohammed."

Modeled on the London Missionary Society, the ABCFM sent out its first missionaries to Calcutta, India, in 1812, but other groups soon followed—to Hawaii, Turkey, and Palestine in 1819, to China in 1830, and to Africa in 1833. (By then, other Christian denominations in the United States had founded their own foreign missionary branches.) But "foreign" referred to the non-Christianized condition of the target communities, rather than literally to their residence in another country. From very early on the ABCFM sought "to extend the blessing of civilization and Christianity, in all their variety, to the Indian tribes within the limits of the United States." The most famous of these interventions was among the eastern Cherokees, where ABCFM influence encouraged acculturation and, later, voluntary removal.

As with other benevolent enterprises, the efforts of the ABCFM were funded through the donations of a vast network of local societies across the United States (particularly New England). Local supporters sponsored speakers, solicited donations, and produced a stream of pamphlets and letters to the editor on the importance of carrying Christianity to the "ignorant" people of other lands. By mid-century, the foreign missionary movement may well have been the largest of the undertakings of the Benevolent Empire.

The ABCFM, like other Christian missionary enterprises, consistently linked Christianity with United States culture, and its evangelizing focused as much on teaching the mores of western European society as on the Christian gospel. Making the Christian Bible accessible to non-English speakers involved ABCFM agents in educational and translation projects and sometimes in the creation of a written language for a nonliterate culture. ABCFM schools taught American standards of conduct and dress, as well as the English language. Mission hospitals introduced American medicine. The practice of sending married couples meant that missionary communities replicated American norms of domesticity. In 1817 the Board founded its own school, the Foreign Mission School in Cornwall, Connecticut, for educating converts to return to their own lands as missionaries of Christianity and United States civilization.

Even as it intervened in the cultures of other societies, discouraging traditional customs and replacing them with the social and religious norms of the United States, the ABCFM shaped Americans' views of other parts of the world. Missionaries constantly wrote letters home. In 1821 the ABCFM founded the magazine *Missionary Herald*, which featured the reports of missionaries. The Board also subsidized the publication of missionaries' recollections of their sojourns abroad. These pages came alive with strange and dangerous customs in exotic places, where ignorant people "jabber[ed] in their horrid jargon," worshiped "idol gods," and lived at "the lowest depths of sin and depravity."

American missionaries in Asia sometimes wrote criticisms of other imperial nations, especially Great Britain for its role in creating the Chinese opium trade (although rarely noted was the American participation in that commerce). Occasionally missionaries reflected critically on their own society. Encountering systems of bondage in other cultures, for example, a few ABCFM agents lamented the survival of slavery in the United States.

But the effect of the American mission movement was to portray the non-European world as a lost paradise, awaiting the arrival of its American rescuers. As one missionary to Hawaii wrote, in the non-Christian world even "the fruits and vegetables . . . taste of *heathenism*."

reform, expressed in religious terms and organized through a network of charities and associations, often referred to as the Benevolent Empire.

The Benevolent Empire reflected Americans' love of organizing, a tendency observed by Frenchman Alexis de Tocqueville when he visited the United States in 1831–1832. Americans, Tocqueville wrote, "combine to . . . found seminaries, build churches, distribute books, and send missionaries to the antipodes. . . . [I]f they want to proclaim a truth or propagate some feeling by the encouragement of a great example, they form an association."

Local societies linked up into national umbrella groups. Among the largest of these were the American Bible Society (which distributed Bibles in cities and new settlements), the Female Moral Reform Society (devoted to reclaiming women from prostitution), and the American Board of Commissioners for Foreign Missions (which promoted missions in the West). Every major city fostered Bible groups, asylums to help the poor, houses of industry, orphanages, and humane societies, among other charitable organizations. By 1830, evangelicals had also created a Sunday-school movement and a movement to prohibit the delivery of mail on the Christian Sabbath.

Benevolent societies combined emotional and rational approaches to reform. The method of the Benevolent Empire was moral suasion. Reformers believed that social change came about not from external rules but rather through the gradual internal awakening of individual moral purpose through personal contact, testimony, and (where needed) exhortation. Yet the Benevolent Empire soon resembled a bureaucratic corporation.

Map 12–1 Revival and Reform Social and economic transformation, religious revival, and social reform movements went hand in hand in the antebellum North. The so-called "burned-over district" of New York (the region directly served by the Erie Canal) nurtured numerous millennial sects (including Mormons and Shakers), antimasonry, Finneyite revivals, and antislavery activism, as well as the Seneca Falls woman's rights convention.

Founded in 1816 in New York by wealthy Christian men, the American Bible Society illustrates this paradox. The society consisted initially of a volunteer board of managers who hired out the printing of Bibles. By 1832, the society was run by a professional staff in its own building in Manhattan. However, the society still depended on idealistic young ministers as its traveling agents and local volunteer organizations as its community contacts.

As they pursued their good deeds—distributing Bibles or religious tracts, praying with the sick—evangelicals came into intimate contact with the poor and ministered to their material needs. They arranged fuel deliveries and medical care, helped homeless families find lodging, and organized soup kitchens. Both men and women were engaged in the charitable associations of the early nineteenth century, but voluntary reform offered special opportunities for women. Women had already been active in organizing maternal societies to improve their parenting habits and Bible societies to discuss their moral failings. By the second decade of the nineteenth century, women were becoming active in the Sunday-school movement and founding orphan asylums, homes for wayward girls, and asylums for "respectable" homeless adults. By the 1830s, women were the acknowledged volunteer backbone of the Benevolent Empire.

Reform and the Urban Classes

As well as addressing purely spiritual concerns, the religious organizing of the early nineteenth century also reflected worries about secular life. These concerns focused largely on the cities, where the market revolution and immigration opened huge rifts between the haves and the have-nots.

Wage Dependency and Labor Protest

By 1830, in response to growing markets, master craftsmen had subdivided the production process into smaller, discrete tasks, sending part production (of shoes, hats, or shirts) to outworkers for piece wages. In house, employers relied more and more on apprentices or poorly trained helpers, who worked more cheaply than journeymen. As work was subdivided, workers became more interchangeable, and their wages dropped.

The Panic of 1819 had thrown thousands of people out of work, driving wages down and prices up. The reviving economy of the 1820s did not reverse those trends, which were deepened by depressions in 1829 and 1837. In an 1833 appeal, workers in Manayunk, Pennsylvania, protested 14½-hour days in "overheated" rooms "thick with the dust and small particles of cotton, which we are constantly inhaling to the destruction of our health, our appetite, and strength." "Our wages," they declared, "are barely sufficient to supply us with the necessaries of life."

The lives of outwork seamstresses, of whom there were tens of thousands in the eastern cities, were even more harrowing. Philadelphia philanthropist Mathew Carey estimated the wages of Philadelphia seamstresses at $1.25 a week, but a committee of seamstresses revealed that they were lucky to earn $1.12 a week. After rent, they were left with a little more than a nickel a day for food, clothing, heat, and anything else they needed.

By 1830 the urban Northeast was witnessing the damages of wage dependency and the subdivision of labor. In the largest cities, neighborhoods had become stratified by class. The New York neighborhood of Five Points, once a thriving community of master craftsmen and trade shops, by 1829 was home to prostitutes, beggars, public drunks, thieves, and confidence men. High rents crowded whole working families into single unventilated rooms. Many went homeless or threw up shanties.

The organizing begun in the 1820s exploded in the 1830s, both among craft workers and in occupations long excluded from craft recognition. When the Philadelphia Mechanics' Union dissolved, leadership passed to the New England Association of Farmers, Mechanics, and Other Workingmen, founded in 1831 by, among others, Seth Luther. The association used its newspaper, the *New England Artisan*, for worker self-education and organizing.

In February 1831, protest erupted in an unexpected quarter. With wages in sharp decline, over 1,800 tailoresses (women who worked in specific aspects of the tailoring craft) struck the New York garment industry. The tailoresses had been advised not to strike to avoid harsh public censure and to wait for times to improve. Sarah Monroe, the secretary of the union, resisted the advice: "Long have the poor tailoresses of this city borne their oppression in silence, until patience is no longer a virtue—and in my opinion to be silent longer would be a crime." The women drew up a constitution, elected officers, and stayed out on strike for five months.

>> Freedom and Wage Labor

In the summer of 1832, only months before Andrew Jackson was elected for his second term as president, former Rhode Island carpenter Seth Luther traveled across New England denouncing the political economy of Jacksonian America. Journeying through Maine, New Hampshire, and Massachusetts, Luther condemned the "tyranny," "avarice," and "exclusive privilege" that drove "AMERICAN MANUFACTURE" and gave his sympathetic audiences a chilling picture of the havoc wrought in the lives of the "producing classes." He spoke of the 15-hour days and "the well seasoned strap" of the boss—all for a mere 75 cents a day. He described adults exhausted and brutalized and children made "pale, sickly, haggard . . . from the worse than slavish confinement of the cotton mill." He told of one 11-year-old girl whose leg was shattered by an impatient supervisor wielding a stick of wood, and another child who had a board split over her head by "a heartless monster in the shape of an overseer of a cotton mill 'paradise.'" The mills were turning out vast quantities of cottons and woolens. But here, in the lives of workers, was the true product of "the AMERICAN SYSTEM," he jeered. It created a social order in which "manufactures must be sustained by injustice, cruelty, ignorance, vice, and misery," a system in which "the poor must work or starve" while "the rich . . . take care of themselves."

In some respects, Luther's harangue was simply the labor counterpart of a standard Jacksonian political speech. It rang with denunciations of wealth and special privilege, praised the worth and dignity of common people, demanded reform, and flamed with images of the impending Armageddon. However, Luther was speaking in 1832, not 1828, when the common man had presumably reigned triumphant for four years. Luther's exhortation that workers were free men in name only and must now rededicate their lives to "LIVE FREEMEN and DIE FREEMEN" hinted at deep failures in Jacksonian democracy.

In some respects, Luther's indictment seems unaccountable. Jackson's landslide 1828 election had brought together a remarkably diverse coalition, including southern planters and northern manufacturers, wage workers and entrepreneurs, and political pragmatists and at least some social and religious perfectionists. These groups represented very different interests, but in 1824 and 1828 they had found enough common ground to produce a clear majority behind the Jacksonian Democrats. By 1832, moreover, Jackson had done much to satisfy the voters. He had removed National Republican appointees. He had supported white claims to Indian lands in the West, opening hundreds of thousands of acres to new settlement. He was preparing to take on the Second Bank of the United States. In national presidential politics, the consensus held. Jackson was reelected in 1832, and his vice president succeeded him to the presidency in 1836.

But Jackson's first term had also revealed disturbing, unreconciled tensions within the new democratic political economy. These tensions arose in part from the very strengths of democracy and economic growth. The expansion of personal liberties created a society in which inequities were all the more obvious. Of all groups, white working men had experienced the most dramatic expansion of their political rights (and, in some respects, their economic independence) in the early nineteenth century. Yet, as Luther made clear, by 1832 many American workers (female, as well as male) felt threatened by the new industrial order. By the early 1830s, worker protests had become common, and working men's parties had begun to assume a more clearly oppositional stance. "The dignity of common labor" had become the rallying cry of protest.

Rather than taking to the streets, Americans of more middling means responded to the volatility of industrial society by attempting to withdraw from it. Although this new middle class continued to insist on the dignity of labor, it grew less certain that the laboring classes could claim this dignity. If workers were poor, perhaps they lacked ambition, were negligent, drank too much, or were irreligious. Criticisms soon focused especially on Irish immigrants, whose growing numbers revealed the virulent anti-Catholicism of many native-born Americans, middle class and working class alike.

Deteriorating labor conditions led to protest even in that industrial paradise, Lowell (see Chapter 10). After a decade of rapid expansion, the market stalled in 1834. When prices fell and owners cut wages by 12.5 percent, 800 female operatives walked off their jobs. The protest failed, but two years later, when owners tried to increase the price of company housing, 2,000 operatives went out on strike, forcing owners to rescind the increases. The 1836 victory was fleeting, however. Business was booming, and the owners had a vested interest in keeping the mills open. When business was slow or inventories high, workers would have far less power.

Workers tried to strengthen their position by forming regional and national associations. The most successful national association was the National Trades' Union (NTU), formed in 1834. The NTU survived for a number of years but was unable to effect statewide coordinated actions. In the end, much of its energy went into lobbying for currency reform, worker access to education and free land, and the 10-hour day.

A New Urban Middle Class

Seth Luther framed his criticisms of American industrial society as a struggle between the "producing classes" and the "rich." However, this was not an accurate description. The concept of the "producing classes" was ambiguous, encompassing Americans of many different standards of living and levels of wealth. For Luther, the term meant primarily urban households dependent on wage labor. Luther sometimes distinguished among the "poor," the "rich," and the "middling classes." Americans were proud of their great "middling" ranks of solid farmers and artisans. But the composition of the category

Five Points, in New York City Once the site of a thriving community of craft shops and smaller retailers, Five Points had become one of New York City's poorest neighborhoods and, as this drawing suggests, a symbol of urban poverty, immorality, and crime.

had changed by the 1830s, as had its relation to the group Luther now called the "working classes."

These new middling classes were difficult to define exactly. Like the new working classes, the middling classes were primarily urban based. Middle-class households tended to receive their income as fees and salaries, rather than wages, and their paid workers held jobs that required mental, rather than physical, labor. These included doctors, lawyers, ministers, middle managers, agents, supervisors, tellers, clerks, shopkeepers, editors, writers, and schoolteachers.

The relationship of these urban households of moderate means to the new industrial economy was complicated. On the one hand, they were not immune to catastrophic economic reversal, whether sudden unemployment, business failure, or bad speculation. At the same time, the new middle class was created by and benefited from the industrial transformation. The paid occupations on which middle-class families depended had expanded enormously. These jobs brought annual salaries ranging roughly from $1,000 to $1,500, compared with the $300 to $400 an average working man might earn. Middle-class families also tended to have access to other resources through family, friends, and business connections.

The middle class celebrated the new political economy, the expansion of democracy, and the growth of individual opportunity even as it deplored the special privilege of the wealthy. Deeply religious and committed to the doctrines of personal agency, they were churchgoers who both donated to and participated in the causes of the Benevolent Empire.

Individuals who aspired to urban middle-class status took far greater pains to distinguish themselves from the urban poor than from the rich. This was especially evident in their understanding of personal responsibility and material success. In sermons and tracts, children's books, and novels, members of the new middle class described the industrial economy as a test of personal character. Success demonstrated superior individual industriousness and self-discipline; failure signified the opposite. These beliefs took their toll on middle-class families that failed, bringing on social and psychological censure. Nevertheless, middle-class writers continued to hone the idiom of the "common man" into the more class-based language of the "self-made man" of business. From this point of view, the middle class was the repository of moderation in a changing world, the heir of Jefferson's idealized "husbandmen."

Meanwhile, middle-class families struggled to distinguish themselves from the working class. Middle-class parents recoiled from manual labor and urged their sons to become "a rich merchant, or a popular lawyer, or a broker." They expressed a new value for education, even for their daughters. Whereas workers crowded into smaller and smaller homes, the emerging middle class expressed itself in increasingly elaborate residential spaces. The ideal middle-class home, the "cottage," offered a private sitting room for the family and a separate "public" parlor for guests. The parlor was a stage on which the family could proclaim its success through a display of costly furnishings and decorations.

To emphasize their distance from the industrial world, the new urban middle class insisted on a "natural" division of temperament and capability between men and women. Although men were required to confront the degradations of labor, women were intended by nature to remain at home to restore the sensibilities of husbands and raise children protected from the ravages of industrialization.

This view of women as the primary influence on children represented a dramatic change in attitude. It was, however, largely inaccurate, as many middle-class women pursued paid labor. They took in boarders, did fancy sewing, opened schools, and worked in family-owned businesses. They all worked unpaid at the daily labor of cooking, cleaning, washing, ironing, preserving food, sewing, and caring for children. Domestic womanhood became the primary symbol of middle-class respectability and a bulwark against the contradictions of the new industrial society.

Immigration and Nativism

Facing enormous changes, even economically secure Americans were alert for sources of potential danger. Many labor leaders and utopians felt that industrialists were posing that danger. More common, however, was the tendency to focus anxieties on the poor, deemed incapable of achieving republican virtue. Immigrants became natural targets, and especially the Catholic Irish.

In spite of the difficulties facing wage workers, the robust economy drew increasing numbers of immigrants from Europe, 90 percent of whom came from England, Germany, or Ireland. The largest group by far was Irish. Plagued by chronic poverty and harsh British rule, almost 60,000 Irish immigrants arrived in the 1820s, 235,000 in the 1830s, and 845,000 during the potato famines of the 1840s. Through most of the period, the Irish accounted for more than one-third of all immigrants.

Their customs and their poverty made Irish immigrants conspicuous. Unable to afford land, they remained crowded in the seaports where they arrived. Desperate, they often had to accept jobs and conditions that native-born workers scorned. With no other place to go, one boss observed, the Irish could "be relied on at the mill all year round."

Not all of the Irish went into mills. Many built roadways, dredged river bottoms, and built canals. Irish women cooked and did laundry for the camps or hired out as domestic workers in middle-class households.

Most of all, the Irish were distinguished by their Catholic religion. By 1830, immigration had virtually doubled the number of Catholics in the country. Not all Catholics were Irish, but many were, making the Irish visible targets of long-standing anti-Catholic prejudices. Anti-Irish stereotypes represented Catholics as given to superstition and unthinking obedience. Funded by the new middle class and supported by Protestant ministers, anti-Catholic newspapers charged the Catholic hierarchy with "tyrannical and unchristian" acts "repugnant to our republican institutions."

By the early 1830s, anti-Catholicism spilled over into street violence. Organizations such as the New York Protestant Association sponsored "public discussions" on the immorality of monks, the greed of priests, and the pope's alleged designs on the American West. The debates would deteriorate into small riots. Anti-Catholicism was especially strong in Massachusetts. In 1834, the associated Congregational Clergy of Massachusetts issued a frantic challenge to Protestants to rescue the republic from "the degrading influence of Popery." Sermons and editorials whipped up a frenzy of anti-Catholic fear. The hysteria was aimed at a convent in Charlestown, Massachusetts, in which, purportedly, nuns were brainwashing innocent Protestant students. On the night of August 11, 1834, a cheering mob burned the convent to the ground. Anti-Catholicism was beginning to serve as a bond among Americans who otherwise had little in common with one another.

Internal Migration

The constant stream of internal migrants also heightened the sense of turmoil in antebellum American society. Strong internal migration signaled growth and opportunity, but it also produced a steady flow of individuals who seemed to have no settled stake in American society.

Many of these were westward settlers, but many were marginalized rural folks seeking employment in the cities. There was both a push and a pull to this movement. Children were pushed out from farming families whose land could no longer support them. They were pulled to the cities by the same conditions that destroyed the artisan tradition: the breakdown of the apprentice system and the subdivision of skills.

In the cities, these young people often lived in rented rooms without adult guidance. Young men joined neighborhood fire companies that served as gathering places for fun and sport. Young women navigated the city unescorted. Young people used their earnings to buy the things unavailable in the countryside: new shoes, clothing of the latest cut, hats, and canes. Migrants usually traveled fairly short distances to the nearest large towns and cities and swelled the populations of the midsized cities in which most American manufacturing took place. Reading, Pennsylvania, was a hub for regional manufacturing, transportation, and trading. In the 1840s, Reading's population doubled to 15,000 people. Nearly half of its unskilled laborers had come from within 25 miles, from areas with poor land and big families.

The constant migration of Americans westward provoked alarm among the eastern, urban middle class. Moralistic observers worried that this migration was draining ambitious, upright citizens from the East Coast, leaving the dregs of society behind. Observers also worried about the influence of the West on future American citizens. The West lacked the institutions that easterners associated with civilization and civic responsibility. There were few schools and churches and too many unattached young men, saloons, and brothels. Moreover, westward migration stood for the materialism and greed that easterners were beginning to worry about. The desire for money drove some families on an almost endless migration. One family, the Shelbys, had made four moves west by 1850, when they ended up in Oregon.

Into this troubling land were being born more and more of the nation's young. Once families had begun to pour in, fertility rates in the newly settled areas became far higher than they were in the older, coastal regions. Easterners were alarmed by the specter of a generation of children growing up in the wilderness without proper social constraints. The values of self-reliance, industry, and civic virtue, which only a decade before had seemed to capture the essence of American nationalism, appeared in danger of disappearing. By the 1820s, these fears were being focused on the growing waves of European immigrants.

Self-Reform and Social Regulation

In his address to working men in 1832, Seth Luther explained that he would uncover "principles and practices which will, if not immediately eradicated and forsaken, destroy all the rights, benefits, and privileges intended for our enjoyment, as a free people." Earlier reformers had been far more optimistic. Faced with deep divisions and seemingly impossible obstacles to an ideal industrial society, reformers began to turn away from broad programs of social perfection to endeavors that centered on self-control and external restraint.

A Culture of Self-Improvement

Answering criticisms from fellow senators that only the rich and well connected enjoyed the benefits of the new American industrial order, in 1832 Henry Clay rose to defend the entrepreneurial class. "In Kentucky," he asserted, "almost every manufactory known to me is in the hands of enterprising and self-made men, who have acquired whatever wealth they possess by patient and diligent labor." Clay's emphasis on personal enterprise captured a perspective increasingly shared by ambitious Americans by the 1830s. Success or failure was less a matter of external injustice and constraint than of individual striving. Those who truly worked hard—who were industrious and clever and frugal—would succeed.

The culture of self-improvement was particularly popular among members of the new middle class. The emphasis on self-creation helped to resolve their ambivalence about industrial society: middle-class families had escaped the worst ravages of wage labor not because they were lucky or had some special advantage but because they worked harder.

The culture of self-improvement also embraced the body as well. From the 1820s to the 1840s, health reform became a national obsession, as Americans experimented with new diets, clothing, exercise programs, abstinence, and hydropathy, the cleansing of the body through frequent bathing and drinking of water.

Middle-class men and women crowded lectures and devoured writings that espoused the philosophy of self-culture. By 1831 the lyceum movement claimed several thousand local organizations under a national association and sponsored such speakers as the writer Ralph Waldo Emerson, Daniel Webster, and later Abraham Lincoln. Meanwhile, middle-class readers supported a publishing bonanza in novels, periodicals, and tracts devoted to self-improvement.

These publications promoted a variety of images of the self-made American. In his Leatherstocking Tales, James Fenimore Cooper celebrated the pioneer. Novels like Catharine Sedgwick's *Rich Man, Poor Man* romanticized urban poverty and suggested that hard work put "true wealth" (virtue) within the reach of even the most humble family.

Although in most cases the myth of the self-made American was decidedly male, it also had important implications for women. On the one hand, it highlighted the importance of childrearing. Periodicals such as the *Ladies Magazine* and *Godey's Lady's Book* and advice books such as Lydia Maria Child's *The Mother at Home* and William Alcott's *The Young Mother* instructed women on the development of the proper mental and moral habits in the young. On the other hand, a generation of female novelists appropriated the themes of self-culture to emphasize female self-reliance. In her 1827 novel *A New-England Tale*, Sedgwick told the story of a young orphan left penniless by an improvident wealthy father and a pampered mother. Jane, the protagonist, learns that hard work builds both economic independence and strength of character and is appropriately rewarded with a prosperous husband, children, and a safe middle-class home.

Some writers mounted a determined assault on the new American political economy. Transcendentalists such as Ralph Waldo Emerson, Margaret Fuller, and William Ellery Channing believed in the power of the independent mind not only to understand the material environment but also to achieve a spiritual wholeness with the world. They saw that, in contemporary America, self-improvement was often cultivated only for immediate material gain. In his essay "Self-Reliance" (1841), Emerson tried to distinguish true independence of mind from slavish rushing after privilege and celebrity. Although Emerson

Lyceum Movement Americans' enormous interest in self-improvement in the antebellum years was reflected in their enthusiasm for public lectures, known as the lyceum movement. This cartoon gently spoofed a lecture by James Pollard Espy, a meteorologist. As the drawing suggests, women were prominent in lyceum audiences.

was a professional man, not a laborer, in many respects his critiques echoed the themes of Seth Luther.

Temperance

Of the many movements for regulating the body, the largest by far—and the longest lived—was the temperance movement. By the 1840s hundreds of thousands of Americans had taken the pledge to swear off demon rum.

Prior to the nineteenth century, liquor played a central role in the lives of Americans. The Puritans (even ministers) had insisted on having their supply of wine, beer, and hard cider, and in craft shops, workers took rum breaks from their labor.

Some religious groups, especially the Quakers and the Methodists, had opposed the drinking of hard liquor in the eighteenth century, but it was only in 1808, in Saratoga, New York, that the first temperance society was formed. Within the next five years, at least four more temperance societies were established in New England.

In the 1820s, the temperance movement was taken over by evangelicals who saw demon rum as the enemy not just of piety but of the self-control essential to the perfection of society. Evangelists began to depict drinking as a sign of social disorder. In a series of six sermons preached in 1825, Lyman Beecher effectively changed the debate over alcohol. He did not call for absolute abstinence, and he urged his followers to form voluntary associations to drive the demon rum from American society. The following February saw the formation of the American Society for the Promotion of Temperance (ASPT). The ASPT quickly set about organizing local chapters across the country. By 1834 there were at least 5,000 state and local temperance societies.

The Common School Movement

By the 1830s, workers, members of the new middle class, and elite philanthropists all identified education as a critical arena for reform. As in other reform movements, however, the motives of different groups varied widely.

Since the founding of the nation, educational opportunities for the sons and daughters of prosperous parents had steadily increased. Children from wealthy urban families had private tutors, followed (for boys) by training in private seminaries and academies. By the 1820s, young women from prosperous northern families could choose from a growing number of seminaries. Meanwhile, subscription schools offered basic education to rural children.

These schools were out of reach for working-class children. Labor reformers linked this lack of schooling directly to the larger process of industrial oppression. In their 1831 constitution, the Working Men's Association of New York placed the demand for "a system of equal, republican education" above every other goal, because education "secures and perpetuates every political right we possess." Seth Luther blasted industrialization for preventing workers "from a participation in the fountains of knowledge." Reformers had founded charity schools in many eastern cities, but workers saw these as inferior. Only free public education, workers argued, could defy "the siege of aristocracy."

Many middle-class parents were also unable to afford private academies. In 1830, fathers in Utica, New York, called for a public school system that would permit children to "keep pace with the age in its improvements" and "calculate their own profits in the world."

Middle-class parents were anxious about daughters, as well as sons. They worried that traditional housewifery skills would be of little use to daughters who faced an increasingly complex market culture and new domestic technologies. Most of all, they worried that their daughters might not marry or might marry into families that would face financial ruin. Concerned that expanded suffrage would introduce volatility into the American electoral process, reformers often supported expanded public education as "the great bulwark of republican government," in the words of New York governor De Witt Clinton. If white working men and their sons were to vote, it was important that they first be educated.

This convergence of interests led to a growing demand for more common schools. Nevertheless, broad segments of the public resisted the idea. In Cincinnati, wealthy property owners opposed paying taxes to send poor children to school. Other skeptics considered the whole idea an invasion of their rights as free citizens. States were often left to passing simple enabling legislation such as Pennsylvania's 1834 act that made public schools a local option.

In 1837 the Massachusetts legislature went further, creating a state Board of Education and appointing educational reformer Horace Mann as its first secretary. Mann addressed the anxieties of more prosperous Americans. On the one hand, he reassured middle-class parents that relying on an extrafamilial institution was both right and natural, given the changing society. On the other hand, he assured them that nothing else need change about the industrial society on which they depended. Poverty, he wrote, was not decreed by God nor required by American society. Only the lack of education barred the poor from prosperity, and benevolence and education would "disarm the poor of their hostility toward the rich."

Whites were less concerned about the potential hostility of the small free African American community. Until the 1850s, free African American children were excluded from public common schools, and tax monies were not used to establish schools for them. Education for free black children came almost entirely from the work of the free African American community. In the North, the efforts bore fruit, but in the South, opposition to the education of slaves hardened. In fact, many enslaved and free African American southerners did learn to read and write, but usually surreptitiously.

Penal Reform

In the first years of the republic, with memories of British injustice still fresh, Americans tended to think of crime as a problem of bad laws, not flawed people. Fair laws would nurture good republican character, and good republican citizens would respect laws they had had a hand in passing.

Yet by the 1820s eastern cities were incarcerating thousands of citizens—some for debt but many for robbery, larceny, fraud, vagrancy, and disorderly conduct. To many Americans—especially members of the middle class—it seemed that good laws were not sufficient to create a good citizenry. Like salvation, law-abiding behavior was a function of individual effort. Where individuals failed to obey the law, the community must devise some mechanism for its own protection.

The most popular solution from the 1820s on was the establishment of state prison systems, where deviant individuals could be kept apart from the community but could also be rehabilitated. State and city prisons soon began to replace older charity institutions. The two primary models, devised by New York and Pennsylvania, were variants on a single principle: The first step in making prisons places of real reform was to prevent inmates from influencing one another.

The New York version became most widely associated with the penitentiary at Ossining, New York, known as Sing Sing. There, prisoners worked side by side all day but were prevented from talking or even looking at one another. They slept in separate cells. The Pennsylvania model called for absolute isolation of the prisoners.

Visitors often toured these prisons and frequently applauded them, but they also noted the exaggerated hopes that Americans seemed to invest in them. The French visitor Alexis de Tocqueville observed of American reformers: "They have caught the monomanie of the penitentiary system, which to them seems to remedy for all the evils of society."

Electoral Politics and Moral Reform

Frustrated with the seeming resistance of social problems to moral suasion, reformers turned increasingly to electoral politics for solutions. The effect was to fragment and weaken party organization rather than to consolidate it. The political landscape became littered with specialized and often largely local parties, demonstrating the inability of the major parties to address basic social conflicts.

Nowhere was possession of the vote more important than among newly enfranchised white male workers. During the struggles of the 1820s and 1830s, laboring people believed that many of their problems would be remedied only through electoral action. As long as the economic power of employers was backed by laws that oppressed workers (debt laws that imprisoned them, bankruptcy laws that took their property, conspiracy laws that made union organizing illegal), strikes and petitions would never be enough.

By the late 1820s workers had begun to mobilize politically. In 1827 a group of workers in Philadelphia formed the Mechanics' Union of Trade Associations. Within a year that group became the Philadelphia Working Men's Party, a new political party dedicated to "the interests and enlightenment of the working classes." Over the next five years, under various names, the movement spread through most of the nation, becoming strongest in northern cities.

Workers were at a political crossroads. On the one hand, the formation of the Working Men's Party implied that workers were still optimistic that change was possible and that working men thought of themselves as citizens with the right and power to affect the makeup of the republic in such issues as public education, broadened incorporation laws, an end to imprisonment for debt, and banking reform. On the other hand, the organization of a separate political party indicated that workers remained deeply skeptical of the responsiveness of existing parties. Workers were moving toward a distinct identity within the new political economy.

In the winter of 1835/1836 anger at the legal system came to a head. With inflation and unemployment running high, New York City journeymen tailors went out on strike. The leaders of the union were arrested, tried, convicted on conspiracy charges, and fined. The labor press denounced the courts as "the tool of the aristocracy, against the people!" Nearly 30,000 people (the largest crowd in American history to that date) protested the convictions. The protesters resolved to meet the following fall in Utica, New York, to organize a "separate and distinct" political party to represent workers' interests. The 93 "workers, farmers, and mechanics" who met in Utica six months later voted to form the Equal Rights Party.

Labor movements in other states also began to focus on legislative reform. The 10-hour day, a long-standing demand, reemerged in the late 1840s as a central point of labor organizing. Workers in New England supported candidates friendly to the 10-hour day, petitioned legislatures for laws setting work hours, and testified before legislative committees. Female workers testified as well, using their life stories to create sympathy for the cause. It was male workers, however, who had the power to vote representatives out of office.

Other reform movements also began to focus on electoral strategies. The Female Moral Reform Society, which had long worked to redeem prostitutes from their sins, shifted strategies and began working for the passage of rent laws and property protections for women. This growing emphasis on legal reform grew out of an enhanced sense of connection between the reformer and the recipient of her aid.

Throughout the 1840s, temperance workers turned increasingly toward the passing of state laws. Among some temperance advocates (especially females), the shift was motivated by concern for legal protections for the wives and families of alcoholic men. But the use of legal strategies also expressed a growing belief on the part of middle-class, native-born reformers that alcoholism was a problem of the unruly immigrant working classes. As they identified drinkers as fundamentally different from themselves, temperance workers grew less interested in aiding drinkers directly and more willing to take recourse to legal controls.

Abolition and Women's Rights

Many of the antebellum reform movements generated widespread controversy and passionate disagreement. But no others touched the central nerve of society like the organized abolition movement after 1830 and the women's rights movement. Race and gender, it seemed to many Americans, were defining their nation and society.

Antislavery Becomes Abolition

Although some whites thought that African Americans had already become too militant in their own cause, black organizing continued to grow more assertive over the 1830s. Most black abolitionists did not counsel armed insurrection, but a growing number wrote and lectured on slavery and the condition of African Americans in the republic. The year 1829 had also seen the publication of Robert Alexander Young's *The Ethiopian Manifesto: Issued in Defense of the Black Man's Rights in the Scale of Universal Freedom* and David Walker's *Appeal to the Colored Citizens of the World*, both of which argued for a common, transnational black identity. In 1832 Maria Stewart, a free black woman in Boston, urged African Americans to take their destinies into their own hands. "If they kill us," she said of white opponents, "we shall but die."

These entreaties found responsive audiences. From 1830 until 1835 (and less regularly thereafter), free African Americans met in annual conventions to coordinate antislavery efforts and secure to free African American men "a voice in the disposition of those public resources which we ourselves have helped to earn." This National Negro Convention movement consistently framed its goals in the idiom of "manhood," calling for "the speedy elevation of ourselves and brethren to the scale and standing of men." Nevertheless, African American women worked to raise funds for the antislavery press and to raise awareness by inviting antislavery speakers to address their societies. In 1832 African American women formed female antislavery societies in Salem, Massachusetts, and Rochester, New York.

Although white opposition and criticism persisted, by the 1840s militant abolitionism had grown common in African American communities. In 1841 escaped slave Frederick

Douglass would deliver his first public abolitionist speech in Nantucket, Massachusetts; four years later he would publish his blunt autobiography of the brutalities of slavery, *Narrative of the Life of Frederick Douglass, An American Slave, Written by Himself*. In 1843 former slave and itinerant preacher Isabella Baumfree changed her name to Sojourner Truth and became a powerful and popular antislavery speaker throughout New England. Also in 1843, Henry Highland Garnet delivered "An Address to the Slaves of the United States of America," in which he called 4 million American slaves to open rebellion: "[A]rise, arise!" he cried, "Strike for your lives and liberties. Now is the day and the hour. . . . Rather die freemen than live to be slaves."

Although many whites in the North disliked the institution of slavery, most were reluctant to confront an issue with such power to ignite violence and division. It took the growth of the perfectionist impulse to dislodge northern complacency. The most dramatic break came in the person of William Lloyd Garrison, whose commitment to perfectionism led him to found his own abolitionist newspaper, *The Liberator*, in Boston in 1831. In the first issue Garrison announced his absolute rejection of any compromise with slavery: "I will not equivocate—I will not excuse—I will not retreat a single inch—and I will be heard." Garrison's approach was known as immediatism—by which abolitionists meant not the immediate abolition of slavery, but the immediate beginning of the process that would lead to slavery's ultimate abolition. Immediatists rejected all forms of compromise with slavery, public or personal. Immediatist white antislavery activism centered in Boston and tended to attract individuals, like Garrison, who were only peripherally linked to the mainstream Benevolent Empire. Most were urban professionals from liberal Protestant backgrounds, such as the author Lydia Maria Child, wealthy lawyer Samuel Sewall, Wendell Phillips (scion of an old Massachusetts family), and Henry and Maria Weston Chapman (he a merchant, she the former principal of a young ladies' high school). In 1831, under Garrison's leadership, they formed the New England Anti-Slavery Society.

Other antislavery workers were more willing than the Garrisonians to risk contact with the imperfect world. One of these was Theodore Dwight Weld, an early supporter of the Colonization Society. After his conversion in the Finneyite revivals of 1825 and 1826, however, he began to doubt that the Society would ever risk alienating its southern constituency. By the 1830s Weld was a committed abolitionist, and in 1834 he became a full-time antislavery organizer.

There were quick converts to the new, energized antislavery movement, especially in urban areas of the Northeast, upstate New York, and Pennsylvania and in western states heavily settled by New Englanders, especially Ohio. Quakers and liberal Congregationalists were particularly active. Local antislavery societies formed throughout New England by 1832. Although Garrison envisioned an abolition movement integrated by race and gender, local societies were generally segregated both ways. By the end of 1833, local and state organizations had grown strong enough to support a national society, the American Anti-Slavery Society, which included six African Americans on its original board.

Abolitionism and Antiabolition Violence

The American Anti-Slavery Society dedicated itself to the abolition of slavery without compensation for owners and to the admission of African Americans to full citizenship. Society members pledged to pursue their goals through nonviolent moral suasion, exhorting individuals to undertake voluntary self-reform and the reform of society.

Although it was nonviolent, moral suasion did not exclude confrontation. In 1835, in the wake of Virginia's unwillingness to take any action against slavery, the Society ratcheted up its challenge to American society, especially the South. The Society dramatically increased its publication of antislavery pamphlets from 100,000 to 1 million pieces. Roughly 20,000 tracts, fliers, and periodicals were mailed to southern destinations, and agents and lecturers spread out across the North.

The response, in the North as well as the South, was immediate and fierce (see Map 12–1). In the South, anger and panic turned violent. With the memory of Nat Turner still fresh, slave owners denounced the campaign. Southern communities offered rewards for prominent abolition leaders, dead or alive. Vigilante committees were appointed to police free African American neighborhoods, to patrol waters for runaway slaves, and to search post offices for offending materials. In Charleston, South Carolina, a mob broke into the post office, stole abolitionist literature, and burned it publicly.

Even before the 1835 campaign, northerners had begun to express their disapproval of abolitionists. In 1833, whites had boycotted a Connecticut school for young women when its principal, Prudence Crandall, admitted two African American scholars. When Crandall admitted an entirely African American student body, white citizens lobbied for laws to bar black students from the state, threatened Crandall, and burned the school to the ground.

The postal campaign unleashed a new fury in the North. Anti–African American and antiabolitionist riots tore through St. Louis, Pittsburgh, Cincinnati, and Philadelphia, and abolitionist meetings were regularly broken up by mobs. In Boston in 1835, a crowd captured William Lloyd Garrison and dragged him through the streets on a rope.

Antiabolitionist mobs also targeted newspapers. Rioters in Alton, Illinois, destroyed abolitionist newspaper editor Elija Lovejoy's press four times in 1837. In the last attack, they murdered Lovejoy himself.

Many white northerners who opposed slavery were distressed by the violence. A few northern state legislatures admonished radical abolitionists, although none passed laws restricting abolitionist activity. Many antislavery activists chastised what they saw as the extreme fringe of their own movement, worried that the abolitionists would "inflame the passions of the multitude, including the women and children," in the words of the *Boston Courier*.

Abolitionists were undeterred and even began to find more converts. Antiabolition violence suggested to some moderates that proslavery forces would stop at nothing—the flagrant violation of civil rights, the destruction of property, or murder. They were alarmed when, in his annual address to Congress in 1835, President Jackson asked for measures curtailing antislavery organizing, including closing the mails to abolitionist literature. Congress refused, but northerners were shocked by the idea that the president would go so far to protect southern interests.

Congress's refusal to interfere with the mails was followed by other, less encouraging decisions. Opponents of slavery had long petitioned Congress to end slavery in the nation's capital. Seeking to mollify southerners, in June 1836 the House of Representatives resolved that antislavery petitions to Congress be automatically tabled. The resolution, known as the "gag rule," was renewed by succeeding Congresses until 1844.

The American Anti-Slavery Society was quick to capitalize on the passage of the gag rule. In July the society published *An Appeal to the People of the United States*, charging that the gag rule violated the right of petition. That summer, female antislavery leaders organized a systematic drive to obtain signatures on antislavery petitions. They traveled across the North, speaking in private parlors and in public halls, and within two years collected some 2 million signatures, more than two-thirds of which were women's.

The petition campaign called attention to the gag rule, to congressional support of slavery, and to the ability of proslavery forces to abridge the rights of all Americans. It also provided moderate northerners with a nonconfrontational avenue of protest. Thanks to a growing awareness of slavery, the American Anti-Slavery Society grew from 225 local auxiliaries in 1835 to more than 1,500 by the end of the decade.

Immediatist sentiment often criticized the North, as well as the South, especially those northern reformers willing to compromise with slavery. Perhaps the North had already lost its moral bearing in the rush to industrial prosperity.

The new interest in electoral politics divided abolitionism. For moderate abolitionists, the passage of the gag rule had raised questions about the effectiveness of Garrison's antipolitical stance. They also flinched at the increasingly aggressive tactics of Garrison's movement and at the visible participation of women and African Americans.

These tensions were palpable in 1840 at the American Anti-Slavery Society's national convention. Participants quickly divided over whether women should participate in deliberations and whether the organization should work to elect abolitionist candidates to office. The Garrisonian branch took control of the convention. When Abby Kelley was elected to a previously all-male committee, anti-Garrisonians walked out. The exodus freed the renegades, led by philanthropists Arthur and Lewis Tappan, to launch an abolitionist political party. By the end of the year, the new Liberty Party, formed on the platform that the Constitution barred the federal government from creating slavery in any new states or territories, had nominated abolitionist James Birney for the presidency.

By definition, electoral reform excluded females. Still, some women were early advocates of the new electoral strategies. Laboring women worked for bankruptcy reform, 10-hour laws, and an end to conspiracy trials. Middle-class women advocated temperance laws and supported antislavery candidates. In the 1830s few of those women intended to claim electoral rights for themselves.

The Gender Limits of Antebellum Activism

Women from all classes and ranks in antebellum society were beginning to chafe under cultural and legal restrictions on their full autonomy as Americans. The young women workers who marched at Lowell called themselves "daughters of freemen" and edged closer to claiming an independent status as citizens, as did the tailoresses, who were tired of waiting for chivalry to improve their lot. Educated women and women who worked as authors, editors, and educators participated actively in the public discourse and profoundly influenced public opinion. Were they to be regarded as mere subordinates to fathers and husbands?

For many women, the growing importance of suffrage and electoral tactics to reform movements created a new consciousness of their precarious status. Reform work permitted women to participate in shaping the new democratic order and to perfect skills useful in civic culture. They ran meetings, kept track of money and records, and honed their skills at public speaking. Elite women involved in charities also learned to make use of the new institutions of the market revolution. Because married women could not hold property or make contracts in their own names, most women would have had trouble accumulating the money to fund asylums and schools. But *these* married women, wives and daughters of wealthy and influential men, could use their social position to obtain donations, endorsements, and even special charters (comparable to those granted to male entrepreneurs) that permitted a group of married women to function legally as males.

Reform women soon learned that there were limits to their authority. Even women who were involved in the mildest of reform activities (e.g., as members of the American Bible Society) were rebuked for "acting out of their appropriate sphere." Women engaged in more controversial activities such as labor reform or abolition work were heckled and hounded by mobs.

In 1837, in her *Essay on Slavery and Abolitionism*, Catharine Beecher attacked female abolitionists for violating the bounds of "rectitude and propriety" and for being motivated by unwomanly "ambition." The same year, the Massachusetts clergy criticized Sarah and Angelina Grimké (members of the southern planter class who were touring the North in the abolitionist cause) for daring to take "the place and tone of man as public reformer."

By the late 1830s women involved in abolition work were subjected to growing criticism from within. Although Garrison remained a staunch ally, other leaders, such as the Tappan brothers, believed that outspoken, assertive women were embarrassing the movement. For women who had given years of their labor and had endangered their lives in the cause of abolition, these attacks were galling. Disappointing, too, was the willingness of such men to abandon the old moral reform strategies, which embraced gender equality. The turn toward electoral reform reduced women to second-class status in the movement. They could still raise money, lobby, and speak, but they could not perform the new essential act of reform, voting.

After the 1840 split of the American Anti-Slavery Society, abolitionist women spearheaded a drive for an organized woman's rights movement. In Seneca Falls, New York, on July 14, 1848, five women (including the seasoned Quaker abolitionist Lucretia Mott and the much younger Elizabeth Cady Stanton) placed an advertisement in the *Seneca County Courier* stating, "A convention to discuss the social, civil and religious condition and rights of woman will be held in the Wesleyan Chapel, Seneca Falls, New York, on Wednesday and Thursday, the 19th and 20th of July current, commencing at 10 A.M."

The response was overwhelming. On July 19, 300 people (including perhaps 40 men, among them the famous abolitionist Frederick Douglass) showed up. The group debated, voted on, and passed a Declaration of Sentiments (modeled after the Declaration of Independence) and a list of resolutions. They demanded specific social and legal changes, including a role in lawmaking, improved property rights, equity in divorce, and access to education and the professions. All of the resolutions passed unanimously but one: a demand for the vote. Even as reform became ever more tied to electoral strategies, some reformers considered suffrage too radical for women.

Conclusion

When Andrew Jackson took office in 1828, he declared his mission to be "reform." Jackson, of course, meant reform of America's political society and, specifically, personal revenge on the politicians who had earlier denied him the presidency. By the time Jackson left office in 1836, and in the years after, Americans had taken the cause of reform into their own

>> Timeline

▼**1822**
Denmark Vesey conspiracy

▼**1826**
General Colored Association of Massachusetts formed
American Society for the Promotion of Temperance formed

▼**1827**
Russwurm and Cornish found *Freedom's Journal*

▼**1828**
Andrew Jackson elected president
Tariff of 1828
Calhoun writes *South Carolina Exposition and Protest*

▼**1829**
David Walker publishes *An Appeal to the Colored Citizens of the World*

▼**1830**
National Negro Convention movement begins

▼**1831**
Nat Turner leads rebellion in Virginia
William Lloyd Garrison begins publication of *The Liberator*
New England Anti-Slavery Society founded
New England Association of Farmers, Mechanics, and Other
    Workingmen founded
New York Protestant Association founded
Lyceum movement begins

▼**1832**
Tariff of 1832
Jackson reelected
South Carolina passes Nullification Resolution
Maria Stewart lectures in Boston

▼**1833**
Congress passes Force Bill
American Anti-Slavery Society founded

▼**1834**
Anti–African American riots in major cities
Anti-Catholic mob burns Ursuline Convent in Charleston,
    Massachusetts
Lowell operatives go on strike
National Trades' Union formed   *continued*

360 Chapter 12: Reform and Conflict

>> Timeline *continued*

▼1835
American Anti-Slavery Society begins postal campaign
Lyman Beecher publishes *A Plea for the West*

▼1836
Congress passes "gag rule"

▼1837
Abolitionist editor Elija Lovejoy murdered in Alton, Illinois
Bread riots in New York City
Massachusetts creates first State Board of Education; Horace Mann
   appointed secretary

---

hands. For some, it was a purifying mission, returning the nation to its founding promises of justice and equality. For others, it was an impossible task, tearing apart the fabric of the democracy. In the nation's short history, the West had always functioned as the republic's social and cultural release. Soon that symbol of reconciliation and prosperity would become the site of America's insoluble conflicts.

Review Questions

1. What conditions gave rise to labor protest in the 1820s and 1830s? What forms did that protest take?

2. What conditions gave rise to the early women's rights movement?

3. Did the rise of perfectionism and the Benevolent Empire reflect a new democratic impulse or a desire for social control?

4. Why did some reformers abandon the tactic of "moral suasion" over time?

For further review materials and resource information, please visit www.oup.com/us/ofthepeople

13

Manifest Destiny
1836–1848

>> Mah-i-ti-wo-nee-ni Remembers Life on the Great Plains

Mah-i-ti-wo-nee-ni was born in the mid-1830s in the Black Hills. Her father was Cheyenne, and her mother was Lakota (or Sioux). Her homelands had been a part of Jefferson's 1803 Louisiana Purchase and would later become the states of South Dakota and Wyoming. In the 1830s, however, the Great Plains were Indian country.

By the time Mah-i-ti-wo-nee-ni was born, contact with whites had been reshaping the life of Great Plains Indians for more than two centuries. The Cheyennes had once been a semiagricultural people who "planted corn every year . . . then went hunting all summer," returning in the fall to gather the crops. The reintroduction of the horse by the Spanish in the sixteenth century had enabled Plains Indians to become more efficient hunters and more effective raiders. Over time, the Cheyennes had given up farming and had organized their economic life around the hunt, foraging other food as they went, as whole villages migrated to seasonal hunting grounds. Competing for game, they sent out raiding parties to steal horses or take captives for exchange. Mah-i-ti-wo-nee-ni recalled a time in her childhood (probably in 1840) when the Cheyennes and the Arapahoes traveled south to meet in a great peace council with their traditional enemies, the Kiowas, Comanches, and Apaches.

By the 1830s, the proximity of white Americans was beginning to affect the Cheyennes. At the time of the great southern peace council, massive overland migration to the Pacific was already under way. In the West, many Americans believed, the nation renewed its virtues and purified the republican model of government. In the mid-1840s, Americans coined a phrase for this linking of land to liberty. Taking the continent was their "manifest destiny."

American settlement of the West implied a different destiny for Mah-i-ti-wo-nee-ni and her people, however. First came missionaries, exhorting Indians to convert to

continued

>> **AMERICAN PORTRAIT** *continued*

Christianity. The settlers followed, trampling Indian crops, destroying villages, spreading disease, and decimating the buffalo. At first the U.S. agents among the Cheyennes wished merely to trade gifts of kettles, coffeepots, knives, and blankets for promises to permit settlers to cross Cheyenne lands. Soon, the U.S. government wanted the land itself. Although the nomadic Cheyennes long resisted removal, by 1877, after years of struggle and compromise, Mah-i-ti-wo-nee-ni and her people were forcibly displaced south into Indian Territory.

Because much of the land Americans sought to settle lay within the boundaries of the nation of Mexico, the manifest destiny of white Americans also implied a distinct destiny for Mexicans. Claiming mistreatment by the Mexican government, white American settlers in the Mexican province of Coahuila y Tejas formed the Republic of Texas and sought entry into the United States. In 1846 the United States provoked a war with Mexico to claim large portions of that nation's northern territories.

That war gained the United States secure access to the Pacific Ocean. But Americans also paid the costs of the manifest destiny. Each stage of expansion reignited controversies over the institution of slavery. Whereas many white Southerners claimed a basic constitutional right to own slaves and felt betrayed by Northern opposition, Northern reformers inveighed against the immorality of the institution. They flooded the mails with abolitionist tracts and Congress with antislavery petitions. This collision of interests and ideals flared within a national political system ill equipped to respond to it effectively. American politicians continued to seek compromises between slave-owning and non-slave-owning interests, but the party structure was in disarray, with no strong leader to hold it together. By 1848, some Americans were prepared to give up on their government altogether.

Common Threads

>> How did the expansion of slavery in the 1820s and 1830s affect U.S. foreign policy in the 1840s?

>> How did settlers' preconceptions of other cultures affect their attitudes toward expansion?

>> How did the Democratic Party change between 1828 and 1848?

>> Was "manifest destiny" consistent with the Monroe Doctrine of 1823 or a repudiation of it?

>> How important were the politics of slavery in the 1840s compared with the previous decade and the decade following?

The Decline of Jacksonianism

Andrew Jackson had governed on a philosophy of federalism, in which a strong presidency had been necessary to combat, rather than support, the growth of a powerful central government. He had backed territorial expansion, the powers of individual states, and the claims of settlers and had opposed federal control of those processes. By 1836, people in new territories sought admission to the Union, settlers were launching the largest westward migration in the history of the nation, and Jackson's Democratic Party seemed to have reduced the old Republican dynasty (now regrouped as Whigs) to whining observers. But there were costs to Jackson's successes: his hatred of strong central government had thrown the nation's banking system into chaos, his zeal for territorial expansion had helped nurture a strong abolition movement in the North, and his own Democratic Party had grown too diverse to remain stable. Jackson would be succeeded in 1837 by a Democrat known for his political acumen, Martin Van Buren—but the "Little Magician" would lose reelection by a landslide in 1840 and fail again when he ran on a third-party ticket in 1848.

Political Parties in Crisis

The expansion of white male suffrage and the translation of moral-reform agendas into electoral politics energized American politics in the 1830s and 1840s. In 1840, 66 percent of the electorate voted in Massachusetts, 75 percent in Connecticut, and 77 percent in Pennsylvania. Yet the capacity of major political parties to accommodate a wide range of conflicting interests and beliefs was limited.

Increasingly fractured since the election of 1824, the Republican Party had struggled to reorganize in opposition to Andrew Jackson. Jackson's war on the national bank had offered the immediate occasion. Although unable to save the bank, Henry Clay and the anti-Jacksonians narrowly passed a Senate resolution in 1834 censuring Jackson for assuming "authority and power not conferred by the Constitution and the laws." (Jackson had refused to turn over a paper on the bank that he had read to his cabinet.) In the debate before the censure, Clay identified his own anti-Jackson position as "Whiggish" (meant to evoke memories of the English "Whigs" who opposed royal tyranny in the eighteenth century). That label stuck as the name of the new political party.

Former National Republicans in the urban Northeast and upper West made up the bulk of the new Whig Party. Some of these were beginning to doubt the wisdom of uncontrolled territorial expansion, which seemed to promote political corruption, economic disorder, sectional conflict, and the extension of slavery. They feared the disruptive power of wildcat settlers, wage workers, the urban poor, and immigrants. Whigs supported market expansion guided closely by a strong, interventionist central government. They continued to embrace the elements of the earlier "American System": a new national bank, a strong protective tariff, and government-sponsored internal improvements.

By 1834, some former Democrats were also disenchanted with the party of Jackson. Prosperous shopkeepers and middling merchants began to see their own interests as distinct from those of the urban laboring classes and were attracted by the Whig emphasis on discipline and order. Some southerners were still angry over the tariff and the nullification crisis. Some small farmers and shopkeepers wiped out by the Depression of 1837 blamed Jackson for their hard times. Workers, who had little trust for the merchant classes at the core of the new Whig Party, tended to form splinter parties or to stay with the Democrats.

Through the 1830s the Whigs were a loose and disorganized opposition. Unable to decide on a single candidate, in 1836 they ran four regional challengers, hoping to deny Van Buren a majority in the Electoral College. The Whig field included William Henry Harrison (governor of Indiana Territory and victor at the Battle of Tippecanoe, nominated by Pennsylvania Antimasons), Senator Hugh Lawson White (Jackson's disenchanted replacement in the Senate, nominated by unhappy Democrats in Tennessee), Senator Daniel Webster (former National Republican and famous orator, nominated by the Massachusetts legislature), and Willie P. Mangum (a protest candidate of the South Carolina Nullifiers).

Jackson's vice president, Martin Van Buren, seemed well positioned for the race. Van Buren was instrumental in creating a successful Democratic coalition, so he was surely the one to hold it together. Van Buren had been constantly at Jackson's side, as secretary of state and as vice president. Few politicians seemed better situated to inherit Jackson's popularity. What was more, Van Buren seemed perhaps uniquely positioned to bridge the growing gulf between northern antislavery and southern proslavery Democrats: his popularity in New York appeared strong enough for him to risk alienating some of the antislavery vote in the effort to gain southern support, a risk he took by publicly declaring himself "the inflexible and uncompromising opponent of any attempt on the part of Congress to abolish slavery in the District of Columbia" or to interfere with slavery "in the states where it exists."

The election was close. Van Buren won part of New England (but not Massachusetts or Vermont). He took his home state of New York, Pennsylvania, Virginia, and North Carolina. And he took far-west states, most of them slave states: Michigan, Illinois (technically free but

popularly proslavery, especially in the south), Missouri, Arkansas, Louisiana, Mississippi, and Alabama. He won 58 percent of the electoral vote (after the weighting of the Three-Fifths Compromise in the South) and a bare majority (51 percent) of the popular vote. A shift of fewer than 2,000 votes in Pennsylvania would have denied Van Buren an Electoral College majority and thrown the election to the House of Representatives.

Martin Van Buren One of the most powerful politicians of his time, Martin Van Buren was also one of the first to extol the virtues of party competition.

Van Buren and the Legacy of Jackson

In his 1837 inaugural address, Van Buren announced that the nation had arrived at a "singularly happy!" condition. Less optimistic, Missourian Thomas Hart Benton observed that in Van Buren's victory "the rising was eclipsed by the setting sun." Benton was closer to the truth. Van Buren's struggle to unite Jackson's party enough to get elected was only the first of the challenges he inherited.

The signs of the Panic of 1837 were already visible when Van Buren was inaugurated that March. Jackson's pet banks had ensured that western land speculation would be built on easy credit. His hard-money measures that had effectively drained the nation of specie did not end the bubble of credit. It simply diverted its source to European financiers, who got higher interest in the United States than in their home countries. When European banks responded to specie shortages in their own countries by increasing interest on deposits and tightening credit, the Europeans called in their American loans. The sudden collapse of credit was exacerbated by crop failures in 1835 and 1837, which put farmers at greater risk for defaulting on their loans and reduced American exports.

As credit evaporated, interest rates rose, paper money depreciated, and debt mounted. The credit-dependent cotton market began to collapse, taking with it several large import-export firms in New York and New Orleans. After years of high inflation, the failures ignited a run on the overextended banks, as depositors tried to hoard their savings before the hard currency was paid out for mercantile debts. "[E]ven during the Embargo, & war that followed," merchant John Perkins Cushing reported in May of 1837, ". . . there was nothing like the complete prostration of commercial credit & confidence that has taken place within the last two months."

A strong federal hand might have stemmed the damage, but Van Buren shared Jackson's view that the federal government should not manage currency. Van Buren's announcement on May 4 that he intended to maintain the Specie Circular in force ensured continued pressure on banks. On May 10, 1837, frightened depositors drained $650,000 from their reserves, and New York City banks closed. Only a show of military force prevented a riot.

Coinciding with large waves of German and Irish immigration, the depression hit the East Coast hard. Wages declined faster than prices. Unemployment was widespread, and losses touched even the prosperous middle classes. Troubled times remained until 1843. While Democrats scrambled to avoid political responsibility, the new Whig Party began to look ahead optimistically to 1840.

Although an additional infusion of federal funds to state banks in 1837 might only have fed the frenzy, Van Buren's decision to delay the scheduled distribution added a new confusion. In an effort to return stability to the nation's monetary system, Van Buren proposed that the Treasury Department establish its own financial institutions to receive, hold, and pay out government funds. The institutions would exist solely to manage government accounts and would not issue paper currency or make loans to business.

The proposal for an independent treasury met with substantial opposition. Predictably, Whigs objected that removing government holdings from circulation would reduce capital investment. But many Democrats also thought the new system would retard growth. The independent treasury did not pass until 1840, enacted as an entirely separate, specie-based system, able neither to receive nor to pay out paper currency.

Van Buren's challenges spilled over from domestic to international crises. Twice, the fears and frustrations of Americans along the Canadian border almost brought the United States and Canada/Great Britain to blows. Americans and Canadians had long argued over who owned the rich timber reserves in the Aroostook Valley on the border of Maine and New Brunswick. When Americans heard rumors in 1838 that Canadian lumberjacks were infiltrating the region and taking trees at will, the Democratic governor of Maine declared that Maine was under invasion and demanded federal protection. Van Buren sent in the army under General Winfield Scott. Aware that the economy could not support a war, he also instructed Scott to offer terms for a truce. If Canada would acknowledge Maine's predominant interest in the valley, the United States would respect existing Canadian settlements pending final disposition of the area.

Meanwhile, Americans along the northern New York border were picking sides in an internal Canadian rebellion against Great Britain (1837–1838). Although the United States was technically neutral, disgruntled unemployed American workers saw the rebels embodying the spirit of the American Revolution and were drawn to support them against wealthy Canadians and the British government. Recruited by the rebels, sympathetic New Yorkers raised funds and offered ships to transport men and arms to Canada. On December 29, 1837, Canadian pro-British troops crossed the river into Schlosser, New York, captured the *Caroline* (owned by American William Wells), towed it out into the middle of the river, and set it afire. A few months later, Americans retaliated by sinking a British ship. The United States and Britain exchanged diplomatic demands until 1840, when Alexander McLeod, a Canadian deputy sheriff, got drunk in a New York tavern and began bragging he had killed an American during the *Caroline* incident. New York authorities immediately arrested him and local mobs clamored for blood, while Britain protested that McLeod's status was an international matter, beyond New York's jurisdiction, and threatened to break diplomatic relations. Van Buren, fighting for reelection as the anti-big-government Democratic candidate, was not ready to intervene. Only with the election of a Whig president and Congress in 1840 was McLeod released.

The Political Economy of the Trans-Mississippi West

Jackson had embodied the restless energy and assumed right of white Americans to settle ever deeper in the North American continent. Manifest destiny, the belief that white Americans had a providential right to as much of North America as they wanted, had been a core belief and policy since the founding of the republic. It was implicit in the Northwest Ordinance, in scores of Indian treaties, in the Louisiana Purchase, in the Transcontinental Treaty, in the 1824 Monroe Doctrine, and in the Removal Act of 1830. But only in 1845 did the phrase enter the American vocabulary, when journalist John O'Sullivan proclaimed that it is "[o]ur manifest destiny . . . to overspread the continent allotted by Providence for the free development of our yearly multiplying millions." As the United States' treatment of Native Americans had long made clear, the manifest destiny of the nation was for many Americans racial, as well as territorial and political.

Manifest Destiny in Antebellum Culture

On the simplest level, manifest destiny was a political slogan and a crass claim for property, a way of asserting that Americans wanted and would have the continent all the way to the Pacific. But most Americans resisted such a naked statement of their ambitions and framed—and deeply understood—their aspirations in the language of democracy and freedom. This land was intended by Providence as the physical home of a unique national greatness. In antebellum culture, this understanding of the singularity of North America was often articulated through a linked pair of evocative images: first, the image of the awesome power and natural majesty of the American wilderness and, second, the image of the wilderness giving way to an even nobler state of cultivation on the arrival of American settlers.

Both images were evident in antebellum landscape painting, particularly in the work of a group of artists known as the Hudson River School. Like most Americans of the era, the Hudson River painters were influenced by the Romantic movement sweeping Europe, which emphasized the power and beauty of untamed nature. For example, the canvases of Thomas Cole, the leader of the Hudson River School, depicted wilderness bluffs surrounded by ageless forests presumedly untouched by American settlers. Ancient trees spiked toward the heavens and wild waterfalls cascaded over crags far above the ground in Cole's *Falls of Kaaterskill* (1826), with a massive gathering storm that underscores the unchecked power of the American wilderness. In these landscapes, the only human figures are usually Native Americans, additional emblems of the primitive beauty of the scene.

Cole and other Hudson River painters often combined these visual celebrations of the American landscape with images of American settlement. In these latter paintings, the arrival of the European Americans seemed to bring to fruition the innate grandeur of nature. Cole's *Landscape* (1825) suggested this harmonious blending of destinies, as did *West Rock, New Haven* (1849), by Connecticut native Frederick Church. The Hudson River paintings sometimes suggested bittersweet sadness at the passing of the wilderness, even as they celebrated the coming of ordered fields and farm towns.

Antebellum poets and novelists also took up the theme of the land, also often envisioning it as a shifting scenery in which the majesty of the wilderness seemed merely to await transformation at the hands of American pioneers. James Fenimore Cooper's Leatherstocking Tales narrated European American settlement of the New York backcountry as a grand myth of manifest destiny, in which settlement tamed the land even as the land itself became the agent through which the newcomers were forged into a new, ennobled society. In *The Last of the Mohicans*, Cooper described the New York backcountry of 1757 as "an impervious boundary of forests" torn by dangerous rapids and rugged passes. By 1793, the fictional time of *The Pioneers*, that same landscape had become "a succession of hills" and "narrow, rich cultivated dales" dotted by "beautiful and thriving villages" and "neat and comfortable farms." In the same spirit, poet William Cullen Bryant visited the Illinois plains in the 1830s and saw not an austere landscape but a vision of "gardens" and "fields, boundless and beautiful." The uniting of the national culture and the land was the "manifest destiny" not only of American citizens but also of the land itself.

Jefferson had imagined this relationship of the people to the land chiefly in terms of the yeoman farmer, with the craftsman a secondary "handmaid." In the wake of innovations in travel and machinery design in the early nineteenth century, however, images of

Thomas Cole's *The Hunter's Return* One of the foremost landscape artists of his time, Thomas Cole romanticized nature and the simple life of the independent farmer.

trade and manufacturing began to make their way into ideas about the abundance of the land. Americans would unleash the richness of the continent not only through farming but also through commerce. De Witt Clinton's prediction that the Erie Canal would help make New York City the emporium of the world captured this new vision in the politics of trade. Commerce, Clinton insisted in 1819, would not only collapse regional differences but also "increas[e] the stock of human happiness—by establishing the perpetuity of free government—and by extending the empire of improvement, of knowledge, of refinement and of religion. . . ." The American wilderness, first cultivated into a homestead, would become a huge highway for the transportation of goods and culture.

To this image of North America as a transportation network, Americans added the image of North American power harnessed into manufacturing output. The proof of America's greatness lay not only in the riches coaxed from the land but also in the seemingly endless array of manufactured goods. Reviewing an exhibit of goods manufactured in Massachusetts in 1839, one magazine correspondent argued that manufacturing "blended harmoniously together" the interests of all Americans. The enjoyments of abundant market goods did not extend to all people, however, and the politics of the marketplace too often became fetid with the stench of greed.

Texas

By the terms of the 1819 Transcontinental Treaty, the United States had given up claims to Spanish lands south of the forty-second parallel. Nevertheless, within a few years Americans began to enter the region.

>> Culture and Politics in Manifest Destiny: Tejanos in Texas

When white Americans rebelled against Mexico in 1836, they cited among their justifications not only specific policies of the Mexican government but also what they viewed as the inferiority of the culture of the Mexicans among whom they lived. They called Tejanos immoral, lazy, and "unmanly" largely because Tejanos were not interested in the aggressive forms of development favored by the immigrants. They were right in at least one respect: Tejano culture was distinctly different from the culture the immigrants brought with them, and most Tejanos neither welcomed nor respected the ways of the newcomers. Chief among those distinctive qualities of Tejano culture were a striking sense of community and of the collective good that contrasted starkly to the individualism prized by American culture and, more fundamentally, a racial fluidity that challenged the basis of southern American expansionism.

By 1836, there were three major regions of Tejano settlement in northern Mexico: the northernmost Nacogdoches region (inland and closest to Louisiana) and the Bexar-Goliad and Rio Grande regions farther south and closer to the coast of the Gulf of Mexico. The three bore some differences, but they shared a heritage that melded together Spanish, Mexican, and native influences to suit the land and the circumstances of survival in a hard and isolated region.

Settlement had come slowly. Although the earliest Spanish foray was in 1716, Spanish authorities (and most Mexican officials, after the national revolution) valued the region as a *frontera*—a boundary land where priests could missionize "heathen" Indians and where soldiers in armed garrisons (*presidios*) could keep out Lipan Apache and Comanche raiding parties. Semiarid, largely void of vegetation, and removed from the comforts of established society, the land offered colonists few rewards. Mortality rates ran high, especially among males (who were required to serve as *ciudadanos armadas*, a sort of armed civilian reserve, in exchange for land) and children. As late as 1821, when Mexico achieved independence, the region held fewer than 2,500 settlers.

As was the case among the settlers, land ownership was central to Tejano culture. By the beginning of the nineteenth century some families and groups of families had left the towns to establish ranches along the rivers that flowed to the Gulf of Mexico, and a class system, based on the private ownership of property, began to take shape. At one extreme were a few wealthy families, settled on large ranches in elaborate houses and employing numerous servants and workers. At the other extreme were the mission Indians, technically free but often held in conditions of semibondage.

Yet the Tejano culture's strong sense of obligation to the collective mediated the impulse toward stark individualism and rough Jacksonian entrepreneurialism. This *continued*

AMERICAN LANDSCAPE *continued*

principle of social life may have resulted from the influence of the Tlaxcalan Indians (originally part of the Aztec empire), who held strongly to the principle of *calpulli*—the close-knit tribal unit. It may have been nurtured by the defensive needs of the far-flung early settlements. Certainly, it was fostered by the challenges of the semiarid environment. Water projects were the work of the entire community, and ranches laid out in thin plots running away from the riverbeds ensured each landowner access to water rights.

This sense of shared obligation may also have sprung from (and may have supported) the racial fluidity of Tejano society. Most of the settlers came from the northern Coahuila province, where intermarriage among native people, Mexicans, and Spaniards had long been common. Although the Spanish authorities had frowned on it, over time the soldiers in the *presidios* had also intermarried with the colonists and with local Indians. The result was a community in which most people claimed racially mixed heritages and in which race did not directly correspond to status and rights in the way it did in the southern United States.

Most alarming to the white American settlers, locals opposed slavery and repeatedly petitioned their government to stop allowing white Americans to establish the institution in Texas. There had been African American slaves in the region for at least 300 years, but in such small numbers that the institution had little social or economic importance before the early nineteenth century. The number of slaves increased after 1800, when slave traders began to use Texas as an entry to the U.S. market. Especially after Mexico gained its independence, Tejanos condemned the trade as antirepublican.

The clash of white American and Tejano cultures in Texas, then, spoke to both the past and the future of republicanism in the United States. Against the growing competitive individualism of American society, Tejano society represented a powerful sense of obligation to the commonweal that had once been the essence of American republicanism. Against the increasingly racialized politics of the United States, Tejanos insisted on a culture in which race would not directly determine status and individual rights.

Many of these immigrants were specifically invited; some were not. The Spanish saw their northern region as a buffer zone against the Lipan Apaches and Comanche Indians and between New Spain and the United States. After independence, the Mexican government expanded those policies by offering land grants to Americans in return for the promise to bring settlers to bolster the sparse population. The first American to accept the invitation was Stephen F. Austin, who began settling a colony on the banks of the Brazos and Colorado rivers in 1821. By 1830 there were more than 20,000 Americans (including 1,000 slaves) living in the northeastern province of Mexico, bordering Louisiana.

Conflict between immigrant Americans and resident Tejanos was inevitable. Tejanos resented the influx of Americans, who were often awarded lands that already belonged to Tejanos or that included Tejano communities. Tejanos complained that the *empresarios* (American landholders) were "nothing more than money-changing speculators" who had no respect for existing claims and did not control their settlers or squatters who used the American colonies to hide stolen livestock.

Although they were happy to take advantage of the cheap prices Mexico offered, many Americans had never fully acknowledged the right of Mexico to these lands. Viewing the region as the natural next frontier for American plantation agriculture, southerners had denounced the 1819 treaty and lobbied John Quincy Adams and Andrew Jackson to purchase the tract free and clear. By 1839 some Americans were convinced that Texas was destined to become the "land of refuge for the American slaveholders."

The immigrants themselves criticized the Mexican government in the language of republicanism. They objected to high taxes, but then so did everybody. They objected to being required to convert to Catholicism in order to intermarry with Mexicans and control their Mexican wives' property, but those laws were not really enforced. They

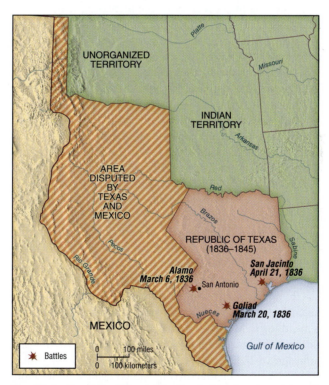

Map 13–1   Republic of Texas After the decisive American victory at San Jacinto that resulted in the independence of Texas, the border dispute between Texas and Mexico continued until it was resolved by the Mexican War a decade later.

objected to having to adopt the Spanish language. But beneath these objections were more fundamental issues, including a deep discontent—which many Mexicans shared—with the autocratic Mexican government.

Southerners who moved to Texas had a particular complaint—the Mexican government's erratic policies on slavery. There had been a few African American slaves in the region for at least 300 years. The number of slaves increased after 1800, when slave traders began to use Texas to enter the U.S. market. After independence, Mexican critics condemned the trade as antirepublican. But like the young United States, the new and unstable Mexican government took an erratic course, now banning slavery altogether, now allowing slaves to enter the nation but mandating gradual abolition.

By the mid-1820s, however, the immigrants had developed a cotton economy dependent on slave labor that they were determined to preserve. They regarded Mexican inconsistency and resistance as evidence of betrayal. In 1824 Stephen Austin, never a devoted supporter of slavery, devised regulations for his colony with harsh provisions for slaves who tried to escape or free people who abetted runaways. By 1830 Austin had concluded that "Texas must be a slave country. Circumstances and unavoidable necessity compels it. It is the wish of the people there. . . ." "The people," in Austin's view, included only white U.S. immigrants and others who agreed with their goals.

But slavery was not the major reason for the increasing tension between Texas and the Mexican government. After 1830 the government took steps to stem immigration and put troops on the United States–Mexican border. Immigrants saw these measures as obstructions to their rightful claims. The rise of General Antonio López de Santa Anna provided the occasion for registering their complaints. But when Santa Anna dissolved the Mexican Congress and made himself dictator in 1834, Texans—both Anglo and Tejano—sharpened their criticisms. Casting themselves as the quintessential republicans, they and several other Mexican states joined in the rebellion. Hoping to secure U.S. statehood, Texas declared itself a sovereign republic on March 2, 1836.

Four days later the huge Mexican army, led by Santa Anna, attacked and wiped out 187 Texas patriots barricaded in a mission called the Alamo. It was a costly and fleeting victory. Santa Anna's army suffered 1,544 casualties and created martyrs for the rebels' cause. Led by Sam Houston, the rebels retreated east, gathering recruits as they went. On April 21 they surprised Mexican troops on the San Jacinto River and scored a huge victory, capturing Santa Anna himself. Bargaining for his life and freedom, Santa Anna declared Texas a free nation. Ecstatic Texans drew up a constitution, made Sam Houston their first president, and called for annexation to the United States.

With the nation in economic crisis and his own party bickering over who was responsible, the last thing Van Buren wanted as president was a bitter battle over Texas and slavery. He doubted that the Constitution permitted annexation, which he feared would be construed as meddling in Mexico's internal affairs. Anticipating Texas's application for admission, abolitionists had made opposition to annexation a central issue in their massive petition campaign of 1837–1838, expanding the controversy widely in the North. John Quincy Adams had delivered a stirring speech against annexation in the House, and some senators were publicly denouncing slavery in general and especially in Texas. Southerners had responded with their own states' rights petitions. In the end, Van Buren did not submit Texas's request for statehood to Congress.

Pacific Bound

For most white Americans, however, Texas was not the fulfillment of America's manifest destiny. That goal lay in the rich lands beyond the plains. By the time Van Buren left office, the Mississippi River had become the staging ground for a massive migration west.

The migration began as a trickle of missionaries in the 1830s. In 1831 rumors reached the East of four young Indians who had appeared in St. Louis, exhausted and sick, imploring that religious teachers be sent to their people. Two years later, the Methodist *Christian Advocate and Herald* published a letter from a Wyandot Indian who claimed that Western tribes hungered for instruction in Christianity. True or not, such stories enabled missionaries to claim they had been invited into Indian communities. In 1834 the Methodist Missionary Society sent the Reverend Jason Lee west to found a mission in the Willamette Valley of Oregon Territory. Two years later, the American Board of Commissioners for Foreign Missions sent six people (including two women) to settle permanent missions in Oregon.

For their first mission, the board selected Marcus and Narcissa Prentiss Whitman, a doctor and a Sunday-school teacher. In 1836, the Whitmans established their mission among the Cayuse Indians near Fort Walla Walla on the Columbia River. Their fellow missionaries Henry and Eliza Hart Spalding founded a mission 125 miles away among the Nez Percés.

At first, the Whitmans seemed to thrive. Marcus Whitman preached and doctored among the Cayuse and taught the men agriculture, and Narcissa taught school and oversaw the operation of the large mission. Over the following decade, however, as white immigration swelled, the Cayuse came to view the missionaries as the cause of the influx of white people and new diseases. In 1847, after a deadly measles epidemic, a Cayuse band attacked the mission, killing Marcus and Narcissa Prentiss Whitman and a number of other white people.

By then, migrants to the West Coast were so numerous that the roads of Iowa "were literally lined with long blue wagons . . . slowly wending their way over the broad prairies," leaving deep, rutted tracks. In the years of heaviest migration, watering holes were so overused and sanitary conditions so poor that the road west became a breeding ground for typhoid, malaria, dysentery, and cholera.

Most of the migrants were farming families of moderate means, pushed out of the Midwest by the hard times of 1837. Men often made the decision to leave with little warning to their families. Sarah Cummins remembered returning home from school one day in Illinois to discover that her father had sold the farm and that "as soon as school closes we are to move." Preparations for the trip took up to half a year, and families could expect to spend another half a year on the trail.

Travelers funneled through St. Louis, crossed Missouri to rendezvous with wagon trains near St. Joseph or Independence, Missouri, and then followed one of two main routes west. The northern route, known as the Oregon Trail, zigzagged northwest roughly parallel to the Rocky Mountains. The Santa Fe Trail headed southwest out of Independence along the Arkansas River through the future state of Kansas before reaching Mexican lands. At Santa Fe, the trail divided, feeding immigrants west along the Old Spanish Trail or south to Chihuahua, Mexico.

Map 13–2   Major Overland Trails The overland trails to the west started at the Missouri River. The Santa Fe Trail was a conduit for traders and goods to Mexico. The Oregon Trail traveled through Wyoming and branched off to California and Oregon.

Most overland migrants traveled in families, in groups of families, and occasionally in entire communities. If they lacked team animals, families pulled their possessions in two-wheeled handcarts. For the most part, wagons carried supplies, not people. Most migrants walked west. Moreover, wagons broke down, were washed away in river crossings, or had to be emptied to ease the burden on the animals.

Past the plains, wagon trains sometimes went days without finding water or game. Women and men drove the wagons and herded the cattle, collected firewood, and caught small animals for food. When broken equipment or sickness slowed families, the trains were often forced to leave them behind, lest the others not clear the Rocky Mountains before winter. The harrowing dangers of that possibility were immortalized in the story of the ill-fated Donner Party, caught in the Sierra Nevadas by an early winter. For four months the group was trapped by snow, slowly starving. When relief finally arrived in mid-February 1847, "the dead were lying about on the snow, some even unburied, since the living had not strength to bury their dead," according to one survivor. Of the 87 persons snowed in, 42 died. It was not a risk worth taking, even if it meant leaving people behind on the plains.

For migrants who reached the west, the rewards were not always immediately apparent. "My most vivid recollection of that first winter in Oregon," one woman recalled, "is of the weeping skies and of Mother and me also weeping." As soon as they were settled, though, many newcomers proclaimed Oregon "this best country in the world." The climate was hospitable to crops of wheat, flax, and corn and to apple and pear orchards. Lumber was plentiful, and the streams were full of fish. Farther south was California, where, after 1848, rumors of "inexhaustible" gold strikes began to filter north and east.

Nations of the Trans-Mississippi West

American settlers felt they were journeying through national territories. Indigenous communities, such as Mah-i-ti-wo-nee-ni's friends and family, viewed the settlers as trespassers in Indian country.

Most wagon trains departed from Missouri, which meant that settlers first crossed Indian Territory, where Native Americans had been guaranteed refuge from white intrusion. Between Independence, Missouri, and the Rocky Mountains lay the Indian nations of the prairies and Great Plains: the Blackfoot and Crow to the northwest; the Sioux, Pawnee, Arapaho, and the two great nations from which Mah-i-ti-wo-nee-ni claimed heritage, the Shoshone and the Cheyenne, through the northern and central Plains; and the Kiowa, Apache, Comanche, and Navajo in the Southwest. Along the Pacific were the Yakima, Chinook, Cayuse, and Nez Percé Indians, and to the south, in California, Pomo, Chumash, Yuma, and many other tribes.

Because most of this vast territory was part of Mexico, and because Great Britain laid claim to Oregon, crossing to utopia meant transgressing the boundaries of those nations, as well.

Penny novelists would depict this contact as a violent confrontation in which warlike Indians massacred well-meaning migrants. In fact, of the more than 250,000 settlers who crossed the plains between 1840 and 1860, fewer than 400 were killed by Native Americans. About the same number of deaths were inflicted by white migrants on the Indians.

Prior to massive migration in the 1840s, official U.S. policy toward the Indians had been one of removal, by force or by pressured sale of lands and physical relocation. Even in the 1830s observers saw no evidence that Americans recognized a boundary short of the Pacific Ocean. Alexis de Tocqueville noted that "when it promises these unlucky people a permanent asylum in the West," the U.S. government "is well aware of its inability to guarantee this." By the late 1830s, as the last of the eastern "removals" were completed, federal policy toward Indians began to shift. Removal and resettlement

Map 13–3 Major Trans-Mississippi Indian Communities, ca. 1850 Most of the Indians living in the Indian Territories in the 1830s and 1840s had been "removed" from areas east of the Mississippi River. The territory was located west of Arkansas, Missouri, and Iowa. The section to the South (now Oklahoma) was home to Cherokees, Choctaws, Creeks, and Seminoles from the Old Southwest. The northern part (now Kansas and Nebraska), was inhabited by Indians from the Old Northwest.

continued to be the primary stated goal, and many western tribes were confined to reservations or moved to Indian Territory. But later removal policies aimed more overtly at individual rather than tribal ownership of reservation lands. Disrupting the land customs of Indians was, of course, what many Americans had long sought, bringing Native Americans into the "civilized" political economy of the United States through individual ownership of property. Allotment became the official policy toward all Indians by the end of the century.

By the mid-1830s, when white Americans started crossing the Mississippi River in huge numbers, most of these nations had already tasted the effects of expansionism. The Comanches (the largest of the southwestern nations) and the Apaches had been at war with European Americans for several centuries, having fought the Spanish, the Mexicans, and, since the 1820s, both the Mexicans and the U.S. settlers in Texas. All of the Plains Indians, especially the Sioux, the Kiowas, and the Comanches, had felt the impact of eastern Indians displaced or officially relocated west. The Sioux had been at war for decades with the Indians of the old Northwest Territory, who were being pushed across the Mississippi River.

For the western Indians, the effects of the migration of the 1840s were social, cultural, and economic. Although the number of deaths from warfare was low, deaths from disease were far higher and took especially high tolls on the children and the old, wiping out both the elders who carried a community's history and collective wisdom and the young people who represented its future. Contact gradually altered the Indians' social organization and gender division of labor. As it became harder to claim and protect planting grounds, tribes shifted to more nomadic ways of life. The relative importance of women's foraging and planting diminished, and the relative importance of men's skills as hunters and warriors increased.

By 1840, the northern grasslands and southern plains supported a complex economy of hunting and foraging. Indians consumed corn, melons, berries, wild sweet potatoes, turnips, and fowl and small game, harvested in a seminomadic way of life and traded through networks. At the center of this economy stood the bison, supplying food and material for clothing, shelter, and trade.

This way of life was threatened as the bison declined in number. Settlers' need for food had only a minor impact on the buffalo. More deadly was their fascination with hunting and killing such a huge creature, regardless of whether they needed its meat and hides. Recreational hunting parties, as well hunters intent on wiping out the Indians' means of support, took their toll. As early as 1842 the Teton Sioux had complained to federal agents that the heavy migrations were harming their hunting grounds. By 1846 the Sioux were demanding that the U.S. government stem the migrations and prevent the migrants from killing animals indiscriminately. When the government ignored the complaints, the Sioux prevented wagon trains from passing until migrants had paid a toll in money, tobacco, or supplies.

In the mid-1840s the energies of the federal government were primarily engaged in Texas, where American nationalists were demanding action against Mexico. In the northern plains, the government constructed a chain of forts intended as quarters for armed rifle units called dragoons, who would, theoretically, protect overland migrants from the Indians. The strategy was not very effective, as Indians continued to exert control over white migration through northern Indian Country.

Comanche Village In 1834-1835, western artist George Catlin observed the importance of the buffalo to Plains Indians. Here he depicted Comanche women dressing buffalo robes and drying buffalo meat. Notice the presence of horses in the village, a sign of European influence on western Indian life.

Slavery and the Political Economy of Expansion

As Americans poured west, expansion became a source of national political controversy. The problem was not the principle of manifest destiny, which few questioned. By the late 1830s, expansion was linked in the public debate with the extension of slavery and raised other problems. Southerners viewed northerners as unfaithful to a 50-year-old compromise ratified in the Constitution. Northerners looked with envy on the wealth of the new Southwest (Louisiana, Mississippi, Alabama, and Arkansas) and worried about the political leverage of a new slave state the size of Texas.

Log Cabins and Hard Cider: The Election of 1840

Approaching the election of 1840, the major parties were in a balancing act. Both hoped to exploit regional differences but without raising the divisive issues associated with slavery. Whigs considered Van Buren vulnerable, both because of the continuing effects of the Depression of 1837 and because he was a northerner who seemed to be blocking the annexation of Texas. Henry Clay, leader of the Whigs, also opposed the annexation, but he calculated that southern Democrats would choose a Kentuckian over a New Yorker. Aware of Van Buren's liabilities in the South, Democrats sought to keep slavery out of the debates, although Van Buren was willing to have northerners see him as the alternative to a southern president. A number of northern Whigs were suspicious of Clay's ties to the South.

Slavery haunted the election. In June 1839 the USS *Washington* had intercepted the ship *Amistad* in American coastal waters. Although Spanish owned, it was under the control of its cargo of kidnapped Africans, who were attempting to sail it home to Sierra Leone. Tricked by the ship's pilot, they had sailed instead into Long Island Sound. The case became the center of heated controversy, as pro- and antislavery forces argued over whether the Africans should be returned to slavery. Ultimately the case reached the U.S. Supreme Court, where John Quincy Adams agreed to argue the case for the captives. He would insist that because the international slave trade was illegal in the United States, the Africans must be returned to their homes.

Meanwhile, Van Buren received the Democratic nomination, but in an effort to skirt the explosive sectional issues, the Whigs turned to William Henry Harrison, an outspoken advocate of cheap western land and the hero of the battle of Tippecanoe. Harrison had run strongest against Van Buren in 1836. To bolster the appeal of their slate, for their vice presidential candidate the Whigs chose a former Democrat, John Tyler of Virginia, a strong advocate of states' rights and (at the time) a Clay supporter.

Harrison was a "sentimental" candidate who the Whigs hoped would evoke feelings of military glory and westward expansion. Avoiding tough issues, they crafted a Jackson-like campaign for "Tippecanoe and Tyler, too." When Harrison was derided as a country bumpkin content with sitting on his porch drinking cider, the Whigs took up the image with gusto. In the "Log Cabin and Hard Cider Campaign," the Whigs celebrated Harrison as a simple man of the people (like Jackson). In fact, Harrison was from a wealthy old Virginia family, but he could be linked to the West, and, as Daniel Webster observed, Harrison's main appeal was the vague "hope of a better time."

The turnout was large, and the popular results were close, but the Electoral College was a different story. Harrison, who had taken every large state but Virginia, triumphed with 234 electoral votes to Van Buren's 60. The Democrats held New Hampshire, Illinois, Missouri, Arkansas, Alabama, Virginia, and South Carolina.

On March 9, 1841, five days after Harrison took the oath of office, the Supreme Court announced its decision in the *Amistad* case. Speaking for the court, Justice Joseph Story—a longtime opponent of slavery—declared that those on board the *Amistad* were "kidnapped Africans, who by the laws of Spain itself were entitled to their freedom." The case quickly became a cause célèbre among abolitionists, but its impact was far broader. Heavy newspaper coverage aroused the sympathy even of moderate opponents of slavery, widening the antislavery debate and increasing interest in the new Liberty Party.

 Table 13-1 The Liberty Party Swings an Election

Candidate	Party	Actual Vote in New York	National Electoral Vote	If Liberty Voters Had Voted Whig	Projected Electoral Vote
Polk	Democratic	237,588	170	237,588	134
Clay	Whig	232,482	105	248,294	141
Birney	Liberty	15,812	0	—	—

And Tyler, Too

Whig jubilation at their presidential victory was short lived. Harrison fell ill shortly after his inauguration and died on April 4, 1841, the first president to die in office. Harrison was followed in office by his vice president, John Tyler, whom most observers assumed would serve as a caretaker president until the next general election. He soon proved them wrong, succeeding to the full stature and authority of the presidency.

Tyler's ascendancy threw the Whig Party into chaos, for once in office he reverted to his Democratic roots. Much about Tyler was reminiscent of Jackson. He opposed the American System and favored slavery and the annexation of Texas, and he was willing to use the full power of the executive to enforce those views. Unlike Jackson, Tyler strongly advocated extreme southern states' rights positions.

Tyler's attention was first drawn to diplomatic troubles with Britain. In 1841 the slave crew of the U.S. ship *Creole*, en route from Virginia to New Orleans, had seized control of the vessel and forced it into the port of Nassau, where, by British law, the crew was freed. To no avail, white southerners demanded the return of the crew. Meanwhile, northern anti-British feeling flared over the question of the Oregon Territory, a vaguely defined expanse between northern California and Alaska that Britain and the United States had agreed in 1818 to occupy jointly. By 1842, reports of the North American Pacific Coast as a "storehouse of wealth in all its forests, furs, and fisheries" had stirred both immigration and the American desire to claim the Oregon Territory.

In 1842 U.S. Secretary of State Webster and British emissary Ashburton concluded the Webster-Ashburton Treaty, which drew a boundary between the United States and Canada from Maine to the Rocky Mountains (Oregon was left undivided), established terms of extradition between the two nations, and created a joint effort to restrict the international slave trade. Great Britain also agreed not to interfere with foreign vessels.

Tyler's success in foreign relations was overshadowed by his 1841 break with his own party. Led by Henry Clay, Whigs in Congress passed legislation that embodied their platform, including tariff bills, a national bank bill, and a bill to distribute federal surpluses to states. Tyler vetoed almost every initiative. He denounced federal distribution as inappropriate when the federal government was in deficit. At last, in 1842, Congressional Whigs offered lower tariff increases and detached the tariff from the question of distribution. Needing federal funds, Tyler signed the bill. Tyler supported the repeal of the independent treasury, a Whig goal, but this, too, proved a bitter victory for the Whigs, because Tyler vetoed the national bank with which the Whigs wanted to replace the independent treasury.

Tyler was soon a president without a party. As early as January 1843, there were calls in the House of Representatives for his impeachment. That year, when Tyler vetoed the bill rechartering the national bank, his entire cabinet resigned, except Webster.

"His Accidency," as opponents dubbed Tyler, proved resilient. Tyler interpreted Democratic gains in the 1842 elections as support for his positions, particularly on the national bank. Urged on by extreme states' rights advocates in Virginia and South Carolina, Tyler took up the cause of the annexation of Texas. After Daniel Webster resigned from the cabinet, Tyler fell almost entirely under the influence of southerners committed to Texas.

Texas did all it could to press for annexation. It allowed Great Britain to serve as an intermediary in Texas's efforts to win official recognition from Mexico and hinted that, as an independent republic, Texas might abolish slavery. The idea of an alliance between

Texas and Great Britain reawakened old anti-British sentiments, and the prospect of a non–slave republic so nearby filled southerners with dread.

Seeking to capitalize on these anxieties, in 1843 President Tyler secretly opened negotiations with Texas for admission to the Union, expecting to justify the treaty as necessary protection against British influence. In 1844, Tyler submitted a treaty of annexation to Congress. He hoped that potential opposition would be countered by expansionist interests. He was wrong. Even before the treaty was submitted, John Quincy Adams and 12 other Whigs denounced it as constitutionally unauthorized and warned that it would bring the nation to "dissolution." Abolitionists labeled the move a naked power grab by slave owners. Even moderate northerners worried that annexing Texas would cause war with Mexico, without yielding the North any tangible gains. Some southerners worried that Texas would compete with the depleted cotton and sugar lands of the South.

By then, other election-year dramas were afoot. John Calhoun still longed for the presidency and felt he had a good chance against Tyler, another southerner, if he could deny Van Buren the Democratic nomination. To that end, Calhoun wrote a note to the British minister that the U.S. goal in Texas was to protect slavery against British abolitionists. As Calhoun hoped, the note became public. The explicit association of Texas and slavery drove Van Buren away from endorsing the treaty, weakening his position in the South. An overwhelmingly sectional vote defeated the treaty in Congress, but Calhoun believed a Democratic victory in 1844 would revive it.

Occupy Oregon, Annex Texas

By the fall of 1844 the American political party system was in disarray. Harrison's impressive victory in 1840 had not signaled a broad endorsement of Clay or the American System, any more than Van Buren's victory in 1836 had signaled a strong hard-money, antibank sentiment. To the contrary, between 1836 and 1844 the party system seemed most successful at polarizing American interests.

Nowhere was that state of affairs more evident than in the 1844 Democratic convention in Baltimore. Van Buren's supporters believed the party owed him the nomination, yet his liabilities were legion. In the South, proslavery, proannexation Democrats led by Calhoun were vowing to have "a slaveholder for President next time regardless of the man." Andrew Jackson was disappointed with Van Buren's refusal to endorse annexation and encouraged former Tennessee governor James K. Polk to run. In the North, workers and entrepreneurs hard hit by years of deflation were disenchanted with the "Little Magician." Van Burenites were unable to block a convention rule requiring a candidate to receive a two-thirds vote to secure the nomination. Van Buren could not marshal that level of support, but neither could Tyler, Calhoun, or Lewis Cass, a compromise candidate. Finally, on the eighth ballot the convention fell back on Jackson's choice, James Polk. Tyler accepted renomination by a renegade group of supporters who styled themselves Democratic Republicans.

The 1844 Democratic Party ran on the platform of manifest destiny, calling for "the reoccupation of Oregon and the reannexation of Texas." It was an odd formulation, given that the United States had several times officially denied possession of Texas and had yet to occupy Oregon fully. The platform went even further on Oregon. Although the U.S. claim to Oregon had never extended beyond the forty-ninth parallel, the Democrats now declared their willingness to go to war to gain the entire region ("Fifty-four forty or fight!"). Their

Table 13-2 Personal Income Per Capita by Region: Percentages of United States Average

	1840	1860	1880
United States	100	100	100
Northeast	135	139	141
North Central	68	68	98
South	76	72	51
West	—	—	190

Note: Source: Richard A. Easterlin, "Regional Income Trends, 1840–1950," in Seymour E. Harris (ed.), *American Economic History* (New York; McGraw-Hill, 1961), p. 528.

strategy incorporated war fears over Texas into a broader assertion of national destiny.

Meanwhile, in 1844 Henry Clay secured the Whig nomination. Clay was certain that opposition to the extension of slavery was strong enough to block a Texas-Oregon compromise and that Americans would not support a war with Mexico. Clay ran primarily as a supporter of the American System as the necessary means for stabilizing economic growth.

The election results suggested a nation teetering on the edge of political division. Polk, annexation, and manifest destiny won, but by only 38,000 of more than 2.5 million votes cast. More striking, James G. Birney of Ohio, the candidate of the new, explicitly antislavery Liberty Party, drew 62,000 votes, most of them taken from Clay. Had Birney not run, the election might have been a dead heat.

Both Tyler and Congress read the election as a referendum on the Democratic platform and specifically on Texas. Early in 1845, with Tyler still in office, a bill approving annexation passed the House. To move it through the Whig-dominated Senate, Senator Robert Walker of Mississippi suggested that the Senate version include the option of negotiating a whole new treaty. Only days away from the presidency, Polk was said to favor this approach, and Whigs thought a revised treaty might get them out of a politically costly position. The Senate approved the amended treaty. The Whigs expected Tyler to concede the decision to the incoming president, but in the last hours of his presidency he sent notice to Texas that (contingent on its own agreement) the republic was annexed to the United States of America. Mexico immediately severed relations with the United States.

War with Mexico

The annexation of Texas was the ostensible cause of the outbreak of war with Mexico in April 1846, but not the only cause. In Polk's eyes, the annexation of Texas was a piece of a larger acquisition: not only Oregon but also present-day New Mexico, Arizona, and California. Polk would have been happy to make these acquisitions peacefully, but he was willing to go to war.

Polk took a two-track approach to foreign relations. In December 1845 he announced his decision to withdraw from negotiations over Oregon, and he called on Congress to terminate the United States–Great Britain Convention of Joint Occupancy. Compromise would be an abandonment of American "territorial rights . . . and the national honour," he insisted, and would be unthinkable. Beyond the combative rhetoric, Polk informed his advisors that he was prepared to hear a compromise offer from England. When one came, proposing a boundary at the forty-ninth parallel, Polk submitted it to Congress. By June 1846 the deal had been struck.

>> Lt. Rankin Dilworth in the War with Mexico

Rankin Dilworth was only 18 years old when he entered the United States Military Academy at West Point. By the time her son applied to the academy, his mother had been widowed twice, and Dilworth may well have seen the army as his one opportunity to get ahead in life. He was apparently an average cadet, graduating in the middle of his class in 1844, one year behind Ulysses S. Grant, future general of the Union army and president of the United States. But in 1844 neither Grant nor Dilworth was contemplating duty in a civil war. If Dilworth had his sights fixed on anything, it was surely the West, where American territorial ambitions were creating countless opportunities for military advancement.

By the spring of 1846, those opportunities were near at hand. Barracked outside of St. Louis, Dilworth's company was ordered to southern Texas, where hostilities had already broken out between United States troops and the Mexican army. They traveled by boat down the Mississippi and across the Gulf of Mexico to Matamoros, Mexico. From there, they marched up the Rio Grande to Carmargo, Texas, where Dilworth's unit joined with American forces under General Zachary Taylor. From Carmargo, the combined unit proceeded to Monterrey. From April 28 to September 19, 1846, Dilworth kept an almost daily record of that journey.

The diary suggests that, officer or not, Dilworth was shadowed by nostalgia for home. Viewing a beautiful church in Reynosa made him wonder "if I will ever go to church again where I hear the English language spoken." That night, he dreamed he was in church at home "without a thought of camps or bivouacs, with smiling happy faces around me." Awakened by the call to guard duty, "in an instant," he wrote, "I found myself on the hot sandy plaza of Reynosa, many, many miles from those I love."

Still, Dilworth found much to occupy his attention in the journey south. He took a keen interest in Mexico. Waxing romantic, he compared Mexico to "a magnificent flower garden" dotted with plots of "limes, oranges, lemons, [and] pomegranates." He admired young Mexican women, one of whom he declared "the handsomest female that I have seen since I parted with E. M. M." (his sweetheart back home). Dilworth's descriptions sometimes betrayed the flippant cultural superiority so much a part of American expansionism of the 1840s. "The inhabitants present all shades from pure Indian to the white person," he wrote on one occasion. "Their intelligence is in the same scale."

Dilworth's diary also recorded the daily, and sometimes needless, hardships that would eventually make the campaign infamous in army annals. Swollen with untrained volunteers and newly trained officers (like Dilworth himself), the Mexican campaign was a tutorial in bad luck and bad judgment. Dilworth wrote about tents that collapsed in violent rainstorms, marches through mud so thick that it added 10 pounds to the weight of each boot, and temperatures so hot that soldiers died of heat prostration. He wrote of arrogant and inept officers who could not even march their troops in the right

continued

AMERICA AND THE WORLD *continued*

direction. On September 19 near Monterrey, Dilworth encountered an old friend in a different unit. The friend asked Dilworth if he had "heard the 'Elephant' groan," an expression used by the troops to express bitterness and disappointment. Dilworth did not record his reply. Nor did he add any further entries in the diary. On September 21, General Taylor ordered an assault on Monterrey, dividing his small band into two groups to attack the city from opposite sides. The western troops won with relative ease, but the eastern forces lost their way in thick cane fields before being caught in deadly Mexican crossfire. Along the city's narrow streets, they were easy targets for sharpshooters. Remarkably, inch by inch, house by house, Taylor's troops carried the day. On September 24, 1846, Mexican general Ampudia offered surrender.

None of this mattered to Rankin Dilworth. During the first day's assault a "twelve-pounder cannon ball" had torn off one of his legs. On September 27, at 24 years of age, he died. His family was unable to pay the costs of having his body returned to Ohio. Lieutenant Rankin Dilworth was buried in Monterrey, Mexico.

In Oregon, Polk threatened war but quickly accepted peace. However, what Polk really wanted in the Mexican borderlands, Thomas Hart Benton claimed, was "a little war," big enough to justify grabbing the Southwest but not so big as to break the budget. Texas provided the excuse.

As a condition of his surrender and release, the Mexican General Santa Anna had agreed to the Rio Grande as the boundary between Texas and Mexico, a boundary that would have run northward to include present-day New Mexico as well as western Texas. The Mexican government had instead drawn the border at the Nueces River, recognizing only about half the territory claimed by Texans. Polk intended to set the boundary at the Rio Grande, and he may have intended to secure not only the disputed Texas territory but also large portions of northern Mexico.

Polk once again played a double game. As late as September, he appealed for a peaceful resolution. That month, he dispatched former Louisiana congressman John Slidell to Mexico to offer to purchase New Mexico and Texas for $30 million. The Mexican government refused to receive Slidell.

Meanwhile, Polk prepared for war. In the spring of 1845 he had sent 1,500 soldiers, under the command of General Zachary Taylor, allegedly to protect Texas against a possible invasion by Mexico. When Texas approved union with the United States, Polk reinforced Taylor's troops and ordered them to approach the Rio Grande, while also sending an army under Stephen Kearny into the northern part of the disputed territory. In August 1846, Kearny occupied Santa Fe. At the same time, Polk ordered the U.S. squadron in the Pacific closer to the California coast and directed the U.S. consul in California, Thomas Larkin, to encourage local disaffection with the Mexican government. When American settlers in the Sonoma Valley staged a rebellion in June and July, the representatives of the United States claimed California. Kearny later crossed into California to solidify the claim.

By then, Polk's brinkmanship on the Rio Grande had produced results. Mexican troops had crossed the river to drive out Taylor's force, and American soldiers had been killed and wounded. In May 1846, Congress declared that "a state of war exists" between the two nations.

The United States entered the war unprepared. Although 100,000 volunteers signed up, at the outbreak of hostilities the United States Army had only 7,500 troops. Perhaps Polk shared the expansionist view of Mexico as a "miserable, inefficient" nation. Mexico (and New Spain before it) had always been less interested in its northern provinces than in other parts of the nation. Moreover, after a coup, the Mexican government was unstable. With California guarded by John C. Frémont and the naval squadron, the United States could bring its military power to bear on Mexico City.

Finding the right leader proved tricky. Taylor, the obvious choice, was a popular Whig. Polk finally settled on Winfield Scott, who also harbored Whig ambitions. In the late winter of 1847, a squadron of 200 ships conveyed Scott's army of 10,000 soldiers to Veracruz, which surrendered in April. Scott's troops fought their way to the outskirts of Mexico City, which fell after six days on September 14.

For all the success of the American campaign, support for the war steadily eroded. From the beginning, the war raised the question of slavery. Northern Democrats saw the war as a transparent ploy to extend slavery. Antislavery activists spoke out against the war, and opposition grew as stories of U.S. military atrocities filtered back east.

Nebel, *Storming of Chapultepec—Quitman's Attack.*

Chapultepec Carl Nebel's depiction of the American attack on the Chapultepec fort, near Mexico City, during the Mexican-American War, September 13, 1847.

In spite of the unpopularity of the war, a defeated Mexico was so weak that Polk thought of extracting greater concessions. His minister in Mexico, Nicholas P. Trist, opposed this proposal, however. In 1848 Trist negotiated the Treaty of Guadalupe Hidalgo, recognizing the Rio Grande as the border of Texas and granting the United States the territory encompassed in the present states of New Mexico, Arizona, Colorado, Utah, and Wyoming, as well as California. In return, the United States paid Mexico $15 million and assumed war claims of American citizens against Mexico. The Senate approved the treaty on March 10, 1848. The following May 25, Mexico concurred.

Although Polk's presidency was dominated by the war with Mexico, the tariff and the independent treasury haunted domestic politics. In each case, Polk was victorious. Like Jackson, Polk opposed protective tariffs, which he saw as benefiting industrialists at the expense of farmers and republican values. Although Whigs in Congress pushed for higher tariffs to support domestic manufacturing, the 1846 tariff eliminated flat duties and reduced overall levels. Also like Jackson, Polk opposed the national bank. In 1846 he persuaded Congress to reinstate Van Buren's independent treasury to handle the federal government's financial transactions. Meanwhile, he vetoed Whig attempts to enact legislation supporting internal improvements.

Jackson and Polk shared a broad understanding of politics and the use of political machinery. Like Jackson, Polk framed policy battles as battles between good and evil,

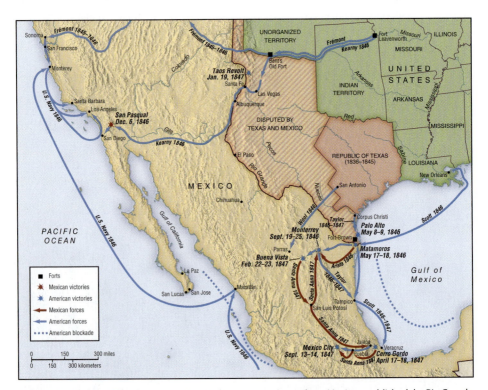

Map 13–4   Mexican War General Zachary Taylor's victories in northern Mexico established the Rio Grande as the boundary between Texas and Mexico. Colonel Stephen Kearny's expedition secured control of New Mexico. General Winfield Scott's invasion by sea at Veracruz and his occupation of Mexico ended the war.

>> Timeline

▼1834
First missionaries arrive in Oregon Territory

▼1836
Martin Van Buren elected president
Equal Rights Party formed
Whig Party runs candidates for president
Texas declares independence

▼1838
"Aroostook" War
Anti-Slavery Petition campaign at height

▼1839
Amistad mutiny

▼1840
Independent Treasury Bill
Anti-Slavery Society splits
Liberty Party nominates James Birney for the presidency
Large-scale overland migration to West Coast begins
Whig candidate William Henry Harrison elected president

▼1841
John Tyler succeeds Harrison in office
Creole Mutiny

▼1842
Webster-Ashburton Treaty

▼1844
James Polk is elected president

▼1845
The United States annexes Texas

▼1846
The United States declares war on Mexico

▼1848
Independent woman's rights movement begins at Seneca Falls,
   New York
Treaty of Guadalupe Hidalgo
Teton Sioux tax white settlers passing through their lands

between individual opportunity and elite finance and capital. At the same time, also like Jackson, Polk exercised executive power as the tool of the people's will. He was convinced that the president, not the legislature (Whig controlled by his final years in office), represented the people's will. Before he left office, virtually every important item on his political agenda had been accomplished. Lost in that flush of victory was the steady erosion of popular support for the Democratic Party.

Conclusion

In 1820, Fanny Wright noted that many observers worried about the differences between the American North and South, but Wright was optimistic. If all else failed, she declared, the western states, settled by migrants from North and South, would always be "powerful cementers of the Union."

By the end of the 1840s, it was clear that Wright's confidence had been misplaced. The war with Mexico revealed just how far apart the North and South had grown. By 1848, the northern states were deeply implicated in a political economy of free labor. The southern states, meanwhile, had grown ever more committed to the political economy of slavery. The Mexican War signaled the beginning of an era in which differences between the North and South would seem undeniable and intractable—and symbolized in the West.

In 1848, Henry David Thoreau spoke to an audience in Concord, Massachusetts, about his refusal to pay poll taxes, which he said supported the institution of slavery and its expansion in the war with Mexico. Thoreau declared himself ready to separate from his government—indeed, to see the Union itself destroyed—rather than support the United States in the West. "How does it become a man to behave toward this American government today?" he asked. "I answer, that he cannot without disgrace be associated with it. I cannot for an instant recognize that political organization as my government which is the slave's government also."

Review Questions

1. What was the depression of 1837 and what were its origins?

2. Why were Whigs cautious about westward migration?

3. Why was the annexation of Texas so controversial?

4. Did the territorial additions of the 1840s represent a departure (in method or intent) from earlier acquisitions?

For further review materials and resource information, please visit www.oup.com/us/ofthepeople

The Politics of Slavery

1848–1860

>> Frederick Douglass

Frederick Douglass denounced the war with Mexico as "disgraceful, cruel, and iniquitous." Northern support for what he saw as a slaveholders' war reinforced Douglass's conviction that the U.S. Constitution had created an unholy union of liberty and slavery. The only solution was for New England to secede. "The Union must be dissolved," Douglass wrote, "or New England is lost and swallowed up by the slave-power of the country."

Douglass had been urging disunion for several years, ever since he became the most compelling antislavery voice in America. His authority derived from his extraordinary intelligence, his exceptional skill as a public speaker, and above all from his personal experience. Frederick Douglass was not simply an abolitionist; he was also the most famous runaway slave in America.

He was born Frederick Augustus Washington Bailey in Talbot County, Maryland, in 1818. At the age of seven he was sent to Baltimore, where he became a skilled caulker in the shipyards. There he hired out his labor, paying his master three dollars each week and keeping the rest himself. He grew to resent the arrangement, and for the rest of his life he would associate freedom with the right to earn a living. When his master ended their arrangement and demanded that the slave hand over all his earnings, Frederick planned his escape.

On May 3, 1838, he dressed as a sailor and boarded a northbound train using borrowed papers. By September he was calling himself Frederick Douglass and was living and working in New Bedford, Massachusetts. He began attending antislavery meetings. He subscribed to William Lloyd Garrison's fiery abolitionist newspaper, *The Liberator*. In 1841 he was invited to speak during an abolitionist convention and stunned his listeners with an eloquent recital of his experience as a slave. Garrison was in the audience, and he invited Douglass to speak for the American Anti-Slavery Society. For the next several years Douglass was a leading spokesman for the Garrisonian wing of the abolitionist movement.

continued

>> AMERICAN PORTRAIT *continued*

The Garrisonians felt that the Constitution was hopelessly corrupted by its compromises with slavery. They saw no point in pursuing political reforms, advocating instead the separation of the North from the South. The Garrisonians rejected all violent efforts to overthrow slavery, including slave rebellion, in favor of moral persuasion of their opponents. Frederick Douglass initially believed all of these things.

The Mexican War was a turning point for Douglass. By the late 1840s, he saw growing numbers of northerners join the Free-Soil Party, fighting the expansion of slavery, and wondered why this could not become a political coalition against slavery itself. During the 1850s Douglass moved further from the Garrisonians: he openly supported slave rebellion, realized that political action was necessary to eliminate slavery, and came to doubt the wisdom of dismissing the Constitution as a proslavery document.

Douglass moved closer to mainstream northern politics because antislavery sentiment had reentered the mainstream. Since the 1820s, the major parties had studiously avoided the topic of slavery. But the annexation of Texas in the 1830s spurred some abolitionists to push slavery back into national politics, first by flooding the South with antislavery literature and Congress with antislavery petitions and then by organizing a Liberty Party dedicated to halting slavery's expansion—a position known as "free soil." By 1848 a Free-Soil Party was attracting hundreds of thousands of votes.

Even as Garrison and his followers were urging withdrawal from politics, other abolitionists were successfully shoving antislavery back into the political mainstream. By the middle of the 1850s the Whig Party collapsed in the North and was replaced by the new Republican Party, openly hostile to slavery and sworn to restricting its expansion. Soon after, the Democratic Party split into northern and southern wings. For the first time in American history the political mainstream could accommodate a radical abolitionist like Frederick Douglass. By 1861 he was urging the president to uphold the Constitution by suppressing the South's attempt to secede.

Common Threads

>> In previous chapters you read about the development of the American economy and the expansion of slavery. Notice the ways in which these developments became sources of tension between the North and South during the 1850s.

>> The conflict between Whigs and Democrats during the 1830s and 1840s is sometimes called "the first party system." How did this change in the 1850s?

>> Do you think that by 1860 the Civil War was "irrepressible"?

The Political Economy of Freedom and Slavery

The politics of slavery reemerged at a moment of tremendous economic growth. As the depression of the 1840s lifted, the American zeal for internal improvements revived. The canals built between 1800 and 1830 were widened during the 1840s and 1850s to accommodate the new steamboats. Railroad construction, which had collapsed during the 1840s, came back stronger than ever in the 1850s. On the eve of the Civil War, the United States boasted more miles of railroad track than the rest of the world combined. No less spectacular was the rapid adoption of the telegraph. Invented by Samuel F. B. Morse in 1844, the telegraph made virtually instantaneous communication possible across oceans and continents. By 1860, there were 50,000 miles of telegraph wire in America. The first transcontinental line was completed in 1861.

These developments might have inhibited the growth of sectionalism. An efficient transportation and communication network helped integrate the United States into a single national market. But market integration only tied together two different societies based on two very different systems of labor. By the 1850s the differences between North and South overwhelmed the connections that bound them together.

A Changing Economy in the North

The 1850s were booming years for northern farmers, now connected firmly to the national market. It took less than a week to ship meat and grains from midwestern cities to the East Coast. Because of the dramatic reduction in transportation costs, northern farmers could devote more time and effort to producing crops for sale rather than for subsistence at home. Thanks also to inventions like the steel plow, seed drills, and the McCormick reaper, northern farmers increased production of goods for market, quadrupling productivity between 1820 and 1860.

Farmers could grow more crops for sale because more Americans were living in cities and working for wages, producing little of their own food, clothing, or shelter. Yet so productive was American agriculture that the proportion of farmers declined. In 1820, 75 percent of the labor force was devoted to agriculture. By 1860 the figure was 57 percent. Wage labor in the North grew so rapidly that native-born workers could not fill the demand for labor in the cities and factories. In the mid-1840s the number of Europeans coming to the United States jumped sharply, and 3 million arrived in the decade between 1845 and 1854. More than two-thirds were Irish or German, many of them Roman Catholic. By 1855 a larger proportion of Americans was foreign born than at any other time in the nation's history.

Many immigrants, especially the Irish, came to America impoverished and congregated in the growing cities and factory towns of the North. By 1860 immigrants made up more than one-third of the residents in northern cities with populations of at least 10,000. Impoverished immigrants became wage laborers in numbers that far outstripped their proportions in the population. Men worked in unskilled jobs on the docks, at construction sites, or on railroads and canals and in the coal mines and iron foundries of Pennsylvania. Women worked as seamstresses, laundresses, or domestic servants. In the textile mills and shoe factories of New England, Irish families worked together.

Industrialization was not the only reason for the growth of wage labor. By the 1850s a growing white-collar middle class also lived off their wages. As industrial production increased, businesses opened large downtown stores to sell their goods. Between 1859 and 1862, for example, A. T. Stewart built a huge dry goods store covering a full square block in lower Manhattan. The financial needs of these enterprises were met by an expanding number of banks, insurance companies, and accounting firms that employed armies of white-collar workers.

Economic growth in the North during the 1850s rested on important social changes. A rural society became more urban. Industry was replacing agriculture as the driving economic force. Wage laborers were replacing small farmers and craftsmen. A Protestant nation saw its first great wave of Catholic immigrants. Machines made it possible for one person to cultivate more acres than ever before. A political economy based on new sources of wealth and new forms of work was being born.

The Slave Economy

It made sense for the wealthy South Carolina planter James Henry Hammond to declare in 1858 that "Cotton is king." It had been a prosperous decade for southern slaveholders. Recovering from the doldrums of the 1840s, the price of cotton remained steady, and the price of slaves rose sharply. Southern states threw themselves into railroad construction, building a substantial network. Steamboats plied the South's rivers. Telegraph wires sped news of cotton prices from New York to New Orleans and deep into the plantation belt. Southerners boasted of their commitment to progress and prosperity. Slavery was thriving. So why shouldn't Hammond confidently defy slavery's critics?

ONTWARD BOUND.
The Quay of Dublin.

The South had changed in many ways during the previous century. It had expanded across half the continent. Cotton had become its most profitable crop. The Atlantic slave trade was over, and a native-born, largely Christian slave population had grown up. There were important signs of social change, especially in the upper South. The immigrant workers Frederick Douglass met on the Baltimore docks faced the same process of economic development as the dock workers of New England. The steady sale of slaves from the upper to the lower South reduced the political influence of slaveholders in such states as Maryland, Kentucky, and Delaware. Indeed, among whites across the South the proportion of slaveholding families had been declining for decades, from one in three in 1830 to one in four by 1860.

Contemplating Emigration to America In this 1854 caricature, an impoverished Irishman on the Dublin docks contemplates booking passage to America in hopes of economic prosperity.

As slavery expanded, it brought commerce but not economic development. The slave economy had always been intensely commercial, more so than northern capitalism, but its profits were concentrated among slaveholders who were, by 1860, among the richest group of Americans. That wealth enabled slaveholders to monopolize the best lands to the detriment of small farmers. Moreover, slaveholders reinvested their profits not in machinery that increased productivity but in more slaves. As a result, slaveless farmers in the South were much poorer than their northern counterparts, and the southern economy was far less developed than the northern.

The Importance of the West

Both the North and the South coveted western lands. By 1850 many northerners believed that slavery, if allowed to expand into the West, would deprive free laborers of an important source of prosperity and independence. But slaveholders had come to believe that their prosperity depended on the spread of the slave economy into the West. The disposition of the land acquired in the war with Mexico forced Americans into a sustained public debate over the future of slavery.

Slavery had expanded more than halfway across the continent of North America in about half a century, and white southerners viewed territorial expansion as a sign of progress. The westward movement of the southern frontier demonstrated the continued strength of the slave economy. Halting that movement would undermine southern prosperity. It was an insult to the moral decency of white southerners, an obstacle to their economic vitality.

Map 14–1 Slavery's Expansion The westward expansion of the slave economy created political turmoil from 1820 until the Civil War. Sustained by an extensive internal slave trade that sold thousands of humans each year, slavery's expansion represented one of the greatest forced migrations in history.

But above all else it was an infringement on the slaveholders' inalienable rights of property, which included the constitutional right to carry their property with them wherever they saw fit. So argued slavery's defenders with increasing vehemence in the 1850s.

But the economic growth of the North created equally strong ties between the East and the West. Mountains and rivers generally ran north and south, but turnpikes, canals, and especially railroads tended to run east and west, linking northeastern cities to the western frontier. Of the approximately 20,000 miles of railroads built in the 1850s, few crossed the Mason-Dixon line to link the northern and southern economies (see Map 14–2).

Map 14–2 Railroad Expansion This map shows that there were two distinct patterns of railroad development in the United States. In the North, rail lines connected the western states to the eastern seaboard. In the South, railroads tied the inland plantation districts to the coastal ports. Few lines connected the North to the South.

For northerners, the West was essential to prosperity. The public lands of the West "are the great regulator of the relations of Labor and Capital," Horace Greeley explained, "the safety valve of our industrial and social engine." This safety-valve theory was repeated regularly in the North, even though there was not much truth in it. To move west, buy land, and establish a farm required resources far beyond the means of many, perhaps most, wage laborers. Nevertheless, to many northerners, westward expansion was critical to their entire social order. It was no wonder that the westward expansion of slavery caused so much anxiety in the North.

Northern and southern expansion were incompatible. The slaveholders were "settlers with means," bringing their wealth and their slave laborers with them. They easily bought up the best lands, usually river bottoms with the most productive soil and the readiest access to markets. Slaves provided a reliable source of labor, making it easier for slaveholding pioneers to clear land, build homes, and start producing profitable crops. Slaveless farmers could not compete with this. Without slaves labor was scarce on the frontier, and farm families could rely only on their own labor and any help neighbors could offer. Because the size of free farms was restricted by the amount of labor a family could perform, the best lands were more widely dispersed among settlers wherever slavery was excluded. Free farmers quickly saw the expansion of slavery as a threat to their own prospects in the West.

Slavery Becomes a Political Issue

Westward expansion forced the issue of slavery back into the political mainstream in the late 1840s. During the heyday of the "second party system," Whigs and Democrats had tacitly agreed to suppress open debates over slavery, but the Mexican War made it hard to maintain that silence. For nearly 15 years, national politics would focus on one crucial question: Should Congress restrict the movement of slavery into the West? Behind that question lay a larger moral issue, the wrong and the right of "property in man."

Wilmot Introduces His Proviso

On August 8, 1846, David Wilmot, a Democratic congressman from Pennsylvania, attached to an appropriations bill an amendment banning slavery from all the territories acquired in the war with Mexico. The aim of the famous Wilmot Proviso was to preserve western lands for white settlement. "I plead the cause and rights of the free white man," Wilmot insisted.

Initially, northern Whigs and Democrats joined in support of the proviso, whereas their southern counterparts opposed it. Reintroduced in the next session of Congress, however, the proviso went down to defeat. Nevertheless, it paralyzed Congress for several years in the late 1840s, when conditions in the West demanded federal legislation. Mormon settlers had been pouring into the basin of the Great Salt Lake, and they required some form of government. The discovery of gold in California brought a rush of settlers and much disorder to the mining camps of the Sierra foothills and the boomtown of San Francisco. Territorial governments required congressional action, but Congress was frozen by sectional differences.

By 1850, four positions had hardened. At one extreme were antislavery northerners favoring a Wilmot-like solution to ban slavery in all the territories. At the other extreme were the southern followers of John C. Calhoun, who argued that Congress had no right to interfere with the property rights of slaveholders in the territories. In between were two compromise positions. Some wanted to extend the Missouri Compromise line and push the North-South division all the way to the Pacific Ocean. Finally, there was popular sovereignty, later supported by Stephen A. Douglas of Illinois, that gave settlers the right to decide for themselves whether they would have slavery in their territory.

The four positions disrupted the major parties. In the presidential election of 1848 antislavery men bolted both the Democrats and the Whigs for the Free-Soil Party. With the Wilmot Proviso as their platform, Free-Soilers won 14 percent of the northern vote. Meanwhile, proslavery fire-eaters threatened to walk out of the Democratic convention. The Whigs survived to elect President Zachary Taylor, a hero of the war with Mexico. The triumph was short-lived, however. In 1849 President Taylor urged New Mexico and California to apply directly for admission to the Union, bypassing the usual territorial stage. California's application for statehood came with a constitution that prohibited slavery, provoking a fight over whether new slave states should be admitted to the Union. The House of Representatives, with a strong northern majority, reaffirmed the Wilmot Proviso, condemned the slave trade in Washington, D.C., and almost abolished slavery in the District of Columbia. The Senate, with a strong southern wing, blocked all such measures.

This was no ordinary stalemate. Fistfights broke out in the halls of Congress. Representatives challenged each other to duels. Threatening secession, proslavery partisans called for a southern-rights convention to meet at Nashville in June 1850. The stage was set for one of the most dramatic debates in congressional history.

A Compromise Without Compromises

Into this stalemate marched the "great triumvirate" of distinguished old senators, Henry Clay of Kentucky, Daniel Webster of Massachusetts, and John C. Calhoun of South Carolina. Clay, instrumental in securing the Missouri Compromise of 1820, tried one last time to save the Union. He devised a series of eight resolutions designed to balance the conflicting interests of North and South. Under two measures, California would be admitted as a free state, but the rest of the Mexican territories would have no conditions regarding slavery attached to their applications for statehood. The second pair of resolutions limited the number of slave states that could be carved out of Texas Territory but in return required the federal government to assume Texas's debt. The third pair abolished the slave trade in Washington, D.C., but protected slavery itself from federal interference. The final two provisions favored the South: a formal promise not to interfere in the interstate slave trade and a new fugitive slave law.

Clay gathered all eight provisions into a single package, derided by critics as the Omnibus Bill. His goal was simple: to gain enough support from centrists in each party to override both southern fire-eaters and northern Free-Soilers.

The congressional debate over Clay's package in the spring and summer of 1850 included a series of extraordinary speeches. Appealing for sectional harmony, Daniel Webster eloquently supported the compromise measures. Calhoun, by contrast, spoke very much as a southern man. He warned that the bonds of unity had been snapped by the North's continued agitation of the slavery question. If the right of property in slaves was not enforced, the Union would be severed. In response, New York's William H. Seward ar-

Senator Stephen A. Douglas The "Little Giant" from Illinois, became the leading advocate of "popular sovereignty" as a solution to the crisis over slavery in the 1850s.

THE LITTLE GIANT.. IN THE CHARACTER OF THE GLADIATOR.

gued that the Constitution gave Congress every right to restrict slavery in the territories.

The sectional hostilities exposed in the debate suggest why Clay's Omnibus Bill was doomed. Antislavery senators voted against the bill for its provisions protecting slavery. Proslavery senators opposed it for its restrictions on slavery. On July 31, after months of wrangling, the Senate killed the package. Exhausted and angry, Clay gave up and left Washington. The old generation had failed to resolve the crisis.

From then on national politics would be dominated by a new generation of congressional leaders. Seward of New York was one of them. Another was Senator Stephen A. Douglas, the "Little Giant" from Illinois who used his adroit parliamentary skills to rescue the compromise. He broke the omnibus package up into five separate bills, each designed to win different majorities. Antislavery and moderate congressmen joined to admit California as a free state. Proslavery congressmen voted with moderates to pass a fugitive slave law. By similar means, Congress settled the Texas border, determined that New Mexico and Utah would apply for statehood under the principle of popular sovereignty, and abolished the slave trade in the District of Columbia. Although proslavery and antislavery forces never compromised on a single issue, the five bills that Douglas and his allies steered through Congress came to be known as the Compromise of 1850.

Douglas's efforts were aided by the untimely death of the president. Zachary Taylor's replacement, Millard Fillmore, was more sympathetic to sectional reconciliation and called the Compromise of 1850 the "final settlement" of the slavery question. For the next few years moderate politicians avoided all discussion of slavery. In the short run, the compromise apparently worked. A southern-rights convention at Nashville fizzled, and the radical edge of the southern-rights movement was blunted. But fire-eaters in the South and Free-Soilers in the North insisted that the day of reckoning had only been postponed. And in the North, opposition to one feature of the compromise, the fugitive slave law, came with unanticipated intensity.

The Fugitive Slave Act Provokes a Crisis

The Fugitive Slave Act was one of the least debated features of the 1850 compromise. The Constitution had a fugitive slave clause, and a law enforcing the clause had existed since 1793. Why, then, did the new Fugitive Slave Act provoke such an uproar? Many northern states had passed laws to restrain fugitive slave catchers by guaranteeing the rights of due process to accused runaways. The 1850 statute took jurisdiction over fugitive-slave cases away from northern courts and gave it to federal commissioners who were paid $10 if they ruled that a black captive should be returned to slavery but only $5 if they ruled that the captive was legitimately free. Abolitionists naturally charged that this amounted to a bribe to send captives into slavery.

The Fugitive Slave Act sent terror through northern African American communities. Slaves who had run away decades earlier now risked being captured and sent back to the South. Even free-born blacks feared being kidnapped into slavery, unable to prove their freedom in a court of law. In the North, vulnerable African Americans moved to the far West, the upper North, or Canada. A convention of blacks denounced the Fugitive Slave Act as "the most cruel, unconstitutional, and scandalous outrage of modern times."

White abolitionists were no less vehement. Even white northerners who cared little about the fate of blacks were upset. The South seemed to be imposing its laws and institutions on the North. Appalled by the act, Harriet Beecher Stowe published the great antislavery novel *Uncle Tom's Cabin* in 1852. The astonishing success of Stowe's novel was a measure of northern anxiety. In vivid prose, Stowe drew a sentimental portrait of a slave mother and her infant child as they fled from a master who had contracted to sell them apart. Few readers missed the point. Anyone who helped Eliza save her child violated the Fugitive Slave Act of 1850.

Many northerners did tolerate violations of the Fugitive Slave Act. Fillmore vowed to enforce the law with federal marshals if necessary, but Frederick Douglass, far from his earlier pacifism, advocated violent resistance. "A half dozen or more dead kidnappers carried down South," he suggested, "would cool the ardor of Southern gentlemen."

Anthony Burns Burns was a fugitive slave whose owners were attempting to return him to the South. His 1854 trial created an uproar across the North, but especially in Boston, where the trial was held.

The Election of 1852 and the Decline of the Whig Party

White southerners were outraged by the North's unwillingness to obey the Fugitive Slave Act. The Democratic Party made enforcement of the Compromise of 1850 its rallying cry in 1852. The Democrats, torn by sectional divisions, nominated Franklin Pierce, a northerner felt to be sympathetic to southern interests. The Democratic platform pledged to silence discussion of slavery by strict federal enforcement of the Compromise of 1850, "the act for reclaiming fugitives included."

The Whigs found no such unifying principle. White southerners abandoned the party because of its antislavery advocates, and northern voters punished the Whigs who supported the Compromise of 1850. Henry Clay wrote the Fugitive Slave Act. Daniel Webster backed it. Millard Fillmore signed and aggressively enforced it. All were Whigs. The Whig Party convention in Baltimore nominated Winfield Scott of Virginia after 52 ballots and despite nearly unanimous southern opposition. Southern delegates secured a platform that reaffirmed the party's commitment to the Compromise of 1850, forcing the Whigs to run a candidate who was objectionable in the South on a platform that was objectionable in the North.

Southern defections all but assured a major Whig defeat in the election. Pierce won 254 electoral votes to Scott's 42. The Democratic candidate won 27 out of 31 states. Severely

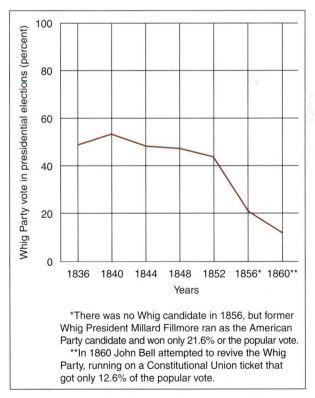

*There was no Whig candidate in 1856, but former Whig President Millard Fillmore ran as the American Party candidate and won only 21.6% or the popular vote.
**In 1860 John Bell attempted to revive the Whig Party, running on a Constitutional Union ticket that got only 12.6% of the popular vote.

Figure 14–1   The Decline of the Whig Party

weakened by the these results, the Whigs were unable to meet a political challenge that erupted in the early 1850s: hostility to immigrants, also known as nativism.

Nativism and the Origins of the Republican Party

The politics of nativism destroyed a Whig Party weakened by sectionalism. From 1852 through 1854 the nativist American Party gained surprising strength. Hostility to immigrants, however, was not enough to rally northerners concerned about slavery. What, then, would replace the Whig Party in the North? A new political force, the Republican Party, was dedicated to halting slavery's westward expansion.

The Nativist Attack on Immigration

For a while the arrival of large numbers of Catholic immigrants stirred nearly as much animosity among Yankee Protestants as did slavery. In the early 1850s the Catholic Church was known for its conservatism. The pope expressed a contempt for "progress," and the Vatican condemned the liberal revolutions sweeping Europe in 1848 that were widely supported by Americans.

Anti-Catholicism had about it a strong odor of middle-class condescension. Nativism appealed to shopkeepers, independent craftsmen, and clerks, people for whom the Protestant ethic of steadiness and sobriety was a scriptural injunction. They disdained a working class of Irish and German immigrants who drank heavily, lived in squalor, and lacked economic independence. But it was immigrant voting, particularly among Irish Catholics, that most troubled nativists: the Irish voted Democratic.

The Democrats' appeal to Irish Catholics was double-edged. On the one hand, the party's populist rhetoric attracted immigrants stung by the snobbery of Yankee Whigs. At the same time, as Democrats stepped up their racist invective, Irish Americans heaped contempt on African Americans with whom they competed for jobs and housing. Democrats cultivated this sentiment, using racism to welcome Irish voters into politics at a time when many were working to keep immigrants out. The consequences for sectional politics were significant. The Democrats argued that abolition would force white workers into economic competition with an inferior race. Supported by the Irish voting bloc, the Democratic Party sponsored new restrictions on the civil rights of free African Americans in many northern states.

In the elections of 1854, those who believed that immigration was the greatest threat to their way of life voted for the American Party. (They were often called "Know-Nothings" because of their origins in a secret organization whose members insisted they "knew nothing" about it.) Voters caring more about the threat of slavery voted for the Free-Soil Party. American Party candidates won 25 percent of the vote in New York and 40 percent in Pennsylvania; in Massachusetts, they took control of the state legislature.

In 1854 nativism seemed likely to eclipse slavery as the great issue of American politics. But slavery and nativism were never entirely separate issues. Middle-class Yankees often viewed the struggle against Catholicism as inseparable from the struggle against slavery. Both were said to represent authoritarianism, ignorance, and a rejection of the "modern" values of individualism and progress. Given the close ties between nativism and antislavery sentiment, it was unclear which issue would prevail. The question was decided on the plains of Kansas and Nebraska (see Map 14–3).

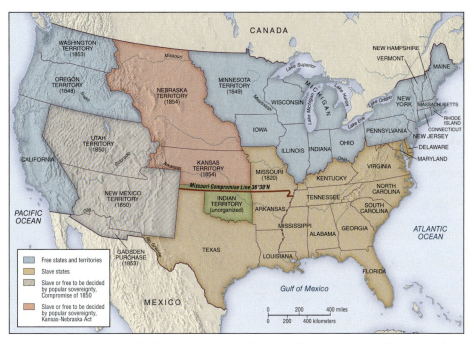

Map 14–3 The Kansas–Nebraska Act of 1854 Stephen Douglas's Kansas–Nebraska Act carved the Kansas Territory out of the larger Nebraska Territory. Because Missouri was already a slave state, the map indicates that slaveholders could move west and settle in Kansas. But because Kansas lay north of the 1820 Missouri Compromise line, many northerners wanted slavery restricted from the territory.

The Kansas-Nebraska Act Revives the Slavery Issue

In 1853, the House of Representatives passed a bill banning slavery in Nebraska Territory on the grounds that it fell north of the Missouri Compromise line. Southerners killed the Nebraska Bill in the Senate. The next year Stephen Douglas reintroduced it, this time organizing the territory on the principle of popular sovereignty.

No one was satisfied with Douglas's proposal. Northerners were outraged that the 1850 agreement to extend the Missouri Compromise line was so quickly scuttled. Militant southerners, suspicious of attempts to regulate slavery in the territories, demanded that the Missouri Compromise be repealed. Douglas withdrew the bill and reintroduced it in 1854 with a new twist. He split Nebraska Territory in two, Kansas to the west of the slave state of Missouri and Nebraska to the north of Kansas. Both were to be organized on the principle of popular sovereignty, and Kansas was expected to become a slave state and Nebraska a free state. To win southern congressional support, the final version of Douglas's bill repealed the Missouri Compromise of 1820.

Debate over the bill was ferocious: Southerners denied that Congress had the right to regulate slavery in the territories. Northerners noted that the federal government had been regulating slavery in the territories since the 1780s.

In the end, the Kansas-Nebraska Act became law. Yet, as with other southern victories, it increased support for northern antislavery politicians. It persuaded many northerners that

AMERICA AND THE WORLD

>> Slavery as a Foreign Policy

The Franklin Pierce administration's disastrous support for the Kansas-Nebraska Act undermined its ability to pursue the expansionist policies of its Democratic predecessors. To be sure, Pierce blustered about America's right to more Mexican territory and to parts of the Caribbean, particularly Cuba. But all of Pierce's expansionist efforts were southward, promising the expansion of slavery. This was hardly an accident. Southerners dominated Pierce's cabinet, and he appointed slaveholders to crucial diplomatic posts.

Pierce sent a South Carolinian, James Gadsden, to Mexico with instructions to spend up to $50 million to acquire a large portion of northern Mexico. Mexico's leader resisted the extravagant offer. Gadsden returned with a treaty giving the United States just enough territory for a transcontinental railroad across the southern tier of the nation. But even this was too much for most northern senators. For the first time in American history, Congress rejected land ceded to the United States. The Gadsden Purchase ended up with only a small piece of land for $10 million on the southern border of the United States.

The expansionist Pierce fared even worse in Cuba. He appointed Pierre Soulé, a Louisianan, as minister to Spain. Soulé was instructed to negotiate the purchase of Cuba, with the understanding that if Spain refused to sell he should encourage the Cubans to rebel. To Soulé the Spanish government offered an extraordinary response. It proposed to free millions of Cuban slaves and arm them for the defense of the island against a possible American invasion.

The United States responded with the Ostend Manifesto, which declared that Cuba was "naturally" a part of the United States and urged Spain to accept an offer of $120 million for the island. If Spain refused, the United States would "wrest" the island by force.

The Ostend Manifesto was issued in 1854 at the height of northern reaction against the Kansas-Nebraska Act and was denounced as another example of slavery's insatiable hunger for expansion. Expansionism was now hopelessly tainted by its association with slavery. As Pierce's secretary of state, William L. Marcy, admitted, "the Nebraska question" had shattered the Democratic Party in the North "and deprived it of that strength which was needed and could have been more profitably used for the acquisition of Cuba."

popular sovereignty was a proslavery swindle, even though Douglas believed it would produce mostly free states. For that reason southerners came to mistrust popular sovereignty as well. Douglas had paid a heavy price for his victory. In the 1854 elections the number of northern Democrats in Congress fell from 91 to 25. The fallout from the Kansas-Nebraska Act would split the Democratic Party in two, destroy the credibility of popular sovereignty, and damage expansionism as a political program.

One of the most important results of the struggle over the Kansas-Nebraska Act was the emergence of Abraham Lincoln. Douglas was widely denounced in his home state of Illinois for having helped open Kansas to slavery, facing hostile voters and the sharp criticism of Lincoln, his longtime political rival. Lincoln had largely left public life, but the Kansas-Nebraska Act brought him out of semiretirement. He followed Douglas around the state, demanding the restoration of the Missouri Compromise. In Peoria, on October 16, 1854, Lincoln gave a speech summing up his arguments against slavery and had it published. He pronounced slavery "a great moral wrong," insisted on the humanity of blacks, and denounced the dehumanization of slaves. He said slavery was founded on greed, selfishness, and unrestrained self-interest. With this remarkable speech, Lincoln reemerged as one of the state's leading antislavery politicians.

Kansas Begins to Bleed

Under the terms of the Kansas-Nebraska Act, the people in Kansas would determine whether their territory would enter the Union as a slave state or a free state. Elections for the territorial legislature were set for March 1855. Hoping to secure an antislavery victory, the New England Emigrant Aid Company sent settlers opposed to slavery. By election day proslavery settlers still would have won a fair fight. But when the polls opened, proslavery partisans from Missouri crossed the border and cast thousands of phony ballots. This undermined the legitimacy of the newly elected proslavery legislature. To make matters worse, the new legislature made it a crime to question slavery in Kansas, made it a capital crime to protect fugitive slaves, and expelled the few antislavery members who had been elected.

Free-state settlers repudiated the proslavery government. In January 1856, free-staters elected a governor and legislature of their own. By the spring of 1856, Kansas had two competing governments, a proslavery one in Lecompton and an antislavery one in Topeka. Free-state settlers were now in the majority. Nevertheless, sheriffs and federal marshals, backed up by "border ruffians" from Missouri, tried several times to enter the town of Lawrence to arrest free-staters. They tried again May 21, 1856, but most of the free-staters had fled. The frustrated Missourians destroyed two printing presses and burned the Free State Hotel to the ground. Although little blood was shed, the eastern press blasted the "sack of Lawrence" as the latest example of proslavery violence. Kansas, they said, was bleeding.

Three days after the sack of Lawrence, Kansas really did begin to bleed, when John Brown launched his famous raid on proslavery settlers at Pottawatomie Creek. Brown was an awesome and in many ways a frightening man, a religious zealot convinced it was his personal mission to cleanse the nation of the sin of slavery. The wrath of God, not moral persuasion or political organization, was Brown's solution to the problem of slavery.

The day after he learned of the sack of Lawrence, Brown organized a band of seven men to take revenge, among them four of his sons and a son-in-law. Armed with swords, Brown's troops went into battle late on May 24. They shot James Doyle in the head, split open the skulls of two of his sons, and then hacked up the bodies. They committed similar atrocities at two other settlers' cabins. Then they went back to their camp, having stolen several horses along the way.

As blood flowed in the western territories, another battle erupted on the floor of Congress. Prompted by the sack of Lawrence, abolitionist senator Charles Sumner of

AMERICAN LANDSCAPE

>> **Lawrence, Kansas**

Eli Thayer was more interested in making money than in spreading freedom when he secured a charter for the Massachusetts Emigrant Aid Society in April of 1854. But one month later, Congress passed the Kansas-Nebraska Act, and Thayer's organization became the focus of an effort to fill Kansas with northern settlers who opposed the spread of slavery. Within a year Thayer's organization had a new name, the New England Emigrant Aid Company, and a treasurer with deep pockets and an even deeper desire to halt the spread of slavery. He was Amos Lawrence, and when the settlers reached the prairie, they named their settlement after him. Within a year everybody was talking about Lawrence, Kansas.

Lawrence quickly became the center of the "free-state" movement in Kansas, and settlers established two antislavery newspapers, the *Kansas Free State* and the *Herald of Freedom*. If the goal of the New England Emigrant Aid Company was to overwhelm Kansas with free-state settlers who could outvote the proslavery forces, then their campaign failed. When elections for the territorial legislature were held on March 30, 1855, a flood of "border ruffians" crossed into Kansas from Missouri, casting thousands of ballots for candidates who favored slavery. "There are eleven hundred coming over from Platte County to vote," boasted Senator David Rice Atchison, the unofficial leader of the proslavery forces, "and if that ain't enough we can send five thousand—enough to kill every God-damned abolitionist in the territory."

The free-state settlers and their supporters quickly declared the elections and the new legislature frauds and set up a "government" of their own. Charles Robinson, the "governor" of the free state and the Emigrant Aid agent in Lawrence, wrote stormy letters of protest. He also asked for arms and ammunition. "We want 200 of Sharp's rifles & two cannon for Lawrence people," Robinson wrote. From New York, the pastor of Brooklyn's Plymouth Church, the Reverend Henry Ward Beecher, obliged by organizing a campaign to send the rifles ("Beecher's Bibles") to the frontier. Over the next year the free-state settlers armed themselves in preparation for battle. Meanwhile, the proslavery state government grew increasingly impatient with the growing abolitionist stronghold at Lawrence. In April 1856, Sheriff Jones was shot in the back while in Lawrence, and proslavery forces sprang into action. Several free-state leaders were indicted for "treason." Robinson was arrested. A grand jury recommended that the town's Free State Hotel be demolished and antislavery newspapers be shut down. The U.S. marshal for Kansas urged all "law abiding" settlers to converge on Lawrence so that he could serve warrants on the free-state leaders.

Sheriff Jones led a posse of 750 men bent on destroying the "hotbed of abolitionism" under a flag emblazoned with the words "Southern Rights." They invaded the offices of both newspapers and tossed the presses into the river. They ransacked the Free State Hotel, fired their cannon at it, then set it on fire. The mob pillaged several houses and burned down Robinson's house. Only one person was killed, but the town was largely demolished. Newspapers around the country dubbed the attack the "sack of Lawrence."

At stake in the battle over Lawrence were competing conceptions of democracy. Southerners had built an aggressive slaveholders' democracy in which white men were as proud of their freedom as they were jealous of their property rights in slaves. For the free-state settlers, slav-

ery and democracy were fundamentally incompatible. Thus the war on the Kansas prairie was a prelude to the civil war that would erupt nationwide a few years later.

The sack of Lawrence did not discourage the free-state settlers who lived there. They rebuilt their town, attracted ever more settlers to their cause, and within a few years were in the majority. For proslavery partisans Lawrence survived as a symbol of the abolitionism they so despised. During the Civil War they attacked Lawrence again, and again the town survived.

Massachusetts delivered a two-day harangue exposing the "Crime Against Kansas." Deliberately provocative, the speech was filled with sexual metaphors. Proslavery forces, Sumner said, had set out to "rape" the virgin territory of Kansas. He accused Senator Andrew Butler of South Carolina of consorting with a "polluted . . . harlot, Slavery." Two days later, Congressman Preston S. Brooks, a nephew of Butler's, brutally attacked Sumner with his cane.

Across the South, Brooks was hailed as a hero. Southern congressmen prevented his expulsion from the House. Northerners, shocked by the South's reaction to the Sumner-Brooks affair, responded by voting for a new Republican Party dedicated to halting the expansion of the "slave power."

A New Political Party Takes Shape

The election of 1856 presented Americans with a clear choice. A candidate's position on the Kansas-Nebraska Act betrayed a widening circle of convictions—about slavery's expansion, about the relative value of wage labor and slave labor, and about the morality of human property itself. At stake was the fundamental conflict between slave and free societies. In the past the Whigs and Democrats had avoided sectional issues by running candidates who appealed to both the North and the South. In 1856 a new major party, the Republicans, appealed exclusively to northern voters.

The First Sectional Election

In 1856 antislavery brought together the Democratic Party's opponents in the North in the new Republican Party. Its first presidential candidate was John C. Frémont.

The Republican Party platform called for a prohibition on the expansion of slavery into any western territories, and on this nearly all Republicans were agreed. But a party of former Whigs and Democrats had trouble unifying on anything else, and decades of partisan rivalry left a lingering mistrust. Former Whigs wanted the federal government to sponsor a transcontinental railroad and to set high tariffs to protect industries. They proposed a homestead act to encourage small farmers to settle the West and supported the creation of land grant colleges to foster innovation in agriculture. But Republicans who had once been Democrats were suspicious of such "whiggish" plans for big government. They believed that the "money power" they had long opposed as Jacksonian Democrats had been transformed into a "slave power" that now threatened the freedom of northern whites. Opposition to slavery's expansion in the western territories was what held Republicans together.

The Democrats faced an even more daunting challenge: to find a candidate acceptable to both the northern and southern wings of the party. They turned to James Buchanan of Pennsylvania, "a northern man with southern principles." Where the Republicans promised to interfere with slavery in the territories, the Democrats pledged "non-interference by Congress with slavery," thereby keeping the principle of popular sovereignty alive without actually endorsing it. Northern and southern Democrats could thus unite around a candidate committed, above all else, to ending public discussion of slavery. After decades of silencing discussion of slavery by emphasizing white supremacy, by the 1850s the Democrats' resort to racist appeals became desperate. Antislavery politics was back in the mainstream, and the Democrats were splitting apart along sectional lines. A newly intensified racism was all that held the Democratic Party together.

Nevertheless, by 1856 Buchanan and the Democrats could claim to be the only ones who could prevent the breakup of the Union. Southern leaders repeatedly warned that if Frémont and the Republicans won, the South would secede. The Democrats played on widespread fears of disunion. The "grand and appalling issue" of the campaign, Buchanan wrote, is "Union or Disunion."

For the first time, Americans were asked to decide in a presidential election whether the Union was worth preserving. Would the Union be based on a society whose wealth came from the labor of slaves or from the progress of free labor?

The Labor Problem and the Politics of Slavery

Northern Democrats warned that a Republican victory would flood the North with emancipated slaves, "side by side in competition with white men." The interest of northern workers therefore required the preservation of southern slavery within the Union. The most articulate spokesman for this view was Stephen Douglas. Douglas did not repudiate the promise of equality in the Declaration of Independence. Instead, he argued that it was never intended for an "inferior race" of blacks.

Republicans insisted that slavery degraded all labor, black and white, and that the expansion of slavery threatened the well-being of free labor in the North. Republicans held that slavery destroyed the work ethic by withholding from slaves any incentive to diligence and industry and by encouraging a disdain for hard work and self-discipline among the masters. By stifling the economic progress of the South, slavery was said to deny opportunities to poor whites as well. An inefficient workforce and an aristocratic ruling class would doom the South to economic backwardness. In contrast, Republicans depicted the North as a society in which labor was free and hard work was rewarded. The

Protestant virtues of thrift, sobriety, and diligence were cultivated, opportunities for up-ward mobility were many, and progress was manifest.

Southern spokesmen did not deny that in theory slave labor was less efficient than free labor. But they made a racial exception to this general rule. Blacks, they argued, did not respond to the incentives of free labor the way whites did. And whites, in turn, could not work efficiently in hot climates such as the South. Slavery solved this dual problem. It was the only way to get blacks to work productively in an otherwise unproductive cli-mate. The proof, the slaveholders argued, was the booming, expanding slave economy. The southern labor system provided a poor white man with the opportunity to rise up the social ladder by acquiring land and slaves "as soon as his savings will admit." Southern Democrats hailed slavery for preserving the economic independence of free whites in terms reminiscent of the Republican defense of wage labor as a stepping stone to self-employment. Slave property was, in this view, a reward for the same virtues of thrift and industry that Yankees thought they alone embraced.

But for many northerners the only possible explanation for the South's apparent pros-perity was the existence of a "slave power" that kept slavery artificially alive by opening the door to its continual expansion. Many Republicans believed that "property in man" was immoral and violated the basis of human equality. But other Republicans were at-tracted to the "slave power" theory because it allowed whites to feel threatened by slavery without having to sympathize with the plight of the slaves. The greater evil was not the oppression of the slave but the power of the slaveholder.

The Republicans did not succeed in the short run. In 1856, Buchanan won five north-ern states and all but one of the slave states, winning 45 percent of the popular vote and 174 electoral votes. Frémont swept the upper North and Ohio, winning 114 electoral votes. The surprise was not that Frémont lost, but that he did so well. All the Republicans needed to win four years later was Pennsylvania and either Illinois or Indiana. Never be-fore had a sectional party done so well in a presidential election. The slavery issue would not disappear until slavery itself did.

The Dred Scott Decision

In 1857 Democrat James Buchanan was inaugurated as president. His efforts to silence the slavery issue proved a disastrous failure. By the end of 1858 the nation's most promi-nent Republican, William Seward, had declared the sectional conflict between North and South "irrepressible." When Buchanan left office in 1861 his party was in disarray, a Re-publican had been elected his successor, and the Union had collapsed.

Within days of the inauguration, the Supreme Court, dominated by southern Dem-ocrats, issued one of the most controversial decisions in American history. The case stretched back to 1833, when John Emerson, an army surgeon from Missouri, was as-signed to Fort Armstrong, Illinois, and took a slave named Dred Scott with him. Emerson spent two years in Illinois and two more years at Fort Snelling in Wisconsin Territory (now Minnesota). Slavery was illegal in Illinois and Wisconsin Territory. Back in Missouri in 1846, Scott sued his owners, claiming that several years of residence on free soil made him legally free. After losing his suit in 1854, Scott appealed to the U.S. Supreme Court. By then two questions stood out: First, was Dred Scott a citizen, such that his suit had standing in a court of law? Second, did the laws of the free state of Illinois or the free ter-ritory of Wisconsin prevail over the master's property right?

The justices could have upheld the lower court's decision against Scott. But instead the majority decided, with some inappropriate coaxing from Buchanan, to render a sweeping decision covering some of the most explosive issues of the day.

The majority decision against Scott did not create the uproar. The problem was Chief Justice Roger Taney's provocative and partisan opinion. Taney argued, first, that Dred Scott was not a citizen because he was black. Since before the republic, he reasoned, African Americans had "been regarded as . . . so far inferior that they had no rights which the white man was bound to respect." Because their ancestors had been slaves in 1776, Taney reasoned, blacks could not be citizens in 1857. The problem was that Taney was wrong about 1857 and 1776: free blacks were discriminated against throughout America, but were nowhere denied all the rights of citizenship. They held property, entered into contracts, brought suits in court, and exercised the rights of speech, press, and assembly.

Second, Taney ruled that slaves were property, like any other property, and the Constitution "expressly affirms" the right of property in slaves. Dred Scott's residence in Wisconsin Territory could not make him a free man, because the Missouri Compromise, which excluded slavery from the territory, was an unconstitutional infringement on the right of property. Nor could his residence in Illinois make Scott free, because the right of property included the right of "sojourn."

Taney's decision made the southern defense of slavery into the law of the land. Neither Congress nor western settlers could legally exclude slavery from the territories, because any such exclusion would trample on the slaveholders' sacred rights of property. The only human beings who fell into the category of "property" were black slaves. In a thoroughly political ruling, Taney had declared unconstitutional both the northern Democrats' policy of popular sovereignty and the northern Republican policy of free soil. The one political position left standing by the Court was that of the southern slaveholders. Owning slaves was a right of property, and only blacks could be slaves.

The Lecompton Constitution Splits the Democratic Party

When the Court undermined popular sovereignty as a viable political position, it contributed to the sectional division of the Democratic Party. But the cause of the final Democratic rupture was again Kansas. In 1858 Congress had to choose between two different constitutions accompanying the territory's petition for admission to the Union. The so-called Lecompton Constitution was drawn up by proslavery partisans, representing a minority of Kansas residents. Free-staters, knowing they were in the majority, submitted their constitution to a popular referendum, whereas supporters of the Lecompton Constitution sent their document directly to Congress. Buchanan supported the proslavery minority. But the leading northern Democrat in the Senate, Stephen Douglas of Illinois, rejected the Lecompton Constitution because it violated his principle of popular sovereignty.

Douglas was in a difficult position. Southern Democrats assailed popular sovereignty as an affront to their rights of property in slaves. Northern critics pointed out that the Dred Scott decision had rendered popular sovereignty meaningless. In their famous 1858 debates, Lincoln shrewdly forced Douglas to confront the issue at Freeport, Illinois. Given the Dred Scott decision, Lincoln asked, can the people of a territory legally exclude slavery? In what became known as the Freeport Doctrine, Douglas argued that the people of a territory could exclude slavery simply by refusing to pass the laws necessary to protect it. That way no master would dare go there with his human property. Douglas's logic infuriated southern Democrats and split the party into northern and southern wings in 1860.

The Irrepressible Conflict

By the late 1850s the conflict between the North and the South began to seem irrepressible to more and more Americans. Northern Democrats, led by Douglas, tried desperately to preserve a middle ground that would prevent the Union from breaking apart. Similarly, the Whigs in the Border States struggled to devise yet another compromise to save the Union. But the middle ground was giving way to the irreconcilable positions of the Republican Party in the North and the Democratic Party in the South.

More than ever, the Democratic Party in the South was the voice of the slaveholding class, its sole purpose the defense of the inalienable right of property in slaves. On most matters southern Democrats were staunch advocates of state's rights as a defense of slavery against a strong central government. They opposed protective tariffs and federal support for internal improvements (railroads, canals, turnpikes), and they were suspicious of efforts to reestablish a national bank. But when it came to the protection of slave property, southern Democrats supported a strong central government. In response to Douglas's "Freeport Doctrine," Mississippi Senator Jefferson Davis proposed a federal slave code that would be imposed on any western territory that refused to protect slave property.

Meanwhile northern Republicans were moving in the opposite direction, questioning not only the constitutional right of property in slaves but also the sanctity of property rights themselves. Whigs once revered the rule of law and the authority of the courts. But their Republican descendants, disgusted by the proslavery bias of the Supreme Court, began denouncing the "superstitious reverence" for judges. Republicans also questioned the primacy of property rights. The most powerful Republican in the 1850s, New York Senator William Seward, declared that "property . . . has always a bias toward oppression." And in 1859 Abraham Lincoln praised Thomas Jefferson for elevating human rights over property rights. He repeatedly denounced the Dred Scott decision and argued that there was no such thing as a constitutional right of property in slaves.

As the 1860 elections approached, the business of Congress was again stalled by the bitter division over slavery. So deep were the divisions that the House of Representatives was unable to elect a speaker. After several northern congressmen endorsed an inflammatory antislavery book published by Hinton Rowan Helper, infuriated southern legislators tied Congress up in knots.

For years the conflict between the North and the South over slavery was said to be "irreconcilable." Frederick Douglass often said that Liberty and Slavery were at war with one another and that there could be no peace until one or the other was vanquished, until either slavery or freedom was the law everywhere in the land. George Fitzhugh, the most extreme proslavery theorist, had long argued the same thing. By the late 1850s, such talk had drifted into the mainstream. Southern politicians began to claim that the slave states were no longer safe within the Union. In Illinois, Abraham Lincoln opened his 1858 race for the U.S. Senate with a speech declaring that "a house divided against itself cannot stand." The most famous expression of this sentiment came in a speech by William Seward in 1858. The division over slavery, he said, "is an irrepressible conflict between opposing and enduring forces, and it means that the United States must and will, sooner or later, become either entirely a slaveholding nation, or entirely a free-labor nation."

By the time of Seward's speech emotions were running so high, North and South, that it was easy to miss the substance of the disagreement. In truth, slaveholders had little choice but to take the position they did. Their economy, society, and political power rested on their property rights in slaves. And despite the overheated rhetoric, the principles on which the slaveholders stood were in their own way reasonable and logical. Slaves *were* property, and property rights were supposed to be sacred. At the same time, it made perfect sense for northerners to defend the superiority of free labor. Their own way of life, and the prosperity of their economy, rested on the principle of free labor—that no human being could rightfully own another. The aggressive expansion of slavery and the disproportionate power of the slaveholders in national politics seemed to threaten freedom everywhere. The northerners no less than the southerners had to defend themselves.

But if the conflict between the North and South was irrepressible, that did not mean that civil war was inevitable. The slide from dissension to armed conflict began in late 1859.

The Retreat from Union

Between 1859 and 1860 both the North and the South rejected the sanctity of the Union. In the South the retreat from unionism was a reaction to John Brown's raid on Harpers Ferry. Brown's death was greeted as a martyr's execution in much of the North, leading many southerners to conclude that a union of the North and the South was no longer viable. In 1860, with the election of Abraham Lincoln, the North ceased compromising with slavery for the sake of maintaining the Union.

John Brown's War Against Slavery

In the fall of 1858 the mysterious John Brown reemerged to launch another battle in his private war against slavery. By the late 1850s Brown had concocted a plan to invade Virginia and free the slaves. Friends told Brown his plan was unworkable. Frederick Douglass advised him to give it up. But Brown found financial support from a group of well-connected Bostonians dazzled by his appeal to action rather than words. Brown rented a farm in Maryland, near the town of Harpers Ferry in western Virginia, where a small federal arsenal was located. He apparently planned to capture the arsenal and distribute the guns to local slaves, inciting a rebellion. On the evening of October 16, 1859, Brown and 18 followers crossed the Potomac River with a wagonload of guns and seized the armory. Brown ordered his men to scour the countryside to liberate slaves and take slaveholders prisoner. They found Colonel Lewis Washington, a member of the first president's family, and took him back to Harpers Ferry as a hostage. Mission accomplished, Brown sat back and waited for the slaves to rise.

The slaves did not rise, but the military did. Marines were sent from Washington, D.C., led by Lieutenant Colonel Robert E. Lee and his assistant, Lieutenant J. E. B. Stuart, later to become leading Confederate generals. On the morning after Brown seized Harpers Ferry, the militia surrounded the arsenal. The next day Stuart ordered Brown to surrender, and when Brown refused, 12 marines charged in with bayonets. Two of Brown's men and one marine were killed, and Brown was wounded. The rebellion was over in less than two days.

The entire raid was "absurd," Abraham Lincoln later said. "It was not a slave insurrection," he added. "It was an attempt by white men to get up a revolt among slaves, in

Lincoln-Douglas Debate Poster In 1858 a little-known Illinois Republican, Abraham Lincoln, ran against Stephen A. Douglas for the U.S. Senate. Their seven campaign debates, one of them pictured here, brilliantly spelled out the differences between Democrats and Republicans over slavery. Though Lincoln lost the election, he did so well in the debates that his party nominated him for the presidency two years later.

which the slaves refused to participate." The condemnation of Brown by northerners and the embarrassment of Brown's supporters initially calmed southern outrage. Over the next weeks, however, northern opinion changed from contempt to admiration. Brown's eloquent statements and dignified behavior in prison, at his trial, and on the gallows moved many northerners to extraordinary demonstrations of sympathy. On December 2, the day Brown was hanged, northern churches tolled their bells. Militia companies fired salutes. Public buildings across the North were draped in black. Although mainstream politicians disavowed Brown and his raid, white southerners were shocked to see John Brown become a hero to many northerners. The Baltimore *Sun* said the South could not "live under a government, the majority of whose subjects or citizens regard John Brown as a martyr and a Christian hero, rather than a murderer and robber." In the end, though, it was not John Brown's raid that led the South to secede from the Union. It was the election of Abraham Lincoln.

Northerners Elect a President

In February 1860, as the nation's focus shifted from John Brown to the coming presidential election, Abraham Lincoln traveled to New York to speak to influential eastern Republicans sizing up possible candidates. Speaking in the newly opened Cooper Institute—later known as Cooper Union—Lincoln extended the argument he had made during his debates with Stephen Douglas. When southerners defended their right of property in slaves, Lincoln argued, they were presuming a constitutional right that did not exist. Instead, the Constitution protected slavery in narrow ways and only in the states where it already existed. Moreover, if the slave states seceded from the Union, they would forfeit whatever constitutional protection slavery did have. By making a radical claim—that there was no constitutional right of property in slaves—and by tying it to a threat to interfere with slavery if the South seceded, Lincoln established his antislavery credentials among leaders of the Republican Party. The Cooper Union Address helped Lincoln win his party's nomination, but it also proved to southern Democrats that his election would be a direct threat to slavery.

Lincoln could not hope to win any votes in the South, and he was attacked as a "sectional" candidate. But by 1860 no major party candidate could appeal to both the North and the South. There were, in effect, two different presidential elections that year. In the slave states a southern Democrat ran against a Constitutional Unionist. In the free states a northern Democrat ran against a Republican. On the surface, slavery in the territories remained the dominant issue. Below the surface, the future of the Union was about to be determined.

The Democratic Party met in April in Charleston, South Carolina, the center of extreme secessionist sentiment. Southern fire-eaters demanded federal recognition of slavery in all the territories as part of the Democratic platform. But Stephen Douglas, the leading candidate for the nomination, insisted on a reaffirmation of popular sovereignty. Douglas had a bare majority of the delegate supporters, enough to push his platform through, but not enough to win the party's nomination. When Douglas's plank was passed, 49 delegates from eight southern states walked out. The convention was deadlocked. After 57 ballots, the Democrats adjourned, agreeing to reconvene in Baltimore a month and a half later.

The delay only made matters worse. In Baltimore, 110 southerners nominated their own candidate, giving the Democrats two presidential aspirants in 1860. Stephen Douglas ran in the North advocating popular sovereignty and insisting that the Union itself hung in the balance of the election. John Breckinridge, the southern candidate, ran on a platform calling for federal recognition of slavery in all the territories. Another candidate, John Bell of Tennessee, tried to revive the Whig Party by running on a Constitutional Unionist ticket. No candidate had much chance of winning.

The Republicans were far more united. Sensing victory, tens of thousands of Republicans poured into Chicago. The leading candidate for the nomination was William H. Seward of New York. But his strength was limited to the uppermost states in the North. In the border states, such as Pennsylvania, Indiana, and Illinois, Seward's antislavery politics were seen as too radical, and he faced opposition even in his home state of New York. The party needed a candidate with impeccable antislavery credentials but moderate enough to carry the critical states of the lower North. That candidate was Abraham Lincoln. Not only was Lincoln from Illinois, but he also tempered his radical critique of slavery with a constitutional restraint that made him acceptable to moderates and conservatives. Unlike conservative Republicans, Lincoln did not race-bait much, and he opposed nativist restrictions on immigration. Unlike party radicals, Lincoln had supported enforcement of the Fugitive Slave Act, denounced John Brown's raid on Harpers Ferry, and insisted that the federal government could not interfere in states where slavery already existed. Still, Lincoln made clear his view that slavery was immoral, that owning slaves was not a constitutionally protected property right, that Congress had the right to restrict slavery's expansion into the territories, and that the entire slave system should be placed "in the course of ultimate extinction." No major party had ever run a candidate dedicated to such a proposition.

Throughout the campaign, Lincoln and the Republicans scoffed at secessionist threats from the South, as did Breckinridge the Democrat and Bell the Constitutional Unionist. But Douglas was so convinced that the election of Lincoln would result in secession and war that he actively campaigned as the only candidate who could hold the Union together. When Lincoln's victory became clear, Douglas made a series of speeches in the slave states—"not to ask for your votes for the Presidency," he told his audiences, "but to make an appeal to you on behalf of the Union."

Lincoln won every free state except New Jersey. Douglas got the second largest number of votes but took only one state, Missouri. Breckenridge took 11 slave states, although his support was concentrated in districts with the lowest proportions of slaves. The slaveholders continued to vote their traditional Whig sympathies, supporting John Bell's Constitutional Unionist candidacy.

Lincoln did not campaign in the South; his name was not even on the ballot in most of the slave states. He won by appealing exclusively to voters in the North (see Map 14–4), which allowed Lincoln to run on a platform dedicated to slavery's "ultimate extinction." Antislavery forces in the North were doubly vindicated: not only did the Republican victory show wide appeal for an antislavery platform, but it also suggested that a dynamic economy based on free labor was bound to grow faster than a slave society. In their own way, white southerners agreed. They concluded that no matter what assurances Lincoln gave them, the future of slavery in the Union was doomed.

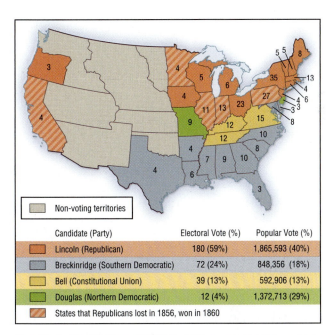

Candidate (Party)	Electoral Vote (%)	Popular Vote (%)
Non-voting territories		
Lincoln (Republican)	180 (59%)	1,865,593 (40%)
Breckinridge (Southern Democratic)	72 (24%)	848,356 (18%)
Bell (Constitutional Union)	39 (13%)	592,906 (13%)
Douglas (Northern Democratic)	12 (4%)	1,372,713 (29%)
States that Republicans lost in 1856, won in 1860		

Map 14–4   The Election of 1860 By 1860, no presidential candidate could appeal to voters in both the North and the South. By then, the northern population had grown so rapidly that a united North could elect Lincoln to the presidency without any southern support.

>> Timeline

▼**1838**
Frederick Douglass escapes from slavery

▼**1844**
Samuel F. B. Morse invents the telegraph

▼**1846**
David Wilmot introduces his "proviso"

▼**1847**
Treaty of Guadalupe Hidalgo

▼**1848**
Zachary Taylor elected president

▼**1850**
Taylor dies; Millard Fillmore becomes president Compromise of 1850

▼**1852**
Uncle Tom's Cabin published in book form
Franklin Pierce elected president

▼**1854**
Gadsden Purchase ratified
Kansas-Nebraska Act
Ostend Manifesto

▼**1856**
"Bleeding Kansas"
Sumner-Brooks affair
James Buchanan elected president

▼**1857**
Dred Scott decision

▼**1858**
Lincoln-Douglas debates

▼**1859**
John Brown's raid on Harpers Ferry

▼**1860**
Abraham Lincoln elected first Republican president

▼**1861**
South secedes from Union, Civil War begins

Conclusion

Frederick Douglass had misgivings about Lincoln but sincerely hoped that the Republicans would win the 1860 elections. "Slavery is the issue—the single bone of contention between all parties and sections," he insisted. Slavery and freedom had guided the nation along two diverging pathways. The North was developing an urban, industrial economy based on the productive energy of wage labor. In the South, a prosperous slave economy depended on a system of commercialized agriculture in which laborers were commodities as much as the cash crops they produced. The political tensions arising from these differences finally pushed the nation into civil war. And as the war progressed, the same differences in political economy would shape the destiny of the Union and Confederate forces.

Review Questions

1. What were the major differences between the northern and southern economies by the 1850s?

2. How did the war with Mexico provoke a conflict over slavery?

3. What did the Republican Party stand for?

4. What was the Kansas-Nebraska Act and why was it so important?

5. What were the major issues in the Lincoln-Douglas debates?

For further review materials and resource information, please visit www.oup.com/us/ofthepeople

A War for Union and Emancipation

1861–1865

15

AMERICAN PORTRAIT

>> Edmund Ruffin

Edmund Ruffin was born in 1794 into one of the wealthiest planter families in eastern Virginia. By the age of 20 he was the master of a substantial plantation on the James River. Yet from his youth Edmund Ruffin was discontented and angry. He coveted a political career, but his contempt for democracy thwarted him. In 1823 he was elected to the Virginia state senate, but he was unwilling to forge the alliances and make the compromises that would bring him political influence. Before his term expired, Ruffin resigned his seat, "tired and disgusted with being a servant of the people." He never held public office again.

During the 1830s and 1840s Ruffin retreated to his plantations, publishing the results of his experiments in crop rotation, drainage, and new fertilizers. His work paid off in improved productivity, higher profits, and public esteem. But Ruffin, more interested in politics than farming, used his fame as an agricultural reformer to spread his proslavery message. By 1850 Ruffin was urging Virginians to secede from the Union to preserve slavery.

Ruffin moved from reformer to secessionist through the logic of political economy. A more productive slave economy, he reasoned, would protect the South from the growing power of the industrializing North. Inspired by other proslavery authors, Ruffin set all the world's peoples on a sliding scale from the most savage to the most civilized. The only way for barbaric peoples to rise above savagery, Ruffin claimed, was for the powerful and industrious to force these shiftless people to work, usually by enslaving them. Slavery thus spurred both civilization and prosperity.

But Ruffin's defense of slavery left several important questions unanswered: Who, for example, should be enslaved? It was both morally objectionable and socially disruptive for equals to enslave equals. Southern slavery escaped this problem, Ruffin believed, because whites only enslaved racially inferior blacks. And what of the abolitionist claim that slavery was less efficient than wage labor? Ruffin agreed that in principle slaves lacked the motive of self-interest that made wage laborers more efficient, but he pointed to exceptional conditions in the United States. As long as western lands could absorb the surplus labor of the North, free laborers would work on their own farms at their own pace. But slaves were compelled to labor on precious cash crops grown in climates where, Ruffin believed, only African Americans could work. As long as these exceptional conditions prevailed, slavery would be as efficient as free labor.

Once the West filled up, Ruffin argued, free men and women would be forced to sell their labor at miserably low wages. Eventually, the misery of free laborers would give rise to socialism and anarchy. Thus northerners would pay the price of perpetual social unrest for their wealth and prosperity. Southern whites, by contrast, had struck the perfect balance between material well-being and social peace. By enslaving an "inferior" race, they could raise the general level of civilization without the disruptions associated with wage labor.

Edmund Ruffin had always believed that slavery was the issue dividing the North from the South. Ironically, as war approached, it was northerners who clung to the belief that the Union could be held together with slavery intact. Most northerners started out thinking that the war could be fought only to restore the Union but came to see it as a struggle to rid the nation of slavery as well. Edmund Ruffin was not surprised that the northern crusade to preserve the Union eventually became a crusade for the abolition of slavery.

Common Threads

>> **What made the South secede from the Union?**

>> **In what ways did the military strategies of the North and South reflect the differences between the two regions?**

>> **What was the relationship between emancipation and war?**

>> **Why did the South lose the Civil War? Why did the North win?**

>> **What happened to the slaves who were freed by the war?**

From Union to Emancipation

Southerners made it clear that they were going to war to preserve their rights of property in slaves. In 1861 Confederate president Jefferson Davis justified secession on the grounds that northern Republican rule would make "property in slaves so insecure as to be comparatively worthless." Southerners talked in general about defending "states' rights" or "property rights," but they were referring specifically to the right of the states to maintain slavery and to the right of individuals to hold property in slaves. These were among the cherished principles that white southerners believed they had inherited from the Founding Fathers of the nation. Slavery had been legal in every one of the thirteen colonies represented in the Declaration of Independence. In declaring their own independence, white southerners believed they were affirming rather than rejecting the legacy of the American Revolution. Their rights and prosperity were no longer safe in the Union the Founders had created. So they made a confederacy of their own in which slavery could survive unharmed, forever.

But the Union was a sacred thing for most northerners, a beacon of liberty in a world of tyranny. To break the Union apart would be treason, but it would also prove that democratic republics could not hold themselves together. If the Union collapsed, "the last best hope" of the oppressed peoples of the world would go down with it. Northerners understood that slavery was the *cause* of the war, but most at first supported war to restore the Union, not to destroy slavery. Some did not care enough about the plight of African Americans to support a war for their freedom. Those who did usually agreed with Lincoln and the Republicans that the federal government had no authority to interfere with slavery where it already existed. In his inaugural address of March 1861, Lincoln reasserted his intention to leave slavery alone in the South. But he also denied that there was a constitutional right to property in slaves and warned that, by seceding, the South risked losing whatever federal protection slavery did enjoy. Like most northerners, Lincoln would fight to restore the Union. After the war began, however, more and more Yankees began asking a question: What would be the point of restoring the Union without also destroying slavery, the very thing that had torn the Union apart?

The South Secedes

As the news of Lincoln's election flashed across telegraph wires, the South Carolina state legislature called a secession convention. On December 20, 1860, the state withdrew from the Union on the grounds that northerners had elected a president who denied the existence of a right of property in slaves. "They have encouraged and assisted thousands of slaves to leave their homes," South Carolina declared, "and those who remain have been incited . . . to servile insurrection." Within weeks, Mississippi, Florida, Alabama, Georgia, Louisiana, and Texas followed suit (see Map 15–1). Then, as quickly as it had begun, the secession movement came to a halt. The slave states of the upper South refused to leave the Union simply because Lincoln was elected. Ardent secessionists began to suspect that the South was not unified in its opposition to the North.

The upper South was dominated by cooperationists rather than secessionists. Cooperationists were committed to remaining in the Union provided that the Lincoln administration "cooperated" with the South. Thus even after Lincoln's inauguration Virginia, Arkansas, and Missouri would not secede. The state legislatures of Kentucky and Delaware refused to authorize secession conventions, and in Tennessee and North Carolina the voters refused. Lincoln and many Republicans hoped that if they moved cautiously they could keep the upper South in the Union and thereby derail the secession movement. But cooperationism turned out to be a weak foundation for a rebuilt Union. Cooperationist loyalty required the federal government to meet certain demands for the protection of slavery.

Cooperationist demands were the basis of several last-minute attempts at sectional compromise. The most famous was a series of constitutional amendments proposed by

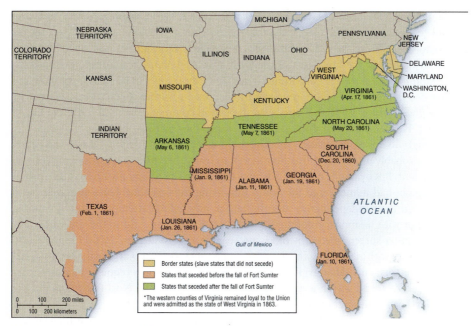

	Border states (slave states that did not secede)
	States that seceded before the fall of Fort Sumter
	States that seceded after the fall of Fort Sumter

*The western counties of Virginia remained loyal to the Union and were admitted as the state of West Virginia in 1863.

Map 15–1   The Secession of the Southern States The South seceded in two stages. During the "secession winter" of 1860–1861, the lower South states seceded in reaction to the election of Abraham Lincoln. The following spring the upper South seceded in response to Lincoln's attempt to resupply Fort Sumter. The border slave states of Maryland, Delaware, Kentucky, and Missouri never left the Union.

Senator John J. Crittenden of Kentucky. The Crittenden Compromise would have restored the Missouri Compromise line and guaranteed federal protection of slavery south of that line in all territories currently held or later acquired by the United States. It would have prohibited Congress from abolishing slavery in Washington, D.C., and from regulating the interstate slave trade. Finally, it called for the compensation of masters unable to recover fugitive slaves from the North.

Each of these concessions was unacceptable to the Republicans, especially the one protecting slavery in future territories. This struck Republicans as an open invitation for southerners to expand the slave power into Central America, South America, and the Caribbean. And once the lower South seceded, the Republicans concluded that *any* compromise amounted to surrender to southern blackmail. They began making nationalist appeals to rally all northerners around the preservation of the Union. By early 1861 northern Democrats who cared little about slavery still refused to compromise with southern states that had left the Union. The Crittenden proposals—like every other compromise scheme—fell on deaf ears throughout the North.

The conflict over slavery had become irreconcilable. By the spring of 1861 most southerners agreed with Edmund Ruffin that there should be no more compromise with the North. Even "cooperationists" insisted that the southern states had a right to secede and should do so if Lincoln committed any act of overt "coercion." It was also clear that the confrontation would come at one of the two Union forts still in the seceded states—Fort Pickens in Pensacola, Florida, or Fort Sumter in Charleston Harbor. Realizing that Pickens was indefensible, Jefferson Davis sent the flamboyant P. G. T. Beauregard to Charleston Harbor to prepare defenses against the impending Union invasion. Out of respect for his long years of service to the cause, Ruffin was invited to South Carolina and given the privilege of firing one of the first shots of the Civil War. At 4:30 in the morning on April 12, 1861, Ruffin aimed a rifle at Fort Sumter and began shooting. For 33 hours Confederates bombarded the fort, located on an island in Charleston Harbor, to block its resupply by the U.S. government. With no alternative, the Union commander raised the white flag of surrender. Fort Sumter fell to the Confederates, and the Civil War began.

Though he hoped for peace, Lincoln had long since concluded that a war was inevitable. He probably understood that his attempt to resupply Fort Sumter would provoke an armed assault. But by announcing in advance that he was sending only nonmilitary provisions, Lincoln had maneuvered the South into firing the first shot. For southerners who had declared their independence months earlier, any federal attempt to supply Sumter, with food or with weapons, amounted to a declaration of war. And so the war came. The day Fort Sumter surrendered, Lincoln issued a call to the states for 75,000 militiamen to report for duty within 90 days. The governors of Tennessee, Virginia, North Carolina, Arkansas, Kentucky, and Missouri refused to comply with Lincoln's request. Two days later Virginia seceded, and within a month Arkansas, Tennessee, and North Carolina did the same. Northern hopes of holding on to the upper South had vanished.

But the South remained divided. Four slave states (Kentucky, Maryland, Delaware, and Missouri) never joined the Confederacy. In the mountains of western North Carolina and eastern Tennessee, unionist sentiment remained strong during the war years. Virginia was literally torn apart. The western third of the state voted overwhelmingly against secession, and when the eastern slaveholders decided to leave the Union, western counties formed their own state government. (In 1863 the state of West Virginia was admitted to the Union.) Where slavery was weak, support for secession was weak also. Where slavery thrived, so did the sentiment for secession. Yet despite these internal divisions, support for secession was remarkably widespread in the South, and over the next four years white southerners would put up a long, hard fight to sustain the independence of the Confederacy.

Civilians Demand a Total War

Most Americans expected the war to last only a few months. Lincoln's first call for troops asked volunteers to enlist for 90 days, although he hedged his bets by calling for three-year enlistments as well. Confederate soldiers initially signed up for 12 months but were later required to serve "for the duration" of the war. Although both sides began with relatively limited military and political goals, the conflict descended into a "hard" war that produced shocking numbers of military casualties, horrifying massacres of black prisoners, and the deliberate destruction of the homes and farms of southern whites. In the end, hard war would also mean the unconditional surrender of Confederate armies and the end of southern slavery.

In the weeks following Fort Sumter, enthusiasm for war overflowed in the Union and the Confederacy. Military victory was not enough. In the spring of 1861, one southern woman prayed that "God may be with us to give us strength to conquer them, to exterminate them, to lay waste to every Northern city, town and village, to destroy them utterly." In 1862 southern troops burned the town of Chambersburg, Pennsylvania, to the ground, and in 1864 Jefferson Davis sent Confederate agents to New York City, where they set fire to 10 hotels, hoping to send the city up in flames.

Northerners felt no differently toward southerners. Even before fighting began, Ohio senator Benjamin Wade talked of "making the south a desert." After Fort Sumter, one northern judge argued that the North should "restore New Orleans to its native marshes, then march across the country, burn Montgomery to ashes, and serve Charleston in the same way. . . . We must starve, drown, burn, shoot the traitors."

The military was more hesitant, and neither side was prepared for battle nor sought it. For several months Union and Confederate commanders concentrated on building up their armies. The entire U.S. Army had only 16,000 troops scattered across the continent. Under aged war hero General Winfield Scott, Union strategy was initially designed to use the North's naval superiority to blockade the entire South, but there was almost no navy, either. Yet, as spring became summer, civilians in the North and the South demanded more. "Forward to Richmond!" cried Horace Greeley, echoing northern sentiment for a swift capture of the new Confederate capital.

Slaves Take Advantage of the War

In the South the enthusiasm for battle was compounded by fantasies of a race war between African Americans and whites. The lower South seceded while still in the grip of the insurrection panics that followed John Brown's raid on Harpers Ferry. Few slaves actually joined with Brown, but that did little to calm the fears of southern whites. Such fears were usually exaggerated, but by 1861 they were not.

As the war began, slaves struggled to collect war news. House servants reported conversations at the masters' residences to field hands in the slave quarters. Every neighborhood had one or two literate slaves who got hold of a newspaper. News of the war spread along what the slaves called the "grapevine telegraph."

Shortly after Lincoln was inaugurated, several slaves in Florida escaped to Fort Pickens, claiming their freedom. In Virginia, scarcely a month after Fort Sumter, Union commander Benjamin F. Butler refused to return three runaway slaves on the grounds that they would have been put to work on Confederate military fortifications. Butler called the runaways "contrabands" of war, and the label stuck. As the number of contrabands mounted, Butler demanded that his superiors clarify Union policy. "As a military question it would seem to be a measure of necessity to deprive their masters of their services," he wrote on May 27, 1861. Immediately realizing the importance of Butler's idea , Lincoln called his cabinet together to discuss the matter on May 30. After the meeting, Secretary of War Simon Cameron telegraphed Butler that his proposal to retain "contraband" slaves "is approved." The Fugitive Slave Act was effectively nullified.

But emancipation was still a long way off. For every runaway who made it to Union lines, hundreds were still trapped in slavery on southern farms and plantations, and most would remain trapped until the war was over. War disrupted slave life, but if slavery survived the war, the plantations would recover. It had happened many times before in the long history of human slavery; it had even happened in America. Southern slave society had weathered the upheaval of the American Revolution, and slaveholders vowed that slavery would outlast the Civil War as well. The slaves were determined to win their freedom, but their masters had the guns. To succeed, the slaves would need allies—the U. S. government and the Union army. But that would take time.

Escaping Slaves Designated "contrabands" of war, these Virginia slaves are escaping to Union lines in August 1862. The Lincoln administration took office with a promise not to interfere with southern slavery, but runaways like those pictured here helped push the Union toward a policy of emancipation.

Military Strategy and the Shift in War Aims

No single military strategy defined either the Confederate or Union war efforts, as there was wide disagreement among leaders on both sides about the best way to win the war. But in general the South pursued a defensive strategy. If Confederate armies could hold off Union attacks, using interior lines to move men to different theaters of war, they might be able to wear down the North until it gave up the fight. Throughout the war Confederate commanders moved their armies like chess pieces across the southern playing field to engage larger Union armies: from the Shenandoah Valley to Manassas, from New Orleans to Shiloh, from northern Virginia to Tennessee. It was a mostly successful strategy. But the Confederates also pursued a more aggressive if less successful strategy. Robert E. Lee invaded the North twice, for example, in September of 1862 and July of 1863, and both times his armies were defeated.

A more aggressive Union strategy took some time to develop. At the outset General Winfield Scott proposed a gigantic siege of the entire South, choking the Confederacy by an increasingly successful blockade. Critics derided this as "the anaconda plan." But the naval squeeze of the South remained a key element of northern strategy, and some of the most successful northern commanders were admirals, such as David Farragut and Andrew Foote. Lincoln had much more trouble with his generals than with his admirals, particularly in the Army of the Potomac that fought most of the major battles in the East. The problems began with George McClellan, who replaced Scott as general in chief and who developed a strategy for capturing the Confederate capital of Richmond, Virginia. Eventually Lincoln realized that capturing territory was no replacement for defeating armies, and until the last year of the war he struggled with a succession of eastern generals who could not see their goal to be the destruction of the Confederate armies. It was not enough to drive Robert E. Lee's army out of Maryland or Pennsylvania, Lincoln insisted; the army itself had to be destroyed. The capture of Richmond, too, was a strategic fantasy so long as Lee's armies were waiting somewhere nearby. Not until 1863, with Grant's capture of the Confederate armies trapped in Vicksburg, did Lincoln feel he had a general who shared his strategic commitment to the unconditional surrender of Confederate armed forces. By then, Lincoln had also embraced a final strategy, "hard war," aimed at undermining the morale of southern civilians. The most revolutionary piece of the hard-war strategy was emancipation.

The first test of Union and Confederate military strength came on July 21, 1861, near a creek called Bull Run at the town of Manassas Junction, Virginia, 25 miles from Washington. Everyone knew the battle was coming. Spectators with picnic baskets followed the Union army out of Washington to watch from the surrounding hillsides. Among the southerners who came to watch was Edmund Ruffin.

The Confederates stretched a defensive line eight miles along Bull Run and waited for the attack. Along their interior lines, the Confederates made the first strategic use of the railroad to shift reinforcements quickly from the Shenandoah Valley to the Manassas battlefield. The battle itself, fought by poorly trained and untested troops, resembled a brutal struggle between two armed mobs more than a well-executed set of maneuvers. Still, the arrival of Confederate reinforcements proved crucial. And the first battle of Bull Run did establish at least one new military reputation. A southern officer named Thomas J. Jackson, perched on his horse "like a stone wall," inspired his men to drive back the Union advance. The green Union troops retreated. Heading east toward Washington, frightened spectators clogged the road in panic, and the retreat turned into a rout. It would not be the last time "Stonewall" Jackson would give the Union army grief.

Most southerners were ecstatic, even overconfident, after their victory. By contrast, the chaos in the Union ranks shocked the North into realizing that this would be no 90-day war. To discipline the Union troops, Lincoln put George B. McClellan in command of the Army of the Potomac.

The defeat also prompted northerners to start thinking about emancipation. When the war began, the Republicans were pledged to leave slavery undisturbed. Butler's contraband policy was the first crack in that pledge, and the Union defeat at Bull Run drove the first wedge into it. Only weeks before Bull Run, Congress had passed a resolution reaffirming that the aim of the war was only the restoration of the Union. Even radical Republicans held their tongues. But the humiliating Union defeat changed all of that. Churches and civic associations across the North began sending petitions declaring that the war could not be won without destroying the slave system that had caused the war. Union soldiers began saying such things in their letters and diaries. The radicals argued that emancipation was a "military necessity."

Signaling this shift, the Republican-dominated Congress passed a Confiscation Act within weeks after Bull Run. For the first time, the federal government committed itself to confiscating any property, including slaves, used to prosecute the war against the United States. Strictly speaking, neither confiscated nor contraband slaves were emancipated.

Most Republicans, the radicals included, worried that the Constitution prohibited the government from permanently confiscating property, slaves included. Technically, confiscated slaves would have to be returned to their owners once the war ended. But Lincoln signed the act anyway, and more than a few northern commanders began enforcing the law somewhat liberally.

By the fall of 1861 the Union army was relying on the labor of fugitive slaves to support the northern effort, thus stretching the definition of "military necessity." In his first annual message in December, Lincoln urged Congress to pass legislation encouraging the four border states still in the Union to sell their slaves to the federal government, which would then "liberate" them, along with the contrabands. As 1862 began, the nature of the Civil War was already changing.

Also among the North's war aims was its determination to keep England and France from recognizing the Confederate government, which in turn hoped to keep Europeans from respecting the Union blockade of southern ports. A diplomatic crisis loomed in late 1861 when a Union navy captain intercepted a British ship, the *Trent*, in Havana and forced two Confederate commissioners to disembark before allowing the *Trent* to sail on. The commissioners had slipped through the blockade and were headed for Europe, hoping to secure diplomatic recognition of the Confederacy. When the British protested, the administration wisely released them. "One war at a time," Lincoln said.

Mobilizing for War

By the end of the first summer, both sides realized that the conflict would last for more than a few months and would demand every resource the North and South could command. But in 1860 neither side had many military resources to command. By the end of the war approximately 2.1 million men had served in the Union armed forces and another 900,000 in the Confederacy. To raise and sustain such numbers was an immense political and social problem. To feed, clothe, and arm them was an equally immense technological problem. To pay for such armed forces was an immense economic problem. The Civil War became a test of the competing economies of the North and the South (see Figure 15–1).

The Confederate States of America

By the spring of 1861 secessionists had persuaded 11 states to leave the Union. In a constitutional convention in Montgomery, Alabama, they drafted a basic charter for their new government, the Confederate States of America, with its capital at Richmond, Virginia. They selected as president an experienced politician and Mississippi planter, Jefferson Davis.

The Confederate constitution varied in interesting ways from the U.S. Constitution. The Confederate chief executive served a single, six-year term and had a line-item veto, for example. But the most important differences had to do with slavery. The slaveholders preferred their markets the same way they preferred their power over the slaves—without restraints. The free market in slaves captured this dual preference perfectly. So it made sense that the Confederate constitution defined slaves as property and protected slavery as an inviolable right of property. It also made sense that the Confederacy's constitution

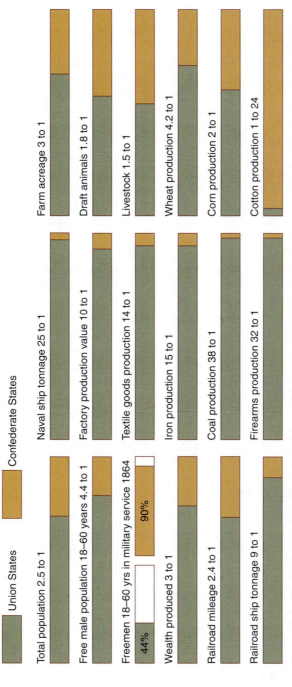

Figure 15–1   The Productive Capacities of the Union and Confederacy   Not only did the northern economy dwarf the South's industrial capacity, it also outpaced southern agricultural production in everything but cotton.

Union States
Confederate States

Total population 2.5 to 1

Free male population 18–60 years 4.4 to 1

Freemen 18–60 yrs in military service 1864

44%   90%

Wealth produced 3 to 1

Railroad mileage 2.4 to 1

Railroad ship tonnage 9 to 1

Naval ship tonnage 25 to 1

Factory production value 10 to 1

Textile goods production 14 to 1

Iron production 15 to 1

Coal production 38 to 1

Firearms production 32 to 1

Farm acreage 3 to 1

Draft animals 1.8 to 1

Livestock 1.5 to 1

Wheat production 4.2 to 1

Corn production 2 to 1

Cotton production 1 to 24

outlawed protective tariffs and severely restricted the government's power to build rail-roads, canals, and turnpikes. This was the fundamental charter of a highly commercial-ized slave society.

There were also several political differences between the United States of America and the Confederate States of America. The most striking was the absence of a two-party system in the South. The Whig Party had collapsed in the North during the early 1850s, and the Republican Party took its place. Throughout the war, the northern Democrats represented a strong but loyal opposition to the Lincoln administration. In the South, by contrast, the Democratic Party ruled without opposition after the Whigs collapsed.

A consistent source of tension was the South's commitment to states' rights, which often conflicted with the need to mount a concerted defense of the new nation. This led to conflicts between Jefferson Davis and several state governors, in particular Joseph E. Brown of Georgia and Zebulon Vance of North Carolina. Brown and Vance were loyal Confederates, but in their zeal to protect their states, they frequently locked horns with the Confederate president.

It is not clear how any of these political and constitutional differences affected the outcome of the war. Southerners realized soon enough that their devotion to the free mar-ket would lose them the war. In the end the Confederacy would sustain itself with a com-mand economy the likes of which the United States has never seen, before or since. Abra-ham Lincoln was certainly more personable than his Confederate counterpart and better able than the prickly Davis to slough off his critics. But Lincoln's critics were, if anything, more threatening than Davis's. Northern opponents of the war were sometimes violent, though more often they expressed their opposition through the Democratic Party. Like Davis, Lincoln had to deal with obstreperous states, and at least a few northern gover-nors seemed determined to undermine the Union war effort. Both presidents suspended habeas corpus and jailed dissidents to counteract the threat of internal subversion. And whatever its weaknesses, the Confederate government managed to survive for four years against a massive Union invasion. In the end, the Confederacy failed because its armies, not its politics, were weaker than the Union's.

Union Naval Supremacy

The conviction that commerce ruled the world came naturally to the leaders of southern slave society. At the start of the war Confederate strategists believed they could bring their enemies to heel by starving them of cotton. By withholding their most valuable cash crop from the market, they would cripple northern industry and force England to recognize Confederate independence.

The Yankees knew better. From the outset northern strategists hoped to use their superior naval forces to prevent the Confederacy from selling its cotton abroad. By the closing months of 1861, the Union navy controlled vast stretches of the Atlantic and Gulf coasts. By early 1862, Union forces were in a position to enforce their blockade, except for a magnificent new weapon designed to thwart Union naval supremacy.

The South refitted an old Union ship, the *Merrimac*, with thick iron plates that ren-dered it all but impervious to conventional weapons. Rechristened the *Virginia*, the iron-clad ship sailed into Union-controlled waters at Hampton Roads, Virginia, on March 8, 1862, and wrought havoc on helpless northern ships. But that night the Union's own ironclad, the *Monitor*, arrived from New York. For most of the next day the "battle of the ironclads" raged on, with neither vessel dominating. The standoff left the Union navy in control of the coast and better able to enforce its blockade. After the battle the *Virginia* slipped up the James River to assist in the defense of Richmond, but in May the Confederates destroyed the ironclad rather than allowing it to be captured by Union forces.

Beyond the blockade, the greatest achievements of the Union navy came in those rare but crucial occasions when it launched joint operations with the army. This was not easy, with no Pentagon and no Joint Chiefs of Staff to coordinate the two branches of the military. Any joint army-navy ventures would depend on the commanders involved or on the direct participation of President Lincoln—the only person who could issue orders to both branches of the armed services. There were successful joint operations early in the war—at Port Royal in November 1861, the capture of New Orleans in early 1862, and the collaboration between U. S. Grant and Andrew Foote in the capture of Forts Henry and Donelson a few months later. But just as often, communication broke down and the results—in the unsuccessful effort to capture Charleston and in the Red River campaign of 1864—were disastrous. Still, by the end of the war the Union had built one of the largest and most modern navies in the world, not to be matched in American history until World War II.

Southern Military Advantages

The Union dominated the naval war, but on land the Confederates had several advantages. More southerners had gone to military academies than had northerners, and early on they brought skill and discipline to the Confederate army that the Union could not match. The South's greatest advantage, however, was that it was defending its own territory. It did not have to invade the North, destroy the Union army, or wipe out the North's industrial capacity. Closer to their sources of supply, southern armies operated in the midst of a friendly civilian population, except for the slaves.

By contrast, the North had to fight an offensive war. It had to invade the South, destroy the Confederate armies, capture and retain a huge territory, and wipe out the South's capacity to fight. Northern soldiers fought on unfamiliar ground surrounded by a hostile civilian population, not counting the slaves.

The Union required longer lines of supply and much larger provisions. An invading northern army of 100,000 men had to carry with it 2,500 wagons and 35,000 animals. It consumed 600 tons of supplies a day. The further it penetrated southern territory, the more men were needed to maintain increasingly tenuous supply lines. The more territory Union troops conquered, the more they were shifted from battle duty to occupation forces. As a result, many major battles were fought by roughly even numbers of Union and Confederate troops.

Even in battle the defensive posture of the Confederate army was an advantage. Forts and cities on high ground (such as Vicksburg and Fredericksburg) could defend against large numbers of invading troops. In the invasion of northern Virginia in 1864, Confederate general Robert E. Lee repeatedly held off much larger Union forces.

Besides his commitment to destroying enemy armies rather than capturing territory, Lincoln developed a second basic strategy for overcoming the South's advantage in operating from interior lines. To take advantage of the North's superior numbers, Lincoln wanted his generals to launch coordinated attacks on different southern armies at different times. This strategy had worked in New Orleans. Once Farragut's naval forces had breached Confederate defenses on the lower Mississippi River, the army was able to capture New Orleans without a fight because the southern troops had been pulled from the city to meet Grant's army at Shiloh. But Lincoln found that launching coordinated attacks was easier on paper than it was in practice. Until the end of the war the commander in chief was frustrated by Union generals who did not press their armies forward in time, allowing Confederates to continue shifting their own forces to meet Union assaults that came one after another rather than all at once.

The Slave Economy in Wartime

Secessionists argued that slavery gave the South several clear military assets. Because they were agricultural workers, the slaves could be shifted easily from cash crops to foodstuffs. With this single stroke, the Confederacy could feed its civilians, supply its armies, and cripple the enemy by starving the industrial world's mills of desperately needed cotton. With slaves at home doing the work, a very high proportion of white men were able to serve in the southern military. Within the Confederate armies slaves and free blacks were impressed into nonmilitary service as construction workers, teamsters, nurses, and cooks, freeing up more white soldiers to fight. In all of these ways slavery reduced the North's advantage in the number of military-age men.

The relative backwardness of the slave economy had certain military advantages. Because of slavery the South had remained a largely rural society. Southern country boys could shoot guns and ride horses better than shopkeepers and factory workers in the Yankee armies. In the first years of the war the southern cavalry was far superior to its northern counterpart, and many white southerners assumed that one average Confederate could easily whip two Yankees.

But the southerners assumed incorrectly. They overestimated England's dependence on American cotton and underestimated the strength of Britain's economic ties to the North. The English refused to break the blockade of the South or grant diplomatic recognition to the Confederacy. King Cotton diplomacy failed, and so did the slave economy. If slavery freed 60 percent of southern men for military service, it kept from military service the 40 percent of the population that was enslaved. With masters and their sons off to war, farm productivity collapsed, and in the end the rural South had trouble feeding itself. It also became harder to control the slaves left behind and, when Union armies approached, harder still to keep slaves from running off. Even the superiority of the southern cavalry gave way as the growing use of rifles made traditional cavalry charges deadly.

Above all, slavery diminished the South's industrial strength. Ninety percent of the nation's factories were in the North. Furthermore, the bulk of the Confederacy's industrial capacity was located in the upper South, which was overrun by Union forces early in the war. Even if its arms and supplies were severely restricted, the South did manage to produce enough rifles, gunpowder, and ammunition. Generally well armed, the Confederate soldier was not well fed or well clothed and often fought in rags and barefoot.

Slavery also crippled the South's ability to finance its war. The cotton crop was systematically embargoed. Because slaves earned no income, they could not be taxed as northern workers were, and white southerners remained true to the Jacksonian tradition of resistance to taxation. To finance its military campaign, the South began to print money in huge quantities. By 1865 a Confederate dollar had the purchasing power that one Confederate cent had had in 1861.

In the North, prospering farms and growing factories generated substantial taxable income. In addition to the $600 million raised from taxes on incomes and personal property, the government eventually sold $1.5 billion worth of Union bonds and also floated war bonds. The North also supplemented its tax revenues by printing money, the famous "greenbacks," which became legally acceptable as currency everywhere in the country. To ease the flow of so many dollars, the Republicans passed the National Bank Act in 1863. This law rationalized the monetary system, making the federal government what it remains today, the only printer of money and the arbiter of the rules governing the nation's banks.

On balance the southern slave economy did remarkably well. The Confederacy staggered through the war with ragged soldiers, starving civilians, makeshift factories, and inflated currency. But as long as it could sustain its armies in the field, the Confederacy survived. Johnny Reb and Billy Yank had the ammunition they needed to fight. The question was, did they have the will to fight on and the commanders they needed to win the war?

What Were Soldiers Fighting For?

Political, military, and economic differences are the tangible reasons that armies win or lose wars, but there are also important psychological reasons. Southern soldiers fought from a variety of motives, but above all, they fought to protect their homes and their families from Yankee invasion. Most Confederate soldiers took for granted that they were fighting to preserve slavery, and they saw the threat to slavery in personal terms, even when they themselves owned no slaves. In the southern economy slavery was the only real avenue of advancement. To own a slave was a symbol of mastery, but more than that, it was the source of prosperity.

The defense of homes and slaves gave southern patriotism a concrete and individualistic flavor. The "spirit of 1776" loomed large in the letters and diaries of Confederate soldiers, who saw themselves fighting to preserve the rights and liberties that their forefathers had won from Great Britain. But the right they fought for was the right to own slaves, and the liberty they defended was freedom from government interference with slavery.

Nevertheless, class distinctions affected the levels of patriotism in the Confederate army. Slaveholders and their sons were far more likely to express patriotic sentiments than were soldiers from yeoman families. Troops from states in which slavery was relatively unimportant, such as North Carolina, were less enthusiastic about the war than were troops from states such as South Carolina in which slavery was strong.

Class divisions were less severe in the Union army. Impoverished immigrants sometimes joined the military to secure a steady income or a substantial bounty. But Catholic immigrants were less likely to fight than native-born Protestants. The most common motivation among northern soldiers was also patriotism. They, too, thought of themselves as the proud protectors of America's revolutionary heritage, but their patriotism was more abstract. Unlike the Confederates, Yankee troops were not fighting to protect their homes and families. Rather, they were fighting in defense of northern society in general, for an idealized notion of what America meant. The Union as a "beacon of liberty" throughout the world was a common theme in the letters and diaries of northern soldiers.

Most northern soldiers believed that slavery had caused the war, but only a few were motivated by antislavery principles, and many denied that they were risking their lives to free slaves. As civilian soldiers, they reflected shifts in northern public opinion against slavery. Antislavery views became more common beginning in late 1861, and soldiers' views changed with the tides of war. There were racist backlashes among Yankee troops, but there was also growing support for the abolition of slavery. By the end of the conflict most northern soldiers believed that to restore the Union and destroy the Confederacy they would have to abolish slavery as well.

The Civil War Becomes a Social Revolution

By 1862 the North and the South had built up powerful military machines. At the same time, the North's war aims were shifting to include the abolition of slavery and the destruction of the southern social system. In the spring and summer of 1862, Republicans in Congress and the Lincoln administration adopted the view that emancipation was a military necessity. Within a year they would point to the abolition of slavery to justify the increasingly bloody war. Throughout the South a civil war erupted within the Civil War. As the Union army swept through the South gathering up thousands of slaves fleeing for freedom, the South unleashed a campaign of violence and intimidation aimed at thwarting the unfolding process of emancipation. The outcome of this civil war on the ground depended on the fate of the Union and Confederate armies on the field of battle.

Union Victories in the West

In early February 1862, the Union army and navy joined in an aggressive strike deep into Confederate Tennessee. Assisted by the naval bombardment under the direction of Andrew Foote, Ulysses S. Grant's Union forces captured Fort Henry on the Tennessee River and, shortly thereafter, Fort Donelson on the Cumberland River (see Map 15–2). To the shock of Confederate officers at Fort Donelson, Grant insisted on "unconditional and immediate surrender."

The war's growing ferocity became clear eight weeks later, at the battle of Shiloh. General P. G. T. Beauregard, the hero of Fort Sumter and Manassas, caught Grant's troops off guard at a peach orchard at Shiloh Church in southern Tennessee. The Confederate's surprise attack on April 6 forced the Union lines steadily backward, although the line did not break. Beauregard telegraphed Richmond with news of his victory. But on the morning of April 7, Confederate troops were stunned by a Union counterattack that pushed Beauregard's army back over the ground it had taken the day before. When the Confederates finally retreated, the two armies had suffered an astounding 23,741 casualties, dwarfing all previous losses but foreshadowing things to come. The Civil War was quickly becoming a fight for the total destruction of the enemy.

With Confederate forces busy at Shiloh, New Orleans had few defenses beyond two forts on the Mississippi River 75 miles south of the city. But they were impressive forts. It took six days of Yankee bombardment before Union commander David Farragut attempted to break through. In the middle of the night of April 24, his fleet pushed upriver through a blaze of burning rafts and Confederate gunfire that lit up the sky. Within a few days the Confederates evacuated both forts, and New Orleans fell to Union forces.

Union victories in the West gave rise to northern optimism that war would be over by summer. Republicans seized the mood to enact a bold legislative agenda. During the first half of 1862 Congress and President Lincoln substantially reorganized the structure

Map 15–2   The War in the West in 1862 As Union armies floundered in the East, northern troops in the West won a decisive series of battles. Here the nature of the war changed. First, General Ulysses S. Grant demanded "unconditional surrender" of the southern troops at Forts Henry and Donelson. Then a bloody battle at Shiloh foreshadowed the increasing brutality of the war. Finally, the western theater produced two of the Union's most effective generals, Grant and William Tecumseh Sherman.

of national government in the North. Lincoln appointed Edwin M. Stanton as secretary of war and named Henry Wager Halleck as general in chief of the Union forces. Stanton was not much of a military strategist, and Halleck, who was said to be, was paralyzed when it came to giving orders to commanders in the field. But both were effective bureaucrats, and, with the help of the Quartermaster General Montgomery Meigs and a brilliant railroad engineer named Henry Haupt, they built a powerful war-making machine that kept the huge, far-flung Union armies well supplied.

Congress was also active. For years Democratic majorities had blocked passage of laws that Republicans considered essential. Now the Republicans had the votes and the popular support to push their agenda through Congress. They began with a critical financial reform. To sustain the integrity of the currency, the Republicans passed a Legal Tender Act protecting northern greenbacks from inflationary pressure. To maintain military manpower, they instituted the first draft in United States history. In addition, in 1862 they established a system of land-grant colleges designed to promote agricultural development and passed a Homestead Act offering land at low prices to settlers in the West. Finally, the Republicans financed the construction of the nation's first transcontinental railroad. Together these laws reflected the Republican Party's commitment to the active use of the government to preserve the Union and promote capitalist development.

The Confederate government also reformed its bureaucracy to sustain its military struggle. Southern leaders realized that it was a mistake to withhold the region's cotton from the world market. A year into the war the Confederate economy was showing signs of the weakness that would lead it to the brink of complete financial collapse. As a remedy the Confederate Congress passed a comprehensive tax code, but with disappointing results. In April 1862 the Confederacy established a national military draft. By centralizing taxation and conscription, however, Jefferson Davis's government created powerful resistance from advocates of states' rights. Thus, whereas victories in the West allowed northern Republicans to enact an expansive legislative agenda, the Confederate government had trouble winning popular support for its own centralizing measures, despite the success of its troops in the Peninsula campaign of 1862.

Southern Military Strength in the East

In the Peninsula campaign, the Union army sought to capture the Confederate capital, Richmond, as Lincoln expected George B. McClellan to do as commander of the Army of the Potomac. McClellan's great strength was his ability to administer and train a huge army, instilling discipline and restoring troop morale after the defeat of Bull Run. But McClellan was reluctant to fight, exaggerating the size of his opponents' forces and demanding more troops before he would take the offensive. Throughout the fall and winter of 1861 and 1862, McClellan stubbornly resisted Lincoln's suggestions to attack. Vain and arrogant, McClellan held all politicians in contempt, and none more than the president.

Under intense pressure, and with his own reputation at stake, McClellan did devise an elaborate strategy to capture Richmond. He very slowly moved his huge army of 112,000 men up the peninsula between the York and James rivers. Instead of directly attacking Richmond, however, McClellan dug in at Yorktown, overestimating the size of his enemy. The Confederates quickly learned to manipulate McClellan's weaknesses. They moved small numbers of soldiers back and forth to make him think there were more enemy troops than there really were and planted fake cannons along their lines. Then, during the night of May 4, 1862, the outnumbered Confederates withdrew toward Richmond. When McClellan discovered their escape, he declared it a Union victory.

The Army of the Potomac inched its way toward Richmond, but it never took the offensive. Instead, it was the Confederates, initially led by General Joseph E. Johnston, who forced Union troops into battle. The southerners attacked the divided Union forces at Seven Pines on May 31, and both sides took heavy losses. Far more serious were the brutal battles of the Seven Days beginning in late June. During this campaign Johnston was wounded and replaced by Robert E. Lee, who repulsed but did not destroy McClellan's larger army. Still, Lee had saved Richmond and sent the Union army back to new fortifications at Harrison's Landing, where McClellan sat until he was finally ordered to bring his big army back to Washington, D.C. There McClellan did for his troops what he did best: He revived their sagging morale and whipped them back into shape. But he still would not do the fighting. Defying the desperate orders of Lincoln and Halleck, McClellan let Union general John Pope take the offensive alone. Hampered by generals loyal to McClellan, Pope led his troops to a disastrous defeat at the second battle of Bull Run (August 29–30), while McClellan's huge army stood by.

By the fall of 1862, the Union and Confederate forces had reached a military stalemate. The North had scored tremendous victories in the West. In the East, however, Robert E. Lee turned out to be one of the most skillful and daring commanders of the war. Stonewall Jackson, Lee's "right arm," had also proven himself brilliantly aggressive.

Having turned back the Union invasion on the peninsula and defeated the Union army in a second battle at Bull Run, Lee decided to invade the North. He hoped the Confederacy could win the war in the East before losing it in the West. Lee marched his confident troops across the Potomac into Maryland, where he was met by McClellan's army at Sharpsburg, beside Antietam Creek, on September 17.

McClellan nearly lost Antietam. He had Lee's plans in advance, but he took his time and squandered the advantage. Once engaged, McClellan launched his troops in consecutive assaults rather than a single simultaneous maneuver, allowing the Confederates to shift their men around the battlefield as fighting moved to different locations. He held back his reinforcements, missing a chance to break the center of the vulnerable Confederate line. The delay gave Confederate reinforcements time to arrive and turn back an attack on Lee's right. But the Union troops fought with astonishing determination, and Lee's men suffered staggering casualties. His invasion blocked, Lee quickly retreated back into Virginia. It might have been even worse for the South, but despite intense pressure from Washington, McClellan refused to send his fresh reserves after the disoriented southerners as they fell back across the Potomac. When McClellan boasted that his army had forced the Confederates off "our soil," Lincoln fumed, "It's *all* 'our soil.'" The point was not to send Lee's army back to Virginia but to defeat it. The president had run out of patience and after the fall elections fired McClellan. A total of 4,800 soldiers died and 18,000 more were wounded at Antietam, the single bloodiest day of the war. Nevertheless, Antietam was a Union victory, and Lincoln used it to announce an important shift in northern war aims.

Emancipation as a Military Necessity

By the summer of 1862, northern public opinion was shifting in favor of emancipation. Slave laborers were sustaining the Confederacy, feeding southern troops, building their fortifications , and driving mules for rebel regiments. Emancipation took on a double character for many northerners. It was both a military necessity and a moral good.

Union advances in the plantation South in early 1862 had produced a flood of runaway slaves pouring across northern lines. As slaves escaped from their masters, Union commanders responded in a variety of ways. Some put the contrabands to work behind Union lines. Others sent the runaways back into slavery, to the horror of African Americans and the dismay of northern radicals. To clarify the situation, in March 1862 Congress prohibited the use of Union troops to return fugitives to the South. Union commanders and soldiers interpreted the law as an invitation to sweep even larger numbers

Map 15–3 The Battle of Antietam In September 1862, southern General Robert E. Lee led the Confederacy's first invasion of the North. He was stopped at Sharpsburg, Maryland, by Union troops under the command of George B. McClellan. Antietam was the bloodiest single day of the war, but it was an important turning point for the North. It gave Lincoln the victory he was waiting for to announce the preliminary Emancipation Proclamation.

of slaves off their farms and plantations. During the first year of the war, slaves drifted into Union lines in small numbers. By the middle of 1862 they were coming in by the thousands. A new phase in the process of emancipation had begun.

In April Congress moved further by abolishing slavery in Washington, D.C. For the first time, the federal government exercised the power to emancipate slaves. In June 1862

AMERICA AND THE WORLD
....

>> The Diplomacy of Emancipation

"The Emancipation Proclamation," Henry Adams wrote from London, "has done more for us here than all our former victories and all our diplomacy. It is creating an almost convulsive reaction in our favor." Adams was part of the American legation that had been struggling since the war began to prevent England and other European nations from formally recognizing the Confederate States of America. It was unlikely that England would do so, and unlikely that France would do it if England did not. But there were powerful elements in Britain who openly hoped for Union defeat and called for diplomatic recognition of the Confederacy. With every northern military reversal, the South's supporters grew more vocal. The Emancipation Proclamation tilted the diplomatic balance irreversibly in favor of the North. Huge pro-Union rallies across England declared their support for Union and freedom. At Exeter Hall in London one of the largest such rallies "has had a powerful effect," Richard Cobden declared. "It has closed the mouths of those who have been advocating the side of the South. Recognition of the South, by England, whilst it bases itself on slavery, is an impossibility."

There was a similar reaction across Europe. As soon as Lincoln proclaimed the emancipation of the slaves as one of the war aims of the Union, nearly all diplomatic support for the Confederacy was silenced. After January 1, 1863, only the complete military victory of the South over the North could have won substantial diplomatic recognition for the Confederacy. Whatever the Emancipation Proclamation meant for slavery in the South, it signaled the diplomatic triumph of the North.

Congress prohibited slavery in the western territories. The following month a second Confiscation Act was passed, declaring "forever free" the slaves of any "traitors" engaged in rebellion against the United States. Congress also passed a militia act making it possible for "persons of African descent" to join the Union army.

But there was only so much Congress could do. Many Republicans, even radicals, worried that Congress had no constitutional right to liberate the slaves coming into Union lines. If such an authority existed, it resided in the war powers of the commander in chief. Congress could confiscate slaves, but only President Lincoln could emancipate them. Lincoln believed that because slaves were not "property" under the Constitution, he could free slaves by virtue of his war powers. The only question was when to invoke those powers.

Lincoln had always hated slavery, but he did not want to risk an antiwar backlash by moving ahead of public opinion. But public opinion was changing. He was searching for a dramatic gesture to break the military stalemate and convince European powers to side

Tredegar Iron Works in Richmond, Virginia, 1865 This was the South's largest industrial plant. Because the South lagged so far behind the North in industrial capacity, protecting the Tredegar works was essential to the Confederate war effort.

with the Union, and an Emancipation Proclamation would certainly be dramatic. Then, too, something had to be done to clarify the status of the thousands of slave refugees now pouring into Union lines.

On July 22, 1862, Lincoln told his cabinet that he had decided to issue an Emancipation Proclamation. But Secretary of State William Seward warned the president that recent military losses in Virginia would make such a proclamation seem like an act of desperation to the rest of the world. Lincoln agreed. He would wait for a battlefield victory to make his proclamation public. Antietam was that victory. On September 22, five days after Lee was turned back, Lincoln issued a preliminary proclamation threatening to free the slaves in areas still in rebellion 100 days later. One month later he proposed a plan of gradual emancipation in all areas under Union control. Nobody expected any of the seceded states to return to the Union, and on January 1, 1863, Lincoln issued his Emancipation Proclamation.

Reactions were swift and predictable. Jefferson Davis, the president of the Confederate States of America, denounced Lincoln's proclamation as the most despicable act "in the history of guilty man." Abolitionists and free blacks rejoiced and celebrated proclamation day at gatherings across the North. Other northerners, particularly Democrats, were enraged by the idea that the war was being fought to free the slaves, and some northern soldiers were embittered. "I came out to fight for the restoration of the Union . . .," one northern soldier wrote, "not to free the niggers." But most Union troops already knew that for the war to end the South had to be destroyed, and with it the institution of slavery.

Company E, 4th United States Colored Infantry, at Fort Lincoln, Washington DC, 1865 African Americans serving in the Union Army symbolized the revolutionary turn the Civil War took once emancipation became the policy of the North. Despite overwhelming loss of life among the African American troops, their bravery impressed many northerners and helped change white attitudes about the goals of the Civil War.

The proclamation itself was both a reaction and a spur to emancipation. Thousands of slaves had been escaping to Union lines throughout 1862, but it took Lincoln's proclamation to clarify their status as free. The proclamation also increased the pace of emancipation in the South. In low-country South Carolina and New Orleans, slaves celebrated their freedom on January 1, 1863, even though those areas were under Union occupation and were therefore technically unaffected by the proclamation. Union advances across the South helped more slaves to flee, especially from plantations from which the master and his sons were away in the army. It made no difference whether a master had been kind or cruel; the slaves left anyway. "We were all laboring under a delusion," one South Carolina planter confessed. "I believed that these people were content, happy, and attached to their masters."

Emancipation in Practice: Contraband Camps and Black Troops

The shift in Union policy solved the biggest obstacle to emancipation: it gave the slaves somewhere to go when they left their farms and plantations. There had always been runaway slaves, but with nowhere to go, most ended up returning to their masters. The U.S. government now gave them options. In areas occupied by Union troops early in the war, such as the Sea Islands off South Carolina, the masters had abandoned their plantations

>> Freedman's Village, Arlington, Virginia

When Mary Lee's father died in 1857, her husband, Robert E. Lee, became executor of the family's plantation at Arlington, Virginia, across the Potomac River from Washington, D.C. The will stipulated that the slaves at Arlington were to be freed, but because the estate was burdened with debts, Lee had the will revoked and took charge of the plantation himself. He began selling off slaves, and within a few years he had broken up all but one of the slave families on the plantation. Expecting to be freed, the slaves were instead worked harder than ever. Lee, they complained, was a "hard taskmaster" and "the worst man I ever saw." They began running away.

When the Civil War broke out, the areas surrounding Washington, D.C.—including Arlington—came under the control of the Union army almost immediately. When Congress abolished slavery in the nation's capital on April 12, 1862, large numbers of contraband slaves began escaping into the city from nearby Virginia and Maryland. After Lincoln issued his Emancipation Proclamation on January 1, 1863, the contraband camps in Washington were soon overcrowded and overwhelmed. In May Union officials decided to move the contrabands to a new location, Freedman's Village, to be constructed on the Lee estate at Arlington. Freedman's Village would serve two distinct purposes. First, it would remove the freed people from the crowded, unhealthy camps in the city, where diseases spread rapidly. Second, Freedman's Village was also designed as a model for the dozens of contraband camps springing up across the South as more and more slaves came into Union lines and were freed.

By 1864 Freedman's Village had 50 homes and as many as 2,000 residents. There was a hospital, a laundry, a kitchen, a home for elderly slaves, and a schoolhouse. The buildings were neatly arranged around the pond, and the Village became a destination for dignitaries and journalists. But there were complaints from the freed people about the rigid rules they were expected to follow. To pay for the camp the residents were expected to work in adjoining fields. They earned $10 per month but had to pay back half for the upkeep of the camp. That was hardly enough, they complained, to set them on the road to economic independence. Yet despite attempts by the government to close Freedman's Village down, the freed people resisted, and the camp remained open until the end of the century.

By then, however, Arlington had been transformed yet again. On June 15, 1864, the quartermaster general of the Union armies, Montgomery Meigs, wrote to the secretary of war, Edwin M. Stanton, suggesting that "the land surrounding the Arlington Mansion, now understood to be the property of the United States, be appropriated as a National Military Cemetery." Stanton approved the proposal, and within weeks the bodies of Union soldiers were being laid to rest at Arlington. Meigs saw to it that the graves were laid out "encircling" the mansion house, and, in the garden once cultivated by Lee's mother-in-law, Meigs placed a mass grave of unknown soldiers who had died at Manassas. By June of 1864 there were 2,600 Union soldiers buried at Arlington National Cemetery.

No one missed the symbolism. By 1863 Robert E. Lee was the Confederacy's most daunting military commander. To northerners, he was a symbol of treason as well.

What could be more appropriate than to turn his family's plantation first into a model village for former slaves and then into a national grave for fallen Union soldiers? The cemetery would survive, but Freedman's Village would disappear, and with it the hope for the future it once represented.

and their slaves were, in Lincoln's words, "thus liberated." In occupied regions where the masters remained, such as West Virginia and southern Louisiana, Lincoln required those states to emancipate their slaves as a precondition for admission or readmission to the Union. For slaves who left their farms and plantations, the Union provided two options: contraband camps and the Union army.

As the number of slave refugees grew, Union commanders began constructing massive contraband camps across the South. Yet the Union was unprepared for the huge numbers pouring into the makeshift camps. Diseases, especially smallpox, raged through the camps. Food and shelter were in short supply. For some slaves the filth and disorder of the camps were so terrible that they went back to their farms and plantations. Over time, however, the army and northern volunteers learned to organize the camps more efficiently. Just across the Potomac River from Washington, D.C., on the Arlington estate that had been owned by Robert E. Lee's family, the government built a model contraband camp known as "Freedman's Village." It had a school, a hospital, and a cemetery that was the nucleus for what would later become Arlington National Cemetery.

But most contraband camps were temporary, set up quickly as Union troops moved through an area and just as quickly taken down. The camps were transfer points—the first place slaves went before the army shipped them off to permanent camps or to cities outside the war zones. The camps were a major development in the history of emancipation. For the first time the slaves, particularly women, children, and the elderly, had somewhere to go once they escaped from their masters.

The second place for slaves to go, at least for young men, was the Union army. Although they had fought in the American Revolution and the War of 1812, blacks had never been allowed in the regular army. The Militia Act of 1862 finally allowed black troops. Lincoln was at first reluctant, but by the end of the year he became an active supporter of black enlistment. His final Emancipation Proclamation not only declared all rebel slaves free, it also sanctioned the enlistment of African Americans in the Union army. "The bare sight of 50,000 armed and drilled black soldiers upon the banks of the Mississippi," he said in March 1863, "would end the rebellion at once." Before the war was over, 186,000 blacks had joined, 134,111 of them recruited in the South.

For African Americans, especially for former slaves, the experience of fighting a war for emancipation was exhilarating. In a society with increasingly sharp distinctions between men and women, slaves who became soldiers often felt as though they were becoming men. "Now we sogers are men," one black sergeant explained, "men the first time in our lives."

Black Union troops were an astonishing spectacle for those still enslaved, but to white southerners, this was the "world turned upside down." As African American troops marched through the streets of southern cities, whites shrieked in horror and could barely control their rage and indignation. But southern whites were not alone in their opposition to the revolutionary turn the Civil War had taken.

Although they made up nearly 10 percent of the Union army, black soldiers were never treated as the equals of white soldiers. Few African American officers were commissioned, and black soldiers were paid less than whites. They were often held back from combat for fear that Confederates would kill them if captured. But blacks performed respectably in combat and changed the minds of many northern whites. Black soldiers were among the most aggressive in spreading emancipation still further across the Confederacy. Moreover, their numbers tipped the balance of northern and southern forces decisively in favor of the Union army, thereby contributing critically to the defeat of the Confederacy.

The War at Home

African American troops could not end the rebellion "at once," as Lincoln hoped. The war persisted for two more years, and as body counts rose and hardships mounted, civilians in the North and the South began to register their discontent.

The Care of Casualties

At Shiloh, 24,000 men had fallen in two days of fighting. Almost as many fell during a single day of fighting at Antietam. The following year 50,000 men would die or suffer wounds at Gettysburg. At the battles of Chickamauga and Franklin, Tennessee, Confederate troops would suffer appalling losses. And in Grant's struggle against Lee in the spring of 1864, both sides would lose 100,000 men in seven weeks. Casualties, partly due to inept leadership and inadequately prepared troops, were mostly the result of military technology outpacing battlefield tactics. Generals ordered traditional charges on enemy lines even though newly developed rifles and repeating carbines made such assaults almost suicidal.

If new military technology multiplied the casualties, primitive medical practices did even more damage. Of the 620,000 soldiers who died, two out of three were felled by disease. Thousands of soldiers were killed by contaminated water, spoiled food, inadequate clothing and shelter, mosquitoes, and vermin. Crowded military camps bred dysentery, diarrhea, malaria, and typhoid fever. Nobody knew what "germs" were nor that sterilization made any difference. No one knew what caused typhoid fever or malaria. There were no antibiotics, and liquor was often the only anesthesia. The only cure for gangrene was amputation, so field hospitals were littered with piles of sawed-off arms and legs.

In one area, nursing, the Civil War advanced the practice of medicine. The Civil War overturned long-standing prejudices against the presence of women in military hospitals.

Hundreds of southern women volunteered their services to Confederate forces. In the North the thousands of women who volunteered their services to the Union army had to overcome barriers against them. In mid-1861, however, northern reformers persuaded Lincoln to recognize the services of the United States Sanitary Commission. A private organization led by men but staffed by thousands of women, the "Sanitary" helped reform the Army Medical Bureau. It established the first ambulance corps for the swift removal of wounded soldiers from the battlefield, pioneered the use of ships and railroad cars as mobile hospital units, and made nursing a respectable profession for women after the war ended.

But these heroic efforts could not undo the fact that the Civil War had caused unprecedented bloodshed. As the war dragged on, and as the aims of the war shifted, Americans voiced their opposition to the policies of the Lincoln and Davis administrations.

Northern Reverses and Antiwar Sentiment

Lincoln struggled for years to find a commander who could stand up to great southern generals such as Robert E. Lee and Stonewall Jackson. For failing to crush Lee's army after Antietam, Lincoln fired McClellan and gave command of the Army of the Potomac to a reluctant Ambrose Burnside. But Burnside could not match Lee's brilliant, unorthodox strategy. At Fredericksburg, Virginia, on December 13, 1862, Lee's army defeated Burnside's men in a calamitous slaughter. Lincoln quickly replaced Burnside with "Fighting Joe" Hooker, a braggart who was scarcely better at fighting than Burnside had been. At Chancellorsville, Virginia, in May 1863, Lee overwhelmed Hooker's forces in one of the bloodiest Union defeats of the war.

Northern military reverses fueled a wave of opposition to emancipation. Northern Democrats had always favored compromise with the South on slavery and continued to argue that the restoration of the Union was the only legitimate aim of the war. In the elections of 1862, Peace Democrats (known as Copperheads) took control of the legislatures

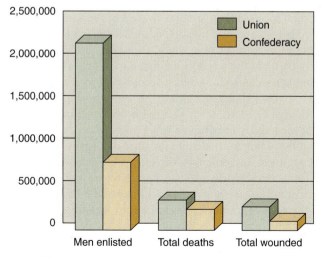

Figure 15–2   Casualties of War

in Illinois and Indiana and threatened to withhold troops. In southern Illinois troops deserted in droves in early 1863, after the Emancipation Proclamation was issued. Democrats were scandalized when the War Department authorized the formation of African American regiments in early 1863.

The beginning of military conscription in March 1863 further outraged northern Democrats. Because northern draftees could escape conscription by paying a $300 commutation fee, many working-class men, especially Irish immigrants, complained that the rich could buy their way out of combat. But although the Irish were underrepresented in the Union army and there were ways for working men to pay the commutation fee, the taint of inequity was so strong that Congress abolished commutation.

Drafting white men to fight for black emancipation provoked anger. Dissent became so widespread that Lincoln claimed the constitutional authority to suspend habeas corpus. The Peace Democrats' leading spokesman, Clement L. Vallandigham, attacked the president's "despotic" measures. If forced to choose between loss of freedom for whites and continued enslavement of African Americans, he said, "I shall not hesitate one moment to choose the latter alternative."

In 1862 whites protesting the drift toward emancipation rioted in several northern cities. In New York City, Irish Democrats rioted in the streets at the opening of a draft office. Working-class immigrants had suffered most from wartime inflation and were most susceptible to competition from African Americans. Their frustration exploded into the New York City draft riots, which began on July 13, 1863, and lasted several days.

Rioters assaulted well-dressed men and attacked the homes of leading Republicans, but they mostly targeted blacks. White mobs lynched a dozen African Americans and set fire to the Colored Orphan Asylum. More than 100 people died, most of them rioters. Violent northern opposition to the war later subsided, partly because the draft riots had discredited the Copperheads but also because of the improving military fortunes of the Union army.

Gettysburg and the Justification of the War

As criticism of the Lincoln administration swelled in the summer of 1863, Lee sensed an opportunity to launch a second invasion of the North. On July 1 the opposing armies converged on the small town of Gettysburg, Pennsylvania. For three days they fought the most decisive battle of the war. On the first day it looked as though the South was on its way to another victory. Confederate troops pushed the Union enemy backward through the town streets and onto the hills to the south. Now in command of the heights, Union general George Gordon Meade secured a two-mile line of high ground during the night. On the second day Lee ordered two flanking attacks and a third assault on the Union center, but the Union line held. On the third day, against the advice of his trusted general James Longstreet, Lee ordered a direct attack by George Pickett's troops on the fortified Union center. Pickett's charge was a devastating loss for the southern troops. On July 4 the Confederates began the retreat back toward the Potomac River, where rising waters trapped them for more than a week. Lincoln furiously urged Meade to go after Lee's trapped army and finish the job. But by the time Meade launched an attack, the river had subsided, and Lee's army escaped. Again, Lincoln was mortified by the insufficiently aggressive instincts of his generals.

Gettysburg—The Aftermath The bodies of dead soldiers litter the battlefield at Gettysburg. Shortly thereafter workers rushed to bury the corpses in time for the dedication of the battlefield as a military cemetery. Lincoln's powerful address promised "a new birth of freedom—and that government of the people, by the people, for the people, shall not perish from the earth."

As northerners celebrated Lee's defeat, news came of another Union victory in the West. For months the Mississippi River town of Vicksburg, Mississippi, had proved invincible, frustrating General Grant. After a series of failed maneuvers Grant laid siege to the town. He cut Vicksburg off from all supplies and waited until its soldiers and civilians were starved into submission. For six weeks the people of Vicksburg lived in caves, bombarded by sharpshooters during the day and by cannon fire at night. They subsisted on mules and rats. On June 28, Confederate soldiers inside the city threatened mutiny, and less than a week later, Vicksburg surrendered. His experience with McClellan had led Lincoln to distrust sieges, and at first he was dubious about Grant's plans. But when Vicksburg surrendered, so did a large Confederate army holed up inside it. Lincoln joyfully pronounced Grant's Vicksburg campaign "brilliant." The Confederate commander at Port Hudson surrendered shortly thereafter. The Mississippi River was now opened to Union navigation, and the Confederacy was split in two. Vicksburg and Gettysburg were the greatest Union victories of the war.

Despite his disappointment with Meade, Lincoln came to realize the significance of the Union victory at Gettysburg. In November, he went to Gettysburg to speak at the dedication of a military cemetery at the battlefield. There he articulated a profound justification of the Union war effort. The Civil War, Lincoln said, had become a great test of democracy and of the principle of human equality. The soldiers who died at Gettysburg had dedicated their lives to those principles, the president noted. It remained only "for us the living" to similarly "resolve that these dead shall not have died in vain—that this nation, under God, shall have a new birth of freedom—and that government of the people, by the people, for the people, shall not perish from the earth."

With the Gettysburg Address, Lincoln took brilliant advantage of the North's improving military fortunes to elevate the meaning of the war beyond the simple restoration of the Union. After 1863, antiwar sentiment in the North diminished substantially. In the South it exploded.

Discontent in the Confederacy

The South was divided over secession from the very beginning. Four slave states—Maryland, Delaware, Kentucky, and Missouri—never even joined the Confederacy. The entire western portion of Virginia "seceded" from the state and rejoined the Union as

Map 15–4 The Battle of Gettysburg, July 1–3, 1863 In three extraordinary days in Gettysburg, Pennsylvania, the Union Army turned back Lee's second invasions of the North. The Union victory, combined with equally important successes in the West at the same time, turned the tide of the war in the North's favor. At the dedication of a military cemetery at Gettysburg a few months later, Lincoln articulated his most profound justification for waging war against the South.

the new state of West Virginia. Brutal guerilla warfare broke out in the mountains of eastern Tennessee and western North Carolina, where hostility to the Confederacy was widespread.

Although most whites in the seceded states remained loyal to the Confederacy, many attacked the government of Jefferson Davis. Although formed in the name of states' rights, the Confederate government became a huge centralized bureaucracy that taxed white southerners far beyond anything in their prewar experience. The Confederate government burned private stores of cotton and impressed slaves into service, enraging the slaveholders for whom the war was being fought in the first place.

The government in Richmond was forever wrestling with the states for control of military enlistments. The South relied much more heavily on draftees than did the North. A "planter's exemption" designed to thwart emancipation allowed the sons of wealthy slaveholders to purchase replacements, an action that generated tremendous hostility. Ordinary southerners complained of a "rich man's war but a poor man's fight." The most important resistance came from Georgia, where powerful politicians launched a vitriolic assault on the Confederate government. Faced with swelling internal opposition, Davis followed Lincoln's course and suspended habeas corpus in many parts of the Confederacy.

Southerners, military and civilian, suffered proportionally far more casualties than did northerners. Deprivation and physical destruction were common experiences in the Civil War South. Confederate money was becoming worthless, and the army swallowed up much of the food supply. Bread riots erupted in a dozen southern cities in 1863. By 1864 life for millions of southerners had become miserable and desperate. Women wrote desperate letters to their husbands and sons in the Confederate armies, begging them to come home and rescue their families from the threat of starvation.

The War Comes to a Bloody End

In the face of bread riots, war weariness, and disloyal slaves, a crippled Confederacy nonetheless sought desperately to maintain itself. At the same time, northern society seemed stronger than ever. Amidst the most ferocious fighting ever witnessed on North American soil, the commander in chief ran for reelection to the presidency and won.

Grant Takes Command

During the summer of 1863, Union forces under William S. Rosecrans pushed Braxton Bragg's Confederate troops out of central Tennessee. Bragg retreated east to Chattanooga, a critical rail terminal. Prodded by Washington, Rosecrans began moving his army toward Chattanooga in mid-August, later joined by Ambrose Burnside. Outnumbered and almost surrounded, Bragg abandoned Chattanooga and retreated into Georgia. Jefferson Davis sent reinforcements and ordered Bragg to return to the offensive. At the same time, Union general George Thomas reinforced Rosecrans and Burnside. On September 19 the two armies discovered each other at Chickamauga Creek in eastern Tennessee. In two days, the bloodiest battle of the western theater ended in the Union troops' retreat and almost total rout.

Weeks after their defeat at Chickamauga, Union armies were still stuck in Chattanooga unable to feed themselves. A frustrated President Lincoln swiftly reorganized the command of the western theater, putting General Grant in charge of all Union armies west of the Appalachians. In November 1863 Grant and William Tecumseh Sherman rescued the Union troops trapped at Chattanooga. Together with General Thomas, they dislodged the Confederates from the city. Two days later, Union forces routed the enemy at Lookout Mountain, driving Confederate troops into Georgia. The war in the West was nearly over.

Lincoln at last had a general who would fight. In March 1864 he put Grant in charge of the entire Union army. Grant decided on a simple two-pronged strategy: he would take control of the Army of the Potomac and confront Lee's Army of Northern Virginia while Sherman would hunt down and destroy Joseph E. Johnston's troops in Georgia. In these two engagements the Civil War reached its destructive heights. "From the summer of 1862, the war became a war of wholesale devastation," John Esten Cooke explained. "From the spring of 1864, it seems to have become nearly a war of extermination."

The Theory and Practice of Hard War

McClellan, Burnside, and Hooker had all withered under Lee's assaults. When Grant got to Virginia in early 1864 to do battle with Lee, he did not wither. The two generals hurled their men at one another, often directly into the lines of fire. The result was a series of unspeakably bloody encounters beginning in the spring of 1864. The first battle took place on May 5 and 6, in a largely uninhabited stretch of thick woods. Appropriately called the Wilderness, the terrain made it difficult to see for any distance and impossible for armies to maintain strict lines. Soldiers and commanders alike were confused by the woods and smoke, by the roar of gunfire, and by the wailing of thousands of wounded. Entire brigades got lost. In two days of fighting, the Union army suffered 17,000 casualties, the Confederates 11,000; and there was more to come.

Grant's goal was to break through Lee's defensive line and capture Richmond. With smoke still billowing in the Wilderness, Grant marched his army south hoping to outflank Lee at Spotsylvania Court House. As usual, Lee kept one step ahead, and from May 10 to May 12 the bloodbath was repeated. There were another 18,000 Union and 12,000 Confederate casualties. Still Grant pushed his men further south. Determined to break through Lee's defenses, Grant waged a series of deadly skirmishes culminating in a frightful assault at Cold Harbor on June 3. Bodies piled on top of bodies until finally Grant had to call a halt. Seven thousand Union men were killed or wounded at Cold Harbor, most of them in the first 60 minutes of fighting. The armies moved south yet again, but when Lee secured the rail link at Petersburg (critical to the defense of Richmond), Grant settled in for a prolonged siege. The brutal Virginia campaign had not ended the war. More than 50,000 Union men were killed or wounded, but Grant had not destroyed Lee's army or taken Richmond. The war was at a standoff, and Lincoln was up for reelection in November.

Three other military achievements saved the election of 1864 for the Republicans. The first, in late August, was the Union capture of Mobile Bay, the last major southern port still controlled by the Confederates. The entire southern coastline was now virtually sealed. Next came General Philip Sheridan's Union cavalry raid through the Shenandoah Valley in September and his defeat of the Confederate cavalry's raid into Maryland. Ordered by Grant to wipe out the source of supplies for Lee's army, Sheridan's men swept through the Shenandoah Valley, burning barns and killing animals. Sheridan's campaign demonstrated that the Union army now had a cavalry that could match and defeat the Confederacy's. Meanwhile, General Sherman took Atlanta, providing Lincoln and the Republicans with a third piece of good news. On September 1, as the election campaign was heating up in the North, Sherman telegraphed Lincoln: "Atlanta is ours, and fairly won."

After Atlanta, Sherman came to believe that the South's civilians had to be subdued along with its armies. He would not attack civilians directly, but he would systematically destroy their homes and farms—even whole towns and cities. The white South, Sherman concluded, would remain rebellious until forced to taste the bitter reality of civil war.

"War is cruelty," he told the citizens of Atlanta who petitioned him for mercy, "and the only way the people of Atlanta can hope once more to live in peace and quiet at home, is to stop the war."

But Sherman was merely the theorist of this type of warfare. Lincoln was its administrator. It was Lincoln who demanded unconditional surrender. It was he who determined to destroy the southern social order by emancipating all the slaves. He allowed Grant to pursue his relentless military campaigns. And now he was sanctioning the systematic destruction of the homes, the property, and even the food supplies of southern civilians. If this was not "total" war, it was something very close to it.

Northern Democrats were horrified by the destructive turn the war had taken. In 1864 they nominated George McClellan, the general Lincoln had fired, for president on a platform advocating compromise, a swift end to the war, and a negotiated settlement with the South. Lincoln's policy of hard war was the major issue of the campaign. The fact that McClellan won 45 percent of the votes suggested that many in the North disapproved of the administration's policy. But by election day Mobile was in Union hands, Sheridan had laid waste to the Shenandoah Valley, and Sherman had taken Atlanta. The majority of northern voters could smell a Union victory, and Lincoln won convincingly. All Confederate attempts to offer anything less than unconditional surrender were rejected. Lee's hopes were dashed, and the siege of Petersburg continued.

Sherman Marches and Lee Surrenders

A week after Lincoln's reelection, Sherman's men burned half of Atlanta to the ground, turned east, and marched toward the sea. Confederate general John Bell Hood tried to distract Sherman by moving west toward Alabama and then up into Tennessee, but Union troops led by George Thomas destroyed Hood's forces in devastating battles at Franklin and Nashville, Tennessee. There was almost nothing left of the Confederate army between the Mississippi River and the Appalachian mountains.

Meanwhile Sherman's troops raged through the Georgia countryside. In late December, Sherman telegraphed Lincoln and presented him with Savannah as a Christmas gift. From Savannah, Sherman's men marched northward into South Carolina, the birthplace of secession. There, Union soldiers brought the practice of hard war to its ferocious climax. They torched homes and barns, destroyed crops, and slaughtered livestock. With Charleston in Union hands and the state capital of Columbia in flames, Sherman moved northward. By then events in Virginia were bringing the war to a conclusion. Lee's army was fatally weakened when Union forces closed off Petersburg's last line of supply. On April 2, 1865, the Army of the Potomac broke through the Confederate defenses and forced Lee to abandon Petersburg. The next day Confederate leaders abandoned Richmond. Lee moved his tired and hungry troops westward in one last attempt to elude Grant's force, but when he reached Appomattox Court House, Lee surrendered, and the war was over.

The Meaning of the Civil War

Despite the draft riots, Copperheads, wartime inflation, and terrible loss of life, the Civil War years had been good for the North's economy. Mechanization allowed northern farmers to increase wheat production, despite losing one-third of the farm labor force to the army. Huge orders for military rations propelled the growth of the canned-food industry. The railroad boom of the 1850s persisted through the war. By contrast, the slave economy was crushed. Much of the South lay in ruins. Thousands of miles of railroad track had been destroyed. One-third of the livestock had been killed; one-fourth of the young white men were dead. In 1860 the North and the South had identical per capita incomes and nearly identical per capita wealth. By 1870 the North was 50 percent wealthier than the South.

The redistribution of political power was equally dramatic. Until 1860, slaveholders and their allies had controlled the Supreme Court, dominated the presidency, and exercised disproportionate influence in Congress. The Civil War destroyed the slaveholding class and with it the slaveholders' political power.

Union victory strengthened the advocates of a stronger, more centralized national government. The growth of this "nationalist" sentiment can be traced in the speeches of Abraham Lincoln. When the Civil War began, he emphasized the restoration of the "Union." By the end of the war Lincoln was more likely to talk of saving the "nation."

But all of this paled beside the destruction of slavery. Emancipation was not what the North intended in 1861, but it clearly was by the end. For in truth, the war had not been enough to destroy slavery. When Lincoln was reelected in November 1864, perhaps half a million slaves had been freed. That meant there were 4 million slaves still in place. Emancipation had been justified as a military necessity, and once the war ended it was not clear that emancipation would continue. Some things had to be done to make sure that it would.

A thirteenth amendment would have to be added to the Constitution, outlawing slavery forever. Lincoln supported such an amendment; it was the only thing he asked to be included in the 1864 Republican Party platform. Once reelected he and the Republicans scrambled to get it through Congress before the war ended and support for emancipation evaporated. Congress finally passed the amendment and sent it to the states in January of 1865. It was not ratified until December, but in the intervening months most of the slaves were in fact emancipated. How?

Three of the four border states finally emancipated their slaves on their own. Kentucky was the stubborn holdout. When Lee surrendered, many slaves and slaveholders spontaneously concluded that slavery itself was finished and began making new arrangements. Officers of the Freedmen's Bureau, an agency of the U.S. Army, stayed on when the war ended and enforced emancipation on farms and plantations across the South. Most important, the southern states themselves were required to enact emancipation to be readmitted to the Union. As they did so, in the fall of 1865, millions of slaves across the South were finally liberated. The Thirteenth Amendment sealed the process, liberating the slaves in Kentucky.

Emancipation had not been easy. It took runaway slaves forcing the Union's hand. It took Union troops determined to use slave liberation to put down the southern rebellion. It took tens of thousands of former slaves to put on blue uniforms and point their guns at their former owners. It took determined antislavery politicians. It took a genuine shift in northern public opinion. It had to overcome sustained and violent resistance by the Confederates. And it took nearly five years. But when it was over, the domestic slave trade was gone, the slave auction houses were shuttered, and nobody claimed the fruits of a slave's labor as a right of property.

Atlanta in Ruins Much of Atlanta lay in ruins after General Sherman captured and burned the city. The Northern general had made a conscious decision to make war "hell" for the Southern civilians who supported the war.

Six hundred thousand men died during the Civil War. If anything justified the slaughter, emancipation did. Yet even Lincoln was stunned by the price the nation had paid. He wondered whether the bloodshed was a form of divine retribution for the unpardonable sin of slavery. In his second inaugural address, in March 1865, he prayed that the "mighty scourge of war may speedily pass away." But, Lincoln added, "if God wills that it continue, until all the wealth piled up by the bond-man's two hundred and fifty years of unrequited toil shall be sunk, and until every drop of blood drawn with the lash, shall be paid by another drawn with the sword, as was said three thousand years ago, so still it must be said, 'the judgments of the Lord, are true and righteous altogether.'"

The bloody war had ended, but there was more blood to be shed. On the evening of April 14, 1865, a disgruntled southern actor named John Wilkes Booth assassinated Abraham Lincoln at Ford's Theater in Washington, D.C.

Conclusion

The president who had led the nation through the Civil War would not oversee the nation's reconstruction. Lincoln had given some thought to the question of how to reincorporate the defeated southern states into the Union, but when he died neither he nor his fellow Republicans in Congress had agreed on any particular plan. Would the Union simply be restored as swiftly as possible? Or would the South be reconstructed,

>> Timeline

▼1860
South Carolina secedes

▼1861
Lower South secedes
Abraham Lincoln inaugurated
First shots fired at Fort Sumter
Upper South secedes
North declares runaway slaves "contraband"
First battle of Bull Run
McClellan takes command of Army of the Potomac
First Confiscation Act
Trent affair

▼1862
Battles of Fort Henry and Fort Donelson
"Battle of the Ironclads"
Battle of Shiloh
Union capture of New Orleans
Slavery abolished in Washington, D.C.
Homestead Act
Confederacy establishes military draft
Peninsula campaign
Slavery prohibited in western territories
Second Confiscation Act, Militia Act,
    and Internal Revenue Act all passed
    by northern Congress
Second battle of Bull Run
Battle of Antietam
Preliminary Emancipation Proclamation
Battle of Fredericksburg

▼1863
Emancipation Proclamation
Union establishes military draft
Battle of Chancellorsville
Battle of Gettysburg
Vicksburg surrenders
New York City draft riots
Battle of Chickamauga
Gettysburg Address
Battle of Lookout Mountain

>> Timeline *continued*

▼1864
Wilderness campaign
Battle of Cold Harbor
Siege of Petersburg begins
Sherman captures Atlanta
Philip Sheridan raids Shenandoah Valley
Lincoln reelected
Sherman burns Atlanta and marches to the sea
Battles of Franklin and Nashville

▼1864–1865
Sherman's march through the Carolinas

▼1865
House of Representatives approves Thirteenth Amendment
Lincoln's second inauguration
Lee surrenders to Grant at Appomattox
Lincoln assassinated

continuing the revolution begun during the Civil War? At the moment Lincoln died, nobody was sure of the answer to these questions. They would emerge over the next several months and years, as the freed people in the South pressed to expand the meaning of their freedom.

**For further review materials and resource information,
please visit** www.oup.com/us/ofthepeople

16

Reconstructing a Nation

1865–1877

>> John Dennett Visits a Freedmen's Bureau Court

John Richard Dennett arrived in Liberty, Virginia, on August 17, 1865, on a tour of the South reporting for the magazine *The Nation*. The editors wanted accurate weekly accounts of conditions in the recently defeated Confederate states, and Dennett was the kind of man they could trust: a Harvard graduate, a firm believer in the sanctity of the Union, and a member of the class of elite Yankees who thought of themselves as the "best men" the country had to offer.

At Liberty, Dennett was accompanied by a Freedmen's Bureau agent. The Freedmen's Bureau was a branch of the U.S. Army established by Congress to assist the freed people. Dennett and the agent went to the courthouse because one of the Freedmen's Bureau's functions was to adjudicate disputes between the freed people and southern whites.

The first case was that of an old white farmer who complained that two blacks who worked on his farm were "roamin' about and refusin' to work." He wanted the agent to help find the men and bring them back. Both men had wives and children living on his farm and eating his corn, the old man complained. "Have you been paying any wages?" the Freedmen's Bureau agent asked. "Well, they get what the other niggers get," the farmer answered. "I a'n't payin' great wages this year." There was not much the agent could do, but one of his soldiers volunteered to go and tell the blacks that "they ought to be at home supporting their wives and children."

A well-to-do planter came in to see if he could fire the blacks who had been working on his plantation since the beginning of the year. The planter complained the workers were unmanageable now that he could no longer punish them. The sergeant warned the planter not to beat his workers as if they were still slaves. In that case, the planter responded, "Will the Government take them off our hands?" The agent suspected that the planter was looking for a way to discharge his laborers at the end of the growing season but before they had been paid. "If they've worked on your crops all the year so far," the agent told the planter, "I guess they've got a claim on you to keep them a while longer."

Next came a "good-looking mulatto man" representing a number of African Americans worried that they would be forced to sign five-year contracts with their employers. "No, it a'n't true," the agent said. They also wanted to know if they could rent or buy land to work for themselves. "Yes, rent or buy," the agent said. But with no horses, mules, or ploughs, the former slaves wanted to know "if the Government would help us out after we get the land." The agent had no help to offer, except for a note from the bureau authorizing them to rent or buy their own farms.

The last case involved a field hand who came to complain that his master was beating him with a stick. The agent told the field hand to go back to work. "Don't be sassy, don't be lazy when you've got work to do; and I guess he won't trouble you." The field hand left but came back a minute later and asked for a letter to his master "enjoining him to keep the peace, as he feared the man would shoot him, he having on two or three occasions threatened to do so."

Most of the cases Dennett witnessed centered on labor relations, which often spilled over into other matters, including the family lives of the freed people, their civil rights, and their ability to buy land. The freed people preferred to work their own land but lacked the resources to rent or buy farms. Black workers and white owners who negotiated wage contracts had trouble figuring out each other's rights and responsibilities. The former masters wanted to retain as much of their old authority as possible. Freed men wanted as much autonomy as possible, whereas freed women were forced to seek the patriarchal protection of their husbands.

The Freedmen's Bureau was in the middle of these conflicts. Most agents tried to ensure that freed people were paid for their labor and were not brutalized as they had been as slaves. Southern whites resented this intrusion, and their resentment reached sympathetic politicians in Washington, D.C. The Freedmen's Bureau became a lightning rod for the political conflicts of the Reconstruction period.

Conditions in the South raised several questions for lawmakers in Washington. How far should the federal government go to protect the economic well-being and civil rights of the freed people? What should the federal government require of southern states to be readmitted to the Union? Politicians disagreed violently on these questions. At one extreme was Andrew Johnson, who, as president, believed in small government and a speedy readmission of the southern states and looked on the Freedmen's Bureau with suspicion. At the other extreme were radical Republicans, who believed that the federal government should redistribute confiscated land to the former slaves, guarantee their civil rights, and give African American men the vote. They viewed the Freedmen's Bureau as too small and weak to be effective. In between were moderate Republicans who at first tried to work with the president. But as reports of violence and the abusive treatment of the freed people reached Washington, Republicans shifted toward the radical position.

It went back and forth this way: policymakers in Washington responded to events in the South, and events in the South were shaped in turn by policies from Washington. What John Dennett saw in Liberty, Virginia, was a good example of this. The

continued

>> **AMERICAN PORTRAIT** *continued*

Freedmen's Bureau agent listened to the requests of former masters and slaves, his responses shaped by the policies established in Washington. But those policies were, in turn, shaped by reports on conditions in the South sent back by Freedmen's Bureau agents like him and by journalists like John Dennett. From this interaction the politics of Reconstruction, and with it a "New South," slowly emerged.

Common Threads

>> In what ways did emancipation and wartime Reconstruction overlap?

>> When did Reconstruction begin?

>> Did Reconstruction change the South? If so, how? If not, why not?

>> What brought Reconstruction to an end?

Wartime Reconstruction

For several years emancipation overlapped with Reconstruction. Emancipation began early in the war and was not completed until the very end of 1865. Experiments with Reconstruction began during the war, long before emancipation was complete. Indeed, what is known as "Presidential Reconstruction" was also the crucial phase in the completion of emancipation. Congress and the president often had very different ideas about how to reconstruct the defeated Confederacy, but on one thing they agreed from the very beginning. Until the Thirteenth Amendment was ratified in December of 1865, state emancipation was the most legally secure means of abolishing slavery. Congress and the president therefore agreed that before any southern state could be readmitted to the Union, it had to emancipate its own slaves.

After that, however, came other contentious questions. What system of free labor would replace slavery? What civil and political rights should the freed people receive? During the war Congress and the Lincoln administration responded piecemeal to developments in regions of the South under Union control. A variety of approaches to Reconstruction emerged.

Experiments with Free Labor in the Lower Mississippi Valley

In November 1861, several of the Sea Islands off South Carolina were occupied by Union troops. The slaveholders fled the advancing Union army, leaving behind between 5,000 and 10,000 slaves. Were they free? Or merely contrabands of war? In December, responding to concerns about the status of contrabands, President Lincoln declared them "liberated." So began the first notable "rehearsal for Reconstruction." By the end of the war the abandoned plantations of the Sea Islands had been reorganized. Slave families were given small plots of their own to cultivate, and in return for their labor they would receive a "share" of the year's crop. When the masters returned after the war to reclaim their lands, the labor system evolved into what would become known as "sharecropping."

Southern Louisiana also came under Union control early in the war. The sugar and cotton plantations around New Orleans provided another major experiment in the transition from slave to free labor. Unlike in the Sea Islands, however, Louisiana's planters did not abandon their plantations, and tens of thousands of slaves were involved. Union commanders faced a dilemma. The plantation workers were no longer slaves, but their masters were still in place, so the plantations could not be broken up. And sugar plantations could not be effectively organized into small sharecropping units. The unusual labor system that emerged played an important role in the politics of Reconstruction.

Union general Nathaniel Banks, hoping to stem the flow of black refugees to Union lines and prevent the shocking numbers of deaths among blacks in the camps, issued stringent regulations designed to put the freed people back to work quickly. The Banks Plan required freed people to sign yearlong contracts to work on their former plantations, often for their former owners. Workers would be paid either 5 percent of the proceeds of the crop or three dollars per month. The former masters would provide food and shelter,

Freed People Planting Sweet Potatoes Slaves in parts of coastal South Carolina were freed early in the Civil War. Here the freed people on Edisto Island in 1862 are shown planting sweet potatoes rather than cotton. In other parts of the South the former slaves returned to the cultivation of cash crops.

Charlotte Forten Born to a prominent African American family in Philadelphia, Charlotte Forten was one of many northern women who went to the South to become a teacher of the freed slaves. Forten helped found the Penn School on St. Helena's Island in South Carolina.

and African American workers were forbidden to leave the plantations without permission. So harsh were these regulations that to many critics Banks had simply replaced one form of slavery with another. But as harsh as it was, the Banks Plan was not slavery, and most of the freed people returned to work fully aware of the difference. The Banks Plan was implemented throughout the lower Mississippi Valley, especially after the fall of Vicksburg in 1863.

The Banks Plan touched off a political controversy. Established planters had the most to gain from the plan, which preserved much of the prewar labor system. Louisiana Unionists, who had remained loyal to Washington, formed a Free State Association to press for more substantial changes. Lincoln publicly supported the Free State movement and issued a Proclamation of Amnesty and Reconstruction to undermine the Confederacy by cultivating the support of southern Unionists. The Proclamation contained, in outline, the first plan for reconstructing the South.

The most important thing Lincoln's plan did was to require Louisiana to abolish slavery as the price for readmission to the Union. The precedent for such a precondition had been established earlier the same year for West Virginia. Lincoln quickly applied that precedent to the seceded states, beginning with Florida and Louisiana. But the attempt to establish a loyal government in Florida foundered, so Louisiana became the first great experiment in wartime Reconstruction.

Lincoln's Ten Percent Plan Versus the Wade-Davis Bill

Beyond requiring the abolition of slavery, Lincoln's Ten Percent Plan promised full pardons and the restoration of civil rights to all those who swore loyalty to the Union, excluding only a few high-ranking Confederate military and political leaders. When the number of loyal whites in a former Confederate state reached 10 percent of the 1860 voting population, they could organize a new state constitution and government. Abiding by these conditions, Free State whites met in Louisiana in 1864 and produced a new state constitution. It abolished slavery, but it also denied blacks the right to vote.

By the spring of 1864 such denials were no longer acceptable to radical Republicans. Unionists were active in many parts of the South immediately after the war, and they developed strong ties to leading radicals in Congress, such as Thaddeus Stevens of Pennsylvania and Charles Sumner of Massachusetts. Most radicals favored federal guarantees of the civil rights of former slaves, including the right to vote, and were prepared to use the full force of the federal government to enforce congressional policy in the South. Although the radicals never formed a majority in Congress, they gradually won over the moderates to many of their positions. When Congress took control of Reconstruction after the elections in 1866, the process became known as "radical Reconstruction."

The radicals were particularly strong in New Orleans, thanks to the city's large and articulate community of free blacks. In the spring of 1864 they sent a delegation to Washington to meet with President Lincoln and press the case for voting rights. The next day Lincoln wrote to the acting governor of Louisiana suggesting a limited suffrage for the most intelligent blacks and for those who had served in the Union army. The suggestion was ignored. Free blacks in New Orleans and former slaves then demanded civil and political rights and the abolition of the Banks labor regulations. Radicals complained that Lincoln's Ten Percent Plan was too kind to former Confederates and that the Banks Plan was too harsh on former slaves.

Swayed by events in Louisiana, congressional radicals rejected Lincoln's plan. In July 1864 Congressmen Benjamin F. Wade and Henry Winter Davis proposed a different Reconstruction plan. Under the Wade-Davis Bill, Reconstruction could not begin until a majority, rather than merely 10 percent, of a state's white men swore an oath of allegiance to the Union. In addition, the Wade-Davis Bill guaranteed full legal and civil rights to African Americans, but not the right to vote. Lincoln pocket-vetoed the bill because it required Louisiana to emancipate its slaves as a condition for readmission to the Union. Lincoln believed that only he, as commander in chief, could emancipate slaves as a necessity of war. He included an emancipation provision in his own plan for Louisiana Reconstruction.

The Louisiana experience made several things clear. The radical Republicans were determined to press for more civil and political rights for blacks than moderates initially supported; however, the moderates showed a willingness to move in a radical direction. Equally important, any Reconstruction policy would have to consider the wishes of southern blacks.

The Freed People's Dream of Owning Land

Freedom meant many things to the former slaves. It meant that they could move about their neighborhoods without passes, that they did not have to step aside to let whites pass them on the street. Following emancipation, southern blacks withdrew from white churches and established their own congregations, and during Reconstruction the church emerged as a central institution in the southern black community. Freedom also meant literacy. Even before the war ended, northern teachers poured into the South to set up schools. When the fighting stopped, the U.S. Army helped recruit and organize thousands more northern women as teachers. As a result, hundreds of thousands of southern blacks became literate within a few years.

More important, former slaves went out of their way to have their marriages secured by the law. In 1865 marriage became an urgent necessity for many recently freed slaves, particularly women. Under slavery black women were valued in part for their labor and in part for their ability to reproduce more slaves. With emancipation black women and their offspring were no longer valuable as property, and some planters, hoping to avoid the expense of caring for them, began expelling women and children from their plantations in late 1865. Desperate women quickly realized that their best hope for survival was the patriarchal protection of their husbands. Once married, their husbands would demand sharecropping contracts that allowed their families to live with them on the plantations. For the first time in their lives black women across the South became what the law called "domestic dependents." Emancipation moved black women—no longer human property—out of slavery and into patriarchy.

The freed people also wanted land, without which they saw no choice but to work for their old masters. As the war ended, many African Americans had reason to believe that the government would help them become landowners. In early 1865, Union general William Tecumseh Sherman discovered how important land was to the freed people on the Sea Islands off the Carolinas . "The way we can best take care of ourselves is to have land," they declared, "and turn it out and till it by our own labor." Persuaded by their arguments, Sherman issued Special Field Order No. 15 granting captured land to the freed people. By June, 400,000 acres had been distributed to 40,000 former slaves.

Congress seemed to be moving in a similar direction. In March 1865, the Republicans established the Bureau of Refugees, Freedmen and Abandoned Lands, commonly known as the Freedmen's Bureau. The bureau became involved in the politics of land redistribution and controlled the disposition of 850,000 acres of confiscated and abandoned Confederate lands. In July 1865, General Oliver Otis Howard, the head of the bureau, directed his agents to rent the land to the freed people in 40-acre plots that they could eventually purchase. Many agents believed that to reeducate them in the values of thrift and hard work, the freed people should be encouraged to save money and buy land for themselves. From the bureau's perspective, redistributing land was like giving it away to people who had not paid for it.

The former slaves, however, felt they had more than earned a right to the land. "The labor of these people had for two hundred years cleared away the forests and produced crops that brought millions of dollars annually," H. C. Bruce explained. "It does seem to me that a Christian Nation would, at least, have given them one year's support, 40 acres of land and a mule each." Even Abraham Lincoln seemed to agree. But in April 1865 Lincoln was dead, and Andrew Johnson became president of the United States.

Presidential Reconstruction, 1865–1867

When Andrew Johnson took office in April 1865, it was still unclear whether Congress or the president would control Reconstruction policy and whether that policy would be lenient or harsh. As with so many Democrats, Johnson's sympathy for the common man did not extend to African Americans. Determined to reconstruct the South in his own way and blind to the interests of the freed people, Johnson grew increasingly bitter and resentful of the Republicans who controlled Congress.

The Political Economy of Contract Labor

In the mid-nineteenth century, Congress was normally out of session from March until December. Taking office in April 1865, Johnson hoped to use the recess to complete the Reconstruction process and present it to lawmakers in December. At the end of May the president offered amnesty and the restoration of property to white southerners who swore an oath of loyalty to the Union, excluding only high-ranking Confederate military and political leaders and very rich planters. He named provisional governors to the seceded states and told them to organize constitutional conventions. To be readmitted to the Union, the seceded states were first required to abolish slavery, preferably by ratifying the Thirteenth Amendment. Johnson also required the states to nullify their secession ordinances and repudiate their Confederate war debts. These terms were far more lenient than those Lincoln and the congressional Republicans had contemplated. They did nothing to protect the civil rights of the former slaves.

Johnson's leniency encouraged defiance among white southerners. Secessionists had been barred from participating in the states' constitutional conventions, but they participated openly in the first elections held late in the year after Johnson issued thousands of pardons. Leading Confederates thus assumed public office in the southern states. As required, the former Confederate states began abolishing slavery, and in the fall of 1865 the last great wave of emancipation spread across the South. Right up to the end of the war most slaveholders hoped to retain their slaves, even if they were forced to rejoin the Union. When the last holdouts—and there were many thousands of them—were finally forced to accept emancipation, they were furious and resentful. As the new state governments were coming into existence, a wave of violence spread across the South.

Blacks who had been freed earlier were not immune to the reaction. Back in power, white southerners demanded the restoration of all properties confiscated or abandoned during the war. In September 1865 Johnson ordered the Freedmen's Bureau to return all confiscated and abandoned lands to their former owners, and in late 1865 former slaves were being forcibly evicted from the 40-acre plots they had been given by the Union army or the Freedmen's Bureau.

Alongside their emancipation ordinances, the Johnsonian state governments enacted a series of "Black Codes" that severely restricted the civil rights of freed people. In many states the Black Codes *were* the emancipation statutes. Vagrancy statutes, for example, allowed police to arrest and fine virtually any black man. If he could not pay the fine, the "vagrant" was put to work on a farm, often the one operated by his former master. Even more disturbing to the former slaves were apprenticeship clauses that allowed white officials to remove children from their parents' homes and put them to work as "apprentices" on nearby farms.

Presidential Reconstruction left the freed people with no choice but to sign labor contracts with white landlords that restricted their personal, as well as their working, lives. In one case, a South Carolina planter contractually obliged his black workers to "go by his direction the same as in slavery time." Contracts required blacks to work for wages as low

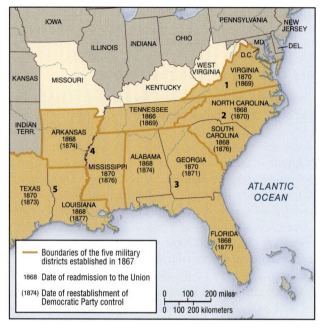

Map 16–1   Reconstruction and Redemption By 1870 Congress had readmitted every southern state to the Union. In most cases the Republican Party retained control of the "reconstructed" state governments for only a few years.

as one-tenth of the crop, and cotton prices were falling. It is no wonder that contract labor seemed little different from slavery.

Resistance to Presidential Reconstruction

In September 1865, blacks in Virginia issued a public appeal for assistance. They declared that they lacked the means to make and enforce legal contracts, because the Black Codes denied African Americans the right to testify in court in any case involving a white person. Many planters blocked the development of a free labor market by agreeing among themselves to hire only their former slaves and by fixing wages at a low level. Finally, there were many cases of black workers who had obeyed the terms of their contracts being "met by a contemptuous refusal of the stipulated compensation."

Across the South whites reported a growing number of freed people unwilling to accept the humiliating conditions of the contract labor system. Some blacks refused to perform specific tasks, whereas others were accused of being "disrespectful" to their employers or to whites in general. Most important, thousands of freedmen declined to sign contracts at the end of the year.

As white backlash and black defiance spread, reports of violence flooded into Washington. A former slave named Henry Adams claimed that "over two thousand colored people" were murdered around Shreveport, Louisiana, in 1865. Near Pine Bluff, Arkansas in 1866, a black community was burned to the ground by whites. Blacks were assaulted for not speaking to whites with the proper tone of submission, for disputing the terms of labor contracts, or for failing to meet the standards white employers expected. Through relentless intimidation, whites prevented blacks from buying their own land or attending political meetings to press for civil rights.

Northerners read these reports as evidence that whites were resisting emancipation and that "rebel" sentiment was reviving in the South. When Congress returned in December 1865, moderate Republicans were already suspicious of presidential Reconstruction. Radicals argued that the contract system made a mockery of their party's commitment to free labor and insisted that the only way to protect the interests of the freed people was to grant them the right to vote.

Congress Clashes with the President

Increasingly distressed by events in the South, Republican moderates in Congress were radicalized. They accepted the need for a more active government in the South and endorsed voting rights for black men. President Johnson, meanwhile, became obsessed with fears of "negro rule" in the South. When he insisted on readmitting southern states clearly controlled by unrepentant Confederates, Congress refused. Instead, the Republicans formed a Joint Committee on Reconstruction to propose the terms for readmission, reflecting Congress's determination to follow its own course.

In February 1866 Congress voted to extend the life of the Freedmen's Bureau and empowered the bureau to set up its own courts, which would supersede local jurisdictions. The bureau's record during its first year had been mixed. In the area of labor relations, the bureau too often sided with the landowners and against the interests of the freed people. It emancipated thousands of slaves. It provided immediate relief to thousands of individual freed people, and it assisted in the creation of schools. The bureau's effectiveness varied with the commitments of its agents. Some agents sided instinctively with the former masters. The more idealistic agents often acted under difficult circumstances to protect the freed people from racist violence, unfair employers, and biased officials. Thousands of freedmen and freedwomen looked to the bureau as their only hope for justice; for the same reason, thousands of southern whites resented the bureau, and they let Andrew Johnson know it.

To the amazement of moderate Republicans, Johnson vetoed the bill to extend the life of the Freedmen's Bureau, claiming that the legislation would increase the power of the central government at the expense of the states. He invoked the Jacksonian ideal of the free market, insisting that the "laws that regulate supply and demand" were the best way to resolve the labor problem in the South. Republicans fell just short of the two-thirds vote needed to override the veto. Johnson reacted by attacking the Republicans in Congress and questioning the legitimacy of the Joint Committee on Reconstruction.

Origins of the Fourteenth Amendment

In March 1866 Congress passed a landmark Civil Rights Act. It overturned the Dred Scott decision by granting United States citizenship to Americans regardless of race. This marked the first time that the federal government intervened in the states to guarantee due process and basic civil rights. But Johnson vetoed the Civil Rights Act of 1866. Alongside the usual Jacksonian rhetoric about limited government, Johnson justified his veto on

The Freedmen's Bureau Led by President Andrew Johnson, attacks on the Freedmen's Bureau became more and more openly racist in late 1865 and 1866. This Democratic Party broadside was circulated during the 1866 election.

racist grounds. He doubted that blacks "possess the requisite qualifications to entitle them to all the privileges and immunities of citizens of the United States."

Johnson's actions and rhetoric forced moderate Republicans to confront him. The Republican Congress overrode Johnson's veto of the Civil Rights Act and passed another Freedmen's Bureau Bill. Again Johnson vetoed it, but this time Congress overrode his veto.

To ensure the civil rights of the freed people, the Joint Committee on Reconstruction proposed a Fourteenth Amendment to the Constitution. The most powerful and controversial of all the Constitution's amendments, it guaranteed citizenship to all males born in the United States, regardless of color (see Table 16–1). Although the amendment did not guarantee blacks the right to vote, it based representation in Congress on a state's voting population. This punished southern states by reducing their representation if they did not allow blacks to vote.

By mid-1866, Congress had refused to recognize the state governments established under Johnson's plan, and it had authorized the Freedmen's Bureau to create a military justice system to override the local courts, thereby guaranteeing the former slaves basic rights of due process. Finally, it made ratification of the Fourteenth Amendment by the former Confederate states a requirement for readmission to the Union. Congress and the president were now at war, and Andrew Johnson went on a rampage.

AMERICAN LANDSCAPE

>> Race Riots in Memphis and New Orleans

A few weeks after Congress passed the Civil Rights Act, white mobs in Memphis rioted for three days. In the year since the war had ended, the city's black population had multiplied four times over as former slaves fled the countryside for better opportunities in the city. But whites in Memphis grew increasingly hostile to the presence of so many blacks. "Would to God they were back in Africa, or some other seaport town," the Memphis *Argus* complained, "anywhere but here." Under President Andrew Johnson's terms for a newly reconstructed government, the old Memphis elite had been displaced by Irish politicians at least as hostile to freed people as the old guard. Conflict between whites and blacks broke out on the streets of Memphis.

In this atmosphere of heightened racial tension one incident sparked a riot. On May 1, 1866, after two hack drivers— one black, one white—had a traffic accident, police arrested the black man. A group of black veterans tried to prevent the arrest. A white crowd gathered and began rioting in the streets. Over the next three days white mobs burned hundreds of homes, destroyed churches, and attacked black schools. Five black women were raped, and nearly 50 people, all but two of them black, were killed.

Three months later, white mobs in New Orleans rioted as well. Once again both the state and city governments were falling into the hands of former Confederates. But the New Orleans massacre had a more explicitly political dimension. Its well-established community of free blacks had, by the middle of 1866, grown disillu-

sioned with the direction Reconstruction was taking in Louisiana and New Orleans. A group of radicals sought to bring the state's 1864 constitutional convention back into session. They proposed giving blacks the vote, stripping "rebels" of the franchise, and establishing an entirely new state government. The convention was scheduled to meet on July 30.

But as the delegates met, white mobs set out to stop them. Led by police and firemen, many of them Confederate veterans, whites first attacked a parade of about 200 blacks marching to the Mechanics' Institute to support the delegates. At the convention hall, the mobs began shooting and killing the delegates trying to escape through the windows, even after they raised the white flag of surrender. When the mob finally dispersed, 34 blacks and 3 white supporters had been killed, and another 100 had been injured.

The Memphis and New Orleans massacres quickly became political issues in the North, thanks in large part to Johnson's reaction. In late August the president undertook an unprecedented campaign tour designed to stir up voters' hostility to Congress, but his trip backfired. He blasted congressional Republicans, blaming them for the riots, and suggested that radical congressman Thaddeus Stevens should be hanged. Republicans charged in turn that Johnson's own policies had revived the rebellious sentiments that led to the massacres.

The elections of 1866 became a referendum on competing visions of what American democracy should mean. For President
continued

AMERICAN LANDSCAPE *continued*

Johnson "democracy" meant government by local majorities, which often meant white supremacy. For African Americans and a growing number of Republicans in Congress, genuine democracy demanded a firm foundation of equal civil and political rights. The results were "overwhelm-ingly against the President," the *New York Times* noted, "clearly, unmistakably, decisively in favor of Congress and its policy." The Republicans gained a veto-proof hold on Congress, and Republican moderates were further radicalized. Congressional Reconstruction was about to begin.

 Table 16-1 Reconstruction Amendments, 1865–1870

Amendment	Main Provisions	Congressional Passage (2/3 majority in each house required)	Ratification Process (3/4 of all states including ex-Confederate states required)
13	Slavery prohibited in United States	January 1865	December 1865 (27 states, including 8 southern states)
14	1. National citizenship for all men and women born in the U.S.	June 1866	Rejected by 12 southern and border states, February 1867
	2. State representation in Congress reduced proportionally to number of voters disfranchised		Radicals make readmission of southern states hinge on ratification
	3. Former high ranking Confederates denied right to hold office		Ratified July 1868
	4. Confederate debt repudiated		
15	Denial of franchise because of race, color, or past servitude explicitly prohibited	February 1869	Ratification required for readmission of Virginia, Texas, Mississippi, Georgia. Ratified March 1870.

Congressional Reconstruction

Johnson's outrageous behavior during the 1866 campaign, capped by a Republican sweep of the elections, ended presidential Reconstruction. Congressional Reconstruction would be far different. It was an extraordinary series of events, second only to emancipation in its impact on the history of the United States.

Origins of the Black Vote

The Congress that convened in December 1866 was far more radical than the previous one, evidenced clearly by the emerging consensus among moderate Republicans that southern blacks should be allowed to vote. Radical Republicans and black leaders had been calling for such a policy for two years, but moderate Republicans initially resisted the idea. At most, moderates contemplated granting the vote to veterans and to educated blacks who had been free before the war. Not until early 1867 did the majority of Republicans conclude that the only way to avoid a lengthy military occupation of the South was to put political power into the hands of all male freedmen.

Andrew Johnson finally pushed the moderate Republicans over the line. Ignoring the results of the 1866 elections, Johnson urged the southern states to reject the Fourteenth Amendment. Frustrated Republicans finally repudiated presidential Reconstruction. On March 2, 1867, Congress assumed control of the process by passing the First Reconstruction Act. It reduced the southern states to the status of territories and divided the South into five military districts directly controlled by the army (see Map 16–1). Before the southern states could be readmitted to the Union, they had to draw up new "republican" constitutions, ratify the Fourteenth Amendment, and allow black men to vote. The Second Reconstruction Act, passed soon after, established the procedures to enforce black suffrage by placing the military in charge of voter registration. Johnson vetoed both acts, but in both cases Congress immediately overrode him. This was congressional Reconstruction at its most radical, and for this reason it is often referred to as "radical Reconstruction."

Radical Reconstruction in the South

Beginning in 1867 the constitutions of the southern states were rewritten, thousands of African Americans began to vote, and hundreds of them assumed public office. Within six months 735,000 blacks and 635,000 whites had registered to vote across the South. Blacks formed electoral majorities in South Carolina, Florida, Mississippi, Alabama, and Louisiana. In the fall these new voters elected delegates to conventions that drew up progressive state constitutions that guaranteed suffrage for all men, mandated public education systems, and established progressive tax structures.

The governments elected under congressional authority were based on an unstable political coalition. Northern whites were prominent in the southern Republican Party. Stereotyped as greedy carpetbaggers, they included Union veterans who stayed in the South, idealistic reformers, well-meaning capitalists, and opportunists on the make. More important to the Republican coalition were southern whites, or scalawags. Some of them lived in up-country regions that resisted secession and the Confederacy. Others had been Whigs before the war, hoping to regain some former influence. But new black voters were the backbone of the Republican Party in the South. They were a varied lot. Elite black artisans and professionals did not always share the interests of poor black farmers and farm laborers, but most African Americans were united by a shared interest in securing civil rights.

Although in the long run class and race divisions weakened the party, in the late 1860s and early 1870s the southern Republicans launched an impressive experiment in interracial democracy in the South. Racist legend paints these years as a dark period of

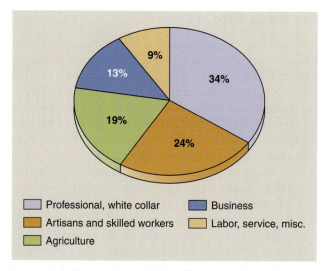

Figure 16–1 Occupations of African American Officeholders During Reconstruction Although former slaves were under-represented among black officeholders, the Reconstruction governments were among the most broadly representative legislatures in U.S. history.

"negro rule" and military domination, but military rule rarely lasted more than a year or two, and only in South Carolina did blacks ever control the legislature. Blacks who held office were largely members of the prewar free African American elite of teachers, ministers, and small businessmen rather than sharecroppers or farm workers. These Reconstruction legislatures were more representative of their constituents than most legislatures in nineteenth-century America.

Achievements and Failures of Radical Government

Once in office, southern Republicans had to cultivate a white constituency and at the same time serve the interests of the blacks who elected them. To strengthen this biracial coalition, Republican politicians emphasized government support for economic development. Republican legislatures granted tax abatements for corporations and spent vast sums to encourage the construction of railroads. They preached a "gospel of prosperity" that promised to benefit ordinary white southerners.

In the long run, the gospel of prosperity did not hold the Republican coalition together. Outside investors were unwilling to risk their capital on a politically unstable region. By the early 1870s, black politicians questioned the diversion of scarce revenues to railroads and tax breaks for corporations. Instead, they demanded public services, especially universal education. But more government services meant higher property taxes at a time of severe hardship. White small farmers had been devastated by the Civil War. Unaccustomed to paying high taxes and believing strongly in limited government, they grew increasingly receptive to Democratic appeals for restoration of "white man's government." Thus southern Republicans were unable to unite the diverse interests of their constituents.

Despite powerful opposition at home and lukewarm support from Washington, D.C., radical governments in the South boasted several important achievements. They funded the construction of hospitals, insane asylums, prisons, and roads. They introduced home-stead exemptions that protected the property of poor farmers. Republican legislatures established public school systems that were a major improvement over their antebellum counterparts. The literacy rate among southern blacks rose steadily. Nevertheless, public schools for southern blacks remained inadequately funded and sharply segregated.

The Political Economy of Sharecropping

Congressional Reconstruction made it easier for the former slaves to negotiate the terms of their labor contracts. Republican state legislatures abolished the Black Codes and passed "lien" laws that gave black workers more control over the crops they grew. Workers with grievances had a better chance of securing justice, as southern Republicans became sheriffs, justices of the peace, and county clerks and as southern courts allowed blacks to serve as witnesses and sit on juries.

The strongest card in the hands of the freed people was a shortage of agricultural workers in the South. After emancipation thousands of blacks sought opportunities in towns and cities or in the North. And even though most blacks remained in the South as farmers, they reduced their working hours in several ways. Black women still worked the fields, but they spent more time nursing their infants and caring for their children. And the children went to school when they were able. The resulting labor shortage forced white landlords to renegotiate their labor arrangements with the freed people.

The contract labor system that had developed during the war and under presidential Reconstruction was replaced with a variety of regional arrangements. On the Louisiana sugar plantations, the freed people became wage laborers. But in tobacco and cotton regions, where most freed people lived, a new system of labor called *sharecropping* developed. Under this system, an agricultural worker and his family typically agreed to work for one year on a particular plot of land, with the landowner providing the tools, seed, and work animals. At the end of the year the crop was split, perhaps one-third going to the sharecropper and two-thirds to the owner.

Sharecropping shaped the economy of the postwar South by transforming the production and marketing of cash crops. Landowners broke up their plantations into family-sized plots, worked by sharecroppers in family units with no direct supervision. Each sharecropping family established its own relationship with local merchants to sell crops and buy supplies. Merchants became crucial to the southern credit system, because most southern banks could not meet the banking standards established by Congress during the Civil War. Storekeepers, usually the only people who could extend credit to sharecroppers, provided sharecroppers with food, fertilizer, animal feed, and other provisions during the year until the crop was harvested.

These developments had important consequences for white small farmers. More merchants fanned out into up-country areas inhabited mostly by ordinary whites, areas now served by railroads sponsored by the Reconstruction legislatures. With merchants offering credit and railroads offering transportation, small farmers started to produce cash crops. Thus Reconstruction accelerated the process by which southern yeomen abandoned self-sufficient farming in favor of cash crops.

Sharecropping spread quickly among black farmers in the cotton South. By 1880, 80 percent of cotton farms had fewer than 50 acres, and the majority of those farms were operated by sharecroppers (see Map 16–2). Sharecropping had several advantages for

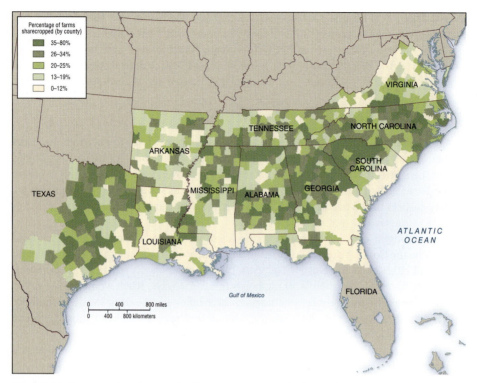

Map 16–2   Sharecropping By 1880 the sharecropping system had spread across the South. It was most common in the inland areas, where cotton and tobacco plantations were most common before the Civil War.

landlords. It reduced their risk when cotton prices were low and encouraged workers to increase production without costly supervision. Further, if sharecroppers changed jobs before the crop was harvested, they lost a whole year's pay. But there were also advantages for the workers. For freed people with no hope of owning their own farms, sharecropping at least rewarded their hard work. The bigger the crop, the more they earned. It gave them more independence than contract labor.

Sharecropping also allowed the freed people to work in families rather than in gangs. Freedom alone had rearranged the powers of men, women, and children within the families of former slaves. Parents gained new control over their children. They could send sons and daughters to school, or put them to work. Successful parents could give their children an important head start in life. Similarly, African American husbands gained new powers.

The marriage laws of the mid-nineteenth century that defined the husband as the head of the household were irrelevant to slaves, because their marriages had no legal standing. With emancipation these patriarchal assumptions of American family law shaped the lives of freed men and women. Once married, women often found that their property belonged to their husbands. The sharecropping system further assumed that as head of the household the husband made the economic decisions for the entire family. Men signed most labor contracts, and most contracts assumed that the husband would take his family to work with him.

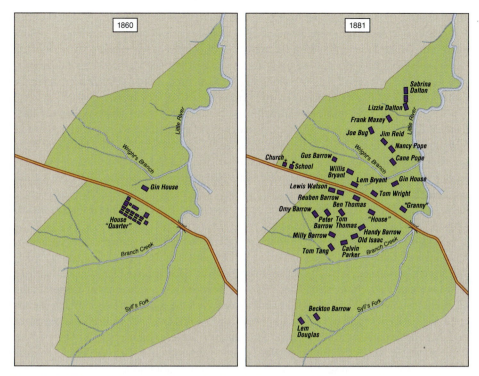

Map 16–3   Effect of Sharecropping in the South: The Barrow Plantation in Oglethorpe County, Georgia Sharecropping cut large estates into small landholdings worked by sharecroppers and tenants, changing the landscape of the South.

Sharecropping shaped the social system of the postwar South. It influenced the balance of power between men and women. It established the balance of power between landowners and sharecroppers. It tied the southern economy to agriculture, in particular to cotton production, impeding the region's overall economic development. Yet amid these changes, the Republican Party was retreating from its commitment to the freed people.

The Retreat from Republican Radicalism

By the late 1860s fractures in the Republican coalition were weakening the party's commitment to radical Reconstruction. By 1868 the Republicans were presenting themselves as the party of moderation. The success of this appeal brought the last major achievements of Reconstruction.

The Impeachment and Trial of Andrew Johnson

Throughout 1866 and much of 1867, President Johnson waged a relentless campaign against Congress and the radicals. Inevitably, this conflict led to a struggle over control of the military in the South. The First Reconstruction Act placed the entire South under direct military power. The Freedmen's Bureau was a branch of the U.S. Army. Judicial authority was vested in the provost marshals. The military also oversaw voter registration. But as the commander in chief of the military, Johnson removed dozens of Freedmen's Bureau officials who enforced the Civil Rights Act of 1866. He replaced Republican provost marshals with men hostile to Congress and contemptuous of the former slaves. In short, Johnson went out of his way to undermine the will of Congress.

Radicals called for Johnson's impeachment, but moderates and conservatives resisted. Instead, Congress hoped to restrain the president by refining the Reconstruction Acts and by using the Tenure of Office Act of March 2, 1867. This act prohibited the president from removing officials whose appointments required Congressional approval, such as Secretary of War Edwin M. Stanton, who was sympathetic to the Republicans. A related statute required that all presidential orders to the military pass through General Ulysses S. Grant. Republicans hoped that this would prevent the president from removing military officials who enforced the Reconstruction Acts.

Congress's actions only provoked the president. In his veto messages and public pronouncements Johnson indulged in blatant racist pandering. He played on fears of "amalgamation," "miscegenation," and racial "degeneration." He expressed fear for the safety of white women, when the evidence suggested that black women were most in danger. In the off-year elections of 1867, northern Democrats played the race card successfully. Democratic victories erased many of the Republican gains of 1866 and inspired the president to defy congressional restraints. As a deliberate provocation, Johnson asked Secretary of War Stanton to resign on August 5, 1867. Stanton refused, and the president appointed General Grant as interim secretary of war. Stanton would not budge, so in February 1868 Johnson fired him. For this the House of Representatives voted to impeach the president and put him on trial in the Senate.

For all the animosity that Johnson had aroused by his obnoxious behavior, the senators trying him took their job seriously. Many were concerned that the Tenure of Office Act, which Johnson was accused of violating, was in fact unconstitutional. Others wondered whether his technical breach of the law was serious enough to warrant his removal from office. These and other doubts, along with Johnson's promise of good behavior in the future, led the Senate to acquit the president by a single vote.

Republicans Become the Party of Moderation

While Andrew Johnson was on trial in the Senate, voters in Michigan voted overwhelmingly to reject a new state constitution that granted blacks the right to vote. Coming on the heels of Democratic victories in 1867, the Michigan results were read by Republicans as a rejection of radical Reconstruction.

During the 1868 elections Republicans repudiated the radicals' demand for nationwide black suffrage, arguing that the black vote was a uniquely southern solution to a uniquely southern problem. The northern states should be free to decide this issue for themselves. Congress readmitted six southern states to the Union, demonstrating that Republican policies had restored law and order to the South. By nominating General Ulysses Grant as their presidential candidate, the Republicans confirmed their retreat from radicalism. "Let Us Have Peace" was Grant's campaign slogan.

By contrast, the Democrats nominated Horatio Seymour, who ran a vicious campaign of race-baiting. The Democratic platform denounced the Reconstruction Acts

AMERICA AND THE WORLD
....

>> Reconstructing America's Foreign Policy

Before the Civil War, Republicans associated expansionism with the slave power and the Democratic Party. But with the triumph of nationalism, the Republicans equated overseas expansion with the spread of liberty. In 1867 Secretary of State William Seward negotiated the purchase of Alaska from Russia. The acquisition ignited expansionist dreams of eventual U.S. control of all of North America, including Canada and Mexico, and "all the West Indian Islands."

The administration was equally adroit in its negotiations with Great Britain over the settlement of the so-called *Alabama* claims. In 1872 the English accepted responsibility for having helped equip the Confederate navy during the Civil War and agreed to pay over $15 million for damage to American shipping by the *Alabama* and other southern warships built in England.

In 1870, a diverse coalition came together to support the annexation of the island nation of Santo Domingo. The Grant administration strongly supported the treaty, and Republicans who had once objected to any scheme associated with slavery now endorsed annexation. It would, they claimed, allow "our neighbors to join with us in the blessings of our free institutions." Thus the abolition of slavery in the United States was said to have purified the motives for American expansion. Even Frederick Douglass endorsed the annexation of Santo Domingo as a way to help the island's inhabitants rise out of their grinding poverty. But Grant's aggressive foreign policy was not uncontested. Grant tried to bulldoze the treaty through Congress but was thwarted by Senator Charles Sumner of Massachusetts, the powerful chairman of the Foreign Relations Committee. Sumner took a principled stance against imperial ventures in general, but he was particularly concerned with protecting the independence of the black republic of Haiti, which shared the island with Santo Domingo. A handful of Republicans, including Carl Schurz and Oliver P. Morton, also opposed the treaty, but most of the party sided with Grant. Yet Sumner succeeded in having the treaty rejected, by a 28–28 tie vote, thanks to the opposition of Senate Democrats. They opposed annexation for racist reasons: they objected to incorporating into the United States an island populated by dark-skinned peoples of an inferior race. The prewar alignments on expansionism were reversed by the Civil War. Republicans spearheaded American imperialism, and Democrats largely opposed it.

and promised to restore white rule to the South. Seymour suggested that a Democratic president might nullify the governments organized under congressional Reconstruction. Whereas the Republicans promised order and stability, the Democrats seemed to promise continued disruption. Northern fears were confirmed by the election violence that swept the South, incited by southern Democrats to keep black voters from the polls.

The Ku Klux Klan, which systematically intimidated potential black voters, was one of several secretive organizations dedicated to the violent overthrow of radical Reconstruction and the restoration of white supremacy. They included the Knights of the White Camelia, the Red Shirts, and the Night Riders. In addition to harassing and attacking African Americans, these organizations worked in the main to restore the political power of the Democratic Party in the South. They intimidated white Republicans, burned homes of black families, and lynched African Americans who showed signs of political activism. In 1868 the Ku Klux Klan served as the paramilitary arm of the southern Democratic Party.

As a means of restoring white supremacy, the Klan's strategy of violence backfired. As a wave of disgust swept across the North, the Republicans regained control of the White House, along with 25 of the 33 state legislatures, and quickly seized the opportunity to preserve the achievements of Reconstruction.

The Republicans reinforced their moderate image by attempting to restore law and order in the South. Congressional hearings produced vivid evidence of the Klan's violent efforts to suppress the black vote. Congress responded with a series of Enforcement Acts designed to "enforce" the recently enacted Fifteenth Amendment (see the following section). After some hesitation, the Grant administration used the new laws to prosecute the Klan and diminish political violence throughout the South. As a result the 1872 presidential elections were relatively free of disruption.

Reconstructing the North

Although Reconstruction was aimed primarily at the South, the North was affected as well, especially by the struggle over the black vote. The transformation of the North was an important chapter in the history of Reconstruction.

The Fifteenth Amendment and Nationwide African American Suffrage

Before the Civil War, blacks in the North were segregated in theaters, restaurants, cemeteries, hotels, streetcars, ferries, and schools. Most northern blacks could not vote, either because they were expressly denied the privilege or because of discriminatory property requirements that blacks alone were required to meet. The Civil War galvanized the northern black community to fight racial discrimination, with some success. In 1863 California removed the ban on black testimony in criminal courts. Two years later Illinois did the same. During the war, many northern cities abolished streetcar segregation. But faced with black voting, northern whites retained their racial prejudices. In 1865 voters in three northern states (Connecticut, Wisconsin, and Minnesota) rejected constitutional amendments to enfranchise African American men. In 1867, even as Congress was imposing the black vote on the South, black suffrage was defeated in Ohio, Minnesota, and Kansas.

The shocking electoral violence of 1868 persuaded many northerners that, given the chance, southern whites would quickly strip blacks of the right to vote. In Iowa and Minnesota, voters finally approved black suffrage. In 1869 Republicans passed the Fifteenth Amendment to the Constitution, which prohibited the use of "race, color, or previous condition of servitude" to disqualify voters anywhere in the United States. By outlawing voter discrimination on the basis of race, the Fifteenth Amendment protected the most radical achievement of congressional Reconstruction.

The Fifteenth Amendment brought Reconstruction to the North by overturning state laws that discriminated against black voters. In addition, Congress required ratification of the amendment in those southern states still to be readmitted to the Union. Virginia, Mississippi, and Texas did so and rejoined the Union. On March 30, 1870, the Fifteenth Amendment became part of the Constitution. For the first time, racial criteria for voting were banned everywhere in the United States, North as well as South.

Women and Suffrage

The issue of black voting divided northern radicals, especially feminists and abolitionists, who had long been allies in the struggle for emancipation. Signs of trouble appeared as early as May 1863 at the convention of the Woman's National Loyal League in New York City. The League had been organized to assist in defeating the slave South. One of the convention's resolutions declared that "there never can be a true peace in this Republic until the civil and political rights of all citizens of African descent and all women are practically established." For some delegates, this went too far. They argued that it was inappropriate to inject the issue of women's rights into the struggle to restore the Union.

By the end of the war, radical pressure for black suffrage in addition to emancipation caused a rancorous debate among reformers. Abolitionists argued that, although they supported women's suffrage, the critical issue was the protection of the freed people of the South. This, abolitionist Wendell Phillips argued, was "the Negro's Hour." Some women's rights activists felt betrayed. For 20 years they had pressed their claims for the right to vote. They were loyal allies of the Republicans and were now abandoned by them. It would be better, Elizabeth Cady Stanton argued, to press for "a vote based on intelligence and education for black and white, man and woman." Because voting rights based on "intelligence and education" would have excluded virtually all the freed slaves, as well as the working-class Irish, Germans, and Chinese, Stanton's remarks revealed a strain of elitism that further alienated abolitionists.

Not all feminists agreed with Stanton, and as racist violence erupted in the South, abolitionists argued that black suffrage was more urgent than women's suffrage. "I have always championed women's right to vote," argued Frederick Douglass, "but it will be seen that the present claim for the negro is one of the most urgent necessity."

Stanton was unmoved by such arguments. Supporters of women's suffrage opposed the Fifteenth Amendment on the ground that it subjected elite, educated women to the rule of base and illiterate males, especially immigrants and blacks. Abolitionists favored universal suffrage, not the "educated" suffrage that Stanton was calling for. The breach between reformers weakened the coalition of radicals pushing to maintain a vigorous Reconstruction policy in the South.

The Rise and Fall of the National Labor Union

Inspired by the radicalism of the Civil War and Reconstruction, industrial workers across the North organized dozens of craft unions, Eight-Hour Leagues, and working men's associations, all designed to protect northern workers who were overworked and underpaid. They called strikes, initiated consumer boycotts, and formed consumer co-operatives. In 1867 and 1868 workers in New York and Massachusetts campaigned to enact laws restricting the workday to eight hours. Soon, workers began electing their own candidates to state legislatures.

Founded in 1866, the National Labor Union (NLU) was the first significant post-war effort to organize all "working people" into a national union. William Sylvis, an iron molder, founded the NLU and became its president in 1868. He denied any "harmony of interests" between workers and capitalists. On the contrary, every wage earner was at war with every capitalist, whose "profits" robbed working people of the fruits of their labor.

Under Sylvis's direction the NLU advocated a wide range of political reforms, not just bread-and-butter issues. Sylvis believed that through organization American workers could take the "first step toward competence and independence." He argued for a doubling of the average worker's wages. He supported voting rights for blacks and women. Nevertheless, after a miserable showing in the elections of 1872, the NLU fell apart. By then Reconstruction in the South was also ending.

The End of Reconstruction

National events had as much to do with the end of Reconstruction as did events in the South. Reacting to a nationwide outbreak of political corruption in the late 1860s and 1870s, influential northern liberals, supporters of Reconstruction, abandoned the Republican Party in disgust in 1872. The end of Reconstruction finally came after electoral violence corrupted the 1876 elections. Republican politicians in Washington, D.C., responded with a sordid political bargain that came to symbolize the end of an era.

Corruption as a National Problem

Postwar America witnessed an extraordinary display of public dishonesty. Democrats were as prone to thievery as Republicans. Northern swindlers looted the public treasuries. In the South, both black and white legislators took bribes. Corruption, it seemed, was endemic to postwar American politics.

If corruption was everywhere in the late 1860s and 1870s, it was largely because there were more opportunities for it than ever before. The Civil War and Reconstruction had swollen government budgets. Never before was government so active in collecting taxes and disbursing vast sums for the public good. Under the circumstances, many government officials traded bribes for votes, embezzled public funds, or used insider knowledge to defraud taxpayers.

The federal government set the tone. In the most notorious case, the directors of the Union Pacific Railroad set up a dummy corporation called the Credit Mobilier, awarded it phony contracts, and protected it from inquiry by bribing influential congressmen. The Grant administration was eventually smeared with scandal as well. Although personally honest, the president surrounded himself with rich nobodies and army buddies

William Marcy Tweed The boss of New York's notoriously corrupt "Tweed Ring" was parodied by the great cartoonist, Thomas Nast. Nast's portrayal of the bloated public official became an enduring symbol of governmental corruption.

TWO GREAT QUESTIONS.

rather than respected statesmen. Grant's own private secretary was exposed as a member of the "Whiskey Ring," a cabal of distillers and revenue agents who cheated the government out of millions of tax dollars every year.

State and city governments in the North were no less corrupt. Wealthy businessmen curried favor with politicians whose votes would determine where a railroad would be built and which land would be allocated for rights of way. State officials accepted gifts, received salaries, and sat on the boards of corporations directly affected by their votes. Municipalities awarded lucrative contracts to build schools, parks, libraries, water and sewer systems, and mass-transportation networks, creating temptations for corruption. The Tweed Ring alone bilked New York City out of tens of millions of dollars. By these standards the corruption of the southern Reconstruction legislatures was relatively small.

But corruption in the South had particular significance for Reconstruction. Southern Republicans of modest means depended heavily on the money they earned as public officials. They were responsible for the collection of unusually high taxes and for economic development projects. For many, the lure of corruption proved overwhelming. The Republican governor of Louisiana grew rich while in office by "exacting tribute" from railroads seeking state favors. Corruption on a vast scale implied petty corruption as well: some legislators sold their votes for as little as $200.

Opponents of Reconstruction often used attacks on corruption to undermine Republican policies. Their strategy helped galvanize opposition, destroying Republican hopes of attracting white voters. Finally, corruption in the South stirred a backlash against active government nationwide, weakening northern support for Reconstruction. The intellectual substance of this backlash was provided by influential liberal Republicans, many of whom had strongly supported radical Reconstruction.

Liberal Republicans Revolt

The label "liberal Republicans" covered a small but influential group of intellectuals, politicians, publishers, and businessmen from the northern elite who were disgusted by postwar corruption and discouraged by the failure of radical Reconstruction to bring peace to the South.

Liberal philosophy was deeply suspicious of democracy. Liberals argued that any government beholden to the interests of the ignorant masses was doomed to corruption. They believed that public servants should be chosen on the basis of intelligence, as measured by civil-service examinations, rather than by patronage appointments through corrupt party machines. To liberals, party politics was the enemy of good government.

Liberals grew increasingly alienated from the Republican Party and from President Grant. Above all, they resented the fact that the Republican Party had changed as its idealistic commitment to free labor waned and its radical vanguard disappeared. To emerging Republican leaders, getting and holding office had become an end in itself.

As Republicans lost their identity as moral crusaders, liberal reformers proposed a new vision of their own. In 1872 they supported Horace Greeley as the Democratic presidential candidate. The liberal plank in the Democratic platform committed the party to universal equality before the law, the integrity of the Union, and support for the Thirteenth, Fourteenth, and Fifteenth Amendments. At the same time, liberals demanded "the immediate and absolute removal of all disabilities" imposed on the South, as well as a "universal amnesty" for ex-Confederates. Finally, the liberals declared their belief that "local self-government" would "guard the rights of all citizens more securely than any centralized power." In effect, the liberals were demanding the end of federal efforts to protect the former slaves.

In the long run, the liberal view would prevail, but not with the voters of 1872. The liberals' biggest liability was their presidential candidate. Horace Greeley's reputation and Republican background were too much, and Democrats refused to vote for him. Grant was easily reelected, but Republicans saw the returns as evidence that Reconstruction was becoming a political liability.

The 1874 elections confirmed the lesson. Democrats made sweeping gains across the North, and an ideological stalemate developed. For a generation, neither party would clearly dominate American politics. The Republicans would take no more risks in support of Reconstruction.

During his second term, Grant did little to protect black voters from violence in the South. Not even the Civil Rights Act of 1875 undid the impression of waning Republican zeal. Ostensibly designed to prohibit racial discrimination in public places, the act lacked enforcement provisions. The bill's most important clause, prohibiting segregated schools, was eliminated from the final version. Southern states ignored even this watered-down statute, and in 1883 the Supreme Court declared the last major piece of Reconstruction lawmaking unconstitutional.

A Depression and a Deal "Redeem" the South

Angered by corruption and high taxes, white voters in the South answered the Democratic Party's appeal for restoration of white supremacy. As the number of white Republicans fell, the number of black Republicans holding office in the South increased, even as the Grant administration backed away from civil rights. But the persistence of black officeholders only reinforced the Democrats' determination to "redeem" their states from Republican rule. Democrats had taken control of Virginia in 1869, North Carolina in 1870, Georgia in 1871, and Texas in 1873. Then panic struck.

In September 1873 America's premier financial institution, Jay Cooke & Company, went bankrupt after overextending itself on investments in the Northern Pacific Railroad. Within weeks hundreds of banks and thousands of businesses went bankrupt. And the country sank into a depression that lasted five years. Unemployment rose to 14 percent as corporations slashed wages. To protect their incomes, railroad workers tried to organize a nationwide union and attempted to strike several times. The strikes failed.

As the nation turned its attention to labor unrest and economic depression, the Republican Party's commitment to Reconstruction all but disappeared. Democrats regained control of the governments of Alabama and Arkansas in 1874. In the few southern states where black Republicans clung to political power, white "redeemers" used violence to overthrow the last remnants of Reconstruction.

Mississippi established the model in 1875, and it became known as "the Mississippi Plan." Confident that Washington would no longer interfere in the South, Democrats launched an all-out campaign to regain control of the state government. Crude appeals to white supremacy reduced the dwindling number of scalawags. To defeat black Republicans, White Leagues

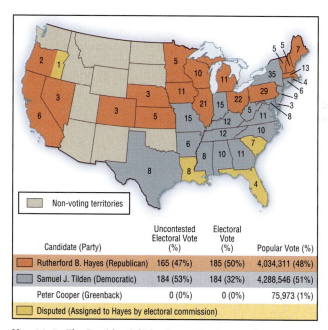

Candidate (Party)	Uncontested Electoral Vote (%)	Electoral Vote (%)	Popular Vote (%)
Rutherford B. Hayes (Republican)	165 (47%)	185 (50%)	4,034,311 (48%)
Samuel J. Tilden (Democratic)	184 (53%)	184 (32%)	4,288,546 (51%)
Peter Cooper (Greenback)	0 (0%)	0 (0%)	75,973 (1%)
Disputed (Assigned to Hayes by electoral commission)			

Non-voting territories

Map 16–4   The Presidential Election, 1876 In 1876 the Democratic presidential candidate, Samuel Tilden, won the popular vote but was denied the presidency because the Republicans who controlled Congress chose to interpret voting irregularities in Louisiana, South Carolina, Oregon, and Florida in a way that gave their candidate, Rutherford B. Hayes, all of the disputed electoral votes.

used violence and intimidation to keep blacks from the polls. Republicans were beaten, forced to flee, and in several cases murdered. Washington ignored African American pleas for protection. In the end enough blacks were kept from the polls and enough scalawags voted their racial prejudices to put the Democrats in power. Mississippi was "redeemed."

The tactics used in Mississippi were repeated elsewhere the following year, with dramatic consequences for the presidential election of 1876. Amidst a serious economic depression, and with an electorate tired of Reconstruction, the Democrats stood a good chance of winning the presidency. The Democratic candidate, Samuel J. Tilden, won 250,000 more votes than the Republican, Rutherford B. Hayes (see Map 16–4). But electoral fraud in South Carolina, Louisiana, Florida, and Oregon threw the results into doubt.

If all of the electoral votes from those states went to Hayes, he would win, but if even a single electoral vote went to Tilden, he would win, the first Democrat to win the presidency in 20 years. The outcome was determined by an electoral commission with a Republican majority, which awarded every disputed electoral vote to the Republican Hayes, casting doubt on the legitimacy of his presidency. What he did shortly after taking office suggested that he had won thanks to a "compromise" with the Democrats to end Reconstruction in the South. There is no proof that such a deal was ever actually made. Nevertheless, Hayes ordered the federal troops guarding the Republican statehouses in South Carolina and Louisiana to leave. This order marked the formal end of military occupation of the South and the symbolic end of Reconstruction. By late 1877, every southern state had been redeemed by the Democrats.

The following year the Supreme Court began to issue rulings that further undid the achievements of Reconstruction. In *Hall v. DeCuir* (1878) the Supreme Court invalidated a Louisiana law prohibiting racial segregation on public transportation. In 1882, the justices declared unconstitutional a federal law protecting southern African Americans against racially motivated murders and assaults. More important, in the Civil Rights Cases of 1883, the Supreme Court declared that the Fourteenth Amendment did not pertain to discriminatory practices by private persons. The Supreme Court thus completed the retreat from Reconstruction.

Conclusion

Inspired by an idealized vision of a society based on equal rights and free labor, Republicans expected emancipation to transform the South. Freed from the shackles of the slave power, the region would soon become a shining example of democracy and prosperity. If the results were less than Republicans expected, the achievements of Reconstruction were still impressive. Across the South, African American men and women carved out a space in which their families could live more freely than before. Black men by the tens of thousands elected to office some of the most democratic state legislatures of the nineteenth century. Thousands more black workers repudiated an objectionable contract-labor system in favor of a new compromise known as sharecropping. Furthermore, Reconstruction added three important amendments to the Constitution that transformed civil rights and electoral laws throughout the nation.

Nevertheless, the Republicans quickly washed their hands of Reconstruction. They left southern blacks unprotected in a hostile world. Sharecropping offered them little hope

>> Timeline

▼**1863**
Lincoln's Proclamation of Amnesty and Reconstruction

▼**1864**
Wade-Davis Bill

▼**1865**
General Sherman's Special Field Order No. 15
Freedmen's Bureau established
Lincoln's second inaugural
Lincoln assassinated; Andrew Johnson becomes president
General Howard's Circular 13
President Johnson orders the Freedmen's Bureau to return confiscated lands to former owners
Joint Committee on Reconstruction established by Congress

▼**1866**
Congress renews Freedmen's Bureau; Johnson vetoes renewal bill
Civil Rights Act vetoed by Johnson
Congress overrides presidential veto of Civil Rights Act
Congress passes Fourteenth Amendment
Congress passes another Freedmen's Bureau Bill over Johnson's veto
Republicans sweep midterm elections

▼**1867**
First and Second Reconstruction Acts
Tenure of Office Act

▼**1868**
Johnson fires Secretary of War Stanton
House of Representatives impeaches Johnson
Senate trial of Johnson begins
Acquittal of Johnson
Fourteenth Amendment ratified
Ulysses S. Grant wins presidential election

▼**1869**
Congress passes Fifteenth Amendment

▼**1870**
Fifteenth Amendment ratified

▼**1872**
"Liberal Republicans" leave their party
Grant reelected

continued

>> **Timeline** *continued*

▼**1873**
Financial "panic" sets off depression

▼**1875**
"Mississippi Plan" succeeds
Civil Rights Act of 1875 enacted

▼**1876**
Disputed presidential election

▼**1877**
Electoral commission awards presidency to Rutherford B. Hayes

of real economic independence. Democratic redeemers excluded blacks from the substance of power. Tired of Reconstruction, Americans turned their attention to the new problems of urban, industrial America.

Review Questions

1. What were the three major phases of Reconstruction?

2. What made congressional Reconstruction "radical"?

3. How did Reconstruction change the South?

4. How did Reconstruction change the North?

5. What were the major factors that brought Reconstruction to an end?

**For further review materials and resource information,
please visit www.oup.com/us/ofthepeople**

17

The Triumph of Industrial Capitalism

1850–1890

>> Rosa Cassettari

In 1884 Rosa Cassettari left the Italian village of Cuggiono, near Milan, to meet her husband Santino, a miner in Union, Missouri. Theirs had been an arranged marriage, and Rosa was reluctant to go, especially because she had to leave behind her infant son. "It is wonderful to go to America even if you don't want to go to Santino," Rosa's friends told her at the train station in Milan. "You will get smart in America. And in America you will not be so poor." Along with millions of others, Rosa entered a stream of migrants coming from the far corners of Europe. At Le Havre, France, she embarked on a ship for America. "All us poor people had to go down through a hole to the bottom of the ship," she remembered. But she was going to "America! The country where everyone would find work! Where wages were so high that no one had to go hungry! Where all men were free and equal and where even the poor could own land!"

Rosa's first taste of America did not live up to her dreams. In New York she was cheated and forced to make the long trip to Missouri with nothing to eat. At Union she found a shabby collection of tents and shacks. Life in the mining camp lived up to her fears rather than her hopes. With no doctors or midwives available, Rosa gave birth to a premature child alone on the floor of her cabin. Santino was an abusive husband and a cruel father. Rosa had to supplement his earnings by cooking for 12 additional miners.

Yet Rosa was impressed by many things about America. Poor people did not behave humbly in the presence of the rich, for example, and Rosa wore decent clothing and ate meat every day, things she could never do back in Europe.

When Rosa discovered that Santino planned to spend all their savings to open a house of prostitution, she separated from him. With the help of her immigrant friends, Rosa moved to Chicago with her two children. She took a job at a place called Hull House, where the social workers were so impressed by her life story that they wrote it down and published it as *Rosa Cassettari's Autobiography*.

continued

>> **AMERICAN PORTRAIT** *continued*

Rosa was one of millions of men and women who were moving around the world in the late nineteenth century. They moved from the countryside to the city or from town to town. They moved from less developed regions to places where industrialization was well under way. The hub of all of the movement was a core of industrial capitalist societies, and at the center of the core was the United States. Migrants were on a worldwide trek, but more of them came to the United States than went to any other nation.

Constant human migration, global in its extent, had become a hallmark of industrial capitalism. Common laborers moved from place to place because jobs were unsteady, or they moved when work was finished. African American sharecroppers in the South moved at year's end, eventually into cotton-growing districts, into towns and cities, or out of the South. White tenant farmers moved into mill towns. Native Americans were pushed off their lands throughout the trans-Mississippi West, making room for a flood of white settlers. And all across America the children of farmers abandoned the rural life for mill villages and for huge cities such as New York, Chicago, and Philadelphia.

They went looking for work, and that meant working in a bureaucracy under the control of professional managers. It meant working with new and complicated machines, with polluted air, dirty rivers, or spoiled land. Most of all, industrial capitalism meant wage labor. Working people had been freed from the things that once tied them to the land, such as feudal dues, slavery, and even independent farming. But wage labor released men and women to move about from community to community, from country to country, and finally from continent to continent. To watch Rosa Cassettari as she traveled from Cuggiono to Missouri and then Chicago is to witness one small part of a global process set in motion by the triumph of wage labor.

Common Threads

>> In what ways were the problems of Reconstruction and the problems of industrialization similar?

>> What made "big business" different from earlier enterprises?

>> Does the new social order of the late nineteenth century look more like what came before it or more like what came later on?

The Political Economy of Global Capitalism

The economic history of the late nineteenth century was sandwiched between two great financial panics in 1873 and 1893. Both were followed by prolonged periods of high unemployment and led directly to tremendous labor unrest. The years between the two panics saw a general decline in prices that placed a terrible burden on producers. Farmers found that their crops were worth less at harvest time than they had been during planting season. The more that manufacturers increased production to maintain profits, the lower the prices for their products fell. In search of an inexpensive workforce, industrialists turned to an international labor market. Amidst financial panics and nationwide strikes, depressions and deflation, Americans experienced a dramatic economic transformation. When it was over, the United States had become the leading capitalist nation on earth.

The "Great Depression" of the Late Nineteenth Century

On July 16, 1877, workers for the Baltimore and Ohio Railroad struck at Martinsburg, West Virginia. Within days the strike spread to the Pennsylvania Railroad, the New York Central, the Great Western, and the Texas Pacific. Governors ordered the strikers to disperse and asked for federal assistance. Federal troops were sent to major cities, but confrontations between workers and armed forces only fanned the flames of insurrection. "Other workingmen followed the example of the railroad employees," explained Henry Demarest Lloyd, a prominent social critic. "At Zanesville, Ohio, fifty manufactories stopped work. Baltimore ceased to export petroleum. The rolling mills, foundries, and refineries of Cleveland were closed. . . . Merchants could not sell, manufacturers could not work, banks could not lend. The country went to the verge of a panic." A strike in one key industry now threatened the entire nation.

The railroad strike of 1877 was fueled by an economic depression that began with the Panic of 1873 (see Chapter 16) and spread throughout the developed world. Immigrant arrivals in New York—200,000 every year between 1865 and 1873—fell to less than 65,000 in 1877. Although employment recovered in the 1880s, prices and wages continued to fall. Then in 1893 another panic struck. Once again several major railroads went bankrupt, and more than 500 banks and 15,000 businesses shut down. From 1873 to 1896 a "great depression" blighted much of the globe.

The world was shrinking, and most Americans knew it. In 1866 a telegraph cable was laid under the Atlantic Ocean. From that moment, Americans could read about events in Europe in the next morning's newspaper. Railroads slashed distances across Europe and the United States. Steamships brought distant ports into regular contact. Midwestern farmers sold their wheat in Russia. Chinese workers laid the tracks of the Union Pacific Railroad. Eastern Europeans worked the steel mills of Pittsburgh. The political economy of capitalism was tying the world's nations together.

The clearest sign of this linkage was the emergence of an international labor market. As economic change swept through the less developed world, men and women were freed from their traditional ties to the land and hurled into a global stream of wage laborers. Irish women went to work as domestic servants. African Americans took jobs as railroad porters. Wage laborers built and maintained the transportation network, the steel mills, and the petroleum refineries; slaughtered beef in Chicago; sewed ready-made clothing in factories; and staffed department store sales counters.

America Moves to the City

Between 1850 and 1900 the map of the United States was redrawn thanks to the appearance of dozens of new cities (see Figure 17–1). Of the 150 largest cities in the United States in the late twentieth century, 85 were founded in the second half of the nineteenth

Map 17–1 Patterns of Global Migration, 1840–1900 Emigration was a global process by the late nineteenth century. But more immigrants went to the United States than to every other nation combined. *Source:* London Times Atlas.

century. In 1850 the largest city in the United States was New York, with a population of just over half a million. By 1900 New York, Philadelphia, and Chicago each had more than a million residents.

The industrial city was different from its predecessors. By the middle of the nineteenth century the modern "downtown" was born, a place where people shopped and worked but did not necessarily live. Residential neighborhoods separated city dwellers from the downtown districts and separated the classes from one another. Streetcars and commuter railroads brought middle-class clerks and professionals from their homes to their jobs and back, but the fares were beyond the means of the working class. The rich built their mansions uptown, but workers had no choice but to remain within walking distance of their jobs.

Cities became more crowded, unsanitary, and unsafe. Yellow fever and cholera epidemics were frequent. Fires periodically wiped out entire neighborhoods. In October 1871 much of Chicago went up in flames. Along with fires and epidemics, urban life was

AMERICA AND THE WORLD

>> The Global Migration of Labor

Nineteenth-century migrants tended to leave areas already in the grip of social and economic change. Rosa Cassettari, for example, had worked in a silk-weaving factory in Italy. At first, the largest numbers emigrated from the most developed nations, such as Great Britain and Germany. Later in the century, as industrial or agricultural revolution spread, growing numbers of immigrants came from Scandinavia, Russia, Italy, and Hungary (see Map 17-1). As capitalism developed in these areas, small farmers were forced to produce for a highly competitive international market. The resulting upheaval sent millions of rural folk into the worldwide migratory stream.

Improvements in transportation and communication were a sign that capitalism was spreading; they also made migration easier. In 1856, more than 95 percent of immigrants came to America aboard sailing vessels. By the end of the century, more than 95 percent came in steamships. The Atlantic crossing took one to three months under sail, but only 10 days by steam. Beginning in the 1880s, fierce competition among steamship lines lowered the cost of a transatlantic ticket. Many immigrants went back and forth across the Atlantic, particularly workers in seasonal trades such as construction.

But the great migrations were also related to political upheaval. In China, for example, the Taiping Rebellion of 1848 was accompanied by an economic disaster rivaling the Irish potato famine of the same decade. This combination of economic and political disruption sent some 300,000 Chinese to the Pacific Coast of North

America between 1850 and 1882. They labored in mines and panned for gold and helped build the transcontinental railroad. Desperate for employment and willing to work for low wages, the Chinese soon confronted racist hostility from American and European workers and union officials. In 1882 Congress responded by passing the Chinese Exclusion Act, banning further immigration from China.

A similar combination of economic and political forces lay beneath European immigration. The revival of employment in the 1880s spurred a revival of movement. After 1890, immigration from northern and western Europe fell off sharply, as capitalist development made labor scarce in those areas. But by then agrarian crisis and political disruption had set off a wave of emigration from eastern and southern Europe. In Austria-Hungary, for example, the revolution of 1848 brought with it economic and political changes that resulted, by the 1880s, in a profound agrarian crisis. In southern Italy, citrus fruits from Florida and California arrived on the market, and protective tariffs thwarted the sale of Italian wines abroad. Desperate Italian farmers started coming to the United States.

Jewish immigration was propelled by a different combination of politics and economics. The assassination of Czar Alexander II in 1881 was followed by a surge of Russian nationalism. Anti-Jewish riots (called *pogroms*) erupted in 1881-1882, 1891, and 1905-1906, during which countless Jews were massacred. Anti-Semitic laws forced Russian Jews to live within the *continued*

AMERICA AND THE WORLD *continued*

so-called Pale of Settlement along Russia's western and southern borders, and the May Laws of 1882 severely restricted Russian Jews' religious and economic life. In the 1880s, Russian Jews began moving to America in significant numbers.

Most immigrants came to America looking for work. Some came with education and skills; some were illiterate. Most came with little more than their ability to work, and they usually found their jobs through families, friends, and fellow immigrants. Letters from America told of high wages and steady employment. Communities of immigrant workers provided the support that newcomers needed. Some immigrants settled directly on farms, but the overwhelming number lived in cities.

marred by poverty and crime. Immigrant slums appeared in most major cities of America, as well as in mill towns and mining camps. In 1890 Jacob Riis published *How the Other Half Lives*, his famous exposé of life in the immigrant slums of New York. He described a dark three-room apartment inhabited by six people. The two bedrooms were tiny, the beds nothing more than boxes filled with "foul straw." Such conditions were a common feature of urban poverty in the late nineteenth century.

Yet during these same years urban reformers set about to make city life less dangerous and more comfortable. Professional fire departments were formed in most big cities by

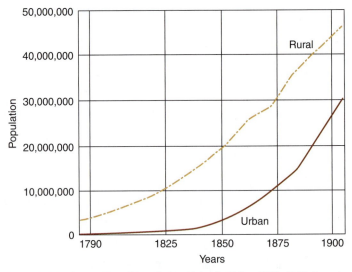

Figure 17–1   Proportion of Population Living in Cities, 1790–1900 A growing proportion of Americans lived in cities, but not until the twentieth century did city dwellers outnumber rural Americans.

The Lower East Side of Manhattan This busy street scene is from an area swollen with largely Jewish immigrants.

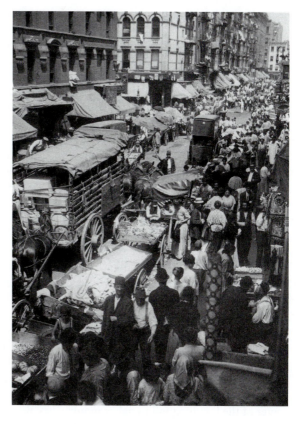

the 1860s. Professional police departments appeared around the same time, greatly reducing urban violence. In 1866 New York City set up the first board of health.

In the second half of the nineteenth century American cities undertook the colossal task of making urban life decent and safe. To a large degree they succeeded: cities provided clean drinking water, efficient transportation, and great museums, public libraries, and parks. And so the city, which the Jeffersonian tradition had long associated with corruption and decay, was increasingly defended as an oasis of diversity and excitement.

Annie Aitken, who moved from Scotland to Pittsburgh, Pennsylvania, in 1840, would have agreed. Aitken was prospering in the United States, while her sister Margaret's family in Scotland was sinking fast. Margaret's husband, Will, had been a traditional handloom weaver whose livelihood was destroyed by the rise of textile mills. With Aitken's encouragement, in 1848 Will and Margaret Carnegie and their two sons, Tom and Andrew, left Scotland and moved to Pittsburgh. Annie Aitken let her sister's family live rent free in a small house she owned. Her nephew, Andrew, took a job in a textile mill for $1.20 a week. Fifty years later, Andrew Carnegie sold his steel mills to J. Pierpont Morgan for $480 million.

The Rise of Big Business

Before the Civil War the only enterprises in the United States that could be called "big businesses" were the railroads. Indeed, railroads became the model for a new kind of business—big business—that emerged during the 1880s. Big businesses had massive bureaucracies managed by professionals rather than owners and were financed through a national banking system centered on Wall Street. They marketed their goods and services across the nation and around the world and generated wealth in staggering concentrations, giving rise to a class of men whose names—Carnegie, Rockefeller, Morgan, and Vanderbilt—became synonymous with American capitalism.

The Rise of Andrew Carnegie

Andrew Carnegie was an immigrant, whereas most businessmen were native born. His childhood in Scotland was marked by poverty, whereas most of America's leading men of business were raised in relative prosperity. Certainly, few working families in the late nineteenth century could hope to match Carnegie's spectacular climb from rags to riches. Nevertheless, Andrew Carnegie was the perfect reflection of the rise of big business. In the course of his career, Carnegie mastered the telegraph, railroad, petroleum, iron, and steel industries and introduced modern management techniques and strict accounting procedures to American manufacturing. Other great industrialists and financiers made their mark in the last half of the nineteenth century—Henry Clay Frick, Collis P. Huntington, George M. Pullman, John D. Rockefeller, and Cornelius Vanderbilt—but none of their lives took on the mythic proportions of that of the Scottish lad who came to America at the age of 12 and ended up the richest man in the world.

"I have made millions since," Carnegie once wrote, "but none of these gave me so much happiness as my first week's earnings." Young Andrew might have been happy to earn a wage, but he was not content with his job in a mill. He enrolled in a night course to study accounting, and a year later he got a job as a messenger boy in a telegraph office. So astute and hardworking was Andrew that by 1851 he was promoted to telegraph operator, and he soon displayed the leadership ability that marked his career. He recruited talented, hardworking men and organized them with stunning efficiency.

The most successful businessmen in Pittsburgh, such as Tom Scott, a superintendent for the Pennsylvania Railroad, noticed Carnegie's talents. In 1853, Scott offered Carnegie a job as his secretary and personal telegrapher. Carnegie stayed with the company for 12 years during a time when rail construction soared and railroads were at the center of the booming industrial economy. They would become the steel industry's biggest customer. Petroleum refiners shipped their kerosene by rail. Mining corporations needed railroads to ship their coal and iron. Ranchers shipped their cattle by rail to the slaughterhouses of Chicago, and meat packers distributed butchered carcasses in refrigerated railroad cars. His position at the Pennsylvania Railroad gave Carnegie an unrivaled familiarity with the workings of big business.

By the mid-1850s, the largest factory in the country, the Pepperell Mills in Biddeford, Maine, employed 800 workers, whereas the Pennsylvania Railroad had more than 4,000 employees. If an engineer arrived late, or if a fireman came to work drunk, trains were wrecked, lives were lost, and business failed. The railroads thus borrowed the disciplinary methods and bureaucratic structure of the military to ensure that the trains ran safely and on time.

The man who introduced this organizational discipline to the Pennsylvania Railroad was Tom Scott, the man who hired Andrew Carnegie. J. Edgar Thomson, the Pennsylvania's president, was a pioneer of a different sort. He established an elaborate bookkeeping system providing detailed knowledge of every aspect of the Pennsylvania's operations. Scott used the data to reward managers who improved the company's profits and eliminate those who failed.

Carnegie succeeded. After Scott was promoted to vice president in 1859, Carnegie took his place as superintendent of the western division, where he helped make the Pennsylvania a model of efficiency. By 1865 it had 30,000 employees and had expanded east to New York City and west to Chicago. It was the largest private company in the world.

Map 17-2   The Growth of Railroads, 1850–1890 Railroads were more than a means of transportation; they were also America's first "big business." Railroad management established the model for running huge industrial corporations, and the growth of railroads sustained the initial growth of the iron and steel industries.

Carnegie's experience gave him a keen understanding of the modern financial system. Railroads dwarfed all previous business enterprises in the amount of investment capital they required and in the complexity of their financial arrangements. Railroads were the first corporations to issue stocks through sophisticated trading mechanisms that attracted investors from around the world. To organize the market in such vast numbers of securities, the modern investment house was developed. J. Pierpont Morgan grew rich selling railroad stocks and from his association with Andrew Carnegie, for there was no shrewder investor in America.

Carnegie Becomes a Financier

Carnegie began making money from money in 1856. On Tom Scott's advice he borrowed $600 and invested it in Adams Express Company stock, which soon began paying handsome dividends. Carnegie had become a successful capitalist, and for the next 15 years he made a series of moves that earned him several more fortunes.

Carnegie invested in the Woodruff Sleeping Car Company in the late 1850s and, a decade later, used his position to help George Pullman win near-monopoly control of the industry—and make millions in the bargain. Carnegie brokered a similar deal that created the Western Union monopoly of the telegraph industry. He made millions in shady deals on the international financial markets. More substantially, he created the Keystone Bridge Company, which built the first steel arch bridge over the Mississippi River and provided the infrastructure for the Brooklyn Bridge. With Keystone, Carnegie perfected a model of managerial organization that was the envy of the industrial world.

By 1872 Carnegie was tired of financial speculation and ready for something new. He was 37 years old and had proven himself a master of the railroad industry, a brilliant manager, and a shrewd financial manipulator. Now Carnegie wanted to create an industry of his own. "I wished to make something tangible," he explained. He would make iron and steel.

Carnegie Dominates the Steel Industry

In 1865 Carnegie acquired a controlling interest in the Union Iron Company. His first goal was to speed the flow of materials to his Keystone Bridge Company. This was an important innovation. Iron manufacturing in America had always been decentralized, with each stage of production handled by a different manufacturer. But Carnegie forced Union Iron and Keystone Bridge to coordinate their operations, eliminating middlemen and making production more efficient. Carnegie also forced Union Iron to adopt the managerial techniques and accounting practices he had learned at the Pennsylvania Railroad. By keeping a strict account of all costs, Carnegie could locate the most wasteful points in the production process and reward the most efficient workers. Carnegie introduced modern management techniques to American industry, but it was in steel rather than iron that Carnegie would prove the worth of those techniques.

As with so many industries, the development of steel was driven by the development of railroads. Traditional iron rails deteriorated rapidly under the loads of larger and heavier trains. J. Edgar Thomson, head of the Pennsylvania Railroad, began experiment-

The Eads Bridge The steel arches of the Eads Bridge across the Mississippi River at St. Louis were both an engineering marvel and a triumph of Andrew Carnegie's managerial skills.

Chinese Laborers Building Railroad This 1877 picture of a Southern Pacific Railroad trestle shows the crude construction methods used in building the first railroad across the Sierra Nevada.

ing with steel rails in 1862. Steel was also a better material for locomotives, boilers, and railroad cars. In the 1860s two developments cleared the path for the transition from iron to steel. First, Henry Bessemer's patented process for turning iron into steel became available to American manufacturers. Second, iron ore began flowing freely from deposits in northern Michigan.

Andrew Carnegie was uniquely situated to take advantage of these developments. At Union Iron he learned to run a mill efficiently, and he had access to investment capital. In 1872 Carnegie built a steel mill, the Thomson Works. Despite a worldwide depression, the steel mill was profitable from the start.

Big Business Consolidates

In the late nineteenth century the names of a handful of wealthy capitalists became closely associated with different industries: Gustavus Swift in meat packing, John D. Rockefeller in oil refining, Collis P. Huntington in railroads, J. P. Morgan in financing, and Andrew Carnegie in steel (see Map 17–3). These powerful individuals, sometimes called "robber barons," represented a passing phase in the history of American enterprise. Most big

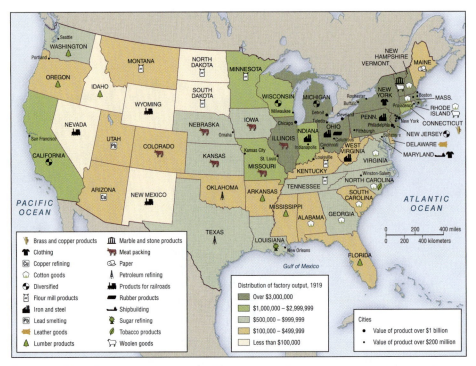

Map 17–3   Major American Industries, ca. 1890 An industrial map of late nineteenth-century America shows regions increasingly defined not by their crops but by their major industries.

businesses were so big that no single individual or family could own them. They were run by professionally trained managers, and the highest profits went to companies with the most efficient bureaucracies. Because the businesses were so big and their equipment so expensive, they had to operate continuously. In an economic slowdown an average factory could close its doors for a while, but big businesses could not.

Beginning in the 1880s big businesses developed strategies designed to shield them from the effects of ruinous competition. The most common strategy was vertical integration, the attempt to control as many aspects of a business as possible, from the production of raw materials to the sale of the finished product. Carnegie integrated the steel industry, from the extraction of iron ore to the production and distribution of steel. He bought iron mines to produce his own ore and railroads to ship the ore to his mills and the finished product to market. His Keystone Bridge Company then purchased the steel.

In 1882 John D. Rockefeller devised a new solution to the problem of ruinous competition by forming the Standard Oil Trust. Rockefeller had founded Standard Oil in 1867 in Cleveland, Ohio. Like Carnegie, Rockefeller hired the best managers and financiers to build and run the most efficient modern refineries, but he was more willing than Carnegie to use ruthless tactics to wipe out his competitors. Rockefeller extracted preferential shipping rates from the railroads, gaining a critical advantage in a savagely competitive business. In 1872 Rockefeller began imposing on the national oil refining industry the same control that he had already achieved in Ohio. As president of the National Refiners'

Association he formed cartels with the major operators in other states. But the cartels were too weak to eliminate independent refiners.

Rockefeller set out to control the entire oil industry by merging all of the major companies together under Standard Oil. In 1882 the Standard Oil monopoly was formalized as a "trust," an elaborate legal device by which different producers came together under the umbrella of a single company that could police competition internally. In 1889 the New Jersey legislature passed a law allowing corporations based in that state to form "holding companies" that controlled companies in other states. Thus the trust gave way to the holding company, with Standard Oil of New Jersey its most prominent example. Within a decade many of the largest industries in America were dominated by massive holding companies.

Rockefeller's Standard Oil monopoly was a notorious example of how big business had changed the American economy. Rockefeller himself came to represent a powerful new class of extraordinarily wealthy businessmen. Their names—Carnegie, Rockefeller, Morgan, Harriman, and others—soon became associated with the upper class of the new social order of industrial America.

A New Social Order

Many Americans believed that classes were not supposed to exist in the United States the way they existed in Europe. Yet the reality of class divisions was so obvious that it had become part of public discussion. It was hard not to notice the conspicuous gap between the astonishing wealth of Andrew Carnegie and the daily struggles of Rosa Cassettari.

Lifestyles of the Very Rich

Between 1850 and 1890 the proportion of the nation's wealth owned by the 4,000 richest families nearly tripled. At the top of the social pyramid rested some 200 families worth more than $20 million each. Concentrated in the Northeast, especially in New York, these families were known throughout the world for their astonishing wealth. Spread more evenly across America were the several thousand millionaires whose investments in cattle ranching, agricultural equipment, mining, commerce, and real estate made them wealthy capitalists.

As a group America's millionaires had a lot in common. Most traced their ancestry to Great Britain. Most were Protestant, usually Episcopalians, Presbyterians, or Congregationalists. By the standards of their day they were unusually well educated. Except in the South, America's upper class voted Republican.

The upper classes lived in spectacular houses in neighborhoods that became famous for their wealth: Fifth Avenue in Manhattan, Nob Hill in San Francisco, Rittenhouse Square in Philadelphia, and Boston's Back Bay. Wealthy suburbs (Brooklyn Heights, Philadelphia's Main Line, and Brookline, Massachusetts) became privileged retreats. The richest families also built

> The most valuable class in any community is the middle class, the men of moderate means, living at the rate of a thousand dollars a year or thereabouts.
>
> WALT WHITMAN
> 1858

rural estates that rivaled the country homes of England and the chateaus of France, such as a string of spectacular summer homes along the Newport, Rhode Island, shoreline.

The leading figures in New York's high society competed with one another to stage the most lavish balls and dinner parties. The competition reached a climax on March 26, 1883, when Mrs. William Vanderbilt staged a stupendous costume ball that challenged Mrs. William Astor's long-standing position as the queen of New York's upper class. It was left to the new middle class to preserve the traditional virtues of thrift and self-denial.

The Consolidation of the New Middle Class

In 1889 *The Century Dictionary* introduced the phrase "middle class" in the United States. The new term reflected a novel awareness that American society had become permanently divided.

Professionals were the backbone of the new middle class of the nineteenth century. All professions defined what it meant to be a member of their tribe, organized themselves into associations, and set educational standards for admission. By these means professionals could command high salaries and enjoy prestige and a comfortable standard of living. Between 1870 and 1890 some 200 societies were formed to establish and maintain the credentials of their members. Even the management of corporations became professionalized, as business schools were created to teach the science of accounting and the art of management. Some professionals succeeded in having their standards written into law. In most states, by 1900, doctors and lawyers could practice legally only when licensed under the auspices of professional associations.

Behind the new professional managers marched an expanding white-collar army of cashiers, clerks, and government employees. They were overwhelmingly men, and they earned annual incomes far beyond those of independent craftsmen and factory workers. They also enjoyed much better opportunities for upward mobility. A beginning clerk might make only $100 a year, but within five years his salary could be closer to $1,000. At a time when the average annual income of a skilled factory worker in Philadelphia was less than $600, over 80 percent of the male clerks in the Treasury Department earned over $1,200 a year.

As it developed, the middle class left the messy uncertainties of the central city. Improved roads and mass-transit systems allowed middle-class families to escape the urban extremes of great wealth and miserable poverty. Middle-class residents idealized the comfortable domestic life that tree-shaded suburbs afforded.

Only the most successful craftsmen matched the incomes and suburban lifestyles of white-collar clerks. Butchers might earn more than $1,600 annually, for example, but shoemakers averaged little more than $500. A shoemaker who owned a small shop maintained the kind of independence cherished by middle-class Americans, yet his income scarcely distinguished him from skilled factory workers. The manual crafts were a bridge between the remnants of the independent middle class and the growing industrial working class made up of men and women like Rosa Cassettari.

The Industrial Working Class Comes of Age

"When I first went to learn the trade," John Morrison told a congressional committee in 1883, "a machinist considered himself more than the average workingman; in fact he did not like to be called a workingman. He liked to be called a mechanic." Morrison identified one of the great changes in nineteenth-century America. Before the Civil War, skilled urban laborers were referred to as artisans and mechanics. "Today," Morrison explained, the mechanic "is simply a laborer." Big businesses replaced mechanics with semiskilled or unskilled factory laborers. For traditional mechanics, this felt like downward mobility.

Because most factory workers and common laborers were migrants (or children of migrants) from small towns and farms, few experienced factory work as a degradation of their traditional skills, as John Morrison did. But industrial labor was a harsh existence for all factory operatives, who worked long hours in difficult conditions performing repetitious tasks with little job security.

The clothing industry is a good example of the lives of urban workers. The introduction of the sewing machine in the 1850s gave rise to sweatshops where work was subdivided into simple, repetitive tasks. One group produced collars for men's shirts, another produced cuffs, and another stitched the parts together. Jobs were defined so that workers could be easily replaced. Workers learned this lesson quickly. They were young; often they were women or children who moved constantly into and out of different jobs. But even among men, factory work was at best insecure and unsteady, subject to the business cycle that swung hard and often.

At the bottom of the hierarchy of wage earners were the common laborers, whose job was physical exertion. Their numbers grew throughout the century until by 1900 common laborers accounted for a third of the industrial workforce. Hundreds of thousands worked for railroads and steel companies.

Common laborers were difficult to organize into effective unions. A large proportion were immigrants and African Americans, and ethnic differences and language barriers often frustrated alliances. Even the kind of work common laborers performed inhibited the growth of effective unions. It was rarely steady work. Men who laid railroad tracks or dug subway tunnels generally moved on when they finished. Common labor was often seasonal, so unskilled workers changed jobs frequently. Common laborers were unusually mobile and easily replaceable, and they increasingly came from parts of the world where the idea of organized labor was unknown. Even when they did organize, common laborers faced the biggest, most powerful, best organized corporations in the country.

Much of the wage work done by women fell into the category of common labor. In 1900 women accounted for nearly one of every five gainfully employed Americans. In northern middle-class homes, young Irish women worked as domestics, jobs held in the South by African American women. A smaller proportion of women held white-collar jobs, as teachers, nurses, or low-paid clerical workers and sales clerks behind department store counters.

The same hierarchy that favored men in the white-collar and professional labor force existed in the factories and sweatshops. In the clothing industry, for example, units dominated by male workers were higher up the chain of command than those dominated by women. Indeed, as the textile industry became a big business, the proportion of women working in textile mills steadily declined. The reverse trend affected white-collar workers. As department stores expanded in the 1870s and 1880s, they hired low-paid women, often Irish immigrants, with none of the prospects for promotion still available to men. White-collar work was not a signal of middle-class status for women as it was for most men in the late nineteenth century.

The story was somewhat different for married women and their children. As few as 1 in 50 working-class wives and mothers took jobs outside the home, supplementing the

Women Workers in a New York City Hat Factory, ca. 1900 In the hierarchy of wage laborers, women were the lowest paid and the least skilled.

family income by taking in boarders or doing laundry. Most working-class families survived by sending their children to work. Even in the families of the highest paid industrial workers, 50 percent of the children worked. Among the poorest working-class families, three out of four children worked. The rich sent their daughters to finishing schools and their sons to boarding schools, middle-class parents sent their children to public schools, and working-class families sent their children to work. This was especially true in the South, where sharecropping was becoming a form of wage labor. Child labor was a clear sign of class distinction.

Sharecropping Becomes Wage Labor

As the southern economy recovered from the devastation of the Civil War, many observers predicted a bright future for the region. Optimists saw a wealth of opportunities from untapped natural and human resources, a South freed from the inefficient slave labor system and ripe for investment.

Americans were building railroads at an exuberant clip, but southerners built them faster. By 1890 impressive steel mills were coming to life in Birmingham, Alabama. The Piedmont Plateau (along the eastern foothills of the Appalachian Mountains from Virginia to Georgia) was dotted with textile mills bigger and more efficient than those in New England. Southerners were migrating from the countryside to the towns, expanding cotton production into new areas, cultivating the rich soil of the Mississippi Delta. Yet for ordinary southerners, especially African Americans, there was no great prosperity in the New South.

After the war most blacks returned to work on land they did not own (see Chapter 16). In place of the master-slave relationship emerged a new labor relationship between landlords and sharecroppers. A powerful class of merchants arose to supply the credit that kept this system alive. At first it was unclear how much power the landlords, the merchants, and the sharecroppers each had. The most important question was who owned the cotton crop at the end of the year: the sharecropper who produced it, the landlord who owned the farm, or the merchant who loaned the supplies to bring the crop in. The answer would be decided in the state legislatures and courts where the credit laws were written and interpreted.

Legal resolution in favor of the landlord came by the middle of the 1880s. The courts defined a sharecropper as a wage laborer. The landlord owned the crop and paid his workers a share of it as a wage. Landlords also won a stronger claim on the crop than the merchant creditors. Under the circumstances, merchants were reluctant to loan money to sharecroppers. Many left plantation districts and moved up-country, doing business with white yeomen farmers. Trapped in a cycle of debt, white farmers in the 1880s began losing their land and falling into tenancy. Meanwhile, in the "black belt" (where most African Americans lived and most of the cotton was produced), successful landlords became merchants while successful merchants purchased land and hired sharecroppers of their own. By the mid-1880s, black sharecroppers worked as wage laborers for the landlord-merchant class across much of the South.

Sharecropping differed in two critical ways from the wage work of industrial America. First, sharecropping was family labor, depending on a husband and father who signed the contract and delivered the labor of his wife and children to the landlord. Second, because sharecropping contracts were yearlong, the labor market was restricted to a few weeks at the end of each year. If croppers left before the end of the year, they risked losing everything.

The political economy of sharecropping impoverished the South by binding the region to a single crop—cotton—that steadily depleted the soil even as prices fell. Yet for most southern blacks there were few alternatives. Over time a small percentage of black farmers purchased their own land, but their farms were generally tiny and the soil poor. The skilled black artisans who had worked on plantations before the Civil War moved to southern cities, where they took unskilled, low-paying jobs. Industrialization was not much help for African Americans. Northern factories were segregated, as were the steel mills of Birmingham, Alabama, and the Piedmont textile mills. Black women worked as domestic servants to supplement their husbands' meager incomes. Wage labor transformed the lives of southern blacks, but it did not bring prosperity.

Hoping to escape the poverty and discrimination of southern life, a number of former slaves moved west. One group, the Exodusters, began moving to the Kansas prairie during the mid-1870s. By 1880 more than 6,000 blacks had joined them, searching for cheap land for independent farms. Like white farmers, the Exodusters fought with cattlemen, and blacks who settled in cow towns such as Dodge City and Topeka found the same discrimination they had known in the South. Still, some of the Exodusters did buy land and build farms. Their experience was similar to that of other Americans escaping west from the constraints of urban and industrial America.

Clearing the West for Capitalism

The Homestead Act, passed by Congress during the Civil War, was designed to ensure that the West would be settled by hardworking, independent small farmers. And millions of farmers did settle in the West during the second half of the nineteenth century. Their movement has become the stuff of legend.

But these hardy individuals did not settle an empty prairie. Waiting in the West were native peoples, some helpful and many hostile. And far from escaping the world of industrial capitalism, the settlers brought it with them. By the time the director of the U.S. Census declared the frontier "closed" in 1890, the political economy of the American West was composed of railroad tycoons and immigrant workers, commercial farmers, and impoverished Native Americans.

The Overland Trail

"Left home this morning," Jane Gould wrote in her diary on April 27, 1862. Along with her husband, Albert, and their two sons, Jane loaded a covered wagon in Mitchell, Iowa, and joined a group of migrants on the Overland Trail to California (see Map 17–4). It would be a long and difficult journey. Albert got sick shortly after they left, and Jane had to nurse him, drive the wagon, and care for the children. The Overland Trail was littered with the remnants of earlier wagon trains, including discarded furniture, dried bones, and lonely graves. In early October the Goulds reached their new home in the San Joaquin Valley. Five months later, Jane's husband died.

In popular images the West was a haven for rugged men who struck out on their own, but most migrants went in family groups, and the families were mostly middle class. Few poor people could afford the expense of the journey and still hope to buy land and set up a farm in the West.

The journey across the Overland Trail became safer over the years. In the late 1840s the U.S. government began building forts to protect migrants from Indians and to serve as resting points for wagon trains. By the 1850s Mormon settlers in Utah had built Salt Lake City into a major stopping point. Also during the 1850s, the government began to

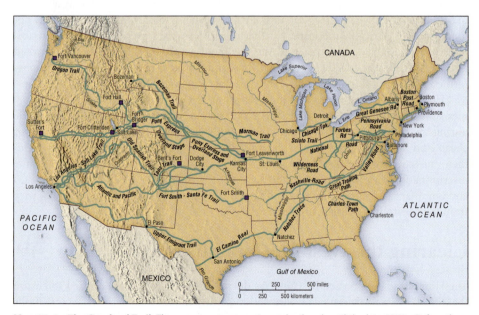

Map 17–4 The Overland Trail There was no transcontinental railroad until the late 1860s. Before then, and even thereafter, most settlers moved west on a series of well-developed overland trails.

pursue a long-term solution to the growing problem of Native American–white relations in the West.

The Origins of Indian Reservations

In 1851 more than 10,000 Native Americans from across the Great Plains converged on Fort Laramie in Wyoming Territory. All the major Indian peoples were represented: Sioux, Cheyenne, Arapaho, Crow, and many others. They came to meet with government officials who hoped to develop a lasting means of avoiding Indian–white conflict. Since the discovery of gold a few years earlier, white migrants had been crossing through Indian territory on their way to California, most of them already prejudiced against the Indians. U.S. officials wanted to prevent hostility between whites and Indians from breaking out into violence and to restrain the conflicts among Indians themselves. They proposed the creation of a separate territory for each Indian tribe, with government subsidies to entice the Indians to stay within their territories. This was the beginning of the reservation system, and for the rest of the century the U.S. government struggled to force the Indians to accept it.

From the start, the reservation system was corrupt and difficult to enforce. Agents for the Bureau of Indian Affairs cheated Indians and the government alike, sometimes reaping huge profits. But the reservations failed mostly because not all Indians agreed to stay within their designated territories, leading to armed confrontations and reprisals.

By the late 1860s the tensions between Indians and whites were at a fever pitch, as Senator James R. Doolittle of Wisconsin discovered on a fact-finding mission through the West. In Denver he asked an audience of whites whether they preferred outright extermination of the Indians to a policy of restricting Indians to reservations. The crowd roared its approval for extermination. Army officers agreed. The government "must act with vindictive earnestness against the Sioux," General William Tecumseh Sherman declared.

Doolittle and his colleagues resisted the calls for extermination, opting instead for a more comprehensive reservation policy. The policy was based on two treaties that divided the Great Plains into two huge Indian territories. The Medicine Lodge Treaty, signed in Kansas in 1867, organized thousands of Indians across the Southern Plains. In return for government supplies, most of the Southern Plains peoples agreed to restrict themselves to the reservation. The Northern Plains Indians did not agree so readily. A treaty was drafted, but a band of holdouts demanded further concessions. Inspired by their leader Red Cloud, the Indians insisted that the U.S. abandon forts along the Bozeman Trail. When the government agreed, Red Cloud signed the Fort Laramie Treaty in 1868.

Red Cloud respected the treaties for the rest of his life, but they nevertheless failed. Most white settlers still preferred extermination to reservations, and not all the Plains Indians approved of the treaties. Nor did the U.S. Army abide by the reservation policy. Within weeks of Red Cloud's signature on the Fort Laramie Treaty, the Seventh Cavalry, led by Colonel George Armstrong Custer, massacred Cheyennes at Washita, Oklahoma. As long as the U.S. Army sustained the settlers' hunger for extermination, Indian "policy" was made on the battlefield.

By 1870 it was clear that western Indians would not voluntarily retire to reservations and that the military could not force them into surrender. If any further evidence of the Indian resistance was needed, it came in South Dakota, where, after discovery of gold in the Black Hills, thousands of whites poured onto Indian territory. When the Lakota Sioux refused to cede their lands to the miners, the government sent in the army, led by General Custer. Custer was an arrogant man, and he made two critical mistakes. First, he divided

Indian Village Routed, Geronimo Fleeing from Camp Oil on canvas by Frederic Remington, 1896.

his army in two, and, second, he failed to keep them in communication with each other. Custer and hundreds of his men were slaughtered at Little Bighorn, Montana, in 1876 by 2,000 Indian warriors led by Sitting Bull and Crazy Horse.

The Destruction of Indian Subsistence

Custer's Last Stand did not improve the fortunes of the Plains Indians. By the 1870s whites had learned that they could best undermine Native American society by depriving Indians of their sources of subsistence, especially the bison. "Kill every buffalo you can," a U.S. Army colonel urged one hunter. "Every buffalo dead is an Indian gone." Federal authorities did not sponsor the mass killing of the bison; they merely turned a blind eye. Railroads joined in, sponsoring mass kills from slow-moving trains on the prairies. Some 13 million bison in 1850 were reduced, by 1880, to only a few hundred.

Their subsistence destroyed, Chief Sitting Bull and his starving men finally gave up in 1881. The Sioux war ended in 1890 with a shocking massacre of 200 Native American men, women, and children at Wounded Knee, South Dakota.

In the Northwest in 1877 the Nez Percés, fleeing from Union troops, began a dramatic trek across the mountains in an attempt to reach Canada. The Nez Percés eluded the troops and nearly made it over the Canadian border. However, hunger and the elements forced Chief Joseph and his exhausted people to agree to go to their reservations.

Reformers who advocated reservations over extermination always believed that the Indians should be absorbed into the political economy of capitalism. By "confining the Indians to reservations," explained William P. Dole, Lincoln's Commissioner of Indian Affairs, "they are gradually taught and become accustomed to the idea of individual property." Most white settlers considered Native Americans an inferior race worthy of destruction. Dole believed that "Indians are capable of attaining a high degree of civilization," but Dole, like other reformers, equated civilization with the cultivation of "individual property." Accordingly, reformers set out to destroy Native American society. They introduced government schools on reservations to teach the virtues of private property, individual achievement, and social mobility.

The reformers' influence peaked in 1887 when Congress passed the Dawes Severalty Act, the most important piece of Indian legislation of the century. Under the Dawes Act, reservation land was broken up into separate plots and distributed among individual families. The goal was to force Indians to live like white farmers. But the lands allotted were generally so poor, and the plots so small, that their owners quickly sold them. By the early twentieth century virtually no reservations were left, except for a few in the desert Southwest. With the Indians subdued, the path was cleared for the capitalist transformation of the West.

The Economic Transformation of the West

A few hundred civilians died in Indian attacks during the late nineteenth century. More than 5,000 died building the railroads. Lawless violence and wild speculation were part of the western experience, as were struggling families, temperance reformers, and hardworking immigrants. By 1900 the West provided Americans with the meat and bread for their dinner tables, the wood that built their homes, and the gold and silver that backed up their currency. The West was being drawn into the political economy of global capitalism.

Cattlemen: From Drovers to Ranchers

The cowboy is the mythic figure of the American West: a rugged loner who scorned society for the freedom of the trail. Like many myths, this one has elements of truth. Cowboys were usually unattached men. They worked hard, but they played just as hard, spending their earnings on a shave, a new suit of clothes, and a few good nights in town. Civil War veterans, emancipated slaves, displaced Indians, and Mexican vaqueros all became cowboys. Their pay was poor, their work was dangerous and unsteady, and their chances of reaching real independence were slim.

Longhorn cattle were as much a part of western legend as the cowboys who drove them. With the destruction of the bison and the westward spread of the railroads, it became possible to drive huge herds of Texas longhorns north onto the Great Plains. With relatively little capital, cattle herders could make substantial profits. Cowboys drove gigantic herds, sometimes numbering half a million, to a railroad town from which the cattle could be shipped, such as Abilene, Wichita, or Dodge City, Kansas. Cattlemen sold half of their stock to eastern markets and the other half in the West, to Californians, or to the government for feeding soldiers and Indians on reservations.

But the Texas longhorn had several drawbacks. Most seriously, it carried a tick that devastated many of the other grazing animals. It also took a long time to fatten up and never produced good beef. Investors began to breed hybrid cattle that did not carry the deadly tick, that fattened up quickly, and that produced higher quality meat. By the early 1880s investors were pouring capital into mammoth cattle-herding companies. By then the Great Plains were becoming seriously overstocked. The depleted grazing lands left the cattle weak from malnutrition, and in the late 1880s several severe winters devastated the sickly herds.

AMERICAN LANDSCAPE

>> Mining Camps in the West

Rosa Cassettari's experience in the mining camps of Missouri was not unique. But it is overshadowed by the more famous mining camps of California and the Far West. Mining fever began in 1848 when James Marshall discovered gold close to John Sutter's mill on the American River near what is now Sacramento, California. Thousands of prospectors poured into California during the 1850s, panning for gold wherever rumors of a vein hit, pulling up stakes and creating boomtowns and ghost towns with dizzying speed. Eventually, word of new discoveries pulled prospectors eastward from California. Tens of thousands of miners flooded into Colorado in 1859. Meanwhile prospectors in Nevada discovered the largest single vein in American history, the Comstock Lode, which would yield 350 million dollars worth of gold and silver during the 1860s and 1870s. Similar rushes transformed parts of Idaho in 1862 and Montana in 1864.

Western mining camps were extraordinary places, peopled by settlers from a variety of backgrounds. In the gold-country camps of the Sierra Nevada mountains, native-born Yankees lived among British subjects, Chinese immigrants, Mexicans, Spaniards, and African Americans. This was a male-dominated world of violence and vigilantism. Alone or in small groups, they would pan for gold in the beds of the rivers and streams that poured out of the mountains. This was known as placer mining. Once the surface gold had been captured, miners would shovel dirt into boxes or sluices to capture gold and silver by running water over it. Only a few miners struck it rich this way, but their stories captured the imaginations of thousands.

Marcus Daly, for example, came to America as a penniless Irish immigrant and struck it rich in the gold fields of California. But his biography says less about the lives of individual miners than it does about the larger transformation in the mining frontier. With the wealth he accumulated on his own, Daly persuaded a group of San Francisco investors to back his plans to dig a deep silver mine at Butte, Montana. They did not find silver, but they struck one of the largest veins of copper in the world. The Anaconda mine made Daly and his partners rich, but it also symbolized how western mining had changed. Daly managed a large group of engineers and wage laborers. Anaconda extracted and smelted its own ore, then shipped its high-grade copper around the world to cities and industries needing copper wire to harness the power of electricity. By 1883 the United States was the largest producer of copper on earth.

The world of the placer miners disappeared almost as quickly as it arose. Miners eventually moved from west to east, following new strikes in Idaho, Montana, Nevada, and Colorado. But as the surface riches were exhausted, the remaining veins of gold and silver proved too deep for any one prospector to reach. It took heavy machines to get at the ore buried deep underground, and machinery required capital investments beyond the means of ordinary miners. Most of the wealth taken from the Comstock mines, for example, was extracted by corporations using powerful tools. So mining corporations steadily bought up the settlers' claims and created a more permanent industrial presence in the West.

Yet the mining camps, however brief their existence, represented a temporary alternative to the permanent inequalities of the industrial economy. As rough and violent as they were, the camps were also experiments in spontaneous democracy in which men came together, governed themselves, and agreed on the rules by which they would live.

Open-range herding became so environmentally destructive that it was no longer economically feasible. Long drives also became increasingly difficult as farmers fenced in the plains. By the 1890s huge cattle companies were giving way to smaller ranches that raised hybrid cattle. The western railroad network was by then so extensive that it was no longer necessary to drive herds hundreds of miles to reach a railhead. Cowboys became ranch hands who worked for regular wages, like miners and factory workers.

In the mid-1880s, more than 7 million head of cattle roamed the Great Plains, but their numbers declined rapidly, and in their place came sheep. Although sheep proved even more ecologically destructive than cattle, by 1900 sheepherding had largely replaced the cattle industry in Wyoming and Montana and was spreading to Nevada. Sheepherding had one other advantage: it did not interfere with small farmers as much as cattle driving did.

Commercial Farmers Subdue the Plains

Between 1860 and 1900, the number of farms in America nearly tripled, thanks largely to the economic development of the West. On the Great Plains and in the desert Southwest, farmers took up former Indian lands. In California, white settlers poached on the estates of Spanish-speaking landlords, stripping them of their natural resources and undermining their profitability. Over time Hispanic ranchers gave way to European American farmers. The Hispanic population of Los Angeles fell from 82 percent in 1850 to 19 percent in 1880. A similar pattern occurred in New Mexico and Texas.

This ethnic shift signaled profound changes in the ecology and political economy of the West, driven by the exploding global demand for western products. Cattle ranchers were feeding eastern cities. Lumber from the Pacific Northwest found its way to Asia and South America. By 1890 western farmers produced half of the wheat grown in the United States, and they shipped it across the globe.

But farming in the arid West was different from farming in the East. To begin with, the 160-acre homesteads envisioned by eastern lawmakers were too small for the economic and ecological conditions of western agriculture. To produce wheat and corn for the international market, western farmers needed costly equipment and extensive irrigation. To make these capital investments, they mortgaged their lands. For mechanized, commercial agriculture to succeed on mortgaged land, western farms had to be much bigger than 160 acres.

Most western agricultural settlement took place not on government-sponsored homesteads but through the private land market. By some estimates speculators bought up nearly 350 million acres of western lands from state or federal governments or from Indian reservations. Railroads were granted another 200 million acres by the federal government. The more farmers there were who settled in the West, the more agricultural produce could be shipped back East. Railroads set up immigration bureaus and offered settlers cheap transportation, credit, and agricultural aid. The Great Plains filled with settlers from the East Coast and from Ireland, Germany, and Scandinavia. In 1890 the director of the Bureau of the Census reported that the frontier had at last been filled.

Changes in the Land

The trans-Mississippi West was no Garden of Eden waiting for lucky farmers. The climate, particularly in the Great Plains and the desert Southwest, was too dry for most kinds of farming. The thick, hard sod on the plains ripped traditional plows like paper; only steel would do the job. With little wood or stone available, farmers lived first in dugouts or sod houses. Fierce winters gave way to blistering summers, each rocked by harsh winds. Yet settlers seemed determined to overcome, and to overwhelm, nature itself. To build fences where wood was scarce, manufacturers invented barbed wire. Windmills dotted the prairie to pump water from hundreds of feet below ground. Powerful machinery tore through the earth, and new strains of wheat were cultivated to withstand the brutal climate.

The western environment was transformed. Wolves, elk, and bear were exterminated as farmers brought in pigs, cattle, and sheep. Tulare Lake, covering hundreds of square miles of California's Central Valley, was sucked dry by 1900. Mines sent tons of earth and rock down the rivers of the Sierra Nevada, threatening entire cities with flooding. The skies above Butte, Montana, turned grey from pollutants released by copper-smelting plants. Sheepherding destroyed the vegetation on the eastern slopes of the Rocky Mountains and the Sierra Nevada.

By the turn of the century, the bison were all but gone, and the Indians had been confined to reservations. Corporate mines, huge cattle ranches, and mechanized farms now dominated the West. The frontier was gone, replaced by commercial farmers whose lives were shaped by European weather, eastern mortgage companies, commodity brokers, and railroad conglomerates. Cowboys sold their labor to cattle companies owned by investors in Boston and Glasgow. Mining and lumber corporations employed tens of thousands of wage laborers. Big cities sprang up almost overnight. San Francisco had 5,000 inhabitants in 1850, but by the time the Gold Rush was over, in 1870, it had 150,000. Denver was incorporated in 1861 with a population just below 5,000. After the railroad came, Denver had more than 100,000 inhabitants in 1870. The West was well on its way to becoming a part of an urban, industrial nation.

Conclusion

Rosa Cassettari and Andrew Carnegie never met, but together their lives suggest the spectrum of possibilities in industrializing America. Both were immigrants who, caught up in the political economy of industrial capitalism, made their way to the United States. Yet the same grand forces touched the two immigrants in different ways. Cassettari moved to a

>> Timeline

▼1848
Taiping Rebellion spurs Chinese emigration to United States
Revolution in Austria-Hungary
Andrew Carnegie emigrates to United States

▼1851
Fort Laramie Treaty establishes Indian reservations

▼1856
St. Paul's boarding school opens

▼1857
Henry Bessemer develops process for making steel

▼1862
Pacific Railroad Act
Homestead Act

▼1865
First transatlantic telegraph cable begins operation

▼1867
Medicine Lodge Treaty

▼1868
Second Fort Laramie Treaty
Washita Massacre

▼1871
October: Great Chicago fire

▼1872
Edgar Thomson Steel Works open near Pittsburgh

▼1873
Financial panic, followed by depression

▼1876
Custer's Last Stand at Little Bighorn

▼1878
American Bar Association founded

▼1881
Czar Alexander II of Russia assassinated   *continued*

>> **Timeline** *continued*

▼**1882**
Chinese Exclusion Act
John D. Rockefeller forms Standard Oil trust
Edison Electric Company lights up New York buildings

▼**1887**
Dawes Severalty Act

▼**1890**
Jacob Riis publishes *How the Other Half Lives*
Massacre at Wounded Knee, South Dakota
Director of U.S. Census declares frontier "closed"

▼**1893**
Financial panic, followed by depression

Missouri mining camp before making her way to Chicago—the city that opened the West to the dynamism of industrial capitalism. Carnegie migrated, almost overnight, from pre-industrial Scotland to the heart of the Industrial Revolution in America—Pittsburgh, with its railroads, oil refineries, and steel mills. Cassettari struggled all her life and achieved a modest level of comfort for herself and her children. She did as well as most immigrants could hope for, and in that sense her biography reflects the realities of working-class life in industrial America. Cassettari's experience with failure impelled her to move on in search of something better. It was success, however, that made Carnegie itch for something different. By 1890, having made his millions, he remade himself by becoming a patron of culture. He moved to New York and traveled the world, befriending the leading intellectuals of his day. He built libraries and endowed universities. He had helped create an industrial nation. Now he set out to re-create American culture.

Review Questions

1. What were the major features of "global" capitalism in the late nineteenth century?

2. Describe the new social order of industrial America.

3. How did western Indians respond to westward expansion?

4. How was the West absorbed into the national and international market?

**For further review materials and resource information,
please visit www.oup.com/us/ofthepeople**

18

Cultural Struggles of Industrial America

1850–1895

>> Anthony Comstock's Crusade Against Vice

Anthony Comstock devoted most of his adult life to putting the owners of brothels, gambling dens, abortion clinics, and dance halls out of business. "You must hunt these men as you hunt rats," Comstock declared, "without mercy." There was little in his background to foreshadow such zeal. As a young man Comstock moved from rural Connecticut to New York City, where he worked as a clerk in a dry goods store, a familiar career for native-born Protestant men in the middle of the nineteenth century. Fame came to him in 1873 when the United States Congress enacted a statute that bore his name. The Comstock Law banned the production, distribution, and public display of obscenity. Thereafter, Comstock spent much of his life chasing down and prosecuting pornographers, prostitutes, and strippers.

Comstock and other citizens were genuinely disturbed by the corruption that kept police departments from enforcing obscenity laws. To overcome this obstacle, reformers established private organizations with quasi-official authority. Among the most influential was Anthony Comstock's New York Society for the Suppression of Vice, known as the SSV. Founded in 1873, the SSV was dedicated to "the enforcement of laws for the suppression of the trade in, and circulation of, obscene literature and illustrations, advertisements, and articles of indecent or immoral use." As head of the society, Comstock was appointed a special agent of the U.S. Post Office. With other SSV leaders, Comstock disregarded the rights of due process by entrapping his victims. But Comstock and others defended their actions by pointing out that the established legal procedures were ineffective in preventing the sale of smut.

Comstock's chief concern was the protection of children. In his most famous book, *Traps for the Young* (1883), he warned that obscenity was enticing American youngsters into deviant ways by artificially nourishing youthful appetites and passions until they exerted "a well-nigh irresistible mastery over their victim." The evils that trapped America's

continued

>> **AMERICAN PORTRAIT** *continued*

children were concentrated in the cities that, in the late nineteenth century, attracted millions of young people. Urban life was relatively anonymous and was also driven by vast amounts of cash. In the last third of the nineteenth century, most urban Americans had more money to spend and more time to spend it than ever before. And if industrial workers enjoyed increased leisure time, white-collar employees enjoyed even more. The big city offered bawdy new entertainments that violated long-established standards of respectability. Pornography was not a new thing, but it was now more widespread than ever before.

For Comstock, cities were cesspools of vice and corruption, the breeding ground for immigrant slums thought to be devoid of "culture." At the time, many educated Americans thought that "culture" referred only to the great works of Western art, literature, and music, which they believed were healthy alternatives to the sordid realities of urban and industrial America. Ironically, the best artists and writers of the late nineteenth century were "realists" who wanted art to reflect the gritty truths of everyday life. While Anthony Comstock tried to suppress the vices of the city, realists embraced them, translating them into compelling fiction and dramatic canvases.

In the second half of the nineteenth century, cultural clashes were as much a part of industrial capitalism as were class conflict and political upheaval. Rural Americans were ambivalent about urban culture, attracted by its freedom but repelled by its licentiousness. Native-born Protestants, often genuinely concerned with helping immigrants, were also suspicious of immigrant folkways. Defenders of high culture resisted the lure of popular culture. Amateur sportsmen sniffed at spectator sports. Victorian moralists assailed the collapse of traditional gender distinctions. Yet these struggles reflected the efforts of Americans to absorb the dramatic social transformations that accompanied the rise of industrial capitalism.

Common Threads

>> How did American culture in the late nineteenth century reflect the rise of big cities and big business?

>> What, if anything, is the difference between popular culture and high culture?

>> What was new about artistic realism?

>> Was culture a political issue in the late nineteenth century?

The Varieties of Urban Culture

Americans both loved and hated their cities, and their mixed feelings were reflected in the entertainments they embraced during the second half of the nineteenth century. They swooned over romanticized re-creations of the Plains wars on the western frontier, and they paid good money to watch nostalgic minstrel shows about plantation life in the Old South. But as the economy developed, this love affair with the countryside gave way to popular entertainments that idealized the city as never before. These new entertainments rested more than ever on the technological marvels of American industry. Beginning in the 1880s, electricity lit up the big city, creating new forms of urban "night life." By 1900 electric trolleys and subways brought tens of thousands of Americans into new "downtown" districts (see Figure 18–1). Stores, businesses, and factories defined the older downtowns. But leisure activities attracted tens of thousands to theaters, music halls, concert saloons, baseball stadiums, and sports arenas in the new city centers. City life, long associated with poverty and crime, now came to mean fun and excitement as well.

Minstrel Shows as Cultural Nostalgia

In the late nineteenth century the western frontier became one of the most popular themes in American show business. As rugged pioneers gave way to wage earners, commercial farmers, and industrialists, the mythology of the West grew. The most spectacular example of this was Buffalo Bill Cody's hugely successful Wild West Show, which toured the country parading live Indians before delighted urban spectators. Audiences watched displays of horsemanship and stylized reenactments of the Plains wars. The fascination with a romanticized frontier was one example of a popular nostalgia for ways of life thought to have been simpler than the life of the city. Nowhere was this nostalgia more obvious than in the minstrel shows.

Minstrel shows were the most significant form of public entertainment for most of the nineteenth century. During the 1830s and 1840s white performers in blackface dominated minstrel shows. Although the early minstrels stereotyped plantation slaves as happy and carefree, by the mid-1850s the tone of blackface minstrel shows became viciously racist. As the slavery controversy forced white northerners to take sides on a divisive issue, popular troupes such as New York's Christy Minstrels took the side of the slaveholders. During the Civil War and Reconstruction, minstrel shows attacked white reformers in the North who supported emancipation and black rights. They portrayed blacks with gross

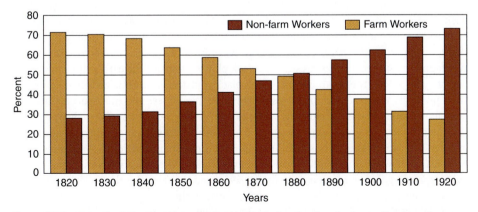

Figure 18–1 Growth of the Non-Farm Sector Underpinning the rise of urban culture was the emergence of a wage-earning labor force. Concentrated in cities, wage earners had cash at their disposal to spend on the amusements cities had to offer.

BILLY KERSANDS.

CALLENDER'S (GEORGIA) MINSTRELS.

Billy Kersands African American minstrels such as Billy Kersands moderated the racism characteristic of the extremely popular white minstrels.

racial stereotypes and subjected abolitionists to ridicule. Yet throughout the period, minstrel shows continued to poke fun at the aristocratic pretensions of cultural elites. Indeed, minstrel shows commonly combined racism with populism, lampooning elites by playing them in blackface wearing fancy clothes and putting on airs.

In the 1870s minstrel shows grew larger and more elaborate. J. H. Haverly led the way. He hired the most players, dressed them in the gaudiest costumes, placed them in the most spectacular sets, and had them perform the widest variety of numbers. He toned down the emphasis on blackface singers and plantation themes and added scantily clad women and off-color routines. By 1881 he had theaters in New York, Brooklyn, Chicago, and San Francisco; three national minstrel troupes; and four touring comedy theaters. Of Haverly's three companies, two were white and one was black. There were other black companies as well. As national minstrel shows ceased offering authentic representations of southern life, blacks often kept the plantation theme alive on stage, operating within the racial stereotypes established by prewar whites in blackface. The most famous black minstrel of the nineteenth century, Billy Kersands, drew huge audiences with his portrayals of ignorant and comical characters. Yet as the plantation theme became the preserve of black players, some of the early criticism of slavery crept back into the productions. When black minstrels romanticized the Old South, their nostalgia was reserved for slaves. Meanwhile, the largest and most successful minstrel shows retained their exclusively white casts and their heavy-handed racism.

As productions grew more ornate and expensive, show business entrepreneurs put smaller local troupes out of business or swallowed them up into national companies. Even as minstrel shows became uniform and somewhat bland, they became more popular than ever, expanding their audiences into the far West and the deep South. By 1890 a handful of huge entertainment moguls controlled the minstrel shows.

Minstrel shows never lost their nostalgic appeal to rural America. However, by the late nineteenth century they looked more and more like vaudeville, an art form born and bred in the big city.

The Origins of Vaudeville

Unlike the minstrels, vaudeville shows did not rely on nostalgia. Rather, vaudeville and its cheaper cousins (concert saloons and dollar theaters) flourished in American cities after elites succeeded in distinguishing serious theater from variety shows. As a ticket to a Shakespeare became too costly for most working people, urban audiences turned to inexpensive houses that offered music, singing, sketches, and variety acts. At first the audiences were rowdy and exclusively male. Yet these concert saloons and variety theaters attracted patrons from up and down the social scale. Even so, there were no blacks.

Increasingly, however, there were women. Beginning in the 1880s, a handful of show business entrepreneurs tried to develop variety theaters that appealed to both men and women. The respectability of a mixed audience was one of the distinguishing signs of vaudeville, which featured a variety of acts appealing to a broad audience. Producers also began offering shows any time of the day or evening. These continuous performances kept prices down, increasing the size of the potential audience. Locating downtown in the heart of the city had the same effect. Theater owners also regulated smoking and banned alcohol consumption to promote the image of family entertainment. Finally, they booked great opera singers or distinguished musicians in an effort to enhance vaudeville's reputation for respectability.

Growing audiences made it possible for vaudeville producers to construct ornate theatrical "palaces" that housed ever more elaborate productions. The high cost of such huge theaters meant that only a handful of companies came to dominate the vaudeville theater industry, much as minstrel companies had become concentrated in the hands of a few owners. By the turn of the century, vaudeville was one of the most popular forms of public entertainment in American cities. But minstrel shows and vaudeville theaters were not the only places Americans went during their leisure time.

Sports Become Professional

As growing numbers of Americans went to the theater to be entertained, still more went to the baseball park or sports arena. For much of the urban population, sports became something to watch rather than something to do.

As the number of spectators increased, baseball and prizefighting became professionalized. Prizefighting had long been a disreputable amusement of shady bars and lower-class streets, but during the 1880s it became an organized sport, attracting a huge national audience. Richard Kyle Fox, owner of the *National Police Gazette*, used his popular magazine and his wealth to transform boxing. Because Fox put up the prize money, he had the power to reform the sport. He made it both more profitable and more respectable, and he introduced standardized rules.

As prizefighting grew in popularity, entrepreneurs sponsored matches at indoor rings where they could control unruly audiences with police and security guards. As prizefighter John L. Sullivan explained in 1892, "the price of admission is put purposely high so as to exclude the rowdy element, and a gentleman can see the contest, feeling sure that he will not be robbed." Although prizefighting never completely lost its aura of disrepute, by the 1890s it was one of the most popular spectator sports in America, second only to baseball.

>> World's Fairs

To celebrate the accomplishments of urban and industrial society, the city of London hosted a spectacular world's fair at the Crystal Palace in 1851. By 1900 there had been expositions in Paris, Vienna, Brussels, Antwerp, Florence, Amsterdam, Dublin, and even Sydney, Australia, all showcases for the technological and cultural achievements of industrial capitalism. Most celebrated the achievements of the host countries and the civic pride of their sponsoring cities, as well as the triumph of technology and the progress of humanity. American fairs were no exception. Several cities—including St. Louis, San Francisco, and Chicago—sponsored world expositions in the late nineteenth and early twentieth centuries.

The first major world's fair in the United States took place in Philadelphia in 1876, timed to commemorate the centennial of American independence. In keeping with the theme of global interaction, the fair's sponsors asked the nations of the world to build pavilions of their own. The pavilions were arranged to reflect not the harmony of nations but the differences among the world's "races." Americans were only beginning to develop such ideas in 1876, but the broad outlines of the racial categories were already evident. France and its colonies, "representing the Latin races," were grouped together, as were England and its colonies, "representing the Anglo-Saxon races," and "the Teutonic races," represented by Germany, Austria, and Hungary. Within 20 years, these racial categories would harden into an elaborate hierarchy that embraced all the peoples of the world.

Nowhere was this hierarchy more visible than at the greatest fair of the century, the World's Columbian Exposition in Chicago in 1893. Built on Lake Michigan south of downtown, the Chicago fair covered 686 acres, and attracted 25 million visitors. The exposition was divided between the White City and the Midway Plaisance. The White City showcased American industrial might and invention and the latest consumer goods. But the Midway Plaisance boasted carnivals, the first Ferris wheel, games, and sideshows. It also featured an ethnographic exhibit illustrating the principles of scientific racism. It portrayed the "races" of the world in a hierarchy from the most civilized (Europeans) to the least civilized (Asians and Africans).

Where earlier entertainments had romanticized preindustrial society and the rural life, the world's fairs celebrated the global economy, industrial enterprise, and urban life. The White City, the heart of the World's Columbian Exposition in Chicago, was an idealized vision of urban life. As the model for civilization, rural simplicity had given way to the majestic city.

Like prizefighters, baseball players became professionals in the last half of the nineteenth century. By the 1860s baseball had become tremendously popular among city dwellers, particularly immigrants and their children, who formed leagues in neighborhoods all across the country. But not until 1869, when the Cincinnati Red Stockings went on tour and charged admission, did baseball become a professional spectator sport, with standardized rules.

Within a decade the owners of eight baseball clubs had formed a National League with all the earmarks of a corporate cartel. It restrained the power of players, restricted the number of teams to one per city, prohibited Sunday games, banned the sale of alcohol at ballparks, hired umpires, and set schedules and admission prices. Chafing under these restrictions, many players jumped to a new American Association that formed in 1882. The owners regrouped, and within a year the two leagues merged and reinstated the restrictions on players. In reaction the players formed a league of their own but were unable to compete with the owners. By the mid-1890s the National League controlled professional baseball.

Baseball idealized the principle of success based purely on merit. Objective statistics identified the best players without respect to their personal background. A model of ordered competition, the baseball meritocracy provided a useful lesson in the way capitalist society was supposed to work. Professional players became working-class heroes, many from factories and slums. But professional baseball reflected the realities and the ideals of American capitalism. The owners' cartel prevented players from taking advantage of the market. In addition, baseball's meritocracy had no place for the merits of black players. Even the seating arrangements in ballparks reflected social divisions: working-class fans in the bleachers, the middle class in the stands, and elites in the box seats.

The popularity of sports was reflected in the growing numbers of participants, as well as spectators. As daily work became more sedentary, especially for white-collar workers, Americans spent more time in physical recreation. During the late nineteenth century, the "sporting life" became an American pastime. The popularity of bicycling exploded, for example, particularly after the invention of the modern "safety bike" in 1888. Within a decade there were 10 million bicycles in the United States. Men joined the YMCA (discussed later). At Harvard, Yale, and Princeton young men took up football, basketball, and rowing. At Smith, Vassar, and Berkeley young women played baseball, basketball, and tennis. Urban neighborhoods fielded Irish, Italian, and German baseball teams. Women began riding bicycles, swimming, and playing golf and croquet.

The sports craze mirrored the inequalities and anxieties of industrial America. Men who believed that independence was a sign of masculinity were worried that wage labor would make them soft and "feminine." A vocal segment of the elite saw athletic activities as an antidote to the supposedly feminizing tendencies of industrial capitalism. Theodore Roosevelt, the product of an old and wealthy New York family who became president of the United States, argued that "the more virile virtues were encouraged by bodily exercise and especially the sports which develop such qualities as courage, resolution and endurance."

As baseball and prizefighting became popular and professional, elites reacted by glorifying the amateur ideal, embracing athletic activity for its own sake rather than for monetary reward. In the late nineteenth century wealthy Americans pursued the sporting life at elite colleges, exclusive racetracks, and private clubs. By the turn of the century, the most exclusive colleges in the Northeast had formed football's Ivy League, a name that became synonymous with elite private universities.

The rigors of sport taught elite men how to face the rigors of business competition, weeded out the weak, and prepared society's leaders for the contest of daily life. This attraction to rugged sports reinforced a self-serving view of American society: in global and competitive capitalism the best nations, like the best men, would rise to the top.

The most significant attempt to spread such values was the founding of the Young Men's Christian Association (YMCA) in 1851. By 1894 there were 261 YMCAs across the nation, sustained by a strong reform impulse. Its founders hoped that organized recreation would distract workers from labor radicalism. Games and classroom instruction would assimilate immigrants to the laws, customs, and language of the United States. The YMCA can be seen as a more mainstream extension of the movement to suppress vice: it hoped to provide wholesome amusements to young men who might otherwise succumb to the temptations of city life.

The Elusive Boundaries of Male and Female

Anthony Comstock saw the city as a place where traditional morality broke down, particularly standards of sexual propriety. In fact, the political economy of industrial capitalism and the triumph of wage labor compelled men and women to rethink traditional conceptions of masculinity and femininity. As they did so, new cities and newfound leisure time offered unprecedented opportunities to test the conventional boundaries of sexual identity.

The Victorian Construction of Male and Female

Until the mid-1700s most European doctors believed that there was only one sex: females were simply inferior, insufficiently developed males. Sometime after 1750, however, scientists and intellectuals began to argue that males and females were fundamentally different, that they were "opposite" sexes. For the first time it was possible to argue that women were naturally less interested in sex than men or that men were "active" whereas women were "passive." Nature itself seemed to justify the infamous double standard that condoned sexual activity by men but punished women for the same thing.

In the nineteenth century, Victorians drew even more extreme differences between men and women. Taking its name from the long reign of Britain's Queen Victoria, the "Victorian" era is often stereotyped as an age of sexual repression and cultural conservatism. Like many stereotypes, the image of the puritanical Victorian is simplistic but not without a grain of truth. Victorian boys were reared on moralistic stories of heroes who overcame their fears, thus prepared for the competitive worlds of business and politics, worlds from which women were largely excluded. To be a "man" in industrial America was to work in the rough-and-tumble world of the capitalist market. Men proved themselves by their success at making a living and therefore at taking care of a wife and children.

Victorian men defined themselves as rational creatures threatened by overwhelming sexual drives. Physical exertion was an important device for controlling a man's powerful sexual urges, just as masturbation was deemed an unacceptable outlet for these drives. Men were urged to channel their sexual energies into strenuous activities such as sports and, conveniently enough, wage labor. Masculinity was defined as the ability to leave home and compete successfully in the capitalist labor market.

Where masculinity became a more rigid concept, femininity became less certain. Women's schools established their own sports programs. Thousands of women took up bicycling, tennis, and other physical activities. Yet the stereotype still persisted that women were too frail for the hurly-burly of business and enterprise. Lacking the competitive instinct of the male, the female was destined to become a wife and mother within the protective confines of the home. Just as men joined social clubs and sports teams, a "female world of love and ritual" developed. Middle-class women often displayed among themselves a passionate affection that was often expressed in nearly erotic terms. But genuinely passionate female sexuality disturbed the Victorians. Evidence of sexual passion among women was increasingly diagnosed, mostly by male doctors, as a symptom of a new disorder called "neurasthenia."

Over time the differences between men and women were defined in increasingly medical terms. Victorian doctors redefined homosexuality as a medical abnormality, a perversion, and urged the passage of laws outlawing homosexual relations. The new science of gynecology powerfully reinforced popular assumptions about the differences between men and women. Leading male physicians argued that the energy women expended in reproduction left them unable to withstand the rigors of higher education. In extreme cases physicians would excise a woman's clitoris to thwart masturbation or remove her ovaries to cure neurasthenia.

On the assumption that motherhood was a female's natural destiny, doctors pressed to restrict women's access to contraception and to prohibit abortion. Before the Civil War many Americans tolerated abortion in the first three months of pregnancy, though they did not necessarily approve of it. This began to change as the medical profession seized control over the regulation of female reproduction. The American Medical Association (AMA, founded in 1847) campaigned to restrict the activities not only of quacks and incompetents but also of female midwives and abortionists in an effort to oppose attempts by women to interfere with pregnancy. The AMA supported passage of the Comstock Law, which outlawed the sale of contraception. Doctors also pushed successfully to criminalize abortion.

Victorians Who Questioned Traditional Sexual Boundaries

In a new economy based on wage labor, many Americans, especially young men, found themselves with cash and leisure time. The anonymity of huge cities gave them the opportunity to defy established standards of sexual behavior. Freed from the constraints of parents and small-town life, wage earners frequented prostitutes in unprecedented numbers, attended sexually provocative shows, read erotic novels, and purchased pornographic prints. Many Americans began to explore unconventional sexual practices.

The major venues of popular amusement flouted Victorian standards of propriety by using sexual titillation to entertain audiences. Can-can girls, off-color jokes, and comedy skits focusing on the war of the sexes were increasingly popular. Even the styles of clothing were a rejection of the stifling Victorian conventions. Both men's and women's

Map 18–1   Houses of Prostitution, 1850–1859 and 1900–1909 One measure of the sexual freedom characteristic of city life was the explosive increase in prostitution. As the demand for prostitution rose, so did attempts to suppress it. *Timothy J. Gilfoyle,* City of Eros *(New York: Norton, 1992), p. 33.*

clothing became simpler, looser, and more comfortable. The sensuous human body became an object of fascination in popular culture. Minstrels, musical variety shows, and the vaudeville theater all glorified female sexuality, while for the first time male sports heroes were openly admired for their physiques.

There were homoerotic themes running through Horatio Alger's novels. Once rescued from rags and gainfully employed, Alger's hero typically set up house with a roommate. These households were fastidiously neat, their inhabitants thrifty and sober. The only difference from an ideal middle-class household was that both inhabitants were male. In one case, two male roommates, both now saved and respectable, "adopted" a little boy, a street urchin named "Mark the Matchboy." But Alger's novels moved beyond homoeroticism to the very different realm of pedophilia. He was expelled from his pulpit as a Unitarian minister in Brewster, Massachusetts, for "the revolting crime of unnatural familiarity with boys." Alger left New England in disgrace and moved to New York, where he developed a keen interest in the problems of young boys who roamed the city streets. Alger's charity work became the basis of his fiction. In most of his novels, the young heroes were dirty but handsome, and their good looks attracted the attention of a wealthy male patron. Alger's novels depicted the relationships between men and boys in terms reminiscent of a seduction.

Immigration as a Cultural Problem

When novelist Henry James returned to the United States in 1907 after a quarter of a century in Europe, he was stunned and disgusted by the pervasive presence of immigrants in New York City. On the streetcars, he confronted "a row of faces, up and down, testifying, without exception, to alienism unmistakable, alienism undisguised and unashamed." James was one of the many native-born Americans who assumed that their culture was Protestant, democratic, and English speaking. They were deeply disturbed, therefore, by the arrival of vast numbers of immigrants who were none of those things and by the way ethnic subcultures seemed to flourish in United States cities. Yet among immigrants and their children, an ethnic identity was often a sign of assimilation into a broader American culture.

Josiah Strong Attacks Immigration

"Every race which has deeply impressed itself on the human family has been the representative of some great idea," Josiah Strong wrote in *Our Country*. Greek civilization was famed for its beauty, he explained, the Romans for their law, and the Hebrews for their purity. The Anglo-Saxons claimed two great ideas: the love of liberty and "pure spiritual Christianity." Published in 1885, Strong's best-selling book was revised, reprinted, and serialized in newspapers across America. Strong appealed to the many native-born Americans who saw themselves as the defenders of Anglo-Saxon culture. Strong was optimistic that as representatives of "the largest liberty, the purest Christianity, the highest civilization," the Anglo-Saxon race would "spread itself over the earth."

But there was a problem. Strong and his followers believed that Anglo-Saxon America was threatened by the arrival of millions of immigrants. By 1900 more than 10 million Americans were foreign born. The typical immigrant, he warned, was not a freedom-loving Anglo-Saxon Protestant but a narrow-minded "European peasant" whose "moral and religious training has been meager or false." Immigrants brought crime to America's cities and, voting in blocks, undermined the nation's politics. "[T]here is no more serious menace to our civilization," Strong warned, "than our rabble-ruled cities."

For Strong, the problem was the fact that immigrants could not be assimilated into the American way of life. They were coming in such huge numbers that assimilation was becoming impossible (see Map 18–2). Worst of all—in Strong's view—the Catholic Church held millions of immigrants in its grip, filling their heads with superstition rather than "pure Christianity." Through its parochial schools, the Catholic Church was training new generations to love tyranny rather than liberty.

Strong and his readers need not have worried. The millions of immigrants adapted quickly to American society. Indeed, Strong misread much of his own evidence. By cultivating the German vote or the Irish vote, for example, political machines brought immigrants into American political culture. Nor were immigrants as slavishly subservient to the Catholic Church as Strong thought. In the end, the church played an ambiguous role in the cultural history of American immigrants.

From Immigrants to Ethnic Americans

Critics such as Strong scarcely noticed the regional and class differences that immigrants brought with them. In the middle of the nineteenth century, most immigrants came with

Immigrants Immigrants often crowded into "tenements," a new form of apartment building that actually improved living conditions for many of America's poor city dwellers.

loyalties to their regions and villages but not to their nationalities. In New York City German-speaking immigrants thought of themselves primarily as Bavarian or Prussian rather than as German. Irish immigrants identified with their home counties more than their native country. Immigrant churches were torn by such regional conflicts.

In the United States, however, these regional differences began to decline. One reason was the growth of secular fraternal organizations, which often began as mutual aid societies designed to help newcomers find jobs and housing. In 1893 mineworkers formed the Pennsylvania Slovak Catholic Union to help cover burial expenses for those killed in the mines. Most often, however, middle-class immigrants or local priests took the lead in forming fraternal organizations, which eventually counted about half of all immigrants as members.

As they grew, fraternal organizations became national in their scope, as immigrants constructed a new "ethnic" identity under a single national rubric. In some cases immigrant businessmen led the drive toward the development of a unified ethnic identity. Marco Fontana, who ran the Del Monte Company in California, encouraged the growth of an "Italian" identity among his workers whose regional loyalties hindered the efficient operation of his enterprises. Eventually, immigrants began to think of themselves as members of ethnic groups that shared the same national ancestry.

It was not merely coincidental that immigrants developed "national" identities in the United States. Nationalism was spreading throughout the Western world during the nineteenth century. While immigrants in America were coming to see themselves as Irish or Italian, the same thing was happening back home in Ireland and Italy. In the United States

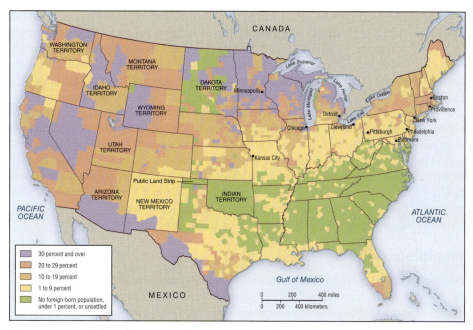

Map 18–2 Population of Foreign Birth by Region, 1880 *Clifford L. Lord and Elizabeth H. Lord,* Lord & Lord Historical Atlas of the United States *(New York: Holt, 1953).*

the Civil War had unleashed a wave of nationalistic fervor, as did a series of liberal revolutions in Europe. As the decades passed, immigrants brought to America an increasingly powerful sense of their ethnic identities.

The Catholic Church and Its Limits in Immigrant Culture

The Roman Catholic Church played a complicated role in the development of ethnic immigrant cultures. Many ethnic communities collected donations to build churches to preserve their Old World traditions. But the church also smoothed the transition into American life by serving as a mutual aid society. Polish churches in Chicago and German parishes in Milwaukee used their women's groups and youth clubs as mutual aid societies for their local immigrants.

The church sometimes unintentionally sped the development of ethnic identities. The Irish became more devout in America as they came to rely on the church to assist them in resisting an overwhelmingly Protestant culture. Through the church, Germans also overcame their regional differences. But the more they came to equate their German identity with Catholicism, the more they resented Irish domination of the church hierarchy. German Catholics worked to establish their own churches and parish schools or to have sermons preached in German. By contrast, the Italians were suspicious of and largely alienated from the official church, the hierarchy of which was largely Irish. By the late nineteenth century North American bishops were trying to standardize Catholicism in America. They published uniform catechisms, established powerful bureaucracies, and tried to suppress the folk rituals of Italian Catholicism.

The church's power was reinforced by the struggle for control over the education of immigrant children. Throughout the nineteenth century, public schools were heavily Protestant. Josiah Strong and other native-born reformers tried to use public education to "Americanize" immigrant children. They taught the Protestant Bible. They shifted the focus away from the classics and toward "practical" education and language training, with the goal of turning immigrants into reliable workers and patriotic citizens. But immigrants fiercely resisted such efforts, and the bulwark of their resistance was the church.

During the second half of the nineteenth century both the Catholic and Lutheran churches established parochial school systems to protect immigrant children from the biases of public education. So comprehensive was the Catholic Church's effort that by 1883 all but two Chicago parishes had their own parochial schools. Ironically, parochial education contributed to assimilation. Schools in Irish Catholic or German Lutheran parishes reinforced the growth of distinctively American ethnic identities tied to an increasingly standardized and Americanized Catholicism or Lutheranism.

Immigrant Cultures

Despite assimilation, the ethnic identities that immigrants developed in America remained distinctive. Irish Americans, for example, fused together songs from various parts of Ireland and added piano accompaniment. Similarly, Polish immigrant bands expanded beyond the traditional violin by adding accordions, clarinets, and trumpets. Hundreds of immigrant theaters offered productions that adjusted traditional plot lines to the New World. Jewish plays told of humble peddlers who outwitted their prosperous patrons. Italian folktales celebrated the importance of the family. In these ways distinctive ethnic identities, adapted to urban and industrial America, developed.

One of the most distinctive features of immigrant culture was family size. At a time when middle-class families had only two or three children, immigrant families remained large, for sound economic reasons. There were no child-labor laws restricting the employment of minors and few compulsory-education laws requiring children to attend school. Immigrant working-class families relied heavily on the incomes of their children, particularly teenagers, to contribute to the well-being of the household.

At the turn of the century, Italian mothers in Buffalo, New York, had an average of 11 children. Among Polish wives the average was closer to eight. In Pennsylvania's coal-mining district, working-class immigrant women had 45 percent more children than native-born women. But the death rate among immigrant children was also high. In 1900, one out of three Polish and Italian mothers had seen one of their children die before his or her first birthday.

As ethnicity developed in the late nineteenth century, class divisions were increasingly difficult to isolate from cultural distinctions. The middle class, for example, was overwhelmingly native born, white, Anglo-Saxon, and Protestant. The working class was, by contrast, African American, foreign born, Catholic, or Jewish. By 1900, 75 percent of manufacturing workers were immigrants or the children of immigrants, closer to 85 percent in large cities. In the South, wage laborers were overwhelmingly black sharecroppers. In this context educated elites constructed a definition of high culture that distinguished the middle classes from the allegedly uncultivated and uncultured working classes.

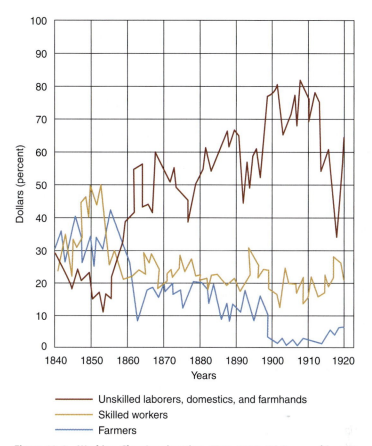

Figure 18–2 Working-Class Immigration, 1840–1920 *U.S. Bureau of Census.*

The Creation of High Culture

During the second half of the nineteenth century many intellectuals sought to isolate and define a tradition, *high culture*, that stretched through Western history from ancient Greece and Rome to the present. By the 1890s high culture embodied principles of social, cultural, and political hierarchy that were firmly installed in museums, libraries, and universities across the United States. A "Western tradition" had been created as an antidote to the new forms of popular culture that had emerged in the same decades.

High Culture Becomes Sacred

The leading advocate of high culture was an Englishman, Matthew Arnold. In *Culture and Anarchy*, published in 1869, Arnold promoted the study of "the best which has been thought and said in the world" as a source of stability amidst the "anarchy" of capitalist society. "Certain things are not disputable," *Harper's Magazine* declared in 1867, proclaiming that authors such as Homer, Shakespeare, and Dante "are towering facts like the Alps or the Himalayas. . . . It is not conceivable that the judgment of mankind upon those names will ever be reversed." American elites looking for firm moral guidelines were establishing a canon of great cultural achievements and turning to it the way earlier generations had looked to holy scripture. Secular culture took on the qualities of the sacred.

Beneath the sacred view of culture was the fear that the modern world had undermined traditional values, especially religious values. Particularly troubling was the apparent decline in religious fervor. Middle-class men and women often confessed to a loss of their own faith.

The middle class never lost its faith entirely. Victorians remained thoroughly Protestant in outlook and deeply suspicious of Roman Catholicism. What they lost was a strong theology and missionary zeal. Victorians moved restlessly from one denomination to another, but few found the spiritual satisfaction or moral guidance they sought. As religious fervor waned, the Victorian middle class looked for comfort in more secular pursuits.

Thomas Wentworth Higginson typified this shift. Nurtured in the reform movements of antebellum New England, Higginson had been an abolitionist and supporter of women's rights. During the Civil War he led a famed regiment of African American troops. Fully engaged in the politics of his day, Higginson was equally at home in the New England literary world, turning to culture for relief from the sordid realities of urban life and industrial capitalism.

In 1871, two years after Matthew Arnold published *Culture and Anarchy*, Higginson made a strikingly similar case. Culture, he explained, "pursues" art and science for their intrinsic worth. It "places the fine arts above the useful arts." It sacrifices "material comforts" for the sake of a "nobler" life. Like Matthew Arnold, Higginson saw culture as a defense against materialism.

Higginson shared the Victorian conviction that culture was an attribute of the middle classes. At the top of the social order stood an increasingly dissolute and unrestrained capitalist class. At the bottom, poor working people lived lives devoid of gentility and refinement. Yet these very classes, the greedy capitalists at the top and the ignorant masses below, seemed to grow in influence as capitalism developed. To counteract this threat, American elites worked to transform cities into centers of high art and cultural distinction.

The Emergence of a Cultural Establishment

In the early nineteenth century Shakespeare was the most popular playwright in America. Traveling through the country in the 1830s, Alexis de Tocqueville observed that "there is hardly a pioneer's cabin but that does not contain a few odd volumes of Shakespeare." Shakespearean plays, and not only a few classics, were performed in theaters more than any others. American audiences were familiar with a substantial body of Shakespeare's work.

A Shakespearean play was usually performed as the centerpiece of an entire evening's entertainment that included music, dancing, acrobats, magicians, and comedians. The show generally ended with a short humorous skit, or farce. Audiences were noisy, enthusiastic, and came from all walks of life. They generally preferred highly melodramatic renditions of Shakespeare in which moral lessons were sharp and clear, the ending was always satisfying, and good always triumphed over evil—in which, instead of committing

AMERICAN LANDSCAPE

>> The Modern University

At the same time that American elites were endowing museums and libraries, they stepped up their commitment to the establishment of distinguished private universities. Cornell, Johns Hopkins, Vanderbilt, Stanford, and the University of Chicago all appeared between the late 1860s and the 1890s. Wealthy businessmen had good reason to endow great universities. The political economy of industrial capitalism rested on technological developments, which in turn depended on up-to-date scientific learning. Research universities played a central role in such developments, training the new business and engineering elite. And finally, corporate philanthropists agreed with many Americans that a great Western nation required great universities.

The new universities reflected a new conception of higher education. Daniel Coit Gilman, the first president of the Johns Hopkins University in Baltimore, created specialized departments of history, English, and the various sciences that were responsible for recommending faculty appointments and promotions and for developing courses. He encouraged the publication of academic journals and established the first American university press in 1878. Gilman had created the modern university with a faculty of specialists dedicated to research and the training of other scholars. His innovations led to the undergraduate major; the system of numbered courses, unit requirements, and electives; and PhD programs with research seminars and dissertations based on original research.

In this new setting, the study of modern literature entered the college curriculum for the first time. Some professors, influenced by German scholarship, emphasized sentence structures, word roots, and forms of publication. This approach appealed to those who sought to make the study of literature into a science, but it was based on assumptions about the intrinsic superiority of western European languages. An Oxford scholar, Friedrich Max Müller, saw "an unbroken chain between us and Cicero and Aristotle." Müller and his American followers created a canon of great works they believed defined culture of the "West." They also defined the study of literature as the preserve of specialists.

Leading scholars in the new "social sciences" of sociology, anthropology, and political science also divided the world into great and inferior nations. At the top stood the so-called Teutonic nations of western Europe and North America. This hierarchy, far from reflecting the biases of its creators, was grounded in the objective methods of pure science—or so anthropologists, sociologists, and professional economists claimed. Science was becoming the model for the production of all human knowledge.

The modern university reflected the inequalities of the age. Only a tiny fraction of Americans attended college, most of them were men, most of the men were native born, and very few of those rose out of the working class. State universities and land-grant colleges welcomed a wider range of

continued

suicide, Romeo and Juliet lived happily ever after. By 1850 Americans were so familiar with Shakespeare that politicians could safely make allusions to his plays without fear of losing an audience.

All of this changed in the second half of the nineteenth century. Shakespeare was redefined as high culture, and performances of his plays were no longer popular entertainment. The entertainments that had once accompanied Shakespearean performances, such as the humorous closing skits, became the basis of the vaudeville theater, and theater audiences became segregated by class. The respectable classes retreated into quiet theaters, where the prices rose beyond the means of ordinary working people.

The same thing happened to opera and to orchestral music. Opera changed from an eclectic, highly popular art form to an elite entertainment. Italian immigrants who began arriving in the United States in the late nineteenth century noticed the difference. Back home opera was widely popular, and certain composers, Verdi in particular, were heroic public figures whose work addressed the national aspirations of millions of Italians. But in America opera had become associated with high fashion and elite culture, and the opening of the opera season became synonymous with the opening of the "social season" among the very rich.

Something similar was happening to orchestral music. In the first half of the nineteenth century local bands sprang up in thousands of communities across America (3,000 of them by 1860) with a repertoire of popular and classical pieces. Beginning in the 1840s, classical music became the preserve of elite symphony orchestras in large cities.

Symphonies and opera companies cost a lot of money. Orchestras needed new halls. Opera companies needed endowments. Serious theater needed generous patrons. Thus great infusions of private wealth were necessary to support lavish arts programs. In the late nineteenth century, the rich formed an alliance with leading performers and intellectuals to create a cultural establishment that endures to this day. Built with and sustained by the patronage of the wealthy, opera houses and symphony halls were the architectural embodiment of high culture.

Great cities required great museums as well. Americans built a stunning array of secular temples devoted to the world's great art, founding museums in New York, Boston, Philadelphia, and Chicago in the 1870s. Spectacular new public libraries appeared at the same time. By 1900 many Americans had come to associate "culture" with impressive institutions in major cities. By this reasoning, for example, the cultural life of Chicago was embodied not in its immigrant neighborhoods or popular theaters but in the Art Institute, Symphony Hall, and the Chicago Public Library.

Social Darwinism and the Growth of Scientific Racism

In 1859 Charles Darwin published his masterpiece of evolutionary theory, *On the Origin of Species*. Several scientists had already suggested that life had evolved over a long period of time, but Darwin offered the first persuasive explanation of how this might have taken place. He argued that a process of "natural selection" favored those biological changes that were most suited to the surrounding environment. In Darwinian theory, natural selection was the single most important explanation for the vast array of life forms on earth. American scientists were remarkably receptive to Darwinism. Asa Gray at Harvard and Joseph Le Conte at the University of California spread the evolutionary word in their influential textbooks on botany and geology. By 1900 virtually all the science textbooks used in American high schools embraced evolution.

Darwin's remarkable influence did not stop with the natural sciences. Social scientists applied the theory of natural selection to social evolution. This combination of social theory with evolutionary science was known as social Darwinism. Social Darwinists argued that human inequality was the outcome of a struggle for survival in which the fittest rose to the top of the social ladder. This theory made the rich seem more fit than the poor; it made blacks seem less fit than whites. To social Darwinists, inequality was the natural order of things. In this way Darwin's theory—one of the greatest scientific discoveries of all time—was twisted into a pseudoscientific defense of the new social order of industrial capitalism.

From the moment Darwin published his findings, the theory of natural selection was invoked to sustain a theory of African racial inferiority. Racists had argued that emancipation would force blacks to compete with their white superiors and that this competition would end in the disappearance of the African race. When the 1890 census seemed to show that the African American population was declining, racial theorists published influential studies claiming to show that blacks were withering under the strain of competition with whites. In an 1892 article, biologist Joseph Le Conte argued that under conditions of free competition with whites, blacks faced either "extinction" or permanent subordination. Only the protection of whites could shield blacks from their natural fate.

Far more influential than the Le Conte article was Frederick L. Hoffman's full-length treatise, *Race Traits and Tendencies of the American Negro*, published in 1896. Hoffman's book quickly established itself as one of the century's most important studies of race relations. Hoffman was a statistician, and the book's many tables and figures gave it the authoritative air of the new social sciences. Those numbers, Hoffman claimed, led to one inescapable conclusion: ever since leaving the protective cover of slavery, blacks had shown clear signs of moral degeneration and were doomed to poverty and social inferiority.

Social scientists such as Hoffman prided themselves on their commitment to the truth as it was revealed in facts and statistics. Like advocates of high culture, sociologists and anthropologists claimed to have isolated the definitive truths of human society. But not all "realists" sought solace in the past or justified the inequalities of the present. The best American artists of the late nineteenth century openly embraced the realities of urban and industrial America.

Artistic Realism Embraces Urban and Industrial America

In the second half of the nineteenth century, artists and writers embraced the world that Anthony Comstock wanted to suppress, that Matthew Arnold wanted to escape, and that Thomas Wentworth Higginson wanted to fix. "This is the age of cities," writer Hamlin Garland declared, "and the problem of our artistic life is practically one of city life." Artists like Garland called themselves "realists" and saw themselves as part of the first major artistic movement that was grounded in urban and industrial America. As writer Fanny Bates put it, the people of the cities "live more in realities than imagination."

The Triumph of Literary Realism

In April 1861 the *Atlantic Monthly* published a powerful story called "Life in the Iron Mills" by a writer named Rebecca Harding. Her story created a sensation. Rarely had the dreary lives of ordinary workers been presented in such relentless detail. In the decades to come, the best writers in America joined the crusade to make fiction realistic. The leading spokesperson for realistic fiction was William Dean Howells, the author of one of the best-known realist novels, *The Rise of Silas Lapham*, and editor of the *Atlantic Monthly*, one of few influential magazines that championed literary realism.

Realists tried to bridge the gap between "high" and "popular" culture by making great literature out of the details of everyday life. To "enjoy the every-day life," Sarah Orne Jewett explained in *Deephaven*, one must "find pleasure in thought and observation of simple things, and have an instinctive, delicious interest in what to other eyes is unflavored dullness." By writing about failed businessmen or runaway slaves, writers such as Howells and Mark Twain hoped to reveal both courage and cowardice in the lives of ordinary men and women. This was the great achievement of Twain's *Huckleberry Finn*.

The characters in realistic novels were flawed men and women who struggled with the moral dilemmas they encountered in their daily lives. In Howells's best novel, Silas Lapham had to decide whether to mislead the men who wanted to buy his failing paint company. Huck Finn had to decide whether to turn in a runaway slave. Yet neither Lapham nor Finn was "heroic" in the way that earlier heroes were. Lapham was an ill-educated social climber who drank too much. Huck Finn was a barely literate seeker of adventure who played hooky, spoke improper English, and spun absurd fantasies. In the end both Silas Lapham and Huck Finn made the right moral decisions, but neither found his decision easy to make, and Lapham suffered for having done so. Thus realism meant not merely the evocation of ordinary life, but the creation of characters who were psychologically complex and therefore more "realistic." For Henry James, psychological realism was the whole point, and his characters—Isabel Archer in *Portrait of a Lady* is a good example—are among the most vivid and compelling in all American literature.

The realist movement shocked the defenders of the genteel tradition of American letters. In 1885 the public library committee of Concord, Massachusetts, banned *Huckleberry Finn* from its shelves, denouncing it as "the veriest trash" and characterizing Twain's masterpiece as "rough, coarse and inelegant, dealing with a series of experiences not elevating, the whole book being more suited to the slums than to intelligent, respectable people."

Realists dismissed such criticism as evidence of the "feminine" taste that prevailed in American letters, and they saw realism as a "masculine" alternative to sentimental writing that appealed to women novel readers. In their commitment to the unvarnished truth, realists thought of themselves as "virile and strong." But female realists also rejected the assumption, common to sentimental fiction, that women's lives should be bounded exclusively by the needs of their husbands and children. "The public demands realism and they will have it," the novelist Willa Cather declared. Louisa May Alcott wanted her female characters to be "strong-minded, strong-hearted, strong-souled, and strong-bodied." Realistic writers challenged the depiction of women as nervous, frail, and fit only for the domestic life.

Other authors, most notably Walt Whitman, pushed the radical possibilities of realism even further. Like most realists, Whitman aspired to "manly" writing. Through his poems he hoped "to exalt the present and the real, to teach the average man the glory of his daily walk and trade." He was the poet of the city, who vividly detailed the "goodness," as well as the "wickedness," of modern urban America. Just as vaudeville flirted more and more openly with sexual titillation, Whitman wrote more and more openly about eroticism, as in this passage from *Leaves of Grass*:

> Have you ever loved the body of a woman?
> Have you ever loved the body of a man?
> Do you not see that they are exactly the same to all in all nations and times
>   all over the earth?
>
> If anything is sacred the human body is sacred,
> And the glory and sweet of a man is the token of manhood untainted,
> And in man or woman a clean, strong, firm-fibred body, is more beautiful
>   than the most beautiful face.

Thus Whitman, like so many realists, fused the themes of popular culture with the forms of "high" art.

Painting Reality

In 1878 New York artist John Ferguson Weir declared that "art, in common with literature, is now seeking to get nearer the reality, to 'see the thing as it really is.'" Like the best writers of the era, the finest painters rejected romanticism. Winslow Homer and Thomas Eakins shifted the emphasis of American painting from sentiment to realism, from unspoiled nature to the facts of social life in urban and industrial America. Realists did not always paint the city, but they generally avoided the romanticized scenes of nature that had been so popular in the early nineteenth century.

Winslow Homer was, in the words of one critic, a "flaming realist—a burning devotee of the actual." A series of Civil War studies, notably *Prisoners from the Front* (1866), presented ordinary soldiers with ragged uniforms and worn, tired expressions. This was a sharp departure from a tradition of painting military men in heroic poses. As an illustrator for *Harper's Weekly*, the first successful mass-circulation magazine in America, Homer also drew realistic scenes of factories, railroad workers, and other aspects of industrial life.

Two of Homer's most enduring contributions were his sensitive depictions of African Americans and his remarkable portrayals of seafaring men struggling against nature. At a time when intellectuals were perfecting theories of black racial inferiority and minstrel shows presented blacks in the grossest stereotypes, Homer represented blacks as varied men and women who worked hard and struggled with dignity against the difficulties of everyday life. In the process, he produced some of his finest paintings.

Thomas Eakins was even more determined to drain his paintings of all romantic sentiment. He wielded his paintbrush with the precision of a scientist. Indeed, in his effort to represent the human body with perfect accuracy, Eakins attended medical school. After studying in Europe, Eakins returned to his native Philadelphia in 1870 and was soon shocking viewers with warts-and-all portraits of his own sisters. Eakins, one critic sniffed, "cares little for what the world of taste considers beautiful."

Eakins established his reputation with a series of lifelike paintings of rowers. A master at rendering scenes with startlingly three-dimensional effects, in 1875 he shocked the art world again with *The Gross Clinic*, a large canvas depicting the gruesome details of a surgical procedure. The selection committee for the 1876 Philadelphia Centennial Exposition rejected *The Gross Clinic* on the grounds that "the sense of actuality about it was . . . oppressive."

Fascinated by the human form, Eakins photographed dozens of naked men and women and used some of them as the basis for full-scale paintings. *The Swimming Hole* (ca.1884) was based on an Eakins photograph. By 1886 the directors of the Academy had had enough. Eakins was fired after he pulled the loincloth from a male model posing before a group of female students.

Critics complained that Eakins was obsessed with nudity, but for Eakins the exact details of the human body allowed a deeper exploration of the characters and personalities

Orchestra Hall in Chicago This is one of many stately auditoriums built to house America's major symphony orchestras in the second half of the nineteenth century. Pictured here are the Chicago Symphony Orchestra and Theodore Thomas, Auditorium Theater, 1897.

of his subjects. Like Winslow Homer's portrayals of blacks, Eakins's women were thoughtful and dignified. *Miss Amelia C. Van Buren* (1891) conveys its subject's intelligence and complexity with no sacrifice of accuracy. Eakins did for painting what Henry James did for literature. Both demonstrated that distinguished works of art could be impressively realistic and at the same time deeply insightful.

Is Photography Art?

As city life became the subject matter of painters and writers, a major technological development—photography—created a new medium of artistic expression. The camera had been invented scarcely a generation earlier, in 1839, by a Frenchman named Louis Daguerre. By the early 1860s photographic technology had improved dramatically, and cameras had become more portable. Mathew Brady knew how to take advantage of it. In the fall of 1862 Brady mounted an exhibit of his Civil War photographs in his New York gallery. This was the first time a large viewing public was able to see realistic pictures of the most gruesome facts of war. His exhibition had electrifying effects. By the 1880s journalists used photographs to heighten the reality, the sense of "truth," conveyed by their stories. The effect of Jacob Riis's *How the Other Half Lives*, published in 1890, was enhanced by the inclusion of dramatic photographs documenting the misery of the urban poor. Photography had become part of the body of factual evidence.

The camera's eye inevitably fascinated realistic writers and artists. In the second half of the nineteenth century photography set the standard for accurate representation. Thomas Eakins, for example, used the camera to freeze images, such as those of horses in motion, which he intended to paint on canvas. Eakins soon became a skilled photographer, producing hundreds of portraits of his subjects. He took numerous photos of the naked human form and was one of the first artists to recognize the artistic element of photography itself. His work raised questions that remain unanswered: Is a painting based on a photograph a work of art? Is photography art?

Some writers applauded the camera's capacity to capture the "truth." Writers as varied as Walt Whitman and Harriet Beecher Stowe used photographic metaphors to describe the effects they hoped to achieve with their words. But others were not persuaded that the photograph could ever be a genuine work of art. The

Walt Whitman One of America's greatest poets, Whitman was a champion of the diversity and excitement of city life.

>> Timeline

▼1851
YMCA is founded
First world's fair is held at Crystal Palace in London

▼1859
Charles Darwin publishes *On the Origin of Species*

▼1861
Rebecca Harding publishes "Life in the Iron Mills"

▼1862
Mathew Brady exhibits Civil War photos at his New York studio

▼1866
New York Athletic Club opens
Horatio Alger expelled from his pulpit in Brewster, Massachusetts

▼1869
Cincinnati Red Stockings charge admission to watch baseball games
Matthew Arnold publishes *Culture and Anarchy*

▼1870
Metropolitan Museum of Art and Boston Museum of Fine Arts are founded

▼1870s
National League is formed; baseball becomes professional

▼1871
Walt Whitman publishes *Democratic Vistas*

▼1873
New York Society for the Suppression of Vice (SSV) founded
Congress enacts the Comstock Law

▼1875
First Harvard-Yale football game is played
Thomas Eakins paints *The Gross Clinic*

▼1876
World's Fair held in Philadelphia
Philadelphia Museum of Art founded
Daniel Coit Gilman becomes first president of Johns Hopkins University

▼1878
Johns Hopkins establishes the first American university press

▼1879
Art Institute of Chicago founded

>> Timeline *continued*

▼**1880s**
Richard Kyle Fox professionalizes prizefighting

▼**1881**
Henry James publishes *Portrait of a Lady*

▼**1883**
Anthony Comstock publishes *Traps for the Young*

▼**1884**
Mark Twain publishes *The Adventures of Huckleberry Finn*
Thomas Eakins paints *The Swimming Hole*

▼**1885**
William Dean Howells publishes *The Rise of Silas Lapham*
Josiah Strong publishes *Our Country*

▼**1888**
Modern "safety" bike invented

▼**1890**
Jacob Riis publishes *How the Other Half Lives*

▼**1891**
Thomas Eakins paints *Miss Amelia C. Van Buren*

▼**1893**
World's Columbian Exposition held in Chicago

▼**1894**
Vaudeville producer B. F. Keith opens the New Theatre in Boston

▼**1896**
Frederick L. Hoffman publishes *Race Traits and Tendencies of the American Negro*

camera captures only "the external facts," *The Galaxy* magazine declared; it "does not tell the whole truth."

Anthony Comstock worried a great deal about the difference between art and photography. Millions of copies of great and not-very-great works of art flooded the market in the late nineteenth century. Photographs of naked men and women suddenly became a new form of readily accessible pornography. "Is a photograph of an obscene figure or picture a work of art?" Comstock asked. "My answer is emphatically, No." Painters of nude portraits use artistry to divert viewers' attention from the nudity. Photographers have no such artistic devices at their disposal, Comstock explained. "A photograph of a nude woman in a lewd posture, with a lascivious look on her face," was to Comstock no work of art, for it lacked "the skill and talent of the artist."

Conclusion

When Comstock asked if photography could be art, he was participating in a larger debate about what counted as culture in the new world created by industrial capitalism. Did it include the popular culture of the city, or was American culture restricted to great libraries, universities, museums, and opera houses? And what was culture supposed to do for people? Americans argued over whether culture should maintain traditional values or boldly face up to the realities of the new political economy.

These cultural struggles easily spilled over into politics. Urban reformers proposed policies to elevate the cultural level of slum dwellers. Elites convinced politicians to subsidize the construction of huge public libraries. Nevertheless, American politics in the late nineteenth century had not yet become cultural politics. The issues that brought Americans into the streets and into the voting booths remained, for the most part, economic issues. Just as American culture was transformed by the rise of cities and industry, the problems of industrial capitalism became the focus of American politics in the late nineteenth century.

Review Questions

1. In what ways was American culture "urbanized" in the late nineteenth century?

2. How did immigration affect American culture?

3. What were the major features of the high cultural establishment that developed in this period?

4. What was "artistic realism?"

5. Did American culture become more repressed or more eroticized in the second half of the nineteenth century?

6. In what ways did American culture reflect the patterns of race relations in the late nineteenth century?

For further review materials and resource information, please visit www.oup.com/us/ofthepeople

19

The Politics of Industrial America

1870–1892

>> Luna Kellie and the Farmers' Alliance

L una Kellie was the daughter of a railroad worker, but as a young girl she dreamed of raising a family on a farm of her own. Born in 1857, Luna grew up in towns along the Northern Pacific Railroad line. Her father did try to make a go of farming in Minnesota, but when the farm failed he moved the family to St. Louis, Missouri. There Luna met and married James T. Kellie. But she still hoped for a large family and a big house, so at the age of 18 Luna moved with her husband and their infant to a homestead in Hastings, Kansas.

Life on the prairie was a far cry from the dreams of Luna Kellie's youth. She gave birth to 12 children, two of whom died. They lived in an 8-by-12-foot sod house dug into a hill. Overworked and exhausted, weakened by the strain of childbirth and constant work, Luna kept dreaming of a better future. She read about the great geysers of Yellowstone and imagined a family trip. "Our trip never materialized," she recalled years later, "but we put in some happiest hours of life planning it."

What Luna Kellie imagined as a life of sturdy independence turned out to be an impoverished and isolated existence. It was an experience common to many American farmers, men and women alike. She tried to find connections with friends and neighbors, but there was not much choice. Her family joined a Methodist church, but Luna's husband became estranged from the church's pastor. Schools were even scarcer than churches, but Luna went out of her way to become active in the school district, where she took part in discussions over whether women should have the right to vote.

Luna Kellie was one of a large number of rural women who became active in the Populist movement.

Luna and her husband were not able to make a go of their farm. Like many rural women, Luna shared the responsibility for managing the farm with her husband. She kept a garden, which helped feed the family and brought in extra income from the sale of chickens and eggs. As Luna taught herself how to maintain the livestock and grow fruit trees, her husband learned how to grow spring wheat. But no matter how hard they worked, a lethal combination

continued

>> **AMERICAN PORTRAIT** *continued*

of declining prices and high interest rates kept them in perpetual debt. After seven years Luna and her husband lost the farm. They struggled to survive by raising chickens, sheep, and livestock.

The more Luna Kellie came to understand the burdens on farmers, the more attracted she was to organized efforts to relieve their plight. She became active in the Farmers' Alliance, the largest and most powerful of all such efforts. She was not alone. Luna Kellie was among the 250,000 women who joined the Farmers' Alliance, making it the largest women's organization in the United States at the time.

For Kellie, the Alliance held out the hope of realizing the dreams of her youth. It advocated education for the young, scientific farming, business methods, and organized cooperation among producers. Its reforms would bring progress and prosperity to rural America. They would break down the isolation of rural life, bringing farmers together in cooperative enterprises and linking rural Americans to the world of cities and industry. In 1892, when the Nebraska Farmers' Alliance affiliated with the National Farmers' Alliance and Industrial Union, Kellie was elected state secretary. She worked as tirelessly on Alliance business as she had on her own farm. She wrote countless letters. She edited and set the type for articles for the Alliance newspaper.

Without ever setting foot outside her home, Luna Kellie found herself at the center of a vast network of farmers who learned from each other by discussing the issues of greatest concern. Those issues started from a basic desire to improve the lives of rural Americans but quickly expanded into broader questions of political reform. By 1892 the Farmers' Alliance had become the backbone for the most important political insurgency of the late nineteenth century, the Populist Party.

Common Threads

>> How did both culture and politics reflect sharp distinctions between men and women? How did culture and politics break those distinctions down?

>> What was the overriding issue of American politics in the late nineteenth century?

>> Was American politics headed for a crisis in the 1890s?

Two Political Styles

There were two distinct political styles in late nineteenth-century America: one was partisan, the other was voluntary. Partisan politics included all the eligible voters who counted themselves as Democrats or Republicans, who attended party parades and electioneering spectacles, and who cast their ballots in record numbers. This was largely a world of men.

The second political style, voluntarism, embraced a vast network of organizations, including women's assemblies, reform clubs, labor unions, and farmers' groups.

The Triumph of Party Politics

In the late nineteenth century American men voted along very strict party lines. Political parties printed and distributed their own ballots, which loyal Republicans and Democrats simply dropped in the appropriate box. Party allegiances and discipline were firm, and campaigns were carefully organized. At no other time in American history did voters ally themselves so tightly to the two major parties.

Never again would so large a proportion of American men participate in presidential elections. From the 1840s through the 1860s an average of 69 percent of those eligible voted in presidential elections. During the final quarter of the century, the average rose to 77 percent. The figures were less impressive in the South, although they followed the same general pattern. Between 1876 and 1892, nearly two out of three southern men voted in presidential elections, compared with 82 percent of men in the North. In the presidential elections of 1896 and 1900, northern voter turnout peaked at 84 percent.

Newspapers played a critical role in maintaining this level of political participation. Most editors were strong party advocates. Papers survived with the help of official advertisements and contracts to print ballots and campaign documents. Editors such as Horace Greeley of the *New York Tribune* and William Cullen Bryant of the *New York Evening Post* became influential party leaders. Papers editorialized relentlessly in favor of their candidates and their party and slanted stories to show their party in the most favorable light. Some papers printed logos boasting of their partisan affiliation. "Republican in everything, independent in nothing," the *Chicago Inter Ocean* declared. Newspapers presented readers a starkly partisan world in which the difference between parties was the same as the difference between good and evil.

Spectacular political campaigns reinforced partisan attachments. The parties organized political clubs and military marching companies to drum up enthusiasm for elections. The clubs and marching groups in turn organized an endless series of competing party parades, where marchers rang bells, set off cannons, raised banners, an unfurled flags. Millions of American men, perhaps a fifth of all registered voters, participated in these huge, boisterous spectacles.

Conspicuously absent from these events were the candidates themselves, particularly in presidential contests. Throughout the nineteenth century it was considered unseemly for presidential candidates to stump for votes. Those who did campaign—for example, Stephen Douglas in 1860, Horace Greeley in 1872, or James G. Blaine in 1884—were notoriously prone to losing the elections.

Masculine Partisanship and Feminine Voluntarism

Party politics was a largely masculine activity in the late nineteenth century. Both major parties functioned like fraternal organizations, and voting was increasingly referred to as a "manly" or a "manhood" right. Denying a man his right to vote was like denying his masculinity. If the public sphere of campaigns and voting was a man's world, the private sphere of home and family was widely understood as a woman's world. In practice, women always participated in popular politics. They decorated the meeting halls, prepared the food, and joined

Figure 19–1   Percent of Eligible Voters Casting Ballots Between 1840 and 1896 a huge proportion—
often 80 percent—of those eligible to vote did so in presidential elections. In the twentieth century turnout
dropped substantially.

the parades dressed as symbolic representations of the Goddess of Liberty or some similarly
feminine icon. Nevertheless, politically active women opted for a different style of politics.

The stereotypes of the public man and the private woman rested on the assumption
that women were destined to remain at home as protectors of the family's virtue. By the
middle of the century, increasing numbers of women used that stereotype to develop their
own form of political activism. Female virtue justified women's support for moral reform
movements such as abolitionism and temperance. Thus many women entered the public
sphere to protect the private sphere. By defining "the family" broadly, women expanded
political activity beyond the confines of the two-party system. In this way, a stereotype
that initially restricted feminine political activity became a justification for women's increasing participation in public crusades.

Women pursued politics as representatives of voluntary associations dedicated to
specific reforms, such as Sabbatarian laws that would prohibit working and drinking alcohol on the Sabbath, or the struggles against slavery, prostitution, and poverty. Because
it grew out of voluntary associations rather than political parties, this style of political
activity is known as "voluntarism." Voluntary associations attracted mostly the educated
members of the middle class, who brought their class biases with them. By upholding the
home as the special preserve of feminine authority, for example, reformers ignored the
fact that working-class families depended heavily on the labor of children.

Sometimes women's associations copied the style of partisan politics, staging mass
marches and rallies. But because many politically active women were critical of the emotional style of mass politics, they concentrated less on rousing voters than on educating
them and lobbying elected officials. Men also joined voluntary associations, but they were
dismissed by mainstream politicians as "namby-pamby, goody-goody gentlemen." In the
late nineteenth century, voluntarism was associated with feminine politics and, party politics was associated with masculinity.

THE AGE OF BRASS.
or the triumphs of Woman's rights

"Women on Top" A satirical cartoon from 1869 belittled the campaign for women's suffrage. Entitled "Women on Top," the image reflected the common assumption that electoral politics was strictly a masculine activity.

The Critics of Popular Politics

The combination of partisanship and voluntarism made American politics more "popular" than ever before, attracting women and men, blacks and whites, immigrants and the native born, working class and middle class. But not all Americans appreciated popular politics. After the Civil War a small but influential group of conservatives reacted with disgust to the American rage for politics. Contemptuous of partisanship, they advocated a new style of nonpartisan politics and questioned the principle of universal suffrage. Because they laid the groundwork for a new style of politics that would prevail in the twentieth century, the critics were ahead of their time.

"Universal suffrage can only mean in plain English the government of ignorance and vice," Charles Francis Adams complained in 1869. Adams spoke for a traditional American elite that saw popular politics as a degradation of public life. To such men, political virtue required economic independence, among voters and public officials alike. The fact that the American working class was made up largely of blacks, Asians, and Catholic immigrants only made matters worse.

But blatantly antidemocratic rhetoric was a losing proposition in the late nineteenth century. Elites hoping to maintain influence avoided direct assaults on the principle of universal suffrage. Instead they became advocates of good government: government run by professionals rather than party bosses and staffed by civil servants rather than party favorites. They became, in short, advocates of *nonpartisan* politics.

Nonpartisan politics was a reaction against the upheavals of urban and industrial development and what elites saw as the twin evils of radicalism and immigration. In the wake of the nationwide strikes of 1877, *The Nation* magazine, a voice of elite opinion, asked whether an "alien" proletariat had transformed universal suffrage from a democratic blessing into a nightmare for the "well-to-do and intelligent" classes. In 1881, supporters of good government organized the National Civil Service Reform League to prevent political parties from filling government positions. Victory came two years later with the establishment of a Civil Service Commission that would assign federal jobs on the basis of merit rather than patronage.

But civil service reform would not stop the phenomenal growth of a largely immigrant working-class electorate. Political opposition to immigration, known as nativism, had enjoyed some success in the 1850s, and in 1882 nativists won a congressional ban on the further immigration of Chinese. Anti-Catholicism spread across the country, especially in the Midwest in the late 1880s. Immigrants were Catholic and working class, and so were seen to pose a double threat. One nativist pointed to the "two lines" of foreign influence threatening the republic. One line led to the radical politics of "agrarianism" and "anarchy," the second to Catholic "superstition." Both led "by different roads to one ultimate end, despotism!"

By the mid-1890s, as immigration from eastern and southern Europe increased, nativist rhetoric grew more racist. The threat was no longer merely from radicals and Catholics but also from darker-skinned peoples from Italy, Russia, and eastern Europe. Social scientists proclaimed the inherent intellectual inferiority of such peoples, giving the imprimatur of science to the most vicious stereotypes. Italians were said to be genetically predisposed to organized violence, Jews to thievery and manipulation. Anti-immigrant parties and nativist societies appeared across America.

As the Number of Immigrants to America Swelled, So Did Opposition to Them This 1891 cartoon blames immigration for causing a host of social and political evils.

Throughout most of the nineteenth century, however, the critics of popular politics remained a vocal minority. Most Americans entered the political arena with deep concerns over the problems of a society rapidly becoming more urban and industrial. Industrial capitalism generated the issues that dominated American public life in the late nineteenth century.

Economic Issues Dominate National Politics

By the late nineteenth century, Americans were used to the idea that government should oversee the distribution of the nation's natural resources. After the Civil War, federal officials distributed public lands to homesteaders and railroads and granted rights to mining, ranching, and timber companies. During those same decades, the rise of big business led many Americans to believe that the government should regulate the currency and also protect American commerce and workers from ruinous foreign competition. Given the even balance of the two major parties, the outcome was a policy that split the difference. High tariffs protected workers, while the gold standard remained largely intact. Meanwhile, the Supreme Court restricted the government's ability to regulate the domestic market. But this was never a stable compromise, and struggles over economic policy occupied national politics throughout the late nineteenth century.

Weak Presidents Oversee a Stronger Federal Government

Starting in the mid-1870s, the Democrats and Republicans had nearly equal electoral strength. From 1876 through 1896 no president took office with an overwhelming electoral mandate, and none enjoyed a full term during which his own party controlled both houses of Congress. After Grant's reelection in 1872, no president was elected to two consecutive terms until 1900.

In some cases, a president took office already tainted by the electoral process itself, as did Rutherford B. Hayes in 1876. Hayes's fellow Republicans were annoyed by his efforts to conciliate the southern Democrats, who were conducting congressional investigations of his election, and frustrated by the president's contradictory position on civil service reform. Hayes forbade his party to raise money from Republican officeholders, and he wrestled with Roscoe Conkling, Republican boss of New York City, for control of the New York Customs House—the most lucrative source of patronage in America. Hayes spoke for civil service reform but acted the role of the party patron by lavishly rewarding his own supporters. Civil service reformers soon turned away from him.

In 1877 Hayes took one important step toward strengthening the presidency. When railroad workers went on strike, Hayes sent federal troops to suppress them. This was an important precedent. Later presidents would often exercise their authority to intervene directly in disputes between workers and employers. But Hayes did nothing to relieve the distress caused by the depression of the 1870s. Millions of Americans were suffering from the sharp fall in wages and prices, yet Hayes vetoed a bill that would have modestly inflated the currency. By 1880 the president was so unpopular that his fellow Republicans happily took him up on his offer not to run for reelection.

The results of the 1880 election were typical of the era. Republican James A. Garfield won by a tiny margin. He received 48.5 percent of the votes, and Democrat Winfield Hancock received 48.1 percent. As usual, the Republicans did best in New England, the upper Midwest, and the West. The Democrats swept the South but also took New Jersey, Nevada, and California. The Republicans generally appealed to southern blacks and to a Protestant, native-born northern middle class. The Democrats counted on strong support from working-class immigrants and southern whites.

As usual, economic issues dominated the 1880 campaign, even though Democrats and Republicans differed little on economic policy. Both parties were addicted to the patronage system, so neither pressed for civil service reform. In theory the Democrats favored lower tariffs than the Republicans. In practice neither party advocated free trade, and both parties had strong "protectionist" blocs (supporting high tariffs to protect American business) as well as members who favored lower tariff rates. Neither party wanted to reverse current deflationary policies. Finally, although Republicans made periodic gestures in support of southern blacks, they had abandoned the freed people of the South. Garfield's victory in 1880 did not foreshadow any major shifts in government policy.

On July 2, 1881, the president was shot by a lunatic who claimed to be a disappointed office seeker. Garfield died two months later, and Chester A. Arthur, the product of a powerful patronage machine, became president. The assassination made it dangerous for the new president to resist the swell of popular support for civil service reform. The Republicans in control of Congress did resist, however, and Democrats swept into office on a tide of resentment against Republican corruption and patronage. The following year Congress passed, and President Arthur signed, the landmark Pendleton Civil Service Act.

The Pendleton Act prohibited patronage officeholders from contributing to the party machine that gave them their jobs. More important, the law authorized the president to establish a Civil Service Commission to administer competitive examinations for federal jobs. Before the century ended, the majority of federal jobs were removed from the reach of the patronage machines. The Pendleton Act was a major turning point in the creation of a stable and professional civil service.

Although Arthur signed the Pendleton Act, he lost his chance of gaining credit as a reformer by distributing lavish patronage to his supporters in a bid for reelection in 1884. He also threw away an opportunity to lead the way on tariff reform. As prosperity returned in the late 1870s and early 1880s, government coffers bulged with surplus revenues from import taxes. Cries for lower tariffs grew louder, but the president succumbed to high-tariff forces in Congress. Arthur was no more successful in his attempts to strengthen the navy or carry out an aggressive foreign policy. To make matters worse, the economy began to slow down again. Arthur approached the 1884 elections a tainted president. His fellow Republicans would not even renominate him.

The Democrats nominated Grover Cleveland. As mayor of Buffalo and governor of New York, Cleveland had a reputation as an honest man and a moderate. Cleveland, the first Democrat elected to the presidency in nearly 30 years, made reconciliation between the North and the South a theme of his administration.

Cleveland's conviction that the federal government should defer to southern whites derived in part from his commitment to local government. Accordingly, Cleveland was not an activist president. During his first two years in office he initiated no new programs, but neither did he thwart congressional moves to strengthen the authority of the central government. Cleveland approved legislation that raised the Agriculture Department to the status of a cabinet office and signed the Dawes Severalty Act of 1887, which placed the federal government in direct control over most Native Americans (see Chapter 17). In the same year, he signed the Interstate Commerce Act, the first federal legislation designed to regulate big business. It empowered an Interstate Commerce Commission to curb monopolistic and discriminatory practices by railroads.

When his fellow Democrats lost control of the House of Representatives in 1886, Cleveland decided to take the lead on an important issue. The issue he chose was the tariff. In December 1887, as his reelection campaign was to begin, Cleveland devoted his annual message to Congress almost entirely to sharp reductions in the tariff. Insisting he was not an advocate of free trade, he said he thought the tariff was too high.

Cleveland merely watched passively as Congress produced a doomed bill that was biased in favor of southern interests. When his own party included only a weak endorsement of tariff reform in the 1888 platform, Cleveland did nothing. Throughout his campaign for reelection, he spoke not one word on the subject. Cleveland had no tariff reform, and little else, to show for his four years in office.

Running skillfully on a protectionist platform, the Republicans won back the White House in 1888. A Republican president, Benjamin Harrison, at last presided over a Republican majority in Congress. Making good on campaign promises, Republicans enacted high tariff rates. The Harrison-McKinley Tariff of 1890 also gave the president the authority to raise or lower tariffs with nations that opened their markets to American businesses, granting him important new authority in the conduct of foreign affairs. Also in 1890 the Republicans passed the Sherman Anti-Trust Act, declaring it illegal for "combinations" to enter into arrangements that would restrain competition. By failing to define "restraint of trade," the Sherman Act left it to the probusiness courts to decide.

The Republicans received little credit for their efforts, and part of the problem was the president himself. Nicknamed "the human iceberg," the pompous Harrison could not rally the people. But the larger problem was rising discontent among voters. In 1890 they put the Democrats back in control of the House of Representatives, and in 1892 they reelected Grover Cleveland president. Once again, however, a president took office without a popular majority. Cleveland was the last of a string of relatively weak presidents (see Table 19–1). But the weakness of the executive did not indicate an inactive central government. In addition

 Table 19-1 Razor-thin Electoral Margins in the Gilded Age

Year	Popular Vote	% of Popular Vote	Electoral Vote
1876	4,036,572	48.0	185
	4,284,020	51.0	184
1880	4,453,295	48.5	214
	4,414,082	48.1	155
	308,578	3.4	—
1884	4,879,507	48.5	219
	4,850,293	48.2	182
1888	5,477,129	47.9	233
	5,537,857	48.6	168

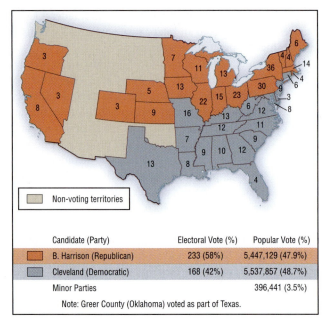

Candidate (Party)	Electoral Vote (%)	Popular Vote (%)
B. Harrison (Republican)	233 (58%)	5,447,129 (47.9%)
Cleveland (Democratic)	168 (42%)	5,537,857 (48.7%)
Minor Parties		396,441 (3.5%)

Note: Greer County (Oklahoma) voted as part of Texas.

Map 19–1   The Election of 1888

to the Pendleton Act, the Interstate Commerce Act, and the Sherman Anti-Trust Act, the government tried to inflate the currency by modestly increasing the amount of silver in circulation. By maintaining high tariffs, politicians protected the wages of workers and the economic security of businesses. Nevertheless, the weakness of the federal government left the impression that the political system could not solve the problems associated with industrial capitalism.

Government Activism and Its Limits

There are two standard themes in the political history of the late nineteenth century. The first theme stresses that government in this era was replete with corruption and bribery. The second theme emphasizes that this was the great age of limited government and unregulated markets. After the retreat from Reconstruction, the government allowed the new industrial economy to grow at its own rapid pace. There is a kernel of truth in each of these themes. Corruption was a real problem in late nineteenth-century politics, and the government's regulatory powers were still weak. The conflicting impulses toward limited and active government can be seen most clearly in one of the most disruptive issues of late nineteenth-century American politics, the regulation of the currency.

Greenbacks and Greenbackers

People have always disagreed over how much money governments should produce and how they should produce it. During the eighteenth century, American colonists complained

AMERICA AND THE WORLD

>> **Foreign Policy and Commercial Expansion**

Capitalist development reshaped American foreign policy just as it dominated domestic politics. In the 1860s William Henry Seward shifted the emphasis of American foreign policy from the acquisition of territory to the expansion of American commerce. As the secretary of state for Abraham Lincoln and Andrew Johnson, Seward advanced policies that promoted industrial expansion. He believed that "political supremacy follows commercial supremacy" and worked to open American markets in Latin America, Canada, and the Pacific region, including Asia. Territorial expansion did not end, but it took a back seat to commercial expansion.

In the late 1860s, as congressional Republicans struggled with President Johnson over Reconstruction, many of Seward's plans got caught in the crossfire. His biggest success came on April 9, 1867, when the Senate ratified the treaty purchasing Alaska for $7.2 million. A few months later, however, the Senate blocked a treaty with Denmark for the purchase of the Virgin Islands. Seward also failed to win approval for a naval base in Santo Domingo and a treaty with Colombia giving the United States exclusive rights to build a canal across the isthmus of Panama. President Grant and Senator Charles Sumner revived long-standing American hopes of annexing Canada, but Canadians seemed intent on cementing their ties to Great Britain.

European powers thwarted U.S. territorial ambitions in Latin America, but so did racist concerns about bringing large numbers of nonwhites into the United States. A rebellion in Cuba in 1868 heightened American interest in annexing the island. But Secretary of State Hamilton Fish had long resisted the idea of absorbing half a million Cubans of "every shade and mixture of color." Similar inhibitions led the Senate to reject President Grant's 1869 treaty with Santo Domingo.

Despite America's territorial efforts, however, Seward believed that commercial expansion would drive American foreign policy in the future. Between 1860 and 1897 American exports tripled, surpassing $1 billion per year. After 300 years of trade deficits, in 1874 America's exports began to surpass its imports. Nearly 85 percent of those exports were agricultural commodities, but the growth of industrial exports was even more spectacular. Iron and steel exports jumped by 230 percent between 1888 and 1898. In the 1880s, U.S. multinational corporations became a fixture of international commerce.

Aggressive secretaries of state reaffirmed Seward's commitment to commercial expansion. In 1886, for example, James G. Blaine worried that European nations were diverting Latin American commerce away from the United States. Concern for access to foreign markets pushed successive administrations to assert America's exclusive right to build a canal across Central America. Hoping to thwart European commercial expansion by forging ties with Latin America, the United States convened the first Pan-American Conference in 1889.

Mexico provided the most vivid demonstration of U.S. commercial expansion.

continued

AMERICA AND THE WORLD *continued*

Although Americans had been buying property in Mexico since before the Civil War, political instability limited investments. In 1876, however, Porfirio Díaz seized power in Mexico and began a reign of 35 years that favored American commercial interests. American investors quickly swarmed into Mexico, building railroads, selling life insurance, and digging oil wells. By 1910 Americans owned 43 percent of all the property in Mexico, more than Mexicans themselves owned.

United States attention also turned toward Asia and the South Pacific. In the 1880s the United States nearly went to war with England and Germany over disputed claims to Samoa. An 1876 treaty gave Hawaiian sugar favored treatment on the American market, prompting a huge influx into the United States (along with a backlash by sugar producers on the mainland). By 1886 two-thirds of Hawaiian sugar was produced on American-owned plantations. By the 1890s American power in Hawaii had grown so great that it provoked among native Hawaiians a backlash that culminated in Queen Liliuokalani's ascension to the throne in 1891. Two years later, Hawaiians favorable to the United States dethroned the queen. Under President William McKinley, Hawaii was annexed to the United States.

The United States treaded somewhat more cautiously in East Asia, where European powers had established ties, and negotiated treaties with Japan and Korea that greatly increased American access to Asian markets.

From 1865 to 1890 a string of powerful secretaries of state compensated for a succession of weak presidents. By the late 1880s America's extensive global interests began to shape military policy. In 1890 Congress approved the construction of the first modern warships, and the Supreme Court extended the president's control over "our international relations." The growing links between commercial and diplomatic interests were reviving the powers of the American presidency.

that there was not enough money in circulation to sustain their economy. In the first half of the nineteenth century, Americans fought over the power the government should give to banks to regulate the amount of money in circulation. After the Civil War, capitalist development sparked another debate over the role of government in the economy.

To support the Union effort during the Civil War, the U.S. government printed $450 million worth of "greenbacks," paper bills backed by the government's word but not by the traditional reserves of gold or silver. When the war ended, most Americans agreed that the greenbacks should be withdrawn from circulation. But after the depression of the 1870s there was a demand to keep the greenbacks in circulation. Those who wanted to return to the gold standard by making greenbacks convertible for "specie"—gold or silver—were called *resumptionists*, that is, they wanted the government to resume specie payments. Those who wanted the government to keep greenbacks in circulation to help inflate the currency were called *greenbackers*.

Supporters of the gold standard associated sound money with sound religion and could compare greenbackers to atheists. Greenbackers were indeed often radical critics of industrial society. They formed a Greenback-Labor Party, which garnered more than 1 million votes and elected 14 members of Congress in the 1878 elections. But the sound-money forces won out, and in 1879 the $300 million in greenbacks still in circulation were made convertible into gold.

Supporters of inflation next took up the issue of "free silver." To counteract the deflationary trend, they argued, the government should add to the amount of money in circulation by allowing the unlimited coinage of silver. In 1878 Congress passed the Bland-Allison Act authorizing the Treasury to mint silver in amounts tied to the amount of gold being minted. When prosperity returned in the 1880s the currency question died down until the arrival of another severe depression in the 1890s.

Growth of the Central Government

Despite the inevitable retrenchment after the Civil War, the size of the central government grew as new bureaucracies were created. Congress consolidated the United States Geological Survey in 1879, established the Interstate Commerce Commission in 1887, and created the Department of Justice in 1870 and the Department of Agriculture in 1889.

The number of civilian federal employees rose from 53,000 in 1871 to 256,000 in 1901 and reflected the emergence of a professional civil service. In 1883, when Congress passed the first civil service law, 13,780 federal jobs were "classified," meaning that applicants had to pass an exam to qualify. Fifteen years later, 89,306 positions were classified, nearly half of the jobs in the national government. This expansion of civil service dried up the patronage well and greatly weakened the power of the Democratic and Republican parties.

By the turn of the century, however, only the rudiments of a modern federal government were in place. The Interstate Commerce Commission lacked the power to enforce its own rulings, so it was forced to rely on courts, dominated by supporters of big business. The weak Sherman Anti-Trust Act threatened few monopolies. Finally, only about 15 percent of the wage-labor force was actually protected by the high tariffs. By 1900 the federal government had developed in important ways, yet it remained small and weak by later standards. Indeed, it was rather the state and municipal governments that responded most aggressively to the problems of urban and industrial society.

States Regulate; Municipalities Reform

Even as Americans called on their government to do more and more, politicians voiced their opposition to the taxes and bureaucracies that active government required. The result was a jarring contradiction. At the state level, politicians enacted policies of retrenchment. In contrast to the steady expansion of the federal government, late nineteenth-century state legislatures passed fewer laws and lowered taxes.

But states also established new regulatory bodies to govern the exploding municipalities of urban and industrial America. During the late nineteenth century, state officials often transferred municipal power from elected officials and party politicians to experts and specialists on unelected boards. Mayors, city council members, and aldermen lost much of their authority over budgets, schools, health, transportation, police, and parks to commissions

Bird's-eye View of Golden Gate Park San Francisco's Golden Gate Park, designed by Frederick Law Olmsted, was one of the most impressive of the great municipal parks built in cities across America in the late nineteenth century.

generally staffed by middle-class professionals who were appointed as "nonpartisans" to their posts. The quality and professionalism of police and fire services increased dramatically over the course of the nineteenth century.

As states retrenched, cities increased their property taxes to pay for streets, sewers, reservoirs, and public transportation. In the late nineteenth century city governments produced some of the great urban achievements of American history, including huge public parks, such as Central Park in New York and Golden Gate Park in San Francisco, and spectacular feats of engineering and architecture. New Yorkers built the Brooklyn Bridge; Chicagoans literally reversed the flow of the Chicago River. Municipal governments greatly enhanced the civility and decency of urban life.

Yet Americans grew dissatisfied with their governments. Some were disgusted by corruption and inefficiency; others were offended by the hoopla of popular politics. To many, government policies seemed inadequate to the demands of urban and industrial America. The powers of government grew slowly, but they were dwarfed by the private power of huge new corporations. Frustrated by piecemeal reforms, middle-class Americans turned to radical campaigns for social and economic transformation.

Middle-Class Radicalism

In the late nineteenth century middle-class radicals argued that economic development had undermined individual liberty and equality. Yet although their attacks on capitalism were severe, their assumptions were surprisingly traditional. They were usually frightened, not motivated, by socialism. They often worried that without substantial reforms, a discontented working class would overthrow the reign of private property. Their radical critiques of industrial society exposed deep wells of discontent among Americans.

Henry George and the Limits of Producers' Ideology

Henry George was born in Philadelphia in 1839 to middle-class parents. Although his formal education was limited, George traveled and read widely. Like many middle-class Americans of his time, he was shocked by the fact that as the nation grew richer the number of poor people grew as well. He studied the problem for many years and in 1879 published his conclusions in a best-selling book called *Progress and Poverty*.

George's explanation rested on what historians have called producers' ideology. He assumed that only human labor could create legitimate wealth and that anything of value, such as food, clothing, or steel rails, came from the world's producing classes. By contrast, stockbrokers, bankers, and speculators made money from money rather than from the goods they produced. Their wealth was therefore illegitimate. From these premises, George divided the world into two classes: producers and predators.

The harmony of capital and labor was a central theme of producers' ideology. Henry George dreamed of a world in which working people owned their own farms and shops, making them both capitalists and laborers, a vision that recalled Thomas Jefferson's ideal society of small farmers and independent shopkeepers. America used to be that way, George believed, but as society "progressed," the land was monopolized by a wealthy few, and producers were forced to work for wealthy landholders. Employers then invested in technology that increased the productivity of their workers but kept the added wealth for themselves. George's solution for the inequities of industrial society was a so-called Single Tax on rents. Because all wealth derived from labor applied to land, he reasoned, rents were an unnatural transfer of wealth from the producers to the landlords. To discourage the landowning class from accumulating land, George suggested prohibitively high taxes on rents and improvements on land. All other taxes would be abolished, including the tariffs protecting big business.

George presented his Single Tax as an alternative to the dangerous socialist doctrines he thought were spreading among the working class. George attacked the socialist idea that there was an inherent conflict between labor and capital. He opposed government regulation of the economy, and he was a fiscal conservative, suspicious of proposals to counteract deflation by putting more money in circulation. Despite his apparent radicalism, George's popularity testified to the strength of middle-class concerns about the political power of the working class.

Edward Bellamy and the Nationalist Clubs

In 1888 Edward Bellamy, a Massachusetts editor, published a best-selling critique of capitalism even more powerful than Henry George's. Bellamy's *Looking Backward* was a utopian

John F. Weir's 1877 Painting *Forging the Shaft: A Welding Heat* This painting graphically depicts the forms of industrial wage labor that Henry George feared. He advocated tax policies that would restore a Jeffersonian economy of small, independent producers.

novel set in the future. The plot revolves around Julian West, who goes to sleep in Boston in 1887 and wakes up in the year 2000. His host, Doctor Leete, introduces West to the miraculous changes that have taken place. Technological marvels have raised everyone's standard of living. Boston has become a clean and orderly city. The great problems of industrial civilization have been solved. This was possible, Doctor Leete explains, because Americans had overcome the "excessive individualism" of the late nineteenth century, which "was inconsistent with much public spirit."

What about "the labor question?" Julian West asks. It had been "threatening to devour society" in 1887 when West fell asleep. Doctor Leete's answer offers Bellamy's critique of capitalism. In the early years of the republic, the doctor explains, workers and employers lived in harmony. Upward mobility was common. This changed when "great aggregations of capital" arose. Like Henry George's, Bellamy's criticism of capitalism was grounded in Jeffersonian ideals. For both authors the triumph of wage labor led to concentrations of wealth that undermined the harmony of capital and labor.

But where *Progress and Poverty* proposed the restoration of the simple virtues of Jeffersonian society, *Looking Backward* imagined a high-tech future filled with consumer goods. In Bellamy's ideal world, production and consumption would no longer be subject to the whims of the market; instead, they would be harmonized by an obscure process of centralized planning. The result would be a consumer's utopia of widespread abundance.

Where Henry George reasserted the values of hard work and self-restraint, Edward Bellamy embraced the modern cult of leisure. For Henry George, technology led to misery and inequality, but for Edward Bellamy, machines would free mankind from the burdens and inequities of the modern world.

In spite of these differences, Bellamy and George shared a profound fear of militant workers. *Looking Backward* catered to a middle class craving for order amidst the chaos of industrial society. Decisions about what to produce were made collectively, and society as a whole owned the means of production. Yet Bellamy was contemptuous of socialism and called his vision "nationalism." Under the social peace of nationalism, there was little or no need for government. This vision inspired thousands of middle-class Americans to form "Bellamy Clubs" or "Nationalist Clubs," particularly in New England.

The Woman's Christian Temperance Union

"Edward Bellamy's wonderful book" also inspired Frances Willard, president of the Woman's Christian Temperance Union (WCTU). She called nationalism "the fulfillment of man's highest earthly dream." Such support would have been impossible 15 years earlier, when "conservatives" pressed the WCTU to restrict its activities to the suppression of liquor. But Willard had grander visions, and so, apparently, did the WCTU's members. In 1879 they elected Willard their national president, a position she held until her death in 1898.

The temperance movement broadened its interests and grew more radical and more popular. It embraced women's suffrage, workers' rights, and "Christian socialism." Still, the WCTU's appeal and its radicalism were restricted by its predominantly prosperous membership and its middle-class Protestant bias against most forms of party politics.

To be sure, the WCTU convened huge rallies, but Willard contrasted these serious, well-disciplined gatherings to raucous party conventions. Unlike the major parties, the WCTU combined education with interest-group pressure. Willard and her associates gave speeches, wrote articles, published books and newspaper columns on the evils of drink, organized petition campaigns, and lobbied officeholders. The crusade against alcohol grew into a wider political campaign to alleviate the problems of a new industrial society. In this sense the WCTU was typical of American politics in the late nineteenth century.

Under Willard's direction the WCTU endorsed women's suffrage and formed an alliance with the country's largest labor union. Willard supported laws restricting the workday to eight hours and prohibiting child labor. The WCTU's attitude toward alcohol also changed. By the 1890s Willard viewed drunkenness as a public health issue rather than a personal sin, a social problem rather than an individual failure. Temperance advocates supported reforms designed to relieve poverty, improve public health, raise literacy, alleviate the conditions of workers, reform prisons, suppress public immorality, and preserve peace. In the end, Willard attributed the evils of liquor to the inequities of corporate capitalism.

Three factors explain the WCTU's success. The first was Frances Willard's paradoxically conservative approach to radical reform. Her justification for female political activism always came back to women's distinctive calling as protectors of the home. The second reason for the WCTU's success was its decentralized structure: local chapters were free to adjust their activities to suit local needs. Finally, the WCTU appealed to middle-class women isolated by a culture that restricted them to the home. Women found in the WCTU a source of camaraderie, as well as political activism, and they made it among the largest women's political organizations in the late nineteenth century. The WCTU had 150,000 adult members compared with 13,000 members of the National American Woman Suffrage Association. The only reform organization to attract more women was the Farmers' Alliance.

AMERICAN LANDSCAPE

>> The "Crusade" Against Alcohol

Just before Christmas in 1873, Dr. Diocletian Lewis arrived in Hillsboro, Ohio, to speak on the evils of alcohol. He had given the speech many times before, but this time the women who came proved unusually responsive. Lewis told them how his mother saved his father from drink by persuading a local saloon keeper to stop selling liquor. The next morning a group of Hillsboro women met for prayer and then marched through the town urging local merchants to stop selling liquor. Inspired by their success, the women kept up the pressure through the winter of 1873–1874.

The Crusade, as it came to be called, quickly spread to more than 900 towns and cities in 31 states and territories. Women closed down thousands of liquor stores and saloons and secured pledges from hundreds of druggists and hotel keepers not to sell alcohol. With the success of the Crusade of 1873–1874, temperance was reborn as a movement dominated by women.

From these almost accidental beginnings there grew one of the late nineteenth century's largest outlets for women's political activism. Under the auspices of the Woman's Christian Temperance Union, women took up causes that stretched well beyond the suppression of alcohol. Voting and office holding were restricted to men, but the WCTU expanded democratic participation to include tens of thousands of women.

For all its success, however, temperance remained a middle-class reform movement concentrated in cities, especially in the North. The WCTU did not attract many immigrants, for example, and its official policy of religious toleration was undermined by the prejudices of middle-class members. For many members, immigrants were the Union's targets rather than its constituents, and the strong Protestant identity of the WCTU limited its appeal among working-class Catholics. A campaign aimed at replacing altar wine with grape juice in Christian services was rejected by both Irish Catholics and German Lutherans. As radical as it was, the WCTU would never reflect the interests of black sharecroppers, white tenant farmers, or immigrant workers. Nevertheless, like the Single-Taxers and the Bellamy Clubs, WCTU reformers reflected a growing sense that the American political system was unable to solve the problems of an industrial political economy.

Discontent Among Workers

Radicalized workers agreed that mainstream politics could not confront the problems of industrial capitalism. They questioned one of the premises of producers' ideology—that American democracy was secured by a unique harmony between capital and labor. Labor agitation often became violent, and employers demanded that government use its police powers to put down strikes. But if the harmony of capital and labor had been destroyed, advocates of the producers' ideology continued to search for a political solution to the labor problem.

The Knights of Labor and the Haymarket Disaster

Between 1860 and 1890 wages overall grew by 50 percent, but the bulk of the growth was confined to elite skilled and semiskilled workers in a handful of industries, such as printing and metalworking. The vast majority of workers suffered directly from deflation and economic instability. By 1880, 40 percent of industrial workers lived at or below the poverty line, and the average worker was unemployed for 15 to 20 percent of the year. To relieve their plight, American workers sought political solutions to economic problems.

The most important labor organization to emerge from the crisis of the 1870s was the Noble and Holy Order of the Knights of Labor. Founded in 1869, the Knights of Labor was inspired by the producers' ideology and admitted everyone from self-employed farmers to unskilled factory workers. The Knights advocated a host of progressive reforms, including the eight-hour day, equal pay for men and women, the abolition of child and prison labor, inflation of the currency to counteract the deflationary spiral, and a national income tax.

By the late 1870s the union needed a strong national organization to hold various locals together. A new constitution required all members to pay dues and allowed the national organization to support local boycotts and thereby boost its credibility among workers. The Knights grew rapidly, from 19,000 members in 1881 to 111,000 in 1885. True to the producers' tradition, leader Terence Powderly favored the consumer boycott over the strike, an approach that proved successful during the recession of 1884, when strikes were being broken. By 1886 membership swelled to more than 700,000.

But the more the Knights of Labor grew, the more the strains among its members showed. The interests of shopkeepers and small-factory owners were very different from those of wage laborers, and the critical issue dividing them was the use of the strike as a weapon of organized labor. Self-employed producers preferred the consumer boycott, as did the Knights' leadership. By contrast, wage laborers saw the strike as their most powerful weapon.

With the return of prosperity, trade unions called for a nationwide strike for the eight-hour day. On May 1, 1886, workers across the country walked off their jobs in one of the largest and most successful labor walkouts in American history. In Chicago 80,000 workers went out on strike. The Chicago strike was largely peaceful until May 4, when, at an anarchist rally at Haymarket Square, someone from the crowd tossed a bomb into a line of police. Eight policemen were killed. The number of civilian casualties was never determined. Although the bomb thrower was never identified, eight anarchists were tried for inciting violence, and four were put to death.

Anarchists—who questioned the legitimacy of all government power—had been active in Chicago for several years. Although they had little influence on the labor movement, their fiery rhetoric advocating the use of violence made them conspicuous. At the Haymarket rally on May 4, anarchist speakers used the same violent rhetoric. Samuel Fielden, for example, urged his listeners to "throttle" and "kill" the legal system or else, he warned, "it will kill you." Haymarket was a turning point in American labor politics. The Knights of Labor had tried to prevent its locals from supporting the May Day walkouts, but it put itself in a bind. Members resented this failure to support the strikes, while a wave of revulsion against labor agitation swept the country. The Knights of Labor never recovered from the Haymarket disaster. Worker agitation later split into two competing wings. Small farmers formed their own organizations, and wage laborers organized separately into industrial trade unions.

Agrarian Revolt

The late nineteenth century was a desperate time for American farmers, especially in the West and South. To compete they had to buy expensive agricultural equipment, often from manufacturers who benefited from tariff protections. Then they had to ship their goods on railroads that charged higher rates to small farmers than to big industrialists. At the market, they faced steadily declining prices.

As the economy became global, southern cotton had to compete against cotton from India and the Near East. Western wheat competed with Russian and eastern European wheat. To keep up, farmers increasingly went into debt, and in a deflationary spiral the money they borrowed to plant their crops was worth more when it came time to pay it back, whereas their crops were worth less. As farmers mortgaged their homes and land, the proportion of owner-occupied farms declined, whereas the number of tenants rose.

Farmers were traditionally opposed to active government, but they began to press for government action. However, farmers were notoriously hard to organize. Scattered over large sections of the country, they were committed to an ideology of economic independence and hostile to government intervention. One of the first attempts to organize farmers was the Patrons of Husbandry, generally called the Grange. The Grange began to attract farmers during the depression of the 1870s and claimed 1.5 million members by 1874. Consistent with producers' ideology, the Grange organized cooperatives designed to eliminate the role of merchants and creditors. By storing grain collectively, farmers held their products back from the market in the hope of gaining control over commodity prices. But inexperience made the Grange cooperatives difficult to organize and sustain. After 1875 their membership dwindled.

The National Farmers' Alliance and Industrial Union, known simply as the Farmers' Alliance, was much more effective than the Grange. Founded in Texas in 1877, the Farmers' Alliance spread rapidly across the South, the West, and the upper Plains states. Its goal was not to restore rural Jeffersonian simplicity but to bring American farmers into the modern world of industry and prosperity. The Alliance focused above all on education, broadly conceived. That meant public schools and the spread of scientific agriculture and sound business practices. The Alliance also built a remarkable network of newspapers and lecturers to help liberate farmers from their rural isolation. The appeal of the Alliance ultimately transcended politics and economics. For rural men and women alike, the Farmers' Alliance offered a chance to escape the isolation of farm life and appealed to their desire to share in the progress and prosperity of American life.

At its core the Alliance was a reform organization calling for a specific set of economic policies. Above all, the farmers wanted to inflate the currency, whether by the circulation of more silver currency or of more paper currency ("greenbacks") or a combination of the two. Inspired by the successes of highly organized corporations, especially railroads, the Alliance also supported a system of cooperative "subtreasuries" that would allow farmers to pool and store their products until the best prices were available. In the meantime the cooperative would sustain them through low-interest loans.

By the late 1880s the Farmers' Alliance had attracted millions of members, concentrated in the southern, western, and Plains states. Created at a huge meeting at Ocala, Florida, in 1890, the Ocala Platform supported a host of new policies that joined economic progress to democratic reform. The platform called for the free coinage of silver, lower tariffs, government subtreasuries, and a constitutional amendment providing for direct election of senators. Finally, the Alliance called for strict government regulation, and if necessary direct government ownership, of the railroad and telegraph industries.

The Farmers' Alliance steered clear of politics and instead judged political candidates by their support of the Ocala Platform reforms. But neither major party demonstrated much support, so Farmers' Alliance members formed their own third parties, with some success on the Great Plains in the election of 1890. Out of these efforts came the most significant third party of the late nineteenth century, the People's Party, otherwise known as the Populists.

The Rise of the Populists

On February 22, 1892, a coalition of reform organizations met in St. Louis, including Single Tax advocates inspired by Henry George, greenbackers who wanted an inflationary currency policy, and representatives of the Knights of Labor and the Farmers'

Kansas Farmers Organizing to Attend a Populist Party Gathering

Alliance. Together they founded the People's Party and called for a presidential nominating convention to meet in Omaha, Nebraska, on July 4. There they nominated General James B. Weaver of Iowa for president and drew up the famous Omaha Platform, a vigorous restatement of the proposals laid out two years earlier by the Farmers' Alliance. Like the Ocala Platform, the Omaha Platform demanded an inflationary currency policy and subtreasuries. The Populists also called for a graduated income tax, direct government ownership of the railroad and telegraph industries, and the redistribution of lands owned by the railroads.

In the 1892 elections Weaver won about 1 million votes, and the Populists elected several senators, representatives, governors, and state legislators. But there was no support among wage earners in the industrial North and East. The Populist platform, for all its talk of the unity of working people, was incompatible with the interests of industrial workers, who favored the protective tariffs that shielded the industrial economy. Inflation would undermine the value of their wages and raise the price of commodities, and income taxes would shift the tax burden from landowners and importers to wage laborers. Conversely, farmers who hired workers had every reason to oppose the eight-hour day and laws restricting child labor.

Southern Populists faced a particularly strong challenge. They could win only with the support of the largest class of impoverished farmers, black sharecroppers. But any attempt to build a multiracial alliance of white and black Populists was met with an avalanche of racial demagoguery from Democratic politicians. White Populists had a hard enough time overcoming their own racial prejudices. The Farmers' Alliance had always been strictly segregated, with a separate Colored Farmers' Alliance. And in fact the economic interests of the two groups were not always compatible. But some cross-racial cooperation was essential for political purposes. Leading black Populists were aware of the limits of any alliance with white reformers. But the *need* for such a coalition tended to contradict the racial prejudices of white farmers. It also made the extremist racial demagoguery of the Democratic Party all but inevitable. Third parties are always hard to sustain, but in the face of such attacks Populism in the South could not survive.

Conclusion

After the Civil War the problems of industrial capitalism placed increasing strain on the political system. The two major parties were so closely matched in electoral strength that neither could risk bold new political and economic programs. So restless workers, desperate farmers, and an anxious middle class turned increasingly to voluntary organizations, labor unions, and farmers' alliances.

The politics of industrial society reached a turning point in the 1890s. During that decade Americans went to the polls in record numbers. Organized farmers made their most radical demands; labor agitation reached a violent climax. And as night follows day, a conservative reaction set in. Movements to restrict the number of voters emerged, particularly in the South. Opponents of immigration made significant strides. The Supreme Court declared systematic racial segregation constitutional. In short, radicalism and reaction reached their peak in the 1890s, as a recognizably modern America was being born.

>> Timeline

▼1867
United States purchases Alaska from Russia
Patrons of Husbandry (the Grange) founded

▼1869
Noble and Holy Order of the Knights of Labor founded
Suez Canal opened

▼1870
Department of Justice created

▼1872
Grant reelected

▼1873
"Crusade" against alcohol begins in Hillsboro, Ohio

▼1874
WCTU is formed

▼1876
Rutherford B. Hayes elected president
Porfirio Díaz seizes power in Mexico

▼1877
Farmers' Alliance founded

▼1878
Bland-Allison Act

▼1879
Frances Willard becomes president of the WCTU
Henry George publishes *Progress and Poverty*

▼1880
James Garfield elected president

▼1881
Garfield assassinated; Chester Arthur becomes president
WCTU endorses women's suffrage

▼1883
Pendleton Civil Service Act

▼1884
Grover Cleveland elected president

▼1886
Nationwide strike for eight-hour day
Riot at Haymarket Square in Chicago

continued

>> **Timeline** *continued*

▼**1887**
Interstate Commerce Act
Four Haymarket anarchists executed
Dawes Severalty Act

▼**1888**
Benjamin Harrison elected president
Edward Bellamy publishes *Looking Backward*

▼**1889**
United States convenes first Pan-American Conference
Department of Agriculture created

▼**1890**
Harrison-McKinley Tariff
Sherman Anti-Trust Act
Ocala Platform

▼**1891**
Queen Liliuokalani assumes the Hawaiian throne

▼**1892**
Omaha Platform of the People's Party
Grover Cleveland reelected

▼**1893**
Queen Liliuokalani overthrown

▼**1898**
Frances Willard dies

Review Questions

1. Describe the two major "styles" of politics in the late nineteenth century.

2. What were the major issues in national politics in this period?

3. What did Henry George, Edward Bellamy, and Frances Willard have in common?

4. What did the Farmers' Alliance stand for?

**For further review materials and resource information,
please visit www.oup.com/us/ofthepeople**

20

Industry and Empire
1890–1900

It was a short distance from the Arlington Hotel to the White House, and although it was icy and dark, J. Pierpont Morgan chose to walk. He pulled his scarf up around a scowling face known to millions of newspaper readers. He had not wanted to come to Washington. There were "large interests" that depended on keeping the currency of the United States sound, he told a Treasury official, and those interests were now in jeopardy. The commander in chief of the nation's bankers was going to meet the president to keep the United States from going bankrupt.

The events leading up to this meeting stretched back five years to 1890, when business failures toppled London's Baring Brothers investment house and triggered a collapse in European stock prices. Depression spread through Britain, Germany, and France. Anxious European investors began selling off their large American holdings. In early 1893 the panic reached the United States. The Philadelphia and Reading Railroad folded in February. Fourteen thousand businesses soon followed, along with more than 600 banks.

Summer brought more bad news from abroad. The government of India stopped minting silver, causing U.S. silver dollars to lose one-sixth of their value. Wall Street went into another tailspin. In New York 55,000 men, women, and girls in the clothing industry were thrown out of work. Banks refused to cash checks, and coins vanished from circulation. Tens of thousands of homeless poor people filled the roads. Breadlines formed. "The world surely cannot remain as mad as it is," the historian Henry Adams observed.

For Grover Cleveland the madness was only starting. The anger of workers and farmers, simmering for decades, was boiling over. The president pledged to keep the dollar on the gold standard, but it was not enough. A wave of strikes swept the country. Unemployed workers battled police on the Capitol grounds. By January 1895 so many panicky investors were cashing government bonds that the Treasury's gold reserve was

continued

>> **AMERICAN PORTRAIT** *continued*

half gone, and it looked as if the remainder might last only two weeks. Reluctantly, Cleveland agreed to open negotiations with Morgan.

Admired and reviled, Morgan was known as the leading financial manipulator of the late nineteenth century. Born to wealth in Hartford, Connecticut, he had been a Wall Street fixture since before the Civil War. Like his contemporaries, steelmaker Andrew Carnegie and oil magnate John D. Rockefeller, Morgan's skill lay in organization. He re-structured railroads, rooting out corruption, waste, and competition and driving down wages. Instead of taking risks, he eliminated them. He convinced leaders of warring firms to strike bargains and share the profits. Cleveland was about to place the Treasury in this man's hands.

The president opened the meeting by suggesting that things might not be so bad; a new bond issue might stabilize the Treasury. No, Morgan replied flatly, the run on gold would continue until European investors regained confidence. If the president agreed, Morgan would arrange a private loan and personally guarantee the solvency of the U.S. Treasury. After a stunned silence, the two men shook hands. News of the deal instantly calmed the bond markets. The crisis was over. The *New York Sun* reported that the deal "revived a confidence in the wealth and resources of this country," but Populist news-papers denounced it as a conspiracy and a "great bunco game."

Culminating two decades of turbulence, the Panic of 1893 permanently trans-formed the American political economy. Businessmen such as Morgan created even larger corporate combinations and placed them under professional managers. They used technology and "scientific management" to control the workplace and push la-borers to work faster and harder. Workers resisted, and the 1890s saw brutal clashes between capital and labor. Looking for jobs and schools, country people moved to the city and found both promise and danger. Social mobility among African Americans aroused fears in whites, and southerners created a system of formal segregation, en-forced by law and terror. Amid growing violence, industrial workers, Native Americans, and African Americans debated how best to deal with the overwhelming forces ranged against them.

The 1890s were also a turning point in American political history. After the 1896 election, many Americans walked away from the electoral process. Others were re-moved from the voter rolls through a process known as "disfranchisement." African American leaders and union organizers urged their followers to turn away from poli-tics in favor of "bread and butter" economic issues. The masculine, public spectacle of nineteenth-century politics with its parades and flag raisings died out. Patriotism, once synonymous with partisanship, now stood for America's global military and economic ambitions. Civic events featured army bands and cannon salutes. News-papers conjured up foreign threats. As Americans became more conscious of their military power, they watched the horizon for threats to their well-being as far away as China.

Americans began to feel that their economy's links to the world—and the changes wrought by manufacturing and rapid communications—separated their times from all that had happened before. Morgan's rescue required transactions on two continents, instantaneously coordinated by telegraph. The speed of industry, trade, and informa-tion, the way machines and technology spanned distance and time created a sense

>> **AMERICAN PORTRAIT** *continued*

that the environment and the future could be controlled. Many felt that those who possessed this newfound control—the modern countries—stood apart from those in other lands whose lives were not guided by science and information.

Between 1890 and 1900 Americans made their country recognizably modern. Those with the means to do so enlarged and refashioned many aspects of work and daily life. Financiers and giant corporations assumed control of the economy. Huge cities grew. The significance of voting declined, and a decade that opened with a global economic catastrophe ended with a dramatic display of the global reach of U.S. power.

Common Threads

>> How did industrial ideals of efficiency and organization change the democratic practice in America during the early 1900s?

>> Did the choices Americans made about how to run their

economy set the United States on a course for overseas conflict?

>> What did it mean to be modern? How did the pace of technological change affect Americans' outlook?

The Crisis of the 1890s

Financial convulsions, strikes, and the powerlessness of government against wealth rudely reminded Americans of how much their country had changed since the Civil War. When Illinois sent Abraham Lincoln to Congress, Chicago's population was less than 5,000; in 1890 it exceeded 1 million. Gone was the America of myth and memory, in which class tensions were slight and upward (or at least westward) mobility seemed easy. Many Americans foresaw the collapse of civilization. Others, however, felt that the United States was passing into a new phase of history that would lead to still greater trials and achievements.

Hard Times

Chicago in 1893 captured the hopes and fears of the new age. To celebrate the 400th anniversary of Columbus's discovery of America, the city staged the World's Columbian Exposition, transforming a lakefront bog into a gleaming vision of the past and the future. Just outside the exposition's gates was the city of the present. In December 1893 Chicago had 75,000 unemployed, and the head of a local relief committee declared that "famine is in our midst." In the nation's second largest city, thousands lived in shacks or high-rise tenements with only a single bathroom on each densely packed floor. Jobs were scarce, and when men gathered at the exposition's gates to beg for work, the police drove them away.

As the depression deepened, the Cleveland administration ordered troops to guard Treasury branches in New York and Chicago. Jobless people banded together into "industrial armies," many with decidedly revolutionary aims. Hundreds heeded the call of Jacob Coxey, an Ohio landowner and Populist. In 1894 Coxey urged the unemployed to march on Washington and demand free silver and a public road-building program that would hire a half million workers. When Coxey set out with 100 followers, reporters predicted the ragged band would disintegrate as soon as food ran out, but well-wishers turned out by the thousands to greet the Coxeyites with supplies for the trip.

Industrial armies set out from Boston, St. Louis, Chicago, Portland, Seattle, and Los Angeles. When Coxey arrived in Washington on May 1 with 500 marchers, Cleveland put the U.S. Army on alert. The march ended ignominiously. In front of the Capitol, police arrested Coxey, and his disillusioned army dispersed. Still, no one could deny that something was seriously wrong and that, as Ray Stannard Baker, a reporter for the *Chicago Record*, noted, " the conditions in the country warranted some such explosion."

The Overseas Frontier

At noon on September 16, 1893, thousands of settlers massed along the borders of the Cherokee Strip, a 6-million-acre tract in northwestern Oklahoma. In the next six hours the last great land rush came to an end, and the line of settlement long marked on census maps ceased to exist.

Frederick Jackson Turner, a historian at the University of Wisconsin, explained the implications of this event. Steady westward movement had placed Americans in "touch with the simplicity of primitive life," he explained, and helped renew the process of social development. The frontier furnished "the forces dominating the American character," and without its rejuvenating influence, democracy itself might be in danger. Turner's thesis resonated with Americans' fears that modernity had robbed their country of its unique strengths and that the end of free lands would put free institutions at risk. "There is no unexplored part of the world left suitable for men to inhabit," Populist writer William "Coin" Harvey claimed.

That assertion turned out to be premature. More homesteaders claimed more western lands after 1890 than before, and well into the next century new "resource frontiers"—oil fields, timber ranges, Alaskan ore strikes—were explored. Irrigation technology and markets for new crops created a boom for dry-land farmers. Nonetheless, the upheavals of the 1890s seemed to confirm Turner's contention that new frontiers lay overseas.

Whereas farmers had always needed to sell a large portion of their output abroad, until the 1890s the market for manufactured goods was almost exclusively domestic. As the volume of manufactured goods increased, the composition of exports changed. Oil, steel, textiles, typewriters, and sewing machines made up a larger portion of overseas trade. Americans still bought nine-tenths of domestic manufactures, but by 1898 the extra tenth was worth more than $1 billion (see Figure 20–1).

As American firms entered foreign markets, they discovered that other nations and empires also used restrictive tariffs to guard their markets and promote domestic manufacturing. Government and business leaders saw that the United States might have to use political or military leverage to open foreign markets to gain a larger share of world trade. Their social Darwinist view of the world—as a jungle in which only the fittest nations would survive—justified the global competition for trade and economic survival.

AMERICA AND THE WORLD

....

>> Singer Sewing Machine Company

Before the Russian Revolution, on St. Petersburg's grandest boulevard, the Nevskii Prospekt, the headquarters of the Singer Sewing Machine Company was Russia's tallest building. Completed in 1904, the six-story Kompaniya Singer tower was topped by an illuminated globe bearing the name Singer in gilded letters. It symbolized the global reach of one of America's preeminent manufacturers.

Isaac Merritt Singer did not invent the sewing machine; he invented a way to market it. Elias Howe, who applied for the first U.S. patent in 1845, invented a device with an oscillating needle that made a locking stitch fed from spools turning on an overhanging arm. It seemed a practical, labor-saving device, but Howe found that tailors and shoemakers who made a living by hand sewing had no use for it. His principal customers viewed the gadget with hostility.

Singer, a machinist from Rochester, New York, made Howe's device smaller, added a decorative cabinet, and sold it as an article for the home. He employed young women to demonstrate the machine in shopfront "sewing centers." Salesmen went door to door, and in the 1880s, Singer introduced buying on the "installment" plan, whereby customers could purchase a new machine by putting down a dollar a week. It was a "psychological fact ," he asserted, that "a woman would rather pay $100" in installments "than $50 outright." By 1867, Singer was the largest manufacturer of sewing machines in the world, producing 43,000 a year.

The federal government aided this growth in two ways. First, the need for military uniforms during the Civil War outstripped the capacities of hand tailors, and Singer promoted machine sewing as a woman's patriotic duty. "We Clothe the Union Army," the company proclaimed. Second, the government imposed a 35 percent tariff on imported sewing machines, preventing European makers from challenging Singer in its home market.

With its domestic base secure, Singer expanded. By 1890, it had an international merchandising network that sold three quarters of the world's sewing machines. The sales formula did not work everywhere. In India, agents complained that they were not allowed to speak to women. Chinese merchants were suspicious of the "iron tailor." A Singer representative in Charkoff, Russia, was ordered to leave on the grounds that he was "a foreign Jew." In Japan, however, the adoption of Western-style military uniforms during the Sino-Japanese War (1894–1895) provided a ready market for the machines among Japanese outfitters. Europe, the Philippines, Mexico, and Russia all became significant markets.

Alarmed by Singer's success, European governments began protecting their colonial and home markets. In 1893, French courts ordered Singer to reveal information about its earnings and stock dividends. Other governments raised import taxes or set quotas to exclude American machines. Singer responded by forming separate national subsidiaries that could claim local, rather than American, origin. When the Spanish-American War broke out in 1898, the Singer offices in Madrid *continued*

AMERICA AND THE WORLD *continued*

flew the Spanish flag and donated to the war fund. The locals were not fooled, however. The newspaper *El Pais* called Singer "an immense octopus whose tentacles encircle Spain and crushes it" in order to "aggrandize the miserable, iniquitous, cowardly disgusting North American nation."

The company prided itself on bringing democracy and fair dealing to the world. In the Middle East, Singer machines carried the brand *Hurriya*, Arabic for "freedom." By the turn of the century, the company had over 4,000 branch offices, located on every inhabited continent, and factories in Austria, Canada, Prussia, Russia, and Scotland.

Growth slowed in the tumultuous twentieth century. The agent in Teheran had to flee a revolution in 1907, and 10 years later Red Guards stormed the St. Petersburg office. The armies of World War I wore factory-made uniforms, and the postwar market for ready-to-wear clothing undercut demand. German bombers destroyed the Scotland plant in 1941, and four years later the Soviet army smashed the Prussian factory.

Singer was a forerunner of the global commerce in consumer goods that the United States would dominate in the late twentieth century. Portable and practical, the machine had universal appeal, and its marketing was infinitely adaptable. In 1891, Singer issued trading cards showing the peoples of the world in native costume. The images were strikingly different from racialized depictions common in that period. Although the fabrics and colors varied, the peoples of other cultures looked very much alike, each with their sewing machine, a global community of consumers.

Recognizing that a strong navy could extend America's economic reach, Congress authorized the construction of three large battleships in 1890. Four years later, an official commission investigated the feasibility of a canal across Central America. A newly organized National Association of Manufacturers urged the government to open foreign markets. The administration created a Bureau of Foreign Commerce and urged U.S. consuls to seize opportunities to extend sales of American industrial products abroad.

Congress also knew that tariff rates could influence the expansion of trade. Before 1890, taxes on imports had been set high to raise revenue and to help domestic manufacturers by making foreign goods unaffordable. The Harrison-McKinley Tariff of 1890 did something different. It allowed the president to use the tariff to punish countries that closed their markets to U.S. goods or to reward them for lifting customs barriers. This "bargaining tariff" used the weight of the U.S. economy to open markets around the world.

The United States began reorganizing to compete in a global marketplace. The struggle required the executive branch to enlarge the military and take on additional authority. It also meant that domestic industries had to produce higher quality goods at less cost to match those from Germany or Japan. Employers and workers had to gear up for the global contest for profits.

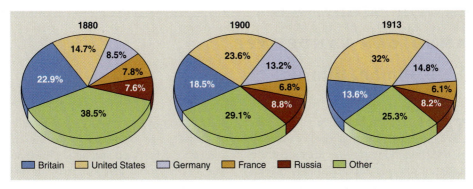

Figure 20-1 Relative Shares of World Manufacturing The United States was a significant industrial power by 1880, but by the turn of the century it moved into a position of dominance.

The Drive for Efficiency

In mines, factories, and mills production relied on the knowledge of skilled workers. Laborers used their knowledge to set work routines, assure their own safety, and bargain with managers who wanted to change the nature of work. As profits stagnated and competition intensified, employers tried to prevent labor from sharing control over production. Employers relied on three allies: technology, scientific management, and federal power. Workers resisted, organizing themselves and enlisting the support of their communities.

Advances in management techniques enabled employers to dictate new methods. Frederick Winslow Taylor, the first "efficiency expert," reduced each occupation to a series of simple, precise movements that could be easily taught and endlessly repeated. To manage time and motion scientifically, Taylor explained, employers should convert traditional workplace skills and knowledge into "rules, laws, and formulae."

Taylor's stopwatch studies determined everything from how much pig iron a man should load into a box car in a day (75 tons) to how he should be paid (3.75 cents per ton). Even office work could be separated into simple, unvaried tasks. "Taylorism" created a new layer of college-educated "middle managers" who supervised production in offices and factories.

Although Taylorism accelerated production, it also increased absenteeism and worker dissatisfaction. Another new technique, "personnel management," promised to solve this problem with tests to select suitable employees, team sports to ward off boredom, and social workers to regulate the activities of workers at home.

As the nineteenth century ended, management was establishing a monopoly on expertise and using it to set the rhythms of work and play, but workers did not easily relinquish control. In the 1890s, the labor struggle entered a new phase. New unions confronted corporations in bloody struggles that forced the federal government to decide whether communities or property had more rights. Skilled workers rallied the labor movement to the cause of retaining control of the conditions of work.

Progress and Force

To accelerate production, employers aimed to seize full control over the workplace. They had private detective agencies, the courts, and federal troops on their side and ready to act. In Pennsylvania and Chicago this antagonism led to bloody confrontations.

AMERICAN LANDSCAPE

>> Pullman, Illinois

When economist Richard T. Ely first saw the industrial town of Pullman in 1885, he thought he was looking at the future. A planned suburb entirely owned by one company and inhabited by its employees, Pullman seemed "a forerunner of better things for the laboring classes." On broad streets named for famous inventors—Watt, Fulton, Morse, and, of course, Pullman—mechanics, shopkeepers, and company officials lived side by side in tidy homes with gas heat and indoor plumbing. Pullmanites shopped under the glass roof of the Arcade, the first indoor shopping mall, and benefited from a library, a theater, and a school provided by their employer. Surrounded by culture and natural beauty, Pullman workers were, by company estimate, 40 percent more refined, thrifty, and wholesome than other workers.

George Mortimer Pullman's name was synonymous with luxury. With the help of Andrew Carnegie, he had become the preeminent maker of passenger railroad cars. By the 1880s every railroad used Pullman sleeping cars, dining cars, and observation cars.

In 1880 he decided to centralize his factories into a single site on Lake Calumet, south of Chicago, and built a model town around the plant. By the next year, there were 1,400 dwellings, public parks, gardens, a hotel, a school, and a church, all designed in a gracious "secular gothic" style. By 1893 it was home to 12,000 residents.

Pullman was not designed as art or charity, but for business. Happy, healthy workers were expected to produce more, and by Pullman's estimate, they did. Modern sewers and plumbing made the air and water safe. The death rate in Pullman was less than half that in nearby neighborhoods. There were no saloons. The theater screened out "immoral" shows.

Other companies rushed to copy Pullman's success. Chocolate makers built Hershey, Pennsylvania, and near Cincinnati producers of floating soap colonized the model town of Ivoryville. But the residents of Pullman were less enthusiastic. Despite low rents and spacious homes, most Pullmanites moved out within a year or two, and even those who stayed saw the arrangement as temporary. Ely noted that "the general complaint seems to be that they were too much under Mr. Pullman's thumb."

Pullman had no newspaper, no clubs, no elected officials. The school board was manned by company executives. When a group of women organized a charity, the company ordered it stopped. Political activity, especially for Democratic candidates, was discouraged. When shopkeeper John P. Hopkins put up a sign for Grover Cleveland, his lease was revoked. The town's one church was for "artistic effect" only. No congregation met there.

After staying several weeks, Ely concluded that "the idea of Pullman is un-American." It was impossible for residents to escape the power of the company, which owned everything. There was not a single piece of privately owned property, and leases could be terminated in 10 days. In the factories, workers assembled sumptuous railroad cars that only reminded them of the wealth they could not attain.

When the Panic of 1893 hit, Pullman laid off 2,000 of his 5,000 employees and cut wages to the others by 25 percent. Rents dropped in Chicago, but not in Pullman. Many residents could not afford rent or food, but there were no charities or municipal agencies to help. There was only the company.

Desperate workers organized in the spring of 1894 and joined Eugene V. Debs's American Railway Union (ARU). On May 11, they struck. George Pullman cut off credit for workers at the stores in the Arcade and then went on vacation. In June, desperate Pullman workers asked the entire ARU to join the strike. The ARU voted to make the strike national; ARU switchmen would refuse to switch Pullman cars onto trains.

The strike shut down 20 railroads in the West and Midwest. Almost no traffic moved through Chicago, the nation's hub. The U.S. attorney general vowed to meet the strike with force, and President Cleveland sent 2,000 troops to Chicago. Fighting broke out between workers and soldiers at the stockyards and in the Illinois Central switchyard. Troops fired into crowds of workers, killing 20 and wounding 60 others. Debs was jailed for "interfering with the mails." The union was broken.

Three years later, George Pullman died of a heart attack. His obituaries mixed praise for his achievements with criticism of his refusal to head off one of the bloodiest labor conflicts in U.S. history. The next year, the city of Chicago absorbed Pullman, and the company town became a neighborhood where voters could choose their own aldermen. Efficient, paternal corporate rule gave way to the messy but democratic politics of a big city. A writer for *The Nation* noted that what working people wanted most was a chance to own a place of their own. "Mr. Pullman," the writer observed, "overlooked this peculiar American characteristic. Hence, in my humble opinion, these tears."

In 1892 Andrew Carnegie's mill at Homestead, Pennsylvania, the most modern steelworks in the world, made armor plating for American warships and steel rails for shipment abroad. In June Carnegie's partner, Henry Clay Frick, broke off talks with the plant's American Federation of Labor–affiliated union and announced that the plant would close on July 2 and reopen a week later with a nonunion workforce. The union contended that Frick's actions were an assault on the community, and the town agreed. On the morning of July 6, 300 armed company guards were raked by gunfire and arrested by townspeople.

The victory was short-lived. A week later the governor of Pennsylvania sent in the state militia, and under martial law strikebreakers reignited the furnaces. The battle at Homestead broke the union and showed that corporations, backed by government, would defend their prerogatives at any cost.

The Pullman strike, centered in Chicago, paralyzed the railroads for two weeks in the summer of 1894. It pitted the American Railway Union (ARU) against 24 railroads and

A TAYLOR SYSTEM MACHINIST "UP-TO-DATE"

An argument without words

Taylorism Corporations used stopwatches and social workers to stretch each machine and worker to full capacity. The method was called "Taylorism."

the powerful Pullman Company over the company's decision to cut pay by 30 percent. Eugene V. Debs, the charismatic president of the ARU, urged strikers to obey the law, avoid violence, and respect strikebreakers. When Cleveland sent in the army over the governor's protests, enraged crowds blocked tracks and burned railroad cars. Police arrested hundreds of strikers. Debs went to jail for six months and came out a socialist. Pullman and Homestead showed that the law was now on the side of the proprietors.

Newspapers, magazines, and novels portrayed Pullman and Homestead as two more battles in an unending war against the savage opponents of progress, with the forces of government rescuing civilization from the unions.

The business elite's cultural influence allowed it to define the terms of this contest, to label its enemies as enemies of progress. Workers did not object to efficiency or modernization, but they wanted a share of its benefits and some control over the process of change. With state and corporate power stacked against them, their goals appeared beyond reach.

Just as the massacre at Wounded Knee in 1890 had ended the armed resistance of Native Americans, the violence at Homestead and Chicago marked a new phase in the struggle of industrial workers.

Corporate Consolidation

In a wave of mergers between 1897 and 1904, investment bankers consolidated leading industries under the control of a few corporate giants, and J. P. Morgan led the movement. His goal was to take industry away from the industrialists and give it to the bankers.

Bankers, he felt, had better information about the true worth of an industry and so could make better decisions about its future. They could create the larger, leaner firms needed to take on foreign competitors.

Morgan's greatest triumph was the merger of eight huge steel companies, their ore ranges, rolling mills, railroads, and shipping lines into the colossal U.S. Steel. The 1901 merger created the world's largest corporation. Its capital amounted to 7 percent of the total wealth of the United States (by comparison, the largest U.S. firm in 2008, Exxon Mobil, had assets valued at only six tenths of 1 percent of gross domestic product). U.S. Steel's investors (Morgan especially) earned profits "greatly in excess of reasonable compensation," according to one government report.

Bankers outnumbered steelmakers on U.S. Steel's board, and they controlled the company. *McClure's* magazine reported that the new company was "planning the first really systematic effort ever made by Americans to capture the foreign steel trade."

A Modern Economy

Grover Cleveland's bargain with Morgan revived the industrial economy, but farm prices, wages, and the president's popularity remained flat. Cash-strapped farmers in the West and South disliked the president's hard-money policies and cozy relationships with plutocrats such as Morgan. Calling out troops to crush the Pullman strike cost Cleveland the support of northern workers. The escalating cycle of economic and political crises, farmer and labor insurgencies, middle-class radicalism, and upper-class conservatism fractured political parties. Democrats, Republicans, and Populists all called for stronger government action, but each party split over what action to take. In 1896 the "currency question" dominated a watershed election that transformed the two major parties and destroyed the third.

The year 1896 was the last time presidential candidates openly debated great economic questions in terms that had been familiar to voters since Thomas Jefferson ran for president in 1800; 1896 was also the first recognizably modern presidential election, the first time a successful candidate used the advertising and fund-raising techniques of twentieth-century campaigns.

Currency and the Tariff

The soundness of the dollar, which Morgan and Cleveland worked so hard to preserve, was a mixed blessing for Americans. Based on gold, the dollar helped sell American goods in foreign markets, especially in Europe, where currencies were also based on gold. The United States traded on a much smaller scale with countries—such as Mexico and China—that used silver. Gold, however, was valuable because it was scarce, and many Americans suffered from that scarcity. The low prices and high interest rates Populists complained of were a result of the gold standard.

Increasing the money supply would reduce interest rates and make credit more available. There were two ways to put more money in circulation: the government could print paper "greenbacks," or it could coin silver. "Free silver" advocates generally favored coining a ratio of 16 ounces of silver for each ounce of gold. Both Populists and western mining interests pushed silver. The Republican and Democratic parties officially endorsed the gold standard, but by 1896 each party had a renegade faction of silverites. In the 1890s, the crucial political issues—jobs, foreign trade, the survival of small farms, and the prosperity of big corporations—boiled down to one question: Would the dollar be backed by gold or silver? The election of 1896 was "the battle of the standards."

The Cross of Gold

A dark mood hung over Chicago as delegates arrived at the Democratic convention in July 1896. They had come to bury Cleveland and the party's commitment to the gold standard along with him. The draft platform denounced Cleveland for imposing "government by injunction" during the Pullman strike. When the platform came before the full convention, delegates had to decide whether the party would stand for silver or gold and who would replace Cleveland as the candidate for president.

Both questions were decided when a former congressman from Nebraska, William Jennings Bryan, mounted the stage. He was an electrifying speaker. "You come and tell us that the great cities are in favor of the gold standard," he said. "Destroy our farms, and the grass will grow in the streets of every city in the country!" Bryan spoke in the rhythmic cadence of a camp preacher. "We will answer their demand for a gold standard by saying to them"—he paused, stretching out his arms in an attitude of crucifixion—"You shall not press down upon the brow of labor this crown of thorns. You shall not crucify mankind upon a cross of gold!" The hall exploded with cheers. Bryan won the nomination handily.

Two weeks later the Populists, meeting in St. Louis, also nominated Bryan. The Ocala and Omaha platforms, which imagined comprehensive changes in the money system and American institutions, had been reduced to a single panacea: silver. Republicans overwhelmingly adopted a progold plank, drafted with the approval of J. P. Morgan, and nominated William McKinley, the governor of Ohio and a supporter of industry. The parties could hardly have offered two more different candidates or two more different visions of the future.

The Battle of the Standards

In one of the most exciting electoral contests since the Civil War, the candidates employed new techniques in radically different ways. McKinley ran like an incumbent: he never left his home. Instead, delegations came to him. Some 750,000 people from 30 states trampled McKinley's grass and listened to speeches affirming his commitment to high tariffs and sound money. The speeches were distributed as newspaper columns, fliers, and pamphlets across the country. The campaign used public relations techniques to educate the electorate on the virtues of the gold standard. Posters reduced the campaign's themes to pithy slogans like "Prosperity or Poverty," or "Vote for Free Silver and Be Prosperous Like Guatemala."

The genius behind the campaign was a Cleveland coal-and-oil millionaire named Marcus Hanna who bankrolled his publicity blitz with between $3 million and $7 million raised from industrialists. The combination of big money and advertising revolutionized presidential politics.

With only $300,000 to spend, Bryan ran like a challenger even though his party occupied the White House. He logged 29,000 miles by rail and buggy and made more than 500 speeches in 29 states. Oratorical ability had won Bryan the nomination, but audiences were unaccustomed to hearing a candidate speak for himself, and many considered it undignified. "The Boy Orator has one speech," wrote an unsympathetic Republican, John Hay. "He simply reiterates the unquestioned truths that . . . gold is vile, that silver is lovely and holy."

Despite the scorn of eastern newspapers, industrialists feared the prospect of a Bryan presidency. Factory owners threatened to close shop if Bryan won. Just before election day, the global markets that McKinley praised returned the favor. Crop failures abroad doubled the price of wheat in the Midwest, raising farm incomes and alleviating the anxieties that drove farmers to Bryan. Bryan won the South and West decisively, but McKinley won the populous industrial Northeast and several farm states in the upper Midwest, capturing the Electoral College by 271 to 176.

The election of 1896 changed the style of campaigns and shifted the political positions of both major parties. By pushing currency policies to improve the lives of workers and farmers, Bryan's Democrats abandoned their traditional Jacksonian commitment to minimal government. The Republicans recognized that voters would judge the president on his ability to bring them prosperity. Electoral democracy now had a distinctly economic cast. As president, McKinley asserted his leadership over economic policy, calling Congress into special session to pass the Dingley Tariff Act, which levied the highest taxes on imports in American history. He extended presidential power even more dramatically through an expansionist foreign and military policy.

In the election of 1896 basic economic questions—who is the economy supposed to serve? what is the nature of money?—were at stake in a closely matched campaign. No

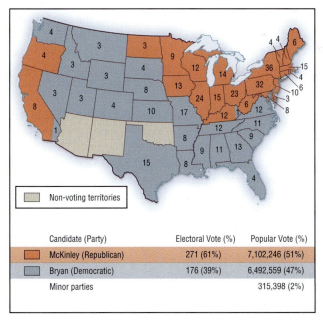

Candidate (Party)	Electoral Vote (%)	Popular Vote (%)
McKinley (Republican)	271 (61%)	7,102,246 (51%)
Bryan (Democratic)	176 (39%)	6,492,559 (47%)
Minor parties		315,398 (2%)

Non-voting territories

Map 20–1   The Election of 1896 William McKinley's "front porch campaign" carried the northern industrial states, along with the key farm states of Iowa and Minnesota, securing a narrow victory over Bryan.

wonder voter turnout hit an all-time high. Administrative agencies took over those issues after the turn of the century, but Americans long remembered that raucous campaign when the nation's economic future was up for grabs. As late as the 1960s, schoolchildren still recited the Cross of Gold speech.

The Retreat from Politics

The economy improved steadily after 1895, but this latest business panic left lasting marks on corporate and political culture. Industrial workers made a tactical retreat in the face of a new political and legal climate. In the South, depression, urbanization, and the modernizing influence of railroads accelerated the spread of legalized racial segregation and disfranchisement. What was happening in the South and the nation was part of a nationwide decline of participatory politics. With the slackening of both agrarian unrest and resistance to corporate capitalism, politics lost some of its value. Voter participation declined, and Americans felt less of a personal stake in elections. Disaffected groups—such as labor and African Americans—had to devise new ways to build community and express resistance.

The Lure of the Cities

In the South as in the North, people left the countryside and moved to towns and cities. By 1900 one out of six southerners lived in town. Except for Birmingham, Alabama, southern cities were not devoted to manufacturing but to commerce and services. Doctors' offices, clothing and dry goods stores, and groceries could be found near warehouses in which cotton was stored, ginned, and pressed and near the railway station, from which it was shipped to textile mills.

The growth of villages and towns in the South was the product of rural decay. Crop liens, which gave bankers ownership of a crop before it was planted, and debt drove people from farms. The young and the ambitious left first, while older and poorer residents stayed behind.

While white newcomers settled on the outskirts of towns, African Americans moved into industrial districts along the railroad tracks. Cities grew more segregated, and by 1890 most blocks in the larger cities were either all black or all white. Still, towns offered things that were missing in the country, such as schools. A Little Rock, Arkansas, resident noted that newly arrived African American parents were "very anxious to send their children to school." Jobs were often available, too, although more frequently for women than for men. Men looked for seasonal labor at farms or lumber camps outside towns. This meant families faced a tough choice between poverty and separation.

Despite setbacks, newcomers gained a place for themselves in urban life. By 1890 every southern city had an African American business district with churches, insurance companies, lawyers, doctors, undertakers, and usually a weekly newspaper. Benevolent and reform organizations, sewing circles, and book clubs enriched community life. African American professionals such as lawyers, doctors, and nurses were limited to working within their community. Jobs on the bottom rung of the corporate ladder—clerk, salesman, telephone operator, stenographer, railroad conductor—were reserved for whites.

Mary Church Terrell (1863–1954) Activist, suffragist, and educator, Terrell tried to unite the struggles for women's rights and civil rights. "A white woman has but one handicap to overcome," she wrote. "I have two—both sex and race."

Inventing Jim Crow

In June 1892 Homer Plessy boarded the East Louisiana Railway in New Orleans for a trip to Covington, Louisiana. Having purchased a first-class ticket, he attempted to board the whites-only car and was arrested under a Louisiana law that required African Americans and whites to ride in "equal but separate accommodations." Before Judge John H. Ferguson could try the case, Plessy's lawyer appealed on the grounds that the separate-car law violated the Constitution's Fourteenth Amendment.

When *Plessy v. Ferguson* came before the Supreme Court in April 1896, the state of Louisiana argued that the law was necessary to avoid the "danger of friction from too intimate contact" between the races. In separate cars, all citizens enjoyed equal privileges. Plessy's lawyer, Albion Tourgée, replied that the question was not "the equality of the privileges enjoyed, but the right of the state to label one citizen as white and another as colored." In doing so, the government gave unearned advantages to some citizens and not to others. The issue for Tourgée was not racial conflict or even prejudice, but whether the government should be allowed to divide people arbitrarily. The court upheld the "separate but equal" doctrine, and the decision provided legal justification for the system of official inequality that expanded in the twentieth century. Informal segregation had existed since the Civil War, and unwritten local customs usually governed the public interaction of whites and African Americans—at work, in business, or when traveling. By the 1890s those informal customs were being codified in law. Railroads, as symbols of progress, were a chief point of contention.

The political and economic tensions created by the depression helped turn racist customs into a rigid caste division. Competition for jobs fed racial antagonisms, as did the migration into cities and towns of a new generation of African Americans, born since the war, who showed less deference to whites. New notions of "scientific" racism led intellectuals and churchmen to regard racial hostility as natural. Angry southern voters deposed the governing coalitions of landowners and New South industrialists and replaced them with Populist "demagogues."

Between 1887 and 1891 nine states in the South passed railroad segregation laws. Trains included separate cars for African Americans, called "Jim Crow" cars after the name of a character in a minstrel show. Soon Jim Crow laws were extended to waiting rooms, drinking fountains, and other places where African Americans and whites might meet.

Lynchings Were Public Spectacles When 17-year-old Jesse Washington was killed in Waco, Texas, in 1916, a crowd of several thousand, including the mayor, police chief, and students from Waco High, attended the event on the lawn of city hall. Afterward, the murderers posed for a photograph and sold their victim's teeth for $5 apiece.

Segregation was also enforced by terror. The threat of lynching poisoned relations between the races, and African Americans learned that they could be tortured and killed for committing a crime, talking back, or simply looking the wrong way at a white woman. Between 1882 and 1903, nearly 2,000 African American southerners were killed by mobs. Victims were routinely tortured, flayed, castrated, gouged, and burned alive, and members of the mob often took home grisly souvenirs such as a piece of bone or a severed thumb.

Many African American southerners fought segregation with boycotts, lawsuits, and disobedience. Ida Wells-Barnett, a Nashville journalist, organized an international antilynching campaign (see Chapter 21). Segregation was constantly negotiated and challenged, but after 1896 it was backed by the U.S. Supreme Court.

The Atlanta Compromise

When Atlanta invited African American educator Booker T. Washington to address the Cotton States Exposition in 1895, northern newspapers proclaimed a new era of racial progress. The speech made Washington the most recognized African American in the United States. Starting with 40 students and an abandoned shack, Washington had built Tuskegee Institute into the preeminent technical school for African Americans. Washington was a guest in the stately homes of Newport and at Andrew Carnegie's castle in Scotland. When Atlanta staged an exposition to showcase the region's industrial and social progress, the organizers asked Washington to speak.

Washington's address stressed racial accommodation. It had been a mistake, he argued, to try to attain equality by asserting civil and political rights and stated that progress "must be the result of severe and constant struggle rather than artificial forcing." He urged white businessmen to employ African American southerners "who have, without strikes and labor wars, tilled your fields, cleared your forests, built your railroads and cities." Stretching out his fingers and then closing them into a fist, he summarized his approach to race relations: "In all things that are purely social, we can be as separate as the fingers, yet one as the hand in all things essential to mutual progress." The largely white audience erupted into applause.

Washington's "Atlanta Compromise" stressed the mutual obligations of African Americans and whites. African Americans would give up the vote and stop insisting on social equality if white leaders would keep violence in check and allow African Americans to succeed in agriculture and business. White industrialists welcomed this arrangement, and African American leaders felt that for the moment it might be the best that could be achieved.

Disfranchisement and the Decline of Popular Politics

After the feverish campaign of 1896, elections began to lose some of their appeal. Attendance fell off at the polls, from79 percent of voters in 1888 down to 65 percent in 1896. The public events surrounding campaigns also drew thinner crowds, and apathy seemed to have become a national epidemic.

In the South, the disappearance of voters was easy to explain. As Jim Crow laws multiplied, southern states disfranchised African Americans (and one out of four whites) by requiring voters to demonstrate literacy, property ownership, or knowledge of the Constitution in order to register. Louisiana added the notorious grandfather clause, which denied the vote to men whose grandfathers were prohibited from voting.

Whites saw disfranchisement and segregation as modern, managed race relations. Demonizing African Americans enforced solidarity among white voters otherwise divided by local or class interests.

No new legal restrictions hampered voting in the North and West, but participation fell there, too. This withdrawal from politics reflected the declining importance of political pageantry and the disappearance of intense partisanship. For American men, the cliffhanger contests of the late nineteenth century provided a sense of identity that strengthened ethnic, religious, and neighborhood identities.

A developing economy with new patterns of social and cultural life undermined partisanship, but so did the new style of campaigns. The emphasis on advertising, education, and fund-raising reduced the personal stakes for voters. Educated middle- and upper-class voters liked the new style, feeling that raucous campaigns were no way to decide important issues. They sought to influence policy more directly, through interest groups rather than parties. Unintentionally, they discarded traditions that unified communities and connected voters to their country and its leaders.

 Table 20-1 The Spread of Disfranchisement

	State	Strategies
1889	Florida	Poll tax
	Tennessee	Poll tax
1890	Mississippi	Poll tax, literacy test, understanding clause
1891	Arkansas	Poll tax
1893, 1901	Alabama	Poll tax, literacy test, grandfather clause
1894, 1895	South Carolina	Poll tax, literacy test, understanding clause
1894, 1902	Virginia	Poll tax, literacy test, understanding clause
1897, 1898	Louisiana	Poll tax, literacy test, grandfather clause
1899, 1900	North Carolina	Poll tax, literacy test, grandfather clause
1902	Texas	Poll tax
1908	Georgia	Poll tax, literacy test, understanding clause, grandfather clause

Organized Labor Retreats from Politics

Workers followed organized labor as it turned away from political activity and redefined objectives in economic terms. As traditional crafts came under attack, skilled workers created new organizations that addressed immediate issues: wages, hours, and the conditions of work. The American Federation of Labor (AFL), founded in 1886, built a base around skilled trades and grew from 150,000 members to more than 2 million by 1904. The AFL focused on immediate goals to improve the working lives of its members. Its founder, Samuel Gompers, was born in London's East End and apprenticed as a cigar maker at the age of 10. After his family moved to New York, Gompers joined the Cigar Makers' International Union.

Although affiliated with the Knights of Labor, the cigar makers were more interested in shortening work hours and increasing wages than in remaking the economy. High dues and centralized control allowed the union to offer insurance and death benefits to members while maintaining a strike fund. Gompers applied the same practices to the AFL. His "pure and simple unionism" made modest demands, but it still encountered fierce resistance from corporations, which were backed by the courts.

In the 1895 case of *In re Debs*, the Supreme Court allowed the use of injunctions to criminalize strikes. The court then disarmed one of labor's last weapons, the boycott. In *Loewe v. Lawlor* (1908), known as the Danbury Hatters case, the court ruled that advertising a consumer boycott was illegal under the Sherman Anti-Trust Act.

Gompers believed that *industrial unions*, which drew members from all occupations within an industry, lacked the discipline and shared values needed to face down corporations and government, whereas unions organized around a single trade or craft would be stronger. However, because the AFL was organized by skill, it often ignored unskilled workers, such as women or recent immigrants. Because employers used unskilled newcomers to break strikes or to run machinery that replaced expert hands, Gompers excluded a large part of the labor force. Organizers recruited Irish and German workers while ignoring Italian, African American, Jewish, and Slavic workers. The union attacked female workers for stealing jobs that rightfully belonged to men.

Other unions were built to represent the immediate interests of their members. Under Eugene V. Debs, railroad workers merged the old railroad brotherhoods into the ARU in 1893. The United Mine Workers (UMW), founded in 1890, unionized coal mines in Pennsylvania, Ohio, Indiana, and Michigan. The ARU and the UMW were industrial unions that tried to organize all of the workers in an industry. These new unions faced determined opposition from business and its allies in government. "Our government cannot stand, nor its free institutions endure," the National Association of Manufacturers declared, "if the Gompers-Debs ideals of liberty and freedom of speech and press are allowed to dominate."

American Diplomacy Enters the Modern World

The Republican victory in 1896 gave heart to proponents of prosperity through foreign trade. Before the turn of the century, the new president announced, the United States would control the world's markets. "We will establish trading posts throughout the world as distributing points for American products," Senator Albert Beveridge forecast. "Great colonies, governing themselves, flying our flag and trading with us, will grow about our posts of trade." McKinley sought neither war nor colonies, but many in his party wanted both. Called "jingoes," they included Assistant Secretary of the Navy Theodore Roosevelt; John Hay, the ambassador to London; and Senators Beveridge and Henry Cabot Lodge. Britain, France, and Germany were seizing territory around the world, and jingoes believed the United States needed to do the same for strategic, religious, and economic reasons. Spain was the most likely target, clinging feebly to the remnants of its once-vast empire in Cuba, the Philippines, Guam, and Puerto Rico. Under Cleveland, the United States had moved away from confrontation with Spain, but McKinley pushed for the creation of an American empire that stretched to the far shores of the Pacific.

Sea Power and the Imperial Urge

Few men better exemplified the jingoes' combination of religiosity, martial spirit, and fascination with the laws of history than Alfred Thayer Mahan. A naval officer and strategist, he argued that world leadership had belonged to the nation that controlled the sea. Published in 1890, his book *The Influence of Sea Power upon History, 1660–1783* became an instant classic.

Mahan connected naval expansion and empire to the problem of overproduction that the United States faced. A great industrial country needed trade; trade required a merchant fleet; and merchant shipping needed naval protection and overseas bases. Colonies could provide markets for goods and congregations for Christian missionaries, but, more important, they allowed naval forces to protect sea lanes and project power in Asia, Latin America, and Africa.

Mahan urged the United States to build a canal across Central America for better access to Asian markets. He urged the building of naval bases along routes to Latin America and the Far East. Congress and the Navy Department began implementing these recommendations even before McKinley took office.

Mahan was not the only prophet who recalled the Roman Empire. Brooks Adams's *The Law of Civilization and Decay* (1895) detailed the effects of the closed frontier: greater concentration of wealth, social inequality, and eventual collapse. To repeal this "law" the United States needed a new frontier in Asia, where it could regenerate itself through combat. Sharing the social Darwinist belief (see Chapter 18) that nations and races were locked in a savage struggle for survival, Mahan and Adams expected the United States to win the approaching conflict.

If subduing continents with the cross, Constitution, and Gatling gun appealed to anyone, it was Theodore Roosevelt. Roosevelt paid keen attention to the forces that were magnifying the power of some nations and diminishing others. Imperialism seemed to him the essential characteristic of modernizing countries. A frontiersman, writer, soldier, and politician, Roosevelt was acutely conscious of how modern forces—globalized trade, instant communications, modern navies, and imperialism—had altered the rules of domestic and international politics. He sought to position the United States at the center of these modernizing currents, a place that would have to be earned, he felt, both on foreign battlefields and at home, where the gains of the nineteenth century had not yet been translated into the social and moral advancement that marked a true civilization.

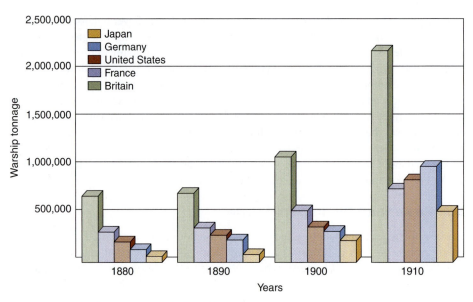

Figure 20–2   Warship Tonnage of the World's Navies Naval strength was the primary index of power before World War I. The United States held onto third place in the naval arms race, while Germany and Japan made significant gains. *Paul Kennedy,* Rise and Fall of the Great Powers *(New York: Random House, 1987), p. 203.*

The Scramble for Empire

For jingoes, China was the ultimate prize in the global contest for trade and mastery. It had more people than any other country, hence more customers and more souls for Christ. The number of American missionaries in China doubled in the 1890s, many of them from the Student Volunteer Movement, which had chapters on nearly every college campus. Even though no more than 1 or 2 percent of U.S. exports had ever gone to China, manufacturers believed that China could absorb the output of America's overproductive factories. James B. Duke founded the British-American Tobacco Company based on "China's population of 450 million people, and assuming that in the future they might average a cigarette a day." In 1890 Standard Oil began selling kerosene in Shanghai. Fifteen years later, China was the largest overseas market for American oil. Mahan had predicted that China would be the arena for the coming struggle for industrial and military supremacy, and by 1897 he seemed to be right.

In 1894 Japan declared war on China and soon occupied Korea, Manchuria, and China's coastal cities. When the fighting was over, Western powers seized slices of Chinese territory. In 1897, German troops captured the port of Qingdao on the Shandong Peninsula. An industrial area, Shandong was the center of American missionary activity, investment, and trade. To Americans, the invasion of Shandong presaged an imperial grab for territory and influence. In the 1880s European powers had carved up Africa. Now it appeared that the same thing was about to happen in China. The McKinley administration watched events in China carefully, but in the winter of 1897/1898 it had more pressing concerns closer to home.

Missionaries in China Thanks to the work of missionaries in China, Mark Twain observed, "the people who sit in darkness . . . have become suspicious of the blessings of civilization."

War with Spain

While other European powers were expanding their empires, Spain was barely hanging onto the one it had. Since the 1860s its two largest colonies, Cuba and the Philippines, had been torn by revolution. Between 1868 and 1878 Cuban nationalists fought for independence. Spain ended the war by promising autonomy but not independence. U.S. officials wanted an end to Spanish rule, but the McKinley Tariff and the Panic of 1893 ruined Cuba's chief export industry, sugar. Under a crushing debt, Spain reneged on its promise, and in 1895 the rebellion resumed. The rebels practiced a "scorched earth" policy, dynamiting trains and burning plantations in an attempt to force Spain out.

Spain retaliated with a brutal campaign of pacification, killing nearly 100,000 civilians, but it was no use. The Spanish army was disintegrating. Cuban rebels, in control of the countryside, prepared a final assault on the cities. U.S. officials, many of whom wanted to annex the island, now worried that Cuba would gain full independence. McKinley explored the options of either purchasing it from Spain or intervening on the pretext of ending the "strife." William Randolph Hearst's *New York Journal* and other newspapers favored the latter, inciting readers with lurid stories of Spanish atrocities and Cuban rioting. Cuba sold newspapers. McKinley moved quickly toward confrontation. When riots erupted in the Cuban capital he ordered a warship to Havana. Theodore Roosevelt sent one of the newest battleships, the USS *Maine*. The arrival of the *Maine* reduced tensions for a while, but on February 15 an explosion ripped through the ship, killing almost the entire crew of 266. Navy investigators later concluded that boilers had exploded accidentally, but the newspapers blamed both Spanish and Cuban treachery. Hearst printed a full-page diagram of the ship being destroyed by a "sunken torpedo."

McKinley hesitated, mindful of the budget and events in China, but Roosevelt ordered Commodore George Dewey's Asiatic Squadron to ready an attack on the Philippines. Congress appropriated $50 million for arms. Spanish emissaries tried to gain support from other European countries, but they were rebuffed.

In March the economic picture brightened, and McKinley sent Spain an ultimatum demanding independence for Cuba. On April 11 he asked Congress for authorization to use force, and Congress passed a declaration of war. Expansionists such as Roosevelt, Mahan, and Adams would not have succeeded if war had been less popular. Corporate interests favored it, immigrants and southerners saw it as a way to assert their patriotism, and newspapers found it made good copy. "We are all jingoes now," declared the *New York Sun*.

Neither side had many illusions about the outcome. Fighting Spain, novelist Sherwood Anderson wrote, was "like robbing an old gypsy woman in a vacant lot at night after the fair," but the war opened with a cliffhanger that even Hearst could not have invented. On May 1 news arrived that Dewey's forces were fighting the Spanish fleet in Manila Bay in the Philippines. The war had begun not in Cuba, but instead half a world away. There the information stopped. The telegraph cable from Manila had been cut. Official Spanish reports alleged that the Americans had suffered a "considerable loss of life." Dewey's squadron contained only two modern cruisers, but all of its ships were steel-hulled in contrast to Spain's wooden vessels. For six anxious days Americans awaited word from the far edge of the Pacific.

It arrived early on May 7. The *New York Herald*'s Hong Kong correspondent had been at the battle. Dewey destroyed Spain's entire fleet of 12 warships without a single serious casualty. The country went wild with relief and triumph. New York staged a parade on Fifth Avenue. A Dewey-for-president movement began. In Washington, McKinley consulted a map to see where the Philippines were. Roosevelt quit his job and ordered up a uniform.

The war in Cuba unfolded more modestly. The navy bottled up Spain's ships in the Bay of Santiago de Cuba and American warships cut the fleet to pieces as it attempted to escape. "Don't cheer, men," an officer ordered the gun crews. "Those poor devils are dying."

In the years before the war, Congress had poured money into the navy but not the army, and it took some time before soldiers could be trained and equipped. Recruits were herded into camps in Florida without tents, proper clothing, or latrines. There were few medical supplies or doctors. In these unsanitary camps, soldiers died of dysentery and malaria. Of the 5,462 U.S. soldiers who died in the war with Spain, 5,083 succumbed to disease, a scandal that forced the government to elevate the status of the surgeon general and to improve sanitation and disease prevention in the military.

The army landed on the Cuban coast and marched inland to engage Spanish defenders. Roosevelt came ashore with the First Volunteer Cavalry, known as the "Rough Riders." He recruited, trained, and publicized the regiment and wrote its history. An assortment of outlaws, cowboys, Ivy League athletes, New York City policemen, a novelist, and a Harvard Medical School graduate, its membership combined frontier heroism with eastern elite leadership. The regiment traveled with its own film crew and a correspondent from the *New York Herald*.

Spanish forces stubbornly resisted around the city of Santiago. At San Juan Hill, 500 defenders forced a regiment of the New York National Guard to retreat. The all–African American 9th and 10th Cavalry fought alongside the Rough Riders. "The negroes saved that fight," a white soldier reported. The capture of Santiago effectively ended Spanish resistance. When fighting ended in August, U.S. troops occupied Cuba, Guam, Puerto Rico, and the city of Manila. The war had lasted only four months.

As American and Spanish diplomats met in Paris to conclude a peace treaty, McKinley had to decide which occupied territories to keep as colonies. Congress, not wanting to inherit the island's $400 million in debt, had already resolved not to annex Cuba. McKinley decided that Guam and Puerto Rico would make ideal naval bases.

The president also seized the opportunity to annex the island nation of Hawaii. In 1893 American sugar planters, led by Sanford Dole, overthrew the islands' last queen, Liliuokalani, and petitioned for annexation (see Chapter 19). They were motivated by the Harrison-McKinley Tariff, which would ruin the planters unless they could reconnect Hawaii's trade to the United States. Annexation was their best chance, and they had a powerful ally in the U.S. Navy. Mahan had identified Pearl Harbor, on Oahu, as a vital base. McKinley decided to take up Dole's annexation offer.

The Philippines were more of a problem. Its 7,000 islands were far from the United States and had a population of several million. The United States needed a naval base and supply station close to the China coast, but holding just one island would be impossible if another power controlled the others. Shortly after Dewey's victory, British and German warships anchored in Manila Bay, clearly intending to divide up the territory the United States did not claim. McKinley felt trapped.

McKinley did not take into account the fact that the Philippines had already declared independence. With Dewey's encouragement, rebels under the command of Emilio Aguinaldo had liberated the countryside surrounding Manila and laid siege to the city. At Malolos, north of Manila, a national assembly, including lawyers, doctors, professors, and landowners , issued a constitution. By the time the U.S. Army arrived in 1899, Filipinos had overthrown the Spanish and rallied to their new government.

Spain recognized Cuban independence and surrendered most of its empire to the United States for free, but it gave up the Philippines only after the United States agreed to pay $20 million, or, as an American satirist calculated, $1.25 for every Filipino. The treaty was signed December 10, 1898.

The Anti-Imperialists

Many prominent Americans opposed both the annexation of new colonies and the approaching war with the Philippines. During the treaty fight in Congress in January 1899, they tried to mobilize opinion against the treaty. The movement included ex-presidents Grover Cleveland and Benjamin Harrison; William Jennings Bryan; labor unionists, including Samuel Gompers and Eugene Debs; writers such as Mark Twain and Ambrose Bierce; and industrialists, including Andrew Carnegie. The anti-imperialists advanced an array of moral, economic, and strategic arguments. Filipinos and Hawaiians, they said, had sought American help in good faith and were capable of governing themselves. The islands could not be defended, and U.S. forces would be exposed to attack at Pearl Harbor or Manila. Carnegie argued that imperialism took tax dollars and attention away from domestic problems. White supremacists asked whether Filipinos would become citizens or be allowed to vote and emigrate to the mainland.

The most moving objections came from those who believed imperialism betrayed America's fundamental principles. To Mark Twain imperialism was only the newest form of greed: "There is more money in it, more territory, more sovereignty, and other kinds of emolument, than there is in any other game that is played." Opponents of annexation organized an Anti-Imperialist League and lobbied for the rejection of the Paris Treaty.

Congress responded to anti-imperialist objections, banning Philippine immigration, placing the colonies outside the tariff walls, and promising eventual self-government. Jingoes had a military victory on their side. Anti-imperialists could not offer a vision

Map 20–2   Spanish-American War, Caribbean   Spanish American War, Pacific

comparable to naval supremacy, the evangelization of the world, or the China market. On February 6, 1899, the U.S. Senate ratified the Paris Treaty and annexed the Philippines. A day earlier, on the other side of the world, the Philippine-American War began.

The Philippine-American War

McKinley believed he had annexed islands full of near savages "unfit for self-rule," but the Philippines by 1899 had an old civilization with a long tradition of resistance to colonialism. When Magellan discovered the islands in 1521, he found a literate population linked by trade ties to India, Japan, and China. The Spanish converted most Filipinos to Catholicism and established schools and a centralized government. Manila's oldest university was older than Harvard. By 1898 much of the upper class, the *illustrados*, had been educated in Europe.

Dewey gave Aguinaldo his word that America desired no colonies. Aguinaldo continued to trust the Americans despite the arrival of fresh U.S. troops. On February 4 an argument between American and Filipino sentries ended in gunfire. Aguinaldo was despondent: "No one can deplore more than I this rupture. I have a clear conscience that I endeavored to avoid it at all costs."

Kansas volunteers drove the Filipino armies into the mountains. Aguinaldo adopted a guerilla strategy, which proved effective. Some 4,000 Americans were killed during the war and another 3,000 wounded out of a total force of 70,000. Frustrated by guerilla conflict, American soldiers customarily executed prisoners, looted villages, and raped Filipino women. An American general on the island of Samar ordered his soldiers to kill everyone over the age of 10. "No cruelty is too severe for these brainless monkeys," a soldier wrote home. "I am in my glory when I can sight some dark skin and pull the trigger."

The army's preferred mode of torture was "the water cure," in which water was forced down a prisoner's throat until the abdomen swelled, and then forced out again by kicking. Military officials argued that Filipinos were "half-civilized" and that force was the best language for dealing with them.

Newspaper accounts of torture and massacres fueled American opposition to the war, just as U.S. forces scored some victories. Recognizing that they were fighting a political war, U.S. officers took pains to win over dissidents and ethnic minorities. In 1901 this strategy began to pay off. When American troops intercepted a messenger bound for Aguinaldo's secret headquarters, Brigadier General Frederick Funston devised a bold (and, under the rules of war, illegal) plan. He dressed a group of Filipinos loyal to the American side in the uniforms of captured Filipinos, and, posing as a prisoner, Funston entered Aguinaldo's camp and kidnapped the president.

After three weeks in a Manila prison, Aguinaldo issued a proclamation of surrender. When resistance continued in Batangas Province for another year, the U.S. Army responded by imposing the same reconcentration policies the United States had condemned in Cuba, with the same result. Perhaps a third of the province's population died of disease and starvation. On July 4, 1902, President Theodore Roosevelt declared the war over.

The American flag flew over the Philippines until 1942, but the colony never lived up to its imperial promise. Instead of defending American trade interests, U.S. troops were pinned down in garrisons, guarding against uprisings and the threat of Japanese invasion. The costs of occupation far exceeded the profits generated by Philippine trade. The colony chiefly attracted American reformers and missionaries, who built schools, churches, and agricultural colleges. Some colonists sought statehood, but Americans liked their colonial experiment less and less. Labor unions feared a flood of immigration from the islands, and farmers resented competition from Philippine producers; in 1933 Congress voted to phase out American rule.

The Open Door

As Americans celebrated their victories, European powers continued to divide China into quasi-colonial "concessions." An alarmed imperial court in Beijing began a crash program of modernization, but reactionaries overthrew the emperor and installed the conservative "dowager empress" Ci Xi. In the countryside, Western missionaries and traders came under attack from local residents led by martial artists known as Boxers. Many Americans feared that the approaching disintegration of China would mean the exclusion of U.S. trade.

Secretary of State John Hay watched events in China carefully. "The inherent weakness of our position is this," he wrote McKinley. "We do not want to rob China ourselves, and our public opinion will not allow us to interfere, with an army, to prevent others from robbing her. Besides, we have no army." Seeking some way to keep China's markets open, McKinley turned to William Rockhill, a legendary foreign service officer who had lived in China and had been the first westerner to visit Tibet. He, in turn, consulted his friend

Map 20–3 **The Imperial World** Modern imperialism reached its apex between 1880 and 1945. Most of Africa, the Middle East, and Asia, a third of the world's population, was absorbed into global empires linked by telegraph and steamship to centers of government and commerce in London, Paris, Tokyo, and Washington, D.C.

Alfred Hippisley, an Englishman returning from service with the British-run Chinese imperial customs.

Rockhill, Hippisley, and Hay drafted an official letter known as the Open Door Note. Sent to each of the imperial powers, it acknowledged the partitioning of China into spheres and observed that none of the powers had yet closed its areas to the trade of other countries. The note urged the powers to declare publicly their intention to continue this policy. The Open Door was mostly bluff. The United States had no authority to ask for such a pledge and no military power to enforce one. The foreign ministers of Germany, Japan, Russia, Britain, and France replied cautiously at first, but Hay adroitly played one power off another, starting with Britain and Japan. Once the two strongest powers in China had agreed, France and then Russia and Germany followed. The United States had secured access to China without war or partition, but the limits of Hay's success soon became apparent.

In early 1900, the antiforeign Boxer movement swept through Shandong province. Armed Chinese attacked missions and foreign businesses, destroyed railroads, and massacred Chinese Christians. Empress Ci Xi recruited 30,000 Boxers into her army and declared war on all foreign countries. The Western powers rushed troops to China, but

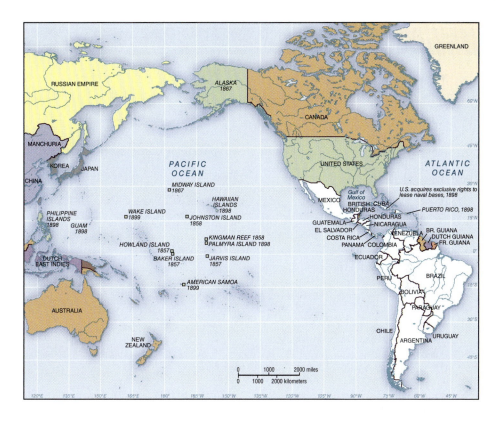

before they arrived Chinese armies attacked Western embassies in Beijing. A British, Russian, Japanese, and French force gathered at Tianjin to march to the rescue. European powers appeared all too eager to capture the Chinese capital.

Without consulting Congress, McKinley ordered American troops into battle on the Asian mainland. Five thousand soldiers rushed from Manila to Tianjin. Hay issued a second Open Door Note, asking the allies to pledge to protect China's independence. Again, the imperial powers reluctantly agreed rather than admit their secret plans to carve up China. On August 15, 1900, U.S. cavalry units reached Beijing, along with Russian Cossacks, French Zouaves, British-Indian sepoys, German hussars, and Japanese dragoons. After freeing the captive diplomats, the armies of the civilized world looted the city. The United States was unable to maintain the Open Door in China for long. Russia and Japan established separate military zones in northeast China, but the principle of the Open Door, of encouraging free trade and open markets, guided American foreign policy throughout the twentieth century. It rested on the assumption that, in an equal contest, American firms would prevail, spreading manufactured goods around the world, and American influence with them. Under the Open Door, the United States was better off in a world without empires, a world in which consumers in independent nations could buy

>> Timeline

▼1890

Global depression begins.

United Mine Workers founded.

Battle of Wounded Knee ends Indian wars.

Harrison-McKinley Tariff passed.

Alfred T. Mahan publishes *The Influence of Sea Power upon History, 1660–1783*.

Standard Oil markets kerosene in China.

▼1892

Homestead strike

▼1893

Financial crisis leads to business failures and mass unemployment.

World's Columbian Exposition, Chicago

Cherokee Strip land rush

American sugar planters overthrow Queen Liliuokalani of Hawaii.

▼1894

Coxey's Army marches on Washington.

Pullman strike

U.S. commission charts canal route across Nicaragua.

▼1895

Morgan agrees to Treasury bailout.

National Association of Manufacturers founded.

Brooks Adams publishes *The Law of Civilization and Decay*.

Booker T. Washington gives "Atlanta Compromise" address.

Revolution begins in Cuba.

Japan annexes Korea and Taiwan.

▼1896

Plessy v. Ferguson declares "separate but equal" facilities constitutional.

Mary Church Terrell founds National Association of Colored Women.

William McKinley elected president.

▼1897

Germany captures Qingdao on China's Shandong Peninsula.

McKinley issues formal protest to Spain.

▼1898

USS *Maine* explodes in Havana's harbor.

United States declares war on Spain.

Dewey defeats Spanish fleet at Manila Bay.

In the Treaty of Paris, Spain grants Cuba independence, cedes Guam, Puerto Rico, and the Philippines to the United States.

Aguinaldo proclaims Philippine independence.

>> **Timeline** *continued*

▼1899

Senate votes to annex Puerto Rico, Hawaii, and the Philippines.

Philippine-American War begins.

Hay issues first Open Door Note.

▼1900

Hay issues second Open Door Note.

U.S. Army joins British, French, Russian, German, and Japanese forces in capture of Beijing.

Great Exposition of Paris showcases American technology.

William McKinley reelected.

▼1901

Aguinaldo captured.

McKinley assassinated; Theodore Roosevelt becomes president.

▼1902

Roosevelt declares Philippine-American war over.

---

what they wanted. Just one year after the Spanish-American War, Hay rejected imperial expansion in favor of trade expansion. This new strategy promised greater gains, but it placed the United States on a collision course with the empires of the world.

Conclusion

In the turbulent 1890s the social and economic divisions among Americans widened. The hope that a solution to these divisions could be found outside the United States was short-lived. Imperialism promised new markets and an end to the cycle of depression and labor strife. The United States conquered an overseas empire and challenged other empires to open their ports to free trade, but the goal of prosperity and peace at home proved elusive.

In many ways social Darwinism became a self-fulfilling prophecy, as competition rather than compromise prevailed. Workers and businessmen, farmers and bankers, middle-class radicals and conservatives, whites and African Americans saw each other as enemies. Racial segregation showed that middle ground, on which whites and African Americans could meet on equal terms, had disappeared. Americans now had to decide what was politically possible and devise new bargaining strategies.

Economic recovery and military victory closed the decade on an optimistic note. Prosperity, power, and technology seemed to have rewritten the rules of human affairs to America's advantage. In the American exhibit at the Paris Exposition of 1900, Henry Adams contemplated a 40-foot dynamo—a "huge wheel, revolving within arm's length"— and felt as if he had crossed a "historical chasm." The machine's mysterious silent force, emanating from "a dirty engine house carefully kept out of sight," seemed a metaphor for the modern age.

Review Questions

1. What new techniques and practices made U.S. industries more efficient?

2. What motivated Americans to seek an empire?

3. Why did some observers find the Pullman experiment "un-American"?

4. Which cities were the main centers of industry and culture in the 1890s?

5. How did the concept of individual rights evolve in reaction to new economic conditions? Name key figures who articulated a concept of democratic rights, and describe their ideas.

6. Contrast the arguments for empire with the rhetoric of the anti-imperialists. Which dangers to the nation and democracy did each side stress?

7. Why was the issue of currency so important to Americans in 1896? What was at stake?

For further review materials and resource information, please visit www.oup.com/us/ofthepeople

AMERICAN PORTRAIT
....

>> **Alice Hamilton**

On an October morning in 1902, three friends, Maude Gernon of the Chicago Board of Charities, Gertrude Howe, kindergarten director at Hull-House, and Dr. Alice Hamilton, a professor of pathology at Northwestern University, stood over sewer drains catching flies. The prey was abundant, and the women trapped dozens in test tubes. Hamilton organized the expedition in the midst of a typhoid epidemic. The disease ravaged Chicago's 19th Ward, a working-class neighborhood where Hull-House stood. To find out why, Hamilton investigated the surrounding tenement houses, which often had illegal outdoor privies rather than indoor plumbing. It was then that she noticed the flies. Army doctors in the Spanish-American War found a link between flies and poor sanitation and the spread of typhoid. Hamilton examined the flies under a microscope and confirmed that they carried the typhoid bacillus.

Her report in the *Journal of the American Medical Association* touched off a furor. Hull-House attacked the Board of Health for failing to enforce the sanitary codes, and an inquiry revealed that landlords bribed inspectors to overlook the outhouses. Investigations found that drinking water was pumped straight from Lake Michigan, without purification, and that broken pumps channeled raw sewage into the water mains. Through bribery and neglect, city government was responsible for an epidemic that killed hundreds of people.

Hamilton, who grew up affluent in Fort Wayne, Indiana, attended medical school at the University of Michigan, later studying bacteriology and pathology at Leipzig and Munich. Despite her training, it was difficult for her to find work, but in Chicago she found support at Hull-House, a "settlement house" founded by women who wanted to live among the poor. Hamilton lived there for 22 years. A specialist in occupational health, she noticed a "strange silence on the subject" of job-related disease. Her early research linked the working conditions of Jewish garment workers to the tuberculosis that frequently claimed their lives.

continued

After the typhoid scandal, Hamilton began looking into stories of poisoning among workers at the National Lead Company. Clouds of metallic dust filled the plant, and employees left work glistening with lead. The company refused to admit its high absenteeism had anything to do with the work. One foreman told Hamilton that lead workers "don't last long at it. Four years at the most, I should say, then they quit and go home to the old country." "To die?" she asked. "Well," he replied, "I suppose that is about the size of it." Using hospital records, she documented a pattern of chronic lead poisoning. Confronted with these findings, the company agreed to install ventilators and create a medical department. Hamilton pushed for state laws on occupational disease, and in 1911 Illinois became the first state to pass legislation giving workers compensation for job-related disability. Hamilton's activism was not unique. She was one of millions of people in the early twentieth century who reshaped democracy through a new type of politics. Responding to the challenges of immigration, industrialization, and urbanization, Americans agitated for change. They worked outside the two-party system, forming their own organizations. Women, who did not have the vote, took the lead and created a new style of activism.

Some activists feared the uncontrolled power of corporations, whereas others feared the uncontrolled passions of the poor. Both called themselves "progressives," and they shared certain ideas about democracy. They optimistically believed in people's ability to improve society, but they were pessimistic about the ability of people, particularly nonwhite people, to improve themselves. Science and religion, they felt, supported these beliefs and justified the supervision of human affairs by qualified experts.

Although reformers accepted modern industry, they were outraged by the trail of disease, waste, and corruption the factory system left behind. They sought a middle ground between revolutionary socialism and uncontrolled corporate capitalism. Finally, they belonged to a movement with national reach. Progressivism, as it came to be called, was the first and perhaps the only reform movement experienced by all Americans. Popular magazines carried its agitation into every town and county.

Common Threads

>> What political problems arose from the transition to an urban, industrial, and national society?

>> How did women's activism on social issues change the style and content of politics?

>> Why did party politics decline at the same time that national interest groups emerged?

>> How did the new interventionism transform the administration of cities and states?

>> In what ways did progressivism enlarge the president's powers over foreign policy and the economy?

Toward a New Politics

Progressivism displaced the intensely partisan politics of the late nineteenth century. The political and economic crises of the 1890s left Americans disillusioned with traditional parties. A growing socialist movement threatened more radical action if moderate reform failed. Protestant churches spoke out against capitalism's abuses, and new interpretations of Christian ethics lent a moral urgency to reform. The dangers of urban life, some of which Alice Hamilton encountered, gave educated, affluent Americans a sense that civic problems needed to be dealt with immediately. Women took leading roles, using pressure groups to extend their influence while also seeking the vote.

Egged on by the press, progressives organized to solve the problems of the new industrial world. Although they sometimes idealized smaller towns and bygone eras, progressives recognized that large-scale industrial capitalism was here to stay. They worked as troubleshooters to make an erratic and brutal system more predictable, efficient, and humane. In pushing for reform, they were willing to enlarge the power of the state and to use it to tell people what was good for them. As reform gained momentum, mayors, governors, and presidential candidates identified themselves and their agendas as progressive.

The Insecurity of Modern Life

Most people who lived in cities at the turn of the century had grown up in the country. They remembered living in communities where people knew each other, where much of what they ate and wore was made locally. In the modern city, water, fuel, and transportation were all supplied by large, anonymous corporations. Unknown executives made decisions that affected the livelihoods, savings, and safety of thousands of people. City dwellers felt more sophisticated than their parents but also less secure.

City living carried risks. Inspecting a Chicago market, journalist Upton Sinclair found milk laced with formaldehyde, peas colored green with copper salts, and sausage doctored with toxic chemicals. Dozens of patent medicines—including aspirin, cocaine, and heroin—were sold as remedies for everything from hay fever to cancer.

Tenement blocks housing hundreds of people often had no fire escapes or plumbing. Tragedy reminded New Yorkers of these dangers on March 25, 1911, when fire engulfed the Triangle Shirtwaist Company on the top three floors of a ten-story building. Five hundred Jewish and Italian seamstresses were trapped; many jumped from ledges in groups, holding hands. In all, 146 died. Such episodes demonstrated that an unregulated economy could be both productive and deadly.

Government added to the problem. Regulation often created kickbacks and bribery. In 1904 and 1905, journalist Lincoln Steffens uncovered corruption in state after state. In New York, insurance companies paid off elected officials in return for favorable legislation. In San Francisco boss Abraham Ruef ruled the city with a slush fund from public utilities. The Minneapolis police, along with the mayor's office, protected brothels and gambling dens in return for bribes. Elections made the system less accountable, not more. By creating a demand for campaign funds and jobs, elections became invitations to graft.

The rising middle class found public and corporate irresponsibility infuriating. In stately Victorian "streetcar suburbs," business managers, accountants, engineers, lawyers,

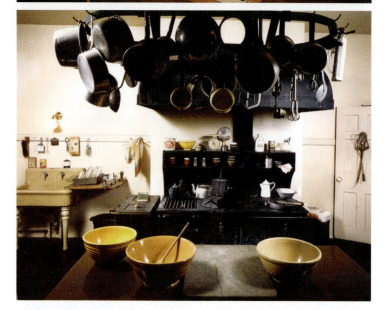

A Tale of Two Kitchens The house where Woodrow Wilson was born in 1856 (above) used food, fuel, water, and lighting supplied locally or even just outside the door. The kitchen in the house where he died in 1924 (below), used gas and electricity from hundreds of miles away, as well as food and appliances that came from national suppliers.

and doctors became aware of themselves as a class, but one trapped between two groups, the rich and the masses of wage laborers. Because of education and experience, members of the middle class had their own ideas on how organizations, such as utility companies, cities, and states, should run. Modern corporations needed clear lines of authority, an emphasis on efficiency, and reliable sources of information. Yet these virtues were frustratingly absent from civic life.

The Decline of Partisan Politics

Participation in elections declined by choice and coercion. Nationally, 79 percent of the electorate voted in 1896, but four years later only 73 percent voted, and by 1904 the total fell to 65 percent. Literacy tests accounted for much of the decline in the South, but in all regions the old spectacular style of electioneering, with parades, and rallies, gave way to campaigns that were more educational and less participatory. Worse for the parties, the voters split their tickets. The ethnic and sectional loyalties that led to straight party ballots in the late nineteenth century seemed to be weakening.

Increasingly, Americans participated in politics through associations. Voluntary and professional societies took over functions that once belonged to the parties: educating voters and even making policy. These "interest groups" worked outside the system to gather support for a cause or proposal. Many were patterned after corporations, with a board of directors and state and local chapters. Built on the idea that reform was a continuous process, they strove for permanence. Some, such as the National Association for the Advancement of Colored People (NAACP), the Salvation Army, and the Sierra Club, are still prominent.

Social Housekeeping

The mounting clamor for change aroused political strength in unexpected places. Women's social clubs had been nonpolitical before the turn of the century. Dedicated to developing public talents such as art, speaking, reading, and conversation, they were highly organized, with local, state, and national chapters. A General Federation of Women's Clubs was formed in 1890. Within 10 years the urgency of social problems led many clubs to campaign for free kindergartens, civil service reform, and public health.

A growing cohort of professional women energized reform. The first generation of graduates from the new women's colleges had reached adulthood, and some, like Alice

Figure 21–1 Voter Participation, 1896–1920 After the intense partisanship and high-stakes elections of the 1890s, campaigns became more "educational," and voters lost interest.

Hamilton, had attained advanced degrees at a time when few men went to college. These "new women," as historians have called them, had ambitions and values different from those of their mothers' generation. About half did not marry. With career paths closed to them, educated women found careers by finding problems that needed solving. Florence Kelley, trained as a lawyer, became Illinois's first state factory inspector and later directed the National Consumers League. Margaret Sanger, a New York public health nurse, distributed literature on birth control and sex education when it was illegal to do so. Sophonisba Breckinridge, with a doctorate from the University of Chicago, led the struggle against child labor. Female activists "discovered" problems, publicized them, lobbied for new laws, and then staffed the bureaus and agencies administering the solutions.

Women's professional associations, unions, business clubs, ethnic and patriotic societies, and foundations changed the practice of democracy. What was once considered charity or volunteer work became political. Some groups, such as the Young Women's Christian Association (YWCA, 1894) and the International Council of Nurses (1899), had a global reach. The experiences of women's groups taught activists the importance of cooperation, organization, and expertise. When women's clubs built a playground and donated it to the city, they increased their stake in the political system. They gave themselves new reasons to demand full citizenship.

The women's suffrage movement grew quietly in the early years of the century. Women had gained the vote in four states—Colorado, Wyoming, Utah, and Idaho—but between 1896 and 1910 no other states adopted a women's suffrage amendment. The movement was stubbornly opposed by the Catholic Church, machine politicians, and business interests.

Competing suffrage organizations joined forces under the National American Woman Suffrage Association (NAWSA). Led by Carrie Chapman Catt and Anna Howard Shaw, NAWSA developed a strategy based on professional lobbying and publicity. Suffragists appealed to clubwomen and middle-class reformers by cultivating an image of Victorian respectability and linking suffrage to moderate social causes, such as temperance and education. At first, NAWSA's strategy paid off. After 1910, five states adopted suffrage amendments, but the opposition rallied and defeated referenda in three states.

Frustrated with the glacial pace of progress, Alice Paul's National Woman's Party adopted more radical tactics, picketing the White House and staging hunger strikes. Despite setbacks, women led the transformation of politics through voluntary organizations and interest groups and were on the threshold of even greater gains.

Evolution or Revolution?

Founded in 1901, the Socialist Party's swelling membership seemed to confirm its claims that the future would be revolutionary rather than progressive. In 1912, Eugene V. Debs, the party's candidate for president, won almost a million votes, or 6 percent of the total. "Gas and water" Socialists, who demanded public ownership of utilities, captured offices in many smaller cities. In the Plains states, socialism drew strength from primitive Baptist and Holiness churches and held revival-style tent meetings. In stronghold Oklahoma, almost one-quarter of the electorate voted Socialist in 1914.

Although tinged with religion, Socialists' analysis of modern problems was economic. They maintained that the profit motive distorted human behavior, forcing people to compete for survival as individuals instead of joining to promote the common good. Driven by profits, corporations could not be trusted with the welfare of consumers or workers. Socialists demanded the collective ownership of industries, starting with ones that most directly affected people's lives: railroads and city utilities. Socialists had faith that America could make the transition without violence and that socialism was surely "coming like a prairie fire," a Socialist newspaperman told his readers. "Social Gospel" clergymen preached this coming millennium. Washington Gladden, a Congregationalist pastor from Ohio; Walter Rauschenbusch, a Baptist minister from New York; William Dwight Porter Bliss, who founded the Society for Christian Socialists; and George Herron, an Iowa Congregationalist, were among the prominent ministers who interpreted the Bible as a call to social action. Their visions of the Christian commonwealth ranged from reform to revolution, but they all believed that corporate capitalism was organized sin and that the church had an obligation to stand against it.

When the Industrial Workers of the World (IWW) talked about revolution, they meant class war, not elections. Founded in 1905, the IWW (known as the "Wobblies" unionized some of the most rugged individuals in the West: miners, loggers, and even rodeo cowboys (under the Bronco Busters and Range Riders Union). Gathering unskilled workers into "one big union," the Wobblies challenged the AFL's elite unionism and the Socialists' gradualism. With fewer than 100,000 members, the union and its leader, William "Big Bill" Haywood, had a reputation for radicalism. In Lawrence, Massachusetts, and Paterson, New Jersey, IWW strikers clashed with police and paraded under red flags with thousands of marchers. To an anxious middle class, these activities looked like signs of approaching class warfare.

Conservatives and reformers alike felt the hot breath of revolution on their necks, and socialism's greatest influence may have been the push it gave conservatives to support moderate reform. Theodore Roosevelt warned that without reform the United States would divide into two parties, one representing workers, the other capital.

The failure of the two parties to deal with urgent problems created a chance to redefine democracy. As the new century began, Americans were testing their political ideals, scrapping old rules, and getting ready to fashion new institutions and laws to deal with the challenges of modern society.

The Progressives

Historians have found it difficult to define the progressives. They addressed a wide variety of social problems with many different tactics but appealed to a broad audience. A rally to end child labor, for instance, might draw out young lawyers, teachers, labor unionists, woman suffragists, professors, and politicians. A series of overlapping movements, campaigns, and crusades defined the era from 1890 to 1920.

Progressivism was a political style, a way of approaching problems. Progressives had no illusions that wage labor or industrialism could be eliminated or that it was possible to re-create a rural commonwealth. Big cities and big corporations, they believed, were permanent features of modern life, but progressives were convinced that modern institutions could be made humane, responsive, and moral.

In choosing solutions, progressives relied on scientific expertise as a way to avoid the clash of interests. Those raised during the Civil War knew democracy was no guarantee against mass violence. Rival points of view could be reconciled more easily by impartial authority. Like the salaried managers many of them were, progressives valued efficiency and organization. No problem could be solved in a single stroke, but only by persistent action.

Sure that science and God were on their side, progressives did not balk at imposing their views on other people, even if democracy got in the way. Such measures as naming "born criminals" to be put on probation *before* committing a crime were called "progressive." To southern progressives "scientific" principles justified racial segregation. Progressives demanded more democracy when it led to "good government," but if the majority was wrong, in their view, progressives handed power to unelected managers. The basic structure of American society, they felt, should not be open to political debate.

Above all, progressives shared an urgency. "There are two kinds of people," Alice Hamilton learned from her mother, "the ones who say, 'Someone ought to do something about it but why should it be I?' and the ones who say, 'Somebody must do something about it, then why not I?'" Hamilton and other progressives never doubted which kind they were.

Social Workers and Muckrakers

Among the first to hear the call to service were the young women and men who volunteered to live among the urban poor in "settlement houses." Stanton Coit established the first on New York's Lower East Side in 1886, but the most famous was Hull-House, which opened in Chicago three years later. Its founders, Jane Addams and Ellen Starr, bought a run-down mansion at the center of an inner-city ward thick with sweatshops, factories, and overcrowded tenements. The women of Hull-House opened a kindergarten and a clinic, took sweatshop bosses to court, investigated corrupt landlords, criticized the ward's powerful alderman, and built the city's first public playground.

Addams drew together at Hull-House a remarkable group of women with similar backgrounds. Florence Kelley organized a movement for occupational safety laws. Julia Lathrop headed the state's Children's Bureau. All three women were raised in affluent Quaker homes during or shortly after the Civil War, and their parents were all abolitionists. Like Alice Hamilton, all three attended college and traveled or studied in Europe.

> I've come here to write the **Uncle Tom's Cabin** of the labor movement.
>
> UPTON SINCLAIR,
> Chicago, 1904

As the fame of Hull-House spread, women (and some men) organized settlement houses in cities across the country. By the turn of the century there were more than 100, and by 1910 more than 400. Reformers often began by using social science techniques to survey the surrounding neighborhoods, gathering information on the national origins, income, housing conditions, and occupations of residents. Addams released *Hull-House Maps and Papers*, a survey of the 19th Ward, in 1895. One of the most ambitious research projects was the Pittsburgh Survey, a massive investigation of city living and working conditions published between 1909 and 1914. Its data confirmed that the causes of poverty were social, not personal, contradicting a common belief that the poor had only themselves to blame. Settlements did "social work" rather than charity.

Surveys also used maps, photographs, and even three-dimensional models. In 1900, housing reformers exhibited a scale cutaway model of a New York tenement block, show-

The Hull-House Choir in Recital, 1910 Chicago, according to Lincoln Steffens, was "loud, lawless, un-lovely, ill-smelling, new; an overgrown gawk of a village." Addams and other settlement workers sought to tame this urban wilderness through culture and activism.

ing how airless, overcrowded rooms contributed to disease and crime. Shelby Harrison, director of surveys for the Russell Sage Foundation, explained that the survey itself was reform, stimulating popular action with "the correcting power of facts."

This statistical outlook motivated settlement workers to attack urban problems across a broad front. Social workers labored to make food safe, repair housing, and sponsor festivals and pageants. Working conditions, especially for women and children, drew special attention, but employers, landlords, and city bosses were not the only targets: working-class vices—gambling, saloons, and brothels—were also attacked. The loudest voice of progressivism came from a new type of journalism introduced in 1902. In successive issues, *McClure's* magazine published Lincoln Steffens's investigation of graft in St. Louis and Ida Tarbell's "History of the Standard Oil Company," sensational exposés of the crimes of the nation's political and economic elite. As periodicals competed for readers, the old partisan style of journalism gave way to crusades, celebrities, and "sob sister" features. The new 10-cent magazines, such as *Everybody's*, *Cosmopolitan*, and *McClure's*, had audiences and budgets big enough to pay for in-depth investigations. The result was a type of reporting Theodore Roosevelt disdainfully called "muckraking." Readers loved it, and an article exposing some new corporate or public villainy could easily sell half a million copies.

Muckrakers named names. Upton Sinclair described the grisly business of canning beef. Ray Stannard Baker investigated railroads and segregation. Samuel Hopkins Adams catalogued the damage done by narcotics in popular medicines. Tarbell exposed Standard Oil's camouflaged companies, espionage, sweetheart deals, and predatory pricing. Her series shattered the notion that industrial giants competed in a free market and pushed the Justice Department to sue Standard Oil in 1906 for conspiracy to restrain trade.

The 10-cent magazines projected local problems onto a national canvas. Newspapers had covered municipal corruption before, but Steffens's series in *McClure's* revealed that bribery, influence peddling, and protection rackets operated in nearly every major city. Magazines also reported on progressive victories, allowing solutions adopted in Toledo or Milwaukee to spread quickly. Muckraking declined after 1912, the victim of corporate advertising boycotts and declining readership, but while it lasted, "public opinion" became a force that could shake the powerful.

Dictatorship of the Experts

For doctors, lawyers, and engineers, reform offered a chance to apply their skills to urgent problems, and the Progressive Era coincided with the rise in influence of the social sciences and the professions. Experts could mediate potentially violent conflicts and eliminate the uncertainties of democracy. Scientific advances seemed to justify this faith. In just a generation, antiseptic techniques, X-rays, and new drugs created a new understanding of disease. Electric light, recorded sound, motion pictures, radio, and flight confirmed science's ability to shape the future.

Social workers copied doctors, diagnosing each case with clinical impartiality. Newly professionalized police forces applied the techniques of fingerprinting, handwriting analysis, and psychology to law enforcement. Dietitians installed bland but nutritionally balanced meals in school cafeterias. Reformers tried (but failed) to simplify spelling and bring "efficiency" to the English language.

Trust in science sometimes led to extreme measures. One was the practice of eugenics, an attempt to rid society of alcoholism, poverty, and crime through selective breeding. "If the knowledge [of eugenics] were applied, the defective classes would disappear within a generation," the president of the University of Wisconsin predicted. Persuaded that genetics could save the state money, the Indiana legislature passed a law in 1907 authorizing the forced sterilization of "criminals, idiots, rapists, and imbeciles." Patients with epilepsy, psychiatric disorders, or mental handicaps who sought help at state hospitals were surgically sterilized. Criminals received the same treatment. Seven other states also adopted the "Indiana Plan."

The emphasis on expertise hid a thinly veiled distrust of democracy. Professional educators, for example, took control of the schools away from local boards and gave it to expert administrators and superintendents. They certified teachers and classified students based on "scientific" intelligence tests. To reformers, education was too important to be left to amateurs, such as teachers, parents, or voters.

Progressivism created new social sciences and made universities centers of advocacy. Sociology was a product of the progressive impulse. The study of government became political science, and "scientific" historians searched the past for answers to modern problems. John R. Commons, Richard Ely, and Thorstein Veblen used economics to study how modern institutions developed and functioned. Legal scholars such as Louis Brandeis and Roscoe Pound called for revising the law to reflect social realities.

This stress on expertise made progressive-era reforms different from those of earlier periods. Instead of trying to succeed at a single stroke—by passing a law or trouncing a corrupt politician—progressives believed in process and established organizations and procedures that would keep the pressure on and make progress a habit.

AMERICA AND THE WORLD

>> The Calorie

Just after breakfast on March 23, 1896, Professor Wilbur Atwater sealed a student in an airtight chamber in the basement of Wesleyan University's Judd Hall. The apparatus was described by the press as resembling a meat locker, lined with copper and zinc. Atwater carefully recorded the change in temperature inside the cell while the student, A. W. Smith, rested, lifted weights, and ate measured portions of bread, baked beans, hamburger, milk, and potatoes. The device was a calorimeter, a tool previously used to measure the efficiency of engines and explosives.

The press was riveted by the story of the "prisoner of science," but the results were even more startling. Atwater proved a theory European scientists had advanced 50 years earlier: that the human body had the thermodynamic properties of a machine. Both its intake—food—and its output—physical or mental exertion—could be measured in uniform units called calories. The discovery had immense military and industrial implications, allowing rations and wages to be calculated for maximum energy-producing efficiency. Congress voted funds to build a calorimeter in Washington, and government scientists proved another fact: all people, regardless of climate or race, need exactly the same number of calories to thrive. When it came to food, all men were created equal, after all.

Before the calorie, it was no more possible to measure appetite than to measure beauty or intelligence. Eating habits varied widely among cultures and individuals, and dietary knowledge was rudimentary. The calorie opened the way for the systematic study of nutrition.

World War I provided the first practical applications. After Germany's invasion of 1914 devastated Belgium, a wealthy mining engineer, Herbert Hoover, organized American charities to prevent famine. The Belgium Relief used the calorie to ration food supplies. When the United States entered the war, Hoover mobilized the country's food supply to feed the Allied armies. He prized wheat, "the largest supply of calories available" for the war effort. American families were told how to count calories and save wheat by cleaning their plates and avoiding "overeating." Restaurants listed calorie counts on their menus.

After victory in 1918, Europe's ports opened to American relief shipments, and Hoover's organization commanded the food supply from central Europe east to Moscow. The calorie briefly even became a unit of currency. Immigrants could send a check from New York to relatives in Poland or Lithuania to be cashed at food banks for a fixed number of calories. The newly formed League of Nations discussed using the calorie to rationalize the world's food supply, perhaps eliminating famines permanently.

Calorie consciousness revolutionized global cuisine in the interwar years. The discovery that Japanese sailors could eat just as much as their British counterparts prompted the Imperial Navy to provision its ships with high-calorie pork and chicken dipped in batter (tempura). These new recipes, popularized as the national

continued

....

cuisine, became what we know today as Japanese food. But while nationalists used calories to assert entitlement to a full plate, newspapers urged women to count calories to stay thin. Despite doctors' warnings, "dieting" became a global fad.

To many people, counting took the pleasure out of eating. Dutch historian Johan Huizinga saw the calorie as a peculiarly American "Taylorism of the mind." Indian leader Mahatma Gandhi rejected the calorie as another imperial ploy to control the world's hungry masses. He made hunger and self-denial into weapons in the independence struggle.

Nutrition was seen as a solution to economic and political problems. A 1936 League of Nations report proposed that the global agricultural depression could be solved if surplus calories in the industrial countries could be exported to countries, such as China, with caloric deficits. The proposal led in 1942 to the creation of the Food and Agriculture Organization, the first component of the United Nations system.

Since ancient times, societies have always kept a close eye on food supplies, but the calorie made food and nutrition an international concern. It implied that humanity had a single appetite and that those who had food had obligations to those who did not, even if they were on opposite sides of the world.

Progressives on the Color Line

In her international crusade against lynching, Ida B. Wells-Barnett pioneered some of the progressive tactics of research, exposure, and organization. A schoolteacher in Memphis, Wells-Barnett documented mob violence against African Americans and mobilized opinion in the United States and Britain. Cities that condoned extralegal executions soon faced a barrage of condemnation from church groups and women's clubs. As her Afro-American Council grew, Wells-Barnett joined forces with white suffragists, social workers, and journalists, but her cause was not fully embraced. Many reform groups sympathized with white southerners or wanted to avoid dividing their membership over race.

Reformers debated how much progress non-Anglo-Saxons were capable of, but they were inclined to be pessimistic. Eugenics gave white supremacy the endorsement of science. A new technology, the motion picture, showed its power to rewrite history from a racial viewpoint in D. W. Griffith's classic *Birth of a Nation* (1915), which romanticized the Klan's campaign of terror during Reconstruction. Policy was often based on racial assumptions. Trade schools, not universities, were deemed appropriate for educating Filipinos and Hawaiians. Progressives took Native American children from their families and placed them in boarding schools. Electoral reform in Texas meant disfranchising Spanish-speaking voters.

Wells-Barnett was not alone in finding doors through this wall of racial ideology. William Edward Burghardt DuBois documented the costs of racism in *The Philadelphia Negro* (1898). The survey spoke the progressives' language, insisting that discrimination

Ida B. Wells-Barnett with Her Children Ida Wells-Barnett, journalist and activist, made lynching an international issue through her writing and speaking tours.

was not just morally wrong but inefficient, because it took away work and encouraged alcoholism and crime. DuBois transformed the politics of race as profoundly as Addams transformed the politics of cities.

Raised in Massachusetts, DuBois learned Latin and Greek in public schools. At 17, he went to Fisk University in Tennessee, where he "came in contact for the first time with a sort of violence that I had never realized in New England." He also had his first encounter with African American religion and gospel music, which was "full of the voices of the past." DuBois later studied at Harvard and Berlin.

DuBois and Booker T. Washington espoused opposing visions of African Americans' place in the United States. Both emphasized the importance of thrift and hard work. DuBois, however, rejected Washington's willingness to accept legal inequality. DuBois came to believe that the Atlanta Compromise (see Chapter 20) led only to disfranchisement and segregation. He disliked the way Washington's influence with white philanthropists silenced other voices. Five years after the Atlanta speech he opened a sustained attack on Washington's "Tuskegee Machine."

In *The Souls of Black Folk* (1903), DuBois argued that the strategy of accommodation contained a "triple paradox": Washington had urged African Americans to seek industrial training, build self-respect, and become successful in business, while asking them to stop striving for higher education, civil rights, or political power. How could a people train themselves without higher education or gain self-respect without having any of the rights other Americans enjoyed—or succeed in business without the power to protect themselves or their property? Economic, political, and educational progress had to move together. Like other progressives, DuBois insisted on the importance of process and organization. African Americans could not stop demanding the vote, equality, or education.

In July 1905, DuBois and 28 African American leaders met on the Canadian side of Niagara Falls (no hotel on the U.S. side would admit them) to organize a campaign against racial violence, segregation, and disfranchisement. The Niagara Movement was one of several such organizations. In 1909, Wells-Barnett, Addams, and other reformers created the National Association for the Advancement of Colored People to carry on the fight in the courts. In 1915 the NAACP won a Supreme Court decision outlawing the grandfather clause, which denied the vote to descendants of slaves; but another 40 years passed before it succeeded in overturning *Plessy v. Ferguson.*

Progressives in State and Local Politics

Progressives were of two minds about the public. Walter Lippmann, a journalist and re-former, could write fondly of "the voiceless multitudes" and contemptuously of the "great dull mass of people who just don't care." Progressives' tactics betrayed this split vision. Their reforms made city government less democratic and more "businesslike." Reforms at the state level, however, expanded voters' power to initiate legislation and remove of-ficeholders. In both cases, the changes enlarged the influence of small-town and urban-middle-class reformers while reducing that of immigrants and the working class.

Redesigning the City

The machine politicians who ran American cities adapted well to change. To immigrants and factory workers, the local boss was one of the few people looking out for the average person. He rushed to fire scenes to aid homeless victims. He distributed turkeys in poor neighborhoods at Christmas. He could be counted on to post bail or find someone a job. Jane Addams acknowledged that she could not compete with Johnny Powers, the popular local ward boss, this "big manifestation of human friendliness, this stalking survival of village kindness."

Powers and other aldermen sheltered the brothels, saloons, and gambling dens that, in Addams's view, exploited honest workers. Hull-House organized to beat Powers in 1895, and in defeat the reformers revealed their frustrations with democracy. The reform-ers nominated an Irish bricklayer, William Gleeson, who they thought would appeal to the 19th Ward's working-class voters. But voters said they wanted someone grander to represent them, such as Powers, with his big house and diamond buttons. Gleeson was trounced. Addams was "puzzled, then astounded and indignant" at the outcome.

With officials like Powers in charge, corporations could do what they liked if they padded the right wallets. "If you want to get anything out of the council," the head of the Chicago Chamber of Commerce advised, "the quickest way is to pay for it—not to the city, but to the aldermen." City machines lost their appeal by providing not too few services but too many. As tax burdens grew, wealthier voters clamored for reform. Progressives set out to replace paternalism with efficient, scientific administration.

After the depression of 1893, many groups sprang up to criticize municipal govern-ment, which often resembled the federal system in miniature. A mayor, elected by the whole city, presided over a council of representatives from each neighborhood, or ward. This system diluted the influence of the "better classes" and allowed a few powerful wards to rule the city. In 1899 Louisville's Conference for Good City Government proposed a new model, later known as the "strong mayor" system. It gave more power to the mayor and required each council member to represent the whole city. Two years later, after a hurricane and tidal wave destroyed Galveston, Texas, the devastated city tried an even bolder plan. The recovery would be run by a commission of five elected officials, each managing a city department. Des Moines, Iowa improved on Galveston's design, and by 1911 some 160 cities had commission governments.

The commission resembled a corporate board of directors. Professionalism and accountability, the keys to business success, could make a city run, too. This philosophy led Detroit voters to elect Ford Motor Company's chief efficiency expert, James Couzens, as mayor. Other cities, led by Dayton, Ohio, tried to improve on the city-commission plan by placing local government in the hands of an unelected "city manager."

Middle- and upper-class professionals led this revolution in city government, and they gained the most from it. The new officials could explain where tax money was spent, but there were no turkeys at Christmas. Getting a job from the city meant filling out the proper forms. Reform administrations targeted urban "vice," which included most working-class recreations. Voters also learned that efficiency did not lower taxes. Budgets grew along with the public's demand for services.

Reform Mayors and City Services

While commissioners rewrote the rules, a new breed of reform mayors cleaned up their cities. Samuel "Golden Rule" Jones, a Welsh immigrant who earned a fortune in the oil fields, won election three times as independent mayor of Toledo. He enacted the eight-hour day for city employees, pushed for public ownership of city utilities, and staged free concerts in the parks. Like Tom Johnson in Cleveland and Hazen Pingree in Detroit, Jones worried less about saloons and more about utilities. Milwaukee, Schenectady, and other cities bought or regulated the private monopolies that supplied lighting, garbage removal, water, and streetcars.

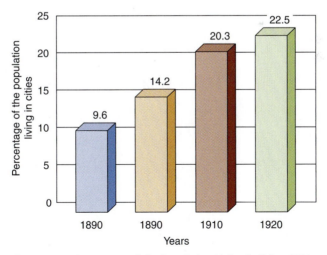

Figure 21–2   Percentage of the Population Living in Cities, 1890–1920 Cities and towns underwent dramatic growth around the turn of the century. Offices, department stores, and new forms of mass entertainment—from vaudeville to professional sports—drew people to the city center. Railroads and trolleys allowed cities to spread outward, segregating residents by class. *Kennedy,* Rise and Fall of the Great Powers, *p. 200.*

The reform mayors' efforts to humanize the city were supported by architects and engineers who looked to improve urban life through the arrangement of public space. A City Beautiful movement sought to soften the urban landscape with vistas, open spaces, and greenery. The District of Columbia, with its commission government, broad avenues, and parks, furnished a model of city planning, and Congress sought to make it a model of municipal reform as well by introducing a model child-labor law, slum-clearance plan, and school system. The new urban spaces performed social and educational functions as well, especially to Americanize and uplift immigrant city dwellers. New York enacted zoning laws in 1916, and "city planners" joined the ranks of specialists by organizing themselves as a profession.

Progressivism and the States

State reform varied by region. The East mimicked the agenda of urban reform. New York's progressive governor, Charles Evans Hughes, passed laws prohibiting gambling and creating a state commission to regulate utilities. In southern states, progressivism often meant

Daniel Burnham's City Plan for Chicago, 1909 Through comprehensive planning, Burnham sought to save cities from "the chaos incident to rapid growth." He drafted designs for Washington, Cleveland, San Francisco, and Manila.

refining the techniques of segregation and disfranchisement. Lynching and mob assaults on African Americans were weekly occurrences in the Progressive Era. White leaders justified segregation and violence in terms used to justify urban reform in the North: the "better classes" had an obligation to rein in the excesses of democracy.

States in the West and Midwest produced the boldest experiments. Oregon introduced the secret ballot, voter registration, and three measures originally proposed by the Populists: the initiative, recall, and referendum. The initiative allowed voters to place legislation on the ballot by petition; the referendum let the legislature put proposals on the ballot; and the recall gave voters the chance to remove officials from office before the end of their terms. Other states soon adopted all or part of the "Oregon system."

The best known of the progressive governors was Robert M. "Fighting Bob" La Follette, whose model of state government came to be known as the "Wisconsin Idea." Elected in 1900, La Follette pushed through a comprehensive program of social legislation. Railways and public utilities were placed under public control. One commission designed a "scientific" distribution of the tax burden, including an income tax, whereas others regulated hours and working conditions and protected the environment. Wisconsin also implemented the direct primary, which allowed party nominees to be chosen directly by voters rather than by party caucuses.

Few machine politicians had as much personal power as the reform governors did. Wisconsin papers would call La Follette a "demagogue," but the reform governors brought policy making out of the "smoke-filled rooms." By shaking up city halls and state houses, progressives made the public less cynical and government more responsive to reform. They knew, however, that social problems did not respect political boundaries: national corporations and nationwide problems had to be attacked at the federal level, and that meant capturing the White House.

The President Becomes "The Administration"

If Theodore Roosevelt stood at the center of the two great movements of his age, imperialism and progressivism, it was because he prepared himself for the part. The Roosevelt family was wealthy and one of the oldest in New York, but Theodore embarked instead on pursuits that were unusual for a man of his class. After graduating from Harvard in 1880, he married, started law school, wrote a history of the War of 1812, bought a cattle ranch in the Dakota Territory, and, most surprisingly, ran for the state legislature.

For Roosevelt's family and friends, government was no place for gentlemen. Roosevelt himself described his colleagues as "a stupid, sodden, vicious lot, most of them being equally deficient in brains and virtue." Avoiding the "rough and tumble," he argued, only conceded high offices to those less fit to lead. Roosevelt's flair for publicity got him noticed, and in 1886 the Republican Party nominated him for mayor of New York. He finished third, behind the Tammany nominee and the Socialist candidate.

A turn as head of New York's board of police commissioners from 1895 to 1897 deepened Roosevelt's commitment to reform. The commission supervised an army of 38,000 policemen. Roosevelt's crackdown on saloons and corruption in the police department earned him a reputation as a man who would not be intimidated, even by his own party's bosses, and when McKinley won the presidency he named Roosevelt assistant secretary of the navy.

The Spanish-American War catapulted him to national fame, and in quick succession he became governor of New York, vice president, and then president of the United States.

Roosevelt believed that to restore democracy—"genuine democracy"—America needed a mission, "a genuine and permanent moral awakening." In the White House, he sought great tasks—duties to be carried out, principles to be upheld, isthmuses to be cut, and lands to be conserved—to inspire a common purpose and test the national will. In the process, he rewrote the president's job description, seizing new powers for the executive branch and turning the presidency into "the administration."

The Executive Branch Against the Trusts

Roosevelt approached politics the way Jane Addams approached poverty: studying it, living in its midst, and carefully choosing his battles. His fear of radicalism was borne out in September 1901. President William McKinley was shaking hands at the Pan American Exposition in Buffalo, New York, when a man thrust a pistol into his chest and fired twice. The assassin, Leon Czolgosz, came from the Cleveland slums and claimed to seek vengeance for the poor.

> Theodore Roosevelt began the work of turning the American mind in the direction which it had to go in the Twentieth Century.
>
> WALTER LIPPMANN

At age 42, Roosevelt was the youngest man to attain the presidency. He was the first president to call himself a progressive, and the first, according to Lippmann, "who realized clearly that national stability and social justice had to be sought deliberately and had consciously to be maintained." Unsatisfied merely to lead his party, he set out to remake the executive as the preeminent branch of government, initiating legislation, shaping public opinion, and protecting the national interest at home and abroad. "I believe in power," he explained. Instead of asking Congress for legislation, he drafted bills and lobbied for them personally. He believed government should intervene in the economy to protect citizens or to save business from itself. McKinley had already planned against the trusts, but his plans were not as bold as his successor's.

Challenging the corporations would not be easy. Roosevelt took office less than a decade after J. P. Morgan rescued the federal Treasury. In 1895, the Supreme Court gutted the Sherman Act, one of the few laws allowing federal action against monopolies. The underfunded Interstate Commerce Commission possessed few powers. Roosevelt told Congress "publicity is the only sure remedy which we can now invoke." He used it to the limit, putting Wall Street on notice in his first inaugural when he asserted that trusts "are creatures of the State, and the State not only has the right to control them, but it is duty bound to control them." In 1903 Roosevelt established a Department of Commerce and Labor that required annual reports, making corporate activities transparent.

The Justice Department revitalized the Sherman Act with vigorous prosecutions, and Roosevelt selected cases for maximum publicity value. Attorney General Philander Knox filed suit against J. P. Morgan's holding company, Northern Securities. Morgan expected the matter to be settled in the usual way, and his attorney asked how they might "fix it up." "We don't want to fix it up," Knox replied. "We want to stop it." When the Court handed Roosevelt a victory in 1904, Americans cheered.

With this case, Roosevelt gained an undeserved reputation as a "trust buster." He did oppose serious abuses, but he distinguished between good and bad trusts and believed that government should encourage responsible corporations to grow. He agreed with such progressive writers as Herbert Croly, editor of *The New Republic*, who imagined a central government staffed by nonpartisan experts who would monitor big corporations to assure efficiency and head off destructive actions.

Not all progressives agreed. Brandeis and Woodrow Wilson envisioned a political economy of small, highly competitive firms kept in line by regular use of the Sherman Act. To Roosevelt, there was no future in a small-business economy. Only large combinations could compete on a world scale, and government's obligation was not to break them up but to regulate them. He secured passage of the Hepburn Act (1906), which allowed the commission to set freight rates and banned "sweetheart" deals (of the kind Standard Oil enjoyed) with favored clients. The Elkins Act (1910) regulated telephone, telegraph, and cable communications. The Pure Food and Drug Act (1906) responded to Upton Sinclair's exposé of the meatpacking industry by making it a crime to ship or sell contaminated or fraudulently labeled food and drugs. Under Roosevelt, the federal government gained the tools to counterbalance the power of business. It grew to match its responsibilities. The number of federal employees almost doubled between 1900 and 1916.

The Square Deal

Roosevelt's exasperation with big business reached a peak during the coal strike of 1902. The United Mine Workers represented 150,000 miners in the coal fields of eastern Pennsylvania. The miners, mostly Polish, Hungarian, and Italian immigrants, earned less than $6 a week, and more than 400 died yearly to supply the coal to run railroads and heat homes. Seventy percent of the mines were owned by six railroads, which in turn were controlled by the usual financiers, including Morgan and Rockefeller. The owners refused to deal with the union, declaring it a band of outlaws. When the miners struck in May, they had the public's sympathy. Editorials, even in Republican newspapers, urged the president to take the mines away from the owners.

The "gross blindness of the operators" infuriated Roosevelt. Coal was the only fuel for heating, and a strike might cause hundreds to freeze. After failing to get the sides to negotiate, he invited union officials and the operators to Washington so that he could personally arbitrate. John Mitchell, head of the mine workers, eagerly accepted the offer, but the owners refused.

For Roosevelt this was the final straw. He prepared the army to move into the coal fields and put the mines under government control. The owners capitulated, agreeing to submit the dispute to a federal commission. The result was a compromise: miners received a 10 percent increase in pay and a nine-hour workday, but owners did not have to recognize the union.

Roosevelt's direct action made the federal government a third force in labor disputes. For the first time a strike was settled by federal arbitration, and for the first time a union had struck a strategic industry without being denounced as a radical conspiracy. The government would no longer automatically side with the corporations. "We demand that big business give the people a square deal," Roosevelt explained. " In return, we must insist that when anyone engaged in big business honestly endeavors to do right, he shall be given a square deal."

Conserving Water, Land, and Forests

When Roosevelt felt important issues were at stake, he pushed the limits of his office. He enraged Congress by stretching the definitions of presidential power, especially in the area of conservation. When Congress sent him a bill to halt the creation of new national forests in the West, Roosevelt first created or enlarged 32 national forests, then signed the bill. To stop private companies from damming rivers, he reserved 2,500 of the best hydropower sites by declaring them "ranger stations." Behind his program was Gifford Pinchot, the chief forester of the United States, who saw conservation as a new frontier. Unsettled, undeveloped lands were growing scarce, and Pinchot convinced the president of the value in managing resources more efficiently. Forests, deserts, and ore ranges were to be used wisely, scientifically, and in the national interest.

One of Roosevelt's first victories was the Newlands Reclamation Act (1902), which gave the Agriculture Department authority to build reservoirs and irrigation systems in the West. In the next four years, 3 million acres were "reclaimed" from the desert and turned into farms. To prevent waste, Roosevelt put tighter controls on prospecting, grazing, and logging. Big lumber and mining companies accepted rationalized resource administration, but small-scale prospectors and ranchers were shut out of federal lands. Naturalists like John Muir also resisted, pointing out that nature was to be appreciated, not used.

By 1909, conservation had become a national issue and created a new constituency of hikers, sightseers, and tourism entrepreneurs. By quadrupling the acreage in federal

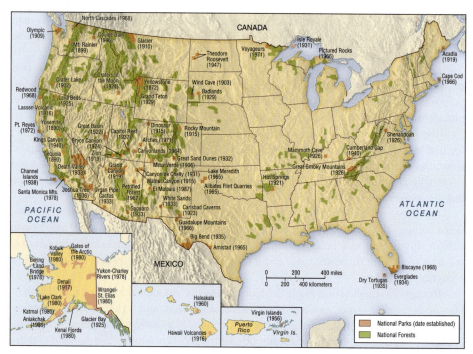

Map 21–1   Growth of Public Lands Responding to a national conservation movement, Roosevelt set aside public lands for use as parks and managed-yield forests. The National Park Service was founded in 1916.

AN AMERICAN LANDSCAPE

>> The Hetch Hetchy Valley

When landscape painter Albert Bierstadt visited in 1875, he saw a panorama of waterfalls. The canyon walls towered 2,500 feet above a wide, forested meadow populated by herds of elk. Twenty-five years later, San Francisco's mayor James Phelan beheld the cliffs and the pure glacier water pouring into the Tuolumne River and saw his city's answer to the problems of "monopoly and microbes."

The Hetch Hetchy Valley hypnotized naturalists and engineers equally because of its magnificence and its location. It was only 152 miles from San Francisco, close enough both to lure visitors and to channel its waters to the city. A village of less than a thousand in 1848, the City by the Bay was, by 1900, the nation's ninth largest, with 340,000 people. Only water kept it from growing larger.

Hemmed in by ocean on three sides, San Francisco faced a chronic scarcity of water. As the Gold Rush swelled the population, entrepreneurs bought up all available water supplies and formed the Spring Valley Water Company, which monopolized the city's water for 60 years. Water tycoons supported the political machine led by "Boss" Abe Ruef. The company's water was neither cheap nor safe, causing occasional outbreaks of cholera and typhus.

When voters elected Phelan and a reform ticket in 1897, they expected something to be done about water. The Republican mayor proposed to dam the Hetch Hetchy and build an aqueduct across the Central Valley, breaking the monopoly and making water an abundant, safe public utility.

Many obstacles stood in the way. The city's board of superintendents, controlled by Ruef, sided with Spring Valley and blocked plans for a city reservoir. But it was even harder to get permission from the federal government. Hetch Hetchy was located in Yosemite National Park, one of the first nature preserves, created in 1890 to save its peaks and waterfalls. The parks system was new, and the philosophy of conservation—how to preserve natural resources, and for what purposes—was evolving rapidly. Phelan found an ally in Gifford Pinchot, who filled the newly created office of chief forester.

Pinchot's father had made millions in the lumber trade. Gifford argued that the job of forestry was "to grow trees as a crop." He and Phelan agreed that the two main threats to any resource were inefficient use and monopoly control. The few hikers who might enjoy Hetch Hetchy's magnificence were less important than the need "to supply pure water to a great center of population."

Natural and political disasters worked to Phelan's advantage. After the 1906 San Francisco earthquake and fire vividly demonstrated the need for a water supply, Congress allowed the city to apply to use part of Yosemite's land. The following year, a lurid scandal led to a bribery conviction for Ruef and disgrace for his followers. But just as the way seemed clear, a public outcry urged the secretary of the interior to save the Hetch Hetchy.

continued

AMERICAN LANDSCAPE *continued*

Behind the campaign was the 1,000-member Sierra Club and its ascetic founder, John Muir. A wilderness explorer and naturalist, Muir was popular for his writings on the transcendent, spiritual aspects of the natural world. "Dam Hetch Hetchy!" he remonstrated. "As well dam for water tanks the people's cathedrals and churches." Historians have characterized the debate between Muir and Pinchot as a contest between rival concepts of environmentalism—conservation for use versus preservation for nature's sake—but the two men also represented opposing interpretations of democracy and the dangers it faced.

"Conservation is the most democratic movement this country has known for generations," Pinchot believed. The Hetch Hetchy project would replace unbridled corporate power with management of natural resources for the public good.

Democratic values were scientific values: efficiency, expertise, and "the greatest good, for the greatest number, for the longest time." For Muir, nature was a refuge where democratic values could survive amid the culture of self-interest and scientific progress. The valley had to be preserved not just to save the trees but also to "save humans for the wilderness." Only there could people share the nonmaterial values in which democracy took root.

The Sierra Club did not advocate leaving the area pristine. They imagined making Hetch Hetchy a retreat for harried city dwellers, managed by the park service. The public outcry surprised dam advocates, but they managed to cast the "nature lovers" as unwitting tools of the water and power monopolies.

The Roosevelt administration wavered, but in 1913, Phelan got his dam. Muir died a year later. Today the Hetch Hetchy aqueduct delivers 300 million gallons of water a day to San Francisco. But the battle for the valley gave birth to a modern environmental movement. When municipal and mining interests encroached on the Yosemite and Yellowstone preserves in the following decades, they were opposed by a national constituency that saw both activism and wilderness as national legacies.

reserves, professionalizing the forest service, and using his "bully pulpit" to build support for conservation, Roosevelt helped create the modern environmental movement.

TR and Big Stick Diplomacy

Imperial and commercial expansion put new strains on foreign and military policy after the turn of the century. U.S. investors wanted Washington to protect their overseas factories and railroads against civil wars and hostile governments. Diplomatic and military budgets grew to meet these demands. Diplomats were no longer political cronies but trained professionals, and diplomacy was no longer a matter of weathering "incidents" but of making policy.

Roosevelt's view of world affairs flowed from his understanding of the past and the future. Global trade and communications, he believed, united "civilized" nations. His foreign policy aimed to keep the United States in the mainstream of commerce, imperialism, and military (particularly naval) modernization. He felt a duty to interfere with "barbarian" governments in Asia, Latin America, or Africa that blocked progress. The United States was obliged, he felt, to overthrow governments and even to seize territory when it was acting in the interests of the world as a whole.

Building an interoceanic canal topped Roosevelt's list of foreign-policy priorities. A canal would be a hub of world trade and naval power in the Atlantic and Pacific, and Roosevelt aimed to prevent France or Britain from building it. He negotiated a deal to buy out a failed French venture in the Colombian province of Panama.

A civil war in Colombia complicated his plans. In 1902 American diplomats brokered a peace between modernizers led by José Marroquín and traditionalists who fiercely opposed the canal. Marroquín favored it but knew war would erupt again unless the Americans gave Bogotá full control over the canal. For Roosevelt, control was not negotiable.

In the spring of 1903 Panamanian senators, upset by the rejection of the U.S. offer, began planning to secede. Panama had had revolutions before, but the United States had always stepped in to preserve Colombia's sovereignty. Together with Philippe Bunau-Varilla, who represented the French company, the Panamanians lobbied U.S. officials to support their plot. Bunau-Varilla predicted a revolution for November 3, thereby ensuring that the rebels, the Colombian army (which had been bribed into surrendering), and U.S. warships would all be on hand.

The revolution went off without a hitch, and Roosevelt presented the new Panamanian government a treaty that gave less and took more than the one offered to Colombia. Congress launched an investigation. "I took the canal and let Congress debate," Roosevelt said, "and while the debate goes on the canal does also." The canal, a 50-mile cut built under the direction of George W. Goethals at a cost of $352 million and more than 5,600 lives, opened in 1914.

With construction under way, Roosevelt acted to protect the canal from other powers. Poverty in the region created opportunities for imperial governments to establish bases on Panama's doorstep. In 1902 Germany almost invaded Venezuela over an unpaid loan, but Roosevelt stepped in to mediate. When the Dominican Republic later reneged on its loans, four European nations laid plans for a debt-collecting expedition.

Roosevelt went before Congress in December 1904 and announced a policy later known as the Roosevelt Corollary. It stipulated that when chronic "wrongdoing or impotence" in a Latin American country required "intervention by some civilized nation," the United States would do the intervening. In Roosevelt's view, white "civilized" nations acted; nonwhite "impotent" nations were acted on. The next month the United States took over the Dominican Republic's customs offices and began repaying creditors. The economic intervention turned military in 1916, when the United States landed marines to protect the customs from Dominican rebels. U.S. troops stayed in the Dominican Republic until the early 1920s.

By enforcing order and efficiency in the Caribbean, Roosevelt extended progressivism beyond the borders of the United States. The movement spread to the Far East, too. In 1906 a U.S. federal court was created in Shanghai, China, to control prostitution in the American community there.

Taft and Dollar Diplomacy

Enormously popular at the end of his second term, Roosevelt chose his friend, William H. Taft, to succeed him. Taft gained national attention as a circuit judge whose decisions enlarged federal power to regulate trusts. As governor general of the Philippines, he brought reform to Manila. Taft easily defeated William Jennings Bryan in the 1908 election, and as president he began consolidating Roosevelt's gains. He sent to the states constitutional amendments for the direct election of senators and the income tax. He increased antitrust enforcement and levied the first tax on corporations. Satisfied that his legacy would continue, Roosevelt left for a tour of Africa.

In the Caribbean, Taft put the Roosevelt Corollary into action. The United States bought up the debts of Honduras and Nicaragua. Taft persuaded New York banks to refinance Haiti's debt to prevent German intervention there. Taft intended "dollar diplomacy" to replace force as an instrument of policy, but in most cases, dollars preceded bullets. For Caribbean nations, American protection meant high import taxes. A revolt usually followed. Marines went into Honduras and Nicaragua in 1912 and stayed until 1933.

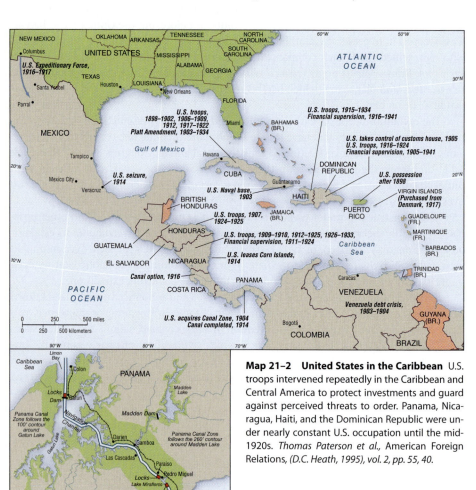

Map 21–2 United States in the Caribbean U.S. troops intervened repeatedly in the Caribbean and Central America to protect investments and guard against perceived threats to order. Panama, Nicaragua, Haiti, and the Dominican Republic were under nearly constant U.S. occupation until the mid-1920s. *Thomas Paterson et al.,* American Foreign Relations, *(D.C. Heath, 1995), vol. 2, pp. 55, 40.*

Dollar diplomacy also aimed to harness economic power for diplomatic purposes. Taft mobilized a consortium to finance China's Chinchow-Aigun railway. Railroads were instruments of power in North China, and Taft felt he could drive a wedge between the imperial powers—Britain, Russia, and Japan—and compel them to resume open-door trade. Instead, they joined forces against the United States and the Open Door. Despite the setback, Taft still believed that economic power, not military force, was what mattered.

Taft disappointed both conservatives and progressives in his party. He first urged Congress to reduce the tariff, but then signed the Payne-Aldrich Tariff in 1909, which raised rates on key imports. Taft's secretary of the interior, Richard Ballinger, sided with ranchers and miners who opposed Roosevelt's resource-management policies. When Pinchot, the chief forester, fought back, Taft fired him. When the Ballinger-Pinchot affair revealed the party's divisions, Roosevelt felt his country needed him back.

Rival Visions of the Industrial Future

After Roosevelt returned in 1910, Pinchot, La Follette, Croly, and others trooped to his home at Sagamore Hill to complain about Taft. The former president denied any interest in the Republican nomination, but he could not keep his pledge. Roosevelt reentered politics because his views had evolved and because politics was what he knew best. Just 54 years old, his energy undiminished, he took more radical positions on corporations, public welfare, and labor than he had while president. The election of 1912 would define the future of industrial America.

The New Nationalism

At a sun-baked junction in Osawatomie, Kansas, in August 1910, Roosevelt declared, "the essence of any struggle for liberty . . . is to destroy privilege and give the life of every individual the highest possible value." He laid out a program he called the New Nationalism. It included the elimination of corporate campaign contributions, regulation of industrial combinations, an expert commission to set tariffs, a graduated income tax, banking reorganization, and a national workers' compensation program. "This New Nationalism regards the executive power as the steward of the public welfare." The message drew cheers.

Roosevelt had the newspapers, whereas Taft had the delegates. The nomination fight tested the new system of direct primaries. Taft's control of the party machinery helped him in states that chose delegates by convention, but in key states Roosevelt could take his campaign to the voters. At the convention in Chicago in June 1912, Taft's slim but decisive majority allowed him to control the platform and win over undecided delegates. Grumbling that he had been robbed, Roosevelt walked out.

Roosevelt returned to Chicago in August to accept the nomination of the newly formed Progressive Party. The delegates were a mixed group. They included Hiram Johnson, the reform governor of California; muckraking publisher Frank Munsey; imperialist senator Albert Beveridge; and J. P. Morgan's business partner George W. Perkins. The party platform endorsed the New Nationalism, along with popular election of senators, popular review of judicial decisions, and women's suffrage. Women were delegates, and Jane Addams seconded Roosevelt's nomination. The gathering had an evangelical spirit.

"Our cause is based on the eternal principles of righteousness," Roosevelt said. "We stand at Armageddon and we battle for the Lord."

The 1912 Election

In Baltimore the Democrats nominated a former college professor and governor of New Jersey. Like Roosevelt, the young Woodrow Wilson defied his family's expectations by pursuing a political career. He took an unusual route. Obtaining a doctorate in government from Johns Hopkins University in 1886, he published his first book, *Congressional Government*, at the age of 28. It advocated enlarging the power of the executive branch. As a professor and later president of Princeton University, he became a well-known lecturer and commentator for new national political magazines such as *Harper's* and the *Atlantic Monthly*. In 1910 he was elected governor of New Jersey and enacted sweeping progressive reforms. For Democrats, smarting from losses under Bryan's leadership, Wilson offered a new image and the ability to unite the South and the East under a progressive program.

With Roosevelt in the race, Wilson had to stake his own claim to the progressive constituency. With the help of Louis Brandeis, Wilson devised a program called the New Freedom. It challenged Roosevelt on his approaches to the economy and politics. Simply regulating the trusts, Wilson argued, would not help consumers, workers, or small entrepreneurs. Instead, it would create a paternalistic bureaucracy. Wilson wanted a lean, strong government and antitrust laws to encourage a return to competition and economic mobility. Both agreed on the importance of a strong executive, but they had different economic formulas. Roosevelt appealed to a collective, national interest, whereas Wilson stressed the needs of individual consumers and investors. The New Nationalism was evangelical, aiming to inspire people to work for the common good. Wilson appealed to reason and self-interest.

On Election Day, the split in the Republican Party gave Wilson a plurality. He won 42 percent of the popular vote, compared with 27 for Roosevelt, 23 for Taft, and 6 for Debs. Although his margin was thin, Wilson could interpret Taft's loss and the large combined vote for the progressive candidates as a mandate for change. "What the Democratic Party proposes," he told his followers, is "to do the things the Republican Party has been talking about doing for sixteen years."

The New Freedom

Within a year and a half of his inauguration, Wilson produced one of the most coherent and far-reaching legislative programs ever devised by a president. Drawing on his long study of congressional politics, he seized the advantage of his party's majority and exercised an unprecedented degree of personal control through the majority leaders in both houses. The New Freedom advocated lower tariffs, increased competition, and vigorous antitrust enforcement. Three monumental bills passed through Congress in rapid succession.

The first bill was the Underwood-Simmons Tariff (1913), which made the first deep cuts in tariff rates since before the Civil War. The bill overturned a cornerstone of Republican economic policy, the protectionist tariff. It helped farmers and consumers by lowering prices and increasing competition, but Wilson argued that its real beneficiaries would be manufacturers. Lower tariffs would help persuade other countries to reduce taxes on imports from the United States, opening new markets for American-made

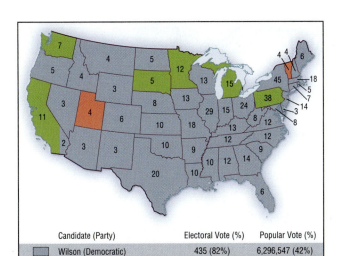

Candidate (Party)	Electoral Vote (%)	Popular Vote (%)
Wilson (Democratic)	435 (82%)	6,296,547 (42%)
Roosevelt (Progressive)	88 (17%)	4,118,571 (27%)
Taft (Republican)	8 (1%)	3,486,720 (23%)
Debs (Socialist)		900,672 (6%)

Map 21–3   The Election of 1912 The election pitted rival visions of progressivism against each other. The decentralized regulation of Wilson's "New Freedom" had more appeal than Roosevelt's far-reaching "New Nationalism."

goods. Wilson created an expert Tariff Commission in 1916 to improve tariff bargaining. The most-favored-nation policies it implemented (and which remain in place) induced European powers to open their empires to American goods. The Singer, Ford, and Camel brand names began appearing in markets from Caracas to Mandalay.

Wilson next targeted the banking system. When Steffens and Lippmann investigated banking for *Everybody's* magazine in 1908, they found that its structure was "strikingly like that of Tammany Hall," with a similar concentration of power, lack of accountability, and extra-legal maneuvering. The Federal Reserve Act of 1913 set up a national board to supervise the system and created 12 regional reserve banks throughout the country. Banks were now watched to ensure that their reserves matched their deposits. The system's real advantage was the flexibility it gave the currency. The board could put more dollars into circulation when demand was high and retire them when it subsided. Regional banks could adjust the money supply to meet local needs. The system broke Wall Street's stranglehold on credit and opened new opportunities for entrepreneurship and competition.

Finally, Wilson attacked the trusts. He established the Federal Trade Commission (FTC), an independent regulatory commission assigned to enforce free and fair competition. It absorbed the functions of Roosevelt's Bureau of Corporations, but with more authority, including the right to subpoena corporate records and issue cease-and-desist orders. The Clayton Antitrust Act (1914) prohibited price fixing, outlawed interlocking directorates, and made it illegal for a company to own the stock of competitors. To enforce these provisions citizens were entitled to sue for triple the amount of the actual damages

>> Timeline

▼1889
Hull-House founded

▼1890
General Federation of Women's Clubs founded

▼1893
Illinois passes eight-hour day for women

▼1895
National Association of Manufacturers organized

▼1900
Robert La Follette elected governor of Wisconsin

▼1901
Socialist Party of America founded
Galveston introduces commission government
McKinley assassinated; Theodore Roosevelt inaugurated president

▼1902
Newlands Reclamation Act funds construction of dams and irrigation systems
Alice Hamilton investigates Chicago's typhoid epidemic
McClure's publishes first episodes of Ida Tarbell's "History of the Standard Oil
   Company" and Lincoln Steffens's "The Shame of the Cities"
Roosevelt settles anthracite strike

▼1903
Roosevelt establishes Department of Commerce and Labor
Panama declares independence from Colombia
W. E. B. DuBois publishes *The Souls of Black Folk*

▼1904
Justice Department sues Standard Oil under the Sherman Anti-Trust Act
U.S. Supreme Court orders Northern Securities Company dissolved as an
   illegal combination
Roosevelt reelected president
The Roosevelt Corollary announced

▼1905
U.S. takes over Dominican customs
Industrial Workers of the World founded
Roosevelt mediates end to Russo-Japanese War

▼1906
Hepburn Act passed, allowing the Interstate Commerce Commission
   to set freight rates
Pure Food and Drug Act requires accurate labeling

>> **Timeline** *continued*

▼1907
Indiana passes forcible-sterilization law

▼1908
William H. Taft elected president
Supreme Court upholds maximum-hours laws for women in *Muller v. Oregon*

▼1909
Payne-Aldrich Tariff goes into effect
NAACP founded

▼1910
Taft fires chief forester Gifford Pinchot
Elkins Act authorizes Interstate Commerce Commission to regulate
   electronic communications
Roosevelt announces the New Nationalism

▼1911
Triangle Shirtwaist Company fire

▼1912
U.S. troops occupy Nicaragua
Woodrow Wilson elected president

▼1913
Federal Reserve Act reorganizes banking system
Underwood-Simmons Tariff

▼1914
Panama Canal completed
Clayton Act strengthens antitrust enforcement

▼1916
New York City enacts zoning laws
Federal workers' compensation, child-labor, and eight-hour-day laws passed

they suffered. In 1916 Wilson produced more reform legislation, including the first national workers' compensation and child-labor laws, the eight-hour day for railroad workers, and the Warehouse Act, which extended credit to cash-strapped farmers.

These programs furthered Wilson's goal of "releasing the energies" of consumers and entrepreneurs, but they also helped business. Businessmen headed many of the regulatory boards, and the FTC and Federal Reserve Board helped stabilize unruly markets. The New Freedom brought reform without the elaborate state machinery of the New Nationalism or European industrial nations. The New Freedom linked liberal reform to individual initiative and free markets.

Conclusion

By 1900 America's political economy had outgrown the social relationships and laws that served the rural republic for most of the nineteenth century. Squeezed between corporate elites and the large, transient immigrant communities that controlled urban politics, middle-class reformers created a new style of political participation. They experimented with new forms of political decision making and vested the state with responsibility for the quality of life of its citizens. Progressives challenged but never upset the system. Science and the pressure of informed opinion, they believed, could produce managed, orderly change without open conflict.

The progressive presidents took this movement to the national stage. Roosevelt and Wilson touted their programs as attacks on privilege, but both presidents helped position the federal government as a broker among business, consumer, and labor interests. In less than two decades, the federal government overcame its reputation for corruption and impotence and moved to the center of economic and social life. The concept of a "national interest" greater than individual and property rights was now firmly ingrained; so, too, was the need to protect it. The president's leadership now extended beyond the administration to Congress and public opinion. These achievements created a modern central government just as military, diplomatic, and economic victories made the United States a global power. War and its aftermath would curtail the progressive movement, as support for a strong central government would be tested by events unfolding in Europe.

Review Questions

1. Were the progressives' goals conservative or radical? How about their strategies?

2. Why did reformers feel that privately owned utilities caused corruption?

3. What were the Oregon system and the Wisconsin Idea?

4. Theodore Roosevelt has been called the first modern president. In what ways did he change the presidency?

5. Did the progressives' emphasis on research and documentation indicate their respect for public opinion or not?

6. Choose one level of government—local, state, or federal—and describe three key progressive reforms.

For further review materials and resource information, please visit www.oup.com/us/ofthepeople

A Global Power
1914–1919

>> Walter Lippmann

Walter Lippmann had just arrived in Brussels in July 1914 when the trains suddenly stopped running. At the station, "crowds of angry, jostling people" were trying to leave the city. This looked, he confided in his diary, like the beginning of a war. Four weeks earlier, Austria-Hungary's crown prince, Archduke Ferdinand, had been shot in the Serbian city of Sarajevo. Austria threatened to attack unless Serbia found and punished the terrorists. Russia mobilized to come to Serbia's defense. As stock markets tumbled and banks collapsed, Lippmann found himself caught in a conflict between the world's most powerful states: Austria and Germany on one side, Russia, France, and Britain on the other. As land borders closed, he escaped across the channel to England.

In the twilight of August 4, he stood with an anxious crowd outside the House of Commons, as Britain's foreign minister, Sir Edward Grey, asked Parliament for a war resolution. In Berlin, the Reichstag declared war on France. "We sit and stare at each other and make idiotically cheerful remarks," Lippmann wrote, "and in the meantime, so far as anyone can see, nothing can stop the awful disintegration now."

Twenty-four years old, Lippmann had come of age in the Progressive Era. As a student at Harvard, he came to believe that reason and science would allow his generation to "treat life not as something given but as something to be shaped." After graduation, he set out to become a journalist, studying under Lincoln Steffens and helping to start a magazine called the *New Republic*. "It was a happy time, those last few years before the First World War," he later remembered; "the air was soft, and it was easy for a young man to believe in the inevitability of progress, in the perfectibility of man and of society, and in the sublimation of evil."

The European war crushed those hopes. Just days after Lippmann left Belgium, German armies sliced through the neutral nation in a great maneuver designed to

continued

encircle the French army, but before the ring could be closed, reserve troops from Paris, many of them rushed to the front in taxicabs, stopped the German advance at the Marne River. By November, the Western Front had stabilized into the bloody stalemate that would last the next four years, taking between 5,000 and 50,000 lives a day. The machine gun defeated all attempts to break through the enemy's trench lines. Colossal artillery, poison gas, submarine warfare, aerial bombardment, and suicide charges would each be used in desperate bids to break the deadlock, and all would fail.

The carnage horrified Americans. German soldiers terrorized Belgian civilians in retaliation for guerilla attacks, killing over 5,000 hostages and burning the medieval city of Louvain. The gruesome tragedy of modern war made Americans feel both fortunate and guilty to be so uninvolved. "We Americans have been witnessing supreme drama, clenching our fists, talking, yet unable to fasten any reaction to realities," Lippmann told his readers. For three years, Americans watched a civilization they had admired sink into barbarism. They recoiled from the war's violence and the motives behind it, and they debated what, if anything, they could do to stop it.

When the United States entered the fight in 1917, it mobilized its economy and society to send an army of a million to Europe. The war disrupted and culminated the progressive movement. In the name of efficiency, the state stepped in to manage the economy as never before, placing corporations under federal supervision but allowing them profits and some autonomy. The war transformed controversial items on the progressive agenda—women's suffrage, prohibition of alcohol, restrictions on prostitution—into matters of national urgency. The federal government punished political dissenters. On the battlefield, American forces brought swift triumph, but not a new stability. Defeated powers collapsed into revolution and anarchy. New ideologies threatened American ideals. The experience of war brought home the dangers of a modern, interdependent world, but it also revealed the United States' power to shape the global future.

Common Threads

>> As a progressive, Wilson was committed to order, efficiency, and gradual reform. How did his policies toward Mexico and Europe reflect this commitment?

>> Both the Philippine-American War of 1899 and U.S. involvement in World War I in 1917 provoked dissent at home. Why did the government tolerate opposition in the first case but suppress it in the second?

>> How did the repression of the war years set the stage for the Red Scare and the Ku Klux Klan?

The Challenge of Revolution

Like other progressives, Wilson saw threats arising from rapid change in the industrial world. Revolution, militarism, and imperial rivalries threatened global stability just as surely as labor wars, reckless corporations, and corrupt officials threatened the republic. Wilson opposed radicalism at home and abroad, and he tried to foster orderly change. Stability, like reform, was a process, not a goal but Wilson believed it had to be forced on those who resisted.

Imposing order, the president believed, was both a duty and an opportunity. An expanding commercial power such as the United States had talent, technology, and capital to share. "Prosperity in one part of the world ministers to prosperity everywhere," he declared, but only in safe markets. Imperialism and revolution endangered the trade necessary for peace in the world and growth at home. It was the government's duty to safeguard goods and investments in order to secure American prosperity and its benefits for the world.

This combination of idealism and self-interest, humanitarianism and force, produced a seemingly contradictory foreign policy. Wilson renounced "dollar diplomacy" only to use Taft's tactics himself in China. He atoned for U.S. imperialism but intervened repeatedly in Central America. Secretary of State William Jennings Bryan negotiated a series of "cooling-off" treaties that required arbitration before resorting to war, but Wilson seldom submitted his own policies to arbitration. He believed the United States had a mission to promote democracy, yet he considered many peoples—including Filipinos—unready to govern themselves.

These contradictions are explained by Wilson's view of history. As he saw it, modern commerce and communications were creating a global society with new rules of international conduct. Meanwhile, relics of the past—militarism and revolution—threatened to "throw the world back three or four centuries." Resolving the struggle between the past and the future would require "a new international psychology," new norms and institutions to regulate conflict. Wilson's sympathies lay with Britain and France, but with Europe aflame, the United States, the sole voice of reason, had to remain aloof. "Somebody must keep the great economic processes of the world of business alive," he protested. He was also preoccupied with matters closer at hand. In April 1914, American troops invaded Mexico in an attempt to overthrow its revolutionary government.

> We intend to teach the Mexicans to elect good men.
>
> WOODROW WILSON

The Mexican Revolution

In May 1911, rebels took control of Mexico City, ending over three decades of enforced order and rapid industrialization under the dictatorship of Porfirio Díaz. Díaz and a clique of intellectuals and planners known as the *científicos* had made Mexico one of the world's leading oil exporters. They confiscated communal lands, forcing Indians to farm as tenants on commercial *haciendas*. Foreign investment poured in, and by 1911 Americans owned 40 percent of the property in the country. Mexicans grew to resent foreign business and the regime's taxes. When Francisco Madero's revolt broke out, the army folded, Díaz fled to Spain, and power changed hands in a nearly bloodless coup.

The fall of Díaz hardly troubled the United States: Madero held an election to confirm his presidency. But in February 1913, two weeks before Wilson's inauguration, General Victoriano Huerta seized power and had Madero shot. Mexican states raised armies and revolted against Huerta's regime, beginning one of the twentieth century's longest and bloodiest civil wars. In the mountains south of Mexico City, Emiliano Zapata led a guerilla resistance. Meanwhile, along Mexico's northern border, Venustiano Carranza organized a constitutionalist army.

Wilson denounced Huerta, gave arms to Carranza's soldiers, and sent 7,000 marines to occupy Mexico's largest port, Veracruz, in April 1914. The invasion radicalized the revolution, unifying all sides against the United States. When Carranza deposed Huerta a few months later, he promised to nationalize U.S. oil fields. Wilson pressured Carranza to resign while providing arms to his enemy, Francisco "Pancho" Villa. Villa briefly seized the capital at the end of 1914, but Carranza drove Villa's army north toward the border. Reluctantly, Wilson recognized the Carranza government and cut ties to Villa. Stung by Wilson's betrayal, Villa crossed the border and attacked the 13th Cavalry outpost at Columbus, New Mexico, killing 17 Americans and stealing horses and guns.

Furious, Wilson sent 10,000 troops under General John J. Pershing into Mexico. Pershing never found Villa, but the invasion again unified Mexicans against the United States. Rather than declare war, Wilson ordered Pershing home. After three years of trying to bring

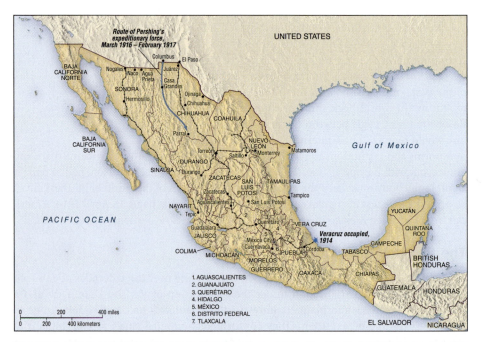

Map 22–1   Mexican Invasion Routes to Veracruz General John Pershing led 10,000 troops, together with observation aircraft and a convoy of trucks, 419 miles into Mexico on a fruitless hunt for Francisco Villa's band. Federal forces loyal to Carranza confronted Pershing near Parral, bringing the U.S. advance to a halt.

democracy and stability to Mexico, Wilson had nothing to show for his efforts. He failed to tame nationalism and revolution in Mexico. The civil war still raged, and American property was more in danger than ever.

Bringing Order to the Caribbean

In principle, Wilson opposed imperialism, but his desire to bring order to neighboring countries led him to use force again and again. He sent the marines into more countries in Latin America than any other president. Marines quashed a revolution in Haiti in 1915, then occupied the country. They landed in the Dominican Republic the following year to supervise an election and stayed to fight a guerilla war until 1924. Wilson kept marines in Honduras, Panama, and Nicaragua and briefly sent troops into Cuba.

Progressive senators wondered why Wilson busted trusts and reorganized banks at home but put the marines at their service abroad. Senators Robert La Follette and George Norris argued that revolutions might be necessary in some countries to protect the many against the few. On August 29, 1914, some 1,500 women, dressed in black, marched down Fifth Avenue in New York City to oppose wars in the Caribbean and Europe. Peace advocates, such as Jane Addams, saw signs of a country being drawn toward war.

A One-Sided Neutrality

As German armies crossed Belgium in August 1914, Wilson declared a policy of strict neutrality. The war took him by surprise, and like Addams he found it "incredible" that civilized nations could display such savagery. His first worry was that America's immigrant communities would take sides. Shortly after the crisis began, 450 steelworkers from Gary, Indiana, enlisted in the Serbian army. Irish Americans, who wanted independence for their homeland, sided with Germany against England. The Allies (Britain, France, Italy, and Russia) and the Central powers (Germany, Austria-Hungary, and Turkey) each used propaganda to manipulate U.S. opinion.

Wilson sent his closest aide, Colonel Edward House, to Europe with offers to broker a peace agreement. Privately the president believed that a German victory would be a catastrophe. Protected by Britain's control of the seas, the United States had expanded its influence during the previous century. In an Allied defeat, he said, "the United States, itself, will have to become a military nation, for Germany will push her conquests into South America." With Europe and possibly Asia controlled by a single power, the United States would be vulnerable and alone.

Modern warfare and commerce made true neutrality difficult. The belligerent powers desperately needed everything the United States had to export. As purchasing agent for France and Britain, J. P. Morgan's firm soon became the world's largest customer, buying more than $3 billion worth of armaments, food, textiles, steel, chemicals, and fuel. U.S. loans to the Allies grew to $2.5 billion by 1917, but the Central powers received only $127 million in credit. Trade with the Central powers meanwhile sank from $170 million to less than $1 million by 1916. An Allied victory would make the United States the world's leading creditor, whereas defeat might mean financial collapse. The United States had not formally taken sides, but the American economy was already in the war on the side of the Allies.

Wilson's response to the British and German naval blockades reinforced the tilt toward the Allies. Both sides violated the "freedom of the seas," Britain with mines and warships,

Germany with submarines. Wilson considered Britain's violation justifiable, but not Germany's. Britain's surface fleet was able to capture civilian ships as required by international law, but a German *Unterseeboot*, or U-boat—a small, fragile submarine—could not do that without giving up the stealth and surprise that were its only weapons.

The *Lusitania*'s Last Voyage

Germany used advertisements in American newspapers to warn against travel on ships bound for the war zone. The State Department was divided. Robert Lansing, the department's counselor, condemned submarine attacks as an offense against law and morality, but Bryan wanted to bar Americans from traveling on belligerent ships. Wilson sided with Lansing and declared that Germany would be held to "strict accountability" for American lives or property.

On the afternoon of May 7, 1915, submarine U-20 sighted the luxury liner *Lusitania* off the coast of Ireland and fired a torpedo that detonated against the starboard side. In 18 minutes the *Lusitania* broke apart and sank. Of almost 2,000 passengers aboard, 1,198 drowned, including 94 children and 124 Americans. The newspapers reacted with rage and horror, but Wilson's advisers again disagreed on how to respond. Bryan wanted to balance a protest with a denunciation of Britain's violation of neutral rights. Wilson ignored him and demanded that submarine warfare stop altogether. He hinted that unless his demands were met, the United States would break relations.

Public opinion was equally divided. Lippmann told a friend in England that "the feeling against war in this country is a great deal deeper than you would imagine by reading editorials." When Germany promised not to attack passenger liners without warning, Wilson accepted this pledge as a diplomatic triumph. It momentarily restored calm, but official and public opinion had turned against Germany. The *Lusitania* crisis, Lippmann predicted, "united Englishmen and Americans in a common grief and a common indignation" and might "unite them in a common war."

The Drift to War

The *Lusitania* disaster divided progressives on the issue of the war. Peace advocates such as Addams, Bryan, and La Follette urged a stricter neutrality. Others believed war, or preparations for war, were justified. Theodore Roosevelt clamored for it. He endorsed the preparedness campaign mounted by organizations such as the National Security League and the American Defense Society. Thousands marched down New York's Fifth Avenue under an electric sign declaring "Absolute and Unqualified Loyalty to Our Country."

Preparedness leagues, headed by businessmen and conservative political figures, called attention to the state of the armed forces, equipped only for tropical wars and lacking trucks, planes, and modern arms. The preparedness campaign appropriated patriotic rituals once reserved for elections. Wilson himself led the parade in Washington in 1916, wearing a red tie, white trousers, and a blue blazer. Hundreds of young Americans, positive that a German victory would mean the defeat of civilization, went to Paris to enlist. The French army soon had an American Volunteer Corps and a squadron of American fliers, the Lafayette Escadrille, whose exploits filled American newspapers. Magazines featured the poems of Alan Seeger, a Harvard graduate who joined the foreign legion. While

>> Plattsburg Training Camp

Dawn rose over Lake Champlain as a special train pulled onto a siding near the old army barracks at Plattsburg, on the lake's New York side. The passengers, young men in their 20s and early 30s, some in civilian clothes, others already in uniform, filed from the cars and stood at attention on the platform. These were no ordinary recruits. They included diplomat and Morgan partner Willard Straight; congressman Thomas Miller; Raynal C. Bolling, a top executive at United States Steel; southern plantation owners; Ivy League professors; the editor of *Vanity Fair*; and the mayor of New York.

They were there for four weeks of push-ups, marches, and intensive military training, although none had actually enlisted in the army. Drill sergeants called them "tourists," but the recruits saw themselves as the bearers of a new martial spirit. The camp was conceived in New York's Harvard Club by an alliance of generals, businessmen, and professors. Leonard Wood, commander of the army's eastern division, wanted to create an army reserve that could be used in a foreign war. University presidents suggested that he organize a summer military camp for college students. Students needed the discipline and exercise, and the army needed educated commanders. Private businessmen provided funds, and the first college camps bivouacked at Gettysburg, Pennsylvania, and Monterey, California, in the summer of 1913.

When war erupted in Europe the following summer, young business leaders clamored for a camp of their own. Over a thousand people jammed the Harvard Club on June 14, 1915, five weeks after the *Lusitania* disaster, to hear Wood announce the Businessmen's Military Training Camp at Plattsburg. Word spread through alumni and professional societies, and 1,300 of "the best and most desirable men" signed up. Young men from the wealthiest and most prestigious families shelled out $30 for a khaki uniform and mess kit.

The press sniped at this new fashion for militarism, but Willard Straight replied that the camp's organizers "do not propose to militarize the American nation. They seek rather to civilize the American military." Harvard was out to show West Point how to run an army, but two weeks of close-formation drill was enough to give the "tourists" a new respect for professional soldiers. The recruits answered reveille at 5:55 A.M. Calisthenics and drill began at 7:25 and went until supper. Top college athletes found it grueling. Regular infantry marched 30 miles in a day, but at the end of four weeks the recruits could barely manage 10.

At evening campfires, recruits discussed politics and war. Theodore Roosevelt, who had three sons and a nephew at the camp, came one evening to denounce "the professional pacifist, the poltroon, and the college sissy" trying to keep the country out of war. Some recruits agreed with Roosevelt that the United States must be prepared for war, but others saw preparedness as a way to avoid war. They agreed that young Americans, and particularly the rich, could benefit from military drill.

continued

AMERICAN LANDSCAPE *continued*

Over the previous decades, the upper class had detached itself from American society, retreating into exclusive schools, neighborhoods, and enclaves, a process known as "social closure." Aloofness undermined its claim to leadership in a democratic society, especially in the military. The regular army came from the rural South and West, from farming and working-class families. Few in the corporate elite sent their sons to West Point and almost none to the enlistment depots. The heroes of the coming war would become the elected leaders of the future, and Plattsburg was Wall Street's chance to claim a share of military glory.

Recruits talked about the wholesome, democratic influence of military training. It instilled "discipline, manliness, and that comradeship in a high common purpose," one observed. A millionaire looked like anyone else in uniform, and a journalist remarked that "each reservist left his worldly goods, his 'pull,' his record of past performances at home." Just as in sports, the only standard was how well one per-

formed now, and the camp included a large number of college athletes. Not surprisingly, recruits saw what one described as the "obvious parallel between a football team and an army." War, he wrote, was the "real game."

In articles and and memoirs, the recruits remembered the emotions stirred by watching the flag lowered at sunset to the strains of a bugle sounding retreat. "I do not believe that anyone in the camp," John J. McCloy, an Amherst College student who would become an adviser to five presidents, told a friend, "no matter how tired or blue he felt, ever 'stood retreat' without having a tiny thrill run up his spine." Like McCloy, many of the young men at Plattsburg fought in World War I, served the federal government in World War II, and ran law firms, industries, embassies, and government agencies during the cold war. For them, Plattsburg was the beginning of America's adventure in world leadership, a place where, as historian Kai Bird wrote, "the upper class elite underwent a conversion experience of patriotism."

Americans slept "pillowed in silk and scented down," Seeger wrote, "I've a rendezvous with death/At midnight in some flaming town." Wilson felt that to shape the world after the war, Americans would have to meet that rendezvous.

The Election of 1916

Although Wilson believed the United States would need to enter the fight, he campaigned for reelection under the slogan "He kept us out of war." The preparedness issue reunited Theodore Roosevelt and the Republicans behind Supreme Court Justice Charles Evans Hughes, who attacked Wilson for failing to defend American honor in Mexico and Europe. Woman suffragists campaigned against Wilson and picketed the White House with signs asking, "Mr. President? How long must women wait for liberty?" Although the

Republicans remained dominant, Hughes was an inept campaigner. He won New York, Pennsylvania, and Illinois but lost in the South and West. Wilson won narrowly, whereas Republicans controlled the House and the Senate. Still, reelection freed Wilson to pursue a more vigorous foreign policy. As Lippmann realized, "What we're electing is a war president—not the man who kept us out of war."

The Last Attempts at Peace

After the election, Wilson launched a new peace initiative. Looking for an opening after years of stalemate, he asked each of the belligerent powers to state its war aims. Each insisted on punishing the other and enlarging its own territories. Before Congress in January 1917, the president called for a "peace without victory," based on self-determination of all nations and the creation of an international organization to enforce peace.

Germany toyed with accepting Wilson's proposals but decided to wait. With the defeat of Russia in 1917, it could shift armies from the eastern front to France. U-boats again torpedoed British passenger liners and American merchant ships. In late February, British intelligence officers showed the U.S. ambassador in London a telegram from the German foreign minister, Arthur Zimmermann, plotting an alliance with Mexico. With the Zimmerman Telegram revealed, if Wilson did not declare war now, Roosevelt declared, he would "skin him alive."

Americans disagreed then, as historians do today, on why the United States went to war. Critics pointed to the corporate interests that stood to gain. Publicly and in private, Wilson stressed two considerations: the attacks on American ships and the peace settlement. The treaty conference would settle scores of issues affecting American interests. Unless it went to war, Wilson told Jane Addams, the United States would have to shout "through a crack in the door."

War Aims

Rain was falling on the evening of April 2, 1917, as Wilson went to ask Congress for war. Some on Pennsylvania Avenue cheered and waved flags, whereas others stared silently at the president's limousine. The war, Wilson told the assembly, was in its last stages. American armies could bring it to a merciful end. The United States had tried to stand apart, but it had failed. Neutrality had provided no safety for travelers or trade. The only hope for avoiding even more dangerous future wars was for the United States to dictate the peace, to establish a "concert of free peoples." This would be a war to end all wars, to make the world safe for democracy.

In urging the vote for war, the president explicitly rejected the aims of the Allies. "We have no quarrel with the German people," he said, but with the kaiser and all other emperors and autocrats who blocked his road to a new world order. Wilson realized, however, that imperial France and Britain did not stand for democracy or self-determination, either. The United States would fight with Britain and France as an "associated power."

Edward House assembled a secret committee, known as the Inquiry, to draft a peace proposal both generous enough to show "sympathy and friendship" to the German people and harsh enough to punish their leaders. Made up of economists, historians, geographers, and legal experts, with Lippmann as its secretary, the Inquiry produced a set of 14 recommendations that redrew the boundaries of Europe, created a league of nations, and

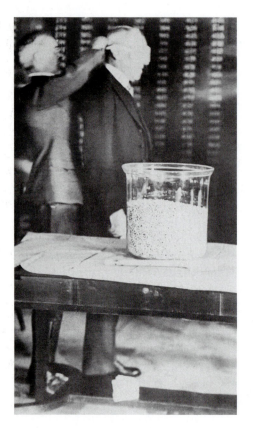

Wilson and the Draft Lottery The American Expeditionary Force (AEF) was the first U.S. army chosen primarily by conscription. The selective service registered 24 million men and chose 3 million of them—some through a draft lottery—to enlist.

based peace on the principles of freedom of the seas, open-door trade, and ethnic self-determination.

The Fight in Congress

During the ovation after Wilson's speech to Congress, one senator stood silently, his arms folded. La Follette told his colleagues that if this was a war for democracy, it should be declared democratically. The country had voted for the peace candidate for president, and there were strong reasons to suspect a declaration would fail a national vote. Representatives found that voters opposed American entry, often by two to one. Midwestern farmers, William Allen White reported from Iowa, "don't seem to get the war."

Prowar representatives blocked La Follette's move for a referendum and brought the declaration to a vote on April 6, when it passed 82 to 6 in the Senate and 373 to 50 in the House. Divisions resurfaced over questions of how to pay for the war and who would fight in it. Wilson wanted universal conscription, the first draft since the Civil War. The 1917 draft law deputized 4,000 local boards to induct men between 18 and 45. Both supporters and opponents believed the draft would mold citizens. It would "break down distinctions of race and class," said one representative, turning immigrants into "new Americans." La Follette countered that the new Americans would be like the new Germans, indoctrinated by the army.

Newspapers and politicians denounced the antiwar progressives as traitors. They had too few votes to stop conscription, but they did create an exemption for conscientious objectors and reduced some taxes used to pay for the war. Opposition voices were soon silenced by patriotic calls for unity. "I pray God," Wilson avowed, "that some day historians will remember these momentous years as the years which made a single people of the great body of those who call themselves Americans."

Mobilizing the Nation and the Economy

News of the war declaration, carried in banner headlines on Easter Sunday, 1917, set the nation abuzz with activity. Wilson recognized that he was asking for an unprecedented effort. Raising an army of over 3 million, supplying it with modern equipment, and transporting it across submarine-infested waters were herculean feats. By midsummer, there were more men at work building barracks than had been in both armies at Gettysburg. Americans would send to Europe 1.8 million tons of meat, 8.8 million tons of grain, and 1.5 million tons of sugar. Factories that produced sewing machines and automobiles would retool to make howitzers and tanks.

The strain war placed on the American people and economy were severe. Wilson and others feared that it could widen political divisions and destroy 15 years of progressive achievements. Others felt that sharing the sacrifices of war would consolidate the gains. "We shall exchange our material thinking for something quite different," the General Federation of Women's Clubs predicted. "We shall all be enfranchised, prohibition will prevail, many wrongs will be righted." Lippmann hoped war would bring a new American revolution.

Enforcing Patriotism

Authorities dealt severely with dissent. Suspicions about the loyalties of ethnic communities and rumors of German saboteurs fed the hysteria. There had already been mysterious explosions. On July 30, 1916, across the river from New York City, the largest arms storage facility in the country blew up. Thousands of pounds of shells and guns bound for Russia were lost. Four days after Wilson declared war, saboteurs struck again, blowing up a munitions factory near Philadelphia and killing 112 workers, mostly women and girls. Federal agents rounded up many aliens, but the fear of internal enemies persisted.

Congress gave the president sweeping powers to suppress dissent. The Espionage Act (1917) and the Sedition Act (1918) effectively outlawed opposition to the war and used the postal service to catch offenders. Although there was no link between the labor movement and sabotage, unions were the prime target. The Justice Department raided the Chicago offices of the Industrial Workers of the World and sent 96 leaders to prison on charges of sedition. William D. "Big Bill" Haywood was sentenced to 20 years. Eugene V. Debs, leader of the Socialist Party, received 10 years for telling Ohioans they were "fit for something better than slavery and cannon fodder."

States also passed laws criminalizing "unpatriotic" activity. Indiana's Council for Defense licensed citizens to raid German homes, prevent church services in German, and make sure German Americans bought war bonds. Towns, schools, and clubs with German-sounding names changed them. East Germantown, Indiana, became Pershing. Hamburgers became "liberty sandwiches." Schools in the Midwest stopped teaching German altogether. Americans who had once proudly displayed their ethnicity now took pains to disguise it.

Pacifist faiths had their own ordeals. Some sects had come to America to avoid conscription in Germany or Russia. Many could not comply with the conscientious objector statute, which required submission to military control. Fifteen hundred Mennonites fled to Canada to avoid being placed in camps. Thirty-four Russian Pentecostals were arrested in Arizona, turned over to the army, court-martialed, and sent to Leavenworth.

The government's propaganda effort was managed by the Committee on Public Information (CPI) under former muckraker George Creel. It made films, staged pageants, and churned out ads, billboards, and press releases. The CPI sold the war by telling Americans they were fighting to save their own homes. One poster showed German bombers over a shattered, headless Statue of Liberty. Like Wilson, propaganda distinguished between

Germany and the German people. CPI leaflets in German offered "Friendly Words to the Foreign Born." It cast immigrants as potential patriots and women as symbols of progress and sacrifice. Creel drafted Charles Dana Gibson, whose "Gibson Girl" ads personified glamour, to depict women as mothers, nurses, and patriotic consumers. As advertising mobilized American thought for the war effort, it also advanced progressive agendas.

Regimenting the Economy

The first prolonged conflict between industrial nations, World War I introduced the term "total war." By 1917 all of the resources, manpower, and productive capacities of the combatants had been mobilized. It soon became clear that the economy of the United States would have to be organized in new ways.

The navy planned a vast shipyard on Hog Island, near Philadelphia, with 250 buildings, 80 miles of railroad track, and 34,000 workers. It would be larger than Britain's seven largest shipyards combined, but in April 1917, Hog Island was 847 acres of swamp. Steelmaker Charles M. Schwab, in charge of the project, signed contracts for machinery, cement, steel, and timber. Materials were loaded on trains headed east. The result was the Great Pile Up, the biggest traffic jam in railroad history. Without enough workers to unload, cars began to back up on sidings in Philadelphia and then all the way back to Pittsburgh and Buffalo, their loads dumped on the outskirts of cities. Schwab begged the railroads to cooperate, to no avail. The voluntary system had failed, and on January 1, 1918, Wilson nationalized the railroads.

The Hog Island fiasco demonstrated the need for supervision of the economy. Wilson created a War Industries Board (WIB) to regulate prices, manufacturing, and transport. The job was enormous, and Wilson found the overseer he needed in Bernard Baruch, a Wall Street financier, who believed in regulation by "socially responsible" businessmen. He recruited corporate executives for top positions and paid them a dollar a year. The president of the Aluminum Company of America became chairman of the WIB's aluminum committee, and a former top executive of John Deere headed the agricultural implements section.

The dollar-a-year men regimented the economy and put business to work for government, but they also guaranteed profits and looked after their own interests. One of their innovations, the "cost-plus" contract, assured contractors the recovery of costs plus a percentage for profit. Under these arrangements, the Black and Decker Company made gun sights, Akron Tire made army cots, and the Evinrude Company stopped making outboard motors and turned out grenades. Each company built up revenues to launch new product lines after the war. Standardization also helped industry. The WIB set standard designs and sizes for everything from shirts to lug nuts. One steel executive observed, "We are all making more money out of this war than the average human being ought to."

Not all businesses submitted willingly to "war socialism." The Ford Motor Company had just set up a national dealer network, and it refused to stop making cars. When other automakers followed suit, the board threatened to cut off the industry's supply of coal and steel. After long negotiations, the automakers agreed to cut production by three-fourths. The delay hurt. When American troops went into battle, they had a grand total of two tanks.

The war economy was a culmination of two movements: Wall Street's drive for corporate consolidation and the progressives' push for federal regulation. Businessmen saw that the WIB could rationalize the economy. These "New Capitalists" wanted to end cutthroat

Hog Island Shipyard Building the massive shipyard at Hog Island was a major feat. The railroad network broke down under the strain, leading Wilson to nationalize the railroads.

competition and make business predictable. They encouraged workers to identify with the company through stock sharing and bonus plans. The WIB's example of government-industry cooperation would serve as a model in national crises to come.

The Great Migration

The war economy gave Americans new choices and opportunities. As factories geared up, they faced a shortage of labor. The draft took eligible employees from the cities, and the usual source of new workers—Europe—was sealed off by a screen of U-boats. Employers did find a ready supply in the South. In small towns and rural junctions, labor recruiters arrived offering free rides to the North and well-paid employment on arrival. Manufacturers came to rely on the labor of former sharecroppers. Westinghouse employed 25 African Americans in 1916; by 1918 it employed 1,500. The Pennsylvania Railroad recruited 10,000 workers from Florida and Georgia. In some northern cities, a thousand migrants were arriving each week. This massive movement from the rural South to the urban North and West came to be called the Great Migration.

Lynchings, intimidation, and a declining southern economy encouraged migration. Almost half a million people came north during the war years—so many that some counties emptied out, creating panic among whites left behind. Mississippi alone lost 75,000 workers. "We must have the Negro in the South," the Macon, Georgia, *Telegraph* pined. "It is the only labor we have. . . . If we lose it, we go bankrupt." Southern states banned recruiters. In some places violence provoked migration. "Every time a lynching takes place in a community down south," one observer noted, "you can depend on it that colored people will arrive in Chicago within two weeks."

African American workers moved into jobs at the bottom of the pay scale: janitors, domestics, and factory hands. Rent, groceries, and other necessities were substantially more expensive in the cities. Still, African American workers could earn wages 70 percent higher than what they were used to at home. Almost no one went back, and the new arrivals adapted to the rhythms of city life. "South State Street was in its glory then, a teeming Negro street with crowded theaters, restaurants, and cabarets," Langston Hughes wrote of Chicago in 1918. Housing was scarce, and African American renters were limited to overcrowded districts wedged between industrial zones and hostile white neighborhoods. W. E. B. DuBois noted that residential patterns in Philadelphia changed dramatically. At the turn of the century African Americans had lived in many neighborhoods, but by the end of the war they were concentrated in the Seventh Ward. Ghetto neighborhoods were both expensive and decrepit. On Chicago's South Side, rents were 15 to 20 percent higher than in white neighborhoods, and the death rate was comparable to that of Bombay, India. White property owners and real estate agents worked to create the ghettos and enforce their boundaries. On Chicago's South Side, the Hyde Park Property Association organized to "Make Hyde Park White." A real estate agent said that African American homeowners "hurt our values." When discrimination failed, dynamite was used. From 1917 to 1919 there were 26 bombings of African American residences in Chicago. On July 2, 1917, in East St. Louis, an arms manufacturing center in southern Illinois, competition for housing and political offices led a mob of white workers to attack "Black Valley," an African American neighborhood along the Southern Railroad track. Forty-seven people were killed and six thousand left homeless.

After East St. Louis, white mobs found it less easy to attack. When a mob invaded a Washington, D.C., ghetto three years later, residents fought back with guns. "New Negroes are determined to make their dying a costly investment for all concerned," an African American newspaper explained drily. The New Negro, urban, defiant, demanding rather than asking for rights, became the subject of admiring and apprehensive reports. Police kept files on suspected militants, but the mobility and anonymity of northern cities translated into freedom.

Reforms Become "War Measures"

On August 3, 1917, thousands of protestors marched in New York under signs demanding "Why not make America safe for democracy?" In the wake of the East St. Louis outrage, the NAACP urged Congress to outlaw lynching as a "war measure." African Americans were not alone in using the president's language to justify reform. Carrie Chapman

Catt told Wilson that he could enact women's suffrage as a "war measure." Advocates of progessive change demanded that the United States practice at home the ideals it fought for abroad.

Suffragists hitched their cause to the national struggle. Catt's National American Woman Suffrage Association (NAWSA) abandoned its state-by-state lobbying to identify women with the national cause. Members sold liberty bonds and knitted socks for the Red Cross, making it clear they expected a constitutional amendment in return. Alice Paul's National Woman's Party (NWP) picketed the White House with signs quoting Wilson's demand for all peoples to "have a voice in their own governments." When Wilson announced his support in 1918, he cited women's war service as the reason. The Nineteenth Amendment was finally ratified in 1920, "so soon after the war," according to Jane Addams, "that it must be accounted as the direct result of war psychology."

As it had for African Americans, the labor shortage increased opportunities for women. Although most women workers were already in the labor force, many took jobs previously considered "inappropriate" for their sex. Women replaced men as bank tellers, streetcar operators, and mail carriers and in heavy-manufacturing firms. Many of these opportunities vanished when the war ended, but in expanding sectors such as finance, communications, and office work, women made permanent gains. By 1920, more than 25 percent worked in offices or as telephone operators, and 13 percent were in the professions. The new opportunities gave women a source of prestige and enjoyment. Alice Hamilton remarked on the "strange spirit of exaltation among the men and women who thronged to Washington, engaged in all sorts of 'war work' and loving it." Army General Order 13 set standards for women's work, including an eight-hour day, prohibitions on working at night or in dangerous conditions, and provisions for rest periods, lunchrooms, and bathrooms. The government also empowered women consumers, encouraging them to report on shopkeepers who charged above the official price.

Wilson authorized a National War Labor Board to intervene in essential industries. The board set an unofficial minimum wage. For the first time the federal government recognized workers' rights to organize, bargain collectively, and join unions. Unskilled workers earned higher real wages than ever before. When the Smith and Wesson Company refused to acknowledge its workers' right to bargain collectively, the army seized the factory and recognized the union. There were limits, however, for the administration. When skilled machinists at the Remington Arms plant made demands the board considered excessive, Baruch threatened to have them drafted and sent to France.

Prohibition did not please workers, either, but beer, wine, and spirits were early casualties of war. The Anti-Saloon League and the Woman's Christian Temperance Union had built a powerful antiliquor coalition by 1916. Congress would have passed Prohibition without war, but temperance became a patriotic crusade. Military regulations prohibited liquor near army camps. Finally, in 1919 the states ratified the Eighteenth Amendment, banning the "manufacture, sale, or transportation of intoxicating liquors." The Anti-Saloon League celebrated the dawn of "an era of clear thinking and clean living." America was "so dry it couldn't spit," according to Billy Sunday. He overstated the case. By some estimates, after the ban illegal speakeasies in New York outnumbered the saloons they replaced. Bootleggers and smugglers slaked American thirsts, but liquor prices rose and consumption declined. Americans never again drank anything like the average two and a half gallons of pure alcohol per person annually imbibed before Prohibition.

The war also lent patriotic zeal to antivice crusaders. During the Progressive Era, muckrakers exposed the police-protection rackets that allowed gambling dens and brothels to thrive. Within days of the declaration of war, reformers identified prostitutes as enemies of the health of American troops. Gonorrhea afflicted a quarter of the Allied forces in France, and middle-class Americans were appalled. Before 1917, reformers targeted commercial vice as a source of political and social corruption, but afterward they directed their efforts at women as carriers of disease.

The army acted against liquor and prostitution to protect the welfare of soldiers, but it did not challenge racial injustice, even when lives were at stake. At camps in the South, it was often unclear who had more authority, uniformed African American soldiers or white local officials. Clashes could easily turn violent. A riot in Houston in August 1917 began when soldiers from nearby Camp Logan rushed to the aid of an African American woman being beaten by police. Twenty policemen and soldiers were killed, and 54 soldiers received life sentences in the largest court-martial in U.S. history.

After the Houston riot, African American units were dispersed across the country, and the army remained segregated. Worse, many southern communities used military discipline to strengthen their own Jim Crow laws. Encouraged by the army's "work or fight" order, which required draft-age men to either enlist or get a job, states and localities passed compulsory work laws that applied to women and older men. The laws were intended to keep laborers in the fields and servants in the kitchens at prewar wages.

In this "war welfare state," the government mediated among labor, industry, and other organized interests. Social activism became a matter of lobbying federal agencies that could either dictate sweeping changes or use wartime powers to maintain the status quo. Success required organization and an ability to tie one's goals to the government's ambitions.

Over There

When the Senate took up the enormous war budget Wilson submitted in April 1917, the finance committee questioned Major Palmer E. Pierce about what would be done with the money. "Clothing, cots, camps, food, pay," he replied, "and we may have to have an army in France." "Good Lord!" exclaimed Senator Thomas Martin of Virginia. "You're not going to send soldiers over there, are you?" After the horrors of the Somme and Verdun, where men were fed to machine guns by the tens of thousands, it hardly seemed reasonable to send Americans to such a place. "One would think that, after almost four years of war, after the most detailed and realistic accounts of murderous fighting, . . . it would have been all but impossible to get anyone to serve," one veteran later recalled. "But it was not so, we and many thousands of others volunteered."

Americans went to France optimistically believing they could change the war and the peace. Trench warfare was not for them. They planned to fight a war of movement, sweeping in formations across open fields, like those at Antietam and Gettysburg. To a remarkable degree, they got the war they wanted. Europeans watched their civilization destroy itself in the Great War, but Americans saw theirs rising. Soldiers, "doughboys," said so in their letters, echoing the words of their leaders, their newspapers, and the volumes of poetry they carried with them into battle.

Citizens into Soldiers

Enlisting, training, and transporting soldiers began in a rush. Camps housing 400,000 recruits went up in the first 30 days. Conscription went smoothly, and soon 32 camps were housing 1.3 million men. Commander John J. Pershing arrived in France in June with 40,000 men and the first of some 16,000 women who would serve in the American Expeditionary Force (AEF).

Neither the Wilson administration nor the Allies initially anticipated that soldiers would be the United States' main contribution to the war effort. Britain urgently needed financial support, and Wilson advanced $200 million immediately, the first of an eventual $10 billion in loans to the Allies. Funds, food, and ammunition were needed more urgently than men, but that changed in October 1917, when German and Austrian forces smashed through the Italian lines at Caporetto, capturing 275,000 men and finishing the war on that front. When the Bolshevik Revolution curtailed Russian resistance in the east in November, Britain and France saw that by the next spring Germany would be able to mass its armies on the line from Belgium to Switzerland and break through to Paris. The war became a race to the Western Front between the United States and Germany.

Getting troops to the war required ships, but the American merchant fleet was smaller in 1917 than it was during the Civil War. For a time the United States had to cut back draft calls because it lacked ships to transport soldiers. The navy, meanwhile, cured the U-boat problem. The American destroyer fleet drove submarines from the sea lanes with depth charges, allowing the Allies to convoy effectively for the first time. By July 18, some 10,000 troops a day boarded the "Atlantic Ferry" for the ride to France.

The Fourteen Points

In December 1917, the Inquiry sent the president a memorandum titled "The War Aims and the Peace Terms It Suggests." Wilson redrafted it and presented it to Congress on January 8, 1918. The Fourteen Points outlined U.S. objectives, but more fundamentally they offered an entirely new basis for peace. Unlike nineteenth-century wars waged for limited territorial or political objectives, the Great War was a total war, fought for unlimited aims. The principal belligerents—Britain, France, Russia, Germany, and Austria-Hungary— were global empires. Germany hoped both to defeat Britain and take its empire. France wanted to destroy Germany's future as a great power, economically and militarily. Wilson replaced these imperial visions of total victory with a peace based on limited gains for nations, not empires.

The Fourteen Points addressed four themes: national self-determination; freedom of the seas; enforcement of peace by a league of nations; and open diplomacy. The Inquiry's memorandum included maps marked with new European boundaries based on national, ethnic identities. The new state of Poland, for instance, should govern only territories with "indisputably Polish populations." Point three restated the Open Door, urging international free trade, reflecting Wilson's hope of eliminating what he saw as the two leading causes of war, imperial ambition and commercial rivalry. By calling for an end to secret diplomacy, he appealed directly to the people of Europe. The expectation was that the hope of a just peace would weaken the enemy nations' will and inspire the Allies to fight harder. Creel printed 60 million copies and had them distributed around the world. Planes dropped copies over Germany and Austria.

Wilson hoped the Fourteen Points would dispel both the old dream of empire and the new one of socialist revolution. On November 7, two months before Wilson presented the points to Congress, Russian workers overthrew the Provisional Government of Alexander Kerensky. The one-party regime of the Bolsheviks, led by Vladimir Lenin, summoned workers everywhere to rise against their governments and to make peace without indemnities or annexations. "The crimes of the ruling, exploiting classes in this war have been countless. These crimes cry out for revolutionary revenge." In December, Lenin revealed the contents of the secret treaties, unmasking the imperial ambitions of the Allies. He sued for peace based on the principle of self-determination. The Council of People's Commissars allocated 2 million rubles to encourage revolutions around the world and called "upon the working classes of all countries to revolt."

Two world leaders—Lenin and Wilson—now offered radically different visions of the new world order, and Lenin was putting his into effect. The Bolsheviks' contempt for democracy angered Wilson, but he hoped that Russia would stay in the war. Those hopes ended with the Treaty of Brest-Litovsk, signed by Russia and Germany in March 1918. The treaty showed the fearful price of defeat in modern war. Russia lost the Ukraine, Poland, and Finland, most of its iron, steel, and best farmland, and one-quarter of its population. Those assets went into the German war machine, which began transferring 10 divisions a month to the west, its eastern front now secure.

Wilson was the first, but not the last, American president to be haunted by the specter of a German-Russian alliance, uniting the immense war-making resources of Europe and Asia. In Wilson's strategic vision, the great land powers of Eurasia, not Alfred Thayer Mahan's sea powers, most threatened U.S. security. He refused to recognize the Bolshevik government and sent 7,000 American troops to Russia to support anti-Bolshevik forces on the eastern front. U.S. and Japanese forces invaded Siberia from the east. The Bolshevik government now counted the United States among its enemies. Meanwhile, the battle for the control of Europe was about to begin.

The Final Offensive

The German high command knew the spring offensive would be the last. Their exhausted economy no longer could supply food or ammunition for a sustained effort. Bread lines, strikes, and industrial breakdowns foreshadowed the chaos that would follow defeat. Risking everything, the German commander Erich Ludendorff launched his offensive on March 21, 1918. Shock troops hurled the British Fifth Army back to Amiens. In May they penetrated French lines as far as Soissons, 37 miles from Paris. As gaps split the lines, French general Ferdinand Foch and General Douglas Haig of Britain appealed urgently to Pershing to put American troops under British and French command. Pershing opposed the idea. He wanted the American army to play its own part in the war.

Pershing criticized European commanders for remaining on the defensive instead of "driving the enemy out into the open and engaging him in a war of movement." Trained at West Point in Civil War tactics, he imagined himself a General Grant replacing European McClellans and saw trenches as symbols of inertia. Pershing favored massed assaults in which the sheer numbers of American troops would overwhelm the Germans, rifles against machine guns. In seeing Europe's war as a replay of the U.S. Civil War, Pershing revealed a habit of mind that would typify American geopolitical thinking for the next century: the belief that Americans could understand the world through the prism of their own experience. He was not alone in wanting a decisive alternative to trench warfare. Billy Mitchell, head of the army's aviation section, noted that "we could cross the lines of these contending armies in a few minutes in our aeroplanes."

On May 27, German divisions pierced French lines at Château-Thierry and began advancing on Paris at a rate of 10 miles a day. The French government considered whether to abandon the capital or surrender. Bowing to urgent requests, Pershing threw the AEF into the breach. Column upon column of fresh American troops filled the roads from Paris to the front. "We are real soldiers now and not afread [sic] of Germans," John F. Dixon, an African American infantryman from New York, wrote home. "Our boys went on the battlefield last night singing." Ahead lay five German divisions, poison gas, minefields, rolling artillery barrages, and machine guns in interlocking fields of fire. The Germans were stopped, but at a fearful cost. The marine brigade that took Belleau Wood suffered 4,600 casualties, half the force. Without artillery or tanks, they assaulted machine gun nests head-on, with rifles.

By mid-July, the initiative passed to the Allies. On September 12, Foch allowed Pershing to try his tactics against the St. Mihiel salient, a bulge in the French lines which, unknown to the Allies, the Germans had already begun to evacuate. The doughboys raced behind the retreating enemy past their planned objectives. Pershing was delighted.

Map 22–2 Western Front, 1918 On the western front, the opposing armies fought from trenches fortified with earthworks and barbed wire. The parallel trench lines stretched thousands of miles from the North Sea to Switzerland.

The Western Front From 1914 to 1918, the western front was the largest metropolis on earth, in Robert Crowley's phrase, an "unreal city" whose inhabitants—8,000 of whom died each day—worked in an industry of destruction.

St. Mihiel had vindicated his strategy, and he yearned for another chance. It came two weeks later, at the battle of the Meuse-Argonne.

Ten miles northwest of Verdun, the Argonne Forest contained some of the most formidable natural and man-made defenses on the western front. Atop parallel ridges lay three fortified trench lines, *Stellungen*—barriers of concrete pillboxes, barbed wire, artillery, and observation posts. Half a million German troops had defended these fortifications for four years. Against this force, Pershing arrayed the American First Army, 1,031,000 men. The average doughboy at the Meuse-Argonne had a total of four months of training, and some had as little as 10 days. Pershing's battle plan called for overwhelming the German defenses with speed and numbers, reaching the second trench line, 10 miles inside the German front, the first day.

"Moving slowly forward, never heeding the bursting shells, nor gas, we followed a road forking to the left . . . into no man's land. It was soon noticed that we were in the bracket of a German barrage," a soldier wrote from the battlefield. They broke through the first line of German trenches after a day and a half; then the battle turned into a deadly crawl. In two weeks of fighting, 26,277 Americans died. French soldiers reported seeing the American dead lying in rows, cut down by machine guns as they marched in formation. Finally, on November 10, American troops reached their objective and dynamited the rail line connecting the cities of Metz and Sedan. Meanwhile, Germany announced that it would accept the Fourteen Points as the basis for an armistice and negotiations. At 11:00 A.M. on November 11, 1918, the guns fell silent.

American intervention had been decisive. The American economy, two and a half times the size of Germany's, lent its industrial and agricultural strength to the Allies at a crucial moment. American military power also tipped the balance. Pershing failed to transform strategy—it remained a mechanized war of attrition until the end—but by striking the final blow, Americans had the illusion that their way of war had been triumphant. American losses, 116,516 dead, were smaller than those of the British (908,371), the French (1.4 million), or the Germans (1.8 million), but they still show the colossal destructiveness of industrial war. In just six months, the United States suffered twice as many combat deaths as it would in the Vietnam War and almost a third as many as in World War II.

Americans and Europeans fought two vastly different wars on the same battlefields. The Americans' war was swift and victorious, but the Europeans experienced a catastrophe that consumed an entire generation. For Europeans, their faith in modernity and in the ability of science and democracy to create a better future vanished forever. Confidence in the inevitability of progress became a distinctive feature of U.S. culture in the postwar era. In much of the world "American" became almost synonymous with "modern," but not everywhere. In the East another political and economic system shouted its claim to the future.

Revolutionary Anxieties

Americans celebrated the armistice with bonfires, church bells, automobile horns, and uplifted voices. Wilson told Congress that "everything for which America fought has been accomplished," but he observed that the situation in Russia cast doubt on the durability of peace. Even before the armistice, German revolutionaries took power in Bavaria. Over the next months, revolutions broke out throughout eastern Europe. From the trenches of Flanders to the Sea of Japan, not a single government remained intact, and in Moscow the new Soviet state towered above the ruins of the old regimes.

Wilson in Paris

For Wilson, the moment he had planned for in 1917 had arrived—the United States could help set the terms of peace—but war had exhausted the president. Confident that the public would view the nation's victory as his victory, he committed mistakes. Had he remained in Washington, some historians argue, he could have taken credit for the peace while keeping a close eye on his critics. Instead, he went to Paris, staking the treaty's success on his own popularity. He passed up a chance to include in the delegation a prominent Republican, such as Henry Cabot Lodge, who could guide the treaty through Congress.

> The Department of Justice has undertaken to tear out the radical seeds that have entangled American ideas in their poisonous theories.
>
> ATTORNEY GENERAL
> A. MITCHELL PALMER
> 1920

Council of Four Peace Conference Ending World War I The Big Four. From left to right, David Lloyd George of Great Britain, Vittorio Orlando of Italy, Georges Clemenceau of France, and Woodrow Wilson of the United States gather outside Hotel Crillon before the Paris Peace Conference in 1919.

In December 1918, Walter Lippmann, now an army captain, watched Wilson's triumphal entry into Paris. Crowds lined the streets, and as the procession crossed the Pont du Concorde, a great cheer echoed off the walls of the Chamber of Deputies. "Never has a king, never has an emperor received such a welcome," *L'Europe Nouvelle* declared. For the next month, Wilson toured France, Italy, and Britain to cries of "Viva Veelson." "They say he thinks of us, the poor people," a workingman remarked, "that he wants us all to have a fair chance; that he is going to do something when he gets here that will make it impossible for our government to send us to war again. If he had only come sooner!"

By the time Wilson arrived for treaty talks at the Palace of Versailles, two of the Fourteen Points had already been compromised. Britain refused to accept the point on freedom of the seas, which would thwart the use of the Royal Navy in a future conflict. Wilson also undercut his own position on point six, respect for Russia's sovereignty, as American troops were occupying Russian Siberia. Wilson was unable to prevent Britain, France, and Japan from dividing Germany's colonies among themselves and imposing harsh peace terms. Germany had to sign a humiliating "war guilt" clause and pay $33 billion in reparations, enough to cripple its economy for decades. Wilson concentrated on the League of Nations, which might make up for the treaty's other weaknesses and provide some safety against the rising tide of revolution. He took the lead in drafting the League Covenant, which committed each member to submit disputes to arbitration and pledged them to take action against "any war or threat of war."

The Senate Rejects the League

To many observers in the United States the Treaty of Versailles betrayed the goals Americans had fought to attain. "This is Not Peace," declared the *New Republic*. Congress saw the League of Nations less as a way to prevent wars than as a guarantee that the United States would be involved. Americans were "far more afraid of Lenin than they ever were of the Kaiser," Lippmann wrote. To Republican leaders such as Henry Cabot Lodge, the United States' best bet was to look to its own security, keep its options open, and work out its international relations independently rather than as part of an alliance or league.

In March 1919, before the treaty was concluded, Lodge and 38 other senators—more than enough to defeat the treaty—signed a petition opposing the League of Nations. James A. Reed of Missouri said the covenant would turn American foreign policy over

AMERICA AND THE WORLD
··

>> The Influenza Pandemic of 1918

The 57th Vermont Pioneer Infantry marched for hours through the rain on the night of September 29, 1918, from Camp Merritt, New Jersey, to ferries that carried them down the Hudson to Hoboken, where they boarded the U.S.S. *Leviathan* for the trip to France. The 9,000 wet, tired soldiers and 200 nurses aboard the country's largest and fastest troop transport were nervous about U-boats in the Atlantic, but they had a deadlier enemy, one that came on board with the men of the 57th.

Within hours of embarkation, every bed in the ship's infirmary was full, and every patient had symptoms all too familiar to military doctors: aches in the legs and back, nosebleed, and, in extreme cases, the blue lips and ears, the thin, gasping breaths that indicated advanced pneumonia. But though doctors recognized the signs, they knew nothing about how to treat or prevent Spanish influenza. They could only comfort patients and try to separate the sick from the well on the overloaded ship. By the time it arrived in France, 1,700 passengers were down with "the flu." The disease would kill 290.

The 1918 pandemic affected nearly every spot on the globe, killing over 30 million people, far more than died in the world war. Called "Spanish" because the king of Spain was the first well-known figure to die, the flu was first observed at Fort Riley, Kansas, where the virus may have jumped from pigs to humans. War and commerce accelerated its spread. Men from all of Europe and colonial nations in Asia and Africa came together in the trenches and then carried the disease to every continent. In August the flu mutated into an exceptionally lethal strain. Patients showed signs of massive pneumonia and usually died within three days.

It spread westward across North America, following the railroads, and within weeks encircled the world in a fatal embrace, killing 6 million in India and 675,000 in the United States. In Cincinnati, Ohio, and Harbin, China, farmers noticed that the disease killed hogs in the same proportion that it killed humans, roughly one in ten. A steamer from San Francisco put in at Tahiti on November 16, and within the next three weeks 10 percent of the population died. Isolated habitations newly tied to global trade and communications were hit hardest. The virus arrived in Eskimo villages on postal dogsleds and by camel caravan to Arabian towns. Australia closed its ports in a vain effort to shut out the disease.

At the Paris Peace Conference, delegate and Plattsburg veteran Willard Straight died, and President Wilson, Walter Lippmann, Edward House, and the entire American delegation were sick. At the height of the pandemic in Philadelphia, churches, schools, saloons, and theaters were shut; San Francisco required everyone to wear surgical masks in public. Trolley cars were used as hearses, and the dead were interred in mass graves. Katherine Anne Porter, who nearly died, described the "noiseless houses with the shades drawn, empty streets, the dead cold light of tomorrow."

continued

AMERICA AND THE WORLD *continued*

World war aroused a fervid nationalism, but the pandemic revealed that all nations were equally powerless in the face of catastrophe on this scale. Citizens accused their governments of apathy. The British Raj was in "a state of coma," the Bombay *Chronicle* complained. At Cartwright, on Canada's Labrador Coast, a minister wrote bitterly of his "resentment at the callousness of the authorities, who sent us the disease by mail-boat, and then left us to sink or swim." American soldiers in Brest mutinied, demanding to be released from flu-infested Camp Pontanezen.

One of the first acts of the new League of Nations in 1920 was to establish an international health organization to track epidemics. Agents at port cities collected reports of influenza, typhus, smallpox, cholera, and other plagues and sent them by telegraph to centers at Geneva and Singapore, allowing quarantines to be established or lifted when danger passed. Quarantines disrupted trade, and the League wanted to control panic as much as disease. In 1948, the service became the World Health Organization (WHO), an affiliate of the United Nations.

Nearly a century later, air transport and global food-supply chains have made every epidemic into a potential pandemic. Outbreaks of communicable disease—or livestock infections, such as mad cow disease—touch off a global response. In March 2003, a strange pneumonia appeared in China, Canada, Vietnam, and Singapore, reviving memories of the 1918 flu. A WHO doctor, an Italian tending an American patient in a Hanoi hospital, identified it as a new virus: severe acute respiratory syndrome (SARS). The WHO issued travel alerts, established quarantine procedures at airports, and sent epidemiological teams to trace the outbreak to its source. National governments tried to conceal the extent and danger of the disease from the media, but the WHO prevailed, and the outbreak was contained. Still, experts counted us lucky. No cure has yet been found for viral diseases, and had SARS spread at the rate of the Spanish flu, the toll would have numbered in the millions. In April 2009, a lethal flu virus—transferred, like the 1918 strain, from pigs—emerged in Mexico and spread through New York and Toronto to the rest of the world. Once again, the WHO mobilized a global response. For disease trackers, 1918 remains the standard for how destructive a modern plague can be—and might be again.

to foreigners. Editorials feared that American troops would be summoned to settle blood feuds in the Balkans. Wilson expected to fight, but he believed that the Senate would not reject the treaty.

In September, Wilson went "over the heads" of Congress and stumped for the treaty on a nationwide tour. He assured listeners in Sioux Falls that "the peace of the world cannot be established without America." He promised the citizens of Salt Lake City that China's independence would be respected. Traveling more than 8,000 miles and speaking before large audiences without loudspeakers took a toll on his health. After a speech in Pueblo, Colorado, he became so ill that he was rushed back to Washington, where he suffered a stroke that left him partially paralyzed and unable to concentrate for more than a few minutes a day. Mrs. Wilson and the president's physician kept his condition a secret and refused to allow anyone to see him.

With Wilson secluded in the White House, the Senate voted against ratification. To the end, Wilson refused to allow Senate Democrats to accept any modifications. Even Lippmann's *New Republic*, a mouthpiece for Wilson throughout the war, called the treaty's demise "desirable and wholesome." Lodge and the Republicans were not ready for isolation, but they preferred diplomatic strategies based on economic strength rather than a relatively weak military. They also saw Latin America as more critical than Europe to U.S. security. Meanwhile, European governments organized the League of Nations without delegations from the United States or the Soviet Union.

Over the next decade, U.S. influence abroad grew enormously. American automobiles, radios, and movies could be seen in far corners of the globe. The United States still practiced cautious diplomacy in Europe and Asia, to avoid being drawn into what the *New York Tribune* called the "vast seething mass of anarchy extending from the Rhine to the Siberian wastes."

Red Scare

On May 1, 1919, a dozen or more mail bombs were sent to prominent Americans: J. P. Morgan, John D. Rockefeller, senators, cabinet officials, and Supreme Court Justice Oliver Wendell Holmes. None of the packages reached its intended target, but one injured a maid in the home of Senator Thomas Hardwick and another exploded at the residence of Attorney General A. Mitchell Palmer in Washington, nearly injuring Franklin and Eleanor Roosevelt, who lived next door. Investigations later showed that the bombings were the work of lone lunatics, but many people quickly concluded that the United States was under attack. Since the Russian Revolution, newspapers, evangelists, and government officials had fed fears of Bolshevism. Revolution, Palmer alleged, was "licking at the altars of the churches, leaping into the belfry of the school bell, crawling into the sacred corners of American homes."

Revolutions in Europe terrified conservatives in the United States and led them to look for Soviet terrorists, particularly among immigrants and unionized workers. They drew no distinctions among Socialists, anarchists, Communists, and labor unionists; they were all "red." Seattle's mayor called in the army to break a dockworkers' strike. When steelworkers in Gary, Indiana, struck for higher wages and shorter hours in September 1919, Judge Elbert Gary, president of U.S. Steel, denounced them as followers of Russian "anarchy and Bolshevism." During the war they had worked 12 hours a day, 7 days a week, for an average wage of $28 a week. With the help of local loyalty leagues, Gary broke the strike.

Using the patriotic rhetoric of the war, industry leaders labeled strikers as dangerous aliens. They persuaded allies in the courts to take action, and a series of Supreme Court decisions made union activity virtually illegal. In 1919 the Court allowed antitrust suits to be filed against unions and later outlawed boycotts and picketing. Then, in January 1920, a series of crackdowns known as the Palmer raids rounded up and deported

The Sacco and Vanzetti Trial The trial of Sacco and Vanzetti, depicted here by Ben Shahn, came to symbolize the arbitrary injustices of the Red Scare. Their trial became an international cause célèbre.

250 members of the Union of Russian Workers. In one night, 4,000 suspected Communists were arrested in raids across the country.

The most notorious case associated with the "Red Scare" began in May 1920 when Nicola Sacco and Bartolomeo Vanzetti, a shoemaker and a fish peddler, were arrested for robbing a shoe company in South Braintree, Massachusetts. Two men died of gunshot wounds during the robbery, and ballistics experts claimed the bullets came from Sacco's gun. The trial, however, focused less on the evidence than on the fact that the defendants were Italian and anarchists. The state doctored evidence and witnesses changed testimony, but the judge favored the prosecution. The appeals lasted six years, as protests for their release mounted. With the execution approaching, labor parties organized worldwide boycotts of American products. Riots in Paris took 20 lives. Uruguayan workers called a general strike. Governments called on the president to intervene, but on August 23, 1927, Sacco and Vanzetti died in the electric chair.

Americans who had talked in 1917 about making the world safe for democracy now seemed ready to restrict their own freedoms out of fear. Lippmann found it "incredible that an administration announcing the most spacious ideals in our history should have done more to endanger fundamental American liberties than any group of men for a hundred years." By the end of 1920, the terror subsided, but labor unions and social radicals would have to fight the charge of communism for decades to come.

Conclusion

Wilson tried to lead America toward what he called a new world order, in which nations and international law would count more than empires and in which the United States could light the way toward progress, stability, and peace. He failed to recognize that for many Americans this future was filled with terrors, as well as promise. The strains of war had introduced new divisions into American society. Progressivism, which had given coherence and direction to social change, was a spent force. The growth of federal administration, the new powers of big business, internal migrations, and new social movements and values added up to what Lippmann called a "revolutionary world." Many of the changes that began during the war had not fully played out, nor were their consequences apparent, but Americans entered the 1920s with a sense of uneasiness. They knew that their nation was now the world's strongest, but they were unsure about what that might mean for their lives.

>> Timeline

▼1911
Mexican Revolution begins

▼1912
Woodrow Wilson elected president

▼1914
U.S. troops occupy Veracruz, Mexico
World War I begins

▼1915
U.S. troops occupy Haiti (until 1934)
Lusitania sunk

▼1916
U.S. forces invade Mexico in search of Pancho Villa
U.S. forces enter the Dominican Republic
Woodrow Wilson reelected

▼1917
Russian czar abdicates; parliamentary regime takes power
U.S. declares war on Germany
East St. Louis riot
Houston riot
October Revolution overthrows Russian government; Lenin takes power

▼1918
Wilson announces U.S. war aims: the Fourteen Points
Wilson nationalizes railroads
Sedition Act outlaws criticism of the U.S. government
U.S. troops stop German advance
Wilson sends troops to Siberia
Armistice ends fighting on the western front
Influenza pandemic peaks in September

▼1919
Eighteenth Amendment outlaws manufacture, sale, and transport
    of alcoholic beverages
Versailles Treaty signed in Paris
Mail bombs target prominent government and business figures
Gary, Indiana, steel strike
U.S. Senate rejects Versailles Treaty

▼1920
Nineteenth Amendment secures the vote for women
Palmer raids arrest thousands of suspected Communists
Sacco and Vanzetti arrested on charges of robbery and murder

Review Questions

1. Did the war help or hurt the progressive movement?

2. Allied commanders wanted to use American troops as a reserve, but Pershing wanted his soldiers to enter the battle as an army. Why was that so important to him?

3. Did Senate Republicans reject the League of Nations because they wanted the United States to withdraw from the world, or because they wanted to deal with the world in a different way?

4. Managing the pace of change posed a tricky problem for leaders in the early twentieth century. How did Wilson try to control the dynamic of social and political change? What methods of change was he unwilling to accept?

5. Why were American leaders so much more concerned about sedition and dissent during World War I than they were during the Civil War or World War II?

6. How did mobilization for war advance the progressive agenda? In what ways did it set progressives back?

For further review materials and resource information, please visit www.oup.com/us/ofthepeople

The Modern Nation
1920-1928

>> "The Queen of the Waves"

On August 6, 1926, Gertrude Ederle walked across the beach at Cape Gris-Nez on the French coast. Her body and her bright red swimsuit were heavily greased. At 7:00 A.M., the 19-year-old New Yorker plunged into the water and began to swim toward the coast of England.

"Trudy," the daughter of a German immigrant butcher, was a champion distance swimmer who had won medals at the 1924 Olympics, but no woman had ever completed the long, hazardous swim across the English Channel. Only five men had accomplished the feat. Ederle had tried and failed the year before. Exhausted, she had been pulled from the water by her coach.

This time was different. Despite the tides, the chill water, and the threat of sharks, Ederle persevered, spurred on by her competitive instincts, her eagerness to please her mother, and her father's promise to buy her a new car if she succeeded.

Inspired by thoughts of that car, Ederle fought the choppy waves and hunted for a favorable tide. Finally, after 14 hours and 31 minutes in the water, she came ashore at Kingsdown at 9:40 P.M. Ederle had become the first woman to swim the channel and had made the crossing faster than any of the men before her. "I am a proud woman," Trudy announced as she walked up the English beach.

Back home, newspapers trumpeted Ederle's stunning achievement in page-one headlines and analyzed it in editorials. Ederle returned to a tumultuous ticker tape parade in New York. "No President or king, soldier or statesman," reported the *New York Times*, "has ever enjoyed such an enthusiastic and affectionate outburst of acclaim by the metropolis as was offered to the butcher's daughter . . . the 'Queen of the Waves.'" President Calvin Coolidge sent his congratulations. Trudy was overwhelmed with offers to endorse products and to appear on stage and in the movies.

continued

>> AMERICAN PORTRAIT *continued*

Gertrude Ederle's enormous reception said a great deal about the United States in the 1920s. Again at peace, America could enjoy the exploits of a long-distance swimmer. A dynamic industrial economy seemed effortlessly to produce plenty of cars, movies, and prosperity.

Ederle herself exemplified a new national culture, rooted in the needs of the booming consumer economy, that emphasized the importance of pleasure. Breaking with the past, this modern culture celebrated leisure activities such as dancing, channel swimming, and other diversions. Ederle loved playing the ukulele and "all normal pleasures, including a jazzy dance now and then." The new culture glorified the purchase and consumption of material goods such as the car Ederle wanted and the merchandise she advertised. The teenage swimmer embodied still other aspects of the new culture—its fascination with youth, its approval of a more indulgent, child-centered family life, and its infatuation with pleasure-seeking, independent, nontraditional women.

Ederle also exemplified the resurgent individualism that shaped the staunch Republican politics of the 1920s. She seemed to prove that individuals could still achieve great things and find happiness in an increasingly bureaucratized society.

In the euphoria of the ticker tape parade, it was easy to conclude that Americans welcomed the emerging cultural and political order as much as they welcomed Trudy Ederle. In fact, many people were troubled by the changes of the 1920s. The modern order did not reflect the values of millions of Americans. Neither did it speak to troubling social and economic inequalities. The new cultural and political order faced a powerful backlash, just as Ederle faced a hostile tide in the English Channel. Nevertheless, like the swimmer, the new culture and politics seemed to overcome all opposition as the decade moved to a close.

Common Threads

>> How did the Industrial Revolution continue to affect culture and politics, as well as the economy?

>> What differentiated the modern culture of the 1920s from the popular culture of the Gilded Age and the Progressive Era?

>> Why did individualism continue to be such an important force in American life?

>> How did the Republican New Era of the 1920s mark a break from the progressive politics of the 1900s–1910s?

>> What were the long-term implications of a political and cultural order so dependent on material prosperity?

A Dynamic Economy

By and large, the 1920s were a prosperous time for America. After a recession during 1920 and 1921, the economy continued to grow. Consumer prices remained steady throughout the decade, and jobs were plentiful; the unemployment rate went as low as 1.8 percent in 1926. Wages jumped: the nation's net income—the value of its earnings from labor and property—leapt from $64.0 billion in 1921 to $86.8 billion in 1929. This prosperity was driven by a dynamically evolving industrial economy boosted by new technologies, increased efficiency, a maturing automobile industry, and new businesses.

Despite general prosperity, the transformation of the economy involved defeats for organized labor and decline for many farmers. The relative weakness of agriculture and the strength of industry helped to turn the United States into a predominantly urban nation. In the prosperous 1920s, as always, industrial capitalism was a transforming force.

The Development of Industry

Several long-term factors shaped the development of American industry in the 1920s. Searching for more efficient production, businessmen made use of a flood of new technologies and other innovations, plus greater use of technical expertise. More patents were issued for new inventions—421,000 of them—than in any preceding decade. During the 1920s, the number of engineers in the country nearly doubled.

The switch from coal to electricity, under way since the 1910s, was an important innovation. By the end of the 1920s, electricity powered more than two-thirds of American manufacturing plants. Henry Ford's car company pioneered another critical innovation, the system that became known as Fordism, or mass production. By the 1910s, Ford, like other American manufacturers, used interchangeable parts, simple and accurate machine tools, and electric power to speed output at its Highland Park plant in Detroit. However, production was slowed by traditional manufacturing practice. Frames, transmissions, and other key subassemblies waited on stands while teams of workers moved from one stand to another. Eager to meet the rising demand for the popular Model T car, Ford's managers reversed the process by "moving the work to the men." Beginning in 1913, conveyor belts and chains sent subassemblies past groups of stationary workers. Instead of making an entire engine, a worker might tighten a few bolts or install a single part. The results were astonishing: in 1914, Ford produced 300,000 Model Ts; in 1923, more than 2 million. Other manufacturers raced to copy Ford's techniques.

Mass production, electrification, and other innovations spurred an extraordinary increase in productivity for American industry. Output per worker skyrocketed 72 percent from 1919 to 1929.

Along with increased productivity, the rise of several industries drove the economy. Auto production now dominated as textiles, railroads, iron, and steel had earlier. In 1921, there were 9.3 million cars on American roads; by 1929, there were 23 million. Producing all those cars stimulated demand for plate glass, oil, gasoline, and rubber.

Other sectors of the economy also grew rapidly. The demand for processed foods, household appliances, office machinery, and chemicals increased dramatically. Emerging industries such as aircraft demonstrated their potential importance.

Ford Assembly Line Mass production at work: the assembly line at the Ford Motor Company plant in Dearborn, Michigan, 1928.

Arguably the first powered, fixed-wing flight had occurred in December 1903, when Wilbur and Orville Wright's "Flyer" flew 120 feet in 12 seconds over the beach at Kitty Hawk, North Carolina. But the civilian airplane industry did not take off until the 1920s. Aircraft production rose from less than 300 in 1922 to more than 6,000 in 1929. By then, fledgling airlines were flying passengers on scheduled flights.

The Trend Toward Large-Scale Organization

The development of industry reinforced the trend toward large-scale organization that was basic to U.S. capitalism (see Chapter 17). Only giant corporations, with thousands of employees and hundreds of millions of dollars in capitalization, had the financial resources to pay for mass production. A wave of mergers meant that these big businesses controlled more factories and assets than ever. By 1929, corporations produced 92 percent of the nation's manufactured goods.

The largest firms also benefited from more efficient organization. When the recession of 1920 and 1921 left them with too many unsold goods, companies reorganized. Top managers, aided by financial, legal, and other experts, now oversaw semiautonomous divisions that supplied different markets. At General Motors, for example, the Chevrolet division produced huge numbers of relatively inexpensive cars, while the Cadillac division turned out a smaller number of expensive cars. The new system made corporations more flexible, efficient, and responsive to changes in demand.

Corporate growth was not confined to industry. Chains such as A. & P. grocers and F. W. Woolworth variety stores increased their share of retail sales from 4 percent to 20 percent. One percent of the nation's banks managed nearly half of the country's financial assets. By 1929, just 200 corporations held about one-fifth of national wealth.

Giant firms and their leaders had often been targets of hostility and reform during the Progressive Era, but the decade's prosperity led many Americans to soften their attitude toward business. There were fewer calls to break up or regulate giant corporations. Big-businessmen had seemed to be selfless patriots during World War I. Now their companies were apparently creating a new period of economic well-being. To ensure a better image, businessmen paid for public relations campaigns that stressed their commitment to ethical behavior and social service. Basking in the glow of public approval, big business was confident about its role in the nation's destiny.

The Transformation of Work and the Workforce

The quest for productivity had sweeping consequences for American workers. Industrial efficiency was not just a matter of electricity and machines. To speed up production, the managers at Ford and other factories had to change the nature of work.

Accordingly, the spirit of scientific management continued to sweep through American industry. Under ever-tighter supervision, workers were pushed to work faster and harder. In textile mills, for instance, the "stretch-out" required workers to tend more looms than before. Ford's system of mass production shared Frederick Winslow Taylor's determination to simplify and regiment labor. The result was less satisfying work. Instead of making a whole engine, a Ford assembly line worker might spend his day turning a few nuts on one engine after another. In 1913, Ford's labor turnover rate soared to 380 percent as unhappy workers quit their jobs.

As production grew more efficient, about a million jobs were lost in manufacturing, coal mining, and railroading. The growth of other kinds of employment more than compensated for this decrease, however. The ranks of white-collar workers increased 80 percent from 1910 to 1930, or nearly one worker in three. The nation had already begun to evolve from an industrial economy based on manual labor to a postindustrial economy based on sales and service.

Economic development also encouraged the gradual movement of women into the paid workforce. By the end of the 1920s, women, most of them unmarried, made up a majority of clerical workers. In 1900, 22.1 percent of women had worked for pay; by the 1940s, the percentage would reach 27.1.

Despite these changes, women still faced discrimination. Overwhelmingly concentrated in low-wage occupations such as domestic service, factory work, and agriculture, they were paid less than men who did comparable work. Female sales workers, for example, earned between 42 and 63 percent of the wages paid to their male counterparts. Few women held high-level managerial jobs. Moreover, most people continued to believe that a woman's place was in the home, especially if she had children, and many men feared that paid labor would make women too independent. Only economic necessities reconciled American society to women's employment in the 1920s.

The Defeat of Organized Labor

The American labor movement did not respond effectively to the transformation of work and the workforce. In an age of increasing economic organization, workers became less organized. In 1920 nearly one nonagricultural worker in five belonged to a union. By 1929, little more than one in ten did. The labor movement was especially weak in such developing mass-production industries as automobiles and steel and barely addressed the growing ranks of clerks and other white-collar workers.

Prosperity also weakened organized labor. Earning relatively good wages, many workers were less interested in joining unions. To show that unions were unnecessary, corporations promoted welfare capitalism, highly publicized programs ranging from lunch-hour movies to sports teams to profit-sharing plans. Many firms created company unions, but when it became clear that they did not give employees a real voice in management, their membership dwindled.

Although some firms tried to win over their workers with baseball teams and company unions, many others used tougher tactics to battle the labor movement. Management crusaded for the "open shop"—a workplace free of labor organization—and found an ally in the judicial system. Rulings by the U.S. Supreme Court, such as *Duplex Printing Press Co. v. Deering* (1921) and *Bedford Cut Stone Co. v. Journeymen Stone Cutters' Assn.* (1927), made it easier for state and federal courts to grant injunctions to stop unions from striking and exercising their rights. Businesses could sue unions for damages. They also demanded that workers sign "yellow-dog contracts" promising not to join a union.

The labor movement also hurt its own cause. The leadership of the major national organization, the AFL, was increasingly conservative and timid. The heads of the AFL, mostly white males of western European extraction who represented skilled crafts, had little interest in organizing women workers and wanted nothing to do with socialists, radical unionists, or African American workers. The AFL was slow to acknowledge the Brotherhood of Sleeping Car Porters, the assertive union of African American workers organized in 1925 under socialist A. Philip Randolph. Despite pleas from Randolph and others, the AFL failed to organize unskilled workers, many of whom were African Americans or white immigrants from eastern and southern Europe.

Weakened by internal divisions, welfare capitalism, the open-shop crusade, and the courts, the labor movement did not challenge the transformation of industrial labor. Nationwide, the number of strikes and lockouts dropped from 3,411 in 1920 to 604 in 1928. These labor actions often ended in defeat for workers.

The Decline of Agriculture

Against the backdrop of national prosperity, American agriculture continued its long decline. Prices for basic crops such as cotton and wheat fell, and the number of farms dropped.

The larger story of decline obscured important signs of growth and health. Some agricultural sectors were as dynamic as industry and for the same reasons—increased efficiency promoted by new technologies and large-scale organization. Mechanization, including the introduction of powerful tractors, made farm labor more efficient. So did the development of irrigation systems. By the 1920s, the irrigated farms of the Southwest were producing bumper crops of cotton, fruits, and vegetables. The Southwest also witnessed the rise of huge mechanized farms with hundreds and even thousands of irrigated acres. These "factories in the fields" depended not only on size and technology but also on the old-fashioned exploitation of farm labor. In California's Imperial Valley and elsewhere, migrant workers labored in harsh conditions for low pay to create modern agriculture.

Ironically, the dynamic agricultural economy created a problem for many farmers. Midsize farms, too big to be run by their owners alone and too small for mechanization, could not compete with the vast "factories in the fields." Increased efficiency, meanwhile, led to bumper crops that did not always find a good market price. Farmers were hurt by a changing American diet, with declining consumption of bread and potatoes, and by the rise of competitors overseas. Productive American farmers could not export enough of their surplus crops overseas. The resulting glut reduced the price of farm products. As their incomes lagged behind those of urban workers, farmers yearned for the return of high pre–World War I agricultural prices to restore parity between city and country. As a Georgia farmer observed, "The hand that is feeding the world is being spit upon."

The Urban Nation

The woes of agriculture contributed to a long-term shift in the American population. For the first time, according to the census of 1920, a majority of Americans—54 million out of 105 million—lived in urban territory. The census defined "urban territory" as places with as few as 2,500 people, many of them small towns close to country life. Still, the population of the United States was no longer predominantly rural.

The decline of farming spurred this shift. As agricultural prices fell, millions of Americans fled the nation's farms. The total U.S. population increased by 17 million during the 1920s, but the farm population declined by more than 1.5 million.

At the same time, the growth of the industrial economy swelled the population of towns and cities. In the 1920s, factory production was still centered in urban areas and gave many cities their identity. Detroit was becoming the "motor city." Akron was the home of rubber production. Pittsburgh and Birmingham symbolized the steel industry. Most of the new white-collar jobs were located in cities. Corporations also put their headquarters in cities, especially the two largest, Chicago and New York.

The rise of the automobile also contributed to the emergence of the urban nation. The car made it practical for Americans to live in suburbs and drive into the city to work and to shop. In the 1920s, the suburban lifestyle was still reserved mostly for the well-to-do. Elite suburbs, such as Grosse Pointe and Ferndale outside Detroit and Beverly Hills and Glendale outside Los Angeles, grew explosively. The transformation of the countryside into suburbs symbolized the new urban nation.

A Modern Culture

The 1920s saw the full emergence of a modern culture that had been taking shape for decades and that now surrounded Americans with something fundamentally new. Perfectly symbolized by Gertrude Ederle, the new culture extolled the virtues of modernity and pleasure. Rooted in the nation's economic development, the new culture reflected both the needs of businessmen with goods to sell and the desires of Americans with more money and free time than ever. Supported by advertising and installment buying, the culture of leisure and consumption offered spectator sports, movies, popular music, radio, and sex. It also offered new views of gender, family life, and youth and renewed old values of individualism in an increasingly organized society.

The Spread of Consumerism

Encouraged by big business, many Americans now defined life as the pursuit of pleasure and found happiness in leisure and consumption rather than in work. This philosophy of consumerism saturated society by the end of the decade.

> Every morning,
>
> Every evening,
>
> Ain't we got fun/
>
> Not much money,
>
> Oh but honey,
>
> Ain't we got fun
>
> RICHARD A. WHITING,
> RAYMOND B. EGAN,
> AND GUS KAHN,
> 1921

Increased efficiency and profitability enabled American employers to allow their workers higher wages and more leisure hours. Some employers, notably Ford, also raised wages in order to hold on to workers alienated by the drudgery of mass production. And Ford himself increased workers' pay to enable them to buy the products of modern factories. The incomes of workers and other employees reached a new high in the 1920s. Factory workers' real wages rose 19 percent from 1914 to 1923.

Many workers had more time to enjoy their wages. For salaried, middle-class workers, the annual vacation had become a tradition by the 1910s. Although blue-collar workers seldom enjoyed a vacation, they spent less time on the job. Some employers, including Henry Ford, instituted a five-day workweek during the 1920s. More businesses shortened their workdays, and the average workweek fell from 47.4 hours in 1920 to 44.2 in 1929. "The shorter work day brought me my first idea of there being such a thing as pleasure," said one young female worker. "Before this time it was just sleep and eat and hurry off to work."

A change in attitude accompanied these changes in wages and workdays. The work ethic seemed less necessary in a prospering economy. Thanks to Fordism and Taylorism, work was also less satisfying, and people justified pleasure as an essential antidote to labor.

The advertising industry encouraged the new attitude toward pleasure. Although advertising agencies had first appeared in the 1850s and 1860s, the business did not mature until the 1920s. Now, ads appeared everywhere—in newspapers and magazines, on billboards and big electric signs. Major advertising agencies such as J. Walter Thompson and Batten, Barton, Durstine, and Osborn became concentrated in New York City, home to so many corporations. Impressed by successful ad campaigns for Listerine mouthwash and Fleischmann's yeast, big business hired advertising agencies to sell goods and services. Expenditures for advertising leaped from $682 million in 1914 to nearly $3 billion by 1929.

Advertising, like the new culture, optimistically embraced change and trumpeted the new. In advertisements, purchasing the right products solved problems, made up for the drudgery of work, and brought fulfillment. To enthusiastic ad men, advertising was as important as the products it sold. In his best-selling book, *The Man Nobody Knows* (1925), ad pioneer Bruce Barton portrayed Jesus Christ as a great advertiser, whose disciples "conquered the world" by selling a new product, Christianity.

Along with advertising, business used installment loans to encourage Americans to buy goods and services "on time." Credit buying spread so rapidly that total consumer debt more than doubled from 1922 to 1929. The sales of such consumer goods as pianos, washing machines, and automobiles boomed. Americans bought 181,000 automobiles in 1910; they bought 4,455,000 in 1929. Thanks to the availability of another kind of loan, the mortgage, more Americans were able to invest in a home of their own. Spending on new private housing jumped from $2.0 billion in 1920 to $5.0 billion by 1924. Loan-driven spending helped power the economic prosperity of the 1920s.

New Pleasures

The culture of the 1920s offered many pleasures, especially sports, movies, popular music, and radio. Gertrude Ederle was part of a golden age for spectator sports. Although people still played games themselves, they also watched other people's games more than ever before. Tennis, boxing, and auto racing flourished during the decade. The American Professional Football Association, which became the National Football League, played its first season in 1920. Although crowds packed college football stadiums, baseball remained the most popular American sport. Minor-league baseball covered the nation. Meanwhile, the popularity of major-league baseball surged, thanks in part to the exploits of Babe Ruth and his New York Yankees.

Spectator sports enthralled millions, but another passive pleasure, the movies, was the most popular consumer attraction of the 1920s (see Table 23–1.) A novelty in the mid-1890s, silent films had become a big business. In city neighborhoods in the 1900s, crowds packed into stuffy "nickelodeons"—storefront theaters showing short, silent one-reel films for the price of a nickel. The movies became longer and more sophisticated, and theaters became larger and more lavish. Nationwide, weekly attendance doubled from 40 million in 1922 to 80 million in 1929.

Booming attendance fueled the growth of a handful of corporations, including Warner Brothers and RKO, that dominated the film industry. By the 1920s, the center of movie production had shifted from New York to Hollywood, California. Now called "Hollywood,"

 Table 23-1 Spending for Recreational Services, 1909-1929

Year	Total (millions of dollars)	Motion Picture Theaters (millions of dollars)	Spectator Sports (millions of dollars)
1909	377	###	###
1914	434	###	###
1919	806	###	###
1921	911	301	30
1923	1082	336	46
1927	1405	526	48
1929	1670	720	66

Historical Statistics of the United States, Millennial Online Edition (Cambridge: Cambridge University Press, 2008), Table Dh309–318.

= No Data

***The Jazz Singer* Premiere** The dazzling allure of a new pleasure—the "talking picture"—draws a big opening-night crowd to Warners' Theatre, New York City, October 6, 1927.

the film industry grew still bigger toward the end of the decade, when studios learned to synchronize sound and moving images in such films as *The Jazz Singer* of 1927.

It was fitting that one of the first "talking pictures" was about jazz. Popular music in general and jazz in particular played an important role in the new consumer culture. Created by African Americans in the 1910s, jazz was a rhythmically and harmonically innovative music that featured improvised solos and a hot beat. The new music emerged around the country, but its first great center was the streets, brothels, and dives of New Orleans. The Louisiana city was home to the first major jazz composer, Jelly Roll Morton, and to the first jazz superstar, trumpeter and singer Louis Armstrong. As jazz became nationally popular, Morton, Armstrong, and the focus of jazz moved on, as did so many African Americans, to Chicago and New York City (see Chapter 22).

The new music quickly attracted white Americans, especially the young, who yearned for something more daring than the relatively sedate popular music of the day. Even its name—a reference perhaps to speed or sexual intercourse—conjured up pleasure and liberation. Soon white musicians were contributing to the music. For many whites, jazz summed up a period marked by the pursuit of liberating pleasures. The 1920s became known as the "Jazz Age," after the title of a 1922 book of short stories by F. Scott Fitzgerald.

The great popularity of jazz and other musical genres was made possible by the phonograph, originated by Thomas Edison in the 1870s and modified by other inventors. In the 1920s, the electrical recording microphone dramatically improved sound quality and made the new music accessible to millions of Americans.

A newer technological innovation, the radio, also allowed Americans to hear popular music. In 1895, Italian inventor Guglielmo Marconi transmitted the first radio waves; by 1920, commercial radio broadcasting began in the United States. The federal government started licensing radio stations the next year.

Like the movies, radio quickly became corporatized big business. By 1923, there were more than 500 stations and, in 1926, the first permanent radio network, the National Broadcasting Company (NBC). Americans tuned in to broadcasts of live music, news, sports, and soap operas, and by 1925, manufacturers turned out more than 2 million radios a year. Radio, like the movies, disseminated the values of consumerism, as corporations rushed to advertise their products by sponsoring radio programs.

A Sexual Revolution

Along with such new pleasures as radio and movies, the modern culture offered a new attitude toward an old pleasure, sex. By the 1920s, Americans' sexual attitudes and behavior were changing. People openly discussed sex and placed a new emphasis on the importance of sexual satisfaction, primarily in marriage. And there were signs of greater sexual exploration among unmarried young people.

In the nineteenth century, Americans, especially middle-class Victorians, had kept a discreet silence about sex. That silence gave way in the twentieth century. Progressive Era reformers forced the public discussion of such sexual issues as prostitution and venereal disease. The reformers, anxious to control extramarital sexual behavior, hardly wanted to glorify sexual pleasure. But they helped pave the way for an approving depiction of sexuality.

Popular amusements of the 1910s and 1920s were filled with sexual images. The movies explored sexual topics in such films as *The Anatomy of a Kiss* and *A Bedroom Blunder*. Popular music featured suggestive songs about sex, such as "It's Tight Like That" and "I Need a Little Sugar in My Bowl." Popular dances such as the grizzly bear and the turkey trot promoted close physical contact or sexually suggestive steps. As early as 1913, a magazine concluded that "Sex O'Clock" had struck in the United States.

The increased openness about sex reflected the growing belief that sexual pleasure was necessary and desirable, particularly within marriage. Married couples increasingly considered intercourse an opportunity for pleasure, as well as procreation. Experts insisted that healthy marriages required sexual satisfaction for both partners.

The new view of marital sexuality helped change attitudes toward contraception. By the 1910s, a grassroots movement, led by socialists and other radicals, promoted sex education and contraceptives, which were largely illegal. The crusade's best-known figure was the fiery former nurse and socialist organizer Margaret Sanger, who coined the term "birth control." Although Sanger once had to flee the country to avoid prosecution, birth control became respectable—and widely practiced—in the 1920s.

At the same time, most adult Americans still condemned premarital sex. Nevertheless, premarital intercourse apparently became more common. Many couples believed that intercourse was acceptable if they were "in love" and intended to marry. There was also an apparent increase in "petting"—sexual contact short of intercourse.

While changing some of their attitudes about sexual behavior, most heterosexual Americans still condemned homosexuality. Nevertheless, a sexual revolution was under way.

Changing Gender Ideals

Shifting sexual attitudes were tied to new gender ideals. By the 1920s, Americans' sense of what it meant to be female was changing. Since the late nineteenth century, Americans had been talking about the independent, assertive "New Woman" who claimed the right to attend school, vote, and have a career. The "New Woman" of the 1920s was now a sexual being, too, a fun-loving individual with desires of her own.

The sexual nature of women was central to a new movement, known as feminism, that had emerged in the 1910s. The feminists, like earlier female reformers, were generally white, well-educated, Protestant, urban women. Concentrated in New York's Greenwich Village, feminists broke with older reformers by insisting on sharing the sexual opportunities that men had presumably long enjoyed. Unlike the older generation of activist women, feminists were unwilling to give up marriage and children for careers outside the home. Feminism insisted on women's right to pleasure and satisfaction in all phases of life, from the most public to the most intimate.

Small in number, the feminists commanded a great deal of attention. Several of their ideas and practices were too radical for many American men and women, such as some feminists' decision to retain their maiden names in married life or to explore sexual relationships outside of marriage. Most fundamentally, many Americans were unwilling to accept the feminist insistence on full equality with men.

American culture proved rather open to a more liberated view of female sexuality. The most popular image of the American woman of the 1920s was the vivacious young "flapper," with her short skirt, bound breasts, and bobbed hair. The flapper was likely to wear cosmetics and to smoke cigarettes—practices once associated only with prostitutes.

Notions of masculinity were also changing. With the growing emphasis on female needs and desires, men were urged to be attentive and responsive and to focus on the home. As the world of work became less satisfying, experts told men to look for fulfillment in family life. The family man of the 1920s was no longer to be a distant, stern patriarch but a companion to his wife and a doting friend to his children.

In practice, many men still defined themselves in terms of their work rather than their domestic life, and society still regarded women as the primary caretakers of children. Despite the change in domestic values, many men were still relative outsiders in the home.

The Family and Youth

Changing gender ideals were directly related to a reconsideration of family life and youth. Although whole families still labored together in fields and mills, most Americans no longer regarded the family as a group of productive workers. Child-labor laws increasingly made sure that boys and girls went to school rather than to work. The family became primarily a unit of leisure and consumption. The home was where men, women, and children found pleasure and fulfillment, gathered around the radio.

Reflecting modern cultural values, parents became more likely to indulge their children, who enjoyed more toys, possessions, and spending money than had earlier generations. The automobile gave young people more mobility, too. With their new freedom, they began to create their own separate culture. One sign was the dramatic spread of petting among high-school youth, newly free from parental control.

>> "Flaming Youth" on Campus

During the 1920s, college and university campuses were laboratories for "flaming youth," as male and female college students created a distinctive youth culture. Campus life reflected central features of the larger society: the desire for individual freedom and the need to cope with organization. The world of the "advance guard of the younger generation" also reflected the uneven development of American democracy in the Jazz Age.

Traditionally for the elite, higher education was anything but democratic. In 1899, only 238,000 students—some 2 percent of Americans ages 18 to 24—enrolled in colleges and universities. Only 85,000 of those students were women. But as the dynamic economy demanded educated white-collar workers, more middle-class families found the means to send their sons and daughters to college. By 1929, 1.1 million students—7.2 percent of 18- to 24-year-olds—were enrolled. Thanks to changing attitudes toward women, 480,000 of those students were female. The development of public-supported colleges and universities made this growth possible. From 1919 to 1922, enrollments doubled from 3,000 to 6,000 at the University of Illinois and from 4,000 to 8,000 at the Ohio State University. The public schools were at the forefront of a more democratic student culture.

That culture celebrated independence. "To me the Jazz Age signifies an age of freedom in thought and action," explained a coed at the University of Denver. Liberated from the traditional constraints of home and workplace, college students could pursue their desires. "We were big-eyed with wanting," said the songwriter Hoagy Carmichael, then a student at Indiana University, "with making fun."

Students held "petting parties." They forced college officials to tolerate racy new dances such as the toddle, the shimmy, the Charleston, and the black bottom. By the end of the decade, about two out of three students defied Prohibition (see Chapter 22) by drinking on and off campus. Public drunkenness was no longer a scandal. Women students engaged in the "unladylike," sexually suggestive practice of smoking. "College," sniffed a dean at Princeton, "has unfortunately become a kind of glorified playground . . . a paradise of the young."

Students' quest for pleasure shaped their politics. Although Carmichael and his friends cared little about most public issues, they believed strongly in individual rights. Students regarded sex and other satisfactions as a private matter. College newspapers criticized Prohibitionists and other reformers who wanted to regulate individual behavior.

Even as they reflected the individualist values of modern culture, college students adapted to the growing power of organization. Collegiate life became more crowded and more bureaucratic. Students turned to organizations in the 1920s, when the number of fraternities and sororities shot up. By 1930 about one student in three belonged to one; Hoagy Carmichael joined Kappa Sigma. Greek houses often included most student *continued*

Most adults accepted this situation partly because they admired and envied youth-
fulness. The modern culture, unhappy with work and anxious for fun, glorified sexually
adventurous, fast-living young people. The title of the 1923 novel *Flaming Youth* became a
catchphrase for the youth culture of the 1920s.

The Celebration of the Individual

The emphasis on the individual, so evident in changing views of sex, gender, family, and
youth, was fundamental to the modern culture. In addition to Gertrude Ederle and Babe
Ruth, Americans admired a host of sports heroes and heroines, and the movie industry
increasingly showcased the distinctive personalities of its stars. Individualism was basic to
the "New Woman," too.

The resurgence of individualism was not surprising. The belief in the importance of
the individual was deeply ingrained in American culture. Paradoxically, the development
of industrial capitalism intensified the importance of both individuals and organizations.
As corporations grew larger and produced more, they needed to stimulate consumerism,
the gratification of individual needs and desires.

There were serious obstacles to true individualism in the 1920s. Powerful organizations, including corporations, controlled individual life. Even the most famous individual
exploit of the decade depended on organization. On May 20–21, 1927, Charles A. Lindbergh flew the *Spirit of St. Louis* from New York City to Paris. This first nonstop solo
crossing of the Atlantic made Lindbergh an international symbol of individual achievement, but his feat relied on businessmen who put up the money and a corporation that
built the plane. Organization and individualism, the new and the old, were interdependent in the 1920s.

The Limits of the Modern Culture

The modern culture had clear limits in the 1920s. For millions of Americans, much of the
consumer lifestyle was out of reach. Many Americans, including artists and intellectuals,
chose not to define themselves by the pursuit of pleasure, leisure, and consumption. For

them modern society, with its emphasis on the new, including the "New Negro," the "New Woman," and the "New Era," represented an unwelcome abandonment of old values. In different ways, fundamentalist Christians, immigration restrictionists, and the Ku Klux Klan demanded a return to an earlier United States. Mexican Americans, African Americans, and others found that the new culture, like the old, treated them like second-class citizens.

The Limits of Prosperity

Despite the aura of prosperity, low incomes and poverty persisted in the 1920s. As late as 1928, six out of ten families made less than the $2,000 a year required for the "basic needs of life." Despite the housing boom, most American household heads did not own their own homes.

The towns and cities of the increasingly urban nation were still divided by social class. In *Middletown* (1929), their pioneering study of a small midwestern city in the 1920s, Helen and Staughton Lynd discovered that the "division into the working class and business class . . . constitutes the outstanding cleavage." The working class of "Middletown"—in fact Muncie, Indiana—had less money and leisure to enjoy the new culture. About a third of the city still did not own automobiles.

The "Lost Generation" of Intellectuals

Many artists and intellectuals felt alienated from the United States of the 1920s. For white, mostly male writers and artists who came of age during World War I, the conflict represented a failure of civilization, a pointless exercise in destruction. Its aftermath left them angry, alienated, and rootless. In a nation supposedly devoted to individualism, they did not feel free. They were, as the writer Gertrude Stein described them, a "Lost Generation." Some of them, such as Stein and her fellow writer Ernest Hemingway, left the United States for Paris and other places in Europe.

However prosperous and peaceful, the postwar years did not reassure the Lost Generation that American life had changed much. In such works as *Winesburg, Ohio* (1919), novelist Sherwood Anderson portrayed a still-repressive society that denied people real freedom and individuality. The acid-tongued H. L. Mencken, editor of the *American Mercury*, condemned a provincial culture still dominated by the "booboisie" and its rural values.

Still other American artists and intellectuals feared their country had changed too much. Although excited by the potential of the machine, they criticized the routinized work and superficial pleasures of modern life. In his 1922 novel *Babbitt*, Sinclair Lewis satirized a midwestern Republican businessman whose consumerism made him a conformist, not an individualist. F. Scott Fitzgerald, in such fiction as *This Side of Paradise* (1920) and *The Great Gatsby* (1925), conveyed the sense of loss and emptiness in the lives of fashionable "flaming youth" in the "Jazz Age."

From a different angle, 12 southern intellectuals, including Allen Tate, Robert Penn Warren, Donald Davidson, and John Crowe Ransom, attacked the modern culture in *I'll Take My Stand: The South and the Agrarian Tradition* (1930). Their essays offered a defense of rural culture and a critique of a consumer society that demeaned work and exalted individualism.

Artists and intellectuals did not set off a mass rebellion against modern culture, but they did express a widespread ambivalence and uneasiness. In different and contradictory ways, they laid out an agenda for Americans as they came to terms with modern, consumer society.

Fundamentalist Christians and "Old-Time Religion"

For many Americans of faith, the modern culture promoted a sense of deep, unsettling change. "The world has been convulsed," declared *Presbyterian Magazine*. "The most settled principles and laws of society have been attacked." The new culture was troubling because it was so secular and seemed to define life in terms of material satisfaction rather than spiritual commitment. Many Protestants, feeling betrayed by their own churches, resented the influence of liberal Protestants who had tried to accommodate religion to science and scholarship.

Fundamentalists, or opponents of liberalism, took their name from *The Fundamentals*, a series of essays by conservative Protestant theologians that appeared beginning in 1909. Fundamentalists emerged across the country but were strongest in rural areas and in the South and West. By the end of World War I, fundamentalists dominated the Southern Baptist Convention and were fighting liberals for control of northern churches.

Fundamentalists rejected liberalism above all for its willingness to question the historical truth of the Bible. The fundamentalist movement urged a return to biblical, patriarchal, and denominational authority, to what came to be called "old-time religion."

The high point in the fundamentalist-liberal battle came in a courtroom in Tennessee in 1925. That year, a high-school biology teacher, John Scopes, defied a new state law banning the teaching of "any theory that denies the story of the divine creation of man as taught in the Bible, and that teaches instead that man has descended from a lower order of animals." Scopes's trial became a national media event. The chief lawyer for the prosecution was William Jennings Bryan, the former Democratic presidential candidate who had become a leading crusader for fundamentalism. While Bryan was a champion of rural America, Scopes's attorneys—Clarence Darrow and Dudley Field Malone—represented the city and modern culture. (Malone had helped finance Gertrude Ederle's swim across the English Channel.) In a dramatic confrontation, Darrow called Bryan to the stand and forced him to concede that the Bible might not be literally accurate. Although Scopes was convicted and fined, the fun-

Scopes Trial The battle between liberalism and fundamentalism: Clarence Darrow, lawyer for John Scopes in his 1925 trial for teaching evolution, confronts chief prosecutor William Jennings Bryan on the witness stand.

damentalists lost some credibility, and Bryan died soon after. Other southern and western states later passed antievolution laws, but similar measures failed in the more urbanized Northeast.

The Scopes trial did not end the war between fundamentalism and liberalism. Fundamentalists were numerous. Their hostility to liberal Protestantism and modern culture would affect American life for decades to come.

Nativists and Immigration Restriction

While fundamentalist Christianity sought a return to old-time religion, a resurgent nativist movement wanted to go back to a supposedly more homogenous America. As mass migration from Europe resumed after World War I, nativist feeling revived among Americans from western European backgrounds. Thanks to the Russian Revolution and the domestic Red Scare, they associated immigrants with anarchism and radicalism and derided southern and eastern Europeans as inferior races that would weaken the nation.

In 1921, Congress overwhelmingly passed a law temporarily limiting the annual immigration from any European country to 3 percent of the number of its immigrants living in the United States in 1910. This quota sharply reduced the number of new immigrants from southern and eastern Europe, but nativists wanted tougher action. Congress responded with the National Origins Act of 1924. This limited the annual intake from a European country to 2 percent of the number of its immigrants living in the United States in 1890, when there were few southern and eastern Europeans in America. The act excluded Japanese immigrants altogether. The legislation worked: immigration fell from 805,000 arrivals in 1921 to 280,000 in 1929 (see Table 23–2).

The Rebirth of the Ku Klux Klan

Nativism and fundamentalism helped spur another challenge to the new order of the 1920s. In 1915, the Ku Klux Klan, the vigilante group that had terrorized African Americans in the South during Reconstruction, was reborn in a ceremony on Stone Mountain, Georgia. It enjoyed explosive growth after World War I. The "Invisible Empire" borrowed

 Table 23-2 The Impact of Nativism: Immigration, 1921-1929

	Arrivals (in thousands)		
Origin	**1921**	**1925**	**1929**
Eastern Europe and Poland	138	10	14
Southern Europe	299	8	22
Asia	25	4	4
Mexico	31	33	40
Total	805	294	280

Source: *Historical Statistics of the United States*, (Cambridge: Cambridge University Press), I, 401.

Itemized groups do not add up to totals.

the rituals of the nineteenth-century Klan, including its white robes and hoods and its symbol of a burning cross. The new Klan was still driven by a racist hatred of African Americans, but it took on new targets, including Jews, Roman Catholics, immigrants, religious liberalism, and change in general.

The Invisible Empire condemned big business and modern culture, charging that they valued "money above manhood." The Klan condemned pleasure, "the god of the young people of America," and was hostile to the new gender ideals, birth control, freer sexuality, and the independence of youth. Klansmen and Klanswomen yearned for an earlier America in which white Protestant males controlled women, youth, and other groups and had nothing to fear from big business.

The Klan's tactics blended old and new. Seeing themselves as a secret army of vigilantes, some Klan members supported the age-old tactics of moral regulation—intimidation, flogging, and sometimes lynching—to scare people into good behavior. At the same time, much of the Invisible Empire repudiated violence and used the latest advertising techniques to boost its membership.

For several years, the Klan proved extraordinarily successful. Despite its extremist views, the Invisible Empire had a mainstream membership, in every region, in cities and the countryside. At its peak, there were perhaps 3 to 5 million secret members. Because so many politicians feared or sympathized with it, the Klan had considerable political influence. It helped to elect governors, senators, and other officials from both major parties.

At the height of its power, however, the Klan collapsed when its leaders were revealed to be caught up in financial scandal, alcohol, pornography, adultery, kidnapping, and murder. Most people realized they had nothing to fear from such Klan targets as Communists, unions, and Jews. Millions of Americans, however uneasy about the new culture, had no desire to support prejudice, lawbreaking, and violence in a futile attempt to go back to the past. The Klan's membership dropped precipitously in the late 1920s.

Mexican Americans

Despite the efforts of immigration restrictionists and the Klan, the United States became more diverse than ever. Up to a million and a half Mexicans entered the United States legally or surreptitiously between 1890 and 1929. Many left to avoid the upheaval of the Mexican Revolution of 1910 (see Chapter 22) and to escape the agricultural changes driving the rural poor from the land. The dynamic U.S. economy created opportunities for impoverished Mexican immigrants, as did, ironically, the restrictionist immigration legislation of the 1920s. Unable to get enough European or Asian workers, employers turned eagerly to Mexico as a source of cheap seasonal labor. In particular the Southwest's rapidly developing economy needed Mexican workers for mines, railroads, construction gangs, and, above all, farms.

Like many immigrants from Europe, many Mexican migrants did not plan to stay in the United States. They traveled back and forth to their homeland or returned permanently. Gradually, many chose to stay as they developed economic and family ties in the United States. The National Origins Act, which made it costly, time-consuming, and often humiliating for Mexicans to cross the border, also encouraged migrants to remain in the United States. As a result, the official Mexican population of the United States rose from 103,000 in 1900 to 478,000 by 1920. At the turn of the century, the majority of immigrants

Mexican American Workmen Laborers pause for the camera while making adobe bricks at the Casa Verdugo, Glendale, California, ca. 1920.

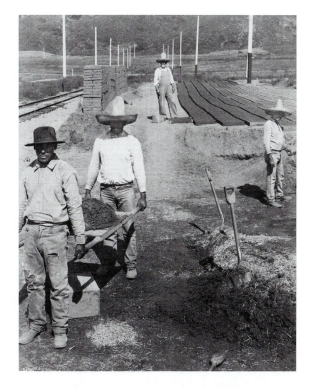

lived in Texas and Arizona, but California, with its booming agriculture, rapidly became the center of the Mexican population. Los Angeles, growing phenomenally in the early twentieth century, attracted perhaps 190,000 Mexicans by 1930.

Mexican immigrants, like so many other ethnic groups in the United States, wrestled with questions about their national identity. Were they still Mexicans, or had they become Americans or some unique combination of the two nationalities? In varying degrees, the migrants clung to old identities and adapted to their new home. Mexican Americans, eager to hold on to the advantages they had won by birth and residence in the United States, feared that newcomers would compete for jobs and cause native-born whites to denigrate all Mexicans alike. The immigrants, in turn, often derided Mexican Americans as *pochos*—bleached or faded people—who had lost their true Mexican identity.

Nevertheless, ethnic Mexicans created a distinctive culture in the United States. For all their differences, they shared a sense of common origins and common challenges. In a white-dominated society, they saw themselves as *La Raza*—The Race—set apart by heritage and skin color.

Poverty and discrimination also contributed to a sense of common identity. In many towns and cities, ethnic Mexicans were effectively segregated in certain neighborhoods—*barrios*—in poor conditions. Largely ignored by national corporations, Mexican Americans supported their own businesses and listened to their own Spanish-language radio programs. Anglo-American prejudice also drove Mexicans together. Many whites stereotyped them as a lazy and shiftless race who would take jobs from native-born workers and who could not be assimilated into American life. Still other white Americans, drawing on the reform agenda of the Progressive Era, wanted to "Americanize" ethnic Mexicans by teaching them English and middle-class values.

Their sense of shared identity encouraged Mexican Americans to struggle for economic progress and equal rights. In 1928, farm workers in California created La Unión de Trabajadores del Valle Imperial (Imperial Valley Workers Union) in a successful fight for higher wages. A year later, Mexican American businessmen and professionals formed the League of United Latin American Citizens (LULAC) in Texas.

African Americans and the "New Negro"

Like Mexican Americans, African Americans found the new cultural terrain of the United States appealing but unsatisfying. They enjoyed and helped to create the new culture, but it did little to affect racial discrimination. South and North, African Americans still lived with economic and political inequality.

Although discrimination had not changed, many African Americans insisted that they had. It was the decade of both the "New Woman" and the "New Negro." In 1900, Booker T. Washington titled one of his books *A New Negro for a New Century*. By the 1920s, the increased use of "New Negro" reflected a fresh sense of freedom as African Americans left the rural South for cities. It was also the product of frustration as African Americans encountered inequality along with opportunity. The "New Negro" was assertive in the face of mistreatment. "The time for cringing is over," said an African American newspaper.

The "New Negro" was also defined by a deep sense of racial difference. Applauding their distinctive life and culture, African Americans spurred the Harlem Renaissance. Harlem, the section of upper Manhattan in New York where many African Americans had moved, became a center of artistic and intellectual creativity. Novelists such as Zora Neale Hurston, Jessie Fauset, Claude McKay, Jean Toomer, and Dorothy West; poets such as Langston Hughes, Sterling Brown, and Countee Cullen; and artists such as Aaron Douglas and Augusta Savage produced a new birth of African American creativity. In different ways, these women and men explored and celebrated the nature of American blackness in 1920s America and its origins in Africa.

The militancy of the "New Negro" was reflected in the development of the NAACP, which turned increasingly to African American leadership. Its key figure, W. E. B. DuBois, became more critical of whites and more determined that white colonizers return Africa to Africans. The NAACP also pushed the cause of African American civil rights more aggressively and attacked the white primary system that denied African Americans any say in the southern Democratic Party. The NAACP continued a longtime antilynching campaign, which bore fruit in the 1920s, as southern whites were increasingly embarrassed by vigilante justice.

For a time, the NAACP's efforts were overshadowed by the crusades of Marcus Garvey. A Jamaican immigrant to New York City, Garvey founded the Universal Negro Improvement Association (UNIA), which became the largest African American activist organization of the 1920s. Less interested in political rights and integration, Garvey focused on African American pride and self-help and on Africa. He exalted "a new Negro who stands erect, conscious of his manhood rights and fully determined to preserve them at all times." Garvey urged African Americans to develop their own businesses and become economically self-sufficient. Like DuBois, he insisted that the imperial powers give up their control of Africa. Sure that blacks could never find equality in a white-dominated nation, Garvey believed African Americans should return to Africa.

Unlike the mostly middle-class NAACP, Garvey's UNIA developed a vast following among the African American working class. In 1919, he launched an economic self-help project, the Black Star Line, which, he promised, would buy ships and transport passengers and cargo from the United States to the West Indies, Central America, and Africa. Many of his followers invested in the venture, but it collapsed due to mismanagement.

Garvey was indicted for mail fraud in connection with the project. In 1927, he was deported to Jamaica, and the UNIA lost its mass following.

As the fate of the UNIA suggested, militancy could be costly for African Americans. The NAACP also saw its membership drop dramatically during the decade. Nevertheless, African Americans' struggles laid the groundwork for more successful struggles in the future.

A "New Era" in Politics and Government

The economic and cultural transformations of the 1920s shaped American democracy in important but contradictory ways. Modern culture helped empower ordinary people and transform the style of politics. But organized groups—big business above all—affected public life more decisively while a succession of conservative Republican presidents monopolized the White House during the decade. In a society fascinated by all things "new," the Republicans claimed to represent a "New Era" in politics and government. But the Republican ascendancy of the 1920s mostly meant the return of an older vision of minimalist government, individualism, and a less internationalist foreign policy. The mix of old ideology and new political styles failed to galvanize the democratic system: the prosperous 1920s became an age of apathy and low voter turnout.

The Modern Political System

In some ways, the cultural changes of the 1920s stimulated equality and reinforced the idea that the individual could make a difference in politics, too. The emphasis on female freedom and empowerment encouraged women to exercise their newly won right to vote.

The modern culture also hastened the emergence of a political style taking shape since the late nineteenth century. Copying big business, politicians used advertising to appeal to the electorate. In the Gilded Age, voters had been active participants in political campaigns. Now, citizens were political consumers choosing candidates just as they chose mouthwash or automobiles.

The shift to advertising was necessary, too, because the major parties' control over the media had dramatically decreased. Once partisan, many newspapers now took a more independent stand. The new radio stations and movie theaters had no political affiliations at all. With the decline of partisanship, political ad campaigns focused more on individual candidates than on their parties.

Economic and cultural change also benefited big business and other organized groups. Congress was besieged by lobbyists from corporations, business groups, professional organizations, and single-issue pressure groups such as the Anti-Saloon League. Organizations employed a political style that used supposedly objective facts to educate legislators and voters. Unorganized Americans had less chance of influencing the political process.

The new, less partisan politics did a poor job of mobilizing voters. Nationwide, voter turnout fell from 79 percent in the presidential election of 1896 to just 49 percent in 1920 and 1924. A number of factors accounted for this drop-off: African Americans in the South had been effectively disfranchised, and newly enfranchised women were less likely to vote than men; but white male turnout dropped dramatically, too.

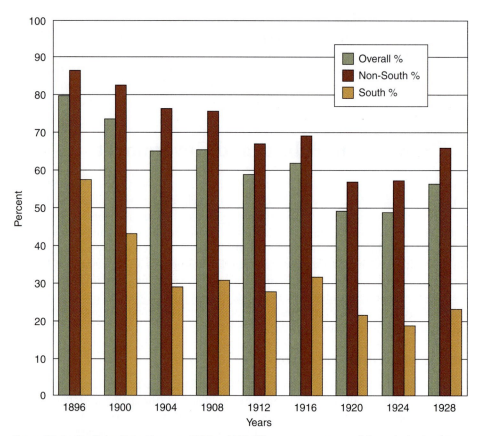

Figure 23–1 **Declining Voter Turnout, 1896 to 1928** Why was turnout so much lower in the South?

The Republican Ascendancy

The chief beneficiaries of the new politics were the Republicans. Determined to regain the White House in 1920, the Republican Party chose an uncontroversial, conservative ticket. Handsome and charismatic, presidential nominee Warren G. Harding of Ohio had accomplished little during a term in the Senate. His running mate, Governor Calvin Coolidge of Massachusetts, was best known for his firm stance against a strike by the Boston police.

The Republican ticket was not imposing, but neither was the opposition. The Democratic presidential nominee, Governor James M. Cox of Ohio, was saddled with the unpopularity of the Wilson administration. His running mate, Franklin Roosevelt of New York, was a little-known cousin of former president Theodore Roosevelt who had served as assistant secretary of the navy.

While the Democrats ran an ineffective campaign, the Republicans made excellent use of advertising. Harding cleverly appealed to the reaction against Wilson's activist government, offering a return to "normalcy" after years of unsettling progressive innovations.

Harding won a huge victory with 60.3 percent of the popular vote, a new record; he won 37 states for a total of 404 electoral votes. The Republican Party substantially increased its majorities in Congress.

The Harding administration was plagued by revelations of fraud and corruption, some involving the so-called Ohio Gang of cronies from Harding's home state. The director of the Veterans' Bureau, caught making fraudulent deals with federal property, went to prison. One of the Ohio Gang, fearing exposure of the group's influence-peddling schemes, committed suicide.

A shaken Harding died suddenly of a misdiagnosed heart attack in August 1923, but the troubles continued. Congressional hearings revealed that former secretary of the interior Albert B. Fall had apparently accepted bribes in return for leasing U.S. Navy oil reserves at Teapot Dome, Wyoming, and Elk Hills, California. Teapot Dome, as the scandal came to be called, earned Fall a fine and a jail term. In 1924, Harding's attorney general resigned because of his role in the Ohio Gang.

The scandals damaged Harding's reputation but did not seriously harm his party or his successor, Calvin Coolidge. The former vice president—so reserved in public that he was called "Silent Cal"—was well suited to the political moment. The picture of rectitude, Coolidge restored public confidence in the presidency.

In 1924, Coolidge easily won the presidency against the Democrat John W. Davis, a colorless, conservative corporate lawyer from West Virginia, and Wisconsin's Senator Robert M. La Follette, the standard-bearer of the new Progressive Party. The choice, insisted Republicans, was either "Coolidge or Chaos." Holding on to the White House and to their majorities in Congress, the Republicans continued their ascendancy.

The Politics of Individualism

The Republicans practiced the politics of individualism. Eager to serve big business, they denounced the activist, progressive state and called for less government and more individual freedom. Coolidge declared, "The chief business of the American people is business."

Despite such slogans, Republicans sometimes used government power to spur economic development. The Federal Highway Act of 1921 provided federal matching grants to improve roads, and the Fordney-McCumber Tariff of 1922 restored high protective taxes on imports.

These measures were exceptions, however. Above all, the Harding and Coolidge administrations called for "economy"—reduced government spending and lower taxes. The Republicans also condemned budget deficits and pledged to reduce the national debt; they succeeded on all counts. Federal expenditures dropped from $6.4 billion in 1920 to $3.1 billion in 1924. Congress repeatedly cut income and other taxes, but the federal government still produced annual budget surpluses and reduced its debt.

Republicans' commitment to minimal government was obvious in their lax enforcement of Progressive Era legislation. Under Harding and Coolidge , the federal government made only weak attempts to carry out Prohibition. The Republicans also allowed regulatory commissions to atrophy. The Interstate Commerce Commission (ICC) and the Federal Trade Commission (FTC) were effectively controlled by the businesses they were supposed to regulate.

Herbert Hoover, the secretary of commerce for both Harding and Coolidge, had a more activist view of the government's role in the economy. Sensitive to business interests, Hoover used the Commerce Department to promote "associationalism"—organized cooperation among business trade groups. However, businessmen did not trust one another enough to make voluntary cooperation effective, and Hoover did not advocate federal action to force cooperation. Afraid of too much government, Hoover believed above all in what he called "American individualism."

Republican Foreign Policy

After America's intense involvement in international affairs during World War I, the 1920s were a period of relative withdrawal. But even without a foreign policy crisis, the United States, the world's greatest economic power, played an active role around the globe.

In the aftermath of World War I, Americans were eager to reduce the size of the military and to avoid new conflict. Horrified by the "Great War," women's groups and religious organizations joined a surging international peace movement. Activists' calls for disarmament helped push the Harding administration to organize the Washington Naval Conference of 1921–1922. In the first international arms-reduction accord, the United States, Great Britain, and Japan agreed to scrap some of their largest warships and, along with France and Italy, promised to limit the tonnage of their existing large ships, abandon gas warfare, and restrict submarine warfare.

The peace movement was less successful in its second goal, outlawing war. In 1928, the United States and 14 other countries signed the Kellogg-Briand Pact forswearing war as an instrument of national policy. Enthusiastically received, the measure lacked an effective mechanism to stop a nation from going to war. U.S. membership in a world court, the third major goal of the peace movement, was not achieved in the 1920s. Too many Americans believed that the court, like the League of Nations, would undermine U.S. sovereignty.

Meanwhile, the United States became an increasingly active member of the world economy. American investment grew substantially overseas during the 1920s, American bankers made major loans around the world, and Ford and other American companies exported their products around the world. More U.S. corporations became multinational firms by building plants overseas.

The growth of American economic activity abroad complicated the priorities of the Harding and Coolidge administrations. In the 1920s, the United States had more interests than ever to protect overseas, but Americans were wary of policies that might lead to war. Many were also uneasy about imperialism, the nation's military role in its own possessions and in supposedly sovereign nations.

The Harding and Coolidge administrations tried to pull back from some of the imperial commitments made by presidents Taft and Wilson in the 1910s. U.S. Marines withdrew from the Dominican Republic in 1924. They also withdrew from Nicaragua in 1925 but returned the next year when the country became politically unstable.

The Harding and Coolidge administrations also attempted to promote a stable world for American business. During the 1920s, the United States helped negotiate an increase in Chinese sovereignty to reduce the chances of conflict in Asia. The United States also tried to stabilize Europe after World War I. With the quiet approval of Republican presidents,

>> "Jazz-band partout!"

Even as political leaders pulled back from an activist foreign policy, American culture spread across the world in new ways. The rapid diffusion of jazz epitomized the powerful global impact of the new, modern culture emerging in the United States. In 1920, a popular French song proclaimed *"Jazz-band partout!"*—"Jazz band everywhere!": "They're jazz bands by day, by night/ They're jazz bands everywhere/ It's all the rage in Paris, it makes men crazy."

Jazz itself was the product of globalization, of the encounter between the musical cultures that Europeans and Africans had brought to the Americas. As World War I ended, jazz became an agent of U.S. musical globalization. African American musicians had been part of the American army sent to France in 1917. The pioneering "Hell Fighters" band of the 369th Infantry Regiment, led by Lt. James Reese Europe, helped introduce the French to the new music. After the war, American jazz groups and musicians began to tour overseas. Both the white musicians of the Original Dixieland Jazz Band and the African American musicians of Will Marion Cook's Southern Syncopated Orchestra visited England in 1919. Sam Wooding's band for the Chocolate Kiddies revue began a tour in 1925 that took African American jazz to Germany, Scandinavia, Spain, the Union of Soviet Socialist Republics, and South America. Meanwhile, phonograph records carried the excitement of this swinging, hot music throughout the world.

The new sounds from America had a strong but complicated impact overseas. Noble Sissle, one of James Reese Europe's musicians, described a jazz "spasm" at a Hell Fighters concert in France: "The audience could stand it no longer; the 'jazz germ' hit them and it seemed to find the vital spot, loosening all muscles and causing what is known in America as an 'eagle rocking fit.'" Jazz seemed at once primitive and modern to the French. On one hand, it conjured up fantasies about African American sensuality and the mysteriousness of the African jungle. On the other, jazz conveyed the excitement of modern life in the industrial age. "The jazz band is the panting of the machine," said a French critic. Above all, jazz seemed quintessentially American, and, as a French writer observed, " helped us finally to discover and to understand the United States." After playing to enthusiastic French audiences, Noble Sissle happily predicted that "American music would one day be the world's music."

That was a worrisome prospect for some French musicians and writers. "[D]oes the whole world," one complained, "have to be American?" A number of French artists feared that jazz would silence French music, especially the French song, or *chanson*. But the *chanson* did not die. Just as white and black Americans had absorbed each other's music, so French musicians reinterpreted American jazz. By the mid-1930s, the greatest jazz-guitar player in the world was a French Gypsy, Django Reinhardt,

continued

whose many records incorporated French popular music, as well as the distinctive, traditional sounds of the Gypsies.

Jazz was indeed *partout*. The music was one sign of the internationaliza-

tion of the new American culture in the 1920s. It was a reminder, too, that the United States could not simply remake the world in its own image, musical and otherwise.

American businessmen intervened to help resolve the controversial issue of how much Germany should pay in reparation to the Allies.

Extending the "New Era"

With their cautious foreign and domestic policies so popular, Republicans faced no serious challenge as the decade came to a close. The Democrats were also hurt by the backlash against modern culture. The Democratic Party depended on support not only from nativists, fundamentalists, and Klansmen, but also from their frequent targets—urban Catholics and Jews. The antagonism among these constituencies helped doom the Democrats' chances in the 1924 and 1928 elections.

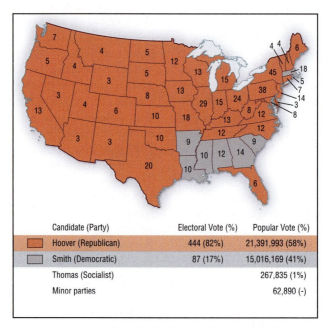

Candidate (Party)	Electoral Vote (%)	Popular Vote (%)
Hoover (Republican)	444 (82%)	21,391,993 (58%)
Smith (Democratic)	87 (17%)	15,016,169 (41%)
Thomas (Socialist)		267,835 (1%)
Minor parties		62,890 (-)

Map 23–1   The Election of 1928 Herbert Hoover's landslide victory extends the Republican "New Era."

>> Timeline

▼1913
Introduction of assembly line at Ford Motor Company

▼1918
End of World War I

▼1919
Black Star Line founded by Marcus Garvey
Original Dixieland Jazz Band and Will Marion Cook's Southern Syncopated
    Orchestra bring jazz to England

▼1920
Commercial radio broadcasting
Warren G. Harding elected president

▼1922
Fordney-McCumber Tariff
Sinclair Lewis, *Babbitt*

▼1923
Calvin Coolidge succeeds Harding as president

▼1924
Teapot Dome scandal
National Origins Act

▼1925
Founding of the Brotherhood of Sleeping Car Porters
Bruce Barton, *The Man Nobody Knows*
Scopes trial

▼1926
Gertrude Ederle's swim across the English Channel

▼1927
Charles Lindbergh's solo transatlantic flight

▼1928
Kellogg-Briand Pact
Herbert Hoover elected president

In 1928, the Democrats nominated Al Smith, the governor of New York, for president. The first Irish Catholic presidential nominee of a major party, Smith displeased fundamentalists and nativists. Moreover, his brassy, urban style—his campaign theme song was "The Sidewalks of New York"—alienated many rural Americans. Smith represented a new generation of urban, ethnic Democrats ready to use activist government to deal with social and economic problems. Their brand of urban liberalism would be influential in later years, but Smith could not galvanize a majority of voters in 1928.

Meanwhile, Herbert Hoover, the Republican nominee, polled 58.2 percent of the popular vote and carried 40 states for a total of 444 electoral votes—the Republicans' largest electoral triumph of the decade. Republicans also increased their majorities in the House and Senate. The New Era would continue.

Conclusion

The Republicans' victory in 1928 underscored the triumph of modern culture. Just as Gertrude Ederle overcame the tides in the English Channel, the "New Era" swept past the challenges of nativists, fundamentalists, and Klansmen. As Hoover prepared to take office, the appeal of the modern culture, rooted in the industrial economy, appeared undeniable. It offered a renewed sense of individual worth and possibility. It promised new freedom to women and youth. It held out an alluring vision of material pleasures—a life devoted to leisure and consumption—to all Americans.

Nevertheless, the modern culture and its Republican defenders were vulnerable. The political "New Era" of the 1920s was especially dependent on the state of the economy. Perhaps more than ever before in their history, Americans equated happiness with the capacity to pay for pleasures. What would happen if Americans lost their jobs and their purchasing power? The new culture and the "New Era" had survived the dissent of alienated and excluded Americans in the 1920s. It would not survive the sudden end of prosperity.

Review Questions

1. What caused the transformation of the industrial economy in the 1910s and 1920s? How did that transformation benefit or harm different economic groups such as big business, workers, and farmers?

2. Why did the modern culture emerge in the 1920s and not before?

3. How did views of sexuality, gender, family, and youth change in the 1920s? Why was individualism so important to the modern culture?

4. Why was there such a widespread backlash against the modern culture of the 1920s? Why did the backlash fail?

5. Why did the Republican Party dominate the emerging political system of the 1920s? How did Republican policies reflect the economic and cultural changes of the decade?

6. Did the United States become more or less democratic a nation in the 1920s?

7. How would the emergence of consumer culture shape the United States beyond the 1920s?

A Great Depression and a New Deal

1929–1940

24

AMERICAN PORTRAIT

>> Margaret Mitchell

Margaret Mitchell wrote her first and only book, *Gone with the Wind*, to earn extra money, and she was more than a little surprised when it became an immediate runaway best seller in June 1936. Stores sold out before the first shipments arrived. Crowds of fans gathered outside her Atlanta apartment. In four days, almost 1,200 letters from admiring readers arrived.

Most wrote to tell Mitchell how she had renewed their faith in themselves. For an urban, industrial society in the depths of the century's worst economic crisis, *Gone with the Wind* conjured up a rural past in which Americans struggled and triumphed. Mitchell's determined heroine, Scarlett O'Hara, survived the collapse of her world in the Civil War through sheer force of will. "I'm going to live through this," Scarlett resolved, "and when it's over, I'm never going to be hungry again." Her eventual triumph reaffirmed the values of self-reliance and individualism at a time when many wondered whether those values still mattered.

In 1936 the Great Depression—the worst economic collapse in United States history—was nearly seven years old. The stock market crash in October 1929 preceded an uninterrupted four-year decline in nearly every sector of the economy. On farms hard work was rewarded with failure and poverty. In cities and towns there was little work to be found. Since the time of Andrew Jackson, Americans had believed that democracy rested on shared values of individualism, private property, and a capitalist market economy. Now, with millions unemployed, these principles were openly questioned. Politicians had few answers, and Americans felt alone and vulnerable.

The popularity of *Gone with the Wind* suggests that even in the depths of the Depression Americans still clung to the promise of individual opportunity. "We Americans have all been taught, from childhood, that it is a sort of moral obligation for each of us to rise, to get up in the world," the writer Sherwood Anderson explained. Steeped in individualism, impoverished Americans blamed themselves for the economy's failure. "It's my own fault," explained a wheat farmer who worked hard his whole life only to

673

>> **AMERICAN PORTRAIT** *continued*

lose his farm. "I wasn't smart enough." *Gone with the Wind* echoed the advice of books, newspapers magazines, radio shows, and movies that encouraged Americans to confront the Great Depression by working harder than ever.

While millions were heartened by Scarlett's old-fashioned individualism, others turned to updated versions of American values. Another bestseller of 1937 was Dale Carnegie's *How to Win Friends and Influence People*, a book that told readers how to become rich and famous. Carnegie, born poor on a Missouri farm, reinvented himself by moving to New York and adopting the last name of a steel tycoon. He sprinkled his writings with the names of celebrities ("Arnold Reubens . . . originator of the four-decker sandwich") who overcame setbacks by following a few simple steps. Where Scarlett O'Hara was the lone heroine overcoming adversity as an individual, Carnegie's hero was a team player, an "organization man" who knew how to manipulate others for himself.

One figure best captured the tension between old and new versions of American individualism. In 1938 *Action Comics* introduced Superman, who in his first year thwarted two European wars, foiled evil businessmen and insane scientists, and rescued helpless politicians by the planeload. Superman's dual identity reflected the split personality of Dale Carnegie's mild-mannered manipulator. Clark Kent, reared in rural Kansas, was a big-city organization man, a reporter for a large daily paper. But beneath his grey flannel suit he was Superman, who could right society's wrongs in a single bound. In one issue, he turned his super strength against the Depression, tearing Metropolis's slums apart with his bare hands and forcing officials to rebuild. The "man of the future" revived the fantasy of the rugged individual able to remake society on his own terms.

Society's emphasis on individual responsibility affected the way voters and politicians responded to the economic disaster. For the first four years of the Depression, the federal government offered solutions based on individuals' willingness to help each other and themselves. But the persistence of the Depression strained the public's faith, and in 1933 the administration undertook a series of experiments to help individuals. The experiments, known collectively as the "New Deal," permanently changed the relationship between Americans and their government. Voters relied on elected officials not just to represent their interests but also to protect their livelihoods. Yet by the late 1930s the ingrained suspicion of big government began to revive, and the New Deal ground to a halt. Margaret Mitchell and her character Scarlett ended the decade in triumph. In 1939 she was immortalized in the film version of *Gone with the Wind*, which swept the 1940 Academy Awards.

Common Threads

>> **Contrast government's response to the Depression against its actions in earlier "panics" in 1893 and 1877.**

>> **How did Franklin D. Roosevelt's Democratic Party differ from the** one that nominated William Jennings Bryan or Woodrow Wilson?

>> **How did the New Deal redefine what it meant to be "liberal" or "conservative"?**

The Great Depression

In the fall of 1929 declining confidence in the stock market shook the economy. By Thursday, October 24, panic had set in as brokers rushed to unload their stocks. Prices rallied briefly, but on October 29, "Black Tuesday," stock values lost over $14 billion, and within the month the market stood at only half its precrash worth. Hundreds of corporations and thousands of individuals were wiped out. On Wall Street, the symbol of prosperity in the 1920s, mounted police had to keep angry mobs away from the stock exchange. Although the crash did not cause the depression, it did expose underlying weaknesses and shatter the confidence President Herbert Hoover relied on for recovery. His optimistic speeches would ring false over the years of unemployment, hunger, and homelessness.

Causes

No single factor explains the Great Depression. Politicians, bureaucrats, and business leaders had no clear idea why things had gone so wrong. Economists and historians still debate the issue today. Yet, even without a definitive account, it is clear that structural flaws in the national and international economies and ill-conceived government policies were at fault.

> Now everyone will get back to work instead of cherishing the idea that it is possible to get rich overnight.
>
> ALFRED P. SLOAN,
> CHAIRMAN,
> GENERAL MOTORS,
> October 27, 1929

In the 1920s the base of the economy had begun to shift. No longer was it driven by steel, coal, textiles, railroads, and other heavy industries. New industries that sold complex consumer goods such as automobiles became the driving force. In addition to cars, sales of radios, clothing, processed foods, and a whole range of consumer products grew dramatically. This shift toward a new consumer-oriented economy was fueled by favorable business conditions, job growth, and plentiful consumer credit. The limits of this market had, however, been reached even before the great crash. When the stock market fell, the collapse of purchasing power caused by mass unemployment and the loss of savings slowed the transition to the new economy.

A rickety credit and financial system added to the problems of the late 1920s. Even in good times banks failed by the hundreds. For rural banks these failures could be traced to low farm prices, but financial institutions everywhere suffered from inept and even criminal management. Banks were virtually unregulated, and in the booming 1920s many bet depositors' money on stocks or large, risky loans. Bank failures magnified the impact of the crash; many thousands lost money they thought was safe.

Like banks, corporate finance was free from regulation and given to misrepresentation, manipulation, and corrupt insider deals. Few could be sure whether investments were going into sound companies or worthless paper.

Government missteps and poor policies also had a role. The Republican administrations of the 1920s were focused on reducing government interference in the economy, lowering taxes on the wealthy, and reducing spending. They did little to address the banking mess, the problems of farmers, or the growing reliance on credit. The Federal Reserve could have dampened speculation in stocks or, after the Depression began, expanded the currency to promote growth. Concerned more about a strong dollar than about stable employment, the Harding and Coolidge administrations cut spending and the money supply, worsening the eventual collapse.

The Depression was magnified by an international economy still reeling from the effects of World War I. Under the peace terms, Germany owed $33 billion in reparations to Britain and France, who in turn owed billions in debts to the United States. Only U.S. bank loans to Germany made these huge payments possible, so throughout the 1920s funds that could have created jobs and industries went instead into this financial merry-go-round. The cycle was broken by the depression in the United States. European nations tried to protect themselves by devaluing their currencies and raising trade barriers. The result was a steady economic decline that made payments on reparations or loans impossible. The cycle reached a breaking point in 1931, and the international financial system came crashing down, bringing with it many more American banks and further deepening the crisis.

Descending into Depression

The statistics describing the Great Depression were alarming. Between 1929 and 1933 every index of economic activity steadily worsened. The gross national product shrank from $104.4 billion in 1929 to $74.2 billion in 1933. The combined incomes of American workers fell by more than 40 percent. Bank failures increased, from 640 in 1928 to 2,294 in 1931. A *New York Times* index of business activity dropped from 114.8 in June of 1929 to 63.7 in March of 1933. Both exports and imports fell by more than two-thirds.

As business activity collapsed, joblessness skyrocketed. Periods of unemployment had always been a feature of capitalist economies, even in good times. What distinguished the Great Depression was the extent and duration of unemployment. At the lowest point of the slump in the early 1930s, between 20 and 30 percent of wage earners were out of work. In some cities the jobless rate was much higher, with Chicago and Detroit near 50 percent, Akron 60 percent, and Toledo a crushing 80 percent. In 1933, the Bureau of Labor Statistics estimated that as many as one in three workers, more than 12,600,000 Americans, were unemployed.

Behind the grim statistics lay terrible human costs. In the spring of 1930, as the first Depression winter came to an end, breadlines appeared in major cities. The unemployed could be seen in the thousands, Sherwood Anderson wrote, "creeping through the streets of American cities, eating from garbage cans." Unemployed men and women stood outside factory gates desperately seeking work, at soup kitchens hoping for a meal, and at homeless shelters already overflowing.

The basic necessities—food, clothing, and shelter—were suddenly hard to get. Schoolteachers reported that growing numbers of students were listless from hunger. Hospitals began receiving patients suffering from nutritional disorders, including children with rickets, a disease caused by a lack of vitamin D. *Fortune* magazine ran an article on Americans who had starved to death. Embarrassed mothers sent children to school in rags. Men wrapped newspapers beneath their shirts as protection from the cold. Desperate families, their savings gone, unable to pay the rent, "doubled up" with relatives. More and more tenants were evicted; more and more banks foreclosed on mortgages. Apartments stood vacant and homes went unsold, yet by 1932 more than a million homeless men, women, and children occupied shantytowns or slept in doorways and alleys. Hoboes were everywhere, searching for something to eat, somewhere to live, someplace to work.

Table 24-1 Labor Force and Unemployment, 1929–1941 (Numbers in Millions)

| Year | Labor Force | Unemployment | |
		Number	% of Labor Force
1929	49.2	1.6	3.2
1930	49.8	4.3	8.7
1931	50.4	8.0	15.9
1932	51.0	12.1	23.6
1933	51.6	12.8	24.9
1934	52.2	11.3	21.7
1935	52.9	10.6	20.1
1936	53.4	9.0	16.9
1937	54.0	7.7	14.3
1938	54.6	10.4	19.0
1939	55.2	9.5	17.2
1940	55.6	8.1	14.6
1941	55.9	5.6	9.9

Source: *United States Department of Commerce*, Historical Statistics of the United States (1960), p. 70.

Farmers faced both economic and environmental disaster. Farmers in the Plains states and the West aggressively increased production in the 1920s and then saw the markets for corn, wheat, beef, and pork collapse. Between 1929 and 1932, farmers' income dropped by two-thirds. Then the drought struck. Between 1930 and 1936, the rains all but stopped in large parts of the South, the Southwest, and the Great Plains. Exposed by decades of wasteful farming practices, the earth dried up and blew away. Spectacular dust storms carried topsoil hundreds of miles through the air, giving a new

Effects of the Dust Bowl Drought and modern agriculture churned the Great Plains into silica powder that was carried by windstorms. Over half the patients in Kansas hospitals in 1935 suffered from dust pneumonia.

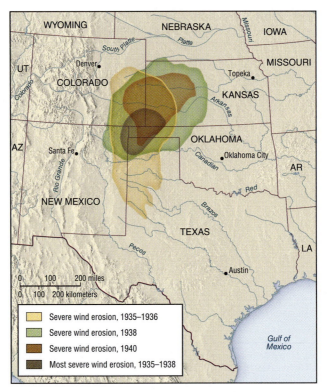

Map 24–1   Extent of Dust Bowl The Dust Bowl of the 1930s eventually spread across thousands of square miles of the Southern Plains.

name—the Dust Bowl—to much of the Southern Plains. Dust and depression ripped thousands of farm families from the land in Texas, Kansas, Oklahoma, and Arkansas, sending these "Okies," "Arkies," and "Texies" off to California in search of work.

The Great Depression affected nearly everyone in America, but it was most severe for those already disadvantaged. Although the shock of the Dust Bowl affected many poor white farmers, the larger agricultural depression was even more devastating for share-croppers on the southern cotton lands, workers in the wheat fields of the Midwest, and the vast migrant labor pools that traveled the East and West coasts picking fruits and vegetables. In cities, African Americans, who held the least secure jobs, found themselves pushed from menial service tasks and unskilled work by desperate white workers.

By 1932 private charities, the major social safety net before the Depression, failed to meet the needs of desperate citizens. Ethnic organizations such as the Bohemian Charitable Association or Jewish Charities in Chicago now found themselves overwhelmed. Arthur T. Burns, the president of the Association of Community Chests and Councils, flatly declared, "the funds we have are altogether inadequate to meet the situation."

Public monies were just as scarce. Only eight states provided any form of unemployment insurance; most of it was meager. The few state welfare agencies were poorly funded and now stretched beyond their limits. Entire cities faced insolvency as their tax bases dwindled. Many states were forbidden by their constitutions to borrow for social welfare expenditures. Frustrated Americans looked to the federal government for a solution, but there was little help beyond pensions for veterans. There was no social security for the elderly and disabled, no federal unemployment insurance for those who lost their jobs, and no food stamps to relieve hunger.

The federal government was under unprecedented pressure to do something, anything, to relieve the Depression. Even bankers and businessmen abandoned their resistance to a strong central government. The president of Columbia University suggested that a dictatorship might provide more effective leadership. Others warned of social revolution. Most of the pleas for action were aimed at the administration, and Herbert Hoover himself came to symbolize the failures of government. The newspapers that jobless men wrapped themselves in were called "Hoover shirts"; shantytowns were "Hoovervilles." In the popular imagination, Hoover and the Great Depression became inseparable.

Hoover Responds

In many ways, Hoover was ideally qualified to handle this emergency. He had experience with natural and human catastrophes. Orphaned at a young age, Hoover worked hard to educate himself. Trained as an engineer at Stanford University, he roamed the world building and managing mining operations and was a millionaire by his mid-20s. Like other young progressives, Hoover sought to use business skills to solve social problems. He won

A Hooverville in Seattle, Washington As the Depression deepened, the homeless settled in "Hoovervilles" on the edge of city centers.

fame as an administrator of emergency relief, saving Belgium from starvation during World War I and overseeing rescue efforts during the Great Mississippi Flood of 1927.

He brought to the presidency a well-developed theory of the role of government in a modern economy. Hoover believed that complex societies required accurate economic information, careful planning, and large-scale coordination. His political philosophy, associationalism, envisioned a federal government empowered to gather information and encourage voluntary cooperation among businesses but forbidden to intervene further. He feared that an overbearing government would crush the creativity essential to a capitalist economy. This voluntarist dream fit well with America's dominant ideology, and Hoover easily won the presidency in 1928.

Hoover acted quickly. One of his first achievements was the Agricultural Marketing Act of 1929, designed to raise farm incomes and rationalize production. Since the turn of the century, farmers had been plagued by a "paradox of plenty." They produced more food and fiber than Americans could consume, so the more farmers grew, the less they earned. The bill established a Federal Farm Board to create cooperatives for purchasing and distributing surplus crops. It issued $500 million in loans to stabilize prices but did not limit production or dictate prices.

When the market crashed, Hoover's initial response reflected his overall vision. His goal was to get business to promise to cooperate to maintain wages and investment. In 1931, as 25 banks a week were failing, he encouraged formation of the National Credit Corporation, in which banks were urged to pool resources to stave off collapse. Rather than distribute unemployment insurance or poor relief, he tried to persuade companies not to lay off workers and to contribute to charities for the homeless and unemployed. But the breadth and depth of the Depression overwhelmed Hoover's schemes. Crop prices fell so low that farmers blockaded cities and demanded compensation for their crops.

Hoover had never failed before, and he worked tirelessly to fight the Depression. By 1932, he reluctantly agreed to more aggressive government action, even at the risk of deficit spending. He proposed a Reconstruction Finance Corporation (RFC) authorized to loan $2 billion to revive large corporations. Plans to increase government revenues and distribute farm surpluses to the needy were also enacted. But it was too little, too late. The Depression was three years old and showed no signs of lifting.

Hoover's policies did not simply fail to relieve the Depression; rather, they increased its severity. Unable to control his own party, Hoover watched Congress pass the Hawley-Smoot Tariff in 1930. The tariff raised import duties to record levels, stifling hopes that international trade might help the economy and damaging the weak nations of Europe. Despite misgivings, he signed the bill into law. At the same time, Hoover opposed other measures that might have relieved poverty or stimulated recovery. He vetoed massive public works bills sponsored by congressional Democrats. Finally, Hoover's stubborn commitment to the gold standard and a balanced budget choked off hopes of a turnaround.

Hoover, whose popularity had plummeted as the Depression deepened, reinforced his reputation as a protector of the privileged by his response to the Bonus Marchers in 1932. In 1924 Congress had issued the veterans of World War I a "bonus" to be paid in 1945. But as the Depression threw millions out of work, veterans asked to have their bonuses paid early. In the summer of 1932, veterans formed a "Bonus Expeditionary Force" to march on Washington. Arriving on freight cars and buses, over 20,000 Bonus Marchers and their families encamped on Capitol grounds. Hoover ordered the army to remove the marchers. Against orders, General Douglas MacArthur attacked with tanks and mounted cavalry. Major George S. Patton, saber drawn, galloped through the encampment, setting fire to its miserable tents and shacks. Among those he attacked was Joseph T. Angelino, who won the Distinguished Service Cross in 1918 for saving Patton's life. Photographs of government brutality shocked Americans. Hoover's silence solidified his reputation for callousness.

As Congress struggled to relieve unemployment and suffering, Hoover dismissed the "futile attempt to cure poverty by the enactment of law." Arrogant and aloof, he questioned the integrity and motives of everyone who disagreed with his policies. By the end of his term the "Great Humanitarian" had become sullen and withdrawn. It was a dispirited Republican Convention that met in Chicago to nominate Hoover for reelection in 1932.

The First New Deal

When the Democratic Convention chose a presidential candidate in 1932, Franklin Delano Roosevelt flew from Albany, New York, to Chicago to accept the nomination in person, a dramatic gesture in an age new to air travel and personal politics. "I pledge myself," he told the enthusiastic crowd, "to a new deal for the American people." The phrase stuck, and the reforms enacted between 1933 and 1938 have since come to be known as the New Deal. The programs came in two great waves, the "first" and "second" New Deals. The first New Deal began with the Hundred Days, a burst of executive and legislative activity following FDR's inauguration, and continued through 1934.

The Election of 1932

The Depression reached its lowest depths as the 1932 election approached, and the Republicans seemed headed for disaster. Their inability to develop a legislative program to attack the Depression had already cost them control of the House. But to take advantage of the situation, Democrats had to overcome serious internal divisions.

Throughout the 1920s the Democratic Party had been split between the ethnically diverse, wet (anti-Prohibition), urban wing concentrated in the North and the East and the Anglo-Saxon Protestant, rural southern and western wings. Ideological divisions on many issues separated northeastern business Democrats from western populists and urban progressives from southern conservatives.

The leading candidate for the Democratic nomination, New York's Governor Franklin D. Roosevelt, had the background to overcome many of these divisions. He came from an upstate rural district, and his interest in conservation endeared him to many westerners. He had built ties to southern Democrats while serving as Wilson's assistant secretary of the navy and as a sometime resident of Warm Springs, Georgia. As governor of New York his strong record of support for progressive social reforms appealed to urban liberals.

Roosevelt turned out to be the ideal candidate. As a distant cousin of Theodore Roosevelt, he had a recognizable name. FDR also had immense personal charm. Despite having been crippled by polio since 1921, he was a tireless campaigner and would become one of the most visible of modern presidents. He was an American aristocrat, raised in wealth and educated at Groton and Harvard. Yet he spoke in clear, direct language that ordinary Americans found persuasive and reassuring.

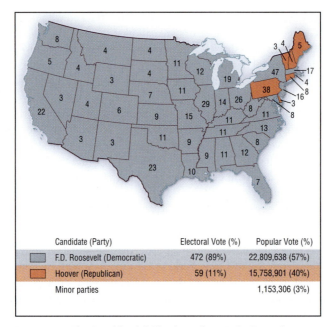

Candidate (Party)	Electoral Vote (%)	Popular Vote (%)
F.D. Roosevelt (Democratic)	472 (89%)	22,809,638 (57%)
Hoover (Republican)	59 (11%)	15,758,901 (40%)
Minor parties		1,153,306 (3%)

Map 24–2 The Presidential Election of 1932 By November 1932 most American voters blamed the Depression on Hoover and the Republicans. The Democrats, led by Franklin Delano Roosevelt, swept into office by huge electoral margins.

During the campaign, Roosevelt simultaneously embraced old orthodoxies and enticed reformers with hints of more radical changes. He promised to cut government spending and provide government relief for the poor. FDR did not say how he would do both, but it hardly mattered. In November 1932, the Republicans were swept out of office in a tide of popular repudiation. FDR and the Democrats took control of the government with the promise of "a new deal" for the American people.

Roosevelt worked hard to develop a program to fight the Depression. While governor of New York, FDR had recruited intellectuals who provided him with an influential diagnosis of the Great Depression. Known as the "Brains Trust," they attempted to convince Roosevelt that the Depression was caused by the economy's fundamental defects. The core issue was the maldistribution of wealth. Because the rich held on to too large a share of the profits of American industry, the economy was producing much more than Americans could consume.

Roosevelt never fully bought the ideas of the Brains Trust nor allowed any one group to dominate his thinking. FDR's comfort with experimentation and chaos would hold his administration together and enable it to confront the complexities of the Depression. Where Hoover had retreated into dogmatism, FDR endorsed "bold, persistent experimentation." Above all, he ordered his officials, "try something." And rather than trying to unite his followers behind a single idea or policy, Roosevelt seemed to enjoy watching his advisers feud while he orchestrated their final compromises. The president, an adviser said, was "the boss, the dynamo, the works."

FDR Takes Command

In the weeks before the inauguration, the ailing American banking system took a sharp turn for the worse. In mid-February the governor of Michigan declared an eight-day bank holiday. In one of the most important manufacturing states, nearly a million depositors could not get their money. Stock prices dropped when the news came, and the rich began shipping their gold to safer countries. Panic struck, and funds flew out of bank tellers' windows. On the morning of the inauguration New York and Illinois joined most of the other states in calling a bank holiday. The New York Stock Exchange and Illinois Board of Trade also closed. To many, it seemed like the end of the American economy.

With commerce at a standstill, the nation turned to the new president, and Roosevelt did not disappoint. "First of all," he declared, "let me assert my firm belief that the only thing we have to fear is—fear itself, nameless, unreasoning, unjustified terror." Such words could easily have sounded empty, but in the midst of a frightening financial collapse they revitalized the nation almost overnight.

Roosevelt knew reassuring words alone would not end the crisis. On his first day in office, he declared a national bank holiday to last through the end of the week. He instructed his new secretary of the treasury to draft emergency legislation and called Congress into special session. When Congress convened on March 9, the drafting team had barely finished the bill, but Congress was ready to act. Breaking all precedent, the House unanimously shouted its approval of the bill after less than a half hour of debate; the Senate voted to do the same with only seven dissents, and the president signed it into law that night. The Emergency Banking Act was a modest reform. It gave the treasury secretary the power to determine which banks could safely reopen and which had to be reorganized. It also enabled the RFC to strengthen sound banks by buying their stocks.

On Sunday night, a week after taking office, FDR went on national radio to deliver the first of his many "fireside chats." Sixty million people tuned in to hear Roosevelt explain, in his resonant, fatherly voice, his response to the banking crisis. He assured Americans that their money would be "safer in a reopened bank than under the mattress." The government was not fully sure how solid most banks were, but the gamble worked. The next day, 12,756 banks reopened, the run stopped, and deposits started flowing into the system. The immediate crisis was over.

Once the banking crisis had been resolved in March 1933, Roosevelt wanted to ensure that the financial system would remain sound for the long run. He moved to restrict banks' speculations while guaranteeing their

FDR Photographed During One of His Fireside Chats Hoover broadcast his speeches on radio, but Roosevelt's "fireside chats" took advantage of the intimacy of the new medium.

profitability. The Glass-Steagall Banking Act of 1933 imposed conservative banking practices nationwide. Chancy loans, stock investments, and shady business practices were outlawed, and close federal oversight guaranteed bank stability until Glass-Steagall was repealed in 1999. In addition, the new Federal Deposit Insurance Corporation protected deposits. The Banking Act of 1935 reorganized the Federal Reserve under more centralized and democratic control. Together, these laws established the credibility of the U.S. banking system. One reason the banking system had become so vulnerable was its ties to the unregulated securities markets. So in 1933 the administration sponsored a Truth in Securities Act that required all companies issuing stock to disclose accurate information to all prospective buyers. In 1934 Congress passed the Securities and Exchange Act. Whereas the 1933 law regulated companies, the 1934 legislation regulated the markets, prohibiting inside trading and other forms of manipulation. It gave the Federal Reserve Board the power to control the supply of credit and established the Securities and Exchange Commission, which quickly became one of the largest and most effective regulatory agencies in the country.

Federal Relief

Roosevelt's unemployment programs departed sharply from Hoover's relief strategies. In May, Congress passed a bill providing a half billion dollars for relief and creating the Federal Emergency Relief Administration (FERA) to oversee it. Local and state agencies dispensed the funds. Headed by Harry Hopkins, a shrewd social worker and Roosevelt confidant, FERA distributed money at a rapid rate. As winter came on, Hopkins convinced Roosevelt that only a massive new federal program could avert disaster. At FDR's request, Congress created the Civil Works Administration (CWA), which employed 4 million men and women. During the winter, the CWA built or renovated over half a million miles of road and tens of thousands of schools and other public buildings. The CWA was eliminated in the spring—Roosevelt did not want the nation to get used to a federal welfare program—but FERA continued to run programs on a smaller scale.

Of all the relief programs, Roosevelt was most enthusiastic about one, the Civilian Conservation Corps (CCC). FDR believed that life in the countryside and service to the nation would have a positive moral impact on the young men of the cities and on those Depression "wild boys" roaming the nation. For the CCC, these young men built roads and trails in the national parks. By the time the program ended in 1942, it had transformed America's public lands and employed over 3 million teenagers and young adults.

The Farm Crisis

I don't want on the relief if I can help it," a Louisiana farm woman wrote to the first lady, Eleanor Roosevelt, in the fall of 1935. "I want to work for my livin'." But she was desperate. She asked Mrs. Roosevelt to send money to save the family cow "for my little children to have milk." The doctor was no longer able to give her sick child medicine "unless we pay him some for he is in debt for it." The landlord was threatening to evict them. She had turned to the first lady because of Mrs. Roosevelt's reputation for caring about the poor, but political realities would limit what the first lady, or her husband, could do to help.

Eleanor Roosevelt Eleanor Roosevelt wrote a syndicated newspaper column, personally inspected government projects, and acted as a presidential adviser, all new roles for a first lady.

By the spring of 1933, farmers were desperate. Prices of commodities such as corn, cotton, wheat, and tobacco had fallen so low that it was not even worth the cost of harvesting. The banking crisis left farmers without access to necessary credit, and millions faced foreclosure, homelessness, or dust storms.

FDR saw a stark "imbalance" between city and country as a root cause of the Depression. While the land remained the only real source of wealth, modern cities absorbed all of the countryside's water, produce, talent, and people. The Dust Bowl was a result of this ecological distortion. His aim was to restore a more even pattern of development, with small manufacturing towns, suburbs, and farms linked to centers of culture and commerce. The New Deal program that came closest to fulfilling these goals was the Tennessee Valley Authority, or TVA. In his campaign, Roosevelt had endorsed a proposal to develop the Muscle Shoals property along the Tennessee River. Congress created the TVA within the first Hundred Days. The TVA was a "corporation clothed with the power of government but possessed of the flexibility and initiative of a private enterprise." According to its administrator, it aimed to change the environment, the economy, the way of life, and the "habits, social, economic, and personal" of a region that spanned nine states.

One of the most ambitious projects of the entire New Deal, the TVA was also astonishingly successful. The dams built by the TVA controlled flooding, created reservoirs for irrigation, and provided cheap hydroelectric power. Electricity improved life for millions of farm families and made it possible for industry to move into new areas, bringing jobs to some of the poorest parts of the country. The TVA took responsibility for soil conservation, reforestation, improved navigation, and the manufacture of fertilizer and aluminum. During the Roosevelt administration, the poor Tennessee–North Carolina border region went from growing cotton to manufacturing aircraft and components for nuclear weapons. Average incomes in the area increased tenfold. As a comprehensive, centrally planned development scheme, the TVA came closest to the Brains Trusters' vision of how a modern "democracy on the march" should work.

Headed by Henry Wallace, founder of the Pioneer Hi-Bred Corn Company, the Agriculture Department was an idea factory in the first Hundred Days. An emergency farm bill gave Wallace powers to control production, buy up surpluses, regulate marketing, and levy taxes. Conservation and reclamation projects drained swamps, irrigated deserts, and sheltered the Great Plains from windstorms. The Agricultural Adjustment Act

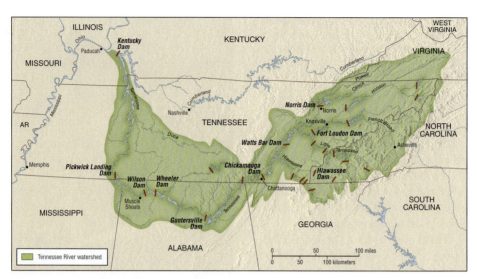

Map 24–3   TVA Projects The Tennessee Valley Authority (TVA) was one of the most ambitious of all New Deal projects. A network of dams provided electricity, irrigation, and flood control to many of the poorest regions of the South.

(AAA) turned agriculture into a regulated industry. After 1933, farmers, once fiercely independent, essentially worked for the federal government. The New Deal farm system permanently altered the American diet by making processed grains, grain-fed meat, sugar, and dairy products cheap and plentiful relative to unsubsidized fresh vegetables, fruits, and fish.

In many respects, however, the New Deal did little for the rural poor. Price supports and production controls helped farmers who owned their own land, whereas soil conservation, irrigation, and rural electrification tended to benefit independent commercial farmers. Subsistence farmers and the landless poor—Mexican migrant workers in the Far West and tenants and sharecroppers, black and white, in the cotton South—gained little. An unintended consequence of New Deal production limits was to take work away from the poorest Americans, pushing them to migrate from the country to industrial cities.

Native Americans suffered an especially severe form of rural poverty. Shunted onto reservations in the late nineteenth century, the majority of American Indians by 1930 were landless, miserably poor, and subjected to the corrupt paternalism of the Bureau of Indian Affairs. Alcoholism, crime, and infant mortality plagued reservations. John Collier, FDR's commissioner of Indian affairs, was determined to correct the situation, and the Indian Reorganization Act of 1934 gave him the power to try. Collier reversed decades of federal attempts to assimilate Native Americans into the mainstream. Under the New Deal, forced land sales ended, and reservations were enlarged. Tribal democracy replaced bureaucratic authority. But Congressional opponents, even western liberals, resented attempts to preserve traditional culture. Indians themselves were divided over policies and goals, and what worked for Pueblo communities might not work for the Navajo. As a result, although the New Deal relieved some poverty among Native Americans, it did not develop a satisfactory long-term solution.

The Blue Eagle

FDR had no fixed plan for industrial recovery and preferred to wait for business interests to agree on one before acting. Congress, however, moved independently to pass a bill aimed at spreading employment by limiting the workweek to 30 hours. Heading off what he thought an ill-conceived plan, Roosevelt offered his last proposal to become law in the first Hundred Days: the National Industrial Recovery Act. It mandated that business, labor, and government officials negotiate a "code" restructuring each industry into a national cartel. The code would set trade practices, wages, hours, and production quotas. The hope was to raise prices by limiting production while protecting the purchasing power of workers. The NIRA reversed decades of antitrust law. The act protected organized labor by guaranteeing unions the right of collective bargaining. Finally, $3.3 billion was earmarked for jobs creation through a Public Works Administration.

The NIRA was a bold idea, but it suffered from many of the same problems as Hoover's earlier schemes. It brought together hundreds of industries to draw up their codes, but the process tended to be dominated by business. Few strong unions existed, and smaller businesses were shut out, leaving the largest corporations to write the codes in their interest. For a time in 1933 and 1934 the Blue Eagle banner, the symbol of compliance with the codes, flew proudly in the windows of shops and factories. Dissatisfaction with the program soon dampened enthusiasm, and by 1935 the eagle had come to roost atop a shaky and unpopular agency.

The Second New Deal

The first Hundred Days had been extraordinary by any standard. Congress had given the president unprecedented power to regulate the economy. The financial system had been saved from collapse. Federal relief reached the unemployed. The agricultural economy was given direct federal support. The TVA had created a "yardstick" for public utilities. A bold experiment in industrial planning had been attempted. Almost everyone was dazzled, but not everyone was pleased. Critics noted that much of this legislation was poorly drafted, overly conservative, or just self-contradictory. If Hoover had been too rigid, FDR struck even his admirers as hopelessly flexible. By 1935 the New Deal was besieged by critics from all directions. But Roosevelt responded to political criticism and judicial setbacks by keeping Congress in session throughout the hot summer of 1935. The result was another dramatic wave of reforms known as the second New Deal.

Critics Attack from All Sides

In May 1935 one of William Randolph Hearst's emissaries traveled to Washington to warn Roosevelt that the New Deal was becoming too radical. Hearst was one of the most powerful newspaper publishers in America and, like many businessmen, had "no confidence" in Roosevelt's advisers. But by 1935 Roosevelt was losing patience with the business community. Saving capitalism was always one of Roosevelt's goals, but shortsighted capitalists never appreciated his efforts. They had their own reasons for detesting the New Deal, and they proved more potent critics than all of Roosevelt's radical opponents combined.

The fate of the Communist Party illustrates the difficulties radicals faced during the New Deal. On the one hand, the 1930s were the "heyday of American Communism,"

AMERICAN LANDSCAPE

>> Angola, Louisiana

"Angola was a pleasant place to live back then," Patsy Spillman remembers of her childhood in the 1930s. "You could get inmates as cooks, yard boys, house boys; you could have two or three of them if you wanted." "It was wonderful," her sister JoAn agrees. "We had servants, and we didn't want for anything." There were occasional problems. Once, a convict put rat poison in the girls' milk. The Himel family down the road had their throats slit by a prisoner attempting to escape. JoAn and Patsy were the daughters of John Spillman, a guard "captain" at the Louisiana State Penitentiary at Angola. Their home was a plantation house inside the prison.

Apart from the striped uniforms, Angola in the 1930s resembled a pre–Civil War plantation, 18,000 treeless acres of cotton and sugarcane bounded on one side by the Tunica Hills and on the other three by levees holding back the Mississippi River. Inmates, organized into work gangs, slept in military-style "camps" and rose before dawn to chop cotton and cane and refine sugar in the prison's own mill. Guards, all of them white, flogged prisoners, most of them black, with a leather strap an average of three times a day between 1928 and 1940. "Angola was probably the closest thing to a feudal system in America," one warden observed, "the guard captains being the lordly aristocrats and the inmates as the downtrodden serfs."

The prison's main purpose was to turn a profit, not to reform prisoners or even to keep them alive. With the economy in crisis, voters and legislators wanted to lower property taxes while increasing state spending on roads, education, and jobs. To save money, Governor Huey Long demanded that the prison system be self-supporting, or even return revenue to the state. Democratic pressures created the system of convict slavery at Angola.

Before 1928, many southern states had a "convict lease" system that allowed planters and private businesses to rent chain gangs of prisoners. In the 1930s that system disappeared, as Long and other governors realized that the state could as easily reap the proceeds for itself. With two-thirds of American workers unemployed, convict laborers nationwide produced $75 million a year in shirts, shoes, cement, license plates, and other goods and services. Inmates at Angola were treated as state property and used to repair roads, tend gardens at the governor's mansion, and even to perform minstrel shows. Prisoners worked 60 hours a week for two cents a day. They grew their own food, slept in unheated barracks, used the same bucket for a toilet and to hold drinking water, and had no medical care. Epidemics regularly swept through the camps. In the 1930s, an average of 41 prisoners died each year.

No walls stood between the prisoners and the outside. The prisoners guarded themselves. Fewer than 20 free captains, along with 600 armed "trusty" convicts, guarded over 4,000 prisoners. Trusties were rewarded for shooting prisoners who stepped over the "deadlines" that surrounded work areas. Mounted teams hunted escapees with dogs. Survivors were "hotboxed" in airless cells at the notorious Red Hat camp, where they received only bread and water. Desperation drove prisoners to keep trying. On September 10, 1933, 12 prisoners took advantage of a Sunday baseball game to shoot a captain and two trusties and steal a car. They were captured in hours. The next year, 15 Red Hats working an okra field brandished wooden pistols and disarmed two trusties, but other guards shot them down.

The system established in the 1930s has proven surprisingly resilient. Voters continue to demand that prisons turn a profit. When the population topped 4,000 inmates in the 1950s, the prison was deemed overcrowded. Today it has 5,100; over half are lifers, and 87 are awaiting execution. Prisoners still work five days a week, raising soybeans and cattle instead of sugar, for two cents an hour. The prison now serves the local tourist economy. Vacationers can explore a museum on the site of the old Red Hat camp and attend an annual rodeo, where convicts ride bulls. In 1976, inmates started a newspaper, *The Angolite*, which won a Pulitzer Prize for reporting on prison life. Its editor likes to quote the essayist William Hazlitt, who wrote that "We are all, more or less, slaves of opinion."

as perhaps a quarter of a million disillusioned Americans joined the Communist Party (CPUSA). The Communists organized labor unions and took the lead in defending the Scottsboro Boys, nine young African American men falsely accused of raping two white women in Alabama. On the other hand, the party's appeal was greatest after 1935, when, on orders from the Soviet Union, it adopted a "popular front" strategy in support of the New Deal. The Communists were most popular when they surrendered their revolutionary aims. Most of those who joined had left the party by the end of the decade.

Populist radicals gave Roosevelt more trouble. Father Charles Coughlin was a Catholic priest in Detroit who attracted listeners to his weekly radio show by blaming the Depression on international bankers and Wall Street. His solution was to nationalize the banking system and inflate the currency. At first the radio priest defended Roosevelt and blamed the New Deal on Communist and Jewish influence. But by 1935 Coughlin turned on the president. He formed his own organization, the National Union for Social Justice, to pressure Congress for further reforms.

A California physician, Dr. Francis Townsend, offered an agenda appealing to older Americans devastated by the Depression. Through a transaction tax of 2 percent, the government would fund retirement pensions of $200 per month. By requiring elderly retirees to spend all of their pensions each month, the program was supposed to pump money into the economy and stimulate a recovery. Huey Long's "Share Our Wealth" program was more comprehensive than Townsend's and more popular than Coughlin's. As governor of Louisiana, Long slapped steep taxes on the oil industry that he used for roads, schools, hospitals, and Louisiana State University. In the process, he amassed nearly dictatorial powers, controlling the legislature and the state police. At first, Long

was a loyal but critical supporter of FDR, but by 1934 he was proposing his own alternative to the New Deal.

Long believed that the Depression was caused by the maldistribution of income. His program for recovery called for the radical redistribution of wealth through confiscatory taxes
on the rich and a guaranteed minimum income of $2,500 per year. Townsend's, Coughlin's,
and Long's plans all contained truths about the American economy. The currency did need to
be inflated. Elderly Americans were indeed desperate, and wealth was unequally distributed.
Roosevelt eventually defused these movements by adopting parts of their programs.

The business community's rising hostility concerned FDR as he prepared for his 1936
campaign. It would be years before bankers admitted that the New Deal had saved the
financial system. Wall Street never admitted it. And most industrialists became vocal critics of the NIRA. As criticism grew, a conservative U.S. Supreme Court moved to strike
down many of the key laws of the first Hundred Days. On May 27, 1935, in *Schechter
Poultry Corporation v. United States*, the Court invalidated the NIRA. The case had been
brought by a small poultry company but was financed by larger companies out to kill the
Blue Eagle. The justices ruled the NIRA unconstitutional in a way that made it difficult
for Congress to regulate the national economy to any significant degree. Roosevelt feared
the setback would undo most of his achievements, and his fears were borne out in January
1936, when the Court overturned the Agricultural Adjustment Act.

The Second Hundred Days

FDR loved a good fight. No longer concerned about attracting support from business, he
welcomed criticism and shot right back. After 1935 the rhetoric became noticeably more
radical. When the Supreme Court invalidated the NIRA, Roosevelt kept Congress in session through a sweltering summer and forced through a raft of legislation in a "second
Hundred Days," which began the second New Deal.

A few of the new proposals were meant to salvage pieces of the NIRA and AAA or to
silence radical critics. Hoping to undermine the "crackpot ideas" of Huey Long, Roosevelt
proposed a Revenue Act to encourage a "wider distribution of the wealth." It raised estate
and corporate taxes and pushed personal income taxes in the top bracket up to 79 percent.
Despite the political motives behind the bill, it made economic sense. Before the 1935 Revenue Act, most New Deal programs had been financed by regressive sales and excise taxes.
Thereafter, programs were funded with progressive income taxes that fell most heavily on
those best able to pay.

The first New Deal had been preoccupied with the emergency of 1933. The second
New Deal left a more enduring legacy. The administration finished its program to ensure
the long-term security of the financial system and extend the relief programs that had
helped so many to survive. It created a social security system that anchored the American
welfare state for the rest of the century. With organized labor it created a new and powerful Democratic Party coalition. By the time Congress adjourned in late August 1935, the
most important achievements of the New Deal were in place.

Social Security for Some

Bolstered by big Democratic gains in the 1934 elections, FDR pursued a massive effort
to fund work relief by sponsoring the Emergency Relief Appropriations Bill. Providing

nearly $5 billion, more than the entire 1932 federal budget, the bill rejuvenated the relief programs of the first New Deal and created a new Works Progress Administration (WPA), headed by Harry Hopkins. The WPA lasted for eight years, employing as many as 3.3 million Americans. WPA workers built bridges, schools, libraries, sewer systems, the Blue Ridge Parkway, and more than 800 airports. The WPA commissioned artists to decorate post offices and historians to collect the stories of mill workers and former slaves. At Indiana University, the WPA paid undergraduates to build a student union. WPA lexicographers wrote a Hebrew-English dictionary. The program was hugely popular.

Critics of the WPA complained with some justice about meaningless "make-work" jobs and unqualified workers. Political corruption was a more serious problem. WPA officials, especially at the local level, often used the agency as a patronage machine, favoring loyal party regulars with contracts and jobs. In many states, particularly in the South, officials openly discriminated against African Americans. The WPA was never able to employ all those who needed work, but for millions of Americans it provided immediate relief from the very real prospect of hunger and misery.

The New Deal also created a permanent system of long-term economic security. In 1932 there were no national programs of unemployment insurance, workers' compensation, old-age pensions, or aid to needy children, and the states were only slightly more able to care for citizens. Most Americans had little or no protection from economic calamity.

The Social Security Act of 1935 took a critical first step toward providing such protection. It established matching grants to states that set up their own systems of workers' compensation, unemployment insurance, and aid to families with dependent children. More important, the federal government itself created a huge social security system that guaranteed pensions to millions of elderly Americans. FDR insisted that it be funded as an insurance plan, with payroll taxes paid by employees and employers. He hoped that this would protect the system from the political attacks that welfare programs typically encountered.

Most New Dealers hoped to go much further. Secretary of Labor Frances Perkins wanted to include agricultural laborers and domestic servants, mostly women and African Americans, in the new social security system. But that would have provoked enough opposition from southern conservatives to kill the entire program. The administration also preferred federal- rather than state-run programs. There was, however, no federal bureaucracy in place to run such programs, and there was fierce opposition to the idea of taking such programs away from the states.

Local and factional opposition limited the New Deal's plans for nationalized social welfare and economic security. Welfare and insurance programs were weaker in the South than in the North and weaker for women and African Americans than for white men. Despite such strong opposition, the New Deal accomplished a great deal. By 1939 every state had a program of unemployment insurance and assistance to the elderly. Almost overnight the social security system became the federal government's first huge social welfare bureaucracy. More Americans than ever before were now protected from the ravages of unemployment, disability, poverty, and old age.

Labor and the New Deal

During the 1930s unions took a new role in America's political economy. The number of Americans organized in unions leaped by the millions, and by 1940 nearly one in four nonfarm workers was unionized. Labor organizations were able to enroll workers in core industries, including steel, rubber, electronics, and automobiles. Unions also became key players in the Democratic Party. None of the leading New Dealers, Roosevelt included, had anticipated this in 1932, but in critical ways the New Deal fostered the growth of organized labor and its inclusion in the Democratic electoral coalition.

Unlike past administrations, Roosevelt's had never demonstrated outright hostility toward unions. Rather, through the 1930s FDR moved from grudging acceptance to open support for organized labor. Across the country, workers responded to the change. Unions were now allowed to run organizing drives, and labor began to flex its muscle with a spontaneous wave of strikes. Mill workers in the South launched brave, but doomed, strikes against textile manufacturers. Dockworkers in San Francisco organized a successful general strike throughout the city. At the same time, the NIRA inspired a talented group of national leaders, in particular John L. Lewis of the United Mine Workers, Sidney Hillman of the Amalgamated Clothing Workers, and David Dubinsky of the International Ladies' Garment Workers.

Employers fought back against this new militancy. They used all the methods to intimidate workers—espionage, blacklisting, and armed assault—that had once worked so well. But when it became clear that the federal government would now protect workers seeking to organize and bargain collectively, employers formed company unions to thwart workers' independent action. By 1935 the employers seemed to be winning, particularly when the Supreme Court declared the NIRA, and its protection of union rights, unconstitutional. In 1935 worker militancy declined, and the unionization drive seemed stalled. But the hopes of organized labor were kept alive by an influential and imaginative liberal senator from New York named Robert Wagner.

Wagner took the lead in expanding the NIRA's limited labor protections into the National Labor Relations Act, also known as the Wagner Act. Although he had few ties to organized labor, Wagner believed workers had a basic right to join unions. He also hoped that effective unions would stimulate the economy by raising wages, thereby building consumer purchasing power. Like the NIRA provisions, the Wagner Act guaranteed workers the right to bargain collectively with their employers, but it also outlawed company unions, prohibited employers from firing workers after a strike, and restricted many other antiunion tactics. Most important, the Wagner Act created the National Labor Relations Board (NLRB) to enforce these provisions. In the summer of 1935 FDR declared the Wagner Act "must" legislation, and the bill became law.

While Wagner and his colleagues moved in Congress, John L. Lewis and Sidney Hillman took another course. In 1935 they pressed the conservative leadership of the American Federation of Labor to accept the principle of industrial unions, which would organize workers in an entire sector of the economy, such as steel. AFL traditionalists rejected the idea and held fast to the notion that workers should be organized by their crafts, not by whole industries. Thwarted by AFL leadership, Lewis, Hillman, and their allies formed a rival organization that eventually became the Congress of Industrial Organizations (CIO).

The CIO began organizing some of the most powerful and prosperous industries in the country. The government's new attitude toward organized labor played an important role in the CIO's initial success. For example, when the United Automobile Workers initiated a series of "sit-down strikes" against General Motors, neither Roosevelt nor the Democratic governor of Michigan sent in troops to remove workers from the factories they were occupying. This clear message to the leaders of industry helped to win the strike against America's most powerful corporation. The NLRB also protected the new unions from an employer counterattack during the recession of 1937.

By the late 1930s a crucial political alliance had formed. A newly vigorous labor movement had become linked to a reinvigorated national Democratic Party. Thanks to this alliance, American industrial workers entered a new era. Having won the ability to organize with the help of the government, industrial workers used their power to increase wages, enhance job security, improve working conditions, and secure their retirements. Organized labor now had a stake in preserving the system from collapse. As much as the banking and financial reforms of the first New Deal, the successful unionization of industrial workers helped stabilize American capitalism.

The New Deal Coalition

Roosevelt believed that to overcome his varied opposition and win reelection he needed to create a coalition far broader than that of 1932. By 1936, the Democratic Party was transformed in fundamental ways. For the first time since the Civil War, a majority of voters identified themselves as Democrats, and the Democrats remained the majority party for decades to come. FDR achieved this feat by forging a powerful coalition between the competing wings of the party. In the end, however, the same coalition that made the New Deal possible also limited its progressivism.

The rural South had been overwhelmingly Democratic for a century, but urban voters in the North became the party's new base. This shift was well under way during the 1920s, when Al Smith's two presidential bids attracted ethnic blue-collar voters. FDR offered prominent ethnic Americans an unprecedented number of federal appointments. Jews and Catholics (Italian, as well as Irish) served Roosevelt as advisers, judges, and cabinet officers. More important, thousands of working-class city dwellers found jobs with the CWA, the WPA, or the CCC. Those New Deal programs generated a flood of patronage appointments that endeared Roosevelt to local Democratic machines. Finally, the unions reciprocated FDR's support for labor. The CIO alone poured $600,000 into Roosevelt's campaign, replacing the money no longer forthcoming from wealthy donors, and its members formed an army of campaign volunteers. By 1940, the Democratic Party became the party of the urban working class.

The New Deal's programs also explain a dramatic shift of allegiance among African American voters. Since Reconstruction, southern blacks had supported the party of Lincoln, but as they migrated to the urban North they gained voting strength and abandoned the Republican Party. By 1936 northern blacks voted overwhelmingly for FDR, even though the Democrats were weak on the issue of civil rights. The New Deal included no legislation against discrimination, and FDR silently allowed Congress to reject antilynching laws. New Deal agencies did offer more assistance to poor, unemployed African Americans than previous federal programs, and some leading New Dealers supported equal rights. Mary McLeod Bethune, a prominent African American educator and close friend of Eleanor Roosevelt, served the New Deal as director of the National Youth Administration's Office of Negro Affairs, which gave jobs and training to some 300,000 young African Americans. Besides controlling her own Special Negro Fund, Bethune convinced other New Deal administrators to open their programs to blacks. With perhaps a million African American families depending on the WPA by 1939, black voters had solid reasons for joining the New Deal coalition.

A similar logic explains why women reformers threw their support to the Democrats in the 1930s. Once again, FDR had no feminist agenda, and New Deal programs discriminated against women by offering lower pay and restricting jobs by sex. But women also benefited in unprecedented numbers from New Deal welfare and jobs programs. For the first time in American history, a woman, Frances Perkins, was appointed to the cabinet.

The most prominent female reformer associated with the New Deal was Eleanor Roosevelt. She was in many ways the last great representative of a woman's reform tradition that flourished in the Progressive Era. She had worked in a settlement house and campaigned for suffrage and progressive causes. Eleanor and Franklin made a remarkable political couple. Millions of Americans read Eleanor's opinions in her weekly newspaper column, "My Day." She became for many the conscience of the New Deal, the person closest to the president who spoke most forcefully for the downtrodden. Her well-deserved reputation for compassion also protected her husband. Liberals who might have been more critical of the New Deal instead relied on Eleanor Roosevelt to push the president toward more progressive reform. At the same time, conservatives who were charmed by FDR's personality blamed the faults of the New Deal on his wife. "It was very simple," one southern journalist explained. "Credit Franklin, better known as He, for all the things you like, and blame Eleanor, better known as She, or 'that woman,' for all the things you don't like."

Although four years of the New Deal had not lifted the Depression, the economy was making headway. Jobs programs had put millions of Americans to work; the banking crisis was over; the rural economy had been stabilized. Based on this record and the backing of his powerful coalition of southern whites, northern urban voters, the labor movement, and many other Americans, FDR won reelection by a landslide in 1936. He captured over 60 percent of the popular vote and, in the Electoral College, defeated his Republican opponent Alf Landon in every state but Maine and Vermont. Landon, the governor of Kansas, even lost his home state. The new Democratic coalition also won sweeping command of the Congress, and Roosevelt now stood at the peak of his power.

Crisis of the New Deal

In 1937 it seemed as if Roosevelt was unbeatable, but within a year the New Deal was all but paralyzed. A politically costly fight to "pack" the Supreme Court at last gave FDR's conservative opponents a winning issue. A sharp recession encouraged the New Deal's enemies and provoked an intellectual crisis within the administration. In 1938, when the Republicans regained much of their congressional strength, the reform energies of the New Deal were largely spent. Within a year the nation turned its attention to rising threats from overseas.

Conservatives Counterattack

With conservative opponents vanquished, it seemed as if New Dealers could finish the job begun in 1933. Administration progressives such as Frances Perkins hoped that existing legislation could now be strengthened.

FDR seemed poised to launch the next great wave of New Deal reforms, but one apparently immovable barrier stood in the way: the U.S. Supreme Court. The court had already struck down the NIRA and the AAA, and recent rulings made it seem that neither social security nor the Wagner Act were safe from the court's nine "old men." Roosevelt wanted to change the court. He had not yet had the opportunity to appoint any new justices, and pundits joked that the elderly judges refused to die. Sure that a constitutional amendment supporting his program would take too long or fail, FDR launched a reckless and unpopular effort to "reform" the Court. He proposed legislation that would allow the president to appoint a new justice for every sitting member of the court over 70 years of age. This "court packing" plan, as opponents labeled it, would have given the president as many as six new appointments.

Conservatives had long complained of FDR's "dictatorial" powers, and the court plan seemed to confirm their warnings. They skillfully cultivated congressional allies, giving Democrats the lead in opposing the court reform. Even his allies refused to campaign for the president's bill, and it took all of FDR's political power and prestige to keep it before a hostile Congress. By the end of the summer of 1937, the bill was defeated.

Ironically, Roosevelt won his point. Several justices soon retired, giving FDR the critical appointments he needed, and the Supreme Court backed away from its narrow conception of the role of the federal government. Nevertheless, FDR's court plan proved a costly mistake, and its defeat emboldened his opponents. In November 1937 the administration's critics issued a Conservative Manifesto calling for balanced budgets, states' rights, lower taxes, and the defense of private property and the capitalist system, themes that would rally conservatives for the remainder of the century. Behind the manifesto lay some hard political realities that drove the conservatives into opposition.

Southern congressmen, for example, desired to preserve white privilege. The new federal programs disturbed entrenched systems of political and economic dominance. Southern conservatives blamed the New Deal. "You ask any nigger in the street who's the greatest president in the world. Nine out of ten will tell you Franklin Roosevelt," one white southerner declared. "That's why I think he's so dangerous."

In the rural South and West there were fears that the New Deal was growing too close to the urban working class in the Northeast. Against this trend, conservatives appealed to the deeply rooted American suspicions of central government. Still, conservatives were not strong enough to block all New Deal legislation. Farm-state representatives needed Roosevelt's support. In late 1937 the administration succeeded in passing housing and farm tenancy reforms. In 1938 Congress passed the Fair Labor Standards Act, requiring the payment of overtime after 40 hours of work in a week, establishing a minimum wage, and eliminating child labor. Even with flagging support, FDR could enact proposals blocked during the Progressive Era.

The 1938 congressional elections gave conservatives the strength they needed to bring New Deal reform to an end. The president campaigned against leading conservatives, but he failed. Republicans gained 75 seats in the House and were now strong enough in the Senate to organize an effective anti–New Deal coalition with southern Democrats. By then, a jolting recession had created a crisis of confidence within the New Deal itself.

The Liberal Crisis of Confidence

During the 1936 campaign Roosevelt was stung by conservative criticism of his failure to balance the budget. He had leveled the same charge against Hoover four years earlier, but the demands of the Depression made it difficult and dangerous to reduce government spending. Deficit spending seemed to help resuscitate the economy.

AMERICA AND THE WORLD

>> **The Global Depression**

In 1930, mulberry trees covered the hills of the Japanese islands of Hokkaido and Honshu. In parts of Japan, two-thirds of the cultivated land was fodder for the silkworms that produced Japan's leading export. Over 2 million families depended on silk, which went chiefly to the United States to be made into the fashionable stockings worn by American women.

The silk market was the one bright spot in Japan's economy after World War I. Chinese consumers had boycotted Japan to protest land grabs during the war. In 1923, an earthquake followed by fires and a tidal wave leveled Tokyo and Yokohama. Japan was not alone: in much of the world, economies stagnated in the 1920s under the burden of war reparations and war loans. One of the worst hit was Italy, where unemployment contributed to the rise of Benito Mussolini's fascist government in 1922. But the New York Stock Exchange crash triggered a global depression. As the world's leading creditor, producer, and consumer, the United States exported its financial disaster to the world.

Countries tied to a single commodity or to the American market suffered most. After the crash, American women stopped buying stockings, and the price of silk dropped by three-quarters. By 1931, Japanese silk farmers were broke; by 1932, they were starving. Similar catastrophes hit the rubber plantations of Malaya and the coffee farms of Guatemala. International prices for Australian wool, Cuban sugar, Canadian wheat, and Egyptian cotton plummeted. Brazil, unable to export coffee, used it to fuel locomotives. In Rwanda a famine aggravated by the loss of tin exports killed 40,000. In China, 25 million people fled when the Yangtze River broke its banks in 1935.

The disruption of trade intensified conflict in India, Africa, and other areas under imperial rule. Unable to collect taxes at the ports, colonial governments imposed taxes or monopolies that shifted burdens onto the rural poor. The distress of the peasantry intensified demands for independence in India, and Mohandas Gandhi's *satyagraha*, civil resistance, reached a peak in 1932, when 32,500 nonviolent protestors filled the jails. The French government of Indochina (Vietnam) forced rice farmers to pay taxes in gold. Uprisings against French rule increased as the Depression wore on, as did insurgencies against the U.S. colony in the Philippines. In the industrial countries, jobless people stood in breadlines and lived in shanties. More than 2 million workers were unemployed in Britain. When American loans to Germany dried up in 1930, two out of every five Germans were out of work. This catastrophe, the worst economic crisis in memory, silenced the voices of political moderates. Voters demanded extreme action. Each country now looked out for itself, marshaling scarce resources and forming self-contained economies known as autarkies. Brazil and Argentina restricted trade and steered investment into industry. The Soviet Union, already cut off from the capitalist world, built "socialism in one country." Japan merged its colonies in Taiwan, Korea, and Manchuria into a "Greater East Asia

Co-Prosperity Sphere." The 1932 Ottawa Accords merged Britain, its empire, Canada, and Australia into a self-contained economic bloc. In Germany autarky was the policy of the National Socialist (Nazi) Party led by Adolf Hitler.

Autarky exacted heavy demands on citizens, requiring them to sacrifice prosperity, liberty, and lives for the nation. Efficiency was more important than democracy, and regimes became more ruthless and less free. Even to Americans, dictatorships had a high-tech sheen. "If this country ever needed a Mussolini," Senator David A. Reed remarked, "it needs one now." FDR and other American leaders drew the connections between global trade, autarky, repression, and war. "If goods don't cross borders," Secretary of State Cordell Hull observed, "armies will." As another global war loomed, they recognized it as a contest between dictatorship and democracy, but also as a conflict between economic systems. The outcome would mean either autarky or a New Deal for the world.

Hoping to silence conservative critics, Roosevelt ordered a sharp cutback in relief expenditures in 1937. On top of an ill-timed contraction of the money supply and the removal of $2 billion from the economy by the new social security taxes, the measure had a disastrous effect. Once again, the stock market crashed and industrial production plummeted. Even the relatively healthy automobile, rubber, and electrical industries were seriously hurt. Opponents carped about the "Roosevelt Recession" and accused the administration of destroying business confidence.

Among the president's advisers, the competition between the budget balancers and the deficit spenders intensified. This was an important turning point in the New Deal and in twentieth-century American politics. Until 1938, the orthodoxy that associated economic health with balanced budgets was entrenched in government and the business community. The recession of 1937–1938 converted young New Dealers to the newer economic theories associated with John Maynard Keynes, the great English economist. During periods of economic stagnation, Keynes argued, the government needs to stimulate recovery through deficit spending. The goal of fiscal policy was no longer to encourage production, but rather to increase the purchasing power of ordinary consumers. Roosevelt never fully embraced these theories, but more and more members of his administration did. Moreover, the breathtaking economic revival created by massive government expenditures in World War II seemed to validate Keynesian economics. Until the 1980s, presidents of both parties subscribed to Keynesian theory, although they differed on what kind of government programs federal spending should buy.

Conclusion

The New Deal did not bring an end to the Depression, and this was undoubtedly its greatest failure. Nevertheless, FDR achieved other important goals. "I want to save our system," he said in 1935, "the capitalistic system." By this standard, the New Deal was a smashing

>> Timeline

▼**1929**
Stock market crash

▼**1930**
Hawley-Smoot Tariff enacted

▼**1931**
National Credit Corporation authorized

▼**1932**
Franklin Roosevelt elected president

▼**1933**
FDR declares a bank holiday
First Hundred Days
Emergency Banking Act passed
Economy Act passed
Civilian Conservation Corps (CCC)
United States goes off the gold standard
Agricultural Adjustment Act (AAA)
Emergency Farm Mortgage Act
Tennessee Valley Authority (TVA)
Truth in Securities Act
National Industrial Recovery Act (NIRA)
Glass-Steagall Banking Act
Farm Credit Act

▼**1935**
Second Hundred Days
NIRA declared unconstitutional
National Labor Relations Act
Social Security Act

▼**1936**
AAA overturned
Gone with the Wind published
FDR reelected

▼**1937**
FDR announces "court packing" plan
Economy goes into recession

▼**1938**
Second Agricultural Adjustment Act
Fair Labor Standards Act
New Deal opponents win big in Congress

▼**1939**
Administrative Reorganization Act
British actress Vivien Leigh stars in *Gone with the Wind*

success. By allowing Americans to survive the worst collapse in the history of capitalism while preserving core freedoms, the New Deal reaffirmed democracy at a time when most of the industrialized world chose dictatorship. The New Deal also created a system of security for the vast majority of Americans. National systems of unemployment compensation, old-age pensions, and welfare programs were born during the 1930s. Farm owners received new protections, as did the very soil of the nation. Workers were granted the right to organize, hours of labor were limited, child labor ended, and wages were held above the bare minimum. The financial system was stabilized and strengthened. America was a safer place at the end of the 1930s, but the world had become more dangerous. After 1938 the Roosevelt administration was increasingly preoccupied with the threatening behavior of nations that had responded poorly to the challenge of the Great Depression.

Review Questions

1. Did the stock market crash cause the Great Depression?

2. How did Roosevelt's philosophy of government differ from Hoover's?

3. What setbacks caused FDR to launch a second New Deal?

4. Compare the American response to the Depression with that of Britain, Germany, and Japan. Why did other industrial countries choose different paths?

5. What were Franklin Roosevelt's attributes as a leader? What aspects of his style inspired confidence or animosity?

6. Histories of the Depression focus on national statistics and large-scale programs. How could you retell the story of the 1930s from a local, personal perspective?

For further review materials and resource information, please visit www.oup.com/us/ofthepeople

"Who is this guy Randolph," Joseph Rauh wondered, and "what the hell has he got on the President of the U.S.?" It was June 1941 and Rauh, a government attorney, had just been instructed to draft a presidential order prohibiting discrimination on grounds of "race, color, creed, or national origin" in defense industries. It was a radical departure from decades of official support for legalized racism. It would use the economic muscle of the federal government to overturn job segregation and, in the process, make enemies for President Franklin Roosevelt. Rauh was enthusiastic, but he couldn't understand why FDR, with his reliance on southern votes, would even consider it. The president was bending to pressure, Rauh learned, from African Americans led by a charismatic organizer named A. Philip Randolph.

Raised in Florida and educated at New York's City College, Randolph had founded the largest African American labor union, the Brotherhood of Sleeping Car Porters, in 1925. Porters traveled the railroads as baggage handlers and valets, and during the Depression Randolph's influence extended into every station and depot reached by the Brotherhood's magazine, the *Messenger*.

In 1941, it looked to Randolph like only a matter of months before the United States entered the war raging in Europe and Asia. He believed, according to FBI informants, "that Negroes make most fundamental gains in periods of great social upheaval." War would create a chance to achieve equality, but only if African Americans demanded it. "The Negro sat by idly during the first world war thinking conditions would get better," he told an audience in Oklahoma City. "That won't be the procedure during the duration of this conflict."

In January 1941, Randolph called for African Americans to march to Washington to demand an end to job discrimination. Only 3 percent of workers in war industries were people of color. "The administration leaders in Washington will never give the Negro

>> AMERICAN PORTRAIT *continued*

justice," he declared, "until they see masses, ten, twenty, fifty thousand Negroes on the White House lawn." The March on Washington Movement (MOWM) was largely bluff, but Roosevelt and the FBI believed it enough to try to head it off.

A protest march would embarrass the government, and Roosevelt had the power to accept Randolph's demands. Leveraging federal defense contracts, the president could desegregate a large portion of the economy without even asking Congress. He opened negotiations with Randolph through Eleanor Roosevelt. The organizers agreed to cancel the march in return for a presidential directive—Executive Order 8802—establishing a Fair Employment Practices Committee to assure fairness in hiring.

It was a victory for civil rights and for Randolph personally. If the Emancipation Proclamation had ended physical slavery, the New York *Amsterdam News* declared, E.O. 8802 ended "economic slavery." Within a year, thousands of African Americans would be working at high-tech jobs in aircraft factories and arms plants. Randolph had recognized that war created an opening for changing the economic and political rules of the game. War touched all Americans. Millions were sent, to serve and fight, everywhere from the Arctic to the tropics. Millions of others left home to work in plants producing war materiel. Government stepped in to run the economy and created new relationships with corporations, labor, the states, and universities. The war stimulated revolutionary advances in science, industry, and agriculture. The United States itself became the foremost military and economic power in a world destroyed by war.

These changes enlarged the discretionary powers of the presidency and the federal government. Americans willingly accepted personal sacrifices and greater federal authority as part of the price of victory. As the March on Washington Movement proved, the president's enhanced powers could enlarge freedom and opportunity, but they could also restrict individual liberties. Many Japanese Americans spent the war imprisoned in "relocation centers," and the FBI placed Randolph's name on a list of persons to be placed in "custodial detention" in the event of a national emergency. The war unsettled the economy and society, enlisting all Americans in a global crusade and arousing both idealism and fear.

Common Threads

>> What strategic and domestic issues were at stake in the debate over American entry into the war?

>> Did the war consolidate or overturn New Deal reforms?

>> In what ways did the war generate economic opportunities and highlight issues of civil rights?

Island in a Totalitarian Sea

Randolph's movement capitalized on a world crisis that reached back to the treaty that ended World War I. The Depression heightened international tensions, turning regional conflicts in Africa, Europe, and Asia into tests of ideology and power. In 1937 Japan attacked China. Two years later, when Germany invaded Poland, France and Britain declared war, beginning World War II in Europe. As with the previous war, Americans had time to reflect on the world crisis. Most blamed it on the failures of the Versailles Treaty and the desperation caused by the global Depression. Nations and empires were solving economic problems with military force.

> If Hitler destroys freedom everywhere else, it will perish here. Ringed around by a world hostile to our way of life, we should be forced to become a great military power.
>
> FORTUNE MAGAZINE, June 1941

Americans were divided, however, on how their country ought to respond, on its role in the world and its responsibilities at home. Isolationists wanted to stay out of war and secure the Western Hemisphere against attack. But Roosevelt and other internationalists believed the United States had to support the nations fighting Germany and Japan. Internationalists saw a free-trading, open-door world economy as a solution to international conflict. Isolationists worried about growing federal power and the ambitions of Britain and the Soviet Union. The threat of fascism forced Americans to ask whether their economy and government could compete in the world.

Both camps knew war would change American society. The future of world politics and the world economy would be shaped by America's choice of allies and aims. In 1940, most Americans feared involvement and opposed aid to the enemies of fascism. When France's defeat left Britain to fight alone, more Americans saw aid to Britain as an alternative to U.S. involvement. Japan's attack on Pearl Harbor ended a debate that divided the nation.

A World of Hostile Blocs

The Depression destroyed the liberal international order based on free trade. For a century, governments had favored policies that increased the movement of goods, people, and investment across borders. The steamship and telegraph accelerated that trend. Movement toward an open-door world slowed during World War I and the 1920s, and then stopped completely with the Depression. World trade shrank from almost $3 billion a year in 1929 to less than $1 billion in 1933. Empires and nations began to restrict the movement of goods, capital, and people and to regiment their societies for self-sufficiency. Everywhere, it seemed, governments became more ruthless and less free.

Dictators offered visions of imperial conquests and racial supremacy. Mussolini promised a new Roman Empire in Africa and the Mediterranean. Japanese schoolchildren learned they belonged to a "Yamato race," purer and more virtuous than the inferior peoples they would one day rule. Hitler urged Germans to defend themselves against the *Untermenschen*, subhumans, in their midst—Jews, Gypsies, homosexuals. He built a state based on racism, total control, and brutality, where secret police, the Gestapo, hunted down enemies of the regime and a Nazi army, the SS, enforced party rule.

Jews were the main target of Nazi terror. In 1935, the Nuremberg Laws stripped Jews of citizenship and outlawed intermarriage with members of the "Aryan race." On the night of November 9, 1938, Nazi stormtroopers and ordinary citizens rampaged throughout Germany, burning synagogues and destroying Jewish shops, homes, and hospitals, killing 100 Jews and arresting 30,000 more. Until *Kristallnacht*, this "night of the broken glass," FDR thought international opinion would restrain Hitler. Now he was no longer sure.

Roosevelt grew apprehensive as Germany, Italy, and Japan, the Axis powers, sought to solve their economic problems through military conquest. Italy invaded Ethiopia in 1935. In July 1937, Japan attacked China. In 1938, Hitler's troops marched into Austria. Roosevelt worried that the Axis would soon control most of Europe and Asia, but American leaders had an even darker fear, one they scarcely breathed: that totalitarianism would outcompete democracy. America's free markets and free labor might be no match for the ruthless efficiency of the fascist states. The United States would have to regiment its own citizens just to keep up and to enlist industry, labor, and agriculture into a "state system," *Fortune* magazine predicted, "which, in its own defense, would have to take on the character of Hitler's system."

The Good Neighbor

Some believed the United States ought to retreat into its own sphere. The Hawley-Smoot Tariff of 1930 blocked most imports, but within a year, FDR reversed course and began pushing trade as the answer to America's economic problems. He reacted mainly to the vision of his single-minded secretary of state, Cordell Hull. A conservative former senator from Tennessee, Hull believed that equal access for all to the world's markets was the cure for dictatorship and depression and the best way to ensure peace. In a world of empires and blocs, Hull turned an old foreign policy tradition, the Open Door, into a bold plan for peace and prosperity.

Roosevelt and Hull slowly began to reopen markets in Latin America. FDR expanded Hoover's "Good Neighbor" policy, encouraging trade and renouncing the use of force. A new Export-Import Bank financed transactions, and tariffs were lowered. Hull surprised the 1933 Pan American Conference by approving a declaration that no nation had the right to intervene in the affairs of another. Good Neighbor policies undermined German and Japanese economic ventures, and Latin American governments invited the FBI to track down Axis agents on their soil.

In 1938, after absorbing Austria, Hitler demanded part of Czechoslovakia's territory. Fearing that a small war over the territory would escalate into a larger war, Czechoslovakia's allies, Britain and France, agreed to negotiations. In a meeting at Munich in September they yielded to Hitler's demands. FDR cabled Hitler a last-minute appeal for restraint but accepted the final decision. After World War II, the term "Munich" came to symbolize the failed attempts to appease aggressors, but in 1938 Americans were unsure how best to guard their freedoms in a hostile world.

America First?

As the Axis threat grew, Roosevelt pushed for a buildup of U.S. forces, but Congress and the public disagreed. Disillusioned by the last war, the public wanted to stay out of the conflicts in Europe and Asia. Polls indicated that more than 70 percent believed the

Charles Lindbergh Charles Lindbergh and the America First Committee campaigned against involvement in Europe's war. With Britain's defeat likely, they urged neutrality and defense of the Western Hemisphere as the only chance to keep America safe.

United States had been tricked into World War I. Half a million students pledged their refusal to serve in another war. Senator Gerald P. Nye charged that the munitions industry was lobbying for war. Pacifists, economic nationalists, and veterans groups, backed by the *Chicago Tribune* and the Hearst newspapers, composed a powerful isolationist constituency.

From 1935 to 1937, Congress passed annual Neutrality Acts prohibiting loans and credits to nations engaged in war. The action took place against the backdrop of the Spanish Civil War in which Fascist forces, aided by Germany and Italy, fought against democratic Loyalist forces aided by the Soviet Union. Some 3,000 Americans volunteered to fight with the Loyalists. For that reason, Congress decided to stay out of the conflict; the Neutrality Acts also restricted the president's ability to aid the enemies of fascism.

In late 1939, Roosevelt's worst nightmare come true, as the United States became an island in a world dominated by force. The Soviet Union signed a nonaggression treaty with Germany. The full terms of the Nazi-Soviet pact were secret, leading diplomats to fear the worst, a totalitarian alliance stretching from the Rhine to the Pacific. In September, German armies struck Poland, using tanks and dive-bombers in a *Blitzkrieg*, or "lightning war." Hitler and Soviet leader Josef Stalin split Poland between them. Britain and France declared war on Germany.

The following April, Nazi armies invaded Denmark and Norway. On May 10, 1940, Hitler launched an all-out offensive in the West. Tank columns pierced French lines in the Ardennes Forest and headed toward the English Channel. France, Belgium, and the Netherlands were defeated; Britain faced the German onslaught alone. Roosevelt now had to consider the possibility of a British surrender, placing the Royal Navy, control of the Atlantic, and possibly even Canada in Hitler's hands. The German air force, the *Luftwaffe*, was already dueling for control of the skies over England.

Determined to shore up this last line of defense, Roosevelt used his powers as commander in chief to bypass the Neutrality Acts. In June 1940, he submitted a bill to create the first peacetime draft in American history. He declared army weapons and supplies "surplus" so they could be donated to Britain. In September 1940, he traded Britain 50 old destroyers for leases to naval bases in Canada, Bermuda, and the Caribbean.

The isolationists were now isolated. Sympathy for Britain grew as radio audiences heard the sounds of air attacks on London. Two-thirds of the public favored the draft, but isolationists were not finished. In September 1940, the America First Committee launched a new campaign that urged Americans to turn from Europe and prepare for their own defense. Charles A. Lindbergh and Senator Burton Wheeler headlined America First rallies. The only reason for United States involvement, Lindbergh argued, "is because there are powerful elements in America who desire us to take part. They represent a small minority . . . but they control much of the machinery of influence and propaganda."

Roosevelt worried that the 1940 election would become a referendum on intervention. Isolationist senator Robert Taft was a leading contender for the nomination, but the Republicans chose Wendell L. Willkie, an anti–New Deal internationalist who endorsed the draft and expressed sympathy for Britain. With defense and foreign policy off the table, FDR won an unprecedented third term by a 5-million-vote margin.

Means Short of War

British prime minister Winston Churchill could now broach the delicate but urgent issue of war finances. Britain had been buying arms on a "cash and carry" basis but was now out of funds. The Neutrality Act prohibited new loans, but without arms Britain would have to surrender. FDR gave his cabinet a weekend to devise a plan, and the following Monday he produced the answer himself. Instead of loaning money, the United States would lend arms and equipment. Roosevelt compared the idea to lending a garden hose to a neighbor whose house was on fire. "There would be a gentleman's obligation to repay," but because there would be no loans, it would not violate the Neutrality Act. Lend-Lease, as the program was called, put the U.S. "arsenal of democracy" on Britain's side and granted FDR unprecedented powers to arm allies. The Lend-Lease bill, H.R. 1776, passed the Senate by a two-to-one margin in 1941.

Repayment took the form of economic concessions. Hull saw Lend-Lease as a chance to crack one of the largest autarkic blocs, the British Empire. He insisted that in return for aid, Britain had to discard the Ottawa Accords and open its empire's door to American trade. Churchill's economic adviser, John Maynard Keynes, reluctantly agreed. Later that year Churchill and Roosevelt met aboard the cruisers *Augusta* and *Prince of Wales* to issue a declaration of war aims, the Atlantic Charter. It ensured all nations, "victor and vanquished," equal access to the trade and raw materials of the world.

In June 1941, Hitler stunned the world again with a lightning invasion of the Soviet Union. Three million men and 3,000 tanks slashed through Soviet defenses toward Moscow and Leningrad. Secretary of War Henry Stimson predicted that in three months the Axis would control Europe and Asia, but George C. Marshall, the army's chief of staff, saw that this might be a turning point. If the Soviet army could hold the area between Moscow and the Black Sea, the Germans would have a long winter. Roosevelt shared his optimism. The eastern front took pressure off Britain and gave the Allies a real chance to defeat Hitler. Roosevelt extended Lend-Lease aid to Moscow. The German columns advanced steadily, but they were no longer moving through Poland or France. "Even when encircled, the Russians stood their ground and fought," a Nazi general reported.

German U-boats worked to cut Britain's lifelines, sinking half a million tons of shipping a month. To help the British, Roosevelt fought an undeclared naval war against Germany in the western Atlantic. The U.S. Navy convoyed merchant ships as far as Iceland, where British destroyers took over. FDR said he was offering "all aid short of war," but it was not far short. In September a U-boat fired torpedoes at the USS *Greer*, and the destroyer threw back depth charges. When Roosevelt ordered patrols to expel German and Italian vessels from the western Atlantic, he had crossed the line from neutrality to belligerency and seemed to be seeking an incident that would make it official.

Japan, meanwhile, moved into Southeast Asia. In 1939, the Japanese had adopted a "go south" strategy to capture oil fields in the Dutch East Indies and encircle China. Because the Philippines, a U.S. territory, blocked the invasion route, the question for the Japanese was not whether to declare war on the United States, but when. In July 1941, Japan established bases in French Indochina. Roosevelt saw this as a threat, but, preoccupied with Europe, he wanted to forestall war in the Pacific. U.S. diplomats opened talks with Japan while Marshall dispatched a fleet of B-17s in an attempt to deter an attack. When Japanese troop convoys moved into the South China Sea, Hull ended negotiations and cut off U.S. oil exports, Japan's only source of fuel. On November 27, Marshall warned commanders in Hawaii and the Philippines to expect "an aggressive move by Japan" in the next few days. The Philippines, Thailand, and Malaya were the likely targets.

On Sunday afternoon, December 7, Americans listening to the radio heard that aircraft "believed to be from Japan" had attacked U.S. bases at Pearl Harbor in Hawaii. At 7:40 A.M. Hawaii time, 181 planes had bombed and strafed airfields on Oahu, destroying

Pearl Harbor Japan's attack on the U.S. Navy's principal Pacific base at Pearl Harbor brought the United States into World War II. For Japan, it was the opening phase of a campaign to capture European and American colonies in Southeast Asia.

or damaging more than 200 planes on the ground. Bombers then attacked the 96 ships of the U.S. Pacific Fleet anchored next to each other. Three torpedoes struck the battleship *Oklahoma*, capsizing it with 400 crew members aboard. Alongside her the *Maryland* went down. A bomb exploded in the *Arizona*'s forward magazine, breaking the ship in half and killing over a thousand men. In the Philippines, Japanese bombers also caught American planes on the ground. The following day, President Roosevelt appeared before Congress to ask for a declaration of war against Japan. Only one representative, Montana's Jeannette Rankin, voted no. On December 11, Germany honored its alliance with Japan and declared war on the United States.

Some historians have argued that Roosevelt knew of the approaching attack but withheld warnings in order to draw the United States into war. In fact, naval authorities at Pearl Harbor anticipated an attack but doubted that Japan could project air and sea power across the Pacific in secrecy. When Japanese planes destroyed American aircraft on the ground in the Philippines nine hours after the Pearl Harbor attack, Douglas MacArthur said Germans must have flown the bombers. Such preconceptions blinded commanders to the warning signs.

Turning the Tide

For the Allies there was only bad news in the first half of 1942. Japanese invaders walked over the larger British and Dutch armies in Southeast Asia and captured the American islands of Guam and Wake. In February, the "impregnable" fortress of Singapore surrendered with most of the Australian and Indian armies still inside. Japan's Combined Fleet ruled the seas between Hawaii and India, striking at will. MacArthur abandoned Manila and staged an Alamo-style defense of the Bataan Peninsula and the fortress island of Corregidor.

But the tide was beginning to turn. The Soviets stopped the German advance outside Moscow. On April 18, Colonel James Doolittle's B-25 bombers raided Tokyo. Roosevelt wanted to hold the line in the Pacific while coming to the aid of Britain and the Soviet Union as soon as possible. This meant stopping Japan, creating an American army, and sending it to other side of the Atlantic. None of those jobs would be easy.

> Through the haze
> I saw Marines
> stumble and pitch
> forward as they got
> hit. I then looked
> neither right nor
> left but just straight
> to my front. The
> farther we went, the
> worse it got.
>
> EUGENE B. SLEDGE,
> Battle of Peleliu,
> September 1944

Midway and Coral Sea

"We can run wild for six months or a year," Admiral Isoroku Yamamoto prophesied before the victorious attack on Pearl Harbor, "but after that I have utterly no confidence." Panic-stricken Americans imagined enemy landings in California, but Japan was never so ambitious. It called for fortifying a defensive screen of islands in the western Pacific and holding the Allies at

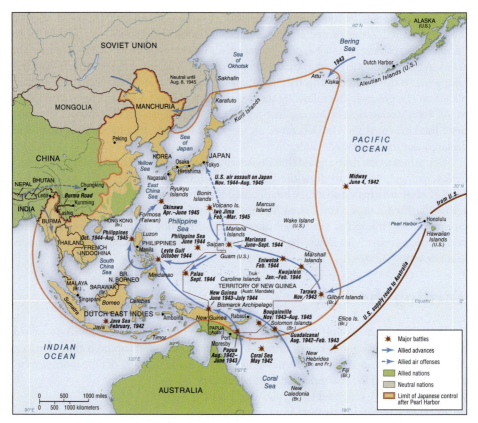

Map 25–1 **World War II in the Pacific, 1942–1945** Japan established a barrier of fortified islands across the western Pacific. U.S. forces penetrated it westward from Hawaii and from Australia northward through the Solomon Islands to the Philippines.

bay until they sued for peace. "The fact that the Japanese did not return to Pearl Harbor and complete the job was the greatest help for us," Chester W. Nimitz, the U.S. Pacific commander, later remembered.

After the Doolittle raid, the Japanese realized their error and laid plans to lure the U.S. Pacific Fleet into battle. The increase in radio traffic helped Commander Joseph Rochefort, who had already partly broken the Japanese codes. In late April, he was able to tell Nimitz that Japan was planning an attack on Port Moresby on the island of New Guinea. Nimitz dispatched two carriers, *Lexington* and *Yorktown*, to intercept the Japanese carrier force. The Battle of Coral Sea was the first between carrier task forces, an entirely new type of sea battle. Sailors never saw the enemy's ships, only their aircraft, which struck with devastating speed. Planes from *Yorktown* turned back the Japanese transports while *Lexington's* torpedo and dive-bombers sunk the carrier *Shoho*. The Japanese fatally crippled *Lexington* and tore a hole in *Yorktown's* deck. The two sides pulled back after fighting to a draw.

Yamamoto next chose to attack the U.S. fleet directly. Sending a diversionary force toward the Aleutians, he aimed his attack at Midway, the westernmost island of the

Hawaiian chain. Yamamoto gambled that Nimitz would divide his forces, allowing the Combined Fleet to crush the remnant guarding Hawaii. But trusting Rochefort's code breakers, Nimitz knew the real target was Midway. He also learned from Coral Sea that aircraft, not battleships, were the winning weapons. He hastily assembled task forces around the carriers *Hornet* and *Enterprise* and reinforced airfields on Midway and Oahu. Crews worked night and day to repair *Yorktown*. The American fleet was still outnumbered, but surprise was now on its side.

When Japanese aircraft met stiff resistance from Midway's guns on the morning of June 4, they returned to their carriers and prepared for an unplanned second attack. With bombers, bombs, and fuel littering their decks, Japan's four carriers were vulnerable, their defending Zeros busy intercepting U.S. torpedo bombers. At that moment dive-bombers from *Yorktown* and *Enterprise* burst out of the clouds. They destroyed three carriers in a matter of minutes. The mighty Combined Fleet ceased to exist. Midway put Japan on the defensive and allowed the United States to concentrate on building an army and winning the war in Europe.

Gone with the Draft

The German army that overran France in May 1940 consisted of 136 mechanized divisions of 17,000 men each. The United States had only five divisions and was still using horse cavalry. "Against Europe's total war," *Time* observed, "the U.S. Army looked like a few nice boys with BB guns." Military officials drew up plans for a 10-million-man force. As in World War I, the United States had to find ways to house, equip, and transport the army, but this time it would be five times larger. By December 1941, 2 million men and 80,000 women had enlisted. A year later the total exceeded 5 million.

Buses rolled into the new boot camps and unloaded recruits, called selectees, in front of drill instructors. Basic training aimed to erase the civilian personality and replace it with an instinct for obedience and action. Eugene Sledge left college to join the marines and found himself at a camp in San Diego. "Your soul may belong to Jesus," his drill instructor bellowed, "but your ass belongs to the Marines." After 13 weeks of calisthenics, close-order drill, marches, and rifle practice, Sledge was assigned to the infantry.

Recruits hungered for a weekend pass, but in the South and West, where many bases were located, there was little to do. The War Department joined several charities in creating the United Services Organization (USO) to provide a "home away from home" with meals, dances, and wholesome entertainment. Still, wherever they were on leave, soldiers often fought with each other and with the locals. Distinctions of apparel and race could stimulate violence. Southerners lynched African American soldiers for wearing their uniforms. In 1943, riots erupted in Harlem after police arrested an African American soldier in uniform. The same year, sailors in Los Angeles attacked Mexican American shipyard workers who wore distinctive "zoot suits." In both cases the clothes signified a disruption of the established social order, a process accelerated by the war.

Army leadership struggled to preserve racial traditions amid wartime changes. Like the multiethnic armies of Britain and France, the U.S. Army consisted of segregated units, some with special functions. The Japanese American 442nd Regimental Combat Team and the marines' Navajo "code talkers" became well known. African Americans served in the army in segregated units, and until 1942 were excluded from the navy altogether.

The 99th Pursuit Squadron Known as the Black Eagles, they trained at the Tuskegee Institute and engaged the Luftwaffe in the skies over North Africa.

Roosevelt ordered the services to admit African Americans and appointed an African American brigadier general, Benjamin O. Davis, but injustices remained. Even blood plasma was segregated in military hospitals.

Two issues aroused the most anger among African Americans: exclusion from combat and the treatment of soldiers at southern bases. Many GIs in uniform experienced the indignity of being refused service at restaurants where German prisoners of war were allowed to eat. Mutinies and race riots erupted at bases in Florida, Alabama, and Louisiana, where African American soldiers were housed separately and denied furlough privileges. The army responded by sending African American GIs to the war theaters.

Though desperately short of infantrymen, the army kept African Americans out of front-line units and assigned them to menial chores. Combat symbolized full citizenship, and the NAACP pressed Roosevelt to create African American fighting units. An African American infantry division, the 92nd, fought in Italy; three air units—among them the 99th Pursuit Squadron, known as the Tuskegee Airmen—flew against the *Luftwaffe;* and one mechanized battalion, the 761st Tanks, received a commendation for action in the Ardennes. Most African Americans went into the line individually as replacements, and racially mixed units aroused few complaints in the field. Resistance to desegregation came mainly from Washington.

With manpower in short supply, the armed forces reluctantly enlisted women. The Women's Army Corps (the WACs) was created in 1942, while the navy signaled its reluctance in the title of its auxiliary, the Women Accepted for Volunteer Emergency Service (WAVES). Eventually more than 100,000 women served as mechanics, typists, pilots, cooks, and nurses, an unusually low rate of mobilization. Nearly every other warring country enlisted women for industry and combat, leaving the state to perform traditionally female jobs: caring for children, the sick, and the elderly. This government role came to be accepted in Europe, Canada, and Australia, but in the United States "welfare" continued to be associated with poor relief.

The Winning Weapons

During World War II weapons technology advanced with blinding speed. Entering the war late, the United States gained a technological edge. American factories produced models using the latest innovations, but many of these would not see combat until 1943 or later.

Until then, troops had to make do with inferior weapons. Marines landed on Guadalcanal wearing World War I–era helmets and carrying the 1903 Springfield rifle. Japan's Zero was faster and lighter than any American fighter. After 1943, the advantage began to pass to the Americans. The M1 rifle was the finest infantry weapon in the war. Artillery was precise and lethal, and American crews were skilled in the devastating "time-on-target" technique, which delivered shells from several directions simultaneously. The elegant P-51 Mustang, a high-speed ultra-long-range fighter, could escort bombers from Britain to Berlin. It dominated the skies after D-Day. American four-engine bombers—the B-17 Flying Fortress and the B-24 Liberator—were superior to German or Japanese counterparts. In 1944, the B-29 Superfortress, with its 10-ton bomb load and unrivalled range, took to the skies over the Pacific and incinerated one Japanese city after another. American tanks, however, remained inferior to their German counterparts throughout the war, owing to the army's failure to recognize the importance of this weapon.

Quantity often trumped quality, however, and the results were impressive. When Allied troops landed in France in 1944, they enjoyed a superiority of 20 to 1 in tanks and 25 to 1 in aircraft. When Roosevelt set a production target of 50,000 aircraft in 1940, the Germans considered it a bluff, but American factories turned out almost 300,000 planes during the war. Sometimes, sheer American numbers defeated Axis skill. An American soldier in Salerno asked a captured German lieutenant why he had surrendered. "The Americans kept sending tanks down the road," the German replied. "Every time they sent a tank, we knocked it out. Finally, we ran out of ammunition, and the Americans didn't run out of tanks."

Americans also developed secret weapons. The War Department funded defense laboratories at Johns Hopkins, MIT, Harvard, and other universities, forging a permanent link between government, science, and the military. American and British scientists invented one of the first "smart" bombs, the proximity fuse. American and British scientific collaboration also produced improvements in sonar and radar, penicillin, and the atomic bomb.

The Manhattan Project that produced the atomic bomb was the war's largest military-scientific-industrial enterprise. In 1939, Albert Einstein warned Roosevelt that the Germans might invent a nuclear weapon. The National Academy of Sciences concluded that a weapon of "superlatively destructive power" could be built, and General Leslie R. Groves was put in charge of the project, which eventually employed 600,000 people and cost $2 billion. World War II's marriage of technology and war changed warfare, and it also changed science. Researchers and inventors had once worked alone on their own problems. Now they worked in teams at government-funded laboratories on problems assigned by Washington.

The Second Front

To reassure Britain and the Soviet Union, FDR adopted a "Europe First" strategy, holding the line against Japan while directing the main effort at Nazi Germany. The Allies had little in common except that Hitler had chosen them as enemies. Britain was struggling to preserve its empire. The Soviet Union had once been allied with Germany and had a nonaggression pact with Japan. Roosevelt needed to keep this shaky coalition together long enough to defeat Hitler. His greatest fear was that one or both of the Allies would make a separate peace or be knocked out of the war. Stalin and Churchill each had their own opinions about how to use American power, and their conflicting aims produced bitter disputes over strategy.

As the Nazis closed in on the Soviet oil fields during 1942, Stalin pleaded with Britain and the United States to launch an invasion of France. Roosevelt and Marshall also wanted a second front against Germany in northern Europe. But to the British, the idea of a western front evoked the horrors of the trench warfare of World War I and the losses it could no longer sustain. Instead, Churchill wanted to encircle the Nazis and attack the "soft underbelly" of the Axis from the Mediterranean.

Concerned about U-boats and the inexperience of American troops, FDR reluctantly accepted Churchill's plan. A month after Pearl Harbor he had promised Stalin a second front "this year." In late 1942, he postponed it to the spring of 1943. Finally, in June 1943, he told Stalin it would not take place until 1944. The delays reinforced Stalin's suspicions that the capitalist powers were waiting for the USSR's defeat.

Instead of invading Europe, the Americans chose a softer target, North Africa, where troops under Lt. Gen. Dwight Eisenhower landed in Algeria and Morocco on November 8, 1942. As they moved east to link up with British forces attacking into Tunisia, German tank divisions under General Erwin Rommel burst through the Kasserine Pass and trapped American columns in high, rocky terrain. Panicky troops fled, blowing up their ammunition stores. Once through the pass, Rommel had a chance to encircle and defeat the Allied forces, but his Italian commanders ordered him to advance in another direction. The Americans and British regrouped for a counterattack.

Ernie Pyle, the popular war correspondent, reassured readers that despite the rout, "there was never at any time any question about the American bravery." Eisenhower was not so sure. He sacked the commander responsible for Kasserine and replaced him with Maj. Gen. George S. Patton. The army increased basic training from 13 to 17 weeks and reviewed its doctrine and weapons. For Patton, Kasserine showed that firepower delivered by air, tanks, and artillery was more reliable than infantry. His preference for technology over bravery became ingrained in American strategy.

On May 7, Allied forces captured Tunis and Bizerte and took 238,000 German and Italian prisoners. Rommel escaped to fight again in France a year later. There he would

Map 25–2   World War II in Europe, 1942–1945 While the Soviets reduced the main German force along the eastern front, the British and American allies advanced through Italy and France.

encounter a different American army, larger, more experienced, and equipped with the newest weapons. As it mobilized, the United States was changing, too.

Organizing for Production

To defeat totalitarian regimes, Americans had to gear their economy for war. Big government and corporations made possible the "miracle of production" that was winning the war and raising living standards. During the height of the Depression, FDR did not use deficit spending to stir the economy (a technique economists call a "Keynesian stimulus"), but during the war, half the money the federal government spent was borrowed, and nobody complained. The economy boomed. War contracts created 17 million new jobs.

Industrial production doubled. The employment dial reached "full" in 1942 and stayed there until Japan surrendered.

War industries worked by a new set of rules. Contractors depended on the government for financing, materials, and labor. New war plants, built at taxpayer expense, went up in towns with little industry. As industry moved, workers moved with it into the new boomtowns, organizing themselves into a powerful political and economic force.

A Mixed Economy

The Roosevelt administration added new war agencies to control prices, assign labor, and gear up industry. It dusted off methods from World War I—dollar-a-year men and "cost plus" contracts—and added new incentives, such as tax breaks, federal loans, and subsidies. "You have to let business make money out of the process," Secretary of War Henry Stimson explained, "or business won't work." Sometimes it didn't, and the government seized at various times the steel industry, the railroads, the coal mines, and a department store chain.

Output soared. A Ford plant at Willow Run, Michigan, turned out a fleet of B-24s larger than the whole *Luftwaffe*. Cargo ships, which took more than a year to build in 1941, were coming out of the Kaiser Shipyards in an average of 56 days. Entirely new industries such as synthetic rubber and Lucite (a clear, hard plastic used for aircraft windshields) appeared overnight. Industrial techniques applied to agriculture—mechanization and chemical herbicides and pesticides—raised output with fewer farmers. Corporations patriotically increased their market share. Coca-Cola's mobile bottling plants followed the front lines, creating a global thirst for their product. Wrigley added a stick of gum to each K ration and made chewing gum a national habit.

Business leaders regained the prestige lost during the Depression. Major corporations such as General Electric, Allis-Chalmers, and Westinghouse ran parts of the super-secret Manhattan Project. Edwin Witte, a member of the National War Labor Board, called this partnership "a mixed economy, which is not accurately described as either capitalism or

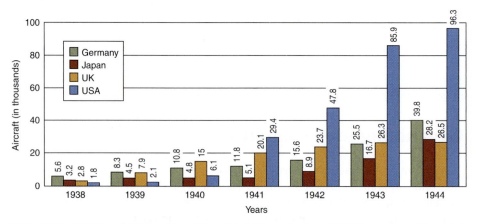

Figure 25–1   Number of Military Aircraft Produced U.S. production of military equipment lagged at first, but once in high gear it dwarfed the rest of the world. *I. C. B. Dear,* The Oxford Companion to World War II *(Oxford University Press, 1995), p. 22.*

socialism." Most business was still small; 97 percent of manufacturing came from firms with just a few hundred employees. During the war, Congress and the administration drew a line between large high-tech firms, its partners in defense, and "small business" that needed tax breaks and loans. "Small business" acquired its own federal agency and lobbying groups, while major corporations such as Boeing and General Electric negotiated long-term contracts with the federal government. World War II permanently divided the economy into separate "government" and "market" sectors, each with its own rules and ways of dealing with Washington.

Industry Moves South and West

Although Detroit got its share, the bulk of war contracts went to states in the South and Southwest and on the Pacific Coast, shifting industry's center of gravity. Airplanes flown in World War I came from Dayton and Buffalo, but the B-29 Superfortress was made in Seattle, Omaha, Wichita, and Marietta, Georgia. The Manhattan Project's largest facilities at Oak Ridge, Tennessee, Hanford, Washington, and Los Alamos, New Mexico, also broke the historic concentration of industry in the Northeast and Midwest.

There were several reasons for this shift. Like other industries moving to the huge hydroelectric grids created by the New Deal, aluminum plants went up along the Tennessee and Columbia rivers to tap abundant power from federal dams. The government also encouraged construction in the middle of the country to lessen the danger of enemy attacks. Corporations moved south and west to find low-wage nonunion workers. Powerful southern and western senators, who controlled military appropriations, steered new development into their states.

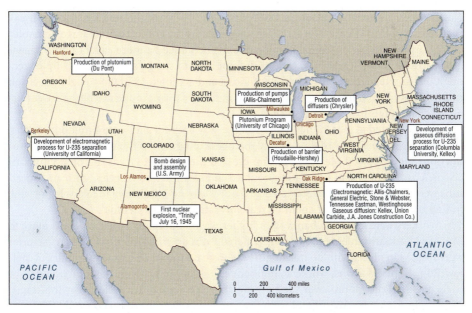

Map 25–3   The Manhattan Project   The Manhattan Project created a new kind of collaboration between industry, government, and science. Much of the new infrastructure was located in the South and West.

The results were visible. The population of the West increased by 40 percent. San Diego doubled in size in 1942. Los Angeles, Houston, Denver, Portland, Seattle, and Washington, D.C., became boomtowns. Whereas "old" industries such as automobiles and steel remained strong above the Mason-Dixon Line, the Sunbelt states became home to the gleaming industries of the future: plastics, aluminum, aircraft, and nuclear power.

Few objected to government direction of the economy when it meant new jobs and industry in poor regions. A 1942 Gallup poll showed that two-thirds of Americans wanted the government to register all adults and assign them to war work as needed. The Office of Price Administration enlisted women consumers to enforce price ceilings by informing on their local grocers. Citizens started scrap drives, bond drives, blood drives, and victory gardens. The war effort was so popular that the administration did not worry much about propaganda. Roosevelt and other leaders—many of them former Progressives—had learned a lesson from World War I: in gaining public support, inducements worked better than coercion.

New Jobs in New Places

As it had during World War I, the need for workers pushed up wages, added new employees to the workforce, and set people on the move. It also swelled the ranks of organized labor from 10 million to almost 15 million between 1941 and 1945. Enlisted as a partner in the war effort, unions grew because of a federally mandated "maintenance of membership" policy, by which new employees automatically joined the union. Through the National Defense Mediation Board (NDMB), the administration encouraged cooperation, a process begun by the New Deal. When wildcat locals of the United Auto Workers struck North American Aviation plants in Los Angeles in 1941, Stimson sent the army to break the strike, but the NDMB then forced management to accept the union's wage demands. Using carrots and sticks, federal administrators encouraged a more collaborative, managerial style of union leadership. Unions did not have to struggle for membership or recognition; in return, they curbed militant locals and accepted federal oversight. Decision making moved from one-story brick "locals" in factory towns to the marble headquarters of national unions in Washington, DC.

People moved to jobs, rather than the other way around, and some 4 million workers, and with them another 5 million family members, migrated to the new sites of war production. Some 200,000 Mexican *braceros* crossed the border to harvest crops. San Francisco's African American population doubled in a year. In Los Angeles, African Americans were arriving at a rate of 300 to 400 a day. By leaving Mississippi to take a factory job in California, a sharecropper could increase his salary six- or sevenfold.

Workers were generally happy with higher wages, but many lacked a decent place to live. New York, with plenty of housing, suffered from unemployment while new factories were located in places with no housing. There were no rooms to rent within miles of Willow Run. In many towns, workers "hot bedded"—slept in shifts in boardinghouses—or lived in cars. Frustrations over the housing shortage sometimes boiled over into racial conflict. In 1943, two days of mob violence erupted in Detroit over who would take possession of 1,000 new units of federal housing. Housing remained a chronic problem during the war and for several years afterward.

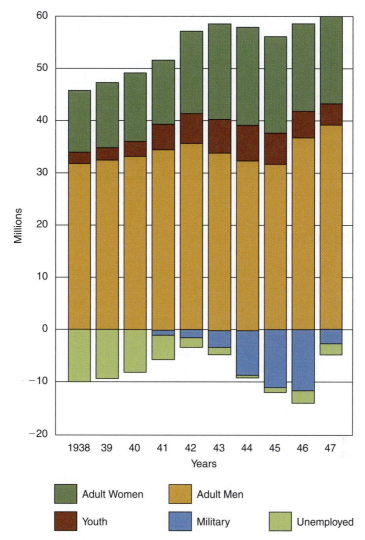

Figure 25–2   Makeup of U.S. Labor Force, 1938–1947 *Dear,* Oxford Companion to World War II, *p. 1182.*

Women in Industry

"Rosie the Riveter," the image of the glamorous machinist laboring to bring her man home sooner, was largely a creation of the Office of War Information. Some 36 percent of the wartime labor force was female, but that was only slightly higher than the peacetime figure. Few women left housework to take a job in a factory solely for patriotic reasons. Instead, the war economy shifted women workers into new roles, some from service jobs into industry and others from factory jobs to better-paid positions.

The number of manufacturing jobs for women grew from 12 million to 16.5 million, with many women moving into heavy industry as metalworkers, shipwrights, and assemblers of tanks and aircraft, jobs that had been off-limits before. Women worked coke ovens, blast furnaces, and rolling mills. For many women, the war and its demands offered the first real chance for mobility.

Even so, employers did not offer equal pay or help to women trying to juggle job and family. Unions either refused women membership or expelled them when the war ended. The Lanham Act provided the first federal support for day care, but the 2,800 government centers were not nearly enough. "Latchkey children," left home alone while their mothers worked, were said to be a major problem. Experts saw female labor as necessary during the war but dangerous in the long run. "Many of them are rejecting their feminine roles," a social worker complained. After the war, women were expected to yield their jobs to returning servicemen. They were also blamed for neglecting their duties and encouraging juvenile delinquency.

Between Idealism and Fear

In the movies Americans marched to war (and war plants) singing patriotic tunes by George M. Cohan, but in real life this war was noticeably free of high-minded idealism. Americans had already fought once to end all wars and to keep the world safe for democracy. They were not ready to buy that bill of goods again. Journalist John Hersey asked marines on Guadalcanal what they were fighting for. "Scotch whiskey. Dames. A piece of blueberry pie. Music," they replied. Things were no clearer at home, where to writer Dwight Macdonald the war seemed to represent "the maximum of physical devastation accompanied by the minimum of human meaning."

If Americans weren't sure what they were fighting for, they knew what they were fighting against: totalitarianism, gestapos, and master races. Throughout the war and after, totalitarianism was a powerful symbol of what America and Americans ought to oppose. The president of the U.S. Chamber of Commerce denounced the New Deal as "fascist" and "totalitarian." Labor unions and civil rights groups used the same words against their enemies, but wartime rhetoric also held Americans to a higher standard of tolerance. "All races and religions; that's America to me," sang Frank Sinatra in *The House I Live In* (1945).

Wartime leaders struggled to fill the inspirational vacuum with some of the century's most stirring restatements of the democratic creed. Winston Churchill spoke of protecting the liberty and culture of the "English-speaking peoples." In his State of the Union address in January 1941, Franklin Roosevelt aspired to a world based on the "Four Freedoms": freedom of speech, freedom of worship, freedom from want, and freedom from fear. A month later, *Life* magazine published an essay by its founder, Henry Luce, entitled "The American Century." It was a powerfully optimistic vision of globalized democracy and abundance, "a sharing with all people of our Bill of Rights, our Declaration of Independence, our Constitution, our magnificent industrial products, our technical skills." In response, Vice President Henry Wallace proclaimed that in the "Century of the Common Man," nations would "measure freedom by standards of nutrition, education and self-government." He equated democracy—as American leaders would do after the war—with schools, jobs, food, and a New Deal for the world.

African Americans sought their four freedoms in an atmosphere of increasing racial hostility. Detroit was just one city in which rapid growth touched off racial conflict. In

Maryland, Michigan, New York, and Ohio, white workers engaged in "hate strikes" to prevent the hiring of African American workers. Over 3,000 white employees of a naval shipyard burned African American neighborhoods in Beaumont, Texas, in June 1943. Curfews, rumors of riots, and white citizens' committees kept many other cities on edge.

African Americans responded by linking their struggle for rights at home to the global war against fascism. Thurgood Marshall, chief counsel for the NAACP, compared the Detroit rioters to "the Nazi Gestapo." In 1942, the *Pittsburgh Courier* launched the "Double V" campaign to connect the fight against racism to the one against fascism. "Defeat Hitler, Mussolini, and Hirohito," it urged, "by Enforcing the Constitution and Abolishing Jim Crow." NAACP membership grew tenfold during the war. In Chicago, students and activists inspired by the nonviolent tactics of Mohandas Gandhi organized the Congress of Racial Equality (CORE), which desegregated restaurants and public facilities in the North. The NAACP won a legal victory in the Supreme Court case of *Smith v. Allwright* (1944), which invalidated all-white primary elections.

The experience of war may have been the greatest catalyst to change. Many African Americans returned from combat determined not to accept discrimination any longer. Amzie Moore came home to Cleveland, Mississippi, after serving in the army and was elected head of the local NAACP chapter. "Here I am being shipped overseas," he said of his service in the Pacific, "and I been segregated from this man who I might have to save or he save my life. I didn't fail to tell it." The war prepared Moore and his generation for the struggle ahead.

Japanese Internment

Idealism was no match for fear, and in the days after Pearl Harbor, panicky journalists, politicians, and military authorities perpetrated an injustice on American citizens of Japanese descent. Ominous signs reading "Civilian Exclusion Order" went up in California and the Pacific Northwest in February 1942. They instructed "Japanese aliens and non-aliens" to report to relocation centers for removal from the Pacific Coast "war zone." The Western Defense Command of Lt. Gen. John L. DeWitt and the *Los Angeles Times*, believing the Japanese planned to invade the West Coast, aroused the public against the Japanese "menace." FBI investigators found no suspicious plots and told the president so, but the press continued to print rumors. Responding to the press, DeWitt, and the California congressional delegation, Roosevelt ordered the relocation.

Internees and lawyers challenged the legality of confining American citizens without charge or trial. Fred Korematsu, a welder from San Leandro, California, took a new name and had his face surgically altered in a futile attempt to stay out of the camps. When he was arrested, the American Civil Liberties Union used his case to challenge the evacuation order. Supreme Court Justice Hugo Black upheld the policy as justified by "military necessity." In January 1947, the Western Defense Command praised the evacuation program and suggested that it could be used as a model for the treatment of suspect populations during the next national emergency.

No Shelter from the Holocaust

The United States might have saved more of the victims of Hitler's "final solution" had it chosen to do so. A combination of fear, anti-Semitism, and a desire to avoid unwanted

>> Manzanar

Jeanne Wakatsuki's internment began with a Greyhound bus ride from Los Angeles across the Mojave Desert. A mile from her destination, she saw "a yellow swirl across a blurred, reddish setting sun. The bus was being pelted by what sounded like splattering rain. It wasn't rain. This was my first look at something I would soon know very well, a billowing flurry of dust and sand churned up by the wind through Owens Valley." Its lakes and rivers emptied by the Los Angeles aqueduct, Owens Valley was a man-made desert.

Temperatures ranged from 115 degrees in summer to well below freezing in winter. On an alkali flat beneath the towering Inyo Range, workmen were building the Manzanar Relocation Camp, 600 wood and tar paper barracks that would soon house more than 10,000 people. Each family received 20 square feet of floor space and an iron cot and army blanket for each member. Prisoners made the other furnishings themselves, filling burlap bags with straw for mattresses, crafting chairs and tables from spare lumber.

The prisoners fed themselves. They planted tomatoes, turnips, radishes, watermelons, and corn. They raised cattle, pigs, and poultry, making the camp self-sufficient in both meat and vegetables. The flowers and greenery they planted softened the dry land. Prisoners opened shops, laundries, a newspaper, a clinic, and a cemetery. They practiced medicine and law. The Manzanar Co-Op sold $1 million of retail and mail-order goods in 1944.

Manzanar was like a small city, but one surrounded by wire and armed guards. Camp administrators created a network of informants to spy on inmates. In December 1942, four prisoners beat up a man suspected of being an informant. When one was arrested, a group of prisoners demonstrated to demand his release. Nervous guards fired into the crowd, killing two young men and wounding eight others. "You can't imagine how close we came to machine-gunning the whole bunch of them," a camp official explained. "The only thing that stopped us, I guess, were the effects such a shooting would have had on the Japs holding our boys in Manila and China."

It was the last "uprising" at the camp. Administrators censored the newspaper, prohibited expressions of Japanese culture, and required all meetings to be conducted in English. The community within the camp remained forever divided. Young men denounced their elders for respecting the law even when it was unjust. Administrators separated the angry from the docile and drew up blacklists.

Defiance was severely punished. Over 8,000 internees who would not renounce the emperor were sent to a camp at Tule Lake, California, and 263 men who refused military service went to federal prison. Still, the majority of draft-eligible men in the camps served in the armed forces, many in intelligence and combat roles. The separation of the loyal from the disloyal and the placement of so many in positions of trust removed all justification for continuing to hold loyal Japanese Americans, apart from the political embarrassment their sudden release would cause.

Those who could leave—students admitted to universities, workers with contracts elsewhere, those who joined the armed forces—did so, leaving only the very old and the very young. "What had to be endured was the climate, the confinement, the steady crumbling of family life," Wakatsuki wrote in her memoir, *Farewell to Manzanar*. "In such a narrowed world, in order to survive, you learn to contain your rage and your despair, and you try to re-create, as well as you can, your normality, some sense of things continuing."

burdens led American leaders to dismiss the Holocaust as someone else's problem. The State Department, worried that spies and saboteurs would sneak in with the refugees, erected a paper wall of bureaucratic restrictions. Refugees found it easier to get a visa from China than from the United States. In 1939, the *St. Louis* steamed from Hamburg with 930 Jewish refugees aboard. American immigration officials refused to let the refugees ashore because they lacked proper papers—papers that only their Nazi persecutors could have furnished. The ship and its passengers returned to Germany.

Nazi Germany's systematic extermination of the Jews made news in the United States. Stories in the *New York Times* as early as 1942 described the deportations and concluded that "the greatest mass slaughter in history" was under way. At Auschwitz, Poland, in the most efficient death camp, 2,000 people an hour could be killed with Zyklon-B gas. Jewish leaders begged the War Department to bomb the camp or the rail lines leading to it. The city of Auschwitz was bombed twice in 1944, but John J. McCloy, the assistant secretary of war, refused to target the camp, dismissing it as a humanitarian matter of no concern to the army. Roosevelt knew of the Holocaust, but his inaction, according to historian David Wyman, was "the worst failure of his presidency."

When American soldiers entered Germany in 1945, they saw clearly why they were fighting. On April 15, Patton's Third Army liberated the Buchenwald death camp. Correspondent Edward R. Murrow described the scene to radio listeners in the United States: the skeletonlike survivors, the piles of the dead, the ovens. "I pray you to believe what I have said about Buchenwald," he said. "I have reported what I saw." Eisenhower had photographs and films taken, and he brought German civilians from nearby communities to witness the mass burial, by bulldozer, of the corpses. Many GIs doubted anyone would believe what they had witnessed. "We got to talk about it, see?" one told reporter Martha Gellhorn. "We got to talk about it if anyone believes us or not."

Americans entered the First World War flushed with idealism and became disillusioned in victory's aftermath. The Second World War reversed this trajectory. Americans slowly came to see the power of their shopworn ideals against the hatred and bigotry that afflicted all nations, including their own. Rose Mclain wrote her husband in the Pacific to promise "that our children will learn kindness, patience, and the depth of love . . . that they shall never know hate, selfishness and death from such [a war] as this has been."

Closing with the Enemy

"The Americans are so helpless," Joseph Goebbels, Hitler's propaganda minister, said in 1942, "that they must fall back again and again upon boasting about their maté-riel." After the North Africa campaign, the United States made good on its boasts. The American army was small—only 5 million compared with Germany's 9 million—but it was amply supplied and agile, emphasizing speed and firepower. In 1944 and 1945 the United States carried the war to Japan and into the heart of Europe with a singular destructiveness. As the war drew to a close, Americans began to anticipate the difficul-ties of reconstructing the postwar world and to create institutions to structure a global economy at peace.

Taking the War to Europe

Using North Africa as a base, the Anglo-American Allies next attacked northward into Italy, knocking one of the Axis powers out of the war. In Sicily, where the Allies landed in July 1943, Patton applied the mobile, aggressive tactics he had advocated since 1940. Slic-ing the island in half and trapping a large part of the Italian army, he arrived at Messina too late to block the Germans' escape. The defeat shook Italy. Parliament deposed Mus-solini and ordered his arrest. German troops took control and fiercely resisted the Allied landings at Salerno in September, and winter rains stopped the Anglo-American offensive south of Rome. American troops finally broke through to Rome on June 5, 1944.

The next day, D-Day, finally began the second front the Soviets had asked for. Early on the morning of June 6, 1944, the massive Allied invasion armada assembled off Eng-land's Channel coast and launched the assault on France's Normandy coast on beaches designated Juno, Gold, Sword, Utah, and Omaha. Hitler had fortified the beaches with an "Atlantic Wall" of mines, obstacles, heavy guns, and cement forts. Americans waded ashore on the lightly held Utah Beach without much difficulty, but on Omaha the small boats headed straight into concentrated fire. The boats unloaded too soon, and men with full packs plunged into deep water. Floating tanks overturned and sank with crews inside. Commanders briefly considered calling off the attack, but soldiers in small groups began moving inland to outflank German batteries. By the end of the day, they held the beach.

Eisenhower's greatest fear was another Italy. The hedgerow country behind the beaches contained the most defensible terrain between the Channel and Germany. Each field and pasture was protected by earthen mounds topped with shrubs, natural walls that isolated troops. When GIs crossed a hedgerow, "the Germans could knock off the first one or two, cause the others to duck down behind the bank and then call for his own mortar support," according to one infantryman. "The German mortars were very, very efficient." However, just as had happened on Omaha Beach, the defects of the generals' strategy were compensated for by the initiative of ordinary soldiers. On their own, tankers hand-built devices to help their tanks cut through the thick hedgerows. By the end of the month

Mitchel Jamieson's *Burial Grounds* **(1944)** Wartime censors carefully spared the American audience from images of the anonymous, mass death of modern war, but scenes such as this one in Normandy always followed major battles.

the U.S. advance broke through German defenses and captured the critical port city of Cherbourg.

Once in open country, highly mobile American infantry chased the retreating enemy across France to the fortified German border. There, in the Ardennes Forest, Hitler's armies rallied for a final desperate counterattack. Thirty divisions, supported by 1,000 aircraft, hit a lightly held sector of the American lines, broke through, and opened a "bulge" 40 miles wide and 60 miles deep in the Allied front. Two regiments were forced to surrender, but the 101st Airborne, encircled and besieged at Bastogne, held on to a critical road junction, slowing the German advance until Allies brought in reinforcements. The Battle of the Bulge lasted a month and cost more than 10,000 American dead and 47,000 wounded, but the German army had lost the ability to resist.

Island Hopping in the Pacific

To get close enough for a knockout blow at Japan, the United States had to pierce the barrier of fortified islands stretching across the western Pacific. The army and the navy each had a strategy and bickered over supplies and the shortest route to Tokyo. MacArthur favored a thrust from Australia through the Solomon Islands and New Guinea to retake the Philippines. Nimitz preferred a thrust across the central Pacific to seize islands as staging areas for an air and land assault on Japan.

By November 1943, MacArthur's American and Australian forces had advanced to Bougainville, the largest of the Solomon Islands and the nearest to the Japanese air and naval complex at Rabaul. Jungle fighting on these islands was especially vicious. Each side treated the other without mercy, killing prisoners, mutilating the dead, and fighting with "a brutish, primitive hatred," according to Eugene Sledge, whose marine comrades kept gold teeth and skulls as trophies. Air attacks pulverized Rabaul in early 1944, opening the way for an advance into the southern Philippines.

Meanwhile, Nimitz launched a naval attack on Japan's island bases. With 11 new aircraft carriers, the Fifth Fleet attacked Tarawa, a tiny atoll with 4,500 Japanese troops protected by bunkers and hidden guns. Coral reefs snagged landing craft, forcing troops to wade ashore under heavy fire. Americans were shocked by the losses, more than 3,000 dead and wounded, for such a small piece of territory, but it was only one of many island battles. "Island hopping" from Tarawa to the Marshall Islands and the Marianas, American forces bypassed strongly held islands and moved the battle closer to Japan.

The Allied capture of Saipan, Tinian, and Guam in July 1944 brought Japan within range of B-29 bombers. General Curtis LeMay landed his 21st Bomber Command on Saipan in January 1945 and began a new kind of air offensive against Japanese cities. LeMay experimented with low-level attacks using high explosives (to shatter houses) and incendiaries (to set fire to the debris). The proper mix could create a "firestorm," a flaming tornado hundreds of feet high. On the night of March 9, 1945, 334 bombers lit a fire in Tokyo that destroyed 267,000 buildings. The heat was so intense that the canals boiled and 83,000 people died from flames and suffocation. LeMay went on to burn more than 60 percent of Japan's cities. Americans felt the attacks justified, but, as historian Ronald Spector has written, bomber crews "realized that this was something new, something more terrible than even the normal awfulness of war."

Building a New World

As the war progressed across Europe and the Pacific, Allied leaders met to discuss their visions of the world after victory. In Casablanca in 1943, Roosevelt and Churchill agreed to demand the unconditional surrender of the Axis powers to give the Allies a free hand to set the terms of peace. No country planned for peace as thoroughly as the United States. The State, War, and Navy departments undertook a comprehensive survey of the world, examining each country and territory to determine its importance to the United States. Planners had only sketchy ideas about future threats, but based on experience they believed that American security would depend on having a functioning international organization, a global system of free trade, and a worldwide network of American military bases.

The weak League of Nations stood little chance of maintaining the peace in the 1930s. Roosevelt envisioned a stronger organization led by regional powers acting as "policemen" within designated spheres of influence. The new organization would disband empires, placing "trusteeships" over colonial territories preparing for self-government. The world after victory would be a world of nations, not empires or blocs. In September 1944, delegates from 39 nations met at the Dumbarton Oaks estate in Washington, D.C., and sketched out a plan for a United Nations (UN) organization comprising a general assembly, in which all nations would be represented, and an executive council made up of the United States, China, the Soviet Union, Britain, and France.

To American leaders, the lesson of the 1930s had been that without prosperity there could be no peace. They wanted to remove the economic conditions that caused

AMERICA AND THE WORLD

>> Bretton Woods

As Allied armies struggled for control of Normandy in late June 1944, 300 economists, diplomats, and translators from 44 nations converged on the Mount Washington Hotel in Bretton Woods, New Hampshire. Army MPs were still painting the lobby as they arrived. The hotel had closed during the Depression, but a new owner, David Stoneman, reopened it in 1944. With most big hotels converted into barracks, this remote, run-down resort was one of the few places where the United States could host a global conference.

Roosevelt and Churchill convened the conference to deal with the staggering economic problems that would follow the war. International trade had collapsed; several major world currencies—the franc, the mark, and the yen—were or soon would be valueless; Britain and the Soviet Union were near bankruptcy; and two-thirds of the world's gold reserves were held by one country, the United States. Allied leaders also recognized that the postwar peace would require a global system in which every nation could control its economic future.

Preventing a renewed Depression required each nation to combat unemployment, applying all its financial resources to self-recovery. Reporter I. F. Stone noted that the new international economy would have to go beyond the gold standard and accommodate this "positive governmental interference." Every nation would need a welfare state, and no nation could be allowed to fail. "Prosperity is indivisible," Treasury Secretary Henry Morgenthau warned at the opening session.

The use of gold as an international currency had expanded trade in the nineteenth century, but in the twentieth century it amplified economic and political troubles by sharply reducing consumption and employment in debtor countries. By the 1930s, the world economy had broken into rival blocs, each settling accounts using a different metal or currency (sterling, gold, the yen). To create an indivisible prosperity, the conferees at Bretton Woods needed to find substitutes for gold and empire: a new way to settle international debts, encourage trade expansion, and still allow national governments to pursue full employment.

Two strong personalities vied to shape the postwar order. John Maynard Keynes, the brilliant British economist, wanted to create a global currency unit, the "bancor," that would allow a centralized world bank to expand or shrink the money supply as needed. The chief American delegate, Harry D. White, held that a world currency would be unnecessary if every lira, zloty, and balboa could be converted into U.S. dollars. Convertibility was the economic equivalent of a military alliance, and the United States should "attract other currencies into its orbit of influence."

The conference debated these proposals for a month. The United States' massive gold reserves gave it a strong hand. White's assistant, Dean Acheson, settled a debate over the location of the new world *continued*

AMERICA AND THE WORLD *continued*

financial institutions—in Washington—by explaining simply "you fellows will have to give way in this matter, you know, if the fund is to go through." The conference's final resolutions were nearer to White's vision than to Keynes's.

The International Monetary Fund (IMF) would manage international accounts. It fixed the relationship between gold and the dollar at $35 an ounce and pegged all other currencies to the dollar at fixed rates of exchange. The system brought predictability to international trade: the profits of Mexican wheat farmers no longer depended on the value of the peso but only on the value of wheat. The International Bank for Reconstruction and Development (later known as the World Bank) would promote growth and trade, Keynes explained, and "raise the standard of life and condition of labor everywhere."

The "Bretton Woods institutions" possessed broad powers to manage the global movement of capital. The IMF kept the system of fixed exchange rates until 1973, after which it managed the float

of currencies against one another. IMF and World Bank loans have financed an expanding repertoire of development projects and reforms. By the 1990s, an international antiglobalization movement criticized the Bretton Woods institutions for enforcing trade rules at the expense of local business, cultural diversity, and the environment. In 1944, however, critics of the new system objected that the plan gave national governments far too much leeway at the expense of stability. After the straitjacket of the gold standard, the new rules seemed slack.

Contention between global and local interests began right in the lobby at the Mount Washington. When delegates told the reservations clerk they needed three more days to straighten out the planet's finances, Stoneman told Morganthau that he had a hotel to run, other guests had booked rooms, and the conferees would have to leave. Morgenthau replied that the army could always seize the hotel. The hotel keeper gave in. Score one for the forces of globalization.

desperate people to follow dictators into war. A true victory, they imagined, would create an open-door world, in which goods and money could move freely, eliminating the need or justification for conquest. In 1943, before the UN existed as an organization, the United States created the United Nations Relief and Rehabilitation Administration (UNRRA) to provide food and medicine to areas retaken by the Allies. The Bretton Woods Conference set conditions for a postwar expansion of trade. The army established schools at universities where officers studied languages and discussed strategies for instilling a democratic culture in enemy nations. The invasion of Italy provided a first test of these techniques, and the United States drew on its resources as an immigrant nation to staff units with Italian-speaking officers.

Military planners were not ready to stake America's future security entirely on trade or international organizations. Pearl Harbor had shown that oceans offered no protection against aggression. Military leaders could imagine aircraft and rockets striking deep into the American heartland without warning. Beginning in 1943, they laid plans for a global system of military bases from the Azores to Calcutta to Manila, encircling the vast Eurasian land mass. Planners could not say who the next enemy would be, but with such an extensive base network, the United States could act against any challenger before it could strike. Britain and the Soviet Union looked upon this plan warily, suspecting that they might be its targets, but American leaders were willing to take diplomatic risks to attain the security they felt they required.

The Fruits of Victory

Despite rumors of his failing health, Americans elected Franklin Roosevelt to a fourth term in 1944 by a margin of 53.5 percent to 46 percent for the challenger Thomas E. Dewey. On April 12, 1945, less than three months after his inauguration, Roosevelt died suddenly of a cerebral hemorrhage at Warm Springs, Georgia. "Mr. Roosevelt's body was brought back to Washington today for the last time," reporter I. F. Stone wrote on April 21, 1945. "The marching men, the solemn bands, the armored cars, the regiment of Negro soldiers, the uniformed women's detachments. . . . In that one quick look thousands of us said goodbye to a great and good man, and to an era." In Paris, French men and women offered condolences to American GIs. Flags flew at half-staff on Guadalcanal, Kwajalein, and Tarawa. Roosevelt died just days before Allied troops in Europe achieved the great victory for which he had struggled. On April 25, American and Soviet troops shook hands at Torgau in eastern Germany. On April 30, with Soviet soldiers just a few hundred yards away, Hitler committed suicide in his Berlin bunker. On May 8, all German forces surrendered unconditionally.

Harry S. Truman, the new vice president and former senator from Missouri, was now commander in chief. Shortly after taking office, aides informed him that the Manhattan Project would soon test a weapon that might end the war in Asia. The first atomic explosion took place in the desert near Alamogordo, New Mexico, on July 16, 1945. Truman, meeting with Churchill and Stalin at Potsdam, Germany, was elated by the news. He informed Stalin while Churchill looked on, watching the expression of the Soviet leader. The bomb had been developed to be used against the Axis enemy, but by the time Truman learned about it, American leaders already saw it as a powerful instrument of postwar diplomacy.

As American forces neared the Japanese home islands, defenders fought with suicidal ferocity. On Okinawa, soldiers and civilians retreated into caves and battled to the death. GIs feared the invasion of Japan's home islands, where resistance could only be worse. Then on August 6, a B-29 dropped an atomic bomb on Hiroshima. Two days later the Soviet Union declared war on Japan, and Soviet armies attacked deep into Manchuria. On August 9, the United States dropped a second atomic bomb, this time on Nagasaki. It detonated 1,900 feet above Shima Hospital. In a fraction of a second, the hospital and nearly a square mile of the city ignited. Bricks and granite melted in the nuclear fire. People were vaporized, some leaving shadows on the pavement. In the ruins of Hiroshima, a French Red Cross worker saw "not a bird or an animal. . . . On what remained of the station facade the hands of the clock had been stopped by the fire at 8:15. It was perhaps the first time in the history of humanity that the birth of a new era was recorded on the face of a clock."

V-J Day Jubilant crowds greeted V-J Day in New York. Many soldiers newly returned from Europe were on their way to the Pacific.

Conclusion

Emperor Hirohito announced Japan's unconditional surrender on August 14. In New York, crowds celebrated, but everywhere there was silence and reflection. Thirty million people had been killed; great cities lay in ruins. At the end of the war, the United States' economic, scientific, and military mastery reached a pinnacle never attained by any of the great empires of history. Two-thirds of the world's gold was in American treasuries; half of the world's manufactured goods were made in the United States. At its height, imperial Britain controlled 25 percent of the world's wealth. In 1945, the United States controlled 40 percent. America's air force, almost 80,000 planes, dominated the skies; its fleet had more ships than the navies of all its enemies and allies combined. Then there was the atomic bomb. The rest of the world looked to see how the United States would use its formidable wealth and power.

The war's sudden end meant Americans had to reconvert to a "peacetime" economy, preferably one more stable and prosperous than the depression economy of the 1930s. A. Philip Randolph predicted government would have to take a larger role in raising wages and stimulating key industries, such as housing, if returning soldiers were to find jobs and goods to buy. The postwar future looked tenuous. America could either succumb to "a native variety of fascism" or open an era of expanding rights, democracy, and material abundance.

>> Timeline

▼1933
Hitler becomes chancellor of Germany
President Roosevelt devalues the dollar
The United States recognizes the Soviet Union

▼1934
Reciprocal Trade Act passed
Export-Import Bank created

▼1935
Congress passes first Neutrality Act

▼1937
War begins in Asia

▼1938
Munich agreement gives Hitler Sudetenland

▼1939
War begins in Europe

▼1940
Germany defeats France, Netherlands, Belgium
Destroyers-for-bases deal between the United States and Britain

▼1941
Lend-Lease passed
Executive Order 8802 ends discrimination in defense industries
Roosevelt and Churchill sign Atlantic Charter
Germany invades the Soviet Union
Japan attacks the United States at Pearl Harbor
United States declares war on Axis powers

▼1942
Philippines falls to Japan
Internment of Japanese Americans begins
Battles of Coral Sea and Midway turn the tide in the Pacific
Allies land in North Africa

▼1943
Allies land in Sicily
Churchill and Roosevelt meet at Casablanca
U.S. troops advance to Bougainville
Marines capture Tarawa   *continued*

>> Timeline *continued*

▼1944
U.S. troops capture Rome
Allied landings in Normandy
U.S. troops capture Saipan
Bretton Woods Conference
Roosevelt reelected for fourth term

▼1945
Roosevelt dies
Harry S. Truman becomes president
Germany surrenders
Truman meets Churchill and Stalin at Potsdam
Atomic bombs dropped on Hiroshima and Nagasaki
Japan surrenders

Review Questions

1. Which was more important to victory at Midway, planning or luck?

2. Why did the population of the West grow so rapidly during the war?

3. Contrast isolationist and internationalist viewpoints. Did they imagine different futures for the United States?

4. Thurgood Marshall worried about the emergence of "gestapos" in America. What did he mean?

5. According to American leaders, what caused World War II? How did their answers to that question affect their plans for the postwar world?

6. The government used propaganda and repressive laws to control domestic opinion during World War I. Why was there no repeat of those policies in World War II?

7. Some historians blame Roosevelt for luring the United States into war. How might that historical view be rooted in the isolationist/internationalist debate?

For further review materials and resource information, please visit www.oup.com/us/ofthepeople

The Cold War

1945–1952

>> Esther and Stephen Brunauer

Esther Caukin and Stephen Brunauer were an American success story. Born in California in 1901, Esther benefited from the growing opportunities for women in the twentieth century. She graduated from Mills College, earned a doctorate from Stanford, and became an administrator for the American Association of University Women. In 1931, she married Stephen Brunauer, a successful chemist who had come to the United States from Hungary. The Brunauers were patriots who hated fascism. In the 1930s, Esther tried to educate Americans about the threat from Adolf Hitler's Germany. When World War II came, she went to work in the U.S. State Department. Stephen also worked for the government as an explosives expert in the navy. After the war, he traveled to Hungary to gather scientific intelligence for the government and to help Hungarian scientists emigrate to the United States. With fascism defeated and their careers launched, the Brunauers had succeeded. Like most Americans, they could have looked forward to a happy, prosperous future. But then it all went wrong.

In 1947 a congressman accused Esther of being one of the "pro-Communist fellow travelers and muddle heads" in the State Department. One of her speeches, he said, was "echoing Soviet propaganda." That year, a federal agency refused to let Stephen attend a meeting about atomic energy because he had once, as a student in the 1920s, belonged to the Young Workers' League, a group with Communist ties. Somehow, even though they hated Communism as much as they hated fascism, the Brunauers found their patriotism questioned.

Then things got worse. On March 13, 1950, Senator Joseph McCarthy of Wisconsin charged Esther and Stephen with espionage and links to known Communists. Esther, McCarthy testified, had engaged in "Communist-front activities"; Stephen had access "to some of the topmost secrets" of the U.S. military and was "a grave security risk of the highest order." McCarthy demanded federal records in order to

continued

find out whether the Brunauers were Communists who had betrayed their country. Stephen immediately denied he had ever been a Communist. "I am a loyal American," Esther insisted.

Two weeks later Esther took the witness stand to defend herself and her husband before the subcommittee. Rejecting McCarthy's charges, she accused the senator of betraying American values of fairness with his sudden and unfounded attack. Esther revealed how much McCarthy's accusations had already hurt her family. They had received threatening telephone calls day and night. "Get out of this neighborhood, you Communists," one caller warned, "or you will be carried out in a box." Esther offered letters of support from a senator, a former senator, and a college president. Dismissing McCarthy's charges, the college president, who was a brother of General Dwight D. Eisenhower, maintained that it was "un-American" to call Esther a "Communist sympathizer."

A majority of the subcommittee agreed. In July, the subcommittee's report concluded that McCarthy's charges against the Brunauers were "contemptible," "a fraud and a hoax." But the damage had been done. Despite the subcommittee report, the State Department and the navy were no longer willing to risk keeping such controversial people on the job. In 1951 the navy suspended Stephen from his position, and the State Department suspended Esther from hers. Esther fought her suspension but was charged with "close and habitual association" with her husband. In 1952, the State Department fired her as a "security risk." The real reason for her dismissal, Esther told the press, was "political expediency." Their careers destroyed, the Brunauers left Washington to try to rebuild their lives out of the spotlight in Illinois.

How had it happened? How had the optimism of 1945 degenerated into suspicion? Like the Brunauers, Americans lived in a country and a world saved from ruin. At home, the economic boom of World War II had swept away the Great Depression. Abroad, the United States had helped to destroy the threat of fascism. Americans should have expected the postwar world to be stable and safe.

Within two years, however, a tense peacetime confrontation with the Soviet Union disrupted American life. Convinced that the Soviets intended to expand their power and spread Communism across Europe, U.S. leaders challenged their former allies. While this "cold war" developed, Americans also faced the task of maintaining prosperity in peacetime. Organized labor, women, and African Americans struggled to preserve and extend their rights and opportunities. President Harry Truman and the Democratic Party struggled to preserve power and implement a liberal agenda.

However unsettling, the cold war was not an aberration. The confrontation with Communism was deeply rooted in the core values of American democracy at the close of World War II. Truman and other leaders saw the Soviet system as inimical to free institutions, civil rights, and the capitalist system revived by the New Deal. Moreover, they worried that if a Communist coalition became too strong, the United States would have to defend itself by regimenting the economy and restricting individual rights—turning America into a "garrison state." To contain Soviet expansion, the U.S. government took unprecedented peacetime actions—massive foreign aid, new alliances, a military buildup—that helped to transform the political economy in the 1940s and beyond.

>> **AMERICAN PORTRAIT** *continued*

Although dramatic, the new policies did not prevent the cold war from widening and intensifying. By 1950, the nation was fighting a hot war on the other side of the world in Korea. By then, too, Americans knew that the Soviet Union had nuclear weapons that could devastate the United States. In turn, the Truman administration stepped up military spending and developed more powerful nuclear weapons. As the cold war seemed to spiral out of control, fear gripped American society. A frenzied search for Communist subversives at home threatened civil liberties and destroyed the careers of Esther and Stephen Brunauer. They suffered more than most people, but in one way or another, the cold war unsettled the lives of all Americans for years to come.

Common Threads

>> Why did friction over Germany, Poland, and the Mediterranean turn into a cold war affecting the entire world?

>> How did the need for constant vigilance interfere with democratic values?

>> The specter of the Depression hung over postwar economic planners. How did they try to avoid another decline as they reconverted the war economy?

Origins of the Cold War

In a span of two years, the United States and the Soviet Union went from a wartime alliance to the protracted rivalry known as the cold war. The sweeping, long-term consequences of the cold war made it particularly important for Americans to understand the origins of the conflict. From the outset, the United States and the Soviet Union tried to pin the blame for the cold war on each other. For a long time, Americans wanted to believe that the Soviet Union, authoritarian and expansionist, was solely responsible. However, historians have gradually offered a more critical perspective, and they generally agree that actions by both countries caused the cold war.

Ideological Competition

There is less agreement about the precise sources of the conflict. Ideological, political, military, and economic factors all clearly played a role. Ever since the founding of the Soviet Union toward the end of World War I, Soviets and Americans were ideological adversaries with different political systems. The Soviet Union was committed to Communism and socialism, the United States to democracy and capitalism. Despite their differences, the two countries fought as allies in World War II. Wartime decisions, especially about the postwar world, laid the groundwork for animosity after 1945. In peacetime, the Soviet Union and the United States were the only countries strong enough to threaten each other, and World War II showed that with modern arms both sides could strike with devastating suddenness. Moreover, they had different political, military, and economic ambitions. By 1947 those different goals produced open antagonism. With the United States' vow to combat the spread of Communism, the cold war was under way.

The Union of Soviet Socialist Republics (USSR) emerged from the Russian Revolution of 1917 and the civil war that followed. Vladimir Lenin's Bolshevik Party introduced a socialist economy in which the state—the government—owned factories and farms. At home, the Soviet Union practiced forms of economic and social regimentation Americans recognized from Nazi Germany and imperial Japan, limiting individual rights, including freedom of speech and religion, and achieving a self-contained autarkic economy. Abroad, the new nation endorsed the revolutionary overthrow of capitalism.

The Soviets' Marxist ideology obviously set them at odds with American ideals. The vast majority of Americans favored a capitalist economy, in which private citizens owned property. They celebrated individualism, freedom of speech, freedom of religion, and democratic government based on free elections. Communists believed all modern societies would eventually eliminate religion and private property and set the collective good over the rights of the individual.

Nevertheless, open conflict was not inevitable. Although American leaders hated Communism, the USSR was weak and hemmed in by powerful neighbors, Germany in the west and Japan in the east. It posed no military threat to the United States in the 1920s and 1930s and could even be helpful to American interests. President Franklin Roosevelt, eager to promote trade and restrain Japanese expansion, officially recognized the Soviet Union in 1933.

Uneasy Allies

World War II demonstrated that, despite differences, the United States and the Soviet Union could become allies. After the German invasion of the USSR and the Japanese attack on Pearl Harbor, the United States and the Soviets were thrown together in the war against fascism. They were uneasy allies at best. For many Americans, the lesson of the war was that the United States could not tolerate aggression. No new dictator should ever be able to take over other European countries unopposed, as Hitler did, nor should any single power be allowed to dominate Eurasia. By 1945 some Americans already equated the Soviets with the Nazis by denouncing "Red Fascism."

Different experiences drove each country to protect itself from future disasters. American leaders believed autarkic trade blocs had caused both the Great Depression and the war that followed, and they resolved to rebuild the world economy as a single system, with reduced trade barriers and uniform rules. Soviet leaders feared a repeat of the last two wars, when Poland and Eastern Europe had been staging areas for invasions that claimed millions of Russian lives. But the lessons they drew from war led to opposite solutions: American leaders favored an interdependent system, with open borders allowing goods, information, and people to move freely; Soviet leaders felt only a closed system and tight controls would give it real protection.

Wartime decisions also aggravated tensions. In 1943 the American government created ill feeling by excluding the Soviets from the surrender of Italy. The delay of the Allied

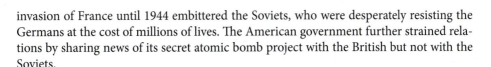

invasion of France until 1944 embittered the Soviets, who were desperately resisting the Germans at the cost of millions of lives. The American government further strained relations by sharing news of its secret atomic bomb project with the British but not with the Soviets.

Decisions about the postwar world led to trouble as well. At a conference in Yalta in the Soviet Union in February 1945, Franklin Roosevelt, Josef Stalin, and British prime minister Winston Churchill proposed a self-contradictory vision of the postwar world. The "Big Three" supported national self-determination, the idea that countries should decide their own futures. They agreed that countries should act collectively to deal with world problems and laid plans for the United Nations, which would encourage states to cooperate for security. But they also believed powerful nations should dominate other nations within a "sphere of influence." In these areas—Latin America and the Pacific for the United States; Africa and the Middle East for Britain; and Eastern Europe for the Soviet Union—each power could act independently and limit the self-determination of smaller states. Clearly, spheres of influence and unilateral action conflicted with democracy, self-determination, and collective action.

The conflict was made apparent when the three leaders dealt with the future of Poland, the Soviets' neighbor to the west. Despite talk of self-determination and democracy, Stalin wanted to install a loyal Polish government that would not become a gateway for another invasion. Churchill and Roosevelt favored a self-governing Poland under its prewar leaders. Stalin agreed to elections but believed that Roosevelt had given him a free hand in Poland. This lack of clarity set the stage for future misunderstandings.

From Allies to Enemies

The United States' ambitions for global security appeared threatening to the Soviet Union. To prevent a future Pearl Harbor, the Pentagon erected a circle of air and naval bases around Europe and Asia. Thanks to the Bretton Woods agreement, the United States led a global economy that worked to the disadvantage of controlled, socialist economies. To Roosevelt these steps were not antagonistic, but to Stalin their effect was to block his ambitions with bombers and dollars.

Disagreements over Germany sharpened these suspicions. The United States wanted defeated Germany to rejoin the world economy. The Soviets wanted the country that attacked them twice in 50 years divided and weakened forever. In the end, the Big Three agreed to split it into four zones of occupation. The United States, the USSR, Great Britain, and France would each administer a zone. Although Berlin lay within the Soviet zone, the four powers would each control a section of the capital. The Big Three also agreed that eventually Germany would be reunified but did not indicate when or how.

The uncertainties and contradictions of Yalta led to disagreements even before the war ended. When Vice President Harry Truman succeeded Roosevelt in April 1945, he objected to the Soviets' attempt to take tight control of Poland. Promising to "stand up to the Russians," the new president met in Washington with the Soviet Foreign Minister, V. M. Molotov. Truman "gave it to him straight 'one-two to the jaw.'" "I have never been talked to like that in my life," Molotov answered. "Carry out your agreements," snapped Truman, "and you won't get talked to like that."

When Truman met with Stalin and the British prime minister in Potsdam in July, relations were more cordial. Because Soviet troops occupied most of Eastern Europe and

Map 26–1 Cold War in Europe, 1950 Five years after World War II, the cold war had divided Europe into hostile camps, with NATO members allied to the United States and Warsaw Pact signers tied to the Soviet Union.

much of Germany, Truman could do little about Stalin's actions there. There was no progress on planning the future reunification of Germany. But Truman learned during the meeting of the successful test of the atomic bomb in Nevada. The new weapon would increase U.S. influence everywhere in the world.

National Security

After the war, relations between the United States and the Soviet Union deteriorated. Although Stalin was still committed to overthrowing capitalism, his immediate concerns were in Eastern Europe and along the southern border with Turkey and Iran. The Soviet leader also wanted to keep Germany and Japan from menacing his country again. As an added measure of security, the USSR built a completely self-reliant economy. The United States, by contrast, did not have to worry about securing its borders or supplies. Armed with nuclear weapons, it was stronger than any rival. But American leaders feared that impoverished and vulnerable states would voluntarily align themselves with Soviet power. Every election in Europe, coup in the Middle East, or uprising in Asia had the potential to build a Communist war machine. Recalling the collapse of empires and alliances in the late 1930s, they could imagine the United States suddenly alone and vulnerable.

The Truman Doctrine

To avoid this scenario, American leaders favored the quick reconstruction of nations, including Germany and Japan, within a world economy based on free trade. They also needed military bases to keep future aggressors far from American shores. The opposing interests of the Soviet and U.S. systems soon translated into combative rhetoric. In February 1946 Stalin declared capitalism and Communism incompatible. A month later, Winston Churchill, the former British prime minister, spoke at Fulton, Missouri. Introduced by Truman, Churchill ominously declared that "an Iron Curtain has descended across the Continent" of Europe. Central and Eastern Europe, he warned, "lie in the Soviet sphere." Churchill called for an alliance against this menace.

In February 1946, George Kennan, an American consul in Moscow, sent the State Department a long telegram. The Soviet leadership, he wrote, believed "there can be no permanent peaceful coexistence" between capitalism and socialism. Stalin's regime was sure that capitalist nations, beset by internal problems, would attack socialist nations. Acting on this fear, the USSR would, Kennan insisted, try to destabilize other nations and align them with the Communist bloc. The Communist system had to expand to survive.

More concerned than ever, Truman took aggressive steps to counter apparent Soviet expansion in the Mediterranean. The USSR had been pressing Turkey for control of the Dardanelles, a key waterway. Meanwhile, in Greece, a civil war pitted Communist guerrillas against a monarchist government backed by Britain. By 1947 the British could no longer afford the war and wanted to pass the burden to the Americans. Truman told Congress on March 12, 1947, that the world faced a choice between freedom and totalitarianism. He announced what became known as the "Truman Doctrine." The United States must "support free peoples who are resisting attempted subjugation by armed minorities or by outside pressures." The speech, said *Life* magazine, was "a bolt of lightning." Congress voted overwhelmingly to send aid to Greece and Turkey.

The crisis marked a turning point. In 1947, Walter Lippmann coined the term "cold war" to describe the American-Soviet confrontation. There was no formal declaration of war, but with the Truman Doctrine, confrontation had certainly begun. Dividing the world into good and evil, the United States would support "free peoples" and oppose Communism. Former allies were now bitter antagonists.

Was the confrontation inevitable? There is no way for historians to prove it was, but the United States and the Soviet Union realistically could not have avoided friction. They had a history of hostility, and both possessed great military power. It is also not clear that the form confrontation took—the cold war—was inevitable. It was the product of choices, such as Truman's decision to aid Greece, and perceptions, such as Kennan's judgment about Soviet expansion. Those choices and judgments were not the only ones that could

Iron Curtain In Winston Churchill's image, an "iron curtain" divided Europe, but soon similar barriers would mark the frontiers of containment in Asia and the Middle East.

have been made, and Americans, with good reason, would wonder for decades whether the cold war could have been different.

Containment

As the United States implemented diplomatic, economic, and military strategies for containing Soviet expansion, the scope of the confrontation widened to include the entire world. In 1949 China's civil war ended in a Communist victory. In 1950, five years after the end of World War II, the United States went to war again, this time to save a non-Communist regime in South Korea. The cold war spread and became more dangerous. When the Soviets exploded their atomic bomb, the United States also increased military spending and built a hydrogen bomb. As the arms race spiraled, the cold war seemed out of control.

Committed to opposing Soviet and Communist expansion, the Truman administration had to learn just how to fight the cold war. It would be, in George Kennan's words, "a long-term, patient but firm and vigilant containment of Russian expansive tendencies."

The term *containment* aptly described American policy for the cold war. The United States worked to hold back the Soviets for the next 40 years, but "containment," as Kennan described it in 1947, was still a vague concept. Truman and his successors had to decide where and when to contain the Soviet Union and what combination of diplomatic, economic, and military programs to use.

Containment would not , however, rely primarily on the United Nations. Like the United States, the Soviet Union had a veto over actions by the United Nations Security Council and used it to frustrate American efforts. The United Nations would become another arena for rivalry, not an instrument of American policy.

Truman and his advisors revolutionized American policies on foreign aid, overseas alliances, and national defense. Fearing a ruined and impoverished Europe would embrace Communism, they were determined to help rebuild. In June 1947, Truman's new secretary of state, General George C. Marshall, proposed a "European Recovery Plan" to combat "hunger, poverty, desperation and chaos" and to promote "political and social conditions in which free institutions can exist." The Soviets declined to join and refused to allow Eastern European countries to participate, but 16 nations eagerly supported what became known as the "Marshall Plan."

AMERICAN LANDSCAPE

>> Dhahran

In the years after World War II an American city grew in the Arabian Desert. Starting with just 92 pioneers in 1942, Dhahran grew into a city of over 5,000 Americans, working and living in air-conditioned offices, clubhouses, movie theaters, and homes that looked, according to the *New York Times*, as if they had been lifted from Florida by magic carpet.

The clean, modern facilities inside the American zone contrasted sharply with the ragged tents and desert heat outside. Dhahran was like thousands of compounds built all over the world during the cold war to house the expatriates who staffed the corporate headquarters, military bases, and embassies that looked after America's interests.

America's interest in Arabia was oil. In the 1930s, U.S. companies struck a bargain with Ibn Saud, patriarch of a nomadic clan, securing rights until 2005 to any petroleum found in an area twice the size of Texas. When a huge reserve was found near Dhahran in 1938, pipelines and refineries sprang up overnight, making the oil consortium, known as ARAMCO, into the largest U.S. private overseas investment. And as the company grew, so did the power of its partner, Ibn Saud. By the late 1940s, Americans began to refer to the territory as "Saudi Arabia."

Before World War II, the Saud family was one of several Bedouin clans vying for control over the Arabian Peninsula. With oil wealth, Saud created a centralized monarchical state, using radio to spread Wahabism, a puritanical faith that rejected liberal, pluralist Islamic practices in favor of Koranic literalism and a strict, punitive code of Sharia justice. Saud permitted no labor unions, prohibited music and the education of women, and forced nomadic Arabs into settlements.

Oil money financed these policies, but ARAMCO officials refrained from criticism. The king's relationship with the company was, the crown prince explained, "founded on mutual profit, with both parties respecting the rights of the other."

In the cold war, security for the company and the Saudi regime became vital U.S. interests. The U.S. Pacific Fleet consumed nearly three-quarters of ARAMCO's oil, and the remainder fueled European construction under the Marshall Plan. If rebels or the Soviets cut off Saudi oil, Defense Secretary James Forrestal warned, Americans would be reduced to driving four-cylinder cars. With its tennis courts and ranch homes, Dhahran looked like a suburb of Houston or Miami. It had its own PTA and scout troop, a country club, libraries, and television station. It resembled American cities in another way, too. It was racially segregated. Outside the American colony, ARAMCO built an "intermediate camp" for 2,000 Italian and Palestinian skilled workers. Beyond lay the "coolie camp," a squalid settlement of huts housing the 14,000 Arabs who drilled the oil, laid the pipe, and paved the roads.

Each settlement had its own electrical and water systems, schools, and clinics, except for the Arab camp, which had none of those things. The American

continued

AMERICAN LANDSCAPE *continued*

colony had the country's only swimming pools and hospitals—no Arabs allowed. Americans could live, work, and shop entirely in air-cooled surroundings, but Arabs dug ditches and hauled loads in temperatures averaging 120 degrees in the shade for a starting wage of 90¢ a day. Friendships between Arabs and Americans were few.

Arabs resented being third-class citizens in their own country, but complaints were not tolerated in Saud's kingdom. Americans drank liquor and appeared in public unveiled, flouting Sharia laws that Saud's religious police sternly enforced in the Arab community. Bedouin shepherds complained that pipelines fenced them in. Literate Arabs resented United States support for Israel. By the early 1950s, occasional flashes of violence unsettled the community. In 1953, Dhahran erupted in a general strike as 13,000 Arabs walked off the job to protest the arrest of workers attempting to organize a union. Americans met the challenge and kept the oil flowing. Together with Saud's U.S.-trained police they broke the strike.

ARAMCO and the king responded to the strike with paternalism and force. The company raised wages to over a dollar a day and built a hospital and concrete dormitories for Arab workers. Saud built a modern military equipped with U.S. jets and tanks. More Saudis took white-collar positions in the company, but the number of Americans living in the country grew. Executives hoped the American example would make Saudi society more tolerant, progressive, and democratic, but the company adapted readily to the kingdom's autocratic customs. ARAMCO refused to hire Jews for fear of offending their hosts. It helped the king seize lands from rival tribes and from neighboring Yemen.

An opportunistic partnership between an American industry and an antidemocratic monarchy had become a permanent alliance. The cold war created many such relationships, and U.S. officials worried that so many of America's allies were dictators and kings. But the Soviet threat, they believed, did not allow the United States to choose its friends. That time would come when the danger had passed.

"The Marshall Plan saved Europe," Truman boasted. From 1948 to 1952, $13 billion went to boost agricultural and industrial output, increase exports, and promote economic cooperation. Whole cities were rebuilt. By 1950, participating countries had already exceeded prewar production. Prosperity helped stabilize Western European governments, bind them to the United States, and weaken Communist parties. Containment required more than aid. It also demanded the kind of military alliances that the United States had historically avoided as dangerous entanglements. But challenged by the cold war, leaders now saw alliances as a way of preventing, rather than provoking, armed conflict. In 1949, the United States joined 10 Western European nations and Canada to form the North Atlantic Treaty Organization (NATO). Under NATO, an attack on any member nation would be treated as an attack on all. To strengthen the American commitment to Western Europe, Congress appropriated $1.3 billion in military aid for NATO countries, and

Truman ordered American troops to the Continent. General Dwight D. Eisenhower, the commander of the Allied invasion of France in World War II, became the supreme commander of NATO forces.

Containment also required vigilance. In 1947 Congress passed the National Security Act, creating a Central Intelligence Agency (CIA) to gather and assess information for the president and a National Security Council (NSC) to advise him on military and political threats. The act placed the army, navy, and air force under a single command, the Joint Chiefs of Staff, and a single cabinet secretary, the secretary of defense. The term "national security" provided a blanket justification for responses to all kinds of threats, actions such as election rigging, proxy wars, and other "covert operations." Congress passed a new Selective Service Act creating a draft for men between 19 and 25.

Taking Risks

Containment entailed risks. There was always the chance that simmering conflict could boil over into world war. One particularly dangerous hot spot was Berlin. In 1948, the Americans, British, and French began to unify their zones of occupation in Germany into a single unit under a new currency, the deutschmark. Faced with an anti-Communist western Germany, Stalin sealed off his own German zone of occupation. On June 24, the Soviets cut road and rail transport into Berlin, the jointly occupied German capital. "We stay in Berlin, period," Truman snapped, calling what he felt was Stalin's bluff. But 2.5 million Berliners were at risk of running out of food and coal. Sending an armed supply convoy through the Soviet blockade could provoke a shooting war.

Instead, Berlin was supplied by air power. American transport planes carried 2,500 tons of food and fuel a day. Along with this massive airlift, the Truman administration sent to Britain two squadrons of B-29 bombers, the kind that dropped the atomic bombs on Japan. In May 1949 the Soviets ended the blockade. Tested, the strategy of containment had worked: Soviet expansion had seemingly been deterred. But the risks were clear.

Those risks became even clearer later that year. In early September, American planes found radioactivity in the air over the Pacific, evidence that the Soviet Union had exploded an atomic bomb. The U.S. nuclear weapon monopoly was over. Suddenly, confrontation with the Soviets had potentially lethal consequences. It was now, a Republican senator somberly observed, "a different world."

Global Revolutions

The cold war soon spread from Europe to shape the politics of the world. Civil and post-colonial strife in Asia, Africa, the Middle East, and Latin America came to be seen as part of the conflict between the nuclear superpowers.

In China, the nationalist government of Jiang Jieshi had waged a civil war against Mao Zedong's Communist rebels since the 1920s. Both sides joined forces to fight the Japanese in World War II, but whereas combat strengthened the Communists, it weakened Jiang's corrupt and unpopular regime. When Japan surrendered, U.S. forces helped Jiang regain control of Chinese cities. Truman urged a permanent settlement, but the civil war resumed. Congressional Republicans saw China as a key cold war battleground, but Truman doubted the United States could influence the outcome. He sent the nationalists $2 billion in aid but refused to send troops. In December 1949 the defeated nationalists

AMERICA AND THE WORLD

>> Underdevelopment

As the cold war unfolded, a second global drama, in some ways more consequential, played out in Asia, the Middle East, and Africa. Subjugated peoples struggled for and claimed independence, and European colonial systems crumbled. By the end of the 1940s, for the first time in history, a majority of the world's people lived in nations instead of empires.

Decolonization ripped apart systems of authority and trade. After years of conflict, new nations often gained little but freedom. They inherited economies without industry or markets, governments with no schools, roads, or tax collectors, and restless citizens living in deep poverty. The Truman administration recognized the need to help manage this movement toward nationalism.

In the fourth point of his 1949 inaugural address, Truman announced a "bold new program for making the benefits of our scientific advances and industrial progress available for the improvement and growth of underdeveloped areas." The "Point Four" program was the United States' first global foreign aid program, but Truman's real innovation was in redefining terms. By calling the new nations "underdeveloped," he asserted that nations were entitled to growth, that all nations would one day be fully developed.

National leaders eagerly accepted the new terms and sent delegations to ask for technical assistance. "America's attitude is our salvation," an Afghan prince declared. "We are free of the threat of great powers using our mountain passes as pathways to empire. Now we can concentrate our talents and resources on bettering the living conditions of our people."

While nationalists struggled for freedom from outside interference, development obliged every responsible government to open the door to foreign experts. Countries that had earlier expelled foreign advisers welcomed economists from the World Bank and the Ford Foundation. UN commissions on food, health, and education measured each nation's progress toward the universal benchmarks of a fully modern state. Development directed nationalist energies into economic channels and away from political actions that might endanger U.S. interests. Nationalist leaders remarked on how material changes altered the spiritual and cultural outlook of people. Hydroelectric dams were the temples of modern India, declared Prime Minister Jawaharlal Nehru at the dedication of an enormous water project modeled on the TVA. "When we undertake a big work, our minds open out a little." Some contended that development might replace the cold war with a peaceful competition to modernize the world under rival economic theories.

Others argued that poverty went beyond aid, technical knowledge, or even states of mind. A Brazilian delegate at the first Point Four conference explained that poverty was caused by the terms of trade: Latin American agricultural exports declined in value, while manufactured imports from the United States increased in price.

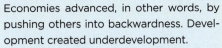

Economies advanced, in other words, by pushing others into backwardness. Development created underdevelopment.

But the success of the Marshall Plan and Japan's reconstruction gave Americans tremendous confidence in their ability to make over whole societies. In the 1950s, social scientists devised theories of "nation building." For their own convenience, specialists divided the world into three parts, each with its set of problems: a democratic, developed "first world," a Communist "second world," and the underdeveloped "third world," with most of the nations and two-thirds of the people on earth.

If the United States could ease the third world's ascent, it could strengthen its own security. Military strategies against guerilla insurgencies increasingly employed development techniques to stabilize governments and win (in Mao Zedong's phrase) the "hearts and minds" of the people.

Aid officials often said that development and democracy went together. As peasants became consumers and workers, they would demand more choice in their lives and their leaders. By giving of its resources and know-how, America could "export democracy." But development programs seldom asked ordinary people what kind of progress they wanted. Aid reinforced a centralized state, channeling funds to unelected commissions and experts who made decisions that affected millions of people.

By the 1960s, "nation building" had become central to U.S. containment strategy. The long U.S. struggle in Vietnam, which began with military aid in 1950 and ended with defeat in 1975, would test the theory that stimulating development would increase democracy and security. That idea, Henry Kissinger later concluded, was "clearly wrong."

But by then, a system of national and international institutions to guide the development of nations was already in place. Around the world national success was judged by the statistical yardstick of economic growth. Although few fully accepted Truman's hunch that prosperity would guarantee peace, even fewer were ready to reject it entirely. Underdevelopment had taken a permanent place on the agenda of global problems.

fled the Chinese mainland for the island of Taiwan, and Republicans angrily blamed the administration for the "loss" of China.

With most of Asia now in Communist hands, American strategists began to rethink containment. Before 1949, the danger zones were in the world's industrial heartlands, Europe and Japan. Now it seemed brushfire wars could spread nearly anywhere. Peasants had manned Mao's armies, and the rural "third world" seemed especially vulnerable. To contain Latin America, Truman organized the Rio Pact, through which the United States would provide training, weapons, and advisors for Latin American militaries. The Organization of American States (OAS), created in 1948, promoted stability and economic development from its headquarters in Washington.

Territories formerly of little strategic interest, such as Southeast Asia and Africa, became vital to security. Although the Truman administration favored self-determination, it tolerated Latin American dictatorships, European colonial dominion, and South Africa's white supremacist rule because these undemocratic regimes opposed Communism.

Korea

Working to hold off Communism at so many points, it was probably not surprising that the United States was eventually drawn into war. Nevertheless, the news that U.S. troops were fighting in Korea startled Americans in 1950, because the conflict was so far from areas considered strategically important. But the Korean War was firmly rooted in the logic of the cold war.

Korea, a peninsula bordering China and the Soviet Union, had been liberated from the Japanese in 1945. American and Soviet troops jointly occupied the territory, splitting it into two zones at the 38th parallel. The United States opposed the popular nationalist Kim Il Sung, a Communist, and acted unilaterally to install a regime in the South under Syngman Rhee, an anti-Communist. By 1948, Korea had two governments, each claiming jurisdiction over the whole. In June 1950, after incidents along the 38th parallel, Kim's army, led by Soviet-made tanks, invaded the South.

Truman responded boldly. By itself, South Korea was not important, but the administration believed the Soviet Union was behind the North Korean attack. After the "loss" of China, Truman could not afford another Communist victory in Asia. He secured United Nations approval for international action. Troops from 15 countries eventually fought in the UN force, but nine-tenths came from the United States. Was America at war, then? Claiming the conflict was only a "police action," Truman never asked Congress for a declaration of war. For the first time, but not the last, a president sent troops to battle in the cold war without regard for the Constitution.

At first, the fighting did not go well. Ill-prepared U.S. troops fell back toward the coast. But in the summer, General Douglas MacArthur used the U.S. Navy's control of the seas to put troops ashore at Inchon, deep behind enemy lines. North Korea's main armies were cut off and destroyed. Within weeks, the South had been reclaimed.

Then Truman and his advisers made a fateful decision. Rather than just contain Communism, they wanted to roll it back. Truman gave the order to invade North Korea and reunify the peninsula. MacArthur, who privately wanted war with the Chinese Communists, pushed ever closer to China. Fearing an invasion, the Chinese issued warnings, sent their forces into North Korea, and, on November 25, unleashed a massive attack on UN troops. MacArthur's shattered army pulled back to defend South Korea.

The Korean "police action" became a stalemate. A frustrated MacArthur wanted to fight aggressively, but the chastened Truman administration gave up reunification and accepted the 38th-parallel division. That was too much for MacArthur, who broke the military's unwritten rule against public criticism of civilian leaders. "There is no substitute for victory," MacArthur lectured in 1951. Fed up, Truman fired his popular general in April as the war dragged on.

The Korean stalemate underscored hard truths of the cold war. Containment could mean sacrificing American lives in minor, nondecisive wars. As nuclear war was not an option, U.S. troops had to be prepared, as the saying went, to "die for a tie"—to fight for something less than victory. In this kind of conflict, leaders had to convince allies, undecided nations, and citizens at home that, despite setbacks, the West would eventually win. Psychology was more important than territory.

Map 26–2   **The Korean War, 1950–1953** The shifting lines of advance mark the back-and-forth struggle that would end with stalemate and the permanent division of Korea.

NSC-68

Before Korea, the Truman administration tried to balance its international and domestic agendas. But by the 1950s, containment became the first priority. The administration escalated efforts against revolutionary movements even in peripheral areas, such as Southeast Asia. Colonial struggles, such as the Vietnamese rebellion against their French overlords, were seen as critical challenges.

In April 1950, the National Security Council approved a secret guideline known as NSC-68. Citing a growing list of threats and the "possibility of annihilation," it called for the United States to triple defense spending, impose order in postcolonial areas, and seek more powerful weapons. Truman worried about the cost, but the Korean War convinced him. By 1952, defense expenditures had nearly quadrupled, to $44 billion. Meanwhile, the armed forces grew—to 3.6 million by 1952—along with the list of combat theaters, now including Vietnam. Truman ordered the building of "the so-called hydrogen or su-perbomb." Successfully tested in November 1952, the thermonuclear bomb was far more powerful than the atomic bomb, but it did not stop the arms race. Less than a year later, the USSR had its own "H-bomb."

Although it remained top secret until the 1970s, NSC-68 profoundly changed the U.S. economy and political system. The military buildup was paid for with deficit financ-ing, and federal borrowing generated jobs and growth, particularly in the South and West. To fight the cold war, Americans accepted things they had long feared: secrecy, debt, alli-ances, a massive standing army, and centralized direction of the economy. Each of these magnified the role of the federal government.

The Reconversion of American Society

While the cold war intensified, domestic policy focused on restoring the economy and society to a peacetime footing. "Reconversion" was welcomed by a nation tired of war, but it was also a cause for worry. Americans feared a return to the desperate conditions of the 1930s. Labor, women, and African Americans, especially, wanted to hold on to and extend wartime gains.

The Postwar Economy

As World War II ended, the economy threatened to slide back into depression. Millions of unemployed servicemen came home at a time when government was cutting spending. The disaster never happened. Unemployment did rise in 1946 but never approached the double-digit rates of the 1930s. Despite brief downturns, the economy was vibrant. Its re-silience reflected several factors, including veterans' choices, the federal role, the transfor-mation of industry, and U.S. economic dominance. Returning veterans did not strain the economy, partly because half of them went to school rather than work. Under the GI Bill of 1944 the federal government paid veterans for up to three years of education. Federal spending also helped prevent a return to the economic troubles of the 1930s. With World War II over, federal expenditures decreased dramatically, but spending was still far greater than it was during the 1930s. The GI Bill showed how spending stimulated the economy. Pumping nearly $14.5 billion into education, the bill encouraged colleges and universities to expand. As veterans swelled enrollments, institutions hired new faculty, and entire new systems, such as the State University of New York, were created.

Reconversion accelerated the economic change started by World War II. In the late 1940s, industrial production was still concentrated in the Northeast and Midwest, but new military spending was helping to shift factories and population South and West. In the 1940s, the population of the western states grew by 50 percent, compared with 10 percent in the East. The nature of the economy was changing, too. Oil and natural gas replaced coal as the chief source of power. New industries, such as plastics, electronics, and aviation, were growing rapidly.

Finally, the dominance of the United States in the world economy helped reconversion. At the end of World War II, the U.S. economy was roughly the size of the European and Soviet economies combined. As late as 1950, America, with only 6 percent of the world's population, accounted for 40 percent of the value of all the goods and services produced in the world. Demand for American exports created jobs but also stoked inflation. Production caught up, and in the late 1940s, the economy began a prolonged peacetime boom.

The Challenge of Organized Labor

Organized labor had never been more powerful than at the end of World War II. One-third of nonagricultural civilian workers belonged to unions. The Democratic Party paid attention to influential unions, such as the Congress of Industrial Organizations (CIO), and after pledging not to strike during World War II, organized labor was eager to test its clout. Workers wanted wage increases to cope with inflation and as a reward for their contribution to wartime profits. In Europe and Japan, unions were gaining control over the way corporations did business, and some American unions also wanted a role in management. Not surprisingly, corporations were reluctant to give up any of their power or profits. Along with conservatives in Congress, they branded the unions as agents of Communism.

The result was a huge wave of strikes as soon as the war ended in August 1945. In 1946, 2 million machinists, longshoremen, and other workers around the country called a record 4,985 strikes. "[L]abor has gone crazy," an anxious Truman told his mother.

Significant work stoppages hit automobile factories, coal mines, and railroad yards. Late in 1945, the United Auto Workers (UAW) struck General Motors (GM) for a 30 percent raise in hourly wages, access to the company's books, and more say in company decisions. GM rejected union interference in management decisions. When the strike finally ended after 113 days, the UAW won only some of its wage demands. It marked a turning point for labor. Unions never again demanded to participate in management, but instead focused on pay and benefits.

The coal and railroad strikes were even more contentious. Members of the United Mine Workers (UMW) and the railway unions refused to accept federal arbitration. As the coal supply dwindled, power systems suffered "brownouts," and railroad passengers were stranded. The situation tested the strong relationship, forged in the New Deal, between the Democratic Party and organized labor. Truman ordered federal takeovers of the mines and the railroads. "Let Truman dig coal with his bayonets," snarled John L. Lewis, leader of the UMW. But the strikes ended in May. Many Americans applauded the president's action and believed that Lewis and other union leaders had become too powerful and demanding.

Counting on this unhappiness with unions, probusiness Republicans in Congress soon moved to limit the power of organized labor. In 1947, a coalition of Republicans and conservative, mostly southern Democrats passed the Taft-Hartley Act, a sweeping modification of federal labor law. The bill made it easier for employers to hire nonunion workers and to oppose the formation of unions. It also limited unions' right to organize and engage in political activity. Most humiliating , it compelled union leaders to swear that they did not belong to the Communist Party.

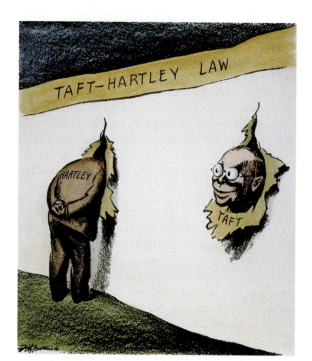

Containment on the Home Front Although Congress passed the Taft-Hartley Act in 1947 to forestall an impending coal strike, United Mineworkers leader John L. Lewis ignored the act and struck anyway.

Despite these setbacks, workers and unions prospered. Landmark contract negotiations between the UAW and GM offered a model of labor relations. In 1948 the UAW won guaranteed cost-of-living adjustments, known as COLAs, and an annual wage increase tied to rises in worker productivity. In the so-called Treaty of Detroit, signed in 1950, the UAW won other increases and a pension plan in a long five-year contract. In return for pensions and protection against inflation, autoworkers gave management stable, predictable labor relations over the long term.

The Treaty of Detroit ended a difficult period for organized labor. Thanks to lucrative contracts, many workers were more secure than ever before, but reconversion also limited the power of organized labor and the support of the Democratic Party. Aggressive strikes produced mixed results, public hostility, and government interference. With the end of the strike wave, unions effectively abandoned their demand to participate in management.

Opportunities for Women

Reconversion also posed special challenges to the status of American women. During World War II, the shortage of male labor had expanded women's opportunities for employment. Working women prized the income and the sense of satisfaction they gained from performing jobs traditionally monopolized by men. But employers and government officials encouraged the belief that women should surrender jobs to returning veterans. The number of women in the labor force dropped 13 percent from 1945 to 1946, but reconversion did not send female workers home for good. Three-quarters of the women who wanted to stay at work after the war managed to find jobs.

Most women, of course, needed to earn a living for themselves or their families. By 1953 the number of women in the workforce matched the level of 1945. The number in nontraditional jobs increased, too. More women than ever before were skilled craftspersons, forepersons, physicians, and surgeons.

The number of married women in the postwar labor force was especially notable, as economic necessity overcame cultural prejudice against working mothers and married women. By 1947 there were more married women than single women in the wage labor force.

The armed forces, like civilian employers, initially cut back the number of women in the ranks when the war ended, but Congress granted women permanent status in the armed forces and merged the separate women's military organizations, such as the Women's Army Corps, into the regular armed services.

Despite these gains, women still faced discrimination. The majority had to settle for traditionally female, low-paying jobs in offices, stores, and factories. Women's hourly pay rose only half as much as men's pay in the first years after the war. In the military, women were largely confined to noncombatant roles such as nursing. There were no women generals.

In the larger society there was little interest in women's rights. After a meeting with female activists, Truman dismissed a constitutional amendment guaranteeing equal rights for women as a "lot of hooey."

Despite the lack of support for women's rights, women's opportunities were gradually expanding in the postwar years; the combination of women's desires and the economy's needs was slowly promoting the feminization of the labor force.

Civil Rights for African Americans

Like women, African Americans had made significant gains during World War II. They filled new roles in the military and higher-paying jobs in the civilian economy and pushed their demand for civil rights. Like women, African Americans sought to preserve and extend these rights and opportunities in the face of substantial resistance.

Several factors, including economic change, legal rulings, and wartime experiences, stimulated the postwar drive for equal rights and opportunities. By the end of the war, the transformation of the southern economy was undermining the system that segregated African Americans and denied them the right to vote. As mechanization reduced the need for field hands, African Americans left for the region's growing cities and for the North and West. One of the basic rationales for segregation—the need for an inexpensive, submissive labor force in the fields—was disappearing. The developing southern economy also attracted whites from other regions who were less committed to segregation and disfranchisement. Meanwhile, by migrating to northern and western cities, African Americans increased their votes and political influence.

In fighting the Nazis during the war and the Communists afterward, the United States dedicated itself to universal freedoms. The United Nations Declaration on Human Rights committed member states to guarantee rights to education, free movement, assembly, and personal safety. African Americans appealed to the UN, the courts, and the press to have the United States recognize these commitments.

During the 1940s, a series of U.S. Supreme Court decisions struck at racial discrimination and encouraged African Americans to challenge inequality. In *Smith v. Allwright* in 1944, the court had banned whites-only primary elections. In *Morgan v. Virginia* in 1946, the court ruled that interstate bus companies could not segregate passengers. In *Shelley v. Kraemer* in 1948, the court banned restrictive covenants, the private agreements between property owners not to sell houses to African Americans and other minorities. These and other court decisions weakened discriminatory practices and suggested that African Americans might have a judicial ally in the struggle for justice.

Slain American Civil Rights Activist Medgar Evers (1925–1963) Medgar Evers fought for democracy in France and Germany and then returned to fight for it again in Mississippi.

African Americans' war experiences also encouraged them to demand more and to expect justice from the country they fought for. "Our people are not coming back with the idea of just taking up where they left off," an African American private wrote. "We are going to have the things that are rightfully due us or else."

That kind of determination spurred civil rights activism after the war. In the South, African Americans increasingly demanded the right to vote after *Smith v. Allwright*. The National Association for the Advancement of Colored People (NAACP) set up citizenship schools in the South to show African American voters how to register. The campaign was driven, too, by individual actions. In July 1946 Medgar Evers, a combat veteran who had just reached his 21st birthday, decided to try to vote in the Democratic Party's primary election in Decatur, Mississippi.

Such activism was resisted by whites deeply committed to disfranchisement and segregation. A white mob kept Evers from voting in 1946. In Georgia, whites killed an African American voter. More often, they manipulated registration laws to disqualify voters. A voter seeking to register might have to answer such questions as "How many bubbles are there in a bar of soap?" Still, African American voter registration in the South, only 2 percent in 1940, rose to 12 percent by 1947. The result was the election of a few African American officials and improved service from local government.

Alongside the campaign for voting rights, civil rights activists fought segregation across the country. The interracial Congress of Racial Equality (CORE) took the lead in protesting public discrimination. To test the Supreme Court's decision in *Morgan*, CORE sent an integrated team on a bus trip through the upper South, where they met with violence and arrests. Activists hardly dented segregation in the South in the 1940s but had more success promoting antidiscrimination laws in the North. By 1953, fair-employment laws had been adopted in 30 cities and 12 states.

Activists also pressured Truman to support civil rights. In the spring and summer of 1946, picketers marched outside the White House with signs that read, "SPEAK, SPEAK, MR. PRESIDENT." Racial discrimination was an embarrassment for a nation claiming to represent freedom and democracy in the world, but support for civil rights was a risk for a politician dependent on white support. Nevertheless, Truman took significant steps.

In the fall of 1946, Truman supported a presidential committee report, *To Secure These Rights*, that called for strong federal action against lynching, vote suppression, job discrimination, and civil rights violations, including segregation in the armed forces. Furious white southern politicians and newspapers said Truman was "stabbing the South in the back."

African Americans, meanwhile, kept the heat on Truman. To protest discrimination in the military, A. Philip Randolph, the head of the Brotherhood of Sleeping Car Porters, proposed a boycott of the draft. In July 1948 Truman responded with Executive Order 9981, creating a committee to phase out discrimination in the military. He also established the Fair Employment Board, which moved more slowly against discrimination in federal hiring.

During the Truman years, the most publicized blow to racial inequality came not from the White House but the baseball diamond. When the Brooklyn Dodgers called up infielder Jackie Robinson from the minor leagues in 1947, he became the first African American to play in the major leagues since the late nineteenth century. A strong, self-disciplined former soldier, Robinson took taunts and beanballs on the field and death threats in the mail. Fast, powerful, and exciting, he finished the season as the National League's Rookie of the Year. Robinson's success paved the way for increasing numbers of African American players in the majors over the next several years.

Robinson's success also spelled the end of the Negro Leagues, created when African Americans were banned from the major leagues. Integration would sometimes undermine distinctly African American institutions. Nonetheless, the achievements of Robinson, Larry Doby, and other pioneering African American players sent a powerful message for civil rights and underscored the limits of reconversion. On the whole, African Americans preserved and sometimes expanded their wartime gains while still encountering injustice and inequality. In one respect, African Americans, women, and organized labor shared a common experience in the first years after World War II. For each of these groups, struggling for rights and opportunities, reconversion turned out to be better than feared and worse than hoped. They all confronted the limits of their power to change the society around them.

The Frustrations of Liberalism

During the Great Depression, New Deal liberalism of had reshaped American democracy, thrusting the federal government more deeply than ever into economic and social life. But the liberal Democratic agenda of federal activism, which stalled during World War II, met more frustration afterward. Liberals and the Democratic Party strained to provide answers for a nation no longer facing an economic or military emergency. Harry Truman struggled to prove that he was a worthy successor to Franklin Roosevelt.

The Democrats' Troubles

Many Americans were skeptical about their accidental president. Liberals who wondered whether Truman shared their ideals were incensed when he fired FDR's trusted aide Henry Wallace after Wallace criticized Truman's policy toward the USSR. Conservatives and moderates also had their doubts. During the Depression, Americans had been willing to endorse government interventions in the economy, but they felt less need for government and more need for individual freedom in a prosperous peacetime.

The president was more liberal than the liberals expected. Shortly after he took office in 1945, he presented a legislative program that included proposals on education, employment, insurance, social security, and civil rights. Yet a full-employment bill, giving the federal government responsibility for securing jobs and prosperity, met overwhelming conservative and moderate opposition. Watered down by Congress, the resulting Employment Act of 1946 created a presidential Council of Economic Advisors but did nothing to increase the economic role of the federal government.

Truman and the liberals suffered an even sharper defeat over the president's sweeping proposal for a national health insurance system that would guarantee medical care to all Americans. Under the plan, the federal government would manage the insurance system and set doctors' and hospitals' fees. Conservatives and the medical profession promptly condemned the proposal. The bill failed, and so did most of Truman's domestic proposals.

Nevertheless, the federal role in national life continued to grow. Medical care offered a notable example. The Veterans Administration established a vast network of federal hospitals to care for returning soldiers. In 1946, the Hill-Burton Act appropriated federal money for new hospitals. That same year, Congress created a research lab in Atlanta, later called the Centers for Disease Control, to monitor infectious diseases. Congress also established the National Institute of Mental Health in 1949.

As Truman struggled with domestic and foreign policy, he became increasingly unpopular. "To err is Truman," went the joke. "Had Enough?" asked Republicans. Many had. In the 1946 congressional elections, the voters gave the Republicans a majority in the House of Representatives and the Senate for the first time in 16 years.

Truman's Comeback

The 1946 elections seemed to presage a defeat for Truman in two years, but the president managed a stunning comeback. It began with the Republican majority that took control in Congress in 1947. Led by Senator Robert Taft of Ohio, they hoped to replace New Deal liberalism with a different understanding of American democracy. Refuting "the corrupting idea" that prosperity, equality, or opportunity can be legislated, Taft wanted "free Americans freely working out their destiny." The Taft-Hartley Act was a blow to liberals and the administration, but Republicans found themselves trapped by Americans' ambivalence about liberalism. Few were enthusiastic about such innovations as national health insurance, but there was little sentiment to roll back the New Deal and its benefits. Besides Taft-Hartley, the Eightieth Congress did not accomplish much, and soon Truman was campaigning against a "do-nothing Congress."

Still, things looked bad for Truman. By March 1948 his approval rating was 35 percent. His party was also splitting apart. On the left, his former secretary of commerce Henry Wallace was running for president as a "Progressive." On the right, Democratic governor Strom Thurmond of South Carolina was running as a "Dixiecrat," appealing to white supporters of segregation. Truman seemed certain to lose in November. Or so his Republican opponent, Governor Thomas E. Dewey of New York, thought. Dewey believed an uncontroversial campaign would do the trick, but Truman pulled the New Deal majority back together. The president reached out to African Americans, labor, farmers, senior citizens, and other beneficiaries of New Deal liberalism. "Give 'em hell, Harry," the crowds shouted, and he did, driving home his vision. "The Democratic Party puts human rights and human

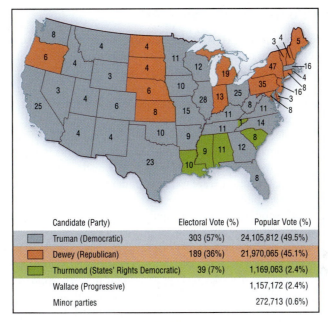

Candidate (Party)	Electoral Vote (%)	Popular Vote (%)
Truman (Democratic)	303 (57%)	24,105,812 (49.5%)
Dewey (Republican)	189 (36%)	21,970,065 (45.1%)
Thurmond (States' Rights Democratic)	39 (7%)	1,169,063 (2.4%)
Wallace (Progressive)		1,157,172 (2.4%)
Minor parties		272,713 (0.6%)

Map 26–3   The 1948 Presidential Election Segregationist and progressive candidates were expected to undermine the Democratic majority, but the Roosevelt coalition returned Truman to the White House for a second term.

welfare first," he declared. "These Republican gluttons of privilege . . . want a return of the Wall Street economic dictatorship."

On election day, Wallace and Thurmond received only a million votes each. Dewey attracted fewer votes than he had four years before. Leading Roosevelt's coalition, Truman won the presidency with only 49.5 percent of the vote (see Map 26–3). The Democrats recaptured the House and the Senate, but the triumph did not last long. Like Taft two years before, Truman soon discovered that a victory did not mean a mandate. In his State of the Union address in January 1949, Truman declared that "every individual has a right to expect from our Government a fair deal." But his "Fair Deal" legislation stalled in Congress. Despite Truman's comeback, the liberal vision could not dominate the politics of cold war America.

Fighting the Cold War at Home

Beyond the battles over domestic policy, the cold war increasingly intruded into every aspect of life. Billions of dollars in defense expenditures stimulated economic growth, but fear, doubt, and insecurity pervaded the late 1940s. Americans added a new fear of nuclear weapons to their old fear of immigrants, and society succumbed to a largely irrational dread of hidden traitors in Hollywood, Washington, the universities, and the public library. To fight the cold war at home, anti-Communist crusaders such as Joe McCarthy hunted for disloyal Americans. By the 1950s, McCarthyism was capable of destroying the lives of thousands of Americans, including Esther and Stephen Brunauer.

Doubts and Fears in the Atomic Age

Despite triumph in World War II, American culture was dark and pessimistic in the late 1940s. The rise of fascism, the Holocaust, and the bombings of Hiroshima and Nagasaki raised questions about the direction of progress and the goodness of humankind. The cold war did nothing to calm those concerns. Even the welcome prosperity of the reconversion period did not soothe this sense of doubt. People felt small and powerless in an age of big corporations, big unions, big government, and superbombs.

Americans revealed their unease in a variety of ways. Not long after the announcement of the Truman Doctrine in 1947, people began seeing lights in the sky, and. "flying saucers" were reported over 35 states and Canada. In a nuclear-armed world, columnist Joseph Alsop observed, the saucer scare was a reminder that "man-made horrors are quite real, quite imminent possibilities."

Meanwhile, Hollywood films explored popular fears. In 1946, *The Best Years of Our Lives* traced the difficult, sometimes humiliating readjustment of three returning veterans. The same year, *It's a Wonderful Life* told the story of a small-town banker forced to accept the disappointment of his unfulfilled dreams. Both films expressed reservations about the morality of capitalism and the chances of achieving happiness in the modern world. A new genre, film noir, offered an even darker view of individuals trapped in a confusing, immoral world.

As the greatest source of fear, nuclear weapons dominated the popular imagination. Many Americans dealt with their anxiety about the Atomic Age in a variety of ways, including dark attempts at humor. Americans drank "atomic cocktails" and danced the "Atomic Polka." American women wore the new "bikini," the explosively scanty bathing suit named for the Pacific atoll where the United States tested the H-bomb. The Soviets' development of the atomic bomb and the hydrogen bomb was impossible to laugh away.

Americans' fear was also reflected in the hardening of attitudes toward foreigners. In 1945, the nation welcomed the foreign wives of American servicemen by passing the War Brides Act, but as the cold war intensified, other potential migrants met a hostile reception. The Immigration and Nationality Act of 1952 tightly restricted immigration, particularly from Asia. It kept out Communists and homosexuals and allowed the deportation of American citizens suspected of disloyalty.

The Anti-Communist Crusade

Americans may have feared disloyalty most of all. Many believed the real Communist threat came from within. Historians debate the origins of this second "Red Scare." Some trace the anti-Communist crusade to a conservative reaction against the rise of labor, African Americans, women, and other disempowered groups. Others blame the Truman administration for using fear to justify unprecedented military activity and spending. Although anti-Communism had deep roots in American culture, politicians in both parties gave domestic anti-Communism its particularly dangerous form.

The crusaders had to search hard for local Communists. The Communist Party of the United States of America (CPUSA), a legal political party, was tiny and losing followers. Infiltrated by FBI and police informants, it never received more than 0.3 percent of the popular vote. Just to be sure, the Truman administration charged 12 party leaders with violating the Smith Act, which criminalized membership in "a group advocating . . . the overthrow of the government by force." In 1949, 11 were convicted and sent to jail.

George Tooker, *The Subway* (1950) Modernist painter George Tooker captured the claustrophobic anxiety of the McCarthy era in paintings like *The Subway* and *Government Bureau* (1956). In popular fiction and noir films, social conformity only thinly concealed a mounting hysteria.

Open Communists posed less of a threat than secret ones, and in fact, self-professed former Communists and spies were considered the most reliable informants on America's presumed hidden network of traitors. The hunt for these "subversives" was led by the House of Representatives' Un-American Activities Committee (HUAC). In 1947 HUAC held hearings on supposed Communist plots in Hollywood. The film industry cooperated, but eight screenwriters, a producer, and a director cited their First Amendment rights and declined to testify. The "Hollywood Ten" were convicted of contempt of Congress and sent to jail for up to a year. Film studios got the message and "blacklisted"—refused to hire—writers, directors, and actors even remotely suspected of Communist ties. Avoiding controversial subjects, studios put out overwrought anti-Communist movies such as *The Red Menace* and *I Was a Communist for the FBI*.

Afraid of looking "soft" on Communism, the Truman administration declared there was a real problem with domestic Communism. "Communists," said Truman's attorney general, Tom Clark, "are everywhere . . . and each carries with him the germs of death for society."

In 1947, the president created an "employee loyalty" program. Any civil servant could lose his or her job by belonging to any of the "totalitarian, Fascist, Communist or subversive" groups listed by the attorney general. The program had little regard for due process. People accused of disloyalty could not challenge evidence or confront their accusers and were presumed guilty until they proved their innocence. Although only about 300 employees were discharged, the loyalty program helped create the impression of a serious problem in Washington.

The Hunt for Spies

There was, in fact, spying going on inside the government. The Soviet Union, like the United States, carried out espionage abroad. The Canadian government found evidence of a spy ring that had passed American atomic secrets to the Soviets during World War II. Through interceptions of Soviet communications, the CIA knew about the spy ring but chose not to share this information with Congress, prosecutors, or even the president.

Thanks to the Canadian evidence, the FBI began to suspect that Alger Hiss, an aide to the secretary of state, was a Soviet agent. Hiss was quietly eased out of his job. Then, in 1948, HUAC took testimony from Whittaker Chambers, a *Time* magazine editor who claimed to have been a Soviet agent in the 1930s. Chambers accused Hiss of passing secret documents. The patrician Hiss denied the charges and said he had never even met Chambers. He seemed more credible than the rumpled Chambers, an admitted perjurer, but Congressman Richard Nixon of California, a Republican member of HUAC, forced him to admit that he had known Chambers under an alias. With help from the FBI, Chambers charged that Hiss had given him secret information in the 1930s. When Chambers produced microfilmed photographs of the secret documents, Hiss could not explain them. Under the statute of limitations, it was too late to try Hiss for spying, but not too late to indict him for lying to Congress. Hiss's perjury trial ended in a hung jury in 1949, but a second jury convicted him in 1950, and he served almost four years in federal prison. The case was a triumph for Republicans and conservatives and a blow to Democrats and liberals.

As the Hiss case ended, another scandal stoked Americans' fears. In early 1950, British authorities arrested Klaus Fuchs, a physicist who had worked at the U.S. nuclear research facility in Los Alamos, New Mexico. The investigation led to David Greenglass, who worked on the atomic bomb project, and his brother-in-law, Julius Rosenberg. Julius, a former member of the CPUSA, and his wife Ethel were convicted of conspiring to steal atomic information in a trial controversial for its anti-Semitic overtones and because the act protecting atomic secrets became law after the spying allegedly took place. Though they had two young sons, both Rosenbergs were sentenced to death. Ignoring appeals for clemency, the federal government electrocuted the Rosenbergs in 1953.

There now seems little doubt that the USSR obtained American nuclear secrets, but the impact was probably not as great as conservatives feared or as small as liberals insisted. Most likely, espionage sped up work on an atomic bomb the Soviets would have eventually produced anyway.

The Rise of McCarthyism

Two weeks after Hiss's conviction, one week after Truman's announcement of the decision to build the hydrogen bomb, and days after the arrest of Klaus Fuchs, Senator Joseph McCarthy of Wisconsin spectacularly took command of the anti-Communist crusade. Speaking to the Republican Women's Club of Wheeling, West Virginia, the previously obscure senator claimed to have names of 205 Communists working in the State Department. In fact, McCarthy had no new information, only a handful of old accusations, including the ones against the Brunauers.

Nevertheless, McCarthy was instantly popular and powerful. Frightened by new dangers, many people wanted to believe in a senator bold enough to fight back. Some shared McCarthy's resentment of privileged elites—New Dealers, diplomats, scientists—whom he derided as "egg-sucking phony liberals" and "bright young men . . . born with silver spoons in their mouths." For some Americans—immigrants, midwesterners, Catholics, and fundamentalists—support for McCarthy was a way to prove their patriotism. " Even

Democratic legislators voted for the Internal Security Act of 1950, which forced the registration of Communist and Communist-front groups, provided for the deportation of allegedly subversive aliens, and barred Communists from defense jobs. Refusing to "put the Government of the United States in the thought control business," Truman vetoed the bill, but Congress overrode his veto.

Eventually, McCarthy went too far. Angry that one of his aides, David Schine, had not received a draft deferment, he launched an investigation of the army. The secretary of the army, Robert T. Stevens, refused to cooperate and claimed McCarthy had tried to get preferential treatment for Schine. In April 1954, before a television audience of 20 million people, McCarthy failed to come up with evidence of treason in the army. When he tried to smear an army lawyer as a Communist, the senator was exposed. "Have you no sense of decency, sir, at long last?" asked the army's chief counsel, Joseph Welch. It was an electric moment. The Senate hearings came to no judgment, but Americans did. McCarthy's popularity plummeted. By year's end, the Senate condemned him for "unbecoming conduct."

The fall of McCarthy did not end McCarthyism. Schools forced teachers to sign loyalty oaths. Faculty members at several universities lost their jobs, and deans gave the names of suspect students to the FBI. Communism had become a useful charge to hurl at anything that anybody might oppose—labor unions, civil rights, even modern art. To protect themselves, groups policed their own membership. Labor unions drove out Communist leaders and unions. The Cincinnati Reds renamed their team the "Redlegs."

Americans became more careful about what they said out loud. Many had come to believe, along with McCarthy, that the civility of democracy, the attention to rights and fairness exposed America to a ruthless adversary not bound by similar codes of conduct. Even as the Senate was censuring McCarthy, James Doolittle, the heroic World War II aviator, handed the CIA a report on counterespionage and countersubversion. It explained that the goal of America's enemy is "world domination by whatever means and at whatever cost." "If the United States is to survive," it concluded, "long-standing American concepts of 'fair play' must be reconsidered."

Conclusion

By the time Esther Brunauer lost her job in 1952, the cold war had disrupted American life. To contain Communism, the United States had transformed the economy. American society dealt with the unfinished business of reconversion, including the role of government and the rights and opportunities of labor, women, and African Americans. Despite these changes, the cold war had widened and intensified. Just seven years after dropping the first atomic bomb on Japan, Americans were again at war in the Far East and were forced to live with the threat of nuclear annihilation. They lived, too, with the frenzied search for subversives. America seemed to be out of control.

As Esther and Stephen Brunauer returned to Illinois to find peace and rebuild their lives, other Americans needed peace as well. They wanted the fighting in Korea to end. Anxious to avoid a nuclear holocaust, they wanted the confrontation with the Soviets to stabilize. Meanwhile, American society adjusted to a postwar economy, sorting out the role that government, labor, race, and gender would have in the new cold war order.

>> Timeline

▼1945
Yalta conference
Harry S. Truman inaugurated
Potsdam Conference
Industrial strikes break out

▼1946
Winston Churchill's "Iron Curtain" speech
George Kennan's "long telegram" on Soviet expansionism
Employment Act of 1946
Morgan v. Virginia
Election of Republican majorities in House and Senate

▼1947
Announcement of Truman Doctrine
Beginning of Federal Employee Loyalty Program
CORE's "Journey of Reconciliation"
Integration of major league baseball by Jackie Robinson
HUAC Hollywood hearings
Rio Pact
Taft-Hartley Act
National Security Act
Presidential commission reports on civil rights

▼1948
Shelley v. Kraemer
Congressional approval of Marshall Plan
Truman's Executive Order 9981
Beginning of Berlin crisis
Selective Service Act
Truman elected president

▼1949
Formation of North Atlantic Treaty Organization
Communist takeover of mainland China

▼1950
NSC-68
Alger Hiss's conviction for perjury
Joe McCarthy's speech in Wheeling, West Virginia
Treaty of Detroit
Beginning of Korean War
Internal Security Act of 1950

▼1951
Truman fires General Douglas MacArthur

>> Timeline *continued*

▼**1952**
Immigration and Nationality Act
Test of hydrogen bomb

▼**1953**
Execution of Ethel and Julius Rosenberg

▼**1954**
Army-McCarthy hearings

Review Questions

1. How did the National Security Act change the executive branch?

2. Why did Truman see Korea as important enough to defend?

3. Why were struggles in the workplace more intense in the late 1940s than during the Depression or World War II?

4. McCarthyism attacked government, science, education, theater, and Hollywood. Does this pattern reveal anything about the nature of American anxiety in the 1950s?

5. Two-thirds of the world's peoples gained their independence between 1945 and 1961. How did the cold war affect this movement toward nationhood?

6. In the 1950s and 1960s, historians debated the question of who started the cold war. In the 1990s, it became more interesting to ask *when* it started. Why the change, and what questions might historians today ask?

For further review materials and resource information, please visit www.oup.com/us/ofthepeople

>> Gene Ferkauf

At the end of World War II, Harry Ferkauf owned two luggage stores in midtown Manhattan in New York City. A Jewish immigrant from Eastern Europe, he haggled with customers over prices in the old way and made a decent living. Having barely kept his business alive during the Depression, he did not want or expect much more

Harry's son, Eugene, who managed one of the stores, did not accept the old limits. After the war, Gene began offering discounts on luggage, watches, and other goods. Father and son argued frequently over Gene's strategy. In 1948, Gene quit and put all his savings into his own discount store on East 46th Street. Gene envisioned a new kind of store, where customers could buy appliances and other goods, without haggling, at low, fixed prices. Discounting his merchandise by a quarter and even a third, Gene could not make much from a single sale. But if he sold enough televisions and refrigerators, he would earn more than his father ever had. On opening day, crowds filled the small shop and spent $3,000. Harry, who usually took in about $50 a day, was impressed.

In a few years, Gene had five successful discount stores in and around New York City. The business was called "E. J. Korvettes"—E for Eugene, J for his partner Joe Zwillenberg, and Korvettes after the quick Canadian warships of World War II. Korvettes appealed to a new, more optimistic generation than the one that had survived the Depression. Eager to buy televisions and other appliances, these younger people were unafraid to go into debt. Prosperous, they were leaving their parents' neighborhoods in the city for new suburbs. Gene Ferkauf understood these people; he was one of them. He, too, moved from his small $75-a-month apartment in Brooklyn to a $75,000 "mansion" in Jamaica, Queens.

Gene had made it big. Adding to the stores in New York City, Korvettes built suburban stores in several states. In 1955, the partnership became a corporation. Gene had left his father's world behind.

>> **AMERICAN PORTRAIT** *continued*

Gene Ferkauf's success reflected one of the central developments in American society after World War II. Along with the cold war, economic prosperity transformed the nation. Just as Gene left his father's world behind, American society left behind the economic limits and constraints of the Great Depression and the war. The 1950s marked the culmination of the nation's emergence as a full-fledged consumer society. Gene Ferkauf profited because mainstream culture celebrated consumption and pleasure instead of work and self-restraint and because televisions and suburbs defined the consumer lifestyle.

The emergence of consumer society strongly affected American culture and politics. The prosperous 1950s helped to produce a more homogeneous, seemingly more harmonious nation, with decreasing class differences, changing gender relations, and a baby boom. Enjoying the benefits of consumerism, American voters demanded less from government. In later years, American culture would look back nostalgically at the 1950s as a prosperous golden age, not one that had real conflicts, failures, and limits. In different ways, many Americans chafed against the conformity and constraints of the 1950s. Consumer society did not benefit every group; nor did it solve the problem of racial inequality or end the cold war. By the close of the decade, many Americans worried about the inadequacies of the consumer society, even as they enjoyed its benefits.

Common Threads

>> Did the character of the cold war change from the 1940s to the 1950s?

>> Why did consumerism change the way Americans lived?

>> Why did diversity and individuality survive in the 1950s?

>> What was the impact of the Eisenhower administration on democracy?

>> How would the emerging discontents of the 1950s affect society and politics in the next decades?

Living the Good Life

Much of the consumer lifestyle was in place by the 1920s (see Chapter 23), but only in the 1950s did consumer values and habits finally dominate the American economy and culture. Never before had so many Americans had the chance to live the good life.

They tended to define that "good life" in economic terms. A dynamic, evolving economy offered more leisure and income. Sure of prosperity, Americans had the confidence to spend more of their time and money in the pursuit of pleasure. Millions of people lived the dream of a home in new suburbs, bought flashy automobiles, purchased their first televisions, and enjoyed a new openness about sex.

Economic Prosperity

Consumerism could not have flourished without prosperity. Despite three short recessions, the 1950s were a period of economic boom. The gross national product—the value of all the country's output of goods and services—grew solidly at an average of 3.2 percent a year.

> See the USA in your
>
> Chevrolet
>
> America is asking
>
> you to call
>
> Drive your Chevrolet
>
> through the USA
>
> America's the
>
> greatest land
>
> of all.
>
> ~~~~~~~~~~~
> CHEVROLET
> COMMERCIAL JINGLE,
> 1950

Several major factors spurred this economic growth. The shortage of consumer goods during and just after World War II had left Americans with money to spend. Because of the cold war, federal spending for defense and foreign aid helped stimulate the demand for American goods and services. Robust capital spending by businesses also helped ensure economic growth. The industrial economy was also evolving. Traditional heavy manufacturing—steel and automobiles—was still crucial to prosperity, but newer industries, such as electronics, chemicals, plastics, aviation, and computers, became increasingly important.

The emergence of the computer business was especially significant for the long run. In 1946, two engineers at the University of Pennsylvania, J. Presper Eckert Jr. and John William Mauchly, completed the first fully electronic digital computer. The Electronic Numerical Integrator and Computer (ENIAC) weighed more than 30 tons and filled a large room. Then Eckert and Mauchly produced the more advanced UNIVAC 1 (Universal Automatic Computer), which was used to count census data in 1951 and presidential election returns in 1952.

As tiny solid-state transistors replaced bulky vacuum tubes, computers became smaller, more powerful, and more common. By 1958, American companies were producing $1 billion worth of computers a year. Because computers were still so large and expensive, they were used mostly by universities, corporations, the Department of Defense, and other agencies. By 1961, there were about 10,000 computers in use, and the nation was on the brink of the digital age.

As American industry evolved, the nation's distribution and service sectors played a larger role than ever before. While the number of manufacturing jobs barely changed, employment in retail stores such as E. J. Korvettes increased 19 percent. Jobs in the service sector, such as restaurants, hotels, repair shops, hospitals, and universities, jumped 32 percent. The United States had begun to develop a postindustrial economy, less dependent on production and more dependent on service and consumption.

Economic prosperity greatly benefited big business. New corporations such as E. J. Korvettes emerged and grew. Thanks to a wave of mergers, established corporations became still larger. By 1960, corporations earned 18 times as much income as the rest of the nation's businesses combined.

The New Affluence All the groceries consumed by a white-collar DuPont Chemical worker, his wife, and their two children in 1951.

Prosperity also boosted corporations' confidence and popularity. Even liberals, once critical of corporate power, now celebrated the benefits of large-scale business enterprise. "What is good for the country is good for General Motors, and vice versa," Charles Wilson, the head of GM, supposedly announced.

American workers enjoyed high employment, low inflation, and rising incomes. Less than 5 percent of the workforce was out of a job at any one time. Wages rose dramatically. Factory workers' average hourly pay more than doubled between 1945 and 1960, while consumer prices rose less than 2 percent per year. The percentage of Americans living in poverty fell from as much as 30 in the late 1940s to 18 in 1959.

Americans also had more leisure time. By the 1950s, the 40-hour workweek was commonplace. Many workers now looked forward to two- or three-week paid vacations. As life expectancy increased and the economy boomed, more and more Americans expected to retire at age 65 and live comfortably off their pensions and social security.

Workers' well-being produced labor peace, which in turn stimulated prosperity. After the contentious 1940s, workers and employers were more likely to resolve differences without strikes and lockouts. When the relatively aggressive Congress of Industrial Organizations (CIO) merged with the American Federation of Labor (AFL) to become the gigantic AFL-CIO in 1955, the union movement seemed to become more bureaucratic and complacent. "American labor never had it so good," crowed a trade union leader.

The Suburban Dream

For growing numbers of people, the good life meant a house in the suburbs. Most Americans had never owned their own homes. Suburbs had been mainly for the well-to-do. But entrepreneurship, new construction methods, inexpensive land, and generous federal aid made possible affordable-housing developments outside the nation's cities. Along with Gene Ferkauf and his family, much of America moved to the suburbs in the 1950s.

William J. Levitt's pioneering development, Levittown, illustrated the suburban housing boom. Levitt came back from World War II with an optimistic vision of the future. He wanted to make houses affordable for middle-class and working-class people. Drawing on his military experience and on the assembly-line techniques of automaker Henry Ford, he intended to build houses so efficiently that they could be sold at remarkably low prices. Levitt bought 1,000 acres of cheap farmland not far from a Korvettes on New York's Long Island. He put up simple houses, with prefabricated parts, no basements, and low price tags. The original Cape Cod–style house cost $7,990, ideal for young couples financing their first home.

Like Korvettes, Levittown quickly became a huge success. Buyers signed 1,400 contracts for houses on a single day in 1949. The development grew to 17,500 dwellings housing 82,000 people. Levitt soon built more Levittowns, as did imitators all around the country.

The federal government helped develop the suburbs. To make home ownership more affordable, the government allowed buyers to deduct mortgage interest payments from their federal income taxes and guaranteed loans to millions of military veterans. To make commuting practical, the National System of Defense Highways Act of 1956 encouraged the construction of freeways connecting cities and suburbs.

Under such favorable conditions, the United States quickly became a nation of suburban homeowners. As the rate of home ownership increased 20 percent between 1945 and 1960, nearly one-third of Americans lived in places like Levittown. The suburban dream had become an everyday reality.

The Pursuit of Pleasure

The consumer society depended on Americans' eagerness to pursue pleasure. Businesses made sure that nothing would prevent them from buying goods and services. If their wages and salaries were not enough, consumers could borrow. In 1950, the Diners Club introduced the credit card for well-to-do New Yorkers. By the end of the decade, Sears Roebuck credit cards allowed more than 10 million Americans to spend borrowed money. In 1945, Americans owed only $5.7 billion for consumer goods other than houses. By 1960, they owed $56.1 billion.

In the 1950s, discount stores such as Korvettes made shopping seem simpler and more attractive, and so did another new creation, the shopping mall. In 1956, Southdale, the first enclosed suburban shopping mall, opened outside Minneapolis. Consumers ate more easily, too. The first McDonald's fast-food restaurant opened in San Bernardino, California, in 1948. Taken over by businessman Ray Kroc, McDonald's began to grow into a national chain in the mid-1950s.

To get to McDonald's, the Southdale Mall, Korvettes, or Levittown, Americans needed cars. In the 1950s, automobiles reflected a new sense of affluence and self-indulgence. Big,

AMERICAN LANDSCAPE

>> Levittown, New York

For many Americans, the first Levittown epitomized the virtues and defects of suburbia, consumerism, and democracy in post–World War II America. The new community seemed to be a democratic triumph, a visual reminder of equality and upward mobility. The male heads of Levittown households tended to be prosperous blue-collar workers, veterans of World War II seeking middle-class status for their growing, baby-boom families. As an observer noted, Levittown was a "one-class community," where most households had an annual income of about $3,500 to $4,000.

From another angle, Levittown seemed less democratic, notable for who didn't live there. Amid the young families, there were few teenagers or senior citizens. There were hardly any African Americans, either.

Levittown's homogeneity was no accident. The developer, William Levitt, had planned it that way. Its first four-room Cape Cod houses came in only five very similar models. All the houses and streets appeared to be the same. Even Levitt admitted that he had once gotten lost in the look-alike streets of his suburb. The uniform style and cost of the houses attracted only one class of residents. So-called restrictive covenants—special clauses in housing deeds—ensured that those residents would be white.

Levitt also tried to impose uniform behavior on his residents. Community rules forbade putting up fences or hanging out the wash on weekends. Some residents helped promoted conformity. They wrote the local newspaper to attack neighbors who broke the rules. A nonconformist could expect to be labeled a "commie" or a "Russkie."

The design of the community and its houses reflected the domestic values of the period. The small Cape Cod homes encouraged family "togetherness." With so little private space, family members congregated around the kitchen table or in front of the TV. Wives were expected to spend weekdays doing tasks at home, rather than working at a paying job. Because it was supposed to be the center of women's lives, the kitchen was placed at the front of the house.

Levittown's design also supported men's domestic role. Former apartment dwellers found they had to spend time at home mowing their new lawns. With few traditionally masculine public places—bars, firehouses, and ball fields—the child-centered community promoted family togetherness away from home with plenty of playgrounds and swimming pools. Despite the power of conformity, Levittown demonstrated the strength of individuality in America. Over time, the suburb became less homogeneous, and Levitt offered houses with more variety. In 1949, new ranch-style houses replaced the Cape Cod model. New features were added, including carports. Residents remodeled their houses to express individual tastes. They built garages and patios and added rooms, gardens, signposts, and distinctive paint jobs. They put up fences. "The houses take on the *continued*

AMERICAN LANDSCAPE *continued*

personalities of their owners," wrote a suburban resident.

Levittown was a product of 1950s America. This pioneering suburb revealed the power of domesticity and conformity, but it also demonstrated the limits of democracy and the persistence of individuality in the consumer society.

high-compression engines burning high-octane gasoline powered ever-bigger cars stuffed with new accessories—power steering, power brakes, power windows, and air conditioning. Unlike the drab sedans of the Depression, the new models featured "Passion Pink" and "Horizon Blue" interiors and two- and even three-tone exteriors studded with shiny chrome.

Automakers used that chrome to solve one of the main problems of a consumer society—getting people who already had plenty to want to buy even more. How could Detroit persuade Americans to trade in cars that were running just fine for new ones? The answer was what General Motors' chief designer called "dynamic obsolescence," the feeling that last year's model was somehow inadequate. So the automakers changed chrome, colors, and tailfins from year to year (see Table 27–1).

Icons of the Consumer Society The first enclosed mall in the United States—Southdale, outside Minneapolis, Minnesota.

Table 27-1 Automobiles and Highways, 1945–1960

Year	Factory Sales (in 1,000s)	Registrations (in 1,000s)	Miles of Highway Completed (in 1,000s)
1945	69.5	25,796.9	3,035
1946	2,148.6	28,217.0	5,057
1947	3,558.1	30,849.3	15,473
1948	3,909.2	33,355.2	21,725
1949	5,119.4	36,457.9	19,876
1950	6,665.8	40,339.0	19,876
1951	5,338.4	42,688.3	17,060
1952	4,320.7	43,823.0	22,147
1953	6,116.9	46,429.2	21,136
1954	5,558.8	48,468.4	20,548
1955	7,920.1	52,144.7	22,571
1956	5,816.1	54,210.9	23,609
1957	6,113.3	55,917.8	22,424
1958	4,257.8	56,890.5	28,137
1959*	5,591.2	59,453.9	32,633
1960	6,674.7	61,682.3	20,969

*Denotes first year for which figures include Alaska and Hawaii.

Source: *Historical Statistics of the United States, Millennial Online Edition* (Cambridge University Press, 2008), Table Df347–352 and Table Df213–217

The cars of the 1950s reflected a driver's identity and affluence. General Motors' line rose up the socioeconomic ladder, from the ordinary Chevrolet to the more prosperous Pontiac, Oldsmobile, and Buick all the way up to the sumptuous success symbol, the Cadillac.

Automobiles also spoke to gender identities. Designed to appeal to women, car interiors seemed like living rooms. The exterior offered men power and sexuality. While the back of a 1950s car could look like the afterburner of a jet, the front spoke to something else. The chrome protrusions on 1950s Cadillac bumpers and grilles were known as "Dagmars," after the name of a large-breasted female television star. A car, as a Buick ad promised, "makes you feel like the man you are."

It was not surprising that the chrome on a Cadillac would make Americans think of a television star. In the 1950s, television became a central part of American life. As TV sets became less expensive and sales boomed, there were new opportunities for broadcasters. By 1950, the Federal Communications Commission (FCC) had licensed 104 TV stations, mostly in cities. By 1960, 90 percent of the nation's households had a television (see Table 27–2). In 15 years, TV had become a part of everyday life.

From its early days, television reinforced the values of consumer society. Advertisements for consumer products paid for programming created mainly for pleasure and diversion. Nightly national news broadcasts lasted only 15 minutes. There were operas, documentaries, and live dramas in what some critics consider television's golden age, but

Table 27-2 Television, 1941–1960

Year	Television Stations	Households with Television Sets (in 1,000s)
1941	2	—
1945	9	—
1950	104	3,875
1955	458	30,700
1960	579	45,750

Source: George Thomas Kurian, *Datapedia* (Lonham, MD: Bernan Press, 1994), pp. 299–300.

most of the broadcast day was filled with variety shows, sports, westerns, and situation comedies. As television undermined the popularity of radio and movie theaters, the three major broadcasting companies quickly created TV networks and dominated the new industry.

American culture also became more open about sexuality. Dr. Alfred C. Kinsey commanded enormous public attention with two pioneering academic studies—*Sexual Behavior in the Human Male* (1948) and *Sexual Behavior in the Human Female* (1953). Kinsey surprised Americans by reporting more sexual activity outside of marriage than had been thought. The Supreme Court contributed to sexual openness by overturning a ban on a film version of D. H. Lawrence's often erotic novel, *Lady Chatterley's Lover*, in 1959. The new sexual candor was epitomized by *Playboy* magazine, first published by Hugh Hefner in December 1953. Featuring pictures of bare-breasted women, *Playboy* presented sex as one part of a hedonistic lifestyle of flashy cars, expensive stereos, and fine liquor.

A Homogeneous Society?

The spread of consumerism reinforced a sense of sameness in America, that the United States was becoming a homogeneous society in which people bought the same products, watched the same TV shows, worked for the same corporations, and dreamed the same dreams. Critics worried that Americans had sacrificed their individuality for conformity. Declining class differences and a renewed emphasis on religion and family strengthened the feeling that people were becoming more alike.

Nevertheless, the United States remained a heterogeneous society. Although class and ethnic differences among whites decreased, race remained a powerful divider. Despite fears of conformity, the nation still encouraged difference and individuality.

The Discovery of Conformity

In the years after World War II, sociologists and other writers discovered an increasing uniformity in American society, for a variety of reasons. During the frenzied search for domestic Communists, people did not want to risk accusations by appearing different or unusual. As corporations merged and small businesses disappeared, more Americans worked for the same giant companies. Levittown and the other new suburbs intensified the sense of sameness. In 1957, one writer described suburbanites as "people whose age, income, number of children, problems, habits, conversations, dress, possessions, perhaps even blood types are almost precisely like yours."

Some observers believed that Americans actually wanted to be like one another. In *The Lonely Crowd* (1950), sociologist David Riesman argued that instead of following their own internal values, Americans adjusted their behavior to meet the expectations of the people around them. In *The Organization Man* (1956), William H. Whyte Jr. suggested that conformist white-collar workers in big corporations were making the United States more like the Soviet Union.

The Decline of Class and Ethnicity

The apparent decline of social class differences reinforced the sense of homogeneity. By the 1950s, the old upper class—the families of the Gilded Age—no longer ran American industry and finance. Thanks to taxes and the Depression, the largest American fortunes were smaller than at the beginning of the twentieth century. As sociologist C. Wright Mills argued in *The Power Elite* (1956), an interlocking group of military, political, and economic managers ran the nation's institutions. They did not have the bold swagger or the dynastic ambitions of the Gilded Age robber barons.

Meanwhile, the ranks of American farmers continued to shrink. As agriculture became more efficient and corporatized, the number of farms fell from more than 6 million in 1944 to 3.7 million in 1959. Although manual and service workers remained the largest occupational group, they seemed a less distinctive social class. In an era of labor peace, well-paid blue-collar workers appeared content with American society. Labor leaders endorsed consumerism and anti-Communism, and some observers argued that American workers had become middle class in their habits and values. The middle class itself was burgeoning. By 1960, the white-collar sector made up 40 percent of the workforce.

Even ethnic differences no longer seemed significant. Whites from different national and religious backgrounds mixed together in the new suburbs. The rate of intermarriage between ethnic groups increased. Anxious to prove their loyalty during the cold war, newer Americans were reluctant to emphasize their origins. Ethnicity had apparently disappeared in the melting pot of the consumer society.

Many Americans, especially powerful ones, had long wanted to believe theirs was a unified society devoted to middle-class values. In the 1950s, there was probably more basis for this belief than ever before.

The Resurgence of Religion and Family

A renewed emphasis on religion and family contributed to the homogeneity of American society. Political leaders, fighting the cold war, encouraged religiosity. Freedom of religion, they insisted, set the United States apart from allegedly godless Communist nations. To underscore this commitment to religion, the federal government put the words "In God We Trust" on all currency. Meanwhile, religion adapted itself to the consumer society. Charismatic preachers such as Roman Catholic bishop Fulton J. Sheen and Protestant evangelist Billy Graham used television to bring religion to Americans in a new way.

Americans became more involved with organized religion. In 1945, 45 percent of the nation belonged to one religious denomination or another; by 1960, that figure had reached 61 percent. Weekly church attendance increased, too, reaching a peak of 49 percent in 1958. By 1960, there were 64 million Protestants, 42 million Roman Catholics, and fewer than 6 million Jews (see Table 27–3).

American culture also celebrated what *McCall's* magazine christened family "togetherness." Manufacturers promoted TV viewing as a way of holding families together. Detroit called its big automobiles "family" cars.

"Togetherness" meant the nuclear family, with a mother, a father, and plenty of children. After decades of decline, the birthrate rose in the 1940s. Beginning in 1954, Americans had more than 4 million babies a year. Thanks to new drugs, nearly all these infants survived. Antibiotics reduced the risk of diphtheria, typhoid fever, influenza, and other infections. The Salk and Sabin vaccines virtually wiped out polio. As a result, the average number of children per family went from 2.4 in 1945 up to 3.2 in 1957, and the population grew by a record 29 million people to 179 million.

Like the religious revival, the "baby boom" of the 1940s and 1950s is somewhat difficult to explain. For more than 100 years, Americans had reduced the size of their families to ease financial and economic burdens. Cold war economic prosperity may have per-

Table 27–3 Religious Revival and Baby Boom, 1945–1960

Year	Membership of Religious Bodies (in 1,000s)	Live Births (in 1,000s)
1945	71,700	2,858
1946	73,673	3,411
1947	77,386	3,817
1948	79,436	3,637
1949	81,862	3,649
1950	86,830	3,632
1951	88,673	3,823
1952	92,277	3,913
1953	94,843	3,965
1954	97,483	4,078
1955	100,163	4,104
1956	103,225	4,218
1957	104,190	4,308
1958[1]	109,558	4,255
1959[2]	112,227	4,245
1960	114,449	4,258

[1]Includes Alaska.

[2]Denotes first year for which figures include Alaska and Hawaii.

Source: George Thomas Kurian, *Datapedia* (Lanharn, MD: Bernan Press, 1994), pp. 37, 146.

suaded couples that they could afford to have more children. But prosperity alone did not explain why American culture became so much more child centered during these years. In his book *Common Sense Book of Baby and Child Care* (1946), pediatrician Benjamin Spock urged parents to raise their children with less severity and more attention, warmth, tenderness, and fun. It outsold every other book in the 1950s except the Bible.

Maintaining Gender Roles

As many social differences seemed to disappear, American culture nevertheless reemphasized the distinctions between the sexes. During the baby boom, women were expected to be helpful wives and devoted mothers. Men were encouraged to define themselves primarily as family providers.

The 1950s underscored the differences between genders in a variety of ways. Blue became the color for boys and pink the color for girls. Standards of beauty highlighted physiological differences between women and men. Voluptuous actresses such as Dagmar, Jayne Mansfield, and Marilyn Monroe defined femininity.

Nevertheless, gender roles grew more similar during the 1950s. Society stressed a man's domestic role more than before. Husbands were urged to do some housework and to spend more time nurturing their children, although few men lived up to the new ideal.

Female roles evolved more dramatically. To help pay for the consumer lifestyle, many wives had to find jobs. In 1940, 15.6 percent of married women were in the paid workforce. By 1960, that percentage had nearly doubled to 31.0, and women made up more than one-third of the labor force, mostly in clerical and sales positions. To a degree, American culture supported the expanding role of women outside the home. In the cold war competition with the Soviets, Americans celebrated the supposedly greater freedom and opportunity for women in the United States. Nevertheless, women had little help coping with their jobs and bigger families. Congress voted an income tax deduction for child-care costs in 1954, but little first-class child care was available. At work, women were expected to watch men get ahead of them. Women's income was only 60 percent of men's in 1960.

American culture strongly condemned women and men who strayed outside conventional gender norms. *Modern Woman: The Lost Sex*, a 1947 best seller by Marynia Farnham and Ferdinand Lundberg, censured feminism as a "deep illness" of "neurotically disturbed women" with "penis envy." Psychologists and other experts demonized lesbians and gay men. As police cracked down on gay bars, unmarried men risked accusations of homosexuality. The dominant culture expected males to be heterosexual husbands and fathers. Those roles, in turn, made men more likely to conform to social expectations.

Persisting Racial Differences

In spite of the many pressures toward conformity, American society remained heterogeneous. Although suburbanization broke down ethnic differences among whites, it intensified the racial divide. The suburbs were 95 percent white in 1950. As whites moved into Levittown and other suburbs, African Americans took their place in cities. By 1960, more than half of the black population lived in cities, typically kept out of white neighborhoods.

Living on their reservations, Native Americans were also set apart. In 1953, Congress tried to "Americanize" the Indians by approving the termination of their special legal status as sovereign groups and, with it, of the traditional rights and reservations of more than 11,000 Native Americans. The new policy was intended to turn them into members of the consumer society.

It did not turn out that way. As reservations became counties in the 1950s and early 1960s, Indians had to sell valuable mineral rights and lands to pay taxes. Tribes still faced poverty, unemployment, and social problems. Encouraged by the federal government's new Voluntary Relocation Program, about one in five Native Americans moved to the city. Some tribes, including the Catawba, the Coquille, the Klamath, and the Menominee, began long legal fights to reclaim tribal status. But whether they lived on reservations or on crowded city blocks, a quarter of a million Indians remained largely separate and ignored.

The increasing migration of Puerto Ricans also reinforced the multiracial character of American society. Beginning in the 1940s, a large number of Puerto Ricans, who were U.S. citizens, left their island for more economic opportunity. By 1960, there were 887,000 Puerto Ricans on the mainland, two-thirds of them concentrated in the East Harlem section of New York City. They found opportunities but also separation and discrimination in their new homes. Mexican immigration also added to racial diversity. After 1945, increasing numbers of Mexicans left their impoverished country for the United States, particularly the booming Southwest. Congress, bowing to the needs of southwestern employers, continued the Bracero Program, the supposedly temporary agreement that had brought hundreds of thousands of laborers, or *braceros*, to the wartime United States. Meanwhile, illegal Mexican migration increased dramatically.

Like other Mexican migrants before them, the newly arrived met a mixed reception. As in the years before World War II, Mexicans already living in the United States worried that the new migrants would compete for jobs, drive down wages, and feed American prejudice. Many white Americans did deride them as *mojados*, or "wetbacks," because so many had supposedly swum the Rio Grande River to enter the country illegally. Mexican Americans feared that the federal government would use the Internal Security Act of 1950 and the Immigration and Nationality Act of 1952 to deport Mexicans and break up families. The government's intention became clear in 1954 with Operation Wetback, which sent more than 1 million immigrants back to Mexico in that year alone.

About 3.5 million Mexican Americans were living in the United States by 1960. The great majority worked for low wages in the cities and on the farms of the Southwest. Many lived in *barrios* apart from whites. Because of Operation Wetback and other instances of prejudice, some Mexican Americans became more vocal about their rights. The League of United Latin American Citizens denounced the impact of the Immigration and Nationality Act. More outspoken was the American GI Forum, an organization of Mexican American veterans formed when a Texas funeral parlor would not bury a deceased comrade. Such assertiveness made it harder to ignore the presence of Mexican Americans in the consumer society.

The experiences of Hispanics, Mexican Americans, Native Americans, and African Americans underscored the continuing importance of race in the United States. Mostly living apart, whites and nonwhites faced different conditions and different futures. Prosperity and consumerism did not change that reality. As long as race was so potent a factor, the United States would never be a homogeneous society. In the 1960s, white Americans would have to face that fact.

The Plight of Mexican "Wetbacks" Illegal immigrants taken off freight trains in Los Angeles, after two days without food or water, in 1953. They were probably sent back to Mexico.

The Survival of Diversity

Along with race, other forces ensured the survival of diversity, especially in regional differences. As in the past, internal migration and the expansion of national boundaries promoted change. During the 1950s, more than 1.6 million people, many of them retired, moved to Florida. As a result, the state increasingly played a distinctive national role as a center for leisure and entertainment.

Other Americans moved westward. During the 1950s, more than 3 million people moved to California, which earned a reputation as the pioneer state of the consumer society, home of the first Disney amusement park and the first McDonald's.

The admission of two new states highlighted the continuing diversity of the United States. In 1959, Alaska and Hawaii became, respectively, the 49th and 50th states in the Union. Racially and culturally diverse, climatically and topographically distinctive, they demonstrated that America was not simply a land of corporations and Levittowns.

Popular music also exemplified this continuing diversity. Big swing bands gave way to such popular singers as Frank Sinatra and Patti Page. Jazz split into different camps—traditional, mainstream, and modern. Country music featured cowboy songs, western swing, honky-tonk, bluegrass, and the smooth "Nashville sound." A range of African American musical forms, including blues, jazz, and vocal groups, became known as "rhythm and blues" (R & B). Gospel music thrilled white and black audiences. Mexican

Americans made Tejano music in Texas, and Polish Americans danced to polka bands in Illinois.

R & B collided with country music to create rock and roll. By 1952, white disc jockey Alan Freed was playing R & B on his Cleveland radio show, "Moondog's Rock 'n' Roll Party." In 1954, a white country group, Bill Haley and the Comets, recorded the first rock-and-roll hit, "Rock Around the Clock." Early rock and roll produced both African American and white heroes—Chuck Berry, Fats Domino, Jerry Lee Lewis, and Buddy Holly, among others.

The biggest rock-and-roll sensation of all was a young white singer and guitar player, Elvis Presley. Born in Mississippi and raised in near poverty in Memphis, Presley drew on a variety of genres to create a distinctive personal style. "Who do you sound like?" he was asked. "I don't sound like nobody," he said.

Because of Presley and other musicians, the sound of American popular music was anything but homogeneous. Because of the distinctiveness of Florida, California, Alaska, Hawaii, and other states, the United States was hardly monolithic. In these ways, at least, American society avoided uniformity after World War II.

The Eisenhower Era at Home and Abroad

Prosperity encouraged Americans to demand less from government in the 1950s. In a period of social change and international tensions, most people wanted reassurance rather than boldness from Washington. The politics of the decade were dominated by President Dwight D. Eisenhower, whose middle-of-the-road domestic program, "Modern Republicanism," appealed to a prosperous electorate wary of government innovation. But Eisenhower's anti-Communist foreign policy did little to diminish popular anxieties about the cold war and laid the groundwork for future trouble in the Middle East and Southeast Asia.

"Ike" and 1950s America

Eisenhower, a charismatic military hero with a bright, infectious grin, would have been an ideal public figure in almost any era of American history, but the man known as "Ike" was especially suited to the 1950s. The last president born in the nineteenth century, he had successfully accommodated the major changes of the twentieth. Raised on the individualistic values of the rural Midwest, Eisenhower adopted the bureaucratic style of modern organizations. He succeeded in the military not because he was a great fighter but because he was a great manager, a classic "organization man." As a commander in World War II, Eisenhower worked to keep fractious allies together. After the war, he deepened his organizational experience as president of Columbia University and as the first commander of NATO armed forces. Just as he accommodated the rise of big organizations, Eisenhower accommodated America's expanding commitment abroad. Ike was raised among people who often feared American involvement in the world's problems. But his military career rested on accepting an activist role for the United States around the world.

Eisenhower easily fit the dominant culture of the 1950s. He was an involved, loving husband and father. In a society pursuing pleasures, he was famous for his hours on the golf course. His wife, Mamie, wore the "New Look" fashions inspired by designer Christian Dior and avidly watched television soap operas.

Nominated for president by the Republicans in 1952, Eisenhower ran against Adlai Stevenson, the liberal Democratic governor of Illinois. Running a moderate, conciliatory campaign, Eisenhower avoided attacks on the New Deal and promised to work for an end to the Korean War. Meanwhile, his tough-talking running mate, Senator Richard Nixon of California, accused Stevenson of being soft on Communism. Eisenhower handily won 55 percent of the popular vote and 442 electoral votes. The Republican s took control of the White House and both houses of Congress for the first time in 20 years.

Modern Republicanism

Eisenhower's Modern Republicanism attempted to steer a middle course between traditional Republican conservatism and Democratic liberalism. With a conservative's faith in individual freedom, the president favored limited government and balanced budgets, but Eisenhower the organization man believed that Washington had an important role to play in protecting individuals. He also knew that most Americans did not want to give up such liberal programs as Social Security and farm subsidies.

Accordingly, the Eisenhower administration limited the reach of the government by decreasing regulation of business and cutting taxes for the wealthy. The Submerged Lands Act of 1953 turned over offshore oil resources to the states for private exploitation. The Atomic Energy Act of 1954 allowed private firms to sell power produced by nuclear reactors.

Nevertheless, the administration did little to undermine the legacy of the New Deal and the Fair Deal. Eisenhower went along with increases in Social Security benefits and farm subsidies. Despite his belief in balanced budgets, his administration produced several budget deficits. Federal spending helped fuel the consumer economy.

Modern Republicanism frustrated liberals, as well as conservative "Old Guard" Republicans, but "the public loves Ike," a journalist observed. "The less he does the more they love him."

Eisenhower's popularity was confirmed at the polls in 1956. In a repeat of 1952, Eisenhower and Nixon again defeated Adlai Stevenson, this time in an even bigger victory, with 58 percent of the popular vote and 457 electoral votes.

An Aggressive Cold War Strategy

Like Truman before him, Eisenhower was committed to opposing Communism at home and around the world. The president helped the crusade against alleged Communist subversives and tolerated its excesses. He refused publicly to criticize the tactics of Senator Joseph R. McCarthy and declined to stop the execution of the convicted spies, Julius and Ethel Rosenberg, in 1953. Eisenhower denied the security clearance that J. Robert Oppenheimer, the former director of the Manhattan Project, needed to work on federal nuclear projects. Thousands of other alleged security risks also lost their federal jobs during the Eisenhower era.

Whereas Truman had pledged only to contain Communist expansion, Eisenhower and his advisers talked of rolling back Soviet power in Europe and freeing "captive peoples" from Communism. Secretary of State John Foster Dulles threatened "instant,

The "New Look" of Defense in the Eisenhower Era A ceremony honors the production of the 1,000th B–47 Stratojet, the long-range bomber capable of delivering nuclear weapons in an attack on the Soviet Union.

massive retaliation" with nuclear weapons in response to any Soviet aggression. To support this threat, the U.S. military adopted the "New Look" strategy, named after Mamie Eisenhower's favorite fashions, that de-emphasized conventional armies and increased the nuclear arsenal with long-range bombers, missiles, and nuclear-powered submarines.

The president also used the CIA to counter Communism by stealthier means. At his direction, the CIA carried out secret activities once considered unacceptable. At home, the agency explored the possible uses of lysergic acid diethylamide—the dangerous hallucinogenic drug known as LSD—by using it on hundreds of unwitting Americans. Abroad, the agency gave secret aid to pro-American regimes and ran secret programs against uncooperative governments.

In August 1953 a covert CIA operation, code-named Ajax, orchestrated a coup that removed Mohammad Mossadeq, the nationalist prime minister of oil-rich Iran. Eisenhower and Dulles feared that this "madman," who had nationalized Iran's oil fields, would shut out U.S. business and open the way for Communism and the Soviet Union. The young Iranian monarch, Shah Mohammad Reza Pahlavi, who had ceded power to Mossadeq, now reclaimed it. The shah accepted $45 million in U.S. aid, turned his back on the Soviets, and made low-priced oil available to American companies.

In 1954, PBSUCCESS, a secret CIA operation modeled on Ajax, overthrew another foreign leader. Eisenhower and Dulles worried that a "Communist infection" in the Central American nation of Guatemala could spread to the United States–controlled Panama Canal and to Mexico. In fact, the Soviet Union had made no effort to help Guatemala's new president, Jacobo Arbenz Guzmán, who supported redistribution of land and threatened the interests of a powerful American corporation, United Fruit. In June, PBSUCCESS used misleading "disinformation," a force of Guatemalan exiles, and CIA-piloted bombing raids to persuade Arbenz Guzmán to resign.

More openly, Eisenhower intensified efforts to shape perceptions of American culture and values abroad. In 1953, the administration created the United States Information Agency (USIA), overseen by the State Department. Active in 76 countries by 1960, the agency published pamphlets, promoted the exchange of visitors with other nations, broadcast Voice of America radio around the world, and worked with the CIA on propaganda and psychological warfare. The growth of the USIA underscored the fact that the cold war was about culture and ideas, as well as about military power.

Avoiding War with the Communist Powers

Despite tough talk, the Eisenhower administration tried to avoid direct confrontation with the two major Communist powers, the People's Republic of China and the Soviet Union. Eisenhower knew he had to end the Korean conflict. As he promised in his 1952 campaign, Eisenhower traveled to Korea to end the military stalemate that ultimately killed 33,629 Americans. A cease-fire agreement in July 1953 left the United States without a victory and North and South Korea divided. It was, Eisenhower declared, "an acceptable solution."

Ending an old war with one Communist power, Eisenhower avoided a new conflict with the other. In October 1956, Hungarians, spurred on by American broadcasts, rose up against their pro-Soviet government. The Soviet Union sent troops to break the rebellion. Despite talk of "captive peoples" and "massive retaliation," Eisenhower did not intervene.

Fundamentally, Eisenhower would not break with Truman's policy of containment. Cautious about military confrontation with the Soviets and the Chinese, Eisenhower declined to unleash nuclear weapons that would "destroy civilization." Although he sent CIA agents to conduct covert operations, the president was more reluctant than Truman to send American soldiers into open battle.

At the same time, Eisenhower, like Truman, knew the cold war was an economic and political war, waged by foreign aid and propaganda. In front of a model American kitchen in Moscow in 1959, Vice President Richard Nixon and Soviet leader Nikita Khrushchev argued the merits of their two systems. Not surprisingly, Nixon turned this "Kitchen Debate" into a celebration of the prosperity and freedom of the consumer society.

The administration took modest steps to improve relations with the Soviets. Responding to the Soviets' interest in "peaceful coexistence," Eisenhower told the United Nations that he wanted to pursue disarmament and the peaceful use of atomic power. He proposed an "Atoms for Peace" plan in which an international agency would explore nonmilitary uses for nuclear materials. The Soviets dragged their feet.

In 1955 Eisenhower took one more step when he joined Khrushchev in Geneva for the first meeting between an American president and a Soviet leader since World War II. Eisenhower's proposal for "Open Skies"—a plan to allow each side to fly over the other's territory—sparked some optimism about better relations. That optimism ended by May 1960, when the Soviets shot down an American U-2 spy plane flying over the USSR. After the United States denied the affair, Khrushchev triumphantly produced the captured pilot, Francis Gary Powers, along with pieces of the plane. The rivalry would continue.

>> Popular Music as a Cold War Weapon

By the 1950s, music, like other forms of popular entertainment, had long served as a vehicle for spreading American culture around the world. It was only natural, then, for the United States government to make popular music a weapon in the cold war against Communism.

The State Department used jazz, a uniquely American improvised music, to sell a democratic image of the United States. In 1955, the Voice of America began broadcasting *Music U.S.A.*, hosted by Willis Conover, worldwide. "Jazz is a cross between total discipline and anarchy," Conover explained. "It's a musical reflection of America." Conover also believed that jazz, largely created by African Americans, "corrects the fiction that America is racist."

Music U.S.A. became a hit, reaching almost 30 million people in 80 countries. "Conover's daily two-hour musical program has won the United States more friends than any other activity," declared an Egyptian weekly in 1959. Conover saw the show's popularity as a sign of the spread of American values. "[P]eople in other countries love jazz because they love freedom," he observed. "Jazz also helps them to believe that America is the kind of country that they want to believe it is."

Washington sent well-known jazz musicians on international concert tours overseen by the State Department. The most popular touring jazzman was Louis "Satchel Mouth" Armstrong, who became known as "Ambassador Satch." Beginning in 1956, the African American trumpeter and singer won over white audiences in Europe and black audiences in Africa. "I feel at home in Africa," Armstrong proclaimed. "I'm African-descended down to the bone." "Through his superb jazz musicianship," a Kenyan newspaper wrote, "Satchmo has given expression to the often inarticulate feelings of his people, once oppressed, but now . . . moving rapidly towards full and equal citizenship of the great country he represents."

Armstrong's message and music disturbed the Soviet Union, whose leaders worried both about the impact of jazz around the world and on the loyalties of its own young people. Soviet composers, visiting the United States in 1959, denounced Armstrong's music as "vulgar" and "unnatural." When cheering throngs welcomed "this son of our African race" to the Congo in 1960, the Soviets charged that Armstrong was there only to "distract" the African nation from the reality of white European power.

Armstrong usually played his propaganda part to perfection. But during the Little Rock crisis in 1957, the goodwill ambassador rebelled against his role; he was outraged by white treatment of black students and by Eisenhower's reluctance to intervene. "The way they are treating my people in the South, the government can go to hell," Armstrong fumed. "It's getting so bad, a colored man hasn't got any country." Armstrong refused to represent the United States on a trip to Moscow. "The people over there ask me what's wrong with my country." He demanded, "What am I supposed to say?"

As the State Department discovered, jazz, in the person of Louis Armstrong, really was the sound of democratic freedom and therefore impossible to control completely. "[M]usic," Armstrong concluded, "is stronger than nations."

Crises in the Third World

Although Eisenhower worried most about Western Europe, his administration increasingly focused on the threat of Communist expansion in Africa, Asia, Latin America, and the Middle East. These relatively rural, unindustrialized regions, which made up the so-called third world, were enmeshed in the confrontation between the "first world" of industrialized non-Communist nations and the "second world" of industrialized Communist countries. Plagued by poverty, violence, and civil war, many third world societies struggled against imperial domination.

Under Khrushchev, the Soviet Union tried to exploit third world discontent and conflict. Anxious to preserve America's influence and access to natural resources, the Eisenhower administration countered Soviet moves with the tools of containment—aid, trade, and alliances. Eisenhower offered increased foreign aid and trade opportunities to third world countries. He pursued closer military ties, including defense pacts with the Philippines, South Korea, and Taiwan.

This approach was sorely tested in Southeast Asia. When Eisenhower took office in 1953, the United States supported France's war to hold on to Vietnam and its other Southeast Asian colonies. Despite vast American aid, the French could not defeat the nationalist forces of the Viet Minh, led by the Communist Ho Chi Minh and helped by the mainland Chinese. By 1954, the Viet Minh had surrounded French troops at Dien Bien Phu. Unwilling to fight another land war in Asia, Eisenhower refused to send American troops and rejected the use of atomic bombs. France surrendered in May.

In 1954, peace talks at Geneva produced an agreement to cut Vietnam, like Korea, in half. Ho Chi Minh's forces would stay north of the 17th parallel; his pro-French Vietnamese enemies would stay to the south. The agreement called for a popular election to unite Vietnam in 1956. Certain that Ho Chi Minh and the Communists would win the election, the United States refused to sign the agreement. The president feared that a Communist Vietnam would deprive the West of raw materials and encourage Communism elsewhere. Comparing the nations of Asia and the Pacific to "a row of dominoes," Eisenhower explained that the fall of the first domino—Vietnam—would lead to the fall of the rest, including Japan and Australia.

Instead, the Eisenhower administration worked to create an anti-Communist nation south of the 17th parallel. To protect South Vietnam, the United States joined with seven nations to create the Southeast Asia Treaty Organization (SEATO) in 1954 (see Map 27–1).

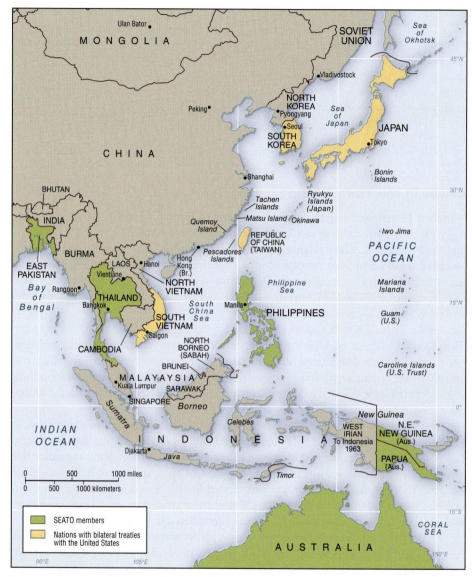

Map 27–1 **America's Cold War Alliances in Asia** Members of SEATO (the Southeast Asian Treaty Organization) and signers of other treaties with the United States. Through these pacts, the Eisenhower administration hoped to hold back the threat posed by Communist mainland China.

To ensure South Vietnam's loyalty, the Eisenhower administration backed Ngo Dinh Diem, an anti-Communist who established a corrupt, repressive government, with military advisers and hundreds of millions of dollars.

By thwarting the Geneva Accords and installing an unpopular regime in the South, Eisenhower ensured that Vietnam would be torn by civil war. In the short run, however, he had avoided war and seemingly stopped the Asian dominoes from falling.

Map 27–2 America's Cold War Alliances in the Middle East Located between the members of NATO and SEATO, the members of CENTO (the Central Treaty Organization) joined with the United States to deter the threat of international Communism sponsored by the Soviet Union to the north.

Eisenhower soon confronted another crisis in the Middle East. Gamal Abdel Nasser, who had seized power in Egypt in 1954, emerged as a forceful spokesman for Arab unity and nationalism. Fearing that Nasser would open the way for Soviet power in the region, John Foster Dulles withdrew an offer to aid the Egyptians. Nasser struck back by taking over the British- and French-owned Suez Canal in 1956. In retaliation, Britain and France, with Israel's cooperation, moved against Nasser. As Israeli troops entered Egypt in October, Britain and France prepared to take back the Suez Canal. Eisenhower, fearing the invasion would give the Soviets an excuse to move into the Middle East, threatened the British, French, and Israelis—U.S. allies—with economic sanctions. They soon withdrew.

The Suez crisis was a pivotal moment. Before a joint session of Congress in January 1957, Eisenhower promised that the U.S. would intervene to protect any Middle Eastern nation threatened by "power-hungry Communists." He implemented this "Eisenhower Doctrine" by sending troops to Lebanon the next year. In 1959, the United States joined with Turkey and Iran to create a Middle Eastern defense alliance known as the Central Treaty Organization (CENTO) for its geographical position between NATO and SEATO.

Eisenhower had helped to stabilize the Middle East and Southeast Asia temporarily, but he had also drawn the United States more deeply into these crisis-prone regions and increased the odds of future trouble. In the 1960s and 1970s, the United States would have to deal with this legacy.

Challenges to the Consumer Society

Along with crises abroad, American society confronted challenges at home. In different ways, a rebellious youth culture, the alienated beat movement, a nascent environmental movement, and the divisive civil rights struggle upset the stability of the Eisenhower era.

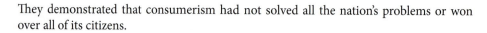

They demonstrated that consumerism had not solved all the nation's problems or won over all of its citizens.

Rebellious Youth

"Never in our 180-year history," declared *Collier's* magazine in 1957, "has the United States been so aware of—or confused about—its teenagers." In the 1950s, the emergence of a distinct youth culture, built around rock and roll, cars, comic books, and premarital sex, troubled many adults. The youth culture culminated a trend apparent since the 1920s and 1930s. As more and more teenagers attended high school, they were segregated in their own world and developed their own values and practices. In the 1950s, young people claimed rock and roll as their music. They wore blue jeans; they read comic books and teen magazines. Expressing their individuality, boys modified cars into customized "hot rods." Teens were attracted to alienated and rebellious movie characters, such as the troubled son played by James Dean in *Rebel Without a Cause* (1955) and the motorcycle-gang leader played by Marlon Brando in *The Wild One* (1953). Adults worried about teenage defiance and juvenile delinquency.

Many young people were rebellious, but not nearly as much as adults feared. Juvenile delinquency did not actually increase after World War II, and neither did rates of sexual intercourse among teenagers. Girls never played a strongly visible role in male-dominated youth culture. Most young people never questioned the political system, and youth culture exaggerated rather than rejected the values of adult, consumer society.

The early career of Elvis Presley illustrated the boundaries of youthful rebellion. Presley's appeal rested on an unsettling combination of rock-and-roll music and open sexuality. Presley's style—his sensual mouth, disheveled "duck's ass" haircut, and gyrating hips—amplified the music's sexuality.

Despite his appeal to teenagers, Presley was always polite and soft spoken and devoted to his parents. Buying a pink Cadillac and other luxury cars, he was caught up in the consumer culture. Like millions of other Americans, Presley joined the suburban migration when he bought his house, Graceland, on the outskirts of Memphis. He was a new version of the old American dream of upward mobility.

Still, many adults blamed Presley, rock and roll, and mass media for the spread of violence, lust, and degeneration among young Americans. One popular television program showed Presley only from the waist up. To get rid of blue jeans and other teenage fashions, high schools imposed dress codes. There was a crusade against comic books, teen magazines, and movies that were supposedly "brainwashing" teenagers. In well-publicized hearings from 1954 to 1956, the Senate's Subcommittee to Investigate Juvenile Delinquency focused attention on the corrupting power of the mass media.

The campaign against youth culture had little impact in a society of free speech and consumerism. Mass culture did not stop catering to teenagers with spending money. Many adults found youth culture appealing.

The Beat Movement

A smaller and older second group of rebels was much more critical of American society. The beat movement, which emerged in New York City in the 1940s, expressed a sense of both alienation and hope. The term "beat" referred to a feeling of exhaustion and also to a state of transcendence, the "beatific." Worn down by contemporary culture, the beats searched for a way beyond it.

Uptown at Columbia University and downtown in Greenwich Village, Allen Ginsberg, Jack Kerouac, John Clellon Holmes, William Burroughs, and others wanted, as one of them put it, "to emote, to soak up the world." Beats explored their sexuality, sampled mind-altering drugs, and pursued the spirituality of Eastern religions. In a society of bright colors, "beatniks" declared their alienation from consumerism by wearing black. Kerouac captured their spirit in his novel about a trip across America, *On the Road* (1957). In San Francisco, another center of beat culture, Allen Ginsberg published his long poem, "Howl" (1956), which gave voice to alienation: "I saw the best minds of my generation destroyed by madness, starving hysterical naked. . . ."

Though few in number, the beats attracted a great deal of attention with their dark vision of America. Their movement signaled a new dissatisfaction with consumer society, conventional sexual mores, and politics as usual.

The Rebirth of Environmentalism

A rebirth of environmental consciousness was also evidence of concern about consumerism. By the late 1950s, Americans were more concerned about the environment than at any time since the beginning of the twentieth century. The environmental threat was obvious in the cities. A well-publicized pall of smog seemed to hang perpetually over car-choked Los Angeles. Americans could no longer ignore the fact that their automobiles, the symbol of the consumer society, were polluting the air.

The environmental threat was obvious in the countryside, too. Even as they filled new suburban developments built on old farms, some Americans lamented the disappearance of open land. They began to criticize society's attitude toward the natural world. In the mid-1950s, environmentalists, led by the Sierra Club and the Wilderness Society, blocked construction of the Echo Park Dam in the upper Colorado River because it would have flooded a national park, the Dinosaur National Monument. A new environmental movement to protect wilderness lands emerged from the battle.

The Struggle for Civil Rights

The African American struggle for civil rights also challenged the Eisenhower era. By the 1950s, segregation was under increasingly effective attack in the courts and on the streets. Focusing on public schools, the NAACP assaulted the discriminatory legacy of the Supreme Court's *Plessy v. Ferguson* ruling of 1896 (see Chapter 20). In 1951 the NAACP's special counsel, Thurgood Marshall, combined five school lawsuits, including Oliver Brown's challenge to the constitutionality of a Kansas state law that allowed cities to segregate their schools. Because of the law, Brown's eight-year-old daughter, Linda, had to ride a bus 21 blocks to a "colored only" school, even though there was a "white only" school just three blocks from home. When the Brown case reached the Supreme Court in December 1952, Marshall attacked the *Plessy* argument that justified "separate but equal" facilities for whites and African Americans. Because of segregation, Marshall argued, Linda Brown and other African Americans received both an inferior education and a feeling of inferiority. He concluded that segregation violated the citizenship rights guaranteed by the Fourteenth Amendment.

In May 1954, the Court, led by new Chief Justice Earl Warren, handed down its ruling in *Brown v. Board of Education, Topeka, Kansas.* Overturning *Plessy,* the justices ruled unanimously that public school segregation was unconstitutional under the Fourteenth Amendment. "Separate but equal has no place," Warren announced. African Americans and white liberals were jubilant over what an African American newspaper called "a second emancipation proclamation." Marshall foresaw the end of school segregation before the close of the decade.

It did not work out that way. When the Supreme Court ruled on the enforcement of its decision in 1955, the justices turned to local school boards, dominated by whites, to carry out integration. Federal district courts were to oversee the process, which should occur with "all deliberate speed." School segregation would have to end, but not right away.

Taking heart from the enforcement ruling, many whites refused to give up Jim Crow. As one white southerner put it, a "reasonable time" for the end of segregation would be "one or two hundred years." In 1956, 101 congressmen signed a "Southern Manifesto" calling on their home states to reject the *Brown* ruling. Amid calls for massive resistance to desegregation, White Citizens' Councils formed to resist desegregation in southern states, some of which passed laws intended to stop school integration. There was violence, too. In October 1955, white Mississippians brutally killed Emmett Till, a 14-year-old black boy from Chicago, who had supposedly whistled at a white woman.

African Americans were ready to fight even harder against segregation. In Montgomery, Alabama, the NAACP wanted to test the state law that segregated the city's buses. On December 1, 1955, Rosa Parks, a 42-year-old African American tailor's assistant

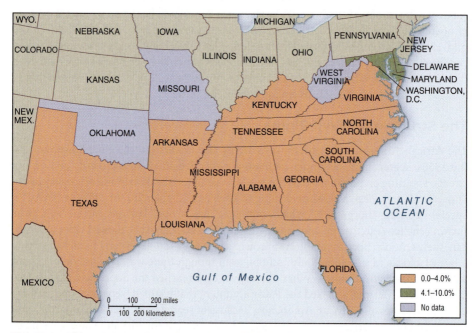

Map 27–3   African Americans Attending Schools with White Students in Southern and Border States, 1954 The small percentages indicate just how successfully segregation had separated the races before the Supreme Court ruled in *Brown v. Board of Education, Topeka, Kansas* in 1954.

An Unlikely Criminal Arrested for refusing to give up her bus seat to a white passenger, Rosa Parks poses for her official "mug shot" in December 1955.

and NAACP official "tired of giving in," boarded a bus to go home from work. Local custom required her to give her seat to a white passenger and move to the back of the bus, but when the bus driver told her to move, Parks refused. As she said, "my feet hurt." More than that, she wanted to find out "once and for all what rights I had as a human being and a citizen." The angry driver thought she had none; he had Parks arrested.

Seizing on Parks's arrest, African Americans began to boycott the bus system. Twenty-six-year-old Martin Luther King Jr., pastor of the Dexter Avenue Baptist Church, agreed to lead the boycott. The son of a noted Atlanta preacher, King was already developing a brilliant oratorical style and a philosophy of nonviolent protest against segregation.

The boycott met immediate resistance. The city indicted the leaders, and African American homes and churches were bombed. In November 1956, however, the U.S. Supreme Court ruled Alabama's bus-segregation law unconstitutional. By then, the boycott had cost the city dearly, and the white community had lost the will to resist. The city settled with the boycotters and agreed to integrate the buses. "We just rejoiced together," one of the boycotters remembered. "We had won self-respect."

Montgomery showed that a combination of local activism and federal intervention could overcome Jim Crow. It established a charismatic new leader with a powerful message and brought forward a new civil rights organization, the Southern Christian Leadership Conference. To one journalist, Montgomery "was the beginning of a flame that would go across America."

The flame did not travel easily. In 1957, the school board of Little Rock, Arkansas, accepted a federal court order to integrate Central High School, but in September the state's segregationist governor, Orval Faubus, called out National Guard troops to stop black students from enrolling. Even after meeting with Eisenhower, Faubus would not remove the troops. When he finally did, an angry mob of whites made it impossible for the African American students to stay. "Two, four, six, eight," cried the mob, "we ain't going to integrate."

Little Rock created a dilemma for the president. Not a believer in racial equality, Eisenhower wanted to avoid the divisive issue of civil rights. He privately opposed the *Brown* ruling and gave only mild support to the weak Civil Rights Act of 1957, which did not protect African Americans' right to vote. The president knew, however, that his government was being defied in Little Rock and humiliated around the world. So Eisenhower sent in troops of the Army's 101st Airborne. With that protection, nine African American students went to Central High.

Like Montgomery, Little Rock demonstrated that a combination of federal action, however reluctant, and African American courage could triumph. The Central High crisis showed, too, how the cold war helped tip the balance against segregation. Competing with the Soviets for support from the multiracial third world, no president could afford the embarrassment of racial inequality at home. Segregation and discrimination were, the president concluded, "troublesome beyond imagination."

An Uneasy Mood

Youth culture, the beat movement, the environmental movement, and the civil rights struggle brought an uneasy mood to America by the end of the 1950s. Many worried that the consumer society was flawed. Some intellectuals believed that "softheaded high living" had left the nation "cultureless." For the critic Lewis Mumford, automobiles were "fantastic and insolent chariots" and suburbs "a low-grade uniform environment from which escape is impossible." Consumerism itself could seem like a trap. In his best seller *The Hidden Persuaders* (1957), Vance Packard played on the fears that advertisers were manipulating Americans.

Americans were troubled, too, by signs of corruption in the consumer society. In 1958, they learned that record companies had paid Alan Freed and other disc jockeys to play particular records on the radio. The same year, they were shocked by revelations that TV quiz show contestants had secretly been given the answers to questions in advance.

Americans also wondered whether they could meet the challenge of the cold war. In October 1957, the Soviet Union sent *Sputnik*, the world's first satellite, into orbit, setting

off a wave of fear in the United States. If the Soviets could send up a satellite, they could be ahead in nuclear weapons and economic growth, too. Americans felt suddenly more vulnerable.

Sputnik intensified concerns about American education. A diverse and growing student population and rising parental demands had strained the nation's schools. Now Americans worried that the schools were not preparing children to compete with the Soviets in science and technol-

"The Helicopter Era" Cartoonist Herblock lampoons President Dwight Eisenhower's apparent lack of involvement in the nation's problems.

ogy. In 1958, Congress passed the National Defense Education Act. To win what Senator Lyndon Johnson called the "battle of brainpower," the measure promoted instruction in science, math, and foreign languages, supported construction of new schools, and offered loans and fellowships to students.

Sputnik forced Washington to accelerate the space program. The first U.S. satellite launch collapsed in flames—*Flopnik*, the press called it. In January 1958 the government successfully launched its first satellite, *Explorer I*. Later that year, Congress created the National Aeronautics and Space Administration (NASA) to coordinate space exploration. These initiatives did not completely wipe away Americans' worry that, as one magazine railed, "the whole kit and caboodle of our American way of life—missiles and toasters, our freedoms, fun, and foolishness—is about to go down the drain."

Eisenhower did little to change the national anxiety. Slowed by poor health, he seemed old and out of ideas. In 1960, he even had to create a Commission on National Goals to help figure out what the country should do. At the end of his term in January 1961, Eisenhower fed the uncertain mood with a somber farewell address. Noting that cold war spending had built up the military and the defense industry, he warned against allowing this "military-industrial complex" to gain too much power or "endanger our liberties or democratic processes." It was a stunning admission that the cold war might destroy rather than save democracy in America.

Eisenhower's difficulties were a sign of new stresses on American society. Most Americans were not about to give up the benefits of prosperity, but many worried whether consumerism and Modern Republicanism were enough to meet the challenges of the cold war world.

Conclusion

Along with the cold war, the triumph of consumerism dramatically affected the United States in the 1950s. The booming consumer economy gave Americans a new sense of security and affluence during the unsettling confrontation with Communism. Breaking with the past, they moved to the suburbs, had record numbers of children, bought televisions at E. J. Korvettes, and defined life as the pursuit of material pleasures. Consumerism helped promote homogeneity and conformity and spurred the victory of Dwight Eisenhower and his moderate approach to government. For a moment, it seemed as if America had achieved stability and harmony in a dangerous world, but that feeling did not last. At the close of the 1950s, many Americans wanted more for themselves and their country. They questioned whether consumer society could provide prosperity, democracy, and security for all its citizens. The next decade would offer an unsettling answer.

Review Questions

1. How did the consumer society of the 1950s differ from the modern culture of the 1920s?

2. Compare and contrast Modern Republicanism with the New Era and other Republican domestic policy programs of the 1920s to 1940s. Was Modern Republicanism a break with the party's past?

>> Timeline

▼**1947**
Levittown suburban development
Announcement of Truman Doctrine

▼**1948**
First McDonald's fast-food restaurant
Alfred Kinsey, *Sexual Behavior in the Human Male*

▼**1950**
Diners Club credit card

▼**1951**
UNIVAC 1 computer

▼**1952**
Dwight D. Eisenhower elected president

▼**1953**
First suburban E. J. Korvettes store
Korean cease-fire

▼**1954**
"Baby boom" birthrate over 4 million per year
Supreme Court school desegregation decision, *Brown v. Board of Education,*
   Topeka, Kansas
Army-McCarthy hearings
Creation of divided Vietnam in Geneva peace talks

▼**1955**
Formation of AFL-CIO

▼**1955–56**
Montgomery, Alabama, bus boycott

▼**1956**
National System of Defense Highways Act
William H. Whyte Jr., *The Organization Man*
Suez crisis
Reelection of President Eisenhower

▼**1957**
Eisenhower Doctrine
School desegregation crisis, Little Rock, Arkansas
Jack Kerouac, *On the Road*
Soviet *Sputnik* satellite launch

>> Timeline *continued*

▼1958
National Defense Education Act
TV quiz show scandals

▼1959
Alaska and Hawaii statehood
Nixon-Khrushchev "Kitchen Debate" in Moscow

▼1960
President Eisenhower's Commission on National Goals
Soviet downing of U.S. U-2 spy plane
John F. Kennedy elected president

▼1961
Eisenhower's farewell address on "military-industrial complex"

3. Why did the civil rights movement make progress in the 1950s?

4. What was Eisenhower and Dulles's strategy for fighting the cold war? Was it successful?

5. Why did social-class differences decrease after World War II? Did class still matter?

6. On balance, did the domestic and international events of the 1950s leave Americans more or less well off than before? Did the decade make American democracy stronger?

**For further review materials and resource information,
please visit www.oup.com/us/ofthepeople**

The Rise and Fall of the New Liberalism

28

1960–1968

AMERICAN PORTRAIT

....

>> Lt. Fred Downs

On the night of January 10, 1968, Second Lieutenant Fred Downs of the U.S. Army looked up at the stars over the coast of South Vietnam. Only 23, he was thousands of miles from the Indiana farm where he had grown up. His job now was to lead a platoon of American soldiers in the war to protect anti-Communist South Vietnam from Viet Cong insurgents and the North Vietnamese Army. Downs faced his duty with absolute confidence. "I knew we would never be beaten," he declared.

Still, the months in Vietnam had tested Downs severely. The hot sun "cooked" him by day, the rain drenched him by night, and leeches sucked his blood. He worried about stepping on land mines and booby traps. He worried whether he could trust the South Vietnamese. He worried whether his country was fighting the war the right way. Downs was wounded four times, but he put aside his worries and kept fighting.

Much of the time, Lt. Downs and his men went out hunting for the enemy on "Search and Destroy" missions. To his frustration, the Viet Cong and the North Vietnamese were hard to find. When he did get close to them, the result was a "deadly game of hide and seek." Downs shot and killed Viet Cong and North Vietnamese soldiers with his rifle. He stabbed a soldier to death in the throat with a bayonet. He killed women. He watched his own men die.

Despite all his experiences, Downs never lost his confidence. "My men thought I was invulnerable," he reported. "I did too." On the night of January 10 he saw "no clouds on my horizon." "Nothing would happen to me," he believed.

Fred Downs's story mirrored the experience of his country in the 1960s. With growing confidence in its wealth, power, and wisdom, the United States cast aside the cautious politics of the 1950s and began bold new projects at home and abroad, new solutions for the problems of consumer society, civil rights, and the cold war. Increasingly the nation turned to a vigorous liberalism that pledged to confront Communism abroad and reform life at home. To save South Vietnam, Lt. Downs and hundreds of

>> **AMERICAN PORTRAIT** *continued*

thousands of other soldiers were sent around the world. To create a "Great Society" in the United States, the government tried to wipe out poverty, heal race relations, protect consumers and the environment, and improve education and health care.

By 1968, these efforts had torn the nation apart. As the 1960s ended, the confidence that sustained Fred Downs and his country would be gone.

Common Threads

>> How did the prosperity of the 1950s shape the politics of the 1960s?

>> What was the impact of the civil rights movement on other groups?

>> How did the new liberalism, the new conservatism, and the New Left define democracy?

>> How did anti-Communism shape U.S. foreign policy?

>> How would desires for rights and worries about limited resources continue to shape American society beyond the 1960s?

New Ideas, New Leaders

The discontents at the close of the 1950s created an opportunity for new ideas and new leaders in the 1960s. Buoyed by the nation's power and prosperity, Americans faced the new decade with urgency and optimism. From right to left, activists, intellectuals, and politicians offered conflicting solutions for domestic and international problems.

Grassroots Activism for Civil Rights

By 1960, a new generation of African Americans was impatient with the slow, "deliberate speed" of the desegregation ordered by the Supreme Court in *Brown v. Board of Education* (see Chapter 27). Young blacks were ready to go beyond court cases and boycotts and try new tactics. In 1960, grassroots activists, committed to peaceful civil disobedience, spurred a wave of sit-ins and the formation of a new civil rights organization.

The sit-ins began in Greensboro, North Carolina. On February 1, four black male students from North Carolina Agricultural and Technical College politely insisted on being served at the whites-only lunch counter of the local Woolworth store. When the white waitress refused their order, the students, who would become known as the Greensboro 4, stayed all afternoon. Returning the next day with about 30 male and female colleagues, the four were again denied service. Soon hundreds of African American students, along with some white students, were besieging lunch counters. Under pressure, Woolworth and other large stores agreed to serve African Americans. "I felt," concluded Franklin Mc-Cain, one of the Greensboro 4, "as though I had gained my manhood."

The new tactic spread quickly across the South and North. There were wade-ins at whites-only beaches, kneel-ins at whites-only churches, and even paint-ins at whites-only art galleries. The demonstrations forced whites to open up facilities to black patrons and spawned a new organization, the Student Nonviolent Coordinating Committee (SNCC). The SNCC (pronounced "Snick") brought together white and African American young people eager to create "a social order permeated by love." Demonstrating that ordinary people could confront the powerful, the sit-ins energized the civil rights movement and inspired Americans to confront other problems.

The New Liberalism

Out of power during the 1950s, liberal intellectuals and politicians, mostly Democrats, had been forced to reconsider their ideas and plans. By the 1960s, the liberals were offering a fresh agenda that responded to the civil rights movement, consumerism, and the cold-war confrontation with Communism.

A powerful faith in economic growth drove the new liberalism. To meet its domestic and international challenges, the United States, liberals believed, had to expand its

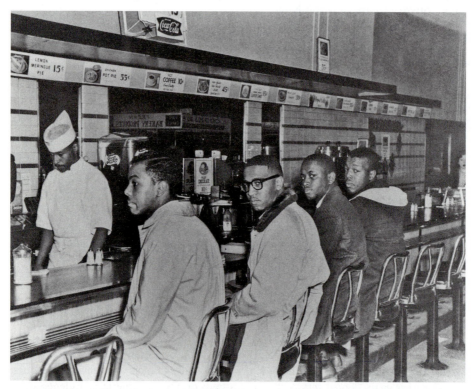

The Greensboro Sit-Ins, February 2, 1960 African American college students at the whites-only lunch counter of Woolworth on the second day of protest in Greensboro, North Carolina. The first two students from the left, Joseph McNeill and Franklin McCain, had helped start the sit-ins the day before.

economy more rapidly. By manipulating its budget, the federal government could keep the economy growing. The right amount of taxes and expenditures would ensure full employment, strong consumer demand, and a rising gross national product.

Growth alone would not make America great, the liberals cautioned. A society devoted mainly to piling up personal wealth and spending it on consumer goods was fundamentally flawed. Economic growth should create a better life for all Americans. Because the private sector could not solve pressing problems, the federal government had to deal actively with poverty, racial inequality, pollution, housing, education, world Communism, and other problems.

Like the liberals of the 1930s and 1940s (see Chapter 24), 1960s liberals believed in employing government to correct problems created or ignored by the private sector. Nevertheless, the new liberalism differed from the old in important ways. New Dealers had worried most of all about restoring prosperity in the Great Depression; the new liberals almost took prosperity for granted. The old liberals had feared that big business and class conflict posed dangers for the United States. Their successors generally saw racial divisions as the country's greatest domestic problem.

The New Conservatism

Conservatives had been out of power even longer than the liberals. In the 1930s, Herbert Hoover's failure to halt the Great Depression had discredited the conservative faith in minimalist government; then Hitler's aggression had undercut the conservative belief in isolationism.

By 1950, conservative ideas had already begun a quiet resurgence. In 1951, conservative intellectual William F. Buckley's book, *God and Man at Yale*, attacked his alma mater for its liberalism and denial of individualism. Two years later, Russell Kirk published *The Conservative Mind* to prove that there was a conservative tradition in America. In 1955, Buckley and Kirk founded the magazine *National Review* as a forum for conservative ideas, especially vigorous anti-Communism.

Conservatives soon had a new political hero in outspoken Senator Barry Goldwater of Arizona. With a western belief in individual freedom and fear of federal power, Goldwater was a blunt opponent of New Deal liberalism. A major general in the Air Force Reserve, he also advocated a more aggressive stance toward Communism.

By 1960, the growing conservative movement had its own younger generation of activists. That year, the Young Americans for Freedom gathered at Buckley's estate in Sharon, Connecticut, to adopt a manifesto. The Sharon Statement called for government to protect individual liberty by preserving economic freedom and maintaining a strong national defense.

The New Left

At the opposite end of the political spectrum, another young group, inspired by civil rights activism and troubled by student life on campus, rejected both conservatism and liberalism. By the early 1960s many students felt confined and oppressed in overcrowded and impersonal colleges and universities, where their lives were regulated by rules that governed eating in dining halls, drinking alcohol, keeping cars on campus, and socializing in dorm rooms. Female students were subject to particularly strict rules, including curfews.

Some of these youth created the New Left, a radical movement that attempted to create a more democratic nation. The key organization of the New Left was Students for a Democratic Society (SDS), which emerged in 1960 to produce "radical alternatives to the inadequate society of today." During its national convention at Port Huron, Michigan, in 1962, SDS approved an "Agenda for a New Generation." An answer to the Sharon Statement, the Port Huron Statement argued that American society denied people real choice and real power in their lives. The answer, SDS claimed, was "participatory democracy." The members of SDS did not believe that liberalism would promote real democracy in America. SDS did not expect much help from the old left of socialists and Communists, with their Marxist faith in the revolutionary power of the working class. Instead, students would lead the way by fighting for control of their schools. The message began to resonate: SDS membership rose from 2,500 to 10,000 in late1965.

The Presidential Election of 1960

As so often in American politics, new ideas did not immediately transform mainstream politics. The presidential election of 1960 offered a choice between a vaguely liberal Democratic future and a moderate Republican status quo. The Democratic nominee, Senator John F. Kennedy of Massachusetts, was open to the liberals' agenda and shared their optimism. Only 42 when he announced his candidacy, Kennedy was energetic and charismatic. Although he had compiled an undistinguished record in Congress, he exuded an enormous sense of promise.

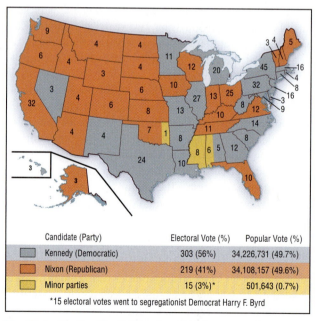

Candidate (Party)	Electoral Vote (%)	Popular Vote (%)
Kennedy (Democratic)	303 (56%)	34,226,731 (49.7%)
Nixon (Republican)	219 (41%)	34,108,157 (49.6%)
Minor parties	15 (3%)*	501,643 (0.7%)

*15 electoral votes went to segregationist Democrat Harry F. Byrd

Map 28–1 The Presidential Election, 1960 Democrat John F. Kennedy's clear margin in the electoral vote belies just how narrowly he outpolled Republican Richard M. Nixon in the popular vote.

Kennedy gave voice to that promise during the campaign. Americans, he explained, stood "on the edge of a New Frontier—the frontier of the 1960s—a frontier of unknown opportunities and paths, a frontier of unfulfilled hopes and threats." The United States needed to foster economic growth, rebuild slums, end poverty, improve education for the young, and enhance retirement for the old.

In contrast, Kennedy's Republican opponent, Vice President Richard Nixon of California, favored balanced budgets, limited government, and qualified acceptance of New Deal programs. Nixon embraced neither the bold programs and dynamic economic growth of the new liberalism nor the soaring individualism and strident anti-Communism of the new conservatives.

Despite Kennedy's stirring rhetoric and apparent triumph in televised debates, the election was the closest in history. Kennedy managed to keep much of the Democratic New Deal coalition of liberals, workers, and African Americans together, but he won by less than 120,000 votes (see Map 28–1). However narrowly, the voters had turned to a Democrat, influenced by liberal ideas, who was eager to explore the New Frontier.

The New Frontier
Style and Substance

Kennedy voiced the confident liberal faith in America's unlimited power and responsibility. "Let every nation know," he declared in his inaugural address in January 1961, "that we shall pay any price, bear any burden, meet any hardship, support any friend, oppose any foe to assure the survival and the success of liberty. This much we pledge—and more." He perfectly captured the optimistic spirit of the early 1960s.

So did the president's space program. The exploration of space, the ultimate frontier, seemed like an ideal occupation for confident Americans in the 1960s. Moreover, the space race allowed Kennedy to reject cautious Eisenhower policies and confront the Soviet challenge. In April 1961 the Soviet Union sent up the first astronaut to orbit Earth. The next month, NASA managed only to launch astronaut Alan Shepard for a brief, suborbital flight. Once again Americans feared "that the wave of the future is Russian."

Insistent on "beating the Soviets," the president boldly pledged to land "a man on the moon before the decade is out." Apollo, the moon project, got underway with 60,000 workers and billions of dollars. Meanwhile, in February 1962 astronaut John Glenn became the first American to orbit Earth. That year the United States launched Telstar, the first sophisticated communications satellite. The space program mixed practical achievements such as Telstar with more symbolic gestures such as manned space flights.

That mixture of style and substance epitomized the administration. The president maintained a dynamic image, but his administration, hampered by a weak mandate, did not venture too far out onto the liberal New Frontier.

For liberals, the persistence of poverty amid prosperity was a chief failure of the consumer society and a global embarrassment. Liberals argued that the government had to help the poor become productive workers; they contended that the battle against poverty should include improved housing, education, health, and job opportunities, as well as job training.

Kennedy supported some modest antipoverty measures. In 1961 he signed into law the Area Redevelopment Act to help revive depressed areas. He also signed the Omnibus

Housing Act to clear slum housing and renew inner cities. But these measures were not enough to wipe out poverty.

Civil Rights

Grassroots activism for civil rights posed a critical challenge for the Kennedy administration. In one place after another, attempts to break down segregation and promote African American voting met with resistance.

After the Supreme Court outlawed the segregation of interstate bus terminals, a small group of African American and white "Freedom Riders" traveled south on buses to test the decision in the spring of 1961. The Freedom Riders met with beatings from white citizens and harassment from local authorities. Only then did the Kennedy administration send federal marshals to protect them.

In 1961, when SNCC started a voter-registration drive in Mississippi, white people struck back. SNCC workers were beaten and shot. When SNCC tried to register black voters in Albany, Georgia, members of this Albany Movement were beaten and arrested. Martin Luther King Jr., leader of the Southern Christian Leadership Conference (SCLC), came to Albany and was arrested, too, but segregation still ruled in the city.

SNCC activists resented the lack of presidential support. Kennedy understood that racial inequality damaged the United States' image abroad, but he also knew that the civil rights issue could split the Democratic Party.

The defiance of southern whites gradually pushed Kennedy toward action. In 1962 the governor of Mississippi, Ross Barnett, disregarded a federal court order by preventing a black student from enrolling at the University of Mississippi. When federal marshals escorted the student, James Meredith, to school, white students pelted them with rocks and Molotov cocktails. After the rioting killed two people and wounded more than 100 marshals, Kennedy called in federal troops to stop the violence and allow Meredith to enroll.

Two confrontations in Alabama forced the president's hand in 1963. In April, Martin Luther King Jr. and the SCLC tried to end segregation in Birmingham, perhaps the most segregated city in America. The city's Public Safety Commissioner, Eugene "Bull" Connor, was a stereotypical racist white southern law enforcement officer. King and local allies planned to boycott department stores and overwhelm the jails with arrested protesters. In the next days, Connor's officers arrested demonstrators by the hundreds. Ignoring a judge's injunction against further protests, King ended up in solitary confinement. In a powerful statement, "Letter from Birmingham Jail," he rejected further patience: "We must come to see . . . that 'justice too long delayed is justice denied.'" With King out on bail, the SCLC pushed harder, with demonstrations by thousands of African American students.

Goaded by the new protests, Connor turned fire hoses on demonstrators, set dogs on them, and hit them with clubs. Shocking pictures of the scenes increased the pressure on the white leadership of Birmingham and on President Kennedy. The Justice Department arranged for a deal in which the SCLC gave up the demonstrations and local businesses gave up segregation and promised to hire African Americans. However, soon thereafter the Ku Klux Klan marched outside the city, and bombs went off at the home of King's brother and at SCLC headquarters. After African Americans rioted in the streets, Kennedy was forced to send federal troops to keep the peace.

A second confrontation in Alabama drew the president still deeper into the civil rights struggle. The segregationist governor, George Wallace, defied federal officials and tried to stop two black students from enrolling at the University of Alabama. In an eloquent televised address, Kennedy finally admitted that there was "a moral crisis" and called for sweeping civil rights legislation.

On August 28, a march on Washington brought together a crowd of nearly 200,000 people, including 50,000 whites, at the Lincoln Memorial to commemorate the 100th anniversary of the Emancipation Proclamation and to demand "jobs and freedom." Demonstrators joined hands to sing the stirring civil rights anthem, "We Shall Overcome." Martin Luther King Jr. moved the nation with his vision of racial harmony. "I have a dream," he said, "that one day . . . little black boys and black girls will be able to join with little white boys and white girls as sisters and brothers." King looked forward to "that day when . . . black men and white men, Jews and Gentiles, Protestants and Catholics, will be able to join hands and sing . . . 'Free at last! Free at last! Thank God Almighty, we are free at last!'"

Kennedy's address and the March on Washington marked a turning point. The surging grassroots movement for racial equality had created broad-based support for civil rights and finally forced the federal government to act.

Flexible Response and the Third World

Although Kennedy shared Eisenhower's commitment to containing Communism, Kennedy believed the nation could afford to spend more money on the military. He also abandoned the doctrine of massive retaliation, Eisenhower's threat to use nuclear weapons

"I Have a Dream" Martin Luther King Jr. at the Lincoln Memorial, Washington, D.C., August 28, 1963.

against any Soviet aggression. Kennedy preferred the strategy of flexible response, or the threat of different military options, not just nuclear weapons, to counter the Soviets. While spending generously on nuclear weapons, the Kennedy administration also built up conventional ground forces and Special Forces—the highly trained troops, known as Green Berets, who could fight in guerilla wars.

Kennedy was more willing than Eisenhower to intervene in the third world. This was partly a reflection of Kennedy's confidence about American power and partly a response to Soviet actions. In January 1961 Nikita Khrushchev announced Soviet support for "wars of national liberation," insurgencies against established governments in Asia, Africa, and Latin America.

To counter the appeal of Communism, Kennedy supported modernization for Africa, Asia, and Latin America; that is, the development of capitalist, democratic, independent, and anti-Communist regimes along the lines of the United States. In 1961, his administration created the Peace Corps to send young volunteers to promote literacy, public health, and agriculture around the world. The Peace Corps reflected not only the idealism and anti-Communism of the Kennedy years but also an arrogant sense of superiority. Not surprisingly, the organization was not always welcomed by the people it was supposed to help. To promote the modernization of Latin America, Kennedy announced the formation of the Alliance for Progress in 1961. Over the next eight years, this venture provided $20 billion for housing, health, education, and economic development in the Western Hemisphere.

The Kennedy administration sometimes helped to thwart third-world independence and democracy in the name of anti-Communism by intervening in the domestic affairs of supposedly independent countries. In the Republic of the Congo, the CIA engineered the election of an anti-Communist leader, and it secretly tried to manipulate elections in Chile, as well. The United States also backed antidemocratic, but anti-Communist, regimes in Argentina, Guatemala, Haiti, and Honduras.

Similarly, Kennedy wanted to bring down Fidel Castro, whose Cuban revolution was an example for the rest of Latin America. The president inherited a plan from the Eisenhower administration for a CIA-directed invasion of the island by anti-Communist Cuban exiles. To conceal U.S. responsibility, Kennedy canceled air cover to protect the invaders. As a result, nearly all 1,500 exiles who landed at the Bay of Pigs in April 1961 were killed or captured. Embarrassed, Kennedy turned to the CIA, which launched "Operation Mongoose," an unsuccessful secret campaign to kill or depose Castro. The Cuban leader, aware of the plot, declared himself a Communist and turned to the Soviets for help.

Two Confrontations with the Soviets

Kennedy faced two direct confrontations with the Soviet Union. In 1961, Khrushchev threatened to stop Western traffic into West Berlin, which was surrounded by Soviet-dominated East Germany. In response, Kennedy called up reserve troops, asked Congress to increase defense spending, and hinted at a preemptive nuclear strike against the Soviets. Khrushchev backed down, but the East German government built a barbed-wire and concrete fence between East Berlin and West Berlin. By halting the embarrassing flight of East Germans to freedom in West Berlin, the so-called Berlin Wall defused the crisis and became a symbol of cold war Europe, a visible "iron curtain" that separated Communists and non-Communists.

In 1962 Kennedy entered a more dangerous confrontation with the Soviet Union. On October 15 photos from a spy plane showed that the Soviets were building launch sites in Cuba for nuclear missiles that could strike the United States. On October 22, after tense secret meetings, Kennedy put ships in place to intercept Soviet vessels bound for Cuba. That night, a somber Kennedy told a television audience about the missiles and demanded their removal. Fearing a nuclear war, Americans waited for the Soviets' response. Khrushchev, unable to confront the United States in its own hemisphere, backed down. The Soviets withdrew the missiles in exchange for the removal of obsolete American missiles from Turkey.

The Cuban Missile Crisis both eased and intensified the cold war. Faced with a nuclear conflict, neither side found the prospect appealing. To ensure communication in a crisis, a teletype "hotline" was installed between the White House and the Kremlin. In 1963 the two powers also approved a Limited Test Ban Treaty halting above-ground tests of nuclear weapons, even as the Soviets and the Americans remained more determined to stand firm against each other.

Kennedy and Vietnam

Kennedy inherited a deteriorating situation in South Vietnam in 1961. Ngo Dinh Diem's anti-Communist government faced increasing attacks from the Viet Cong guerrillas determined to overthrow his regime. Diem also faced the Viet Cong's new political organization, the National Liberation Front, which was trying to mobilize his Communist and non-Communist opponents. In addition, he faced the continuing hostility of Ho Chi Minh's

The Tension of the Cuban Missile Crisis Customers in a store watch President John F. Kennedy address the nation, October 22, 1962.

Communist government in North Vietnam, which was secretly sending soldiers and supplies into South Vietnam.

Like Eisenhower, Kennedy tried to shore up the Diem government with financial aid and advisers. This included sending the Special Forces to train the South Vietnamese Army. Before Kennedy took office, there were 900 American troops filling noncombat roles in South Vietnam. By late 1963, there were more than 16,000. Despite this support, Diem's regime spiraled downward. His army could not stop the Viet Cong. A cold, unpopular ruler, he alienated his people. Losing confidence in Diem, the Kennedy administration did nothing to stop a military coup that resulted in his murder in November.

What Kennedy would have done next will never be known. On a trip to Dallas, Texas, on November 22, 1963, the president was shot while riding in an open limousine at 12:33 P.M. Two bullets tore through Kennedy's throat and skull, and doctors pronounced him dead half an hour later. That afternoon, police arrested Lee Harvey Oswald for the shooting. A quiet former Marine, Oswald had spent time in the Soviet Union. Two days later, as police transferred him from a jail, Oswald was shot and killed by Jack Ruby, the troubled owner of a local nightclub.

Americans were shocked and numbed. Some could only believe the assassination was the product of a dark conspiracy, but there was never proof of such a plot. The presidency of John Kennedy, little more than 1,000 days long, left a sad sense of unfulfilled promise. To many Americans, Kennedy's White House seemed like "Camelot," the seat of the mythical English King Arthur. The reality was less magical. Kennedy gave voice to the new liberalism, but he seldom translated liberal ideas into action. Some wanted to believe that Kennedy, if he had lived, would not have escalated the Vietnam War. Yet there was no compelling evidence that he intended to withdraw American troops.

The Great Society

After Kennedy's death, Lyndon B. Johnson and the Democratic-controlled Congress carried out most of the liberal agenda. A flood of new laws addressed poverty, race relations, consumer and environmental protection, education, and health care. At the same time, the liberal majority on the Supreme Court afforded new protections for individual rights. By the mid-1960s, the principles of the new liberalism, turned into law, were transforming American government and society.

Lyndon Johnson's Mandate

The new president, Lyndon Johnson, seemed far different from his slain predecessor. Born to modest circumstances in rural Texas, he had made his fortune largely through political connections. Never an eloquent public speaker or a charismatic figure, he was an especially effective legislator who knew how to bully and cajole Senate colleagues into a deal.

Still, there were fundamental similarities between Johnson and Kennedy. Both were products of the Democratic Party that had engineered the New Deal, won World War II, and fought the cold war. Both shared the liberals' expansive sense of American might. "Hell, we're the richest country in the world, the most powerful," Johnson declared. "We can do it all."

Johnson stressed continuity with his predecessor. Yet the situation had changed: Kennedy's death left Americans more willing to accept innovation. The presidential election of 1964 strengthened Johnson's mandate. The contest offered voters a clear choice between competing visions. Embracing the new liberalism, Johnson stood for activist government, growth economics, and civil rights. His Republican opponent, Barry Goldwater, stood unequivocally for the new conservatism. "We have gotten where we are," he declared, "not because of government, but in spite of government."

It was no contest. Democrats painted Goldwater as a dangerous radical who would gut popular programs and perhaps start a war. Appearing as a statesman and man of peace, Johnson won 61.1 percent of the popular vote, 44 states, and 486 electoral votes. Moreover, the Democrats increased their majorities in the House and Senate. It was a greater victory than Johnson's hero, Franklin Roosevelt, had ever enjoyed.

"Success Without Squalor"

With his mandate, Johnson moved to enact a legislative program that rivaled Roosevelt's New Deal. In May 1964, he had called for the creation of the "Great Society"—"a society of success without squalor, beauty without barrenness, works of genius without the wretchedness of poverty." To create that society, his administration pushed through liberal laws to wipe out poverty, end segregation, and enhance the quality of life for all Americans.

Johnson, like many Americans, was disturbed by the persistence of poverty: nearly one in five Americans was poor. Declaring "unconditional war on poverty," the administration won Congressional approval in 1964 of the Economic Opportunity Act, which created an independent federal agency, the Office of Economic Opportunity (OEO), to spend nearly $1 billion on antipoverty programs. The OEO managed Volunteers in Service to America (VISTA), whose workers taught literacy and other skills in impoverished areas. It ran the Job Corps, which taught job skills to poor youth, and implemented Community Action Programs (CAPs), which encouraged the urban poor to organize themselves. By supporting the "maximum feasible participation" of the poor, the CAPs, unlike other poverty programs, had the potential to redistribute power away from local officials.

In 1965 and 1966 Congress continued the war on several fronts. It established an expanded food stamp program and created Head Start, which provided early schooling, meals, and medical exams for impoverished preschool-aged children. To protect the rights of the poor, the Legal Services Program brought lawyers into slums. To improve urban life, the Model Cities Program targeted 63 cities for slum clearance and redevelopment. Congress also created the Department of Housing and Urban Development in 1965 and the Transportation Department in 1966 partly to help manage antipoverty programs.

To improve the quality of life, the Great Society took a major step toward national health insurance when Congress created Medicare in 1965. This program provided the elderly with coverage for doctors' bills, surgery, and hospitalization. Congress also created Medicaid to help the states provide medical care to the nonworking poor.

The Johnson administration confronted the growing issue of consumer protection. In 1965, Ralph Nader published a disturbing book, *Unsafe at Any Speed*, charging that car manufacturers cared more about style and sales than about safety and that executives at General Motors had ignored safety defects in the Chevrolet Corvair. General Motors attempted to discredit Nader rather than promise to improve the Corvair. In response,

Congress passed the National Traffic and Motor Vehicle Safety Act of 1966, which set the first federal safety standards for automobiles, and the Highway Safety Act, which required states to establish highway safety programs.

The president and Congress adopted the liberals' belief in using the federal government to support education. The Elementary and Secondary School Act of 1965 channeled $1.3 billion into school districts. The Higher Education Act of 1965 offered federally insured student loans.

The Great Society included programs for cultural enrichment. In 1965 Congress established the National Endowment for the Arts to fund the visual and performing arts and the National Endowment for the Humanities to support scholarly research. The Public Broadcasting Act of 1967 established the nonprofit Corporation for Public Broadcasting, which would support such commercial-free cultural and educational television shows as *Sesame Street*.

Protection of the environment was a natural issue for liberals. In 1962, the best-selling book *Silent Spring* sensitized Americans to the ecological threat posed by the consumer economy. The author, marine biologist Rachel Carson, warned that, like nuclear weapons, environmental contamination from pesticides threatened human survival.

During Johnson's presidency, more than 300 pieces of legislation led to the expenditure of more than $12 billion on environmental programs. In 1963 the Clean Air Act encouraged state and local governments to set up pollution control programs. Two years later, amendments established the first pollution emission standards for automobiles. The Air Quality Act of 1967 further strengthened federal authority to deal with air pollution. Meanwhile, the Water Quality Act of 1965 and the Clean Waters Restoration Act of 1966 enabled governments to fight water pollution. The Wilderness Act of 1964 created a system of lands protected from development.

Preserving Personal Freedom

The new liberalism contained a paradox: liberals wanted both to enhance the power of the federal government and to expand individual rights. Their concern for individual rights was apparent in their support for civil rights for African Americans and in a series of decisions by the Supreme Court, led by Chief Justice Earl Warren.

In *New York Times v. Sullivan* in 1964, the Supreme Court encouraged free speech by making it more difficult for public figures to sue news media for libel. In addition, two decisions protected the rights of people accused of crimes. In 1963 the court ruled in *Gideon v. Wainwright* that governments had to provide lawyers to poor felony defendants. Three years later, *Miranda v. Arizona* required police to inform individuals of their rights when they were arrested, including the right to remain silent and the right to an attorney.

The Warren Court also protected sexual and religious freedom. Throwing out a state law that banned the use of contraceptives in *Griswold v. Connecticut* in 1965, the court affirmed individuals' right to privacy and in effect kept government out of the bedroom. In *School District of Abington Township v. Schempp* (1963), the court prohibited state and local governments from requiring public school students to say the Lord's Prayer or read the Bible.

The Supreme Court's rulings were controversial. Some people charged that the court was "driving God out" of the classroom. Others believed that the court had gone too far to protect the rights of alleged criminals. Some conservatives demanded the impeachment of Chief Justice Warren. Through its rulings, the liberal majority on the court substantially increased individual freedom, but few people had yet thought much about the tension caused by expanding both individual rights and government power.

By 1967 the Great Society's programs added up to a major change in American democracy. Government claimed more authority than ever to manage many Americans' daily lives. The Great Society brought a massive expansion of the size, cost, and power of the federal government (see Table 28–1).

That expansion would be controversial for years to come. Some measures—Medicare in particular—proved to be enormously expensive. Conservatives did not welcome an enlarged federal government, and some corporations resented the regulation of business in the name of consumer protection. Despite these concerns, the attempts to improve the quality of life represented some of the major accomplishments of the new liberalism. The war on poverty was at least a partial success. Mainly because of an economic boom, the percentage of people living in poverty decreased to 13 percent by 1970. But 25 million Americans were still poor. Moreover, poverty was unevenly distributed. About a third of African Americans and a quarter of Americans of Spanish origin were impoverished as the 1970s began.

The Death of Jim Crow

Meanwhile, the battle for civil rights had become still more intense. In the 10 weeks after the Birmingham confrontation in 1963, 758 demonstrations led to 14,733 arrests across the United States. When a bomb killed four African American girls in a Baptist church in Birmingham in September, some African Americans rioted, and the police killed two more children.

The violence continued in 1964: CORE, SNCC, SCLC, and the NAACP had created the Council of Federated Organizations (COFO) to press for African American voting rights in Mississippi. Robert Moses, an African American schoolteacher, led the COFO crusade uniting young African American and white activists to register black voters and start "Freedom Schools" for African American children. The effort, known as Freedom Summer, met hostility from whites. Two white activists, Michael Schwerner and Andrew Goodman, and one African American activist, James Chaney, were found shot to death near Philadelphia, Mississippi. Eventually a white deputy sheriff, a local Klan leader,

 Table 28-1 Expanding the Federal Government, 1955–1970

Year	Civilian Employees (thous.)	Total Spending (millions)	Defense (millions)	Space (millions)	Health (millions)	Education and Manpower (millions)
1955	2,397	$68,509	$40,245	$74	$271	$573
1960	2,399	$92,223	$45,908	$401	$756	$1,060
1965	2,528	$118,430	$49,578	$5,091	$1,704	$1,284
1970	2,982	$196,588	$80,295	$3,749	$12,907	$1,289

Source: *Historical Statistics of the United States* (1976), II, 1102, 1116.

>> "The Long Cool Summer" of Greenville, Mississippi

The dramatic pictures of brave marchers, menacing dogs, ominous police, and murdered activists can make the civil rights movement seem like a continuously violent confrontation. But civil rights, like much social change, was also a more quiet process, a slow dance in which blacks and whites gradually, haltingly created and accepted a new, more democratic order. That was the case in Greenville, Mississippi, in the "Freedom Summer" of 1964, when civil rights workers fanned out across the state to ensure the voting rights of African Americans. Although there was turbulence and violence in much of the state, Greenville witnessed what the local newspaper, *The Delta Democrat-Times*, described as "The Long Cool Summer."

Like the rest of Mississippi, Greenville, a city of 41,000 in the rich cotton-growing delta, was segregated. Although African Americans made up half the population, they faced second-class social and economic status. "I don't like it," a young black man declared, "when the white man works an easy job for $25 a day and I work a mean one for $3." African Americans lived with second-class political status, too: thanks to literacy requirements and poll taxes, black voters had long been effectively disfranchised. Few African Americans were registered to vote; the city had no black elected officials.

Freedom Summer—the voting rights drive led by the Council of Federated Organizations (COFO), a coalition of leading civil rights groups—was intended to change that. In the spring of 1964, COFO's white and black activists moved into Greenville. The arrival of these outsiders, mostly in their 20s, touched off a wave of speculation and anxiety among the city's whites. The enactment of the federal Civil Rights Act of 1964, banning segregation, intensified fears of demonstrations, confrontations, and bloodshed. "There are many of us . . . who are today dismayed by the attitude, actions and statements of some of the young men and women who are temporarily within the state," declared the *Democrat-Times*. "At times it would appear that nothing less than a calculated attempt to provoke wholesale violence is their aim."

Despite these fears, local officials urged "patience and self-control." In fact, COFO's strategy focused not on demonstrations but on voter registration. "If you get the vote you don't have to shoot a gun," a COFO leader insisted. "You can pull a trigger with a vote and kill off a politician." To encourage black activism, COFO set up two summer "freedom schools" in Greenville.

In July, COFO began to bring African Americans to the county courthouse to register to vote. The first day, 100 took the preliminary registration test; the turnout was so large that 35 would-be voters were still outside when the office closed for the day. The next day, another 45 began the registration process. And so the COFO drive went on. "There was no sustained violence, no bombings, no riots, no murders and no unruly mass demonstrations," the *Democrat-Times* reported, ". . . rowdies of both races never felt free to follow the course tolerated in other state communities."

Why were the African Americans of Greenville able to begin reclaiming their democratic rights with so little upheaval? Certainly, the nonconfrontational tactics of COFO made a difference. The city's growth and relative prosperity probably made whites more secure about sharing power. At least some whites accepted that American democracy demanded the registration of African Americans. "This is their undeniable right," the *Democrat-Times* conceded, "and what they seek is entirely within the American political pattern." The paper also pointed out that Southern whites faced "inevitable changes" because of the federal government and the national civil rights movement; for many whites, it probably seemed pointless to disrupt the quiet lines of would-be black voters.

There was one final, ironic explanation for the long cool summer of Greenville. As the editor of the *Democrat-Times* noted, most of the city's whites didn't care enough to exercise their right to vote. The paper suggested that Greenville also needed a voting drive for whites "to make our democratic republic more truly democratic." Paradoxically, blacks won the vote in Greenville because whites cared so little about their own rights.

and five other whites were convicted of "violating the rights" of Chaney, Goodman, and Schwerner. The violence continued in Mississippi throughout Freedom Summer. Homes and churches were burned, and three more COFO workers were killed.

Lyndon Johnson could not escape the events in Mississippi. In the summer of 1964, the Mississippi Freedom Democratic Party (MFDP) sent a full delegation to the Democratic National Convention in Atlantic City, New Jersey. The MFDP delegates, including the eloquent Fannie Lou Hamer, hoped at least to share Mississippi's convention seats with the whites-only delegation. Hamer, the daughter of sharecroppers, had been jailed and beaten for trying to register African American voters. Afraid of alienating white southerners, Johnson offered the delegates two seats in the convention. "We didn't come all this way for no two seats," Hamer retorted. The MFDP delegation went away empty-handed.

Johnson and the Democratic Party were clearly not ready to share power with African American activists, but they were ready to end legalized segregation. In July, Congress adopted the Civil Rights Act, which outlawed racial discrimination in public places and also set up an Equal Employment Opportunity Commission (EEOC) to stop discrimination in hiring and promotion. Even the schools gradually became integrated. In 1964 hardly any African American students attended integrated schools; by 1972 nearly half of African American children did.

However, across the South, most African Americans still could not vote. In January 1965 the SCLC and SNCC tried to force the voting rights issue with protests in Selma, Alabama. Predictably, the demonstrations produced violent opposition and helpful publicity. The sight of state troopers using tear gas, cattle prods, and clubs on peaceful marchers built support for voting rights.

Seizing the moment, Johnson called for the end of disfranchisement, and Congress passed the Voting Rights Act of 1965. This powerful measure forced southern states to give up literacy tests used to disfranchise black voters and empowered federal officials to make sure that African Americans could register to vote. In three years, Mississippi saw African American registration increase from 6 percent to 44 percent of eligible voters.

Together with the Civil Rights Act of 1964, the Voting Rights Act transformed the South. These twin achievements of the civil rights movement and the Great Society effectively doomed Jim Crow and laid a foundation for African American political power. However, the struggle for racial equality was far from over.

The American War in Vietnam

The war in Vietnam was the decisive event for the new liberalism and the nation in the 1960s. American participation in the conflict reflected the liberals' determined anti-Communism and their boundless sense of power and responsibility. Driven by these beliefs, Johnson made the fateful decision to send American troops into battle in 1965. When the war did not go according to plan, Americans divided passionately over the conflict, and the economy faltered. By the end of 1967 the war was destroying the Great Society.

Johnson's Decision for War

Like Kennedy, Johnson was a committed cold warrior with an optimistic view of American power. He kept flexible response in place and was equally willing to undermine the independence of third-world countries. In 1965, Johnson sent 22,000 troops to the Dominican Republic to stop an increasingly violent struggle for political power. He violated the sovereignty of this Caribbean nation without obtaining evidence of a Communist threat and without consulting Latin American countries as required by treaty.

At first, Johnson followed Kennedy's policy in Vietnam. The new president believed in the domino theory, the idea that the fall of one country to Communism would lead to the fall of others. The president also felt he could not turn his back on commitments made by Kennedy, Eisenhower, and Truman. As one weak government followed another, Johnson sent more aid and advisers to South Vietnam and stepped up covert action against the North.

This secret activity helped Johnson get Congressional approval to act more aggressively. On August 2, 1964, a U.S. destroyer, the *Maddox*, was cruising a few miles off the coast of North Vietnam in the Gulf of Tonkin. When three North Vietnamese torpedo boats unsuccessfully attacked the *Maddox*, the American ship sank two of the boats and damaged a third. Two days later the *Maddox*, along with a second U.S. destroyer, fired at a nonexistent North Vietnamese attack. Johnson ordered retaliatory air strikes and asked Congress for the power to protect American military personnel. With only two dissenting votes, Congress approved what became known as the Tonkin Gulf Resolution, which gave the president the authority, without a declaration of war, to use military force to safeguard South Vietnam. Even though Johnson knew there had been no real threat to the United States, he had misled Congress to obtain a "blank check" to fight in Southeast Asia.

He soon cashed it. After American soldiers were killed in a Viet Cong attack on a U.S. base in February 1965, Johnson authorized air strikes against North Vietnam itself. In March the United States began Operation Rolling Thunder, a series of bombing raids on military targets in North Vietnam.

When the raids failed, Johnson had a disagreeable but clear choice. If he wanted to save both South Vietnam and his reputation, he had to commit ground troops to battle; otherwise, he would be blamed for the loss of South Vietnam to Communism. In July 1965, Johnson gave the order to send 180,000 soldiers to fight in South Vietnam without a declaration of war.

Johnson's decision was the ultimate expression of the new liberalism. The president went to war not only because he opposed Communism but also because he had faith that American wealth and wisdom could transform a weak, divided South Vietnam into a strong, united, modern nation. Although cautious about going to war, Johnson believed that the United States could afford to fight, and win, a war abroad and still build the Great Society at home. It was a fateful choice.

Fighting a Limited War

Johnson and his advisers believed the United States did not need all its power to save South Vietnam (see Map 28–2). Instead of another total war like World War II, Vietnam was to be a limited war in which the U.S. forces, led by General William Westmoreland, would use conventional weapons against military targets. The goal was not to take over territory through "unconditional surrender" but rather to kill enough enemy soldiers to persuade the North Vietnamese and the Viet Cong to give up. Relying on superior technology, Westmoreland expected the United States to prevail by the end of 1967.

Westmoreland's strategy turned out to be poorly suited to the realities of Vietnam. As Fred Downs discovered, the North Vietnamese and the Viet Cong usually escaped by hiding in tunnels, fleeing through the jungle, fighting mainly at night, or retreating into Cambodia, Laos, and North Vietnam. Their strategy was to live long enough for a frustrated U.S. military to leave South Vietnam.

American troops fought well. Yet at the close of 1967, too many North Vietnamese and Viet Cong were still alive and committed to the overthrow of South Vietnam. Meanwhile, 9,000 U.S. troops died in 1967 alone. Even with half a million troops in his command, Westmoreland had not won the war on schedule. He had not lost the war, either. But the United States was running out of time to win (see Table 28–2).

The War at Home

The war in Vietnam had a divisive impact back home. An impassioned antiwar movement, led by SDS and other student radicals, emerged to condemn American policy. Communism in Southeast Asia, they believed, did not pose a real threat to the United States. But the misguided cold war had led liberals to support an antidemocratic regime. The war also revealed how undemocratic America had become. Johnson, the New Left pointed out, had ignored the Constitution by sending troops into battle without a declaration of war. In addition, the selective service law was forcing a repugnant choice on young men: they could either fight this illegal war or obtain deferments to stay in school and prepare for empty lives as corporate employees in the consumer society.

Map 28-2 America's War in Vietnam, 1965–1968 The many military bases suggest how much power the United States had to commit to South Vietnam; the many major battles show how hard American troops had to fight to protect the South Vietnamese regime from the Viet Cong and from the North Vietnamese soldiers who traveled the Ho Chi Minh Trail.

Table 28-2 The Escalating War in Vietnam, 1960–1968

Year	U.S. Troops	U.S. Battle Deaths	S. Vietnamese Battle Deaths	N. Vietnamese and Viet Cong Battle Deaths (estimated)
1961	3,164	11	(three-year	12,000
1962	11,326	31	total =	21,000
1963	16,263	78	13,985	21,000
1964	23,310	147	7,457	17,000
1965	184,000	1,369	11,403	35,382
1966	385,000	5,008	11,953	55,524
1967	486,000	9,378	12,716	88,104
1968	536,000	14,589	27,915	181,149

Sources: Michael Clodfelter, *Vietnam in Military Statistics*, 46, 57, 209 and 258; Fox Butterfield, ed., *Vietnam War Almanac*, 50, 54, 57, 64, 102, 132, 158, 192; Shelby Stanton, ed., *Vietnam Order of Battle*, 333.

A growing number of liberals and Democrats shared at least some of the radicals' analysis. These "doves" acknowledged that the United States was backing an antidemocratic government in a brutal and apparently unnecessary war. The conflict appeared to be a civil war rather than some plot to expand Soviet or Chinese influence. Meanwhile, the war had shattered many liberals' and Democrats' overconfident view of the Great Society. The United States, confessed Senator J. William Fulbright of Arkansas in 1966, was a "sick society" suffering from an "arrogance of power."

Some African Americans viewed the conflict as a painful illustration of American racism. A disproportionate number of poor African Americans, unable to go to college and avoid the draft, were being sent to kill nonwhites abroad on behalf of a racist United States. First the SNCC and then Martin Luther King Jr. condemned the war. Refusing to be drafted, boxer Muhammad Ali was sentenced to jail and stripped of his championship in 1967.

The growing opposition to the war produced large, angry demonstrations. In 1965 students and faculty staged "teach-ins" at college campuses to question American policy in Vietnam. In April, 20,000 people gathered at the Washington Monument to protest the war. Some young men risked jail by returning or burning their draft cards. On campuses, students protested the presence of recruiters for defense contractors. In October 1967 during Stop the Draft Week, radicals in Oakland, California, tried to shut down an Army draft induction center, fought with police, and briefly took over a twenty-five-square-block area of the city. Meanwhile, nearly 100,000 people rallied in Washington, D.C., to protest the war.

Despite the protests, most Americans supported the war. To many people, the demonstrators were unpatriotic. "America—Love It or Leave It," read a popular bumper sticker. "Hawks," mostly conservative Republicans and Democrats, wanted Johnson to fight harder. Nevertheless, by October 1967 support for the war in one public opinion poll had fallen to 58 percent, while only 28 percent approved of the war.

Bad economic news contributed to the public mood. Massive government spending for the war and the Great Society had overstimulated the economy. With jobs plentiful, strong consumer demand drove up prices, which in turn put upward pressure on wages. Anxious about inflation, the Federal Reserve shrunk the money supply, making it harder for businesses to get loans. When interest rates reached their highest levels since the 1920s, there were fears of a financial panic.

By the end of 1967 the war had put enormous stress on the Great Society. It undermined liberals' commitment to anti-Communism and their confidence in American power and wisdom. By dividing the nation, the conflict also undermined support for the Great Society. By weakening the economy, furthermore, the Vietnam War made it harder to pay for the Great Society. The United States could not, as Johnson believed, "do it all." The new liberalism had reached its crisis.

The Great Society Comes Apart

Even as Congress enacted the liberals' agenda, many Americans were expressing new dissatisfactions that liberalism could not accommodate. The Black Power movement, the youth rebellion, and a reborn women's movement exposed the limits of the liberal vision. In 1968 the strain of new demands, the Vietnam War, and economic realities tore apart the Great Society and destroyed the fortunes of Lyndon Johnson, the Democratic Party, and the new liberalism.

The Emergence of Black Power

For many African Americans, the Great Society's response to racial inequality was too slow and too weak. Even as the civil rights movement reached its climax, a wave of more than 300 race riots from 1964 to 1969 dramatized the gap between the promise of the Great Society and the reality of life in black America. When a white policeman shot a 15-year-old African American in Harlem in July 1964, angry African Americans burned and looted buildings. In August 1965 friction between white police and African American citizens touched off a riot in the poor Watts section of Los Angeles. In five days more than 1,000 fires burned, and 34 people died. The wave of riots peaked in Detroit in July 1967 when 43 people died (see Map 28–3).

To many, the riots were, in the words of an official report on Watts, "senseless," but the disturbances flowed from real frustrations. Despite successful challenges to legalized segregation in the South, African Americans still lived with poverty and discrimination all across the country. Northern cities, the center of the riots, had been largely ignored by Martin Luther King Jr. and other civil rights leaders. The riots signaled that the civil rights movement and the new liberalism, for all their accomplishments, had not addressed some of the most difficult problems of racial inequality.

For years King and other activists had relied on nonviolent demonstrations and ties to white liberals to achieve integration, but that approach proved ineffective in the North. In 1965, King joined marches in Chicago protesting the de facto segregation of the city's schools. King faced the determined opposition of Mayor Richard Daley. Reluctant to challenge the powerful political boss, the Johnson administration did not give King real support. In 1966, King returned to lead the "Chicago Movement" to wipe out slums and win access to better housing in white neighborhoods. "Go back to Africa," white demonstrators chanted. Daley accepted a compromise on fair housing but repudiated it as soon as

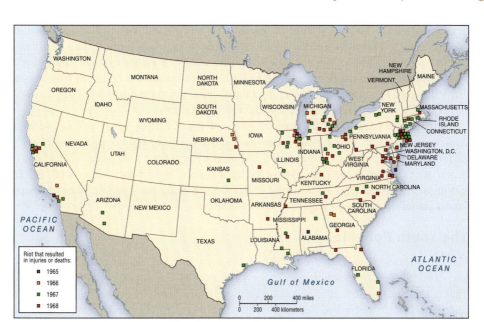

Map 28–3   Race Riots, 1965–1968 The clusters of riots in the Northeast, Midwest, and California emphasize that race was not just a southern issue in the 1960s. *Mark C. Carnes et al.,* Mapping America's Past, *p. 217*

King left town. Under the leadership of 24-year-old Jesse Jackson, Operation Breadbasket threatened demonstrations and boycotts against businesses that refused to hire African Americans. The project produced few results; King's nonviolent tactics had failed.

African Americans already had the example of a different approach to the problem of black-white relations. The Nation of Islam believed that whites were devils and African Americans were God's chosen people. The Black Muslims, as they were known, preached separation of the races and the self-reliance of African Americans. One of the Muslims' most powerful preachers was Malcolm X, a former pimp, drug pusher, and convict who angrily rejected integration and nonviolence. Malcolm X moderated his views before being gunned down, apparently by Muslims, in 1965. But he was best known for his militant call "for the freedom of the 22 million Afro-Americans by any means necessary."

By the mid-1960s, many African Americans were willing to follow at least some of Malcolm X's example. Rejecting integration, they now asserted a separate African American identity that declared, "Black is beautiful." Some African Americans wore African robes and dashikis, explored African language and art, and observed the holiday of Kwanzaa, based on an African harvest festival. Instead of working with white liberals and depending on the federal government, some African American activists insisted that blacks create their own institutions. In 1966, SNCC ousted its white members.

In rejecting nonviolence and integration, a number of African American activists adopted a more militant stance. "What we gonna start saying now is Black Power!" Stokely Carmichael told a rally in Mississippi. The new slogan had different meanings for different people. The most radical interpretation came from the Black Panthers, who were first organized in Oakland, California, by Huey P. Newton and Bobby Seale. Dressed in black clothes and black berets, the Panthers armed themselves to protect their neighborhoods from white police. Newton, admiringly described by an associate as "the baddest motherfucker ever to step foot inside of history," went to jail after a shootout with police. The Panthers also founded schools and promoted peaceful community activism, but they were best known in the media for their aura of violent militance.

Particularly because of the violent image of the Panthers, many people, African American and white, were hostile to the new slogan. For King and his allies, Black Power all too obviously meant repudiation of nonviolent integration. For many whites, Black Power stirred fears of violence. For white leaders such as Richard Daley, Black Power meant giving up political authority to African Americans. For Lyndon Johnson, Black Power obviously meant a rejection of his Great Society.

The Youth Rebellion

The anti-Vietnam War movement was part of a broader rebellion against adult authority and expectations. The battle began at the University of California at Berkeley in 1964. That fall, the university's administration banned political speaking and organizing at the one street corner where had been allowed. When a civil rights activist was arrested for defying the ban in October, hundreds of students sat down around the police cars, trapping the officers for 32 hours. After the stand-off, students created the Free Speech Movement (FSM) to pursue greater student involvement in the educational process. When the university refused to accept that demand, students took over the main administration building. Speaking that day, the student leader Mario Savio reflected the ideas of the New Left. "We have an autocracy which runs this university," he exclaimed. "[W]e're a bunch of raw material[s] that . . . don't mean to end up being bought by some clients of the University, be they the government, be they industry, be they organized labor, be they anyone! We're human beings!" The administration eventually succumbed to faculty protests and a student boycott of classes and agreed to new rules on free speech.

Americans had never seen anything quite like the Berkeley protests. Here were privileged students condemning society, storming a building, and being dragged off by the police. Many people were infuriated; some younger Americans were inspired.

As campus activism flourished, young people were also creating the rebellious lifestyle that became known as the "counterculture." Less politically oriented than the New Left, the counterculture challenged conventional social values. By the mid-1960s, many younger Americans were condemning conformity, careerism, materialism, and sexual repression as they groped toward an alternative lifestyle.

The counterculture rested on the enjoyment of rock music, drugs, and sexual freedom. Beginning in 1964, the sudden popularity of the Beatles, the Rolling Stones, and other British bands brought back a rebellious note to rock and roll. The Beatles' irreverent attitude toward authority, symbolized by their long hair, helped create "Beatlemania" in the United States. Rock also became more socially and politically conscious in the 1960s. Bob Dylan, Simon and Garfunkel, and other musicians rooted in folk music sang about racism, nuclear weapons, and other issues.

Rock music often sang of the virtues of drugs and sex. The use of marijuana, the hallucinogen LSD, and other drugs increased during the 1960s as a way of flouting adult

Mario Savio A crowd estimated at 3,500 gathers outside an administration building at the University of California, Berkeley, for a protest sponsored by the Free Speech Movement, led by Mario Savio (center), January 1965.

convention and escaping everyday reality for a more liberated consciousness. Sex offered a similar mix of pleasure and defiance. On campuses across the country, students demanded greater freedom, including the repeal of rules that restricted the mixing of male and female students in dorms. By the end of the decade, many students were living together before marriage.

Many young people hoped that the counterculture would weave sex, drugs, and rock into a new lifestyle. Novelist Ken Kesey joined with his followers, the Merry Pranksters, to set up a commune, complete with "Screw Shack," outside San Francisco. By 1965 Kesey had created the "acid test," which fused drugs, rock, and light shows into a multimedia experience and helped establish the popularity of "acid rock," the "San Francisco sound" of the Jefferson Airplane and the Grateful Dead.

The purest form of the countercultural lifestyle was created by the hippies, who appeared in the mid-1960s. Hippie culture centered in the Haight-Ashbury section of San Francisco. Rejecting materialism and consumerism, hippies celebrated free expression and free love. They wanted to replace capitalism, competition, and aggression with cooperation and community. One group of hippies, the Diggers, gave away clothes and food and staged the first "Human Be-In" at Golden Gate Park "to shower the country with waves of ecstasy and purification."

The power of youth rebellion was was easy to exaggerate. There were not many full-time hippies. The countercultural lifestyle quickly became conformist consumerism, defined by the right clothes and records.

The counterculture also had roots in the orthodox culture it attacked. By the close of the 1950s, adults themselves had become ambivalent about consumerism, conventional morality, and institutional authority. Sexual freedom for youth was encouraged partly by the greater sexual openness of mainstream culture, the Supreme Court's *Griswold* decision, and the introduction of the oral contraceptive (the "pill") in 1960. Americans chafed at the authority of religious denominations. The "pop art" paintings of Andy Warhol and Roy Lichtenstein, the productions of the Living Theater, the essays of Susan Sontag, and the novels of Thomas Pynchon broke with formal, artistic conventions.

Nevertheless, the counterculture was a disruptive force in the 1960s. Like the Black Panthers, hippies deeply influenced young people and adults and encouraged Americans to question conventional values and authority and seek a freer way of life.

The Rebirth of the Women's Movement

By the 1960s American women were reacting against the difficult social roles enforced on them after World War II. More women than ever went to college, but they were not expected to pursue long-term careers. More women than ever worked outside the home, but they were still expected to devote themselves to home and family. Women also had to put up with the continuing double standard of sexual behavior, which granted men more freedom to seek sexual gratification outside marriage. Women began to question their second-class status. In part, they were inspired by the example of the civil rights movement.

Two best-selling books reflected these complaints. In *The Feminine Mystique* (1963), Betty Friedan described "the problem that has no name," the growing frustration of educated, middle-class wives and mothers who had subordinated their own aspirations to the needs of men. Meanwhile, Helen Gurley Brown rejected unequal sexual opportunities in *Sex and the Single Girl* (1962). Neither Friedan nor Brown challenged male sexual ethics or male careerism. Instead, both wanted equal opportunity for women, in and out of marriage. Brown explained, coyly, that "nice, single girls do."

Women's complaints received attention but little action from men. In 1961 Kennedy appointed the Presidential Commission on the Status of Women, chaired by Eleanor Roosevelt. The commission's cautious report, *American Women*, documented gender discrimination but reaffirmed women's domestic role. In 1963 Congress passed the Equal Pay Act, which mandated the same pay for men and women who did the same work, but the measure, full of loopholes, had little impact. . A year later, Title VII, a provision of the Civil Rights Act of 1964, prohibited employers from discriminating on the basis of sex in hiring and compensation. Yet the EEOC did little to enforce the law.

In 1966 Betty Friedan and a handful of other women, angry at the inaction of the EEOC, formed the National Organization for Women (NOW). Although frustrated with the Great Society, Friedan and the founders of NOW expressed essentially liberal values. They saw NOW as "a civil rights organization" and wrote a women's "Bill of Rights" that focused on government action to provide rights and opportunities. NOW also demanded access to contraception and abortion.

NOW's platform was too radical for many women and not radical enough for others. Some younger women, particularly activists in the civil rights movement and the New Left, wanted more than liberal solutions to their problems. By the fall of 1967, activists were forming new groups dedicated to "women's liberation." Influenced by the New Left, radical feminists blamed the capitalist system for the oppression of women, but a growing number of radicals saw men as the problem. Like African Americans in the Black Power movement, radical women talked less about rights and more about power. Their slogan was "Sisterhood Is Powerful!" Radical feminists also rejected collaboration with male liberal politicians.

Few in number, radical feminists nevertheless commanded public attention. In September 1968 New York Radical Women organized a protest against the annual Miss America pageant in Atlantic City, New Jersey. The pageant, they said, was an act of "thought control" intended "to make women oppressed and men oppressors; to enslave us all the more in high-heeled, low-status roles." The protesters threw bras, girdles, makeup, and other "women-garbage" into a "Freedom Trash Can." Then they crowned a sheep "Miss America." Not surprisingly, men and many women were generally uncomfortable with radical feminism. Onlookers at the Miss America protest called the women "lesbians" and "screwy, frustrated women."

Conservative Backlash

The rebellions against the Great Society strengthened the conservative movement. Just two years after humiliating defeat in the presidential election of 1964, conservatives won new national prominence. Two politicians became focal points for many Americans' resentment against feminism, civil rights and Black Power, the counterculture and the antiwar movement, and the new liberalism.

George Wallace, former governor of Alabama, increasingly combined his hostility to civil rights and federal power with a populist appeal to working-class and middle-class whites. In 1964, he ran for the Democratic presidential nomination, calling for "law and order." Encouraged by his success in Northern primaries that year, Wallace prepared to mount an independent campaign aimed at the "average man—your taxi driver, your steel and textile worker" in 1968. Now he played on anger over the youth rebellion and the antiwar movement, as well as the civil rights movement. "If I ever get to be President and any of these demonstrators lay down in front of my car," Wallace vowed, "it'll be the last car they ever lay down in front of."

Meanwhile, former actor Ronald Reagan became a major conservative force in the Republican Party. A lifelong liberal Democrat, he had moved to the right and supported Goldwater in 1964. Two years later, Reagan ran for governor of California, vowing to "clean up the mess at Berkeley" with all its "Beatniks, radicals and filthy speech advocates" and its "sexual orgies so vile I cannot describe them." He opposed high taxes, Medicaid, and other liberal activism and favored escalation of the war in Vietnam.

1968: A Tumultuous Year

In 1968 the stresses and strains of the Great Society produced the most tumultuous year in the United States since World War II. In January, the Viet Cong and North Vietnamese launched bold, sometimes suicidal attacks all over South Vietnam on the first day of Tet, the Vietnamese new year. Although U.S. and South Vietnamese forces inflicted punishing losses on the attackers, the Tet Offensive shocked Americans. If the United States was

>> International Student Protest, 1968

The unrest had built on campus almost from the moment it opened in 1964. Many students hated the sterile, modern buildings, erected in the midst of a big-city slum. They also chafed at the many rules: no cooking in the dorms, no changes to the furniture, no males in females' rooms. The campus represented, one student critic complained, "an assembly-line conception of educational organization." As the student body grew from 2,000 to more than 12,000 by the fall of 1967, the Vietnam War escalated half a world away. When six local leaders of the antiwar movement were arrested, radical students rushed into the university administration building and occupied the dean's office.

The protest took place not in the United States but on the suburban Nanterre campus of the University of Paris. The student movement of the 1960s was, in fact, a global phenomenon. In Europe, Asia, and Latin America, as well as the United States, mostly middle-class students criticized the authority of universities and governments, demanded more freedom, and condemned the Vietnam War. The wave of protest surged and reached its crest in the spring of 1968. In Western Europe, even in authoritarian, pro-Soviet Eastern Europe, students protested against universities and police. In Japan, students protested the Vietnam War. In Brazil, students confronted their universities' rigid governance and the nation's repressive military regime.

There were significant differences among these protest movements. In the United States, the New Left rejected the old left and did not see organized labor as an ally. In Western Europe, students were influenced by socialism and eager to make common cause with workers and unions. In France, the result was a general strike of students and workers unlike anything seen in the United States. While American protesters seldom criticized the Soviet Union, East European students condemned their own Communist governments and the USSR.

Nevertheless, important commonalities united the movements. They generally shared origins in uneasiness about the cold war and the repressiveness of modern, bureaucratized society, dominated by big organizations. The movements reflected a powerful yearning for freedom and free expression. The simultaneity of these largely separate national protests was a product of rapid communication in this age of satellites and television: students learned quickly what was going on elsewhere around the globe. The rise of student movements was a reminder, too, of the global influence of the United States: America's war in Vietnam angered students abroad, and America's student movement set the example for protest around the world.

Finally, the international protests produced a common reaction—a frightened backlash from educators and other authorities. Tear gas, water hoses, and clubs were common sights in 1968. As in the United States, the result of protest was often the triumph of conservatism and the status quo. The harshest backlash came in Czechoslovakia: the Soviets invaded, killed and wounded more than seven hundred, and ended any loosening of authority. But in the long run, the international student movements also signaled a persisting, even growing, demand for freedom and democracy in the face of great organizations and worldwide superpower competition.

winning the war, how could the North Vietnamese and the Viet Cong have struck so daringly? More Americans now began to believe the war was unwinnable.

The Tet Offensive doomed Johnson's increasingly troubled administration. The president needed to send reinforcements to Vietnam, but he knew public opinion would oppose the move. As it was, he could not even pay for more troops. The economy would no longer support both the war and the Great Society. The political situation was bad, too. On March 12 Senator Eugene McCarthy of Minnesota, a longshot antiwar candidate with little money, nearly beat Johnson in New Hampshire's primary. Four days later, Senator Robert Kennedy of New York, the younger brother of John Kennedy, announced his own candidacy for the nomination. The charismatic Kennedy, opposed to the war, would be a formidable opponent. Besieged by the war, the economy, and the campaign, Johnson went on television the night of March 31. He announced a halt to the bombing of much of North Vietnam and indicated his willingness to talk peace with the North Vietnamese. He then announced that he would not run again for president.

Johnson painfully accepted new limits to the Great Society. Despite liberal pressure, Johnson did not have the money or the clout for new welfare programs, new initiatives to improve race relations, or even much of the space program, that symbol of liberal dreams. The Great Society was coming back down to earth.

Meanwhile, the upheaval and violence tore the nation. In the first six months of 1968, students demonstrated

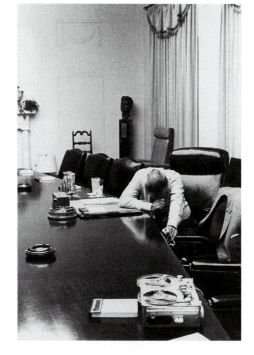

The Anguish of Vietnam President Lyndon Johnson listens to a tape-recorded report on the state of the American effort in South Vietnam, 1968.

at 101 colleges and universities. On April 4, a white man assassinated Martin Luther King Jr. in Memphis, Tennessee, where he had gone to support striking sanitation workers. King's assassination set off riots in more than 100 cities. Forty-one African Americans and five whites died.

The violence soon spread to the presidential campaign. After winning the California Democratic primary on the evening of June 5, Robert Kennedy was shot in a Los Angeles hotel by Sirhan Sirhan, a troubled Palestinian. Kennedy's death the next morning left McCarthy to contest the nomination with Vice President Hubert Humphrey, who still supported the Vietnam war. Humphrey won the nomination at the Democratic convention in Chicago in August, but the party was deeply divided. Outside the convention hall, Mayor Daley's police battled in the streets with antiwar demonstrators.

The Republican Party nominated Richard Nixon, who had lost to John Kennedy in 1960. A critic of the Great Society, Nixon promised to end the war and unify the country. Like the more conservative Reagan and Wallace, Nixon tried to exploit social divisions with promises to speak for "the forgotten Americans, the nonshouters, the nondemonstrators."

Unlike 1960, Nixon won this time. Although Humphrey made it close by repudiating Johnson's Vietnam policy, the vice president could not overcome the troubles of the Great Society. Nixon, running strongly in every region, attracted 43.4 percent of the popular vote to Humphrey's 42.7 percent and Wallace's 13.5 percent. Although the Democrats retained control of Congress, the party's eight-year hold on the White House had been broken.

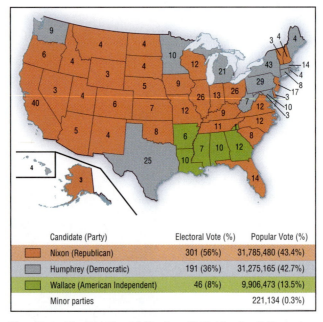

Candidate (Party)	Electoral Vote (%)	Popular Vote (%)
Nixon (Republican)	301 (56%)	31,785,480 (43.4%)
Humphrey (Democratic)	191 (36%)	31,275,165 (42.7%)
Wallace (American Independent)	46 (8%)	9,906,473 (13.5%)
Minor parties		221,134 (0.3%)

Map 28–4 The Presidential Election, 1968 Like the 1960 election, this was another close contest with widespread consequences. But this time, former vice president Richard M. Nixon was the winner.

>> Timeline

▼1955–56
Montgomery, Alabama, bus boycott

▼1957
Soviet Sputnik satellite launch

▼1960
Greensboro, North Carolina, lunch counter sit-ins
Sharon Statement
John F. Kennedy elected president

▼1961
First U.S. suborbital space flight, by Alan Shepard
Freedom Rides

▼1962
Port Huron Statement
Integration of University of Mississippi
Cuban Missile Crisis

▼1963
Birmingham, Alabama, civil rights protests
Civil rights march on Washington, D.C.
Assassination of John F. Kennedy

▼1964
Civil Rights Act of 1964
Lyndon Johnson's "War on Poverty"
Free Speech Movement
Tonkin Gulf incidents
Lyndon Johnson's landslide election as president

▼1965
U.S. escalation of Vietnam War
Voting Rights Act of 1965
Water Quality Act
Watts race riot

▼1966
National Organization for Women (NOW)

▼1967
Air Quality Act
Stop the Draft Week

continued

>> **Timeline** *continued*

▼**1968**
Tet Offensive in Vietnam
Assassinations of Martin Luther King Jr. and Robert F. Kennedy
Richard Nixon elected president

▼**1975**
Surrender of South Vietnam to North Vietnam

Conclusion

The upheavals of 1968 marked the end of illusions about limitless American power. John Kennedy's confident nation—able to "pay any price, bear any burden, meet any hardship, support any friend, oppose any foe"—had vanished. By 1968 the economy could no longer "pay any price." The United States could not support its friends in South Vietnam. The government could not create the Great Society. Instead, generation, race, and gender deeply divided the nation. The assassinations of King and Robert Kennedy dramatized the breakdown of democracy.

1968 was a tumultuous year for Lt. Fred Downs, too. On the morning of January 11, he stepped on a mine. The explosion threw him into the air, ripped through his ear drums, tore away pieces of his legs and hips, mutilated his right hand, laid bare the bones of his right arm, and blew off his left arm at the elbow. Horrified, Downs looked at his wounds. "I felt," he recalled, "the total defeat of my life."

Back in the United States, Downs had to deal with the loss of his arm, his confidence, and his plans. He had to learn how to use a prosthetic arm and accept the breakup of his marriage. He also had to learn how to deal with a divided, angry America. On the street, a man pointed to the hook sticking out of Downs's left sleeve. "Get that in Vietnam?" the man asked. Downs said he had. "Serves you right," the man snapped, and walked away. The United States, like that man, would have a difficult time coming to terms with the events of the 1960s.

Review Questions

1. How did the new liberalism differ from the liberalism of the New Deal and the Fair Deal? How did the new conservatism differ from the old?

2. Compare and contrast the New Frontier and the Great Society. Did their goals differ?

3. Why was the civil rights movement able to attain its major goals by the mid-1960s?

4. How did the United States fight the Cold War in the 1960s? Was America winning by the end of the decade?

5. Compare liberal and radical feminism. Were these movements incompatible with each other?

6. Compare the Black Power movement, the New Left, and the counterculture. Did any of these want radical change for the United States?

For further review materials and resource information, please visit www.oup.com/us/ofthepeople

29

Living with Less
1968–1980

>> "Fighting Shirley Chisholm"

At the end of the 1960s, Shirley Chisholm, an African American congresswoman from Brooklyn, New York, worried about her country. Amid the upheaval of the Great Society, the United States "sometimes seemed to be poised on the brink of racial and class war." Blacks, women, the poor, and the young demanded change, but the political system resisted. "Our representative democracy is not working," Chisholm declared. "It is ruled by a small group of old men."

It was not in Chisholm's nature to give in. Born to working-class West Indian parents in Brooklyn, she had pushed her way to a master's degree and a career as an educator. Running as "Fighting Shirley Chisholm," she won election to Congress from a poor, mostly black and Puerto Rican district in 1968. In January 1972, she became the first black and first female candidate for the Democratic presidential nomination. "You've never had anyone looking like me running for President," Chisholm declared. "Other kinds of people can steer the ship of state besides white men."

Chisholm's campaign continued the 1960s battle for rights. She wanted to create a coalition of African Americans, women, and the young "to get their share of the American dream and participate in the decision-making process that governs our lives."

Chisholm campaigned hard in several primaries. But with little money and organization, she had little chance. She had to fight to win equal time on television. Black male politicians withheld their support, and black voters wondered whether an African American could really win. Her female and black supporters squabbled.

The campaign ended in defeat in California, but it enhanced her reputation. In November, she won reelection to Congress with a huge majority. An exhausted Chisholm did not regret her presidential bid. "I ran for the Presidency in order to crack a little more of the ice which has congealed to nearly immobilize our political system and demoralize people," she explained.

>> **AMERICAN PORTRAIT** *continued*

Shirley Chisholm's failed campaign was part of a collision between Americans' aspirations for equality and new political, economic, and cultural realities. As the struggle for rights and opportunities expanded in the 1970s, the nation's economy and global influence continued to weaken. The United States no longer seemed a land of unlimited possibilities. Americans worried whether the nation could afford to meet everyone's needs in an age of dwindling jobs and resources. As a magazine concluded, Americans were "Learning to Live with Less."

The result was not the "racial and class war" that Chisholm feared. But neither did the liberal Great Society give way to a stable new order dominated by one party or ideology. Instead, workers, employers, politicians, and families struggled with the consequences of limited resources and power. While Americans puzzled over the relationship between the economy and government and between the nation and the world, the political system broke down in scandal and failure.

Common Threads

>> **How did economic problems continue to shape American life from the 1960s to the 1970s?**

>> **Why did liberalism continue to influence politics in the 1970s?**

>> **How did a sense of limits drive Richard Nixon's foreign and domestic policies?**

>> **Did American society become more democratic in the 1970s?**

>> **What were the ways the Vietnam syndrome would affect the United States after the 1970s?**

A New Crisis: Economic Decline

During the social, political, and military crises of the 1960s, Americans had largely taken the economy for granted. Prosperous and growing, the United States seemed destined to remain the world's preeminent economic power. But the economy had faltered as the Great Society came apart. The failings of business, government, and economists, a shortage of oil, intensifying foreign competition, and the multinational strategies of giant corporations combined to weaken the foundations of prosperity. By the end of the 1970s, the United States seemed to be in critical economic decline.

Weakness at Home

Signs of economic weakness were almost everywhere in the 1970s. Although the economy continued to grow, corporate profits and workers' productivity fell off. Unemployment increased; inflation, which usually dropped when unemployment rose, also increased. At best, the economy seemed stagnant. The unprecedented combination of high unemployment and high inflation led to the coining of a new word—*stagflation*—to describe the nation's predicament (see Table 29–1).

Corporations were partially responsible for the weak economy. Corporate leaders had tended to maximize short-term profits at the cost of the long-term health of their companies. Some companies had not put enough of their earnings into research, development, and new equipment. As a result, some American products seemed less innovative and reliable. Detroit's automobiles, so attractive and advanced in the 1950s, now struck consumers as unglamorous, inefficient, and poorly made. Ford's new Pinto sedan had to be recalled because its fuel tank was prone to explode.

Long an emblem of security and stability, corporations now appeared as vulnerable as the Pinto. In 1970, the Penn Central Railroad became the largest corporation in American history to go bankrupt. That year, only federal aid saved Lockheed Aircraft from also going under. The federal government also played a part in the nation's predicament. Massive federal spending had stimulated the economy from the 1940s to the 1960s but did not have the same effect in the 1970s. Some analysts claimed that Washington had diverted too much of the nation's talent and resources from the private sector to military projects during the cold war. In addition, the government's huge expenditures for the Vietnam War promoted inflation.

Economists did not give federal policy makers much help. In the 1960s, liberal economists had been sure they understood the secret to prosperity. The new problem of stag-

 Table 29-1 Stagflation in the 1970s

Year	Inflation % Change	Unemployment % Change	Combined* % Change
1970	5.9	4.9	10.8
1971	4.3	5.9	10.2
1972	3.3	5.6	8.9
1973	6.2	4.9	11.1
1974	11.0	5.6	16.6
1975	9.1	8.5	17.6
1976	5.8	7.7	13.5
1977	6.5	7.1	13.6
1978	7.7	6.1	13.8
1979	11.3	5.8	17.1
1980	13.5	7.1	20.6

*"Combined" means annual percentage changes of inflation and unemployment.

Source: *Statistical Abstract of the United States*, 1984, pp. 375–76, 463; tables 624–25, 760. (1971 inflation data from *Statistical Abstract*, 1973, p. 348, table 569.)

flation left them baffled. "The rules of economics," admitted the chairman of the Federal Reserve, "are not working quite the way they used to."

The Energy Crisis

An emerging energy crisis intensified economic problems. By 1974, the nation had to import over a third of its oil, particularly from the Middle East. The energy needs of the United States and other western countries empowered the Organization of the Petroleum Exporting Countries (OPEC), a group of third world nations that had joined together to get higher prices for their oil. In October 1973, war broke out between Israel and a coalition of Arab nations, including Egypt and Syria. Arab members of OPEC refused to send petroleum to the United States and other nations that supported Israel in the conflict. OPEC soon raised oil prices nearly 400 percent.

The effect of the oil shortage spread well beyond gas stations. In some states, truck drivers blockaded highways to protest the high cost of fuel and low speed limits. Lack of fuel grounded some airline flights. Heating oil for homes and businesses was in short supply. Some people could not afford to heat their homes. Although the Arabs ended the oil embargo in March 1974, the underlying energy problem remained.

Competition Abroad

Weakened by trouble at home, the United States was vulnerable to increasingly tough competition from abroad. Thanks to American aid after World War II, Japan and Western European countries rose to create efficient, up-to-date industries. By the 1970s, these nations rivaled the United States, even in the American market.

The Energy Crisis Motorists crowd around an open gas station, New York City, December 1973.

The rise of Japan was the most dramatic. For decades, Americans had derided Japanese goods. By the 1970s, Japan's modern factories turned out high-quality products. Japanese televisions and other electronic goods filled American homes. Japanese cars—small, well made, and fuel efficient—attracted American buyers worried about the high price of gas.

Because of such competition, the United States fell back in the global economic race. In 1950, the nation had accounted for 40 percent of the value of all the goods and services produced around the world. By 1970 that figure was down to 23 percent. By the end of the 1970s, the United States imported more manufactured goods than it exported.

The Multinationals

Multinational corporations—firms with factories and other operations in several nations—played a key role in the economic crisis. Taking advantage of new technologies and lower trade barriers, U.S. and West European corporations had moved aggressively into global markets after World War II. Multinationals accounted for about 15 percent of the world's annual gross product, and the biggest had annual sales larger than the annual product of some countries.

U.S. firms made up the majority of the largest multinationals in the 1970s. As Americans struggled, U.S. multinationals still earned large profits because of their lucrative overseas units. Not surprisingly, these American firms rapidly expanded abroad. In 1957, just 9 percent of American investments went abroad; by 1972, the figure had reached 25 percent.

The multinationals' most controversial foreign investment was the transfer of manufacturing from the United States to nations with lower wages and less restrictive labor laws. As corporations shifted production to plants in Mexico or Asia, American plants closed, with stunning job losses. The combination of overseas production and foreign competition was devastating. In 1954, U.S. companies had made 75 percent of the world's televisions. Twenty years later, they produced less than 25 percent—and almost all of that production took place in Mexico and overseas.

Multinational executives argued that investment abroad increased jobs and prosperity in the United States. Capital invested in Mexico and Asia came back home, they insisted, as dividends to stockholders and tax payments to the government.

The Impact of Decline

Economic decline began to reshape life in the United States in the 1970s. It seemed as if the Industrial Revolution were being reversed. As factories closed, Americans witnessed the deindustrialization of their country. Huge steel plants, the symbol of American industrial might, stood empty. In the 1970s, most new jobs were in the sales and retail sectors, intensifying a 20-year trend toward a service-centered economy. America, a union official lamented, was turning into "a nation of hamburger stands."

For workers, the effects of deindustrialization were crushing. Heavy industry had been the stronghold of the labor movement. By the late 1970s, less than one in four workers belonged to a union, and organized labor lost power and influence.

The loss of unionized industrial jobs eroded workers' incomes. After rising from the 1950s into the 1960s, workers' spendable income began to drop. To keep up, more and more women took full-time jobs outside the home: the percentage of women in the

AMERICA AND THE WORLD
···
>> Carl Gerstacker's Dream

In February 1972, Carl A. Gerstacker, chairman of the multinational Dow Chemical Company, confessed his secret fantasy to an audience of executives, economists, and policy makers at a White House conference. "I have long dreamed of buying an island owned by no nation," Gerstacker revealed. But this sober executive did not plan to escape to his island for a life of leisure. Instead, Gerstacker wanted to take Dow Chemical along. "If we were located on such truly neutral ground," he explained, "we could then really operate in the United States as U.S. citizens, in Japan as Japanese citizens, and in Brazil as Brazilians." The multinational would effectively be on its own, free to do as it pleased without interference from the U.S. government.

Gerstacker's audience probably agreed. By the 1970s, the leaders of American multinationals felt surprisingly few ties to their home country. "We are not an American company," a U.S. oil executive told a congressional committee. So unattached to the United States or any other country, multinational leaders did not believe their companies should let patriotism interfere with business. As Carl Gerstacker concluded, giant corporations were becoming not so much multinational or international as "anational" and "nationless."

Multinational leaders seemed to prefer a world with no nations at all. Eager for a unified global economy, they felt that governments only got in the way. They imposed tariffs, limited trade, taxed profits, dictated working conditions, nationalized resources, and started wars. "The world's political structures are completely obsolete," fumed Jacques Maisonrouge, a French-born vice president of IBM. "The multinational corporation today is a force that can serve global needs of mankind far better than the medieval concept of nation states," proclaimed José Béjarano, vice president of the Latin American division of Xerox. Of course, heads of the multinationals conveniently forgot how often their firms had turned to the U.S. government for diplomatic and military support when other nations threatened their investments.

Few Americans shared the vision of men like Béjarano. The United States and other nation-states, all fueled by intense patriotism, were not about to disappear—or leave the multinationals alone. As Gerstacker acknowledged, U.S. tax laws made it impossible for Dow Chemical to move to its island paradise. For their impact on the world around them, the multinational executives were ahead of their time. With the certainty of a prophet, John J. Powers, president of the drug company Pfizer, insisted a unified global economy "is no idealistic pipe dream but a hard-headed prediction." Time would tell.

>> Youngstown, Ohio

For more than 75 years, workers made steel in open-hearth furnaces at the Campbell Works of the Youngstown Sheet and Tube Company. Opened at the start of the twentieth century, the huge mill was one of the plants that gave Youngstown, in northeast Ohio, its reputation as a "Steel City." In exchange for hard labor, the Campbell Works also gave generations of Youngstown's workers a chance for prosperity. The city, a resident observed, "was a place in which the American Dream seemed to have come true for many working-class families."

The dream came to a sudden end in 1977. By then, the mill was an inefficient "antique" that made steel more slowly and expensively than new mills. On September 19 the parent company of Youngstown Sheet and Tube, Lykes Corporation, announced it was closing down the Campbell Works and transferring some production to a new facility in Illinois. As many as 5,000 workers would lose their jobs. Once a symbol of American industrial might, the Campbell Works had instantly become a symbol of deindustrialization and decline on that "Black Monday" in 1977.

The announcement stunned employees. To many, it was like another Pearl Harbor. Some workers realized right away that their way of life was gone. On the way home, they threw their hard hats and work boots into the Mahoning River.

The Lykes Corporation refused to reopen the mill. The company claimed that the low price of foreign steel, especially from Japan, and the high cost of U.S. environmental regulations made it impossible to operate the mill at a profit. A coalition of workers and churches tried to buy the mill but failed. Congress and President Jimmy Carter refused to help. Carter, an angry worker grumbled, "ought to run for president of Japan."

There was no way to save the Campbell Works. The workers lost their jobs, and much more. "Our fathers worked here and our grandfathers worked here," said a union official. "Now I face the prospect of this turning into a ghost town." The optimistic future of the American Dream was gone. "They used to tell us: 'Get out of high school, get a job in a mill and you're fixed for life,'" said a steelworker. "Now I know better."

A quarter of the labor force at Campbell Works moved away from Youngstown. Many of them went to the booming Sunbelt. About half stayed in Youngstown and found new jobs, but many of those jobs did not pay nearly as well as the ones at the Campbell Works. The rest of the workforce stayed on but found no work at all.

Other Youngstown residents also suffered because of the closing of the mill. Business dropped in the taverns where steelworkers had gone for drinks after work and in stores and services. "It will kill our business," a Youngstown merchant predicted.

The Campbell Works shutdown was just the beginning of deindustrialization in Youngstown. By 1980, the "Steel City" was dotted with the decaying hulks of empty mills. "There are going to be a few more Youngstowns before it's over," an economist predicted.

workforce, 36 percent in 1960, rose to 50 percent in 1980—the highest level in American history to that time. Many Americans could not find work, however. As the huge baby boom generation came of age, the economy did not produce enough jobs. The unemployment rate, as low as 2.8 percent in 1969, jumped up to a high of 9 percent in 1975.

Economic decline accelerated the transformation of America's regions. The energy crisis and deindustrialization sped up the shift of people and power from north to south and east to west (see Map 29–1). With its cold, snowy winters, the North was especially vulnerable to the oil embargo and higher energy prices. America's Snowbelt now seemed a less attractive place to live and do business. In the 1970s, empty, decaying factories made the Northeast and the Midwest America's "Rustbelt."

> **All I want is my damn job back.**
>
> MARY FARMER KINNEY,
> a laid-off African American autoworker in Hamtramck, Michigan, 1979

Fleeing deindustrialization and high prices, many northerners moved south to the band of states ranging from Florida to California. As this Sunbelt boomed, farms became suburbs, and cities such as Orlando, Houston, Phoenix, and San Diego boomed. Texas and the southwestern states, rich in oil and natural gas reserves, profited from the energy crisis. The Sunbelt was home to new high-technology businesses: aerospace firms,

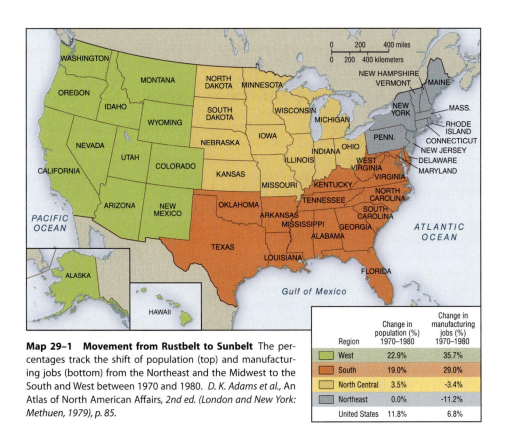

Map 29–1 Movement from Rustbelt to Sunbelt The percentages track the shift of population (top) and manufacturing jobs (bottom) from the Northeast and the Midwest to the South and West between 1970 and 1980. *D. K. Adams et al., An Atlas of North American Affairs, 2nd ed. (London and New York: Methuen, 1979), p. 85.*

Region	Change in population (%) 1970–1980	Change in manufacturing jobs (%) 1970–1980
West	22.9%	35.7%
South	19.0%	29.0%
North Central	3.5%	-3.4%
Northeast	0.0%	-11.2%
United States	11.8%	6.8%

electronics companies, and defense contractors. The Sunbelt was also at the cutting edge of the service economy, which was focused on leisure and consumption. More retirees moved to Florida than to any other state. Tourists flocked to California's Disneyland and Florida's Disney World. They gambled their money in Las Vegas.

Confronting Decline: Nixon's Strategy

Richard Nixon was the first president to confront the decline of America's prosperity and power. He recognized that the failed war in Vietnam marked the end of America's cold war pretensions and that the American economy had weakened. Despite his long opposition to Communism and the New Deal, Nixon was a pragmatist, open to new realities and approaches.

A New Foreign Policy

The president and his national security advisor, Henry Kissinger, still regarded Communism as a menace and saw the cold war rivalry between the United States and the Soviet Union as the defining reality of the modern world. However, Nixon and Kissinger understood that the relative decline of American power dictated a new approach to the cold war.

The twin pillars of the new foreign policy were the Nixon Doctrine and détente. In July 1969, the president announced that the United States "cannot—and will not—conceive all the plans, design all the programs, execute all the decisions and undertake all the defense of the free nations of the world." America would continue to provide a nuclear umbrella, but its allies would have to defend themselves against insurgencies and invasions. This Nixon Doctrine was a repudiation of the interventionist Truman Doctrine of 1947 (see Chapter 26).

The United States also pursued a new relationship with the Soviet Union and the People's Republic of China. Nixon and Kissinger wanted to lessen the cost of the rivalry with these two Communist nuclear powers. Separate agreements with the two nations might keep them from combining forces against the United States. Nixon and Kissinger therefore worked to establish *détente*, the relaxation of tensions.

At the start of Nixon's presidency, the United States had not recognized the legitimacy of the People's Republic of China. Instead, America supported the Communists' bitter foes, the Nationalist Chinese regime on Taiwan. In February 1972, Nixon became the first American president to go to mainland China. He gave the Chinese leaders what they most wanted—a promise that the United States would eventually withdraw its troops from Taiwan. The two sides also made clear they opposed any Soviet attempt to dominate Asia.

Nixon's trip brought American policy in line with the reality of the 1970s and underscored the gradual end of anti-Communist hysteria in America. By design, the trip also left the Soviets with the frightening possibility of a Chinese-American alliance.

Nixon did not want a confrontation with the Soviets, the only power that could destroy America with nuclear weapons. The United States no longer had clear military superiority. Instead, he sought détente. Above all, he wanted the Soviets to agree to limit their long-range or strategic nuclear arsenals. The Soviets also wished to reduce the cost and danger of the cold war and to counter Nixon's overture to the Chinese. Moreover, the Soviets needed American grain to feed their people.

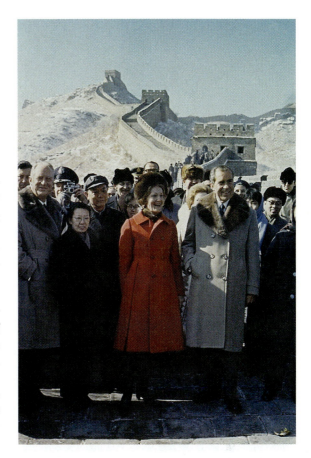

Détente at the Great Wall of China, 1972 President Nixon, with his wife, Pat, became the first American president to visit mainland China.

The two sides began talks on the Strategic Arms Limitation Treaty (SALT I) in 1969. In May 1972, three months after his trip to China, Nixon became the first American president to travel to Moscow, where he signed the SALT treaty, limiting for five years the number of each nation's nuclear missiles. An Anti–Ballistic Missile (ABM) treaty sharply limited the number of defensive missiles the two sides could deploy. Although they did not stop the arms race, the treaties symbolized the American and Soviet agreement that "there is no alternative to . . . peaceful coexistence."

Ending the Vietnam War

Nixon and Kissinger sought better relations with the Soviet Union and the People's Republic of China in part to pressure the North Vietnamese to accept a peace agreement and end the Vietnam War. Nixon knew the United States could not win the war. Meanwhile, the war divided the American people and undermined American prestige and power around the world. But Nixon did not want to the United States to look weak.

To appease public opinion, Nixon began to bring American soldiers home in 1969. With U.S. forces reduced, Nixon needed a new strategy to persuade North Vietnam to accept the existence of South Vietnam. He turned to a policy known as "Vietnamization," in which the South Vietnamese were encouraged to defend themselves. But the South Vietnamese military alone could not beat back the Communists.

Accordingly, Nixon turned to U.S. airpower to support South Vietnamese troops and intimidate the North Vietnamese. In March 1969, he authorized B-52 raids on North Vietnamese sanctuaries in Cambodia. Because bombing this neutral country might outrage American and world opinion, the raids were kept secret. Neither raids nor secret negotiations with North Vietnamese diplomats succeeded.

Meanwhile, news of the secret bombings leaked out. In October, millions of Americans participated in Moratorium Day, a dramatic break from business as usual, to protest the

The Vietnam War Comes to Cambodia Cambodian landscape devastated by the 1969 bombings that President Nixon tried to keep secret.

war. In November, more than 250,000 people staged a "March Against Death" in Washington. That month, Americans learned about one of the most troubling episodes of the war. On March 16, 1968, U.S. soldiers had killed between 200 and 500 unarmed South Vietnamese women, children, and old men in the hamlet of My Lai. This atrocity led to the 1970 court-martial and eventual conviction of Lieutenant William Calley Jr. for mass murder.

Demonstrations did not stop the president from using violence to force a peace agreement. When General Lon Nol, the new pro-American leader of Cambodia, appealed for aid to stop a Communist insurgency, a joint United States–South Vietnamese force invaded Cambodia to look for North Vietnamese troops in April 1970. The Cambodian invasion sparked demonstrations on campuses across the country. On May 4, National Guard troops fired at unarmed protestors at Kent State University in Ohio. Four students died. Ten days later, state police killed two African American students at Jackson State College in Mississippi. These deaths intensified the outrage over Cambodia. Students went out on strike at about 450 campuses.

Some Americans, angered by these protests, mobilized in support of the president and the war. In New York City, construction workers attacked student demonstrators. "The country is virtually on the edge of a spiritual—and perhaps physical—breakdown," New York's mayor lamented.

As American troop withdrawals continued, the war and the peace negotiations dragged on. Meanwhile, the *New York Times* began publishing the so-called Pentagon Papers, a secret government history of American involvement in Vietnam. The documents, which revealed that the Johnson administration had misled the country, further undermined support for the war. The Nixon administration tried unsuccessfully to persuade the Supreme Court to block publication of the papers.

Unable to secure a peace agreement, Nixon pressed North Vietnam harder for a settlement. When the North Vietnamese army invaded South Vietnam in March 1972, the president ordered Operation Linebacker, an aerial attack on North Vietnam. When negotiations stalled, he intensified the air raids in December. On January 27, 1973, negotiators signed a peace agreement in Paris. For the United States, at least, the Vietnam War was over.

Nixon had promised "peace with honor," but the agreement did not guarantee the survival of South Vietnam. The cease-fire came at a heavy cost. Twenty thousand Americans and more than 600,000 North and South Vietnamese soldiers had died since Nixon took office in 1969. The number of civilian casualties will never be known. Nixon had ended U.S. participation in the Vietnam War, but his critics asked whether so flawed an agreement had been worth four years of fighting.

Chile and the Middle East

Détente, a practical accommodation with Soviet power, did not mean that the Nixon administration accepted the rise of potentially hostile regimes. To stop the spread of socialism and Communism, Nixon, like the presidents before him, was willing to subvert a democratically elected government and tolerate an authoritarian one. In 1970, he ordered the CIA to block the election of Salvador Allende, a Marxist, as president of Chile. Allende was elected anyway. "I don't see why we need to stand by and watch a country go communist due to the irresponsibility of its own people," Kissinger fumed. The CIA then helped destabilize Allende's regime by aiding right-wing parties, driving up the price of bread, and encouraging demonstrations. When a military coup deposed Allende in 1973, the United States denied responsibility and offered financial aid to the new military dictator, General Augusto Pinochet.

In the Middle East, the Nixon administration also displayed both its hostility to Communism and its inability to shape events decisively. In October 1973, on Yom Kippur, the holiest day of the Jewish calendar, Egypt and Syria attacked Israel in revenge for their defeat in the Six-Day War of 1967, when Israel occupied territory in Egypt, Syria, and Jordan. After the United States sent critical supplies to Israel, Arab countries responded with the oil embargo. Meanwhile, the Soviets supplied the Arabs and pressed for a role in the region. Determined to keep out the Soviet Union, Nixon put American nuclear forces on alert. Kissinger mediated between the combatants, who agreed to pull back their troops in January 1974. The embargo ended, but American weakness was obvious. Supporting Israel, the United States still needed the Arabs' oil. Nixon and Kissinger held back the Soviets but could not bring peace to the Middle East.

Taming Big Government

The problem of decline, addressed in Nixon's foreign policy, proved more difficult to handle at home. Nixon took office with the conventional Republican goals of taming big government. He wanted a balanced budget and a reduction in federal power.

So Nixon cut spending for programs, including defense. The fate of the space program epitomized the new budgetary realities. On July 20, 1969, a landing module touched down on the moon. When astronaut Neil Armstrong set foot on the surface, the United States had beaten the Soviets to the moon. There still seemed no limit to what Americans could do. There were, however, limits to what the space program could do. Congress slashed NASA's budget.

In 1969, Nixon called for a New Federalism, which would return "a greater share of control to state and local governments and to the people." Three years later, the administration persuaded Congress to pass a revenue-sharing plan that allowed state and local governments to spend funds collected by the federal government.

Nixon took the same pragmatic approach to domestic problems that he did to foreign affairs. He left popular New Deal and Great Society programs largely intact. Despite his budget cuts, the government kept spending vast amounts of money. By 1971, the cost of big government, combined with the unsettled economy, had produced a huge, un-Republican budget deficit.

The president did try to reform the federal welfare system put in place by the New Deal. Like many Republican conservatives, Nixon believed that welfare made the federal bureaucracy too large and the poor too dependent. His administration tried to replace the largest federal welfare program, Aid to Families with Dependent Children, with a controversial system inspired by presidential aide Daniel Patrick Moynihan, a Harvard sociologist. Moynihan's Family Assistance Plan would have provided poor families a guaranteed minimum annual income, but it also would have required the heads of poor households to accept any jobs available. Opposed by both liberals and conservatives, the program failed to pass Congress.

Meanwhile, the administration went along with several liberal initiatives expanding federal regulatory powers. By the 1970s, many Americans worried that corporations did not protect workers, consumers, or the environment. A grassroots environmental movement grew rapidly, particularly on college campuses. and on April 22, 1970, tens of millions of Americans celebrated the first Earth Day with teach-ins, demonstrations, and cleanup campaigns. Liberals in Congress responded to popular opinion with three new federal regulatory agencies: the Environmental Protection Agency (EPA), the Occupational Safety and Health Administration (OSHA), and the Consumer Product Safety Commission. These agencies enhanced the government's power over corporations, as did laws to safeguard coastlines and endangered species and limit strip-mining of coal, air and water pollution, and pesticide use.

An Uncertain Economic Policy

Nixon believed government should not interfere much in the economy. But high inflation, rising unemployment, and falling corporate profits tested his commitment to Republican orthodoxy. He was unable to persuade business to control price increases and organized labor to limit wage demands.

Meanwhile, the U.S. dollar was in crisis. Since the Bretton Woods conference (see Chapter 25), many nations had tied the value of their currencies to the dollar. The value of the dollar, in turn, had been supported by the U.S. commitment to give an ounce of gold in return for 35 dollars. This commitment to the gold standard had stabilized the international financial system and helped spur global economic development for decades. But by the 1970s, the weakening U.S. economy had undermined the dollar: strong European economies had too many dollars and too little confidence in the United States, and the U.S. government didn't have enough gold. If other countries demanded gold for their dollars, Washington would be unable to pay, and panic would follow.

Confronting inflation, monetary crisis, and economic weakness, Nixon announced his New Economic Policy in August 1971. To prevent the breakdown of the monetary system, the president took the United States off the gold standard by ending the exchange of gold for dollars. To strengthen U.S. producers against foreign competitors, Nixon lowered the value of the dollar and slapped new tariffs on imports; now American goods would sell more cheaply abroad and foreign goods would cost more in the United States. To slow inflation, he authorized a freeze on wages and prices.

The New Economic Policy did strengthen the international monetary system and help U.S. producers. But wage and price controls did not solve the underlying problems that caused inflation. The cost of the Vietnam War and the Arab oil embargo continued to drive up prices. Deindustrialization continued, too.

Refusing to Settle for Less: Struggles for Rights

Despite the troubled economy, many Americans, like Shirley Chisholm, refused to settle for less. In the late 1960s and 1970s, African Americans and women continued their struggles for the rights and opportunities they had long been denied. Their example inspired other disadvantaged groups to demand recognition. Mexican Americans, Native Americans, and gays and lesbians organized and demonstrated for their causes. But other Americans, worried about preserving their own advantages in an era of limited resources, were often unwilling to support these new demands. At times, the result was almost the "racial and class war" that Chisholm dreaded.

African Americans' Struggle for Racial Justice

As the civil rights struggle continued, attention focused on two relatively new and controversial means of promoting racial equality—affirmative action and mandatory school busing. First ordered by the Johnson administration, affirmative action required businesses, universities, and other institutions receiving federal money to provide opportunities for women and nonwhites. Supporters viewed the policy as a way to make up for past and present discrimination. Opponents argued that affirmative action was itself a form of discrimination that reduced opportunities for whites, particularly white men.

Nixon, despite his commitment to limited government, generally supported affirmative action. His administration developed the Philadelphia Plan, which encouraged the construction industry to meet targets for hiring minority workers. In 1978, the Supreme Court offered qualified support for affirmative action with its decision in *Regents of the University of California v. Allan Bakke*. The justices ruled that the medical school of the University of California at Davis could not deny admission to Bakke, a white applicant with better grades and test scores than some minority applicants accepted by the school. Although the court barred schools from using fixed admissions quotas for different racial groups, it did allow race to be used as an admissions criterion. By the end of the 1970s, affirmative action had become an important means of increasing diversity in schools and other institutions.

School busing was more controversial than affirmative action. By the late 1960s, the Supreme Court had become impatient with delays in integrating the nation's schools. Even in the North, with no de jure or legal segregation, there was still extensive de facto segregation. In *Swann v. Charlotte-Mecklenburg Board of Education* in 1971, the court upheld the mandatory busing of thousands of children to desegregate schools in the Charlotte,

North Carolina, area. But many Americans opposed busing, because they did not want integration or did not want children taken out of neighborhood schools.

Nixon sided with the opponents of busing. Privately ordering his aides to enforce busing less vigorously, he publicly called for a "moratorium" on new busing plans. Some communities implemented busing peacefully. Others faced protest and turmoil. In 1974, a federal court ordered busing in Boston. When the white-dominated local school committee refused to comply, a federal judge imposed a busing plan on the community. Working-class and lower-middle-class whites formed Restore Our Alienated Rights (ROAR) and other organizations to protest plans to bus students between the predominantly African American neighborhood of Roxbury and the largely Irish American neighborhood of South Boston. In "Southie," whites taunted and injured black students. Although violence spread through the fall, the busing plan went into effect. With busing and affirmative action, the civil rights movement seemed to have reached its limits: many Americans were unwilling to go any further to ensure racial equality.

Women's Liberation

By the 1970s, the movement for women's liberation was flourishing. Many women came together in "consciousness-raising" groups to discuss a broad range of issues in their lives. To commemorate the 50th anniversary of the women's suffrage amendment to the Constitution, thousands marched in the Women's Strike for Equality on August 26, 1970.

The women's liberation movement, like the struggle for African American equality, was diverse. Liberal feminist groups, such as the National Organization for Women (NOW), concentrated on equal public opportunities for women. Radical feminists focused on a broader range of private and public issues. Oppression, they insisted, took place in the bedroom and the kitchen, as well as the school and the workplace. Some radical feminists, influenced by the New Left, blamed women's plight on capitalism; others traced it to men. Cultural feminists insisted that women's culture was different from and superior to male culture and felt that women should create their own separate institutions. Some lesbian feminists went further to argue that women should avoid heterosexual relationships.

Linking the private and personal with the public and political, the women's movement fought on many fronts. More women who married decided to keep their own names rather than adopt their husbands'. Rather than identifying themselves by marital status, many women abandoned the forms of address "Miss" or "Mrs." for "Ms." Women's liberation made its mark on the media. In 1972, Gloria Steinem began the feminist magazine *Ms.* On television, popular sitcoms portrayed independent women.

In the 1970s, feminists focused especially on three public issues—access to abortion, equal treatment in schools and workplaces, and passage of the equal rights amendment (ERA) to the Constitution. Long effectively outlawed, abortions were generally unavailable or unsafe. In *Roe v. Wade* in 1973, the Supreme Court ruled a Texas antiabortion law unconstitutional on the grounds that it violated the "right to privacy" guaranteed by the Ninth and Fourteenth Amendments. With this decision, abortion became legal and widely available.

Like the civil rights movement, the women's movement demanded equal treatment in schools and workplaces. At first reluctant, the Nixon administration opened up federal employment to women and pressed colleges and businesses to end discriminatory practices. In 1972, Congress approved Title IX of the Higher Education Act, which required schools and universities receiving federal funds to give equal opportunities to women and men in admissions, athletics, and other programs.

The women's movement also continued the struggle to enact the ERA. "Equality of rights under the law," the amendment read, "shall not be denied or abridged by the United States or by any State on account of sex." In 1972 Congress passed the ERA. If 38 states ratified the amendment within 7 years, it would become law. But after 28 states ratified within a year, the ERA met heavy opposition. To male critics, feminists were a "small band of braless bubbleheads." Fearing that equal rights would end their femininity and their protected legal status, conservative women, such as activist Phyllis Schlafly, campaigned effectively against the ERA. Although more states ratified the amendment, some rescinded their votes, and the ERA never became law.

The ERA's defeat underscored the challenges to the women's movement. Women still did not have full equality, but they had more control over their bodies, more access to education, and more opportunity in the workplace.

Mexican Americans and "Brown Power"

In the 1960s and 1970s, Mexican Americans, the nation's second largest racial minority, developed a new self-consciousness. Proudly identifying themselves as Chicanos, they organized to protest poverty and discrimination.

Despite efforts to keep out Mexican immigrants, the Mexican American population grew rapidly. By 1980, at least 7 million Americans claimed Mexican heritage. The great majority lived in Arizona, California, Colorado, New Mexico, and Texas, most in urban areas, and more than 1 million in Los Angeles. Winning more skilled and white-collar

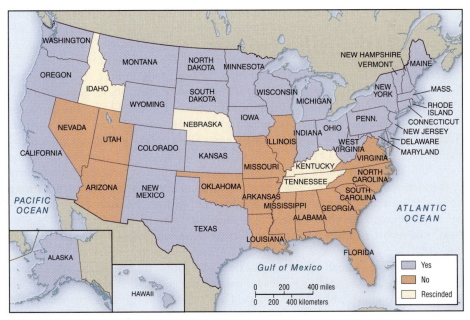

Map 29–2   The Equal Rights Amendment (ERA) Despite substantial support in state legislatures across the country, the ERA faced crippling opposition in the mountain West and the South.

jobs, Mexican Americans still earned much less as a group than did Anglos (white Americans of non-Hispanic descent). One in four Mexican American families lived in poverty in the mid-1970s.

Stereotyped as lazy and shiftless, Mexican Americans faced racism and discrimination. Schools in their neighborhoods were underfunded. In some California schools, Mexican American children could not eat with Anglo children. California and Texas prohibited teaching in Spanish.

Gerrymandering diluted the political power of Mexican American voters. Despite its large Mexican American population, Los Angeles had no Hispanic city council member at the end of the 1960s. The justice system often treated Mexican Americans unfairly.

Poverty and discrimination marked Mexican American life. In cities, many Mexican Americans crowded into *barrios*, run-down neighborhoods. In the countryside, many lived without hot water or toilets. Infant mortality was high and life expectancy low. Nationwide, almost half the Mexican American population was functionally illiterate.

Encouraged by the civil rights movement, Mexican Americans protested against poverty and injustice for migrant farm workers. In the fertile San Joaquin Valley of California, the Mexican Americans who labored for powerful fruit growers earned as little as 10¢ an hour and lived in miserable conditions. César Chávez, a former migrant worker influenced by Martin Luther King Jr.'s nonviolent creed, helped them organize what became the United Farm Workers of America. In 1965 the union went on strike. The growers, accusing Chávez of Communist ties, called for police, strikebreakers, intimidation, and violence. Chávez's nonviolent tactics, which included a 25-day hunger strike in 1968, gradually appealed to liberals and other Americans. He also led a successful nationwide consumer boycott against grapes. Under this pressure, the growers began to settle with the union.

While King inspired Chávez, the nationalism of the Black Power movement spurred other Mexican Americans. In New Mexico, Reies López "Tiger" Tijerina, a former preacher, created the Alianza Federal de Mercedes (Federal Alliance of Land Grants) to take back land that the United States had supposedly stolen from Mexicans.

Mexican American activism flourished in the late 1960s. In East Los Angeles, the Brown Berets, a paramilitary group, showed the influence of the Black Panthers. In California in 1969, college students began the Movimiento Estudiantil Chicano de Aztlán (Chicano Student Movement of Aztlán, known by its initials, MEChA, or the word for "match" in the Spanish of Mexican Americans). MEChA was meant to kindle social change for Chicanos. In Crystal City, Texas, a boycott of Anglo businesses led to the formation of La Raza Unida ("The Unified Race"), a political party that won control of the local school board in 1970. These protests and organizations reflected a strong sense of pride and a powerful desire to preserve the Mexican American heritage. Activists asserted group identity by referring to Mexican Americans as "Chicanos." "A Chicano," said reporter Rubén Salazar, "is a Mexican-American with a non-Anglo image of himself."

Demanding bilingual education, Mexican American studies, equal opportunity, and affirmative action, activists fought for empowerment, for what some called "Brown Power." On the whole, white Americans paid less attention to Chicano activism than to African Americans' struggles. But Mexican American activists made important gains, including the end of state bans on teaching in Spanish.

Asian American Activism

Asian Americans also pressed for rights and recognition. Like Mexican Americans, they confronted a history of discrimination in the United States and faced denigrating stereotypes and hurtful epithets.

The small size of the Asian American population limited organization and protest, but the Immigration Act of 1965 made possible waves of new Asian immigration. By 1980 America was home to more than 3 million Asian immigrants, including 812,000 Chinese, 781,000 Filipinos, and 716,000 Japanese. Overall, there were 3.7 million Americans of Asian descent, mostly in the Pacific states and in cities.

Asian American activism followed the pattern of other minority movements. By the late 1960s, Asian Americans demonstrated a new ethnic self-consciousness and pride. Many Asian Americans saw themselves not only as Chinese or Japanese, but also as members of a broader, pan-Asian group.

In 1968, the Asian American Political Alliance (AAPA) emerged on the campus of the University of California at Berkeley to unite Chinese, Japanese, and Filipino students. In response to demands by Asian American students, colleges and universities established Asian studies courses and programs by the end of the 1970s. Beyond campuses, in 1974 protests forced the hiring of Chinese American workers to help build the Confucius Plaza housing complex in New York City's Chinatown. In San Francisco, activists brought suit against the public school system on behalf of 1,800 Chinese pupils. In *Lau v. Nichols* in 1974, the Supreme Court declared that school systems had to provide bilingual instruction for non-English-speaking students.

In the 1970s, Japanese groups demanded compensation for the U.S. government's internment of Japanese Americans during World War II. In 1976 Washington rescinded Executive Order 9066, the 1942 directive that led to internment, but did not make a more comprehensive settlement until 1988.

Asian Americans, like Chicanos, made only limited gains by 1980. However, with a new consciousness and new organizations, Asian Americans had also forced real social change.

The Struggle for Native American Rights

After many years of decline and stagnation, the Indian population had grown rapidly since World War II (see Map 29–3). By 1970, there were nearly 800,000 Native Americans, half of whom lived on reservations. Divided into about 175 tribes and other groups, Native Americans were united by poverty and persistent discrimination. They had the lowest average family income of any ethnic group and faced high unemployment rates and substandard schools.

Native American life was shaped by the unique relationship with the federal government. Many resented the Bureau of Indian Affairs (BIA) for patronizing and exploiting tribes. Like African American and Mexican American separatists, some Native Americans saw themselves as a nation apart. Calling themselves "prisoners of war," they struck an aggressive stance, expressed in such slogans as "Custer Had It Coming" and "Red Power."

Beginning in the 1960s, a Native American movement emerged to protest federal policy, combat stereotypes, unite tribes, and perpetuate their cultures. Native Americans called for an end to employment discrimination and to the sale of Indian lands and resources to corporations. Activists staged "hunt-ins" and "fish-ins" to protest lost hunting and fishing

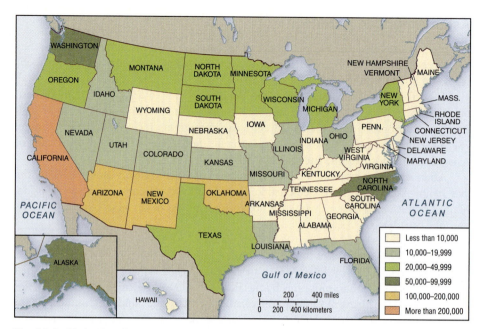

Map 29–3 Native American Population, 1980 After rapid growth in the years following World War II, the Native American population remained largest west of the Mississippi River and, above all, across the Southwest. But there were substantial numbers of Native Americans in every region. *Data from Statistical Abstract of the United States, 1973 (Washington, D.C.: U.S. Bureau of the Census, 1973), p. 348; and Statistical Abstract of the United States, 1984 (Washington, D.C.: U.S. Bureau of the Census, 1984), pp. 375–376, 463, 760.*

rights. They also condemned the use of Indian symbols by schools and sports teams and demanded Indian-centered school curricula.

Some Indians favored more radical action. Copying the Black Panthers, a group of red-beret-clad Native Americans in Minneapolis formed an "Indian Patrol" to defend against the police. The patrol evolved into the American Indian Movement (AIM), which spread to other cities. In 1969, AIM activists occupied the abandoned federal prison on Alcatraz Island in San Francisco Bay. They unsuccessfully offered the government "$24 in glass beads and cloth" for the prison, which they planned to convert into a Native American center. In 1972 and 1973, AIM took over BIA headquarters in Washington and the BIA office in Wounded Knee, South Dakota, where federal troops had massacred Indians in 1890.

The Native American rights movement made few gains. The Indian Self-Determination Act of 1975 did allow Native Americans more independence on the reservations, but Native Americans were still divided about their relationship to the government. Many tribal leaders wanted to continue selling off their lands through the BIA, but were assailed by AIM for accepting Bureau authority. Despite such divisions, the movement had forced Americans to confront the inequitable treatment of Indians more directly than at any time since the Great Depression.

Homosexuals and Gay Power

Singled out for persecution in the McCarthy era, most homosexual men and women had learned to conceal their sexual identity in public. Mainstream American culture ridiculed homosexuals as "faggots," "queers," and "dykes," and the medical profession treated homosexuality as an illness. In the late 1960s, that began to change.

A catalyst for change was the struggle of women, racial minorities, and students. Another was a police raid on the Stonewall Inn, a gay bar in New York City's Greenwich Village, in June 1969. Such raids were commonplace, but this time gay men resisted. The next night, the police beat and arrested gay protestors, who yelled, "Gay Power!"

Stonewall became a rallying cry for gay activism. The Gay Liberation Front, the Student Homophile League, and other organizations appeared. Activists picketed companies that discriminated against gays, and homosexuals socialized more openly. On the first anniversary of Stonewall, 10,000 gay men and lesbians paraded up New York's Sixth Avenue. "Two, four, six, eight!" marchers chanted. "Gay is just as good as straight!" The gay movement began to have an effect. In 1974, the American Psychiatric Association decided that homosexuality was not a "mental disorder" and that homosexuals deserved equal rights.

The emerging gay, Native American, and Chicano movements, along with the ongoing crusades of women and African Americans, made a deep impact on American society. Women, gays, African Americans, Native Americans, and Chicanos did not win full equality, but these groups made important gains despite the troubled economic climate .

Backlash: From Radical Action to Conservative Reaction

By the close of the 1960s, American society shook with demands for peace in Vietnam and equal rights at home. Some activists believed the United States would be torn apart and remade by the "racial and class war" that Shirley Chisholm feared, but the revolution never came. Radical movements fell apart. Many Americans abandoned activism for their private concerns; others angrily rejected protest movements. Encouraging this backlash, President Nixon won reelection in 1972.

"The Movement" and the "Me-Decade"

By the end of the 1960s, women, minorities, student protesters, and antiwar activists seemed to be creating a single coalition, known simply as "the Movement." In August 1969, a crowd of nearly half a million mostly young people gathered for a music festival on a dairy farm near Woodstock in upstate New York. For three days, they created a temporary utopia dedicated to love, equality, and an end to the Vietnam War. What activist Abbie Hoffman called the "Woodstock Nation" briefly symbolized the possibility of a true mass-based coalition for radical change.

Nevertheless, the Movement stalled. "We had the dream and we are losing it," an activist lamented the same year. The different protest groups never merged and were often hostile to each other. Black activists, for instance, criticized white activists for neglecting poverty and other working-class problems.

In addition, Movement groups fell apart. Plagued by internal divisions, SDS held its last convention in 1969. The violent Weathermen called for "Days of Rage" in the "pig city" of Chicago in October 1969, but only a few hundred protestors showed up. Transient radical groups bombed or burned corporate headquarters and other "establishment" targets but succeeded only in giving the New Left and the Movement a bad name. The FBI infiltrated Black Panther chapters to discredit the organization. Panther leaders fled the country, went to jail, or died at the hands of police. Radical feminist groups also declined as women focused on liberal demands, such as the ERA.

Some protest movements lost their targets. After the demonstrations of 1970, the antiwar movement declined as the United States pulled out of Vietnam. The student movement declined as young people lost some of their grievances. In 1971, the voting age was lowered to 18, after ratification of the Twenty-sixth Amendment.

The revolution also failed because many people turned away from activism and political engagement. Some were disillusioned by the failure of the Great Society and the duplicity of the Johnson and Nixon administrations. Others were disappointed by radicalism's limited victories. Still others joined therapeutic and religious movements concerned with inner needs rather than political change.

To the writer Tom Wolfe, the 1970s were the "Me-Decade," a time in which Americans had become self-absorbed and narcissistic. The cause, explained the historian and social critic Christopher Lasch, was the crisis of capitalism in "an age of diminishing expectations." Fears about the self-absorbed Me-Decade were as exaggerated as hopes for the revolutionary Movement. People did not stop working for change, but in a time of economic decline and political disappointment, many Americans felt they could not afford the expansive liberal dreams of the 1960s. They had to look out for themselves.

The Plight of the White Ethnics

The "new American revolution" was a victim of anger, as well as apathy. Most lower-middle-class and working-class whites rejected the Movement. They decried radical feminism and resented the students and protestors who had avoided serving in Vietnam. They also rejected the new liberalism of the 1960s. Feeling threatened by urban renewal, welfare, and court-ordered busing, many whites believed the Great Society did too little for them and too much for minorities and young radicals. Most of all, they feared lost jobs and a lower living standard amid deindustrialization. "I work my ass off," said an ironworker. "But I can't make it."

The media painted an unflattering portrait of these Americans as frustrated racists and reactionaries. In reality, they were not all so racist or forlorn. They took renewed pride in the ethnic heritage that set them apart from other Americans. "White ethnics" were self-consciously German American or Irish American, like the opponents of busing in Boston. They were "PIGS"—Poles, Italians, Greeks, and Slavs.

White ethnics tapped their heritage to affirm an alternative set of values—their own counterculture. For them, ethnicity meant a grounding in family, neighborhood, and religion in place of the individualistic American dream and the centralizing federal government. In response, some colleges and universities created ethnic studies programs. In 1972, Congress passed the Ethnic Heritage Studies Act to "legitimatize ethnicity" and promote the study of immigrant cultures. Most important, white ethnics formed a large potential voting bloc, attractive to politicians.

The Republican Counterattack

Nixon tried to join white ethnics and white southerners in a Republican counterattack against radicalism, liberalism, and the Democratic Party. The president condemned protestors and demonstrations. "Anarchy," he said, "this is the way civilizations begin to die." Nixon ordered IRS investigations to harass liberal and antiwar figures. He used the FBI to infiltrate and disrupt the Black Power movement, the Brown Berets, and the New Left. He made illegal domestic use of the CIA against the antiwar movement.

Nixon also called for support from "the great silent majority of my fellow Americans." With his "southern strategy," the president reached out to Sunbelt voters by opposing busing, rapid integration, crime, and radicalism. He also tried to create a more conservative, less activist Supreme Court. In 1969, he named the cautious Warren Burger to succeed Earl Warren as chief justice. To fill another vacancy, Nixon nominated first a conservative South Carolina judge, Clement Haynsworth, who had angered civil rights and union leaders, and then Judge G. Harrold Carswell of Florida, a former avowed white supremacist. Both nominations failed, but Nixon had sent an unmistakable message to the "silent majority" and to white southerners.

The counterattack paid off in the 1972 presidential election. The Republican ticket of Nixon and Vice President Spiro Agnew benefited from unforeseen occurrences. Only George Wallace, the segregationist governor of Alabama, rivaled Nixon's appeal to the "silent majority." But Wallace's campaign for the Democratic nomination ended when a would-be assassin's bullet paralyzed him from the waist down. In addition, the Democratic vice-presidential nominee, Senator Thomas Eagleton of Missouri, had to withdraw after revelations about his treatment for depression.

Nixon did not really need good luck in 1972. The Democrats chose a strongly liberal senator, George McGovern of South Dakota, for president. McGovern's running mate was another liberal, Sargent Shriver, a brother-in-law of the Kennedys. The Democratic ticket—which endorsed busing and affirmative action and opposed the Vietnam War—alienated white ethnics, white southerners, and organized labor.

Nixon won 49 out of 50 states and nearly 61 percent of the popular vote, but the victory was deceptive: the Democrats still controlled both houses of Congress.

Nevertheless, the 1972 election was a sign that the traditional Democratic coalition was breaking up. Nixon's triumph, along with the failure of the Movement, the rise of the white ethnics, and the self-absorption of the Me-Decade, showed that the glory days of liberalism and radicalism were over.

Political Crisis: Three Troubled Presidencies

Nixon's triumph turned out to be his undoing. The discovery of illegal activities in his campaign led to the revelation of other improprieties and, finally, to his resignation. Nixon's successors, Gerald Ford and Jimmy Carter, could not master the problems of a divided nation discovering the limits of its power. Unable to handle the conflicting issues of rights and economic decline, the three troubled presidencies of the 1970s intensified the sense of national crisis. At the decade's end, Americans wondered whether their democracy still worked.

Watergate: The Fall of Richard Nixon

Nixon's fall began when five men were caught breaking into the offices of the Democratic National Committee in the Watergate complex in Washington, DC, just before 2:00 A.M.

on June 17, 1972. The five burglars had ties to Nixon's campaign organization, the Committee to Re-Elect the President (CREEP). They were attempting to repair an electronic eavesdropping device that had been planted in the Democrats' headquarters.

At first, Watergate had no impact on the president. He won reelection easily, but a disturbing story gradually emerged. Two reporters for the *Washington Post*, Bob Woodward and Carl Bernstein, revealed payments linking the five burglars to CREEP and to Nixon's White House staff. The burglars went on trial with two former CIA agents, who had directed the break-in for CREEP. Facing heavy sentences, the burglars admitted in March 1973 that "higher-ups" had planned the break-in and orchestrated a cover-up. One of those higher-ups, presidential counsel John Dean, revealed his role in the Watergate affair to a grand jury. By the end of April, the president had to accept the resignations of his most trusted aides, H. R. "Bob" Haldeman and John Ehrlichman. To investigate Watergate, Nixon named a special federal prosecutor, Archibald Cox.

In the end, the president was trapped by his own words. A Senate committee, chaired by Sam Ervin of North Carolina, began hearings on Watergate in May 1973. A White House aide told the committee that conversations in the president's Oval Office were routinely recorded on secret tapes. Claiming "executive privilege," Nixon refused to turn over tapes of his conversations after the break-in. When Archibald Cox pressed for the tapes, Nixon ordered him fired on Saturday, October 20, 1973. Attorney General Elliot Richardson and a top aide refused to carry out the order and resigned. A third official finally fired Cox. Nixon's "Saturday Night Massacre" set off a storm of public anger. Nixon had to name a new special prosecutor, Leon Jaworski. The Democratic-controlled House of Representatives began to consider impeachment against the president. "I am not a crook," Nixon insisted.

By 1974, it became clear that the Nixon administration had engaged in a shocking range of improper and illegal behavior. Infuriated by news leaks in 1969, Henry Kissinger had ordered wiretaps on the phones of newspaper reporters and his own staff. Two years later, the White House had created the "Plumbers," an inept group of operatives to combat leaks such as release of the Pentagon Papers. In 1972, Nixon's men had also engaged in dirty tricks to sabotage Democratic presidential aspirants. Nixon's personal lawyer had collected illegal political contributions, "laundered" the money to hide its source, and then transferred it to CREEP.

Nixon himself had ordered the secret and illegal bombing of Cambodia. He had impounded (refused to spend) money appropriated by Congress for programs he disliked. He had secretly approved the use of federal agencies to hurt "political enemies."

As a result of Watergate and other scandals, many of Nixon's associates had to leave office. No fewer than 26, including former attorney general John Mitchell, went to jail. Vice President Spiro Agnew was found to have accepted bribes as the governor of Maryland in the 1960s. In 1973 Agnew accepted a plea bargain deal and resigned. He was replaced by Republican Congressman Gerald R. Ford of Michigan.

Under pressure to release his tapes, Nixon tried to get away with publishing edited selections. Revealing a vulgar, rambling, and inarticulate president, the transcripts only fed public disillusionment. In July 1974 the House Judiciary Committee voted to recommend to the full House of Representatives three articles of impeachment—obstruction of justice, abuse of power, and defiance of subpoenas.

Nixon wanted to fight the charges, but the Supreme Court ruled unanimously that he had to give his tapes to the special prosecutor. They showed that Nixon himself had participated in the Watergate cover-up as early as June 23, 1972. The president had conspired to obstruct justice and had lied repeatedly to the American people. Almost certain to be impeached, Nixon agreed to resign rather than face a trial in the Senate. On August 9, 1974, he left office in disgrace. "My fellow Americans, our long national nightmare is over," the new president, Gerald Ford, declared. "Our constitution works."

Gerald Ford and a Skeptical Nation

At first, Gerald Ford was a welcome relief for a nation stunned by the misdeeds of Richard Nixon. Modest and good-humored, the new president seemed unlikely to abuse authority. But Ford also seemed stumbling and unimaginative in the face of declining prosperity and power. Moreover, he had no popular mandate. Ford was the first unelected vice president to succeed to the presidency. His vice president, former New York governor Nelson Rockefeller, had not been elected, either.

Ford had to govern a nation skeptical about politicians. Johnson's deceitful conduct of the Vietnam War and Nixon's scandals raised fears that the presidency had grown too powerful. To reestablish its authority, Congress passed the War Powers Act of 1973, which allowed the president to send troops to hostilities overseas for no more than 60 days without congressional consent. In 1975 Congress held hearings on CIA secret operations. Amid revelations about the agency's improper roles in domestic spying and the assassination of foreign leaders, Congress created permanent committees to oversee the agency. Ford had to ban the use of assassination in American foreign policy.

Soon after taking office, Ford himself fed the public's skepticism about the presidency by offering Nixon a full pardon for all crimes committed as president. Ford's popularity dropped immediately, and his presidency never fully recovered.

Ford's handling of economic issues did help his popularity. A moderate Republican, he did not want a too active federal role in managing the economy. But, like Nixon, he could not stop some liberal initiatives, as Congress strengthened the regulatory power of the Federal Trade Commission and extended the 1970 Clean Air Act.

Ford had no solutions for deindustrialization and stagflation. Believing inflation was the most serious problem, he did little to stop rising unemployment, which topped 9 percent. His anti-inflation program, known as WIN for "Whip Inflation Now," mainly encouraged Americans to control price increases voluntarily, but inflation continued.

In foreign affairs, Ford had to accept limits on American power. Despite the 1973 cease-fire, the fighting continued in Vietnam. Ford promised to protect South Vietnam, but Congress cut his requests for monetary aid to Saigon. Sending American troops back to South Vietnam was out of the question. When the North Vietnamese invaded early in 1975, panicked civilians fled southward. As Saigon was overrun, the last Americans evacuated in helicopters. Thousands of loyal South Vietnamese fled with them, but many more were left behind. On April 30, 1975, South Vietnam surrendered. There was nothing Ford could do to prevent the final, ignominious failure of America's 20-year-long Vietnam policy.

The president could also do nothing to save the pro-American government of Cambodia from Communist insurgents, the Khmer Rouge, in April 1975. Ford did act the next month when the Khmer Rouge captured an American merchant ship, the *Mayaguez*, off Cambodia. At the cost of 41 deaths, United States marines rescued the 39-man crew. Despite the rescue, the United States no longer wielded much power in Southeast Asia.

The policy of détente with the Soviet Union, meant to help America cope with its limited power, was also in trouble. The United States and the Soviets failed to agree to a second Strategic Arms Limitation Treaty (SALT II). Critics of détente, including Democratic Senator Henry Jackson of Washington, claimed that the policy sapped American defenses and overlooked human rights violations by the Soviets. In 1974, Jackson added to a trade bill an amendment linking commerce to freedom for Soviet Jews to emigrate. The Jackson-Vanik Amendment helped sour the Soviets on détente. Ford further alienated conservatives when he signed an agreement in Helsinki, Finland, accepting the post–World War II boundaries of European nations.

Ford's troubles affected the polls. The Democrats made large gains in the 1974 congressional elections. Two years later, Ford won the Republican nomination for president, replacing Rockefeller with a more conservative vice-presidential nominee, Senator Robert Dole of Kansas. The Democrats chose former Georgia governor Jimmy Carter, a moderate promising efficiency rather than liberal reform.

With low turnout, Carter took 50.1 percent of the vote to Ford's 48 percent. The Democrat won an Electoral College majority by carrying the Northeast and taking back almost all the South from the Republicans. The outcome was less an endorsement of Carter than a rejection of Ford, who became the first sitting president to lose an election since Herbert Hoover during the Great Depression in 1932.

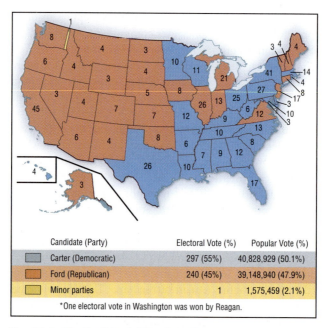

Candidate (Party)	Electoral Vote (%)	Popular Vote (%)
Carter (Democratic)	297 (55%)	40,828,929 (50.1%)
Ford (Republican)	240 (45%)	39,148,940 (47.9%)
Minor parties	1	1,575,459 (2.1%)

*One electoral vote in Washington was won by Reagan.

Map 29–4   The Presidential Election, 1976 Jimmy Carter managed to reestablish the Democratic party's appeal to white southerners.

"Why Not the Best?": Jimmy Carter

As he took office in 1977, Jimmy Carter seemed capable and efficient. A graduate of the Naval Academy, he had served as an engineer in the nuclear submarine program and successfully managed his family's peanut farm before entering politics. Carter's perfectionism was captured in the title of his autobiography, *Why Not the Best?*

Carter responded more energetically and imaginatively than Ford to the nation's problems. But Carter came to be seen as a weak, uncertain leader. More important, he faced the same intractable problems that had bedeviled Ford.

Like his predecessor, Carter had trouble putting to rest the recent past. He met angry criticism when he pardoned Americans who had resisted the draft during the Vietnam War.

Carter also faced increasing popular resentment of government. Many Americans believed that regulation and taxation had gotten out of hand. When the Endangered Species Act of 1973 forced a halt to the construction of a Tennessee dam because it threatened the survival of the snail darter, a small local fish, it seemed as if the federal government worried more about fish than about people's need for electricity and recreation.

The West was the stronghold of antigovernment sentiment in the 1970s. Assailing Washington bureaucrats, the Sagebrush Rebellion demanded state control over federal lands in the West. Businessmen in the West also wanted more exploitation of oil, forests, and other resources on federal lands. Meanwhile, California became the center of an anti-tax movement in 1978. Angered by high taxes and local government spending, California voters passed Proposition 13, which sharply reduced property taxes.

As always, antigovernment sentiment was inconsistent. Many of the same people who attacked taxes and regulation expected aid and benefits from Washington. When Chrysler faced bankruptcy in 1979, the government saved the automaker with a $1.5 billion loan guarantee. When Carter moved to cancel federal water projects in the West in 1977, he faced protest from the heart of the Sagebrush Rebellion.

Carter was most successful when he moved to limit government. By the 1970s, some economists were advocating deregulation of businesses as a way to lower costs, increase competition, and improve services. In 1978, the government removed price controls on the airline industry. In the short run the move lowered fares, but in the long run it drove some airlines out of business.

Deregulation marked a changing balance of political power. Big business, under attack since the 1960s, now lobbied effectively against regulation, organized labor, and taxes. Liberals, meanwhile, failed to convince Congress to create the Consumer Protection Agency or to make labor organization easier. In 1978, Congress diluted the liberal Humphrey-Hawkins Bill asserting federal responsibility for full employment. When Carter tried to raise business taxes, Congress instead cut taxes on capital gains and added more tax loopholes.

Carter attempted, with mixed results, to adjust the economy to the realities of living with less. His voluntary wage and price controls did not stop soaring inflation. After fuel shortages forced schools and businesses to close in the harsh winter of 1976/1977, Carter addressed the energy crisis. The president told Americans that "the energy shortage is permanent" and urged them to conserve. His energy plan included a new Department of Energy, taxes on gas-guzzling automobiles and large consumers of oil, tax incentives to stimulate oil and gas production, and development of nuclear power. Conservatives complained the program expanded government authority, whereas liberals and environmentalists objected to its support for nuclear power and oil-company profits. A weakened plan, passed in 1978, did encourage conservation.

Nuclear power, a key part of Carter's energy plan, lost much of its appeal. In March 1979 a nuclear reactor at Three Mile Island, Pennsylvania, nearly suffered a catastrophic meltdown. As 100,000 frightened residents fled their homes, the reactor had to be permanently closed. Around the country, utilities scrapped plans for new nuclear power plants.

Three Mile Island fed broader anxieties about the environmental damage of industrial capitalism. Americans wondered whether their neighborhoods would suffer the fate of Love Canal, near Niagara Falls, New York. There, hazardous waste buried by a chemical company caused so many cases of cancer, miscarriages, and other health problems that residents had to move away. Despite business hostility to regulation, Washington had to create a "superfund" of $1.6 billion to clean up hazardous-waste sites. The administration also took control of 100 million acres of Alaska to prevent damage from economic development.

At first, Carter had success with foreign policy. Continuing Nixon's deescalation of the cold war, Carter announced that "we are now free of the inordinate fear of Communism." Without abandoning détente, he focused on building harmony and supporting human rights and democracy around the world. In 1978, Carter won Senate approval of a treaty yielding ownership of the Panama Canal to Panama at the end of the century, representing a new, more respectful approach to Central and Latin America.

In 1978, Carter also mediated the first peace agreement between Israel and an Arab nation. Bringing together Israeli and Egyptian leaders at the Camp David presidential retreat, Carter helped forge a framework for peace that led to Israel's withdrawal from the Sinai Peninsula and the signing of an Israeli-Egyptian treaty. The agreement did not settle the fate of the Israeli-occupied Golan Heights and Gaza Strip or the future of the Palestinian people, but it did create a basis for future negotiations.

Carter viewed a commitment to human rights and democracy as America's way of recapturing the international respect lost during the Vietnam War. In practice, however, Carter supported authoritarian American allies, such as the rulers of Iran and the Philippines, who abused human rights in their own countries.

Carter's foreign policy suffered from the collapse of détente. The president did reach an agreement with the Soviets on the SALT II treaty, but the Senate was reluctant to ratify it. Then, in December 1979, the Soviet Union invaded its southern neighbor, Afghanistan. In response, Carter withdrew the SALT II treaty, stopped grain shipments to the Soviet Union, forbade American athletes to compete in the 1980 Olympics in Moscow, and increased military spending. These moves did not affect the Soviets' invasion, but détente was over, and the direction of American foreign policy was unclear.

By 1979, Carter was deeply unpopular. He had not stabilized the economy or forged a coherent foreign policy. After pondering the situation at Camp David for 11 days in July, he told a television audience that the nation was suffering a "crisis of spirit." The president offered proposals to deal with the energy crisis but spoke most strongly to the state of the nation. "All the legislation in the world can't fix what's wrong with America," Carter said. "What is lacking is confidence and a sense of community." The speech only seemed to alienate more Americans.

Carter became still more embattled when the Shah of Iran was overthrown by the followers of an Islamic leader, the Ayatollah Ruholla Khomeini, early in 1979. The Shah

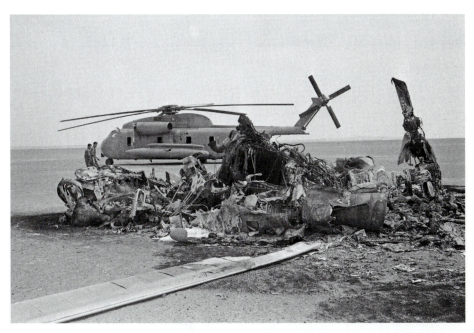

Disaster in the Iranian Desert, April 1980 The wreckage of this Army helicopter, part of the failed attempt to free American hostages in Iran, symbolizes the weakness of the United States at the start of the 1980s.

had long received lavish aid from the United States. Now, Iranian revolutionaries, eager to restore traditional Islamic values, condemned America for imposing the Shah and modern culture on their nation. In the wake of the revolution, oil prices rose. Americans had to contend again with gas lines and inflation.

The situation worsened when Khomeini condemned the United States for allowing the Shah to receive medical treatment in New York. On November 4, students loyal to Khomeini overran the United States embassy in Teheran, the Iranian capital, and took 60 Americans hostage. Carter froze Iranian assets in the United States but could not compel the release of the hostages. The United States seemed helpless. In the spring of 1980, a frustrated Carter ordered a secret military mission to rescue the hostages. On April 24, eight American helicopters headed for a desert rendezvous with six transport planes carrying troops and supplies. When two helicopters broke down and another became lost, the mission had to be aborted. An accident left eight soldiers dead. The hostages remained in captivity And the limits of American power seemed more obvious than ever.

Conclusion

As the 1970s ended, Shirley Chisholm was still deeply worried about her nation. The congresswoman feared that "there was a real crisis . . . in this country. . . . Government was being conducted by crisis." The mixture of economic decline with movements for rights and opportunity had proved too much to handle. To Chisholm, even the changes of the liberal 1960s seemed at risk. "Lots happened in the '60s," she noted sadly. "What's happening today? Every gain has been eroded."

>> Timeline

▼1968
Assassinations of Martin Luther King Jr. and Robert F. Kennedy
Election of Richard Nixon

▼1969
Secret bombing of Cambodia
Stonewall Riot in New York's Greenwich Village
Apollo 11 moon landing
Nixon Doctrine

▼1970
First Earth Day
Invasion of Cambodia

▼1971
United States off gold standard
Ratification of Twenty-sixth Amendment, lowering voting age to 18
Supreme Court busing decision, *Swann v. Charlotte-Mecklenburg Board of Education*

▼1972
President Nixon's trips to the People's Republic of China and the Soviet Union
Strategic Arms Limitation Treaty (SALT I) and Anti–Ballistic Missile (ABM) Treaty
Congressional passage of equal rights amendment
Watergate burglary
Reelection of President Nixon

▼1973
Peace agreement to end Vietnam War
Supreme Court ruling to legalize abortion, *Roe v. Wade*

▼1973-74
OPEC oil embargo

▼1974
Boston busing struggle
Resignation of President Nixon

▼1975
Surrender of South Vietnam to North Vietnam
Helsinki Agreement

▼1976
Announcement of the "Me-Decade" by Tom Wolfe
Jimmy Carter elected president

▼1977
Carter's energy plan

> **>> Timeline** *continued*

▼1978
Camp David peace accords
Supreme Court affirmative action decision, *Regents of the University of California v. Allan Bakke*

▼1979
Accident at Three Mile Island nuclear power plant

▼1979-81
Iranian hostage crisis

▼1980
Ronald Reagan elected president

As always, Chisholm refused to give in to pessimism. "I will continue to do what I'm doing—fighting, fighting, fighting," she vowed, "because I realize that this country is moving to the right." As the 1980s would reveal, Chisholm was correct. After the political uncertainty of the 1970s, the nation would finally deal with economic decline and the other challenges of the decade by embracing a new conservatism. The future lay to the right.

Review Questions

1. How did economic decline affect the lives of Americans?

2. Why was President Nixon's strategy for ending the Vietnam War so controversial?

3. Discuss the foreign policies of the Nixon administration, including détente and the Nixon Doctrine. How did these policies mark a departure from previous American approaches to the cold war?

4. How did the demands of the African American civil rights movement change from the 1960s to the 1970s?

5. Discuss the Republican counterattack of the late 1960s and early 1970s. How did Nixon and his party take advantage of discontent?

6. Analyze the troubled presidencies of Nixon, Ford, and Carter. Did these leaders create their own problems, or did they face impossible situations?

For further review materials and resource information, please visit www.oup.com/us/ofthepeople

30

The Triumph of Conservatism

1980–1991

>> Linda Chavez

"On Election Day 1980," Linda Chavez recalled, "I did something I had never imagined I could do: I voted for a Republican for president." A lifelong Democrat, she rejected her party's nominee, incumbent Jimmy Carter, and pulled the lever instead for the conservative Ronald Reagan.

Chavez admitted she made "an unlikely conservative." The daughter of an Anglo mother and a Mexican American father, Chavez had grown up in the Mexican American neighborhoods of Albuquerque and Denver. Her father, like most Mexican Americans, was a Democrat. Chavez herself was drawn to the party and its causes. As a girl in the early 1960s, she joined the civil rights organization CORE and demonstrated against racial discrimination. Chavez then worked for the Democratic National Committee, a liberal Democratic congressman, two liberal teachers unions, and the Carter administration.

Despite her partisan commitments, Chavez had been changing. As a student at the University of Colorado at Boulder in the late 1960s, Chavez discovered that she did not have to settle for her parents' working-class world. "For the first time," she said, "I realized that I could control my own destiny." Chavez also felt that the university's affirmative action programs shortchanged Mexican Americans by admitting unqualified students, allowing them to founder, teaching them to blame their problems on racism, and then leaving them to drop out.

Those realizations helped Chavez develop a new political outlook in the 1970s. She believed that individuals should take responsibility for their lives. She also rejected affirmative action programs, race-based hiring quotas, busing, and bilingual education as misguided liberal attempts to create equality.

Meanwhile, her stint in the Carter administration left her skeptical about another liberal article of faith. "The federal government was not at all what I expected," Chavez confessed. "Nothing—and almost no one—worked." She was troubled, too, that Carter and the Democrats did not support anti-Communism and a strong defense.

>> AMERICAN PORTRAIT *continued*

In some ways, Chavez felt that she was not the one who had changed. It was her party that had changed by adopting controversial solutions to racial and gender inequality and by abandoning its pledge to contain Communism. In 1976, Chavez stayed home rather than vote for Carter. By 1980, she was ready to vote for Reagan, another longtime Democrat who felt his party had changed.

Linda Chavez was an unusual figure: there were hardly any prominent Mexican American conservatives, male or female. But her change from liberal Democrat to conservative Republican typified a basic shift in the 1980s. Still dealing with economic and political decline, a new majority of Americans, including businesspeople, evangelical Christians, and "Reagan Democrats" like Chavez, adopted a conservative vision of the country. Rejecting the pessimism of the 1970s, they wanted to believe that individual and national success was still possible. The new conservative majority was open to materialism and to a government that left people free to succeed or fail.

The trend toward conservatism had many consequences. Eager to restore old values, Reagan cut taxes, reduced government regulation, and diminished union power to restore economic growth. The president also embraced a conservative social agenda, including attacks on affirmative action and abortion. His foreign policy was dedicated to confronting Communism. Despite scandals, setbacks, and compromises, Reagan and the new conservatism arrested fears of decline and altered America's politics and culture for a generation.

Common Threads

>> How did Ronald Reagan's approach to economic decline differ from that of his predecessor, Jimmy Carter?

>> How did conservatism's emphasis on personal responsibility shape the economic and social policies of the Reagan administration?

>> Why was religion so important to the Reagan Revolution?

>> How would the emergence of microcomputing shape the economy beyond the 1980s?

Creating a Conservative Majority

In the 1970s and 1980s, the conservative movement continued its rise to power. The New Right drew strength from the transformation of the economy, the changing reputation of big business, and the growth of evangelical Christianity. Conservative power became clear in the 1980 presidential election, when voters sent Ronald Reagan to the White House.

The New Economy

Conservatism benefited from the emergence of a postindustrial, computer-centered economy. As deindustrialization continued, technological change pointed the way to national economic revival. Along with other innovations, semiconductors—transistorized integrated circuits attached to small silicon crystals—allowed manufacturers to shrink the computer. By the late 1970s they could put the power of a room-sized mainframe computer into a box that fit on a desktop. In 1981, IBM introduced its first personal computer, or PC. By the end of the 1980s, Americans were buying 7 million PCs a year (see Figure 30–1).

Computers seemed a way out of national economic decline. The microcomputer bolstered older companies such as IBM and created new firms such as Apple and Dell; it enriched new entrepreneurs such as Steve Jobs, a founder of Apple, and Bill Gates, a founder of Microsoft. Asian manufacturers built most consumer-electronics products, but American companies dominated computer hardware and software.

The growth of the computer industry inspired utopian dreams of a high-technology society built on the production of knowledge rather than things. Promoting literacy and education, the computer would lift up the poor and disadvantaged. Unlike the old industrial economy, a computerized economy would cut pollution and the consumption of raw materials. Enabling people to work at home, the microcomputer would eliminate commuting and relieve urban congestion.

The promise of the computer-driven economy helped conservatism. New industries, new companies, and new jobs seemed to confirm conservatives' faith in capitalist free enter-

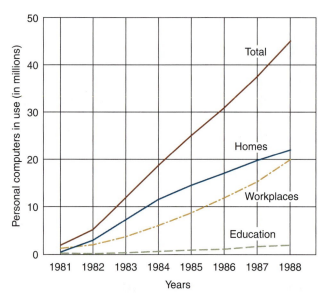

Figure 30–1   The Rise of the Personal Computer The rapid rise in the number of microcomputers in use in homes, workplaces, and schools in the 1980s inspired hopes that the nation's economic decline had ended. Statistical Abstract of the United States, 1989 (Washington, D.C.: U.S. Bureau of the Census, 1990), p. 743; Statistical Abstract, 1993 (Washington, D.C.: U.S. Bureau of the Census, 1994), p. 761.

A Revolution on a Desktop In 1981, the new IBM PC or personal computer conveniently offered the power of an old room-filling mainframe computer.

prise, unaided by government. The new economy also benefited conservatism by stimulating the flow of people, jobs, and political power from the North and East to the South and West. Computing did revive parts of the Rustbelt. In Massachusetts, computer companies sprang up around Boston along Route 128 to replace long-gone textile mills and shoe factories. But computing most benefited the Sunbelt, birthplace of the new conservatism in the 1950s and 1960s. Dell's headquarters were in Texas. Apple was one of many computer firms clustered in the area called Silicon Valley, outside San Francisco. Rustbelt cities such as Pittsburgh and Detroit lost population, while some Sunbelt counties more than doubled in population. These regional shifts had direct political effects. Reapportionment in 1980 gave more congressional seats and electoral votes to the more conservative states of the Sunbelt.

The Rehabilitation of Business

While the 1980s pointed to a utopian future, the decade also recalled the cutthroat capitalism of the turn of the twentieth century. A wave of corporate takeovers and mergers swept the economy. Aggressive investment bankers and entrepreneurs such as Michael Milken and Ivan Boesky used junk bonds—high-risk, high-paying securities—and other techniques to finance takeovers. Executives took golden parachutes, huge payments for selling their companies and losing their jobs. Enormous deals merged some of the largest American corporations. In 1985 General Electric bought RCA for $6 billion. In 1986 alone there were more than 4,000 mergers worth a total of $190 billion. The biggest deal came in 1988 when RJR Nabisco was sold for $25 billion, and the company's president and CEO received a $53 million golden parachute.

The takeover wave and the growth of the computer industry, helped rehabilitate business and its values, under attack in the 1960s and 1970s. Although some observers criticized the concentration of so much economic power, others saw the takeovers as a sign of economic vitality. They argued that the mergers created larger, more efficient, more competitive companies and praised takeover artists as models of energy and creativity. The media enthusiastically reported on Milken, Boesky, Jobs, and Gates. *Dallas, Dynasty,* and other popular television shows celebrated the fictional sagas of wealthy, freewheeling families. Business was more respectable than at any time since the 1950s.

So were materialism and the pursuit and enjoyment of wealth. "Everybody should be a little greedy," Boesky advised. "Thank goodness it's back," gushed the *New York Times,* "that lovely whipped cream of a word—luxury."

The baby boom generation reflected the new appeal of business. Former 1960s radicals such as Yippie (Youth Independent Party) leader Jerry Rubin took up business careers. By 1983 the media were talking about the emergence of yuppies, young urban professionals in their 20s and 30s. Uninterested in social reform, these optimistic, self-centered baby boomers were supposedly eager to make lots of money and then spend it on BMW cars, Perrier water, and other playthings. Although the transition from Yippies to yuppies was exaggerated, the yuppie stereotype underscored American aspirations to a more conservative, money-centered way of life.

The Rise of the Religious Right

As American culture celebrated materialism, many Americans still turned to spirituality to find meaning in their lives. Their choice of denominations reflected the trend to conservatism. Such mainline Protestant denominations as the United Methodist Church, the Episcopal Church, and the Presbyterian Church, USA, had been losing their share of church members since at least 1940. Meanwhile, evangelical churches boomed (see Map 30–1). By the 1980s, the Southern Baptist Convention was the largest American Protestant denomination. Such smaller evangelical bodies as the Assemblies of God more than doubled in size from the 1960s to the 1980s.

This changing denominational balance had social and political consequences. The mainline churches often took moderate or liberal positions on such issues as civil rights and abortion, but the evangelical churches more often supported conservative positions. Troubled by social change and emboldened by their own growth, evangelicals wanted to spread a conservative message across American culture and politics.

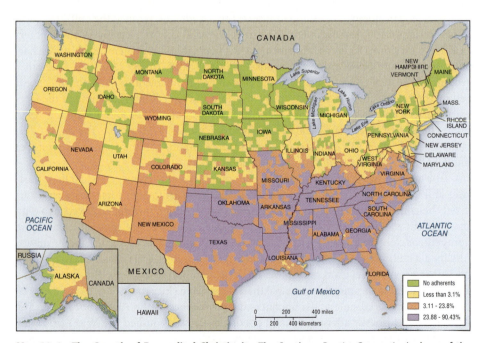

Map 30–1 The Growth of Evangelical Christianity The Southern Baptist Convention's share of the population, by county, reveals its gradual spread beyond its traditional base in the South by 1990. *Peter L. Halvorson and William M. Newman,* Atlas of Religious Change in America, 1952–1990 *(Cincinnati, OH: Glenmary Research Center, 1994), p. 120.*

The Reverend Jerry Falwell Jerry Falwell (left), fundamentalist and leader of the religious right.

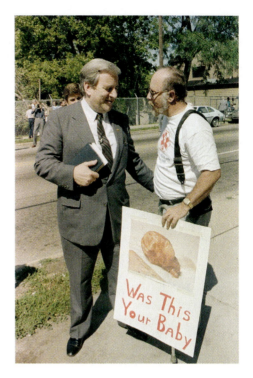

The emergence of "televangelists" was the most obvious result of this impulse. From 1978 to 1989 the number of Christian television ministries grew from 25 to 336. The most successful televangelists also had their own networks, colleges, political groups, and even an amusement park. Pat Robertson, a born-again Baptist from Virginia, hosted *The 700 Club* and ran the Christian Broadcast Network. Jerry Falwell, a fundamentalist who believed in the literal interpretation of the Bible, hosted the *Old Time Gospel Hour* and founded Liberty Baptist College in Virginia. He also organized the Moral Majority, a political pressure group. Deeply conservative, the televangelists condemned women's liberation, abortion, gay rights, and liberal Great Society programs. They wanted prayer in public schools. Earning millions of dollars, they praised low taxes, limited government, and financial success. Determined to win what Falwell called the "war against sin," the televangelists were the spearheads of a religious right ready for politics.

The 1980 Presidential Election

The new conservative majority came together in the presidential election of 1980. Former California governor Ronald Reagan continued his political rise by winning the Republican nomination. Although he chose a moderate running mate, George H. W. Bush of Texas, Reagan ran a conservative campaign. His vision of less government, lower taxes, renewed military might, and traditional social values appealed to business and evangelicals. His genial optimism suggested that the political system could be made to work. As a former Democrat, Reagan reassured Democrats and independents that they too could find a home in the Republican Party.

Meanwhile, the Democratic nominee, incumbent president Jimmy Carter, struggled with a weak economy and the ongoing hostage crisis in Iran. His moderate, sometimes conservative policies had alienated liberal Democrats. His poor economic record had alienated the party's white ethnics. Moderate Republican congressman John Anderson of Illinois, who ran as an independent, drew voters away from Carter. Meanwhile, Reagan focused relentlessly on America's decline during Carter's presidency. In the last presidential debate before election day, Reagan told the audience, "I think . . . it might be well if you would ask yourself, are you better off than you were four years ago?"

Americans answered that question by giving Reagan the presidency. Reagan carried all but four states and the District of Columbia (see Map 30–2). He managed only 50.7 percent

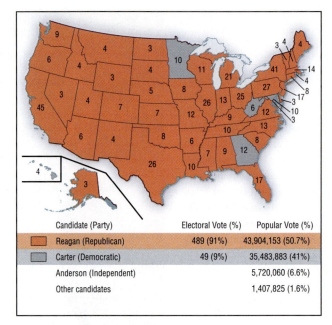

Candidate (Party)	Electoral Vote (%)	Popular Vote (%)
Reagan (Republican)	489 (91%)	43,904,153 (50.7%)
Carter (Democratic)	49 (9%)	35,483,883 (41%)
Anderson (Independent)		5,720,060 (6.6%)
Other candidates		1,407,825 (1.6%)

Map 30–2   The Presidential Election, 1980 As in other elections, a narrow victory in the popular vote translated into a landslide in the electoral college.

of the popular vote, but with Anderson's 6.6 percent, the tally suggested the extent of popular disaffection with Carter and the Democratic Party. The Democrats held on to the House of Representatives, but Republicans won the Senate for the first time since 1962. Sixteen years after the defeat of Barry Goldwater's conservative candidacy, the nation had turned sharply to the right.

The Reagan Revolution at Home

Ronald Reagan shaped American life more decisively than any president since Franklin Roosevelt. Reagan's folksy optimism made him popular, but the Reagan years were more than a triumph of style. With some justice, his supporters believed that his "Reagan Revolution" spurred a sweeping conservative transformation of American economic and political life.

The Reagan Style

The Reagan Revolution was partly a matter of style. Despite the frustrations of the 1960s and 1970s, Reagan exuded optimism. Rather than ask Americans to live with less, he embraced luxury. Reagan's presidency signaled a confident, even opulent, new era. On inauguration day, as if to mark the end of the frustrating 1970s, the Iranian government finally released its American hostages. In his inaugural address, Reagan firmly rejected pessimism. "We are not," the new president declared, "doomed to an inevitable decline." The Reagan inaugural cost five times more than Jimmy Carter's had four years earlier.

Even while Ronald and Nancy Reagan lived lavishly in the White House, the president retained a popular, common touch. After his career in movies and television, he knew how to speak simply and effectively to the American people. He became known as the "Great Communicator."

Reagan also appeared to enjoy and master his job. After the troubled presidencies of the 1970s, Reagan made the presidency seem manageable again. Even though he took office as America's oldest president at the age of 69, he projected vigor and energy.

The president even managed to survive an assassination attempt. On March 30, 1981, John W. Hinckley, a troubled loner, shot and wounded Reagan, his press secretary, and a policeman. Reagan's chest wound was more serious than his spokesmen admitted, but he met the situation with good humor. "Honey," he told his wife, "I forgot to duck." The president's popularity soared.

Shrinking Government

Reagan offered a clear alternative to the New Deal and the Great Society. Above all, he denied that a large, activist federal government could deal with the challenges of American life in the 1980s. So Reagan vowed to reduce the government's size and power.

The president's efforts to shrink the federal government met with mixed success. In his 1982 State of the Union address, Reagan, like the previous Republican president, Richard Nixon, endorsed the New Federalism, a plan to transfer federal programs and tax revenues to the states. Reagan insisted the New Federalism would promote efficiency and economic growth, but governors worried that their states would be saddled with expensive responsibilities. In the end, only a few programs were transferred.

Congress also rebuffed administration plans to save money with tighter qualifications for government benefits and with a line-item veto permitting the president to reject specific spending programs.

Reagan had more success when he attacked social welfare programs. Like other conservatives, Reagan condemned antipoverty programs as a waste of federal resources that sapped the work ethic and the morals of the poor. He wanted reductions in food stamps, school meal programs, and aid to cities. In response, Congress cut funding for urban public housing and ended job training for the unemployed.

Reagan found it nearly impossible to touch Medicare and social security, two expensive and popular programs that benefited most Americans. By the 1980s there was concern that workers' social security payments would eventually not be enough to cover the cost of benefits to retirees. After a long struggle, Congress produced the Social Security Reform Act of 1983, which raised the minimum age for full benefits from 65 to 67 and taxed some benefits. The measure did little to reduce program costs. By 1984, Reagan promised not to cut social security.

Although expenditures for welfare programs continued to rise, the Reagan administration managed to slow the growth of such spending. Benefits did not expand dramatically; there were no costly new programs. Reagan did not reduce the federal government overall, but he did shrink the relative size of some parts of it that he disliked.

Reaganomics

For Reagan and his followers, shrinking the government also meant decreasing Washington's role in the economy. As conservatives, they argued that the nation prospered most when Americans were left free to manage their own businesses and keep their own earnings. The Reagan administration worked to lower taxes, deregulate business, and cut federal support for unions.

"Reaganomics" drew on a new theory known as supply-side economics. In the 1970s, economist Arthur Laffer had offered an alternative to the liberal, Keynesian economics that had guided federal policy since the New Deal. While Keynesians believed that increased consumer demand would spur economic growth, Laffer contended that an increased supply of goods and services was the key to growth. He rejected the Keynesian idea that more government spending put more money in the hands of consumers. To promote prosperity, he believed government should cut, rather than raise, taxes. Leaving more money in the hands of businesses would allow them to produce more goods and services. The increase in supply would stimulate prosperity and increase, rather than decrease, tax revenues.

Supply-side economics was controversial. Liberal critics called it an excuse to let the rich keep more of their money. Even some Republicans doubted that a tax cut would produce more tax revenues. But the supply-side approach fit neatly with conservative dislike for high taxes and big government.

Following supply-side principles, Reagan asked Congress in 1981 to cut taxes dramatically. Impressed by Reagan's popularity and the electorate's conservatism, the Democratic-controlled House joined the Republican-dominated Senate to pass the Economic Recovery Act of 1981 (the Kemp-Roth Bill). An important victory for Reagan, it cut federal income taxes 5 percent the first year and 10 percent in each of the next two years. It benefited the wealthy by making the tax structure less progressive and by reducing the tax rates on the highest incomes and on large gifts and estates.

Like other conservatives, Reagan believed that federal regulations hamstrung American business and prevented economic growth. Accordingly, his administration stepped up the campaign for deregulation begun by Jimmy Carter. The budgets of such key regulatory agencies as the Environmental Protection Agency and the Occupational Safety and Health Administration were cut. The administration also made sure that officials did not strictly enforce regulatory rules and laws. The administration also deregulated the telephone industry. In 1982 the giant American Telephone and Telegraph Company was broken into smaller regional companies, and new firms such as Sprint and MCI were allowed to compete for AT&T's long-distance business.

Reagan moved to lift environmental restrictions on business. His administration made it easier for timber and mining companies to exploit wilderness areas and for oil companies to drill off the Pacific coast. It also opposed environmentalists' demands for laws to protect against acid rain—industrial air pollution that harmed lakes, forests, and crops. Reaganomics also weakened organized labor, already suffering from deindustrialization. Ironically, Reagan, once the head of the Screen Actors Guild, was the first former union official to serve as president. Like most conservatives, Reagan believed that unions obstructed business and limited workers' freedom. He believed the federal government had done too much for organized labor since the New Deal.

Reagan took a strong antiunion stance during a strike by the Professional Air Traffic Controllers Organization (PATCO) in 1981. Despite a law banning strikes by federal workers, PATCO walked out to protest unsafe conditions in the air traffic control system. Reagan fired the striking controllers, refused to hire them back, and replaced them with nonunion workers. His action encouraged business to take a hard line with employees. By the end of the 1980s, unions were weaker than at any time since the Great Depression.

Reaganomics did not quite have the effect its supporters anticipated. Reagan's measures did not prevent a sharp recession, which began in the fall of 1981. As the Federal Reserve Bank fought inflation by raising interest rates, the economy slowed, and unemployment increased. Reaganomics also increased the federal budget deficit. The supply-side theory that tax cuts would boost tax revenues and balance the budget proved incorrect.

By the spring of 1984, the recession had ended. Thanks largely to the Federal Reserve's monetary policy, "stagflation," the combination of stagnant economic growth and high inflation, was over. As employment increased, Reagan's supporters gave the president credit. His critics charged that the deficit, not Reaganomics, had produced the boom and that the deficit would ultimately hurt the economy. In the mid-1980s, however, Reaganomics seemed to be a success.

The 1984 Presidential Election

The changing impact of Reaganomics affected national politics. In the depths of the recession, the Republicans lost 26 House seats in the midterm elections of 1982. But with the return of prosperity, the president was easily renominated in 1984. Reagan ran against a liberal Democratic nominee, former vice president Walter Mondale of Minnesota. Against a popular incumbent, Mondale made bold moves. He chose the first female vice-presidential nominee of a major party, Representative Geraldine Ferraro of New York. To prove his honesty and openness, Mondale made the politically foolish announcement that he would raise taxes as president. The Democrat was also saddled with the record of the Carter administration and the alienation of white working- and middle-class Democrats.

Reagan ran an optimistic campaign emphasizing national renewal. "It's morning again in America," Reagan commercials announced. "And people have a sense of pride they never felt they'd feel again." Mondale would jeopardize all that, the Reagan campaign charged, with tax increases and favors to such "special interests" as labor unions, feminists, and civil rights groups.

Election day revealed both the strength and the weakness of the Reagan Revolution. With his conservative message Reagan won 58.8 percent of the popular vote and lost only the District of Columbia and Mondale's home state of Minnesota. But his personal triumph did not translate into one for his party. Holding on to the Senate, the Republicans lost control of the House of Representatives.

The Reagan Revolution Abroad

Reagan's foreign policy, like his domestic policy, rested on old conservative values. The president rejected the main diplomatic approaches of the 1970s—Nixon's détente with the Soviet Union and Carter's support for international human rights. Instead, the Reagan

Revolution revived the strident anti-Communism of the 1940s and 1950s. The president moved to restore the nation's military and economic power to challenge the Soviet Union and stop Communism in the Western Hemisphere. Communism, however, had little to do with such difficult international issues as conflict in the Middle East, terrorism, and global economic competition. Nevertheless, the Reagan Revolution refocused American policy on the cold war confrontation with Communism.

Restoring American Power

After losing the Vietnam War, the United States had reduced both its armed forces and its willingness to risk military confrontations abroad. Reagan set out to restore American power in the 1980s—and the will to use it.

Like most conservatives, the president did not believe that cutting government spending meant cutting the armed forces. Under Reagan, defense spending more than doubled, from $134 billion in 1980 to more than $300 billion by 1989. Reagan also ordered development of controversial weapons systems. Construction of the B-1 strategic bomber, stopped by Carter, resumed, while development of the B-2 Stealth bomber began. Reagan won congressional approval for the MX Peacekeeper, a nuclear missile with multiple warheads and for work on the neutron bomb, a nuclear weapon. As he built up the military, Reagan faced a growing mass movement against nuclear weapons. In Europe and the United States, millions of people, frightened by nuclear war, called for a halt to new nuclear arms. In June 1982, a crowd of 700,000 in New York's Central Park demanded a nuclear freeze. The National Conference of Catholic Bishops supported the freeze and declared nuclear war immoral. But Reagan rejected the movement as naive and Communist-infiltrated. Peace, he believed, depended on developing more weapons.

The military buildup was also a matter of changing attitudes. In the wake of the Vietnam War, many Americans were reluctant to endorse intervention abroad. They feared becoming entrapped in another costly, losing, possibly immoral battle. This "Vietnam syndrome" threatened Reagan's foreign policy. The president could not afford to let other countries think he would not back up his words with action. Accordingly, Reagan used his speeches to stir up patriotic emotion and to persuade Americans that the Vietnam War had been "a just cause" worth supporting.

By the mid-1980s, Reagan had restored much of America's military power. It remained to be seen, however, whether Americans were willing to use that power abroad.

Confronting the "Evil Empire"

The main purpose of the buildup was to contain the Soviet Union. Suspicion of the Soviets and their Communist ideology was the heart of Reagan's diplomacy. In the early 1980s, Reagan called the USSR the "evil empire" and insisted that failing economies and unpopular regimes doomed the Soviets and their Communist allies. Communism, he predicted, would end up "on the ash heap of history."

Reagan avoided cooperation with the Soviet Union and held no summit meetings during his first term. His administration openly supported the mujahedeen, the Afghan rebels who were resisting the Soviets. More important, he avoided arms-control agreements with the Soviets during his first term. Instead, he used the military buildup to pressure the USSR. Reagan refused to submit the second Strategic Arms Limitation Treaty,

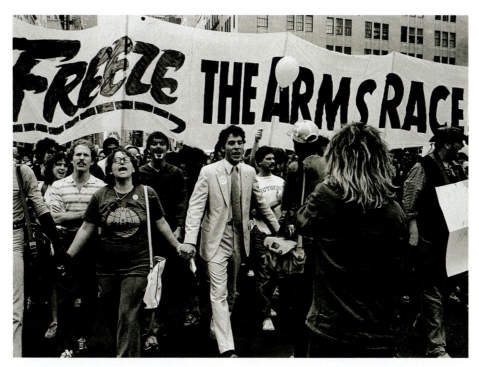

Some of the 700,000 Demonstrators at the Nuclear Freeze Rally in New York City's Central Park, June 1982 For a time, the movement to halt the introduction of new nuclear weapons challenged President Reagan's plans for an arms buildup.

signed by Jimmy Carter, to the Senate for ratification. In response to the United States' deployment of new nuclear missiles in Western Europe, the Soviets walked out of arms-control talks in 1983.

That year, Reagan put even more pressure on the USSR by announcing plans for the Strategic Defense Initiative (SDI), a space-based defense system of lasers and other advanced technology designed to shoot down enemy missiles. Funded by Congress, SDI was such a long way from reality that critics, sure it was science fiction, called the plan "Star Wars," after the epic space movie.

SDI doubly threatened the Soviets. It seemingly made the USSR vulnerable to attack. Since the 1950s, the Americans and the Soviets had relied on the theory of *mutual assured destruction* as a deterrent to war: because a nuclear war would destroy both sides, there was no incentive for either to start one. Now SDI raised the possibility that because the United States could survive a nuclear attack, it might be willing to start a war with the Soviets. The Soviets would then need to develop their own SDI. There was the second threat: the USSR would have to divert scarce resources and perhaps weaken their economy in order to compete with the United States.

While the United States pressed the Soviets, Reagan wanted to avoid open confrontation with the major Communist powers. In 1983, a Soviet fighter plane shot down an unarmed Korean airliner, killing all 269 aboard. Although a U.S. congressman was one of the victims, Reagan responded with restraint. A year later, Reagan traded visits with

864 Chapter 30: The Triumph of Conservatism

the premier of the People's Republic of China and encouraged stronger relations and a nuclear-weapons agreement.

The Reagan Doctrine in the Third World

The Reagan administration also changed American foreign policy toward the third world. Reagan and other conservatives had been impatient with the Carter administration's attempts to promote human rights abroad. The United States, they believed, needed to back anti-Communist, pro-American governments, whether or not they respected human rights. Jeane J. Kirkpatrick, who became Reagan's ambassador to the United Nations, distinguished between totalitarian regimes hostile to the U.S. and authoritarian governments friendly to American interests. Critics claimed this distinction was meaningless and insisted the nation not support antidemocratic governments. The administration adopted Kirkpatrick's view, which became known as the Reagan Doctrine.

The administration applied the Reagan Doctrine aggressively in Central America and the Caribbean (see Map 30–3). Determined to keep Communism out of the Western Hemisphere, the United States opposed the Marxist Sandinista government of Nicaragua and supported the repressive anti-Communist government of neighboring El Salvador.

Encouraged by the Carter administration, the Sandinistas had come to power in the late 1970s by overthrowing the dictatorship of Anastasio Somoza. The Reagan administration believed the Sandinistas were too friendly to the Soviet Union and to leftist rebels

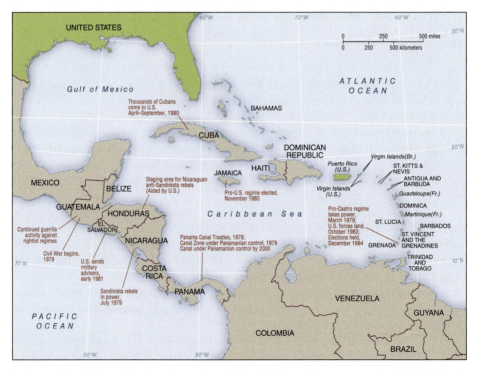

Map 30–3 The Reagan Doctrine in Central America and the Caribbean Events that shaped Reagan's anti-Communist initiative in the Western Hemisphere.

Reagan's Central American Policy The president holds up a T-shirt summing up his approach to the region: "STOP COMMUNISM CENTRAL AMERICA."

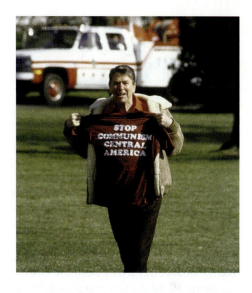

in El Salvador. Reagan halted aid to Nicaragua in April 1981 and directed the CIA to train, arm, and supply the Contra rebels, who opposed the Sandinistas. Many of the Contras had ties to the oppressive Somoza regime, but Reagan praised them as "freedom fighters." Meanwhile, the president strongly backed the right-wing military government of El Salvador, locked in a civil war with pro-Sandinista and pro-Cuban rebels. Employing infamous "death squads," the military government engaged in kidnapping, torture, and murder. Some 75,000 people died in the conflict. Still, Reagan did not want this brutal, undemocratic regime to fall. El Salvador, he explained, was "a textbook case of indirect armed aggression by Communist powers."

Despite such rhetoric, the administration could not persuade Congress to support its Central American policy. Congressional Democrats, like many Americans, did not want war in Central America. They were skeptical about the Communist threat and troubled by the antidemocratic character of the Salvadoran regime and the Contra rebels. In 1983 Congress approved Reagan's Caribbean Basin Initiative, an economic development package, but not military aid for the Salvadoran government. Instead, Congress passed the Boland Amendment, which restricted aid to the Contras and banned efforts to topple the Sandinista regime.

Reagan applied the Reagan Doctrine more successfully in the Caribbean. On October 25, 1983, U.S. troops invaded the small island of Grenada, supposedly to protect about 1,000 Americans, mostly medical students, from a Marxist regime. Reagan feared Grenada would become a Cuban or Soviet base close to U.S. shores. The invading force quickly secured the island and replaced the government with a pro-American regime. Critics charged that Reagan had violated the sovereignty of another state for an easy military victory. To his supporters, the invasion was a welcome demonstration of the Reagan Doctrine and an antidote to the Vietnam syndrome.

The president also applied the Reagan Doctrine in Africa. The Carter administration had condemned the long-standing policy of *apartheid*—racial separation—pursued by the white government of South Africa. Reagan, despite America's struggle with racial segregation, would not take such a strong stance. Rather than impose economic sanctions on South Africa, he endorsed mild diplomatic discussions known as "constructive engagement" while South Africa suffered violence and near civil war. Reagan held back because the South African regime was as an ally against Communism in the region. During the 1980s, the United States supported South African military intervention in Angola, Mozambique, and Namibia against groups aided by Cuba and the Soviet Union. More than a million people died in these conflicts.

The Middle East and Terrorism

The Reagan Doctrine was not much help in dealing with the Middle East and the growing problem of terrorism. Communism and the Soviet Union had little impact on Middle Eastern issues in the 1980s. As before, the United States wanted to ensure its supply of oil and to support its longtime ally, Israel. There was no new Arab oil embargo during the Reagan years, but the administration could not bring peace to the Middle East or end the threat of terrorism.

Reagan found it difficult to build on the Camp David Accords between Israel and Egypt, which were supposed to lead to self-government for the Palestinian Arabs living in the Israeli-occupied West Bank and Gaza Strip. Israel and the Palestine Liberation Organization (PLO), the official representative of the Palestinians, remained at odds. The PLO continued to threaten Israel from bases in neighboring Lebanon. In the spring of 1982, the Israelis invaded Lebanon, which was already convulsed by a civil war between Muslims and Christians.

To end the invasion and stabilize Lebanon, the United States sent marines to join an international peacekeeping force. On October 23, 1983, a terrorist bomb killed 241 Americans at marine headquarters at Beirut. The shocking attack marked a low point of Reagan's administration. The president did not retaliate. He did not want to reward terrorism by withdrawing from Lebanon. Nevertheless, he pulled out the soldiers in 1984, even though there was no peace in Lebanon and no agreement between the Israelis and the PLO.

The attack on the marine headquarters illustrated the growing threat of terrorism. Reagan vowed to make terrorists "pay for their actions," but terrorism proved hard to stop. Acts of terrorism by Palestinians and Libyans drew quick American reprisals in the 1980s. After Palestinians murdered an American passenger on a cruise ship in the Mediterranean in 1985, U.S. planes forced down the Egyptian airliner carrying the escaping terrorists. The Reagan administration believed that Muammar Qaddafi, leader of the North African nation of Libya, supported terrorism. In 1982 U.S. Navy fighter planes shot down two Libyan fighters. After American soldiers died in a terrorist bombing in West Germany in 1986, U.S. jets bombed targets in Libya, among them military barracks and Qaddafi's personal residence, killing one of his daughters. Qaddafi seemed to become less critical of the United States, but the threat of terrorism did not go away.

Reagan also acted to safeguard America's oil supply. During a war between Iran and Iraq, the United States sent warships to protect oil tankers in the Persian Gulf. American intervention was costly. In May 1987 Iraqi missiles struck the U.S. destroyer *Stark*, killing 37 of its crew. Unwilling to help Iran, Reagan accepted Iraq's apology. In July 1988, the U.S. missile cruiser *Vincennes* accidentally shot down an Iranian airliner, killing 290 passengers. An American apology did not quell Iranian anger, but the Iran-Iraq war soon ended, and with it the threat to America's oil supply.

The United States and the World Economy

Middle Eastern oil was only one economic factor shaping Reagan's foreign policy. The president had to deal with strains on the world economy. Like presidents before him, Reagan believed strongly that free trade would boost national economies. He believed, too, that other nations would benefit from cutting taxes, government spending, and regulation. But

AMERICA AND THE WORLD
>> **Japanese Management, American Workers**

Until the 1980s, most American work-ers had missed one of the basic ex-periences of globalization—management by foreigners. But with the weakening of American industry and the rebirth of the Japanese and West European econo-mies, foreign firms began to set up op-erations in the United States in the 1970s and 1980s.

Japanese firms rushed to invest. By 1988, more than 300,000 Americans worked for Japanese companies in the United States. The most publicized Japa-nese ventures came in the auto industry, long dominated by U.S. manufactur-ers. In the 1980s, leading Japanese auto manufacturers set up factories in such places as Marysville, Ohio, Smyrna, Ten-nessee, and Fremont, California. In these and other facilities, Japanese companies set about teaching Americans new ways to work.

The Japanese approach emphasized the importance of the group over the in-dividual and the company as a harmoni-ous family whose members had the same interests. To foster harmony, the Japa-nese eliminated reserved parking spaces for management and time clocks for la-bor. At the Nissan plant in Smyrna, man-agers and workers wore the same blue uniform. The Japanese also tried to im-prove communication with workers and draw them into decision making. To em-power workers and increase efficiency, Japanese companies often gave workers the means to stop production to elimi-nate a problem—something U.S. firms seldom did.

Japanese companies tried to improve factory life. Plants were clean and ef-ficient. At the Nissan factory in Smyrna, workers had basketball hoops and Ping-Pong tables for use during breaks. But the Japanese also banned smoking and radios. Management pushed workers to speed up production and wanted work-ers to be flexible enough to do different jobs in a plant.

Some workers enthusiastically ac-cepted the new approach. "I love it," gushed Nancy Nicholson, a laid-off fac-tory worker who found a job in a Japa-nese plant in Virginia. "They make you feel like a part of a family." Workers ap-preciated that Japanese managers put in long hours and seemed devoted to effi-ciency and quality.

Laboring harder than before, many American workers were not quite so en-thusiastic. They felt the Japanese were hostile to unions, African Americans, and women. Some American managers charged that Japanese employers would not promote them to top jobs. But most employees were glad to have a well-paying job that might last. Japanese ex-ecutives had their own criticisms. They felt that American workers needed too many instructions and too much motiva-tion. Individualistic Americans were not "team players" ready to admit mistakes or work outside their job descriptions. "Americans are too sensitive about fair-ness," complained Kosuke Ikebuchi, af-ter years in the United States. Japanese managers generally concluded that their

continued

American subordinates were less productive than Japanese workers.

Despite such criticism, Japanese companies seemed successful in the United States in the 1980s. Their units made gains in productivity and quality. The General Motors–Toyota plant in Fremont, California, turned out a car in 20 hours, compared with 28 hours at another GM plant. That car was more likely to satisfy buyers than one from an American-run company.

after years of economic decline, the United States could not always impose its will on other nations.

Reagan did force his views on weak, debt-ridden third world countries. By the end of the 1980s, developing nations owed foreign banks more than $1.2 trillion. Mexico was more than $100 billion in debt. American banks would lose heavily if those nations defaulted on loans. American producers stood to lose if those countries could not afford to buy U.S. goods. The Reagan administration refused to protect American banks from defaults, instead forcing debtor countries to adopt freer trade, deregulation of business, and austerity programs in return for new loans.

The Reagan administration had much less power to dictate trade policy with Japan. As Japanese exports flowed into the United States, Americans increasingly resented Japan's control of its home market. Congress, believing Japan discriminated against American goods, pushed for retaliation. Japan placed voluntary quotas on its export of steel and automobiles to the United States. Although the United States devalued the dollar to make American goods cheaper, the trade imbalance continued. In 1988 the president signed the Omnibus Trade and Competitiveness Act, which allowed the government to place high tariffs on Japanese goods if Japan discriminated against American goods. But, as long as Americans wanted Japanese products, retaliation was unlikely. In 1989 a Japanese car, the Honda Accord, was the first international model to become the best-selling automobile in America.

Many Accords had been made in the United States. Even as the administration struggled to open Japanese markets to American goods, Japanese firms increased their direct investment in the United States. Honda built a new factory in Marysville, Ohio, to produce Accords for the American market. As Japanese companies built or took over other facilities, many Americans wondered whether the global expansion of trade really benefited their country after all.

The Battle over Conservative Social Values

For all of Ronald Reagan's success in the early 1980s, the new conservatism met with important opposition. The conservatives' social values were especially controversial. Angered by the changes of the 1960s, many conservatives, like Linda Chavez, wanted to restore supposedly traditional values and practices. The conservative agenda collided head-on with one of the chief legacies of the 1960s—disadvantaged groups' demands for equal rights and opportunities. Many Americans were also unwilling to abandon the social changes of the last generation. Faced with such opposition, conservatives failed to achieve much of their vision.

Attacking the Legacy of the 1960s

The new conservatism was driven by a desire to undo the liberal and radical legacies of the 1960s. Conservatives blamed federal courts for much of the social change over the last generation. In the 1960s and 1970s liberal, activist justices had supported defendants' rights, civil rights, affirmative action, busing, and abortion while rejecting such conservative causes as school prayer.

Determined to take control of the courts, Reagan appointed many staunch, relatively young conservatives to the federal bench and the Supreme Court. In 1981 Sandra Day O'Connor, a fairly conservative judge from Arizona, became the Court's first woman justice. Reagan replaced retiring Chief Justice Warren Burger with conservative William Rehnquist. The appointments of two more conservatives, Antonin Scalia and Anthony Kennedy, seemed to push the Supreme Court away from liberalism.

It did not quite work out that way. In the 1980s the Court followed conservative views in limiting the rights of defendants. Rulings in *United States v. Leon* and *Nix v. Williams* in 1984 made it easier for prosecutors to use evidence improperly obtained by police. However, on other issues, the court took a moderate stance. In *Wallace v. Jaffree* in 1985, the Court invalidated an Alabama law that allowed schools to devote a minute each day to voluntary prayer or meditation.

Prayer was part of the conservatives' plan to reform public education. They believed that the federal government had played too large a role in the schools since the 1960s. Parents, meanwhile, had too little say in the education of their children. Preferring to use market forces rather than government to reform the schools, conservatives wanted to abolish the federal Department of Education. They also wanted to let parents choose the best schools—public or private—for their children and cover part of the cost with federally funded vouchers or tax credits.

Because many Americans worried about the quality of the schools, conservatives had a golden opportunity. But Congress refused to adopt vouchers or abolish the Department of Education.

Drug use was another issue conservatives linked to the 1960s. In the early 1980s, drugs again became a major concern with the spread of crack, a cheap, addictive form of cocaine. The sale and use of crack, especially in the cities, led to crime and violence. In 1986 the president and his wife, Nancy, announced a "national crusade" for a "drug-free" America. Their campaign encouraged young people to "Just Say No" to drugs, implemented drug testing for federal employees, and imposed mandatory minimum sentences for some drug use. The "war on drugs" was controversial. Critics called its rhetoric naive and ineffective. They also condemned new sentencing laws, which put millions in jail, as unfair to African Americans and expensive to taxpayers. Despite the crusade, drug use did not decrease appreciably.

Women's Rights and Abortion

One of the chief legacies of the 1960s was the women's rights movement. The new conservatism condemned feminism and deplored the changing role of women in America.

Many conservatives, especially evangelical leaders, blamed feminists and liberal government for encouraging women to abandon their traditional family role for paid jobs. The conservative movement was especially determined to halt federal initiatives, such as affirmative action programs and the equal rights amendment (ERA), that protected women's rights (see Chapter 29).

The conservative agenda on women's rights met with mixed results. The campaign for the ERA, lagging since the 1970s, ended unsuccessfully, but affirmative action programs to promote the hiring of women continued. So did women's push into the workplace and public life as more families needed two incomes. By 1983 women made up half of the paid workforce. As their economic role expanded, so did their political visibility. Ironically, Reagan gave women new public prominence by choosing Jeane J. Kirkpatrick and Sandra Day O'Connor for important offices.

Women still did not enjoy equality in America. They were generally paid less than men doing the same sort of work, and they had less opportunity to break through the "glass ceiling" and win managerial jobs. Commentators noted the feminization of poverty. Unmarried or divorced women, many with children, made up an increasing percentage of the poor. This unequal suffering, liberals and feminists argued, disproved the conservative claim that women did not need special protection.

For many conservatives, the right to abortion, guaranteed by the Supreme Court in *Roe v. Wade* in 1974, was the most troubling change in the status of women. A growing Right to Life movement passionately denounced abortion as the murder of the unborn, practiced by selfish women who rejected motherhood and family.

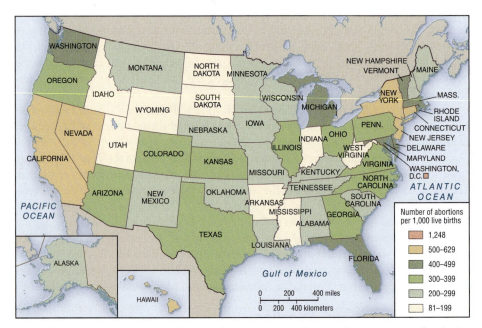

Map 30–4 Abortion in the 1980s The rate of abortions across the United States 14 years after the Supreme Court's decision legalizing abortion in *Roe v. Wade*. *Timothy H. Fast and Cathy Carroll Fast,* The Women's Atlas of the United States, *rev. ed. (1995), p. 166.*

Conservatives failed to narrow abortion rights significantly in the 1980s. Reagan persuaded Congress to stop the use of federal funds to pay for abortions, but a constitutional amendment outlawing abortion stalled in the Senate. Supreme Court rulings made in 1983 and 1986 upheld *Roe v. Wade*.

Gays and the AIDS Crisis

The gay rights movement was another legacy of the 1960s that troubled conservatives. Evangelical leaders such as Jerry Falwell condemned homosexuality on religious grounds. Some people believed that equal rights for gay men and women would promote immorality and corrupt children. In 1977 Anita Bryant, a former Miss America, launched a national crusade, Save Our Children, to protest the passage of a gay rights ordinance in Florida. Voters soon repealed the measure. In San Francisco in 1978, Harvey Milk, the first avowedly gay member of the city's board of supervisors, was assassinated, along with the mayor, by a former supervisor. Many were shocked when the assassin received only a short jail sentence.

Despite such opposition, the gay rights movement made progress in the 1980s. In 1982 Wisconsin became the first state to pass a law protecting the rights of gay men and women. By the end of the decade, most states had repealed sodomy laws that criminalized gay sex. In *Bowers v. Hardwick* in 1986, however, the U.S. Supreme Court dismissed a gay man's right to sexual privacy as "facetious."

The battle over gay rights took place against a tragic backdrop. In 1981 the Centers for Disease Control began reporting cases of acquired immune deficiency syndrome (AIDS), a disease that destroyed the body's immune system and left it unable to fight off infections and rare cancers. By the mid-1980s, researchers had traced AIDS to different forms of the human immunodeficiency virus (HIV) that were transmitted in semen and blood. But no cure had been found. By 1990 there were nearly 100,000 recorded deaths from the AIDS epidemic in the United States (see Figure 30–2).

Because 75 percent of the first victims were gay men, Americans initially considered AIDS a homosexual disease. Some people, including evangelical leaders, believed this "gay cancer" was God's punishment for the alleged sin of homosexuality. It became clear, however, that AIDS could also be transmitted by heterosexual intercourse, by intravenous drug use with shared needles, and by tainted blood transfusions.

Although understanding of AIDS and HIV increased, the specter of "gay cancer" promoted homophobia and slowed the response to the disease. The AIDS Coalition to Unleash Power (ACT UP) and other organizations staged demonstrations and acts of civil disobedience to call attention to the crisis and push for government action. Nevertheless, the Reagan administration did not fund research on AIDS for several years, and the disease continued to spread.

The AIDS epidemic complicated the struggle over gay rights. For some Americans, the disease reinforced the conservative condemnation of homosexuality. For others, the suffering of victims evoked sympathy and compassion. As the 1980s ended, the conservative backlash against gay rights had failed, but the epidemic continued.

African Americans and Racial Inequality

Conservatives were uneasy with another legacy of the 1960s, the expansion of African American civil rights and benefits guaranteed by the federal government. They believed

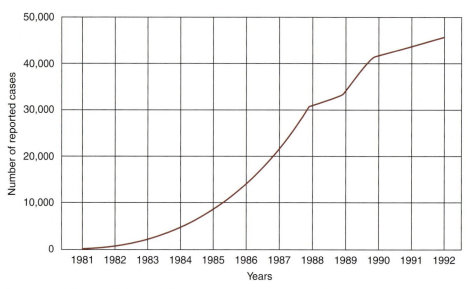

Figure 30-2   The Rapid Rise of AIDS Statistical Abstract of the United States, *1989, p. 111;* Statistical Abstract, *1993, p. 203.*

that the liberal policies of the Great Society hurt, rather than helped, black people and argued that individual initiative, not government action, would promote racial equality. Reflecting these ideas, Reagan opposed renewal of the Voting Rights Act and condemned busing and affirmative action. Like many Republicans, he opposed the creation of a national holiday marking the birthday of Martin Luther King Jr.

The conservatives' tough stance came at a difficult time for racial equality. African Americans' crusade for justice and opportunity generally slowed in the 1970s and 1980s. Despite legal equality, African Americans faced persistent racism and discrimination. Disproportionately clustered in manual occupations, they were particularly hurt by deindustrialization and economic decline . After years of improvement, African Americans' economic status relative to whites stagnated or declined during the Reagan era. African Americans still made less money than whites did for comparable work and had much less chance to attain managerial positions. All African Americans were not affected equally. In the 1980s the African American middle class continued to thrive. Among college-educated Americans, the incomes of black men rose faster than those of whites into the mid-1980s. Middle-class African Americans could afford to move to better housing, often in suburbs and integrated areas. Meanwhile, working-class African Americans found their wages stagnating or falling compared with those of white workers. In the 1970s and 1980s, poverty rates rose faster among African Americans than among whites. In 1985, 75 percent of poor African American children lived in families headed by a single female. Observers feared there was now a permanent African American underclass segregated in inner-city neighborhoods with poor schools and widespread crime.

As in the past, African American culture, driven by the distinctiveness of the black experience, was dynamic and controversial. In the poverty of the Bronx in New York City in the 1970s, young African Americans had begun to create a powerful new music, rap.

Reflecting the city's diversity, pioneering rap artists such as Kool Herc, Afrika Bambaataa, and Grandmaster Flash drew on Caribbean musical styles and the popular dance music disco, as well as on African American expressive traditions. Rap typically featured spoken lyrics over a driving percussive "break" beat, often sampled from other music. Along with graffiti and break dancing, the new sound made up a loose African American cultural movement known as "hip-hop."

Rap was the first new musical form to rival the impact of jazz in the 1920s and rock and roll in the 1950s. Spreading rapidly, rap crossed boundaries of race, class, and nation to appeal to middle-class, white, and international audiences. Commercially successful, rap was also controversial for its often raw look at ghetto life. The subgenre of gangsta rap, with its celebrations of gang life, violence, and misogyny, was especially provocative to conservatives and other Americans. Rap also deeply influenced other genres of music— another instance of the powerful impact of African Americans on American culture.

African Americans also mobilized to fight for equality and opportunity. Across the nation, the number of African American elected officials increased markedly. The Reverend Jesse Jackson, a protégé of Martin Luther King Jr., won wide attention. Preaching self-esteem and economic self-help for African Americans, Jackson was the leader of Operation PUSH—People United to Save Humanity. In 1984 Jackson challenged Walter Mondale for the Democratic presidential nomination. His campaign suggested how far American society had come in accepting African American political participation.

African American activism and the persistence of inequality made it difficult to undo the civil rights revolution. Most Americans seemed to accept that some federal action was essential to redress the imbalance between races. Despite Reagan's opposition, in 1982 Congress voted to extend the Voting Rights Act for 25 years. In 1983 the Supreme Court ruled that Bob Jones University, an evangelical institution, could not retain its tax-exempt status while it prohibited interracial dating and practiced other forms of discrimination. The court also rejected the Reagan administration's bid to set aside affirmative action programs,

The battles over the rights of African Americans, gays, and women underscored the limits of conservatism. Many Americans were not ready to undo the social and cultural legacies of the 1960s. New cultural expressions, such as rap, clashed with conservative values. The result was a stalemate. Disadvantaged groups made relatively little political progress in the 1980s, but conservatives also made little progress in their social and cultural agenda.

"The Decade of the Hispanic"

After the changes of the 1960s and 1970s, the Hispanic experience in the United States took on a quieter, more confident tone in the 1980s. Hispanics were not a homogenous group but a diverse population defined by geographical, cultural, and even linguistic differences. In New York City, Puerto Ricans predominated; in South Florida, Cubans; and in the long arc from South Texas to Southern California, Mexican Americans. In 1980 Hispanics were the nation's fastest growing minority group, with a birthrate 75 percent higher than the national average. Most immigrants to the United States were Hispanic, and demographers predicted that Hispanics would replace African Americans as the nation's largest minority group within a generation.

>> San Antonio

In the 1980s, tourists still came to San Antonio, Texas, to glimpse the past. Strolling the Paseo del Rio, the tree-lined River Walk along the San Antonio River, they visited the Roman Catholic missions erected by the colonizing Spanish in the eighteenth century. Tourists usually stopped at the most famous of the old missions, the Alamo, where a Texian and Tejano garrison died fighting the Mexican army in 1836.

Some hundred and fifty years later, San Antonio was also a place to see the future. By the 1980s, Hispanics, concentrated on the West Side, were a majority of the city's population. Home to nearly a million people, San Antonio was the largest Hispanic-majority city in the nation. Here was a possible glimpse of the future United States.

In San Antonio, the increase in the Mexican American population translated into political power. For decades, an Anglo business elite had controlled the city. But by the 1970s, the emerging Hispanic majority threatened to sweep away Anglo power. COPS—Citizens Organized for Public Service—practiced a divisive, confrontational politics on behalf of Mexican Americans who lacked quality housing, education, and job opportunities. Then, in 1977, the federal government used the Federal Voting Rights Act to destroy a critical tool of elite power, at-large or citywide elections for city council. These elections virtually guaranteed victory for white candidates. Now the city had to adopt single-member council districts,

which meant that the West Side barrios could elect candidates of their own. Five of the eleven positions went that year to Chicanos, who allied with a black councilman for a majority.

However, confrontational politics brought few gains for Chicanos. Then the Democrats nominated a young councilman, Henry Cisneros, for mayor in 1981. An urban planner from the West Side, Cisneros argued that Mexican Americans would flourish only if business flourished, too. Campaigning successfully in the West Side barrios and the Anglo North Side, Cisneros became the first Mexican American mayor of San Antonio since 1842. At a victory party, Cisneros embodied the artful balance behind Chicano power in the city: dressed in a Ralph Lauren suit, he happily broke a traditional piñata.

Reelected three times, Cisneros aggressively pursued his economic vision for San Antonio. Here, again, the city offered a glimpse of the future. Where San Antonio's fragile economy had depended on tourism and military bases, Cisneros wanted to create a "no-smokestack" economy of high technology and tourism. economy. As Advanced Micro Devices, Control Data, and other corporations invested in San Antonio, electronics plants sprang up on the North Side. Sea World and a $200 million shopping plaza opened for tourists and shoppers.

With his term ending, Cisneros designated 1988 "The Year of Emergence," when the nation would have to recognize San Antonio's redevelopment. San

Antonio was still a poor city, above the national average in unemployment and below it in income. Proud of Cisneros, Mexican Americans still lived less well than whites. To some, Cisneros's business

policies had shortchanged the West Side. The community, warned the president of COPS, wanted "development, not exploitation." Only time would tell who was right.

These growing numbers created a new sense in the 1980s that Hispanics mattered and could not be ignored. "We are," a Hispanic Roman Catholic priest declared, "the future."

In this consumer society, the increasing importance of the Hispanic population could be measured in goods and services. Hispanic culture affected the nation's foodways. From the 1970s into the 1980s, more and more Americans discovered "Tex-Mex," the distinctive cuisine of the Tejanos, the Mexican Americans of South Texas. By the 1990s, salsa had passed catsup as the best-selling condiment in the United States.

Meanwhile, American business moved to attract Spanish-speaking consumers. The Coors brewery enthusiastically declared the 1980s "The Decade of the Hispanic." By 1983, Coors and other companies could advertise in the expanding Spanish-language media, including newspapers, magazines, and 67 television stations.

For politicians, the 1980s were also "The Decade of the Hispanic." Republicans, long unable to attract a majority of African Americans, hoped that Roman Catholic Hispanic voters, like Linda Chavez, would respond to the new conservatism's emphasis on values, family, and religion. Reagan's anti-Communism did attract Cuban Americans, so many of whom were refugees from the regime of Fidel Castro. However, most Hispanics, including Mexican Americans, emphasized economic issues. They continued to fight poverty and struggle for opportunity. Unlike Linda Chavez, the Hispanic majority preferred the more activist economic and educational policies of the Democrats.

The increasing importance of Hispanic voters also affected the response to the perhaps 3 million illegal immigrants who had crossed the border from Mexico into the United States. The Immigration Reform and Control Act of 1986, known as the Simpson-Mazzoli Act, penalized Americans who knowingly brought illegal aliens into the country and hired them. But the measure also reflected the sentiments of Mexican Americans and other Americans by offering amnesty to illegal aliens who had arrived since 1981.

From Scandal to Triumph

The stalemate over social values was not the only sign that there were limits to conservatism in the 1980s. Scandals plagued business and religious figures who had helped create the conservative agenda. Policy setbacks, economic woes, and scandals plagued the Reagan administration. For a time, the conservatives' triumph was in doubt, but then the cold war began to end.

Business and Religious Scandals

By the mid-1980s the new conservatism was suffering a series of business and religious scandals. In 1986 Ivan Boesky, the swaggering Wall Street dealmaker, was indicted for insider trading, the illegal use of secret financial information. Rather than go to trial, he agreed to give up stock trading, inform on other lawbreakers, spend two years in jail, and pay a $100 million fine. In 1987 Michael Milken, the junk bond king, was indicted on fraud and racketeering charges. His plea bargain agreement included a 10-year jail sentence and a $600 million fine, the largest judgment against an individual in American history.

Such scandals provoked second thoughts about the celebration of business and materialism. Critics pointed out that Boesky's and Milken's business methods had hurt the economy by saddling corporations with a great deal of debt and little cash to pay for it. Lavish lifestyles no longer seemed so attractive.

Scandal also touched religion. In 1987 Americans learned that televangelist Jim Bakker had defrauded investors in his theme park, Heritage USA, and paid hush money to hide an adulterous liaison with a church secretary. In 1988 Jerry Falwell had to resign from his Moral Majority. That year, televangelist Jimmy Swaggart admitted he "had sinned" with prostitutes.

> At its best, the Reagan Presidency provided a tonic of self-confidence that helped to restore vigor to the national economy and psyche; at its worst, it fostered greed, chauvinism and intolerance.
>
> R. W. APPLE, 1989

Political Scandals

The Reagan administration had its own scandals. Before the end of the first term, more than 20 EPA officials resigned or were fired over charges of favoritism toward lobbyists and polluters. In 1985 Secretary of Labor Raymond Donovan resigned after becoming the first cabinet officer ever indicted. In 1988 Reagan's friend and attorney general, Edwin Meese III, resigned amid questions about his role in the corrupt awarding of government contracts. To critics, the administration's "sleaze factor" stemmed from the president's contemptuous attitude toward government and his eagerness to please business.

In his second term, Reagan faced much more damaging accusations. In October 1986, Sandinista soldiers in Nicaragua shot down a plane attempting to supply the Contra rebels. The plane had been part of a secret effort by the administration to violate the Boland Amendment's ban on aid to the Contras. Then, a Lebanese magazine reported that the United States had traded arms to Iran. Despite Reagan's denials, the government had sold arms to win the release of American hostages held by terrorists in Lebanon. The administration had broken the president's pledge not to negotiate with terrorists and had violated a ban on arms sales to Iran. The arms deal and the Nicaraguan plane crash were connected: the government had illegally used proceeds from the arms sale to pay for supplying the Contras.

The scandal that became known as the Iran-Contra affair had the potential to drive Reagan from office. If the president had ordered or known about the arms deal and the supply effort, he might have faced impeachment. Three separate investigations made clear the president's probable involvement in the Iran-Contra affair, but none turned up enough evidence to impeach him.

Nevertheless, Reagan's reputation was badly damaged. Several of his associates left office and faced jail sentences. Former national security adviser Robert "Bud" McFarlane pleaded guilty to withholding information from Congress. His successor, Rear Admiral John Poindexter, was allowed to resign. Poindexter's aide, Marine Lieutenant Colonel Oliver North, had to be fired. Meanwhile, the director of the CIA, William Casey, died in 1987, the day after he was implicated in the Contra affair. Much of the country concluded that Reagan must have known about his associates' dealings; his popularity dropped.

Setbacks for the Conservative Agenda

Amid the scandals, conservatives faced a series of policy setbacks. The Democratic-controlled House of Representatives was less cooperative during Reagan's second term. Democrats became even more combative after winning majorities in the House and Senate in the congressional elections of 1986.

As a result, Reagan had to compromise more with Congress. In 1985 he called for a Second American Revolution, a comprehensive overhaul of the income tax system. But the Tax Reform Act Congress passed in 1986 did not lower and simplify income taxes nearly as much as the president had wanted.

Reagan also met outright defeat in Congress. In 1988, a coalition of Democrats and Republicans passed a bill compelling large companies to give workers 60 days' notice of plant closings and layoffs. Reagan opposed this liberal measure, but he allowed the bill to become law without his signature.

The president was often defeated on environmental policy at a time of growing concern about environmental hazards. In December 1984 the subsidiary of a U.S. corporation accidentally allowed toxic gas to escape from a pesticide plant in Bhopal, India. The emission killed more than 2,500 people and injured 200,000. In April 1986 an explosion and fire released radioactive material from a nuclear power plant at Chernobyl in the Soviet Union. The accident killed more than 30 people, injured more than 200, and exposed countless others to radioactivity. Suddenly, Reagan's hostility to environmentalism was no longer so appealing. The president had to accept the 1986 extension of the federal Superfund program to clean up hazardous waste. The next year, Congress overrode his veto of a bill renewing the Water Quality Control Act. In 1988 the Reagan administration signed an international agreement setting limits on emissions linked to acid rain.

A Vulnerable Economy

Even the economy, the centerpiece of the Reagan Revolution, became a problem in the president's second term. During the 1980s the gap between rich and poor widened sharply. From 1977 to 1980, the average family income of the highest-paid tenth of Americans rose 27 percent, whereas that of the poorest tenth fell 11 percent (see Figure 30–3). In the 1980s only the rich earned more and kept more. Other Americans faced economic stagnation or decline.

In 1980, 29 million Americans lived below the poverty line. Ten years later, that figure had grown to almost 37 million. Despite Reaganomics, the United States had one of the highest poverty rates among industrialized nations.

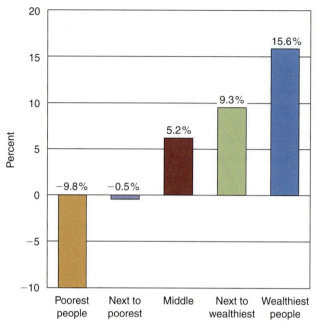

Figure 30–3 Changes in Families' Real Income, 1980–1990 The Reagan Revolution had very different consequences for rich and poor. *Copyright © 1989 by the New York Times Co. Reprinted by permission.*

One of the most visible consequences of poverty was homelessness. In the 1980s the number of homeless Americans increased markedly. The sight of men and women sleeping on sidewalks was common during the Reagan years.

Homelessness, poverty, and inequality produced a spirited debate in the 1980s. Democrats and liberals blamed these problems on Reaganomics. The president, they charged, had done nothing to stop the erosion of high-paying factory jobs. His welfare, housing, and job-training cuts hurt the poor, while his tax cuts and deregulation helped the rich. Conservatives and Republicans maintained that activist, liberal government had hurt manufacturing and weakened the economy. Moreover, welfare programs caused poverty by destroying poor people's work ethic and making them dependent on handouts.

In reality, both liberal and conservative policies had produced flawed economic results. Lyndon Johnson's spending for the Great Society, along with the cost of the Vietnam War, had begun to undermine the economy in the 1960s. His antipoverty programs had been less effective than liberals wanted to admit, but the Reagan Revolution did not end poverty, either. Reaganomics did not reinvigorate manufacturing or boost middle-class incomes.

There were other signs of economic vulnerability by the mid-1980s. Despite Reaganomics, the federal budget deficit did not disappear. Instead, between 1981 and 1986, tax cuts and increased defense spending drove the deficit from $79 billion to $221 billion—a staggering new record.

Like poverty and inequality, the deficit was controversial. Some economists believed the deficit was a sign of great economic weakness; others believed it did not matter. Democrats and liberals blamed Reagan for the red ink. Reagan's supporters blamed Congress for failing to cut the budget.

In fact both the president and Congress were to blame. Neither Republicans nor Democrats wanted to reduce Medicare and social security. Congress enacted the Balanced Budget and Emergency Deficit Control Act of 1985 (the Gramm-Rudman Act), which promised to balance the budget by 1990, but a Supreme Court ruling critically weakened the measure. During Reagan's last years in office, the national debt—the total amount owed by the federal government to its creditors—reached $2.6 trillion.

Along with burgeoning debt, the Reagan years produced a growing international trade deficit. In 1980 the annual value of imports was $25.4 billion greater than the value of the nation's exports. By 1986 that gap had grown to $145.1 billion, as American business lost out to foreign products both at home and abroad. Reaganomics had not solved the problem of America's relative decline in the world economy.

Doubts about Reagan's economic policy increased when the stock market fell unexpectedly on Monday, October 19, 1987, losing 508 points, or 23 percent of its value. It was the biggest one-day decline since "Black Tuesday" in October 1929. The market drop reflected underlying economic problems, including the federal budget deficit, the trade deficit, and deindustrialization, plus lax government regulation of Wall Street. The crash seemed to be a mortal blow to what a journalist called " the Reagan Illusion: the idea that there could be a defense buildup and tax cuts without a price, that the country could live beyond its means indefinitely."

Reagan's Comeback

Remarkably able to withstand defeat, Reagan began his comeback from scandals and economic troubles. Opponents dubbed him the "Teflon president" because nothing seemed to stick to him. That was a tribute to his political skills, as well as many Americans' real affection for him. After a series of disappointing presidencies, Americans seemed unwilling to let Reagan fail.

The economy also helped the president. The stock market crash did not, as feared, lead to depression or recession. The market soon recovered and the economy grew.

Reagan's comeback was probably helped most by the transformation of the Soviet Union. By the mid-1980s the Soviets suffered from a weakening economy, an unpopular war in Afghanistan, and a costly arms race. Mikhail Gorbachev, dynamic and charismatic, became General Secretary of the Communist Party and signaled a new era with a series of stunning reforms. At home, he called for restructuring the economy (*perestroika*) and tolerating more open discussion (*glasnost*). Abroad, he sought to ease tensions with the United States and the West.

Gorbachev's reforms gave the U.S. an opening to thaw cold war tensions. Reagan met with the Soviet leader in a series of summits beginning in November 1985. Visiting West Berlin in June 1987, the president challenged Gorbachev to "tear down" the Berlin Wall, which had symbolized the cold war division of Europe. Meanwhile, it became apparent that the Soviets were changing their foreign policy, as they withdrew their troops from Afghanistan and eased their control over Eastern Europe.

The United States and the Soviets also made real progress on arms control. In December 1987 Reagan and Gorbachev signed the Intermediate-Range Nuclear Forces Treaty

(INF), promising to destroy more than 2,500 intermediate-range missiles. For the first time, the two powers had agreed to give up a weapon altogether.

The INF treaty permanently eased tensions. The cold war suddenly ended. Reagan's presidency ended in 1989; a year later, the United States and the Soviet Union agreed to end production of chemical weapons and reduce existing stockpiles. In 1991, the two nations signed the START (Strategic Arms Reduction Talks) Treaty, which called for each side to reduce its nuclear arsenals as much as 30 percent.

Meanwhile, the Soviet Union weakened. In 1989, Gorbachev could do nothing to stop the collapse of its repressive allies in Eastern Europe, as regimes toppled in Bulgaria, Czechoslovakia, Hungary, Poland, and Rumania. Most dramatically, a new East German government agreed in November to allow travel through the Berlin Wall. As jubilant Berliners dismantled it, the wall's fate epitomized the collapse of Communism. Accepting the transition to democracy, the Soviets withdrew their troops from Eastern Europe.

Powerless to save its allies, the Soviet leadership soon could not save itself. Despite Gorbachev's efforts, the low standard of living, Communist repression, and the unpopular war in Afghanistan made many unhappy. Estonia, Latvia, Lithuania, and other republics chafed under Russia's domination of the USSR. In 1990 Russia chose a charismatic president, Boris Yeltsin, who quit the Communist Party, supported independence for the republics, and challenged Gorbachev. The next year, Gorbachev resigned as party leader and president, and the Soviet parliament suspended the Communist Party. As one republic after another declared its independence, the USSR ceased to exist.

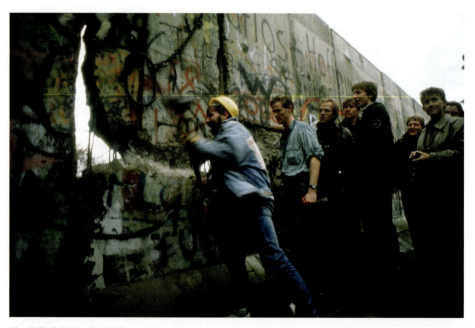

The Fall of the Berlin Wall On November 11, 1989, a man helps dismantle the barrier that divided East and West Berlin and symbolized the division between communism and the west during the cold war.

With the collapse of the Soviet Union, the United States and its allies had won the cold war. Conservatives insisted that Reagan's overpowering defense buildup had forced the Soviets to surrender. Democrats maintained that the buildup and the president's harsh rhetoric had actually slowed the thaw in U.S.-Soviet relations and that America won the cold war because of its long-term strength and strategy. Typically modest, Reagan himself gave credit to American policies reaching back to the 1940s.

Meanwhile, Americans did not celebrate very much as the Berlin Wall came down and the Soviet Union collapsed. The cold war had cost a great deal in money and lives. Many Americans wondered whether Communism had posed a mortal danger to the United States in the first place.

Conclusion

Reagan left office with the highest popularity rating of any president since the beginning of modern polling in the 1930s. His comeback culminated the triumph of the new conservatism, but the nature of that triumph would be debated for years to come. The Reagan Revolution did not solve such basic economic problems as poverty and even worsened some problems, such as inequality and the budget deficit. Much of its conservative social agenda failed to take hold.

Nevertheless, Reagan successfully combated the sense of national decline that had pervaded America in the 1970s. His presidency reinvigorated faith in capitalist innovation, minimal government, and American military power. At the end of the 1980s, business values and evangelical religion claimed a more prominent place in American culture.

The accomplishments of the new conservatism, as Reagan's troubled second term indicated, were fragile. The nation's economic revival was shaky, and Americans were still worried about the future. "I think," a businessman concluded, "the '90s are going to be much trickier than the 1980s."

Review Questions

1. What were the main values and goals of the new conservatism in the 1980s? What role did business and religion play in shaping the conservative movement?

2. What was the Reagan Revolution in domestic policy? How did Reagan's domestic programs reflect conservative values?

3. Describe the aims of Reagan's foreign policy. How did his goals differ from those of earlier presidents during the cold war?

4. What groups resisted the conservative social agenda in the 1980s? Did the desire for equal rights and opportunities conflict with conservatism?

5. What factors limited the triumph of the new conservatism? Did conservatives really succeed in the 1980s?

6. How did the conservatism of the 1980s differ from earlier forms of conservatism in the twentieth century?

>> Timeline

▼1980
Ronald Reagan elected president

▼1981
IBM personal computer
Air traffic controllers' strike
Economic Recovery Act

▼1982
Nuclear freeze rally in New York City
Boland Amendment

▼1983
Strategic Defense Initiative
U.S. invasion of Grenada
Terrorist attack on U.S. Marines in Lebanon

▼1984
Reelection of Ronald Reagan

▼1985
General Electric purchase of RCA
Gramm-Rudman Act

▼1986
U.S. bombing of Libya
Tax Reform Act
Revelation of Iran-Contra affair

▼1987
Stock market crash
Intermediate-Range Nuclear Forces Treaty

▼1988
Omnibus Trade and Competitiveness Act

▼1991
Collapse of the Soviet Union

**For further review materials and resource information,
please visit www.oup.com/us/ofthepeople**

"A Nation Transformed"
1989–2008

>> Tiger Woods

"Hello world," smiled 20-year-old Stanford undergraduate Tiger Woods as he became a professional golfer in 1996. A prodigy ready to take on the world, Woods was a distinctive product of global forces. His father, Earl, was part African American, Native American, and Chinese. A U.S. Army officer, the elder Woods had met Kultida Punsawad in Thailand during the Vietnam War. Kultida, part Thai, Chinese, and Dutch, had become Earl's wife and Tiger's mother.

Tiger quickly succeeded. In 1997, he became the youngest player to win the prestigious Masters Tournament at the Augusta National Golf Club. Setting record after record, Woods became the greatest golfer and the best-paid athlete of his generation.

Observers interpreted Woods's success as a triumph for African Americans. In this notoriously segregated sport, blacks had long been denied admission to elite clubs such as Augusta. Woods's Masters victory, the first for a nonwhite, seemed like one more milestone in the struggle for African American civil rights.

Woods himself fed that perception. "[E]ven though I'm mathematically Asian," he said, "if you have one drop of black blood in the United States, you're black." Yet Woods also defined himself as the sum of all his parents' racial identities, calling himself "Cablinasian"—a mixture of Caucasian, black, Indian, and Asian. "As proud as I am of Tiger Woods, I realize I have to share him," said an African American civil rights activist. "He is part of a new reality. "

Observers welcomed Woods as an emblem of a more diverse nation. "[H]e is many races," said a radio talk show host. "And that's what makes us Americans, because we're the melting pot. We're kind of mutts." The African American television personality Oprah Winfrey dubbed Woods "America's son." Yet he did not always seem American. Representing the nation in the Ryder Cup, Woods, who also had Thai citizenship,

continued

>> AMERICAN PORTRAIT *continued*

felt that he was "playing for the United Nations, not the United States." His parents held up their multiracial son as a transnational man with a globalizing mission. "He can hold everyone together," his mother said. "He's the bridge between the East and the West," Earl Woods said. Marriage to a Swedish model strengthened Tiger's transnational image.

As the world drew together in new ways, Woods's racial and national identities made him "a one-man symbol of globalization in the twenty-first century." Multinational corporations paid him to reach the global marketplace. Woods's greeting, "Hello world," was the slogan of his Nike marketing campaign. He traveled the world to promote everything from cars and video games to laser eye surgery and corporate consulting.

Despite his transnational image, Woods did seem to serve U.S. values and interests. In the Philippines in 1998, he promoted a golf community built on land taken from thousands of peasants. Wanting to keep Woods out of the country, the peasants' lawyer dismissed him and the golf club as "just complete manifestations of U.S.-dictated policies."

So distinctive, Woods epitomized forces changing the United States. As his endorsements reflected, an emerging information economy still manufactured automobiles but leaned toward computing, medical services, and leisure. Like Woods, the nation was economically globalized and culturally diverse. While Woods profited handsomely in a changing world, the United States struggled with the consequences of the information economy, globalization, and diversity. Although conservatism still shaped American democracy, conservatives had less success shaping social and cultural change. America's place in a globalizing world was uncertain, particularly after a devastating terrorist attack in September 2001 and a stunning stock market crash in September 2008. Americans lived, as the commission investigating the attack put it, in "a nation transformed." But the nature of that transformation was uncertain.

Common Threads

>> What were some of the most pervasive consequences of technological change in the last decades of the 1900s? Where and when did these changes begin? How did they unfold?

>> How did the new conservatism of the 1980s continue to influence American politics and culture?

>> Did the African American civil rights movement extend its influence beyond the twentieth century?

>> What were the main uncertainties of a post–cold war, postindustrial, postfeminist, post–civil rights society?

The Age of Globalization

By the end of the twentieth century, Americans increasingly felt enmeshed in global forces. America, of course, had been defined through its history by its relationship to the world. But this global connection entered a new, more self-conscious phase in the 1980s. During the decade, the term *globalization* first came into use to describe the web of technological, economic, military, political, and cultural developments binding people and nations ever more tightly together. The cold war's end, technological advances, the spread of multinationals and other organizations, the creation of transnational economic alliances, and a new wave of immigration all drew the United States deeper into globalization.

> Globalization is not just a trend, not just a phenomenon, not just an economic fad. It is the international system that has replaced the cold-war system.
>
> THOMAS L. FRIEDMAN, 1999

The Cold War and Globalization

For two generations, the cold war had both facilitated and hindered globalization. In some ways, the confrontation between the United States and the Soviet Union linked the world more closely together. Each power had a host of ties to other nations. The United States had established regional military alliances around the world and helped rebuild Asian and European economies through lower trade barriers and the World Bank and the International Monetary Fund.

Still, the cold war inhibited globalization. The United States and the Soviet Union had largely avoided trading with each other. Each power had discouraged its allies from ties with the other side. The collapse of the Soviet Union in 1991 opened the way to further globalization. Now nations and companies could forge new ties more freely across the old cold war divide.

New Communications Technologies

New communications technologies sped up the global flow of news, ideas, and money. The Internet, a product of the cold war, emerged from a Department of Defense search for a means of maintaining communications in the event of a nuclear attack. Aided by the development of the telephone modem and fiber-optic cable, the Internet spread quickly in the 1990s and 2000s. At first, people used the Internet to send and receive electronic messages, but by the middle of the 1990s, computer users also explored the World Wide Web, a rapidly expanding segment of the Internet that blended text, graphics, audio, and video. By 2000, some 304 million people from more than 40 nations were using the global information superhighway to do research, create and exhibit art, listen to music, share photographs and films, and buy and sell online.

Communications satellites also played a critical role in globalization. Following the U.S. deployment of Telstar and other satellites in the 1960s, Canada, Japan, and several other nations had launched their own. In the 1990s, global satellite communications revolutionized

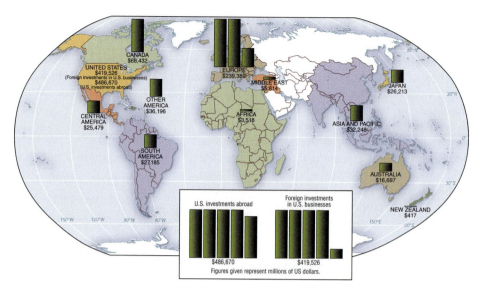

Map 31–1   The Globalization of the U.S. Economy The large worth of U.S. investment in other regions around the world was nearly equaled by the value of foreign investments in the United States in 1992.

the news business. Cable News Network (CNN), founded in 1979 by the entrepreneur Ted Turner, used satellite uplinks to provide live televised coverage of events around the world. Turner wanted CNN to be a "positive force in the world, to tie the world together." CNN's success inspired the creation of satellite news organizations in other countries.

At the same time, mobile and cellular telephones spread especially quickly in many countries outside the United States. In Africa, there were already more than 15 million cell telephone subscribers in the early 2000s.

Multinationals and NGOs

Easily connecting businesses across national borders, communications advances helped stimulate an astonishing increase in the number of multinational corporations. In 1990, there were 3,000 multinationals worldwide. By 2003, the number had mushroomed to 63,000. With some 821,000 subsidiaries, multinationals employed about 90 million people and accounted for perhaps one-fourth of the world's economic output.

Long a leader in the creation of multinationals, the United States was still home to many of the largest and wealthiest firms. By 2003, Wal-Mart was Mexico's largest private-sector employer, with 100,000 workers. But America now faced intense competition from Japan, Europe, and other nations. In 1962, nearly 60 percent of the top 500 multinationals were American; by 1999, the percentage had declined to 36.

Along with multinational companies, private nongovernmental organizations—NGOs—also fostered globalization. Some NGOs, such as the International Red Cross, dated back to the nineteenth century. The World Economic Forum, which brought leaders and experts together each year in Davos, Switzerland, was a product of the 1970s. So were the environmentalist Greenpeace and the humanitarian Doctors Without Borders. By the 2000s, there were more than 10,000 NGOs worldwide.

The Birth of the Internet Sketched in 1969, this crude diagram of the first four nodes of the Advanced Research Projects Agency Network (ARPANET) would lead to the explosive growth of the Internet in the 1990s and 2000s.

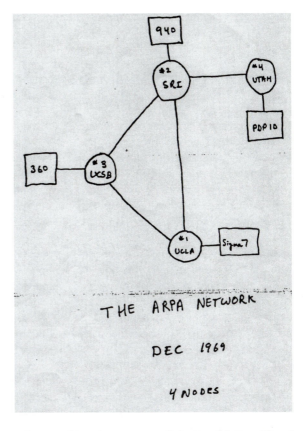

Expanding Trade

After international peace, the most basic necessity for globalization was the easy movement of goods, services, and capital across national boundaries. In the 1990s and 2000s, the United States and other nations, eager to support their multinational corporations and seize their share of the global market, moved aggressively to remove barriers to trade and investment. With the end of the cold war, America established economic relationships with the former republics of the USSR, the European countries of the Soviet bloc, the Socialist Republic of Vietnam, and the People's Republic of China. By 1996, Wal-Mart had a store in Beijing, and McDonald's had restaurants in Russia.

To spur international trade and investment, nations also created regional economic alliances that guaranteed member states trading and investment privileges and lowered or abolished tariffs. In 1991, the member states of the European Economic Community, a pioneering regional trade alliance, signed the Maastricht Treaty to create a single vast unit, the European Union (EU), with its own currency, the euro. With 6.4 percent of global population, the EU produced a third of the world's goods and more than a third of its trade.

The 1990s also witnessed the transformation of the General Agreement on Tariffs and Trade (GATT). A U.S. cold war creation, GATT had drawn together more than 100 nations. Its efforts to liberalize trade through agreements known as "rounds" culminated in 1993 when the Uruguay Round produced a dramatic victory for free-trade policies. GATT was then reborn as a more powerful global body, the World Trade Organization (WTO), whose decisions would be binding on member nations. The United States joined the WTO in 1995.

Moving People

The movement of human beings was critical to globalization. Thanks to regional economic agreements and the end of the cold war, people could cross national borders more

AMERICA AND THE WORLD

>> Globalization's Final Frontier

After covering the earth, globalization also reached into space. Like the United States and the Soviet Union in the cold war, more and more nations translated their hopes, ambitions, and fears into space programs. Like America, other countries found satellites an indispensable part of globalization: they were critical to communications and information gathering and essential to building economies, spying on enemies, and positioning soldiers. A secure military foothold in space might even ensure survival on earth. Outer space became globalization's final frontier.

Dozens of countries had space programs by the 2000s. Reflecting the economic and political integration of Europe, 13 West European nations had formed the European Space Agency in 1975. By the end of the twentieth century, ESA was using the Ariane launch vehicle to send satellites and probes into space. By then, India, Israel, and Japan were also launching satellites, and Brazil was working to develop a launch capability.

The People's Republic of China had the most ambitious of the newer space programs. Despite its developing economy and limited investment in science, China wanted to rival the United States not only in the exploration of space but also perhaps in the development of space-based military capabilities. The Chinese had launched satellites in the 1970s, developed a successful launch vehicle in the 1980s, and begun a manned space program in the 1990s. In October 2003, China became the third nation to put a man in space when the vehicle Shenzhou ("Sacred Vessel"), based on old Soviet technology, carried an astronaut on a 21-hour flight. Meanwhile, the original space powers struggled. The Russians, inheriting the remnants of the Soviet space program, could barely afford to keep it going. Desperate for money, the Russians auctioned space memorabilia and signed up wealthy civilians as the first space tourists.

For most Americans, space no longer seemed exciting or important. With the Soviet Union gone, NASA faced even leaner budgets. In February 2003, the explosion of the shuttle *Columbia*—the second such tragedy—left Americans unsure about the safety and value of the space program.

In space, the United States pursued friendly collaboration with other countries. After partnering with the Soviets on space flights in the 1970s, the American space program joined Canada, Japan, Russia, and other nations in an often troubled effort to build the International Space Station in the 1990s.

The United States also unilaterally pursued its own interests in space. In the 2000s, George W. Bush, like Ronald Reagan before him, favored the development of a space-based system to defend against missile attack. Warily eying the People's Republic of China, policy makers feared an assault on American satellites and potential space weaponry. The globalization of space, like the globalization of the world, was both exhilarating and frightening.

Making Economic Policy in a Global Age World leaders, including President George W. Bush (sixth from the left, front row), meet in Washington, DC, in the midst of a developing economic crisis, November 2008.

easily. Between 1990 and 1994, 4.5 million immigrants came to the United States. By 2000 the immigrant population had reached 26.3 million, about 11 percent of the national total population, the largest percentage since before World War II.

Travel also facilitated globalization by exposing people to other nations and cultures. Thanks to low-cost jet flights and improved living standards, tourism was possibly the largest single global industry by the 1990s.

The Politics of a New Economy

Globalization combined with technological change to create a new, information-centered American economy. This transformation produced a record economic boom in the 1990s; it also produced new insecurity and inequality. The political system responded with generally conservative solutions emphasizing individual responsibility and limited government. Despite unrest over immigration and trade, American leaders remained firmly committed to globalization.

The Information Economy

As deindustrialization continued, the nature of the postindustrial economy became clearer at the close of the twentieth century. By the 1990s, factories employed fewer production workers than in 1955; meanwhile, the service sector accounted for about 70 percent of America's economic activity. The rise of services using sophisticated communications, computing, and biomedical technology encouraged the belief that information would define the twenty-first-century economy.

In the 1990s and 2000s, innovations in electronics continued to transform communications. More and more Americans carried pagers and cellular telephones. High-speed fiber-optic cables and satellite dishes expanded the power and reach of telephone and television systems. By 1999 more than half of the nation's households had at least one computer. The new information economy also spurred the hope that Americans would process data instead of coal and produce knowledge instead of steel.

Advances in genetics and medical technology further sparked hopes for an information-centered economy. At the close of the twentieth century, scientists had made rapid advances in understanding animal and human genomes. Corporations soon began applying this genetic knowledge to agriculture, medicine, and other fields. The result was biomedical technology—the use of organisms and their products to alter health and the environment. By the end of the 1990s, about one-third of the U.S. corn, cotton, and soybean crops were products of genetic engineering. By then, more than 125 genetically engineered drugs had been approved for the treatment of cancer and other diseases.

Computing played a key role in the growth of biomedical technology. It helped researchers pioneer bioinformatics, the application of information science and technology to biological problems, and also drove the development of such tools as magnetic resonance imaging.

A Second Economic Revolution?

The information and industrial economies were fundamentally quite different. Manual, blue-collar labor tended the machines of smokestack America; white-collar, well-educated labor tended the computers of information America. The industrial economy had eaten up fossil fuels, minerals, and other exhaustible resources and produced substantial pollution; the information economy promised less damage to the earth.

In some ways, however, the rise of the information economy repeated the Industrial Revolution. As in the late 1800s and early 1900s, technological change pushed new corporations to the forefront of American capitalism: software firms such as Microsoft and Oracle; hardware firms such as Dell and Intel; e-commerce pioneers such as Amazon.com and eBay; and the search engine giant Google.

Like the Industrial Revolution, the information revolution spurred a wave of corporate consolidation. The ABC television network, already merged with Capital Cities Communications in the 1980s, was taken over by Walt Disney in 1995. That year, media giant Time Warner, the product of a merger in 1989, bought out Turner Broadcasting. Then, in a sign of the growing importance of the Internet, Time Warner merged with Internet service provider America Online in 2000.

The information revolution also paralleled the Industrial Revolution by producing a new, wealthy elite. The most famous of this new group of multibillionaires was Bill Gates, the cofounder of Microsoft, who became the richest American since John D. Rockefeller, the cofounder of Standard Oil, nearly a century before.

Just as the appearance of trains, planes, and machines stimulated artists and intellectuals in the nineteenth and twentieth centuries, so did the appearance of computers a century later. Digital technology made it easy to copy and manipulate text, images, and sounds, a development that encouraged collage and undermined linear narratives. More broadly, some thinkers believed a new, postmodern culture was replacing the modern culture inspired by industrialism. Hard to define, postmodern culture embraced a more skeptical view of accepted truths and dominant ideologies.

Despite the parallels, the information economy was still immature. Machine tools, railroads, and electricity had greatly boosted workers' productivity in the industrial era. Computers, the Internet, and biotechnology had yet to do the same in the 2000s. Moreover, most service positions required little education, used limited technology, and paid less than the best blue-collar jobs of the old economy. By the 2000s, the biggest employer in America was not a software company but rather a low-wage retail store, Wal-Mart.

Boom and Insecurity

For most of the 1990s, globalization and the information revolution seemed to benefit the economy. Productive American workers and a vital service sector produced economic growth for nearly the entire decade, a record. Because of global competition, corporate cost cutting, and low oil prices, inflation was negligible. Interest rates were low; unemployment dropped off to record lows. Excitement about information-related companies drove the stock market to one record high after another. After passing 3,000 for the first time ever in 1991, the Dow Jones industrial average soared past 11,000 in 1999. As memories of the 1987 market crash faded, many Americans no longer felt the need to live with less. Congress repealed the federal 55-mile-per-hour speed limit for interstate highways in 1995, and gas-guzzling sport utility vehicles (SUVs) became popular.

Despite their new SUVs, many Americans faced economic challenges in the 1990s and 2000s. Global competition reduced labor forces aggressively. Corporate downsizing now affected both white-collar and blue-collar workers, and both kinds of jobs were being outsourced overseas. Even jobs in computing and customer service migrated to Ireland, the Philippines, and India, where English was spoken and wages were lower. Outsourcing jolted Americans who believed that college degrees and corporate employment guaranteed middle-class status. "This has been a very nasty journey," admitted an unemployed stockbroker.

The increasing costs of health care also troubled Americans. By the 1990s, the United States was spending a greater proportion of its gross domestic product on health care than were other developed nations. Still, 43 million Americans did not have health insurance in 2003. The United States, almost alone among developed nations, had no national health insurance plan for its citizens. As employers cut costs, they decreased medical benefits for employees. The need for costly medical care would only increase as life expectancy continued to rise and the huge baby boom generation aged.

Americans feared, too, that they could not afford retirement. With the aging of the baby boom generation, there were more Americans over 65 and eligible for social security benefits than ever before (see Map 31–2). Many people believed there would not be enough money to pay pensions in the twenty-first century. Private employers, meanwhile, reduced pension benefits for many retirees.

The Return of Inequality

The insecurities of many working- and middle-class Americans reflected a trend toward economic inequality. Allowing for inflation, the average weekly earnings of American workers in 1998 were less than in 1970. The decline of manufacturing meant the loss of relatively high-paying jobs. Employers were determined to hold down the growth of wages

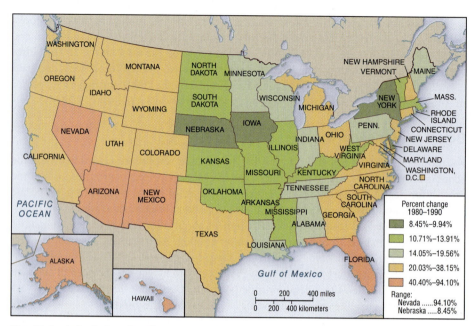

Map 31-2 Aging in America The increase in the percentage of the U.S. population age 65 and over from 1980 to 2008 helped fuel worries about health care and social security.

and salaries in the 1990s. Workers, facing threats from downsizing and outsourcing, were reluctant to demand big wage increases, as were labor unions, which continued to have difficulty organizing workers.

To stay even, Americans borrowed and worked more than before. Many families now had both parents in the paid workforce. In 1960, only a fifth of women with children under six held paid jobs; in 1995, two-thirds worked for pay. Partly because they now held two and even three jobs, many people put in much more time at work. In 1960, Americans worked less—1,795 hours a year—than their counterparts in Britain, France, Germany, and Japan. By 1997–1998, they worked more—1,966 hours a year.

Meanwhile, the wealthy fared exceptionally well. By 1949, the richest 1 percent of American households had seen its share of the nation's wealth dwindle to 20 percent. By 1997, its share had zoomed up to 40 percent, nearly back to the record heights of the 1920s. In 2000, the richest 400 Americans had an average annual income of $174 million, almost quadruple their earnings only eight years earlier.

Several factors spurred the rebirth of great fortunes. The boom of the 1990s, fed by the information revolution, rewarded Bill Gates and other wealthy men and women with vast profits on their stocks and bonds. Tax cuts allowed the rich to keep more of their wealth. A change in public attitudes also helped. In the 1990s, observers noted the emergence of a "winner-take-all" culture that accepted wide differences in earnings.

At the start of the new century, the United States, the richest country in the world, was also the country with the largest gap between rich and poor. Many observers wondered whether strong social class differences, which had decreased in the mid-twentieth century, would once again define the nation and limit democracy.

The Power of Conservatism

Faced with troubling economic change, Americans had relatively little faith in the political system after the upheavals of the 1960s and 1970s. In 1994 only 19 percent felt they could trust government. Partly as a result, most voters did not favor a return to liberal, activist policies. Instead, national politics, although intensely contested, seldom strayed far from the conservative trail blazed by the Reagan Revolution of the 1980s.

In 1988, Reagan's vice president, George H. W. Bush of Texas, easily defeated the colorless liberal Democratic nominee, Governor Michael Dukakis of Massachusetts, to become the nation's 41st president. But hopes of continuing the Reagan Revolution faded as voters left the Democrats in control of the House and Senate. Squabbling with Congress, Bush vetoed 40 bills and even closed down the government briefly in a budget dispute. Yet Bush also alienated conservatives. He supported new environmental controls and federal funding for education. He broke his campaign pledge not to raise taxes.

Running a tired campaign for reelection in 1992, Bush faced a surprisingly strong third-party challenge from a Texas billionaire businessman, H. Ross Perot. But it was Governor Bill Clinton of Arkansas, a moderate "New Democrat," who seemed the best chance for change. Bush's broken tax promise and a weak economy doomed his campaign. Winning with only 43 percent of the popular vote, Clinton had a chance to partner with the Democratic-controlled Congress to move toward liberalism. But when the president proposed a liberal solution to the nation's health care crisis in 1993, Congress rejected the plan as too expensive and too intrusive. A year later, the Democrats lost control of Congress.

Fighting for his political future, Clinton catered to moderates and conservatives. "The era of big government is over," he declared. Through budget cuts and tax increases, he managed to end the budget deficit. In 1996, he signed a welfare bill that significantly reduced federal support for the poor, especially children. The bill limited welfare recipients to five years of assistance over their lifetimes and required heads of households on welfare to find work within two years. Many Democrats and liberals angrily claimed that the president had betrayed the poor.

To keep the economy booming, Clinton blended liberal and conservative financial policies. In 1995, liberals were pleased by the revised Credit Reinvestment Act, originally passed during the Carter administration, to encourage banks to offer "subprime" mortgages—home loans to low-income Americans who would not traditionally qualify for such financing. Clinton also endorsed the conservative goal of easing federal regulation of the financial industry. In 1999, he signed the Financial Services Modernization Act (the Gramm-Leach-Bliley Act), which removed long-standing restrictions and permitted commercial banks, investment banks, and insurance companies to compete for one another's business. Democrats went along in part because Republicans agreed to revise the Credit Reinvestment Act to make it easier for low-income Americans to get credit to buy houses. In the short run, subprime mortgages and deregulation helped sustain the economic boom and President Clinton. But in little more than a decade, these actions would become much more controversial.

Thanks to his move to the right and the continuing economic boom, Clinton easily beat the Republican presidential nominee, Senator Bob Dole of Kansas, in 1996. But Clinton's second term nearly collapsed in scandal over his real estate dealings and his adulterous affairs. In 1998, the House of Representatives voted two articles of impeachment

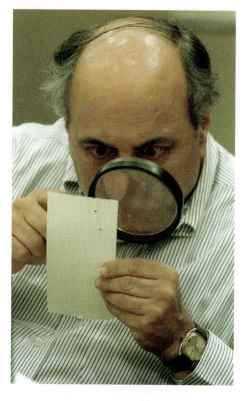

The Disputed Presidential Election of 2000 A judge tries to decide how to count a voter's ballot in Broward County in the crucial state of Florida.

charging the president with perjury and obstruction of justice. Only the second president to go on trial in the Senate, Clinton remained popular. Most Americans seemed willing to separate his private and public lives and wanted to keep him in office. Reflecting popular opinion, the Senate voted to acquit Clinton on both articles of impeachment.

Although Clinton had charted a moderate course between liberalism and conservatism, his scandal-ridden presidency did not guarantee Democratic success. In one of the closest elections in history, his vice president, Al Gore of Tennessee, lost to Governor George W. Bush of Texas, the son of the first President Bush, in 2000. Although Gore won the popular ballot by 550,000 votes, Bush appeared to capture a narrow majority of the Electoral College. But it took the intervention of the Supreme Court to halt a controversial recount of Florida's vote and thereby make him the 43rd president.

Influenced by Reagan's success, the younger Bush was more conservative than his father. In his first term, "Bush 43" pushed successfully for tax cuts to stimulate the economy and weakened regulatory oversight of the financial industry. But Bush also accepted a classic liberal initiative, an expensive drug benefit program for retired Americans.

In 2004, Bush faced another liberal Democrat, Senator John Kerry of Massachusetts, who tried to capitalize on worries over outsourcing and economic change. Yet Bush prevailed with 50.7 percent of the popular vote and a solid electoral majority. Buoyed by his victory, the president promised new conservative initiatives, including a reform of the social security system. His plans went nowhere, particularly after the Democrats won control of both houses of Congress in 2006. Thanks to Bush's tax cuts, drug plan, and military expenditures, the federal government ran a budget deficit again—another disappointment to conservatives, who yearned for a leaner government.

Contesting Globalization

Republican and Democratic leaders generally agreed with big business that globalization represented a triumph for American institutions and values, including capitalism, free trade, and democracy. Despite tough international economic competition, American leaders thought the nation was still better off than in a divided world without free trade. Some

Three Presidents From left, George H. W. Bush ("Bush 41"), his son, George W. Bush ("Bush 43"), and 42nd president Bill Clinton.

Three Presidents From left, George H. W. Bush ("Bush 41"), his son, George W. Bush ("Bush 43"), and 42nd president Bill Clinton.

multinational executives did not see their interests as completely identical with those of the government. But multinationals still depended on a powerful U.S. government to protect their investments around the globe.

In contrast, many middle- and working-class Americans questioned whether globalization made their lives better. In the mid-1990s, the presence of between 2 and 4 million illegal immigrants from Mexico angered many American citizens, particularly in Texas and California. Their argument was familiar: illegal aliens drove down wages and took jobs from native-born Americans who paid higher taxes to provide services and benefits to tax-evading immigrants. Supposedly, Spanish would rival English, and whites would lose political power and cultural influence. In response to such fears in 1994, California voters passed Proposition 187, a referendum denying illegal aliens access to public education and other benefits. Two years later, Congress increased efforts to stop the flow of illegal immigrants.

The anti-immigrant movement did not go much further. Business generally welcomed immigration because it provided workers. Calculating the rapid growth of the Hispanic population, political leaders did not wish to antagonize an increasingly powerful group of voters. Many native-born Americans, themselves descendants of immigrants, believed immigration would invigorate the economy and the culture.

International trade provoked a more complex battle. The U.S. government, faced with the rapid-fire appearance of regional economic alliances, moved to create its own economic bloc. In 1992, the United States joined with Canada and Mexico in the North American Free Trade Agreement (NAFTA). It established the world's largest and richest low-tariff trading zone to promote commerce among the three countries. Fearing more lost jobs, organized labor opposed the agreement. So did many environmentalists, who believed corporations would get around U.S. environmental laws by moving operations to Mexico. But the leadership of both major parties favored the agreement and in 1993, the Senate ratified NAFTA.

Opposition to globalization flared again at a meeting of the WTO in Seattle, Washington, in 1999. Labor unions, environmentalists, consumer activists, women's groups, and other organizations staged parades, meetings, and street theater. Demonstrators charged that the WTO favored corporations and developed nations, damaged the environment, allowed AIDS to spread, and destroyed indigenous cultures. Fears of protest and terrorism led to cancellation of the WTO meetings scheduled for 2001.

Globalization was hard to contest. It would take more than isolated protests to change the behavior of multinationals and governments and divert, let alone halt, the movement of people, ideas, technologies, goods, and capital in the twenty-first century.

A Changing People

Globalization was one of several forces reshaping American society and culture at the turn of the twenty-first century. As Latinos became the largest "minority" group, the time was nearing when people of color, rather than whites, would make up a majority of the nation's population. As the experience of African Americans underscored, race and rights remained divisive issues. Concern about rights also sparked "culture wars" over family and sexual values and the status of women and homosexuals. In general, these struggles moved American society in a liberal direction: the changing population became more tolerant of diversity and more willing to extend rights to disadvantaged groups.

A Diverse Society of Color

The racial and ethnic composition of the United States changed rapidly at the turn of the twenty-first century. In 2001, Americans of Hispanic or Latino origin outnumbered African Americans and became the largest minority group. Thanks to a strong job market, the Hispanic and Latino population had spread well beyond its traditional concentrations in south Florida and the states from Texas to California. Mexican immigrants moved to small midwestern towns and cities where semiskilled and unskilled jobs paid 10 and 15 times more than jobs in Mexico. By 2004, nonwhites made up one-quarter of the population. Americans of Hispanic or Latino origin, white and nonwhite, numbered about 40 million—almost 14 percent of the population. Expecting the number of Hispanics and Asians to triple in the next 50 years, the Census Bureau predicted that the United States would become a diverse society of color, with a nonwhite majority.

As the population changed, the concept of race became more complicated. To many Americans, race was largely a divide between black and white. But the growth of the Hispanic or Latino population confounded this simple division. "White means mostly privilege and black means overcoming obstacles, a history of civil rights," explained Patria Rodriguez in 2003. "As a Latina, I can't try to claim one of these."

Like Tiger Woods and Patria Rodriguez, many Americans felt that mixed racial background was a basic and distinctive part of their identity. In 2000, the Census Bureau let people choose more than one race to describe themselves. Hispanics, epitomizing the complications of race, were allowed to identify themselves both as Hispanic and as members of any race.

African Americans in the Post–Civil Rights Era

As Americans faced the future, the African American experience was a reminder that issues of race and rights remained volatile and unresolved. By the 2000s, half a century after *Brown v. Board of Education*, southern schools were largely desegregated. But thanks to white flight from inner cities, many northern schools were more segregated than ever. Despite continuing inequities, African Americans had made notable gains since *Brown*. In 1957, only 18 percent of black adults had graduated from high school. By 2002, 79 percent had. Yet the African American graduation rate lagged 10 percentage points behind the rate for whites.

African Americans had also made notable economic and political gains. The black middle class continued to grow. But high rates of unemployment and imprisonment

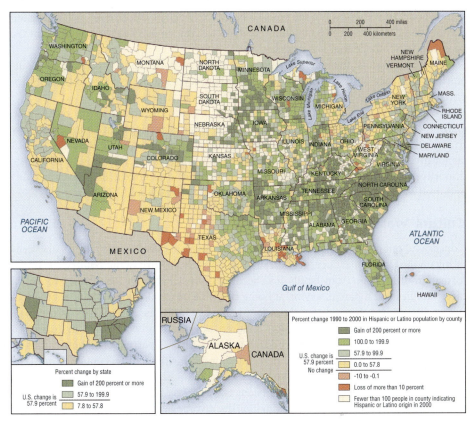

Map 31-3 The Growing Population of Americans of Hispanic or Latino Origin: Percent Change, 1990-2000 Thanks to a strong job market nationwide, the Hispanic and Latino population increased dramatically across the country. *Data Sources: U.S. Census Bureau, Census 2000 Redistricting Data (PL 94-171) Summary File and 1990 Census.*

meant that only about six of every ten African American men were in the paid workforce in 2002. Despite the wealth and fame of Oprah Winfrey, relatively few African Americans ranked among the wealthiest people in the United States. The number of high-profile African American public officials grew, and by 1992 there were more than 10,000 black officeholders nationwide. In 2001, Colin Powell became the first African American secretary of state, and Condoleezza Rice became the first African American (and female) national security advisor. Four years later, Rice became secretary of state.

These and other firsts did not mean the end of racial injustice and conflict. In 1991, white police in Los Angeles stopped a black motorist, Rodney King, for drunk driving and then savagely beat him. Despite a videotape of the beating, an all-white jury acquitted four of the policemen of all charges. The verdict set off a riot in the predominantly African American community of South Central Los Angeles, including the Watts section that had been the center of rioting in 1965. Three days of violence left 51 people dead, 1,800 injured, and nearly 3,700 buildings burned. In the aftermath, Americans debated whether the legal system offered justice to African Americans, while liberals and conservatives blamed each other for the poverty and despair of many black communities. Eventually a federal court convicted two of the police officers for depriving King of his civil rights and another court awarded him $3.8 million in damages. But no one had real solutions for the problems of South Central Los Angeles.

Despite the riots, the federal government took few new steps to deal with racial inequality. In an age of pessimism about government, few Americans believed that any liberal programs could secure equal conditions for African Americans.

At the same time, Americans did not want to undo the achievements of the past. Despite conservative opposition, affirmative action remained legal. In *Gratz v. Bollinger* in 2003, the Supreme Court, reflecting popular uneasiness with racial quotas and formulas for diversity, struck down a system used by the University of Michigan to advantage minority applicants to its undergraduate program. But in *Grutter v. Bollinger*, the court endorsed Michigan's affirmative action program for its law school.

Culture Wars

Concerns about rights also drove a cluster of controversies, known as "culture wars," centering on the family, marriage, gender, and sexuality. By the turn of the century, the transformation of the American family had become unmistakable. In the 1950s, two out of three families had a parent staying at home full-time; in 2000, with so many mothers in the workforce, less than one family in four had a stay-at-home parent. The "traditional" nuclear family of father, mother, and children no longer predominated in American households. Married couples with children made up only 25 percent of all households by 1996 (see Table 31–1). That year, 27 percent of families with children contained one parent, usually a mother, rather than two.

A number of factors led to these changes. Americans were marrying later, having fewer children, and having them later in life. The divorce rate doubled from 1960 to 1990. In the 1990s about half of all marriages were ending in divorce. As women's wages rose, more women could afford to live alone or to head families by themselves.

Many conservatives and Republicans blamed these developments on an alleged moral decline. In their view, the counterculture of the 1960s, liberals, the media, feminists, and gays had undermined "family values." "It is a cultural war, as critical to the kind of nation we will one day be as was the cold war itself," thundered Patrick Buchanan in 1992.

 Table 31-1 The Changing American Family, 1960–2006*

Year	Households	Families	Married-Couple Families	Single-Parent Families	One-Person Households
1960	52,799	44,905	23,358	3,332	6,917
1970	63,401	51,456	25,541	3,271	10,851
1980	80,776	58,426	24,961	6,061	18,296
1990	93,347	66,090	24,537	7,752	22,999
1996	99,627	69,594	24,920	9,284	24,900

Source: U.S. Census Bureau website, http://www.census.gov/population/socdemo/hhfam/rep86/96hh4.txt, http://www.bls.census.gov/population/socdemoc/hhfam/rep96/96hh1.txt and /96fml.txt.

*Numbers given in thousands.

To defend the family, some conservatives argued that single mothers should receive fewer welfare benefits and that divorce should be made more difficult. In response, liberals claimed that the family was not dying but simply adapting to change, as it always had. The different forms of the family, like social diversity in general, could be viewed as a good thing.

Conservatives found the battle for "family values" almost impossible to win. In 1992, George H. W. Bush's vice president, Dan Quayle, attacked the TV sitcom *Murphy Brown* for its positive portrayal of a career woman's decision to have a child out of wedlock. The show stayed on the air; Quayle and Bush lost their reelection bid. A decade later, a Federal Communications Commission crackdown on radio "shock jocks" such as Howard Stern led some radio networks and stations to drop controversial programming, but the business survived, and Stern drew more listeners than ever.

Women in the Postfeminist Era

As the *Murphy Brown* controversy suggested, women were at the center of the culture wars. Women's position in American society had changed dramatically since the 1960s. The percentage of adult women in the workforce rose, as did the percentage of women in high-paying white-collar jobs. Women were more visible in politics. After the 1992 elections, a record 53 women held seats in Congress. In 1993, Janet Reno became the first female attorney general, and Madeleine Albright became the first female secretary of state.

Yet there was a sense of stagnation in the new century. In 2002, women earned on average 77.5 percent as much as men—little better than 10 years before. Women were still more likely than men to live in poverty. Bill Clinton's adulterous affairs dramatized women's insistence that men "just don't get it" about relationships between the sexes. Nearly half of women believed the woman's movement had made their lives better, but the movement was now less visible and less vocal. The 2000s were part of both the "post–civil rights era" and the "postfeminist era."

Still, conservatives could not turn back the clock. Forced to raise troops without a draft, the military, one of the last and most intensely masculine preserves, needed female volunteers. In 1994, the Department of Defense rescinded the "Risk Rule" that kept women out of units in which they could be harmed or captured. As more women entered the military, the armed services repeatedly had to deal with charges of harassment. In 2000, the army admitted that a male general had sexually harassed its highest-ranking woman general.

Conservatives also tried to limit women's access to abortion. At the grassroots level, the Right to Life movement picketed abortion clinics and tried to discourage pregnant women from having abortions. Some radicals resorted to violence, including the murder of clinic workers. Meanwhile, both presidents Bush opposed abortion and named antiabortion judges to the federal courts.

In spite of the protests and political maneuvers, abortion continued in the new century. In *Planned Parenthood v. Casey* in 1992, the Supreme Court narrowly voted to uphold much of a Pennsylvania law limiting access to abortions while also declaring that a woman's right to choose an abortion was "a component of liberty we cannot renounce." President Clinton chose proabortion justices and vetoed antiabortion legislation.

Winning Gay and Lesbian Rights

Homosexuality was one more front in the culture wars. Although most Americans believed businesses should not discriminate on the basis of sexual preference, a majority in the 1990s believed that homosexuality was morally wrong. Every year, there were hundreds of documented instances of violence against gays and lesbians.

As homosexuals pressed for equal rights, evangelical Christians and conservatives fought back. In 1992 Colorado voters passed a referendum forbidding communities to pass laws protecting gay rights, but the state supreme court declared it unconstitutional. In 1996, Congress passed the Defense of Marriage Act, which denied federal benefits to same-sex couples and allowed states to refuse to recognize same-sex marriages from other states.

The military was another battle zone. Officially barred from serving, homosexuals had long concealed their sexual orientation in order to remain in the military. Then, in 1992, a federal court ordered the navy to reinstate an openly gay petty officer who had been discharged. Campaigning for president, Clinton promised to lift the ban on gays in the armed services. As president, he compromised by instituting a "don't ask, don't tell" policy. The military would no longer ask recruits whether they were gay, and gays and lesbians would continue to conceal their sexual orientation.

The tide seemed to turn, however. As AIDS spread more slowly among the gay population and heterosexuals contracted the disease, Americans were less likely to consider it "gay cancer" or God's punishment. Meanwhile, gays became a more accepted presence in society. More television shows positively depicted homosexuality. Openly gay men and women served in Congress. Many businesses, including Disneyland, welcomed gay customers. Leading corporations, including Ford and General Motors, began providing benefits to the partners of gay employees.

Americans, especially younger ones, increasingly accepted the legitimacy of gay relationships. In *Lawrence v. Texas* in 2003, the U.S. Supreme Court struck down state antisodomy laws and effectively legalized gay sexual behavior. After *Lawrence*, there was new support for legalizing same-sex marriage. In 2004, the mayor of San Francisco, flouting state law, issued marriage licenses to same-sex couples. Liberal Massachusetts became the first state to legalize same-sex marriages, and couples flocked there to be married. Despite the support of conservatives and George W. Bush, a constitutional amendment banning gay marriage failed to pass that year. In 2008, the California Supreme Court overturned a state ban on same-sex marriage. But in November, a ma-

The Spread of Same-Sex Marriage
In June 2008, a ruling by the California State Supreme Court allowed same-sex couples, including this one, to marry.

jority of California voters passed a referendum imposing a ban. The struggle over gay rights would continue.

The battles over family values did little to alter the direction of social change in the United States. After a decade of the culture wars, Americans seemed willing to balance conservative economic policy with more liberal social values.

America in the Post–Cold War World

With the end of the cold war, America's role in the world, so clear for nearly half a century, suddenly became unclear. In 1991, the American-led victory in the Persian Gulf War suggested that the United States might serve as an international police officer in a "New World Order," even as Americans remained reluctant about intervention abroad. But then the attacks of September 11, 2001, forced the United States into an ongoing global war on terror.

The New World Order

As the cold war ended, some Republicans called for a less internationalist foreign policy. Echoing conservatives of the 1940s and 1950s, they insisted that the United States should no longer provide financial aid and military protection to other countries. In contrast, internationalists in both the Democratic and Republican parties believed the United States could protect itself and advance its interests only by remaining active in world affairs.

The most powerful internationalist was President George H. W. Bush. A naval aviator in World War II, the elder Bush believed that American isolationism had once encouraged fascist aggression and world war and argued that the United States now had to maintain its overseas commitments. With the help of other powerful countries, America should use foreign aid, military strength, NATO, and the United Nations to maintain a stable international system, a "New World Order," of democracy, capitalism, free trade, prosperity, and the rule of law. Much like Woodrow Wilson and Harry Truman, Bush mixed idealism and self-interest: a free world would be good for other nations and for the United States. But only America could preserve that world.

The New World Order was a vague concept. Just what overseas commitments did America need to make? Was the United States supposed to protect antidemocratic countries in the name of international stability?

There was also a tension between Bush's commitment to international cooperation and the long-standing tendency for the United States to act alone in its own hemisphere. Despite talk of a New World Order, Bush intervened unilaterally in the Central American nation of Panama in 1989. Bush had grown frustrated with General Manuel Noriega, the Panamanian leader who engaged in drug sales to the United States and other illegal activities. After Noriega blocked democratic elections, Bush sent American troops, who captured Noriega and sent him to the United States for prosecution on drug charges in 1989. Bush's action, condemned by Latin American countries, contradicted his rhetoric about international collaboration.

Finally, the New World Order, like the containment of Communism, could be expensive in lives and money. It was unclear whether Americans, remembering the Vietnam War, would endorse armed intervention abroad. With the end of the cold war, many people also wanted a "peace dividend" of savings on foreign aid and military expenditures to be spent on domestic needs.

The Persian Gulf War

The test of the New World Order came soon enough. On August 2, 1990, Iraq, led by President Saddam Hussein, overran Kuwait, its oil-rich but defenseless neighbor to the south. Entrenched in Kuwait, Iraq threatened its much larger western neighbor, oil-producing Saudi Arabia. Hussein's actions clearly jeopardized America's oil supply and its Saudi Arabian ally. The Kuwaiti invasion also challenged Bush's calls for a stable global system.

Comparing Hussein to Adolf Hitler, Bush created an international coalition opposing Iraq. By the end of 1990 over half a million U.S. troops had joined with forces from 36 nations in Operation Desert Shield to protect Saudi Arabia (see Map 31–4). Meanwhile, Bush persuaded the United Nations to authorize military action if the Iraqis did not withdraw by January 15, 1991. He also obtained congressional approval for the use of force.

When Hussein refused to pull back by the deadline, Operation Desert Shield became Operation Desert Storm. Covered live by CNN, coalition missiles and planes struck Iraq on the night of January 17. In response, Hussein launched Scud missiles against America's ally, Israel. The attacks did little damage and failed to provoke Israeli retaliation that might have split the coalition. Ground forces led by U.S. General Norman Schwarzkopf swept into Kuwait, devastated the Iraqi army, and pushed into Iraq in just 100 hours. Fearing

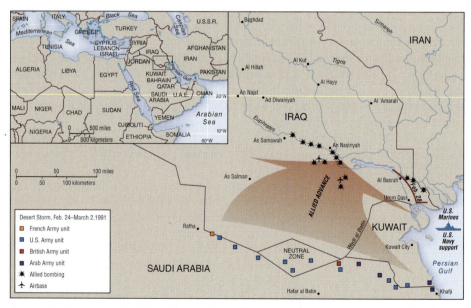

Map 31–4 The Persian Gulf War Operation Desert Storm, the allied attack on the forces of Iraq, tested President George H. W. Bush's vision of a "New World Order" in the oil-rich heart of the Middle East. *Mark C. Carnes et al.,* Mapping America's Past *(New York: Henry Holt, 1996), p. 267;* Hammond Atlas of the Twentieth Century *(New York: Times Books, 1996), p. 166.*

accusations of cruelty, Bush halted the invasion before it reached the Iraqi capital of Baghdad and toppled Hussein.

The Persian Gulf War seemed a great victory for the United States and the New World Order. American technology appeared to work perfectly. Coalition forces suffered only about 220 battle deaths while killing thousands of Iraqis. American leadership and power had halted aggression and restored freedom abroad.

Americans' euphoria did not last. Studies showed that U.S. weapons had not worked quite so well. As many as a quarter of Gulf War veterans suffered major health problems caused by exposure to chemical pesticides and, ironically, ingestion of pills intended to protect them from Iraqi chemical weapons. Despite the destruction of his forces, Saddam Hussein held on to power and ruthlessly repressed the Shiite and Kurdish populations. He would remain a threat to his neighbors and to American interests. The goals of the New World Order had not been fully achieved after all.

Retreating from the New World Order

In the years after the Persian Gulf War, the United States retreated from Bush's vision. Unwilling to maintain cold war spending levels, the nation cut troops, closed bases, and canceled weapons, including Reagan's Strategic Defense Initiative. The Central Intelligence Agency and other intelligence operations struggled with tight budgets, low morale, and public criticism. The foreign aid budget also stagnated.

As U.S. power diminished, the Vietnam syndrome returned: Americans were reluctant to intervene overseas when no critical military or economic interest was at stake. In 1992, a civil war among local warlords hindered international efforts to relieve famine in Somalia, on the eastern horn of Africa. As hundreds of thousands of Somalis died, Bush sent 1,800 marines to a United Nations force protecting the relief efforts. After Clinton took office in 1993, a warlord's forces massacred 32 U.S. troops in the capital city, Mogadishu. Clinton temporarily increased American forces in Somalia, but only until 1994. The chastened president directed that future U.S. peacekeeping operations require a threat to international peace and security or a benefit to "U.S. interests."

The United States was also reluctant to intervene in the violence following collapse of Communist rule in Yugoslavia. As this Balkan country broke apart in the early 1990s, three ethnic groups—Serbs, Croats, and Muslim Slavs—fought a bitter civil war in the newly independent province of Bosnia-Herzegovina. The remnants of the old Yugoslavia, under the harsh leadership of Slobodan Milosevic, aided the Serbs in carrying out "ethnic cleansing," the forcible expulsion of Muslims and Croats from their homes. Faced with the worst mass brutality in Europe since World War II, Bush and Clinton were unwilling to risk American lives. Pressured to stop the slaughter, Clinton allowed U.S. planes and missiles, operating with NATO, to attack Serb forces in 1994. After this devastating assault, the United States brokered a peace agreement in 1995. Clinton committed 20,000 troops to a peacekeeping force, even though most Americans opposed the move.

Yugoslavia posed a challenge again when the Milosevic regime attacked ethnic Albanians in the region of Kosovo. Humiliated by its inability to end the suffering in Kosovo, the Clinton administration finally supported a NATO air offensive against Yugoslavia in March 1999. The 78-day war that ended in June killed between 2,000 and 5,000 people and forced Milosevic to accept a multinational peacekeeping force. NATO suffered no casualties, because Clinton and other leaders were unwilling to risk them. There was no longer any talk about a U.S.-led New World Order.

Al Qaeda and 9/11

As Americans shied away from international commitment, a mortal threat to the United States took shape. In February 1993 an explosive-laden truck blew up in an underground garage beneath New York City's World Trade Center. Six people were killed and more than a thousand injured in the first major international terrorist incident inside the United States. Investigators traced the attack to followers of a radical Islamist spiritual leader from Egypt, Sheikh Omar Abdel-Rahman, who lived in New Jersey. Rahman and over a dozen associates were convicted for the bombing and other plots.

After the attack, most Americans paid little attention to terrorism. U.S. authorities ignored the plotters' connections to a terrorist organization, Al Qaeda, led and financed by a wealthy Saudi Arabian exile, Osama bin Laden. A veteran of the resistance to the Soviet invasion of Afghanistan, bin Laden had made Al Qaeda—Arabic for "base" or "foundation"—into an anti-Western movement dedicated to restoring the supposedly lost glory of Islam. He particularly hated the United States for its support of Israel and its military presence in the Middle East.

Operating out of Sudan and then Afghanistan, Al Qaeda supported Muslim fighters in Bosnia and warlords in Somalia. In 1995 and 1996, the organization was involved in deadly terrorist attacks on U.S. soldiers in Saudi Arabia. In 1996, bin Laden declared jihad—holy war—on the United States.

Although Clinton declared terrorism "the enemy of our generation," Americans paid little attention to it. Al Qaeda attacks continued. In 1998, truck bombs at U.S. embassies in Kenya and Tanzania killed at least 224, including 12 Americans, and wounded 5,000. Blaming bin Laden, the Clinton administration unsuccessfully authorized his assassination and launched missile attacks on Al Qaeda facilities in Sudan and Afghanistan. In 2000, Al Qaeda members slammed an explosive-laden motorboat into the side of the U.S. destroyer *Cole*. Although 17 American sailors died, the president and his advisers did not retaliate (see Map 31–5).

Despite warnings, Clinton's successor, George W. Bush, paid little attention to Al Qaeda. Then, on the morning of September 11, 2001, the most ambitious Al Qaeda plot took place in a clear blue morning sky. Nineteen Middle Eastern members of bin Laden's organization walked through security at East Coast airports and boarded four passenger jets. In flight, the terrorists, brandishing box cutters and Mace or pepper spray, overwhelmed flight attendants and passengers, killed or wounded the pilots, took the controls, and redirected the flights. At 8:46 A.M., American 11 sped into the North Tower of the World Trade Center; 17 minutes later, United 175 hit the Trade Center's South Tower. At 9:37, American 77 struck the west wall of the Pentagon, outside Washington, DC. Aboard United 93, apparently headed toward Washington, there were sounds of struggle, a voice shouted, "Allah is the Greatest," and the jet crashed into an empty field in Shanksville, Pennsylvania, at 10:03. By then, the North Tower of the World Trade Center had collapsed in a cloud of smoke and debris. The South Tower followed at 10:28.

The tragedy, which became known as "9/11," killed the 19 hijackers, 40 people in the crash at Shanksville, 184 at the Pentagon, and 2,751 at the World Trade Center. More

Map 31–5   The Global Reach of Al Qaeda

Americans died on 9/11 than had died in the Japanese attack at Pearl Harbor on December 7, 1941. Only the Civil War battles of Antietam and Cold Harbor had been deadlier days. America suddenly discovered its place in the post–cold war world, and the war on terror had begun.

The War on Terror

In the days after 9/11, stunned Americans felt the attacks had "changed everything." Much stayed the same, but the catastrophe did fundamentally reshape American foreign and security policy. Vowing privately on 9/11 "to kick some ass," President Bush declared publicly that evening, "We will make no distinction between the terrorists who committed these acts and those who harbor them." The United States demanded that the Taliban regime in Afghanistan, which protected bin Laden, turn him over. When the Taliban refused, U.S. and other NATO forces attacked Afghanistan in October. After air strikes against Al Qaeda and Taliban targets, U.S., British, and Australian troops invaded the country to hunt down bin Laden, destroy his camps, and drive out the Taliban.

Afghanistan, weak and impoverished, fell quickly, as the Taliban surrendered the capital, Kabul, and fled their stronghold, Kandahar. Yet bin Laden and many of his men escaped in the remote, mountainous terrain to continue their fight along the border with Pakistan. U.S. and NATO forces remained to protect the new government and find bin Laden.

Meanwhile, the Bush administration reorganized the federal government to combat terror. Within a month of 9/11 he chose the first Director of Homeland Security, Tom Ridge, and gave him responsibility for protecting U.S. borders and infrastructure and for responding to emergencies in the event of a terrorist strike. In 2002, Congress elevated the position to cabinet rank in a new Department of Homeland Security. Two years later, Congress responded to harsh criticism of the CIA and FBI for failing to detect the 9/11 plot by turning over responsibility for the oversight of all U.S. intelligence agencies from the head of the CIA to a new Director of National Intelligence.

More controversially, the Bush administration worked what Vice President Dick Cheney called "the dark side"—practices traditionally condemned by American culture and law. The government maintained a detention center at Guantánamo Bay, Cuba, where "enemy combatants" captured in the war on terror were denied trials and the protections of the Geneva Convention on prisoners of war and, in some cases, evidently tortured. In 2006 and 2008, the U.S. Supreme Court asserted the rights of the Guantánamo detainees and reminded Bush that "a state of war is not a blank check for the president."

Bush also wanted the government to be able to gather more information about its own citizens. In October 2001, Congress hastily passed the USA Patriot Act, which made it easier for the federal government to spy on Americans. It also allowed the attorney general to imprison indefinitely, without trial, noncitizens considered threats to national security.

Opponents condemned the Patriot Act as an unlawful and unequaled deprivation of civil liberties. In 2004, a federal judge declared part of the measure an unconstitutional infringement on First Amendment rights. The Bush administration was able to secure a renewal and expansion of the act.

Bush also rethought the use of American military power. In the past, presidents had rejected preemptive peacetime attacks on other nations. But Bush believed that terrorism presented "a threat without precedent." And since 9/11 demonstrated that enemies did not need "great armies and great industrial capabilities," Bush threatened to strike before a war began and even before a threat emerged. Bush further broke with cold war presidents, including his father, by calling for the United States to act alone when necessary rather than through alliances and the United Nations.

The Bush Doctrine of preemption and unilateral action risked isolating the United States and making it seem selfish, dangerous, and illegitimate. Yet Bush, confident of American power and virtue, was willing to go it alone.

The Iraq War

It was not enough to go after terrorist organizations, Bush said in his State of the Union address in January 2002. The United States must also "prevent regimes that sponsor terror from threatening America or our friends and allies with weapons of mass destruction." He identified Iran, Iraq, and North Korea as an "axis of evil," potentially able to arm terrorists with nuclear, chemical, or biological weapons to threaten the United States directly.

Iraq was the focus of Bush's attention. Saddam Hussein had plotted the assassination of the president's father and seemingly resumed attempts to gain weapons of mass destruction (WMD). In Bush's view, a U.S. missile strike and United Nations economic sanctions and weapons inspections had not deterred Hussein, who had forced the inspectors to withdraw in 1998. After 9/11, Bush shared the view of key advisors that Hussein still had WMD and supported Al Qaeda. Further, some administration members argued that replacing Hussein with a democratic regime would encourage the spread of democracy in the Middle East and make Israel safer.

As Bush moved to confront Iraq, nearly all of America's European allies, as well as Russia, China, and Middle Eastern countries, opposed a unilateral U.S. war. The United States did assemble a "coalition of the willing," but only Great Britain, Australia, and Poland joined the U.S. in committing troops.

AMERICAN LANDSCAPE

>> Gitmo, "The Least Worst Place"

From the camera eye of a satellite miles above, Guantánamo Bay stood out from the rest of eastern Cuba. The inlet was a horseshoe of brown and gray amid the lush green of the island and the bright blue of the Atlantic. To the administration of George W. Bush, Guantánamo Bay was a gray area, too: one of the few places on earth that was American and yet not American, a drab anomaly perfect for one of the most controversial phases of the war on terror.

Guantánamo Bay, 520 miles from Miami, Florida, had been an anomaly for more than a century. After the Spanish-American War of 1898, the U.S. government had taken the spot for a well-protected naval base. The Cuban-American Treaty of 1903 effectively gave America perpetual control over the base. For less than $4,000 a year, the United States could keep the facility until both Washington and Cuba agreed to end the arrangement.

Even when Fidel Castro came to power in 1959, the U.S. base remained. Castro objected to the base but did not try to drive out the United States. So Guantánamo Bay, or "Gitmo," as Americans called it, remained the oldest U.S. overseas naval base and the only one in a Communist country.

Gitmo became less and less valuable over the years. As the cold war ended and the United States closed down military bases, there was no real need for a naval installation so close to the U.S. mainland. Then the war on terror began. The Bush administration needed to put captured Taliban fighters and other "enemy combatants" somewhere safe. It was too risky to leave detainees in unstable Afghanistan or Iraq, but it was also too risky to bring them to the United States, where courts, Congress, and public opinion could interfere in their imprisonment. So the Bush administration looked, in the words of Secretary of Defense Donald Rumsfeld, for "the least worst place" to hold those captured in the war on terror.

They found it at Guantánamo Bay. The U.S. military controlled the base, but U.S. civil law did not apply. Gitmo, with its gray, pebbly beaches, was the perfect gray area for an administration determined to find a way around the law to prosecute the war on terror. Before 2001 was over, detainees began to arrive from Afghanistan. By the end of 2008, some 775 people had been incarcerated at Gitmo. To accommodate them, the U.S. built no fewer than seven separate prison facilities; one of them, known only as "Camp 7," remained secret. Thousands of Americans streamed in to run Gitmo.

For a time, the base provided the Bush administration with the freedom it wanted and needed. CIA, FBI, and military interrogators, apparently copying Chinese Communist techniques from the 1950s, tortured some prisoners. According to detainees, their captors used sleep deprivation and beatings; they also mocked detainees' religious practices by defacing the Qur'an or flushing it down the toilet. Lacking the rights of captured military prisoners under the Geneva Convention, the detainees were deprived of

continued

AMERICAN LANDSCAPE *continued*

the right to trial—a feature of justice in the United States. These conditions took a heavy toll on prisoners; an unknown number committed suicide.

As details of life at Gitmo leaked out, critics of the Bush administration argued that the laws of the United States should apply to prisoners at the base; they deserved the protections of the Geneva Convention and the right to trial. They saw Gitmo as proof that the war on terror, like other wars, had eroded due process, human rights, and other features of democracy, all in the name of battling for democracy.

Even though the U.S. Supreme Court seemed to agree, in its rulings of 2006 and 2008, that it was an assault on democratic values, Gitmo remained open—a swath of gray amid all the green and blue.

On the night of March 19, 2003, Operation Iraqi Freedom began with a hail of Tomahawk cruise missiles aimed at Baghdad in an unsuccessful attempt to kill Hussein. The rest of the attack went almost flawlessly. On March 21, some 1,300 bombs and missiles rained down on Baghdad in a display of "shock and awe" meant to demoralize Iraqi leadership. Meanwhile, ground forces moved into Iraq, the British striking south to seize the port city of Basra and the United States moving east to occupy Baghdad. American technology,

particularly missiles and smart bombs, worked well. The Iraqi army offered little resistance, many of its soldiers simply disappearing into the civilian population. Hussein disappeared, too. By mid-April, his statues were toppling.

Swift and short, the war with Iraq seemed to be everything that the Bush administration had hoped. Only 138 U.S. soldiers had died. Standing before a huge banner declaring "Mission Accomplished" aboard an aircraft carrier on May 1, the president jubilantly announced, "Major combat operations in Iraq have ended." The United States seemed well on the way to winning the war on terror and reshaping the Middle East.

The Fall of Saddam Hussein As the coalition invasion overthrew the Iraqi regime, jubilant Iraqis pulled down the statues of Saddam Hussein, like this one, in the spring of 2003.

America in Crisis

By the 2000s, a new America, "a nation transformed," seemed to have taken shape. The twenty-first-century United States was a globalized, information-based, diverse nation, socially liberal and politically conservative. But the transformation was far from over. The costly war on terror dragged on without victory in either Afghanistan or Iraq. In 2008, financial catastrophe, gradually developing for several years, engulfed the economy. Long-standing monuments of American capitalism teetered on the brink of collapse. So did the conservative policies that had shaped American governance for nearly two generations. In this national crisis, Americans used the presidential election to point their country in a new direction.

Iraq and Afghanistan in Turmoil

The jubilance of "Mission Accomplished" soon gave way to sober realities in Iraq during 2003. Despite an intensive search, no weapons of mass destruction could be found. It was difficult to restart the economy and train new police and defense forces. Rather than embrace their liberators, many Iraqis resented the Americans. Worst of all, a violent insurgency, perhaps orchestrated by Saddam Hussein, tried to destabilize Iraq and drive out the United States.

Although U.S. forces captured Hussein in December 2003, the conflict went badly. Unable to prove that Hussein's regime had ties to Al Qaeda before 9/11, the Bush administration faced charges of fighting a costly, needless war that weakened the hunt for bin Laden in Afghanistan. Bush was further embarrassed by the brutal execution of Hussein and revelations of the humiliation and torture of Iraqis at a U.S. prison in Abu Ghraib. Although sovereignty was handed over to a new Iraqi government, chosen by the United States, in 2004, more than 100,000 American troops remained.

Those forces now confronted "Al Qaeda in Iraq," a new terrorist group loyal to bin Laden, and also a civil war between Shiites and Sunnis. The insurgents' use of IEDs—improvised explosive devices—took a heavy toll on American troops. By the end of 2006, 3,000 U.S. soldiers had died, and Iraq remained in turmoil.

Facing failure, Bush responded in 2007 with a controversial "surge," a temporary increase in troop strength to 130,000. By mid-2008, the surge, along with changes in Iraqi politics, succeeded in decreasing the violence. But more than 4,000 U.S. soldiers and uncounted Iraqis had died, the Iraqi economy still struggled, and the Iraqi government was not truly democratic. American public opinion had largely turned against the war.

Meanwhile, the conflict in Afghanistan had worsened. As the United States focused on Iraq, the Taliban, aided by foreign fighters, had gradually regained strength and the pro–United States government had lost power. Osama bin Laden remained at large, somewhere along the mountainous border with Pakistan. Calling the situation "precarious and urgent," U.S. military leaders admitted they did not have enough troops to commit to Afghanistan, but the United States struck into Pakistan. The American death toll climbed to more than 100 in 2007 and passed 100 again in 2008. By then, over 600 U.S. soldiers had died since 2001 in what was becoming one of America's longest wars. Uncounted thousands of Afghans had died as well.

The wars in Afghanistan and Iraq cost the United States popularity and influence around the globe. Sympathetic to Americans in the months after 9/11, many people no longer supported U.S. military action in the Middle East. The tragic toll of civilian deaths and the use of torture proved particularly costly for America. Critics argued that the callous mistreatment of Middle Easterners was winning converts for Al Qaeda and terrorism. At the same time, as the situation in Afghanistan underscored, the United States had seriously depleted its military power. When Russia invaded neighboring Georgia, a U.S. ally, in the summer of 2008, there was no response the Bush administration could make. The United States no longer seemed like an unstoppable superpower or an unflagging champion of democracy.

The Economy in Jeopardy

The economic boom of the 1990s and 2000s looked a lot like the boom of the 1920s. In both periods, optimistic American consumers, buoyed by good times, borrowed money and bought houses and cars. Investors borrowed money to buy stocks. All that buying spurred the economy and drove the stock market to record heights. But eventually all that borrowing reached its limits: new credit ran out, and many Americans found themselves unable to meet their debts. In both periods, business leaders and government officials paid too little attention to dangerous financial practices until it was too late.

By the early 2000s, the housing industry was developing a classic "bubble," an unrealistic inflation of prices. As Americans—some of them aided by subprime mortgages—bought houses in record numbers, homes began to be seen as great investments whose value would just keep on increasing. Some people then bought houses they could not really afford, and many used houses as collateral for loans. Banks made loans they should not have made. Moreover, financial institutions managed to obscure the reality of bad mortgage loans by folding those loans into complex, risky new financial instruments, known as Collateralized Debt Obligations (CDOs), that they sold around the world. As a result, firms that bought CDOs were vulnerable to trouble in housing but did not understand the danger.

The trouble began in 2005, when U.S. house prices stagnated and then began to fall. As the housing bubble burst, many homeowners discovered they were not as wealthy as they thought they were. Some, particularly those with subprime loans, had trouble making their payments; foreclosures—banks' repossession of homes for unpaid mortgages—began to increase. As a consequence, the home-construction industry suffered, and it became harder for consumers to get credit.

The most dramatic consequences befell financial institutions. In the spring of 2008, the investment bank Bear Stearns, involved in subprime mortgage loans and other risky practices, nearly collapsed despite federal help. Only a takeover by banking giant JPMorgan Chase saved the firm from bankruptcy. In the summer, the nation's largest mortgage lender, IndyMac Bank, failed; the federal government stepped in to guarantee depositors' money. Then, Washington had to take over two key private corporations that bought and sold mortgages from banks—the Federal National Mortgage Association, known as "Fannie Mae," and the Federal Home Loan Mortgage Corporation, known as "Freddie Mac."

At the same time, other developments joined to threaten the United States and the global economy. Globalized free trade suffered when the World Trade Organization's round of trade talks held in Doha, Qatar, ended in failure. Oil prices, driven by rising demand from the growing economies of China and India, hit record levels. High oil prices drove up the prices of other goods, including food, and spurred inflation. Rising oil prices also hurt the auto industry, particularly Chrysler, Ford, and General Motors, whose gas-guzzling SUVs became hard to sell. Although felt worldwide, these events particularly hurt the United States, as the global value of the dollar declined and as American consumers, particularly those with big credit card balances, lost confidence. The Dow Jones Industrial Average, which had reached a record high of over 14,000 in October 2007, had declined into the 11,000s in early September 2008.

Despite the signs, most people were still unprepared when disaster struck in mid-September. In a matter of days, the U.S. financial industry nearly collapsed: Lehman Brothers, another investment firm caught up in the subprime debacle, went bankrupt—the most valuable American corporation ever to fail; the Bank of America bought Merrill Lynch, still another near-bankrupt victim of dubious mortgage and other financial practices; and AIG, an insurance giant heavily involved in CDOs, headed toward collapse until it was bought by the Federal Reserve.

Meanwhile, U.S. and foreign stock markets buckled. The Dow Jones lost more than 4 percent of its value on September 15, and another 4 percent two days later. As governments and financial institutions around the world scrambled to save banks, keep the financial system operating, and prop up the stock markets, Americans worried about a repeat of the great crash of 1929. At the end of the month, a panicked Congress approved the Emergency Economic Stabilization Act of 2008, a $700 billion financial package, to try to bail out the U.S. financial industry, ensure the availability of credit to borrowers, and save the nation from depression.

The Presidential Election of 2008

As the economy reeled, Americans went about choosing the 44th president of the United States. The election was proving a milestone in American history. Democratic senator Hillary Clinton of New York, the wife of Bill Clinton, seemed likely to become the first woman major-party presidential candidate. But Clinton's campaign, which emphasized her "experience" and her original support for the Iraq War, met tough resistance from the younger, first-term senator Barack Obama of Illinois. The son of a black Kenyan father and a white American mother, Obama, like Tiger Woods, evoked a more diverse, globalized nation. In contrast to Clinton, he ran on a platform of "change" for America and an end to the Iraq War. Narrowly defeating Clinton in an epic primary battle, Obama became the first African American major-party presidential nominee.

Obama's Republican opponent, Senator John McCain of Arizona, seemed more a candidate of the status quo. The 72-year-old McCain was a generation older than the 47-year-old Obama. But the Republican, drawing attention away from his support of Bush policies, presented himself as a tough-minded, independent "maverick" with the courage to chart a new political course. The surprise selection of Alaska's reform governor Sarah Palin as the second female major-party candidate for the vice presidency underscored McCain's commitment to change.

An intensifying economic crisis in October mortally wounded the Republican cause. Saddled with the unpopular wars and weak economy of the Bush administration, McCain seemed old and uncertain. Meanwhile, many voters were impressed by Obama's cool performance during the crisis, including three televised debates with McCain. On November 4, voters did what had seemed unthinkable even after the civil rights movement of the 1960s: they made an African American the president of the United States. Obama

"Change We Can Believe In" Democratic nominee Barack Obama campaigns for the presidency in 2008.

won a clear victory, with 52.8 percent of the popular vote, the highest percentage in 20 years, and 365 electoral votes. The Democrat seemed to have his mandate for "change."

He would need it. Even before the celebration of Obama's history-making victory ended, the economic crisis deepened. In mid-November, the stock market lurched down again, below the 8,000 mark. Despite the Emergency Economic Stabilization Act, financial institutions were still in peril, and loans were still scarce. With the collapse of vehicle sales, Chrysler, Ford, and GM headed toward bankruptcy. Unemployment rose and consumer spending fell. As the world economy slowed, oil prices did come down, and inflation abated. But now economists began to worry about deflation, the kind of long-term catastrophic decline in prices that intensified the Great Depression.

Conclusion

Whatever the outcome of the crisis of 2008, the United States had reached the end of one era and the beginning of another. In a generation spanning the end of the cold war to the collapse of the economic boom, the United States had completed its transformation into a globalized, information-based, racially diverse nation. The crisis seemed unlikely to change that basic reality.

Much else was already changing. The conservatism that had shaped American politics and government since the age of Ronald Reagan in the 1980s was in retreat. In the midst of economic meltdown in the fall of 2008, the government and the people had spurned conservative ideology and accepted the kinds of dramatic government intervention reminiscent of the New Deal of the 1930s and Great Society of the 1960s. Americans had turned as well to a president who called for change and embodied the social transformation of a globalized nation.

Much else about America's identity had become uncertain. Amid worldwide economic crisis, the nature of global ties could change. As the United States struggled with declining economic and military power and the war on terror, its relationship to the world was at another crossroads. As Americans grappled with the prospect of economic recession or even depression, their attitude toward social and cultural diversity could change.

And the American people prepared to move forward. "America, we have come so far. We have seen so much," Obama declared the night of his election. "But there's so much more to do."

>> Timeline

▼1988
George H. W. Bush elected president

▼1989
Collapse of Communist regimes in Eastern Europe
Invasion of Panama

▼1990
Partial shutdown of federal government

▼1991
Persian Gulf War
Collapse of the Soviet Union
Dow Jones Industrial Average over 3,000 for first time

▼1992
Los Angeles riot after first Rodney King verdict
U.S. troops sent to Somalia
Bill Clinton elected president

▼1993
Terrorist truck bombing of World Trade Center, New York City
Ratification of North American Free Trade Agreement (NAFTA)

▼1994
End of "Risk Rule" for women soldiers

▼1995
Peace treaty in Bosnia-Herzegovina civil war
Opening of World Trade Organization

▼1996
Federal welfare reform
First Wal-Mart in People's Republic of China
Reelection of Bill Clinton as president

▼1998
Terrorist truck bombings of U.S. embassies in Kenya and Tanzania

▼1999
Acquittal of Bill Clinton in Senate impeachment trial
NATO air war against Yugoslavia
Dow Jones Industrial Average over 10,000 for first time

▼2000
Terrorist attack on destroyer *Cole*   *continued*

>> Timeline *continued*

▼2001
George W. Bush declared president
9/11 attacks
Invasion of Afghanistan

▼2002
Creation of Department of Homeland Security

▼2003
U.S. Supreme Court gay rights ruling, *Lawrence v. Texas*
"Operation Iraqi Freedom," Coalition invasion of Iraq

▼2004
George W. Bush reelected

▼2007
U.S. military "surge" in Iraq

▼2008
Collapse of Doha world trade talks
U.S. financial crisis
Barack Obama elected president

Review Questions

1. What set apart the globalization of the 1990s and 2000s from earlier linkages between the United States and the world?

2. What were the main features of the postindustrial political economy? Why were Americans anxious about the economy even though it was relatively strong?

3. Why did conservatives enjoy mixed political success in the 1990s and 2000s?

4. How did the foreign and security policies of the two presidents Bush differ? Which was more successful?

5. Did globalization, the information economy, and struggles for rights make it easier or harder for ordinary Americans to control their lives?

For further review materials and resource information, please visit www.oup.com/us/ofthepeople

Appendix A

Historical Documents

The Declaration of Independence

When in the course of human events, it becomes necessary for one people to dissolve the political bands which have connected them with another, and to assume, among the powers of the earth, the separate and equal station to which the Laws of Nature and of Nature's God entitle them, a decent respect to the opinions of mankind requires that they should declare the causes which impel them to the separation.

We hold these truths to be self-evident, that all men are created equal, that they are endowed by their Creator with certain unalienable Rights, that among these are life, liberty and the pursuit of happiness. That to secure these rights, governments are instituted among men, deriving their just powers from the consent of the governed; that whenever any form of government becomes destructive of these ends, it is the right of the people to alter or to abolish it, and to institute new Government, laying its foundation on such principles and organizing its powers in such form, as to them shall seem most likely to effect their safety and happiness. Prudence, indeed, will dictate that Governments long established should not be changed for light and transient causes; and, accordingly, all experience hath shown, that mankind are more disposed to suffer, while evils are sufferable, than to right themselves by abolishing the forms to which they are accustomed. But when a long train of abuses and usurpations, pursuing invariably the same object evinces a design to reduce them under absolute despotism, it is their right, it is their duty, to throw off such government, and to provide new guards for their future security. Such has been the patient sufferance of these colonies; and such is now the necessity which constrains them to alter their former systems of government. The history of the present King of Great Britain is a history of repeated injuries and usurpations, all having in direct object the establishment of an absolute tyranny over these States. To prove this, let facts be submitted to a candid world:

He has refused his assent to laws, the most wholesome and necessary for the public good.

He has forbidden his governors to pass laws of immediate and pressing importance, unless suspended in their operation till his assent should be obtained; and, when so suspended, he has utterly neglected to attend to them.

He has refused to pass other laws for the accommodation of large districts of people, unless those people would relinquish the right of representation in the legislature, a right inestimable to them and formidable to tyrants only.

He has called together legislative bodies at places unusual, uncomfortable, and distant from the depository of their public records, for the sole purpose of fatiguing them into compliance with his measures.

He has dissolved representative houses repeatedly, for opposing with manly firmness his invasions on the rights of the people.

He has refused for a long time, after such dissolutions, to cause others to be elected; whereby the legislative powers, incapable of annihilation, have returned to the People at large for their exercise; the State remaining in the mean time exposed to all the dangers of invasion from without, and convulsions within.

He has endeavored to prevent the population of these States; for that purpose obstructing the laws for naturalization of foreigners; refusing to pass others to encourage their migrations hither, and raising the conditions of new appropriations of lands.

He has obstructed the administration of justice, by refusing his assent to laws for establishing judiciary powers.

He has made judges dependent on his will alone, for the tenure of their offices, and the amount and payment of their salaries.

He has erected a multitude of new offices, and sent hither swarms of officers to harass our people, and eat out their substance.

He has kept among us, in times of peace, standing armies without the consent of our legislatures.

He has affected to render the Military independent of, and superior to, the civil power.

He has combined with others to subject us to a jurisdiction foreign to our constitution and unacknowledged by our laws; giving his assent to their acts of pretended legislation:

For quartering large bodies of armed troops among us;

For protecting them, by a mock trial, from punishment for any murders which they should commit on the inhabitants of these States;

For cutting off our trade with all parts of the world;

For imposing taxes on us without our Consent;

For depriving us, in many cases, of the benefits of Trial by Jury;

For transporting us beyond Seas to be tried for pretended offences;

For abolishing the free System of English Laws in a neighbouring Province, establishing therein an Arbitrary government, and enlarging its Boundaries so as to render it at once an example and fit instrument for introducing the same absolute rule into these colonies;

For taking away our charters, abolishing our most valuable laws, and altering fundamentally the forms of our governments;

For suspending our own legislatures, and declaring themselves invested with power to legislate for us in all cases whatsoever.

He has abdicated government here, by declaring us out of his protection and waging war against us.

He has plundered our seas, ravaged our coasts, burnt our towns, and destroyed the lives of our people.

He is at this time transporting large armies of foreign mercenaries to complete the works of death, desolation and tyranny, already begun with circumstances of cruelty and perfidy scarcely paralleled in the most barbarous ages, and totally unworthy the head of a civilized nation.

He has constrained our fellow citizens taken captive on the high seas to bear arms against their country, to become the executioners of their friends and brethren, or to fall themselves by their hands.

He has excited domestic insurrections amongst us, and has endeavored to bring on the inhabitants of our frontiers, the merciless Indian savages, whose known rule of warfare, is an undistinguished destruction of all ages, sexes and conditions.

In every stage of these oppressions we have petitioned for redress in the most humble terms; our repeated petitions have been answered only by repeated injury. A prince whose character is thus marked by every act which may define a tyrant, is unfit to be the ruler of a free people.

Nor have we been wanting in attentions to our British brethren. We have warned them from time to time of attempts by their legislature to extend an unwarrantable jurisdiction over us. We have reminded them of the circumstances of our emigration and settlement here. We have appealed to their native justice and magnanimity, and we have conjured them by the ties of our common kindred to disavow these usurpations, which, would inevitably interrupt our connections and correspondence. They, too, have been deaf to the voice of justice and of consanguinity. We must, therefore, acquiesce in the necessity, which denounces our separation, and hold them, as we hold the rest of mankind, enemies in war, in peace friends.

We, therefore, the representatives of the United States of America, in general Congress, assembled, appealing to the Supreme Judge of the world for the rectitude of our intentions, do, in the name, and by the authority of the good people of these colonies, solemnly publish and declare, that these united colonies are, and of right ought to be free and independent states; that they are absolved from all allegiance to the British Crown, and that all political connection between them and the state of Great Britain, is and ought to be totally dissolved; and that, as free and independent states, they have full power to levy war, conclude peace, contract alliances, establish commerce, and to do all other acts and things which independent states may of right do. And for the support of this declaration, with a firm reliance on the protection of Divine Providence, we mutually pledge to each other our lives, our fortunes and our sacred honor.

The Constitution of the United States of America

We the People of the United States, in Order to form a more perfect Union, establish Justice, insure domestic Tranquility, provide for the common defence, promote the general Welfare, and secure the Blessings of Liberty to ourselves and our Posterity, do ordain and establish this Constitution for the United States of America.

Article I

Section 1

All legislative Powers herein granted shall be vested in a Congress of the United States, which shall consist of a Senate and House of Representatives.

Section 2

The House of Representatives shall be composed of Members chosen every second Year by the People of the several States, and the Electors in each State shall have the Qualifications requisite for Electors of the most numerous Branch of the State Legislature.

No Person shall be a Representative who shall not have attained to the Age of twenty five Years, and been seven Years a Citizen of the United States, and who shall not, when elected, be an Inhabitant of that State in which he shall be chosen.

Representatives and direct Taxes shall be apportioned among the several States which may be included within this Union, according to their respective Numbers, which shall be determined by adding to the whole Number of free Persons, including those bound to Service for a Term of Years, and excluding Indians not taxed, three fifths of all other Persons. The actual Enumeration shall be made within three Years after the first Meeting of the Congress of the United States, and within every subsequent Term of ten Years, in such Manner as they shall by Law direct. The Number of Representatives shall not exceed one for every thirty Thousand, but each State shall have at Least one Representative; and until such enumeration shall be made, the State of New Hampshire shall be entitled to choose three, Massachusetts eight, Rhode-Island and Providence Plantations one, Connecticut five, New York six, New Jersey four, Pennsylvania eight, Delaware one, Maryland six, Virginia ten, North Carolina five, South Carolina five, and Georgia three.

When vacancies happen in the Representation from any State, the Executive Authority thereof shall issue Writs of Election to fill such Vacancies.

The House of Representatives shall choose their Speaker and other Officers; and shall have the sole Power of Impeachment.

Section 3

The Senate of the United States shall be composed of two Senators from each State, chosen by the Legislature thereof for six Years; and each Senator shall have one Vote.

Immediately after they shall be assembled in Consequence of the first Election, they shall be divided as equally as may be into three Classes. The Seats of the Senators of the first Class shall be vacated at the Expiration of the second Year, of the second Class at the Expiration of the fourth Year, and of the third Class at the Expiration of the sixth Year, so that one third may be chosen every second Year; and if Vacancies happen by Resignation, or otherwise, during the Recess of the Legislature of any State, the Executive thereof may make temporary Appointments until the next Meeting of the Legislature, which shall then fill such Vacancies.

No Person shall be a Senator who shall not have attained to the Age of thirty Years, and been nine Years a Citizen of the United States, and who shall not, when elected, be an Inhabitant of that State for which he shall be chosen.

The Vice President of the United States shall be President of the Senate, but shall have no Vote, unless they be equally divided.

The Senate shall choose their other Officers, and also a President pro tempore, in the Absence of the Vice President, or when he shall exercise the Office of President of the United States.

The Senate shall have the sole Power to try all Impeachments. When sitting for that Purpose, they shall be on Oath or Affirmation. When the President of the United States is tried, the Chief Justice shall preside: And no Person shall be convicted without the Concurrence of two thirds of the Members present.

Judgment in Cases of Impeachment shall not extend further than to removal from Office, and disqualification to hold and enjoy any Office of honor, Trust or Profit under the United States: but the Party convicted shall nevertheless be liable and subject to Indictment, Trial, Judgment and Punishment, according to Law.

Section 4

The Times, Places and Manner of holding Elections for Senators and Representatives, shall be prescribed in each State by the Legislature thereof; but the Congress may at any time by Law make or alter such Regulations, except as to the Places of chusing Senators.

The Congress shall assemble at least once in every Year, and such Meeting shall be on the first Monday in December, unless they shall by Law appoint a different Day.

Section 5

Each House shall be the Judge of the Elections, Returns and Qualifications of its own Members, and a Majority of each shall constitute a Quorum to do Business; but a smaller Number may adjourn from day to day, and may be authorized to compel the Attendance of absent Members, in such Manner, and under such Penalties as each House may provide.

Each House may determine the Rules of its Proceedings, punish its Members for disorderly Behaviour, and, with the Concurrence of two thirds, expel a Member.

Each House shall keep a Journal of its Proceedings, and from time to time publish the same, excepting such Parts as may in their Judgment require Secrecy; and the Yeas and Nays of the Members of either House on any question shall, at the Desire of one fifth of those Present, be entered on the Journal.

Neither House, during the Session of Congress, shall, without the Consent of the other, adjourn for more than three days, nor to any other Place than that in which the two Houses shall be sitting.

Section 6

The Senators and Representatives shall receive a Compensation for their Services, to be ascertained by Law, and paid out of the Treasury of the United States. They shall in all Cases, except Treason, Felony and Breach of the Peace, be privileged from Arrest during their Attendance at the Session of their respective Houses, and in going to and returning from the same; and for any Speech or Debate in either House, they shall not be questioned in any other Place.

No Senator or Representative shall, during the Time for which he was elected, be appointed to any civil Office under the Authority of the United States, which shall have been created, or the Emoluments whereof shall have been increased during such time; and no Person holding any Office under the United States, shall be a Member of either House during his Continuance in Office.

Section 7

All Bills for raising Revenue shall originate in the House of Representatives; but the Senate may propose or concur with Amendments as on other Bills.

Every Bill which shall have passed the House of Representatives and the Senate, shall, before it become a Law, be presented to the President of the United States: If he approve he shall sign it, but if not he shall return it, with his Objections to that House in which it shall have originated, who shall enter the Objections at large on their Journal, and proceed to reconsider it. If after such Reconsideration two thirds of that House shall agree to pass the Bill, it shall be sent, together with the Objections, to the other House, by which it shall likewise be reconsidered, and if approved by two thirds of that House, it shall become a Law. But in all such Cases the Votes of both Houses shall be determined by yeas and Nays, and the Names of the Persons voting for and against the Bill shall be entered on the Journal of each House respectively. If any Bill shall not be returned by the President within ten Days (Sundays excepted) after it shall have been presented to him, the Same shall be a Law, in like Manner as if he had signed it, unless the Congress by their Adjournment prevent its Return, in which Case it shall not be a Law.

Every Order, Resolution, or Vote to which the Concurrence of the Senate and House of Representatives may be necessary (except on a question of Adjournment) shall be presented to the President of the United States; and before the Same shall take Effect, shall be approved by him, or being disapproved by him, shall be repassed by two thirds of the Senate and House of Representatives, according to the Rules and Limitations prescribed in the Case of a Bill.

Section 8

The Congress shall have Power

To lay and collect Taxes, Duties, Imposts and Excises, to pay the Debts and provide for the common Defence and general Welfare of the United States; but all Duties, Imposts and Excises shall be uniform throughout the United States;

To borrow Money on the credit of the United States;

To regulate Commerce with foreign Nations, and among the several States, and with the Indian Tribes;

To establish an uniform Rule of Naturalization, and uniform Laws on the subject of Bankruptcies throughout the United States;

To coin Money, regulate the Value thereof, and of foreign Coin, and fix the Standard of Weights and Measures;

To provide for the Punishment of counterfeiting the Securities and current Coin of the United States;

To establish Post Offices and post Roads;

To promote the Progress of Science and useful Arts, by securing for limited Times to Authors and Inventors the exclusive Right to their respective Writings and Discoveries;

To constitute Tribunals inferior to the supreme Court;

To define and punish Piracies and Felonies committed on the high Seas, and Offences against the Law of Nations;

To declare War, grant Letters of Marque and Reprisal, and make Rules concerning Captures on Land and Water;

To raise and support Armies, but no Appropriation of Money to that Use shall be for a longer Term than two Years;

To provide and maintain a Navy;

To make Rules for the Government and Regulation of the land and naval Forces;

To provide for calling forth the Militia to execute the Laws of the Union, suppress Insurrections and repel Invasions;

To provide for organizing, arming, and disciplining the Militia, and for governing such Part of them as may be employed in the Service of the United States, reserving to the States respectively, the Appointment of the Officers, and the Authority of training the Militia according to the discipline prescribed by Congress;

To exercise exclusive Legislation in all Cases whatsoever, over such District (not exceeding ten Miles square) as may, by Cession of particular States, and the Acceptance of Congress, become the Seat of the Government of the United States, and to exercise like Authority over all Places purchased by the Consent of the Legislature of the State in which the Same shall be, for the Erection of Forts, Magazines, Arsenals, dock-Yards, and other needful Buildings;—And

To make all Laws which shall be necessary and proper for carrying into Execution the foregoing Powers, and all other Powers vested by this Constitution in the Government of the United States, or in any Department or Officer thereof.

Section 9

The Migration or Importation of such Persons as any of the States now existing shall think proper to admit, shall not be prohibited by the Congress prior to the Year one thousand eight hundred and eight, but a Tax or duty may be imposed on such Importation, not exceeding ten dollars for each Person.

The Privilege of the Writ of Habeas Corpus shall not be suspended, unless when in Cases of Rebellion or Invasion the public Safety may require it.

No Bill of Attainder or ex post facto Law shall be passed.

No Capitation, or other direct, Tax shall be laid, unless in Proportion to the Census or enumeration herein before directed to be taken.

No Tax or Duty shall be laid on Articles exported from any State.

No Preference shall be given by any Regulation of Commerce or Revenue to the Ports of one State over those of another; nor shall Vessels bound to, or from, one State, be obliged to enter, clear, or pay Duties in another.

No Money shall be drawn from the Treasury, but in Consequence of Appropriations made by Law; and a regular Statement and Account of the Receipts and Expenditures of all public Money shall be published from time to time.

No Title of Nobility shall be granted by the United States: And no Person holding any Office of Profit or Trust under them, shall, without the Consent of the Congress, accept of any present, Emolument, Office, or Title, of any kind whatever, from any King, Prince, or foreign State.

Section 10

No State shall enter into any Treaty, Alliance, or Confederation; grant Letters of Marque and Reprisal; coin Money; emit Bills of Credit; make any Thing but gold and silver Coin a Tender in Payment of Debts; pass any Bill of Attainder, ex post facto Law, or Law impairing the Obligation of Contracts, or grant any Title of Nobility.

No State shall, without the Consent of the Congress, lay any Imposts or Duties on Imports or Exports, except what may be absolutely necessary for executing it's inspection Laws: and the net Produce of all Duties and Imposts, laid by any State on Imports or Exports, shall be for the Use of the Treasury of the United States; and all such Laws shall be subject to the Revision and Control of the Congress.

No State shall, without the Consent of Congress, lay any Duty of Tonnage, keep Troops, or Ships of War in time of Peace, enter into any Agreement or Compact with another State, or with a foreign Power, or engage in War, unless actually invaded, or in such imminent Danger as will not admit of delay.

Article II

Section 1

The executive Power shall be vested in a President of the United States of America. He shall hold his Office during the Term of four Years, and, together with the Vice President, chosen for the same Term, be elected, as follows:

Each State shall appoint, in such Manner as the Legislature thereof may direct, a Number of Electors, equal to the whole Number of Senators and Representatives to which the State may be entitled in the Congress: but no Senator or Representative, or Person holding an Office of Trust or Profit under the United States, shall be appointed an Elector.

The Electors shall meet in their respective States, and vote by Ballot for two Persons, of whom one at least shall not be an Inhabitant of the same State with themselves. And they shall make a List of all the Persons voted for, and of the Number of Votes for each; which List they shall sign and certify, and transmit sealed to the Seat of the Government of the United States, directed to the President of the Senate. The President of the Senate shall, in the Presence of the Senate and House of Representatives, open all the Certificates, and the Votes shall then be counted. The Person having the greatest Number of Votes shall be the President, if such Number be a Majority of the whole Number of Electors appointed; and if there be more than one who have such Majority, and have an equal Number of Votes, then the House of Representatives shall immediately choose by Ballot one of them for President; and if no Person have a Majority, then from the five highest on the List the said House shall in like Manner choose the President. But in choosing the President, the Votes shall be taken by States, the Representation from each State having one Vote; A quorum for this purpose shall consist of a Member or Members from two thirds of the States, and a Majority of all the States shall be necessary to a Choice. In every Case, after the Choice of the President, the Person having the greatest Number of Votes of the Electors shall be the Vice President. But if there should remain two or more who have equal Votes, the Senate shall choose from them by Ballot the Vice President.

The Congress may determine the Time of choosing the Electors, and the Day on which they shall give their Votes; which Day shall be the same throughout the United States.

No Person except a natural born Citizen, or a Citizen of the United States, at the time of the Adoption of this Constitution, shall be eligible to the Office of President; neither shall any Person be eligible to that Office who shall not have attained to the Age of thirty five Years, and been fourteen Years a Resident within the United States.

In Case of the Removal of the President from Office, or of his Death, Resignation, or Inability to discharge the Powers and Duties of the said Office, the Same shall devolve on the Vice President, and the Congress may by Law provide for the Case of Removal, Death,

Resignation or Inability, both of the President and Vice President, declaring what Officer shall then act as President, and such Officer shall act accordingly, until the Disability be removed, or a President shall be elected.

The President shall, at stated Times, receive for his Services, a Compensation, which shall neither be increased nor diminished during the Period for which he shall have been elected, and he shall not receive within that Period any other Emolument from the United States, or any of them.

Before he enter on the Execution of his Office, he shall take the following Oath or Affirmation:—"I do solemnly swear (or affirm) that I will faithfully execute the Office of President of the United States, and will to the best of my Ability, preserve, protect and defend the Constitution of the United States."

Section 2

The President shall be Commander in Chief of the Army and Navy of the United States, and of the Militia of the several States, when called into the actual Service of the United States; he may require the Opinion, in writing, of the principal Officer in each of the executive Departments, upon any Subject relating to the Duties of their respective Offices, and he shall have Power to grant Reprieves and Pardons for Offences against the United States, except in Cases of Impeachment.

He shall have Power, by and with the Advice and Consent of the Senate, to make Treaties, provided two thirds of the Senators present concur; and he shall nominate, and by and with the Advice and Consent of the Senate, shall appoint Ambassadors, other public Ministers and Consuls, Judges of the supreme Court, and all other Officers of the United States, whose Appointments are not herein otherwise provided for, and which shall be established by Law: but the Congress may by Law vest the Appointment of such inferior Officers, as they think proper, in the President alone, in the Courts of Law, or in the Heads of Departments.

The President shall have Power to fill up all Vacancies that may happen during the Recess of the Senate, by granting Commissions which shall expire at the End of their next Session.

Section 3

He shall from time to time give to the Congress Information of the State of the Union, and recommend to their Consideration such Measures as he shall judge necessary and expedient; he may, on extraordinary Occasions, convene both Houses, or either of them, and in Case of Disagreement between them, with Respect to the Time of Adjournment, he may adjourn them to such Time as he shall think proper; he shall receive Ambassadors and other public Ministers; he shall take Care that the Laws be faithfully executed, and shall Commission all the Officers of the United States.

Section 4

The President, Vice President and all civil Officers of the United States, shall be removed from Office on Impeachment for, and Conviction of, Treason, Bribery, or other high Crimes and Misdemeanors.

Article III

Section 1

The judicial Power of the United States shall be vested in one supreme Court, and in such inferior Courts as the Congress may from time to time ordain and establish. The Judges, both of the supreme and inferior Courts, shall hold their Offices during good Behaviour, and shall, at stated Times, receive for their Services a Compensation, which shall not be diminished during their Continuance in Office.

Section 2

The judicial Power shall extend to all Cases, in Law and Equity, arising under this Constitution, the Laws of the United States, and Treaties made, or which shall be made, under their Authority;—to all Cases affecting Ambassadors, other public Ministers and Consuls;—to all Cases of admiralty and maritime Jurisdiction;—to Controversies to which the United States shall be a Party;—to Controversies between two or more States;—between a State and Citizens of another State;—between Citizens of different States;—between Citizens of the same State claiming Lands under Grants of different States, and between a State, or the Citizens thereof, and foreign States, Citizens or Subjects.

In all Cases affecting Ambassadors, other public Ministers and Consuls, and those in which a State shall be Party, the supreme Court shall have original Jurisdiction. In all the other Cases before mentioned, the supreme Court shall have appellate Jurisdiction, both as to Law and Fact, with such Exceptions, and under such Regulations as the Congress shall make.

The Trial of all Crimes, except in Cases of Impeachment, shall be by Jury; and such Trial shall be held in the State where the said Crimes shall have been committed; but when not committed within any State, the Trial shall be at such Place or Places as the Congress may by Law have directed.

Section 3

Treason against the United States, shall consist only in levying War against them, or in adhering to their Enemies, giving them Aid and Comfort. No Person shall be convicted of Treason unless on the Testimony of two Witnesses to the same overt Act, or on Confession in open Court.

The Congress shall have Power to declare the Punishment of Treason, but no Attainder of Treason shall work Corruption of Blood, or Forfeiture except during the Life of the Person attainted.

Article IV

Section 1

Full Faith and Credit shall be given in each State to the public Acts, Records, and judicial Proceedings of every other State. And the Congress may by general Laws prescribe the Manner in which such Acts, Records and Proceedings shall be proved, and the Effect thereof.

Section 2

The Citizens of each State shall be entitled to all Privileges and Immunities of Citizens in the several States.

A Person charged in any State with Treason, Felony, or other Crime, who shall flee from Justice, and be found in another State, shall on Demand of the executive Authority of the State from which he fled, be delivered up, to be removed to the State having Jurisdiction of the Crime.

No Person held to Service or Labour in one State, under the Laws thereof, escaping into another, shall, in Consequence of any Law or Regulation therein, be discharged from such Service or Labour, but shall be delivered up on Claim of the Party to whom such Service or Labour may be due.

Section 3

New States may be admitted by the Congress into this Union; but no new State shall be formed or erected within the Jurisdiction of any other State; nor any State be formed by the Junction of two or more States, or Parts of States, without the Consent of the Legislatures of the States concerned as well as of the Congress.

The Congress shall have Power to dispose of and make all needful Rules and Regulations respecting the Territory or other Property belonging to the United States; and nothing in this Constitution shall be so construed as to Prejudice any Claims of the United States, or of any particular State.

Section 4

The United States shall guarantee to every State in this Union a Republican Form of Government, and shall protect each of them against Invasion; and on Application of the Legislature, or of the Executive (when the Legislature cannot be convened), against domestic Violence.

Article V

The Congress, whenever two thirds of both Houses shall deem it necessary, shall propose Amendments to this Constitution, or, on the Application of the Legislatures of two thirds of the several States, shall call a Convention for proposing Amendments, which, in either Case, shall be valid to all Intents and Purposes, as Part of this Constitution, when ratified by the Legislatures of three fourths of the several States, or by Conventions in three fourths thereof, as the one or the other Mode of Ratification may be proposed by the Congress; Provided that no Amendment which may be made prior to the Year One thousand eight hundred and eight shall in any Manner affect the first and fourth Clauses in the Ninth Section of the first Article; and that no State, without its Consent, shall be deprived of its equal Suffrage in the Senate.

Article VI

All Debts contracted and Engagements entered into, before the Adoption of this Constitution, shall be as valid against the United States under this Constitution, as under the Confederation.

This Constitution, and the Laws of the United States which shall be made in Pursuance thereof; and all Treaties made, or which shall be made, under the Authority of the

United States, shall be the supreme Law of the Land; and the Judges in every State shall be bound thereby, any Thing in the Constitution or Laws of any State to the Contrary notwithstanding.

The Senators and Representatives before mentioned, and the Members of the several State Legislatures, and all executive and judicial Officers, both of the United States and of the several States, shall be bound by Oath or Affirmation, to support this Constitution; but no religious Test shall ever be required as a Qualification to any Office or public Trust under the United States.

Article VII

The Ratification of the Conventions of nine States, shall be sufficient for the Establishment of this Constitution between the States so ratifying the Same.

The Word, "the," being interlined between the seventh and eighth Lines of the first Page, the Word "Thirty" being partly written on an Erazure in the fifteenth Line of the first Page, The Words "is tried" being interlined between the thirty second and thirty third Lines of the first Page and the Word "the" being interlined between the forty third and forty fourth Lines of the second Page.

Attest William Jackson Secretary

Done in Convention by the Unanimous Consent of the States present the Seventeenth Day of September in the Year of our Lord one thousand seven hundred and Eighty seven and of the Independence of the United States of America the Twelfth In witness whereof We have hereunto subscribed our Names,

G°. Washington
Presidt and deputy from Virginia

Delaware
Geo: Read
Gunning Bedford jun
John Dickinson
Richard Bassett
Jaco: Broom

Maryland
James McHenry
Dan of St Thos. Jenifer
Danl. Carroll

Virginia
John Blair
James Madison Jr.

North Carolina
Wm. Blount
Richd. Dobbs Spaight
Hu Williamson

South Carolina
J. Rutledge
Charles Cotesworth Pinckney
Charles Pinckney
Pierce Butler

Georgia
William Few
Abr Baldwin

New Hampshire
John Langdon
Nicholas Gilman

Massachusetts
Nathaniel Gorham
Rufus King

Connecticut
Wm. Saml. Johnson
Roger Sherman

New York
Alexander Hamilton

New Jersey
Wil: Livingston
David Brearley
Wm. Paterson
Jona: Dayton

Pennsylvania
B Franklin
Thomas Mifflin
Robt. Morris
Geo. Clymer
Thos. FitzSimons
Jared Ingersoll
James Wilson
Gouv Morris

Articles

In addition to, and Amendment of the Constitution of the United States of America, proposed by Congress, and ratified by the Legislatures of the several States, pursuant to the fifth Article of the original Constitution.

(The first ten amendments to the U.S. Constitution were ratified December 15, 1791, and form what is known as the "Bill of Rights.")

AMENDMENT I
Congress shall make no law respecting an establishment of religion, or prohibiting the free exercise thereof; or abridging the freedom of speech, or of the press; or the right of the people peaceably to assemble, and to petition the Government for a redress of grievances.

AMENDMENT II
A well regulated Militia, being necessary to the security of a free State, the right of the people to keep and bear Arms, shall not be infringed.

AMENDMENT III
No Soldier shall, in time of peace be quartered in any house, without the consent of the Owner, nor in time of war, but in a manner to be prescribed by law.

AMENDMENT IV
The right of the people to be secure in their persons, houses, papers, and effects, against unreasonable searches and seizures, shall not be violated, and no Warrants shall issue, but upon probable cause, supported by Oath or affirmation, and particularly describing the place to be searched, and the persons or things to be seized.

AMENDMENT V
No person shall be held to answer for a capital, or otherwise infamous crime, unless on a presentment or indictment of a Grand Jury, except in cases arising in the land or naval forces, or in the Militia, when in actual service in time of War or public danger; nor shall any person be subject for the same offence to be twice put in jeopardy of life or limb; nor shall be compelled in any criminal case to be a witness against himself, nor be deprived of life, liberty, or property, without due process of law; nor shall private property be taken for public use, without just compensation.

AMENDMENT VI
In all criminal prosecutions, the accused shall enjoy the right to a speedy and public trial, by an impartial jury of the State and district wherein the crime shall have been committed, which district shall have been previously ascertained by law, and to be informed of the nature and cause of the accusation; to be confronted with the witnesses against him; to have compulsory process for obtaining witnesses in his favor, and to have the Assistance of Counsel for his defence.

AMENDMENT VII

In Suits at common law, where the value in controversy shall exceed twenty dollars, the right of trial by jury shall be preserved, and no fact tried by a jury, shall be otherwise re-examined in any Court of the United States, than according to the rules of the common law.

AMENDMENT VIII

Excessive bail shall not be required, nor excessive fines imposed, nor cruel and unusual punishments inflicted.

AMENDMENT IX

The enumeration in the Constitution, of certain rights, shall not be construed to deny or disparage others retained by the people.

AMENDMENT X

The powers not delegated to the United States by the Constitution, nor prohibited by it to the States, are reserved to the States respectively, or to the people.

AMENDMENT XI

Passed by Congress March 4, 1794. Ratified February 7, 1795.

Note: Article III, Section 2, of the Constitution was modified by Amendment XI.

The Judicial power of the United States shall not be construed to extend to any suit in law or equity, commenced or prosecuted against one of the United States by Citizens of another State, or by Citizens or Subjects of any Foreign State.

AMENDMENT XII

Passed by Congress December 9, 1803. Ratified June 15, 1804.

Note: A portion of Article II, Section 1, of the Constitution was superceded by the Twelfth Amendment.

The Electors shall meet in their respective states and vote by ballot for President and Vice-President, one of whom, at least, shall not be an inhabitant of the same state with themselves; they shall name in their ballots the person voted for as President, and in distinct ballots the person voted for as Vice-President, and they shall make distinct lists of all persons voted for as President, and of all persons voted for as Vice-President, and of the number of votes for each, which lists they shall sign and certify, and transmit sealed to the seat of the government of the United States, directed to the President of the Senate;—the President of the Senate shall, in the presence of the Senate and House of Representatives, open all the certificates and the votes shall then be counted;—The person having the greatest number of votes for President, shall be the President, if such number be a majority of the whole number of Electors appointed; and if no person have such majority, then from the persons having the highest numbers not exceeding three on the list of those voted for as President, the House of Representatives shall choose immediately, by ballot, the President. But in choosing the President, the votes shall be taken by states, the representation from each state having one vote; a quorum for this purpose shall consist of a member or members from two-thirds of the states, and a majority of all the states shall be necessary to a choice. [And if the House of Representatives shall not choose a President whenever the right of choice shall devolve upon them, before the fourth day of March next following, then the Vice-President shall act as President, as in case of the death or other constitutional disability of the President.—]* The person having the greatest number of votes as Vice-President, shall be the Vice-President, if such number be a majority of the whole number of Electors appointed, and if no person have a majority, then from the two highest numbers on the list, the Senate shall choose the Vice-President; a quorum for the purpose shall consist of two-thirds of the whole number of Senators, and a majority of the whole number shall be necessary to a choice. But no person constitutionally ineligible to the office of President shall be eligible to that of Vice-President of the United States.

*Superceded by Section 3 of the Twentieth Amendment.

AMENDMENT XIII
Passed by Congress January 31, 1865. Ratified December 6, 1865.

Note: A portion of Article IV, Section 2, of the Constitution was superceded by the Thirteenth Amendment.

Section 1.

Neither slavery nor involuntary servitude, except as a punishment for crime whereof the party shall have been duly convicted, shall exist within the United States, or any place subject to their jurisdiction.

Section 2.

Congress shall have power to enforce this article by appropriate legislation.

AMENDMENT XIV
Passed by Congress June 13, 1866. Ratified July 9, 1868.

Note: Article I, Section 2, of the Constitution was modified by Section 2 of the Fourteenth Amendment.

Section 1

All persons born or naturalized in the United States, and subject to the jurisdiction thereof, are citizens of the United States and of the State wherein they reside. No State shall make or enforce any law which shall abridge the privileges or immunities of citizens of the United States; nor shall any State deprive any person of life, liberty, or property, without due process of law; nor deny to any person within its jurisdiction the equal protection of the laws.

Section 2

Representatives shall be apportioned among the several States according to their respective numbers, counting the whole number of persons in each State, excluding Indians not taxed. But when the right to vote at any election for the choice of electors for President and Vice-President of the United States, Representatives in Congress, the Executive and Judicial officers of a State, or the members of the Legislature thereof, is denied to any of the male inhabitants of such State, being twenty-one years of age,* and citizens of the United States, or in any way abridged, except for participation in rebellion, or other crime, the basis of representation therein shall be reduced in the proportion which the number of such male citizens shall bear to the whole number of male citizens twenty-one years of age in such State.

Section 3

No person shall be a Senator or Representative in Congress, or elector of President and Vice-President, or hold any office, civil or military, under the United States, or under any State, who, having previously taken an oath, as a member of Congress, or as an officer of the United States, or as a member of any State legislature, or as an executive or judicial officer of any State, to support the Constitution of the United States, shall have engaged in insurrection or rebellion against the same, or given aid or comfort to the enemies thereof. But Congress may by a vote of two-thirds of each House, remove such disability.

Section 4

The validity of the public debt of the United States, authorized by law, including debts incurred for payment of pensions and bounties for services in suppressing insurrection or rebellion, shall not be questioned. But neither the United States nor any State shall assume or pay any debt or obligation incurred in aid of insurrection or rebellion against the United States, or any claim for the loss or emancipation of any slave; but all such debts, obligations and claims shall be held illegal and void.

Section 5

The Congress shall have the power to enforce, by appropriate legislation, the provisions of this article.

*Changed by Section 1 of the Twenty-sixth Amendment.

AMENDMENT XV
Passed by Congress February 26, 1869. Ratified February 3, 1870.

Section 1.

The right of citizens of the United States to vote shall not be denied or abridged by the United States or by any State on account of race, color, or previous condition of servitude.

Section 2

The Congress shall have the power to enforce this article by appropriate legislation.

AMENDMENT XVI
Passed by Congress July 2, 1909. Ratified February 3, 1913.

Note: Article I, Section 9, of the Constitution was modified by Amendment XVI.

The Congress shall have power to lay and collect taxes on incomes, from whatever source derived, without apportionment among the several States, and without regard to any census or enumeration.

AMENDMENT XVII
Passed by Congress May 13, 1912. Ratified April 8, 1913.

Note: Article I, Section 3, of the Constitution was modified by the Seventeenth Amendment.

The Senate of the United States shall be composed of two Senators from each State, elected by the people thereof, for six years; and each Senator shall have one vote. The electors in each State shall have the qualifications requisite for electors of the most numerous branch of the State legislatures.

When vacancies happen in the representation of any State in the Senate, the executive authority of such State shall issue writs of election to fill such vacancies: *Provided,* That the legislature of any State may empower the executive thereof to make temporary appointments until the people fill the vacancies by election as the legislature may direct.

This amendment shall not be so construed as to affect the election or term of any Senator chosen before it becomes valid as part of the Constitution.

AMENDMENT XVIII
Passed by Congress December 18, 1917. Ratified January 16, 1919. Repealed by Amendment XXI.

Section 1

After one year from the ratification of this article the manufacture, sale, or transportation of intoxicating liquors within, the importation thereof into, or the exportation thereof from the United States and all territory subject to the jurisdiction thereof for beverage purposes is hereby prohibited.

Section 2

The Congress and the several States shall have concurrent power to enforce this article by appropriate legislation.

Section 3

This article shall be inoperative unless it shall have been ratified as an amendment to the Constitution by the legislatures of the several States, as provided in the Constitution, within seven years from the date of the submission hereof to the States by the Congress.

AMENDMENT XIX
Passed by Congress June 4, 1919. Ratified August 18, 1920.

The right of citizens of the United States to vote shall not be denied or abridged by the United States or by any State on account of sex.

Congress shall have power to enforce this article by appropriate legislation.

AMENDMENT XX
Passed by Congress March 2, 1932. Ratified January 23, 1933.

Note: Article I, Section 4, of the Constitution was modified by Section 2 of this amendment. In addition, a portion of the Twelfth Amendment was superceded by Section 3.

Section 1

The terms of the President and the Vice President shall end at noon on the 20th day of January, and the terms of Senators and Representatives at noon on the 3d day of January, of the years in which such terms would have ended if this article had not been ratified; and the terms of their successors shall then begin.

Section 2

The Congress shall assemble at least once in every year, and such meeting shall begin at noon on the 3d day of January, unless they shall by law appoint a different day.

Section 3

If, at the time fixed for the beginning of the term of the President, the President elect shall have died, the Vice President elect shall become President. If a President shall not have been chosen before the time fixed for the beginning of his term, or if the President elect shall have failed to qualify, then the Vice President elect shall act as President until a President shall have qualified; and the Congress may by law provide for the case wherein neither a President elect nor a Vice President shall have qualified, declaring who shall then act as President, or the manner in which one who is to act shall be selected, and such person shall act accordingly until a President or Vice President shall have qualified.

Section 4

The Congress may by law provide for the case of the death of any of the persons from whom the House of Representatives may choose a President whenever the right of choice shall have devolved upon them, and for the case of the death of any of the persons from whom the Senate may choose a Vice President whenever the right of choice shall have devolved upon them.

Section 5

Sections 1 and 2 shall take effect on the 15th day of October following the ratification of this article.

Section 6

This article shall be inoperative unless it shall have been ratified as an amendment to the Constitution by the legislatures of three-fourths of the several States within seven years from the date of its submission.

AMENDMENT XXI
Passed by Congress February 20, 1933. Ratified December 5, 1933.

Section 1

The eighteenth article of amendment to the Constitution of the United States is hereby repealed.

Section 2

The transportation or importation into any State, Territory, or Possession of the United States for delivery or use therein of intoxicating liquors, in violation of the laws thereof, is hereby prohibited.

Section 3

This article shall be inoperative unless it shall have been ratified as an amendment to the Constitution by conventions in the several States, as provided in the Constitution, within seven years from the date of the submission hereof to the States by the Congress.

AMENDMENT XXII
Passed by Congress March 21, 1947. Ratified February 27, 1951.

Section 1

No person shall be elected to the office of the President more than twice, and no person who has held the office of President, or acted as President, for more than two years of a term to which some other person was elected President shall be elected to the office of President more than once. But this Article shall not apply to any person holding the office of President when this Article was proposed by Congress, and shall not prevent any person who may be holding the office of President, or acting as President, during the term within which this Article becomes operative from holding the office of President or acting as President during the remainder of such term.

Section 2

This article shall be inoperative unless it shall have been ratified as an amendment to the Constitution by the legislatures of three-fourths of the several States within seven years from the date of its submission to the States by the Congress.

AMENDMENT XXIII
Passed by Congress June 16, 1960. Ratified March 29, 1961.

Section 1

The District constituting the seat of Government of the United States shall appoint in such manner as Congress may direct:

A number of electors of President and Vice President equal to the whole number of Senators and Representatives in Congress to which the District would be entitled if it were a State, but in no event more than the least populous State; they shall be in addition to those appointed by the States, but they shall be considered, for the purposes of the election of President and Vice President, to be electors appointed by a State; and they shall meet in the District and perform such duties as provided by the twelfth article of amendment.

Section 2

The Congress shall have power to enforce this article by appropriate legislation.

AMENDMENT XXIV
Passed by Congress August 27, 1962. Ratified January 23, 1964.

Section 1

The right of citizens of the United States to vote in any primary or other election for President or Vice President, for electors for President or Vice President, or for Senator or Representative in Congress, shall not be denied or abridged by the United States or any State by reason of failure to pay poll tax or other tax.

Section 2

The Congress shall have power to enforce this article by appropriate legislation.

AMENDMENT XXV
Passed by Congress July 6, 1965. Ratified February 10, 1967.

Note: Article II, Section 1, of the Constitution was affected by the Twenty-fifth Amendment.

Section 1

In case of the removal of the President from office or of his death or resignation, the Vice President shall become President.

Section 2

Whenever there is a vacancy in the office of the Vice President, the President shall nominate a Vice President who shall take office upon confirmation by a majority vote of both Houses of Congress.

Section 3

Whenever the President transmits to the President pro tempore of the Senate and the Speaker of the House of Representatives his written declaration that he is unable to discharge the powers and duties of his office, and until he transmits to them a written declaration to the contrary, such powers and duties shall be discharged by the Vice President as Acting President.

Section 4

Whenever the Vice President and a majority of either the principal officers of the executive departments or of such other body as Congress may by law provide, transmit to the President pro tempore of the Senate and the Speaker of the House of Representatives their written declaration that the President is unable to discharge the powers and duties of his office, the Vice President shall immediately assume the powers and duties of the office as Acting President.

Thereafter, when the President transmits to the President pro tempore of the Senate and the Speaker of the House of Representatives his written declaration that no inability exists, he shall resume the powers and duties of his office unless the Vice President and a majority of either the principal officers of the executive department or of such other body as Congress may by law provide, transmit within four days to the President pro tempore of the Senate and the Speaker of the House of Representatives their written declaration that the President is unable to discharge the powers and duties of his office. Thereupon Congress shall decide the issue, assembling within forty-eight hours for that purpose if not in session. If the Congress, within twenty-one days after receipt of the latter written declaration, or, if Congress is not in session, within twenty-one days after Congress is required to assemble, determines by two-thirds vote of both Houses that the President is unable to discharge the powers and duties of his office, the Vice President shall continue to discharge the same as Acting President; otherwise, the President shall resume the powers and duties of his office.

AMENDMENT XXVI
Passed by Congress March 23, 1971. Ratified July 1, 1971.

Note: Amendment XIV, Section 2, of the Constitution was modified by Section 1 of the Twenty-sixth Amendment.

Section 1

The right of citizens of the United States, who are eighteen years of age or older, to vote shall not be denied or abridged by the United States or by any State on account of age.

Section 2

The Congress shall have power to enforce this article by appropriate legislation.

AMENDMENT XXVII
Originally proposed Sept. 25, 1789. Ratified May 7, 1992.

No law, varying the compensation for the services of the Senators and Representatives, shall take effect, until an election of representatives shall have intervened.

Lincoln's Gettysburg Address

Four score and seven years ago our fathers brought forth on this continent, a new nation, conceived in Liberty, and dedicated to the proposition that all men are created equal.

Now we are engaged in a great civil war, testing whether that nation, or any nation so conceived and so dedicated, can long endure. We are met on a great battle-field of that war. We have come to dedicate a portion of that field, as a final resting place for those who here gave their lives that that nation might live. It is altogether fitting and proper that we should do this.

But, in a larger sense, we can not dedicate—we can not consecrate—we can not hallow—this ground. The brave men, living and dead, who struggled here, have consecrated it, far above our poor power to add or detract. The world will little note, nor long remember what we say here, but it can never forget what they did here. It is for us the living, rather, to be dedicated here to the unfinished work which they who fought here have thus far so nobly advanced. It is rather for us to be here dedicated to the great task remaining before us—that from these honored dead we take increased devotion to that cause for which they gave the last full measure of devotion—that we here highly resolve that these dead shall not have died in vain—that this nation, under God, shall have a new birth of freedom—and that government of the people, by the people, for the people, shall not perish from the earth.

Appendix B

Historical Facts and Data

U.S. Presidents and Vice Presidents

 Table App B-1 Presidents and Vice Presidents

	President	Vice President	Political Party	Term
1	George Washington	John Adams	No Party Designation	1789–1797
2	John Adams	Thomas Jefferson	Federalist	1797–1801
3	Thomas Jefferson	Aaron Burr George Clinton	Democratic Republican	1801–1809
4	James Madison	George Clinton Elbridge Gerry	Democratic Republican	1809–1817
5	James Monroe	Daniel D. Tompkins	Democratic Republican	1817–1825
6	John Quincy Adams	John C. Calhoun	Democratic Republican	1825–1829
7	Andrew Jackson	John C. Calhoun Martin Van Buren	Democratic	1829–1837
8	Martin Van Buren	Richard M. Johnson	Democratic	1837–1841
9	William Henry Harrison	John Tyler	Whig	1841
10	John Tyler	None	Whig	1841–1845
11	James Knox Polk	George M. Dallas	Democratic	1845–1849
12	Zachary Taylor	Millard Fillmore	Whig	1849–1850
13	Millard Fillmore	None	Whig	1850–1853
14	Franklin Pierce	William R. King	Democratic	1853–1857
15	James Buchanan	John C. Breckinridge	Democratic	1857–1861
16	Abraham Lincoln	Hannibal Hamlin Andrew Johnson	Union	1861–1865
17	Andrew Johnson	None	Union	1865–1869
18	Ulysses Simpson Grant	Schuyler Colfax Henry Wilson	Republican	1869–1877
19	Rutherford Birchard Hayes	William A. Wheeler	Republican	1877–1881
20	James Abram Garfield	Chester Alan Arthur	Republican	1881
21	Chester Alan Arthur	None	Republican	1881–1885
22	Stephen Grover Cleveland	Thomas Hendricks	Democratic	1885–1889
23	Benjamin Harrison	Levi P. Morton	Republican	1889–1893

continued

Table App B–1 Presidents and Vice Presidents (cont.)

	President	Vice President	Political Party	Term
24	Stephen Grover Cleveland	Adlai E. Stevenson	Democratic	1893–1897
25	William McKinley	Garret A. Hobart Theodore Roosevelt	Republican	1897–1901
26	Theodore Roosevelt	Charles W. Fairbanks	Republican	1901–1909
27	William Howard Taft	James S. Sherman	Republican	1909–1913
28	Woodrow Wilson	Thomas R. Marshall	Democratic	1913–1921
29	Warren Gamaliel Harding	Calvin Coolidge	Republican	1921–1923
30	Calvin Coolidge	Charles G. Dawes	Republican	1923–1929
31	Herbert Clark Hoover	Charles Curtis	Republican	1929–1933
32	Franklin Delano Roosevelt	John Nance Garner Henry A. Wallace Harry S. Truman	Democratic	1933–1945
33	Harry S. Truman	Alben W. Barkley	Democratic	1945–1953
34	Dwight David Eisenhower	Richard Milhous Nixon	Republican	1953–1961
35	John Fitzgerald Kennedy	Lyndon Baines Johnson	Democratic	1961–1963
36	Lyndon Baines Johnson	Hubert Horatio Humphrey	Democratic	1963–1969
37	Richard Milhous Nixon	Spiro T. Agnew Gerald Rudolph Ford	Republican	1969–1974
38	Gerald Rudolph Ford	Nelson Rockefeller	Republican	1974–1977
39	James Earl Carter Jr.	Walter Mondale	Democratic	1977–1981
40	Ronald Wilson Reagan	George Herbert Walker Bush	Republican	1981–1989
41	George Herbert Walker Bush	J. Danforth Quayle	Republican	1989–1993
42	William Jefferson Clinton	Albert Gore Jr.	Democratic	1993–2001
43	George Walker Bush	Richard Cheney	Republican	2001–2008
44	Barack Hussein Obama	Joseph Biden	Democratic	2008–

Admission of States into the Union

 Table App B-2 Admission of States into the Union

	State	Date of Admission		State	Date of Admission
1	Delaware	December 7, 1787	26	Michigan	January 26, 1837
2	Pennsylvania	December 12, 1787	27	Florida	March 3, 1845
3	New Jersey	December 18, 1787	28	Texas	December 29, 1845
4	Georgia	January 2, 1788	29	Iowa	December 28, 1846
5	Connecticut	January 9, 1788	30	Wisconsin	May 29, 1848
6	Massachusetts	February 6, 1788	31	California	September 9, 1850
7	Maryland	April 28, 1788	32	Minnesota	May 11, 1858
8	South Carolina	May 23, 1788	33	Oregon	February 14, 1859
9	New Hampshire	June 21, 1788	34	Kansas	January 29, 1861
10	Virginia	June 25, 1788	35	West Virginia	June 20, 1863
11	New York	July 26, 1788	36	Nevada	October 31, 1864
12	North Carolina	November 21, 1789	37	Nebraska	March 1, 1867
13	Rhode Island	May 29, 1790	38	Colorado	August 1, 1876
14	Vermont	March 4, 1791	39	North Dakota	November 2, 1889
15	Kentucky	June 1, 1792	40	South Dakota	November 2, 1889
16	Tennessee	June 1, 1796	41	Montana	November 8, 1889
17	Ohio	March 1, 1803	42	Washington	November 11, 1889
18	Louisiana	April 30, 1812	43	Idaho	July 3, 1890
19	Indiana	December 11, 1816	44	Wyoming	July 10, 1890
20	Mississippi	December 10, 1817	45	Utah	January 4, 1896
21	Illinois	December 3, 1818	46	Oklahoma	November 16, 1907
22	Alabama	December 14, 1819	47	New Mexico	January 6, 1912
23	Maine	March 15, 1820	48	Arizona	February 14, 1912
24	Missouri	August 10, 1821	49	Alaska	January 3, 1959
25	Arkansas	June 15, 1836	50	Hawaii	August 21, 1959

Glossary

Antinomianism The belief that moral law was not binding on true Christians. The opposite of Arminianism, antinomianism held that good works would not count in the afterlife. Justification, or entrance to heaven, was by faith alone. See Calvinism.

Arminianism Religious doctrine developed by the Dutch theologian Jacobus Arminius that argued that men and women had free will and suggested that hence they would earn their way into heaven by good works.

Armistice A cessation of hostilities by agreement among the opposing sides; a cease-fire.

Associationalism President Herbert Hoover's preferred method of responding to the Depression. Rather than have the government directly involve itself in the economy, Hoover hoped to use the government to encourage associations of businessmen to cooperate voluntarily to meet the crisis.

Autarky At the height of the world depression, industrial powers sought to isolate their economies within self-contained spheres, generally governed by national (or imperial) economic planning. Japan's Co-Prosperity Sphere, the Soviet Union, and the British Empire each comprised a more or less closed economic unit.

Benevolent Empire The loosely affiliated network of charitable reform associations that emerged (especially in urban areas) in response to the widespread revivalism of the early nineteenth century.

Berdache In Indian societies, a man who dressed and adopted the mannerisms of women and had sex only with other men. In Native American culture, the *berdache,* half man and half woman, symbolized cosmic harmony.

Budget deficit The failure of tax revenues to pay for annual federal spending on military, welfare, and other programs. The resulting budget deficits forced Washington to borrow money to cover its costs. The growing budget deficits were controversial, in part because the government's borrowing increased both its long-term debt and the amount of money it had to spend each year to pay for the interest on loans.

Busing The controversial court-ordered practice of sending children by bus to public schools outside their neighborhoods in order to promote racial integration in the schools.

Calvinism Religious doctrine developed by the theologian John Calvin that argued that God alone determines who will receive salvation and, hence, men and women cannot earn their own salvation or even be certain about their final destinies.

Carpetbagger A derogatory term referring to northern whites who moved to the South after the Civil War. Stereotyped as corrupt and unprincipled, "carpetbaggers" were in fact a diverse group motivated by a variety of interests and beliefs.

Charter colony Settlement established by a trading company or other group of private entrepreneurs who received from the king a grant of land and the right to govern it. The charter colonies included Virginia, Plymouth, Massachusetts Bay, Rhode Island, and Connecticut.

City busting As late as the 1930s, President Roosevelt and most Americans regarded attacking civilians from the air as an atrocity, but during World War II cities became a primary target for U.S. warplanes. The inaccuracy of bombing, combined with racism and the belief that Japanese and German actions justified retaliation, led American air commanders to follow a policy of systematically destroying urban areas, particularly in Japan.

Communist   Member of the Communist Party or follower of the doctrines of Karl Marx. The term (or accusation) was applied more broadly in the twentieth century to brand labor unionists, progressives, civil rights workers, and other reformers as agents of a foreign ideology.

Communitarians   Individuals who supported and/or took up residence in separate communities created to embody improved plans of social, religious, and/or economic life.

Commutation   The controversial policy of allowing potential draftees to pay for a replacement to serve in the army. The policy was adopted by both the Union and Confederate governments during the Civil War, and in both cases opposition to commutation was so intense that the policy was abandoned.

Consent   One of the key principles of liberalism, which held that people could not be subject to laws to which they had not given their consent. This principle is reflected in both the Declaration of Independence and the preamble to the Constitution, which begins with the famous words "We the people of the United States, in order to form a more perfect union."

Constitutionalism   A loose body of thought that developed in Britain and the colonies and was used by the colonists to justify the Revolution by claiming that it was in accord with the principles of the British Constitution. Constitutionalism had two main elements. One was the rule of law, and the other the principle of *consent,* that one cannot be subject to laws or taxation except by duly elected representatives. Both were rights that had been won through struggle with the monarch. Constitutionalism also refers to the tendency in American politics, particularly in the early nineteenth century, to transpose all political questions into constitutional ones.

Consumer revolution   A slow and steady increase over the course of the eighteenth century in the demand for, and purchase of, consumer goods. The consumer revolution of the eighteenth century was closely related to the Industrial Revolution.

Consumerism   An ideology that defined the purchase of goods and services as both an expression of individual identity and essential to the national economy. Increasingly powerful by the 1920s and dominant by the 1950s, consumerism urged people to find happiness in the pursuit of leisure and pleasure more than in the work ethic.

Containment   The basic U.S. strategy for fighting the cold war. As used by diplomat George Kennan in a 1947 magazine essay, "containment" referred to the combination of diplomatic, economic, and military programs necessary to hold back Soviet expansionism after World War II.

Contraband of war   In its general sense, contraband of war was property seized from an enemy. But early in the Civil War the term was applied to slaves running to Union lines as a way of preventing owners from reclaiming them. The policy effectively nullified the fugitive slave clause of the U.S. Constitution. It was a first critical step in a process that would lead to a federal emancipation policy the following year.

Cooperationists   Those southerners who opposed immediate secession after the election of Abraham Lincoln in 1860. Cooperationists argued instead that secessionists should wait to see if the new president was willing to "cooperate" with the South's demands.

Copperhead   A northerner who sympathized with the South during the Civil War.

Deindustrialization   The reverse of industrialization, as factory shutdowns decreased the size of the manufacturing sector. Plant closings began to plague the American economy in the 1970s, prompting fears that the nation would lose its industrial base.

Democratic Republicans   One of the two parties to make up the first American party system. Following the fiscal and political views of Jefferson and Madison, Democratic Republicans generally advocated a weak federal government and opposed federal intervention in the economy of the nation.

Détente   This French term for the relaxation of tensions was used to describe the central foreign policy innovation of the Nixon administration—a new, less confrontational relationship with Communism. In addition to opening a dialogue with the People's Republic of China, Nixon sought a more stable, less confrontational relationship with the Soviet Union.

Diffusion   The controversial theory that the problem of slavery would be resolved if the slave economy was allowed to expand, or "diffuse," into the western territories. Southerners developed this theory as early as the 1800s in response to northerners who hoped to restrict slavery's expansion.

Disfranchisement   The act of depriving a person or group of voting rights. In the nineteenth century the right to vote was popularly known as the franchise. The Fourteenth Amendment of the Constitution affirmed the right of adult male citizens to vote, but state-imposed restrictions and taxes deprived large numbers of Americans—particularly African Americans—of the vote from the 1890s until the passage of the Voting Rights Act of 1964.

Domestic patriarchy   The practice of defining the family by the husband and father, and wives and children as his domestic dependents. Upon marriage a wife's property became her husband's, and children owed obedience and labor to the family until they reached adulthood. In combination with an exclusive male suffrage, domestic patriarchy described the political as well as the social system that prevailed among free Americans until the twentieth century.

Downsizing   American corporations' layoffs of both blue- and white-collar workers in an attempt to become more efficient and competitive. Downsizing was one of the factors that made Americans uneasy about the economy in the 1990s, despite the impressive surge in the stock market.

Dust Bowl   Across much of the Great Plains, decades of wasteful farming practices combined with several years of drought in the early 1930s to produce a series of massive dust storms that blew the topsoil across hundreds of miles. The area in Texas and Oklahoma affected by these storms became known as the Dust Bowl.

E-commerce   Short for "electronic commerce," this was the term for the Internet-based buying and selling that was one of the key hopes for the computer-driven postindustrial economy. The promise of e-commerce was still unfulfilled by the start of the twenty-first century.

Encomienda   A system of labor developed by the Spanish in the New World in which Spanish settlers (*encomenderos*) compelled groups of Native Americans to work for them. The *encomendero* owned neither the land nor the Indians who worked for him, but had the unlimited right to compel a particular group of Indians to work for him. This system was unique to the New World; nothing precisely like it had existed in Europe or elsewhere.

"Establishment"   The elite of mainly Ivy League–educated, Anglo-Saxon, Protestant, male, liberal northeasterners that supposedly dominated Wall Street and Washington after World War II. The Establishment's support for corporations, activist government, and containment engendered hostility from opposite poles of the political spectrum—from conservatives and Republicans like Richard Nixon at one end and from the New Left and the Movement at the other. Although many of the post–World War II leaders of the United States did tend to share common origins and ideologies, this elite was never as powerful, self-conscious, or unified as its opponents believed.

Eugenics   The practice of attempting to solve social problems through the control of human reproduction. Drawing on the authority of evolutionary biology, eugenists enjoyed considerable influence in the United States, especially on issues of corrections and public health, from the turn of the century through World War II. Applications of this pseudoscience included the identification of "born" criminals by physical characteristics and "better baby" contests at county fairs.

Federalists   One of the two political parties to make up the first American party system. Following the fiscal and political policies proposed by Alexander Hamilton, Federalists generally advocated the importance of a strong federal government, including federal intervention in the economy of the new nation.

Feminism   An ideology insisting on the fundamental equality of women and men. The feminists of the 1960s differed over how to achieve that equality: while liberal feminists mostly demanded equal rights for women in the workplace and in politics, radical feminists more thoroughly condemned the capitalist system and male oppression and demanded equality in both private and public life.

Feudalism   A social and political system that developed in Europe in the Middle Ages under which powerful lords offered less powerful noblemen protection in return for their loyalty. Feudalism also included the economic system of *manorialism,* under which dependent serfs worked on the manors controlled by those lords.

Fire-eaters   Militant southerners who pushed for secession in the 1850s.

Flexible response   The defense doctrine of the Kennedy and Johnson administrations. Abandoning the Eisenhower administration's heavy emphasis on nuclear weapons, flexible response stressed the buildup of the nation's conventional and special forces so that the president had a range of military options in response to Communist aggression.

Front   Early twentieth-century mechanized wars were fought along a battle line or "front" separating opposing sides. By World War II, tactical innovations—blitzkrieg, parachute troops, gliders, and amphibious landings—complicated warfare by breaking through, disrupting, or bypassing the front. The front thus became a more fluid boundary than the fortified trench lines of World War I. The term also acquired a political meaning, particularly for labor and the left. A coalition of parties supporting (or opposing) an agreed-upon line could be called a "popular front."

Gentility   A term without precise meaning that represented all that was polite, civilized, refined, and fashionable. It was everything that vulgarity was not. Because the term had no precise meaning, it was always subject to negotiation, striving, and anxiety as Americans, beginning in the eighteenth century, tried to show others that they were genteel through their manners, their appearance, and their styles of life.

Glass ceiling   The invisible barrier of discrimination that prevented female white-collar workers from rising to top executive positions in corporations.

Greenbackers Those who advocated currency inflation by keeping the type of money printed during the Civil War, known as "greenbacks," in circulation.

Gridlock The political traffic jam that tied up the federal government in the late 1980s and the 1990s. Gridlock developed from the inability of either major party to control both the presidency and Congress for any extended period of time. More fundamentally, gridlock reflected the inability of any party or president to win a popular mandate for a bold legislative program.

Horizontal integration More commonly known as "monopoly." An industry was "horizontally integrated" when a single company took control of virtually the entire market for a specific product. John D. Rockefeller's Standard Oil came close to doing this.

Humanism A Renaissance intellectual movement that focused on the intellectual and artistic achievements of humankind. Under the patronage of Queen Isabel, Spain became a center of European humanism.

Immediatism The variant antislavery sentiment that demanded immediate (as opposed to gradual) personal and federal action against the institution of slavery. This approach was most closely associated with William Lloyd Garrison and is dated from the publication of Garrison's newspaper, *The Liberator,* in January 1831.

Imperialism A process of extending dominion over territories beyond the national boundaries of a state. In the eighteenth century, Britain extended imperial control over North America through settlement, but in the 1890s, imperial influence was generally exercised through indirect rule. Subject peoples generally retained some local autonomy while the imperial power controlled commerce and defense. Few Americans went to the Philippines as settlers, but many passed through as tourists, missionaries, traders, and soldiers.

Individualism The social and political philosophy celebrating the central importance of the individual human being in society. Insisting on the rights of the individual in relationship to the group, individualism was one of the intellectual bases of capitalism and democracy. The resurgent individualism of the 1920s, with its emphasis on each American's freedom and fulfillment, was a critical element of the decade's emergent consumerism and Republican dominance.

Industrious revolution Beginning in the late seventeenth century in western Europe and extending to the North American colonies in the eighteenth century, a fundamental change in the way people worked, as they worked harder and organized their households to produce goods that could be sold, so they could have money to pay for the new consumer goods they wanted.

Initiative, recall, and referendum First proposed by the People's Party's Omaha Platform (1892), along with the direct election of senators and the secret ballot, as measures to subject corporate capitalism to democratic controls. Progressives, chiefly in western and midwestern states, favored them as a check on the power of state officials. The *initiative* allows legislation to be proposed by petition. The *recall* allows voters to remove public officials, and the *referendum* places new laws or constitutional amendments on the ballot for the direct approval of the voters.

Interest group An association whose members organize to exert political pressure on officials or the public. Unlike political parties, whose platforms and slates cover nearly every issue and office, an interest group focuses on a narrower list of concerns reflecting the shared outlook of its members. With the decline of popular politics around the turn of the twentieth century, business, religious, agricultural, women's, professional, neighborhood, and reform associations created a new form of political participation.

Isolationist   Between World War I and World War II, the United States refused to join the League of Nations, scaled back its military commitments abroad, and sought to maintain its independence of action in foreign affairs. These policies were called isolationist, although some historians prefer the term "independent internationalist," in recognition of the United States' continuing global influence. In the late 1930s, isolationists favored policies aimed at distancing the United States from European affairs and building a national defense based on air power and hemispheric security.

Joint-stock company   A form of business organization that was a forerunner to the modern corporation. The joint-stock company was used to raise both capital and labor for New World ventures. Shareholders contributed either capital or their labor for a period of years.

Judicial nationalism   The use of the judiciary to assert the primacy of the national government over state and local government and the legal principle of contract over principles of local custom.

Keynesian economics   The theory, named after the English economist John Maynard Keynes, that advocated the use of "countercyclical" fiscal policy. This meant that during good times the government should pay down the debt, so that during bad times, it could afford to stimulate the economy with deficit spending.

Liberalism   A body of political thought that traces its origins to John Locke and whose chief principles are consent, freedom of conscience, and property. Liberalism held that people could not be governed except by their own consent and that the purpose of government was to protect people as well as their property.

Linked economic development   A form of economic development that ties together a variety of enterprises so that development in one stimulates development in others, for example, those that provide raw materials, parts, or transportation.

Manifest destiny   A term first coined in 1845 by journalist John O'Sullivan to express the belief, widespread among antebellum Americans, that the United States was destined to expand across the North American continent to the Pacific and had an irrefutable right to the lands absorbed in this expansion. This belief was frequently justified on the grounds of claims to political and racial superiority.

Market revolution   The term used to designate the period of the early nineteenth century, roughly 1815–1830, during which internal dependence on cash markets and wages became widespread.

Mass production   A system of efficient, high-volume manufacturing based on division of labor into repetitive tasks, simplification, and standardization of parts, increasing use of specialized machinery, and careful supervision. Emerging since the nineteenth century, mass production reached a critical stage of development with Henry Ford's introduction of the moving assembly line at his Highland Park automobile factory. Mass production drove the prosperity of the 1920s and helped make consumerism possible.

Massive resistance   The rallying cry of southern segregationists who pledged to oppose the integration of the schools ordered by the Supreme Court in *Brown v. Board of Education* in 1954. The tactics of massive resistance included legislation, demonstrations, and violence.

Massive retaliation   The defense doctrine of the Eisenhower administration which promised "instant, massive retaliation" with nuclear weapons in response to Soviet aggression.

McCarthyism   The hunt for Communist subversion in the United States in the first years of the cold war. Democrats, in particular, used the term, a reference to the sometimes disreputable tactics of Republican Senator Joseph R. McCarthy of Wisconsin, in order to question the legitimacy of the conservative anti-Communist crusade.

Mercantilism   An economic theory developed in early-modern Europe to explain and guide the growth of European nation-states. Its goal was to strengthen the state by making the economy serve its interests. According to the theory of mercantilism, the world's wealth, measured in gold and silver, was fixed; that is, it could never be increased. As a result, each nation's chief economic objective must be to secure as much of the world's wealth as possible. One nation's gain was necessarily another's loss. Colonies played an important part in the theory of mercantilism. Their role was to serve as sources of raw materials and as markets for manufactured goods for the mother country alone.

Middle ground   The region between European and Indian settlements in North America that was neither fully European nor fully Indian, but rather a new world created out of two different traditions. The middle ground came into being every time Europeans and Indians met, needed each other, and could not (or would not) achieve what they wanted through use of force.

Millennialism   A strain of Protestant belief that holds that history will end with the thousand-year reign of Christ (the millennium). Some Americans saw the Great Awakening, the French and Indian War, and the Revolution as signs that the millennium was about to begin in America, and this belief infused Revolutionary thought with an element of optimism. Millennialism was also one aspect of a broad drive for social perfection in nineteenth-century America.

Modernization   The process by which developing countries in the third world were to become more like the United States—i.e., capitalist, independent, and anti-Communist. Confidence about the prospects for modernization was one of the cornerstones of liberal foreign policy in the 1960s.

Moral suasion   The strategy of using persuasion (as opposed to legal coercion) to convince individuals to alter their behavior. In the antebellum years, moral suasion generally implied an appeal to religious values.

Mutual aid societies   Organizations through which people of relatively meager means pooled their resources for emergencies. Usually, individuals paid small amounts in dues and were able to borrow large amounts in times of need. In the early nineteenth century, mutual aid societies were especially common among workers in free African American communities.

National Republicans   Over the first 20 years of the nineteenth century, the Republican Party gradually abandoned its Jeffersonian animosity toward an activist federal government and industrial development and became a strong proponent of both of these positions. Embodied in the American system, these new views were fully captured in the party's designation of itself as National Republicans by 1824.

Nativism   A bias against anyone not born in the United States and in favor of native-born Americans. This attitude assumes the superior culture and political virtue of white Americans of Anglo-Saxon descent, or of individuals assumed to have that lineage. During the period 1820–1850, Irish immigrants became the particular targets of nativist attitudes.

New Left   The radical student movement that emerged in opposition to the new liberalism in the 1960s. The New Left condemned the cold war and corporate power and called for the creation of a true "participatory democracy" in the United States. Placing its faith in the radical potential of young, middle-class students, the New Left differed from the "old left" of the late nineteenth and early twentieth centuries, which believed workers would lead the way to socialism.

Patriotism   Love of country. Ways of declaring and displaying national devotion underwent a change from the nineteenth to the twentieth centuries. Whereas politicians were once unblushingly called patriotic, after World War I the title was appropriated to describe the sacrifices of war veterans. Patriotic spectacle in the form of public oration and electoral rallies gave way to military-style commemorations of Armistice Day and the nation's martial heritage.

Political virtue   In the political thought of the early republic, the personal qualities required in citizens if the republic was to survive.

Polygyny   Taking more than one wife. Indian tribes such as the Huron practiced polygyny, and hence they did not object when French traders who already had wives in Europe took Indian women as additional wives.

Popular sovereignty   A solution to the slavery controversy espoused by leading northern Democrats in the 1850s. It held that the inhabitants of western territories should be free to decide for themselves whether or not they wanted to have slavery. In principle, popular sovereignty would prevent Congress from either enforcing or restricting slavery's expansion into the western territories.

Postindustrial economy   The service- and computer-based economy that was succeeding the industrial economy, which had been dominated by manufacturing, at the end of the twentieth century.

Principle of judicial review   The principle of law that recognizes in the judiciary the power to review and rule on the constitutionality of laws. First established in *Marbury v. Madison* (1803) under Chief Justice John Marshall.

Producers ideology   The belief that all those who lived by producing goods shared a common political identity in opposition to those who lived off financial speculation, rent, or interest.

Proprietary colony   Colony established by a royal grant to an individual or family. The proprietary colonies included Maryland, New York, New Jersey, Pennsylvania, and the Carolinas.

Public opinion   Not quite democracy or consent, public opinion was a way of understanding the influence of the citizenry on political calculations. It emerged in the eighteenth century, when it was defined as a crucial source of a government's legitimacy. It was associated with the emergence of a press and a literate public free to discuss, and to question, government policy. In the twentieth century, Freudian psychology and the new mass media encouraged a view of the public as both fickle and powerful. Whereas the popular will (a nineteenth-century concept) was steady and rooted in national traditions, public opinion was variable and based on attitudes that could be aroused or manipulated by advertising.

Realism   A major artistic movement of the late nineteenth century that embraced writers, painters, critics, and photographers. Realists strove to avoid sentimentality and to depict life "realistically."

Reconversion   The economic and social transition from the war effort to peacetime. Americans feared that reconversion might bring a return to the depression conditions of the 1930s.

Re-export trade   Marine trade between two foreign ports, with an intermediate stop in a port of the ship's home nation. United States shippers commonly engaged in the re-export trade during the European wars of the late eighteenth and early nineteenth centuries, when England and France tried to prevent each other from shipping or receiving goods. United States shippers claimed that the intermediate stop in the United States made their cargoes neutral.

Republicanism   A set of doctrines rooted in classical antiquity that held that power is always grasping and dangerous and presents a threat to liberty. Republicanism supplied constitutionalism with a motive by explaining how a balanced constitution could be transformed into a tyranny as grasping men used their power to encroach on the liberty of citizens. In addition, republicanism held that people achieved fulfillment only through participation in public life, as citizens in a republic. Republicanism required the individual to display *virtue* by sacrificing his (or her) private interest for the good of the republic.

Requerimiento (the Requirement)   A document issued by the Spanish Crown in 1513 in order to clarify the legal bases for the enslavement of hostile Indians. Each *conquistador* was required to read a copy of the *Requerimiento* to each group of Indians he encountered. The *Requerimiento* promised friendship to all Indians who accepted Christianity, but threatened war and enslavement for all those who resisted.

Safety-valve theory   An argument commonly made in the nineteenth century that the abundance of western land spared the United States from the social upheavals common to capitalist societies in Europe. In theory, as long as eastern workers had the option of migrating west and becoming independent farmers, they could not be subject to European levels of exploitation. Thus the West was said to provide a "safety-valve" against the pressures caused by capitalist development.

Scalawag   A derogatory term referring to southern whites who sympathized with the Republicans during Reconstruction.

Second-wave feminism   The reborn women's movement of the 1960s and 1970s that reinterpreted the first wave of nineteenth- and early twentieth-century feminists' insistence on civil rights and called for full economic, reproductive, and political equality.

Separation of powers   One of the chief innovations of the Constitution and a distinguishing mark of the American form of democracy, in which the executive, legislative, and judicial branches of government are separated so that they can check and balance each other.

Slave power   In the 1850s northern Republicans explained the continued economic and political strength of slavery by claiming that a "slave power" had taken control of the federal government and used its authority to keep slavery alive artificially.

Slave society   A society in which slavery is central to the economy and political structure, in contrast to a *society with slaves,* in which the presence of slaves does not alter the fundamental structures of the society.

Slavery A system of extreme social inequality distinguished by the definition of a human being as property, or chattel, and thus, in principle, totally subordinated to the slave owner.

Social Darwinism Darwin's theory of natural selection transferred from biological evolution to human history. Social Darwinists argued that some individuals and groups, particularly racial groups, were better able to survive in the "race of life."

Stagflation The unusual combination of stagnant growth and high inflation that plagued the American economy in the 1970s.

Strict constructionism The view that the Constitution has a fixed, explicit meaning which can be altered only through formal amendment. Loose constructionism is the view that the Constitution is a broad framework within which various interpretations and applications are possible without formal amendment.

Suburbanization The spread of suburban housing developments and, more broadly, of the suburban ideal.

Supply-side economics The controversial theory, associated with economist Arthur Laffer, that drove "Reaganomics," the conservative economic policy of the Reagan administration. In contrast to liberal economic theory, supply-side economics emphasized that producers—the "supply side" of the economic equation—drove economic growth, rather than consumers—the "demand side." To encourage producers to invest more in new production, Laffer and other supply-siders called for massive tax cuts.

Tariff A tax on goods moving across an international boundary. Because the Constitution allows tariffs only on imports, as a political issue the tariff question has chiefly concerned the protection of domestic manufacturing from foreign competition. Industries producing mainly for American consumers have preferred a higher tariff, while farmers and industries aimed at global markets have typically favored reduced tariffs. Prior to the Civil War, the tariff was a symbol of diverging political economies in North and South. The North advocated high tariffs to protect growing domestic manufacturing ("protective tariffs"), and the South opposed high tariffs on the grounds that they increased the cost of imported manufactured goods.

Taylorism A method for maximizing industrial efficiency by systematically reducing the time and motion involved in each step of the production process. The "scientific" system was designed by Frederick Taylor and explained in his book *The Principles of Scientific Management* (1911).

Universalism Enlightenment belief that all people are by their nature essentially the same.

Vertical integration The practice of taking control of every aspect of the production, distribution, and sale of a commodity. For example, Andrew Carnegie vertically integrated his steel operations by purchasing the mines that produced the ore, the railroads that carried the ore to the steel mills, the mills themselves, and the distribution system that carried the finished steel to consumers.

Virtual representation British doctrine that said that all Britons, even those who did not vote, were represented by Parliament, if not "actually," by representatives they had chosen, then "virtually," because each member of parliament was supposed to act on behalf of the entire realm, not only his constituents or even those who had voted for him.

Voluntarism A style of political activism that took place largely outside of electoral politics. Voluntarism emerged in the nineteenth century, particularly among those

Americans who were not allowed to vote. Thus women formed voluntary associations that pressed for social and political reforms, even though women were excluded from electoral politics.

Waltham system   Named after the system used in early textile mills in Waltham, Massachusetts, the term refers to the practice of bringing all elements of production together in a single factory setting with the application of non-human-powered machinery.

Watergate   The name of the Washington, DC, office and condominium complex where five men with ties to the presidential campaign of Richard Nixon were caught breaking into the headquarters of the Democratic National Committee in June 1972. "Watergate" became the catchall term for the wide range of illegal practices of Nixon and his followers that were uncovered in the aftermath of the break-in.

Whig Party   The political party founded by Henry Clay in the mid-1830s. The name derived from the seventeenth- and eighteenth-century British antimonarchical position and was intended to suggest that the Jacksonian Democrats (and Jackson in particular) sought despotic powers. In many ways the heirs of National Republicans, the Whigs supported economic expansion, but they also believed in a strong federal government to control the dynamism of the market. The Whig Party attracted many moral reformers.

Whitewater   With its echo of Richard Nixon's "Watergate" scandals in the 1970s, "Whitewater" became the catchall term for the scandals that plagued Bill Clinton's presidency in the 1990s. The term came from the name of a real estate development company in Arkansas. Clinton and his wife Hillary supposedly had corrupt dealings with the Whitewater Development Corporation in the 1970s and 1980s that they purportedly attempted to cover up in the 1990s.

Women's rights movement   The antebellum organizing efforts of women on their own behalf, in the attempt to secure a broad range of social, civic, and political rights. This movement is generally dated from the convention of Seneca Falls in 1848. Only after the Civil War would women's rights activism begin to confine its efforts to suffrage.

Photo Credits

Chapter 1: The London Art Archive / Alamy, 1; Lloyd Townsend Mural, Cahokia Mounds State Historic Site. Photo by Art Grossman, 5; Pierpont Morgan Library / Art Resource, NY, 15; Benson Latin American Collection, University of Texas, Austin, 25; The Granger Collection, 27.

Chapter 2: The Bridgeman Art Library, 31; The Bridgeman Art Library, 50; Service Historique de la Marine, Vicennes, France / Bridgeman Art Library, 51; Service Historique de la Marine, Vicennes, France / Bridgeman Art Library, 52; The Art Archive / The British Museum, 54.

Chapter 3: Borough of King's Lynn and West Norfolk, 58; Preservation Virginia, 61; Marilyn Angel Wynn / Nativestock.com, 64; Ira Block / National Geographic Stock / Getty Images, 64; The Bridgeman Art Library, 65.

Chapter 4: Illustration by Walter Rane, 87; North Carolina State Archives, Division of Archives and History, 94; Plymouth County Commissioners, Plymouth Court House, Plymouth, MA / Dublin Seminar for New England Folklife, Concord, MA, 103; © President and Fellows Harvard University, Peabody Museum, 99–12–10 / 53121, 113; Kevin Fleming / Corbis; 115; Giraudon / Bridgeman Art Library, 117.

Chapter 5: Private Collection / Bridgeman Art Library, 121; The Granger Collection, 129; Private Collection / Bridgeman Art Library, 134; Gibbes Museum, Gift of Mr. Joseph E. Jenkins © Image Gibbes Museum of Art / Carolina Art Association, 1968.005.0001, 138.

Chapter 6: Frontispiece from A Narrative of the Captivity of Mrs. Johnson (Bowie, Md.: Heritage Books, Inc., 1990), 153; The Granger Collection, 160; Hulton Archive / Getty Images, 161; The Granger Collection, 171.

Chapter 7: The Granger Collection, 183; Bettmann / Corbis, 187.

Chapter 8: Library Company of Philadelphia, 216; The Granger Collection, 221; The Granger Collection; 223.

Chapter 9: The Granger Collection, 248; American Antiquarian Society, 253; Collection of the New York Historical Society / Bridgeman Art Library, 257; National Portrait Gallery, Smithsonian Institution / Art Resource, NY, 270.

Chapter 10: National Portrait Gallery, Smithsonian Institution / Art Resource, NY, 279; Collection of the New-York Historical Society, acc. 1953.251, 288; Cincinnati Museum Center / Getty Images, 295.

Chapter 11: Bentley Historical Library, University of Michigan, 305; The Granger Collection, 308; The Granger Collection, 312; Woolrac Museum, Oklahoma / Bridgeman Art Library, 325.

Chapter 12: The Granger Collection, 334; The Granger Collection, 337; The Granger Collection, 339; Geoffrey Clements / Corbis, 346; The Granger Collection, 350.

Chapter 13: Smithsonian American Art Museum, Washington, DC / Art Resource, NY, 361; The Granger Collection, 364; The Amon Carter Museum, Ft. Worth, TX, 1983.156., 368; Smithsonian American Art Museum, Washington, DC / Art Resource, NY, 378; Hulton Archive / Getty Images, 385.

Chapter 14: Image © The Metropolitan Museum of art, New York / Art Resource, NY, 389; Collection of the New-York Historical Society / The Bridgeman Art Library, 392; Bettmann / Corbis, 397; Bettmann / Corbis, 398; The Granger Collection, 411.

Chapter 15: The Granger Collection, 416; The Granger Collection, 422; The Granger Collection, 436; The Granger Collection, 437; The Granger Collection, 443; Culver Pictures / The Art Archive, 449.

Chapter 16: Louis Psihoyos / Sciencefaction.com, 455; Photographs and Prints Division, Schomburg Center for Research in Black Culture, The New York Public Library, Astor, Lenox and Tilden Foundations, 456; The Granger Collection, 475.

Chapter 17: The Granger Collection, 481; Bettmann / Corbis, 487; The Granger Collection, 490; Bettmann / Corbis, 491; The Granger Collection, 496; The Granger Collection, 500.

Chapter 18: Bettmann / Corbis, 507; The Granger Collection, 518; Chicago History Museum, 528; The Granger Collection, 529*.

Chapter 19: Nebraska State Historical Society, 533; The Granger Collection, 537; Bettmann / Corbis, 538; Bancroft Library University of California, 546; The Metropolitan Museum of art,

New York / Art Resource, NY, 548; Kansas State Historical Society, 553.

Chapter 20: The Granger Collection, 557; The Granger Collection, 571; The Granger Collection, 572; Yale Divinity School, 577.

Chapter 21: History of Medicine Collection / National Library of Medicine, 587; The Woodrow Wilson Presidential Library and Museum, Staunton, VA, 590; Hulton Archive / Getty Images, 595; www .freepedia.co.uk, 599; Chicago History Museum, 602.

Chapter 22: Brown Brothers, 617; Bettmann / Corbis, 626; Courtesy of the Pennsylvania State Archives, 629; Australian War Museum / The Art Archive, 636; Capt. Jackson / Time & Life Pictures / Getty Images, 638; Digital Image © The Modern Museum of Art / Scala / Art Resource, NY. © Estate of Ben Shahn, Licensed by VAGA, NY, 642.

Chapter 23: Hulton Archive / Getty Images, 645; Hulton Archive / Getty Images, 648; The Granger Collection, 654; Hulton Archive / Getty Images, 660; Title Insurance and Trust / C.C. Pierce Photograph Collection, Special Collections, University of Southern California Libraries, 663;

Chapter 24: Bettmann / Corbis, 673; Hulton Archive / Getty Images, 677; Bettmann / Corbis, 679; Hulton Archive / Getty Images, 683; Popperfoto / Getty Images, 685.

Chapter 25: Bettmann / Corbis, 700; William Shrou / Time & Life Pictures /Getty Images, 704; Bettmann / Corbis, 706; Courtesy National Park Service Museum Management Program and Tuskegee Airmen National Historic Site, TUA131,

710; United States Naval History Center, 723; The Granger Collection, 728.

Chapter 26: Bettmann / Corbis, 731; The Daily Mail, 1946, 738; The Granger Collection, 748; Hulton Archive / Getty Images, 750.

Chapter 27: Courtesy Time Inc., 760; Hagley Museum and Library, Better Living Magazine, 1972.341, 763; Guy Gillette / Time & Life Pictures / Getty Images, 766; Bettmann / Corbis, 773; Bettmann / Corbis, 776; AP Images, 785; A 1957 Herblock Cartoon, copyright by the Herblock foundation, 786.

Chapter 28: Courtesy of Fred Downs, 790; Jacko Moebes / Corbis, 792; Hulton-Deutsch Collection / Corbis, 797; Ralph Crane / Time & Life Pictures / Getty Images, 799; Bettmann /Corbis, 813; Jack Kightlinger / Corbis, 817.

Chapter 29: AP Images, 822; Bettmann / Corbis, 825; AP Images, 831; Tim Page / Corbis, 832; Bettmann / Corbis, 849.

Chapter 30: Courtesy Linda Chavez, 852; AFP / Getty Images, 855; AP Images, 857; Lee Frey / Hulton Archive /Getty Images, 863; Diana Walker / Time & Life Pictures /Getty Images, 865; Stephen Ferry / Getty Images, 880.

Chapter 31: David Cannon / Allsport / Getty Images, 883; Courtesy of the Computer History Museum. 887; Tolga Adanall / MCT / Landov, 889; Robert King / Newsmakers / Getty Images, 894; Paul J. Richards / AFP / Getty Images, 895; Justin Sullivan / Getty Images, 900; AP Images, 908; Jeff Haynes / Reuters / Landov, 912.

Index

Stuyvesant, Peter, 45, 46, 91
Submarines, 622
Submerged Lands Act of 1953, 775
Subprime mortgages, 893, 910, 911
Subsidies
  farm, 775
  for transportation, 312, 313
Subtreasuries, 552–53
Suburbs, 764, 765–66, 771
The Subway, Tooker's, 755, *755*
Sudan, 904
Suez Canal crisis, 781
Suffolk Resolves, 181
Suffrage, 309–10, *310*, 328. *See also* Voting; Women's
      suffrage
  universal, *310*, 473, 537–38
Sugar
  in Barbados, 96
  Hawaii and, 544, 579
  increased demand for, 136–37
  plantations, 10, 45, 96, 283, 285
Sugar Act of 1764, 166, 168, 173, 174
Sullivan, John, 204, 511
Sumner, Charles, 403, 405, 457, 471
Sunbelt, 829, *829*, 855
Sunday, Billy, 631
Sunday School Union, 274
Sunnis, 909
Superfund program for hazardous waste, 848, 877
Superman, 674
Supply-side economics. *See* Reaganomics
Supreme Court
  on abortion, 836, 870–71, 899
  on affirmative action, 835, 898
  on all-white primaries, 719, 749
  on *Amistad* incident, 379
  on banks, 268, 276, 327
  as branch of government, 209, 235
  on busing, 835
  on constitutionality, 245, 250–51
  on contraception, 802, 814
  on contracts, 268
  on discrimination, 749, 750, 873
  film ban by, 768
  on foreign policy, 544
  New Deal and, 690, 692, 694–95
  Nixon, R., and, 843
  on personal freedom, 802–3
  on popular sovereignty, 408
  Reagan, R., and, 869
  on same-sex marriage, 900–901
  on segregation, 478, 554, 571, 572, 783–85, 791, 796
  on slavery, 298, 407–8, 409
  on unions, 574, 641, 650
  on writs of mandamus, 250
Surveyors, 222, 307
Susquehanna River, 158
Susquehannock Indians, 47, 67, 99
Sutter, John, 502
Sutter's mill, 502
Swaggart, Jimmy, 876
Swann v. Charlotte-Mecklenburg Board of Education,
    835–36

Swansea, 102
Sweat houses, 40
Sweatshops, 495, 594
Swedish colonies, 29
Swift, Gustavus, 491
The Swimming Hole (Eakins), 528
Syllabary, Cherokee, 327
Sylvis, William, 474
Syngman Rhee, 744
Syphilis, 19
Syria, 825, 833

Tabasco Indians, 24
Taft, Robert, 705
Taft, William H.
  dollar diplomacy and, 609–11
  election of 1912 and, 612
Taft-Hartley Act of 1947, 747, *748*, 752
Tailoresses' strike, 343, 345
Tailors' strike, 353
Taino Indians, 14, 15, *15*, 16, 19
Taiping Rebellion, 485
Taiwan, 743, 779, 830
Takeovers and mergers, corporate, 855, 890
Taliban, 905, 907, 909
Talleyrand, Charles Maurice de, 244
Tallmadge, James, 299
Tanacharison, 158
Taney, Roger, 328, 408
Tanzania, U.S. embassy in, 904
Tappan, Arthur, 357
Tappan, Lewis, 357
Tarawa, 724
Tarbell, Ida, 595–96
Tariff Act of 1789, 235
Tariff Commission, 613
Tariffs
  of 1816, 318
  of 1824, 318
  of 1828, 329–30, 331
  of 1832, 331
  Dingley Tariff Act, 569
  Fordney-McCumber Tariff of 1922, 667
  Harrison-McKinley Tariff of 1890, 541, 562, 577, 579
  Hawley-Smoot Tariff of 1930, 680, 703
  in industrial America, 540–42, 545, 547
  Payne-Aldrich Tariff of 1909, 611
  on sewing machines, 561
  trade and, 560, 562, 612–13, 703
  Underwood-Simmons Tariff of 1913, 612
  Whig Party on, 380
Task system in slavery, 143, 283, 284, 290
Tate, Allen, 659
Taverns, 140
Taxation. *See also* Excise tax; Income tax; Poll taxes;
      Single Tax; Tariffs
  in England, 167–68
  in English colonies, 90, 92, 104, 106, 155–56, 162,
      166–73
  on houses, 244–45
  Reagan, R., and, 860–61, 877
  of slaves, 101, 127
  on spirits, 217, 236, 240

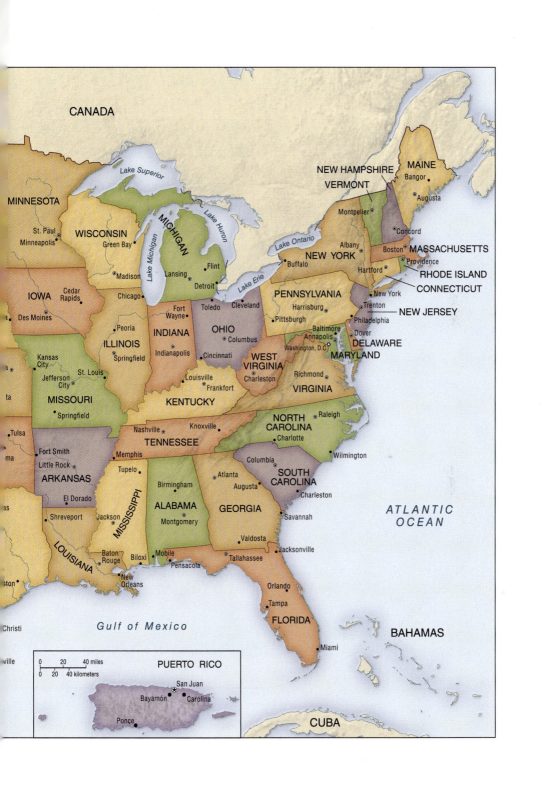

CANADA

MINNESOTA

St. Paul
Minneapolis

WISCONSIN
Green Bay

Lake Superior

MICHIGAN

Lake Huron

Lake Michigan

Madison
Lansing
Flint

IOWA
Cedar
Rapids

Des Moines

Chicago

Detroit

Lake Erie

Lake Ontario

NEW HAMPSHIRE
VERMONT

MAINE
Bangor

Augusta

Montpelier

Concord

Albany
Boston
MASSACHUSETTS
Providence

NEW YORK
Buffalo

Hartford

RHODE ISLAND
CONNECTICUT

PENNSYLVANIA

New York

Harrisburg
Trenton
NEW JERSEY

Peoria

INDIANA

Fort
Wayne

Toledo
Cleveland

OHIO

Columbus

Pittsburgh

Philadelphia
Dover
DELAWARE

ILLINOIS
Springfield

Indianapolis
Cincinnati

Baltimore
Annapolis
Washington, D.C.
MARYLAND

Kansas
City

St. Louis

WEST
VIRGINIA
Charleston

Richmond

Tulsa

Jefferson
City

Louisville
Frankfort

VIRGINIA

MISSOURI
Springfield

KENTUCKY

Raleigh

Nashville
Knoxville

NORTH
CAROLINA
Charlotte

Fort Smith
Little Rock

TENNESSEE

Memphis

Wilmington

Tupelo

Columbia

ARKANSAS

El Dorado

Birmingham

Atlanta
Augusta

SOUTH
CAROLINA

Charleston

Shreveport

Jackson

ALABAMA
Montgomery

GEORGIA

Savannah

ATLANTIC
OCEAN

MISSISSIPPI

LOUISIANA

Baton
Rouge
Biloxi
Mobile
Pensacola

Valdosta
Tallahassee

Jacksonville

New
Orleans

Orlando

BAHAMAS

Tampa

Gulf of Mexico

FLORIDA

Christi

Miami

ville

0   20   40 miles
0   20   40 kilometers

PUERTO RICO

San Juan
Bayamón
Carolina

Ponce

CUBA

ARCTIC OCEAN

Beaufort
Sea

Baffin
Bay

Greenland
(DENMARK)

Greenland
Sea

ICELAND

Bering Sea

Gulf of
Alaska

CANADA

Hudson
Bay

Davis Strait

Labrador
Sea

IRELAND UNITED
KINGDOM

BELGIU

FR.

NORTH PACIFIC
OCEAN

30°N

UNITED STATES

NORTH ATLANTIC
OCEAN

PORTUGAL SPAIN

MOROCCO

MEXICO

Gulf of
Mexico

BAHAMAS

WESTERN
SAHARA
(Morocco)

ALG

MAURITANIA

MALI

CUBA
JAMAICA
BELIZE
HONDURAS

DOMINICAN
REPUBLIC
HAITI

ST. KITTS & NEVIS

Caribbean
Sea

ANTIGUA & BARBUDA
DOMINICA
ST. LUCIA
BARBADOS

CAPE VERDE

SENEGAL
GAMBIA
GUINEA BISSAU

BURKINA
FASO

GUATEMALA
EL SALVADOR

NICARAGUA

ST. VINCENT &
THE GRENADINES
GRENADA
TRINIDAD AND TOBAGO

SIERRA LEONE
LIBERIA

GUINEA
IVORY
COAST
GHANA

COSTA RICA

PANAMA

VENEZUELA

GUYANA
SURINAME
FRENCH GUIANA (Fr.)

TOG

EQU

COLOMBIA

Gulf of
Guinea

0° Equator

ECUADOR

SAO
& PR

PERU

BRAZIL

BOLIVIA

30°S

PARAGUAY

SOUTH ATLANTIC
OCEAN

SOUTH PACIFIC
OCEAN

URUGUAY

CHILE

ARGENTINA

60°S

Weddell
Sea

AN